Oracle Administration and Management

Michael Ault

WILEY COMPUTER PUBLISHING

John Wiley & Sons, Inc.
New York • Chichester • Weinheim • Brisbane • Singapore • Toronto

Publisher: Robert Ipsen
Editor: Robert Elliott
Developmental Editor: Emilie Herman
Managing Editor: John Atkins
New Media Editor: Brian Snapp
Text Design & Composition: Publishers' Design and Production Services, Inc.

Designations used by companies to distinguish their products are often claimed as trademarks. In all instances where John Wiley & Sons, Inc., is aware of a claim, the product names appear in initial capital or ALL CAPITAL LETTERS. Readers, however, should contact the appropriate companies for more complete information regarding trademarks and registration.

This book is printed on acid-free paper. ♾

Published by John Wiley & Sons, Inc.

Published simultaneously in Canada.

This publication is designed to provide accurate and authoritative information in regard to the subject matter covered. It is sold with the understanding that the publisher is not engaged in professional services. If professional advice or other expert assistance is required, the services of a competent professional person should be sought.

Library of Congress Cataloging-in-Publication Data:

ISBN 0-471-21886-3

Printed in the United States of America.

10 9 8 7 6 5 4 3 2 1

To the police, firefighters, and the members of the armed services of the USA who put their lives on the line every day to keep us safe and free. Also, I dedicate this revision to my wife Susan who has continued to offer her love and support through all of my Oracle adventures. Last but not least I dedicate this, as with all my other works, to the greater glory of God.

Contents

Acknowledgments

I would like to acknowledge the following folks from John Wiley and Sons without whom this book would never have made it from a few electronic ghosts on hard drive to the completed paper copy:

Bob Elliott, Senior Editor

John Atkins, Associate Managing Editor

Emilie Herman, Assistant Developmental Editor

Brian Snapp, New Media Editor

Of these folks I would like to single out Emilie with special thanks for her patience during my several personal crises during this rewrite and her compassion and understanding.

Introduction

SO YOU'VE CHOSEN ORACLE . . . NOW WHAT?

With Oracle8 and Oracle*8i,* Oracle Corporation began a trend in database modernization that has culminated in the Oracle9*i* release. Many consider Oracle9*i* to actually be 8.2; I would argue that with the multitude of new features, structures, and capabilities, 9*i* qualifies as a new release.

Oracle's power comes from its ability to give users quick and accurate data retrieval. This is the main strength of a relational system. With Oracle's new object-oriented extensions, it now allows real-world modeling with the power of the relational engine behind the model. This merging of object and relational technology has led to one of the most powerful object-relational databases available. Object-relational databases provide a logical, generally straightforward presentation of data. The tabular relational format, expanded to include the varray, nested table, and object views, as well as to allow storage of methods with data, presents data in a new way that remains familiar to those of us brought up in the relational paradigm. In addition, with Oracle*8i,* the ability to store Java in the database as stored code provided incredible power and flexibility. Greater acceptance of XML (eXtensible Markup Language) has also launched Oracle to the razor's edge of technology. These features, combined with a relational foundation, enable users to query information and easily get the data they need and only the data they need. How is this possible?

It is accomplished through the tabular format of a relational database with the object-oriented extensions added in a clear, straightforward method. The logical collection of *related* data and methods and the data objects' *relationships* to each other form the database. Through its SQL, SQL*Plus, Java, XML and development tools, as well as other tools, Oracle allows developers, users, and administrators to look at their data as never before.

The purpose of this book is to provide administrators responsible for maintaining and administrating the Oracle database with a set of tools to make their jobs easier. Through examples and real-world scenarios, the database administrator or manager will gain valuable insight into the workings of the Oracle database management system. Numerous examples of reports and the SQL, SQL*Plus, and PL/SQL code used to generate them will be given. The interpretation of these reports will also be offered.

Oracle provides a great database administration toolset. Unfortunately, few beginner DBAs have the prerequisite knowledge to put these tools to good use. This book is intended to remedy that. In the chapters to follow, all phases of Oracle database administration and management will be covered, from initial installation to day-to-day maintenance to the all-important backup, recovery, and disaster recovery procedures that could mean the difference between being a successful DBA and being given the boot. In addition, OEM (Oracle Enterprise manager) will be covered. OEM is a GUI tool written in Java that allows easy administration and management of an Oracle database; however, there are times to use it and times not to use it, as you will see in the following chapters.

In previous releases of this book I covered OpenVMS, UNIX, and Windows. In this edition, the VMS coverage will be minimized to allow a new expanded coverage of Linux, an open source version of UNIX.

Brief Overview of Oracle9*i*

Oracle version 9*i* is an *object-relational database management system* (ORDBMS). Oracle9*i* (actually 9.0.1 production release) expands upon the features that were new to Oracle8*i* and makes numerous changes or additions to the Oracle tools. As noted, a traditional RDBMS stores data in tables called *relations*. These relations are two-dimensional representations of data where the rows, called *tuples* in relational jargon, represent records, and the columns, called *attributes*, are the pieces of information contained in the record. Oracle9*i* provides new features in the object-oriented extensions offered in Oracle8*i,* as well as to the Oracle RDBMS. In an object-relational database, columns can represent a single value (as in standard relational databases), a varray (a fixed number of additional records), or a REF to a second table where a variable amount of data can be stored. This takes the two-dimensional relational view and adds a third dimension. Moreover, in an object-relational database, procedures known as methods can be tied to the tables. Methods are above and beyond the old concept of triggers, as explained later in this introduction. In later releases of Oracle8*i*, Java, the newest object-oriented language, can be used to create stored objects in an Oracle8*i* database. Oracle9*i* expands the Java capabilities of Oracle and adds entirely new dimensions to the tuning of the database internals, thereby allowing varying sized database blocks, multiple buffer pools, and a plethora of other new features.

Oracle provides a rich set of tools to allow the design and maintenance of the database. The major Oracle tools are listed here:

RDBMS Kernel. The database engine, the workhorse of Oracle.

SQL. The Structured Query Language, the relational language.

SQL*Plus. Oracle's interface to SQL and the database.

PL/SQL. The Procedural Language SQL, which allows for procedural processing of SQL statements.

SQL*Loader. Allows for data entry from ASCII flat files into Oracle tables.

EXPORT/IMPORT. Allow data and structure information to be removed and inserted from Oracle databases into or out of archives.

INTERMEDIA. Allows access to text-based data stored in Oracle.

Developer2000. Provides for generation of forms, reports and 3GL code based on the inputs to Designer2000.

Designer2000. Allows generation of ERD, FHD, Matrix, and Dataflow diagrams.

Oracle9*i*AS. An application server based on the Apache Web server technology with extensions for Oracle.

SVRMGR. Oracle's replacement tool for SQLDBA. Replaced by SQL*PLUS added functionality in 9*i* releases.

OEM. The Oracle Enterprise Manager, which provides the capability to manage multiple instances across your entire enterprise.

RMAN. Recovery Manager, which provides automated backup and recovery options for Oracle.

Oracle precompilers. Provides interface to most major 3GL languages.

JDBC. Oracle's implementation of the Java Database Connection interface.

SQLJ. Oracle's SQL precompiler for Java, allowing ease of use of SQL from inside Java.

Java. Java is moved into the Oracle kernel in later 8.1 releases and all 9*i* releases.

There are many, many, more!

In order to fully understand the structures that make up an Oracle database, the ability to use these tools is critical. As a database administrator or manager, you will become intimately familiar with at least a few of them.

Oracle is more than just a collection of programs that allow ease of data access. Oracle can be compared to an operating system that overlays the OS of the computer on which it resides. Oracle has its own file structures, buffer structures, global areas, and tunability, above and beyond those provided within the operating system. Oracle controls its own processes, its own records, and consistencies, and cleans up after itself.

Oracle as it exists on your system (with the exception of Windows, which uses a multithreaded process instead) consists of executables, five to nine (or more) detached processes, a global memory area, datafiles, and maintenance files. It can be as small as a couple of megabytes or as large as a massive globe-spanning construction of terabytes. Diagrams showing typical Oracle8*i* and Oracle9*i* environments are shown in Figures I.1 and I.2, respectively; you may want to refer to these diagrams as you read the next sections of this introduction.

Let's look at a typical Oracle system that operates in the UNIX, Linux, or Windows environments. On NT (threads), Linux, or UNIX there may be a minimum of a dozen detached processes for Oracle8*i;* for Oracle9*i,* even more. Five of these are the base Oracle processes (PMON, SMON, DBWR, LOGWR, CKPT), which are launched every time Oracle is started up on a system; additional processes may be started if the database is using archiving (ARC), uses TCP/IP, or is being run in parallel and/or distributed mode. The Oracle job queues, snapshot processes, advanced queuing options, and callout processes all add to the process count. These processes are described here:

DBWR (Database Writer). Handles data transfer from the buffers in the SGA to the database files. There may be multiple database writer processes, as well as database writer slave processes, depending on the release level of Oracle.

LGWR (Log Writer). Transfers data from the redo log buffers to the redo log database files. Where multiple log locations are used, multiple writers can be configured.

SMON (System Monitor). Performs instance recovery on instance startup and is responsible for cleaning up temporary segments. In a parallel environment, SMON recovers failed nodes.

PMON (Process Monitor). Recovers user processes that have failed and cleans up the cache. PMON recovers the resources from a failed process.

ARCH (Archiver Process). Active only if archive logging is in effect. ARCH writes the redo log datafiles that are filled into the archive log datafiles. There may be multiple archiver processes depending on the number of archive log locations specified in the initialization parameters.

RECO (Distributed). Resolves failures.

Transaction Recoverer. Recovers distributed transactions.

LCK*n* (Lock Process). Used for interinstance locking in an Oracle parallel server (OPS) or real application cluster (RAC) environment.

D*nnn* (Dispatcher). Allows multiple processes to share a finite number of Oracle servers. It queues and routes process requests to the next available server. This is used in multithreaded server installations of Oracle.

S*nnn* (Servers). Makes all the required calls to the database to resolve a user's requests. It returns results to the D*nnn* process that calls it. This is a multithreaded server process that is only configured if MTS is being used by the database.

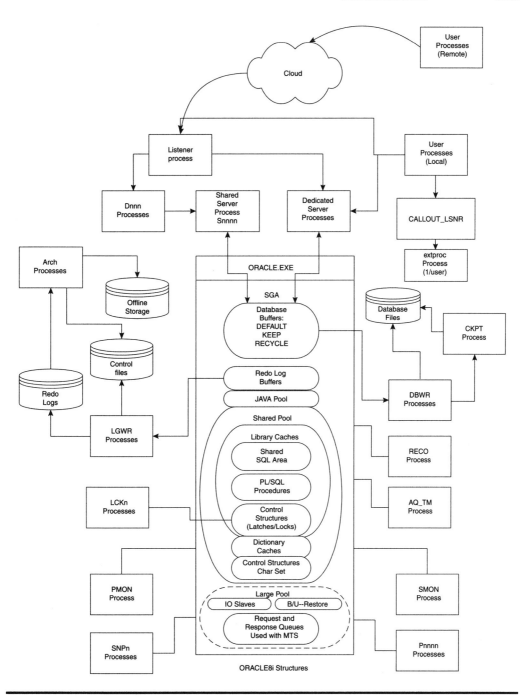

FIGURE I.1   Structures and files for Oracle8*i*.

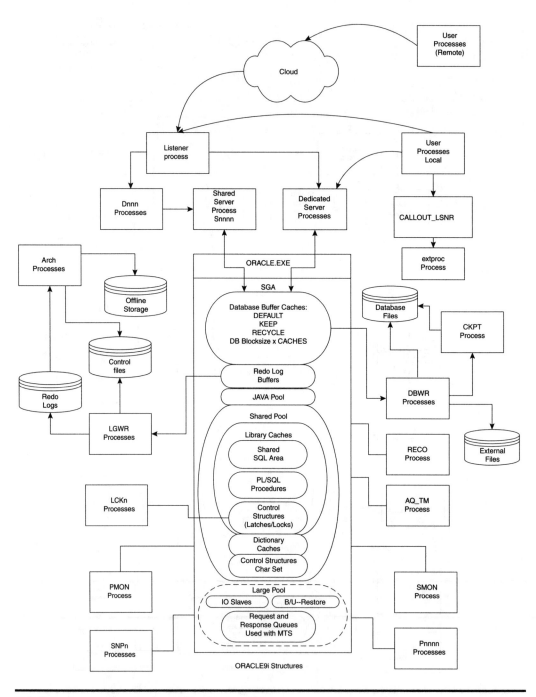

FIGURE I.2   Structures and files for Oracle9*i*.

LISTENERTCPIP server. If you are running TCP/IP, this process, known as the listener process, will be running as well (may have multiple per node). Other communication protocols may also have listener processes.

CKPxx. The checkpoint process that is started to optimize the checkpoint operation for Oracle logging. In releases prior to Oracle8, the process was optional; under Oracle8 and above, it is automatically started.

Snpxx. Snapshot process and job queues. There can be up to 32 configured in 8*i*.

EXTPROC. Callout queues; there will be one for each session performing callouts.

QMNn. Oracle queue monitor processes (new with 8*i*). They monitor the queues used in the Oracle advanced queueing (Oracle AQ). There can be up to 10 QMN processes. These take the place of the single AQ_TXX process in previous releases.

Figure I.3 shows the results of a "ls -ef | grep oracle" command on a SuSE7.2 system running a general configuration Oracle9*i* instance. Notice that the general configuration includes a minimal multithreaded server configuration (the d000-d002 and *s000 processes). If you allow the Oracle Universal Installer to install your database, you will get these by default; if you do not want MTS, you will have to remove the configuration parameters from the initialization file to stop the processes from being configured.

```
                                        Terminal
 File  Sessions  Settings  Help
oracle    3960    1   0 09:04 ?        00:00:02 kdeinit: kicker
oracle    3964    1   0 09:04 ?        00:00:00 kdeinit: klipper -icon klipper -
miniicon klipper
oracle    3965    1   0 09:04 ?        00:00:00 kdeinit: khotkeys
oracle    3968    1   0 09:04 ?        00:00:00 kdeinit: kwrited
oracle    3970  3968   0 09:04 pts/0   00:00:00 /bin/cat
oracle    3972    1   0 09:04 ?        00:00:00 knotes -session 10508a8e23000097
6640408000000019500013
oracle    3973  3948   0 09:04 ?        00:00:02 kdeinit: konsole -icon konsole -
miniicon konsole -caption Terminal
oracle    3974  3973   0 09:04 pts/1   00:00:00 /bin/bash
oracle    3984    1   0 09:06 ?        00:00:00 ora_pmon_galinux1
oracle    3986    1   0 09:06 ?        00:00:00 ora_dbw0_galinux1
oracle    3988    1   0 09:06 ?        00:00:00 ora_lgwr_galinux1
oracle    3990    1   0 09:06 ?        00:00:01 ora_ckpt_galinux1
oracle    3992    1   0 09:06 ?        00:00:04 ora_smon_galinux1
oracle    3994    1   0 09:06 ?        00:00:00 ora_reco_galinux1
oracle    3996    1   0 09:06 ?        00:00:00 ora_s000_galinux1
oracle    3998    1   0 09:06 ?        00:00:00 ora_d000_galinux1
oracle    4000    1   0 09:06 ?        00:00:00 ora_d001_galinux1
oracle    4002    1   0 09:06 ?        00:00:00 ora_d002_galinux1
oracle    4455  3974   0 12:50 pts/1   00:00:00 ps -ef
oracle    4456  3974   0 12:50 pts/1   00:00:00 grep oracle
oracle@tuscgalinux:~ >
  New   Terminal No 1
```

FIGURE I.3   Listing of processes on Linux for Oracle9*i*.

It can be problematic to get a similar listing to the one shown in Figure I.3 for Windows or W2K systems. However, if you download the Resource Kit 4.0 from the Microsoft Web site, it provides several tools that make monitoring multithreaded processes easier. One such tool used for monitoring multithreaded processes is the Pviewer, which allows you to pick a process from the master process list; it will show you all associated threads and their memory usage statistics. An example listing from an Oracle8*i*, 8.1.7 instance on a Windows NT 4.0 server is shown in Figure I.4.

Of course, if you need to see the actual process names, you will have to go inside Oracle and look at the V$SESSION table. An example output from a report on the V$SESSION table on an NT4.0 system is shown in Listing I.1.

On multiuser-capable systems, each user process may spawn several subprocesses, depending on the type of activities being done by that process. Depending on how Oracle is configured, a single parallel query may start dozens of query slave processes for a single user!

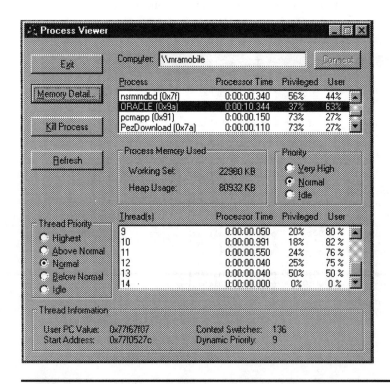

FIGURE I.4   Example screen shot of the PViewer output for NT4.0, SP6a and Oracle9*i*.

Listing I.1   Example output of a report to view Oracle process names.

```
Date: 02/07/02                                              Page:   1
Time: 06:41 PM              Oracle Threads Report           DBAUTIL
                              aultdb1 database

                        Decimal Hex
Process Owner           Thread Thread           PID
------- ----------      ------ ----------  ---------
User    Internal                                 1
PMON    Internal        822 336                   2
DBW0    Internal        849 351                   3
LGWR    Internal        850 352                   4
CKPT    Internal        851 353                   5
SMON    Internal        853 355                   6
RECO    Internal        854 356                   7
User    Internal        855 357                   8
User    Internal        857 359                   9
User    Internal        866 362                  10
User    Internal        867 363                  11
User    DBAUTIL         884 374                  12

12 rows selected.
```

The global memory area, called the System Global Area (SGA), is an area of CPU memory that is reserved for Oracle use only. It contains buffers that are used to speed transaction throughput and help maintain the system integrity and consistency. No data is altered directly on the disk; it all passes through the SGA. The size and configuration of the SGA is defined by a file called the initialization file or INIT.ORA file, which can contain information on each type of buffer or shared pool area in the SGA.

There are also shared programs that make up a typical instance. These can be as few as one (e.g., the ORACLE kernel) or as complex as the entire toolset.

As stated, Oracle can be viewed as an operating system that overlays your existing operating system. It has structures and constructs that are unique to it alone. The major area of an Oracle installation is, of course, the database. In order to access an Oracle database, you must first have at least one *instance* of Oracle that is assigned to that database. An instance consists of the subprocesses, global area, and related structures that are assigned to it. Multiple instances can attach to a single database. Many of an instance's and database's characteristics are determined when it is created. A single Windows, Linux, or UNIX platform can have several instances in operation simultaneously; on Windows, Linux, and UNIX systems, they can be attached to their own database, or may share one. In a shared database environment, called remote application clusters, or RAC, in Oracle9*i*, additional licenses and processes will be required.

The document set for Oracle weighs in at over 60 pounds, and is not light reading by any means. It takes at least a single CD-ROM to contain it all.

Brief Overview of Relational Jargon

Some of you are no doubt wondering what the heck I'm talking about in this book, what with terms like relations, tuples, and attributes. What do they all mean? Ninety percent of any field is learning the jargon—the language specific to that field. With Oracle, the jargon is that of relational databases. Much of this jargon can be attributed to Dr. E. F. Codd, who formulated the rules (called "Normal Forms") for data, as well as the relational algebra upon which relational databases are designed.

You may have already been exposed to such topics as Normal Forms, tuples, and primary and foreign keys. And it is not the intent of this book to give a full course in relational theory. I do, however, attempt to clarify the meaning of this "relational speak," so those without a formal grounding in relational terminology can find the book as valuable as those who are already familiar with it.

I've already mentioned tables, tuples, and attributes, and touched on relationships. Now let's look more closely at relationships, specifically as they apply to relational databases. Stop for a moment and consider the company where you work or perhaps are consulting for. The company has employees, or, let's say, the company employs workers. The reverse is also true: a worker is employed by a company. This is a relationship. A relationship is a logical tie between information that is contained in entities. In this case, the information is from these entities: A, the company, and B, the workers.

Can a worker have more than one job? Of course. Can a company have more than one worker? Yes. So let's restate the relationship: A company may employ one or more workers. A worker may be employed by one or more companies.

This is called a *many-to-many* relationship. Of course, other types of relationships exist. Within a company, a worker usually only works for one department at a time, while a department may have many workers. This is called a *one-to-many* relationship. Generally speaking, most many-to-many relationships can be broken down into one-to-many relationships; one-to-many relationships form a majority of the relationships in a relational database. A relationship is between two *entities*. In our example, "worker" and "company" are entities. An entity is always singular in nature. In most cases, an entity will map into a table. A diagram showing the logical structure of a relational database is called an *entity relationship diagram* (ERD). Figure I.5 shows a simple entity relationship diagram.

Another aspect of a relational database is its functions. Without functions, a database would have no purpose. Functions start at a high level, such as: "Provide a means of tracking and reporting the work history of employees." Functions can be broken down, or if you wish, decomposed, until they are atomic in nature. A fanatic would break down a function until it consisted of operations involving individual attributes, such as add, delete, update, and retrieve.

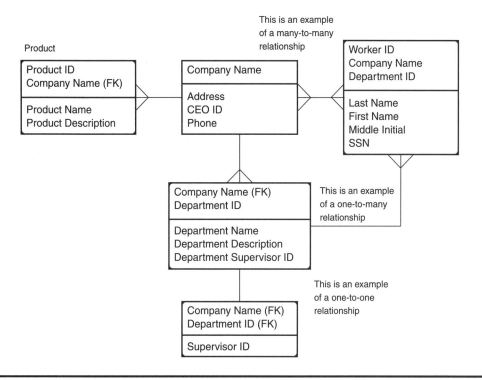

FIGURE I.5   Example of an ERD diagram.

For example, say we wished to retrieve a record (or *tuple*) from a table, update one of its columns (or *attributes*), and then return the row to the table. In one case, it could be considered one function, *update of attribute x*. In a different light, it could be decomposed into the individual retrieves, modifies, and updates of the columns. In most cases, it isn't necessary to go into great and gory detail. The functions a database performs are shown in a function hierarchy diagram. Entities (and hence tables) and relations map into functions. Figure I.6 shows a simple *function hierarchy diagram* (FHD).

The final aspect of a relational database comprises its modules. A module may perform one or more *functions*. A module may map into a form, a report, a menu, or a procedure. For example, a single module representing a form can handle numerous atomic functions, such as add, update, retrieve, and delete, of a table, or even a group of tables, and data records.

Let's summarize: A relational database is made up of entities consisting of attributes. These entities and attributes can be mapped into a table. Each occurrence of an entity adds a row to the table it maps to. These rows are called tuples. Each entity relates to one or more other entities by means of relationships. Relationships must be

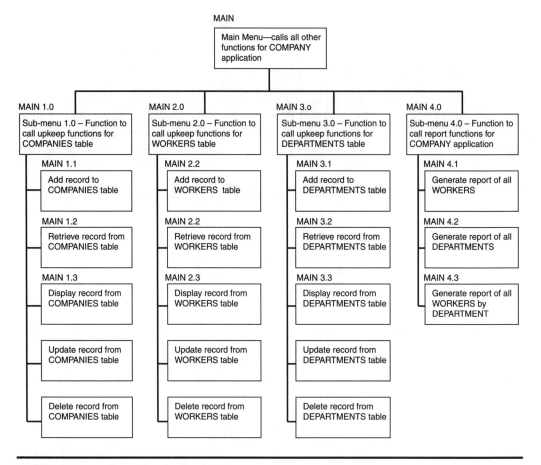

FIGURE I.6   Example of a simple FHD.

valid in both directions and must have degree, such as one-to-many or many-to-many. Relationships must also show *optionality*, such as *may be* or *must be*.

Functions are used to tell what is done with the entities and relations. Entities and relations map into functions. Modules implement functions and map into forms, reports, menus, or procedures.

All of this depends on Dr. Codd's rules. The entire set of rules is complex and, to most of us, rather obtuse at times. Luckily, they have been used to produce the rules of Normalization. These, simply stated, are as follows:

- *Precursor.* Each occurrence of an entity is uniquely identifiable by a combination of attributes and/or relationships.
- *First Normal Form.* Remove repeated attributes or groups of attributes to their own entity.

- *Second Normal Form.* Remove attributes dependent on only part of the unique identifier.
- *Third Normal Form.* Remove attributes dependent on attributes that are not a part of the unique identifier.

In short, to be in third normal form, all attributes in an entity must relate directly to the identifier and only to the identifier. This unique identifier is called the *primary key*. It can be a unique number. such as a Social Security number, or a combination of attributes, called a *concatenated* or *combination key*, such as last name and date of birth. Generally speaking, these primary keys are used to enforce relations by mapping the keys into related entities, where they become *foreign keys.*

For those who want a more detailed discussion of entity relationship diagrams, normalization, and other related (no pun intended) topics, the following books are recommended:

Atre, S. *Data Base: Structured Techniques for Design, Performance, and Management. Second edition.* New York: John Wiley & Sons, 1988.

Barker, Richard. *CASE*METHOD: Entity Relationship Modelling.* Reading, MA: Addison-Wesley, 1990.

Barker, Richard, and Cliff Longman. *CASE*METHOD: Function and Process Modelling.* Reading, MA: Addison-Wesley, 1990.

Barker, Richard. *CASE*METHOD: Tasks and Deliverables.* Reading, MA: Addison-Wesley, 1990.

Braithwaite, Ken S. *Relational Databases: Concepts, Design, and Administration.* New York: McGraw-Hill, 1991.

Date, Chris J. *Introduction to Database Systems*, 6th ed., vol. 1. Reading, MA: Addison-Wesley, 1994.

Brief Overview of Object-Oriented Jargon

No doubt many of you know a great deal more about object-oriented technology than I do or would ever want to know. However, it won't hurt to go over a few of the basic terms and buzzwords in this new paradigm.

The heart of the object-oriented world is, of course, the object. So what is an object? In *Visual Basic 5: Object-Oriented Programming* (Coriolis Press, 1997), Gene Swartzfager explains: "An object is a software package that contains a collection of related procedures and data." A procedure is in turn called a method, and data elements are called attributes. So an object is a software package that contains methods and attributes. Objects, to fall completely into the object-oriented universe, must be independent of each other. This makes them ideal for use as reusable modules since each can be maintained independently of the other, *as long as proper interface and messaging standards are implemented and enforced.* Unfortunately, most shops forget that last little caveat.

Objects communicate via messages. A message usually has three parts: the object name, one of the object's methods (or members), and an attribute list. Objects are contained in classes that define each member of an object's class. A single object is called an *instance* of that object. The only differences between particular instances of objects in a class are the attributes that the particular class objects operate against.

Other terms that bounce around in "object speak" are encapsulation, polymorphism, and inheritance. (I once knew a programmer who suffered from encapsulated polymorphism, but since he had inherited it there was nothing that could be done.) What are these three principles of object-oriented technology?

- *Encapsulation* is simply the feature of an object-oriented program that means it is completely standalone; that is, it is not dependent on another object, nor is another object dependent upon it for its function. Since an encapsulated object is passed attributes and returns attributes with no other external communication required (i.e., no global or public variables, no external calls to other objects or methods) it is said to implement *data hiding* or *binding*.
- *Polymorphism* allows a single method to be used by multiple classes or objects. An example would be overloading of an Oracle PL/SQL function to handle multiple datatypes. An overloaded function (or procedure) in PL/SQL simply has several functions or procedures of the same name and argument structure, except that one of the passed arguments is a different datatype. The user has no idea that multiple functions or procedures exist; he or she simply calls the function or procedure and gets the results back.
- *Inheritance* is just what it appears. We have touched on the concept of classes. Classes can be subdivided into superclasses and subclasses. Inheritance allows subclasses to inherit behaviors from their superclass. Generally speaking, a superclass will be a general class of generic functions with subclasses that exhibit more and more specialized behavior. Oracle9*i* supports limited inheritance.

There are some Oracle-specific definitions for the Oracle object-oriented extensions. These involve how Oracle uses object technology. Let's look at some of these Oracle-specific definitions to complete this discussion of object-oriented jargon.

- *Object type*. Object types (called *abstract datatypes* in early-release documentation) are datatypes that define Oracle objects. An Oracle object is one instance of an Oracle object type. Oracle objects can be persistent, such as tables or views, or may be transient, such as a memory construct in PL/SQL. The CREATE TYPE command is used to create an Oracle object type. Persistent object types will have an object identifier (OID), while nonpersistent object types will not.
- *Object table*. An object table is a table of Oracle object types. If a pre-Oracle8 table is ported to Oracle9*i*, it doesn't automatically become an object table. To get a relational table to behave as if it were an object table, it must be made part of an object view. Only objects represented by true object tables have OIDs. Object tables were referred to as extent tables or typed tables in early Oracle8 documents.

- *Object identifier (OID).* As stated, only objects stored in an object table have an OID. The OID is guaranteed to be globally unique; it consists of a 128-byte hexadecimal value. By itself, an OID cannot be used to locate an object instance; only a REF (discussed in Chapter 5), which contains location data, can be used for locating an object instance.

- *Object.* A single instance of an object datatype, which may or may not have an associated OID. If the object is from an object table, it will have an OID; if it is from Oracle Call Interface variables or PL/SQL variables, it will not.

- *Nested object.* An object is said to be nested if its object type is used to specify a single column in an object table.

- *Nested tables.* The CREATE TYPE command can be used to create a type that is actually a table. This table type can then be used to create a table of that type, which can be used as a column in a second object table. This results in a nested table. Don't worry if this is confusing now; in the next few chapters, you will see examples that should reduce the fog factor.

- *Datatypes.* There are three kinds of datatype in Oracle9*i*: built-in, library, or user-defined. Built-in are the standard NUMBER, DATE, VARCHAR2, LONG, LONG RAW, BLOB, and so on. User-defined are specialized types built by users or VARs; and library types are built by a third party and supplied to the user (generally, a specialized form of the user-defined datatype).

- *Large objects (LOBS).* New in Oracle8 is extended coverage for LOBS. There are several types of LOB: a character LOB (CLOB), binary LOB (BLOB), national character LOB (NCLOB), and a LOB stored externally to the database, a BFILE that is generally to be used for long binary files such as digitized movies or audio tracks.

- *External procedures.* Another Oracle8 feature was the ability to call from PL/SQL procedures that didn't reside in the database. By procedures I mean a 3GL program. Only C and Java are supported. These are also referred to as 3GL callouts.

- *Constructor.* This is an Oracle kernel-generated method to instantiate an Oracle object type instance. It is differentiated from a user-created method in that it is system-created and automatically applied when a call is made to an object type or when an object type is needed and does not have an implicit or explicit SELF parameter (to use a bit of "object speak").

- *Forward type definition.* I prefer to call this a type-in-type. Essentially, it means you can define an object type and then use that type in a second, third, or any number of subsequent type definitions. In this special case, both types refer to each other in their definition. For you C programmers, this is identical to forward declaration. An example of this type of type-in-type definition will be shown in Chapter 5.

- *Object view.* An object view allows normal relational tables to be referenced like objects in an object relational database. The object view process supplies synthesized OIDs for relational rows. Chapter 7 will demonstrate this technique.

- *Universal Modeling Language (UML).* The latest modeling language for use with object-oriented design.

- *Java.* An object-oriented language used to create internal stored objects in Oracle8*i* and Oracle9*i* and external Java scripts, applets and applications.

What Exactly Is a Database Administrator?

A database administrator (DBA) should not be confused with a data administrator (DA). While a data administrator is responsible for administering data via naming conventions and data dictionaries, a database administrator is responsible for administering the physical implementation of a database. This can include or overlap the database management function. In fact, this book will blur the two together since the functions of one are closely related to the other. The DBA provides support and technical expertise to the DA and users.

The DBA position is constantly changing and expanding. It may encompass physical design and implementation, performance monitoring and tuning, even testing and configuration of interface programs such as X Window emulators for use with the database.

The database administrator must have the freedom required to move datafiles in coordination with the system manager to optimize database access. The DBA should work hand in hand with the system administrator to ensure proper use is made of available resources. There is no more sure formula for failure in a company than to have the database administrator and the system administrator at war.

Many shops feel that the DBA must be intimately familiar with their application. I have found through multiple tuning engagements that that simply is not the truth. To be sure, if you are going to design and build the application, you need intimate knowledge, but to maintain and tune, you do not. In fact, I have found in many instances (no pun intended) that too much application-level knowledge may blind a DBA to what is actually happening at the transaction level. In every database, tuning ultimately boils down to the question: Does the transaction perform in the least amount of time in the most efficient manner? Looking at a database at the transaction level is like looking at a forest tree by tree: you need to know the type of tree, but you don't have to know the entire forest.

Here's a list the major jobs of a database administrator, according to the *Oracle9i Database Administrator's Guide* (Release 1, Part No. A90117-01, June 2001, Oracle Corporation):

- Install and upgrade the Oracle server and application tools.
- Allocate system storage and plan future storage requirements for the database system.
- Create primary database storage structures (tablespaces) after application developers have designed an application.
- Create primary objects (tables, views, indexes) once application developers have designed an application.
- Modify the database structure, as necessary, from information given by application developers.
- Enroll users and maintain system security.
- Ensure compliance with Oracle license agreement.

- Control and monitor user access to the database.
- Monitor and optimize the performance of the database.
- Plan for backup and recovery of database information.
- Maintain archived data on tape.
- Back up and restore the database.
- Contact Oracle Corporation for technical support.

In an ideal structure, there is a data administrator who is a direct report to a director or other senior manager. This DA is "off to the side," rather like the executive officer on a Navy ship. Also reporting to this level of management should be the database administrator. The DA and DBA need to work closely together to be sure that the physical and logical structures of the database, through the data dictionary, are closely tied. The database administrator may also hold the database management function, or this may be a separate position. At the next level down are the application administrators, who control individual applications. Then come the application administrators, who may be the development and maintenance staffs, or may be in a separate directorate. This structure is shown in Figure I.7. If the database is sufficiently large, especially under Oracle9*i* due to its more complex security requirements, a security administrator may also be required.

All of these positions must work closely together. The DA must talk to the DBA; the database manager (DBM) and DBA must work closely together to optimize the database system. The application managers need to ensure that their applications meet naming rules and conventions and coordinate their resource utilization with the DBM and DBA.

As can be seen, DBAs are central to the proper running of a database system. They coordinate activities related to the database; assist with design, development, and testing; and provide monitoring and tuning. Given the DBA's importance, let's look at how to find a good DBA.

Selecting a Proper DBA Over the last few years I have been interviewed for, and have interviewed several dozen candidates for, Oracle-related positions. The positions ranged from entry-level developer to senior-level DBA. Many of the interviews were for DBA-level positions. In this period I learned that it is very difficult to hire, or be hired, as a DBA unless you know exactly who or what you are looking for when you use the title "DBA." This section will attempt to clear up the misconceptions about the Oracle DBA position, specify the levels within the DBA position, and give some idea of how to interview and be interviewed for Oracle DBA positions.

To be a full-charge DBA, a candidate must be knowledgeable in all of these areas:

- Design
- Installation
- Configuration management
- Security

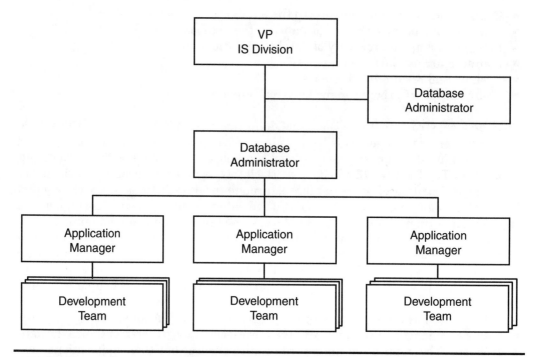

FIGURE I.7   Sample information systems data administration org chart.

- Monitoring and tuning
- Backup and recovery
- Troubleshooting
- Vendor interface

Desirable Personality Traits of a DBA   Many times, managers concentrate on technical qualities and overlook personality. Virtually every category shown in the preceding list means a DBA will have to interface with other personnel, be they vendors, users, developers, or managers. This means the DBA should possess the following personal traits:

- Self-confidence
- Curiosity
- Tenacity
- Tact
- Self-motivation
- Detail-orientation

Of all of these, a recent survey showed tenacity to be the most important. Why are these traits important? I have had several subordinates who lacked self-confidence; they constantly asked my opinion on every decision, major or minor, and showed no initiative. As a novice DBA under a full-charge DBA, this may be all right, but if the person *is* the full-charge DBA, then who is he or she going to depend on to help make decisions if he or she has no self-confidence? Interview questions, therefore, should include problems confronted and how they were solved. The answers should demonstrate self-confidence. One thing to remember is that not knowing an answer is not bad, but not to know where to find an answer is.

The Oracle database system is constantly changing. Not all of these changes are documented. Therefore, curiosity is a requirement to be a good DBA. If DBAs aren't curious, they are passive, and wait for things to be told them. A curious DBA will install the latest version and immediately begin searching out the differences and improvements and how they can be applied to make his or her job better (read easier). Curious DBAs will have multiple reference publications they purchased with their own money and will have read them. One of my interview questions involves what references the candidate has and uses. Needless to say, if he or she responds by citing only the documentation set, and he or she hasn't even read that, then that candidate's stock loses value rapidly. Curiosity will also drive qualified DBAs to understand the Oracle data dictionary and any utilities or packages provided by Oracle. Many of my interview questions deal with these Oracle internals. Lack of knowledge about the data dictionary tables and views and the Oracle-provided utilities and packages is unforgivable in a full-charge DBA.

Troubleshooting requires a bulldog-like tenacity, getting a hold and not letting go until the problem is solved. Many DBAs will give up on a problem that would have been solved with the next solution they tried. As a sysop for the CompuServe ORAUSER forum, I see questions daily that could have been solved by the people asking them, if they were tenacious and curious. I use troubleshooting questions from my own experience and from those of others from the DBAPipeline on the www.revealnet.com and the metalink.oracle.com support forums.

A self-starting employee is important for any position, doubly so for a DBA. A DBA must be able to wade in and make things happen, not just wait for things to happen. Self-starting DBAs obtain or develop their own scripts to monitor such items as table sizes, tablespace usage, SGA usage—in short, all of the items that can get them in trouble if ignored. Interview questions dealing with level of experience in PL/SQL, SQL, and SQL*Plus will show how many scripts the DBA candidate has developed. Some operations in PL/SQL and SQL*Plus are generally only used by DBAs, so questions concerning specific techniques will expose those who have written their own scripts and those who haven't.

Dealing with developers and managers, not to mention users, requires tact. A tactless DBA will make nothing but enemies for your department. Tact has been called the ability to tell someone to go to Hades and have them anxious to make the trip. Many times, developers, managers, and users will make unreasonable requests; the DBA must have tact to field and deflect these requests without burning bridges. How a person acts during the interview process will show his or her level of tact.

The final trait, being detail-oriented, is very important. DBAs who are detail-oriented don't have to be told to cross-check details. It also means they actively document quirks in the installation "just in case." The indications of a detail-oriented person are such things as bringing a Daytimer or scheduler to the interview, showing up ahead of time, and asking questions that indicate the candidate has researched the company he or she is interviewing with. This detail orientation will show up in the candidate's knowledge of the Oracle internals and an understanding of the relationships between the views, tables, and dynamic performance tables. Usually, a detail-oriented person will take the time to research the database on his or her own.

Knowledge Required of a DBA   A good DBA candidate will know all of the areas discussed in the preceding subsection, "Selecting a Proper DBA." DBAs must be familiar with design so that when new tables or indexes are proposed by designers they will know how they should fit into the general schema. Knowledge of a modeling tool such as Designer2000 or ERWin (Platinum Technologies) is a requirement. DBAs should be able to read an ERD diagram with one eye closed, and be able to fight their way through a UML diagram.

The DBA must be familiar with installation and update on the platform that your system is running against. Each platform has its own quirks and idiosyncrasies. A DBA experienced on Windows NT will have difficulty performing an installation on UNIX or DEC VMS. Updates can wreak havoc with production machines if they are done incorrectly. DBA candidates should be able to answer specific questions concerning installation and upgrade of Oracle systems on your platform. During the interview process, they should exhibit the curiosity to ask about your platform and any modifications to the standard installation that exist upon it.

Configuration management involves database sizing, file placement, and specification of storage media. A full-charge DBA will be familiar with system topics such as RAID levels, disk sharing, disk shadowing, solid state disks, optical storage, and their application to the Oracle database environment. On UNIX, they should also be familiar with the cost and benefits associated with use of raw devices and when raw device usage is mandatory.

Understanding Oracle security options is vital to the DBA job. A demonstrated knowledge of system and object-level privileges, roles, and profiles is required for any DBA. Understanding how the operating system security options interface with the Oracle options is also important. Additional requirements such as use of Secure Oracle and implementation of SQLNET are also considerations.

One of the critical aspects of the DBA's job is the monitoring and tuning of the database and any applications. Monitoring and tuning requires a detailed understanding of the Oracle data dictionary, the tkprof, and plan utilities, as well as an understanding of how both the cost-based and rule-based optimizers function. Detailed understanding of what can and can't be done via indexing, use of hints, and SQL statement tuning is vital to a DBA. A DBA candidate should demonstrate knowledge of the following:

- DBA_ views, ALL_ views, and USER_ views
- SYS-owned "$" tables
- dynamic performance tables (V$)

All of these are a part of the Oracle data dictionary. In addition, the DBA candidate should have knowledge of the DBMS_* series of packages and how they can be used to facilitate tuning and script development, and the UTL*.SQL series of utility scripts and their usage in tuning and monitoring.

A DBA candidate must understand all of the backup and recovery options. Use of the import and export utilities and of cold and hot backups are all vital topics that a DBA must understand. Answers to interview questions concerning types of database backups used and how the utilities can be implemented must show level of knowledge in this area. Additional topics to cover in this phase of the interview are recovery scenarios involving partial recovery at the table, tablespace, and database levels.

Troubleshooting is a binary ability. Usually people will either have the knack or they won't. Troubleshooting requires an analytical approach, where the problem is laid out in discrete parts and each is attacked in a methodological fashion until the problem is solved. Troubleshooting also involves being unafraid to admit when you don't know something but having the tenacity to say, "I can look it up." Interview questions on troubleshooting must come from real life and should involve multiple steps and critical thinking to solve. To test their troubleshooting ability, candidates should be asked the most difficult problem they have encountered and how they solved it.

A final bit of knowledge required of a DBA is the ability to communicate clearly, either orally or via written materials. Since a major portion of a DBA job will involve interaction with others on multiple levels within a company environment, DBAs must be able to speak, think, and write clearly and concisely. A review of their resumes with particular attention to any publishing credits will help to determine their abilities in this regard. Presentations at user groups, local or national, magazine articles or articles in local user group publications all show the ability to communicate.

At a professional level, look for experience writing documentation or procedures. Most candidates with advanced degrees such as a master's or Ph.D. will have to have written and communicated to gain that level of education. Ask them to bring their dissertations or examples of their writing to the interview. Candidates should be expected to bring examples of this type of experience to the interview. The ability to speak clearly, to take and give instructions, and to understand complaints is vital. As technically qualified as a candidate may be, if he or she cannot communicate, he or she will not succeed.

What Level of DBA Do You Need?   DBAs range from DBBS level (database baby sitters) to full-charge DBAs. What level do you need? If you place a full-charge, fire-breathing DBA in a job where all he or she has to do is monitor an older version of Oracle and ensure backups are taken, the DBA will soon tire of the job and leave—not to mention that his or her salary requirements will be significantly higher than for more junior people. On the other hand, if you hire a dyed-in-the-wool, don't-want-to-grow DBBS for a position where initiative, drive, tenacity, and troubleshooting skills are critical, you are asking for trouble. Be sure that you get the right candidate for the job. I would rather hire a technically inexperienced DBA who showed all of the personality traits discussed earlier than a DBBS who could rewrite Oracle—if someone told him or her to, that is.

A database baby-sitter usually has a good-looking resume that is full of projects and jobs involving Oracle. However, most of these jobs will have involved third-party applications that were preinstalled and only required monitoring. If they can't answer in-depth questions concerning the DBA_ views or the V$ tables, chances are they are DBBS- rather than DBA-level candidates. Another key indicator is a lack of knowledge about the Oracle utilities, such as import, export, and the tuning tools tkprof and explain plan. A final indicator is lack of knowledge concerning the DBA task-related DBMS_* packages.

If all you need is someone to monitor a third-party database application via a preconfigured monitoring tool, and to take action when the tool tells him or her after a problem has happened, then hire a DBBS. Otherwise, you will waste a DBA and no one will be happy if you get an overqualified person into a low-level job.

If you do need a full-charge DBA, don't hire a DBBS unless he or she shows the curiosity and tenacity to use deep-end learning to pull him- or herself up to the level of a full DBA. Deep-end learning is the analogy for throwing someone into the deep end of the pool to teach him or her to swim. Usually, there won't be time to send such a person to the multitude of classes required to give him or her full knowledge, so he or she will have to learn on the fly. Get the person involved with the Oracle forums and user groups, and purchase whatever references he or she requires. I suggest a full paper copy of the Oracle manuals that is the DBA's alone. An online reference such as the Oracle Administrator product from RevealNet is also a good idea, as it will provide battle-tested solutions to many problems. The Oracle documentation on CD-ROM makes a very convenient and portable way to carry the entire document set, as long as the DBA has a laptop. But, at least to me, nothing replaces a paper manual for ease of use (besides, you can use it even during a power outage—by candlelight!).

Developing Questions for Interviews   Interview questions should be diligently researched, and the expected answers listed. Where open-ended questions are used, the interviewer should have the level of knowledge required to judge the answers' correctness. The questions should be broken into categories, and each should be assigned a point value based on either a scale from, say, 0–5, or according to difficulty. At the conclusion of the interview, technical ability evaluation should be based on the results from these points. Your interview questions should be reviewed by technically competent personnel for accuracy and applicability. Some sample interview questions are included in the downloads for this book at www.wiley.com/compbooks/ault, in the books section, under this title, in Acrobat Reader format.

Prequalification of Candidates   In the past, candidates had two sources for Oracle knowledge: experience and/or Oracle Corporation training classes. Experience speaks for itself and can be judged as to depth and level. Training was only as good as what the candidate put into it. What I mean by this is that the candidates could either gain much from Oracle training, if they took with them to class the will to learn and curiosity, or they could take nothing away from the class, if they practiced passive learning. Since Oracle training is not graded, everyone receives masters certification regardless of participation. Now, many vendors offer Oracle classes. Indeed, with the plethora of classes available, it is difficult, if not impossible, to judge the quality of training a candidate may have received. One item that will assist hiring managers is the Oracle Certification Exams offered by Sylvan Prometric Learning Systems (the Oracle Certified Professional, OCP, program). These exams test candidates' knowledge in all areas of the DBA skill set. The tests were created by battle-tested DBAs and Oracle Corporation. To pass, a candidate will, in almost all cases, have to have had actual experience as an Oracle DBA and knowledge from multiple Oracle references. While obtaining an Oracle certification from these exams is no guarantee that a candidate is fully qualified, it can be used as an acid test to separate the wheat from the chaff.

Always check a candidate's references. Speak to previous employers if possible, and find out about a candidate's past work history. Many people will interview wonderfully but can't function in the job.

Appearance   A candidate who doesn't take the time put the right foot forward by presenting a proper appearance probably doesn't have the wherewithal to perform adequately in the job. Clean, appropriate clothing and proper grooming show that the candidate is willing to make the effort to please the employer. Candidates who are sloppy in appearance and manner will bring this to the job and to their interactions with other parts of the company.

There is no magic formula for determining whether a candidate can perform adequately; nor is there any way to ensure an employer will always properly evaluate a candidate's abilities. However, if proper preparation is done by both the employer and candidate, then successful hiring or acquisition of a proper position can be less a matter of chance.

WHO SHOULD READ THIS BOOK

This book is intended for experienced as well as beginner DBAs. A beginner should start with the introduction and read straight through, trying the various scripts and techniques as they progress from chapter to chapter. An experienced DBA should use this as a reference to be consulted first, right after the documentation that is!

TOOLS YOU WILL NEED

Reading this book without an Oracle database close at hand would be similar to attempting to learn how to ride a bicycle by reading a book—while you might understand the concepts, you would undoubtedly fail at the first opportunity to test your knowledge. Therefore I suggest you obtain a copy of Oracle, preferably Oracle9*i*, and install it on a computer to which you have access.

Oracle9*i* can be downloaded from the Oracle Technet Web site at technet.oracle. com. For a small fee, they will even send you a demonstration CD set. (Unless you have access to a highspeed Internet connection, I suggest this option. Oracle9*i* requires three installation CDs.)

Oracle9*i* runs on everything from Windows NT 4.0 (service pack 6a is required) and Windows 2000 through most flavors of UNIX, including Linux. Linux is easy to use and install (at least Redhat and SuSE are) and will also give you experience with the UNIX command set. Oracle9*i* will install and run fine on a Pentium III, 400 MHz CPU with 256 MB of RAM and about 2 GB of available disk storage. For a Linux installation, a Pentium III, 400 MHz CPU and 512 MB of RAM is suggested, as well as 2 GB of disk storage. A word of caution, some versions of Oracle9*i* don't install easily on Pentium IV–based systems—some fudging with the provided DLLs is required. This process is discussed in notes on the Oracle support Web site, meatlink.oracle.com. (If you don't have access, email me at mikerault@earthlink.net, or just post to the DBAPipeline, OAUG list server, or lazydba list server. Either I or some other helpful DBA will provide them for you.)

I also suggest you download and install the SQL and shell script ZIP files from the book's Web site (www.wiley.com/compbooks/ault). To do this you may need to obtain the WINZIP program from www.winzip.com.

WHAT'S ON THE WEB SITE

I have endeavored to place all of the scripts (and then some, over 400 at last count) in a ZIP format download file. I have included versions for Windows and Unix as well as shell scripts that will provide a template for developing a DBA menu system on most versions of Unix. I have also provided database table, index, and SGA sizing spreadsheets and DBA interview questions.

I will periodically update these scripts and utilities as I increase my knowledge and toolset for Oracle9*i* and other releases as they come down the pike. Again, the URL for the Web site is www.wiley.com/compbooks/ault.

Remember that I don't warrant these scripts to be free of errors; they are merely examples. I have used them in my work and found them useful, but they may not be exactly what you need. Always, no matter who provides it, examine a script in detail and don't run it against your database until you understand what it does. And of course, Wiley cannot be held accountable for the scripts' performance or lack of it either.

SUMMARY

Oracle is probably one of the more complex applications you will ever deal with. Don't expect to learn everything about it in a matter of weeks or even months. Usually, as soon as you have learned something, Oracle will upgrade, change, or drop it from the toolset. Don't despair, this growth and change means job security! It also means Oracle is listening to the users and trying to implement new features while getting rid of old features that may not have been up to snuff.

A number of Web-based resources are available to the Oracle DBA. I'll list a few here to get you started. I'm sure you will find more:

www.wiley.com/compbooks/ault

www.tusc.com

www.revealnet.com

www.orafans.com

technet.oracle.com

www.ioug.org

metalink.oracle.com (if you have a support contract and a CSI number)

These sites have code repositories for database utilities, forums for asking questions, and links to other sites.

CHAPTER 1

Installation of Oracle

Oracle installation is a complex topic. With the new CD-based installs, many of the platform dependencies dealing with installation have been reduced, but you as database administrator (DBA) need to be aware of the differences that apply to your platform. Usually, these differences will be explained in the release documents and platform-specific installation and user's guide provided with your software distribution. However, there are universal topics that involve structure and layout issues, and the purpose of this chapter is to present those topics and give you a general idea of the way to proceed with your installation.

1.1 THINGS TO CONSIDER BEFORE INSTALLATION

Oracle Corporation has devised a standard architecture layout that it suggests should be used when installing Oracle. I have found that this standard layout, known as the *Optimal Flexible Architecture* or OFA for short, to be a logical way of laying out a database. OFA naming and layout standards should be used even in situations where the boundaries blur between disks, volumes, groups, and arrays, as is happening in the arena of RAID (redundant array of independent disks) technology. OFA should be used even when RAID5 or other RAID solutions are present because of the fact that it is a logical way to layout the database. By using OFA you, and subsequent DBAs, can easily locate all files associated with the database. I have seen databases where OFA or an OFA-based arrangement weren't being used; files were placed anywhere it was convenient. This chaos method of database file placement led to bad backups due to missed files, deletion of files that were in use, and, because no one was tracking where files where placed, contention issues.

Optimal Flexible Architecture (OFA)

In accordance with Cary V. Millsap of the Oracle National Technical Response Team, the OFA process involves the following three rules:

1. Establish an orderly operating system directory structure in which any database file can be stored on any disk resource.

   - Name all devices that might contain Oracle data in such a manner that a wild card or similar mechanism can be used to refer to the collection of devices as a unit.
   - Make a directory explicitly for storage of Oracle data at the same level on each of these devices.
   - Beneath the Oracle data directory on each device, make a directory for each different Oracle database on the system.
   - Put a file X (X is any database file) in the directory /u??/ORACLE/sid/type_desig (or on W2K or NT: C:\oracle\sid\type_desig) if and only if X is a control file, redo log file, or datafile of the Oracle database whose DB_NAME is sid. The type_desig specifies the type of file to be placed in the directory at that location and is usually data, index, control, or redo.

TIP   You may wish to add an additional directory layer if you will have multiple Oracle versions running at the same time. This additional layer includes the version level.

---

2. Separate groups of segments (data objects) with different behavior into different tablespaces.

   - Separate groups of objects with different fragmentation characteristics in different tablespaces (e.g., don't put data and rollback segments together).
   - Separate groups of segments that will contend for disk resources in different tablespaces (e.g., don't put data and indexes together).
   - Separate groups of segments representing objects with differing behavioral characteristics in different tablespaces (e.g., don't put tables that require daily backup in the same tablespace with ones that require yearly backup).

3. Maximize database reliability and performance by separating database components across different disk resources. A caveat for RAID environments: Consider spreading datafiles across multiple controller volume groups.

   - Keep at least three active copies of a database control file on at least three different physical arrays.

- Use at least three groups of redo logs in Oracle9*i*. Isolate them to the greatest extent possible on hardware serving few or no files that will be active while the RDBMS (relational database management system) is in use. Shadow redo logs whenever possible.
- Separate tablespaces whose data will participate in disk resource contention across different physical disk resources. (You should also consider disk controller usage.)

Minimum OFA Configuration

The minimum suggested configuration would consist of seven data areas: disks, striped sets, RAID sets, or whatever else comes down the pike in the next few years. These areas should be as separate as possible, ideally operating off of different device controllers or channels to maximize throughput. The more disk heads you have moving at one time, the faster your database will be. The disk layout should minimize disk contention. For example:

AREA1. Oracle executables and user areas, a control file, the SYSTEM tablespace, redo logs

AREA2. Data-datafiles, a control file, tool-datafiles, redo logs

AREA3. Index-datafiles, a control file, redo logs

AREA4. Rollback segment-datafiles

AREA5. Archive log files

AREA6. Export files

AREA7. Backup staging

Of course, this is just a start; you might find it wise to add more areas to further isolate large or active tables into their own areas as well as to separate active index areas from each other.

The structure or UNIX could look like the following:

```
/oracle0/product/oracle/9.0.1/          Top level $ORACLE_HOME
                                             bin/
Standard distribution structure under version
                                             doc/
                                             rdbms/
                                             ...
/oracle0/data/                     Place instance names under type directories
                    ortest1/
                    ortest2/
/oracle0/control/
                    ortest1/
                    ortest2/
/oracle0/redo/
                    ortest1/
                    ortest2/
```

```
/oracle0/admin/
                        ortest1/
                                   bdump/              backup_dump_dest
                                   udump/
user_dump_dest
                                   cdump/
core_dump_dest
                                   pfile/                  initialization file
location (linked back to dbs directory)
                                   create/             Database creation
script storage area
                        ortest2/
                           ...
/oracle1/data/
          /control/
          /redo/
/oracle2/data/
          /control/
          /redo/
...
/oracle27/data/
          /control/
          /redo/
```

Using this type of structure even on a RAID5 volume allows for a logical separation of files for ease in locating and controlling database files. For other platforms just alter the directory syntax; for example, on NT the /oracle0/product/oracle/9.0.1 directory becomes c:\oracle0\product\oracle\9.0.1\.

I have seen several questions posted as to why the standard says to use u01, u02, and so on for mount points. This is based in old UNIX naming conventions and has little actual usefulness in modern structures. Call the mount points whatever you wish as long as it meets your requirements. I suggest using the application name, for example.

1.2 ORACLE STRUCTURES AND HOW THEY AFFECT INSTALLATION

As can be seen from the previous section, an Oracle database is not a simple construct. Much thought must go into file placement, size, number of control files, and numerous other structural issues before installation. It is a testament to the resiliency of the Oracle RDBMS that even if most of the decisions are made incorrectly, the database that results will still function, albeit, inefficiently.

The structures are as follows:

- Oracle executables
- Datafiles—data, index, temporary, rollback
- Redo logs
- Control files
- Export files

- Archive logs
- Placement of any large object (LOB) or BFILE storage structures

Let's examine each of these.

Executables

The Oracle executables are the heart of the system. Without the executables the system is of course worthless since the datafiles are only readable by Oracle processes. The Oracle executables should be on a disk reserved for executables. Disk speed is not a big issue, but availability is a major concern. The executables will require 3 to 4 GB or more of disk space up to three times this for an Oracle applications installation. The installation process will create a directory structure starting at a user-specified ORACLE_BASE directory. There will usually be a subdirectory for each major product installed. If you are looking at Oracle applications such as financials, CRM, or ERM, then this structure could be extremely complex.

Datafiles

Datafiles are the physical implementations of Oracle tablespaces. Tablespaces are the logical units of storage (containers) that would roughly compare to volume groups in an operating system. Each tablespace can have hundreds of tables, indexes, rollback segments, constraints, and other internal structures mapped into it. In return, these are then mapped into the datafiles that correspond to the tablespaces. Only a limited number of datafiles can be associated with a tablespace. The total number of datafiles for the entire database is set by the MAXDATAFILES parameter at creation.

Redo Logs

As their name implies, redo logs are used to restore transactions after a system crash or other system failure. The redo logs store data about transactions that alter database information. According to Oracle, each database should have at least two groups of two logs each on separate physical non-RAID5 drives, if no archive logging is taking place, and three or more groups when archive logging is in effect. These are relatively active files, and, if made unavailable, the database cannot function. They can be placed anywhere except in the same location as the archive logs. Archive logs are archive copies of filled redo logs and are used for point-in-time recovery from a major disk or system failure. Since they are backups of the redo logs, it would not be logical to place the redo logs and archives in the same physical location. The size of the redo logs will determine how much data is lost as a result of a disaster affecting the database. I have found three sets of multiplexed logs to be the absolute minimum to prevent checkpoint problems and other redo-related wait conditions; under archive log, the use of three groups is a requirement.

Control Files

An Oracle database cannot be started without at least one control file. The control file contains data on system structures, log status, transaction numbers, and other important information about the database. When tools such as Oracle's RMAN backup tool are used, the control file can be several tens of megabytes in size. It is wise to have at least two copies of your control file on different disks, three for OFA compliance. Oracle will maintain them as mirror images of each other. This ensures that loss of a single control file will not knock your database out of the water. You should not bring a control file back from a backup, even though this is supported; it is a living file that corresponds to current database status. In both Oracle8*i* and Oracle9*i*, there is a CREATE CONTROL FILE command that allows recovery from loss of a control file. However, you must have detailed knowledge of your database to use it properly. There is also an ALTER DATABASE BACKUP CONTROL FILE TO TRACE command that creates a script to rebuild your control file. In Chapter 15, *Backup and Recovery Procedures for Oracle*, the section titled "Backup and Recovery Plans for Oracle," explains in detail how to protect yourself from the loss of a control file. It is easier to maintain extra control file copies.

Export Files

Export files affect the recoverability of your database should some disaster befall it. Export files, created by the export utility supplied by Oracle, are copies of a database's data and structure at a given point in time. Export files are logical copies of the database, not physical copies. Several types of exports will be covered in Chapter 15. Export files should be stored in a separate location from archive files.

Archive Logs

Archive logs, as stated previously, are archived copies of the redo logs. They provide the capability to recover to a specific point in time for any tablespace in the database. For any application considered to be production- or mission-critical, archive logging must be turned on. These files can be stored to disk, tape, or even optical storage such as WORM (write once, read many). Using operating system backups such as COPY on NT or W2K, or TAR on UNIX, and with the application of archive logs, a database can be recovered quickly after disaster. Archive logs can only be used to recover when cold or hot backups are used for Oracle backup. Archive logs cannot be applied to a recovery using exports files.

After each successful hot or cold backup of an Oracle database, the associated archive and backup files may be removed and either placed in storage or deleted. In an active database archive, logs may average tens of megabytes or gigabytes per day. Clearly, storage for this amount of data needs to be planned for; for example, at one installation doing Oracle development with no active production databases, gigabytes of archives and a like amount of exports were generated in a one-week period. If archive logging is turned on and you run out of archive disk space, the database stops after the last redo log is filled. Plan ahead and monitor disk usage for instances using archive logging.

Large Object (LOB) Storage

Actually a special form of tablespace, the large object (LOB) storage should be on fast disk resources simply due the large required sizes of most LOB data items. LOB storage should be placed away from other types of storage and should contain only LOB (LOB, CLOB, NCLOB, and BLOB) data items. In the 8.0 LOB environment you could specify separate storage for LOB segments and their associated LOB indexes, in 8*i* and greater they are collocated, so don't forget to allow for the LOB and its associated LOB index.

BFILE Storage

A BFILE is a pointer to an external LOB file. Generally, the same considerations given to LOB storage will apply to the storage areas that BFILEs point toward. BFILEs themselves are just internal pointers to external files and don't require storage areas.

1.3 ORACLE AND DISK USAGE

One of the major arguments against relational database systems has been speed. It has been said that relational systems are slow. It has been found, however, that with proper tuning of Oracle applications and operating system, as well as proper file placement, Oracle performance is excellent. In fact I have seen Oracle8*i* deliver subsecond response times even when searching tables containing billions of rows (yes, I said billions). Conversely, if you try to place Oracle on an insufficient number of disks, performance will suffer.

How Many Is Enough?

Some applications will do fine with two disks or volumes. This setup is not great, mind you, but the system will function. Other applications, such as large complex systems involving numerous indexes, data tables, and tablespaces, may require dozens. To reduce disk contention and maximize database reliability, it is suggested that the DBA utilize OFA procedures to place database files. The next subsections cover file placement for some basic disk array layouts.

One Area (Surely You Jest) It is foolish and very dangerous to even consider using a single area to hold all Oracle files for other than DOS, OS/2, WINDOWS NT, or MAC-based single-user databases. Unless you have the latest and greatest EMC array with multiple gigs of storage, hot replacement of disks, and RAID5, a single large area can lead to problems. A single disk failure or crash in a stripe set could completely destroy your system. Since there are no file placement options with one area, let's go on to the next configuration.

Two Areas (Just Barely Adequate)   At least with two areas you can achieve separation of data and indexes and can separate redo logs from archive log files. This gives you some redundancies in recovery options. The file placement is shown here.

> **AREA1.** Oracle executables, index datafiles, redo logs, export files, a copy of the control file
>
> **AREA2.** Data-datafiles, rollback segment datafile, temporary user datafiles, archive log files, a copy of the control file

As you can see, an attempt is made to spread I/O between the two areas. Indexes and data are on separate controllers, as are redo logs and rollback segments. Additional recoverability in case of disk crash is given by having exports on one drive and archive log files on the other. While infinitely better than only one area, having only two areas is still an extremely vulnerable condition and is not recommended. Again, with the most up-to-date storage areas with large caches, extreme striping, and hot replacement of disks, one or two areas is workable.

Three Areas (Nearly There)   With three areas available we improve the chances that the database can be recovered from disk crashes. We can also reduce the disk contention caused by sharing areas between highly active files in flagrant disregard for OFA rules. Let's look at the three-area layout:

> **AREA1.** Executables, redo logs, rollback segments, export files, copy of the control file
>
> **AREA2.** Data-datafiles, temporary user datafiles, a copy of the control file, redo logs
>
> **AREA3.** Archive log files, indexes, a copy of the control file

Again, an attempt is made to spread I/O evenly across the platters. While this is better than one or two areas, there is still contention between redo logs and rollback segments, indexes, and archives.

Four Areas (Just about Right)   Four areas are much better. Now we can spread the read- and write-intensive rollbacks and redo logs. In addition, we can isolate the archives away from the indexes. Let's look at the structure:

> **AREA1.** Executables, redo log files, export files, a copy of the control file
>
> **AREA2.** Data-datafiles, temporary user datafiles, a copy of the control file, redo logs
>
> **AREA3.** Indexes, a copy of the control file, redo logs
>
> **AREA4.** Archive logs, rollback segments

Now we have succeeded in spreading I/O even further. Redo logs and rollback segments have been separated; and because archive logs will not be as active as redo logs, there will be less contention in this configuration. In most installations, exports will be done during off hours, therefore there should be little contention between the redo logs and exports.

Five Areas (Shoehorn Required)   Well, this may not be Nirvana, but it is a minimum configuration. Five areas allow OFA compliance and permit maximum spread of I/O load. Let's look at a five-area spread:

AREA1. Executables, a copy of the control file, redo logs, the SYSTEM tablespace datafiles

AREA2. Data-datafiles, temporary user datafiles, a copy of the control file, redo logs

AREA3. Index datafiles, a copy of the control file, redo logs

AREA4. Rollback segment datafiles, export files

AREA5. Archive log files

Six Areas (Almost Enough)   We are getting closer with six available areas; we can move the exports and temporary areas to their own disk now, eliminating that source of contention, but what about backups?

AREA1. Executables, a copy of the control file, redo logs, the SYSTEM tablespace datafiles

AREA2. Data-datafiles, a copy of the control file, redo logs

AREA3. Index datafiles, a copy of the control file, redo logs

AREA4. Rollback segment datafiles, export files

AREA5. Archive log files

AREA6. Temporary areas, export files

Seven Areas (Oracle Nirvana)   With seven areas we have minimum contention; and by moving export files to tape, we can eliminate one additional source of database lockup.

AREA1. Executables, a copy of the control file, redo logs, the SYSTEM tablespace datafiles

AREA2. Data-datafiles, a copy of the control file, redo logs

AREA3. Index datafiles, a copy of the control file, redo logs

AREA4. Rollback segment datafiles, export files

AREA5. Archive log files

AREA6. Temporary areas, export files

AREA7. Backup staging area

By monitoring AREA5 and periodically removing archive log files to tape we can eliminate another. If we really wanted to push OFA, we could add a couple of areas for redo logs. Of course, if you use the partitioning options of Oracle, then you may need many more areas in order to place the partitions in separate areas.

Other authors recommend larger configurations, and in some cases they are warranted. If you have several large tables, consider placing these, and their indexes, in separate areas. Most of this type of consideration is application-dependent. With some of the giant databases we are now seeing (hundreds of gigabytes aren't uncommon anymore) and with petabyte sizes now available through the latest releases of Oracle, it seems silly to talk about a mere 5, 7, or 100 disks. If you can use RAID0/1 and stripe data across multiple platters, do it. Of course, don't do what one inexperienced system administrator did: try to do RAID5 sets with two disks each.

As previously stated, the more we can spread our tablespaces across multiple disks, the better Oracle likes it. If you have the disk resources, spread Oracle as thin as you can. While a seven-area configuration performs well, and is easy to maintain, the more disk areas the merrier.

Disk Striping, Shadowing, RAID, and Other Topics

Unless you've been living in seclusion from the computer mainstream, you will have heard of disk *striping, shadowing*, and the umbrella term for both of these technologies, *RAID*. Let's take a brief look at these disk storage technologies and how they will affect Oracle.

Disk Striping   Disk striping is the process by which multiple smaller disks are made to look like one large disk. This allows extremely large databases, or even extremely large single-table tablespaces, to occupy one logical device. This makes managing the resource easier since backups only have to address one logical volume instead of several. This also provides the advantage of spreading I/O across several disks. If you will need several hundred gigabytes of disk storage for your application, striping may be the way to go.

There is one disadvantage to striping, however: If one of the disks in the set crashes, you lose them all unless you have a high-reliability array with hot-swap capability. Striping is RAID0.

Disk Shadowing or Mirroring   If you will have mission-critical applications that you absolutely cannot allow to go down, consider disk shadowing or mirroring. As the term implies, disk shadowing or mirroring is the process whereby each disk has a shadow or mirror disk to which data is written simultaneously. This redundant storage allows the shadow disk or set of disks to pick up the load in case of a disk crash on the primary disk or disks; thus the users never see a crashed disk. Once the disk is brought back online, the shadow or mirror process brings it back in sync by a process appropriately called *resilvering*. This also allows for backup since the shadow or mirror set can be broken (e.g., the shadow separated from the primary), a backup taken, and then the set resynchronized. I have heard of two, three, and even higher-number mirror sets. Generally, I see no reason for more than a three-way mirror as this allows for the set of three to be broken into a single and a double set for backup purposes. Shadowing or Mirroring is RAID1.

The main disadvantage to disk shadowing is the cost: For a 200-GB disk "farm," you need to purchase 400 or more gigabytes of disk storage.

Redundant Arrays of Inexpensive Disks (RAID)   The main strength of RAID technology is its dependability. In a RAID5 array, the data is stored, as is parity data and other information about the contents of each disk in the array. If one disk is lost, the others can use this stored information to re-create the lost data. This makes RAID5 very attractive. RAID5 has the same advantages as shadowing and striping but at a lower cost. It has been suggested that if the manufacturers would use slightly more expensive disks (RASMED—redundant array of slightly more expensive disks) performance gains could be realized. A RAID5 system appears as one very large, reliable disk to the CPU. There are several levels of RAID to date:

RAID0. Known as disk striping.

RAID1. Known as disk shadowing.

RAID0/1. Combination of RAID0 and RAID1. May also be called RAID10 depending on whether they are striped and mirrored or mirrored then striped. It is generally felt that RAID10 performs better than RAID01.

RAID2. Data is distributed in extremely small increments across all disks and adds one or more disks that contain a Hamming code for redundancy. RAID2 is not considered commercially viable due to the added disk requirements (10 to 20 percent must be added to allow for the Hamming disks).

RAID3. This also distributes data in small increments but adds only one parity disk. This results in good performance for large transfers; however, small transfers show poor performance.

RAID4. In order to overcome the small transfer performance penalties in RAID3, RAID4 uses large data chunks distributed over several disks and a single parity disk. This results in a bottleneck at the parity disk. Due to this performance problem, RAID4 is not considered commercially viable. RAID3 and -4 are usually used for video streaming technology or large LOB storage.

RAID5. This solves the bottleneck by distributing the parity data across the disk array. The major problem is that it requires several write operations to update parity data. That said, the performance hit is only moderate, and the other benefits may outweigh this minor problem. However, the penalty for writes can be over 20 percent and must be weighed against the benefits.

RAID6. This adds a second redundancy disk that contains error-correction codes. Read performance is good due to load balancing, but write performance suffers because RAID6 requires more writes than RAID5 for data update.

For the money, I would suggest RAID0/1 or RAID1/0, that is, striped and mirrored. It provides nearly all of the dependability of RAID5 and gives much better write performance. You will usually take at least a 20 percent write performance hit using RAID5. For read-only applications RAID5 is a good choice, but in high-transaction/high-performance environments the write penalties may be too high. Table 1.1 shows how Oracle suggests RAID should be used with Oracle database files.

1.4 NEW TECHNOLOGIES

Oracle is a broad topic; topics related to Oracle and Oracle data storage are even broader. This section will touch on several new technologies such as optical disk, RAM disk, and tape systems that should be utilized with Oracle systems whenever possible. Proper use of optical technology can result in significant savings when large volumes of static data are in use in the database (read-only). RAM drives can speed access to index and small table data severalfold. High-speed tapes can make backup and recovery go quickly and easily. Let's examine these areas in more detail.

Optical Disk Systems

WORM (write-once, read-many) or MWMR (multiple-write, multiple-read) optical disks can be used to great advantage in an Oracle system. Their main use will be in storage of export and archive log files. Their relative immunity to crashes and their long shelf life provide an ideal solution to the storage of the immense amount of data that proper use of archive logging and exports produce. As access speeds improve, these devices will be worth considering for these applications with respect to Oracle. They have also shown great benefits in read-only tablespaces and in transportable tablespace sets, a new feature of Oracle8*i* and 9*i*.

TABLE 1.1   RAID Recommendations

RAID	Type of RAID	Control File	Database File	Redo Log File	Archive Log File
0	Striping	Avoid	OK	Avoid	Avoid
1	Shadowing	Recommended	OK	Recommended	Recommended
0+1	Striping and shadowing	OK	Recommended	Avoid	Avoid
3	Striping with static parity	OK	OK	Avoid	Avoid
5	Striping with rotating parity	OK	Recommended if RAID01 not available	Avoid	Avoid

(From Metalink, NOTE: 45635.1)

Tape Systems

Nine-track, 4mm, 8mm, and the infamous TK series from DEC can be used to provide a medium for archive logs and exports. One problem with doing so, however, most installations require operator monitoring of the tape devices to switch cartridges and reels. With the advent of stacker-loader drives for the cartridge tapes, and tape libraries such as those provided by StorageTek, this limitation has all but been eliminated in all but the smallest shops.

Random Access Memory (RAM) Drives

Though RAM drives have been around for several years, they have failed to gain the popularity their speed and reliability would seem to warrant. One reason has been their small capacity in comparison to other storage mediums. Several manufacturers offer solid-state drives of steadily increasing capacities. For index storage, these devices are excellent. Their major strength is their innate speed. They also have onboard battery backup sufficient to back up their contents to their built-in hard drives. This backup is an automatic procedure invisible to the user, as is the reload of data upon power restoration.

The major drawback to RAM drives is their high cost. However, rapid reductions in memory chip costs, along with the equally rapid increase in the amount of storage per chip, may soon render this drawback nonexistent. Use of RAM drives for temporary tablespaces and index tablespaces, as well as for lookup and easily rebuilt tables, could increase processing speeds severalfold. At last check the cost for a RAM drive in the 16-gigabyte capacity range was about $20,000, so beware—they are pricey!

1.5 SYSTEM CONSIDERATIONS

Within each Oracle installation there are several operating system considerations that must be taken into account. These affect how Oracle uses global memory and processes memory areas. The DBAs will be responsible for tuning and maintaining these areas.

What Is an SGA and How Does It Apply to You?

SGA is an abbreviation for *Shared Global Area*. As the term global implies, this area is accessible to all Oracle processes and users. Each instance will have its own SGA. Oracle processes and users must share large amounts of data. If all of the processes had to get the data from the disk, the I/O load would soon render totally unacceptable response times. To prevent this, Oracle uses global memory areas, that is, CPU memory. This memory is dedicated to use for Oracle alone. In Oracle8i, the SGA contains data buffer areas, redo log buffers, and the shared pool (context areas). Each area is important to the database's overall performance. An additional area, the LARGE POOL, is also configured. Under Oracle8i, another area has been added, the Java shared pool area. Oracle9*i* has the capability to divide the database buffer regions into multiple varying block sized areas (2K, 4K, 8K, 16K, and 32K block sizes are supported).

The shared pool context areas and database buffers provide immediate access to data that has been preread from either the data dictionary tables or the data tables. The Oracle kernel process uses an LRU (least recently used) algorithm to write data back to the disks. Data is never altered on the disks directly; it is altered in memory first. In Oracle8, the ability to have areas where LRU aging was turned off, known as the KEEP area, and where LRU aging was accelerated, known as the RECYCLE area, were added.

The redo buffers contain row change information, transaction commit history, and checkpoint history. This data is written into the redo logs and eventually to the archive logs. A commit will force a disk write, as will the filling of a redo log buffer or the reaching of a predefined checkpoint.

For Oracle7 the queue and request areas store data that is being transferred between processes such as servers and other Oracle7 processes. The shared SQL area stores all SQL statements in a parsed form. When a user or process issues an SQL (Structured Query Language) command, the shared SQL area is checked to see if the command already exists in parsed form; if it does, this shared version is used. If the multithreaded server option is utilized, some of the user Process Global Area (PGA; described in the next section) is also placed in the shared pool. Under Oracle8, the LARGE POOL area is an optional extension to the SGA. If configured via its initialization parameters, the LARGE POOL takes over the session-level memory needs for MTS (multithreaded server) or XA sessions. The LARGE POOL is also used for I/O slaves and during Oracle backup and restore operations. Under Oracle8*i*, parallel execution queues are also allocated from the LARGE POOL area. If you will be using the parallel query option, pay particular attention to the section in Chapter 12, *Tuning Oracle Applications*, on tuning the shared, large, and Java pools for Oracle8*i*. In Oracle9*i,* the database buffer areas are allowed to have multiple blocksizes; this promises greater tuning flexibility for mixed-mode databases.

What Is a PGA and How Does It Apply to You?

PGA stands for *Process Global Area*. This is memory reserved for each process that uses Oracle. It contains the context area. Oracle sets this area's size based on the values of the initialization parameters:

OPEN_LINKS. The number of database links allowed open per user.

DB_FILES. The number of database files allowed for the database (up to the value of MAX_DATAFILES).

LOG_FILES. The maximum number of redo log file groups (up to the value of MAX_LOGFILES).

The PGA also contains session-related information if MTS is not used. In environments where MTS is used, the session information is placed in the SHARED_POOL region of the SGA if the LARGE POOL (in Oracle8, 8*i*, and 9*i*) is not configured. This session information consists of the user's private SQL area and other session-specific data. The PGA will always hold the user's stack information. The section of the shared or LARGE POOL allocated for the user is called the UGA, which stands for *Users Global Area*.

Another contributor to the memory footprint of each process is the size of the SORT_AREA_SIZE and SORT_AREA_RETAINED_SIZE parameters. When a process executes a sort memory, the size of SORT_AREA_SIZE is allocated to the user. If SORT_AREA_RETAINED_SIZE is also set, then this amount of memory is reduced to that value and allowed to grow to SORT_AREA_SIZE. If the sort requires more space than is specified in SORT_AREA_SIZE, the sort is broken into SORT_AREA_SIZED chunks, which are swapped out to disk as needed.

1.6 SOME SYSTEM-SPECIFIC NOTES

Each specific operating system contains certain items that a DBA needs to be aware of and take into account when installing Oracle. This section attempts to consolidate these system-specific notes in one location.

UNIX-Specific Notes

There are many different versions of UNIX, including Solaris, AIX, SV4, and the new kid on the block, Linux (while Linux has been around since the early 1990s, it is just now coming to the fore in business uses, hence the new-kid label). This subsection provides general guidelines and some specific suggestions for those systems I have experience with.

Datafiles   On the install for the general-use database, the MAXDATAFILES parameter defaults to a value of 100. On older versions of UNIX there may be a kernel-based limit of 60 open files per process. This can be overcome by altering the OPEN_MAX value in the limits.h file. Under some versions of UNIX this may be different; to make the determination, look under configurable kernel parameters. Another UNIX-specific limit is on the total number of file extents.

System Global Area (SGA)   In some cases, the SGA may exceed the available shared memory segment size; if this occurs, the UNIX administrator must relink or reconfigure the kernel to allow larger programs. There are system-specific shared memory parameters that control the maximum size of the SGA. These should be reviewed under configurable kernel parameters for your version of UNIX. The installation guide for your Oracle system will delineate which parameters to look at for your UNIX system. Under the HP-UX implementation the size of the SGA is limited to the size of swap space on the available disk drives. On a Sun, True64, or HP-UX system, the parameters that control how the SGA grows are SHMMAX, the size of a shared memory area, and SHMSEG, the number of shared memory areas a process can access. On SuSE7.2 and RedHat

Linux you can dynamically set the memory and semaphore processes or load them into the configuration header files and relink the kernel. On systems such as NT and AIX, you have no control over memory and semaphore parameters, as they are automatically set for you.

Rollback Segments Most systems are not using the parallel instance option of Oracle (called real application clusters, or RAC, in Oracle9*i*). Because of this, private, rather than public, rollback segments should be used. This will allow a single rollback segment to be taken offline for consolidation. If you will have large transactions, such as batch updates with numerous updates and adds between commits, a second INIT.ORA file should be created, which brings online a single large rollback segment to be used during batch operations. These limitations may be reduced or mitigated by using the new undo tablespaces in Oracle9*i*.

Raw Devices In Unix and NT/Windows systems there are several types of disk formats used. Generally, the highest performance comes from programs that can directly access the disk. In order to be directly accessed a disk must be configured in what is known as *raw* format meaning no OS buffering or access control is used.

While raw disks provide performance gains over many traditional disk formats they have several limitations that make their use difficult. An example is that only one file may be placed in a raw disk partition at one time, another is that raw disk partitions may require special backup commands. Finally, raw devices can be easily overwritten if the system administrator is not careful.

If you have tuned your application, I/O, and all applicable SGA parameters and still cannot get the performance you want on UNIX or NT, then consider using raw *devices*. Oracle is capable of reading and writing directly to raw devices. This can increase Oracle performance for disk I/O by over 50 percent and ensures that data integrity is maintained. But when raw devices are used, Oracle datafile names are restricted to a specified syntax. Another limitation is that the entire raw partition has to be used for only one file, which can lead to wasted disk space unless the areas are carefully planned. This will require the DBA to keep an accurate map of which devices belong to which tablespaces, log files, and so on.

Another method is to turn off UNIX buffering. Whether the option of removing UNIX buffering is open to you depends on the version of UNIX you are using.

There are also limitations on types of backup that can be used. Many third-party software packages that are designed for use with Oracle support backup of RAW devices. If you don't have one of these packages, I suggest ensuring you have enough formatted (*cooked*) file systems to support a "dd" to a cooked file system followed by a normal backup.

There is some debate as to whether the reported up-to-50 percent increase in speed of access is due to the RAW device usage, or a good deal of it is an artifact of the conversion process from a cooked to a raw system. Generally, a system with bad performance has other problems, such as chained rows and excessive table extents as well as improper placement of indexes, tables, redo, and rollback. The DBA converts to raw by exporting, dropping the database, doing the raw partitions, re-creating the database, and then importing. Usually, files will be better placed due to lessons learned. The chained rows and multiple table extents are eliminated by the export/import; and another major performance problem, brown indexes (the process by which excessive numbers of empty leaf nodes resulting from UPDATE and DELETE operations cause index broadening), is fixed by the import rebuild of the indexes. Voila! The system is 50 percent faster, and RAW gets the credit, when doing all of the above to the database on a cooked file system would have given the same improvements.

If you want to use a shared instance (Oracle's Parallel Server or Real Application Clusters option), you must use raw devices on UNIX since there are no UNIX file systems that support the proper sharing of disks in other than a raw state.

Archives Archive log files are only present if archive logging has been initiated in the database instance. Archive logs are copies of the filled redo logs. Archive logs are used to provide point-in-time recovery to time-of-failure. Archive logs can consume a large amount of disk resource in an active environment. In some situations, I have seen archive logs consume tens of gigabytes of disk area in a single day. I am sure there are installations where it is normal to use hundreds of gigabytes for archive logs.

If you want to be able to recover your database to point-of-failure, you have to use archive logging. The logs should be placed away from the other files in the system on a physically separate disk farm, if possible. In one situation, we had to perform an incomplete recovery after a disk failure because the archive logs were on the same disk farm as the other files and the failed disk had sections striped to datafiles, redo logs, and archive logs.

It is usual to keep all archive logs since at least the last backup in a quickly retrievable state. The storage area can be optical storage, tape, or disk for archive logs. However, I suggest that fast media be used for the initial site to which archive logs are written. The use of fast media for the initial archive log location is required to prevent waits caused by the system cycling back to the redo log being archived before it has been written out completely; this results in a hung database until the archive becomes "unstuck." Once the archive log is written out, it can then be copied to its final location. Once a full cold or hot backup is taken, all previous archive logs can be erased or placed in long-term storage.

If you alter the setting of the COMPATIBLE initialization parameter, it will most likely render all previously generated archive logs as unusable for recovery. Always perform a complete backup after changing the value of the COMPATIBLE parameter. Anytime a startup is performed using the RESETLOGS parameter, all previous archive logs become invalid and may not be used to recover the instance after the startup.

If you are using Oracle parallel server (now called RAC), all archive logs generated from all redo threads must be available to all instances. Usually this is accomplished by using a cron script to copy the archive logs to multiple locations. Another possible solution is to copy the archive logs to a central NFS (Network File System) mounted disk farm; however, if the NFS mount point is lost, you won't be able to recover, so be sure the NFS mount is on a high-reliability server. Never set LOG_ARCHIVE_DEST for archive logs to raw devices; remember that only one file is allowed per RAW area, so each new archive log would overwrite the previous in a raw destination.

In Oracle8*i* and Oracle9*i*, multiple archive log locations are allowed, even on other platforms reachable through the network. This makes administrating standby databases much easier to automate.

1.7 INSTALLATION GUIDELINES

As stated in the introduction to this chapter, installation of Oracle is a complex topic. And though Oracle has automated the process to a large extent, if you don't have your ducks in a row *before* you start, your success is doubtful. Therefore, this section will cover Oracle installation on NT, UNIX, and Linux, and attempt to point out the pitfalls that might trip you up on the path to a proper installation. Note, however, that the product is growing and changing with each release, so this information cannot, nor is it intended to, replace the installation guides provided by Oracle. Instead, this section is intended to provide general guidelines for the DBA who is facing installation or upgrade of the Oracle products.

Generic Installation Issues

In any installation, whether it is on W2K, NT, UNIX, or Linux, there are certain items that must be addressed. These include:

- Disk space availability
- DBA account setup
- Training
- File layout
- Tablespace layout
- Database-specific topics

We will cover these topics in turn and, hopefully, in doing so provide the DBA with the information to arrive at logical answers to installation questions that may arise.

Disk Space Availability More installations are probably messed up due to disk space availability than any other cause. Disk fragmentation doesn't seem to be a problem under UNIX or NT, however I do suggest you defragment any NT system that has been in operation for extended periods of time prior to the Oracle installation unless you are installing to fresh disks. With most modern systems, disk space is allocated dynamically. This means that as a file needs space, it is granted space wherever it is available on a disk. On active systems, where files are created, updated, and deleted or moved to different disks, this results in fragmentation. This can result in problems for the DBA on NT systems since most aren't provided with a disk defragmentation tool.

The Oracle DBA Account   Other than the ADMINISTRATOR on NT, or the ROOT or SUPERUSER account on UNIX, the Oracle DBA account, usually called ORACLE, will be one of the most powerful accounts on the system. This is required due to the Oracle system being more like an operating system than just a set of executables. In order to start up and shut down, create the required files, and allow global sharing of the kernel and perhaps the tools, the Oracle DBA account needs much broader privileges than a normal user account. The account must have the privilege to create directories, files, and other system objects, as well as the ability to place objects in shared memory.

The second-largest contributor to a bad install experience is an underprivileged Oracle DBA account. The account must be set up as stated in the installation documentation for the install to be successful. After the installation, some adjustment of account privileges can be done if the system administrator really doesn't want an account outside of his or her realm of control to have such broad privileges, but no adjustments can be made until the install is complete. In most cases, however, the privileges removed by an overzealous system administrator will have to be periodically reinstated for code relinks, special file work, and, of course, upgrades. This will soon convince most system administrators to set them and leave them. After all, if someone can't be trusted with the required privileges to do his or her job, should the person be trusted with the job in the first place? It is advised that the Oracle DBA be sent to at least an introductory course in system administration so as to know what *not* to do with the privileges. A course in system tuning is also advised.

Training

It has been said that success in a new venture usually depends on three things: training, training, and training. This is especially true in the realm of the Oracle DBA. Oracle Corporation, and many third-party vendors, offer numerous classes at locations across the United States and Europe. There are also many sources for computer-based training (CBT), as well as online resources such as the RevealNet, Inc. Oracle Administrator (which I helped to author and a part of which can be downloaded from the company Web site). These classes are Oracle-specific and address issues that DBAs, developers, and managers need to be aware of and take into account. With most Oracle purchases you can negotiate training units, or TUs. Use them; they are worth their weight in gold. While there have been a few successful seat-of-the-pants Oracle installations, most end up in trouble.

The Oracle Masters programs are especially useful in that they take the guesswork out of which classes you should take. Consult with Oracle training about schedules and classes. For large Oracle installations with large numbers of developers and administrators, Oracle, and vendors such as TUSC, will provide on-site classes that may significantly reduce your training costs. Another good program is the Oracle Certified Professional (OCP) DBA certification program. For a fee, you can go to any Sylvan Learning Center and take a set of examinations that will determine if you have the prerequisite knowledge to be a DBA on Oracle. However, if you don't have at least two years of experience in Oracle and some training, don't waste your money. I have taken these exams; they aren't a piece of cake by any means.

If you have training on-site, don't allow outside interruptions to intrude upon the class. These can be disruptive and are rude to the instructor. Besides, it wastes your training money.

Would you allow a first-time driver to just jump into the car and drive off? It is amazing how many sites turn new and complex systems over to personnel with perhaps a good background in databases but no experience whatsoever in Oracle. Yes, there are generic issues, but there are enough details specific to Oracle alone that training is highly recommended. If it costs $20,000 to fully train a DBA, isn't it worth it? How much money would it cost if the system were down for several days while an inexperienced DBA pored through the manuals and tried to communicate intelligently with the Oracle help line? What if a critical application were destroyed because of something the DBA did or didn't do? At one site, an experienced DBA, new to the Oracle database system, didn't follow the normal database datafile-naming convention recommended by Oracle. Even though backups were taken, they didn't get the one SYSTEM datafile that was named incorrectly. As a result, when an application required recovery due to data corruption, the system couldn't be restored. This resulted in the users abandoning the application and investing hundreds of hours reinventing it on Mac systems.

In my incarnation as a sysop on the DBAPipeline at www.revealnet.com and the lazydba and Metalink forums I assist with, I answer newbie questions on a daily basis that can usually be answered by looking at the manuals. Don't waste support analysts' (and my) time by asking us questions that you can answer yourself. Besides, I have found I learn better if I look it up rather than have someone tell me; I'm sure you have had the same experience. If you ask a question that is easily looked up in Oracle manuals, I may answer "RTFM," which stands for "Read the f****** manual."

Disk Layout

If you've read up to this point, you should realize that disk layout is critical to efficient operation of Oracle systems. There are several questions you need to answer when designing your disk layout:

- What are the sizes of, and available space on, the disks or arrays to be used with Oracle?
- Is this disk or array used for other non-Oracle applications?
- Has the disk been defragmented (if needed)?
- Is this a raw device (if UNIX)?
- What is the speed of the disk or disks in the array; or what is the I/O saturation point of the controller channel?
- Is this a RAM or an optical disk?

Let's look at each of these questions to determine how the answers affect Oracle:

What are the sizes of, and available space on, the disks or arrays to be used with Oracle? Obviously, if there isn't enough space on the disk, you can't use it. If the size is too small to handle projected growth, then you might want to look at another asset. Oracle files can be moved, but not with that section of the database active. If you enjoy coming in before or after hours or on weekends, then by all means put your database files on an inappropriately sized disk asset.

Is this disk or array used for other non-Oracle applications? This question has a many-sided answer. From the Oracle point of view, if you have a very active non-Oracle application, it will be in contention with Oracle for the disk at every turn. If the non-Oracle application, such as a word processing or a calculation program that uses intermediate result files, results in disk fragmentation (on NT) this is bad if the datafile collocated with it has to grow and can't allocate more contiguous space. From the viewpoint of the other application, if we are talking about export files, archive log files, or growing datafiles, an asset we need to operate may be consumed, thus preventing our operation. Look carefully at the applications you will be sharing the disk assets with; talk with their administrators and make logical usage projections.

Has the disk been defragmented (for NT)? This was covered before but bears repeating. A fragmented disk is of little use to Oracle on NT; it will be a performance issue. Oracle needs contiguous disk space for its datafiles. If the disk hasn't been defragmented, have it checked by the system administrator for fragmentation, and defragment it if required.

Is the disk a raw device (for UNIX)? If the disk is a raw device, this restricts your capability for file naming. Be sure you maintain an accurate log of tablespace mapping to raw devices. Map tablespace and other asset locations ahead of time. Remember, an entire raw partition must be used per Oracle datafile; it cannot be subpartitioned without redoing the entire raw setup. If you must use raw, plan it!

What is the speed of the disk? By speed of disk we are referring to the access and seek times. The disk speed will drive disk throughput. Another item to consider when looking at disk speed is whether or not the disk is on a single or shared controller. All of these questions affect device throughput. Generally, datafiles and indexes should go on the fastest drives; if you must choose one or the other, put indexes on the fastest. Rollback segments and redo logs can go on the slowest drives as can archive logs and exports.

Is the disk a RAM or an optical disk? Ultimately, the RAM and optical usage ties back to disk speed. A RAM drive should be used for indexes due to its high speed. It is probably not a good candidate for datafiles due to the RAM drive's current size limitations; this may change in the future. An optical drive, due to its relative slowness, is excellent for archives and exports, but probably shouldn't be used for other Oracle files. A possible exception might be large image files (BLOBs) or large document files. Usually, unless you have a rewritable CD system, the table-spaces placed on a CD-ROM will be read-only. With the storage capacities of most optical drives, they make excellent resources for archive logs and exports. They can conceivably provide a single point of access for all required recovery files, even back-ups. This solves the biggest recovery bottleneck: restoration of required files from tape.

Database-Specific Topics

There are numerous database-specific questions to answer before installation:

- What is the number and size of database tablespaces? What is file placement? How many potential applications? How will extent management for tablespaces be handled (dictionary or local managed)?
- What are the SGA issues?
- What is the number of users, administrative, developer, and application?
- What is the number and placement of control files?
- What is the number and placement of redo logs?
- What is the number and placement of rollback segments? Will new UNDO table-spaces be used?
- Will this database be shared between multiple instances (Oracle RAC)?
- Will this database be distributed?
- Should the tools be linked single-task or independent (two-task)?
- Do we need to plan for external Oracle-managed files or BFILE external files?

Let's examine each of these as they relate to installation of Oracle.

What Is the Number and Size of Database Tablespaces? What Is File Placement, the Number of Potential Applications? These are disk space and create-script-related issues. The number of potential applications will drive the number and size of database tablespaces above and beyond the eight base tablespaces. You will see that these are:

SYSTEM. Contains files owned by the SYS and SYSTEM user.

TOOLS. Contains files usually owned by SYSTEM but that apply to the Oracle developer's toolset; these files contain base information and details of forms, reports, and menus.

ROLLBACK. Contains the private rollback segments; its size will depend on number of rollback segments and expected transaction size. May also be an Oracle-configured UNDO tablespace, which means you will also have to plan for how long UNDO data should be retained to allow for flashback query.

DEFAULT USER. Tablespace in which users can create and destroy temporary, nonapplication-related tables such as those used in SQL*REPORT for intermediate queries.

TEMPORARY USER. Tablespace for sorts, joins, and other operations that require temporary disk space for intermediate operations. If this tablespace is not available, and default tablespace is not set for each user, these tables will be created and dropped in the SYSTEM tablespace, resulting in fragmentation. Additionally, a poorly designed join or overly ambitious SELECT statement could result in filling the SYSTEM area and halting the database.

UNDOTBS. In Oracle9*i* databases created from default templates in the Database Creation Assistant (DBCA), rollback segments are placed in the UNDO tablespace and are now referred to as UNDO segments. Oracle uses automated management of these UNDO segments by default. This UNDOTBS is used by Oracle9*i* to hold UNDO segments.

CWMLITE. This Oracle9*i* tablespace is used to store OLAPSYS schema objects for the new Online Analytical Processing (OLAP) utilities in Oracle9*i* and is created when the default templates in the DBCA are used to create a database.

DRSYS. Used to store CTXUSER and WKSYS schema objects used in advanced indexing options and workspace management utilities and is created when the default templates in the DBCA are used to create a database.

Each application should have its own set of data and index tablespaces. If there are several small applications, you might want to put them in a single large tablespace; but if you can avoid this, it makes application management easier. Each application should also have its own index tablespace. This results in a simple formula for determining the number of tablespaces:

8 + 2 times the number of applications expected

Some applications may require multiple tablespaces, for example where, for performance, you want to separate out large tables from the rest of the application. In one case, a single application generated 13 tablespaces. Most applications aren't as complicated as this and will only require two tablespaces. Of course, the purists will claim each table should be in its own tablespace, but this often is overkill. If you are looking at Oracle Applications installs, there may be over 100 tablespaces configured.

How to size tablespaces is a difficult question to answer because each tablespace will have unique requirements. Here are some general guidelines:

- The SYSTEM tablespace, if you split out the tool tables, should only require 300 to 400 MB of disk space, this has increased dramatically due to increased Java and other stored procedures in the Oracle9*i* system. Under Oracle Application, SYSTEM tablespace can be as large as 2 gigabytes.

- The TOOLS tablespace will depend entirely on the amount of development you expect. At one site with 16 applications being developed, nearly 90 MB were required for the TOOLS tables.
- The ROLLBACK tablespace will again be driven by the number and size of rollback segments you require. The number and size of rollback segments is driven by the number of transactions per rollback segment, the number of users, and the maximum size of nonbatch transactions. With Oracle8*i* and Oracle9*i*, you can create a large rollback segment and leave it offline until it is needed for a large transaction, and then use the SET TRANSACTION USE ROLLBACK SEGMENT command to utilize it after bringing it online. The number of rollback segments is driven by the number of expected transactions and can be estimated by the equation:

NUMBER OF DML TRANSACTIONS / TRANSACTIONS PER ROLLBACK SEGMENT

- The number of transactions will be driven by the number of users and types of database operations they will be doing. In fact, if the Oracle kernel sees a violation of the above formula, it will bring online any available public rollback segments. In Oracle9*i* you should also consider if you wish to use the UNDO tablespace, which takes the place of the rollback segments if it is configured. By default Oracle9*i* sizes the UNDOTBS at 200 megabytes.
- The DEFAULT USER tablespace size will depend upon the number of users you want to assign to it and the estimated size of tables they will be using. In most cases, 10 to 20 MB is sufficient. If you expect heavy usage, assign quotas to each user.
- The TEMPORARY USER tablespace should be up to twice the size of your largest table, if you use RULE-based optimization and up to four times the size of your largest table for COST-based; it is also dependent on the number of users and the size of sorts or joins they perform. An improperly designed join between large tables can quickly fill a temporary area. For example, an unrestricted outside join of 2,000 row tables will result in a 1-million-row temporary sort table. If those rows are each several hundred bytes long, there goes your temporary space. Unfortunately, there isn't much that can be done other than to train developers or ad hoc query generators not to do unrestricted joins of large tables. If a temporary tablespace gets filled, the users who are assigned to it cannot perform operations requiring temporary space; or, worse, the temporary space may be taken from the SYSTEM area. There is a valid argument for having several temporary areas if you have a large number of users. In one instance, a 100-MB temporary tablespace was completely filled by a single multitable outside join using DECODE statements.
- The CWMLITE and DRSYS tablespaces are usually sized at around 20 megabytes by default.
- If you have the disk space, placing the TEMPORARY USER tablespaces on disk assets of their own will improve query and report performance due to reduction of disk contention, especially for large reports or queries using disk sorts.

What Are the SGA Issues? As discussed previously, in UNIX, the parameters controlling shared memory usage are the limiting factor. In any case, before you create the database, serious thought has to be given to how much you expect the SGA to grow over the next year. Overspecifying the shared memory parameters on a UNIX platform will not do any harm and may save you and the system administrator some headaches.

The size of the SGA is controlled by buffer sizes, and the buffer sizes are controlled by the database block size, which is specified at database creation and cannot be changed without rebuilding the database in Oracle8*i* but can vary on Oracle9*i*. This usually defaults to 8 KB. I usually suggest at least 8 KB, although in some cases 16 KB works best. If in doubt, set the block size to the largest supported on your system.

The five major components of the SGA are the database buffers, log buffers, LARGE POOL, Java pool, and the shared pool. The SGA also contains the redo log buffers. The ideal situation would be to size the SGA to hold the entire database in memory. For small systems, this may be a real situation; for most, it is not feasible. However, with the new 64-bit architectures 16 exabytes of storage can be directly addressed; only a few exabytes can hold all of the world's printed, videotaped, and recorded data, so in the future entire databases will reside easily in memory. Therefore, you must decide how much to allocate.

In many cases, especially for development databases, this will be a rough SWAG (scientific wild-assed guess). For systems already designed with detailed data storage estimates, it may be better defined. A general rule of thumb for a pure Oracle system (no other applications) is 50 to 60 percent of available RAM for your SGA. Note that for small databases this may be overkill. In general, I have found that sizing the SGA data block buffers (the product of DB_BLOCK_SIZE and DB_BLOCK_BUFFERS) to 1/50 to 1/100 of the total physical size of the database is a good starting point. Under Oracle8*i* and Oracle9*i*, the new default sizes in the supplied sample initialization file are more realistic, but in general will still be too small for most production databases, so use them with caution.

Oracle provides tools to analyze buffer performance. Unfortunately, they can only be used once a system is operating and running under a normal load; so for our discussion of installation, they are useless.

If you have no idea whatsoever, make the buffer area at least 60 to 100 MB or so (you will usually outgrow the Oracle default rather quickly) for a database that is near 1 gigabyte in total physical size, and up to 400 MB for one that is around 20 gigabytes in size. For databases smaller than 1 gigabyte physical size, the Oracle defaults may be usable. Make the shared pool at least 50 to 100 MB.

We will discuss the actual parameters in the INIT.ORA file that control SGA size when we get to the section on tuning. What you need to know right now is that the default initialization file provided by Oracle has three default ranges: way-too-small, too-small, and small. Unless you are creating a database that will be less than 1 gigabyte in physical size, even the large parameters in the example initialization file are woefully inadequate.

One thing to remember: If you overspecify the shared memory size on UNIX, you may get into a situation known as *swapping*. This is where all or part of your application is swapped out to disk because physical memory just isn't large enough to hold it all. Needless to say, this has a very negative impact on performance. Usually, overspecification of the SGA on UNIX will lead to not being able to start the database.

What Is the Number of Users—Administrative, Developer, and Application?
We've already looked at the responsibilities of the DBA or administrative user; now we need to answer what are the normal responsibilities of the other user types? According to the Oracle8 Server Administrator's Guide, they are:

Developmental Responsibilities

1. Design and develop database applications.
2. Design the database structure for an application.
3. Estimate storage requirements for an application.
4. Specify modifications of the database structures for an application.
5. Keep the database administrator informed of required changes.
6. Tune the application (not the database!) during development.
7. Establish an application's security requirements during development.

Application User's Responsibilities

1. Enter, modify, and delete data, where permitted.
2. Generate reports of data.

All Oracle databases have three types of users: administrative, developmental, and application. As their names imply, administrative users administer and maintain the database itself; developmental users develop applications and systems; and application users use the developed applications and systems.

These three types of users have different needs. The space and disk needs of a developer are usually greater than those of an application user. A developer system may get by with a smaller SGA because, generally speaking, developers will work with a subset of all the data expected, while a production database user will need a larger SGA because the data set is much larger. Administrative users usually have the same quotas as a developmental user, but their privileges are greater.

The number of each of these types of users will tell you about required SGA sizing, disk resource requirements, and required system memory.

What Is the Number and Placement of Control Files?   Control files are probably the smallest and most important files in the Oracle system. They contain the following data:

- Names of the database and redo log files
- Timestamp of database creation

- Begin/end of rollback segments
- Checkpoint information
- Current redo log file sequence number

This data is critical for database operation, and at least one control file is required for database startup. There are methods for rebuilding a control file, but it is much easier to maintain—or rather have Oracle maintain—multiple copies of the control file.

Oracle recommends two copies on separate disk resources. For OFA compliance, three are required. Obviously, if they are on the same platter or are placed in the same stripe set, the same disaster can waste all of them; therefore, they should be placed on different physical disk arrays if possible. More than three copies is a bit paranoid, but if it makes you feel safer, have as many as you wish; only one usable, current file is required for startup.

What Is the Number and Placement of Redo Logs?   Oracle requires at least two groups of one redo log. If you are archiving, three are suggested. In a number of installations, up to six or more have been defined. If you do a lot of update activity and have numerous users, more than six may be required. When a log fills, the next one in the queue is opened, and the previously active log is marked for archive (if you have archiving enabled). The logs are archived on a first-in, first-out basis, so, depending on the speed that the log groups can be written to disk or tape, more than one log group may be waiting to be archived. One redo log group is used at a time, with multiple users writing into it at the same time. The size of the redo logs in a group depends on one critical piece of data: How much data can you afford to lose on a system crash?

You see, the smaller the log group size, the more often it is written to disk and the less data (time-wise) is lost. The larger the log group size, the less often it is written to disk and the more data (time-wise) is lost. For instance, if your log groups are filling every 10 minutes, then you may lose 10 minutes' worth of data should the disk(s) crash that holds that redo log group's files. It has been demonstrated on an active system that a 100-MB redo log group may only last a few seconds. In an inactive or read-only-type situation, a 100-MB redo log may last for hours. It is all dependent on how the database is being used and the size of the redo log group. Remember, a group of three 100-MB redo logs is actually treated as only a single 100-MB redo log (the other two files are mirrors). If you mirror redo logs by placing the group members on separate disks (not just on separate file systems; be sure it is separate physical disks), then your ability to recover from a disk array or controller crash increases manyfold.

You have to balance the needs for restoration and minimal data loss against time to recover data. Obviously, if you have archiving happening every minute and your normal workday is eight hours, you will have 480 logs written to disk daily. Over a five-day workweek, this turns into 2,400 files. If you have to restore from a crash or other disaster, you may have to apply all of these to your last backup to bring the database current to the time of the crash. In one case, a DBA had to apply 9,000-plus files to recover his system because he hadn't looked at how often his redo logs were archiving.

Needless to say, he pays more attention now. The minimum size for redo log groups is 50 KB. By default, the Oracle9i DBCA creates a 100 megabyte redo log

In Chapter 12 on database tuning, we will discuss how to determine if you have a sufficient number of redo log groups and how to optimize your archive process.

What Is the Number and Placement of Rollback Segments?   Another item controlled by the number of data manipulation language users (INSERT, UPDATE, and DELETE commands) and the transaction load on the system is the number of rollback segments. The formula, as stated before, is:

NUMBER OF DML TRANSACTIONS / NUMBER OF TRANSACTIONS PER ROLLBACK SEGMENT

This will yield the number of rollback segments needed. They should be sized to handle the maximum expected data manipulation language (DML) transaction.

The placement of rollback segments is decided based upon resource contention prevention. Put them where they won't cause contention with other Oracle files. Transactions are spread across all active rollback segments. Usually, it is a good idea to locate the rollback segments in a tablespace or tablespaces dedicated to rollback segments. This allows the DBA to easily manage these resources.

The size of rollback segments is based upon three factors:

- Average number of simultaneous active DML transactions.
- Average number of bytes modified per transaction.
- Average duration of each transaction.

The longer a transaction, the larger the rollback segment it will require. One is automatically created when the database is created. This initial rollback segment is for SYSTEM tablespace use. If you have plans for more than one tablespace, you will need a second rollback segment. Of course, this second segment will have to be created in the SYSTEM tablespace. Once the ROLLBACK tablespace is defined, and additional rollback segments are created, the second rollback segment in the SYSTEM tablespace should be placed offline or dropped.

Each rollback segment must be created with a MINEXTENTS value of at least 2 and a MAXEXTENTS based on the number of rollback segments in the tablespace, the size specified for each extent, and the size of the ROLLBACK tablespace. Each of the extents should be the same size; that is, *initial* should equal *next*, and *pctincrease* has to be set to 0 percent (look at the STORAGE statement specification in Appendix B in the download area for an explanation of these parameters). If you intend to do large batch transactions, it may be advisable to create a large rollback segment used only for batch operations. This single large segment can be left offline until needed, then activated and used for a specific transaction using the SET TRANSACTION USE ROLLBACK SEGMENT command.

If you opt to use the UNDO tablespace in Oracle9i, rather than the traditional rollback segments, make sure you size it according to the required transaction load and the desired retention time for flashback queries (more on this in the section on tuning undo tablespaces in Chapter 12).

Will the Tools Be Linked Single-Task or Be Independent (Two-Task)? This question deals with the way the Oracle tools, such as SQLLOADER, IMP, or EXP, address the Oracle kernel. See Figure 1.1 for a graphical demonstration of the concept of single-task versus a two- or multitask structure.

Single Task

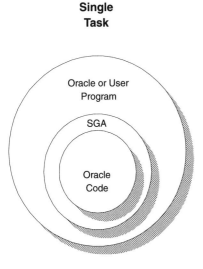

NOTE: For multitier applications additional software or API layers may be present.

Two or Independent Task

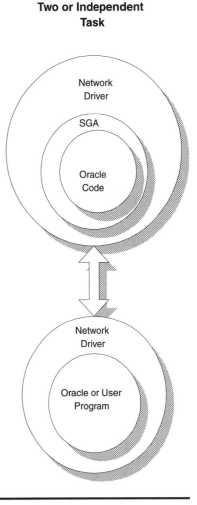

FIGURE 1.1   Single-task versus two-task or multitask structure.

If the tools are linked single-task, they address a specific node's Oracle kernel by default. To access another node or another system, a connect string must be used (connect strings will be covered in Chapter 14, *Managing in a Distributed Environment*). This mode is useful for a single-node database situation and saves on memory and task usage. This is generally used where a client/server architecture is not used. It has been demonstrated that relinking some tools single-task, such as the import and export utilities, will increase their performance by up to 30 percent.

TIP Single-task linking will be allowed only in preOracle9*i* releases, so plan now to remove it from use.

If the tools are linked independent, or two-task, a connect string must always be used. It is called "two-task" because the tools must run as one task while the Oracle executable runs as another. Two-task is generally used in a client/server situation. This allows the following benefits:

- Client machines to perform CPU-intensive tasks, offloading these tasks from the server.
- Movement of tools from one environment to another (such as from a development area to a production one) without relinking.
- The Oracle8*i* server to be relinked without relinking all of the tools.
- Two-task tools can reduce throughput, depending on the machine they are installed upon. The DBA needs to consider the costs versus the benefits when deciding whether to use single- or two-task-linked tools.

Will This Database Be Shared between Multiple Instances? A shared database (RAC) allows a number of instances to access the same database. This allows the DBA to spread the SGA usage for a large database system across the CPUs of several machines. The CPUs must be part of the same CLUSTER. In previous releases this was also known as a *parallel* or *shared database;* in Oracle9*i*, it's known as *Real Application Clusters,* or RAC.

In order to use this option on UNIX, the disks that are shared must be configured as raw devices. This requires what is known as a *loosely coupled system*; a set of clustered Sun, HP, or Windows machines is an excellent example. This parallel server mode has the following characteristics:

- An Oracle instance can be started on each node in the loosely coupled system.
- Each instance has its own SGA and set of detached processes.
- All instances share the same database files and control files.
- Each instance has its own set of redo log groups.
- The database files, redo log files, and control files reside on one or more disks of the loosely coupled system.

- All instances can execute transactions concurrently against the same database, and each instance can have multiple users executing transactions concurrently.
- Row locking is preserved.

Since the instances must share locks, a lock process is started, called LCKn. In addition, the GC_ parameters must be configured in the INIT.ORA files. In Oracle8, Oracle Corporation supplies the required DLM. Under Oracle9i RAC, there are many changes, which we will discuss in Chapter 14, *Distributed Database Management*.

If the answer to the question, Will this database be shared between multiple instances?, is yes, the DBA needs to know how many instances will be sharing this database. This parameter will be used to determine INIT.ORA parameters. This answer is also important when determining the number and type of rollback segments. Rollback segments can either be private and only used by a single instance, or public and shared between all instances that access the database.

The DBA will need to know the names for all instances sharing a database. He or she should also know the number of users per instance. Figure 1.2 illustrates the concepts of shared and exclusive mode; Oracle is usually run in exclusive mode. Essentially, exclusive mode is the "normal" mode for Oracle nonshared databases.

Will This Database Be Distributed? A distributed database, as its name implies, has its datafiles spread across several databases in different locations. This may require that there be DBAs in these distributed locations. The major consideration will be network reliability. This is especially true when two-phase commit is used. Under two-phase commit, if one of your distributed database nodes goes down, you can't update tables that undergo two-phase commit with that node's data.

According to the Oracle9i Distributed Database Administrators Guide (Oracle Corporation, 2001) the DBA needs to consider the following items in a distributed environment:

- The number of transactions posted from each location.
- The amount of data (portion of table) used by each node.
- The performance characteristics and reliability of the network.
- The speed of various nodes and the capacities of its disks.
- The criticality of success if a node or link is down.
- The need for referential integrity between tables.

A distributed database appears to the user to be one database, but is in fact a collection of database tables in separate databases spread across several locations. These databases are, of course, on different computer systems that are connected by a network.

The computers, or nodes in a distributed database environment, will act as both clients and servers depending upon whether they are requesting data from another database on a different node or providing data to a different node as it is requested.

Each site is autonomous, that is, managed independently. The databases are distinct, separate entities that are sharing their data. The benefits of site autonomy are:

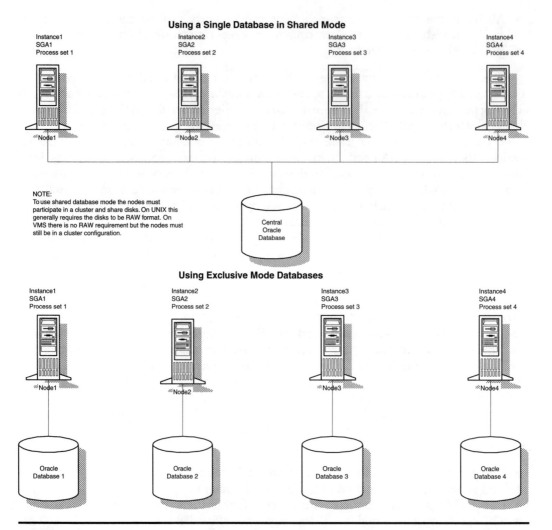

FIGURE 1.2   Shared- versus exclusive-mode databases.

- The various databases cooperating in the distributed environment can mirror the local organization's needs and desires. This is especially useful at sites where there may be two organizations that need to share some, but not all, data. An example would be two aerospace companies cooperating on the space platform. They may need to share data about design but not want to share financial information.
- Local data is controlled by the local database administrator. This limits the responsibility to a manageable level.

- Failure at one node is less likely to affect other nodes. The global system is at least partially available as long as a single node of the database is active. No single failure will halt all processing or be a performance bottleneck. For example, if the Pittsburgh node goes down, it won't affect the Omaha node, as long as Omaha doesn't require any of Pittsburgh's data.
- Failure recovery is on a per-node basis.
- A data dictionary exists for each local database.
- Nodes can upgrade software independently, within reason.

As DBA you will need to understand the structures and limits of the distributed environment if you are required to maintain a distributed environment. The features of a two-phase commit, as well as naming resolution and the other distributed topics, will be covered in Chapter 14. Figure 1.3 shows a distributed database structure.

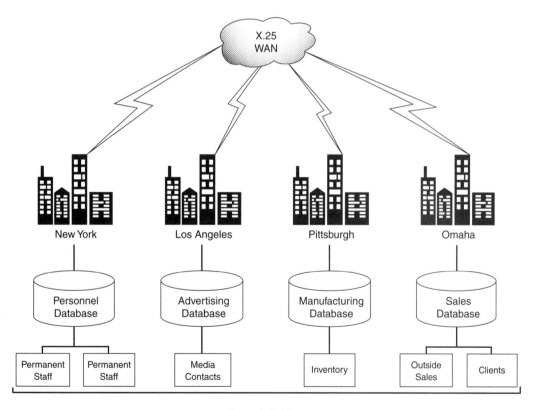

Example Tables

FIGURE 1.3   Example of a distributed database.

1.8 INSTALLING ORACLE

It is strongly suggested that the DBA use the installation guide provided by Oracle for his or her own release of the operating system in use. The following procedure should be regarded only as a general set of guidelines; it is not intended to replace the installation procedures provided by Oracle.

Example Installation of Oracle9*i* Using the Linux Operating System

Before you can successfully install and operate Oracle on the Linux operating system, you must be sure that you meet all the required prerequisites to do so. These prerequisites are specified in the Oracle9*i* installation guide for Linux, which is available online at technet.oracle.com. Always check the latest version of the operating guide, as these requirements may change from release to release and, of course, between different operating systems. Table 1.2 shows the suggested kernel parameters for the UNIX and other systems for Oracle9*i* release 9.0.1, as of 8/13/2001.

As you can see from examining the values for different operating systems in Table 1.2, many parameters are similar, but some vary greatly. Operating systems such as NT, W2K (Windows 2000), and AIX have fewer tunable parameters because they do automatic tuning of their internals.

TABLE 1.2 Sample Changes to UNIX System Shared Memory and Semaphore Parameters

	HP-UX Release	SUN 2.8	Linux 7.1 (SuSE)	Tru64(Compaq)
SHMMAX	0x40000000	4294967295	2147483648	4278190080 (SHM_MAX)
SHMMIN	1	1	1	1024 (SHM_MIN)
SHMSEG	10	10	4096	128 (SHM_SEG)
SHMMNS	1000	1000	256	
SHMMNI	100	100	100	256 (SHM_MNI)
SEMMNI	100	100	100	
SEMMSL		250	100	
SEMOPM			100	
SEMVMX			32767	
MAX_PER_PROC_STACK_SIZE				33554432
PER_PROC_STACK_SIZE				33554432 (no larger than 512MB)

You will need to consult the system administrator or the system specific installation documents to determine how to adjust the parameters on your system. On some, it may be as easy as a change to a configuration file and a reboot; others may require a complete relink and replacement of the kernel executable.

Once the kernel has been properly baseline-tuned, you need to examine the available disk assets and determine which will be used for Oracle. On UNIX or Linux, you (or the system administrator) will need to create mount points to structure the Oracle file systems the way you want. On other systems, such as NT or W2K, you will need to allocate directories for use by Oracle.

Following the disk asset setup, you are ready to install Oracle. This is usually accomplished from one of two possible sources: either you have a distribution CD set or you have downloaded the compressed image files from the technet.oracle.com or Oracle store Web sites.

If you have the distribution CD set, you simply mount the first CD in the CD-ROM drive and use the appropriate command to execute the runInstaller program. The runInstaller program on the UNIX systems will normally be located in the install/os_typ directory on the CD-ROM, where the os_type is the name of the operating system (such as Sun or Linux) and may include a version designation. Do not, on UNIX systems, use the "cd" command to place your user in the top level of the CD-ROM directory structure. The Oracle9*i* and Oracle8*i* (starting with 8.1.7) installation involves multiple CD-ROMs, if you are located in the top-level directory when you launch the runInstaller program, it will lock this directory and you will not be able to unmount the CD-ROM to change to the second or third CDs as requested by the installation procedure. Instead, stay in the Oracle users home directory and simply issue the full path command to run the installer, for example:

```
$ ./cdrom/install/linux/runInstaller.sh
```

The installer will welcome you to the Oracle Universal Installer, or OUI for short. An example of this is shown in Figure 1.4.

If you need to deinstall any older versions of Oracle, you can choose the Deinstall Products button or just choose to see the installed products (if any). Otherwise, choose the Next button. The next screen displayed will be the file source and Oracle Home selection screen. If the defaults are correct, choose Next; or make the needed changes and then select Next. This is shown in Figure 1.5.

The next screen lists the three possible installation options: Oracle9*i* Database 9.0.1.0.0, Oracle9*i* Client 9.0.1.0.0, or Oracle9*i* Management and Integration 9.0.1.0.0. The Oracle9*i* Database 9.0.1.0.0 option installs the complete database suite, the client, and the Management and Integration suites. The Oracle9*i* Client 9.0.1.0.0 option installs the enterprise management tools, networking services, utilities, development tools, and basic client software. The Oracle9*i* 9.0.1.0.0 Management and Integration option installs the management server, management tools, Oracle Internet Directory, Oracle Integration Server, networking servers, utilities, and basic client software. Select the option you desire, then select the next button. This screen is shown in Figure 1.6.

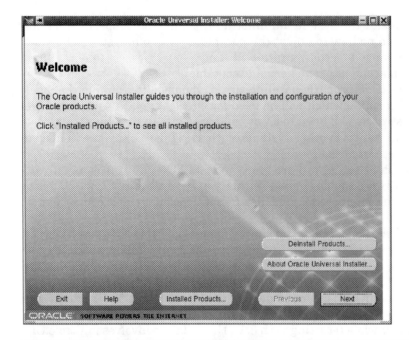

FIGURE 1.4   Oracle Universal Installer Welcome screen.

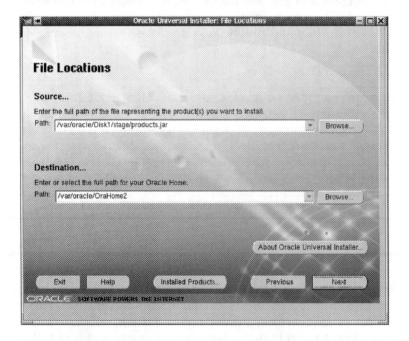

FIGURE 1.5   Oracle Universal Installer File Locations screen.

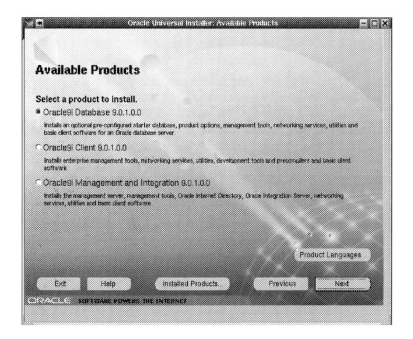

FIGURE 1.6   Oracle Universal Installer Available Products screen.

The next screen shows the options for the types of database that can be installed: Enterprise, Standard, or Custom. Enterprise allows access to virtually all options (except RAC); Standard has a restricted set of options; and Custom allows the options installed to be user selectable. Choose the type of install desired and select the Next button. For our example install we will choose the Enterprise Install. Figure 1.7 shows this screen.

The next screen shows the Database Configuration options. The database configuration options are General Purpose, Transaction Processing, Data Warehouse, Customized, or Software Only. Select the option you wish and then select Next. The Software Only option is the only one where no database is installed; use it when migration of an existing database will be performed as a part of the Oracle9*i* installation. This is shown in Figure 1.8.

The next screen of the installation routine allows you to specify a name for the database if you choose to install a new database. Specify the name and domain name for your database; the program will strip off the domain to specify a system identifier (SID) for the database. The normal format for the domain is sid.domain. Select the Next button when you are satisfied with the SID and domain specification. Figure 1.9 shows this screen.

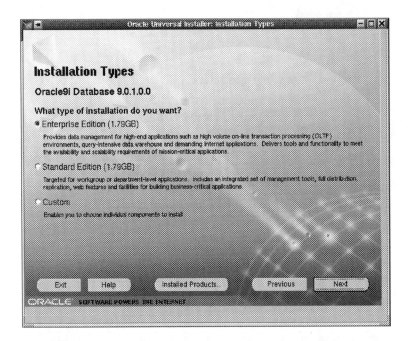

FIGURE 1.7   Oracle Universal Installer Installation Types screen.

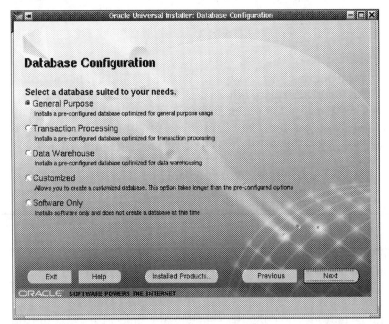

FIGURE 1.8   Oracle Universal Installer Database Configuration screen.

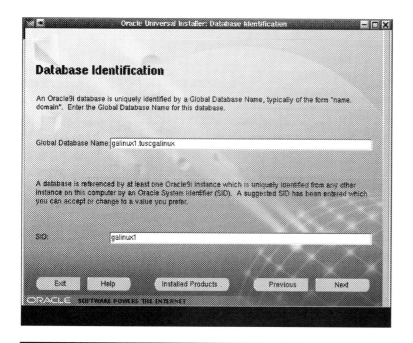

FIGURE 1.9   Oracle Universal Installer Database Identification screen.

Next, you will choose the character set to use in the database that you will be creating (if you choose to create a database). The selections available are:

- Use the default from the settings of the Operations System.
- Use Unicode (UTF8) as the setting (if you wish to support multiple languages in the database you are creating choose this one).
- Choose one of the common character sets from a drop down list.

If your character set of choice is not shown in the drop-down list, you must use the Previous button, then choose Custom database to get a wider selection. When you have made your choice of the database character set, select the Next button. This screen is shown in Figure 1.10.

The next screen allows you to enter the location of the Java Developer Kit (JDK). You must have at least version JDK1.1.8, which is available from www.blackdown.com or the SUN Web site. The standard location for a normal installation of the JDK is /usr/lib/jkd1.1.8; if yours is different, make sure to enter it properly. If you are not sure where your JDK is located, ask your system administrator or start another terminal window and use the *find* command from the root directory to locate it for example:

```
$ cd /
$ find . -name jdk* -print
```

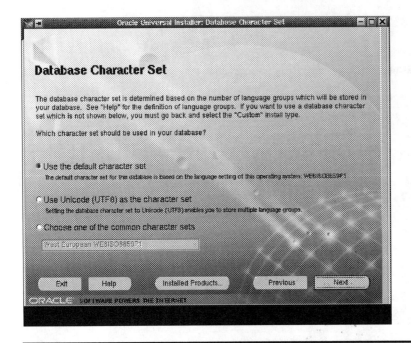

FIGURE 1.10   Oracle Universal Installer Database Character Set screen.

These commands should give you the full path location of the JDK on UNIX or Linux. On Windows, use the *find* drop-down item on the File menu. The JDK screen is shown in Figure 1.11.

The next screen shows a summary of what you will be installing if you proceed. If everything looks correct, select the Install button and installation will commence. This summary screen is shown in Figure 1.12.

The install progress screen (Figure 1.13) will be shown next. It will display a dialog that shows which options and products are being installed and which actions are being performed. Once all install operations are complete, the Setup Privileges dialog box (Figure 1.14) will be displayed. At this point, you will need to start a second display in UNIX or Linux and log in as the root user. In the ORACLE_HOME location, a root.sh script will be created; this script must be run before continuing the installation. Once the script has been run as root, click on the OK button to continue the installation.

The Configuration Tools screen is shown next. It shows the status of the various tools used to configure NET8/9, the Web server and the Oracle database. This is shown in Figure 1.15. When the database configuration assistant starts, you will see a status window showing the results of copying the Oracle base datafiles into your environment. These files are used as a "seed" database to quickly start a new instance. Rather than create a new database, load the database with the various configuration scripts. Next Oracle copies the basic tablespaces from compressed jar files to your system, then uses

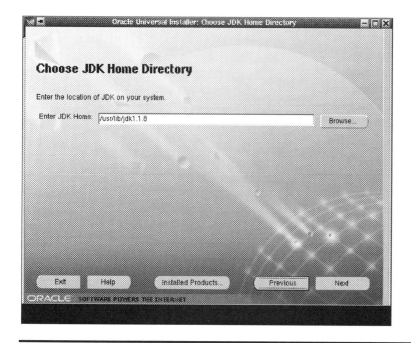

FIGURE 1.11   Oracle Universal Installer JDK Home Directory screen.

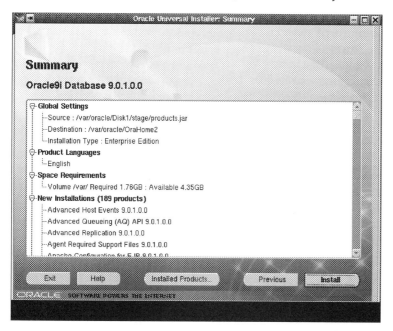

FIGURE 1.12   Oracle Universal Installer Summary screen.

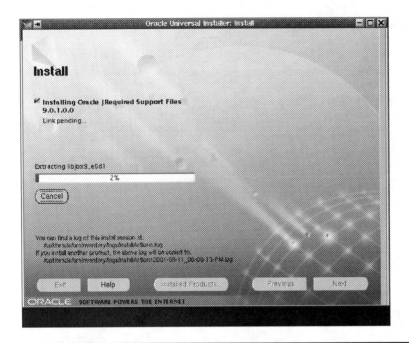

FIGURE 1.13   Oracle Universal Installer Install status screen.

the *control file rebuild* command to give the database the name you have selected. This database configuration assistant is shown in Figure 1.16.

The second screen in the Configuration Assistant allows you to perform password management and selective account lock/unlock tasks against the new database. This is a welcome new feature, as previous Oracle systems set the passwords on critical Oracle accounts the same as the user name and gave little guidance on how to reset the passwords. The password/account management screen is shown in Figure 1.17.

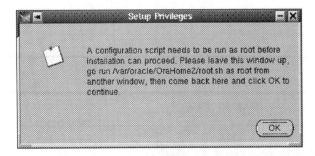

FIGURE 1.14   Oracle Universal Installer Setup Privileges screen.

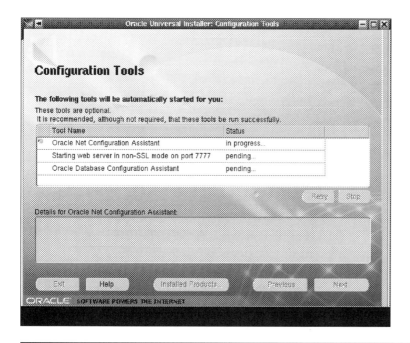

FIGURE 1.15   Oracle Universal Installer Configuration Tools status screen.

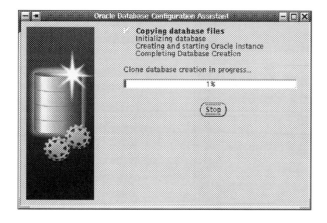

FIGURE 1.16   Database Configuration Assistant file copy screen.

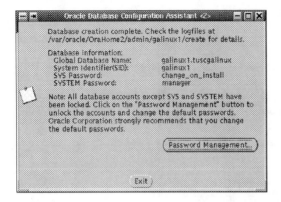

FIGURE 1.17 Database Configuration Assistant password management screen.

If you choose to change the passwords and lock configuration for the default Oracle accounts (which is strongly recommended), select the Password Management button on the screen in Figure 1.17. Selection of this option will display the Password Management dialog box that contains a table of the default accounts, their lock status, and the entry points for their new passwords. Fill in the password management/lock table as needed for your system; then select the OK button. This screen is shown in Figure 1.18.

Once the default account passwords and lock status have been updated, the installation completes, marked by display of the End of Installation screen, shown in Figure 1.19. Select the Exit button from this screen to return to the command line.

User Name	Lock Account?	New Password	Confirm Password
SYS		****	****
SYSTEM		****	****
DBSNMP		****	****
AURORAJISUTILITY$		****	****
AURORAORBUNAUT...		****	****
SCOTT		****	****
OSE$HTTP$ADMIN		****	********
OUTLN	✔		
LBACSYS	✔		
OE	✔		
QS_CS	✔		
QS_CB	✔		
QS_CBADM	✔		

FIGURE 1.18 Oracle Password Management screen.

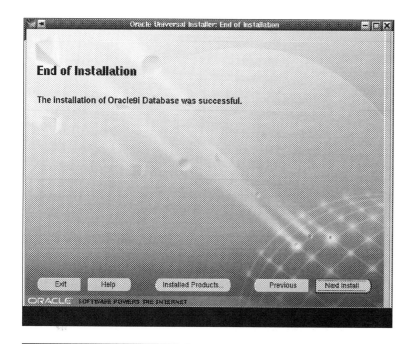

FIGURE 1.19   Oracle Universal Installer End of Installation screen.

The next section of this chapter deals with migration from previous versions of Oracle to Oracle9*i*.

1.9 MIGRATION TO ORACLE9*I*

Once the installation of the new Oracle9*i* software is complete, what do we, as DBAs and application developers, do? We migrate. Of course, we should take the proper steps to ensure that we migrate like graceful geese flying across a sunset rather than lemmings dashing forward over a cliff (see Figure 1.20). Naturally, as DBAs, we prefer the graceful flight across the sunset.

Planning Migration

How do we accomplish this graceful migration? Planning. Planning is the only way to minimize points of possible failure in your migration path from Oracle 6.x, Oracle 7.x, or Oracle8/8*i* to Oracle9*i*. In this section, I will attempt to provide a logical framework for planning your migration and hopefully shine a light on the pitfalls that you should avoid along the way.

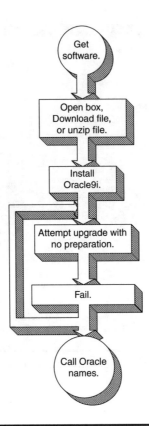

FIGURE 1.20   Usual migration path.

Have you known someone who immediately takes new items (VCRs, computers, TVs) right out of the box, plugs them in, and never reads instructions? Later, they fret because the blankity-blank item won't do what they want (or, more likely, they don't know how to make it do what they want). They didn't prepare to migrate to their new appliance. This preparation should have involved reviewing the installation and operation manuals, performing controlled tests of new features, and then finally bringing the new appliance into full use (see Figure 1.21). The same is true with Oracle9*i*.

Preparing to Migrate

Invariably, other "experts" (using the term loosely) and I will be asked hundreds of questions about installation and migration to Oracle9*i* that could have been answered if the people asking the questions had read the documentation and tested new features

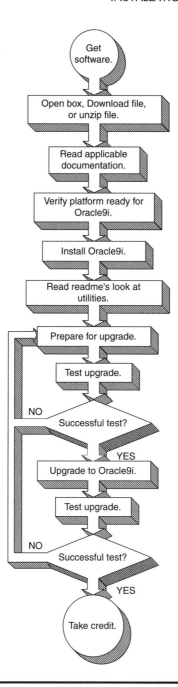

FIGURE 1.21 Proper migration path.

before implementation. The point is, you have to take the time to study the new features sections of the manuals, read the readme.doc, and review utility scripts for "hidden" changes.

Back when the Oracle8 migration was the rage, I mentioned the compatible parameter in one of my columns. A couple of weeks later, Oracle announced a spate of bugs that related to the parameter. Were the two related? Probably. It demonstrated that people who thought they had "migrated" to a new version of Oracle hadn't. Why? Because of the setting of the parameter, they hadn't even tested the new features that depended on a new redo log format! Reading the documentation before they migrated would have prevented this.

How about the person who buys one of those great new sport utility vehicles only to discover it won't fit in their garage? Obviously, they didn't check available resources before "migrating" to a new vehicle. Oracle9i will take up to 150 percent more space for initial load than Oracle8 and up to three times the space of Oracle 7.3. Do you have enough free space? You may want to run both an Oracle9i and an Oracle8i (or earlier release) system in parallel. Do you have enough memory (9i may require twice to three times as much memory as previous releases, 512 megabytes on Linux, for example) or enough CPU? You will require at least 50 meg of free space in an 8i SYSTEM tablespace to upgrade to 9i, or the upgrade will fail. You may also want to take note that the default installation of an Oracle9i database contains a SYSTEM tablespace that is near 350 megabytes in size with only 40 Kilobytes free, you should plan your sizing accordingly.

Getting back to our geese versus lemmings migration analogy: Which chose the better migration path (overlooking hunters in this case . . .)? Don't begin your migration without a clear plan of how to get from your Oracle8i or earlier instance to your Oracle9i instance. Decide on your path, preferably one that doesn't lead you over a cliff! Review the possible methods to migrate your system; choose the best for your situation, and then plan, plan, plan! In Oracle9i migration, you have the choice between export and import, the Data Migration GUI tool, and the migration command-line utility. Of course, there is also the CTAS method, but that is only applicable to real S-and-M fanatics. In a 6.x version database, you must first migrate to Oracle7.3.x and then migrate the 7.3.x database into 9i. In a 7.3.x to 9i, all of the methods are applicable; however, in an 8.1.x to 9i, only the Data Migration Assistant, export and import, unload, and SQLLOADER or CTAS are available. Figures 1.22 through 1.25 show these migration paths.

Finally, how do you know your migration was successful? Do you have a test plan? Did you evaluate your existing system prior to migration to check its performance characteristics? Do you have a standard set of test cases to run against the old database and the new? How will you know that the system is functioning correctly after the migration is "complete?"

Test the Migration Process

I bet the Donner party wished they could have tested their migration plan; and I'll bet the lemmings that dashed off the cliff into the sea did as well. If at all possible, even if

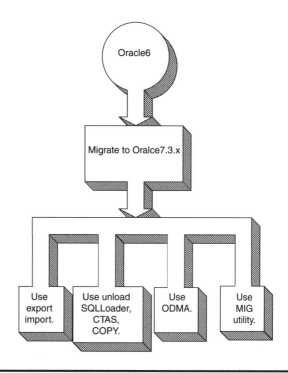

FIGURE 1.22   Oracle6 migration paths.

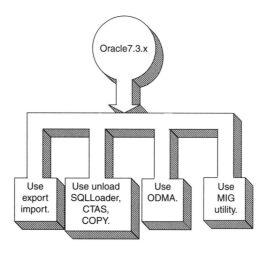

FIGURE 1.23   Oracle7 migration paths.

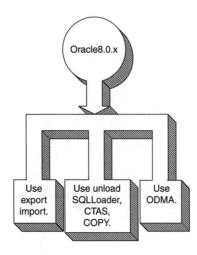

FIGURE 1.24   Oracle8 migration paths.

it is on a small database that you create specifically for the test (in fact, this is the best way), test your migration path. Repeat the test until you are sure exactly what you are doing. I know the bosses will be yelling if you are a bit late with the production migration, but I'll bet the Donner party wished they had been late for their date with history. Hurrying to meet a schedule is probably the best path to meet disaster I know of. When we rush, we forget important steps, overlook potential problems, and just do stupid things.

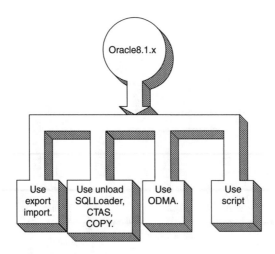

FIGURE 1.25   Oracle8*i* migration paths.

Test the Migrated Test Instance

If you are lucky enough to have the space available to do a nonproduction test migration, be sure to have test plans available to verify that what you ended up with is at least as good as what you started with. Find the causes of any anomalous behavior and fix them before you spend all weekend migrating your production database only to have it malfunction—when the boss is looking of course.

Protect Your Retreat Path

Damn the torpedoes! Full speed ahead! May be fine for Naval engagements but it is no way to migrate an Oracle instance. Protect your retreat path by ensuring you have a complete backup of your Oracle8*i* or earlier release instance.

Ensure you parse out enough time to allow multiple reinstalls and migrations as needed. If you plan the time you need to the nearest second, chances are you won't make your schedule. I'm not saying use the Scottie method (for those non-*Star Trek* aficionados, Scottie was the chief engineer on the Star Ship Enterprise; he would always pad his repair estimates by a factor of 3 or 4, then deliver ahead of schedule). Better to finish early than to have everyone breathing down your neck because you didn't meet your schedule.

Again, cut a full backup or a full export of your source database. I cannot stress this point enough. At worst, having a full backup wastes some disk or tape space for a while; at best, it will save your hide from falling over the cliff with the lemmings.

Prepare the source database as completely as possible. Remove unneeded tables, views, and users. Do space management (why take problems with you?). Consolidate multiple datafiles, or, conversely, split up datafiles that are too big to perform properly. Tune your source as well as you can and have it running at tip-top performance.

Take Flight! (or Fall off the Cliff): Migrate the Source Database

Following the pretested methodology, migrate the source database to its new Oracle9*i* home. Immediately after the migration completes successfully, shut down and perform a complete cold backup. This gives you a starting point should something go awry with subsequent testing. An export will do nearly as well; but don't use a hot backup, because a hot backup will not afford full recoverability at this stage of migration! The backup should contain all datafiles, control files, redo logs, parameter files, and SQL scripts used to build any of the database objects.

The Three Ts: Tune, Tweak, and Test the New Database

Using the knowledge you gained from your thorough review of the documents, readme files, and utility scripts, tune and tweak the new Oracle9*i* instance to optimum performance. Once the database is tuned, test using your predeveloped test cases.

What Next?

Once the database is migrated to the Oracle9*i* instance structure, you need to consider which features you want to implement (after all, if you didn't want the new features, why migrate?) and how you are going to implement them.

Oracle9*i* offers a plethora of new features, including automated rollback (now called undo) segment administration, multiple block sizes in the SGA, and tablespaces, and the ability to change SGA parameters on the fly. You may be shifting to the new release to overcome bugs that were present in the previous release, or only for specific new features that aren't mentioned here.

I want to make a statement here that I'm sure will have some folks shuddering: If you are completely happy with your application, don't force fit it into these new features. Change for the sake of change is foolish. If there is a good, viable reason to implement these new features, by all means do so, but don't be a lemming and just follow the herd over the cliff. Oracle9*i* will function very well with an Oracle8*i* application resting inside of it. Don't feel that you must convert your applications immediately to the new features. Take some time and get familiar with the ride of the new database, and watch for its quirks before you start pell-mell into conversion.

A Detailed Look at the MIG

No, this isn't a new Russian fighter plane. MIG is the migration utility that Oracle has provided to get your Oracle7 database into an Oracle9*i* database. Essentially, there are two main paths and a rocky third to migrate from Oracle7 to Oracle9*i*. These are:

1. For small instances (not more that a gig or two) export the Oracle7 database, build the Oracle9*i* database and import.
2. For large instances (many gigs), use the MIG or the Oracle Data Migration Assistant (ODMA) facility.
3. For those who like pain, unload all Oracle7 tables into flat files, build the Oracle9*i* database using DDL scripts, use SQL loader to reload data. This would also include CTAS and COPY scenarios.

The MIG path of course involves the use of the MIG utility. Oracle9*i* has changes to virtually all database structures if you are upgrading from a release prior to 8. These include:

- Datafile file headers
- Data dictionary
- Controlfile structure
- Rollback segment structure

The MIG utility, properly used, ensures that the existing Oracle7 structures are altered to the new Oracle9*i* structures. This is a one-way path; once started, the only way to go back to the Oracle7 instance you knew and loved is to recover from the backup or export that you dutifully made prior to starting . . . right?

Let's take a more detailed look at the actual procedure to use the MIG utility.

1. You must start at 7.3.x (or higher) release level of Oracle. A version 6 database must be migrated to at least 7.3.x before it can be converted to Oracle9*i*.
2. Back up the source Oracle database, or perform a complete export.
3. Drop any users or roles named "migrate."
4. Resolve all pending transactions in a distributed environment.
5. Bring all tablespaces online, or make sure they are offline normal or temporary, not immediate. Resolve any save undo situations in tablespaces (see migration manual).
6. Shut down normal (not immediate or abort).
7. Install the Oracle9*i* software. Do not do a "complete" install, as this will attempt to build an Oracle9*i* instance and may damage your existing instance beyond recovery. Do a partial, software-only, install.
8. Install the MIG utility into the Oracle7 ORACLE_HOME by using OUI from X-windows on UNIX or its equivalent on your operating system.
9. Unset the TWO_TASK environmental variable on UNIX, or ORA_DFLT_HOLSTER on VMS.
10. Set the following init.ora parameter (or its equivalent location on your system):

```
ORA_NLS33=$ORACLE_HOME/migrate
```

11. Run the MIG utility on the Oracle7 database according to the directions for your system. This creates an Oracle9*i* data dictionary and a binary convert file. You will need 1.5 times the amount of space that your current dictionary occupies as free space in your SYSTEM tablespace area for the new dictionary. If you aren't sure you have the space, run MIG in CHECK_ONLY mode first. You aren't past the point of no return . . . yet. This step obliterates the Oracle7 catalog views, but you can recover them by doing the following if you need to abandon the migration at this point:

    a. Start up the Oracle7 database in normal mode.
    b. Drop the user "migrate."
    c. Rerun CATALOG.SQL.
    d. If using parallel server, rerun CATPARR.SQL.
    e. If using Symmetric Replication, run CATREP.SQL.

NOTE   This will be a 7.3.4 database if you abandon at this point.

---

12. Remove any obsolete initialization parameters from the databases init<SID>.ora file.

    a. Set compatible to 9.0.0.0 or not at all.
    b. Change the locations specified by the control_files parameter to a new location.

13. Remove the old control files; they will re-re-created.

14. From SQLPLUS, issue these commands: CONNECT INTERNAL and STARTUP NOMOUNT.

15. From SQLPLUS, the DBA issues the ALTER DATABASE CONVERT command on the Oracle9*i* side. This command creates a new controlfile, converts all online file headers to Oracle9*i* format, and mounts the Oracle9*i* instance. This is the point of no return.

16. The DBA issues the ALTER DATABASE OPEN RESETLOGS command on the Oracle9*i* side, which automatically converts all objects and users defined in the new dictionary to Oracle9*i* specifications. It also converts all rollback segments to Oracle9*i* format.

17. Finish converting the catalog to a full Oracle9*i* catalog by running cat9000.sql, usually located in the $ORACLE_HOME/rdbms/admin subdirectory on UNIX. Then run catalog.sql, located in the same place. Finally, run catproc.sql to rebuild the PL/SQL and utility packages. If needed, also run any other cat.sql scripts to install any purchased options as required.

18. Shut down and back up your new Oracle9*i*-ready database.

Using Oracle Data Migration Assistant (ODMA)

The Oracle Data Migration Assistant allows an Oracle8 or 8*i* database to be upgraded to 9*i*. This is considered a release-to-release upgrade, not a migration, according to Oracle support. ODMA is a command-line utility written in Java. This means that a compatible JDK or JRE must be installed. For Linux, this would be jdk118_v3 or jre118_v3 from Blackdown or the equivalent Sun release. I also found that, for Linux, the local LANG variable had to be unset or segmentation faults will occur.

Once all the prerequisites are met, you can run ODMA simply by CD'ing to the Oracle bin directory and typing "ODMA" at the command line (see Figure 1.26).

The screen in Figure 1.27 will be displayed once ODMA configures. Most problems with ODMA come from improper settings for PATH, CLASSPATH, and LD_LIBRARY_PATH. If you have multiple databases, each will be shown on the main screen and you can select the one you wish to update.

In the next screen, you have the opportunity to change initialization files, database password entry, and Oracle home location (see Figure 1.28). Following this screen, the Assistant retrieves database information from your system (see Figure 1.29).

Once the database information is retrieved, the options screen is displayed (see Figure 1.30). The allowed options consist only of the capability to move datafiles and to recompile PL/SQL packages (Figures 1.31 and 1.32). Note that you are limited to only one location to which to move the datafiles.

Once you have selected the two options, the conversion is ready to begin. The Assistant reminds you to back up your database, as shown in Figure 1.33.

Once you either back up your database or skip this screen, you are given a summary screen and one more chance to back out as shown in Figure 1.34.

```
oracle@tuscgalinux:/var/oracle/OraHome2 > DISPLAY=:0.0
oracle@tuscgalinux:/var/oracle/OraHome2 > ps -ef|grep oracle
oracle    2292  2269  0 Jul23 ?        00:00:00 /bin/bash --login /usr/X11R6/bin/kde
oracle    2386     1  0 Jul23 ?        00:00:00 kdeinit: dcopserver --nosid
oracle    2388     1  0 Jul23 ?        00:00:00 kdeinit: klauncher
oracle    2390     1  0 Jul23 ?        00:00:13 kdeinit: kded
oracle    2398     1  0 Jul23 ?        00:00:00 kdeinit: kxmlrpcd
oracle    2401     1  0 Jul23 ?        00:00:00 kdeinit: Running...
oracle    2403     1  0 Jul23 ?        00:00:03 knotify
oracle    2407  2292  0 Jul23 ?        00:00:01 ksmserver --restore
oracle    2408  2401  0 Jul23 ?        00:00:04 kdeinit: kwin -session 1054d0ebe2000097566839700000014220000
oracle    2410     1  0 Jul23 ?        00:00:11 kdeinit: kdesktop
oracle    2413     1  0 Jul23 ?        00:00:45 kdeinit: kicker
oracle    2417     1  0 Jul23 ?        00:00:42 kdeinit: klipper -icon klipper -miniicon klipper
oracle    2418     1  0 Jul23 ?        00:00:00 kdeinit: khotkeys
oracle    2421     1  0 Jul23 ?        00:00:00 kdeinit: kwrited
oracle    2423  2421  0 Jul23 pts/0    00:00:00 /bin/cat
oracle    2425     1  0 Jul23 ?        00:00:00 knotes -session 10508a8e230000976640408000000019500013
oracle    2603     1  0 Jul23 ?        00:00:00 kdesud
oracle    3350  2401  0 Jul23 ?        00:00:39 kdeinit: konsole -icon konsole -miniicon konsole -caption Term
inal
oracle    3351  3350  0 Jul23 pts/1    00:00:00 /bin/bash
oracle   13851     1  0 07:39 ?        00:00:00 /opt/oracle/OraHome1/bin/tnslsnr LISTENER -inherit
oracle   13986  3351  0 08:20 pts/1    00:00:00 sqlplus
oracle   13988 13986  0 08:21 pts/1    00:00:00 /bin/bash
oracle   14058 13988  0 08:43 pts/1    00:00:00 ps -ef
oracle   14059 13988  0 08:43 pts/1    00:00:00 grep oracle
oracle@tuscgalinux:/var/oracle/OraHome2 > odma
oracle@tuscgalinux:/var/oracle/OraHome2 > cd bin
oracle@tuscgalinux:/var/oracle/OraHome2/bin > ld od*
odiemap: file not recognized: File format not recognized
oracle@tuscgalinux:/var/oracle/OraHome2/bin > ls od*
odiemap  odiimap  odisrv  odisrvreg  odma
oracle@tuscgalinux:/var/oracle/OraHome2/bin > ./odma
```

FIGURE 1.26   Example invocation of ODMA.

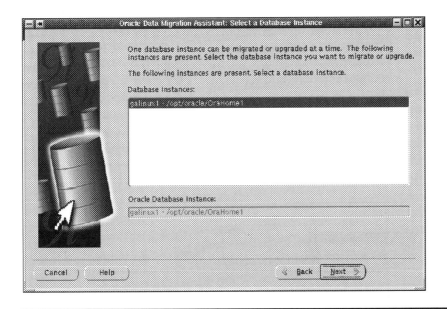

FIGURE 1.27   ODMA main screen.

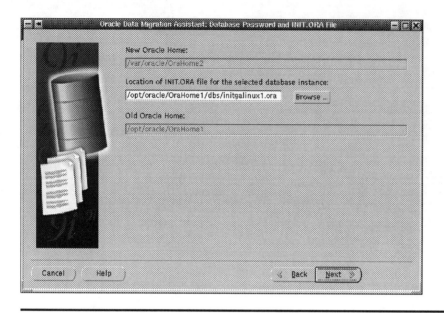

FIGURE 1.28   Home and password screen.

If you choose Yes on the message screen shown in Figure 1.35, the upgrade begins, as shown in Figure 1.36.

Once the upgrade begins, it may take several hours to complete. For example, on a 700-meg, almost-empty 8.1.7 database on SuSE Linux 7.2 with a 450-MgHz CPU, 512-meg memory and a single 30-gig disk, this process took seven hours. Using the U*.sql manual upgrade, this only took three hours; we can only assume that ODMA performs all data block conversions while the manual process waits for dbwr to do them as the blocks are accessed.

Once the upgrade completes, you are given a review screen for log reviews (see Figure 1.37). I had to run the netca (Net Configuration Assistant) to convert my tnsnames.ora and listener.ora before my Java application could connect using JDBC. Just to show you I got it running, Figure 1.38 shows an SQLPLUS startup in the new 9.0.1 instance. You can see my Java application running in Figure 1.39.

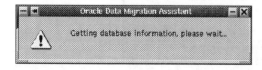

FIGURE 1.29   Message stating database information is being retrieved.

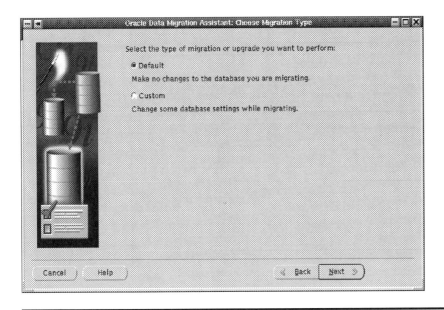

FIGURE 1.30   Choosing between Custom or Default upgrade.

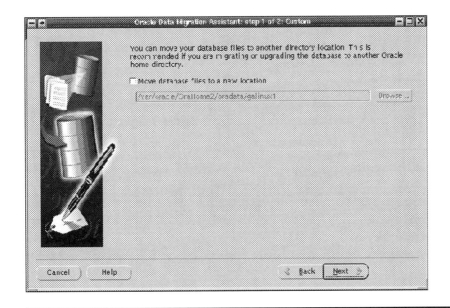

FIGURE 1.31   Moving database files to a new location.

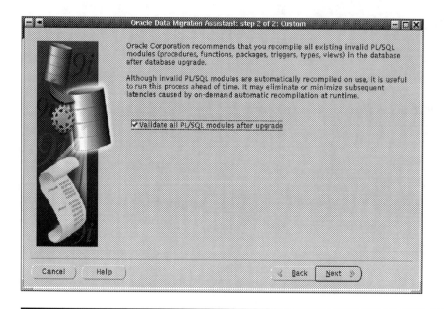

FIGURE 1.32   Recompile PL/SQL modules.

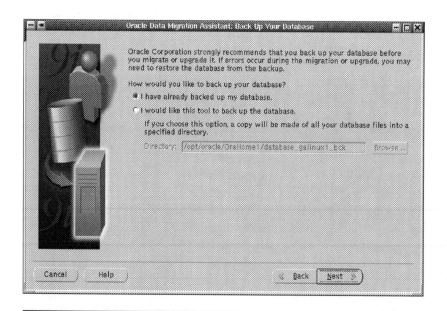

FIGURE 1.33   One more chance to backup.

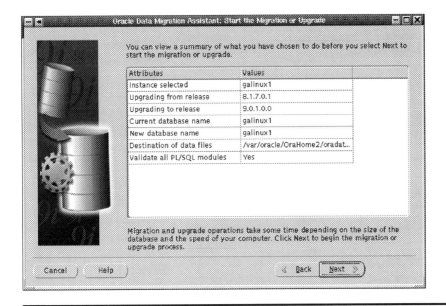

FIGURE 1.34   Summary and last chance to back out.

Pitfalls to Avoid

So what about the pitfalls? What are they? Honestly, it would be impossible to tell you all the possible points of failure, but most will be resource-related, such as not enough space. Let's look at a short list of possible points of failure:

- You don't have enough space in the SYSTEM tablespace when using MIG or ODMA to migrate. The MIG or ODMA will complain and abort if it doesn't have the space to create the new dictionary tables. You will need at least two times the space your current dictionary occupies as free space in the SYSTEM tablespace to use MIG.

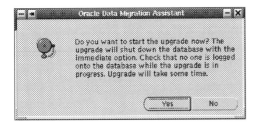

FIGURE 1.35   Last warning.

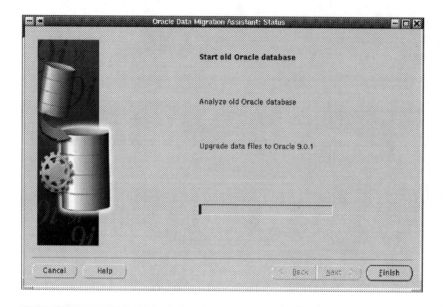

FIGURE 1.36   The screen we've waited for: we are upgrading!

You can run MIG in CHECK_ONLY mode to verify available space (among other nice-to-knows). The Oracle9*i* binaries take up to three times the size of Oracle7 binaries, so make sure there is enough free space on the disk to accommodate them.

■ If you are not using the export/import method, both databases must have matching block sizes, and block size must be at least 2048 bytes. Oracle9*i* will not accept a smaller block size than 2048 bytes.

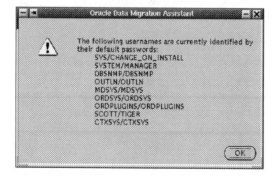

FIGURE 1.37   Review screen for log reviews.

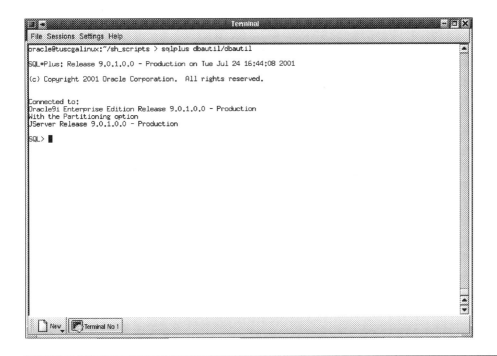

FIGURE 1.38   SQLPLUS screen showing latest version.

- If you are attempting to migrate from a 32-bit machine to a 64-bit machine using MIG, come on, get serious. The only methods that work are export/import or sqlloader. I opt for export/import in this situation.
- Going from one character set to another is verboten (forbidden . . . don't you learn a lot reading this stuff?). For MIG, this isn't a problem, but for the other methods it could be. Be sure to check your NLS parameters.
- Performing migration steps out of order. Obviously, don't do this.
- Not fulfilling the prerequisites for migration (see the first sections above).
- Allowing other users to access the database during migration.
- Database must be at least 7.3.4. I'm not kidding; it checks for this and errors out if it isn't.
- If you are re-creating control files in a different location, be sure permissions are set properly.
- Be sure all tablespaces were either online or in an offline normal or temporary status when the Oracle8 instance shut down. Be sure there is no outstanding undo in any of the tablespaces.

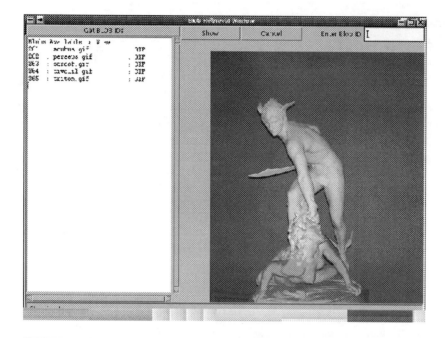

FIGURE 1.39   Java Application Fully Functional!

1.10 SUMMARY

As stated earlier, Oracle9*i* offers numerous new features. It changes the fundamental structures of the database, compared to Oracle8 or earlier versions. The migration to Oracle9*i* is not a simple process of shutting down in one version and starting up in the other; it is a complex operation requiring planning (at least for large databases, which must use the MIG or ODMA utilities). However, according to several DBAs who have done it, as long as you plan properly and *follow directions,* you shouldn't have any problems.

CHAPTER 2

Administration of Oracle
(After the Bloom Is
off the Rose . . .)

If you have reached this point, one of three things has happened: You successfully installed your Oracle system using the guidelines in Chapter 1 and are anxiously awaiting further enlightenment; you failed to successfully install your Oracle system using the guidelines in Chapter 1 but are big-hearted enough to give this book another chance at proving that it's worth the purchase price; or you don't have Oracle yet or have an existing system and just want to see what system administration tools this book can provide. In any case, the next few chapters are the heart of this book and are really what you paid for.

In this chapter we will look at Oracle database-level administration and management in detail. We will cover the tools available to the DBA and administration of the physical database. In the following chapters we will examine object, space, and user administration; techniques for using the tools; tuning issues and solutions; backup and recovery; and security.

As the title of this chapter implies, Oracle administration isn't always a rose garden; sometimes it is the thorns. Hopefully, by using this book, you can avoid some of the thorns that have gouged Oracle DBAs in the past. In writing this and subsequent chapters, use was made of the Oracle documentation set; articles from *Oracle* magazine; IOUG (International Oracle User's Group) presentations; *Oracle Internals* magazine; *DBMS* magazine; Oracle Corporation Support Forums (metalink.oracle.com and technet.oracle.com); the RevealNet Web site (www.revealnet.com) with its DBA and PL/SQL pipelines; www.orafans.com; Internet newsgroups (lazyDBA, OAUG); and my own real-life experiences and those of several Oracle database experts.

In order to make full use of this chapter, it is suggested that the DBA either load the scripts from the Wiley Web site, or load each by hand. The account used to run these scripts should have the DBA_UTILITIES package, included with the scripts, installed and have a default and temporary tablespace other than SYSTEM; the account should not be the SYSTEM account. It is also suggested that a small (generally around 10 MB or less) tablespace be created to hold the temporary tables and permanent tables required to run the various utilities. The DBA_ views should be created and available. The install scripts must be run so the V$ views are available. Once the Web site scripts are downloaded, the file CRE_DBAUTIL_GRANTS.SQL script must be run from the SYS account to provide the needed direct grants. The CREA_DBAUTIL_TABS.SQL script will create the DBA tables and required views. Finally, the DBA_UTILITIES9. SQL (or DBA_UTILITIES8.SQL if you are on 8 or 8*i*) script should be run to create some needed procedures and functions.

This chapter assumes that the DBA is familiar with basic SQL and SQL*Plus commands. As we move along, PL/SQL will also be used, so familiarity with these tools would be helpful. May I suggest Steve Feuerstein's excellent book on PL/SQL, *PL/SQL Programming* (O'Reilly & Associates, 1995), and the companion volume, *PL/SQL Advanced Programming* (O'Reilly & Associates, 1996), as well as *Oracle Provided Packages* (O'Reilly & Associates, 1996) by Feuerstein, Beresniwiecz, and Dunn; and of course *Oracle PL/SQL Tips and Techniques*, Joseph Trezzo, (Oracle Press, Osborne-McGraw Hill, 1999). None of the scripts is overly complex, however, and even if you aren't an SQL virtuoso, you should be able to make some sense of them. Some other good books to have on hand are:

> *Oracle DBA 101* (Oracle Press Editions, Osborne-McGraw Hill, 2000) by Marlene Theriault, Rachel Carmichael, and James Viscusi.
>
> *Oracle Tuning Tips and Techniques* (Oracle Press Editions, Osborne-McGraw Hill, 1999) by Rich Niemiec, Joe Trezzo, and Brad Brown

In any case, when proceeding through this chapter, you should have as references the SQL Language Reference Manual, the SQL*Plus Reference Manual, the Oracle Database Administrator's Guide, the PL/SQL Reference Guide, the Oracle RDBMS Performance Tuning Guide, and the appropriate installation and administration guide for your operating system or the equivalent Oracle9*i* server guides. The Oracle document set is detailed and provides excellent information—if you know where to find the data you need among all of the material provided.

The scripts and procedures presented in this chapter are being used at several sites to manage and administer Oracle databases. Each has been tested under Oracle8, Oracle8*i*, and Oracle9*i*, and under VMS, NT, Windows, and UNIX implementations of Oracle databases. It is suggested that the scripts be called from a centralized menu, either an operating system script or Forms application. A sample script for both KORNE and BASH shell are provided on the Web site. By use of shortcuts, which utilize the location of the scripts as a working directory on Windows-based systems, you can achieve the same results. This provides for a single entry of your Oracle username and password instead of having to invoke SQL*Plus each time you want to run a script. Under NT, I suggest creating an SQLPLUS icon that has as its working or start-in directory the script directory under the SQL script storage directory. The scripts are kept simple for ease of understanding and to ensure that those who may not have the transaction-processing option or other advanced Oracle features implemented may still find this book of use. Only a few of the scripts use PL/SQL; every attempt has been made to follow the KISS principle (Keep it simple, stupid!).

2.1 GENERIC TOOLS AVAILABLE TO ALL DBAS

In almost every Oracle database, the DBA will have access to SQL, SQL*Plus, and, until 9*i*, SVRMGR. Almost all 7.2 and later installations may also have the Oracle Enterprise Manager toolset. In some runtime versions of Oracle, such as are used with some CAD/CAM packages for drawing tracking, only SVRMGR may be provided. The PL/SQL tool is always provided with all post-7.0 Oracle systems as well.

SQL: The Standard RDBMS Language

The Structured Query Language (SQL) is the lingua franca of all relational database management systems (RDBMS). The American National Standards Institute (ANSI) accepted SQL as the standard relational database language in October 1986 (ANSI X3.135-1986). SQL has also been accepted by the International Standards Organization (ISO standard 9075) and by the U.S. government in the Federal Information Processing Standard FIPS-127. A security enhancement has been added and is covered in ANSI SQL Addendum I and issued as X3.135-1989 and 9075-1989. SQL92 is the most recent standard, and Oracle's implementation is entry-level-compliant and has numerous extensions that make it one of the best SQL implementations available. Oracle9*i* SQL is documented in *Oracle9i SQL Reference*, Release 1(9.0.1), Part No. A90125-01, June 2001, Oracle Corporation. The latest SQL standard, simply titled SQL3, was supposed to be approved by 1999; however, not much is being said about it since its initial release in 1999, so it would appear to have stalled. Fortunately, much of the Oracle object features are supposedly SQL3- (SQL99-; described below) and ODMG-standard-compliant.

The latest SQL standard, published by ANSI and ISO, is often called SQL99. The formal names of the new standard are:

ANSI X3.135-1999, "Database Language SQL," Parts 1 ("Framework"), 2 ("Foundation"), 3 ("Bindings")

ISO/IEC 9075:1999, "Database Language SQL," Parts 1 ("Framework"), 2 ("Foundation"), 3 ("Bindings")

The Oracle9*i* server, Oracle precompilers for C/C++ release 8.1, Oracle Precompiler for COBOL, release 8.1, and SQL*Module for ADA release 8.0.4 provide full or partial conformance with the ANSI and ISO standards. The Oracle SQL Reference Manual, Release 1 (9.0.1) provides charts in Appendix B that show which sections of the database are in compliance, and more important, which are not.

NIST testing of database compliance has been suspended, so we have to take the vendors' word (Oracle) about compliance for SQL3.

SQL is considered to be a nonprocedural language, because of the way it processes sets of records and provides automatic data access, or navigation. SQL also uses query optimization; that is, the RDBMS kernel determines the optimum method to reach the desired data so you don't have to. Under Oracle8, Oracle8i, and Oracle9i, a cost-based or a rules-based approach can be used. SQL is designed to be simple to learn and use. Despite this simplicity, SQL provides a rich command set under which virtually any combination of data in a database can be retrieved and reported.

In SQL the major statement is SELECT. SELECT allows the retrieval of data from the database. Multiple SELECTs can be nested into a single statement, and, using NET8, SELECTs can even span databases. SQL also allows insertion, update, and deletion of data, as well as creation, modification, and deletion of database objects such as tables, sequences, indexes, and tablespaces. SQL provides for database security and consistency. Unlike other systems where entirely different command sets govern the different areas of database activities, SQL combines these functions into an integrated command set. All of the SQL for Oracle is shown in the link to the Oracle SQL manual on the Wiley Web site; refer to the appropriate reference manual [Oracle9i SQL Reference, Release 1 (9.0.1), Part No. A90125-01, June 2001, Oracle Corp. as of this writing] for more details on command usage.

SQL is also portable. If two RDBMSs are ANSI-compliant, then an SQL statement that works in one will work in the other, assuming the data structures are the same. This only applies to standard SQL commands; naturally, system-specific extensions won't transport to other systems. A good example of this is the Oracle STORAGE clause.

If the DBA is not familiar with SQL, it is suggested that he or she look through the *SQL Language Reference Manual* and become familiar with the basic commands. The SQL language is utilized through SQL*Plus, Oracle Administrator Toolbar SQL Worksheet, or SVRMGR.

The link to the SQL manual on the Wiley Web page shows the formats for all SQL commands referenced in this book. For more detailed explanations, the DBA should refer to the *SQL Language Reference Manual* for the release of the Oracle database under which he or she is operating.

SQL*Plus: An Oracle Extension to Standard SQL

The SQL*Plus program allows users to access SQL and the Oracle SQL extensions. This combination of commands, SQL, and the Oracle SQL extensions enable users and the DBA to access the database via standard SQL and to format input and output using the SQL*Plus extensions to the language. In Oracle9i, the Server Manager (SVRMGR) program has been completely eliminated in favor of an extended SQL*Plus implementation. The most current documentation as of this writing is SQL*Plus *User's Guide and Reference*, Release 1 (9.0.1), PART# A88827-01, June 2001 Oracle Corporation.

SQL*Plus has a command buffer that stores the current command and allows the user to edit the command using the native system editor or via command-line input. SQL*Plus also allows the user to store, retrieve, and execute SQL/SQL*Plus command scripts, as well as PL/SQL command scripts. It allows use of abbreviated commands and calls to the host system command language. In SQL*Plus, local variables can be assigned as well as providing control of system variables used for format and display control. However, though the new SQL*Worksheet handles standard SQL well, it will not handle the formatting commands from the SQL*Plus extensions.

SQL*Plus can also be used to dynamically create command scripts that can then be used to perform en masse changes to users, tables, or other Oracle objects. This is a very powerful feature that will be used in many of the example scripts. If DBAs are not familiar with SQL*Plus, it is suggested they review the SQL*Plus reference guide to acquaint themselves with the SQL*Plus commands.

SQL*Plus can be accessed once the user has set the appropriate system variables and path, which is done using the ".oraenv" command on UNIX and Linux; in some environments, however, the ORACLE_SID variable may have to be set to point to your database. On NT, the user must either set some environmental variables or use connect aliases (for everything but the prespecified password, I usually set up an SQLPLUS icon for each instance I need to connect to). The format for invoking SQL*Plus is as follows:

```
SQLPLUS   username/password@connect string   @command file
```

or

```
SQLPLUS  /NOLOG
```

where:

username/password. The user's Oracle username and password, which is usually different from the operating system username and password. If the user is assigned an autologin type of account, only the solidus (/) is required.

@connect string. A string that connects the user to databases other than the default database. It can be used with SQL*NET or NET8 over networks to access other systems.

@command file. Allows the user to specify an SQL command file that is run automatically.

/NOLOG. Enables connection without specifying username and password; however you must use the CONNECT username command before the database is available to you. Usually this form is used with a CONNECT SYS AS SYSDBA type connection to perform database maintenance, startup, or shutdown.

If the DBA account is what is known as an OPS$ account (not recommended), the format would be as follows:

```
SQLPLUS  /
```

Since an OPS$ account allows the user to get into the Oracle system without specifying a password if he or she is logging in from his or her normal account, the use of OPS$ accounts should be restricted to "captive"-type users, that is, users who can only access the system via an appropriate secure menu system. Under Oracle8, 8*i*, and 9*i*, the OPS$ format is the default, but the system manager can assign whatever prefix he or she desires by use of the OS_AUTHENT_PREFIX parameter in the INIT.ORA file.

SVRMGR: A Database Administrator's Toolset

As its name implies, SVRMGR (Server Manager) is designed for the DBA and only for the DBA. The SVRMGR program provides access to the database internals and to all database objects. To use SVRMGR, the user must belong to the DBA group under UNIX or Linux, or have the proper group specification in NT or W2K. The SVRMGR product has both a line command version and an X Windows implementation (SVRMGRL and SVRMGRM) on most operating systems where it is appropriate, such as UNIX or NT.

In Oracle7, the use of SVRMGR is covered in the *Oracle7 Server Utilities User's Guide*; in later releases, it is covered in the *Server Manager's User Guide*.

Changes under Oracle9i   In Oracle9*i* Server Manager is no longer supplied.

Changes under Oracle8   Under version 7, SVRMGR was still command-driven. Under Oracle8, the use of pull-down menus and fill-in screens automated many of the more tedious administration tasks, such as the addition of data files, tablespaces, users, dealing with startup/shutdown and with various logs. With Oracle8, SVRMGR and Oracle enterprise monitor (OEM) have come a long way toward being *the* tools to use to administer a database. The addition of customizable monitor screens under the Oracle performance pack looks to be a big help. Unfortunately, the lack of hard-copy reports, one of the major limitations in SQLDBA under version 7, has not been addressed in Oracle8. However, the SPOOL command capability is still usable under SVRMGR, so some output capability is available. In addition, the UTL_FILE package, new for late Oracle7 and Oracle8, provides direct input and output from PL/SQL to operating system files.

Operation of SVRMGR or SQLPLUS /NOLOG   On Oracle9*i*, most of the following will apply to a SQLPLUS /NOLOG login as well as SVRMGR.

- To use SVRMGR, the DBA must have issued the .oraenv command on UNIX or Linux to set environmental variables.
- On NT and other Windows-compliant systems, you will be prompted for username, password, and a connect string.
- If the DBA wants to run SVRMGR against a specific instance, the ORAUSER_ instance file in the directory specified by the ORA_INSTANCE logical on VMS must be run. Under UNIX, this is taken care of by the .oraenv program.

- The user, for some commands under Oracle8, Oracle8*i*, and Oracle9*i* has the OSOPER and OSDBA roles assigned. These roles control the privileges granted, thus allowing limited power to users who must use the CONNECT INTERNAL command under SVRMGR or CONNECT SYS AS SYSDBA under SQLPLUS for shutdown and startup of the database, who but don't need other privileges. The SVRMGR and SQLPLUS command formats follow.

```
SVRMGR{L|M}  (lowercase on UNIX)
SQLPLUS /NOLOG (lowercase on UNIX)
```

Once the SVRMGR or SQLPLUS program is running, the DBA uses the CONNECT command to connect to the appropriate instance.

```
CONNECT username[@db_alias]  or
CONNECT username/password[@db_alias [AS SYSDBA|SYSOPER]
```

The second special form of the CONNECT command can be used by DBAs from accounts with the proper privileges. This form allows the DBA to access all of the structures in the database, including those owned by SYS.

```
CONNECT INTERNAL  [AS SYSOPER|SYSDBA]
```

The INTERNAL user will have the same password as the SYS user, or the password specified during database creation via the ORAPWRD program at installation. In Oracle9*i*, the INTERNAL user is no longer supported; you must switch to using SYS. The DBA is allowed certain commands and privileges while in SVRMGR or under the CONNECT...AS SYSDBA umbrella in SQLPLUS. These also depend on database status, which can be one of the following:

Database STATUS	*Allowed Commands*
CLOSED, not MOUNTED	SHUTDOWN, used for some maintenance activities.
CLOSED, MOUNTED	Used for some maintenance activities.
OPEN, MOUNTED, NORMAL EXCLUSIVE	Normal mode for nonparallel database.
OPEN, MOUNTED, DBA MODE	Used for maintenance.
OPEN, MOUNTED, PARALLEL	Used for parallel instance Oracle.

The DBA tasks include user administration, space administration (physical, such as data files; and virtual, such as tablespace usage), and tools administration. We will cover these tasks in the following sections. In Oracle9*i*, Svrmgrl is discontinued.

Procedural-Level Standard Query Language (PL/SQL)

The PL/SQL language extensions to SQL make doing complex programming tasks in SQL orders of magnitude easier. PL/SQL adds the capability to use cursors (predefined selects), loops, temporary tables, and a number of other high-level language features not available in standard SQL. Stored functions, procedures, packages, triggers, and methods are all built using PL/SQL. The Oracle-provided packages (DBMS_* and UTL*) are also built using PL/SQL and will become your good friends as you use them to explore and master Oracle. In later versions of 8*i* (8.1), Java is available for trigger, procedure, and package work, as well as PL/SQL. PL/SQL is detailed in the latest release of the PL/SQL documentation

As a DBA, you will have to become very familiar with PL/SQL. There are numerous examples in this book to help; I also suggest you keep handy the *PL/SQL User's Guide and Reference,* Release 9.0.1, Part No. A89856-01, June 2001, Oracle Corporation. Another excellent reference is *PL/SQL Advanced Programming*, by Steven Feuerstein (O'Reilly and Associates, 1996); and for sheer ease of use, nothing beats the RevealNet online references (PL/SQL for Developers, PLVision Lite, and PLVision Professional, available at www.revealnet.com/). Another great reference is *Oracle PL/SQL Tips and Techniques* by Joseph C. Trezzo, (Oracle Press, Osborne-McGraw Hill, 1999).

2.2 ADMINISTRATION OF THE DATABASE

A database consists of executables, global areas, and database files. Within the database files exist tables, indexes, sequences, views, clusters, and synonyms. The DBA will be involved in the creation, maintenance, and deletion of these objects on a frequent basis. The commands CREATE, ALTER, and DROP are fairly easy to master. A subset of the CREATE and ALTER command, the STORAGE clause, is also very important for the DBA to understand and use properly.

The CREATE Command

As its name implies, the CREATE statement is used to create databases, tablespaces, tables, clusters, database links, indexes, sequences, views, users, packages, procedures, functions, and rollback segments. It has this general format (any thing in square brackets is optional):

```
CREATE object_type [schema_name.]object_name
create options,
[STORAGE ( storage parameters)]
```

The STORAGE Clause

The STORAGE clause specifies how an object uses the space to which it is allocated. Some objects, including packages, procedures, types, views, libraries, directories, indextypes, and others, don't use the STORAGE clause Let's look at the format of the STORAGE clause.

```
[DEFAULT] STORAGE (INITIAL x [K|M] NEXT x [K|M] MINEXTENTS x MAXEXTENTS x
PCTINCREASE x FREELISTS x FREELIST GROUPS x OPTIMAL x [K|M] BUFFER_POOL
DEFAULT|KEEP|RECYCLE)
```

where:

[DEFAULT]. Is used only in a TABLESPACE specification to specify the default storage used for objects placed in the tablespace when no object-specific storage specification is made.

INITIAL. Specifies the size in bytes of the initial extent of the object. The default is 5 Oracle block sizes (10K for a 2K blocksize, 40K for an 8K blocksize, and so forth). The minimum size is 2 Oracle blocks plus 1 for each freelist specified (freelists default to 1 for tables, 2 for indexes). The maximum is 4 gigabytes on most platforms. All values are rounded to the nearest Oracle blocksize.

NEXT. Indicates the size for the next extent after the INITIAL is used. The default is 5 Oracle blocks, the minimum is 1 Oracle block, the maximum is 4 gigabytes. NEXT is the value that will be used for each new extent if PCTINCREASE is set to 0. If PCTINCREASE is greater than 0, then the next extent will be NEXT, the second extension will be NEXT times 1 plus PCTINCREASE/100, then the size of that extent times 1 plus PCTINCREASE/100 for the next extension, and so forth. The factor of 1 plus PCTINCREASE/100 is only applied to the size of the last extent. The result of the multiplication or the value of NEXT will be adjusted up to minimize fragmentation.

MINEXTENTS. Specifies the number of initial extents for the object. Generally, except for rollback segments, it is set to 1. If a large amount of space is required and there is not enough contiguous space for the table, setting a smaller extent size and specifying several extents may solve the problem. The values for INITIAL, NEXT, and PCTINCREASE are used when calculating the extent sizes for the number of extents requested.

MAXEXTENTS. Specifies the largest number of extents allowed the object. This defaults to the max allowed for your blocksize for Oracle8, Oracle8*i*, and Oracle9*i*. In addition, if UNLIMITED is set, there is no upper limit.

PCTINCREASE. Tells Oracle how much to grow each extent after the INITIAL and NEXT extents are used. A specification of 50 will grow each extent after NEXT by 50 percent *for each subsequent extent*. This means that for a table created with one INITIAL and a NEXT extent, any further extents will increase in size by 50 percent over their predecessor. Under Oracle8, Oracle8*i*, and Oracle9*i*, this parameter is applied only against the size of the previous extent. The DEFAULT value is 50, and this should always be adjusted.

OPTIMAL. Used only for rollback segments, it specifies the value to which a rollback segment will shrink back after extending.

FREELIST GROUPS. Specifies the number of freelist groups to maintain for a table or index. FREELIST GROUPS should be set to the number of instances that will be addressing the table in an OPS or RAC environment. You must allow one block for each FREELIST; the number of FREELISTS * FREELIST GROUPS yields the number of total freelists. If you are using locally managed tablespaces (covered in the tablespace section), and you specify a combination of FREELISTS and FREELIST GROUPS that is too large for the extent sizes specified, the create operation will fail.

FREELISTS. For objects other than tablespaces, specifies the number of freelists for each of the freelist groups for the table, index, or cluster. The minimum value is 1; the maximum is blocksize-dependent. Always specify FREELISTS to the number of simultaneous transactions that will be addressing a single block. Empirical testing has shown little improvements by setting this parameter to greater than 4. INITIAL must be set to the minimum value plus the total number of freelists.

NOTE Both FREELIST GROUPS and FREELISTS are ignored if the tablespace in which the object (index, table, cluster, snapshot, materialized view) resides is in automatic space management mode.

BUFFER_POOL. Specifies the buffer pool in which to place the object when it is used. The choices are DEFAULT (the default value), KEEP, and RECYCLE. KEEP should be used for objects such as indexes or lookup tables that will be referenced multiple times. RECYCLE should be used for objects that are full-scanned and not used all the time (for example, tables with LOB segments or that have to be full table-scanned). The KEEP and RECYCLE pools must be sized properly, and we will discuss this in Chapter 13, *Database Internals Tuning*.

Proper use of the STORAGE clause means that you will have to perform accurate estimates of table and index size before creation. This will be covered in Chapters 4, *Administration of Relational Database Tables*, 5, *Administration of Oracle 9i Object Tables*, and 6, *Administration of Indexes*.

2.3 DATABASE CREATION, ALTERATION, AND DELETION

Like other objects under Oracle, databases themselves can be created, altered, and deleted. Let's look at these different processes.

Database Creation

To create a database, the CREATE command is run under SVRMGR or with 8*i* and 9*i* in SQL*Plus. (The command sqlplus/nolog should be used to avoid annoying prompts for username and password.)

1. The DBA must connect to the Oracle SYS user (or INTERNAL user pre-8*i*) via the command:

```
CONNECT SYS AS SYSDBA
```

2. The instance is started in an unmounted condition. This is accomplished with the following command.

```
STARTUP NOMOUNT PFILE=filename
```

where PFILE=filename refers to the database initialization file (INIT.ORA) you will be using; unless it is located in the directory you are currently in, a path must also be provided. If no PFILE is specified the SPFILE or the default PFILE will be used if no SPFILE is available.

3. The database is created. The format would be:

```
CREATE DATABASE name
     CONTROLFILE REUSE
     LOGFILE GROUP n (filespec)
     MAXLOGFILES      n
     MAXLOGMEMBERS    n
     MAXLOGHISTORY    n
     MAXDATAFILES     n
     MAXINSTANCES     n
     ARCHIVELOG|NOARCHIVELOG
     CHARACTER_SET  charset
     NATIONAL_CHARACTER_SET charset
     DATAFILE (filespec) autoextend_clause
     Extent_management_clause
     Default_temp_tablespace_clause
     UNDO_tablespace_clause
     SET STANDBY DATABASE clause
     Set_time_zone_clause

autoextend_clause:

AUTOEXTEND ON|OFF NEXT n K|M MAXSIZE n|UNLIMITED K|M

Filespec:

'full path file name|logical|system link name' SIZE n K|M REUSE
```

```
extent_management_clause:

EXTENT MANAGEMENT
              DIRECTORY
              LOCAL
                 AUTOALLOCATE
                 UNIFORM
                      SIZE n [K|M]
```

```
Default_temp_tablespace_clause:

DEFAULT TEMPORARY TABLESPACE tablespace [TEMPFILE]
Temp_tablespace_extent_clause
```

```
UNDO_tablespace_clause:

UNDO TABLESPACE tablespace [DATAFILE file_space_clauses]
```

In this code:

DATABASE name. The name of the database, a maximum of eight characters long.

File specifications for data files. Are of the format: 'filename' SIZE integer K or M REUSE. K is for kilobytes, M is for megabytes. REUSE specifies that if the file already exists, reuse it. The AUTOEXTEND option is new with later versions of Oracle7 and all of Oracle8 and is used to allow your data files to automatically extend as needed. (Note: Be very careful with this command, as it can use up a great deal of disk space rather rapidly if a mistake is made during table builds or inserts.) File specifications for log files depend on the operating system.

MAXLOGFILES, MAXDATAFILES, and MAXINSTANCES. Set hard limits for the database; these should be set to the maximum you ever expect.

MAXLOGMEMBERS and MAXLOGHISTORY. Hard limits.

EXTENT MANAGEMENT. Determines whether the extents in the SYSTEM tablespace are managed via the data dictionary (DICTIONARY) or locally via a bitmap in the tablespace (LOCAL). In addition, the extents can be AUTOALLOCATED, to enable the system to manage them as to size; or the UNIFORM clause, with or without a size specification, can be used to force all extents to a uniform size. For versions earlier than 9*i*, you should not make the system tablespace anything other than dictionary-managed.

CHARACTER_SET and NATIONAL_CHARACTER_SET. For Oracle8, Oracle8*i*, and Oracle9*i*, determines the character set that data will be stored in. This value is operating system-dependent.

ARCHIVELOG and NOARCHIVELOG. If you need archive logging, set ARCHIVELOG; if you don't need it right away, set NOARCHIVELOG. I suggest using NOARCHIVELOG to avoid creation of multiple archive logs during initial database creation; you won't recover from a failed build, you will just rebuild. This is one thing to check if the build seems to stall during later steps (running catproc.sql, for example): the archive log location may have filled. This is checked using the alert log stored in the location specified by USER_DUMP_DESTINATION.

Databases are created in EXCLUSIVE mode, and are either EXCLUSIVE or PARALLEL. A database must be altered to PARALLEL mode after creation if you intend to use the oracle parallel or RAC options.

The CHARACTER_SET is used for normal data. Character specifications AF16UTF16, JA16SJISFIXED, JA16EUCFIXED, and JA16DBCSFIXED can be used only as the NATIONAL_CHARACTER_SET. The NATIONAL_CHARACTER_SET specifies the national character set used to store data in columns specifically defined as NCHAR, NCLOB, or NVARCHAR2. The NATIONAL_CHARACTER_SET is usually specified as AF16UTF16 or UTF8 (formally known as UNICODE). You cannot change the national character set after creating the database. If not specified, the national character set defaults to the database character set. There are nearly 300 character sets supported. For a complete list, consult the *Oracle9i Globalization Support Guide* Release 1 (9.0.1) Part Number A90236-01, June 2001, Oracle Corporation.

You must verify that the registry on NT is set with the same character set as the database, or data problems and performance degradation will occur. This applies to all client workstations, including Windows95, 98, NT, as well as Windows2000-based units.

The following clauses are new in Oracle9i:

The default_tablespace_clause. Specifies the default temporary tablespace for all users where one is not specified in the CREATE USER command. In previous releases, the default temporary tablespace was SYSTEM. The SYSTEM tablespace cannot be specified as the DEFAULT TEMPORARY tablespace. The default temporary tablespace must use the database blocksize that was specified for the database at creation.

The UNDO_tablespace_clause. Specifies that an UNDO tablespace will be used instead of a ROLLBACK segment tablespace. An UNDO tablespace is automatically managed by Oracle. If this clause is left off of an Oracle9i (it can only be specified in Oracle9i and later) CREATE DATABASE command, a default tablespace is created called SYS_UNDOTBS. If for some reason the UNDO tablespace cannot be created, the entire CREATE DATABASE clause fails.

The set_timezone_clause. Allows specification of the default time zone for the database. The default time zone is specified either as a displacement from ZULU (Universal Time-Coordinated [UTC] formally Greenwich mean time) of -12:00 to +14:00 or by specifying a region, there are 616 possible regions in an Oracle9i 9.0.1 database. You can find out what regions are available from the V$TIMEZONE_NAMES view. All TIMESTAMP WITH LOCAL TIME ZONE data is normalized to the time zone of the database when data is stored on disk. An invalid zone will default to UTC.

An example database creation script is shown in Source 2.1.

Source 2.1   Example database creation script from the Database Creation Assistant (DBCA).

```
connect SYS/change_on_install as SYSDBA
set echo on
spool /var/oracle/OraHome2/assistants/dbca/logs/CreateDB.log
startup nomount pfile="/var/oracle/OraHome2/admin/galinux2/scripts/init.ora";
CREATE DATABASE galinux2
MAXINSTANCES 1
MAXLOGHISTORY 1
MAXLOGFILES 5
MAXLOGMEMBERS 5
MAXDATAFILES 100
DATAFILE '/var/oracle/OraHome2/oradata/galinux2/system01.dbf' SIZE 325M REUSE
AUTOEXTEND ON NEXT  10240K MAXSIZE UNLIMITED
UNDO TABLESPACE "UNDOTBS" DATAFILE
'/var/oracle/OraHome2/oradata/galinux2/undotbs01.dbf' SIZE 200M REUSE
AUTOEXTEND ON NEXT  5120K MAXSIZE UNLIMITED
CHARACTER SET US7ASCII
NATIONAL CHARACTER SET AL16UTF16
LOGFILE GROUP 1 ('/var/oracle/OraHome2/oradata/galinux2/redo01.log') SIZE
100M,
GROUP 2 ('/var/oracle/OraHome2/oradata/galinux2/redo02.log') SIZE 100M,
GROUP 3 ('/var/oracle/OraHome2/oradata/galinux2/redo03.log') SIZE 100M;
spool off
exit;
```

What the Oracle kernel does when given a CREATE DATABASE command is easy, first the system creates control, redo log, and database files. Next, the system creates the SYSTEM rollback segment in the SYSTEM tablespace, creates and loads data dictionary tables, and mounts and opens the database.

On virtually all platforms you will have a Java-based tool called the Database Configuration Assistant (on UNIX and Linux DBCA in the $ORACLE_HOME/bin directory). This tool will help you create Oracle databases. On NT and W2K, this should be named Database Configuration Assistant and will be in the menu tree: *Start — Programs — Oracle — Oracle_home — Database Administration — Database Configuration Assistant*. Let's look at an example database creation using the Database Creation Assistant on Linux.

At the Linux command line in the Oracle user at the users' home directory we type "dbca." The DBCA command will be effective only if the values for PATH and ORACLE_HOME are set correctly. Generally, if you can run the other Oracle utilities, such as SQL*Plus (the command would be sqlplus), you won't have a problem running DBCA. Figure 2.1 shows the welcome screen for the Database Configuration Assistant tool.

The next screen, shown in Figure 2.2 (reached by selecting the Next button on the welcome screen), allows you to choose between several options:

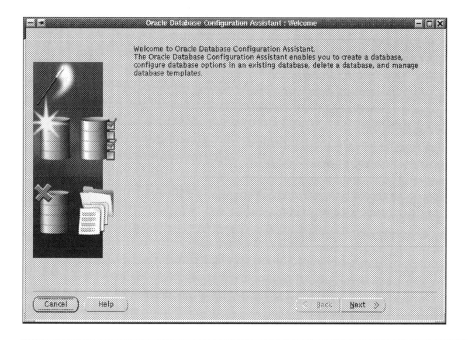

FIGURE 2.1   Welcome screen for the Database Configuration Assistant.

- Create a database.
- Configure database options in a database.
- Delete a database.
- Manage templates.

For this example, we want to create a database. The other options are fairly self-explanatory. In the Oracle9*i* version of the DBCA, the Manage templates option has been added to allow the DBA to manage the precreated or newly created templates used to create databases. The Configure database options allows the DBA to choose from the available databases and perform reconfiguration of the server mode (dedicate or shared), or the options installed. The Delete database option lists the current instances and allows you to delete from them. We have selected the Create a database option for this example. Its radio button is shown as set in Figure 2.2, the Operations screen.

Figure 2.3 shows the selection of the database template to use. We will select New Database, as this will display the most custom options. The other templates use baseline assumptions to provide a minimized set of screens to generate a data warehouse, transaction processing, or general-purpose database. These other templates use already configured database files, which are uncompressed and placed in your filesystems, identically to creating a database from the same options offered in the OUI interface. Note that you have more options in the Oracle9*i* version of the Assistant than the Typical

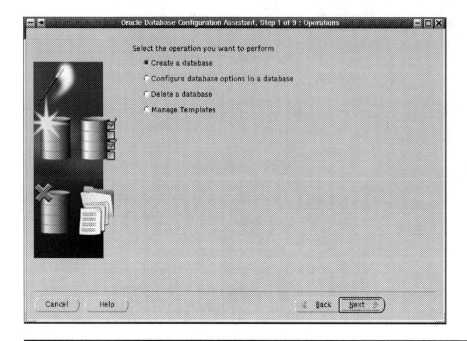

FIGURE 2.2   Database Operations screen.

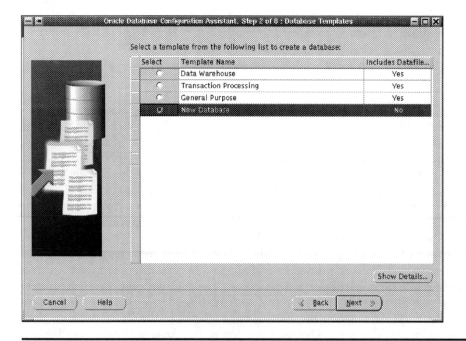

FIGURE 2.3   Database Template Selection screen.

and Custom database options that were provided in the Oracle8*i* version. Now select the Next button to go on to the next step of database creation using the Database Configuration Assistant. The next screen is the Database Identification screen, which is shown in Figure 2.4.

On the Database Identification screen you fill in one value, the SID domain name for your database. If you are unsure of the domain to use, type "sid.world" or simply the SID name. In my system, the domain is my server name, so I used the sid.tuscgalinux or specifically galinux2.tuscgalinux where the database name (SID) is ""galinux1." The screen automatically strips off the domain name (anything after the first period) to create the SID name, and places the SID in the appropriate box for you. Once you have defined the SID and domain and selected the Next button, the Database Options screen (Figure 2.5) is displayed.

The Database Options screen lists all available database options. By default, you will see that the Oracle Spatial, Oracle Ultra Search, and Example Schemas have been selected. I suggest unselecting the Example Schemas unless this is to be a learning database, as they are not needed for a production environment. This screen also allows you to add either custom-designed scripts or choose, via browse capabilities, scripts such as catblock.sql, catparr.sql, or other Oracle-provided scripts not run by catproc.sql. Once you have selected the options to be loaded and have specified any custom scripts that you want run, select the Additional database configurations button; the screen that

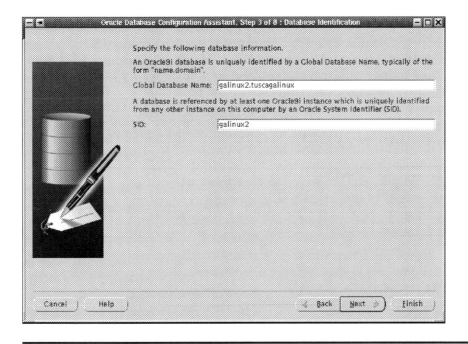

FIGURE 2.4   Database Identification screen.

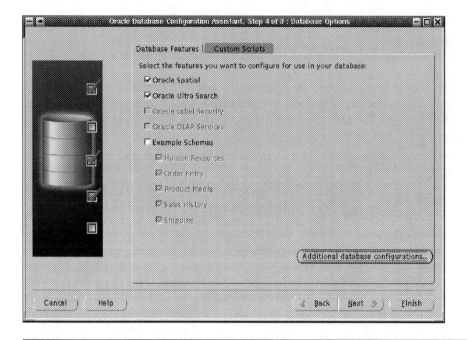

FIGURE 2.5   Database Options.

allows you to select, or deselect, the Oracle JVM and Intermedia options is displayed. This additional option screen is shown in Figure 2.6.

Oracle suggests (and I agree) that you add the JVM and Intermedia to your selection of options; they both provide additional power and functionality that are easy to add now, but may be more difficult in a fully functional production environment. Once you have chosen (or not chosen, as the case may be) the JVM and Intermedia options, select the OK button and then the Next button on the Options screen to display the Database Connection Options screen (Figure 2.7).

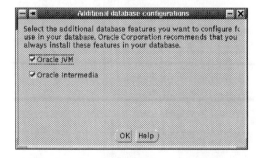

FIGURE 2.6   Additional Configurations screen.

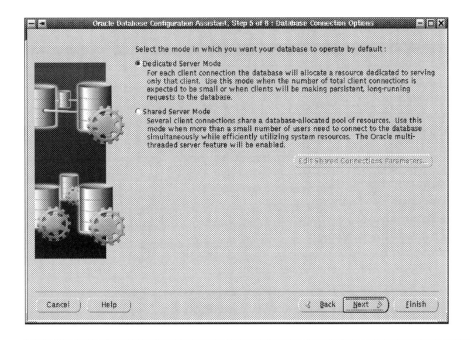

FIGURE 2.7   Database Connection Options screen.

In the Connection Options screen, you choose between using dedicated connections and configuring a multithreaded server (MTS). Generally, if your system isn't serving about 100 connections per CPU to the database, you won't need MTS; however, if you will be using large, complex SQL commands you may need to turn on a minimal MTS configuration to ensure that the large pool is utilized. I have seen cases where not using the large pool will generate ORA-04031 and ORA-1037 errors with large, complex SQL. MTS is used when you either have many connections or when you have a very small amount of memory and many connections. If you have sufficient memory resources to serve the connected users, you will want to use dedicated connections. Make your selection, and then either select Next, if you choose dedicated connections, or configure the MTS (called shared connection) parameters; then select OK and Next. The next screen displayed will be the Initialization Parameters screen, shown in Figure 2.8.

As you can see, this screen allows you to alter the values for key initialization parameters in the general categories of Memory, Archive, DB Sizing, and File Locations, whose screens are shown, respectively, in Figures 2.9, 2.10, and 2.11. You can also specify that you wish to examine and alter all initialization parameters; that brings up the screen shown in Figure 2.12.

Once you have set the initialization parameters as you desire (note, Oracle sets the initialization parameter _unnest_subquery to TRUE, which will dramatically alter the execution plans of statements; set it to FALSE to obtain the explain plans generated in

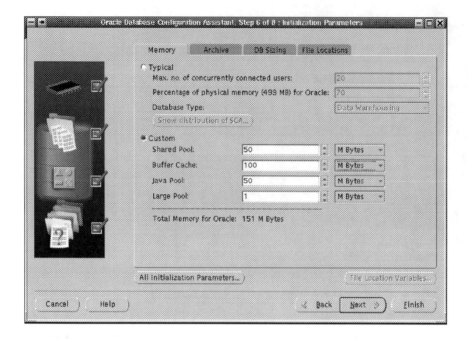

FIGURE 2.8   Database Initialization Parameters screen.

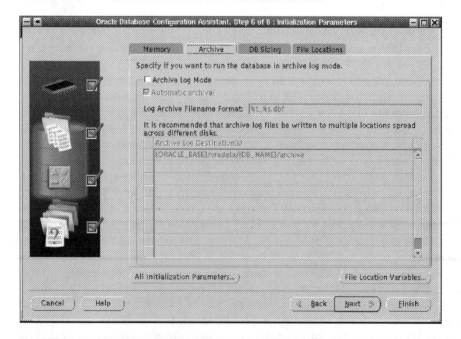

FIGURE 2.9   Database Archive Initialization Parameters screen.

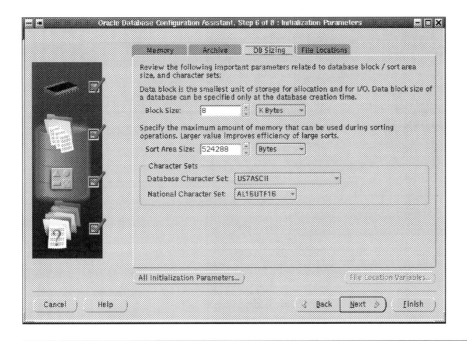

FIGURE 2.10   Database DB Sizing Initialization Parameters screen.

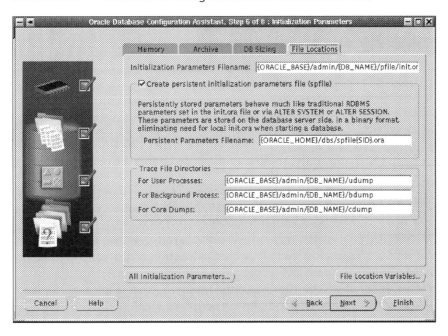

FIGURE 2.11   Database File Locations Initialization Parameters screen.

Name	Value	Included (Y...	Category
optimizer_features_en...	9.0.1		Optimizer
remote_dependencies_...	TIMESTAMP		PL/SQL
parallel_threads_per_c...	2		Parallel Queries
logmnr_max_persistent...	1		Miscellaneous
nls_date_language			NLS
workarea_size_policy	MANUAL		Sort, Hash Joins, Bitm
O7_DICTIONARY_ACCE...	FALSE		Security and Auditing
license_max_sessions	0		License Limits
star_transformation_en...	FALSE		Optimizer
nls_date_format			NLS
lock_sga	FALSE		SGA Memory
fixed_date			Miscellaneous
remote_os_roles	FALSE		Distributed, Replicati
nls_comp			NLS
object_cache_max_size...	10		Objects and LOBs
shared_memory_address	0		SGA Memory
db_recycle_cache_size	0		Cache and I/O
row_locking	always		ANSI Compliance
log_archive_duplex_dest			Archive
sql_trace	FALSE		Diagnostics and Stati
db_block_buffers	0		Cache and I/O
undo_management	AUTO	✔	System Managed Und
oracle_trace_collection...	?/otrace/admin/cdf		Diagnostics and Stati
fast_start_parallel_roll...	LOW		Transactions
global_names	FALSE		Distributed, Replicati
create_bitmap_area_size	8388608		Sort, Hash Joins, Bitm
max_enabled_roles	30		Security and Auditing

FIGURE 2.12   Database All Initialization Parameters screen.

Oracle8*i*, at least in version 9.0.1), select the Next button to display the File Location Variables screen where you can specify the values for ORACLE_BASE, ORACLE_HOME, DB_NAME, and SID; normally, these should not be changed from the displayed values. This screen is shown in Figure 2.13.

Once you have specified any required changes to the file location variables, select the OK button to display the Database Storage screen (Figure 2.14), where you can change the default size of the basic tablespace datafiles (TEMP, INDX, UDOTBS, USERS, TOOLS, DRSYS, SYSTEM). Once you have made any desired changes, you can choose to alter the size of rollback segments, redo logs, or the location of the control files. Select the Next button.

The next screen displayed will be the Creation Options screen (Figure 2.15). Here you can specify whether the database, a template, a script, or all should be created. The Creation Options screen is the final step of input; the rest of the screens show status. Once you have chosen your creation options, select the Finish button to implement

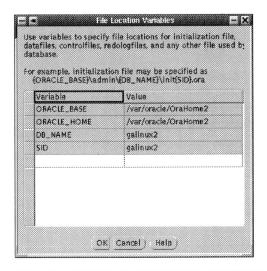

FIGURE 2.13   Database File Location Variables screen.

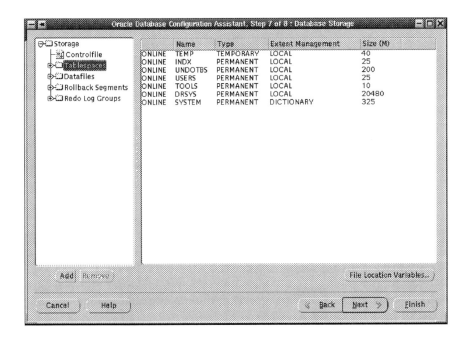

FIGURE 2.14   Database Storage screen.

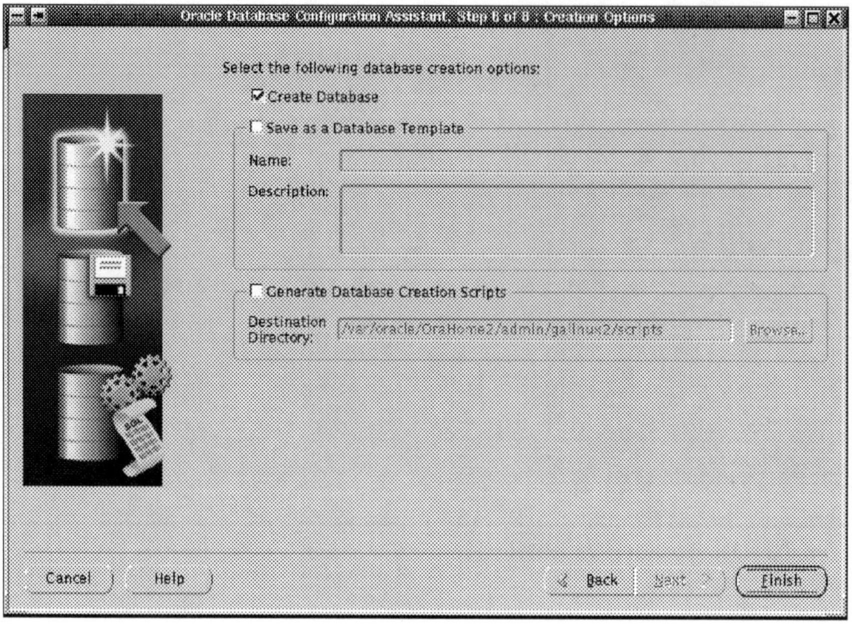

FIGURE 2.15   Database Creation Options screen.

them. I suggest always creating the script so that you can review the creation activity and have a document that describes how the database was created.

The next screen shown, in Figure 2.16, is the Oracle Database Configuration Assistant—Database Creation Script generation status screen. The next tells you the location of the script that was created, as shown in Figure 2.17. Once you have noted the location of the script, select OK.

The next screen displayed shows the various steps being performed and their status. To create a default database as shown in the screens in this section, it took several hours, most of which was taken up by the Java Virtual Machine (JVM) creation on a 400 MgHz, Pentium III, Linux SuSE7.2, with a single 30-gigabyte hard drive with 512 megabytes of memory. The creation status screen is shown in Figure 2.18.

If all goes as anticipated, the next screen (shown in Figure 2.19) will tell you that the database was successfully created. It will also inform you that the default users are locked and that passwords *not* set. I suggest selecting the Password Management button at this point.

The Password Management screen (shown in Figure 2.20) allows you to specify passwords and change the locked status of the default database users. Once the passwords and account status are updated, select the OK button.

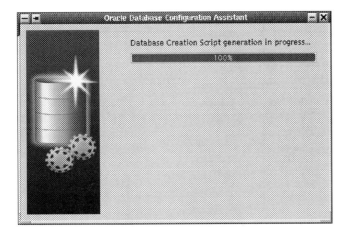

FIGURE 2.16   Creation Script status screen.

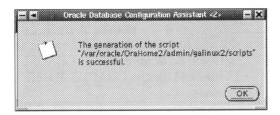

FIGURE 2.17   Script Location screen.

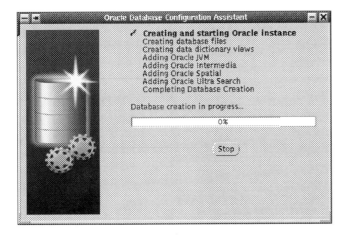

FIGURE 2.18   Database Creation Status screen.

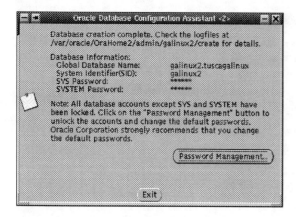

FIGURE 2.19   Successful Database Creation screen.

If you have made it this far, you have successfully created a new Oracle database. Congratulations. If you had problems, you can either restart the process at the beginning after correcting any problems or use the script you hopefully generated earlier to manually create the database. The generated scripts will be located in the $ORACLE_ HOME/admin/sid/scripts directory on UNIX or Linux, and on the ORACLE_HOME\ admin\sid\scripts on NT4.0 or W2K.

User Name	Lock Account?	New Password	Confirm Password
SYS			
SYSTEM			
DBSNMP			
OSE$HTTP$ADMIN			
AURORAORBUNAUT...			
AURORAJISUTILITY$			
OUTLN	✔		
ORDSYS	✔		
ORDPLUGINS	✔		
MDSYS	✔		
CTXSYS	✔		
WKSYS	✔		

FIGURE 2.20   The Password Management screen.

The list of scripts generated during the above database creation contains:

galinux2.sh. Master script that calls the others.

CreateDB.sql. Creates the database.

CreateDBFiles.sql. Creates the additional database tablespaces and files.

CreateDBCatalog.sql. Creates the catalog and procedural options.

JServer.sql. Creates the JVM.

ordinst.sql. Installs the ORDSYS tables, views, and packages for handling Oracle cartridges.

interMedia.sql. Creates the Intermedia option.

context.sql. Creates required support for contexts.

spatial.sql. Creates the spatial option.

ultraSearch.sql. Creates the Ultra Search option.

postDBCreation.sql. Creates the SPFILE; performs a clean shutdown and startup.

There may be more or fewer of these scripts depending on the options you chose to install. If your database creation fails, use these scripts to build the database manually.

Alteration of Databases

Even the best-designed database eventually has to be changed. New log group member files may need to be added, data files may need to be renamed or moved, archive logging status may need to be changed, and so on. These tasks are all accomplished through the use of the ALTER DATABASE command. Let's look at a simplified command format and some of the options.

```
ALTER DATABASE name
     [NO]MOUNT [STANDBY|CLONE] DATABASE
     CONVERT
     OPEN [READ[ ONLY]|WRITE][RESETLOGS|NORESETLOGS]
     ACTIVATE STANDBY DATABASE
     ARCHIVELOG|NOARCHIVELOG
     Recover_clause
     ADD LOGFILE [THREAD n] [GROUP n] file_spec
     ADD LOGFILE MEMBER file_spec [REUSE] TO GROUP n|group_spec
     DROP LOGFILE [GROUP n|group spec] file_spec
     DROP LOGFILE MEMBER file_spec
     CLEAR [UNARCHIVED] LOGFILE [GROUP n|group_spec] file_spec UNRECOVERABLE
DATAFILE
     RENAME file_spec TO file_spec
     CREATE STANDBY CONTROLFILE AS file_name REUSE
     BACKUP CONTROLFILE TO file_name REUSE|TO TRACE RESETLOGS|NORESETLOGS
     RENAME GLOBAL NAME TO database[.domain]
```

```
RESET COMPATIBILITY
ENABLE [PUBLIC] THREAD n
DISABLE THREAD n
CREATE DATAFILE file_spec AS file_name
DATAFILE file_name
          [ONLINE|OFFLINE[ DROP]]
          RESIZE n [K|M]
          AUTOEXTEND CLAUSE
          END BACKUP
CHARACTER SET
NATIONAL CHARACTER SET
Set time zone clauses
DEFAULT TEMPORARY TABLESPACE tablespace
```

where:

DATABASE name. Assigned to a maximum of eight characters. If it is not specified, the value in the INIT.ORA file will be used.

File_spec. A file specification in the format of 'filename' SIZE integer K or M REUSE, with filename an OS-specific full path name; K or M specifies integer as kilobytes or megabytes; and REUSE specifies to reuse the current file if it exists. If SIZE isn't specified, 500K will be used. REUSE is optional.

File_name. A full path filename.

MOUNT. Database is available for some DBA functions, but not normal functions. Either exclusive, which is default, or PARALLEL.

STANDBY DATABASE. With version 7.3 and greater, the command operates against a hot-standby database (see Chapter 15, *Backup and Recovery Procedures for Oracle*).

CLONE. With 8*i* a clone database is used in the recovery of a tablespace to a point in time.

OPEN. Database is mounted and opened for general use, either with RESET LOGS (default) or NORESET LOGS (see Chapter15).

ACTIVATE STANDBY DATABASE. See Chapter 15.

ADD LOGFILE THREAD. Adds a thread or redo to a PARALLEL instance.

ADD LOGFILE MEMBER. Adds a logfile member to an existing group.

CLEAR. Reinitializes an online redo log and, optionally, does not archive the redo log. CLEAR LOGFILE is similar to adding and dropping a redo log except that the command may be issued even if there are only two logs for the thread, and it also may be issued for the current redo log of a closed thread.

CLEAR LOGFILE. Cannot be used to clear a log needed for media recovery. If it is necessary to clear a log containing redo after the database checkpoint, then incomplete media recovery will be necessary. The current redo log of an open thread can never be cleared. The current log of a closed thread can be cleared by switching logs in the closed thread.

If the CLEAR LOGFILE command is interrupted by a system or instance failure, then the database may hang. If so, the command must be reissued once the database is restarted. If the failure occurred because of I/O errors accessing one member of a log group, then that member can be dropped and other members added.

UNARCHIVED. Must be specified if you want to reuse a redo log that was not archived. Note that specifying UNARCHIVED will make backups unusable if the redo log is needed for recovery.

UNRECOVERABLE DATAFILE. Must be specified if the tablespace has a data file offline, and the unarchived log must be cleared to bring the tablespace online. If so, then the data file and entire tablespace must be dropped once the CLEAR LOGFILE command completes.

DROP LOGFILE. Drops an existing log group.

DROP LOGFILE MEMBER. Drops an existing log member.

RENAME. Renames the specified database file.

ARCHIVELOG/NOARCHIVELOG. Turns archive logging on or off.

RECOVER. Puts database into recovery mode. The form of recovery is specified in the recovery clause. (See Chapter 15.)

BACKUP CONTROLFILE. This can be used in two ways: first, to make a recoverable backup copy of the control file ("TO 'filename'") and, second, to make a script to rebuild the control file (" TO TRACE").

CREATE DATAFILE. Creates a new data file in place of an old one. You can use this option to re-create a data file that was lost with no backup. The 'filename' must identify a file that was once a part of the database. The filespec specifies the name and size of the new data file. If you omit the AS clause, ORACLE creates the new file with the same name and size as the file specified by 'filename'.

CREATE STANDBY CONTROLFILE. Creates a control file for use with the standby database.

DATAFILE. Allows you to perform manipulations against the data files in the instance such as resizing, turning autoextend on or off, and setting backup status.

ENABLE and DISABLE threads. Allows the enabling and disabling of redo log threads (only used for parallel databases).

RESET COMPATIBILITY. Marks the database to be reset to an earlier version of Oracle when the database is next restarted. This will render archived redo logs unusable for recovery.

TIP   The RESET COMPATIBILITY option will not work unless you have successfully disabled Oracle9i features that affect backward compatibility.

RENAME GLOBAL_NAME TO. Changes the global name of the database. A rename will automatically flush the shared pool. It doesn't change data concerning your global name in remote instances, connect strings, or db links.

Some examples of the use of ALTER DATABASE are:

- To mount a database PARALLEL:

```
ALTER DATABASE dbname MOUNT PARALLEL
```

- To drop a logfile member:

```
ALTER DATABASE
DROP LOGFILE '/oracle1/ORTEST1/redo/ORTEST1_redo31.log'
```

Re-creation of a Database

Periodically, a DBA may be required to re-create a database. Perhaps the blocksize was incorrectly specified; perhaps it has to be moved from one location to another; or perhaps a DBA has inherited a system and just wants to see how the database was created. I wish I could say there was an easy way to get this information from the database, but unfortunately, unless you have some of the third-party tools, it just isn't so.

Hopefully, you are with a shop that has detailed information on the hows, whens, and whys databases were created. Unfortunately, most shops seem to do this in the SOTP (seat of the pants) mode, so no actual documentation is available. The lesson to be learned here is to always use a script to create anything in the database that is permanent. Source 2.2 shows a sample script to document a database create statement for an Oracle instance. (Note: In this script, the MAX set of parameters are not completely documented, because these are stored in the control file.) To completely document the CREATE command, also document the control file with:

```
ALTER DATABASE BACKUP CONTROL FILE TO TRACE;
```

The file will be located in the directory specified by the BACKGROUND_DUMP_ DEST location specified in the v$parameter table. A sample output from the procedure and SQL script in Source 2.2 is in Listing 2.1. A sample output from the ALTER DATABASE BACKUP CONTROLFILE TO TRACE is shown in Listing 2.2. Another item that must be documented is the initialization parameters for your database; these are located in the v$parameter virtual table. The script db_rct9i.sql from the Wiley Web site will create a template for you to use to re-create your database. An example of the output from DB_RCT9i.sql is shown in Listing 2.1.

Source 2.2   Script to re-create Initialization file.

```
REM
REM NAME        : init_ora_rct.sql
REM FUNCTION    : Recreate the instance init.ora file
REM USE         : GENERAL
REM Limitations : None
REM
SET NEWPAGE 0 VERIFY OFF
SET ECHO OFF feedback off termout off PAGES 300 lines 80 heading off
column name  format a80 word_wrapped
column dbname new_value db noprint
select name dbname from v$database;
DEFINE OUTPUT = 'rep_out\&db\init.ora'
SPOOL &OUTPUT
SELECT '# Init.ora file from v$parameter' name from dual
union
select '# generated on:'||sysdate name from dual
union
select '# script by MRA 08/7/01 TUSC' name from dual
union
select '#' name from dual
UNION
SELECT name||' = '||value name  FROM V$PARAMETER
WHERE value is not null and ISDEFAULT='FALSE';
SPOOL OFF
CLEAR COLUMNS
SET NEWPAGE 0 VERIFY OFF
SET ECHO ON termout on PAGES 22 lines 80 heading on
SET TERMOUT ON
UNDEF OUTPUT
PAUSE Press enter to continue
```

Listing 2.1   Example output from the Database re-creation procedure.

```
CREATE DATABASE GALINUX1
CONTROLFILE REUSE
MAXINSTANCES 1
MAXLOGFILES 50
MAXDATAFILES 100
MAXLOGHISTORY 226
DATAFILE '/var/oracle/OraHome2/oradata/galinux1/system01.dbf' SIZE 340787200
REUSE
AUTOEXTEND ON NEXT  MAXSIZE 34359721984
DEFAULT STORAGE (INITIAL 16384 NEXT 16384
MINEXTENTS 1 MAXEXTENTS 505
PCTINCREASE 50)
LOGFILE
```

continues

Listing 2.1   Continued.

```
GROUP 1 (
'/var/oracle/OraHome2/oradata/galinux1/redo01.log'
) SIZE 104857600,
GROUP 2 (
'/var/oracle/OraHome2/oradata/galinux1/redo02.log'
) SIZE 104857600,
GROUP 3 (
'/var/oracle/OraHome2/oradata/galinux1/redo03.log'
) SIZE 104857600
UNDO TABLESPACE UNDOTBS DATAFILE
'/var/oracle/OraHome2/oradata/galinux1/undotbs01.dbf' SIZE 209715200 REUSE
AUTOEXTEND ON NEXT 5242880 MAXSIZE 34359721984
EXTENT MANAGEMENT LOCAL AUTOALLOCATE
DEFAULT TEMPORARY TABLESPACE TEMP TEMPFILE
'/var/oracle/OraHome2/oradata/galinux1/temp01.dbf' SIZE 41943040 REUSE
EXTENT MANAGEMENT LOCAL LOCAL SIZE 1048576
CHARACTER SET WE8ISO8859P1
NATIONAL CHARACTER SET AL16UTF16
SET TIME_ZONE ='-07:00'
NOARCHIVELOG
;
```

Listing 2.2   Example of output from the ALTER DATABASE BACKUP CONTROL FILE command.

```
/var/oracle/OraHome2/admin/galinux1/udump/ora_9084.trc
Oracle9i Enterprise Edition Release 9.0.1.0.0 - Production
With the Partitioning option
JServer Release 9.0.1.0.0 - Production
ORACLE_HOME = /var/oracle/OraHome2
System name:     Linux
Node name:      tuscgalinux
Release:      2.4.4
Version:      #8 Fri Jul 13 13:48:47 EDT 2001
Machine:      i586
Instance name: galinux1
Redo thread mounted by this instance: 1
Oracle process number: 12
Unix process pid: 9084, image: oracle@tuscgalinux (TNS V1-V3)


*** SESSION ID:(7.1237) 2001-08-23 16:08:41.118
*** 2001-08-23 16:08:41.118
# The following commands will create a new control file and use it
# to open the database.
# Data used by the recovery manager will be lost. Additional logs may
# be required for media recovery of offline data files. Use this
# only if the current version of all online logs are available.
STARTUP NOMOUNT
```

```
CREATE CONTROLFILE REUSE DATABASE "GALINUX1" NORESETLOGS NOARCHIVELOG
    MAXLOGFILES 50
    MAXLOGMEMBERS 5
    MAXDATAFILES 100
    MAXINSTANCES 1
    MAXLOGHISTORY 226
LOGFILE
  GROUP 1 '/var/oracle/OraHome2/oradata/galinux1/redo01.log'  SIZE 100M,
  GROUP 2 '/var/oracle/OraHome2/oradata/galinux1/redo02.log'  SIZE 100M,
  GROUP 3 '/var/oracle/OraHome2/oradata/galinux1/redo03.log'  SIZE 100M
# STANDBY LOGFILE
DATAFILE
  '/var/oracle/OraHome2/oradata/galinux1/system01.dbf',
  '/var/oracle/OraHome2/oradata/galinux1/undotbs01.dbf',
  '/var/oracle/OraHome2/oradata/galinux1/cwmlite01.dbf',
  '/var/oracle/OraHome2/oradata/galinux1/drsys01.dbf',
  '/var/oracle/OraHome2/oradata/galinux1/example01.dbf',
  '/var/oracle/OraHome2/oradata/galinux1/indx01.dbf',
  '/var/oracle/OraHome2/oradata/galinux1/tools01.dbf',
  '/var/oracle/OraHome2/oradata/galinux1/users01.dbf',
  '/opt/oracle/oradata/galinux1/dbautil_index01.dbf',
  '/opt/oracle/oradata/galinux1/dbautil_data01.dbf'
CHARACTER SET WE8ISO8859P1
;
# Recovery is required if any of the datafiles are restored backups,
# or if the last shutdown was not normal or immediate.
RECOVER DATABASE
# Database can now be opened normally.
ALTER DATABASE OPEN;
# Commands to add tempfiles to temporary tablespaces.
# Online tempfiles have complete space information.
# Other tempfiles may require adjustment.
ALTER TABLESPACE TEMP ADD TEMPFILE
'/var/oracle/OraHome2/oradata/galinux1/temp01.dbf' REUSE;
# End of tempfile additions.
#
```

Database Startup and Shutdown

When the instance and database are created using DBCA in Linux or UNIX, the oratab in the /etc or /var/opt/oracle directory is updated to have a listing similar to:

```
galinux1:/var/oracle/OraHome2:N
```

If you manually create the database, you should edit the oratab file to include a similar entry for your database SID.

The listing in the oratab file consists of three parts, divided by colons. The first part is the SID for the instance; in the above example, this is galinux1. The second portion is the value for the ORACLE_HOME symbol for that instance; the final value is either Y or N. The third value determines if the database is started and stopped during startup and shutdown of the host. The oratab is read by the startup files in the init.d directories, and the startup files execute the $ORACLE_HOME/bin/dbstart and $ORACLE_HOME/bin/dbshut files on UNIX.

On NT 4.0, startup and shutdown are generally handled by the oradim program. Whether databases are started or stopped automatically is decided by several registry entries in the HKEY_LOCAL_MACHINE-SOFTWARE-ORACLE-HOMEn registry tree. The registry entries on NT4.0 SP6 are:

ORA_sid_AUTOSTART. Either "TRUE" or "FALSE."

ORA_sid_SHUTDOWNTYPE. One of three options: "i" for immediate, "n" for normal, or "a" for abort; the default is "i."

ORA_sid_SHUTDOWN_TIMEOUT. Set to seconds to wait for Oracle to shut down; defaults to 30, at which time the system shuts down anyway.

The oradim program is used to start, stop, and maintain the databases on NT 4.0 and W2K. By specifying command sets in .CMD files, different actions can be taken in regard to the Oracle database system. For example, the startdb.cmd file for an instance with a SID of TEST, an INTERNAL password of ORACLE, might look like this:

```
c:\orant\bin\oradim      -startup -sid TEST -usrpwd ORACLE
                    -pfile
c:\oracle1\ortest1\admin\pfile\initORTEST1.ora
                    -starttype SRVC, INST
```

A shutdown script for the same instance would look like this:

```
c:\orant\bin\oradim      -shutdown -sid TEST
                    -SURPWD ORACLE
                    -SHTTYPE  SRVC, INST
                    -SHUTMODE a
```

Startup　　The database is open and ready for use after being created. Once the operating system is shut down, or the database is shut down, it must be started before it can be accessed.

UNIX or LINUX Startup　　On UNIX or Linux systems, the DBA has to perform the following steps to ensure the instance and database startup each time the system starts up:

1. Log in as root.
2. Edit the /etc/oratab file. Change the last field for your $ORACLE_SID to Y.
3. Add a line similar to the following to your /etc/init.d/Dbora file or its equivalent on your version of UNIX (it may be in an rc.d directory instead of an init.d directory); be sure you use the full path to the dbstart procedure.

```
su - oracle_owner -c /users/oracle/bin/dbstart
```

An example of a full Dbora script is shown in Listing 2.3.

Listing 2.3   Example Dbora script.

```
#!/bin/sh
#
# /etc/rc.d/init.d/Dbora
# Description: Starts and stops the Oracle database and listeners
# See how we were called.
case "$1" in
  start)
        echo -n "Starting Oracle Databases: "
        echo "-------------------------" >> /var/log/oracle
        date +"! %T %a %D : Starting Oracle Databases as part of system up."
>> /var/log/oracle
        echo "-------------------------" >> /var/log/oracle
        su - oracle -c /users/oracle/9.0.1/bin/dbstart >> /var/log/oracle
        echo "Done."
        echo -n "Starting Oracle Listeners: "
        su - oracle -c "/users/oracle/9.0.1/bin/lsnrctl start" >>
/var/log/oracle
        echo "Done."
        echo ""
        echo "-------------------------" >> /var/log/oracle
        date +"! %T %a %D : Finished." >> /var/log/oracle
        echo "-------------------------" >> /var/log/oracle
        touch /var/lock/subsys/oracle
        ;;
  stop)
        echo -n "Shutting Down Oracle Listeners: "
        echo "-------------------------" >> /var/log/oracle
        date +"! %T %a %D : Shutting Down Oracle Databases as part of system
down." >> /var/log/oracle
        echo "-------------------------" >> /var/log/oracle
        su - oracle -c "/users/oracle/9.0.1/bin/lsnrctl stop" >>
/var/log/oracle
        echo "Done."
        rm -f /var/lock/subsys/oracle
        echo -n "Shutting Down Oracle Databases: "
        su - oracle -c /users/oracle/9.0.1/bin/dbshut >> /var/log/oracle
        echo "Done."
        echo ""
        echo "-------------------------" >> /var/log/oracle
        date +"! %T %a %D : Finished." >> /var/log/oracle
        echo "-------------------------" >> /var/log/oracle
        ;;
  restart)
```

continues

Listing 2.3   Continued.

```
        echo -n "Restarting Oracle Databases: "
        echo "-------------------------" >> /var/log/oracle
        date +"! %T %a %D : Restarting Oracle Databases as part of system
up." >> /var/log/oracle
        echo "-------------------------" >> /var/log/oracle
        su - oracle -c /user/oracle/9.0.1/bin/dbshut >> /var/log/oracle
        su - oracle -c /user/oracle/9.0.1/bin/dbstart >> /var/log/oracle
        echo "Done."
        echo -n "Restarting Oracle Listeners: "
        su - oracle -c "/user/oracle/9.0.1/bin/lsnrctl stop" >>
/var/log/oracle
        su - oracle -c "/user/oracle/9.0.1/bin/lsnrctl start" >>
/var/log/oracle
        echo "Done."
        echo ""
        echo "-------------------------" >> /var/log/oracle
        date +"! %T %a %D : Finished." >> /var/log/oracle
        echo "-------------------------" >> /var/log/oracle
        touch /var/lock/subsys/oracle
        ;;
  *)
        echo "Usage: oracle {start|stop|restart}"
        exit 1
esac
```

To call the above scripts, entries are needed in the appropriate init.d or rc.d directories corresponding to the run level at which Oracle needs to be stopped or started. Usually start in levels 2, 3, and 4, and shut down in 0 and 6.

To accomplish this, you will place links from the rc2.d, rc3.d, rc4.d, rc0.d, and rc6.d subdirectories to the Dbora script. The links are usually of the form SnDbora or KnDbora, where *n* is an integer corresponding to the order of other start or stop calls are present: S means start the database, K means kill it. Typically, you will want an S99Dbora entry in levels 2, 3, and 4 directories, and a K01Dbora entry in levels 0 and 6. The commands lsnrctl, dbstart, and dbshut may have to be full-path'ed depending on your environment. The startup links are formed with these commands:

```
ln -s /etc/init.d/Dbora /etc/init.d/rc2.d/S99Dbora
ln -s /etc/init.d/Dbora /etc/init.d/rc3.d/S99Dbora
ln -s /etc/init.d/Dbora /etc/init.d/rc4.d/S99Dbora
```

Once the script Dbora is in place and the links have been created on Linux, you must run the insserv command to tell the various configuration scripts where the Dbora file is located. The insserv command is available from the root user.

If you get an error on Linux such as:

```
/etc/init.d/Dbora: bad interpreter: Permission denied,
```

this indicates that the program was written in a Windows environment and was not properly converted to UNIX format. I suggest getting a program called dos2unix; at the time of this writing it was available at http://www.bastet.com/software/software.html. Also, be sure you have the proper execute privileges set on the scripts.

Manual Startup   On all systems, manual startup is accomplished via the supplied scripts, through the SVRMGR, or, in the later Oracle8*i* and Oracle9*i* releases, through the SQLPLUS program. To start up a database using SVRMGR or SQLPLUS, use the following procedure. The command used is STARTUP; its format follows.

```
STARTUP  [RESTRICTED] [FORCE] [PFILE=filename] [SPFILE=filename]
         [EXCLUSIVE or PARALLEL] (pre 9i only)
         [MOUNT or OPEN] dbname
         [NOMOUNT]
         [RECOVER]
```

1. Log in to SVRMGR as INTERNAL or in to SQLPLUS as SYS or as "/" using the AS SYSDBA qualifier.
2. Issue one of the following commands:
   a. **STARTUP OPEN dbname PFILE=filename.** This command starts the instance and opens the database named dbname using the parameter file specified by the filename following the PFILE= clause. This starts up the database in the default, EXCLUSIVE mode.
   b. **STARTUP RESTRICT OPEN dbname PFILE=filename.** This command starts the instance and opens the database named dbname using the parameter file specified by the filename following the PFILE= clause. This starts up the database in the restricted-only mode (only users with RESTRICTED SESSION privilege can log in).
   c. **STARTUP NOMOUNT.** This command starts the instance, but leaves the database dismounted and closed. Cannot be used with EXCLUSIVE, MOUNT, or OPEN. Normally, this command is used only when creating a database. There are some maintenance activities that require the database to be in NOMOUNT, but generally it is only used with database creation.
   d. **STARTUP MOUNT.** This command starts the instance and mounts the database, but leaves it closed.
   e. **STARTUP OPEN dbname PARALLEL.** This command starts the instance, opens the database, and puts the database in PARALLEL mode for multi-instance use in pre-Oracle8 versions. In Oracle8, simply setting the initialization parameter PARALLEL_SERVER to TRUE starts the instance in parallel server (shared) mode. In Oracle9*i*, the parameter CLUSTER_SERVER set to TRUE starts RAC. PARALLEL is obsolete in Oracle8. PARALLEL_SERVER is obsolete in Oracle9*i*. It cannot be used with EXCLUSIVE or NOMOUNT or if the INIT.ORA parameter SINGLE_PROCESS is set to TRUE. The SHARED parameter is obsolete in Oracle8.

   f. **STARTUP OPEN dbname EXCLUSIVE.** This command is functionally identical to a, above. It cannot be specified if PARALLEL or NOMOUNT is also specified in pre-Oracle8 versions. EXCLUSIVE is obsolete in Oracle8. If PARALLEL_SERVER—or, in Oracle9*i* CLUSTER_SERVER—is FALSE, the database defaults to EXCLUSIVE.

   g. The FORCE parameter can be used with any of the above options to force a shutdown and restart of the database into that mode. This is not normally done and is only used for debugging and testing.

   h. The RECOVER option can be used to immediately start recovery of the database on startup if desired.

Errors that can occur during a startup include missing files, improperly specified PFILE path or name, or corrupted file errors. If any of these occur, the database will immediately shut down. Using OEM (Oracle Enterprise Manager) you must log in as an account that has been assigned the SYSOPER or SYSDBA roles in order to start up or shut down an instance.

Shutdown   The databases should be shut down before system shutdowns, before full cold backups, and any time system operations require the system to be shut down.

UNIX Shutdown   For UNIX, several things need to be done to ensure shutdown occurs. The following procedure, for the HP-UX version of UNIX, demonstrates these steps:

1. Log in as root.
2. Edit the /etc/oratab file. Make the last field a Y for the $ORACLE_SID you want shut down.
3. Add the following links to your /etc/init.d rcx.d files (where *x* is the run level).

```
ln -s /etc/init.d/Dbora /etc/init.d/rc0.d/K01Dbora
ln -s /etc/init.d/Dbora /etc/init.d/rc6.d/K01Dbora
```

You should alter the shutdown script ($ORACLE_HOME/bin/dbshut) to do a SHUTDOWN IMMEDIATE. This backs out any uncommitted user transactions, logs them out, and then shuts down the database. If a normal SHUTDOWN is performed, the system politely waits for all users to log off of Oracle. If Joe is on vacation and left his terminal up in a form, you could have a long wait. The other shutdown, SHUTDOWN ABORT, should only be used for emergencies, as it stops the database just as it is, with operations pending or not. A SHUTDOWN ABORT will require a recovery on startup. The new command option SHUTDOWN TRANSACTIONAL allows transactions to finish, then logs the user off and performs shutdown.

   The preceding provides for automatic shutdown when the operating system shuts down. For a normal shutdown, execute the dbshut procedure for UNIX. If it has been created, the stop<sid>.cmd script is used to shut down an Oracle instance on NT.

To perform a manual shutdown on all systems, perform the following procedure:

1. Log in to SVRMGR as INTERNAL; if on 9*i*, use the SQLPLUS /NOLOG and log in as either SYS or "/" using the AS SYSDBA qualifier.
2. Issue the appropriate SHUTDOWN command.
   a. **No option means SHUTDOWN NORMAL.** The database waits for all users to disconnect, prohibits new connects, then closes and dismounts the database, then shuts down the instance.
   b. **SHUTDOWN IMMEDIATE.** Cancels current calls like a system interrupt, and closes and dismounts the database, then shuts down the instance. PMON gracefully shuts down the user processes. No instance recovery is required on startup.
   c. **SHUTDOWN ABORT.** This doesn't wait for anything. It shuts the database down now. Instance recovery will probably be required on startup. You should escalate to this by trying the other shutdowns first.
   d. **SHUTDOWN TRANSACTIONAL.** Like SHUTDOWN IMMEDIATE, only it waits for transactions to complete, then boots off any users and shuts down the database.

Killing Oracle User Processes

There are a number of reasons to kill Oracle user processes. (Note: By "killing Oracle processes" I mean killing nonessential database processes.) These nonessential database processes usually consist of terminal sessions that are left connected after real work has been accomplished. These active sessions result in problems when the database has to be shut down for either backup or maintenance operations. As long as there is an active session, a normal-mode shutdown will hang. Coming in on Monday to discover that the database couldn't shut down, and thus couldn't be backed up, is a frustrating experience. Oracle has provided the immediate shutdown mode, but this isn't always reliable and, in some situations, can result in an inconsistent backup. The abort shutdown option will shut down the database, but you then have to restart and perform a normal shutdown before any backup operations, or risk an inconsistent backup. Therefore, it is important for the DBA to know how to kill these processes before operations of this type are accomplished.

Methods of Murder   Other than the aforementioned abort option for the SHUTDOWN command, which after all is rather rude, what are the methods of killing these recalcitrant sessions? Essentially, you can issue an ALTER SYSTEM KILL SESSION or you can issue a manual process kill command such as the UNIX: kill -9 pid from the operating system side. You should do one or the other of these types of kill operations, but not both. If you kill both the Oracle process and the operating system process, it can result in database hang situations, which will force you to perform a shutdown abort.

Killing from the Oracle Side   The DBA can either issue a series of ALTER SYSTEM commands manually or develop a dynamic SQL script to perform the operation. Source 2.3 shows a PL/SQL procedure to perform a kill of a process using the dynamic SQL package of procedures: DBMS_SQL. In Oracle8*i*, a new option is available for the ALTER SYSTEM that allows disconnection of the user process after a transaction completes. The commented-out section in Source 2.3 shows this alternative to a straight kill.

Using the procedure from Source 2.3 the DBA can then create a quick SQL procedure to remove the nonrequired Oracle sessions from the Oracle side. An example of this procedure is shown in Source 2.4. An example of the output from ora_kill.sql (kill_all.sql) is shown in Listing 2.4.

Source 2.3   ORA_KILL.SQL procedure for killing nonessential Oracle sessions.

```
REM
REM ORA_KILL.SQL
REM FUNCTION: Kills nonessential Oracle sessions (those that aren't
REM owned)
REM          : by SYS or "NULL"
REM DEPENDENCIES: Depends on kill_session procedure
REM MRA 9/12/96
REM
SET HEADING OFF TERMOUT OFF VERIFY OFF ECHO OFF
SPOOL kill_all.sql
SELECT 'EXECUTE kill_session('||chr(39)||sid||chr(39)||','||
chr(39)||serial#||chr(39)||');' FROM v$session
WHERE username IS NOT NULL
OR username <> 'SYS'
/
SPOOL OFF
START kill_all.sql

The kill_session procedure Is defined as:

CREATE OR REPLACE PROCEDURE kill_session ( session_id in varchar2,
serial_num in varchar2)
AS
cur INTEGER;
ret INTEGER;
string VARCHAR2(100);
BEGIN
--
-- Comment out the following three lines to
-- not use KILL
--
  string :=
         'ALTER SYSTEM KILL SESSION' || CHR(10) ||
```

```
CHR(39)||session_id||','||serial_num||CHR(39);
--
-- Uncomment the following 4 lines to use DISCONNECT
--
-- string :=
--          'ALTER SYSTEM DISCONNECT SESSION' || CHR(10) ||
-- CHR(39)||session_id||','||serial_num||CHR(39)||CHR(10)||
--' POST_TRANSACTION';
    cur := dbms_sql.open_cursor;
    dbms_sql.parse(cur,string,dbms_sql.v7);
    ret := dbms_sql.execute(cur)   ;
    dbms_sql.close_cursor(cur);
EXCEPTION
    WHEN OTHERS THEN
        raise_application_error(-20001,'Error in execution',TRUE);
        IF dbms_sql.is_open(cur) THEN
          dbms_sql.close_cursor(cur);
        END IF;
END;
/
```

Listing 2.4   Example of a kill.sql script (output from ora_kill.sql).

```
EXECUTE kill_session('10','212');
EXECUTE kill_session('13','1424');
```

Once a session has been killed, its status in the V$SESSION view goes to KILLED, and users will receive an error if they try to reactivate the session. The session entry will not be removed until the user attempts to reconnect. Shutdown immediate and shutdown normal are supposed to be able to handle killed sessions properly, but there have been reports of problems up to version 7.3.2 on some platforms. In 8*i* and 9*i* databases, you may wish to use the more polite kill command, which allows for a transactional kill; that is, it waits to kill the process until after its transaction is over. The format for a transactional kill would be:

```
ALTER SYSTEM DISCONNECT SESSION 'integer1 , integer2'
[POST_TRANSACTION| IMMEDIATE]
```

Killing from the Operating System Side   The other method of removing these unwanted sessions is to kill them from the operating system side. In UNIX environments, this is accomplished with the kill -9 command executed from a privileged user. In other operating systems, there are similar commands. Source 2.4 shows a UNIX shell command script that will remove the nonessential Oracle sessions for all currently active Oracle databases on the UNIX server.

The ora_kill.sh script in Source 2.4 employs a technique used in the dbshut and db-start shell scripts. It uses the /etc/oratab file to determine which databases should be operating. An alternative to using the oratab file would be to do "ps -ef | grep smon", redirecting output into a file, and using awk to strip out the SID names (similar to the technique used below). Each operating instance will have one smon process, so this makes a logical string value to grep out of the "ps -ef" process list.

Killing the sessions from the operating system side will remove their entries from the V$SESSION view. An example of the output from ora_kill.sh (kill.lis) is shown in Listing 2.5.

Source 2.4   Shell script to kill nonessential Oracle processes from the server side.

```ksh
#!/bin/ksh
ORATAB=/etc/oratab
trap 'exit' 1 2 3
# Set path if path not set (if called from /etc/rc)
case $PATH in
    "")      PATH=/bin:/usr/bin:/etc
    export PATH ;;
esac
rm kill.lis
rm proc.lis
touch kill.lis
touch proc.lis
#
# Loop for every entry in oratab
#
cat $ORATAB | while read LINE
do
    case $LINE in
    \#*)            ;;       #comment-line in oratab
    *)
    ORACLE_SID='echo $LINE | awk -F: '{print $1}' -'
    if [ "$ORACLE_SID" = '*' ] ; then
        ORACLE_SID=""
    fi
    esac
    if [ "$ORACLE_SID" <> '*' ] ; then
        proc_name='oracle'$ORACLE_SID
        ps -ef|grep $proc_name>>proc.lis
    fi
done
cat proc.lis | while read LINE2
do
        command='echo $LINE2 | awk -F: 'BEGIN { FS = ",[ \t]*|[ \t]+" }
                            { print $2}' -'
        test_it='echo $LINE2|awk -F: 'BEGIN { FS = ",[ \t]*|[ \t]+" }
                            { print $8}' -'
```

```
    if [ "$test_it" <> 'grep' ] ; then
        command='kill -9 '$command
        echo $command>>kill.lis
    fi
done
rm proc.lis
chmod 755 kill.lis
kill.lis
rm kill.lis
```

Listing 2.5   Example output from the ora_kill.sh script (kill.lis).

```
kill -9 11240
kill -9 11244
kill -9 11248
kill -9 11252
kill -9 11256
kill -9 9023
kill -9 9025
kill -9 9028
kill -9 9030
```

It may be necessary to terminate nonessential Oracle sessions if these sessions are "abandoned" by their users, or if a shutdown must be accomplished regardless of database activity. This termination can be accomplished with one of three methods: a shutdown with the abort option, use of the ALTER SYSTEM kill options, or use of the operating system process killer.

Database Deletion

Databases are deleted by shutting them down and then removing all of their associated files from the system. No command to perform this is provided by Oracle prior to Oracle9*i*. In Oracle9*i*, the DROP TABLESPACE command enables the DBA to drop the operating system files, as well as the logical database structures. The Database Creation Assistant (DBCA) does allow a DBA to remove a database in 8*i* and 9*i*. Let's look at an example using the DBCA on Linux.

The DBCA is started by issuing the DBCA command at the Oracle user in Linux or UNIX (or selecting it from the appropriate menu in Windows or NT). The first screen that is displayed is shown in Figure 2.21. Select the Next button to display the Operations screen (see Figure 2.22). There, select the option Delete a Database and then select the Next button.

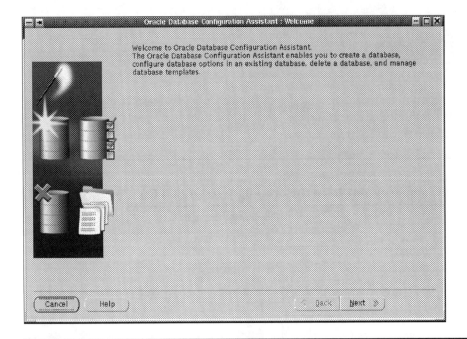

FIGURE 2.21   Welcome Screen of the Database Configuration Assistant.

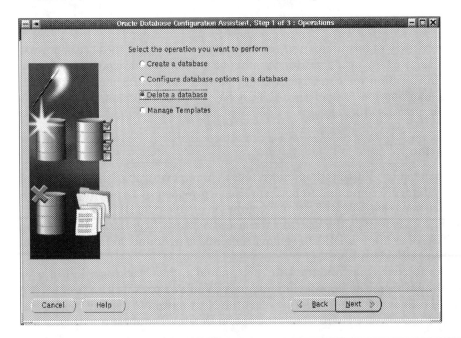

FIGURE 2.22   Operations screen of the Database Configuration Assistant.

The DBCA will display the Database screen next (shown in Figure 2.23). On the Database screen, select the database you wish to delete and then select the Next button.

Once you have made a database selection, the DBCA will show a Summary screen (shown in Figure 2.24) to give you a first chance to abort the deletion, just in case you chose the wrong database SID on the previous screen. Once you have verified that the database being deleted is in fact the one you want deleted, select the OK button to continue with the deletion process.

After you select OK on the Summary screen, the DBCA program gives you one last chance to decide *not* to delete the instance. This screen isn't titled, so I call it the "Are you really, really sure" screen; it's shown in Figure 2.25. If you are really, really sure you want to delete the database, select Yes, and the delete operation will commence. This is the point of no return.

The next screen shown in the DBCA for the database deletion process displays the actual deletion status (Figure 2.26), that is, the progression through the various steps of deleting a database: connect, delete the instance and datafiles, and update network files. Following the final step, the DBCA automatically goes to the completion screen.

The final screen of the deletion process is the Database Deletion Completed screen (shown in Figure 2.27). It asks the question "Do you want to perform another operation?" The choices are Yes, to return to DBCA, or No, exit from DBCA. If you are done deleting databases, choose No.

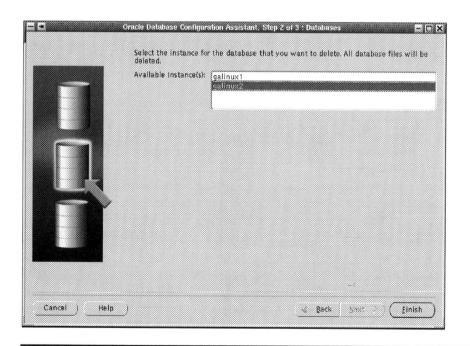

FIGURE 2.23   Database screen of the Database Configuration Assistant.

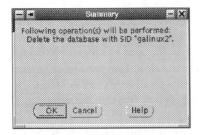

FIGURE 2.24 Summary Screen of the Database Configuration Assistant.

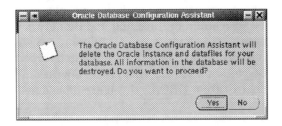

FIGURE 2.25 The "Are you really, really sure?" screen of the Database Configuration Assistant.

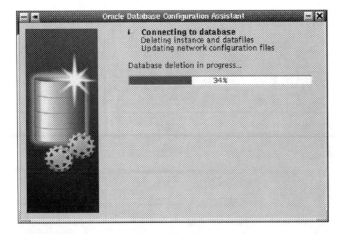

FIGURE 2.26 Database deletion status screen of the Database Configuration Assistant.

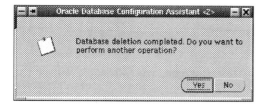

FIGURE 2.27   Database deletion completion screen of the Database Configuration Assistant.

Manual Database Deletion

If you must manually delete a database, first log in as a DBA account, then use the following commands to get a listing of all the datafiles associate with the database:

```
Spool db_files.lis
Select file_name from dba_data_files;
Select file_name from v$log_files;
Select value from v$parameter where name='control_files';
Spool off
```

Once you have your file listing, shut down the database. And I suggest doing a complete, final backup (rest assured, someone will require something from this database sometime in the future) of the database before deleting it.

Once you have backed up the database that you wish to delete, delete the physical files from your list. There are several files that contain data concerning the database and the instance. If deletion is required of both, it is suggested that a UNIX "grep" or "find" command be used to locate the files that contain the instance or database name. On UNIX, the files of concern are oratab, listener.ora, tnsnames.ora, and any user-created scripts or files. On NT, you will need to remove the services and delete the database names from the listener.ora and tnsnames.ora files. The name and related data must be removed from these files, or the files deleted, if the user wishes to reuse the instance name. Generally, the files on UNIX or Linux are in the /etc or /var/opt/oracle directory or (in the case of the network files) in $ORACLE_HOME/network/ admin. If only the database needs to be deleted, and then re-created, edit the CREATE script and rerun it under SVRMGR or SQLPLUS with the database shut down. This will reinitialize the database.

Changing the "dbname" for a Database   Follow these steps to change the dbname for a database:

1. At the operating system command line enter:

```
% svrmgrl or sqlplus /nolog
```

2. Once the server manager or sqlplus command line appears, enter:

```
connect internal (for svrmgrl) or connect / as sysdba or connect sys as
sysdba (for sqlplus)
```

3. When the server manager or sqlplus indicates that you are connected, enter the command:

```
alter database backup controlfile to trace resetlogs;
```

This will write in a trace file, the CREATE CONTROLFILE command that would re-create the control file as it currently exists. This trace file will be located in the USER_DUMP_DEST location specified in the v$parameter table (select value from v$parameter where name='user_dump_dest').

4. Exit and go to the directory where your trace files are located. They are usually in the $ORACLE_HOME/admin/<sid./udump directory, if you haven't explicitly set the location in your initialization file. If user_dump_dest is set in the init<SID>.ora, then go to the directory listed in the user_dump_dest variable. The trace file will have the form "ora_NNNN.trc," with NNNN being a number that will correspond (either in decimal or hexadecimal) to your system process ID.

5. Get the "CREATE CONTROLFILE" command from the trace file and put it in a new file called something like crt_cf.sql.

6. Edit the "crt_cf.sql" file and modify the "CREATE CONTROLFILE" command. Change the word "REUSE" to "SET", and "NORESETLOGS" to "RESETLOGS", and modify the "dbname."

Old line:

```
CREATE CONTROLFILE REUSE DATABASE "old_name" NORESETLOGS ...
```

New line:

```
CREATE CONTROLFILE SET DATABASE "new_name"  RESETLOGS ...
```

Then save the "crt_cf.sql" file.

7. Rename the old control files for backup purposes and so they are not in the way of creating the new ones.

8. Edit initSID.ora so that db_name = "new_name".

9. At the operating system prompt type:

```
% svrmgrl(pre-8i) or sqlplus /nolog (post 8i)
```

10. Once the server manager or sqlplus prompt appears, enter:

```
connect internal (pre-8i) or connect / as sysdba or connect sys as sysdba
(post-8i)
```

11. Once you are connected as INTERNAL or SYS, enter:

```
startup nomount
```

12. Type:

```
@crt_cf
```

13. Once the file stops executing, enter:

```
alter database open;
```

14. Verify that the database is functional; you can check that the database name has been reset with the command:

```
select name from v$database;
```

15. Shut down and back up the database. Make sure any local variables are also changed to reflect the SID (for example, ORACLE_SID).

Other Database Administration Tasks

Let's look at some of the other operations that may need to be performed against a database.

Addition of Log Groups and Log Member Files   The number of redo logs is directly related to the number, size, and length of transactions that are performed in the database. Each transaction that alters the database is recorded in the redo log files. The size of redo logs is governed by the amount of data a database can afford to lose. If a database supports noncritical data, where loss of a few hours' worth of data is not important, then very large redo logs can be used. In a database where each piece of data is critical and loss of even minuscule portions of data could be catastrophic, a very small redo log is in order. If you have larger redo logs, fewer are needed; if you have small redo logs, many may be needed. Under Oracle7, Oracle8-8i and Oracle9i, two groups of at least one redo log each are required; again, three are suggested. Having multiple group members allows the shadowing of log files on multiple drives, thus making redo-log-loss-type failures almost impossible.

Under Oracle7, Oracle8-8i, and Oracle9i, redo logs are members of groups, and each group should be located on a separate drive and can be associated with a single thread of the multithread server. In addition, Oracle allows redo log mirroring, where a redo log can be simultaneously copied to multiple disks at the same time by the LGWR process. This ensures that the loss of a group of log files will not affect operation. Groups are archived together. The MAXLOGMEMBERS parameter in the CREATE DATABASE statement determines the maximum number of redo logs in a group. The MAXLOGFILES parameter in the CREATE DATABASE statement determines the maximum number of groups. The reason that the MAXLOGFILES parameter is MAXLOGFILES and not MAXLOGGROUPS is that it is a carryover from the days before you could have multiple log members, as well as multiple log groups. In those days, a single parameter value controlled the number of files. Rather than change the parameter everywhere it is used, Oracle simply added a second parameter.

Another factor is whether or not you are using archive logging. While a redo log (or log group) is being archived, it cannot be used. If a log switch goes to a redo log (or log group) that is being archived, the database stops. This is why three is the minimum number of logs or log groups recommended for an archive situation: one in use, one waiting to be used, and one archiving. Generally, it is suggested that several be available for use. In several installations where the logs were archived to disk, during heavy-use periods the disk filled, causing archiving to be suspended. Once the available logs filled, the database stopped. In Oracle8*i* and Oracle9*i*, multiplexing of archive logs is supported. Multiplexing of archive logs allows multiple copies to be written to several locations, thus enhancing recoverability.

With multiple logs or log groups, you can have time to respond to this type of situation before the database has to be stopped. This also points out that you should keep a close eye on disk space usage for your archive destination(s). If the redo logs or groups are archived to tape, ensure that the log sizes are such that an equal number will fit on a standard tape to avoid wasting space and time. For example, if you have redo logs that are 1 MB in size on a version 7 database, and your tape has 90-MB capacity, then 90 will fit on the tape (approximately) with little waste. The entire group is archived as a unit with a size equal to that of one of the members.

After operating for a while, DBAs get a feel for how often their databases generate logs. This will tell them how many they will require and what size they will need to be. A check of the alert<SID>.log file located in the background_dump_dest-specified location will tell you how often your system is switching logs. Another location where log history is stored is the v$loghist or v$loghistory view. Unfortunately, there is no convenient formula for determining this; each DBA must determine this for his or her own database(s). To add a redo log, the following command is used:

```
ALTER DATABASE database name
ADD LOGFILE  THREAD y GROUP n (file specification, file specification) SIZE x;
```

or:

```
ALTER DATABASE database name
ADD LOGFILE  MEMBER 'file specification'  REUSE TO GROUP n;
```

or:

```
ALTER DATABASE database name
     ADD LOGFILE  MEMBER 'file specification'  REUSE TO
          ('file specification', 'file specification');
```

where:

n is the group number. If the GROUP n clause is left out, a new group will be added that consists of the specified log files.

x is the size for all members of the group.

y is the thread number to which the group is assigned.

file specification is a system-specific full path filename:

On UNIX, AIX, or Linux:

```
'/oracle1/oracle/ortest/logs/ora_redo11.rdo'  SIZE 1M REUSE
```

(The SIZE parameter is not with the file specification.)

On VMS:

```
'DUA1:[M_ORACLE_1.ORACLE.ORTEST.LOGS]ORA_REDO11.RDO' SIZE 1M
     REUSE
```

On NT:

```
'd:\oracle1\oracle\ortest\logs\ora_redo11.rdo' SIZE 1M REUSE
```

The SIZE clause specifies the size of the new log (it should be the same size as that of all of the other redo logs). M means megabytes; K is kilobytes; and no specification, just a number, means bytes. REUSE tells Oracle that if the file exists, reuse it; however, to be reused, the old and new files must be the same specified size.

Dropping Log Files   The ALTER command is also used to drop redo logs:

```
ALTER DATABASE database name
     DROP LOGFILE   GROUP n --OR--('filename', 'filename');
```

or:

```
ALTER DATABASE database name
     DROP LOGFILE  MEMBER 'filename';
```

where 'filename' is just the filename, no SIZE or REUSE clause.

Addition of Rollback Segments   Another database structure is the ROLLBACK segment. Under pre-9*i* versions and in 9*i* with manually managed undo, ROLLBACK segments can be placed in any tablespace, but it is suggested that they be placed in a tablespace that contains only other rollback segments. This makes administration easier. Rollback segments can be PUBLIC, which means that for a multi-instance database, any instance can use the rollback segment, or PRIVATE, which means only the instance that has the rollback segments named in the ROLLBACK SEGMENTS clause of its INIT.ORA file can use the rollback segment.

Under Oracle9*i*, an UNDO tablespace can be created (is created by default) and should be used to allow Oracle to internally manage UNDO (read rollback) operations. The UNDO tablespace is usually created with the UNDO TABLESPACE clause of the CREATE DATABASE command or can be added after database creation with the

CREATE UNDO TABLESPACE command and addition of the required initialization parameters.

Managing the UNDO Tablespace   There are several initialization parameters that control the UNDO tablespace feature of Oracle9*i*. They are:

> **UNDO_MANAGEMENT.** Can be set to AUTO or MANUAL. In AUTO, the database manages undo operations; under MANUAL, the DBA manages undo operations. The default value is MANUAL, and any UNDO_TABLESPACE specification is ignored. If set to MANUAL, management of rollback segments is identical to pre-9*i* rollback segment management.
>
> **UNDO_TABLESPACE.** A dynamic parameter that specifies which tablespace to use as an UNDO tablespace.
>
> **UNDO_RETENTION.** A dynamic parameter that specifies the length of time to retain undo information for use in flashback queries; the default is 900 seconds.
>
> **UNDO_SUPPRESS_ERRORS.** Either TRUE or FALSE. Used to suppress error messages if manual undo management SQL commands are entered in auto undo management mode.

Creation of the UNDO Tablespace   As stated above, the UNDO tablespace can be created either when the database is created, using the UNDO TABLESPACE clause of the CREATE DATABASE command, or it can be added later, using the CREATE UNDO TABLESPACE command and the appropriate initialization parameters set for it. An example UNDO tablespace creation command is shown here:

```
CREATE UNDO TABLESPACE undo_tbs1 DATAFILE
'/oracle3/oradata/galinux1/data/undo_tbs2.dbf' SIZE 200M AUTOEXTEND ON;
```

Oracle determines the other attributes of the undo tablespace automatically; you only need to specify the datafile clause and size information. The Oracle system will automatically assign an UNDO tablespace with locally managed, auto-allocated extents; the maximum size will be set at approximately one and a half times the specified size. You can specify the autoextend parameters and the extent management parameters in the CREATE UNDO command, but options such as LOGGING will cause an error.

Altering an UNDO Tablespace   An UNDO tablespace can only be altered for the following items:

- Adding a datafile.
- Renaming a datafile.
- Bringing a datafile on- or offline.
- Beginning or ending backup.
- Resizing a datafile.

Dropping an UNDO Tablespace   The UNDO tablespace(s) are dropped using the DROP TABLESPACE command. The UNDO tablespace to be dropped cannot have any currently active transactions.

Switching Active UNDO Tablespaces   Before dropping an UNDO tablespace, you will need to make sure there is a second UNDO tablespace; then you must switch the database to use the new tablespace. The ALTER SYSTEM command is used to switch the database from one UNDO tablespace to another, as shown here:

```
ALTER SYSTEM SET UNDO_TABLESPACE = new_undo_tbsp_name;
```

Of course, if for any reason, the switch cannot be accomplished, an error is issued and no switch occurs. Errors that will prevent a switch are:

- Tablespace to be switched to doesn't exist.
- Tablespace to be switched to isn't an UNDO tablespace.
- Tablespace to be switched to is in use by another RAC instance.

If there are active transactions in the old tablespace, the tablespace goes into PENDING OFFLINE status until the transactions complete. A PENDING OFFLINE tablespace is in a state of LIMBO until its incomplete transactions are finished. A tablespace in PENDING OFFLINE cannot be dropped or used. If the UNDO_TABLESPACE parameter is set to the null string, which in Oracle is represented by two single quotes with no space between them (for example, ALTER SYSTEM SET UNDO_TABLESPACE=") then the existing undo tablespace is taken offline and no new undo tablespace is assigned. The assignment of the UNDO tablespace to the null string would be used if you were switching to MANUAL managed undo.

Assigning Usage Quotas for UNDO Tablespaces   A new feature in Oracle9*i* is the ability to establish quotas on UNDO space for specific types of users. This is accomplished using the DBMS_RESOURCE_MANAGER package. If a resource group is assigned a quota on an UNDO tablespace, and that quota is reached, the current transaction that is generating UNDO is halted and rolled back and no further UNDO transactions will be allowed from that resource group until the usage of UNDO space drops below its quota. If no quota is assigned, a resource group is considered by default to be unlimited. I will cover the use of DBMS_RESOURCE_MANAGER in detail in Chapter 9, *User and Security Administration*.

Retention Periods and UNDO Tablespaces   One of the interesting new features in Oracle9*i* dealing with UNDO tablespaces is the ability to perform flashback queries. Flashback queries allow you to view data that has been updated or deleted as it was before it was updated or deleted. Being able to look back in time is accomplished through the use of the UNDO tablespace retention capability. The DBA can specify how much data, based on an asset retention period, is maintained for flashback query. The default is 900 seconds (15 minutes). The retention period for UNDO tablespaces is set using the UNDO_RETENTION initialization parameter. The information retained for flashback query is persistent between database startups. This persistence of data means that even after a crash and restart the data will still be available. The retention period restarts its countdown after each startup.

The ALTER SYSTEM command can also be used to reset the retention period dynamically. The effect of the ALTER SYSTEM command on retention time is immediate but will only be honored completely if there is enough room in the UNDO tablespace to accommodate the data requirements.

Flashback queries are facilitated using the DBMS_FLASHBACK package, which is covered in Chapter 9. The space required to facilitate flashback is calculated by the formula:

```
UndoSpace = UR * UPS + overhead
```

where:

- UndoSpace is the number of undo blocks required.
- UR is the value of UNDO_RETENTION in seconds.
- UPS is the number of UNDO blocks generated per second.
- Overhead is a small number of blocks used for metadata.

The information for the above calculation is contained in the v$undostat view. A sample SELECT command to get this information about number of transaction UNDO blocks per second since database startup would be:

```
SELECT SUM(undoblks)/((MAX(end_time)-MIN(BEGIN_TIME))*24*3600)
FROM v$undostat;
```

The problem with this SELECT is that it will give an abnormally low value for databases with periods of low activity. It may be better to look at all of the available periods and get values that correspond to high activity times:

```
SELECT undoblks/((end_time-begin_time)*24*3600)) FROM v$undostat;
```

More useful fields from the V$UNDOSTAT view are SSOLDERRCNT and NOSPACEERRCNT. If you get values in either of these columns for your current UNDO tablespace, then you may need either a smaller UNDO_RETENTION parameter value or larger UNDO tablespaces.

Other useful UNDO views are:

V$ROLLSTAT. Shows behavior of undo or rollback segments.

V$TRANSACTION. Contains undo segment usage information.

DBA_UNDO_EXTENTS. Shows the commit time for each extent in the UNDO tablespace.

Manual Rollback Segment Maintenance If you are in pre-9*i* databases, or just like to practice all those hard-earned rollback segment management skills you needed in previous Oracle releases, you can manage the UNDO (read rollback) segments manually. All you need to do is set the initialization parameter UNDO_MANAGEMENT to MANUAL (or don't set it at all) and poof! You are back in pre-9*i* behavior.

The following initialization parameters control rollback segment behavior in pre-9*i* or in 9*i* with manual UNDO management:

UNDO_MANAGEMENT. Must be left unset or set to MANUAL.

ROLLBACK_SEGMENTS. A list of all private rollback segments to be brought online on instance startup.

TRANSACTIONS. Must be set to the number of expected transactions if public rollback segments are used; usually this value is automatically set to 1.1*PROCESSES, so set PROCESSES instead of manually setting TRANSACTIONS.

TRANSACTIONS_PER_ROLLBACK_SEGMENT. Set to the maximum number of concurrent transactions that will be allowed to access a single rollback segment; should usually equal the MINEXTENTS for a public rollback segment. The calculation:

```
TRANSACTIONS/TRANSACTIONS_PER_ROLLBACK_SEGMENT
```

will be used to determine the number of public rollback segments to bring online at database startup. Any offline public rollback segment will be brought online if the above ratio is exceeded.

MAX_ROLLBACK_SEGMENTS. Sets the maximum rollback segments that can be brought online for any instance. This defaults to the above ratio for public rollback segments, 30 for private rollback segments, and requires a database bounce to increase or decrease.

The following subsections discuss rollback segment management for manual mode.

Creating Rollback Segments Manually managed rollback segments are created using the CREATE command. The format for this command follows.

```
CREATE [PUBLIC] ROLLBACK SEGMENT rollback name
    TABLESPACE tablespace name
    STORAGE storage clause;
```

where:

Rollback name is the name for the rollback segment; this name must be unique.

Tablespace name is the name of the tablespace where the segment is to be created.

STORAGE clause specifies the required storage parameters for the rollback segment. It is strongly suggested that the following guidelines be used for this:

INITIAL = NEXT. For an operating database, I usually recommend that the dba_rollback_segs and v$rollstat views be used to determine the settings for INITIAL, NEXT, and OPTIMAL, setting INITIAL=NEXT and both equal to the multiple of the average transaction size as reported in the aforementioned views.

MINEXTENTS = 2 (default on CREATE ROLLBACK). Oracle suggests this be set to 20; however, I believe it should be set based on your database usage characteristics. I generally shoot for four transactions per rollback segment. Remember, only DML transactions and some DDL (that result in tables in the data dictionary receiving updates) require rollback segments.

MAXEXTENTS. A calculated maximum based on the size of the rollback segment tablespace, the size of rollback segments extents, and the number of rollback segments.

OPTIMAL. Reflects the size to which the system will restore the rollback segment after it has been extended by a large transaction. Usually, I set it to MINEXTENTS multiplied by the initial/next values. Another method is to set OPTIMAL as the average of the maximum transaction size times a multiple such as 1.25, as indicated in the dba_rollback_segs and v$rollstat views, and then back-calculate MINEXTENTS.

When a rollback segment is created, it is not online. To be used, it must be brought online using the ALTER ROLLBACK SEGMENT *name* ONLINE; command, or the database must be shut down, the INIT.ORA parameter ROLLBACK_SEGMENTS modified, and the database restarted. In any case, the INIT.ORA file parameter should be altered if the rollback segment is to be used permanently, or it will not be acquired when the database is shut down and restarted.

Altering a Rollback Segment   The rollback segment can be altered using the ALTER command. However, this can result in mismatched extent sizes, so is not recommended. You cannot alter a rollback segment from public to private or private to public; it must be dropped and re-created for this type of change. The format of the command follows:

```
ALTER ROLLBACK SEGMENT name
     STORAGE(storage_clause_changes)
     ONLINE
     OFFLINE
     SHRINK TO n K|M
```

where:

ONLINE brings the rollback segment online.

OFFLINE takes the rollbacks segment offline (after any transactions it has are completed).

STORAGE. This clause cannot contain new values for INITIAL, MINEXTENTS, or PCTINCREASE (which is not allowed for rollback segments).

SHRINK returns a rollback segment that has expanded beyond its OPTIMAL setting to the OPTIMAL size or to the size specified.

Dropping a Rollback Segment Periodically, the DBA will have to drop a rollback segment. This is required when the rollback segment has overextended due to a large transaction, has too many extents in general, or a larger size is desired for all rollback segments. This is accomplished through the DROP command. The format of this command follows:

```
DROP ROLLBACK SEGMENT name
```

A rollback segment must not be in use or online, or it cannot be dropped. Once dropped, it must be removed from the INIT.ORA - ROLLBACK_SEGMENT clause, or the database cannot be restarted.

Moving Database Files Periodically, DBAs will need to move database files, such as the SYSTEM tablespace datafiles or redo logs, from one location to another. This is accomplished through the following procedure:

1. Shut down the database.
2. Use the operating system to copy the file(s) to their new location. (On UNIX, don't move them with the mv command; use cp or dd.)
3. Using SVRMGR, or SQLPLUS in Oracle8*i* and Oracle9*i*, issue the CONNECT INTERNAL or CONNECT SYS command to connect to the database.
4. Using SVRMGR, or SQLPLUS in Oracle8*i*, MOUNT the database, but don't OPEN it.
5. Issue the ALTER DATABASE command to rename the file.

```
ALTER DATABASE database name
        RENAME DATAFILE 'OLD FILE NAME' TO 'NEW FILE NAME';
```

6. Shut down and restart the database.
7. Use SVRMGR or SQLPLUS to look at the view DBA_DATA_FILES to be sure the file is renamed.
8. Delete the old file via the appropriate operating system command. (Be sure the database is started before you delete the file; if the database is running, it will prevent you from deleting files that are still active on VMS and NT. In UNIX, use the "fuser" command against the file to see if it is active.)

2.4 USE OF THE ALTER SYSTEM COMMAND

The ALTER SYSTEM command is used to dynamically alter the Oracle instance under an Oracle7, Oracle8, Oracle8*i*, or Oracle9*i* database. The ALTER SYSTEM command allows the following system-level items to be modified:

- Set or change resource limits.
- Create or terminate shared server or dispatcher processes.
- Switch redo log groups.
- Perform a checkpoint.
- Verify data file access.
- Restrict login to users with RESTRICTED SESSION privilege (replaces DBA mode).
- Perform distributed recovery in single process environment.
- Disable distributed recovery.
- Manually archive redo logs or enable or disable automatic archiving.
- Clear the shared pool in the SGA.
- Terminate a session.

The ALTER SYSTEM command allows the DBA much greater control over the Oracle environment than was possible in previous releases.

ALTER SYSTEM Command Format

The ALTER SYSTEM command's format follows:

```
ALTER SYSTEM
     SWITCH LOGFILE
     CHECKPOINT [GLOBAL|LOCAL]
     CHECK DATAFILES [GLOBAL|LOCAL]
     ENABLE|DISABLE RESTRICTED SESSION
     ENABLE|DISABLE DISTRIBUTED RECOVERY
     Archive_log_clause
     FLUSH SHARED_POOL
     KILL SESSION 'N1,N2'
     DISCONNECT SESSION 'N1,N2' POST TRANSACTION
     SUSPEND|RESUME
     QUIESCE RESTRICTED|UNQUIESCE
     SHUTDOWN [IMMEDIATE] [dispatcher name]
     REGISTER
     SET clause
     RESET clause
```

where:

SWITCH LOGFILE. This switches the active log file groups.

CHECKPOINT. This performs either a GLOBAL (all open instances on the database) or LOCAL (current instance) checkpoint.

CHECK DATAFILES. This verifies access to data files. If GLOBAL is specified, all data files in all instances accessing the database are verified accessible. If LOCAL is specified only the current instance's data files are verified.

ENABLE RESTRICTED SESSION. This only allows users with RESTRICTED SESSION privilege to log on to the database.

DISABLE RESTRICTED SESSION. This allows any user to log on to the instance.

ENABLE DISTRIBUTED RECOVERY. This enables distributed recovery.

DISABLE DISTRIBUTED RECOVERY. This disables distributed recovery.

ARCHIVE LOG clauses:

```
THREAD n
 [SEQUENCE n] [TO 'location']
 [CHANGE n] [TO 'location']
 [CURRENT] [TO 'location']
 [GROUP n] [TO 'location']
 [LOGFILE 'filename'] [TO 'location']
 [NEXT] [TO 'location']
 [ALL] [TO 'location']
 [START] [TO 'location']
 [STOP]
```

FLUSH SHARED_POOL. Flushes SQL and PL/SQL form shared pool if it is not pinned using the DBMS_SHAREDPOOL package.

KILL SESSION 'N1,N2'. Kills the session pid N1=sid and N2=serial number from V$SESSION.

DISCONNECT SESSION 'N1,N2' [IMMEDIATE|POST TRANSACTION]. A nicer form of **KILL**, allows transactions to complete with the **POST TRANSACTION**, same as **KILL** if **IMMEDIATE** is used.

SUSPEND|RESUME. used for suspension of all IO as well as queries, in all instances, allowing you to make copies of the database without having to handle ongoing transactions. Database tablespaces must be in hot backup mode. This is useful for when you don't want the penalties of shutting down, restarting the database and reloading the SGA as you would for a cold backup but don't need the database to be available as it would be during a normal hot backup.

QUIESCE RESTRICTED|UNQUIESCE. Used to restrict access to a database so the DBA can use the SYS or SYSTEM accounts to perform maintenance. No new transactions or connections are allowed in the QUIESCE RESTRICTED mode. Oracle will wait for current transactions to complete and resource to be released before going into QUIESCE.

SHUTDOWN [IMMEDIATE] [dispatcher name]. Used to immediately stop a dispatcher process when you are using MTS for your database. If **IMMEDIATE** is specified the dispatcher is stopped now, if **IMMEDIATE** is not specified it tells the dispatcher to not accept any more connections and to terminate when its last transaction completes.

REGISTER. Causes the instance to register with the listener processes immediately instead of waiting for the next PMON discovery cycle. If not used the registration can take up to 60 seconds or more, which prevents the database from being accessed by remote users.

SET clause. Used to set various initialization parameters dynamically. Allows specification of a comment that is added to the value in the V$PARAMETER file, a new value to which the parameter is reset, the scope of the value change, and whether the change is just for the memory or should be made permanent in the spfile.

RESET clause. Same as for SET clause only applies to specific instances in a RAC cluster.

A Detailed Look at ARCHIVE LOG Clauses

For Oracle8 much of the ARCHIVE LOG command is removed from SVRMGR (except for the pull-down display) and is placed under the ALTER SYSTEM command (shown above). The new command has additional clauses to handle the more complex archive log scheme under Oracle8, Oracle8*i*, and Oracle9*i*. The new syntax handles the threads and groups associated with the new archive logs. The new syntax follows:

```
ALTER SYSTEM ARCHIVE LOG clause;
ARCHIVE LOG clauses:
      THREAD n
        [SEQUENCE n] [TO 'location']
        [CHANGE n] [TO 'location']
        [CURRENT] [TO 'location']
        [GROUP n] [TO 'location']
        [LOGFILE 'filename'] [TO 'location']
        [NEXT] [TO 'location']
        [ALL] [TO 'location']
        [START] [TO 'location']
        [STOP]
```

where:

THREAD. This specifies the particular redo log thread to affect. If this isn't specified then the current instance redo log thread is affected.

SEQUENCE. This archives the redo log group that corresponds to the integer specified by the integer given as the argument.

CHANGE. This corresponds to the SCN (system *change* number) for the transaction you want to archive. It will force archival of the log containing the transaction with the SCN that matches the integer given as the argument to the CHANGE argument.

GROUP. This manually archives the redo logs in the specified group. If both THREAD and GROUP are specified, the group must belong to the specified thread.

CURRENT. This causes all nonarchived redo log members of the current group to be archived.

LOGFILE. This manually archives the group that contains the file specified by 'filespec'. If thread is specified the file must be in a group contained in the thread specified.

NEXT. This forces manual archival of the next online redo log that requires it. If no thread is specified, Oracle archives the earliest available unarchived redo log.

ALL. This archives all online archive logs that are part of the current thread that haven't been archived. If no thread is specified then all unarchived logs from all threads are archived.

START. Starts automatic archiving of redo log file groups. This only applies to the thread assigned to the current instance.

TO. This specifies the location to archive the logs to. This must be a full path specification.

STOP. This disables automatic archiving of redo file log groups. This applies to your current instance.

The ARCHIVE LOG command can still be used under SVRMGR in Oracle versions that support it to LIST the current status of the archive log system.

2.5 THE INIT<SID>.ORA (INITIALIZATION FILE) PARAMETERS

It should be obvious that the most important file regarding database setup and operation is probably the INIT<sid>.ORA, or initialization file. This file contains the assignments for the database initialization parameters.

For Oracle7, version 7.3, there are 154 initialization parameters; for Oracle8, version 8.0.5, there are 184. In Oracle8*i,* there are 194. In Oracle9*i,* version 9.0.1 there are 251. Table 2.1 lists the Oracle9*i* INIT.ORA parameters, their default values, and descriptions. Note that on your platform there may be more or less than this number of parameters.

The Oracle8 and Oracle8*i* initialization parameters, shown in Table 2.2, are invalid for use with Oracle9*i.*

The DBA should review the applicable administrator's and tuning guides before modifying any INIT.ORA parameters.

Oracle 9*i* has expanded the number of initialization parameters that can be altered by use of the ALTER SESSION, ALTER SYSTEM SET, and ALTER SYSTEM SET . . . DEFERRED commands. Table 2.3 shows the initialization parameters that can be altered with the commands listed in Table 2.2.

TABLE 2.1 Oracle9*i* Initialization Parameters

NAME	VALUE	DESCRIPTION
ACTIVE_INSTANCE_COUNT	Null	Number of active instances in the cluster database.
AQ_TM_PROCESSES	0	Number of AQ Time Managers to start.
ARCHIVE_LAG_TARGET	0	Maximum number of seconds of redos the standby could lose.
AUDIT_FILE_DEST	?/rdbms/audit	Directory in which Auditing files are to reside.
AUDIT_TRAIL	NONE	Enable system auditing.
BACKGROUND_CORE_DUMP	partial	Core size for background processes.
BACKGROUND_DUMP_DEST	SD	Detached process dump directory.
BACKUP_TAPE_IO_SLAVES	FALSE	BACKUP Tape I/O slaves.
BITMAP_MERGE_AREA_SIZE	1048576	Maximum memory allow for BITMAP MERGE.
BLANK_TRIMMING	FALSE	Blank trimming semantics parameter.
BUFFER_POOL_KEEP	NULL	Number of database blocks/latches in keep buffer pool.
BUFFER_POOL_RECYCLE	NULL	Number of database blocks/latches in recycle buffer pool.
CIRCUITS	170	Max number of circuits.
CLUSTER_DATABASE	FALSE	If TRUE, start up in cluster database mode.
CLUSTER_DATABASE_INSTANCES	1	Number of instances to use for sizing cluster db SGA structures.
CLUSTER_INTERCONNECTS	NULL	Interconnects for RAC use.
COMMIT_POINT_STRENGTH	1	Bias this node has toward not preparing in a two-phase commit.
COMPATIBLE	9.0.0	Database will be completely compatible with this software version number.
CONTROL_FILES	SD	Control filenames list.
CONTROL_FILE_RECORD_KEEP_TIME	7	Control file record; keep time in days.
CORE_DUMP_DEST	SD	Core dump directory.
CPU_COUNT	SD	Initial number of CPUs for this instance.
CREATE_BITMAP_AREA_SIZE	8388608	Size of create bitmap buffer for bitmap index.
CURSOR_SHARING	EXACT	Cursor sharing mode.
CURSOR_SPACE_FOR_TIME	FALSE	Use more memory in order to get faster execution.
DBLINK_ENCRYPT_LOGIN	FALSE	Enforce password for distributed login always be encrypted.

TABLE 2.1 (*Continued*)

NAME	VALUE	DESCRIPTION
DBWR_IO_SLAVES	0	Number of DBWR I/O slaves.
DB_16K_CACHE_SIZE	0	Size of cache for 16K buffers.
DB_2K_CACHE_SIZE	0	Size of cache for 2K buffers.
DB_32K_CACHE_SIZE	0	Size of cache for 32K buffers.
DB_4K_CACHE_SIZE	0	Size of cache for 4K buffers.
DB_8K_CACHE_SIZE	0	Size of cache for 8K buffers.
DB_BLOCK_BUFFERS	0	Number of database blocks cached in memory.
DB_BLOCK_CHECKING	FALSE	Data and index block checking.
DB_BLOCK_CHECKSUM	TRUE	Store checksum in db blocks and check during reads.
DB_BLOCK_SIZE	8192	Size of database block in bytes.
DB_CACHE_ADVICE	OFF	Buffer cache sizing advisory.
DB_CACHE_SIZE	67108864	Size of DEFAULT buffer pool for standard blocksize buffers.
DB_CREATE_FILE_DEST	NULL	Default database location.
DB_CREATE_ONLINE_LOG_DEST_1	NULL	Online log/controlfile Destination #1.
DB_CREATE_ONLINE_LOG_DEST_2	NULL	Online log/controlfile Destination #2.
DB_CREATE_ONLINE_LOG_DEST_3	NULL	Online log/controlfile Destination #3.
DB_CREATE_ONLINE_LOG_DEST_4	NULL	Online log/controlfile Destination #4.
DB_CREATE_ONLINE_LOG_DEST_5	NULL	Online log/controlfile Destination #5.
DB_DOMAIN	SD	Directory part of global database name stored with CREATE DATABASE.
DB_FILES	200	Max allowable # db files (soft limit).
DB_FILE_MULTIBLOCK_READ_COUNT	8	DB block to be read each I/O.
DB_FILE_NAME_CONVERT	NULL	Datafile name convert patterns and strings for standby/clone db.
DB_KEEP_CACHE_SIZE	0	Size of KEEP buffer pool for standard blocksize buffers.

continued

TABLE 2.1 (*Continued*)

NAME	*VALUE*	*DESCRIPTION*
DB_NAME	SD	Database name specified in CREATE DATABASE.
DB_RECYCLE_CACHE_SIZE	0	Size of RECYCLE buffer pool for standard block size buffers.
DB_WRITER_PROCESSES	1	Number of background database writer processes to start.
DISK_ASYNCH_IO	TRUE	Use asynch I/O for random-access devices.
DISPATCHERS	(PROTOCOL=TCP) (SER=MODOSE), (PROTOCOL=TCP) (PRE=oracle.aurora. server.GiopServer), (PROTOCOL=TCP) (PRE=oracle.aurora. server.SGiopServer)	Specifications of dispatchers.
DISTRIBUTED_TRANSACTIONS	46	Max. number of concurrent distributed transactions.
DML_LOCKS	748	DML locks: one for each table modified in a transaction.
DRS_START	FALSE	Start DR Server framework (DMON process).
ENQUEUE_RESOURCES	968	Resources for enqueues.
EVENT	NULL	Debug event control; default null string.
FAL_CLIENT	NULL	FAL client.
FAL_SERVER	NULL	FAL server list.
FAST_START_IO_TARGET	0	Upper bound on recovery reads.
FAST_START_MTTR_TARGET	300	MTTR target of forward crash recovery in seconds.
FAST_START_PARALLEL_ROLLBACK	LOW	Max number of parallel recovery slaves that may be used.
FIXED_DATE	NULL	Fixed SYSDATE value.
GC_FILES_TO_LOCKS	NULL	Mapping between file numbers and global cache locks (DFS).
GLOBAL_CONTEXT_POOL_SIZE	NULL	Global Application Context pool size in bytes.
GLOBAL_NAMES	FALSE	Enforce that database links have same name as remote database.
HASH_AREA_SIZE	1048576	Size of in-memory hash work area.

TABLE 2.1 (*Continued*)

NAME	VALUE	DESCRIPTION
HASH_JOIN_ENABLED join.HI_SHARED_MEMORY_ ADDRESS	TRUE 0	Enable/disable hash SGA starting address (high-order 32 bits on 64-bit platforms).
HS_AUTOREGISTER	TRUE	Enable automatic server DD updates in HS agent self-registration.
IFILE	NULL	Include file in init.ora.
INSTANCE_GROUPS	NULL	List of instance group names.
INSTANCE_NAME	SD	Instance name supported by the instance.
INSTANCE_NUMBER	0	Instance number.
JAVA_MAX_SESSIONSPACE_ SIZE	0	Max allowed size in bytes of a Java sessionspace.
JAVA_POOL_SIZE	117440512	Size in bytes of the Java pool.
JAVA_SOFT_SESSIONSPACE_ LIMIT	0	Warning limit on size in bytes of a Java sessionspace.
JOB_QUEUE_PROCESSES	0	Number of job queue slave processes.
LARGE_POOL_SIZE	1048576	Size in bytes of the large allocation pool.
LICENSE_MAX_SESSIONS	0	Maximum number of nonsystem user sessions allowed.
LICENSE_MAX_USERS	0	Maximum number of named users that can be created in the database.
LICENSE_SESSIONS_WARNING	0	Warning level for number of nonsystem user sessions.
LOCAL_LISTENER	NULL	Local listener.
LOCK_NAME_SPACE	NULL	Lock name space used for generating lock names for standby/clone.
LOCK_SGA	FALSE	Lock entire SGA in physical memory.
LOGMNR_MAX_PERSISTENT_ SESSIONS	1	Maximum number of threads to mine.
LOG_ARCHIVE_DEST	NULL	Archival destination text string.
LOG_ARCHIVE_DEST_1	NULL	Archival destination #1 text string.
LOG_ARCHIVE_DEST_10	NULL	Archival destination #10 text string.
LOG_ARCHIVE_DEST_2	NULL	Archival destination #2 text string.
LOG_ARCHIVE_DEST_3	NULL	Archival destination #3 text string.
LOG_ARCHIVE_DEST_4	NULL	Archival destination #4 text string.

continued

TABLE 2.1 (*Continued*)

NAME	VALUE	DESCRIPTION
LOG_ARCHIVE_DEST_5	NULL	Archival destination #5 text string.
LOG_ARCHIVE_DEST_6	NULL	Archival destination #6 text string.
LOG_ARCHIVE_DEST_7	NULL	Archival destination #7 text string.
LOG_ARCHIVE_DEST_8	NULL	Archival destination #8 text string.
LOG_ARCHIVE_DEST_9	NULL	Archival destination #9 text string.
LOG_ARCHIVE_DEST_STATE_1	enable	Archival destination #1 state text string.
LOG_ARCHIVE_DEST_STATE_10	enable	Archival destination #10 state text string.
LOG_ARCHIVE_DEST_STATE_2	enable	Archival destination #2 state text string.
LOG_ARCHIVE_DEST_STATE_3	enable	Archival destination #3 state text string.
LOG_ARCHIVE_DEST_STATE_4	enable	Archival destination #4 state text string.
LOG_ARCHIVE_DEST_STATE_5	enable	Archival destination #5 state text string.
LOG_ARCHIVE_DEST_STATE_6	enable	Archival destination #6 state text string.
LOG_ARCHIVE_DEST_STATE_7	enable	Archival destination #7 state text string.
LOG_ARCHIVE_DEST_STATE_8	enable	Archival destination #8 state text string.
LOG_ARCHIVE_DEST_STATE_9	enable	Archival destination #9 state text string.
LOG_ARCHIVE_DUPLEX_DEST	NULL	Duplex archival destination text string.
LOG_ARCHIVE_FORMAT	%t_%s.dbf	Archival destination format.
LOG_ARCHIVE_MAX_PROCESSES	1	Maximum number of active ARCH processes.
LOG_ARCHIVE_MIN_SUCCEED_DEST	1	Minimum number of archive destinations that must succeed.
LOG_ARCHIVE_START	FALSE	Start archival process on SGA initialization.
LOG_ARCHIVE_TRACE	0	Establish archivelog operation tracing level.
LOG_BUFFER	524288	Redo circular buffer size.
LOG_CHECKPOINTS_TO_ALERT	FALSE	Log checkpoint begin/end to alert file.
LOG_CHECKPOINT_INTERVAL	0	Number of redo blocks checkpoint threshold.
LOG_CHECKPOINT_TIMEOUT	1800	Maximum time interval between checkpoints in seconds.
LOG_FILE_NAME_CONVERT	NULL	Logfile name-convert patterns and strings for standby/clone db.
MAX_COMMIT_PROPAGATION_DELAY	700	Max age of new snapshot in .01 seconds.
MAX_DISPATCHERS	5	Max number of dispatchers.
MAX_DUMP_FILE_SIZE	UNLIMITED	Maximum size (blocks) of dump file.

TABLE 2.1 (*Continued*)

NAME	VALUE	DESCRIPTION
MAX_ENABLED_ROLES	30	Max number of roles a user can have enabled.
MAX_ROLLBACK_SEGMENTS	37	Max. number of rollback segments in SGA cache.
MAX_SHARED_SERVERS	20	Max number of shared servers.
MAX_TRANSACTION_ BRANCHES	8	Max number of branches per distributed transaction.
MTS_CIRCUITS	170	Max number of circuits.
MTS_DISPATCHERS	(PROTOCOL=TCP) (SER=MODOSE), (PROTOCOL=TCP) (PRE=oracle.aurora. server.GiopServer), (PROTOCOL=TCP) (PRE=oracle.aurora. server.SGiopServer)	Specifications of dispatchers.
MTS_LISTENER_ADDRESS	NULL	Address(es) of network listener.
MTS_MAX_DISPATCHERS	5	Max number of dispatchers.
MTS_MAX_SERVERS	20	Max number of shared servers.
MTS_MULTIPLE_LISTENERS	FALSE	Are multiple listeners enabled?
MTS_SERVERS	NULL	Number of shared servers to start up at DB start.
MTS_SERVICE	SD	Service name supported by dispatchers.
MTS_SESSIONS	165	Max number of shared server sessions.
NLS_CALENDAR	NULL	NLS calendar system name.
NLS_COMP	NULL	NLS comparison.
NLS_CURRENCY	NULL	NLS local currency symbol.
NLS_DATE_FORMAT	NULL	NLS Oracle date format.
NLS_DATE_LANGUAGE	NULL	NLS date language name.
NLS_DUAL_CURRENCY	NULL	Dual currency symbol.
NLS_ISO_CURRENCY	NULL	NLS ISO currency territory name.
NLS_LANGUAGE	AMERICAN	NLS language name.
NLS_LENGTH_SEMANTICS	BYTE	Create columns using byte or char semantics by default.

continued

TABLE 2.1 (*Continued*)

NAME	VALUE	DESCRIPTION
NLS_NCHAR_CONV_EXCP	FALSE	NLS raise an exception instead of allowing implicit conversion.
NLS_NUMERIC_CHARACTERS	NULL	NLS numeric characters.
NLS_SORT	NULL	NLS linguistic definition name.
NLS_TERRITORY	AMERICA	NLS territory name.
NLS_TIMESTAMP_FORMAT	NULL	Timestamp format.
NLS_TIMESTAMP_TZ_FORMAT	NULL	Timestamp with timezone format.
NLS_TIME_FORMAT	NULL	Time format.
NLS_TIME_TZ_FORMAT	NULL	Time with timezone format.
O7_DICTIONARY_ACCESSIBILITY	FALSE	Version 7 Dictionary Accessibility Support.
OBJECT_CACHE_MAX_SIZE_PERCENT	10	Percentage of maximum size over optimal of the user session's object cache.
OBJECT_CACHE_OPTIMAL_SIZE	102400	Optimal size of the user session's object cache in bytes.
OPEN_CURSORS	300	Max # cursors per session.
OPEN_LINKS	4	Max # open links per session.
OPEN_LINKS_PER_INSTANCE	4	Max # open links per instance.
OPTIMIZER_FEATURES_ENABLE	9.0.1	Optimizer plan compatibility parameter.
OPTIMIZER_INDEX_CACHING	0	Optimizer percent index caching.
OPTIMIZER_INDEX_COST_ADJ	100	Optimizer index cost adjustment.
OPTIMIZER_MAX_PERMUTATIONS	2000	Optimizer maximum join permutations per query block.
OPTIMIZER_MODE	CHOOSE	Optimizer mode.
ORACLE_TRACE_COLLECTION_NAME	NULL	Oracle TRACE default collection name.
ORACLE_TRACE_COLLECTION_PATH	?/otrace/admin/	Oracle TRACE collection path cdf.
ORACLE_TRACE_COLLECTION_SIZE	5242880	Oracle TRACE collection file max size.
ORACLE_TRACE_ENABLE	FALSE	Oracle TRACE enabled/disabled.
ORACLE_TRACE_FACILITY_NAME	Oracled	Oracle TRACE default facility name.
ORACLE_TRACE_FACILITY_PATH	?/otrace/admin/	Oracle TRACE facility path fdf.
OS_AUTHENT_PREFIX	ops$	Prefix for auto-logon accounts.

TABLE 2.1 (*Continued*)

NAME	VALUE	DESCRIPTION
OS_ROLES	FALSE	Retrieve roles from the operating system.
PARALLEL_ADAPTIVE_MULTI_USER	FALSE	Enable adaptive setting of degree for multiple user streams.
PARALLEL_AUTOMATIC_TUNING	FALSE	Enable intelligent defaults for parallel execution parameters.
PARALLEL_BROADCAST_ENABLED	FALSE	Enable broadcasting of small inputs to hash and sort merge joins.
PARALLEL_EXECUTION_MESSAGE_SIZE	2148	Message buffer size for parallel execution.
PARALLEL_INSTANCE_GROUP	NULL	Instance group to use for all parallel operations.
PARALLEL_MAX_SERVERS	5	Maximum parallel query servers per instance.
PARALLEL_MIN_PERCENT	0	Minimum percent of threads required for parallel query.
PARALLEL_MIN_SERVERS	0	Minimum parallel query servers per instance.
PARALLEL_SERVER	FALSE	If TRUE, start up in parallel server mode.
PARALLEL_SERVER_INSTANCES	1	Number of instances to use for sizing OPS SGA structures.
PARALLEL_THREADS_PER_CPU	2	Number of parallel execution threads per CPU.
PARTITION_VIEW_ENABLED	FALSE	Enable/disable partitioned views.
PGA_AGGREGATE_TARGET	0	Target size for the aggregate PGA memory consumed by the instance.
PLSQL_COMPILER_FLAGS	INTERPRETED	PL/SQL compiler flags.
PLSQL_NATIVE_C_COMPILER	NULL	PL/SQL native C compiler.
PLSQL_NATIVE_LIBRARY_DIR	NULL	PL/SQL native library directory.
PLSQL_NATIVE_LIBRARY_SUBDIR_COUNT	0	PL/SQL native library number of subdirectories.
PLSQL_NATIVE_LINKER	NULL	PL/SQL native linker.
PLSQL_NATIVE_MAKE_FILE_NAME	NULL	PL/SQL native compilation make file.
PLSQL_NATIVE_MAKE_UTILITY	NULL	PL/SQL native compilation make utility.
PLSQL_V2_COMPATIBILITY	FALSE	PL/SQL version 2.x compatibility flag.
PRE_PAGE_SGA	FALSE	Prepage SGA for process.
PROCESSES	150	Max user processes.

continued

TABLE 2.1   (*Continued*)

NAME	VALUE	DESCRIPTION
QUERY_REWRITE_ENABLED	FALSE	Allows rewrite of queries using materialized views or function-based, indexes if enabled.
QUERY_REWRITE_INTEGRITY	Enforced	Perform rewrite using materialized views with desired integrity.
RDBMS_SERVER_DN	NULL	RDBMS's Distinguished Name.
READ_ONLY_OPEN_DELAYED	FALSE	If TRUE, delay opening of read-only files until first access.
RECOVERY_PARALLELISM	0	Number of server processes to use for parallel recovery.
REMOTE_ARCHIVE_ENABLE	TRUE	Remote archivelog destinations enabled.
REMOTE_DEPENDENCIES_MODE	TIMESTAMP	Remote-procedure-call dependencies mode parameter.
REMOTE_LISTENER	NULL	Remote listener identification.
REMOTE_LOGIN_PASSWORDFILE	EXCLUSIVE	Password file usage parameter.
REMOTE_OS_AUTHENT	FALSE	Allow nonsecure remote clients to use autologon accounts.
REMOTE_OS_ROLES	FALSE	Allow nonsecure remote clients to use OS roles.
REPLICATION_DEPENDENCY_TRACKING	TRUE	Tracking dependency for replication parallel propagation.
RESOURCE_LIMIT	FALSE	Master switch for resource limit.
RESOURCE_MANAGER_PLAN	SYSTEM_PLAN	Resource mgr top plan.
ROLLBACK_SEGMENTS	NULL	Undo segment list.
ROW_LOCKING	always	Row-locking.
SERIALIZABLE	FALSE	Serializable.
SERIAL_REUSE	DISABLE	Reuse the frame segments.
SERVICE_NAMES	SD	Service names supported by the instance.
SESSIONS	170	User and system sessions.
SESSION_CACHED_CURSORS	0	Number of cursors to save in the session cursor cache.
SESSION_MAX_OPEN_FILES	10	Maximum number of open files allowed per session.
SGA_MAX_SIZE	336356520	Max total SGA size.
SHADOW_CORE_DUMP	partial	Core size for shadow processes.
SHARED_MEMORY_ADDRESS	0	SGA starting address (low-order 32 bits on 64-bit platforms).

TABLE 2.1 (*Continued*)

NAME	VALUE	DESCRIPTION
SHARED_POOL_RESERVED_SIZE	5872025	Size in bytes of reserved area of shared pool.
SHARED_POOL_SIZE	117440512	Size in bytes of shared pool.
SHARED_SERVERS	1	Number of shared servers to start up.
SHARED_SERVER_SESSIONS	165	Max number of shared server sessions.
SORT_AREA_RETAINED_SIZE	0	Size of in-memory sort work area retained between fetch calls.
SORT_AREA_SIZE	524288	Size of in-memory sort work area.
SPFILE	`	Server parameter file.
SQL92_SECURITY	FALSE	Require select privilege for searched update/delete.
SQL_TRACE	FALSE	Enable SQL trace.
SQL_VERSION	NATIVE	SQL language version parameter for compatibility issues.
STANDBY_ARCHIVE_DEST	?/dbs/arch	Standby database archivelog destination text string.
STANDBY_FILE_MANAGEMENT	MANUAL	If auto, then files are created/dropped automatically on standby.
STANDBY_PRESERVES_NAMES	FALSE	Filenames on standby are the same as on the primary.
STAR_TRANSFORMATION_ENABLED	FALSE	Enable the use of star transformation.
TAPE_ASYNCH_IO	TRUE	Use asynch I/O requests for tape devices.
THREAD	0	Redo thread to mount.
TIMED_OS_STATISTICS	0	Internal OS statistic-gathering interval, in seconds.
TIMED_STATISTICS	TRUE	Maintain internal timing statistics.
TRACEFILE_IDENTIFIER	NULL	Trace file custom identifier.
TRACE_ENABLED	TRUE	Enable KST tracing.
TRANSACTIONS	187	Max number of concurrent active transactions.
TRANSACTIONS_PER_ROLLBACK_SEGMENT	5	Number of active transactions per rollback segment.
TRANSACTION_AUDITING	TRUE	Transaction auditing records generated in the redo log.

continued

TABLE 2.1   (*Continued*)

NAME	VALUE	DESCRIPTION
UNDO_MANAGEMENT	AUTO	Instance runs in SMU mode if TRUE, else in RBU mode.
UNDO_RETENTION	900	Undo retention in seconds.
UNDO_SUPPRESS_ERRORS	FALSE	Suppress RBU errors in SMU mode.
UNDO_TABLESPACE	UNDOTBS	Use/switch undo tablespace.
USER_DUMP_DEST	SD	User process dump directory.
USE_INDIRECT_DATA_BUFFERS	FALSE	Enable indirect data buffers (very large SGA on 32-bit platforms).
UTL_FILE_DIR	NULL	utl_file-accessible directories list.
WORKAREA_SIZE_POLICY	MANUAL	Policy used to size SQL working areas (MANUAL/AUTO).

TABLE 2.2   Initialization Parameters Invalid for Use with Oracle9*i*

NAME	NAME
ALLOW_PARTIAL_SN_RESULTS	DISTRIBUTED_RECOVERY_CONNECTION_HOLD_TIME*
ALWAYS_ANTI_JOIN*	
ALWAYS_SEMI_JOIN*	DISTRIBUTED_TRANSACTIONS
ARCH_IO_SLAVES*	FAST_FULL_SCAN_ENABLED*
B_TREE_BITMAP_PLANS*	GC_DB_LOCKS
BACKUP_DISK_IO_SLAVES*	GC_DEFER_TIME*
CACHE_SIZE_THRESHOLD	GC_FREELIST_GROUPS
CLEANUP_ROLLBACK_ENTRIES*	GC_LATCHES
CLOSE_CACHED_OPEN_CURSORS*	GC_LCK_PROCS*
COMPATIBLE_NO_RECOVERY*	GC_RELEASABLE_LOCKS*
DB_BLOCK_CHECKPOINT_BATCH	GC_ROLLBACK_LOCKS
DB_BLOCK_LRU_EXTENDED_STATISTICS	GC_ROLLBACK_SEGMENTS
DB_BLOCK_LRU_LATCHES*	GC_SAVE_ROLLBACK_LOCKS
DB_BLOCK_LRU_STATISTICS	GC_SEGMENTS
DB_BLOCK_MAX_DIRTY_TARGET*	GC_TABLESPACES
DB_FILE_DIRECT_IO_COUNT*	HASH_MULTIBLOCK_IO_COUNT*
DB_FILE_SIMULTANEOUS_WRITES	INSTANCE_NODESET
DISCRETE_TRANSACTIONS_ENABLED*	JOB_QUEUE_INTERVAL*
DISTRIBUTED_LOCK_TIMEOUT*	LARGE_POOL_MIN_ALLOC*

TABLE 2.2   (*Continued*)

NAME	NAME
LGWR_IO_SLAVES*	PARALLEL_DEFAULT_MAX_INSTANCES*
LM_LOCKS*	PARALLEL_SERVER, renamed to CLUSTER_DATABASE
LM_RESS*	
LOCK_SGA_AREAS*	PARALLEL_SERVER_INSTANCES, renamed to CLUSTER_DATABASE_INSTANCES
LOG_ARCHIVE_BUFFER_SIZE*	
LOG_ARCHIVE_BUFFERS*	PUSH_JOIN_PREDICATE*
LOG_BLOCK_CHECKSUM	REDUCE_ALARM
LOG_SIMULTANEOUS_COPIES*	ROW_CACHE_CURSORS*
LOG_SMALL_ENTRY_MAX_SIZE	SEQUENCE_CACHE_ENTRIES
MAX_TRANSACTION_BRANCHES	SEQUENCE_CACHE_HASH_BUCKETS
MTS_LISTENER_ADDRESS	SHARED_POOL_RESERVED_MIN_ALLOC*
MTS_MULTIPLE_LISTENERS	SORT_MULTIBLOCK_READ_COUNT*
MTS_RATE_LOG_SIZE	SORT_READ_FAC
MTS_RATE_SCALE	SORT_SPACEMAP_SIZE
MTS_SERVICE	SORT_WRITE_BUFFER_SIZE
OGMS_HOME*	SORT_WRITE_BUFFERS
OPS_ADMIN_GROUP	SPIN_COUNT*
OPS_INTERCONNECTS renamed to CLUSTER_INTERCONNECTS	TEMPORARY_TABLE_LOCKS
	TEXT_ENABLE
OPTIMIZER_PERCENT_PARALLEL*	

* Parameter has become undocumented parameter.

TABLE 2.3   Initialization Parameters That Can Be Dynamically Altered

NAME	SYSTEM	SESSION
ACTIVE_INSTANCE_COUNT	FALSE	FALSE
AQ_TM_PROCESSES	IMMEDIATE	FALSE
ARCHIVE_LAG_TARGET	IMMEDIATE	FALSE
BACKGROUND_DUMP_DEST	IMMEDIATE	FALSE
BACKUP_TAPE_IO_SLAVES	DEFERRED	FALSE
CONTROL_FILE_RECORD_KEEP_TIME	IMMEDIATE	FALSE
CORE_DUMP_DEST	IMMEDIATE	FALSE

continued

TABLE 2.3 (*Continued*)

NAME	SYSTEM	SESSION
CURSOR_SHARING	IMMEDIATE	TRUE
DB_16K_CACHE_SIZE	IMMEDIATE	FALSE
DB_2K_CACHE_SIZE	IMMEDIATE	FALSE
DB_32K_CACHE_SIZE	IMMEDIATE	FALSE
DB_4K_CACHE_SIZE	IMMEDIATE	FALSE
DB_8K_CACHE_SIZE	IMMEDIATE	FALSE
DB_BLOCK_CHECKING	IMMEDIATE	TRUE
DB_BLOCK_CHECKSUM	IMMEDIATE	FALSE
DB_CACHE_ADVICE	IMMEDIATE	FALSE
DB_CACHE_SIZE	IMMEDIATE	FALSE
DB_CREATE_FILE_DEST	IMMEDIATE	TRUE
DB_CREATE_ONLINE_LOG_DEST_1	IMMEDIATE	TRUE
DB_CREATE_ONLINE_LOG_DEST_2	IMMEDIATE	TRUE
DB_CREATE_ONLINE_LOG_DEST_3	IMMEDIATE	TRUE
DB_CREATE_ONLINE_LOG_DEST_4	IMMEDIATE	TRUE
DB_CREATE_ONLINE_LOG_DEST_5	IMMEDIATE	TRUE
DB_FILE_MULTIBLOCK_READ_COUNT	IMMEDIATE	TRUE
DB_KEEP_CACHE_SIZE	IMMEDIATE	FALSE
DB_RECYCLE_CACHE_SIZE	IMMEDIATE	FALSE
DISPATCHERS	IMMEDIATE	FALSE
DRS_START	IMMEDIATE	FALSE
FAL_CLIENT	IMMEDIATE	FALSE
FAL_SERVER	IMMEDIATE	FALSE
FAST_START_IO_TARGET	IMMEDIATE	FALSE
FAST_START_MTTR_TARGET	IMMEDIATE	FALSE
FAST_START_PARALLEL_ROLLBACK	IMMEDIATE	FALSE
FIXED_DATE	IMMEDIATE	FALSE
GLOBAL_NAMES	IMMEDIATE	TRUE
HASH_AREA_SIZE	FALSE	TRUE
HASH_JOIN_ENABLED	FALSE	TRUE
HS_AUTOREGISTER	IMMEDIATE	FALSE
JOB_QUEUE_PROCESSES	IMMEDIATE	FALSE
LICENSE_MAX_SESSIONS	IMMEDIATE	FALSE

TABLE 2.3   *(Continued)*

NAME	SYSTEM	SESSION
LICENSE_MAX_USERS	IMMEDIATE	FALSE
LICENSE_SESSIONS_WARNING	IMMEDIATE	FALSE
LOG_ARCHIVE_DEST	IMMEDIATE	FALSE
LOG_ARCHIVE_DEST_1	IMMEDIATE	TRUE
LOG_ARCHIVE_DEST_10	IMMEDIATE	TRUE
LOG_ARCHIVE_DEST_2	IMMEDIATE	TRUE
LOG_ARCHIVE_DEST_3	IMMEDIATE	TRUE
LOG_ARCHIVE_DEST_4	IMMEDIATE	TRUE
LOG_ARCHIVE_DEST_5	IMMEDIATE	TRUE
LOG_ARCHIVE_DEST_6	IMMEDIATE	TRUE
LOG_ARCHIVE_DEST_7	IMMEDIATE	TRUE
LOG_ARCHIVE_DEST_8	IMMEDIATE	TRUE
LOG_ARCHIVE_DEST_9	IMMEDIATE	TRUE
LOG_ARCHIVE_DEST_STATE_1	IMMEDIATE	TRUE
LOG_ARCHIVE_DEST_STATE_10	IMMEDIATE	TRUE
LOG_ARCHIVE_DEST_STATE_2	IMMEDIATE	TRUE
LOG_ARCHIVE_DEST_STATE_3	IMMEDIATE	TRUE
LOG_ARCHIVE_DEST_STATE_4	IMMEDIATE	TRUE
LOG_ARCHIVE_DEST_STATE_5	IMMEDIATE	TRUE
LOG_ARCHIVE_DEST_STATE_6	IMMEDIATE	TRUE
LOG_ARCHIVE_DEST_STATE_7	IMMEDIATE	TRUE
LOG_ARCHIVE_DEST_STATE_8	IMMEDIATE	TRUE
LOG_ARCHIVE_DEST_STATE_9	IMMEDIATE	TRUE
LOG_ARCHIVE_DUPLEX_DEST	IMMEDIATE	FALSE
LOG_ARCHIVE_MAX_PROCESSES	IMMEDIATE	FALSE
LOG_ARCHIVE_MIN_SUCCEED_DEST	IMMEDIATE	TRUE
LOG_ARCHIVE_TRACE	IMMEDIATE	FALSE
LOG_CHECKPOINTS_TO_ALERT	IMMEDIATE	FALSE
LOG_CHECKPOINT_INTERVAL	IMMEDIATE	FALSE
LOG_CHECKPOINT_TIMEOUT	IMMEDIATE	FALSE
MAX_DUMP_FILE_SIZE	IMMEDIATE	TRUE
MTS_DISPATCHERS	IMMEDIATE	FALSE

continued

TABLE 2.3   (*Continued*)

NAME	SYSTEM	SESSION
MTS_SERVERS	IMMEDIATE	FALSE
NLS_CALENDAR	FALSE	TRUE
NLS_COMP	FALSE	TRUE
NLS_CURRENCY	FALSE	TRUE
NLS_DATE_FORMAT	FALSE	TRUE
NLS_DATE_LANGUAGE	FALSE	TRUE
NLS_DUAL_CURRENCY	FALSE	TRUE
NLS_ISO_CURRENCY	FALSE	TRUE
NLS_LANGUAGE	FALSE	TRUE
NLS_LENGTH_SEMANTICS	IMMEDIATE	FALSE
NLS_NCHAR_CONV_EXCP	IMMEDIATE	FALSE
NLS_NUMERIC_CHARACTERS	FALSE	TRUE
NLS_SORT	FALSE	TRUE
NLS_TERRITORY	FALSE	TRUE
NLS_TIMESTAMP_FORMAT	FALSE	TRUE
NLS_TIMESTAMP_TZ_FORMAT	FALSE	TRUE
NLS_TIME_FORMAT	FALSE	TRUE
NLS_TIME_TZ_FORMAT	FALSE	TRUE
OBJECT_CACHE_MAX_SIZE_PERCENT	DEFERRED	TRUE
OBJECT_CACHE_OPTIMAL_SIZE	DEFERRED	TRUE
OPEN_CURSORS	IMMEDIATE	FALSE
OPTIMIZER_INDEX_CACHING	FALSE	TRUE
OPTIMIZER_INDEX_COST_ADJ	FALSE	TRUE
OPTIMIZER_MAX_PERMUTATIONS	FALSE	TRUE
OPTIMIZER_MODE	FALSE	TRUE
ORACLE_TRACE_ENABLE	IMMEDIATE	TRUE
PARALLEL_ADAPTIVE_MULTI_USER	IMMEDIATE	FALSE
PARALLEL_BROADCAST_ENABLED	FALSE	TRUE
PARALLEL_INSTANCE_GROUP	IMMEDIATE	TRUE
PARALLEL_MIN_PERCENT	FALSE	TRUE
PARALLEL_THREADS_PER_CPU	IMMEDIATE	FALSE
PARTITION_VIEW_ENABLED	FALSE	TRUE
PGA_AGGREGATE_TARGET	IMMEDIATE	FALSE

TABLE 2.3 *(Continued)*

NAME	*SYSTEM*	*SESSION*
PLSQL_COMPILER_FLAGS	IMMEDIATE	TRUE
PLSQL_NATIVE_C_COMPILER	IMMEDIATE	FALSE
PLSQL_NATIVE_LIBRARY_DIR	IMMEDIATE	FALSE
PLSQL_NATIVE_LIBRARY_SUBDIR_COUNT	IMMEDIATE	FALSE
PLSQL_NATIVE_LINKER	IMMEDIATE	FALSE
PLSQL_NATIVE_MAKE_FILE_NAME	IMMEDIATE	FALSE
PLSQL_NATIVE_MAKE_UTILITY	IMMEDIATE	FALSE
PLSQL_V2_COMPATIBILITY	IMMEDIATE	TRUE
QUERY_REWRITE_ENABLED	IMMEDIATE	TRUE
QUERY_REWRITE_INTEGRITY	IMMEDIATE	TRUE
REMOTE_DEPENDENCIES_MODE	IMMEDIATE	TRUE
RESOURCE_LIMIT	IMMEDIATE	FALSE
RESOURCE_MANAGER_PLAN	IMMEDIATE	FALSE
SERVICE_NAMES	IMMEDIATE	FALSE
SESSION_CACHED_CURSORS	FALSE	TRUE
SHARED_POOL_SIZE	IMMEDIATE	FALSE
SHARED_SERVERS	IMMEDIATE	FALSE
SORT_AREA_RETAINED_SIZE	DEFERRED	TRUE
SORT_AREA_SIZE	DEFERRED	TRUE
SQL_VERSION	FALSE	TRUE
STAR_TRANSFORMATION_ENABLED	FALSE	TRUE
TIMED_OS_STATISTICS	IMMEDIATE	TRUE
TIMED_STATISTICS	IMMEDIATE	TRUE
TRACEFILE_IDENTIFIER	FALSE	TRUE
TRACE_ENABLED	IMMEDIATE	FALSE
TRANSACTION_AUDITING	DEFERRED	FALSE
UNDO_RETENTION	IMMEDIATE	FALSE
UNDO_SUPPRESS_ERRORS	IMMEDIATE	TRUE
UNDO_TABLESPACE	IMMEDIATE	FALSE
USER_DUMP_DEST	IMMEDIATE	FALSE
WORKAREA_SIZE_POLICY	IMMEDIATE	TRUE

While the ALTER SYSTEM command will change the value of the initialization parameter for the instance, it may not change it for all sessions. The DEFERRED clause only alters the parameter for new sessions, not existing sessions. There are some initialization parameters specific to the heterogeneous services option for Oracle8*i* and 9*i*; these are altered using the DBMS_HS package and are not all listed in Table 2.3.

The Server-Side Parameter File   In releases of Oracle prior to Oracle9*i*, any changes to initialization parameters that were performed dynamically where lost when the database was shut down unless the DBA edited the initialization files manually. In Oracle9*i*, the DBA can create what is known as a *server-side parameter file,* or SPFILE, using the CREATE SPFILE command. The SPFILE is a binary file that cannot be edited or browsed; it will be used by Oracle to start up the database once it has been created as long as the SPFILE clause is contained within the STARTUP command; otherwise, it uses the default test init.ora file or the file specified by the PFILE clause.

To create an SPFILE in the platform-specific default location, use the format of the CREATE SPFILE command:

```
CREATE SPFILE FROM init_ora_location_and_name;
```

To create a specifically named and located SPFILE use the form of the CREATE SPFILE command:

```
CREATE SPFILE = spfile_location_and_name
 FROM init_ora_location_and_name;
```

For example:

```
CREATE SPFILE = /u11/oracle/aultdb1/admin/spfile/aultdb1_spfile.ora
FROM /u11/oracle/aultdb1/admin/pfile/init_aultdb1.ora;
```

To make startup easier, it is recommended that you let the file be created in the default location with the default name.

The Undocumented Initialization Parameters("_")

In addition to the Oracle-documented initialization parameters, there are varying numbers of undocumented initialization parameters in every version of Oracle. These undocumented initialization parameters are usually only used in emergencies and only under the direction of a senior DBA or Oracle support. Source 2.5 shows a script for getting the undocumented initialization parameters out of a 7.3, 8.0, 8.1 or 9.0 instance. The undocumented parameters for an Oracle9*i* (9.0.1) database are shown in Table 2.4.

Source 2.5   Script for getting undocumented parameters.

```
REM Script for getting undocumented init.ora
REM parameters from a 7.3, 8.0.x,8.1 or 9.0 instance
REM MRA - TUSC 4/23/97
REM
COLUMN parameter            FORMAT a37
COLUMN description          FORMAT a30 WORD_WRAPPED
COLUMN "Session Value"      FORMAT a10
COLUMN "Instance Value"     FORMAT a10
SET LINES 100
SET PAGES 0
SPOOL undoc.lis
SELECT
    a.ksppinm  "Parameter",
    a.ksppdesc "Description",
    b.ksppstvl "Session Value",
    c.ksppstvl "Instance Value"
FROM
    x$ksppi a,
    x$ksppcv b,
    x$ksppsv c
WHERE
    a.indx = b.indx
    AND a.indx = c.indx
    AND a.ksppinm LIKE '/_%' escape '/'
/
SPOOL OFF
SET LINES 80 PAGES 20
CLEAR COLUMNS
```

Note that each undocumented parameter in the table begins with an underscore (_) character. Those of you who have been around awhile will also notice that some of these "undocumented" parameters used to be documented. You may have seen some used, such as "_offline_rollback_segments" (whose use I document in Chapter15); others you will never use or see used. The point is, you should be aware that there are more parameters than those listed in a user's manual, and that you may need to prompt Oracle support if you see one (for example, "_corrupted_rollback_segments") that may just be helpful in a sticky situation.

Using Oracle's Undocumented Initialization Parameters

Almost every DBA knows about Oracle's documented initialization parameters; most of them are easy to look up and use. However, not everyone knows about the undocumented parameters, and few know how or when to use them. There are many parameters that Oracle will not allow DBAs to use unless specifically directed to by Oracle

TABLE 2.4 Undocumented Initialization Parameters for Oracle 9*i*

Parameter	Description	Instance	Session
_NUMA_instance_mapping	Set of nodes that this instance should run on.	Not specified	Not specified
_NUMA_pool_size	Aggregate size in bytes of NUMA pool.	Not specified	Not specified
_PX_use_large_pool	Use Large Pool as source of PX buffers.	FALSE	FALSE
_abort_recovery_on_join	If TRUE, abort recovery on join reconfigurations.	FALSE	FALSE
_active_standby_fast_ reconfiguration	If TRUE, optimize dlm reconfiguration for active/ standby OPS.	TRUE	TRUE
_adaptive_direct_read*	Adaptive Direct Read.	TRUE	TRUE
_adaptive_fetch_enabled*	Enable/disable adaptive fetch in parallel "group by" operations	TRUE	TRUE
_advanced_dss_features	Enable advanced dss features; enable/disable affinity at runtime.	FALSE	FALSE
_affinity_on	Enable/disable affinity at runtime.	TRUE	TRUE
_all_shared_dblinks	Treat all dblinks as shared.	NULL	NULL
_allocate_creation_order	Should files be examined in creation order during allocation?	FALSE	FALSE
_allocation_update_interval*	Interval at which successful search in L1 should be updated.	3	3
_allow_error_simulation	Allow error simulation for testing.	FALSE	FALSE
_allow_read_only_corruption	Allow read-only open even if database is corrupt.	FALSE	FALSE
_allow_resetlogs_corruption	Allow resetlogs even if it will cause corruption.	FALSE	FALSE
_always_anti_join*	Always use this method for anti-join when possible.	CHOOSE	CHOOSE
_always_semi_join*	Always use this method for semi-join when possible.	CHOOSE	CHOOSE
_always_star_transformation	Always favor use of star transformation.	FALSE	FALSE

TABLE 2.4   (Continued)

Parameter	Description	Instance	Session
_aq_tm_scanlimit	Scan limit for Time Managers to clean up IOT.	0	0
_arch_io_slaves	ARCH I/O slaves.	0	0
_async_bsp	If TRUE, BSP flushes log asynchronously (DFS).	TRUE	TRUE
_async_recovery_claims*	If TRUE, issue recovery claims asynchronously.	TRUE	TRUE
_async_recovery_reads*	If TRUE, issue recovery reads asynchronously.	TRUE	TRUE
_avoid_prepare*	If TRUE, do not prepare a buffer when the master is local.	TRUE	TRUE
_b_tree_bitmap_plans	Enable the use of bitmap plans only for tables with B-tree indexes.	TRUE	TRUE
_backup_disk_io_slaves	Backup disk I/O slaves.	0	0
_backup_io_pool_size	Memory to reserve from the large pool.	1048576	1048576
_bsp_log_flush	If TRUE, flush redo log before serving a CR buffer (DFS).	TRUE	TRUE
_bump_highwater_mark_ count	How many blocks should we allocate per freelist on advancing HW?	0	0
_cgs_send_timeout*	CGS send timeout.	300	300
_check_block_after_ checksum	Perform block check after checksum if both are turned on.	TRUE	TRUE
_cleanup_rollback_entries	Number of undo entries to apply per transaction cleanup.	100	100
_close_cached_open_cursors	Close cursors cached by PL/SQL at each commit.	FALSE	FALSE
_collect_undo_stats*	Collect statistics v$undostat.	TRUE	TRUE
_column_elimination_off	Turn off predicate-only column elimination.	FALSE	FALSE
_column_tracking_level*	Column usage tracking.	1	1
_compatible_no_recovery	Database will be compatible unless crash or media recovery is needed.	0.0.0	0.0.0
_complex_view_merging	Enable complex view merging.	TRUE	TRUE

continued

TABLE 2.4   (Continued)

Parameter	Description	Instance	Session
_controlfile_enqueue_ timeout	Controlfile enqueue timeout in seconds.	900	900
_corrupted_rollback_ segments	Corrupted undo segment list.	NULL	NULL
_cost_equality_semi_join*	Enables costing of equality semi-join.	TRUE	TRUE
_cpu_count*	Current number of CPUs for this instance.	0	0
_cpu_to_io	Divisor for converting CPU cost to I/O cost.	0	0
_cr_grant_global_role*	If TRUE, grant lock for CR requests when block is in global role.	TRUE	TRUE
_cr_grant_local_role*	If TRUE, grant lock for CR using three-way ping when block in local role.	FALSE	FALSE
_cursor_db_buffers_pinned	Additional number of buffers a cursor can pin at once.	51	51
_cursor_plan_enabled*	Enable collection and display of cursor plans.	TRUE	TRUE
_db_aging_cool_count	Touch count set when buffer cooled.	1	1
_db_aging_freeze_cr	Make CR buffers always be too cold to keep in cache.	FALSE	FALSE
_db_aging_hot_criteria	Touch count, which sends a buffer to head of replacement list.	2	2
_db_aging_stay_count	Touch count set when buffer moved to head of replacement list.	0	0
_db_aging_touch_time	Touch count, which sends a buffer to head of replacement list.	3	3
_db_always_check_system_ts	Always perform block check and checksum for system tablespace.	TRUE	TRUE
_db_block_buffers*	Number of database blocks cached in memory: hidden parameter.	8024	8024

TABLE 2.4 (*Continued*)

Parameter	Description	Instance	Session
_db_block_cache_clone	Always clone data blocks on get (for debugging).	FALSE	FALSE
_db_block_cache_map	Map/unmap and track reference counts on blocks (for debugging).	0	0
_db_block_cache_protect	Protect database blocks (true only when debugging).	FALSE	FALSE
_db_block_check_for_debug	Check more and dump block before image for debugging.	FALSE	FALSE
_db_block_granule_interval*	Number of LRU latches.	10	10
_db_block_hash_buckets	Number of database block hash buckets (should be prime).	16057	16057
_db_block_hash_latches	Number of database block hash latches.	1024	1024
_db_block_hi_priority_ batch_size	Fraction of writes for high-priority reasons.	0	0
_db_block_lru_latches*	Number of LRU latches.	8	8
_db_block_max_cr_dba	Maximum allowed number of CR buffers per DBA.	6	6
_db_block_max_dirty_target*	Upper bound on modified buffers/recovery reads.	0	0
_db_block_max_scan_pct*	Percentage of buffers to inspect when looking for free buffers.	40	40
_db_block_med_priority_ batch_size	Fraction of writes for medium-priority reasons.	0	0
_db_block_numa	Number of NUMA nodes.	1	1
_db_block_prefetch_quota	Prefetch quota as a percent of cache size.	10	10
_db_block_trace_protect*	Trace buffer protect calls.	FALSE	FALSE
_db_file_direct_io_count*	Sequential I/O buffer size.	1048576	1048576
_db_file_noncontig_mblock_ read_count	Number of noncontiguous db blocks to be prefetched.	11	11
_db_handles	Systemwide simultaneous buffer operations.	750	750
_db_handles_cached	Buffer handles cached each process.	5	5

continued

TABLE 2.4 (*Continued*)

Parameter	Description	Instance	Session
_db_large_dirty_queue	Number of buffers that force dirty queue to be written.	25	25
_db_no_mount_lock	Do not get a mount lock.	FALSE	FALSE
_db_percent_hot_default	Percent of default buffer pool considered hot.	50	50
_db_percent_hot_keep	Percent of keep buffer pool considered hot.	0	0
_db_percent_hot_recycle	Percent of recycle buffer pool considered hot.	0	0
_db_writer_chunk_writes	Number of writes DBWR should wait for.	0	0
_db_writer_histogram_ statistics	Maintain dbwr histogram statistics in x$kcbbhs.	FALSE	FALSE
_db_writer_max_writes	Max number of outstanding DB writer I/Os.	0	0
_db_writer_scan_depth_pct*	Percentage of LRU buffers for dbwr to scan when looking for dirty buffers.	25	25
_dbwr_async_io	Enable dbwriter asynchronous writes.	TRUE	TRUE
_dbwr_scan_interval	Dbwriter scan interval.	10	10
_dbwr_tracing	Enable dbwriter tracing.	0	0
_default_non_equality_ sel_check	Sanity check on default selectivity for like/range predicate.	TRUE	TRUE
_defer_multiple_waiters	If TRUE, defer down converts when there are waiters (DFS).	TRUE	TRUE
_diag_daemon*	Start DIAG daemon.	TRUE	TRUE
_disable_file_locks	Disable file locks for control, data, redo log files.	FALSE	FALSE
_disable_incremental_ checkpoints	Disable incremental checkpoints for thread recovery.	FALSE	FALSE
_disable_latch_free_SCN_ writes_via_32cas	Disable latch-free SCN writes using 32-bit compare and swap.	FALSE	FALSE
_disable_latch_free_SCN_ writes_via_64cas	Disable latch-free SCN writes using 64-bit compare and swap.	FALSE	FALSE
_disable_logging	Disable logging.	FALSE	FALSE

TABLE 2.4 (*Continued*)

Parameter	Description	Instance	Session
_disable_multiple_block_sizes*	Disable multiple blocksize support (for debugging).	FALSE	FALSE
_disable_sun_rsm*	Disable IPC OSD support for Sun RSMAPI.	TRUE	TRUE
_discrete_transactions_enabled	Enable OLTP mode.	FALSE	FALSE
_dispatcher_rate_scale*	Scale to display rate statistic (100ths of a second).	NULL	NULL
_dispatcher_rate_ttl*	Time-to-live for rate statistic (100ths of a second).	NULL	NULL
_distributed_lock_timeout	Number of seconds a distributed transaction waits for a lock.	60	60
_distributed_recovery_connection_hold_time	Number of seconds RECO holds outbound connections open.	200	200
_dlmtrace*	Trace string of lock types(s).	NULL	NULL
_domain_index_batch_size	Maximum number of rows from one call to domain index fetch routines.	2000	2000
_domain_index_dml_batch_size	Maximum number of rows for one call to domain index DML routines.	200	200
_dss_cache_flush	Enable full cache flush for parallel execution.	FALSE	FALSE
_dump_MTTR_to_trace	Dump high-availability MTTR information to CKPT trace file.	FALSE	FALSE
_dyn_sel_est_num_blocks*	Number of blocks for dynamic selectivity estimation.	30	30
_dyn_sel_est_on*	Dynamic selectivity estimation on.	FALSE	FALSE
_dynamic_stats_threshold	Delay threshold (in seconds) between sending statistics messages.	30	30
_eliminate_common_subexpr	Enables elimination of common subexpressions.	TRUE	TRUE
_enable_NUMA_optimization	Enable NUMA-specific optimizations.	TRUE	TRUE

continued

TABLE 2.4 (*Continued*)

Parameter	Description	Instance	Session
_enable_block_level_transaction_recovery	Enable block-level recovery.	TRUE	TRUE
_enable_cscn_caching	Enable commit SCN caching for all transactions.	TRUE	TRUE
_enable_default_affinity	To enable default implementation of affinity OSDS.	0	0
_enable_kgh_policy*	Temporary to disable/enable KGH policy.	FALSE	FALSE
_enable_list_io	Enable list I/O.	FALSE	FALSE
_enable_multitable_sampling	Enable multitable sampling.	FALSE	FALSE
_enable_type_dep_selectivity	Enable type-dependent selectivity estimates.	TRUE	TRUE
_enqueue_debug_multi_instance	Debug enqueue multi-instance.	FALSE	FALSE
_enqueue_hash	Enqueue hash table length.	375	375
_enqueue_hash_chain_latches	Enqueue hash chain latches.	1	1
_enqueue_locks	Locks for managed enqueues.	2230	2230
_explain_rewrite_mode*	Allow additional messages to be generated during explain.	FALSE	FALSE
_fairness_pi*	If TRUE, allow spontaneous PI buffers.	TRUE	TRUE
_fairness_threshold	Number of times to CR serve before downgrading lock (DFS).	4	4
_fast_full_scan_enabled	Enable/disable index fast full scan.	TRUE	TRUE
_fifth_spare_parameter	Fifth spare parameter: string.	NULL	NULL
_filesystemio_options	I/O operations on filesystem files.	asynch	asynch
_first_spare_parameter	First spare parameter: integer.	NULL	NULL
_force_temptables_for_gsets*	Executes concatenation of rollups using temp tables.	FALSE	FALSE
_fourth_spare_parameter	Fourth spare parameter: string.	NULL	NULL
_full_pwise_join_enabled	Enable full partition-wise join when TRUE.	TRUE	TRUE

TABLE 2.4 (*Continued*)

Parameter	Description	Instance	Session
_gc_bsp_procs	Number of buffer server processes to start (DFS).	0	0
_gc_defer_time	How long to defer down converts for hot buffers (DFS).	3	3
_gc_latches	Number of latches per lock process (DFS).	2	2
_gc_lck_procs	Number of background parallel server lock processes to start.	0	0
_gc_releasable_locks*	Number of global cache locks (DFS).	0	0
_groupby_nopushdown_ cut_ratio	Groupby nopushdown cut ratio.	3	3
_groupby_orderby_combine	Groupby/orderby don't combine threshold.	5000	5000
_gs_anti_semi_join_allowed*	Enable anti-/semi-join for the GS query.	TRUE	TRUE
_hash_multiblock_io_count*	Number of blocks hash join will read/write at once.	0	0
_high_server_threshold	High server thresholds.	0	0
_idl_conventional_index_ maintenance	Enable conventional index maintenance for insert direct.	TRUE	TRUE
_ignore_desc_in_index	Ignore DESC in indexes; sort those columns ascending anyhow.	FALSE	FALSE
_improved_outerjoin_card	Improved outer-join cardinality calculation.	TRUE	TRUE
_improved_row_length_ enabled	Enable the improvements for computing the average row length.	TRUE	TRUE
_imr_active*	Activate Instance Membership Recovery feature.	TRUE	TRUE
_imr_max_reconfig_delay*	Maximum reconfiguration delay (seconds).	300	300
_index_join_enabled	Enable the use of index joins.	TRUE	TRUE
_index_prefetch_factor	Index prefetching factor.	100	100

continued

TABLE 2.4 (*Continued*)

Parameter	Description	Instance	Session
_init_sql_file	File containing SQL statements to execute upon database creation.	?/rdbms/ admin/ sql.bsq	?/rdbms/ admin/ sql.bsq
_insert_enable_hwm_ brokered*	During parallel inserts high-water marks are brokered.	TRUE	TRUE
_inst_locking_period*	Period an instance can retain a newly acquired level 1 bitmap.	5	5
_interconnect_checksum	If TRUE, checksum interconnect blocks (DFS).	TRUE	TRUE
_io_slaves_disabled	Do not use I/O slaves.	FALSE	FALSE
_ioslave_batch_count	Per attempt I/Os picked.	1	1
_ioslave_issue_count	I/Os issued before completion check.	500	500
_ipc_fail_network	Simulate cluster network failure.	0	0
_ipc_test_failover	Test transparent cluster network failover.	0	0
_ipc_test_mult_nets	Simulate multiple cluster networks.	0	0
_job_queue_interval*	Wakeup interval in seconds for job queue coordinator.	5	5
_kcl_debug	If TRUE, record lock escalation history (DFS).	TRUE	TRUE
_kcl_dispatch*	If TRUE, dispatch requests to bsp and lck (DFS).	FALSE	FALSE
_kcl_name_table_latches*	Number of name table latches (DFS).	8	8
_kcl_partition*	If TRUE, dynamically remaster partitioned files (DFS).	FALSE	FALSE
_kcl_use_cr*	If TRUE, use fusion CR buffers (DFS).	TRUE	TRUE
_kdbl_enable_post_allocation*	Allocate dbas after populating data buffers.	FALSE	FALSE
_keep_recovery_buffers*	If TRUE, make recovery buffers current.	TRUE	TRUE
_keep_remote_column_size*	Remote column size does not get modified.	FALSE	FALSE
_kghdsidx_count*	Max kghdsidx count.	1	1

TABLE 2.4 (*Continued*)

Parameter	Description	Instance	Session
_kgl_bucket_count	Index to the bucket count array.	9	9
_kgl_latch_count	Number of library cache latches.	0	0
_kgl_multi_instance_ invalidation	Whether KGL to support multi-instance invalidations.	TRUE	TRUE
_kgl_multi_instance_lock	Whether KGL to support multi-instance locks.	TRUE	TRUE
_kgl_multi_instance_pin	Whether KGL to support multi-instance pins.	TRUE	TRUE
_kkfi_trace	Trace expression substitution.	FALSE	FALSE
_ksi_trace	KSI trace string of lock type(s).	NULL	NULL
_ksmg_granule_size*	Granule size in bytes.	16777216	16777216
_ksu_diag_kill_time*	Number of seconds ksuitm waits before killing diag.	5	5
_large_pool_min_alloc	Minimum allocation size in bytes for the large allocation pool.	16K	16K
_last_allocation_period*	Period over which an instance can retain an active level 1 bitmap.	5	5
_latch_miss_stat_sid	SID of process for which to collect latch stats.	0	0
_latch_recovery_alignment	Align latch recovery structures.	254	254
_ldr_io_size*	Size of write I/Os used during a load operation.	262144	262144
_left_nested_loops_random	Enable random distribution method for left of nested loops.	TRUE	TRUE
_lgwr_async_io	LGWR Asynchronous I/O enabling Boolean flag.	TRUE	TRUE
_lgwr_io_slaves	LGWR I/O slaves.	0	0
_lgwr_max_ns_wt*	Maximum wait time for LGWR to allow NetServer to progress.	30	30
_lgwr_ns_nl_max*	Variable to simulate network latency.	1000	1000
_lgwr_ns_nl_min*	Variable to simulate network latency.	500	500

continued

TABLE 2.4   (*Continued*)

Parameter	Description	Instance	Session
_lgwr_ns_sim_err*	Variable to simulate errors during LGWR-network server testing.	0	0
_like_with_bind_as_equality	Treat LIKE predicates with bind variables as an equality predicate.	FALSE	FALSE
_lm_activate_lms_threshold*	Threshold value to activate an additional LMS.	100	100
_lm_cache_res_cleanup	Percentage of cached resources that should be cleaned up.	25	25
_lm_dd_interval	DD time interval in seconds.	60	60
_lm_direct_sends	Processes that will do direct lock manager sends.	all	all
_lm_dispatch_nonpcm*	Dispatching non-PCM messages to LMS.	FALSE	FALSE
_lm_dispatch_pcm*	Dispatching PCM messages to LMS.	FALSE	FALSE
_lm_dynamic_lms*	Dynamic LMS invocation.	FALSE	FALSE
_lm_dynamic_remastering*	If TRUE, enables dynamic remastering.	TRUE	TRUE
_lm_lms*	Number of background lock manager server processes to start.	0	0
_lm_locks*	Number of locks configured for the lock manager.	12000	12000
_lm_master_weight*	Master resource weight for this instance.	1	1
_lm_max_lms*	Max number of background lock manager server processes.	0	0
_lm_min_lms*	Min number of background lock manager server processes.	0	0
_lm_msg_batch_size*	GES batch message size.	2048	2048
_lm_node_join_opt*	Lock manager node join optimization in reconfig.	FALSE	FALSE
_lm_non_fault_tolerant	Disable lock manager fault-tolerance mode.	FALSE	FALSE
_lm_proc_freeze_timeout*	Reconfiguration: process freeze timeout.	600	600

TABLE 2.4 (*Continued*)

Parameter	Description	Instance	Session
_lm_procs	Number of client processes configured for the lock manager.	127	127
_lm_rcfg_timeout*	Reconfiguration timeout.	180000	180000
_lm_rcv_buffer_size	The size of receive buffer.	32768	32768
_lm_res_part*	Number of resource partition configured for the lock manager.	1289	1289
_lm_ress*	Number of resources configured for the lock manager.	6000	6000
_lm_send_buffers	Number of lock manager send buffers.	10000	10000
_lm_send_queue_length*	KJCT send queue maximum length.	5000	5000
_lm_sync_timeout	Synchronization timeout for DLM reconfiguration steps.	NULL	NULL
_lm_ticket_active_sendback	Flow control ticket active sendback threshold.	NULL	NULL
_lm_tickets*	GES messaging tickets.	1000	1000
_lm_tx_delta*	TX lock localization delta.	16	16
_lm_validate_resource_type*	If TRUE, enables resource name validation.	FALSE	FALSE
_lm_xids	Number of transaction IDs configured for the lock manager.	139	139
_local_communication_costing_enabled*	Enable local communication costing when TRUE.	TRUE	TRUE
_local_communication_ratio*	Set the ratio between global and local communication (0...100).	50	50
_lock_sga_areas	Lock-specified areas of the SGA in physical memory.	0	0
_log_archive_buffer_size	Size of each archival buffer in log file blocks.	2048	2048
_log_archive_buffers	Number of buffers to allocate for archiving.	4	4
_log_blocks_during_backup	Log block images when changed during backup.	TRUE	TRUE
_log_buffers_corrupt	Corrupt redo buffers before write.	FALSE	FALSE

continued

TABLE 2.4 (*Continued*)

Parameter	Description	Instance	Session
_log_buffers_debug	Debug redo buffers (slows things down).	FALSE	FALSE
_log_checkpoint_recovery_ check	Number of redo blocks to verify after checkpoint.	0	0
_log_debug_multi_instance	Debug redo multi-instance code.	FALSE	FALSE
_log_io_size	Automatically initiate log write if this many redo blocks in buffer.	0	0
_log_simultaneous_copies	Number of simultaneous copies into redo buffer (number of copy latches).	2	2
_log_space_errors	Should we report space errors to alert log?	TRUE	TRUE
_log_switch_timeout*	Maximum number of seconds redos in the current log could span.	0	0
_low_server_threshold	Low server thresholds.	0	0
_master_direct_sends*	Direct sends for messages from master (DFS).	31	31
_mav_refresh_consistent_ read*	Refresh materialized views using consistent read snapshot.	TRUE	TRUE
_mav_refresh_double_count_ prevented*	Materialized view MAV refreshes avoid double counting.	FALSE	FALSE
_mav_refresh_opt*	Optimizations during refresh of materialized views.	0	0
_mav_refresh_unionall_tables*	Number of tables for unionall expansion during materialized view refresh.	3	3
_max_exponential_sleep	Max sleep during exponential backoff.	0	0
_max_sleep_holding_latch	Max time to sleep while holding a latch.	4	4
_messages	Message queue resources: dependent on number of processes and buffers.	300	300
_minimal_stats_aggregation	Prohibit stats aggregation at compile/partition maintenance time.	TRUE	TRUE
_minimum_giga_scn	Minimum SCN to start with in 2^30 units.	0	0

TABLE 2.4 (*Continued*)

Parameter	Description	Instance	Session
_multi_join_key_table_lookup*	TRUE if multijoin-key table lookup prefetch is enabled.	TRUE	TRUE
_mv_refresh_delta_fraction*	Delta MV as fractional percentage of size of MV.	10	10
_mv_refresh_eut*	Refresh materialized views using EUT (partition)-based algorithm.	TRUE	TRUE
_mv_refresh_new_setup_disabled*	Materialized view MV refresh new setup disabling.	FALSE	FALSE
_mv_refresh_selections	Create materialized views with selections and fast refresh.	TRUE	TRUE
_mv_refresh_use_stats*	Pass cardinality hints to refresh queries.	TRUE	TRUE
_nchar_imp_cnv*	NLS allow implicit conversion between CHAR and NCHAR.	TRUE	TRUE
_ncmb_readahead_enabled	Enable multiblock read-ahead for an index scan.	0	0
_ncmb_readahead_tracing	Turn on multiblock read-ahead tracing.	0	0
_nested_loop_fudge	Nested loop fudge.	100	100
_new_initial_join_orders	Enable initial join orders based on new ordering heuristics.	TRUE	TRUE
_new_sort_cost_estimate*	Enables the use of new cost estimate for sort.	TRUE	TRUE
_no_objects	No object features are used.	FALSE	FALSE
_no_or_expansion	OR expansion during optimization disabled.	FALSE	FALSE
_ns_max_flush_wt*	Flush wait time for NetServer to flush outstanding writes.	30	30
_number_cached_attributes	Maximum number of cached attributes per instance.	10	10
_offline_rollback_segments	Offline undo segment list.	NULL	NULL
_ogms_home	GMS home directory.	NULL	NULL
_old_connect_by_enabled	Enable/disable old connect-by behavior.	FALSE	FALSE
_oneside_colstat_for_equijoins	Sanity check on default selectivity for like/range predicate.	TRUE	TRUE

continued

TABLE 2.4 (*Continued*)

Parameter	Description	Instance	Session
_open_files_limit	Limit on number of files opened by I/O subsystem.	4294967294	4294967294
_optim_enhance_nnull_detection	TRUE, to enable index [fast] full scan more often.	TRUE	TRUE
_optim_new_default_join_sel*	Improves the way default equijoin selectivity are computed.	TRUE	TRUE
_optim_peek_user_binds*	Enable peeking of user binds.	TRUE	TRUE
_optimizer_adjust_for_nulls	Adjust selectivity for null values.	TRUE	TRUE
_optimizer_choose_permutation	Force the optimizer to use the specified permutation.	0	0
_optimizer_cost_model*	Optimizer cost model.	CHOOSE	CHOOSE
_optimizer_degree	Force the optimizer to use the same degree of parallelism.	0	0
_optimizer_mode_force	Force setting of optimizer mode for user-recursive SQL also.	TRUE	TRUE
_optimizer_new_join_card_computation*	Compute join cardinality using nonrounded input values.	TRUE	TRUE
_optimizer_new_mbio*	Enables the use of new costing I/O with MBIO.	0	0
_optimizer_percent_parallel*	Optimizer percent parallel.	101	101
_optimizer_search_limit	Optimizer search limit.	5	5
_optimizer_undo_changes	Undo changes to query optimizer.	FALSE	FALSE
_or_expand_nvl_predicate	Enable OR expanded plan for NVL/DECODE predicate.	TRUE	TRUE
_oracle_trace_events	Oracle TRACE event flags.	NULL	NULL
_oracle_trace_facility_version	Oracle TRACE facility version.	NULL	NULL
_ordered_nested_loop	Enable ordered nested loop costing.	TRUE	TRUE
_ordered_semijoin	Enable ordered semi-join subquery.	TRUE	TRUE
_parallel_adaptive_max_users	Maximum number of users running with default DOP.	1	1
_parallel_default_max_instances	Default maximum number of instances for parallel query.	1	1
_parallel_execution_message_align	Alignment of PX buffers to OS page boundary.	FALSE	FALSE

TABLE 2.4   (*Continued*)

Parameter	Description	Instance	Session
_parallel_fake_class_pct	Fake db-scheduler percent used for testing.	0	0
_parallel_load_bal_unit	Number of threads to allocate per instance.	0	0
_parallel_load_balancing	Parallel execution load-balanced slave allocation.	TRUE	TRUE
_parallel_min_message_pool	Minimum size of shared pool memory to reserve for PQ servers.	64440	64440
_parallel_recovery_stopat	Stop at position to step through SMON.	32767	32767
_parallel_server_idle_time	Idle time before parallel query server dies.	5	5
_parallel_server_sleep_time	Sleep time between dequeue timeouts (in 1/100ths).	10	10
_parallel_txn_global	Enable parallel_txn hint with updates and deletes.	FALSE	FALSE
_parallelism_cost_fudge_factor	Set the parallelism cost fudge factor.	350	350
_partial_pwise_join_enabled	Enable partial partition-wise join when TRUE.	TRUE	TRUE
_passwordfile_enqueue_timeout	Password file enqueue timeout in seconds.	900	900
_pcm_fast_reconfig*	If TRUE, enable fast reconfiguration for PCM locks.	TRUE	TRUE
_pcm_latches*	Number of PCM resource hash latches to be allocated.	128	128
_pcm_resources*	Number of PCM resources to be allocated.	NULL	NULL
_pcm_shadow_locks*	Number of PCM shadow locks to be allocated.	NULL	NULL
_pct_refresh_double_count_prevented*	Materialized view PCT refreshes avoid double counting.	TRUE	TRUE
_pdml_gim_sampling	Control separation of global index maintenance for PDML.	5000	5000
_pdml_gim_staggered	Slaves start on different index when doing index maintenance.	FALSE	FALSE

continued

TABLE 2.4   *(Continued)*

Parameter	Description	Instance	Session
_pdml_slaves_diff_part	Slaves start on different partition when doing index maintenance.	TRUE	TRUE
_pga_max_size*	Maximum size of the PGA memory for one process.	209715200	209715200
_ping_level*	Fusion ping level (DFS).	3	3
_plsql_dump_buffer_events	Conditions upon which the PL/SQL circular buffer is dumped.	NULL	NULL
_plsql_load_without_compile	PL/SQL load without compilation flag.	FALSE	FALSE
_pmon_load_constants*	Server load-balancing constants (S, P, D, I, L, C, M).	300,192,64 3,10,10,0	300,192,64, 3,10,10,0
_pre_rewrite_push_pred*	Push predicates into views before rewrite.	FALSE	FALSE
_pred_move_around*	Enables predicate move-around.	TRUE	TRUE
_predicate_elimination_ Enabled	Allow predicate elimination if set to true.	TRUE	TRUE
_project_view_columns	Enable projecting out unreferenced columns of a view.	TRUE	TRUE
_push_join_predicate	Enable pushing join predicate inside a view.	TRUE	TRUE
_push_join_union_view	Enable pushing join predicate inside a UNION view.	TRUE	TRUE
_px_async_getgranule	Asynchronous get granule in the slave.	FALSE	FALSE
_px_broadcast_fudge_factor	Set the TQ broadcasting fudge factor percentage.	100	100
_px_granule_size	Default size of a rowid range granule (in KB).	100000	100000
_px_index_sampling	Parallel query sampling for index create (100000 = 100%).	200	200
_px_kxib_tracing	Turn on kxib tracing.	0	0
_px_load_publish_interval	Interval at which LMON will check whether to publish PX load.	200	200
_px_max_granules_per_slave	Maximum number of rowid range granules to generate per slave.	100	100

TABLE 2.4   *(Continued)*

Parameter	Description	Instance	Session
_px_min_granules_per_slave	Minimum number of rowid range granules to generate per slave.	13	13
_px_no_stealing	Prevent parallel granule stealing in shared nothing environment.	FALSE	FALSE
_px_trace*	PX trace parameter.	none	none
_query_cost_rewrite	Perform the cost-based rewrite with materialized views.	TRUE	TRUE
_query_rewrite_1*	Perform query rewrite before and after or only before view merging.	TRUE	TRUE
_query_rewrite_2	Perform query rewrite before and after or only after view merging.	TRUE	TRUE
_query_rewrite_drj*	MV rewrite, and drop redundant joins.	TRUE	TRUE
_query_rewrite_expression	Rewrite with canonical form for expressions.	TRUE	TRUE
_query_rewrite_fpc*	MV rewrite fresh partition containment.	TRUE	TRUE
_query_rewrite_fudge	Cost-based query rewrite with MV fudge factor.	90	90
_query_rewrite_jgmigrate*	MV rewrite with jg migration.	TRUE	TRUE
_query_rewrite_or_error*	Allow query rewrite, if referenced tables are not dataless.	FALSE	FALSE
_query_rewrite_vop_cleanup	Prune frocol chain before rewrite after view merging.	TRUE	TRUE
_realfree_heap_free_threshold*	Threshold for performing real-free, in Kbytes.	64	64
_realfree_heap_max_size*	Minimum max total heap size, in Kbytes.	32768	32768
_recovery_claim_batch_size*	Number of messages to batch in a recovery claim message (DFS).	10	10
_recovery_percentage*	Recovery buffer cache percentage.	80	80

continued

TABLE 2.4   (*Continued*)

Parameter	Description	Instance	Session
_release_insert_threshold	Maximum number of unusable blocks to unlink from freelist.	5	5
_reliable_block_sends*	If TRUE, block sends across interconnect are reliable.	FALSE	FALSE
_reuse_index_loop	Number of blocks being examined for index block reuse.	5	5
_rollback_segment_count	Number of undo segments.	0	0
_rollback_segment_initial	Starting undo segment number.	1	1
_row_cache_buffer_size	Size of row cache circular buffer.	200	200
_row_cache_cursors	Number of cached cursors for row cache management.	10	10
_row_cache_instance_locks	Number of row cache instance locks.	100	100
_scn_scheme	SCN scheme.	NULL	NULL
_second_spare_parameter*	Second spare parameter: integer.	NULL	NULL
_send_close_with_block*	If TRUE, send close with block, even with direct sends.	TRUE	TRUE
_serial_direct_read	Enable direct read in serial.	FALSE	FALSE
_session_idle_bit_latches	One latch per session or a latch per group of sessions.	0	0
_seventh_spare_parameter*	Seventh spare parameter: string list.	NULL	NULL
_shared_pool_reserved_min_alloc	Minimum allocation size in bytes for reserved area of shared pool.	4400	4400
_shared_pool_reserved_pct*	Percentage memory of the shared pool allocated for the reserved section.	5	5
_shrunk_aggs_disable_threshold*	Percentage of exceptions at which to switch to full-length aggregates.	60	60
_shrunk_aggs_enabled*	Enable use of variable-sized buffers for nondistinct aggregates.	TRUE	TRUE
_side_channel_batch_size*	Number of messages to batch in a side channel message (DFS).	100	100
_single_process	Run without detached processes.	FALSE	FALSE

TABLE 2.4   (*Continued*)

Parameter	Description	Instance	Session
_sixth_spare_parameter*	Sixth spare parameter: string list.	NULL	NULL
_skip_assume_msg*	If TRUE, skip assume message for consigns at the master.	TRUE	TRUE
_slave_mapping_enabled*	Enable slave mapping when TRUE.	TRUE	TRUE
_slave_mapping_group_size*	Force the number of slave group in a slave mapper.	0	0
_small_table_threshold	Threshold level of table size for direct reads.	160	160
_smm_auto_cost_enabled*	If TRUE, use the AUTO size policy cost functions.	FALSE	FALSE
_smm_auto_max_io_size*	Maximum I/O size (in KB) used by sort/hash-join in auto mode.	248	248
_smm_auto_min_io_size*	Minimum I/O size (in KB) used by sort/hash-join in auto mode.	56	56
_smm_bound*	Overwrites memory manager automatically computed bound.	0	0
_smm_control*	Provides controls on the memory manager.	0	0
_smm_max_size*	Maximum work area size in auto mode (serial).	0	0
_smm_min_size*	Minimum work area size in auto mode.	128	128
_smm_px_max_size*	Maximum work area size in auto mode (global).	0	0
_smm_trace*	Turn on/off tracing for SQL memory manager.	0	0
_smon_internal_errlimit*	Limit of SMON internal errors.	100	100
_smu_debug_mode*	<debug-flag> Set debug event for testing SMU operations.	0	0
_smu_error_simulation_site*	Site ID of error simulation in KTU code.	0	0
_smu_error_simulation_type*	Error type for error simulation in KTU code.	0	0
_sort_elimination_cost_ratio	Cost ratio for sort elimination under first_rows mode.	0	0
_sort_multiblock_read_count*	Multiblock read count for sort.	2	2

continued

TABLE 2.4   (*Continued*)

Parameter	Description	Instance	Session
_sort_space_for_write_buffers	Tenths of sort_area_size devoted to direct write buffers.	1	1
_sortmerge_inequality_join_off	Turns off sort-merge join on inequality.	FALSE	FALSE
_spin_count	Amount to spin waiting for a latch.	1	1
_sql_connect_capability_override	SQL Connect Capability Table override.	0	0
_sql_connect_capability_table	SQL Connect Capability Table (testing only).	NULL	NULL
_sqlexec_progression_cost	SQL execution progression monitoring cost threshold.	1000	1000
_subquery_pruning_cost_factor	Subquery pruning cost factor.	20	20
_subquery_pruning_enabled	Enable the use of subquery predicates to perform pruning.	TRUE	TRUE
_subquery_pruning_mv_enabled*	Enable the use of subquery predicates with MVs to perform pruning.	TRUE	TRUE
_subquery_pruning_reduction	Subquery pruning reduction factor.	50	50
_system_index_caching*	Optimizer percent system index caching.	0	0
_system_trig_enabled	Are system triggers enabled?	TRUE	TRUE
_table_lookup_prefetch_size*	Table lookup prefetch vector size.	40	40
_table_scan_cost_plus_one	Bump estimated full table scan cost by one.	FALSE	FALSE
_temp_tran_block_threshold	Number of blocks for a dimension before we temp transform.	100	100
_temp_tran_cache	Determines if temp table is created with cache option.	TRUE	TRUE
_test_param_1	Test parmeter 1: integer.	25	25
_test_param_2	Test parameter 2: string.	NULL	NULL
_test_param_3	Test parameter 3: string.	NULL	NULL
_test_param_4*	Test parameter 4: string list.	NULL	NULL
_test_param_5*	Test parmeter 5: deprecated integer.	25	25

TABLE 2.4 *(Continued)*

Parameter	Description	Instance	Session
_test_param_6*	Test parmeter 6: size (ub8).	0	0
_third_spare_parameter	Third spare parameter: integer.	NULL	NULL
_tq_dump_period	Time period for duping of TQ statistics (s).	0	0
_trace_archive*	Start DIAG process.	FALSE	FALSE
_trace_buffer_flushes	Trace buffer flushes if otrace cacheIO event is set.	FALSE	FALSE
_trace_buffer_gets	Trace kcb buffer gets if otrace cacheIO event is set.	FALSE	FALSE
_trace_buffers*	Trace buffer sizes per process.	ALL:256	ALL:256
_trace_cr_buffer_creates	Trace cr buffer creates if otrace cacheIO event is set.	FALSE	FALSE
_trace_events	Trace events enabled at startup.	NULL	NULL
_trace_file_size	Maximum size of trace file (in number of trace records).	65536	65536
_trace_files_public	Create publicly accessible trace files.	FALSE	FALSE
_trace_flush_processes*	Trace data archived by DIAG for these processes.	ALL	ALL
_trace_instance_termination	Trace instance termination actions.	FALSE	FALSE
_trace_multi_block_reads	Trace multi_block reads if otrace cacheIO event is set.	FALSE	FALSE
_trace_options*	Trace data flush options.	text,multiple	text,multiple
_trace_processes*	Enable KST tracing in process.	ALL	ALL
_transaction_recovery_servers	Max number of parallel recovery slaves that may be used.	0	0
_tts_allow_nchar_mismatch	Allow plugging in a tablespace with a different national character set.	FALSE	FALSE
_two_pass*	Enable two-pass thread recovery.	TRUE	TRUE
_unnest_notexists_sq*	Unnest NOT EXISTS subquery with one or more tables if possible.	SINGLE	SINGLE
_unnest_subquery	Enables unnesting of correlated subqueries.	TRUE	TRUE

continued

TABLE 2.4   *(Continued)*

Parameter	Description	Instance	Session
_use_column_stats_for_ function	Enable the use of column statistics for DDP functions.	TRUE	TRUE
_use_ism	Enable shared page tables – ISM.	TRUE	TRUE
_use_new_explain_plan*	If TRUE, use the AUTO size policy cost functions.	FALSE	FALSE
_use_nosegment_indexes	Use nosegment indexes in explain plan.	FALSE	FALSE
_use_realfree_heap*	Use real free-based allocator for PGA memory.	FALSE	FALSE
_use_vector_post	Use vector post.	TRUE	TRUE
_verify_undo_quota*	If TRUE; verify consistency of undo quota statistics.	FALSE	FALSE
_wait_for_sync	Wait for sync on commit MUST ALWAYS BE TRUE.	TRUE	TRUE
_walk_insert_threshold	Maximum number of unusable blocks to walk across freelist.	0	0
_write_clones	Write clones flag.	3	3
_yield_check_interval	Interval to check whether actses should yield.	100000	100000

*Indicates parameter is Oracle9*i* only.

support. DBAs should be aware that use of certain undocumented parameters will result in an unsupported system. I will attempt to identify where parameters should be used only under Oracle support's guidance and where a DBA can safely utilize these high-powered tools.

What's the Difference?   The major difference between the documented and undocumented parameters is that the undocumented parameters begin with an underscore character. In many cases, the undocumented parameters were either documented at one time in previous releases or will be in future releases. Those parameters that have been, or will be, documented are usually those that are safe to use. The undocumented parameters that have never been really documented and the ones that never will be are those for which it is difficult to determine their use safety. When in doubt, get guidance from Oracle support. And always back up the database before using any of the questionable parameters so that you have a way to restore a "supported" version on which you can get help.

So Many Parameters, So Little Time Let's begin this discussion with what an expert has to say on the topic. Rich Niemiec of TUSC cites, in *Oracle Performance Tuning Tips and Techniques* (Oracle Press, 2000), the following 14 undocumented parameters as his favorites:

_ALLOW_RESETLOGS_CORRUPTION. May be only way to start a db backed-up open without setting backup on tablespaces; will result in unsupported system. See detailed section on using _allow_resetlogs_corruption that follows.

_CORRUPTED_ROLLBACK_SEGMENTS. Only way to start up with corrupted public rollback segments. Can be used without fear of desupport.

_ALLOW_READ_ONLY_CORRUPTION. Allows you to open a database even if it has corruption. This should only be used to export as much data from a corrupted database as is possible before re-creating a database. You should not use a database for normal use that has been opened in this manner, as it will not be supported.

_SPIN_COUNT. Sets the number of spins a process will undergo before trying to get a latch. If CPU is not fully loaded, a high value may be best; for a fully loaded CPU, a smaller value may help. Usually defaults to 2000. Can be changed without fear of desupport. Flips from undocumented to documented depending on version.

_LOG_ENTRY_PREBUILD_THRESHOLD. Formerly documented, now is undocumented; is the minimum size of entry in blocks that will be prebuilt for redo log entries; usually set to 30.

_LATCH_SPIN_COUNT. Shows how often a latch request will be taken.

_DB_BLOCK_WRITE_BATCH. Formerly documented, now undocumented; the number of blocks that the db writers will write in each batch; defaults to 512 or DB_FILES*DB_FILE_SIMULTANEOUS_WRITES/2 up to a limit of one-fourth the value of DB_BLOCK_BUFFERS.

_CPU_COUNT. Flips from undocumented to documented. Should be set automatically; but on some platforms, doesn't; set to the number of CPUs. This determines several other parameters.

_INIT_SQL_FILE. The initialization SQL script run by Oracle when a db is created. This should be sql.bsq; if you change it, you may not be supported.

_TRACE_FILES_PUBLIC. Changes the privileges on trace files such that everyone can read them. Should be Okay to change at will.

_FAST_FULL_SCAN_ENABLED. Enables (or disables) fast full index scans if only indexes are required to resolve the queries. Change at will.

_CORRUPT_BLOCKS_ON_STUCK_RECOVERY. Can sometimes get a corrupted db up; you probably won't be supported if done without Oracle support's blessing. Immediately export the tables you need and rebuild the db if used.

_ALWAYS_STAR_TRANSFORMATION. Helps to tune data warehouse queries if you have a properly designed data warehouse.

_SMALL_TABLE_THRESHOLD. Sets the size of table considered a small table. A small table is automatically pinned into the buffers when queried. Defaults to 2 percent in Oracle9*i*.

Niemiec lists another 13 parameters that bear mentioning:

_DEBUG_SGA. Has no noticeable effect.

_LOG_BUFFERS_DEBUG. Slows things down.

_REUSE_INDEX_LOOPS. The blocks to examine for index block reuse.

_SAVE_ESCALATES. Not sure what it does; no measurable effects. According to Steve Adams, Oracle may take an exclusive lock earlier than required to save lock escalations; if this is set to FALSE, it won't. Don't mess with it.

_OPTIMIZER_UNDO_CHANGES. Reverts to pre-6.0.3 optimizer for IN statements. This one is required in certain versions of the Oracle Applications. According to K. Gopalakrishnan of the *India Times*, this parameter has nothing to do with cost-based optimization. In Version 6, somewhere around V6.0.36, if he remembers correctly, Ed Peeler made several changes to the way the optimizer made choices. Many queries in the existing Oracle Applications at that time relied in particular on the old way the optimizer worked to be certain to come up with the intended plan. The code was written prior to hints, so many tricks were used to influence the optimizer to come up with a certain plan and were scattered throughout the code. When the new database release was made, tests showed that many critical applications processes ran catastrophically slower. Fortunately, the old optimizer code had not been stripped out yet, and a way to use the old optimizer code was allowed via the "hidden*" parameter _undo_optimizer_changes (probably so that Oracle could test the old versus the new optimizer internally). So Oracle released this parameter to the applications community. This was long before the cost-based optimizer even existed.

_DSS_CACHE_FLUSH. Enables full cache flush for parallel; effect is not measurable.

_DB_NO_MOUNT_LOCK. Doesn't get a mount lock; no noticeable effect.

_AFFINITY. Defaults to TRUE; enables or disables CPU affinity.

_CORRUPT_BLOCKS_ON_STUCK_RECOVERY. Tried in a corrupt recovery and didn't do anything; no noticeable effect

_CURSOR_DB_BUFFERS_PINNED. Lists additional buffers a cursor can pin; no noticeable effect. The default value is max(db_block_buffers/processes-2,2). One note from Oracle development says that playing around with this parameter will almost always damage performance, so it was made hidden starting in 8.0.3.

_DB_BLOCK_NO_IDLE_WRITES. Disables writes of blocks when the db is idle; may result in an unusable system if used. If you get an instance Crash with the following Error ORA-00600: internal error code, arguments: [kcbbzo_2], [1], [25974], setting this parameter may help. A Ctrl-c during a truncate may cause the DBWR to fail with an ORA-600 [kcbbzo_2], causing the instance to crash.

_DISABLE_LOGGING. Even I won't support you if you set this one. If this parameter is set to TRUE, redo records will *not* be generated, and recovery is *not* possible if the instance crashes or is terminated with shutdown abort.

_IO_SLAVES_DISABLED. Disables I/O slaves, probably not the safest way.

Other Notables Other parameters, covered in various notes on Metalink, *ORACLE8i Internal Services for Waits, Latches, Locks and Memory,* by Steve Adams (Oracle Press, 1999), and other boards include the following:

_DISTRIBUTED_LOCK_TIMEOUT. Sets the amount of time a lock used in a distributed transaction will be held, usually 5. Safe to reset without worry of desupport.

_ROW_CACHE_CURSORS. Maximum number of cached recursive cursors used for data dictionary cache queries. This sets the size of the array in the PGA used for the data dictionary cursors. It takes 28 bytes per cached cursor. Long-running procedures that do a lot of data dictionary lookups can benefit from higher values. If the view K$KQDPG shows excessive overflows of the cache, a small increase may help. This view is for the current process only. The ORADUBUG or DBMS_SYSTEM.SET_EV can be used to grab a trace of a different process. In the resulting trace, find the X$KQDPG structure, count 12 blocks, and use the hexadecimal values to get the values. Recursive calls can be caused by firing of database triggers, execution of SQL statements within stored procedures and functions and anonymous PL/SQL blocks, and enforcement of referential integrity constraints. Setting this value higher may reduce these recursive calls.

_LOG_BLOCKS_DURING_BACKUP. From Oracle support, but we still do not recommend the use of this parameter on production systems. There is a known problem with performance on systems using certain configurations of Veritas with Solaris 2.6. Contact Veritas for further information. Use of this parameter will result in an unsupported system.

_DB_WRITER_SCAN_DEPTH_INCREMENT. Controls the rate at which the scan depth increases if the db writer is idle; defaults to one-eighth the difference between the upper and lower bounds of the scan depth.

_DB_WRITER_SCAN_DEPTH_DECREMENT. Controls the rate at which the scan depth decreases of the db writer is working too hard. The X$KVIT table gives the details of the db writer; you can find the details using the following SELECT statement, courtesy of Steve Adams at www.ixora.com.au:

```
SELECT
Kvitdsc,
```

```
Kvitval
FROM
Sys.x$kvit
WHERE
Kvittag IN ('kcbldq', 'kcbsfs') OR
Kvittag LIKE 'kcbsd_'
/
```

_DB_LARGE_DIRTY_QUEUE. Defaults to one-sixteenth of the write batch size limit. Sets the frequency at which DBWR writes. Should be decreased gradually in one-block increments until buffer waits are eliminated. The cost of reducing this parameter is in CPU usage, so shouldn't be changed without good reason.

_DB_BLOCK_MAX_SCAN_CNT. Defaults to one-fourth of the working set size, rounded down. If this number of blocks is scanned, then the free buffer request fails. The failure of a scan increments the dirty buffers inspected parameter in the V$SYSSTAT view. If there are no free buffer waits, and there are dirty buffers inspected, then there is a potentially serious problem and the parameter should be tuned.

_ENQUEUE_HASH_CHAINS. Derived from the PROCESSES parameter, so is the value for ENQUEUE_RESOURCES, which is directly affected by _ENQUEUE_HASH_CHAINS; therefore, if you explicitly set ENQUEUE_RESOURCES, you will need to adjust _ENQUEUE_HASH_CHAINS to a prime number just less than the value of ENQUEUE_RESOURCES. If the value of _ENQUEUE_HASH is not set to a prime number, long enqueue hash chains could develop. Unless you are receiving ORA-00052 or ORA-00053 errors, this parameter and ENQUEUE_RESOURCES probably don't need adjusting. The default value is equal to CPU_COUNT.

_ENQUEUE_LOCKS. Use V$RESOUCE_LIMIT to see if you need more locks or ENQUEUE_RESOUORCES. A lock takes 60 bytes; a resource, 72 bytes. To increase the enqueue_locks value in v$resource limit, you have to increase the _enqueue_limit value in init.ora.

_USE_ISM. Determines if intimate shared memory is used. On some platforms this can cause problems, and _USE_ISM should be set to FALSE instead of its default of TRUE.

_DB_BLOCK_HASH_BUCKETS. In releases prior to 9*i*, this was set to twice the value of DB_BLOCK_BUFFERS. Unfortunately, this should be set to a prime number to keep the hash chains from getting out of hand; therefore, on releases prior to 9*i*, resetting this to a prime number near the value of twice the DB_BLOCK_BUFFERS is a good idea and will not result in loss of support. According to Steve Adams, _db_block_hash_buckets could be used to set both the number of hash chains and latches in previous releases. From 7.1, it was constrained to prime numbers, and used to default to next_prime(*db_block_buffers* / 4).

Under release 8.1, *_db_block_hash_buckets* it defaults to 2 * *db_block_buffers*, and the *_db_block_hash_latches* parameter must be used to control the number of hash latches if necessary. This parameter is constrained to binary powers so that Oracle can calculate which latch to use with a simple SHIFT operation, rather than a DIVIDE operation. The default number of hash latches depends on *db_block_ buffers*. If *db_block_buffers* is less than 2052 buffers, then the default number of latches is 2 ^ trunc(log(2, *db_block_buffers* - 4) - 1).

If *db_block_buffers* is greater than 131075 buffers, then the default number of latches is 2 ^ trunc(log(2, *db_block_buffers* - 4) - 6). If *db_block_buffers* is between 2052 and 131075 buffers, then there are 1024 latches by default. Sites that have used *_db_block_hash_buckets* to combat *cache buffer chains* latch contention under previous releases should allow the value to default when upgrading to Oracle 8*i*. Remember that contention for these latches is almost always a symptom of one or more blocks being very hot due to unresolved application or SQL tuning problems. Adams may be correct; however, I have seen improvements on 8.1.7 by setting these values as in previous releases.

_DB_BLOCK_HASH_LATCHES. Usually set to 1024, which is usually too small; set it to near 32K (32768) for better performance. Up to release 8.0.

_KGL_LATCH_COUNT. Value defaults to 7. This determines the number of latches that control the shared pool. If you need a large shared pool, or have a large number of items that are placed in the shared pool, set this to a larger prime number. According to Oracle support: In general, on systems that have multiple CPUs and/or when parsing a lot of SQL with few shared cursors, it is recommended to set it to 1. On all other systems it must be set to the default, in which case the latch contention may not be significant compared to the cost of building a new cursor for each SQL statement. However, I tend to agree with Steve Adams: The default is the least prime number greater than or equal to cpu_count. The maximum is 67. It can safely be increased to combat library cache latch contention, as long as you stick to prime numbers. That said, it is only effective if the activity across the existing child library cache latches is evenly distributed as shown in V$LATCH_ CHILDREN.

Here are some undocumented parameters for maximizing DBWR performance:

- Increase _db_block_write_batch (hidden parameter in Oracle8, obsolete in Oracle8*i*).
- Decrease _db_block_max_scan_count, _db_writer_scan_depth, and _db_writer_ scan_depth_increment to decrease the dirty buffer backlog.
- Adjust_db_writer_chunk_writes, which controls the number of writes DBWR should try to group into one batch I/O operation.
- Adjust _db_block_med_priority_batch_size for regular writes.
- Adjust _db_block_hi_priority_batch_size for urgent writes such as when LRUW is full or there are no free buffers or when free buffers are below limit.

Parameters That Must Be Used   Here I attempt to list the specific conditions when the following undocumented parameters must be changed:

_DB_HANDLES. In versions before 8.1.7.2, if set too high, this may cause ORA-04031 because of bug 1397603.

_DB_HANDLES_CACHED. Before 8.1.7.2, may need to be set to 0.

_ELIMINATE_COMMON_SUBEXPR. If left set to TRUE, may cause some queries using IN clauses to return too many rows or bad answers; set to FALSE in 8.1.7.0 and 8.1.7.1.

_IGNORE_DESC_IN_INDEX. May have to set to TRUE on some platforms (such as AIX) in versions 8.1.6 and 8.1.7 if you get ORA-03113 and ORA-07445 errors when you try different management or DML operations on descending indexes. On some platforms may have to use the event-setting "10612 trace name context for-ever, level 1" to reset it.

_INIT_SQL_FILE. This may have to be reset to use 32K block sizes on some platforms, as they will use the sql.bsq.32K file instead of the sql.bsq file.

_MV_REFRESH_SELECTIONS. Is 8.1.7 only, and if you have multilevel joins in your materialized view, setting this to TRUE may allow fast refreshes.

_NEW_INITIAL_JOIN_ORDERS. Set to TRUE when upgrading to 11.5.4 on 8.1.7.

_OGMS_HOME. Used in Oracle Parallel Server. Set explicitly or may default to /tmp, which could result in file loss and inability to start Oracle Parallel Server.

_SQLEXEC_PROGRESSION_COST. For Oracle Application 11.5.4 in 8.1.7, set to 0.

_UNNEST_SUBQUERY. Where you cannot use the UNNEST hint, may improve performance.

_USE_ISM. Set to FALSE on Solaris 2.6 or you may have system crashes and poor performance (depending on Oracle version may be USE_ISM).

_DB_ALWAYS_CHECK_SYSTEM_TS. Always perform block check and check-sum for SYSTEM tablespace; this defaults to TRUE. You may need to set this to FALSE after upgrade from a pre-8*i* version of Oracle. If you need to set this to FALSE to restart the DB, immediately export and rebuild the database, as it de-tected corruption in the data dictionary (probably in the C_TS# cluster, but that is another story).

_DB_CACHE_ADVICE. Will turn on the buffer cache sizing advisory if set to ON to help you perform cache sizing.

Untouchable Parameters   In contrast to parameters that must be changed, there are those that should never be changed. Let's look at a few of them.

_COMPATIBLE_NO_RECOVERY. Usually set to 0.0.0, which defaults to the current version. If you set it to something else and the DB crashes, you may need to do a media recovery instead of just an instance recovery.

_ALLOW_ERROR_SIMULATION. Used by Oracle for internal testing. If you set it, there's no telling what it will do to your instance.

_DB_BLOCK_CACHE_PROTECT. Will cause a db crash rather than let corruption get to the database. It may result in many ORA-0600 errors and other unpleasant things if set in a regular production database. This is for debugging only!

_IPC_FAIL_NETWORK. Simulates network failure; for testing only.

_IPC_TEST_FAILOVER. Tests transparent cluster network failover; for testing only.

_IPC_TEST_MULT_NETS. Simulates multiple cluster networks; for testing only.

_LOG_BUFFERS_CORRUPT. Corrupts redo buffers after write; for testing only.

_MTS_LOAD_CONSTANTS. A complex set of constants that governs the multithreaded server load balancing. It contains six different values dealing with how the load is balanced across servers and dispatchers.

_CPU_TO_IO. The multiplier for converting CPU cost to I/O cost. Change this and you will directly affect the CBO cost calculation.

_LOG_BUFFERS_CORRUPT. Corrupts redo buffers before write; used only for testing. A sure way to bring your database to its knees is to set this to TRUE.

_SINGLE_PROCESS. Run without detached processes; if you want single-user Oracle, this will give it to you.

_WAIT_FOR_SYNC. Wait for checkpoint sync on commit must always be TRUE; if set to FALSE, will cause mismatch between headers and SCN on DB crash or shutdown abort.

_NO_OBJECTS. Tells Oracle that no objects are being used; set to FALSE. If you set it to TRUE, Oracle will probably crash since the data dictionary uses objects.

_PMON_LOAD_CONSTANTS. As with MTS, these are PMON Server load-balancing constants and directly affect the operation of PMON; don't mess with them.

This list contains only those parameters that stand out. There are many more that, if you change them, will have a negative effect on how Oracle behaves. When in doubt, don't touch it!

Recovering Using _ALLOW_RESETLOGS_CORRUPTION Let's now look at a detailed example using _allow_resetlogs_corruption to recover a database. Recovery of a database using the undocumented parameter _allow_resetlogs_corruption should be regarded as a last-ditch, emergency recovery scenario only, and should not be attempted until all other avenues of recovery have been exhausted.

NOTE   Oracle will not support a database that has been recovered using this method unless it is subsequently exported and rebuilt.

Essentially, using _allow_resetlogs_corruption forces the opening of the datafiles even if their SCNs do not match up; then, on the next checkpoint, the old SCN values are overwritten. This could leave the database in an unknown state as far as concurrency.

This type of recovery is usually required when a datafile has been left in hot backup mode through several backup cycles without an intervening shutdown and startup. Upon shutdown and startup, the database will complain that a file (usually file id#1 the SYSTEM tablespace) needs more recovery, and asks for logs past all available archive logs and online logs.

An alternative scenario would be that the database is recovered from a hot backup and the above scenario occurs, or that the database asks for an archive log dated earlier than any that are available (usually for the rollback segment tablespace datafiles). I have also seen this happen when creating a standby database using a hot backup.

A typical error stack would resemble:

```
SVRMGR> connect internal

Connected.

SVRMGR> @sycrectl

ORACLE instance started.

Total System Global Area 113344192 bytes

Fixed Size 69312 bytes

Variable Size 92704768 bytes

Database Buffers 20480000 bytes

Redo Buffers 90112 bytes

Statement processed.

ALTER DATABASE OPEN resetlogs

*

ORA-01194: file 1 needs more recovery to be consistent

ORA-01110: data file 1: '/u03/oradata/tstc/dbsyst01.dbf'
```

Or:

```
ORA-01547: warning: RECOVER succeeded but OPEN RESETLOGS would get error
below

ORA-01194: file 48 needs more recovery to be consistent

ORA-01110: data file 48: '/vol06/oradata/testdb/ard01.dbf'
```

If all available archive logs and all available online redo logs are applied, and the error is not corrected, only then should you consider using the parameter _allow_resetlogs_corruption. Make sure a good backup of the database in a closed state (all files) is taken before attempting recovery using this parameter.

NOTE   It cannot be stressed firmly enough that the database will no longer be supported by Oracle until it is rebuilt after using _allow_resetlogs_ corruption for recovery.

Procedure The following details the recovery process using _allow_resetlogs_ corruption:

1. If no recovery attempts have been made, shut down and back up the database (all files) as-is to provide a fallback position should recovery fail.
2. If recovery attempts have been made, recover the database to the state just before any other recovery attempts were made.
3. Use svrmgrl, sqlplus, or appropriate interface to start up the database in a mounted, but not open, condition:
   a. STARTUP MOUNT
4. Ensure all datafiles are set to END BACKUP status:
   a. SET PAGES 0 FEEDBACK OFF LINES 132
   b. SPOOL alter_df.sql
   c. SELECT 'alter database datafile '||file_name||' END BACKUP;' from v$datafile;
   d. SPOOL OFF
   e. @alter_df.sql
5. Alter the database into open condition:
   a. ALTER DATABASE OPEN;
6. If the database asks for recovery, use an UNTIL CANCEL-type recovery and apply all available archive and online redo logs; then issue the CANCEL and reissue the ALTER DATATBASE OPEN RESETLOGS; commands.
7. If the database asks for logs that are no longer available, or the preceding still resulted in errors, shut down the database.

8. Insert into the initialization file the following line:
   a. _allow_resetlogs_corruption=TRUE
9. Use svrmgrl, sqlplus, or appropriate interface to start up the database in a mounted, but not open, condition:
   a. STARTUP MOUNT
10. Ensure all datafiles are set to END BACKUP status:
    a. SET PAGES 0 FEEDBACK OFF LINES 132
    b. SPOOL alter_df.sql
    c. SELECT 'alter database datafile '||file_name||' END BACKUP;' from v$datafile;
    d. SPOOL OFF
    e. @alter_df.sql
11. Alter the database into open condition:
    a. ALTER DATABASE OPEN;
12. If the database asks for recovery, use an UNTIL CANCEL-type recovery and apply all available archive and online redo logs; then issue the CANCEL and reissue the ALTER DATATBASE OPEN RESETLOGS; commands.
13. Once the database is open, immediately do a full export of the database or an export of the schemas you need to recover.
14. Shut down the database and remove the parameter _allow_resetlogs_corruption.
15. Rebuild the database.
16. Import to finish the recovery.
17. Implement a proper backup plan and procedure.
18. It may be advisable to perform an ANALYZE TABLE...VALIDATE STRUCTURE CASCADE on critical application tables after the recovery and before the export.

NOTE   Uncommitted records that had been written to disk will possibly be marked as committed by this procedure.

Events in Oracle

Another set of parameters that may be useful are events, so I'll discuss events a bit in this subsection. Setting an event means to tell Oracle to generate information in form of a trace file in the context of the event. The trace file is usually located in a directory specified by the initialization parameter USER_DUMP_DEST. By examining the resulting trace file, detailed information about the event traced can be deduced. The general format for an event is:

```
EVENT = "<trace class><event name><action><name><trace name><qualifier>"
```

There are two types of events: *session-events* and *process-events*. Process-events are initialized in the parameter file; session-events are initialized with the ALTER

SESSION... or ALTER SYSTEM command. When checking for posted events, the Oracle Server first checks for session-events then for process-events.

Event Classes There are four traceable event classes:

Class 1: "Dump something." Traces are generated upon so-called unconditioned immediate, events. This is the case when Oracle data has to be dumped; for example, the headers of all redolog files or the contents of the controlfile. These events can not be set in the init<SID>.ora, but must be set using the ALTER SESSION or the DBMS_SESSION.SET_EV() procedure.

Class 2: "Trap on Error." Setting this class of (error-) events causes Oracle to generate an errorstack every time the event occurs.

Class 3: "Change execution path." Setting such an event will cause Oracle to change the execution path for some specific Oracle internal code segment. For example, setting event "10269" prevents SMON from doing free-space coalescing.

Class 4: "Trace something." Events from this class are set to obtain traces that are used for, for example, SQL tuning. A common event is "10046", which will cause Oracle to trace the SQL access path on each SQL-statement.

Table 2.5 itemizes Oracle event classifications.

TABLE 2.5 Event Classifications

Trace Class	Event Name	Action Key Word	"Name"	Trace Name	Trace Qualifier
Dump Something	Immediate	Trace	"name"	blockdump redohdr file_hdrs controlf systemstate	level block# level 10 level 10 level 10 level 10
Trap on error	Error number	Trace	"name"	Errorstack processstate Heapdump	Forever off Level n
Change execution path	Even code corresponding to path	Trace	"name"	context	Forever or level 10
Trace something	10046	Trace	"name"	context	Forever Level n off

The Initialization File Event Settings

The SET EVENTS command in an init<SID>.ora file have generally been placed there at the command of Oracle support to perform specific functions. Usually, these alerts turn on more advanced levels of tracing and error detection than are commonly available. Source 2.6 lists some of the more common events.

The syntax to specify multiple events in the init.ora is:

```
EVENT="<event 1>:<event 2>: <event 3>: <event n>"
```

You can also split the events on multiple lines by using the continuation backslash character (\) at the end of each event and continue the next event on the next line. For example:

```
EVENT="<event 1>:\
<event 2>:\
<event 3>: \
<event n>"
```

For Example:

```
EVENT="\
10210 trace name context forever, level 10:\
10211 trace name context forever, level 10:\
10231 trace name context forever, level 10:\
10232 trace name context forever, level 10"
```

After setting the events in the initialization file, you need to stop and restart the instance. Be sure to check the alert.log and verify that the events are in effect. You can specify almost all EVENT settings at the session level using the ALTER SESSION command or a call to the DBMS_SYSYTEM.SET_EV( ) procedure; doing so does not require an instance bounce for the EVENT to take effect.

The alert.log should show the events that are in effect; for example:

```
   event = 10210 trace name context forever, level 10:10211 trace name
context for ever, level 10:10231 trace name context forever, level 10:10232
trace name context forever, level 10
```

Example Uses of the EVENT Initialization Parameter   To enable block header and trailer checking to detect corrupt blocks:

```
event="10210 trace name context forever, level 10"  -- for tables
event="10211 trace name context forever, level 10"  -- for indexes
event="10210 trace name context forever, level 2" -- data block checking
event="10211 trace name context forever, level 2" -- index block checking
event="10235 trace name context forever, level 1" -- memory heap checking
event="10049 trace name context forever, level 2" -- memory protect cursors
```

And to go with these, the undocumented parameter setting:

```
_db_block_cache_protect=TRUE
```

which will prevent corruption from getting to your disks (at the cost of a database crash).

For tracing of a MAX_CURSORS exceeded error:

```
event="1000 trace name ERRORSTACK level 3"
```

To get an error stack related to a SQLNET ORA-03120 error:

```
event="3120 trace name error stack"
```

To work around a space leak problem:

```
event="10262 trace name context forever, level x"
```

where x is the size of space leak to ignore.

To trace memory shortages:

```
event="10235 trace name context forever, level 4"
event="600 trace name heapdump, level 4"
```

To take a shared pool heapdump to track Ora-04031 as the error occurs, set the following event in your init.ora file:

```
event = "4031 trace name heapdump forever, level 2"
```

For ORA-04030 errors: Take a dump by setting this event in your INIT file and analyze the trace file. This will clearly pinpoint the problem.

```
event="4030 trace name errorstack level 3"
```

The following undocumented SQL statements can be used to obtain information about internal database structures:

- To dump the control file:

  ```
  alter session set events 'immediate trace name CONTROLF level 10'
  ```

- To dump the file headers:

  ```
  alter session set events 'immediate trace name FILE_HDRS level 10'
  ```

- To dump redo log headers:

  ```
  alter session set events 'immediate trace name REDOHDR level 10'
  ```

- To dump the system state:

  ```
  alter session set events 'immediate trace name SYSTEMSTATE level 10'
  ```

- To dump the optimizer statistics whenever a SQL statement is parsed:

```
alter session set events '10053 trace name context forever'
```

- To prevent db block corruptions:

```
event = "10210 trace name context forever, level 10"
event = "10211 trace name context forever, level 10"
event = "10231 trace name context forever, level 10"
```

- To enable the maximum level of SQL performance monitoring:

```
event = "10046 trace name context forever, level 12"
```

- To enable a memory-protect cursor:

```
event = "10049 trace name context forever, level  2"
```

- To perform data-block checks:

```
event = "10210 trace name context forever, level  2"
```

- To perform index-block checks:

```
event = "10211 trace name context forever, level  2"
```

- To perform memory-heap checks:

```
event = "10235 trace name context forever, level  1"
```

- To allow 300 bytes memory leak for each connection:

```
event = "10262 trace name context forever, level 300"
```

You should be noticing a pattern here for tracing events related to error codes: the first argument in the EVENT is the error code followed by the action you want to take upon receiving the code.

Events at the Session Level

Events are also used as the SESSION level using the ALTER SESSION command or calls to the DBMS_SYSTEM.SET_EV() procedure. The general format for the ALTER SESSION command is:

```
ALTER SESSION SET EVENTS 'ev_number ev_text level x';
```

where:

Ev_number is the event number.

Ev_text is any required text (usually "trace name context forever").

x is the required level setting corresponding to the desire action, file, or other required data.

For example, to provide more detailed SQL trace information:

```
ALTER SESSION SET EVENTS '10046 trace name context forever level NN'
```

where NN:

1 is same as a regular trace
4 means also dump bind variables
8 means also dump wait information
12 means dump both bind and wait information

Example Uses of the ALTER SESSION Command to Set EVENT Codes   To coalesce freespace in a tablespace pre-version 7.3:

```
ALTER SESSION SET EVENTS 'immediate trace name coalesce level XX'
```

where:

```
XX is the value of ts# from ts$ table for the tablespace
```

To coalesce freespace in a tablespace defined as temporary:

```
ALTER SESSION SET EVENTS 'immediate trace name drop_segments level &x';
```

where:

```
x is the value for file# from ts$ plus 1.
```

To get the information out of the db block buffers regarding order of LRU chains:

```
ALTER SESSION SET EVENTS 'immediate trace name buffers level x';
```

where:

```
x is 1-3 for buffer header order or 4-6 for LRU chain order.
```

To correct transportable tablespace export hanging (reported on 8.1.6, 8.1.7 on HPUX, a known bug):

```
ALTER SESSION SET EVENT '10297 trace name context forever, level 1';
```

To cause "QKA Disable GBY sort elimination". This affects how Oracle will process sorts:

```
ALTER SESSION SET EVENTS'10119 trace name context forever';
```

- You can disable the Index FFS using the event 10156. In this case, CBO will lean toward FTS or Index scan.
- You can set the event 10092 if you want to disable the hash joins completely.

It is very easy to see how SMON cleans up rollback entries by using the event 10015. You can use event 10235 to check how the memory manager works internally.

CBO is definitely not a mystery. Use event 10053 to give the detail of the various plans considered, depending on the statistics available; be careful using this for large multitable joins, as the report can be quite lengthy! The data density, sparse characteristics, index availability, and index depth all lead the optimizer to make its decisions. You can see the running commentary in trace files generated by the 10053 event.

Seeing Which Events Are Set in a Session   For ALTER SESSION commands that set events, you can use the undocumented dbms_system.read_ev procedure. For example:

```
set serveroutput on
declare
 event_level number;
begin
 for i in 10000..10999 loop
    sys.dbms_system.read_ev(i,event_level);
    if (event_level > 0) then
        dbms_output.put_line('Event '||to_char(i)||' set at level '||
                            to_char(event_level));
    end if;
 end loop;
end;
/
```

To demonstrate how the above PL/SQL can be used, create the script check_param. sql. Note that setting the init<sid>.ora parameter sql_trace sets the event 10046. Other parameters such as timed_statistics, optimizer_mode do not set events.

Within the session issue:

```
SQL> @check_param
PL/SQL procedure successfully completed.
SQL> alter session set sql_trace=true;
SQL> alter session set events '10015 trace name context forever, level 3';
SQL> @check_param
Event 10015 set at level 12
Event 10046 set at level 1
PL/SQL procedure successfully completed.
SQL> alter session set events '10046 trace name context forever, level 12';
SQL> @check_param
Event 10015 set at level 12
Event 10046 set at level 12
PL/SQL procedure successfully completed.
```

```
SQL> alter session set sql_trace=false;
SQL> alter session set events '10015 trace name context off';
SQL> @check_param
PL/SQL procedure successfully completed.
```

Using DBMS_SYSTEM.SET_EV and DBMS_SYSTEM.READ_EV

The DBMS_SYSTEM package contains two useful procedures related to events: SET_EV, used to set a specific event, and READ_EV, used to see the current status of an event. The procedures are defined as follows:

```
DBMS_SYSTEM.SET_EV(
SI    Binary_integer,
SE    Binary_integer,
EV    Binary_integer,
LE    Binary_integer,
NM    Binary_integer);
```

where:

> **SI** is the Oracle SID value.
>
> **SE** is the Oracle serial number.
>
> **EV** is the Oracle event to set.
>
> **LE** is the event level.
>
> **NM** is the name.
>
> For example:

```
EXECUTE SYS.DBMS_SYSTEM.SET_EV(sid,serial#,10046,level,'');
```

> The DBMS_SYSTEM.READ_EV has the following syntax:

```
DBMS_SYSTEM.READ_EV(
IEV   binary_integer,
OEV   binary_integer);
```

where:

> **IEV** is the Oracle event (in value).
>
> **OEV** is the Oracle event setting (out value).
>
> For example:

```
EXECUTE sys.dbms_system.read_ev(i,event_level);
```

Depending on the analyst, day of the week, and phase of the moon, Oracle support will either tell you to use or not to use DBMS_SYSTEM SET_EV and READ_EV.

A list of the Oracle event codes is shown in Table 2.6.

TABLE 2.6   Oracle Event Codes

Code	Description
10000	Controlfile debug event, name 'control_file'.
10001	Controlfile crash event1.
10002	Controlfile crash event2.
10003	Controlfile crash event3.
10004	Controlfile crash event4.
10005	Trace latch operations for debugging.
10006	Testing; block recovery forced.
10007	Log switch debug crash after new log select, thread %s.
10008	Log switch debug crash after new log header write, thread %s.
10009	Log switch debug crash after old log header write, thread %s.
10010	Begin transaction.
10011	End transaction.
10012	Abort transaction.
10013	Instance recovery.
10014	Roll back to save point.
10015	Undo segment recovery.
10016	Undo segment extend
10017	Undo segment wrap.
10018	Data segment create.
10019	Data segment recovery.
10020	Partial link restored to linked list (KSG).
10021	Latch cleanup for state objects (KSS).
10022	Trace ktsgsp.
10023	Create save undo segment.
10024	Write to save undo.
10025	Extend save undo segment.
10026	Apply save undo.
10027	Latch cleanup for enqueue locks (KSQ).
10028	Latch cleanup for enqueue resources (KSQ).
10029	Session logon (KSU).
10030	Session logoff (KSU).
10031	Row source debug event (R*).

TABLE 2.6 (*Continued*)

Code	Description
10032	Sort end (SOR*).
10035	Parse SQL statement (OPIPRS).
10036	Create remote row source (QKANET).
10037	Allocate remote row source (QKARWS).
10038	Dump row source tree (QBADRV).
10039	Type checking (OPITCA).
10040	Dirty cache list.
10041	Dump undo records skipped.
10042	Trap error during undo application.
10044	Freelist undo operations.
10045	Freelist update operations: ktsrsp, ktsunl.
10046	Enable SQL statement timing.
10047	Trace switching of sessions.
10048	Undo segment shrink.
10049	Protect library cache memory heaps.
10050	Sniper trace.
10051	Trace OPI calls.
10052	Don't clean up obj$.
10053	CBO: Enable optimizer trace.
10054	Trace UNDO handling in MLS.
10055	Trace UNDO handling.
10056	Dump analyze stats (kdg).
10057	Suppress filenames in error messages.
10058	Use table scan cost in tab$.spare1.
10060	CBO: Enable predicate dump.
10061	Disable SMON from cleaning temp segment.
10062	Disable usage of OS roles in OSDS.
10063	Disable usage of DBA and OPER privileges in OSDS.
10064	Thread-enable debug crash level %s, thread %s.
10065	Limit library cache dump information for state object dump.
10066	Simulate failure to verify file.
10067	Force redo log checksum errors: block number.
10068	Force redo log checksum errors: file number.

continued

TABLE 2.6 *(Continued)*

Code	Description
10069	Trusted Oracle test event.
10070	Force datafile checksum errors: block number.
10071	Force datafile checksum errors: file number.
10072	Protect latch recovery memory.
10073	Have PMON dump info before latch cleanup.
10074	Default trace function mask for kst.
10075	CBO: Disable outer-join to regular join conversion.
10076	CBO: Enable Cartesian product join costing.
10077	CBO: Disable view-merging optimization for outer-joins.
10078	CBO: Disable constant predicate elimination optimization.
10080	Dump a block on a segment list that cannot be exchanged.
10081	Segment high-water mark has been advanced.
10082	Freelist head block is the same as the last block.
10083	A brand new block has been requested from space management.
10084	Freelist becomes empty.
10085	Freelists have been merged.
10086	CBO: Enable error if kko and qka disagree on oby sort.
10087	Disable repair of media corrupt data blocks.
10088	CBO: Disable new, NOT IN optimization.
10089	CBO: Disable index sorting.
10090	Invoke other events before crash recovery.
10091	CBO: Disable constant predicate merging.
10092	CBO: Disable hash join.
10093	CBO: Enable force hash joins.
10094	Before resizing a data file.
10095	Dump debugger commands to trace file.
10096	After the cross instance call when resizing a datafile.
10097	After generating redo when resizing a datafile.
10098	After the OS has increased the size of a datafile.
10099	After updating the file header with the new file size.
10100	After the OS has decreased the size of a datafile.
10101	Atomic redo write recovery.
10102	Switch off anti-joins.
10103	CBO: Disable hash join swapping.

TABLE 2.6 (*Continued*)

Code	Description
10104	Dump hash join statistics to trace file.
10105	CBO: Enable constant pred trans and MPS with WHERE clause.
10106	CBO: Disable evaluating correlation pred last for NOT IN.
10107	CBO: Always use bitmap index.
10108	CBO: Don't use bitmap index.
10109	CBO: Disable move of negated predicates.
10110	CBO: Try index rowid range scans.
10111	Bitmap index creation switch.
10112	Bitmap index creation switch.
10113	Bitmap index creation switch.
10114	Bitmap index creation switch.
10115	CBO: Bitmap optimization use maximal expression.
10116	CBO: Bitmap optimization switch.
10117	CBO: Disable new parallel cost model.
10118	CBO: Enable hash join costing.
10119	QKA: Disable GBY sort elimination.
10120	CBO: Disable index fast full scan.
10121	CBO: Don't sort bitmap chains.
10122	CBO: Disable count(col) = count(*) transformation.
10123	QKA: Disable bitmap and-equals.
10145	Test auditing network errors.
10146	Enable Oracle TRACE collection.
10200	Block cleanout.
10201	Consistent read undo application.
10202	Consistent read block header.
10203	Consistent read buffer status.
10204	Signal recursive extend.
10205	Row cache debugging.
10206	Transaction table consistent read.
10207	Consistent read transactions' status report.
10208	Consistent read-loop check.
10209	Enable simulated error on controlfile.
10210	Check data block integrity.

continued

TABLE 2.6 (*Continued*)

Code	Description
10211	Check index block integrity.
10212	Check cluster integrity.
10213	Crash after control file write.
10214	Simulate write errors on controlfile.
10215	Simulate read errors on controlfile.
10216	Dump controlfile header.
10217	Debug sequence numbers.
10218	Dump UBA of applied undo.
10219	Monitor multipass row locking.
10220	Show updates to the transaction table.
10221	Show changes done with undo.
10222	Row cache.
10223	Transaction layer: Turn on verification codes.
10226	Trace CR applications of undo for data operations.
10227	Verify (multipiece) row structure.
10228	Trace application of redo by kcocbk.
10230	Check redo generation by copying before applying.
10231	Skip corrupted blocks on _table_scans_.
10232	Dump corrupted blocks symbolically when kcb gotten.
10233	Skip corrupted blocks on index operations.
10234	Trigger event after calling kcrapc to do redo N times.
10235	Check memory manager internal structures.
10236	Library cache manager.
10237	Simulate ^C (for testing purposes).
10238	Instantiation manager.
10239	Multi-instance library cache manager.
10240	Dump DBAs of blocks that we wait for.
10241	Dump SQL generated for remote execution (OPIX).
10243	Simulated error for test percentages of K2GTAB latch cleanup.
10244	Make tranids in error msgs print as 0.0.0 (for testing).
10245	Simulate lock conflict error for testing PMON.
10246	Print trace of PMON actions to trace file.
10247	Turn on scgcmn tracing (VMS ONLY).
10248	Turn on tracing for dispatchers.

TABLE 2.6   (*Continued*)

Code	Description
10249	Turn on tracing for multistated servers.
10250	Trace all allocate and free calls to the topmost SGA heap.
10251	Check consistency of transaction table and undo block.
10252	Simulate write error to data file header.
10253	Simulate write error to redo log.
10254	Trace cross-instance calls.
10256	Turn off multithreaded server load balancing.
10257	Trace multithreaded server load balancing.
10258	Force shared servers to be chosen round-robin.
10259	Get error message text from remote using explicit call.
10260	Trace calls to SMPRSET (VMS ONLY).
10261	Limit the size of the PGA heap.
10262	Don't check for memory leaks.
10263	Don't free empty PGA heap extents.
10264	Collect statistics on context area usage (x$ksmcx).
10265	Keep random system-generated output out of error messages.
10266	Trace OSD stack usage.
10267	Inhibit KSEDMP for testing.
10268	Don't do forward coalesce when deleting extents.
10269	Don't do coalesces of free space in SMON.
10270	Debug shared cursors.
10271	Distributed transaction after COLLECT.
10272	Distributed transaction before PREPARE.
10273	Distributed transaction after PREPARE.
10274	Distributed transaction before COMMIT.
10275	Distributed transaction after COMMIT.
10276	Distributed transaction before FORGET.
10277	Cursor sharing (or not) related event (used for testing).
10281	Maximum time to wait for process creation.
10282	Inhibit signaling of other backgrounds when one dies.
10286	Simulate control file open error.
10287	Simulate archiver error.
10288	Do not check block type in ktrget.

continued

TABLE 2.6   (*Continued*)

Code	Description
10289	Do block dumps to trace file in hex rather than formatted.
10290	Kdnchk—checkvalid event—not for general-purpose use.
10291	Die in dtsdrv to test controlfile undo.
10292	Dump uet entries on a 1561 from dtsdrv.
10293	Dump debugging information when doing block recovery.
10294	Enable PERSISTENT DLM operations on noncompliant systems.
10300	Disable undo compatibility check at database open.
10301	Enable LCK timeout table consistency check.
10320	Enable data layer (kdtgrs) tracing of space management calls.
10352	Report direct path statistics.
10353	Number of slots.
10354	Turn on direct read path for parallel query.
10355	Turn on direct read path for scans.
10356	Turn on hint usage for direct read.
10357	Turn on debug information for direct path.
10374	Parallel query server interrupt (validate lock value).
10375	Turn on checks for statistics rollups.
10376	Turn on table queue statistics.
10377	Turn off load balancing.
10379	Direct read for rowid range scans (unimplemented).
10380	Kxfp latch cleanup testing event.
10381	Kxfp latch cleanup testing event.
10382	Parallel query server interrupt (reset).
10383	Auto parallelization testing event.
10384	Parallel dataflow scheduler tracing.
10385	Parallel table scan range-sampling method.
10386	Parallel SQL hash and range statistics.
10387	Parallel query server interrupt (normal).
10388	Parallel query server interrupt (failure).
10389	Parallel query server interrupt (cleanup).
10390	Trace parallel query slave execution.
10391	Trace rowid range partitioning.
10392	Parallel query debugging bits.
10393	Print parallel query statistics.

TABLE 2.6   (*Continued*)

Code	Description
10394	Allow parallelization of small tables.
10395	Adjust sample size for range table queues.
10396	Circumvent range table queues for queries.
10397	Suppress verbose parallel coordinator error reporting.
10398	Enable timeouts in parallel query threads.
10399	Use different internal maximum buffer size.
10400	Turn on system state dumps for shutdown debugging.
10500	Turn on traces for SMON.
10510	Turn off SMON check to offline pending offline rollback segment.
10511	Turn off SMON check to cleanup undo dictionary.
10512	Turn off SMON check to shrink rollback segments.
10600	Check cursor frame allocation.
10602	Cause an access violation (for testing purposes).
10603	Cause an error to occur during truncate (for testing purposes).
10604	Trace parallel create index.
10605	Enable parallel create index by default.
10606	Trace parallel create index.
10607	Trace index rowid partition scan.
10608	Trace create bitmap index.
10610	Trace create index pseudo optimizer.
10666	Do not get database enqueue name.
10667	Cause sppst to check for valid process IDs.
10690	Set shadow process core file dump type (UNIX only).
10691	Set background process core filetype (UNIX only).
10700	Alter access violation exception handler.
10701	Dump direct loader index keys.
10702	Enable histogram data generation.
10703	Simulate process death during enqueue get.
10704	Print out information about which enqueues are being obtained.
10706	Print out information about instance lock manipulation.
10707	Simulate process death for instance registration.
10708	Print out tracing information for skxf multi-instance comms.
10709	Enable parallel instances in create index by default.

continued

TABLE 2.6 (*Continued*)

Code	Description
10710	Trace bitmap index access.
10711	Trace bitmap index merge.
10712	Trace bitmap index OR.
10713	Trace bitmap index AND.
10714	Trace bitmap index minus.
10715	Trace bitmap index conversion to rowids.
10800	Disable Smart Disk scan.
10801	Enable Smart Disk trace.
10802	Reserved for Smart Disk.
10803	Write timing statistics on OPS recovery scan.
10804	Reserved for ksxb.
10805	Reserved for row source sort.
10900	Extent manager fault insertion event #%s.
10924	Import storage parse error ignore event.
10925	Trace name context forever.
10926	Trace name context forever.
10927	Trace name context forever.
10928	Trace name context forever.
10999	Do not get database enqueue name.

Source 2.7 shows an example of how to use events. As with other powerful and undocumented Oracle features, make sure someone who thoroughly understands the ramifications of using the event or events is present when you attempt usage of the event codes. Improper use of events can result in database crashes and corruption.

The segment header block dump will be in the user session trace file. As with the undocumented initialization parameters, events should be used only under the direction of a senior-level DBA or Oracle support.

2.6 FURTHER DBA READING

For further reading, the DBA should look at the following references:

Oracle9i Database Administrator's Guide, Release 1, 9.0.1, Part No. A90117-01, Oracle Corporation, June 2001.

Source 2.7   Use of SET EVENTS at the session level.

```
How to dump a segment header - by Don Burleson
set heading off;
spool dump_em.sql;

select
'alter session set events ''immediate trace name blockdump level '||
to_char((header_file*16777216)+header_block)||''';'
from
dba_segments
where
segment_name = 'VBAP';

spool off;

cat dump_em.sql
@dump_em
```

Oracle9i SQL Reference, Release 1, 9.0.1, Part No. A90125-01, Oracle Corporation, June 2001.
Oracle9i Reference, Release 1, 9.0.1, Part No. A90190-01, Oracle Corporation, June 2001.
Metalink Notes: 28446.1, 130283.1, 1051056, 134940.16, 121491.1, and 88624.999;
Steve Adam's Web site: /www.ixora.com.au/.

2.7 SUMMARY

This chapter delved into topics of interest when administrating the database itself. Commands such as CREATE and ALTER DATABASE and related topics were demonstrated and discussed. In addition, several techniques were presented that, when used, will ensure database management is done correctly. The chapter also covered how to rename databases and rebuild their control files. You now have an understanding of how Oracle databases are created, modified, and dropped. You have also been exposed to the concept of Oracle undocumented parameters and Oracle events and their usage.

CHAPTER 3

Tablespace Administration

Carrying through with the analogy that Oracle is an operating system, we can say that tablespaces take the place of disks. But with this "disk," you, the DBA, can specify its size and how it will create and store data (via the DEFAULT STORAGE clause) in its files (tables).

3.1 TABLESPACE CREATION

Let's look at the command for creating a tablespace.

```
CREATE [UNDO|TEMPORARY] TABLESPACE tablespace
DATAFILE|TEMPFILE 'file_spec'
            [MINIMUM EXTENT n [K|M]]
            [AUTOEXTEND
                OFF
                ON NEXT n K|M MAXSIZE UNLIMITED|n [K|M]]
            [LOGGING|NOLOGGING]
            [ONLINE|OFFLINE]
            [DEFAULT (storage_clause)] (N/A If TEMPORARY above)
            [PERMANENT|TEMPORARY] (N/A If TEMPORARY above)
            [EXTENT MANAGEMENT
                        DICTIONARY (Must be LOCAL for TEMPFILE)
                        LOCAL
                            AUTOALLOCATE
                            UNIFORM   [SIZE n [K|M]]]
            [SEGMENT SPACE MANAGEMENT MANUAL|AUTO]
```

Keywords and Parameters

Oracle9*i* creates a system-managed UNDO (rollback, for us old-timers) tablespace (this feature is new with this version). If a database is created in UNDO automatic management mode, and no UNDO tablespace is specified in the CREATE DATABASE command, the SYSTEM tablespace will be used. AN UNDO tablespace uses AUTOALLOCATE LOCAL extent management. The database manages an UNDO tablespace, and no other objects can be assigned to it. You can only include the DATAFILE and EXTENT MANAGMEMENT LOCAL clauses for an UNDO tablespace. All UNDO tablespaces are permanent, read/write, and are in logging mode; and the values for MINIMUM EXTENT and DEFAULT STORAGE are system-generated.

tablespace. The name of the tablespace to be created.

DATAFILE. Specifies the datafile or files to comprise the tablespace.

TEMPFILE. IF tablespace is TEMPORARY, must use TEMPFILE; specifies the tempfiles to be used in the TEMPORARY tablespace.

MINIMUM EXTENT integer. Controls freespace fragmentation in the tablespace by ensuring that every in-use and/or free extent size in a tablespace is at least as large as, and is a multiple of, integer.

AUTOEXTEND. Enables or disables the automatic extension of datafile.

OFF. Disables AUTOEXTEND if it is turned on. NEXT and MAXSIZE are set to zero. Values for NEXT and MAXSIZE must be respecified in later ALTER TABLESPACE AUTOEXTEND commands if OFF is specified; they are not persistent values.

ON. Enables AUTOEXTEND.

NEXT. Disk space to allocate to the datafile when more extents are required.

MAXSIZE. Maximum disk space allowed for allocation to the datafile.

UNLIMITED. Set no limit on allocating disk space to the datafile.

LOGGING, NOLOGGING. Specifies the default logging attributes of all tables, index, and partitions within the tablespace. LOGGING is the default. If NOLOGGING is specified, no undo and redo logs are generated for operations that support the NOLOGGING option on the tables, index, and partitions within the tablespace. The tablespace-level logging attribute can be overridden by logging specifications at the table, index, and partition levels.

DEFAULT. Specifies the default storage parameters for all objects created in the tablespace.

ONLINE. Makes the tablespace available immediately after creation to users who have been granted access to the tablespace.

OFFLINE. Makes the tablespace unavailable immediately after creation. If you omit both the ONLINE and OFFLINE options, Oracle creates the tablespace online by default. The data dictionary view DBA_TABLESPACES indicates whether each tablespace is online or offline.

PERMANENT. Specifies that the tablespace will be used to hold permanent objects. This is the default.

TEMPORARY. Specifies that the tablespace will only be used to hold temporary objects; for example, segments used by implicit sorts to handle ORDER BY clauses.

EXTENT MANAGEMENT. The EXTENT MANAGEMENT clause specifies how the extents in the tablespace will be managed. The default extent management is DICTIONARY, which is the standard method used by Oracle7 and Oracle8.0. The LOCAL option has space set aside for a bitmap. LOCAL-managed extents are managed by the tablespace itself, while DICTIONARY-managed extents are managed by the data dictionary processes. The bitmap in a locally managed tablespace is used to track free and used extents. LOCAL management reduces recursive space management caused by rollback, data dictionary, and extent management because LOCAL management requires no dictionary actions and less rollback activity due to data dictionary extensions. LOCAL also allows for automatic mapping of adjacent free extents into a single large extent, eliminating the need for coalescing of freespace. The UNIFORM or AUTOALLOCATE determines how extents are mapped. AUTOALLOCATE, which forces system management of extents, uses the storage clause values for extent management, while UNIFORM uses a default of 1-MB extents. The DEFAULT STORAGE clause is invalid for locally managed tablespaces and cannot be specified; in addition, the MINIMUM EXTENT and TEMPORARY clauses are also prohibited if local extent management is utilized.

SEGMENT SPACE MANAGEMENT MANUAL | AUTO. New in 9*i*, this clause allows permanent, locally managed tablespaces to specify whether Oracle should track the used and freespace in segments using freelists or by use of bitmaps. MANUAL manages the freespace using freelists; AUTO manages the freespace using a bitmap. If AUTO is specified, any specification for FREELISTS or FREELIST GROUPS is ignored for objects stored in the tablespace. You will see this AUTO setting referred to as *automatic segment-space management.* It can be determined for a tablespace by use of the SEGMENT_SPACE_MANAGEMENT column in the DBA_ or USER_TABLESPACES view. Under AUTO, each LOCAL UNIFORM extent must be at least five Oracle blocks in size. If you specify LOCAL ALLOCATE, and the default database blocksize is 16K or greater, extents sizes will automatically be set to 1 megabyte at a minimum. The SYSTEM tablespace cannot be an AUTO type tablespace. LOBs cannot be stored in an AUTO type tablespace.

Say we want to create a data tablespace for the accounts receivable (AR) application in our accounting package. The database for our AR application is called ORACTP, short for Oracle Accounting Production database. Let's look at the actual command to create a tablespace with an initial 500-MB datafile with autoextension to a maximum size of 1 gigabyte (1,024 megabytes). The tables in our AR application will hold a fairly large amount of data, so just in case our developers forget to size their tables (they wouldn't do that, would they?) let's size the default storage to INITIAL 10M NEXT 1M PCTINCREASE 10.

```
CREATE TABLESPACE ar DATAFILE '\ORACLE1\ORACTP\data\oractp_ar01.dbf' SIZE
500M
AUTOEXTEND ON NEXT 200M MAXSIZE 1024M
DEFAULT STORAGE (INITIAL 10M NEXT 1M PCTINCREASE 10)
PERMANENT
ONLINE
LOGGING;
```

I've included the PERMANENT, ONLINE, and LOGGING clauses for illustration only; they are the default if nothing is specified. Why did I specify a PCTINCREASE value? If PCTINCREASE is set to zero, the SMON process will not coalesce freespace. If PCTINCREASE is not specified, it will default to 50 percent; therefore, specifying it at a low value is suggested.

On the other hand, what if we wanted the extents to be locally managed due to the level of dynamic allocation that could happen? The CREATE TABLESPACE clause will change, in that we no longer specify the DEFAULT STORAGE clause, and instead use the EXTENT MANAGEMENT clause with the LOCAL clause. If we want to ensure that uniform extents are generated, we can specify the UNIFORM clause as well. Let's shoot for 2-MB LOCAL UNIFORM extent management.

```
CREATE TABLESPACE ar DATAFILE '\ORACLE1\ORACTP\data\oractp_ar01.dbf' SIZE
500M
AUTOEXTEND ON NEXT 200M MAXSIZE 1024M
LOCAL UNIFORM SIZE 2M
PERMANENT
ONLINE
LOGGING;
```

Now there are two types of temporary tablespaces: a CREATE TEMPORARY TABLESPACE tablespace, which uses TEMPFILES instead of DATAFILES, and a CREATE TABLESPACE tablespace TEMPORARY, which uses DATAFILES. A CREATE TEMPORARY TABLESPACE tablespace has to use LOCAL extent management. A CREATE TABLESPACE tablespace TEMPORARY cannot use LOCAL extent management. TEMPFILEs cannot be backed up using a hot backup; in fact, they don't have to be, and will generate an error if you attempt to place them in backup mode. Let's look at a couple of examples.

First let's create a CREATE TEMPORARY TABLESPACE tablespace:

```
CREATE TEMPORARY TABLESPACE local_temp
TEMPFILE '/oracle1/oradata/ortest1/data/local_temp01.tmp' SIZE 500M
AUTOEXTEND ON NEXT 100M MAXSIZE 1024M
EXTENT MANAGEMENT LOCAL UNIFORM SIZE 2M;
```

CREATE TEMPORARY TABLESPACE tablespaces (CT3s) will not release sort segments until the database is shut down. In tests on 8.1.7.2, this resulted in significant sort area overhead for a busy system. For a 6-gigabyte total size database with 40 concurrent users, 9 doing relatively heavy sorts, more than 16 gigabytes of temporary space was required. This appears to indicate the reuse mechanism isn't quite ready for prime time in CT3s.

Now let's create the equivalent CREATE TABLESPACE tablespace TEMPORARY tablespace:

```
CREATE TABLESPACE TEMP
DATAFILE '/ORACLE01/ORADATA/ORTEST1/DATA/TEMP01.DBF' size 500M
AUTOEXTEND ON NEXT 100M MAXSIZE 1024M
EXTENT MANAGEMENT DICTIONARY
DEFAULT STORAGE (INITIAL 2M NEXT 2M PCTINCREASE 0);
```

CREATE TABLESPACE tablespace TEMPORARY (CT2) releases segments as soon as sorts end. For the same user and sort loads, an equivalent CT2 required 7 gigabytes of space compared to the 16 gigabytes required by the CT3. This reduced space requirement was due to the rapid release of the sort segments and reacquisition by processes requiring sorts.

Sizing of Tablespaces

Tablespaces should be sized to contain all of the objects they are intended to hold. This means that, in order to size a tablespace properly, you will first need to size all of the objects that will be placed in the tablespace. Chapters 4 through 8, on table, cluster, and index management detail the techniques for sizing database objects. If the tablespace will contain large objects (LOBs), it may be difficult to get an accurate size estimate.

The autoextend capability provided since Oracle7 can make some tablespace management easier, but it is no replacement for properly sizing tablespaces. One problem with autoextend is that you have no way of knowing when you will run out of space due to a runaway process (for example, a Cartesian product of 2 million row tables filling the temporary tablespace).

Once you have the sizes of all the objects that will reside in a tablespace, you add these size figures together; I suggest adding 25 to 50 percent additional room to allow for growth. The default storage parameters for a tablespace should never be used, except where the tablespace's purpose is to hold rollback segments.

If a tablespace is built using RAW partitions on either UNIX or NT, I suggest selecting a standard size for the raw partitions, such as 501 MB or 1 GB (plus 1 MB), and create all raw segments this size. The tablespace is then built by mapping the requisite number of raw areas into the tablespace's datafiles. Usually, I use a mix of partition sizes, such as 101 MB, 501 MB, and so on, to allow for sizing of both large (data) tablespaces and small (SYSTEM, USER, TOOLS) tablespaces.

NOTE   I suggest that the raw file sizes be 101, 501, and so on, to prevent writing data into a "zero" block, which can cause problems. Thus, a 100-megabyte datafile is mapped into a 101-megabyte RAW area. This practice may result in small amounts of wasted space, but it helps prevent some RAW problems from happening.

In order to minimize fragmentation issues (Swiss cheese-type fragmentation), it is suggested that several tablespaces (usually three), sized to hold various uniform extent sizes (small, medium, and large, for example), be created; objects that fit into each size model are placed into the appropriate tablespace. This would indicate that you would have three data and three index tablespaces to allow for the various tables and indexes in your application. The new UNIFORM or AUTOALLOCATE tablespace options lend themselves readily to this use of sizing models.

In Oracle9*i*, the concept of *Oracle-managed files* (OMF) is introduced. Essentially, this model forces you to place all of your tablespace datafiles in the same directory. If you use OMF, then you must have a RAID5, a RAID0/1, or a RAID1/0 configuration. Basically, you set the DB_CREATE_FILE_DEST and DB_CREATE_ONLINE_LOG_DEST_X initialization parameters; then Oracle will automatically create the datafiles, controlfiles, and log files in that location. You do not have to specify the tablespace datafile specification during CREATE or ALTER commands using OMF. If a filename is not specified, any file created is placed under the OMF control.

OMF should be used only for low-end or test databases, not for high-performance databases. OMF also should not be used with RAW disks.

3.2 ALTERATION OF TABLESPACES

Periodically, a tablespace may need to have its default storage changed; or require the addition of datafiles to increase its storage volume, a name change, or being taken offline for maintenance; or it may need to have AUTOEXTEND turned off or on; be made temporary, or converted to permanent; or require being placed in backup status for a hot backup. The command used for all of these functions is the ALTER command. Let's look at its format.

```
ALTER TABLESPACE tablespace
      [LOGGING|NOLOGGING]
      [ADD DATAFILE|TEMPFILE file_spec [autoextendclause]]
      [RENAME DATAFILE 'from_file_spec' TO 'to_file_spec']
      [COALESCE]
      [DEFAULT STORAGE storage_clause]
      [MINIMUM EXTENT n K|M]
      [ONLINE|OFFLINE
```

```
                        NORMAL|
                        IMMEDIATE|
                        TEMPORARY]
        [BEGIN|END BACKUP]
        [READ ONLY|WRITE]
        [PERMANENT|TEMPORARY]
```

Keywords and Parameters

tablespace. The name of the tablespace to be altered.

LOGGING, NOLOGGING. Specifies that the creation and logging attributes of all tables, indexes, and partitions within the tablespace are logged in the redo log file. LOGGING is the default. The tablespace-level logging attribute can be overridden by logging specifications at the table, index, and partition levels.

When an existing tablespace logging attribute is changed by an ALTER TABLESPACE statement, all tables, indexes, and partitions created after the statement will have the new logging attribute; the logging attributes of existing objects are not changed.

If the database is run in ARCHIVELOG mode, media recovery from a backup will re-create the table (and any indexes required because of constraints). When running in NOARCHIVELOG mode, all operations that can execute without logging will not generate log entries even if LOGGING is specified.

ADD DATAFILE|TEMPFILE. Adds the datafile specified by filespec to the tablespace. See the syntax description of FILESPEC, next. You can add a datafile while the tablespace is online or offline. Be sure that the datafile is not already in use by another database.

FILESPEC. Specifes the filename (full path), size, and identifies any existing file that should be reused; for example:

```
'c:\oracle1\ortest1\data\system01.dbf' SIZE 100M REUSE
AUTO EXTEND clause:
AUTOEXTEND
          OFF
          ON
                    NEXT n K|M MAXSIZE n K|M | UNLIMITED
```

AUTOEXTEND. Enables or disables the AUTOEXTENDing of the size of the datafile in the tablespace.

OFF. Disables AUTOEXTEND if it is turned on. NEXT and MAXSIZE are set to zero. Values for NEXT and MAXSIZE must be respecified in later ALTER TABLESPACE AUTOEXTEND commands.

ON. Enables AUTOEXTEND.

NEXT. The size in bytes of the next increment of disk space to be automatically allocated to the datafile when more extents are required. You can also use K or M to specify this size in kilobytes or megabytes. The default is one data block.

MAXSIZE. Maximum disk space allowed for automatic extension of the datafile.

UNLIMITED. Set no limit on allocating disk space to the datafile.

RENAME DATAFILE. Renames one or more of the tablespace's datafiles. Take the tablespace offline before renaming the datafile. Each 'filename' must fully specify a datafile using the conventions for filenames on your operating system. This clause associates the tablespace only with the new file, rather than the old one. This clause does not actually change the name of the operating system file. You must change the name of the file through your operating system. TEMPFILEs cannot be renamed.

COALESCE. For each datafile in the tablespace, coalesce all contiguous free extents into larger contiguous extents.

TIP   COALESCE cannot be specified with any other command option.

DEFAULT STORAGE. Specifies the new default storage parameters for objects subsequently created in the tablespace.

storage_clause. Specifies the default storage parameters for any object that is created in the tablespace, without specifying its own storage parameters.

```
DEFAULT STORAGE (
          INITIAL n [K|M]
          NEXT n [K|M]
          PCTINCREASE n
          MINEXTENTS n
          MAXEXTENTS n|UNLIMITED
          FREELISTS n
          FREELIST GROUPS n
          OPTIMAL n [K|M]
          BUFFER_POOL KEEP|RECYCLE|DEFAULT
  )
```

INITIAL. Sets the size in bytes of the initial extent for an object.

NEXT. Sets the size in bytes for any subsequent extents for an object.

PCTINCREASE. A percent increase applied to the last extent created. It may be between 1 and 100.

MINEXTENTS. The number of extents that are created when the object is created.

MAXEXTENTS. The most extents the object may have.

FREELISTS. Sets the number of free extent lists that are created for an object. Set this to the number of simultaneous updates to a block that you expect.

FREELIST GROUPS. Applies only to parallel server instances. Create a freelist group for each instance accessing a table concurrently.

OPTIMAL. Applies only to rollback segments and sets the size a rollback segment will shrink to once it is accessed and after it has grown beyond the OPTIMAL setting. Must be set larger than MINEXTENTS*INITIAL.

BUFFER_POOL. Tells Oracle in which buffer pool to place the object.

MINIMUM EXTENT integer. Controls freespace fragmentation in the tablespace by ensuring that every used and/or free extent size in a tablespace is at least as large as, and is a multiple of, integer.

ONLINE. Brings the tablespace online.

OFFLINE. Takes the tablespace offline and prevents further access to its segments.

NORMAL. Performs a checkpoint for all datafiles in the tablespace. All of these datafiles must be online. You need not perform media recovery on this tablespace before bringing it back online. You must use this option if the database is in NOARCHIVELOG mode.

TEMPORARY. Performs a checkpoint for all online datafiles in the tablespace, but does not ensure that all files can be written. Any offline files may require media recovery before you bring the tablespace back online.

IMMEDIATE. Does not ensure that tablespace files are available and does not perform a checkpoint. You must perform recovery on the tablespace before bringing it back online. The default is NORMAL. If you are taking a tablespace offline for a long time, you may want to alter any users who have been assigned the tablespace as either a default or temporary to use some other tablespace for these purposes. When the tablespace is offline, these users cannot allocate space for objects or sort areas in the tablespaces that are offline. You can reassign users new default and temporary tablespaces with the ALTER USER command.

BEGIN BACKUP. Signifies that an online backup is to be performed on the datafiles that comprise this tablespace. This option does not prevent users from accessing the tablespace. You must use this option before beginning an online backup. You cannot use this option on a read-only or CT3 tablespace. While the backup is in progress, you cannot:

- Take the tablespace offline normally.
- Shut down the instance.
- Begin another backup of the tablespace.

END BACKUP. Signifies that an online backup of the tablespace is complete. Use this option as soon as possible after completing an online backup. If a tablespace is left in BACKUP mode, the database will think it needs recovery the next time the database is shut down and started, and you may not be able to recover. You cannot use this option on a read-only or CT3 tablespace.

READ ONLY. Signifies that no further write operations are allowed on the tablespace.

READ WRITE. Signifies that write operations are allowed on a previously read-only tablespace.

PERMANENT. Specifies that the tablespace is to be converted from temporary to permanent status. A permanent tablespace is where permanent database objects are stored. This is the default when a tablespace is created.

TEMPORARY. Specifies that the tablespace is to be converted from permanent to temporary status. A temporary tablespace is where no permanent database objects can be stored.

READ ONLY I WRITE. Allows you to specify that a tablespace is read-only; the normal default value is READ WRITE. A read-only tablespace doesn't generate redo, rollback, or require backup (after its initial backup, just after its creation). A read-only tablespace can also be made deferrable by using the initialization parameter READ_ONLY_OPEN_DELAYED=TRUE; this means that the tablespace isn't verified to be accessible until the first operation that attempts a read from the read-only tablespace.

At least one of the lines following the ALTER command must be supplied (or else why issue the command?). The definitions for most of the arguments are the same as for the CREATE command. The addition of the COALESCE clause is very welcome, in that for those tablespaces in which SMON doesn't choose to clean up freespace (i.e., any with a default storage PCTINCREASE of 0), the command option forces a scavenge of free segments. There are now four options for the OFFLINE clause: NORMAL (meaning wait for users to finish with it), TEMPORARY (which means do a checkpoint of all of its datafiles), IMMEDIATE (which means *"Now, darn it!"*), and FOR RECOVERY, which allows recovery of the tablespace.

Two other additions are the READ ONLY and READ WRITE options. As their names imply, READ ONLY makes a tablespace read-only in nature; this means no redo will be generated, nor will a rollback against this tablespace; and, of course, you cannot write to it. The READ WRITE is the normal mode and returns a READ ONLY to full service.

PERMANENT and TEMPORARY do the same as in the CREATE clause; that is, PERMANENT means objects such as tables, indexes, and clusters can be assigned to this tablespace, while TEMPORARY means only temporary segments can be placed here.

Note the RENAME DATAFILE option. It is used when you need to: (a) alter the name of a datafile, or (b) relocate a datafile. Option (a) is obvious, but (b) needs some explanation. The procedure for moving a datafile is:

1. Using the ALTER TABLESPACE command, take the tablespace that uses the datafile offline.

   ```
   ALTER TABLESPACE tablespace OFFLINE;
   ```

2. Using the operating system command appropriate for your system, copy the datafile to the new location.

3. Using the ALTER TABLESPACE command, rename the datafile.

   ```
   ALTER TABLESPACE tablespace
   RENAME DATAFILE 'old name' TO 'new name';
   ```

   where 'old name' and 'new name' are full path names.

4. Using the ALTER TABLESPACE command, bring the tablespace back online.

   ```
   ALTER TABLESPACE tablespace ONLINE;
   ```

5. Remove the extra copy of the datafile from its old location using the appropriate operating system command (rm on UNIX; DELETE on VMS).

The OFFLINE qualifiers apply to how user processes are treated as the tablespace is taken OFFLINE. NORMAL tells Oracle to wait for user processes to finish with the tablespace. IMMEDIATE tells the system to take the tablespace offline regardless of who is using it.

When using ALTER to place a tablespace in BEGIN BACKUP, be sure that the backup procedure backs up all the redo and archive logs as well. Immediately after the backup concludes, bring the tablespace back to normal with the END BACKUP command, or the redo logs will get out of sync and the file will not be recoverable without use of Oracle Support and undocumented initialization parameters, should you be required to recover it due to a problem.

3.3 DELETION OF TABLESPACES

At one time or another, such as when consolidating a rollback segment tablespace, the DBA will have to remove, or drop, a tablespace from the Oracle database system. Removing tablespaces is done through the DROP command. Its format follows.

```
DROP TABLESPACE tablespace_name [INCLUDING CONTENTS]
[AND DATAFILES] [CASCADE CONSTRAINTS];
```

The INCLUDING CONTENTS clause is optional, but if it isn't included, the tablespace must be empty of tables or other objects. If it is included, the tablespace will be dropped, regardless of its contents, unless it contains an online rollback segment. The SYSTEM tablespace cannot be dropped.

The AND DATAFILES clause drops any datafiles and tempfiles in the tablespace. Other datafiles and tempfiles are not removed unless both the AND DATAFILES and INCLUDING CONTENTS clauses are included.

The CASCADE CONSTRAINTS clause will cause any constraints from objects inside the tablespace against objects outside of the tablespace to be dropped as well. If there are constraints, and this clause is not included, the DROP command will fail.

You cannot drop any UNDO tablespace that contains active transactions or contains data required to rollback uncommitted transactions. You also cannot drop a tablespace if it contains a domain index or any object created by a domain index. If the tablespace contains a partition from either a table or index, or subpartitions of a table or index but not all of the partitions or subpartitions, then the DROP command will fail even with the INCLUDING CONTENTS clause.

TIP This doesn't remove the physical datafiles from the system in releases prior to Oracle9*i*; you must use operating-system-level commands to remove the physical files.

Let's look at some examples. The command:

```
DROP TABLESPACE ar;
```

This command will drop the tablespace ar if it contains no objects, rollback segments, undo segments, and isn't part of the SYSTEM tablespace.

```
DROP TABLESPACE ar INCLUDING CONTENTS;
```

This command will drop the tablespace ar even if it has contents, as long as the contents aren't partitions, subpartitions, active UNDO or rollback segments, or have constraint to objects outside of tablespace ar and ar isn't a part of the SYSTEM tablespace.

```
DROP TABLESPACE ar INCLUDING CONTENTS CASCADE CONSTRAINTS;
```

This command will drop tablespace ar even if it has contents, as long as the contents aren't partitions, subpartitions, active UNDO or rollback segments, and ar isn't a part of the SYSTEM tablespace.

```
DROP TABLESPACE ar INCLUDING CONTENTS AND DATAFILES
CASCADE CONSTRAINTS;
```

This command will drop tablespace ar even if it has contents, as long as the contents aren't partitions, subpartitions, active UNDO or rollback segments, and ar isn't a part of the SYSTEM tablespace, including datafiles and tempfiles.

3.4 RE-CREATING TABLESPACES

There may be times when the DBA has to drop and re-create tablespaces. For instance, if the physical drive that the tablespaces are on has been damaged, the DBA will have to re-create the tablespaces on another volume or recover from a backup and apply redo logs. If the DBA has good documentation of what the database physical structure was before the incident, there should be no problem. If, on the other hand, the DBA has inherited a legacy system or the system has grown substantially without good documentation, the DBA could have his or her hands full rebuilding it.

The script TBSP_RCT9*i*.SQL on the Wiley Web site can be used to document existing tablespaces and their datafiles. As its name indicates, TBSP_RCT9*i*.SQL is for Oracle9*i* only. Scripts for 8*i* and 8.0 are included in the scripts on the Wiley Web site.

3.5 PERIODIC TABLESPACE MAINTENANCE

Periodic tablespace maintenance includes consolidation of extents, reorganization to push all the freespace in the file to the front, and exports to ensure recoverability. Let's look at these topics.

Consolidation of Extents

As tables, indexes, and clusters are created and dropped in a tablespace, extents are dynamically assigned and deassigned to the objects. Like a disk system that dynamically assigns space to files, this causes fragmentation. Fragmentation results in objects being stored all over the tablespace, requiring more head moves to recover the information to fill users' queries. This reduces response time and makes the system slow. Unless you can exactly specify the required storage and sizing information for each and every table in each tablespace, some of this internal fragmentation will occur. The SMON process automatically consolidates contiguous free extents into single large extents for tablespaces whose default value for the PCTINCREASE storage parameter is greater than zero. This reduces but doesn't eliminate the problem. In Oracle8*i* and Oracle9*i*, you can avoid the overhead associated with either automatic coalescence or manual coalescence by using locally managed tablespaces. In a locally managed tablespace, the tablespace itself tracks its extents through the use of a bitmap, so any contiguous free areas of space are automatically coalesced.

So how do you correct it in earlier versions (and 8*i* or 9*i* with directory-managed tablespaces)? There are two methods. Let's look at each of them.

Method 1: Use of Export and Import This method will consolidate all freespace and will consolidate all tables into single extents. However, the database won't be available, and for large systems, the time required could be extensive.

1. Perform an export on all objects in the tablespace. Remember that you must export each owner's objects for all users who own objects in the tablespace.
2. Drop the tablespace, using the INCLUDING CONTENTS clause.
3. Re-create the tablespace. (If you created a script to create the tablespace, you can just rerun the script; be sure to include all active datafiles. It might be desirable to delete all of a tablespace's datafiles and consolidate them into one large datafile at this time.)
4. Import all of the exports generated in step 1.

A major problem with this method is that it won't work on the SYSTEM tablespace.

Method 2: Use of Commands (Post-7.3)   Method 2 itself is composed of two sub-methods. For versions 7 to 7.3, you can use one of these two submethods. The first is to temporarily set the PCTINCREASE to 1 and await SMON's automatic cleanup. This can take several minutes. The second submethod involves issuing a COALESCE command against the specific tablespace where the fragmentation is happening:

If you create a view against the DBA_FREE_SPACE view that summarizes the fragmentation state of all the tablespaces, a simple procedure can be created that defragments the database on command. For example:

```
rem Name:     view.sql
rem FUNCTION: Create free_space view for use by freespc reports
rem
CREATE VIEW free_space
        (tablespace, file_id, pieces, free_bytes, free_blocks,
         largest_bytes,largest_blks) as
SELECT tablespace_name, file_id, COUNT(*),
    SUM(bytes), SUM(blocks),
    MAX(bytes), MAX(blocks) FROM sys.dba_free_space
GROUP BY tablespace_name, file_id;
```

The SQL procedure becomes:

```
rem
rem NAME: defrg73.sql
rem FUNCTION: Uses the coalesce command to manually coalesce
rem FUNCTION: any tablespace with greater than 1 fragment. You
rem FUNCTION: may alter to exclude the temporary tablespace.
rem FUNCTION: The procedure uses the FREE_SPACE view which is a
rem FUNCTION: summarized version of the DBA_FREE_SPACE view.
rem FUNCTION: This procedure must be run from a DBA user id.
rem HISTORY:
rem WHO          WHAT             WHEN
rem Mike Ault    Created          1/4/96
rem
CLEAR COLUMNS
CLEAR COMPUTES
DEFINE cr='chr(10)'
TTITLE OFF
SET HEADING OFF FEEDBACK OFF ECHO OFF TERMOUT OFF
SPOOL def.sql
SELECT
    'ALTER TABLESPACE '||tablespace||' COALESCE;'||&&cr||
    'COMMIT;'
FROM
    free_space
WHERE
    pieces>files;
SPOOL OFF
@def.sql
HOST rm def.sql
SET HEADING ON FEEDBACK ON TERMOUT ON
TTITLE OFF
```

If there is Swiss cheese fragmentation, the DBA needs to find which objects are bound by freespace in order to plan for the rebuild of these objects. The script in Source 3.1 can be run to determine the bound objects in your database.

Source 3.1   Script to determine bound objects.

```
rem  *****************************************************************
rem  NAME:      BOUND_OB.sql
rem  FUNCTION: Show objects with extents bounded by freespace
rem******************************************************************
START title80 "Objects With Extents Bounded by Free Space"
SPOOL rep_out\&db\b_ob..lis
COLUMN e FORMAT a15        HEADING "TABLE SPACE"
COLUMN a FORMAT a6         HEADING "OBJECT|TYPE"
COLUMN b FORMAT a30        HEADING "OBJECT NAME"
COLUMN c FORMAT a10        HEADING "OWNER ID"
COLUMN d FORMAT 99,999,999 HEADING "SIZE|IN BYTES"
BREAK ON e SKIP 1 ON c
SET FEEDBACK OFF
SET VERIFY OFF
SET TERMOUT OFF
COLUMN bls NEW_VALUE block_size NOPRINT
SELECT blocksize bls
FROM sys.ts$
WHERE name='SYSTEM';

SELECT h.name e, g.name c, f.object_type a, e.name b,
       b.length*&&block_size d
 FROM sys.uet$ b, sys.fet$ c, sys.fet$ d, sys.obj$ e,
      sys.sys_objects f,sys.user$ g, sys.ts$ h
 WHERE b.block# = c.block# + c.length
   AND b.block# + b.length = d.block#
   AND f.header_file = b.segfile#
   AND f.header_block = b.segblock#
   AND f.object_id = e.obj#
   AND g.user# = e.owner#
   AND b.ts# = h.ts#
 ORDER BY 1,2,3,4
/

CLEAR COLUMNS
SET FEEDBACK ON
SET VERIFY ON
SET TERMOUT ON
TTITLE ''
TTITLE OFF
SPOOL OFF
CLEAR BREAKS
```

Bound objects need to be exported, dropped, and rebuilt after a consolidation of freespace. Many times you will have a number of objects, not just one, that are bound because of extensive dynamic extension in the tablespace being monitored. If this is the case, a reorganization of the entire tablespace is in order, which could involve a tablespace-specific export. The script TBSP_EXP.SQL on the Wiley Web site can be used to generate a tablespace-specific export script.

The problem with the script generated by TBSP_EXP.SQL is that it may exceed the limit for the size of an export parfile (this is a parameter file used to automate export processes) if you have a large number of tables under one owner in a single tablespace. The way to correct for this would be to place a counter on the table loop and just export a fixed number of tables per parfile.

Making a Tablespace Read-Only

One of the new features with later versions of Oracle7 and all versions of Oracle8 and Oracle9i is the read-only tablespace. A read-only tablespace, as its name implies, allows read-only access to its information. This is beneficial in several ways:

- Since we are only reading data, no redo or rollback is required for read-only tablespaces.
- Read-only tablespaces only need to be backed up once after they are made read-only, then you can remove them from the backup plan.
- Read-only tablespaces can be left offline until just before they are needed (in Oracle8i or Oracle9i)—for example, on removable media such as CD-ROM or PD CD-ROM—and then brought online only when needed. Finally, read-only tablespaces do not participate in checkpoints.

Normally, you would have two related tablespaces, a data and an index tablespace, that you would want to make read-only. I would suggest dropping and rebuilding the indexes prior to making the index tablespace read-only, as well as correcting any space management problems such as chaining or excessive fragmentation on the data tablespace.

Of course, read-only tablespaces cannot be updated unless they are made readable again through the use of the ALTER TABLESPACE command.

The general procedure for making a tablespace read-only is:

1. Create the tablespace as a normal, permanent tablespace.
2. Populate the tablespace as you would a normal tablespace.
3. Once all data has been added to the tables in the tablespace, alter the tablespace to read-only.
4. Back up the tablespace using normal system backups.

Once a tablespace has been made read-only, you can transfer it to a media such as CD-ROM and then do a rename command on its datafile(s) using the ALTER DATABASE command to relocate them to the CD-ROM, as demonstrated here:

```
SQL> alter tablespace graphics_data read only;

Tablespace altered.

SQL> alter tablespace graphics_data offline;

Tablespace altered.

... Use operating system commands to copy file to new location ...

SQL> alter database rename file
'D:\ORANT8\DATABASE\ORTEST1_GRAPHICS_DATA01.DBF' to
  2* 'H:\ORACLE5\ORTEST1\DATA\ORTEST1_GRAPHICS_DATA01.DBF'
SQL> /

Database altered.

... Here, just to be sure, I rename the actual file I copied from to:
graphics_data01.old using the operating system rename command.

SQL> alter tablespace graphics_data online;

Tablespace altered.
```

In this example, notice that I renamed the file to a location on the h: drive (this happened to be a Panasonic PD CD-ROM drive). In the next example, I will show how to use the new initialization parameter READ_ONLY_OPEN_DELAYED.

Use of READ_ONLY_OPEN_DELAYED with Read-Only Tablespaces

In this section I introduce the new initialization parameter that deals specifically with read-only tablespaces: READ_ONLY_OPEN_DELAYED. This parameter tells Oracle to allow startup of the database even if some or all of the read-only tablespaces are offline or unavailable (for example, someone was using the CD-ROM player to listen to Bruce Springsteen and forgot to slip the CD with your read-only tablespace back in before startup).

At this juncture, I ask you to take a few things on faith because it is rather hard to show in print actual activities. To test this, I first issued the following commands to demonstrate that the read-only tablespace GRAPHICS_DATA was online and had active data (albeit read-only data):

```
SQL> select table_name from dba_tables where tablespace_name='GRAPHICS_DATA';

TABLE_NAME
-----------------
GRAPHICS_TABLE
INTERNAL_GRAPHICS
BASIC_LOB_TABLE

3 rows selected.
```

```
SQL> desc graphics_dba.internal_graphics
 Name                            Null?     Type
 ------------------------------------------------------
 GRAPHIC_ID                                NUMBER
 GRAPHIC_DESC                              VARCHAR2(30)
 GRAPHIC_BLOB                              BLOB
 GRAPHIC_TYPE                              VARCHAR2(10)

SQL> select graphic_id,graphic_desc from graphics_dba.internal_graphics where
rownum<10;

GRAPHIC_ID GRAPHIC_DESC
---------- -----------------------------------
         1 April book of days woodcut
         2 August book of days woodcut
         3 Benzene Molecule Graphic
         4 c20conto.gif
         5 cover11b.gif
         6 December book of days woodcut
         7 February book of days woodcut
         8 harris-c.gif
         9 HIV Virus Image

9 rows selected.
```

I then added the initialization parameter READ_ONLY_OPEN_DELAYED=TRUE (it defaults to FALSE) to the initialization parameter file and shut down the database. Once the database was shut down I opened the PD CD-ROM CD drawer with the PD CD-ROM disk that holds the GRAPHICS_DATA tablespace data file. I then restarted the database.

No error was generated even with the PD CD-ROM drawer open, thus making the GRAPHICS_DATA data file unavailable. I then issued the following commands to see what could be expected for attempting to access the offline tablespace:

```
SQL> select graphic_id,graphic_desc from graphics_dba.internal_graphics where
rownum<10;
select graphic_id,graphic_desc from graphics_dba.internal_graphics

ERROR at line 1:
ORA-01157: cannot identify data file 4 - file not found
ORA-01110: data file 4: 'H:\ORACLE5\ORTEST1\DATA\ORTEST1_GRAPHICS_DATA01.DBF'
```

After verifying that the datafile was in fact not available I simply reloaded the PD CD-ROM cartridge and reissued the command, all with the database online and active:

```
SQL> r
  1* select graphic_id,graphic_desc from graphics_dba.internal_graphics where
rownum<10
```

```
GRAPHIC_ID GRAPHIC_DESC
---------------------------------------
         1 April book of days woodcut
         2 August book of days woodcut
         3 Benzene Molecule Graphic
         4 c20conto.gif
         5 cover11b.gif
         6 December book of days woodcut
         7 February book of days woodcut
         8 harris-c.gif
         9 HIV Virus Image
```

As you can see, the database performs as if nothing were wrong. This means a database can continue to be used even if something has happened to make your read-only tablespaces temporarily unavailable.

TIP Be very careful using READ_ONLY_OPEN_DELAYED=TRUE. If the tablespace that is read-only is not accessed between startups, or if a database crash occurs, the tablespace may be made invalid and become nonrecoverable. Leave the tablespace in this mode (nonaccessed) for as short a time as possible.

Using Transportable Tablespaces

A feature added in Oracle8*i* was the ability to move a tablespace and its datafiles from one database to another. A transportable set of tablespace is one that is self-contained, for example, a set of data and index tablespaces, wherein all internal references between tables and indexes are resolved within that set of tablespaces. However, before you get too excited about this capability, you must be aware of these restrictions and limitations:

- The source and target database must be on the same platform (not the same machine, but the same platform "that is, Sun, version 2.7").
- The source and destination database must have the same blocksize.
- The source and destination database must have the same character set (there is an undocumented event to allow this, but it is not supported).
- There is no way to change the owner of the tablespace objects, so the owner(s) must have users set up in both databases.
- The tablespaces to be moved cannot contain bitmap indexes; these must be dropped before the move and rebuilt afterward.
- There is no way to rename the tablespace in transit; it must not already exist in the target database.
- Tablespaces containing nested tables and varrays cannot be transported.

- Both source and target must have compatibility at least set to 8.1, with the source being the same or earlier version than the target database. The actual versions do not matter as long as the compatibility setpoints are from same or earlier version on the source to the same or later version on the target database.

To check if the set of tablespaces is self-contained, Oracle has provided a stored package called DBMS_TTS that contains another package called TRANSPORT_SET_ CHECK. This procedure is fed the names of the tablespaces in your transport set and verifies that the set is self-contained. For example, to check where AP_DATA and AP_ INDEX tablespaces are a self-contained set, the command would be:

```
EXECUTE DBMS_TTS.TRANSPORT_SET_CHECK('AP_DATA,AP_INDEX', TRUE);
```

The TRUE entry in the TRANSPORT_SET_CHECK call corresponds to whether or not you wish to verify for constraints. Constraints have to be internally consistent, as do tables, indexes, and clusters. If there are violations in the set of tablespaces that prohibit there being a self-contained set, they will be written in human-readable form into the TRANSPORT_SET_VIOLATIONS table.

Once all of the tablespaces in your transport set are verified to be a self-contained set, you set them all to be read-only using the ALTER TABLESPACE command. Once all are set to read-only, a special type of export is performed that creates the data dictionary information for use in the target database. For our example tablespaces, the command to create the data dictionary export, including all triggers, constraints, and grants, would be:

```
Exp transport_tablespace=y tablespaces=ap_data,ap_index triggers=y
constraints=y grants=y file-tts.dmp
```

Obviously, if you set grants, triggers, or constraints to n (no), then they are ignored and not exported. The default setting for the grants, triggers, and constraints options is y (yes).

The next step is to copy the tablespace datafiles and the export file to the target database platform. After the tablespace datafiles have been copied, the original tablespaces can be altered back to READ WRITE mode if desired.

The final step, which consists of these steps, is to "plug in" the tablespaces to the target Oracle8*i* database:

1. Put the target tablespace datafiles into the OFA structure of the target database so the database can find them.
2. Plug in the tablespaces by adding their metadata via an import into the target database from the export file created previously:

```
Imp transport_tablespace=y  datafiles=
(d:\oracle2\ap_db\data\ap_data01.dbf,e:\oracle3\ap_db\data\ap_index.dbf)
file=tss_dmp tablespaces=(ap_data,ap_index) owners=(ap_dba);
```

The datafiles parameter must be specified to tell the target database where to find the transported tablespace datafiles; the tablespace's and owner's parameters are optional. Once the import completes, verify the import log for errors; then you can use the ALTER TABLESPACE command to make the tablespaces READ WRITE again (if desired, they are still in READ ONLY after the import completes). As with other export and import operations, a long list of parameters can be placed into a parameter file and referenced with the PARFILE parameter for ease of use.

Some things to watch for are:

- That rowids may no longer be unique after a transportable set of tablespaces are plugged in, as they are not regenerated.
- REF values are not checked when consistency is verified, so there may be dangling REF values if the REF targets are not self-contained within the transported set of tablespaces.
- BFILE values will be invalid unless the external files they refer to are also moved with the tablespace.
- Triggers, if exported, are exported without validity checks so they may generate an error on import if they are not self-contained in the transport set.
- Snapshot and replication data are not transported.

As long as you operate within these guidelines, transportable tablespaces will make it easier and faster than ever before to move data between databases, because it is much faster to do the data dictionary export and copy the files than to do any data extraction and reloading. Another advantage is that you carry the indexes with the transport set, so they do not have to be rebuilt (however, beware of duplicate rowids causing erroneous results).

3.6 SUMMARY

This chapter examined the commands to create, alter, and drop tablespaces. Tablespaces are roughly equivalent to disks, and provide storage for Oracle objects such as tables, clusters, LOBs, and indexes. The chapter also detailed techniques to maintain and defragment tablespaces, and discussed new options such as delayed verification of read-only tablespaces and transportable tablespaces.

CHAPTER 4

Administration of Relational Database Tables

With Oracle8, the number and complexity of database objects increased substantially. In Oracle8*i* and Oracle9*i,* even more objects were added. However, the basic building block of the database is still the table. We now have three essential table types: the *relational*, the *object-based*, and the *index-only*, or IOT, table. In Oracle7 we had two types of relational tables, standard and clustered; in Oracle9*i,* we have standard, partitioned, object, index-only, nested, global temporary, temporary, locally managed, dictionary-managed, system-managed, clustered tables, and external tables.

The object TYPE definition was added in Oracle8 and expanded in Oracle8*i*. A TYPE can be just a structure of scalar datatypes, an object type, a nested table type, or a varray. In this chapter, we will cover the "standard" relational table, external tables, clusters, and triggers. In the next chapter, we will look at the object extensions to tables. Let's get started.

4.1 THE CONCEPT OF RESTRICTED ROWIDS

Oracle used the concept of the restricted rowid in Oracle7 and earlier releases to uniquely identify each row in each table in the database. This was represented as the pseudocolumn rowid in Oracle7 and earlier releases. Hence, unknown to many DBAs and developers, even nonunique identified tables that violated Third Normal Form always had a unique identifier that could be used for removal of duplicates and other unique-identifier-required operations: the rowid column. Of course, views don't have rowids.

NOTE   In Oracle8, Oracle8*i*, and Oracle9*i*, the concept of rowid is still with us, but the format has been expanded. "Supplied PL/SQL Packages and Types References" from the documentation link on the book's companion Web site documents the DBMS_ROWID set of Oracle-provided packages that provide for rowid manipulation between the old and new formats, and the piece out, as well as the building of rowids.

But what does a rowid contain? To begin to answer that question, in this chapter we will examine the Oracle7 rowid concepts; in the next chapter, we will cover the expanded rowid (Oracle8, Oracle8*i*, and Oracle9*i* types, tables, and such). Though Oracle8*i* did not add to the concept of rowid, it added some datatypes that deal with rowids; Oracle9*i* did not add much to the usage of rowids.

Restricted rowid Format

The restricted rowid in Oracle is a VARCHAR2 representation of a binary value shown in hexadecimal format. You should only need to deal with restricted rowids in versions prior to Oracle8 or in systems that were upgraded from Oracle7 to Oracle8, 8*i*, or 9*i*. Restricted rowids are displayed as:

```
bbbbbbb.ssss.ffff
```

where:

> **bbbbbbbb** is the block ID.
>
> **ssss** is the sequence in the block.
>
> **ffff** is the file ID.

As stated in the introduction to this chapter, this rowid is a pseudocolumn (meaning the DESCRIBE command won't show it) in each table (and cluster). The rowid is unique, except in the case of cluster tables that have values stored in the same block. This makes it handy for doing entry comparisons in tables that may not have a unique key, especially when you want to eliminate or show duplicates before creating a unique or primary key. In *Oracle Performance Tuning,* authors Mark Gurry and Peter Corrigan (O'Reilly & Associates, 1996) show this simple query for determining duplicates using the rowid:

```
DELETE FROM emp E
WHERE E.rowid > ( SELECT MIN (x.rowid)
                  FROM emp X
                  WHERE X.emp_no = E.emp_no );
```

Of course, for your table, this query would have to be modified for the proper table name and column or columns involved in the primary key. And, of course, any operation where you can do a select, update, or delete based on exact rowid values will always out-perform virtually any other similar operation using standard column value logic. The file ID portion of the rowid points to the file with that number, which happens to be the same number given the datafile in the DBA_DATA_FILES view. In the sections to follow, a script called ACT_SIZE.SQL makes use of the rowid to determine the actual number of blocks used by a table. The rowid pseudocolumn is one that any DBA should be aware of and use to advantage. Oracle expanded the rowid in Oracle8 and continues to use the expanded ROWID in Oracle8*i* and Oracle9*i*. Chapter 5, *Administration of Oracle9i Object Tables*, discusses these changes and their implications.

4.2 RELATIONAL TABLE ADMINISTRATION

Tables are the primary storage division in Oracle. All data is stored in tables. Sequences and indexes support tables. Synonyms point to tables. Types and varrays are stored in tables. In short, tables make Oracle work. To create tables, you must have the permission CREATE TABLE or CREATE ANY TABLE. The CREATE TABLE privilege is granted automatically through the CONNECT role. The next subsections describe in detail the administration and maintenance of standard relational database tables.

Tables consist of attributes that are made up of datatypes at one level or another. The allowed Oracle datatypes are:

Datatype. One of the allowed SQL datatypes, which are listed in the SQL reference manual on the technet.oracle.com Web site. The remaining items in this brief list are composed of the other SQL datatypes.

CHAR(size). Character type data, max size 255. Under Oracle7, this was replaced by VARCHAR2. Under Oracle7, 8, 8*i*, and 9*i* CHAR is right-side padded to a specified length. CHAR has a maximum size of 2,000 bytes and a minimum size of 1 byte (which is the default if not specified). Note: There are plans afoot to eliminate the CHAR datatype, so begin converting any that your application may be using to VARCHAR2.

NCHAR(size). Same as CHAR except it is used for multibyte characters. The maximum length that can be stored depends on the number of bytes per character.

VARCHAR2. Variable-length character data of up to 2,000 characters in Oracle7; 4,000 characters in Oracle8, 8*i*, and 9*i*.

NVARCHAR2(size). Same as VARCHAR2, except for multibyte character sets. Maximum length that can be stored is dependent on length of individual character representations.

DATE. Date format, from 1/1/4712 BC to 12/31/4712 AD. Standard Oracle format is (10-APR-93), fixed 7 bytes of internal storage. The DATE datatype can update, insert, or retrieve a date value using the Oracle internal date binary format. A date in binary format contains 7 bytes, as shown here.

Byte:	1	2	3	4	5	6	7
Meaning:	Century	Year	Month	Day	Hour	Minute	Second

Example, for 30-NOV-1992, 3:17 PM:

Byte	1	2	3	4	5	6	7
Value	119	192	11	30	16	18	1

The century and year bytes (bytes 1 and 2) are in excess-100 notation. The first byte stores the value of the year, which is 1992, as an integer, divided by 100, giving 119 in excess-100 notation. The second byte stores year modulo 100, giving 192. Dates before common era (BCE) are less than 100. The era begins on 01-JAN-4712 BCE, which is Julian day 1. For this date, the century byte is 53, and the year byte is 88. The hour, minute, and second bytes are in excess-1 notation. The hour byte ranges from 1 to 24, the minute and second bytes from 1 to 60. If no time was specified when the date was created, the time defaults to midnight (1, 1, 1).

LONG. Only one LONG per table; 2 gig under Oracle7; 4 gig under Oracle8 and 8*i*. Oracle intends to do away with LONG and LONG RAW in favor of LOB datatypes, so it would be wise to begin converting the LONG and LONG RAW columns in your application to LOB datatypes.

RAW(size). Raw binary data, maximum of 2,000 bytes under Oracle7; 4,000 under Oracle8, 8*i,* and 9*i*.

LONG RAW. Raw binary data in hexadecimal format, 2 gig under Oracle7; 4 gig under Oracle8, 8*i,* and 9*i*.

ROWID. Internal datatype, not user-definable; used to uniquely identify table rows. Length of 6 in Oracle7, 10 in Oracle8, 8*i,* and 9*i*.

UROWID[(size)]. Hexadecimal string that represents the unique address of a row in an index-organized table. The optional size parameter is the size of a column of type UROWID. The maximum size is 4,000 bytes; this is also the default size.

NUMBER(p, s). Numeric data, with p being precision and s being scale. Defaults to 38 p, null s.

DECIMAL(p, s). Same as numeric.

INTEGER. Defaults to NUMBER(38), no scale.

SMALLINT. Same as INTEGER.

FLOAT. Same as NUMBER(38).

FLOAT(b). NUMBER with precision of 1 to 126.

REAL. defaults to NUMBER(63).

DOUBLE PRECISION. Same as NUMBER(38).

Note: No scale specification means floating point.

Large Object Datatypes

LOBs are similar to LONG and LONG RAW types, but differ in the following ways:

- Multiple LOBs are allowed in a single row.
- LOBs can be attributes of a user-defined datatype (object).
- The LOB locator is stored in the table column, either with or without the actual LOB value; BLOB, NCLOB, and CLOB values can be stored in separate table-spaces
- BFILE data is stored in an external file on the server.
- When you access a LOB column, it is the locator that is returned.
- A LOB can be up to 4 GB in size. BFILE maximum size is operating system-dependent, but cannot exceed 4 GB.
- LOBs permit efficient, random, piecewise access to, and manipulation of, data.
- You can define one or more LOB datatype columns in a table.
- With the exception of NCLOB, you can define one or more LOB attributes in an object.
- You can declare LOB bind variables.
- You can select LOB columns and LOB attributes.
- You can insert a new row or update an existing row that contains one or more LOB columns, and/or an object with one or more LOB attributes. (You can set the internal LOB value to NULL or empty, or replace the entire LOB with data. You can set the BFILE to NULL or so that it points to a different file.)
- You can update a LOB row/column intersection or a LOB attribute with another LOB row/column intersection or LOB attribute.
- You can delete a row containing a LOB column or LOB attribute and thereby also delete the LOB value. Note that for BFILEs, the actual operating system file is not deleted.

The LOB datatypes themselves are defined as follows:

BLOB. Binary large object, usually used to store graphics, video, or audio data. Maximum length of 4 GB under Oracle8, 8*i,* and 9*i.*

CLOB. Character large object, usually used to store single-byte character objects such as large text files. Maximum length of 4 GB under Oracle8, 8*i,* and 9*i.*

NCLOB. National character large object, usually used to store multibyte character data. Maximum length of 4 GB under Oracle8, 8*i,* and 9*i.*

BFILE. Binary external file locator. This probably varies in size depending on the value of the directory and filename placed into it. In empirical testing, with a directory specification of 'GIF_FILES', which contained the directory value 'e:\Oracle3\Ortest1\Bfiles' and an average name length of 10 for the actual external files, this column showed a length of 40.

Creation of Relational Tables

Tables are *owned* by users. You may hear users referred to as *schemas* and see this term used in Oracle documentation, but as with previous Oracle versions, whether you call them schemas or users makes little difference—the two terms are synonymous. For a given application it is suggested that its tables reside in a single dedicated tablespace or group of tablespaces. This leads to the corollary that all of an application's tables should be owned by a single user, or if you prefer, reside in a single schema. This makes further maintenance, such as exports, imports, synonym creation, table creates, and drops, easier to deal with.

Like the other database objects, tables are built using the CREATE command. This command has changed significantly since early versions of Oracle7. In fact, I can probably say without fear of contradiction that it, and the ALTER TABLE commands, are the most complex, convoluted commands in Oracle8*i*. (For those interested in the command syntax, refer to the Oracle documentation available on the technet.oracle.com Web site or through links on the Wiley Web site.)

Oracle9*i* offers a cornucopia of new table options. Oracle9*i* includes the ability to partition LOBs and types, and to subpartition partitions, as well to specify hash, range, and list partitioning. We will cover the use of types (in the creation of nested tables and varrays) in Chapter 5. Here, we will begin by looking at table-naming conventions, then we will examine the creation of standard tables, standard tables with LOBs, index-only tables (IOT), and partition tables under Oracle9*i*. Then we will move on to examine the use of the ALTER command, as well as the DROP and TRUNCATE commands with Oracle9*i* tables. As a final topic in this chapter, we will cover the use of external tables in Oracle9*i*.

Table-Naming Convention: An Example

Before a table-naming convention is established for a given project, the list of allowed abbreviations and acronyms should be compiled. This will prevent, for example developer A from naming the accounts payable table act_pay and developer B from naming the accounts receivable table accnt_rec.

According to the relational model, table names should always be a plural noun, since they are collections of entities (it logically follows that entity names should be singular in data models). Names should be as short as possible, between 8 and 16 characters. This length restriction is important, because, for column foreign key definitions and constraint naming, the table name is used in conjunction with column names in Designer and Developer products from Oracle.

For example, the table used to track ACCOUNTS PAYABLE in the PITS (Procurement Information Tracking System) application would be:

```
ACCT_PAY
```

assuming the standard abbreviation for ACCOUNT is ACCT and PAYABLE is PAY.

Wherever possible, abbreviations and acronyms should be used to shorten the table name. The TAB_COMMENTS and TAB_COL_COMMENTS tables can be used to store a more detailed name, which can be used in a simple help stored procedure to provide detailed information on the table and its columns. The COMMENT command is used to add comments to the DBA_TAB_COMMENTS and DBA_COL_COMMENTS views; it has the general format:

```
COMMENT ON TABLE|COLUMN [schema.]table|view|snapshot[.column] IS 'text';
```

The importance of short table names cannot be stressed enough. However, using codes like A1, B1, and Z28 for your tables is also to be avoided. Short *meaningful* names are the best.

A specialized type of table is the *intersection table*. An intersection table allows resolution of many-to-many and recursive relationships. Let's say we have a many-to-many relationship between the PARTS table and the VENDORS table (VENDS for short). The resolving intersection table should be named:

```
VENDS_PARTS
```

(assuming the VENDORS table is the driving table for the relationship).

Creation of Simple Relational Tables: An Example

I define simple relational tables as those using standard relational structure, without the use of user-defined types (UDT), partitions, or special storage options such as index-only structure. In many applications the DBA works with, these will be the majority of tables involved.

When creating simple relational tables, the CREATE TABLE command is used, with constraint clauses, simple physical attribute, and a STORAGE clause. The generalized format for the command is:

```
CREATE TABLE [schema.]TABLE
(column datatype [column_constraint],table_constraint)
[physical_attributes_clause]
[storage_clause]
```

In this code, the column datatype [column_constraint] structure can be repeated, as can the table_constraint clause. Usually, the table_constraint clauses follow all column definitions.

Let's look at a very simple table creation command:

```
CREATE TABLE test_dba.test1
(test_col1 NUMBER,
 test_col2 VARCHAR2(10));
```

In this example we created a table called test1 in the schema test_dba. The table test1 would be created in the default tablespace of the specified schema/user owning the table, *not* the default tablespace of the creating schema/user. The table test1 would inherit the storage and physical attributes of the default tablespace of test_dba.

So why is it good or bad to use such a simple command as illustrated here? Actually, it depends on how you have defined the default storage characteristics of the default tablespace and whether or not you want the table created in the default tablespace. If the creation of test1 using the default storage and physical attributes, as well as the default tablespace, is what you desired, then this command is what to use. If, on the other hand, you did not want any of this to occur, then you used too simple a command. Let's look at another "problem" command:

```
CREATE TABLE test_dba.test1
(test_col1 NUMBER PRIMARY KEY,
 test_col2 VARCHAR2(10));
```

This command has the same problems as did the first table creation command we examined. Moreover, there is an added twist: the PRIMARY KEY column constraint will result in the creation of an index, and that index will be stored in the default tablespace for test_dba with the default storage and physical attributes and a system-generated name such as: SYS_C001967. The creation of both the table and its index in the same tablespace results in instant contention for resources between the index and table, hence subsequent performance problems. An additional issue is that both the UNIQUE constraint specification and the PRIMARY KEY specification result in the creation of an index and an additional NOT NULL constraint against the specified column. So how should we specify table test1 to avoid all of these problems?

```
CREATE TABLE test_dba.test1
(test_col1 NUMBER,
 test_col2 VARCHAR2(10),
CONSTRAINT test1_pk PRIMARY KEY(test_col1)
USING INDEX TABLESPACE test_indexes
PCTFREE 30
INITRANS 5
MAXTRANS 255
STORAGE(INITIAL 100k NEXT 100k
        MINEXTENTS 1 MAXEXTENTS UNLIMITED
        PCTINCREASE 0))
PCTFREE 10
PCTUSED 60
INITRANS 5
MAXTRANS 255
STORAGE(INITIAL 1M NEXT 1M
        MINEXTENTS 1 MAXEXTENTS UNLIMITED
        PCTINCREASE 0
        BUFFER_POOL KEEP)
TABLESPACE test_data;
```

Why is this longer format for the CREATE TABLE command better? Let's examine the command and see.

- First, we have isolated the column definitions so that they aren't obscured by layers of added constraint material.
- Next, the constraint is clearly defined after the column definitions with its own storage, physical attributes, and tablespace definition.
- The constraint is named so that, instead of a constraint named SYS_C001967, we have one clearly identified as to table and type of constraint: test1_pk. Note that the automatically defined index will also be named test1_pk, allowing ease of constraint, table, and index tracking.
- Finally, by specifying the tablespaces for both the index generated by the primary key constraint and the table itself, we have assured the physical separation of the index and table, thus eliminating contention for resources.

Notice that we also used the new Oracle8 feature that allows us to specify the buffer pool to which the table blocks should be loaded. In this case, we specified the KEEP pool, meaning we want the tables blocks to be cached in the KEEP section of the db buffer pool. (See Chapter 13, *Database Internals Tuning*, to learn how to use multiple buffer pools.) The other options for the BUFFER_POOL clause are RECYCLE and DEFAULT, with DEFAULT correlating to the old behavior in pre-Oracle8 databases.

A slightly more complex example involves the use of foreign keys. As the name implies, a foreign key references a table outside of the current table. A foreign key must reference a primary or unique key value already in existence in the other table. Building on the preceding examples, look at the definition of our table test1. Notice that in test1 we have specified the primary key column test_col1; let's create a table test2 that has a primary key and a foreign key that references using a foreign key back into table test1.

```
CREATE TABLE test_dba.test2
(test2_col1 NUMBER,
 test2_col2 NUMBER,
 test2_col3 DATE,
CONSTRAINT test2_pk PRIMARY KEY (test2_col1,test2_col2)
USING INDEX TABLESPACE test_index
PCTFREE 30
INITRANS 5
MAXTRANS 255
STORAGE(INITIAL 100K NEXT 100K
 MINEXTENTS 1 MAXEXTENTS UNLIMITED
PCTINCREASE 0),
CONSTRAINT test2_fk1 FOREIGN KEY(test2_col2)
 REFERENCES test_dba.test1(test_col1))
PCTFREE 10
PCTUSED 60
INITRANS 5
```

```
MAXTRANS 255
STORAGE(INITIAL 1M NEXT 1M
 MINEXTENTS 1 MAXEXTENTS UNLIMITED PCTINCREASE 0
 BUFFER_POOL KEEP)
TABLESPACE test_data
/
```

The table test2 is created with a *concatenated* primary key called test2_pk, which comprises the columns test2_col1 and test2_col2. The column test2_col2 is also a foreign key reference back to our original table test1. What a foreign key implies is that for every value entered into test2.test2.col2 there must be a primary key value in test1.test.col1 that matches it exactly. This is the basis for the concept of *referential integrity* in relational databases.

What other types of constraints can we define? We haven't looked at unique value, check, and default value constraints yet. A UNIQUE constraint is nearly identical to a primary key constraint in that it enforces that each value in the unique column be unique and uses a unique index to enforce this constraint. However, in a unique column, NULL values are allowed, while they are forbidden in a primary key. Look at Listing 4.1.

Listing 4.1   Example of a table creation script.

```
SQL> CREATE TABLE test_dba.test3
   2  (test3_col1 NUMBER,
   3    test3_col2 NUMBER,
   4    test3_col3 DATE,
   5   CONSTRAINT test3_pk PRIMARY KEY(test3_col1,test3_col2)
   6   USING INDEX TABLESPACE test_index
   7   PCTFREE 30
   8   INITRANS 5
   9   MAXTRANS 255
  10   STORAGE(INITIAL 100K NEXT 100K
  11   MINEXTENTS 1 MAXEXTENTS UNLIMITED
  12   PCTINCREASE 0),
  13   CONSTRAINT test3_fk1 FOREIGN KEY(test3_col2)
  14   REFERENCES test_dba.test1(test_col1),
  15   CONSTRAINT test3_uv1 UNIQUE (test3_col3)
  16   USING INDEX TABLESPACE test_index
  17   PCTFREE 30
  18   INITRANS 5
  19   MAXTRANS 255
  20   STORAGE(INITIAL 100K NEXT 100K
  21   MINEXTENTS 1 MAXEXTENTS UNLIMITED
  22   PCTINCREASE 0))
  23   PCTFREE 10
  24   PCTUSED 60
```

```
25  INITRANS 5
26  MAXTRANS 255
27  STORAGE(INITIAL 1M NEXT 1M
28  MINEXTENTS 1 MAXEXTENTS UNLIMITED PCTINCREASE 0)
29  TABLESPACE test_data;

Table created.

SQL> desc test_dba.test3
 Name                            Null?     Type
 ------------------------        -----     ------
 TEST3_COL1                      NOT NULL  NUMBER
 TEST3_COL2                      NOT NULL  NUMBER
 TEST3_COL3                                DATE
```

Notice here in the DESCRIBE of the table TEST3 that the column TEST3_COL3 is not specified as a NOT NULL even though it is defined as a uniquely constrained value. The last two constraint types are check and default value. The NOT NULL constraint is a specialized form of the check constraint, in that it checks that the value entered into a column is not null; that is, it must have a valid value. More complex versions of the check constraint can be used to enforce ranges of values for a specific column. Look at Listing 4.2.

Listing 4.2   Second CREATE TABLE example.

```
SQL> CREATE TABLE test_dba.test4
  2  (test4_col1 NUMBER,
  3   test4_col2 NUMBER,
  4   test4_col3 DATE CONSTRAINT test4_ck1
  5   CHECK(test4_col3 BETWEEN
  6  TO_DATE('01-jan-1999 00:00:00','dd-mon-yyyy hh24:mi:ss') AND
  7  TO_DATE('01-jan-2000 00:00:00','dd-mon-yyyy hh24:mi:ss')),
  8  CONSTRAINT test4_pk PRIMARY KEY (test4_col1,test4_col2)
  9  USING INDEX TABLESPACE test_index
 10  PCTFREE 30
 11  INITRANS 5
 12  MAXTRANS 255
 13  STORAGE(INITIAL 100K NEXT 100K
 14  MINEXTENTS 1 MAXEXTENTS UNLIMITED
 15  PCTINCREASE 0),
 16  CONSTRAINT test4_fk1 FOREIGN KEY(test4_col2)
 17  REFERENCES test_dba.test1(test_col1)
 18  ON DELETE CASCADE,
 19  CONSTRAINT test4_uv1 UNIQUE (test4_col3)
 20  USING INDEX TABLESPACE test_index
```

continues

Listing 4.2   Continued.

```
 21  PCTFREE 30
 22  INITRANS 5
 23  MAXTRANS 255
 24  STORAGE(INITIAL 100K NEXT 100K
 25  MINEXTENTS 1 MAXEXTENTS UNLIMITED
 26  PCTINCREASE 0))
 27  PCTFREE 10
 28  PCTUSED 60
 29  INITRANS 5
 30  MAXTRANS 255
 31  STORAGE(INITIAL 1M NEXT 1M
 32  MINEXTENTS 1 MAXEXTENTS UNLIMITED PCTINCREASE 0)
 33* TABLESPACE test_data
SQL> /

Table created.
```

Notice here that the check constraint is a column-level constraint and can't be placed at the table level. The check constraint on the column test4_col3 restricts the dates placed into the field to be between 01-Jan-1999 00:00:00 and 01-Jan-2000 00:00:00.

Also notice in Listing 4.2 the inclusion of the ON DELETE CASCADE clause to the foreign key defined on test4_col2. This clause forces any values in this row to be deleted when the row from the source column in test1.test_col1 is deleted. Note that there is no similar clause to allow updates to be carried forward from the parent table to the child table.

Providing Cascade Update Functionality

A common situation is that a master table may be updated, leaving dependent tables without a link back to the master—in which case, a cascade update option would be a nice one to have. Unfortunately, Oracle Corporation doesn't provide this as a native capability, so a PL/SQL option must be developed.

An example of a situation that calls for a cascade update is where a dependent table is dependent on one or more tables. For example, there may be two types of customer, one who has bought from us before and for whom we have marketing information, and another who is new to us, may buy from us, but may decide to go with another vendor. If we had dependent tables (such as an interaction log that tracks phone calls to and from customers), it would be nice to be able to switch the dependencies from our *new* customer table to our *established* customer table.

Enforcing a Cascade Update   What do we need to enforce a cascade update? One method is to utilize data dictionary tables and views to backtrack foreign key relations and then apply updates along this path. However, this may be a lengthy process and can cause a performance problem. A simpler method is to implement a table-based cascade update. The table would contain the information that a procedure would need to update all tables that are dependent upon a main, or master, table. Therefore, the table would have to contain the master table name, the dependent table(s), and, in case we can't duplicate the exact column name across all of the dependent tables, the column to update. The table DDL script in Listing 4.3 meets these requirements. If required, a fourth column indicating an update order could be added, and the cursor in the UPDATE_TABLES procedure (detailed later) would have to be altered to do an ordered retrieve of the information. Listing 4.3 shows the required CREATE TABLE command.

The table by itself would be of little use. Since the data in the table is dynamic (i.e., multiple tables and columns that would have to be addressed), we must enable our trigger to be able to dynamically reassign these values. The easiest way to do this is to create a set of procedures that utilize the DBMS_SQL Oracle-provided package to dynamically reassign our update variables. Source 4.1 shows the commented code for just such a procedure set, which consists of two procedures: UPDATE_TABLES and UPDATE_COLUMN.

Listing 4.3   Command to create UPDATE_TABLES table.

```
CREATE TABLE update_tables
(
     main_table        VARCHAR2(30) NOT NULL,
     table_name        VARCHAR2(30) NOT NULL,
     column_name       VARCHAR2(30) NOT NULL,
CONSTRAINT pk_update_tables
PRIMARY KEY (main_table,table_name,column_name)
USING INDEX
TABLESPACE tool_indexes)
STORAGE (INITIAL 100K NEXT 100K PCTINCREASE 0)
TABLESPACE tools
/
-- Column definitions are:
-- main_table holds the name of the table that the update
-- cascades from.
-- table_name is the name(s) of the tables to cascade the
-- update into.
-- column_name is the column in the target table(s) to
-- update
```

The Cascade Update Procedures   By using the DBMS_SQL package to dynamically build the table update command on the fly, we can use the same set of procedures for any set of master-dependent tables that have entries in the source table.

The UPDATE_TABLES procedure accepts the master table name, the old value for the column to be updated, and the new value for the column. The procedure uses a standard cursor fetch to retrieve the dependent table names and dependent table column names from the source table, shown in Listing 4.3. If required, the table could be altered to accept an ordering value for each master-dependent set to allow the cascade update to be done in a specific order. Using this information and the new and old values for the column from the trigger call, the UPDATE_COLUMN procedure dynamically rebuilds the table update command to update the appropriate tables. I have created a sample package for cascade updates; it is shown in Source 4.1.

Source 4.1   Cascade update package.

```
-- First create package body
-- Decided to use package so that all procedures will
-- be in one place and very controllable
-- M. Ault 1/14/97 Rev 1.0
--
CREATE OR REPLACE PACKAGE cascade_update AS
--
-- First package is update_column
-- This package actually does the work
-- using DBMS_SQL to dynamically rebuild the
-- UPDATEs at run time for each table.
--
PROCEDURE update_column(
    old_value       IN VARCHAR2,
    new_value       IN VARCHAR2,
    table_name      IN VARCHAR2,
    update_column   IN VARCHAR2
);
--
-- Next procedure is update_tables
-- It is the loop control procedure for
-- the trigger and calls update_column
--
PROCEDURE update_tables(
    source_table    IN VARCHAR2,
    old_value       IN VARCHAR2,
    new_value       IN VARCHAR2
);
--
-- End of PACKAGE HEADER
--
END cascade_update;
/
--
-- Now build package body
-- That actually holds the
-- procedures and code
--
```

```
CREATE OR REPLACE PACKAGE BODY cascade_update AS
PROCEDURE update_column(
     old_value        IN VARCHAR2,
     new_value        IN VARCHAR2,
     table_name    IN VARCHAR2,
     update_column IN VARCHAR2)
AS
--
-- define state variables for dbms_sql procedures
--

     cur              INTEGER;
     rows_processed  INTEGER;

--
-- start processing
-- (dbms_output calls are for debugging
-- commented out during normal run time)
--
BEGIN
DBMS_OUTPUT.PUT_LINE(
'Table name: '||table_name||' Column: '||update_column);
     --
     -- initialize the dynamic cursor location for
     -- the dbms_sql process
     --
     cur:=DBMS_SQL.OPEN_CURSOR;
     --
     -- populate the initialized location with the
     -- statement to be processed
     --
DBMS_OUTPUT.PUT_LINE(
'UPDATE '||table_name||
' SET '||update_column||'='||chr(39)||new_value||chr(39)||
chr(10)||' WHERE '||
update_column||'='||chr(39)||old_value||chr(39)||
' AND 1=1');
     --
     dbms_sql.parse(cur,
     'UPDATE '||table_name||
' set '||update_column||'='||chr(39)||new_value||chr(39)||
chr(10)||' WHERE '||
update_column||'='||chr(39)||old_value||chr(39)||
' AND 1=1',dbms_sql.native);
     --
     -- execute the dynamically parsed statement
     --
     rows_processed:=DBMS_SQL.EXECUTE(cur);
     --
     -- close dynamic cursor to prepare for next table
     --
     DBMS_SQL.CLOSE_CURSOR(cur);
```

continues

Source 4.1   Continued.

```
--
-- END PROCEDURE
--
END update_column;
--
PROCEDURE update_tables(
    source_table  IN VARCHAR2,
    old_value          IN VARCHAR2,
    new_value          IN VARCHAR2) as
--
-- Create the cursor to read records
-- from bbs_siteid_tables
-- Use * to prohibit missing a column
--
    CURSOR get_table_name IS
        SELECT
                *
        FROM
                bbs_update_tables
        WHERE
                main_table=source_table;
--
-- Define rowtype variable to hold record from
-- bbs_siteid_tables. Use rowtype to allow for
-- future changes.
--
    update_rec      update_tables%ROWTYPE;
--
-- start processing
--
BEGIN
--
-- open and fetch values with cursor
--
 OPEN get_table_name;
 FETCH get_table_name INTO update_rec;
--
-- now that cursor status is open and values in
-- variables can begin loop
--
LOOP
--
-- using the notfound status we had to prepopulate
-- record
--
   EXIT WHEN get_table_name%NOTFOUND;
--
-- Initiate call to the update_column procedure
```

```
--
   update_column(old_value, new_value,
    update_rec.table_name, update_rec.column_name);
--
-- Now get next record from table
--
   FETCH get_table_name INTO update_rec;
--
-- processing returns to loop statement

 END LOOP;
--
-- close cursor and exit
--
 CLOSE get_table_name;
--
-- end of procedure
--
END update_tables;
--
-- end of package body
--
END cascade_update;
/
```

The Final Piece: The Trigger

Once the source table and procedures have been built, we need to design a trigger to implement against our master tables and that automatically fires on update to the target master column. The next code section shows an example of this trigger. Notice that the trigger passes the master table name to the UPDATE_TABLES procedure, as well as the old and new values for the column being updated. This allows the UPDATE_TABLES procedure to select only the names and columns for the tables that are dependent upon the master table for which the trigger is implemented. This allows multiple master tables to utilize a single source table.

The calling trigger has to be of the form:

```
CREATE OR REPLACE TRIGGER cascade_update_<tabname>
   AFTER UPDATE OF <column> ON <tabname>
   REFERENCING NEW AS upd OLD AS prev
     FOR EACH ROW
       BEGIN
        cascade_update.update_tables('<tabname>',
           :prev.<column>,:upd.<column>);
       END;
```

Note how the table name is passed to the procedure: this must be done.

This type of combination of table, procedure, and trigger makes it possible to do the cascade update in a controlled, uniform manner. The table storing the update table information is used by multiple tables; thus, the only required operations would involve adding the prerequisite data to the update table and then placing the required trigger on the tables to undergo the cascade update. Triggers are covered in more detail in Chapter 7, *Administration of Other Database Objects*. All of the procedures discussed in this section are included in the DBA Utilities package provided on the companion Web site.

Deferred Constraints

New in Oracle8, and expanded in Oracle8*i*, is the concept of *deferred constraint*. A deferred constraint is one whose enforcement is deferred, or delayed, until it is either manually turned on, or a specific action, such as a transaction end point, is reached. The constraint state clause is used to set a constraint's deferrability. The generalized format for the constraint state clause is:

```
Cons_state_clause:
[NOT] DEFERRABLE [INITIALLY [IMMEDIATE|DEFERRED]]
[INTIALLY|IMMEDIATE] DEFERRED [NOT] [DEFERRABLE]
     [RELY|NORELY]
[ENABLE|DISABLE] [VALIDATE|NOVALIDATE]
          [EXCEPTIONS INTO [schema.]table]
```

If left out, the cons_state_clause, shown here, produces a nondeferrable-enabled constraint with a default index (for UNIQUE and PRIMARY KEY constraints) located in the default tablespace. Constraints are either DEFERRABLE or NOT DEFERRABLE. This means, respectively, that they can be changed in their deferrable status using the SET CONSTRAINTS command or that the SET CONSTRAINTS has no effect upon them. An example would be a large loading operation where the primary and foreign keys may not be in sync until the operation completes. If a constraint is DEFERRABLE, it can be either INITIALLY IMMEDIATE, where the constraint is checked with every DML statement, or INITIALLY DEFERRED, which means it is checked at the end of a transaction.

RELY|NORELY. Applies only to constraints on materialized views. This option specifies to the optimizer whether a materialized view to which this constraint applies is eligible for query rewrite. If all constraints have been validated, the materialized view is eligible for query rewrite. If one or more constraints have not been validated, the materialized view may not be eligible for query rewrite unless RELY is specified for the nonvalidated constraints. (Its eligibility is further dependent on the value of the REWRITE_INTEGRITY parameter.)

ENABLE VALIDATE. Specifies that the existing rows must conform to the constraint; ENABLE NOVALIDATE specifies that future rows must meet the restrictions of the constraint but that existing rows can exist as-is (unless they are updated, in which case they must conform).

DISABLE VALIDATE. Disables the constraint, drops the index on the constraint, and disallows any modification of the table. This option is most useful for unique constraints. The disabled validate state of the unique constraint enables you to load data efficiently from a nonpartitioned table into a partitioned table using the EXCHANGE PARTITION option of the ALTER TABLE command. DISABLE NOVALIDATE means that Oracle ignores the constraint entirely. If you specify neither VALIDATE nor NOVALIDATE, the default is NOVALIDATE. If you disable a unique or primary constraint that is using a unique index, Oracle drops the unique index and forgets all storage specifications for the index that was dropped. The index storage parameters must be respecified if the constraint is reenabled at a future time.

EXCEPTIONS INTO. Allows you to capture the rowids of any rows that do not meet the validation criteria in a table that you specify.

NOTE   You must create an appropriate exceptions report table to accept information from the EXCEPTIONS option of the enable_disable_clause before enabling the constraint. You can create an exception table by submitting the script UTLEXCPT1.SQL, which creates a table named EXCEPTIONS. You can create additional exceptions tables with different names by modifying and resubmitting the script. (You can use the UTLEXCPT1.SQL script with index-organized tables. You cannot use earlier versions of the script for this purpose.)

A Sample Constraint Naming Convention

There are five types of constraints in an Oracle database (version 8*i* and 9*i*); these are:

- Primary key
- Foreign key
- Unique value
- Check value
- Default value

Constraints should be named by function. For primary and foreign key constraints, the constraints should be named the same as their supporting indexes. For example, for a primary key constraint on the ACCT_PAY table:

PK_ACCT_PAY or P_ACCT_PAY or ACCT_PAY_PK, etc.

For the unique value on the vendor code in the ACCT_PAY table, the name could be:

UV_ACCT_PAY_VENDCD or UV_ACCT_PAY_1 or ACCT_PAY_UV_1 (If it is the first unique value) or:

    ACCT_PAY_VENDCD_U (The supporting index would be named the same.)

    Within the 32-character limit imposed by Oracle, this name can be as wordy as you wish.

    For a foreign key constraint, the constraint indicator, the constraint table, and the foreign table should be included in the name. So, for the foreign key to the VEND table from the ACCT_PAY table, the constraint would be:

    FK_ACCT_PAY_VEND

or:

    ACCT_PAY_VEND_FK

    It may not always be possible to include all the column names in a foreign key name. If this is the case, you can make it just a numeric reference or describe the situation:

    FK_ACCT_PAY_8COL_VEND or FK_ACCT_PAY_1

    For other types of constraint, use a simple type indicator, such as CK for check type constraints (e.g., NOT NULL constraints), and DV for default value. Include the table name and the column name. So, for a NOT NULL constraint on the VNDCD column, the naming convention would be:

    CK_ACCT_PAY_VNDCD

    You may also use NN for NOT NULL instead of CK, and reserve CK for special check constraints.

Using LOB Datatypes in Relational Tables: An Example

The LOB datatypes were new to Oracle8. The essential types are BLOB, CLOB, NCLOB, and BFILE. The BLOB is a binary large object, and is generally used for pictures, video, or audio-type information storage. The CLOB is a character large object, and is generally used for character-type information storage such as large text files. NCLOB is the national character large object datatype, and is used for multibyte character large objects. BLOBs, CLOBs, and NCLOBs are all internally stored objects (up to 4,000 bytes inline with outer data; anything longer is stored in a separate tablespace with special storage characteristics). The final LOB datatype is actually a pointer used to tell Oracle where an externally stored LOB datafile of any type is stored; the BFILE is used in concert with a DIRECTORY definition. The next example shows a simple table definition using a LOB datatype.

```
CREATE TABLE internal_graphics (
graphic_id    NUMBER,
graphic_desc  VARCHAR2(30),
graphic_blob  BLOB,
graphic_type  VARCHAR2(10))
LOB (graphic_blob) STORE AS glob_store (
TABLESPACE graphics_data
STORAGE (INITIAL 100K NEXT 100K PCTINCREASE 0)
CHUNK 4
PCTVERSION 10
STORAGE (INITIAL 1M NEXT 1M PCTINCREASE 0)
TABLESPACE graphics_data
/
```

The boldface section of this example shows the LOB storage clause; this is a vital part of any table definition using LOB datatypes. If the LOB storage is not specified, the LOB objects are stored in the default tablespace, and severe performance problems may result. In Oracle8, the LOB index was able to be stored in a different tablespace from the specified LOB datatype storage tablespace. In Oracle8*i* and in Oracle9*i* the LOB indexes are stored with the LOB data objects; the tablespace specification for the LOB index is ignored. Though the preceding example shows only a BLOB definition, CLOB and NCLOB are specified identically.

TIP   Remember that the actual number of characters that can be stored in an NCLOB is: NCLOB / (# bytes per character)

As stated above, in order to use a BFILE, a DIRECTORY must be specified and specific grants must be given to any users needing to access the DIRECTORY. Look at the next example:

```
CREATE TABLE bfile_graphics (
graphic_id     NUMBER,
graphic_desc   VARCHAR2(30),
graphic_bfile  BFILE)
STORAGE (INITIAL 1M NEXT 1M PCTINCREASE 0)
TABLESPACE graphics_data
/
```

Notice that no LOB storage clause is included in the table definition. All BFILE data (simply a pointer) is stored inline, so no LOB storage is required. What *is* required before the BFILE can be used is at least one directory specification that points to the location of the external graphics, text, or audio files. The next example shows how this directory entry is created and how the specifically required grants are done.

```
SQL> CREATE OR REPLACE DIRECTORY gifs_dir AS 'e:\oracle3\ortest1\bfiles';

Directory created.

SQL> GRANT READ ON DIRECTORY gifs_dir TO PUBLIC;

Grant succeeded.
```

Once the directory is specified, and the grants made as required (for simplicity, I granted to PUBLIC), the actual pointers to the external files are built using the BFILENAME function call. First, let's add a column to our table to allow the type of file to be added, along with the other BFILE information:

```
SQL> desc bfile_graphics
 Name                           Null?    Type
 ------------------------------ -------  ---------------
 GRAPHIC_ID                              NUMBER
 GRAPHIC_DESC                            VARCHAR2(30)
 GRAPHIC_BFILE                           BINARY FILE LOB

SQL> alter table bfile_graphics add graphic_type varchar2(10);

Table altered.

SQL> insert into bfile_graphics
  2  values(4,
  3  'April Book of Days Woodcut',bfilename('GIFS_DIR','APRIL.JPG'),'JPEG');

1 row created.

SQL> insert into bfile_graphics
  2  values(8,
  3  'August Book of Days
Woodcut',bfilename('GIFS_DIR','AUGUST.JPG'),'JPEG');

1 row created.

SQL> commit;

Commit complete.
```

As you can see, the required inputs to the BFILENAME function are:

Directory name. The name of the created directory passed in as a text string

BFILE name. The actual BFILE name passed in as a text string

An automated PL/SQL anonymous block to perform the loading of BFILE data is shown in Source 4.2.

Source 4.2   Example of a BFILE loading procedure.

```
CREATE  OR REPLACE PROCEDURE get_bfiles(
 bfile_dir in  VARCHAR2,
 bfile_lis in  VARCHAR2,
 bfile_int_dir VARCHAR2)
AS
 cur        INTEGER;
 bfile_int  VARCHAR2(100);
 sql_com    VARCHAR2(2000);
 file_proc  INTEGER;
 file_hand  utl_file.file_type;
 file_buff  VARCHAR2(1022);
 file_type  VARCHAR2(4);
BEGIN
 bfile_int:=UPPER(bfile_int_dir);
 file_hand:=utl_file.fopen(bfile_dir,bfile_lis,'R');
 LOOP
   BEGIN
   utl_file.get_line(file_hand,file_buff);
   cur:=dbms_sql.open_cursor;
   file_type:=SUBSTR(file_buff,INSTR(file_buff,'.')+1,3);
   file_type:=UPPER(file_type);
   IF file_type='GIF'
     THEN
        file_type:='GIF';
     ELSIF file_type='JPG'
     THEN file_type:='JPEG';
   END IF;
   sql_com:= 'INSERT INTO graphics_table '||CHR(10)||
             'VALUES (graphics_table_seq.NEXTVAL,'||CHR(39)||CHR(39)||
             ', bfilename('||
             CHR(39)||bfile_int||CHR(39)||','
             ||CHR(39)||file_buff||CHR(39)||
             ') ,'||CHR(39)||file_type||CHR(39)||')';
   dbms_output.put_line(sql_com);
   dbms_sql.parse(cur,sql_com,dbms_sql.v7);
   file_proc:=dbms_sql.execute(cur);
   dbms_sql.close_cursor(cur);
   EXCEPTION
    WHEN no_data_found THEN
    EXIT;
   END;
 END LOOP;
 utl_file.fclose(file_hand);
END;
/
```

This procedure depends on a sequence called graphics_table_seq and a single-column list of the files placed in the location specified in the bfile_dir argument; the name of the list file is specified in the bfile_lis argument. The final argument is the internal directory name that corresponds to the actual external file directory. The procedure assumes a three-place file extension of either 'JPG' or 'GIF', and assigns the graphic type field automatically. For example, if we had a file called file.lis that contained a list of all of the graphics files we wanted to load into the bfile_graphics table, our call to this procedure would be:

```
SQL> EXECUTE get_bfiles(
  2    'e:\oracle3\ortest1\bfiles',
  3    'file.lis',
  4    'GIFS_DIR');
```

Once the BFILEs are loaded into the database, they can be used to pull the external graphics or LOB files into internal LOB storage areas or simply to pass the BFILE information to an external program for further processing. An example application that uses Java to display stored BLOB data pulled into a database using the DBMS_LOB routines, can be found in my book *Oracle8 Black Book* (Coriolis Press, 1998). It is more of a development action than an administration topic. In contrast, the process for loading LOB data from a BFILE into an internal LOB is an administration topic. Source 4.3 shows a PL/SQL routine that will use the loaded BFILE information to move the LOB from external to internal storage.

Source 4.3   Example of a PL/SQL procedure to move BFILEs into BLOBs.

```
CREATE OR REPLACE PROCEDURE load_lob AS
id            NUMBER;
image1        BLOB;
locator       BFILE;
bfile_len     NUMBER;
bf_desc       VARCHAR2(30);
bf_name       VARCHAR2(30);
bf_dir        VARCHAR2(30);
bf_typ        VARCHAR2(4);
ctr           INTEGER;
CURSOR get_id IS
SELECT bfile_id,bfile_desc,bfile_type
FROM graphics_table;
BEGIN
  open get_id;
LOOP
    FETCH get_id INTO id, bf_desc, bf_typ;
    EXIT WHEN get_id%notfound;
    dbms_output.put_line('ID: '||to_char(id));
    SELECT bfile_loc
```

```
      INTO locator
      FROM graphics_table
      WHERE bfile_id=id;
   dbms_lob.filegetname(locator,bf_dir,bf_name);
   dbms_output.put_line('Dir: '||bf_dir);
   dbms_lob.fileopen(locator,dbms_lob.file_readonly);
   bfile_len:=dbms_lob.getlength(locator);
dbms_output.put_line('ID: '||to_char(id)||' length: '||
 to_char(bfile_len));
   insert into dual_lob(x) values(empty_blob());
   select x into image1 from dual_lob;
   bfile_len:=dbms_lob.getlength(locator);
   dbms_lob.loadfromfile(image1,locator,bfile_len,1,1);
   IF bf_desc is null THEN
      bf_desc:=bf_name;
   END IF;
   insert into internal_graphics values (id,bf_desc,image1,bf_typ,'GENERAL');
   dbms_output.put_line(bf_desc||' Length: '||to_char(bfile_len)||
    ' Name: '||bf_name||' Dir: '||bf_dir||' '||bf_typ);
   dbms_lob.fileclose(locator);
   delete dual_lob;
 END LOOP;
END load_lob;
/
```

Notice that the code in Source 4.3 pulls the location information from the bfile_ graphics table and then uses the DBMS_LOB package procedures to load the BLOB data into internal storage in the internal_graphics table that we created in the BLOB table example. The anonymous PL/SQL block also uses a table called dual_lob, which must be created; it consists simply of a single row, with a null BLOB, CLOB, and BFILE as its attributes:

```
SQL> desc dual_lob
 Name                              Null?    Type
 ------------------------------   -------   ----------------
 X                                          BLOB
 Y                                          BINARY FILE LOB
 Z                                          CLOB
```

Before LOB datatypes can be utilized in PL/SQL, they must be initialized to a NULL value, which is where this table is used.

Creation of Partitioned Tables: An Example

A partitioned table has to be a straight relational table in Oracle8; in Oracle8*i* and in Oracloe9*i*, though this restriction is removed, you must be careful to allow for all LOB or nested storage to be carried through to all partition storage areas. A partitioned table is used to split up a table's data into separate physical and logical areas. This allows for breaking up a large table into more manageable pieces and for the Oracle8 kernel to more optimally retrieve values.

Let's look at a short example. Assume we have a sales entity that will store results from sales for the past 12 months. This type of table is a logical candidate for partitioning because:

- Its values have a clear separator (months).
- It has a sliding range (the last year).
- We usually access this type of date by sections (months, quarters, years).

The DDL for this type of table would look like this:

```
CREATE TABLE sales (
acct_no                 NUMBER(5),
sales_person            VARCHAR2(32),
sales_month             NUMBER(2),
amount_of_sale          NUMBER(9,2),
po_number               VARCHAR2(10))
PARTITION BY RANGE (sales_month)
    PARTITION sales_mon_1 VALUES LESS THAN (2),
    PARTITION sales_mon_2 VALUES LESS THAN (3),
    PARTITION sales_mon_3 VALUES LESS THAN (4),
        ...
    PARTITION sales_mon_12 VALUES LESS THAN (13),
    PARTITION sales_bad_mon VALUES LESS THAN (MAXVALUE));
```

Here we created the sales table with 13 partitions, one for each month plus an extra to hold improperly entered months (values >12). Always specify a last partition to hold MAXVALUE values for your partition values.

Using Subpartitioning

New to Oracle8*i* was the concept of subpartitioning. Subpartitioning allows a table partition to be further subdivided to allow for better spread of large tables. In the next example, we create a table for tracking the storage of data items stored by various departments. We partition by storage date on a quarterly basis and do a further storage subpartition on data_item. The normal activity quarters have four partitions; the slowest has two, and the busiest has eight.

```
CREATE TABLE test5 (data_item INTEGER, length_of_item INTEGER,
                    storage_type VARCHAR(30),
                    owning_dept NUMBER, storage_date DATE)
    PARTITION BY RANGE (storage_date)
    SUBPARTITION BY HASH(data_item)
    SUBPARTITIONS 4
```

```
   STORE IN (data_tbs1, data_tbs2,
            data_tbs3, data_tbs4)
   (PARTITION q1_1999
      VALUES LESS THAN (TO_DATE('01-apr-1999', 'dd-mon-yyyy')),
    PARTITION q2_1999
      VALUES LESS THAN (TO_DATE('01-jul-1999', 'dd-mon-yyyy')),
    PARTITION q3_1999
      VALUES LESS THAN (TO_DATE('01-oct-1999', 'dd-mon-yyyy'))
      (SUBPARTITION q3_1999_s1 TABLESPACE data_tbs1,
       SUBPARTITION q3_1999_s2 TABLESPACE data_tbs2),
    PARTITION q4_1999
      VALUES LESS THAN (TO_DATE('01-jan-2000', 'dd-mon-yyyy'))
      SUBPARTITIONS 8
      STORE IN (q4_tbs1, q4_tbs2, q4_tbs3, q4_tbs4,
               q4_tbs5, q4_tbs6, q4_tbs7, q4_tbs8),
    PARTITION q1_2000
      VALUES LESS THAN (TO_DATE('01-apr-2000', 'dd-mon-yyyy'))):
 /
```

The items to notice in this code example are that the partition-level commands override the default subpartitioning commands; thus, partition Q3_1999 only gets two subpartitions instead of the default of four, and partition Q4_1999 gets eight. The main partitions are divided based on date logic, while the subpartitions use a hash value, calculated from a VARCHAR2 value. The subpartitioning is done in round-robin fashion, depending on the hash value that was calculated filling the subpartitions equally.

Note that no storage parameters were specified in the example. I created the tablespaces such that the default storage for the tablespaces matched what I needed for the subpartitions. This made the example code easier to write and to visualize the process involved.

Using List Partitioning

List partitioning, new in Oracle9*i*, allows the DBA or designer to place rows into specific partitions based on the value of a particular column; for example:

```
CREATE TABLE world_distributors
   ( distributor_id          NUMBER(6)
   , manager_first_name      VARCHAR2(20)
   , manager_last_name       VARCHAR2(20)
   , office_address          OFFICE_ADDRESS_TYP
   , nls_territory           VARCHAR2(30)
   , office_email            VARCHAR2(30))
   PARTITION BY LIST (nls_territory) (
   PARTITION asia VALUES ('CHINA', 'THAILAND', 'CAMBODIA'),
   PARTITION europe VALUES ('ENGLAND', 'GERMANY', 'ITALY', 'FRANCE'),
   PARTITION north_am VALUES ('UNITED STATES', 'CANADA', 'MEXICO'),
   PARTITION mid_am VALUES ('PANAMA', 'HONDURUS'),
   PARTITION south_am VALUES ('COLUMBIA', 'CHILE', 'BOLIVIA'),
   PARTITION east VALUES ('INDIA', 'PAKISTAN'));
```

List partitioning provides expanded capabilities over RANGE, HASH, or combination partitioning schemes, and can be used in combination with HASH to further spread IO across disk assets. There are, however, a number of restrictions on list partitioning:

- You can specify only one partitioning key in the column list, and it cannot be a LOB column.
- If the partitioning key is an object type column, you can partition on only one attribute of the column type.
- Each partition value in the VALUES clause must be unique among all partitions of the table.
- You cannot list partition an index-organized table.
- The string comprising the list of values for each partition can be up to 4K bytes. The total number of partition values for all partitions cannot exceed (64K-1).
- The MAXVALUE keyword is not applicable to list partitions and cannot be specified.

Using Oracle Global Temporary Tables

The capability of temporary tables was a new feature of Oracle8*i*. A GLOBAL TEMPORARY table is one whose definition is visible to all sessions, but whose data is visible only to the user who is currently using the definition. In addition, a temporary table can have session-specific or transaction-specific data, depending on how the ON COMMIT clause is used in the table's definition. The temporary table doesn't go away when the session or sessions are finished with it; however, the data in the table is removed. GLOBAL TEMPORARY tables are created in the user's TEMPORARY tablespace by default. Listing 4.4 is an example of the creation of both a preserved and deleted temporary table.

Listing 4.4   Example of the creation of a temporary table.

```
SQL>    CREATE GLOBAL TEMPORARY TABLE test6 (
  2        starttestdate DATE,
  3        endtestdate DATE,
  4        results NUMBER)
  5* ON COMMIT PRESERVE ROWS
SQL> /

Table created.

SQL> desc test6
 Name                                      Null?    Type
 ----------------------------------------- -------- --------
 STARTTESTDATE                                      DATE
 ENDTESTDATE                                        DATE
 RESULTS                                            NUMBER
```

```
SQL> CREATE GLOBAL TEMPORARY TABLE test7 (
  2      starttestdate DATE,
  3      endtestdate DATE,
  4      results NUMBER)
  5  ON COMMIT DELETE ROWS
  6  /

Table created.

SQL> desc test7
 Name                              Null?    Type
 ------------------------------    -----    --------
 STARTTESTDATE                              DATE
 ENDTESTDATE                                DATE
 RESULTS                                    NUMBER


SQL> insert into test6 values (sysdate, sysdate+1, 100);

1 row created.

SQL> commit;

Commit complete.

SQL> insert into test7 values (sysdate, sysdate+1, 100);

1 row created.

SQL> select * from test7;

STARTTEST ENDTESTDA    RESULTS
---------------------------------------------
29-MAR-99 30-MAR-99        100

SQL> commit;

Commit complete.

SQL> select * from test6;

STARTTEST ENDTESTDA    RESULTS
---------------------------------------------
29-MAR-99 30-MAR-99        100

SQL> select * from test7;

no rows selected

SQL>
```

Pay particular attention here to these specific items in Listing 4.4: First, notice that with the PRESERVE option, the data is kept after a commit; with the DELETE option, the data is removed from the table when a COMMIT occurs. Even with the GLOBAL option set and select permission granted to public on the temporary table, I couldn't see the data in the table from another session; however, I could perform a describe of the table and insert my own values into it, which then the owner of the temporary table couldn't see.

Creation of an Index-Only Table

Index-only tables have been around since Oracle8. If neither the HASH or INDEX ORGANIZED options are used with the CREATE TABLE command, then a table is created as a standard hash table. If the INDEX ORGANIZED option is specified, the table is created as a B-tree-organized table identical to a standard Oracle index created on similar columns. Index-organized tables do not have rowids.

Index-organized tables have the option of allowing overflow storage of values that exceed optimal index row size, as well as allowing compression to be used to reduce storage requirements. Overflow parameters can include columns and the percent threshold value to begin overflow. An index-organized table must have a primary key. Index-organized tables are best suited for use with queries based on primary key values. Index-organized tables can be partitioned in Oracle8*i* and in Oracle9*i* as long as they do not contain LOB or nested table types. The PCTHRESHOLD value specifies the amount of space reserved in an index block for row data. If the row data length exceeds this value, then the row(s) are stored in the area specified by the OVERFLOW clause. If no overflow clause is specified, rows that are too long are rejected. The INCLUDING COLUMN clause allows you to specify at which column to break the record if an overflow occurs. For example:

```
CREATE TABLE test8
  ( doc_code CHAR(5),
    doc_type INTEGER,
    doc_desc VARCHAR(512),
        CONSTRAINT pk_docindex PRIMARY KEY (doc_code,doc_type) )
  ORGANIZATION INDEX TABLESPACE data_tbs1
  PCTTHRESHOLD 20 INCLUDING doc_type
  OVERFLOW TABLESPACE data_tbs2
/
```

In this example, the IOT test8 has three columns: the first two make up the key value, the third column in test8 is a description column containing variable-length text. The PCTHRESHOLD is set at 20, and if the threshold is reached, the overflow goes into an overflow storage in the data_tbs2 tablespace with any values of doc_desc that won't fit in the index block. Note that you will obtain the best performance from IOTs when the complete value is stored in the IOT structure; otherwise, you end up with an index and table lookup as you would with a standard index-table setup.

Using External Tables in Oracle9*i*

Oracle9*i* has added the capability to use external tables as sources for data in an Oracle database. The data will still reside in the external tables but will be accessible to users from inside the database. The general format for accomplishing this connection between an external data table and the database is:

```
CREATE TABLE [schema.]table_name
[relational_properties]
ORGANIZATION EXTERNAL external_table_clause;
```

where relational_properties are:

```
( column datatype constraint list)
[table constraints]
[logging clauses]
```

and external_table_clause is:

```
([TYPE external_driver_type] external_data_properties) [REJECT LIMIT
n|UNLIMITED]
external_data_properties are:
DEFAULT DIRECTORY directory
[ACCESS PARAMETERS (opaque_format_spec)| USING CLOB subquery]
LOCATION ([directory:]'location specifier')
```

> **TYPE. TYPE access_driver-type.** Indicates the access driver of the external table. The access driver is the API that interprets the external data for the database. If you do not specify TYPE, Oracle uses the default access driver, ORACLE_LOADER.
>
> **DEFAULT DIRECTORY.** Lets you specify one or more default directory objects corresponding to directories on the filesystem where the external data sources may reside. Default directories can also be used by the access driver to store auxiliary files such as error logs. Multiple default directories are permitted to facilitate load balancing on multiple disk drives.
>
> **ACCESS PARAMETERS.** (Optional) Lets you assign values to the parameters of the specific access driver for this external table.
>
> **opaque_format_spec.** Lets you list the parameters and their values.
>
> **USING CLOB subquery.** Lets you derive the parameters and their values through a subquery. The subquery cannot contain any set operators or an ORDER BY clause. It must return one row containing a single item of datatype CLOB. Whether you specify the parameters in an opaque_format_spec or derive them using a subquery, Oracle does not interpret anything in this clause. It is up to the access driver to interpret this information in the context of the external data.

LOCATION. Lets you specify one external locator for each external data source. Usually the location_identifier is a file, but it need not be. Oracle does not interpret this clause. It is up to the access driver to interpret this information in the context of the external data.

REJECT LIMIT. Lets you specify how many conversion errors can occur during a query of the external data before an Oracle error is returned and the query is aborted. The default value is 0.

Use the external table clause to create an external table, which is a read-only table whose metadata is stored in the database but whose data in stored outside database. Among other capabilities, external tables let you query data without first loading it into the database.

Because external tables have no data in the database, you define them with a small subset of the clauses normally available when creating tables.

- Within the relational_properties clause, you can specify only column datatype and column_constraint. Further, the only constraints valid for an external table are NULL, NOT NULL, and CHECK constraints.
- Within the table_properties clause, you can specify only the parallel_clause and the enable-disable clause.
- The parallel_clause lets you parallelize subsequent queries on the external data.
- The enable-disable clause lets you either enable or disable a NULL, NOT NULL, or CHECK constraint. You can specify only ENABLE or DISABLE, and CONSTRAINT constraint_name. No other parts of this clause are permitted.

As for list partitioning, there are restrictions associated with using external tables:

- No other clauses are permitted in the same CREATE TABLE statement if you specify the external_table_clause.
- An external table cannot be a temporary table.
- An external table cannot be indexed
- An external table cannot be analyzed

Creation of an External Table: An Example I have a listing of all of the SQL scripts I use to manage Oracle databases. This listing was generated on a Linux box using the command: ls –l>file.dat. The resulting listing file has been cleaned up using system editors to look like this:

```
'-rw-r--r--';1;oracle;dba;626;Apr 17 18:25;accept.sql;
'-rw-r--r--';1;oracle;dba;11103;Apr 17 18:25;access.sql;
'-rw-r--r--';1;oracle;dba;3295;Apr 18 01:19;act_size8.sql;
'-rw-r--r--';1;oracle;dba;918;Apr 17 18:25;active_cursors.sql;
'-rw-r--r--';1;oracle;dba;63;Aug 21 12:35;afiedt.buf;
'-rw-r--r--';1;oracle;dba;273;Apr 17 18:25;alter_resource.sql;
'-rw-r--r--';1;oracle;dba;5265;Apr 17 18:25;alter_views.sql;
'-rw-r--r--';1;oracle;dba;401;Apr 17 18:25;anal_tab.sql;
```

```
'-rw-r--r--';1;oracle;dba;374;Apr 17 18:25;analyze_all.sql;
'-rw-r--r--';1;oracle;dba;244;Apr 17 18:25;analz_sch.sql;
'-rw-r--r--';1;oracle;dba;989;Apr 17 19:25;auto_chn.sql;
'-rw-r--r--';1;oracle;dba;1861;Apr 17 18:25;auto_defrag.sql;
'-rw-r--r--';1;oracle;dba;167;Apr 17 18:25;awt.sql;
'-rw-r--r--';1;oracle;dba;481;Apr 18 01:20;backup.sql;
'-rw-r--r--';1;oracle;dba;405;Apr 18 01:20;block_usage.sql;
'-rw-r--r--';1;oracle;dba;960;Apr 18 01:21;blockers.sql;
'-rw-r--r--';1;oracle;dba;940;Apr 17 18:25;blockers2.sql;
'-rw-r--r--';1;oracle;dba;1002;Apr 18 01:21;bound2.sql;
'-rw-r--r--';1;oracle;dba;1299;Apr 18 01:22;bound_ob.sql;
'-rw-r--r--';1;oracle;dba;1742;Apr 17 18:25;brown.sql;
```

To match this external file, I created a CREATE TABLE command that matches up the columns in the internal representation with the external file using standard SQLLOADER controlfile syntax:

```
CREATE DIRECTORY sql_dir as '/home/oracle/sql_scripts';
CREATE TABLE sql_scripts (permissions VARCHAR2(20),
filetype NUMBER(3),owner VARCHAR2(20),
group_name VARCHAR2(20), size_in_bytes NUMBER,
date_edited DATE , script_name VARCHAR2(64))
ORGANIZATION EXTERNAL
(TYPE ORACLE_LOADER
DEFAULT DIRECTORY sql_dir
ACCESS PARAMETERS
(FIELDS TERMINATED BY ';' OPTIONALLY ENCLOSED BY "'"
(permissions, filetype,owner,group_name,size_in_bytes,
date_edited DATE(19) "Mon dd 2001 hh24:mi",
script_name))
LOCATION ('file.dat'))
/
```

Here is what it actually looked like during the creation:

```
SQL> get external_table
  1  CREATE TABLE sql_scripts (permissions VARCHAR2(20),
  2  filetype NUMBER(3),owner VARCHAR2(20),
  3  group_name varchar2(20), size_in_bytes number,
  4  date_edited date , script_name VARCHAR2(64))
  5   ORGANIZATION EXTERNAL
  6  (TYPE ORACLE_LOADER
  7  DEFAULT DIRECTORY sql_dir
  8  ACCESS PARAMETERS
  9  (FIELDS TERMINATED BY ';' OPTIONALLY ENCLOSED BY "'"
 10 (permissions, filetype,owner,group_name,size_in_bytes,
 11 date_edited DATE(19) "Mon dd 2001 hh24:mi",
 12 script_name))
 13* LOCATION ('file.dat'))
SQL> /

Table created.
```

```
Elapsed: 00:00:00.37
SQL> DESC sql_scripts
 Name                                   Null?    Type
 ------------------------------------   -------  ----------------
 PERMISSIONS                                     VARCHAR2(20)
 FILETYPE                                        NUMBER(3)
 OWNER                                           VARCHAR2(20)
 GROUP_NAME                                      VARCHAR2(20)
 SIZE_IN_BYTES                                   NUMBER
 DATE_EDITED                                     DATE
 SCRIPT_NAME                                     VARCHAR2(64)

SQL> SET AUTOTRACE ON EXPLAIN
SQL> SET TIMING ON
SQL> SELECT COUNT(*) FROM sql_scripts;

  COUNT(*)
-------------------
       441

Elapsed: 00:00:00.38

Execution Plan
----------------------------------------------------------
   0      SELECT STATEMENT Optimizer=CHOOSE
   1    0   SORT (AGGREGATE)
   2    1     EXTERNAL TABLE ACCESS (FULL) OF 'SQL_SCRIPTS'
```

I then used multiple Linux copy (cp) commands to make three additional copies of the file.dat file, and then used the Linux concatenation (cat) command to combine them with the original to make the file four times larger. Then I renamed the larger file using the Linux move (mv) command to the name of the original file. Without changing a thing inside Oracle, I was able to reselect from the new external table:

```
SQL> /

  COUNT(*)
-------------------
      1764

Elapsed: 00:00:00.37

Execution Plan
----------------------------------------------------------
   0      SELECT STATEMENT Optimizer=CHOOSE
   1    0   SORT (AGGREGATE)
   2    1     EXTERNAL TABLE ACCESS (FULL) OF 'SQL_SCRIPTS'
```

To get an idea of the performance of these external tables I kept quadrupling the size of the external table until I reached 1,806,336 rows. The chart in Figure 4.1 shows the

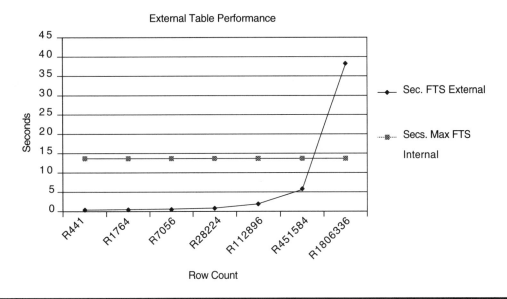

FIGURE 4.1   FTS performance for an external table.

results from the full table scans of the external table compared against a full table scan of an identical internal table created from a SELECT * FROM sql_tables command of the largest external table. The actual data is shown in Table 4.1.

You must remember that external tables cannot be analyzed nor indexed, so the performance will always be for a full table scan. In addition, if you have a syntax error in your SQLLOADER command file section, it will not show itself until an attempt is made to access that row. In my initial specification, I had an error in the date conversion;

TABLE 4.1   FTS Results for External Table in Figure 4.1

Size in Rows	Time for FTS	Internal FTS
441	0.38	
1764	0.39	
7056	0.46	
28224	0.78	
112896	1.86	
451584	5.77	
1806336	38.26	13.68

though I was able to select columns without the dates, and do row counts and value counts, as soon as I did anything that attempted to access the date_edited column, I would get an OCI error. This indicates that you should always verify that you can access all rows before turning over an external table for general use. Also note that, by default, unless you specify no log be generated, a log identical to a SQLPLOADER log will be generated and inserted into each time a user accesses the external table.

> **N**OTE   If you have a multiple file external file, you can use parallel access to speed performance. There is an excellent example of this type of external table access in the Oracle SQL manual, in the CREATE TABLE section.

External tables can also be used to export data out of Oracle. The following example uses the EMP and DEPT tables in the SCOTT schema to show how all employees working in the MARKETING and ENGINEERING departments can be exported in parallel using the default degree of parallelism.

```
#
# Export employees working in the departments 'MARKETING' and
# 'ENGINEERING'
#
CREATE TABLE emp_ext
    (empno NUMBER, ename VARCHAR2(100), ...)
    ORGANIZATION EXTERNAL
    (
        TYPE ORACLE_INTERNAL
        DEFAULT DIRECTORY private2
        LOCATION (export_dir:'/emp_data/emp1.exp',
                  export_dir:'/emp_data/emp2.exp')
    ...)
    PARALLEL
    AS SELECT e.*, d.dname
       FROM emp e, dept d
       WHERE e.deptno = d.deptno
         AND  d.dname IN ('MARKETING', 'ENGINEERING');
```

At this point, you will have an external table that contains all of the records corresponding to the MARKETING and ENGINEERING departments and that can be used by other programs if desired. Once changes are made to the data, it can be reimported to the external table specification and then moved easily from there back into its parent tables. Notice that the TYPE becomes ORACLE_INTERNAL, rather than ORACLE_ LOADER, and that no conversion specification is required.

```
#
# Re-import the employees that are working in the 'ENGINEERING' department
#
```

```
CREATE TABLE emp_import
    PARALLEL
    AS SELECT *
        FROM emp_ext
        WHERE dname = 'ENGINEERING';
```

This example illustrates how the external table feature can help to export (and import) a selective set of records.

Note: As of Oracle9i 9.0.1.1, this feature has *not* been implemented.

Sizing an Oracle Nonclustered Table

The procedures in this section describe how to estimate the total number of data blocks necessary to hold data inserted to a nonclustered table. No allowance is made for changes to PCTFREE or PCTUSED due to insert, delete, or update activity. On the Wiley Web site I have provided Oracle9i relational table and index-sizing spreadsheets.

TIP This sizing example is a best-case scenario, when users insert rows without performing deletes or updates.

Typically, the space required to store a set of rows that undergo updates, deletes, and inserts will exceed this calculated value. The actual space required for complex workloads is best determined by analysis of an existing table and then scaled by the projected number of future rows in the production table. In general, increasing amounts of concurrent activity on the same data block result in additional overhead (for transaction records), so it is important to take into account such activity when scaling empirical results.

Calculating space required by nonclustered tables is a five-step process:

1. Calculate the total block header size.
2. Calculate the available data space per data block.
3. Calculate the space used per row.
4. Calculate the total number of rows that will fit in a data block.
5. With the rows/block data, calculate the total number of data blocks and convert to kilo- or megabytes.

Let's take a more detailed look at the steps.

Step 1: Calculate the Total Block Header Size The space required by the data block header is the result of the following formula:

```
Space after headers (hsize) =
DB_BLOCK_SIZE - KCBH - UB4 - KTBBH - ((INITRANS - 1) * KTBIT) - KDBH
```

where:

> **DB_BLOCK_ SIZE.** The database blocksize with which the database was created. It can be viewed in the V$PARAMETER view by selecting:

```
SELECT value FROM v$parameter WHERE name = 'db_block_size';
```

> **KCBH, UB4, KTBBH, KTBIT, KDBH.** Constants whose sizes you can obtain by selecting from entries in the V$TYPE_SIZE view.
>
> **KCBH.** The block common header; on NT, with a 4-KB blocksize, this is 20.
>
> **UB4.** Short for "either byte 4"; on NT with a 4-KB blocksize, this is 4.
>
> **KTBBH.** The transaction fixed-header length; on NT with a 4-KB blocksize, this is 48.
>
> **KTBIT.** The transaction variable header; on NT with a 4-KB blocksize, this is 24.
>
> **KDBH.** The data header; on NT with a 4-KB blocksize, this is 14.
>
> **INITRANS.** The initial number of transaction entries allocated to the table.

So, for an NT 4.0 platform with a 4-KB blocksize and an INITRANS value of 5, the calculation would be:

```
DB_BLOCK_SIZE - KCBH - UB4 - KTBBH - ((INITRANS - 1) * KTBIT) - KDBH
hsize = 4192 - 20 - 4 - 48 - ((5 - 1)*24) - 14 =
4192 - 182 = 4010 bytes
```

Step 2: Calculate the Available Data Space per Data Block The space reserved in each data block for data, as specified by PCTFREE, is calculated as follows:

```
available data space (availspace) =
CEIL(hsize * (1 - PCTFREE/100 )) - KDBT
```

where:

> **CEIL.** The round fractional result to the next highest integer.
>
> **PCTFREE.** The percentage of space reserved for updates in the table.
>
> **KDBT.** A constant corresponding to the Table Directory Entry size, which you can obtain by selecting the entry from the V$TYPE_SIZE view. For an NT 4.0 platform with a 4-KB blocksize, this is 4 KB.

TIP If you are unable to locate the value of KDBT, use the value of UB4 instead.

So, to carry on our example, assuming a PCTFREE of 20 for our table:

```
CEIL(hsize * (1 - PCTFREE/100 )) - KDBT
CEIL(4010* (1 - 20/100)) - 4 = CEIL((4010*.8) - 4 ) = CEIL(3208 - 4) = 3204
```

Step 3: Calculate the Space Used per Row   Calculating the amount of space used per row is a multistep task. First, you must calculate the column size, including byte lengths:

```
Column size including byte length =
column size + (1, if column size < 250, else 3)
```

I suggest using estimated averages for all variable-length fields, such as numeric, VARCHAR2, and raw. Remember that NUMBER datatypes are stored at a two-to-one ratio in the database (e.g., a NUMBER(30) takes up 15 bytes of storage if each place is filled). The maximum for a NUMBER is 21 bytes. The size for a DATE is 7 bytes. Rowid takes 10 bytes for the extended and 6 bytes for the restricted type of rowid. CHAR always takes its full specified length; VARCHAR2, RAW, and other variable-length fields will use only the space they actually take up.

TIP   You can also determine column size empirically, by selecting avg(vsize(colname)) for each column in the table.

For example, I have a table TEST with a single VARCHAR2(50) column that has eight rows of various lengths. The return from the select SELECT AVG(VSIZE (TEST1)) FROM TEST; is:

```
AVG(VSIZE(TEST1))
---------------------
                29
```

The table also has a number column, TEST2:

```
AVG(VSIZE(TEST2))
---------------------
                 7
```

Then, calculate the row size:

```
Rowsize =
row header (3 * UB1) + sum of column sizes including length bytes
UB1 is 'UNSIGNED BYTE 1' and is 1 on NT 4.0 with a 4 KB block size.
Rowsize =
(3*1) + (8 + 30) = 41
```

Of course, if you have a sample table, the quickest way to get average row size is to analyze it and then select average row size from USER_TABLES:

```
SQL> analyze table test1 compute statistics;
Table analyzed.
SQL> select avg_row_len from user_tables where table_name='TEST1';

AVG_ROW_LEN
-----------
         41
```

Finally, you can calculate the space used per row:

```
Space used per row (rowspace) =
MIN(UB1 * 3 + UB4 + SB2, rowsize) + SB2
```

where:

> **UB1, UB4, SB2.** Constants whose size can be obtained by selecting entries from the V$TYPE_SIZE view.
>
> **UB1.** "Unsigned byte 1," set to 1 for NT 4.0 with a 4-KB blocksize.
>
> **UB4.** "Unsigned byte 4," set to 4 for NT 4.0 with a 4-KB blocksize.
>
> **SB2.** "Signed byte 2," set to 2 for NT 4.0 with a 4-KB blocksize.

This becomes:

```
MIN((1*3) + 4 + 2, 41) + 2, or, 41 + 2 = 43.
```

To determine MIN, take the lesser of either UBI *3 + UB4 + SB2 or the calculated rowsize value.

If the space per row exceeds the available space per data block, but is less than the available space per data block without any space reserved for updates (for example, available space with PCTFREE=0), each row will be stored in its own block.

When the space per row exceeds the available space per data block without any space reserved for updates, rows inserted into the table will be chained into two or more pieces; hence, the storage overhead will be higher.

Step 4: Calculate the Total Number of Rows That Will Fit in a Data Block   You can calculate the total number of rows that will fit into a data block using the following equation:

```
Number of rows in block =
FLOOR(availspace / rowspace)
```

where FLOOR is the fractional result rounded to the next-lowest integer.

For our example, this becomes:

```
FLOOR(3204/43) = 74
```

Step 5: Calculate the Total Blocks Required The next step is to calculate the total blocks required, which involves finding the ratio of total rows divided by the maximum number of rows able to be stored per block. Once we have the number of total blocks, it is a simple matter to multiply this times the blocksize and make the appropriate conversions to get to megabytes or gigabytes as required.

```
Total blocks =
(total table rows) / (rows per block)
Total kilobytes = CEIL((total blocks * block size) / 1024)
Total megabytes =
CEIL((total blocks * block size) / 1048576)      -- (1024^2)
```

For our example, we estimate we will have 42,000 rows in this table over the next year. So, the calculation becomes:

```
((42000/74)*4192)/1024 = 2324k or 3m (rounding up)
```

Of course, you can also use the table-sizing spreadsheet I have provided on the Wiley Web site. A screenshot of this spreadsheet is shown in Figure 4.2.

Table Alteration

Face it, no one designs perfect applications. This means we sometimes have to change things. For tables, this means adding, changing, or dropping columns; adding constraints; or even deleting all of the rows from the table. Let's look at how to accomplish these table changes using the functions of the Oracle8 ALTER TABLE command, which are to:

- Add a column.
- Add an integrity constraint.
- Add integrity constraints to object-type columns.
- Add or modify index-only table characteristics.
- Add or modify LOB columns.
- Add or modify object type, nested table type, or varray type column for a table.
- Add, modify, split, move, drop, or truncate table partitions.
- Add, modify, split, move, drop, or truncate table subpartitions.
- Allow or disallow writes to a table.
- Change the rows per block of storage for a table.
- Drop a column.
- Enable, disable, or drop an integrity constraint or trigger.

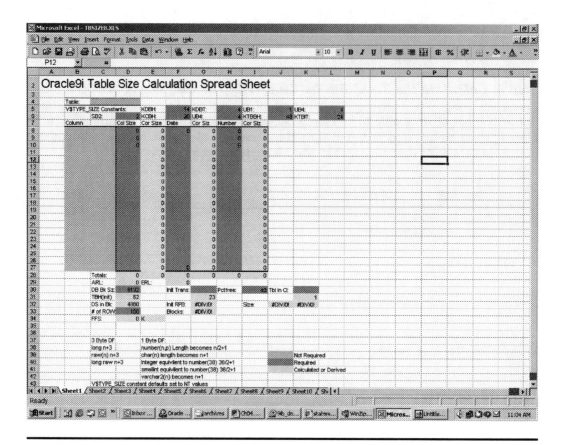

FIGURE 4.2 Screenshot of the table-sizing spreadsheet.

- Explicitly allocate an extent.
- Explicitly deallocate the unused space of a table.
- Modification of the degree of parallelism for a table.
- Modify the LOGGING/NOLOGGING attributes.
- Modify the real storage attributes of a nonpartitioned table or the default attributes of a partitioned table.
- Modify the storage characteristics or other parameters.
- Physically move a table.
- Redefine a column (datatype, size, default value).
- Rename a table or a table partition.

In order to use the ALTER TABLE command in Oracle, the following must be true:

- The table must be in your own schema, you must have ALTER privilege on the table, or you must have ALTER ANY TABLE system privilege.

- To use an object type in a column definition when modifying a table, either that object must belong to the same schema as the table being altered or you must have either the EXECUTE ANY TYPE system or the EXECUTE schema object privilege for the object type.
- If you are using Trusted Oracle in DBMS MAC mode, your DBMS label must match the table's creation label or you must satisfy one of the following criteria:
   a. If the table's creation label is higher than your DBMS label, you must have READUP and WRITEUP system privileges.
   b. If the table's creation label is lower than your DBMS label, you must have the WRITEDOWN system privilege.
   c. If the table's creation label and your DBMS label are not comparable, you must have READUP, WRITEUP, and WRITEDOWN system privileges.

The syntax of the ALTER TABLE command for Oracle is located in the SQL manual for on the Orcle technet Web site.

Adding Columns   If you use the ADD clause to add a new column to the table, the initial value of each row for the new column is null. You can add a column with a NOT NULL constraint only to a table that contains no rows.

If you create a view with a query that uses the asterisk (*) in the select list to select all columns from the base table, and you subsequently add columns to the base table, Oracle will not automatically add the new column to the view. To add the new column to the view, you can re-create the view using the CREATE VIEW command with the OR REPLACE option.

Operations performed by the ALTER TABLE command can cause Oracle to invalidate procedures and stored functions that access the table.

Modifying Column Definitions   You can use the MODIFY clause to change any of the following parts of a column definition:

- Datatype
- Size
- Default value
- NOT NULL column constraint

The MODIFY clause need only specify the column name and the modified part of the definition, not the entire column definition.

Datatypes and Sizes   You can change:

- A CHAR column to VARCHAR2 (or VARCHAR).
- A VARCHAR2 (or VARCHAR) to CHAR, but only if the column contains nulls in all rows or if you do not attempt to change the column size.

- Any column's datatype, or decrease any column's size, if all rows for the column contain nulls. You can always increase the size of a character or raw column or the precision of a numeric column.

Default Values   A change to a column's default value affects only those rows subsequently inserted to the table. Such a change does not alter default values previously inserted.

Integrity Constraints   The only type of integrity constraint that you can add to an existing column using the MODIFY clause with the column constraint syntax is a NOT NULL constraint. However, you can define other types of integrity constraints (UNIQUE, PRIMARY KEY, referential integrity, and CHECK constraints) on existing columns using the ADD clause and the table constraint syntax.

You can define a NOT NULL constraint on an existing column only if the column contains no nulls.

Allocation of Extents   The following statement allocates an extent of 5 KB for the emp table, and makes it available to instance 4:

```
ALTER TABLE emp
   ALLOCATE EXTENT (SIZE 5K INSTANCE 4);
```

Because this command omits the DATAFILE parameter, Oracle allocates the extent in one of the datafiles belonging to the tablespace containing the table.

LOB Columns   You can add a LOB column to a table, modify a LOB index, or modify the LOB index storage characteristics.

The following statement adds CLOB column REFERENCES to the emp table:

```
ALTER TABLE emp ADD (references CLOB)
   LOB (references) STORE AS references_seg (TABLESPACE references_ts);
```

To modify the LOB column RESUME to use caching, enter the following statement:

```
ALTER TABLE emp MODIFY LOB (references) (CACHE);
```

Nested Table Columns   You can add a nested table type column to a table by specifying a nested table storage clause for each column added. The following example adds the nested table column ABILITIES to the emp table:

```
ALTER TABLE emp ADD (abilities ability_list)
   NESTED TABLE abilities STORE AS abilitiesv8;
```

You can also modify a nested table's storage characteristics, using the name of the storage table specified in the nested table storage clause to make the modification. You cannot query or perform DML statements on the storage table; you can only use the storage table to modify the nested table column storage characteristics.

The following example creates table CARSERVICE with nested table column CLIENT and storage table CLIENTV8. Nested table CARSERVICE is modified to specify constraints and to modify a column length by altering nested storage table CLIENT_LIST:

```
CREATE TABLE carservice (mech_name VARCHAR2(30),
                         client   client_list);
  NESTED TABLE client STORE AS clientv8;

ALTER TABLE clientv8 ADD UNIQUE (ssn);

ALTER TABLE clientv8 MODIFY (mech_name VARCHAR2(35));
```

The following statement adds a UNIQUE constraint to nested table ABILITY_ LIST:

```
ALTER TABLE ABILITY_LIST ADD UNIQUE (a);
```

Scoped REFs   A REF value is a reference to a row in an object table. A table can have top-level REF columns or REF attributes embedded within an object column. In general, if a table has a REF column, each REF value in the column could reference a row in a different object table. A SCOPE clause restricts the scope of references to a single table. In the real world, I would say 99 percent of applications would use scoped REFs; I can envision few applications where you would want to access multiple tables from the same column of a single table.

Use the ALTER TABLE command to add new REF columns or to add REF clauses to existing REF columns. You can modify any table, including named inner nested tables (storage tables). If a REF column is created WITH ROWID or with a scope table, you cannot modify the column to drop these options. However, if a table is created without any REF clauses, you can add them later with an ALTER TABLE statement.

TIP   You can add a scope clause only to existing REF columns of a table if the table is empty. The scope_table_name must be in your own schema, or you must have SELECT privilege on the table or the SELECT ANY TABLE system privilege. This privilege is only needed while altering the table with the REF column.

In the following example, an object type dept_t has been previously defined. Now assume that table emp is created as follows:

```
CREATE TABLE emp
  (name   VARCHAR(100),
```

```
   salary      NUMBER,
   dept   REF dept_t) AS OBJECT;
An object table DEPARTMENTS is created as:
CREATE TABLE departments OF dept_t AS OBJECT;
```

If the DEPARTMENTS table contains all possible departments, the dept column in emp can only refer to rows in the DEPARTMENTS table. This can be expressed as a scope clause on the dept column as follows:

```
ALTER TABLE emp
    ADD (SCOPE FOR (dept) IS departments);
```

Note that the ALTER TABLE statement here will succeed only if the emp table is empty.

Modifying Table Partitions You can modify a table or table partition in any of the ways described in the subsections following. You cannot combine partition operations with other partition operations or with operations on the base table in one ALTER TABLE statement. You cannot move a partition with subpartitions; each subpartition must be individually moved.

Add Partition. Use ALTER TABLE ADD PARTITION to add a partition to the high end of the table (after the last existing partition). If the first element of the partition bound of the high partition is MAXVALUE, you cannot add a partition to the table. You must split the high partition.

You can add a partition to a table even if one or more of the table indexes or index partitions are marked UNUSABLE.

You must use the SPLIT PARTITION clause to add a partition at the beginning or the middle of the table.

The following example adds partition jan99 to tablespace yr99 for table sales:

```
ALTER TABLE sales
   ADD PARTITION jan99 VALUES LESS THAN( '990201' )
   TABLESPACE yr99;
```

Drop Partition. ALTER TABLE DROP PARTITION drops a partition and its data. If you want to drop a partition but keep its data in the table, you must merge the partition into one of the adjacent partitions.

If you drop a partition and later insert a row that would have belonged to the dropped partition, the row will be stored in the next higher partition. However, if you drop the highest partition, the insert will fail because the range of values represented by the dropped partition is no longer valid for the table.

This statement also drops the corresponding partition in each local index defined on table. The index partitions are dropped even if they are marked as unusable.

If there are global indexes defined on the table, and the partition you want to drop is not empty, dropping the partition marks all the global, nonpartitioned indexes and all the partitions of global partitioned indexes as unusable.

When a table contains only one partition, you cannot drop the partition. You must drop the table.

The following example drops partition jan98:

```
ALTER TABLE sales DROP PARTITION jan98;
```

Exchange Partition.   This form of ALTER TABLE converts a partition to a nonpartitioned table, and a table to a partition, by exchanging their data segments. You must have ALTER TABLE privileges on both tables to perform this operation.

The statistics of the table and partition, including table, column, index statistics, and histograms, are exchanged. The aggregate statistics of the partitioned table are recalculated. The logging attribute of the table and partition is exchanged.

The following example converts partition feb99 to table sales_feb99:

```
ALTER TABLE sales
  EXCHANGE PARTITION feb99 WITH TABLE sales_feb99
   WITHOUT VALIDATION;
```

Modify Partition.   Use the MODIFY PARTITION options of ALTER TABLE to:

- Mark local index partitions corresponding to a table partition as unusable.
- Rebuild all the unusable local index partitions corresponding to a table partition.
- Modify the physical attributes of a table partition.

The following example marks all the local index partitions corresponding to the apr96 partition of the procurements table UNUSABLE:

```
ALTER TABLE procurements MODIFY PARTITION apr99
  UNUSABLE LOCAL INDEXES;
```

The following example rebuilds all the local index partitions that were marked UNUSABLE:

```
ALTER TABLE procurements MODIFY PARTITION jan98
  REBUILD UNUSABLE LOCAL INDEXES;
```

The following example changes MAEXTENTS for partition KANSAS_OFF:

```
ALTER TABLE branch MODIFY PARTITION kansas_off
  STORAGE(MAXEXTENTS 100) LOGGING;
```

Merge Partition.   New in Oracle8*i*, the MERGE capability promised in 8 was fulfilled. The MERGE option for PARTITIONS in the ALTER TABLE command allows two partitions to be merged into one larger partition.

```
ALTER TABLE branch
MERGE PARTITIONS kansas_off,missouri_off
INTO NEW PARTITION midwest_off
STORAGE (INITIAL 1M NEXT 1M MAXEXTENTS 200);
```

Move Partition or Subpartition.   This ALTER TABLE option moves a table partition or subpartition to another segment. MOVE PARTITION always drops the partition's old segment and creates a new segment, even if you do not specify a new tablespace.

If partition_name is not empty, MOVE PARTITION marks all corresponding local index partitions, all global nonpartitioned indexes, and all the partitions of global partitioned indexes as unusable.

ALTER TABLE MOVE PARTITION or SUBPARTITION obtains its parallel attribute from the PARALLEL clause, if specified. If not specified, the default PARALLEL attributes of the table, if any, are used. If neither is specified, it performs the move without using parallelism.

The PARALLEL clause on MOVE PARTITION does not change the default PARALLEL attributes of table.

The following example moves partition station3 to tablespace ts099:

```
ALTER TABLE trains
   MOVE PARTITION station3 TABLESPACE ts099 NOLOGGING;
```

Merge Partition.   While there is no explicit MERGE statement, you can merge a partition using either the DROP PARTITION or EXCHANGE PARTITION clause. You can use either of the following strategies to merge table partitions.

If you have data in partition PART1, and no global indexes or referential integrity constraints on the table PARTS, you can merge table partition PART1 into the next-highest partition, PART2.

To merge partition PART1 into partition PART2:

1. Export the data from PART1.
2. Issue the following statement:

   ```
   ALTER TABLE PARTS DROP PARTITION PART1;
   ```

3. Import the data from step 1 into partition PART2.

TIP   The corresponding local index partitions are also merged.

Here is another way to merge partition PART1 into partition PART2:

1. Exchange partition PART1 of table PARTS with "dummy" table PARTS_DUMMY.
2. Issue the following statement:

   ```
   ALTER TABLE PARTS DROP PARTITION PART1;
   ```

3. Insert as SELECT from the "dummy" tables to move the data from PART1 back into PART2.

Split Partition. The SPLIT PARTITION option divides a partition into two partitions, each with a new segment, new physical attributes, and new initial extents. The segment associated with the old partition is discarded.

This statement also performs a matching split on the corresponding partition in each local index defined on the table. The index partitions are split even if they are marked unusable.

With the exception of the TABLESPACE attribute, the physical attributes of the LOCAL index partition being split are used for both new index partitions. If the parent LOCAL index lacks a default TABLESPACE attribute, new LOCAL index partitions will reside in the same tablespace as the corresponding newly created partitions of the underlying table.

If you do not specify physical attributes (PCTFREE, PCTUSED, INITRANS, MAXTRANS, STORAGE) for the new partitions, the current values of the partition being split are used as the default values for both partitions.

If partition_name is not empty, SPLIT PARTITION marks all affected index partitions as unusable. This includes all global index partitions, as well as the local index partitions that result from the split.

The PARALLEL clause on SPLIT PARTITION does not change the default PARALLEL attributes of table.

The following example splits the old partition station5, thereby creating a new partition for station9:

```
ALTER TABLE trains
  SPLIT PARTITION STATION5 AT ( '50-001' )
  INTO (
    PARTITION station5 TABLESPACE train009 (MINEXTENTS 2),
    PARTITION station9 TABLESPACE train010 )
  PARALLEL ( DEGREE 9 );
```

Truncate Partition or Subpartition. Use TRUNCATE PARTITION to remove all rows from a partition or a subpartition in a table. Freed space is deallocated or reused, depending on whether DROP STORAGE or REUSE STORAGE is specified in the clause.

This statement truncates the corresponding partition or subpartition in each local index defined on the table. The local index partitions are truncated even if they are marked as unusable. The unusable local index partitions are marked valid, resetting the UNUSABLE indicator.

If global indexes are defined on the table, and the partition or subpartition you want to truncate is not empty, truncation marks all the global nonpartitioned indexes and all the partitions of global partitioned indexes as unusable.

If you want to truncate a partition or subpartition that contains data, you must first disable any referential integrity constraints on the table. Alternatively, you can delete the rows and then truncate the partition.

The following example deletes all the data in the part_17 partition and deallocates the freed space:

```
ALTER TABLE shipments
   TRUNCATE PARTITION part_17 DROP STORAGE;
```

Rename.   Use the RENAME option of ALTER TABLE to rename a table or to rename a partition. The following example renames a table:

```
ALTER TABLE emp RENAME TO employee;
```

In the following example, partition EMP3 is renamed:

```
ALTER TABLE employee RENAME PARTITION emp3 TO employee3;
```

Altering a Table's Subpartitions   Partitioning was complex enough; now, with the addition of subpartitioning, including the ability to do a mixed partition (hash and range), a whole new level of complexity is added to the Oracle ALTER commands. This new layer of complexity deals with subpartitions. Let's examine a few ALTER commands for use with Oracle and table subpartitions.

Modify Partition partition_name or Add Subpartition.   This form of the ALTER TABLE command adds a subpartition. In a table where a new subpartition is added, any local indexes involving the subpartition must be rebuilt. To add subpartitions, the table must already be composite-partitioned (i.e., have subpartitions). An example would be to add four biweekly subpartitions to the sales table for each month (assuming a weekly set of subpartitions already exists):

```
ALTER TABLE sales
   MODIFY PARTITION feb99 ADD SUBPARTITION feb99_biweek1
      TABLESPACE feb_subs;
 ALTER TABLE sales
   MODIFY PARTITION feb99 ADD SUBPARTITION feb99_biweek2
      TABLESPACE feb_subs;
ALTER TABLE sales
   MODIFY PARTITION feb99 ADD SUBPARTITION feb99_biweek3
      TABLESPACE feb_subs;
ALTER TABLE sales
   MODIFY PARTITION feb99 ADD SUBPARTITION feb99_biweek4
      TABLESPACE feb_subs;
```

This example creates four additional subpartitions for the feb99 partition of the sales table.

Exchange Partition or Subpartition.   This form of ALTER TABLE converts a partition or subpartition to a nonpartitioned table, and a table to a partition by exchanging their data segments. You must have ALTER TABLE privileges on both tables to perform this operation.

The statistics of the table and partition, including table, column, index statistics, and histograms, are exchanged. The aggregate statistics of the partitioned table are recalculated. The logging attribute of the table and partition is exchanged.

The following example converts subpartition feb99_biweek1 to table sales_feb99_biweek1:

```
ALTER TABLE sales
  EXCHANGE SUBPARTITION feb99_biweek1 WITH TABLE sales_feb99_biweek1
  WITHOUT VALIDATION;
```

Modify Subpartition. Use the MODIFY SUBPARTITION options of ALTER TABLE to:

- Mark local index partitions corresponding to a table subpartition as unusable.
- Rebuild all the unusable local index subpartitions corresponding to a table subpartition.
- Modify the physical attributes of a table subpartition.

The following example marks all the local index subpartitions corresponding to the apr99 partition of the procurements table as UNUSABLE:

```
ALTER TABLE procurements MODIFY SUBPARTITION apr99_biweek1
  UNUSABLE LOCAL INDEXES;
```

The following example rebuilds all the local index partitions that were marked UNUSABLE:

```
ALTER TABLE procurements MODIFY SUBPARTITION apr99_biweek1
  REBUILD UNUSABLE LOCAL INDEXES;
```

The following example changes MAXEXTENTS for subpartition kansas_off_ sub1:

```
ALTER TABLE branch MODIFY SUBPARTITION kansas_off_sub1
  STORAGE(MAXEXTENTS 100) LOGGING;
```

Move Subpartition. This ALTER TABLE option moves a table subpartition to another segment. MOVE PARTITION always drops the subpartition's old segment and creates a new segment, even if you do not specify a new tablespace.

If subpartition_name is not empty, MOVE SUBPARTITION marks all corresponding local index subpartitions, all global nonpartitioned indexes, and all the partitions of global partitioned indexes as unusable.

ALTER TABLE MOVE SUBPARTITION obtains its parallel attribute from the PARALLEL clause, if specified. If not specified, the default PARALLEL attributes of the table, if any, are used. If neither is specified, it performs the move without using parallelism.

The PARALLEL clause on MOVE SUBPARTITION does not change the default PARALLEL attributes of table.

The following example moves subpartition station3_sub1 to tablespace ts098:

```
ALTER TABLE trains
MOVE SUBPARTITION station3_sub1 TABLESPACE ts098 NOLOGGING;
```

Truncate Subpartition.   Use TRUNCATE SUBPARTITION to remove all rows from a subpartition in a table. Freed space is deallocated or reused depending on whether DROP STORAGE or REUSE STORAGE is specified in the clause.

This statement truncates the corresponding partition in each local index defined on the table. The local index partitions are truncated even if they are marked as unusable. The unusable local index partitions are marked valid, resetting the UNUSABLE indicator.

If there are global indexes defined on the table, and the subpartition you want to truncate is not empty, truncating the subpartition marks all the global nonpartitioned indexes and all the subpartitions of global partitioned indexes as unusable.

If you want to truncate a partition that contains data, you must first disable any referential integrity constraints on the table. Alternatively, you can delete the rows and then truncate the subpartition.

The following example deletes all the data in the subpart_17a subpartition and deallocates the freed space:

```
ALTER TABLE shipments
  TRUNCATE SUBPARTITION subpart_17a DROP STORAGE;
```

Rename.   Use the RENAME option of ALTER TABLE to rename a table or to rename a subpartition. In the following example, partition subemp3a is renamed:

```
ALTER TABLE employee
RENAME SUBPARTITION subemp3a TO subemployee3a;
```

Dropping Table Columns   Prior to Oracle8*i*, if you created a table with a column you later found you didn't need, you had to rebuild the entire table to get rid of it. Not so in Oracle8*i* and Oracle9*i*. Finally, after years of users requesting it, Oracle has added the drop column capability to the ALTER TABLE command. The new ALTER TABLE drop column clause has the following options:

```
SET UNUSED [COLUMN column_name]|[(column_name(s))]
   [CASCADE|INVALIDATE CONSTRAINTS]

DROP [COLUMN column_name]|[(column_name(s))]
   [CASCADE|INVALIDATE CONSTRAINTS]
    [CHECKPOINT integer]

DROP UNUSED COLUMNS|COLUMNS CONTNUE [CHECKPOINT integer]
```

The DROP clause will drop the column(s), dependent constraints, and triggers specified in the command, even if those items also are used with other columns. So be careful to fully understand the implications of using the DROP clause before you use it.

The SET UNUSED clause allows you to deactivate the column without dropping it. This allows a preliminary test of whether the column is really able to be dropped without damaging existing data. It also allows you to cascade the action to dependent constraints.

The INVALIDATE option allows you to invalidate all directly and indirectly dependent objects such as procedures, functions, and so on.

The DROP clause allows either a drop of an active column or columns or just a drop of columns previously marked as unused. As with the UNUSED clause, constraints can be cascaded (values are deleted) and objects invalidated. The DROP clause also allows you to force a checkpoint. Note that a drop of any column in a table with columns marked as UNUSED will result in a drop of all UNUSED columns, as well as the explicitly stated column.

Reclaiming a Column Marked as UNUSED

Oops! You marked the wrong column as UNUSED and now you find that you can't go back . . . or can you? During the testing of this feature, I found a method to reclaim a column marked as UNUSED. Once you DROP a column that has been marked as UNUSED, it is gone for good, but up to the point where it is actually dropped, it can be reclaimed. This is how the technique works (I suggest practicing before doing the reclaim on a production table):

The col$ has obj#, col#, name and property fields, which tie into the columns for each table where obj# will correspond to the obj# in the tab$ table. When a column is marked unused, the col# is set to 0, the name is set to a system-generated name, and the property is set to 32800 from its initial value of 0 (for a normal, nontype column). In the tab$ table, the number of columns is decremented by one in the cols column. The obj$ table stores the link between the object name and owner and the obj#; you then use that obj# to pull relevant data from the tab$ and col$ tables.

In order to reverse the unused state, reset the col# value to its original value, reset the name column to the proper name, and reset the property to 0. In the tab$ table, reset the cols column to the appropriate value.

You will have to flush the shared pool, or even restart to flush the object caches and dictionary caches, to see the column again. To test this process, perform the following steps:

1. Create a small table with two to three columns.
2. Look at the entries for obj$, tab$, and col$ for this table, noting the values for COLS in tab$ and COL#, INTCOL#, PROPERTY, and NAME in col$ (from SYS or INTERNAL user).
3. Add data to the table, and commit.

4. Select from the table to confirm the data and columns.
5. Use ALTER TABLE SET UNUSED to mark a column unused.
6. Select from the table to confirm the column is unavailable.
7. Log in as SYS or INTERNAL, and check tab$ and col$ as before.
8. Update tab$ and col$ to before the ALTER conditions, and commit.
9. Flush the shared pool to get rid of the postcondition SELECT statement parse. Issue a SELECT against the table to confirm the column reappeared.

NOTE   Sometimes you may need to shut down and restart before the column will reappear.

That should do it. Of course, if you actually drop the column, you can't reclaim it. And remember, dropping any column in a table will result in loss of all columns marked UNUSED, whether mentioned in the DROP or not.

Table Statistics and Validity: The ANALYZE Command   To help a DBA determine whether a table's data and indexes have integrity, and to calculate the statistics used by the cost-based optimizer, all versions of Oracle since version 7 provide the ANALYZE command, which is used to analyze the structure of a table and its indexes. The schema object to be analyzed must be in your own schema or you must have the ANALYZE ANY system privilege.

If you want to list chained rows of a table or cluster into a list table, the list table must be in your own schema and you must have INSERT privilege on the list table or the INSERT ANY TABLE system privilege.

If you want to validate a partitioned table, you must have the INSERT privilege on the table, into which you list analyzed rowids, or you must have the INSERT ANY TABLE system privilege.

NOTE   The Oracle syntax for ANALYZE is contained in the SQL reference manual on the Oracle technet Web site.

Some options for the ANALYZE command require a table. This table is named using the INTO clause. Usually, this specifies a table into which Oracle lists the migrated and chained rows. If you omit schema, Oracle assumes the list table is in your own schema. If you omit this clause altogether, Oracle assumes that the table is named CHAINED_ROWS. The script used to create this table is UTLCHAIN.SQL. The list table must be on your local database.

The structure under Oracle9*i* for the table is:

```
CREATE TABLE chained_rows (
owner_name          varchar2(30),
```

```
table_name              varchar2(30),
cluster_name            varchar2(30),
partition_name          varchar2(30),
head_rowid              rowid,
analyze_timestamp        date);
```

To analyze index-only tables, you must create a separate chained-rows table for each index-only table created to accommodate the primary key storage of index-only tables. Use the SQL scripts DBMSIOTC.SQL and PRVTIOTC.PLB to define the DBMS_ IOT package. The tables themselves are built with a call to the BUILD_ CHAIN_ ROWS_TABLE(owner VARCHAR2, iot_name VARCAHR2, chainrow_table_ name VARCHAR2) procedure. Execution of this procedure creates an IOT_CHAINED_ ROWS table for an index-only table. The IOT_CHAINED_ROWS table has the structure:

```
CREATE TABLE iot_chained_rows (
owner_name              varchar2(30),
table_name              varchar2(30),
cluster_name            varchar2(30),
partition_name          varchar2(30),
head_rowid              rowid,
timestamp               date,
test1           varchar2(6) <- This is the primary key
);                              from the table being analyzed
```

Collecting Statistics   You can collect statistics about the physical storage characteristics and data distribution of an index, table, column, or cluster, and store them as histograms in the data dictionary. For computing or estimating statistics, computation always provides exact values but can take longer than estimation, and requires large amounts of temporary tablespace (up to four times the size of your largest table). Estimation is often much faster than computation, and the results are usually nearly exact. You cannot compute or estimate histogram statistics for the following column types:

- REFs
- varrays
- nested tables
- LOBs
- LONGs
- object types

Use estimation, rather than computation, unless you feel you need exact values. Some statistics are always computed exactly, regardless of whether you specify computation or estimation. If you choose estimation, and the time saved by estimating a statistic is negligible, Oracle computes the statistic exactly.

If the data dictionary already contains statistics for the analyzed object, Oracle updates the existing statistics with the new ones.

ANALYZE Myths   Since ANALYZE was introduced, many myths about its use have been circulated. Some of the more harmful ones are:

- You need to ANALYZE entire schema.
- ANALYZE does a full row count no matter what.
- You can sample 5 to 10 percent and get good results.
- You can sample 50 rows and get good results.

Let's take a quick look at these to determine if any are valid.

First, the statement that you need to analyze the entire schema to get good results is not true. You only need to analyze the tables that have changed. Oracle provides the monitoring clause for the CREATE an ALTER TABLE commands, which will place a table into monitored mode; any changes on the table will result in its being analyzed the next time the DBMS_STATS.GATHER_STATISTICS procedure is run. However, this means that if a table undergoes only a few INSERT, UPDATE, and DELETE operations, it will be analyzed. If the table has several million rows, and you only change 10, there is no need to reanalyze it. Source 4.4 shows a procedure that can be utilized to analyze tables based on a percent change in row count.

Source 4.4   Procedure to conditionally ANALYZE tables.

```
-- You may need to comment out the write_out procedure and subsequent
-- calls to it, I like to track what tables need analysis using a
-- dba_running_stats table
--
CREATE OR REPLACE PROCEDURE check_tables (
    owner_name in varchar2,
    pchng IN NUMBER,
    lim_rows IN NUMBER) AS
--
CURSOR get_tab_count (own varchar2) IS
        SELECT table_name, nvl(num_rows,1)
        FROM dba_tables
        WHERE owner = upper(own);
--
tab_name    VARCHAR2(64);
rows        NUMBER;
string      VARCHAR2(255);
cur         INTEGER;
ret         INTEGER;
row_count   NUMBER;
com_string  VARCHAR2(255);
--
PROCEDURE write_out(
  par_name  IN VARCHAR2,
```

```
 par_value IN NUMBER,
 rep_ord   IN NUMBER,
 m_date    IN DATE,
 par_delta IN NUMBER) IS
BEGIN
 INSERT INTO dba_running_stats VALUES(
  par_name,par_value,rep_ord,m_date,par_delta
 );
END;
--
BEGIN
--
-- The next line Is for schemas with many tables
-- If you don't lose the cursors you can exceed
-- open_cursor limits and flood the shared pool
--
DBMS_SESSION.SET_CLOSE_CACHED_OPEN_CURSORS(TRUE);
OPEN get_tab_count (owner_name);
LOOP
BEGIN
        FETCH get_tab_count INTO tab_name, rows;
        tab_name:=owner_name||'.'||tab_name;
        IF rows=0 THEN
        rows:=1;
        END IF;
EXIT WHEN get_tab_count%NOTFOUND;
DBMS_OUTPUT.PUT_LINE('Table name: '||tab_name||' rows: '||to_char(rows));
--
-- Need to have created the get_count procedure in the same schema
--
GET_COUNT(tab_name,row_count);
   IF row_count=0 THEN
        row_count:=1;
   END IF;
DBMS_OUTPUT.PUT_LINE('Row count for '||tab_name||': '||to_char(row_count));
DBMS_OUTPUT.PUT_LINE('Ratio: '||to_char(row_count/rows));
        IF (row_count/rows)>1+(pchng/100) OR (rows/row_count)>1+(pchng/100)
THEN
              BEGIN
     IF (row_count<lim_rows) THEN
           string :=
'ANALYZE TABLE '||tab_name||' COMPUTE STATISTICS ';
     ELSE
          string :=
'ANALYZE TABLE '||tab_name||' ESTIMATE STATISTICS SAMPLE 30 PERCENT';
     END IF;
          cur := DBMS_SQL.OPEN_CURSOR;
DBMS_OUTPUT.PUT_LINE('Beginning analysis');
          DBMS_SQL.PARSE(cur,string,dbms_sql.v7);
          ret := DBMS_SQL.EXECUTE(cur)   ;
```

continues

Source 4.4   Continued.

```
        DBMS_SQL.CLOSE_CURSOR(cur);
        DBMS_OUTPUT.PUT_LINE(' Table: '||tab_name||' had to be
analyzed.');
        write_out(' Table: '||tab_name||' had to be analyzed.',
row_count/rows,33,sysdate,0);
        EXCEPTION
        WHEN OTHERS THEN
        raise_application_error(-20002,'Error in analyze:
'||to_char(sqlcode)||' on '||tab_name,TRUE);
        write_out(' Table: '||tab_name||' error during analyze.
'||to_char(sqlcode), row_count/rows,33,sysdate,0);
        IF dbms_sql.is_open(cur) THEN
            dbms_sql.close_cursor(cur);
          END IF;
        END;
      END IF;
EXCEPTION
WHEN others THEN
null;
END;
COMMIT;
END LOOP;
CLOSE get_tab_count;
END;
```

Notice in the procedure in Source 4.4 that you specify the schema (owner) whose tables you wish to analyze, the percent change (I usually use 10), and the number of rows at which to switch from a COMPUTE to a ESTIMATE SAMPLE 30 PERCENT type of ANALYZE.

In one environment, using a procedure similar to the one in Source 4.4, resulted in analysis times dropping from over four hours to less than an hour.

To test the next myth, that ANALYZE does a full row count no matter whether you use COMPUTE or ESTIMATE, I ran various sample sizes. The tests were run first with a fixed row size and then with a varying row size. Figure 4.3 is a chart of my results on an Oracle8*i*, 8.1.7 database, and the actual numeric results are shown in Tables 4.1 and 4.2.

As you can see, the row counts did change with sample size, as did other key statistics. In general, a sample size of 20 to 30 percent gives the best results on large tables. I don't suggest sampling based on row counts at all.

To understand sampling based on number of rows, let's look at a graph that shows the results as the row count increases from 0 to 5,000 rows for the same table. The graph is shown in Figure 4.4.

As you can see, the results vary widely until a substantial number of rows have been sampled (the graph begins to stabilize at around 2,800 rows).

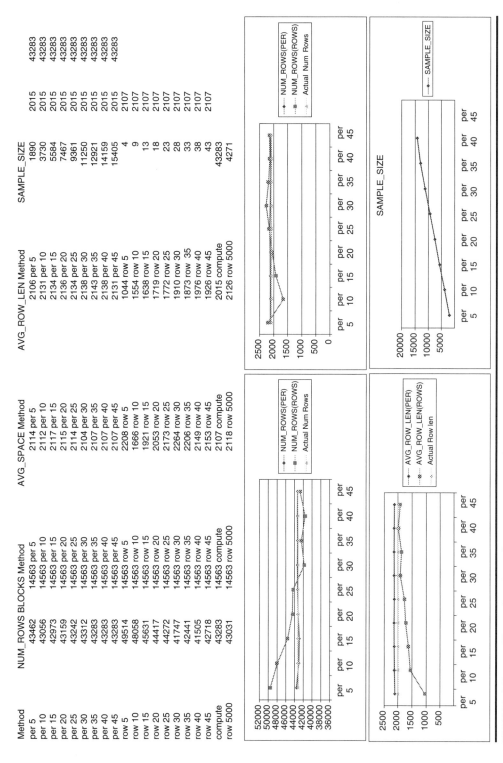

Method	NUM_ROWS	BLOCKS	Method	AVG_SPACE	Method	AVG_ROW_LEN	Method	SAMPLE_SIZE	
per 5	43462	14563	per 5	2114	per 5	2106	per 5	1890	2015
per 10	43056	14563	per 10	2112	per 10	2131	per 10	3730	2015
per 15	42973	14563	per 15	2117	per 15	2134	per 15	5584	2015
per 20	43159	14563	per 20	2115	per 20	2136	per 20	7467	2015
per 25	43242	14563	per 25	2114	per 25	2134	per 25	9361	2015
per 30	43312	14563	per 30	2104	per 30	2138	per 30	11250	2015
per 35	43283	14563	per 35	2107	per 35	2143	per 35	12921	2015
per 40	43283	14563	per 40	2107	per 40	2138	per 40	14159	2015
per 45	43283	14563	per 45	2107	per 45	2131	per 45	15405	2015
row 5	49514	14563	row 5	2208	row 5	1044	row 5	4	2107
row 10	48058	14563	row 10	1666	row 10	1554	row 10	9	2107
row 15	45631	14563	row 15	1921	row 15	1638	row 15	13	2107
row 20	44417	14563	row 20	2053	row 20	1719	row 20	18	2107
row 25	44272	14563	row 25	2173	row 25	1772	row 25	23	2107
row 30	41747	14563	row 30	2264	row 30	1910	row 30	28	2107
row 35	42441	14563	row 35	2206	row 35	1873	row 35	33	2107
row 40	41505	14563	row 40	2149	row 40	1976	row 40	38	2107
row 45	42718	14563	row 45	2153	row 45	1926	row 45	43	2107
compute	43283	14563	compute	2107	compute	2015	compute	43283	
row 5000	43031	14563	row 5000	2118	row 5000	2126	row 5000	4271	

FIGURE 4.3   Chart of statistics from various sample sizes.

TABLE 4.1 Results of Various Sample Sizes for Fixed-Size Row

Method	NUM_ROWS	BLOCKS	Method	AVG_SPACE	Method	AVG_ROW_LEN	Method	SAMPLE_SIZE		
per 5	30165	14477	per 5	4030	per 5	2573	per 5	1105	1992	29515
per 10	29334	14477	per 10	4038	per 10	2671	per 10	2181	1992	29515
per 15	29461	14477	per 15	4035	per 15	2689	per 15	3284	1992	29515
per 20	29442	14477	per 20	4033	per 20	2682	per 20	4359	1992	29515
per 25	29328	14477	per 25	4034	per 25	2684	per 25	5459	1992	29515
per 30	29497	14477	per 30	4035	per 30	2684	per 30	6551	1992	29515
per 35	29481	14477	per 35	4037	per 35	2692	per 35	7646	1992	29515
per 40	29513	14477	per 40	4036	per 40	2691	per 40	8735	1992	29515
per 45	29511	14477	per 45	4036	per 45	2697	per 45	9813	1992	29515
row 5	31849	14477	row 5	4053	row 5	4021	row 5	3	4036	
row 10	37640	14477	row 10	4044	row 10	3020	row 10	8	4036	
row 15	33780	14477	row 15	4050	row 15	2687	row 15	12	4036	
row 20	31126	14477	row 20	4054	row 20	2687	row 20	15	4036	
row 25	35324	14477	row 25	4048	row 25	2757	row 25	19	4036	
row 30	33297	14477	row 30	4051	row 30	2977	row 30	23	4036	
row 35	32263	14477	row 35	4052	row 35	2944	row 35	26	4036	
row 40	32573	14477	row 40	4033	row 40	2859	row 40	31	4036	
row 45	33136	14477	row 45	4015	row 45	2788	row 45	35	4036	
compute	29515	14477	compute	4036	compute	1992	compute	29515		

TABLE 4.2 Results of Various Sample Sizes for Variable-Size Row

Method	NUM_ROWS	BLOCKS	Method	AVG_SPACE	Method	AVG_ROW_LEN	Method	SAMPLE_SIZE		
per 5	43462	14563	per 5	2114	per 5	2106	per 5	1890	2015	43283
per 10	43056	14563	per 10	2112	per 10	2131	per 10	3730	2015	43283
per 15	42973	14563	per 15	2117	per 15	2134	per 15	5584	2015	43283
per 20	43159	14563	per 20	2115	per 20	2136	per 20	7467	2015	43283
per 25	43242	14563	per 25	2114	per 25	2134	per 25	9361	2015	43283
per 30	43312	14563	per 30	2104	per 30	2138	per 30	11250	2015	43283
per 35	43283	14563	per 35	2107	per 35	2143	per 35	12921	2015	43283
per 40	43283	14563	per 40	2107	per 40	2138	per 40	14159	2015	43283
per 45	43283	14563	per 45	2107	per 45	2131	per 45	15405	2015	43283
row 5	49514	14563	row 5	2208	row 5	1044	row 5	4	2107	
row 10	48058	14563	row 10	1666	row 10	1554	row 10	9	2107	
row 15	45631	14563	row 15	1921	row 15	1638	row 15	13	2107	
row 20	44417	14563	row 20	2053	row 20	1719	row 20	18	2107	
row 25	44272	14563	row 25	2173	row 25	1772	row 25	23	2107	
row 30	41747	14563	row 30	2264	row 30	1910	row 30	28	2107	
row 35	42441	14563	row 35	2206	row 35	1873	row 35	33	2107	
row 40	41505	14563	row 40	2149	row 40	1976	row 40	38	2107	
row 45	42718	14563	row 45	2153	row 45	1926	row 45	43	2107	
compute	43283	14563	compute	2107	compute	2015	compute	43283		
row 5000	43031	14563	row 5000	2118	row 5000	2126	row 5000	4271		

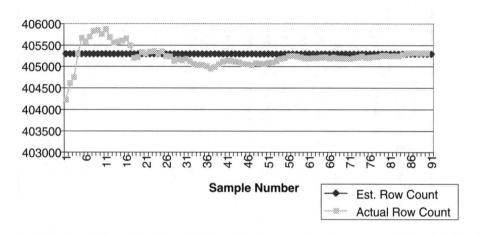

FIGURE 4.4   Graph showing row count for increasing values of rows sampled.

Based on this research, I suggest using COMPUTE or ESTIMATE SAMPLE 20-30 PERCENT to ANALYZE your database tables.

Deletion of a Table's Data

Deletion of a table's data can be done by two methods. The first method uses the DELETE command and can be conditional. A DELETE is also able to be rolled back if you decide, before you commit, that you goofed. The second method is the TRUNCATE command. TRUNCATE is a DDL, not a DML, command, and it's not conditional (it's all or nothing) and cannot be rolled back (yes, you will spend days reentering data if you goof). Let's look at these commands and their options.

The DELETE Command   You can delete data selectively or delete all of a table's data using the DELETE command. The format for this command follows.

```
DELETE hint [FROM] [ONLY]
[TABLE select_clause][(+)]
[schema.]table_name|view_name|materialized_view[@db_link]
 sub_query [WITH READ ONLY|CHECK OPTION [CONSTRAINT con_clause]] alias
[WHERE expr]
[schema.]table_name [PARTITION (partition_name)]
[schema.]table_name [SUBPARTITION (subpartition_name)]
[returning clause]
```

where the clauses have the following definitions:

hint. Any one of the allowed hints.

schema. The schema or owner of the table, view, or partition being deleted from. If this is left off, the user's default schema is used.

Table_name, view_name, or materialized_view. The name of the table, view, or materialized view to be deleted from.

dblink. If the table, view, or partition is in a remote database, this is the dblink to that database.

PARTITION(partition name). Deletes from a specified (partition_name) of a partitioned table.

SUBPARTITION (subpartition_name). Deletes from a specified (subpartition_name) of a subpartitioned table.

TABLE. Used to flatten nested tables. The subquery following the TABLE clause tells Oracle how the flattening should occur.

subquery. Used to tell Oracle how to delete from the table or nested table. If the deletion is from a nested table, the TABLE clause must be included.

alias. Used when a correlated subquery is used to denote table hierarchy in the query/delete commands.

WHERE condition. The condition each deleted row must meet or fail.

Returning_clause. Retrieves the rows affected by the DELETE statement. You can retrieve only scalar, LOB, rowid, and REF types.

TIP   You can use hints in a DELETE statement to optimize delete subquery processing.

The table name can include an alias; if the WHERE clause is left out, all of the rows in the table are deleted. Four examples follow:

```
DELETE FROM PER_DBA.JOBS A WHERE A.JOB_STATUS = 'COMPLETE';
```

This command would delete all rows with the data value COMPLETE in the column JOB_STATUS from the JOBS table owned by the PER_DBA user.

```
DELETE PER_DBA.OLD_JOBS
```

This command would remove all rows from the table OLD_JOBS that belongs to the schema PER_DBA.

To delete specific rows from a nested table, the TABLE clause is specified (I like to think *FROM THE SET* when I see TABLE):

```
DELETE TABLE (SELECT addresses
 FROM clientsv8 c
 WHERE c.customer_name = 'Joes Bar and Grill, Inc.')
 AS a
WHERE a.addrtype=1;
```

In this example, note the use of the alias "AS a"; this is required.

Deleting from a single partition is accomplished by use of the PARTITION clause:

```
DELETE FROM trains PARTITION (roundhouse1)
WHERE
service_date < to_date('01-Jan-1956 00:00:00,
'DD-Mon-YYYY hh24:mi:ss');
```

If you wish to delete from a specific subpartition, this is accomplished with the SUBPARTITION clause:

```
DELETE FROM trains SUBPARTITION (subroundhouse1a)
WHERE
service_date < to_date('01-Jan-1956 00:00:00,
'DD-Mon-YYYY hh24:mi:ss');
```

The TRUNCATE TABLE Command   There is also a way to avoid the use of rollback, thus making deletions much faster: use the TRUNCATE command. One good feature of this command is that it can be used to reclaim the space used by the data that was in the table. As noted in the introduction to this section, TRUNCATE is a DDL command; once issued, the data is gone. A TRUNCATE cannot be rolled back. The format for this command follows.

```
TRUNCATE TABLE|CLUSTER [schema.]table_name|cluster_name
[PRESERVE|PURGE SNAPSHOT LOG]
[DROP|REUSE STORAGE]
```

The DROP|REUSE STORAGE option allows you to shrink the table back to its high-water mark or leave the table at its current size. Both DROP and REUSE qualifiers also apply to whatever index space is regained.

For tables, PRESERVE or PURGE SNAPSHOT options allow control over a table's snapshot logs as well.

Again, the TRUNCATE command is faster than the DELETE command because it is a DDL command and generates no rollback data. When using TRUNCATE on a clustered table, the data must be removed from the entire cluster, not just the one table. Any referential integrity constraints on a table must be disabled before it can be truncated. Like a table DROP, a truncation is not recoverable. If a table is truncated, you cannot roll back if you made a mistake. Use TRUNCATE carefully.

Dropping a Table   To completely remove a table from the tablespace, use the DROP TABLE command. This command's format follows:

```
DROP TABLE [schema.]table_name [CASCADE CONSTRAINTS]
```

Oracle will drop the table regardless of its contents. The only time a drop will fail is when a table's primary key is referenced by another table's foreign key via a restraint clause. The DBA can check for this situation by looking at the DBA_CONSTRAINTS and the DBA_CONS_COLUMNS views. A view called USER_CROSS_ REFS provides this information on a user-by-user basis. Using the CASCADE CONSTRAINTS clause will force a CASCADE DELETE to occur in all child tables.

Rebuilding Tables   The DBA may have to rebuild a table or tables after maintenance, after a physical disk crash, or—the leading cause—due to operational stupidity. If the application designers were thoughtful enough to provide a build script, there is no problem. However, for legacy systems, systems that have been modified and not redocumented, or systems created on the fly, there may be no current build scripts, if there were any to begin with. In this case, the DBA is in trouble. How can this situation be prevented? Require build scripts for each application and keep them up to date. For existing, undocumented systems, the script TAB_RCT9*i*.sql from the Wiley Web site will create a build script for simple existing tables. For very complex tables, I suggest implementing a utility such as TOAD from Quest, Inc. In Oracle9*i*, the DBMS_METADATA can also be used to generate the DDL for any database object. Any rebuild script generator must be run before any loss has occurred. Due to the added complexity of Oracle9*i*, it is doubtful many systems created on the fly will make use of the complex options and types. Over time, I will be revising TAB_RCT9*i*.SQL to handle the more complex Oracle9*i* structures, and newer versions will be made available at the Wiley Web site.

A similar script is referenced for indexes in Chapter 6. The TAB_RCT9*i*.SQL script will rebuild straight-partitioned or subpartitioned Oracle9*i* and Oracle8*i* relational tables only. It will not rebuild tables with types, objects, nested tables, or varrays.

4.3 SUMMARY

This chapter addressed the management of Oracle relational tables for Oracle8, 8*i*, and Oracle9*i*. As the lines continue to blur between relational and object tables, each assumes more of the characteristics of the other. This chapter covered the traditional relational table and the blended Oracle8/8*i* /9*i* table that contains BLOBs, partitions, and other complex structures. It also touched on scripts to rebuild tables, as well as other useful table-related scripts.

CHAPTER 5

Administration of Oracle9*i* Object Tables

As mentioned in Chapter 4, Oracle8 and Oracle8*i* introduced a number of new table objects or types that DBAs have to worry about. Probably the most basic of these is the straight object table. But Oracle8 also introduced nested tables, varray types, REF values, and the entire concept of types. Oracle9*i* has enhanced the concept of TYPE to more closely resemble the full Object-oriented paradigm, adding limited inheritance and polymorphism. Thus, Oracle9*i* has become truly object-relational in context. This chapter addresses these new Oracle8 and Oracle8*i* object tables, the modifications and additions in Oracle9*i*,and the types used to build them.

5.1 THE ROWID CONCEPT IN ORACLE9*i*

Under Oracle8, the concept of OBJECTS was introduced. In Oracle8*i* and Oracle9*i* this concept has been kept and expanded upon. These OBJECTS have identifiers that now are added to the rowid, giving an EXTENDED ROWID format, which is 10 bytes long versus the 6 bytes that was the norm in Oracle7. The Oracle8, Oracle8*i* and Oracle9*i* rowid is a VARCHAR2 representation of a base-64 number (remember that base-64 starts at B, not A; A is used to designate 0). The rowid is displayed as follows:

```
OOOOOO.FFF.BBBBBB.SSS
```

where:

OOOOOO is the data object number.
FFF is the relative file number.
BBBBBB is the block number.
SSS is the slot number.

An example of the new rowid would be:

AAAAVJAAEAAAABEAAA

where:

> **AAAAVJ** is the data object number.
> **AAE** is the relative file number.
> **AAAABE** is the block number.
> **AAA** is the slot number.

The new parts of the rowid are the object number and the relative file number. Multiple files can have the same relative file number because Oracle assigns the number based on a tablespace. This means that these numbers are unique only per tablespace, which means that you cannot derive an absolute address directly from the new rowid. This also means that the new rowid addressing scheme is tablespace-relative.

The new rowid contains the data object number, which increments when an object's version changes. An object's version changes whenever a table is truncated or a partition is moved. The data object number is not related to the object ID.

The rowid can be easily manipulated with the DBMS_ROWID package. If, against Oracle admonitions not to, you used rowid in your Oracle7 application, you will have to familiarize yourself with this package.

- Old rowids (called restricted rowids) will be automatically converted to the new format if:

  - You use export/import to move data.
  - You use the migration utility.
  - You use the ODMA to upgrade to 9*i*.

If you used rowids in your Oracle7 application and stored them as columns in other tables, then these columns will have to be manually changed to the new format using the DBMS_ROWID package. If a column in a table has been designated as a datatype of rowid, it will be altered to accept the new format during migration; this will not affect the data in the column.

5.2 THE CONCEPT OF OBJECT IDENTIFIERS (OID) IN ORACLE9*i*

Oracle8 introduced the concept of objects as they apply to Oracle. Each object in Oracle8, Oracle8*i,* and Oracle9*i* (i.e., table, cluster, etc.) has a 16-byte object identifier. This object identifier (OID) is guaranteed to be globally unique across all databases in your environment. It is a 16-byte, base-64 number that allows for a ridiculously high number of objects to be identified (in the peta-region of countability—a quadrillion? The maximum is $2^{**}128$ (340,283,266,920,938,463,463,374,607,431,768,211,456)).

The OID, as well as being a globally unique identifier, is used to construct REFs for nested tables. In some statements involving nested tables, if you don't specifically tell Oracle to bring back the UNREF value (i.e., translate the OID and get the data), you will get a 42- to 46-byte REF number, as useful as that sounds. The number itself is simply an identifier and contains no "intelligence" such as would be in a rowid. The REF value can vary in size between 42 and 46 bytes of internal storage.

5.3 ORACLE9*i* OBJECT TYPES

Before we can begin to discuss objects in Oracle8, Oracle8*i*, and Oracle9*i*, we have to address object types. As their name implies, an object type is used to define an object. To bridge the gulf between Oracle7 and Oracle9*i*, you can think of an object type as a predefined row that you can then use to build Oracle9*i* objects. The exact format for creating an object table is shown in the SQL reference in the documentation area of the http://technet.oracle.com/ site link on the Wiley Web site. The examples that follow demonstrate how to use Oracle types to create an object table.

Before you can build an object table in Oracle8, 8*i*, or 9*i*, you must define its types. A table can consist of single columns, types, or a mix, as well as varrays (which are discussed later in this chapter). There are only object TYPEs. Under Oracle8*i*, the AUTHID clause was added to the CREATE TYPE command. In Oracle9*i*, the CREATE TYPE command has been extended with the clauses required to support inheritance. Also in Oracle9*i*, type bodies support overloading, thus providing polymorphism. Let's look at a simple type definition and how it is used to build an Oracle9*i* object table. The only instances where the AS OBJECT clause is not used is with varray, TABLE, or incomplete type specifications.

Suppose we want to define a real-world situation, such as a collection of pictures. What are the attributes of pictures? How about topic, date and time taken, photographer, negative number, picture number, and the on-disk location of the actual image? Let's look at the type required to implement this structure:

```
CREATE TYPE picture_t AUTHID CURRENT_USER
AS OBJECT(negative#    number,
          Picture#     number,
          topic        varchar2(80),
          date_taken   date,
          photographer person_t,
             picture   bfile);
```

Notice something odd? What are the person_t and bfile columns? The person_t is another type definition, "person type," which includes:

```
CREATE TYPE person_t AUTHID CURRENT_USER
AS OBJECT ( first_name  varchar2(32),
        last_name    varchar2(32),
        middle_init  varchar2(3),
```

```
        sex          char(1),
        address      address_t);
```

The embedded type address_t inside person_t is:

```
CREATE TYPE address_t AUTHID CURRENT_USER
AS OBJECT (address_line1     varchar2(80),
        address_line2      varchar2(80),
        street_name        varchar2(30),
        street_number      number,
        city               varchar2(30),
        state_or_province  varchar2(2),
        zip                number(5),
        zip_4              number(4),
        country_code       varchar2(20));
```

Do you see the value of these type definitions—and the nightmare? To make things more complex, METHODS can be declared in the type definition; then a type body must also be created. The BFILE definition was a new BLOB (binary large object) definition added in Oracle8 that specifies it as a LOB-stored external to the database.

Anyway, back to the example: Now we want to create our picture object. This becomes:

```
CREATE TABLE pictures OF picture_t (
CONSTRAINT pk_pictures PRIMARY KEY (negative#,picture#)
USING INDEX TABLESPACE indexes);
```

When creating types, the order of creation is critical, unless we use incomplete types (covered in the next section); in the preceding example, the creation order must be: address_t, person_t, picture_t, and then the table pictures. You create from the most atomic-level type to the most inclusive.

The AUTHID CURRENT_USER clause tells the kernel that any methods that may be used in the type specification (in the above example, none) should execute with the privilege of the executing user, not the owner. The default option for the AUTHID is DEFINER, which would correspond to the behavior in pre-Oracle8i releases, where the method would execute with the privileges of the user creating the type.

One of the nice things about this concept of types is that it allows us to create these type primitives, such as person_t, and then use them to define objects. If you must add an attribute to a TYPE, you use the:

```
ALTER TYPE type_name ADD ATTRIBUTE attribute datatype CASCADE;
```

command; the new attribute is added to the TYPE and all dependent TYPEs, as well as any tables that use the TYPE. This promulgation of changes is new in Oracle9i; it was not available in previous versions.

You can specify either CASCADE or INVALIDATE, but if there are dependent TYPEs of TABLEs, you must specify either one or the other. CASCADE cascades the change to all dependent TYPEs and TABLEs, while INVALIDATE marks them as INVALID. Added attributes are placed at the end of the TYPE attribute list. Let's examine a very simple example of this altering of types. Using the PICTURES table, we have already created, let's do an insert without making any changes to any of the TYPEs:

```
SQL> INSERT INTO PICTURES VALUES(1,1,'Test',SYSDATE,
  1  PERSON_T('Michael','Ault','R','M',
  2  ADDRESS_T('','','Mockingbird Lane','1313','Altoona','GA',
  3  30000,9999,'US')),NULL);

1 row created.
```

If you haven't used TYPEs before, you may be wondering what the heck the PERSON_T( ) and ADDRESS_T( ) calls are for. These are called *constructors,* and are created for each TYPE unless you specify NOT INSTANTIABLE as an argument with your CREATE TYPE or ALTER TYPE command. All TYPEs are INSTANTIABLE by default. A constructor method takes all IN values, one for each attribute of the TYPE. If an ATTRIBUTE (such as ADDRESS) is another TYPE, then the call to that constructor is embedded in the call to the master TYPE constructor. Now let's alter the PERSON_T TYPE to include a new column IDENTIFYING_MARKS as a VARCHAR2(255) datatype.

```
SQL> ALTER TYPE person_t ADD ATTRIBUTE Identifying_marks VARCHAR2(255)
CASCADE;

Type altered.
```

Let's try the same type of insert as before, without the new attribute:

```
SQL> INSERT INTO PICTURES VALUES(1,2,'Test',SYSDATE,
  1  PERSON_T('Michael','Ault','R','M',
  2  ADDRESS_T('','','Mockingbird Lane','1313','Altoona','GA',
  3  30000,9999,'US')),NULL);

PERSON_T('Michael','Ault','R','M'
*
ERROR at line 2:
ORA-02315: Incorrect number of arguments for default constructor
```

Since we have added an attribute to PERSON_T, it will be placed after the ADDRESS_T attribute, so we must add a value or a NULL insert at that point in our INSERT command:

```
SQL> INSERT INTO PICTURES VALUES(1,2,'Test',SYSDATE,
  1  PERSON_T('Michael','Ault','R',
  2  ADDRESS_T('','','Mockingbird Lane','1313','Altoona','GA',
  3  30000,9999,'US'),'None'),NULL);

1 row created.
```

Notice the addition of the value 'None' after all of the ADDRESS_T constructor call.

To create a TYPE hierarchy, the UNDER clause is specified in the CREATE TYPE... AS OBJECT command. An example would be if we wanted to create a subtype of EMPLOYEE under the existing PERSON_T TYPE we created in the previous example:

```
CREATE TYPE employee_t AUTHID CURRENT_USER
UNDER person_t (
Emp_Id NUMBER,
Dept_Id NUMBER,
Hire_date DATE);
```

A subtype can only be created on a TYPE that is not a FINAL TYPE. Unless the clause NOT FINAL is specifically added to a CREATE TYPE command, or it is specified through an ALTER TYPE command, then a TYPE is considered to be FINAL. To add the TYPE EMPLOYEE_T as a subtype to our PERSON_T TYPE, we will need to ALTER the PERSON_T TYPE to NOT FINAL. Let's look at an example of this:

```
SQL> ALTER TYPE person_t NOT FINAL CASCADE;

Type altered.

SQL> CREATE TYPE employee_t AUTHID CURRENT_USER
  1    UNDER person_t (
  2    emp_id NUMBER,
  3    dept_id NUMBER,
  4    hire_date DATE);
  5  /

Type created.
```

But what exactly does this do for us? Any subtype inherits the attributes of its parent TYPE. So instead of just containing the attributes emp_id, dept_id, and hire_date, the EMPLOYEE_T TYPE also contains all of the attributes of its parent TYPE PERSON_T:

```
SQL> DESC employee_t
Employee_t extends SYSTEM.PERSON_T
Name                            Null?    Type
------------------------------- -------  ---------------
FIRST_NAME                               VARCHAR2(32)
LAST_NAME                                VARCHAR2(32)
MIDDLE_INIT                              VARCHAR2(3)
SEX                                      CHAR(1)
ADDRESS                                  ADDRESS_T
EMP_ID                                   NUMBER
DEPT_ID                                  NUMBER
HIRE_DATE                                DATE
```

Notice anything odd? The attribute we added, IDENTIFYING_MARKS, is not shown. However, the attribute does show up if you do a describe on a table created with

EMPLOYEE_T, and must be allowed for in any INSERT into a table created from EMPLOYEE_T. An example would be:

```
SQL> CREATE TABLE employees OF employee_t (
CONSTRAINT pk_employees PRIMARY KEY (emp_id,dept_id)
USING INDEX TABLESPACE indexes);

Table created.

SQL> DESC EMPLOYEES

Name                            Null?   Type
------------------------------- ------- ---------------
FIRST_NAME                              VARCHAR2(32)
LAST_NAME                               VARCHAR2(32)
MIDDLE_INIT                             VARCHAR2(3)
SEX                                     CHAR(1)
ADDRESS                                 ADDRESS_T
IDENTIFYING_MARKS                       VARCHAR2(255)
EMP_ID                                  NUMBER
DEPT_ID                                 NUMBER
HIRE_DATE                               DATE

SQL> INSERT INTO employees (EMPLOYEE_T('Michael','Ault','R','M',
  1  ADRESS_T('','','Mockingbird Lane','1313','Altoona','GA',30000,
  2  9999,'US'),'None',1,1,SYSDATE));

1 row inserted.
```

Also note that you don't specify the parent TYPE constructor, just the child TYPE constructor, in this case, EMPLOYEE_T. Any contained types such as ADDRESS_T must still have their constructor methods explicitly called.

This extension to the definitions of TYPEs will enable the simplification of some of the more complex database design into a more manageable real-world view. We will take a deeper look at types when we discuss tables, nested tables, and varrays later in this chapter. Types can be incomplete, complete, varray, nested table, or a combination of complete, varray, and nested table. A varray cannot contain a LOB, and a nested table cannot contain an NCLOB, but can contain BLOB or CLOB datatypes.

The Incomplete Type

The command to create an incomplete type is shown next. Incomplete types are required for circular reference situations. Incomplete types specify no attributes.

```
CREATE OR REPLACE TYPE type_name;
```

An incomplete type would be used where a type references a second type that references the first type (a circular reference such as emp-supervisor). This allows the incomplete type to be referenced before it is completed. However, before a table can be constructed from an incomplete type, it must be completed.

The Varray Type

Varrays are used for small sets of related items. For example, a house has several rooms, and each room has measurements. Let's assume that a house of a certain square footage can't have more than 10 rooms. Thus, a varray to hold this room data would be sized at a limit of 10, so the command to create a varray type would be:

```
CREATE OR REPLACE TYPE [schema.]type_name AS|IS
VARRAY|[VARYING ARRAY] (LIMIT) OF datatype;
```

NOTE   Datatype cannot be of type rowid, LONG, or LONG RAW; it can be a built-in datatype, a REF, or an object-type (excluding LOB datatypes such as BLOB, CLOB, NCLOB, or BFILE). In releases earlier than Oracle9*i*, a varray cannot contain a nested table type or a varray as a direct element; in 9*i*, this is allowed. New in Oracle8*i* was the ability to store varrays out-of-line in LOB storage-specified areas.

A varray should be used when the number of items to be stored in the type is:

- Known and fixed.
- Small (this is a relative term; remember, the data is stuffed into a RAW and stored inline with the rest of the type's data unless a special LOB storage area is specified for the varray under Oracle8*i*).

Since release 8*i*, a varray can be used in a partitioned table. In earlier releases (up to and including 8.0.3), varrays took up an inordinate amount of space. Since Oracle8*i*, you can store them out-of-line in a specified LOB storage area. Nevertheless, I still suggest using nested tables, as the overall storage requirements are lower and the limitations are the same.

Varrays cannot be sparse, they must be contiguous from the first entry to the last item entered; no "holes" are allowed. An example would be when a person or company has multiple addresses. In this case, we could use the address_t type to make a varray since usually the number of addresses will be small (say, a mailing address, a work address, and a home address, for a total of three):

```
CREATE OR REPLACE TYPE address_v AS VARRAY (3) OF address_t;
```

The Nested Table Type

A nested table is used where the same data is repeated for a given entity an unknown number of times, such as the one-to-many relationships between a parent and children.

In applications where storage is at a premium, a nested table may actually be more efficient (at least in early 8.0 releases) than a varray. If you have the time, check both types of objects for storage usage before committing your design to one or the other. Another positive side of nested tables is that they can be sparse.

The command to create a NESTED TABLE type would be:

```
CREATE OR REPLACE TYPE [schema.]type_name IS|AS TABLE OF datatype;
```

A NESTED TABLE should be used when:

- The number of items is large or unknown.
- The storage of the items needs to be managed.

A NESTED TABLE is stored in a STORE TABLE, which must be specified in the CREATE TABLE command for each NESTED TABLE type used. The NESTED TABLE type can be used in partitioned tables after release 8*i*. Some early-release documentation states that Oracle itself specifies the store table name; this is incorrect. Nested tables cannot contain NCLOBs, varrays, or other nested tables. A nested table can contain a BLOB, BFILE, or CLOB datatype. An example would be if we wanted to embed a nested table of pictures into a gallery type:

```
CREATE TYPE picture_nt AS TABLE OF picture_t;
/
CREATE TYPE gallery_t AS OBJECT (
Gallery_id number,
Owner person_t,
Gallery_address address_t,
Contents picture_nt);
/
CREATE TABLE galleries OF gallery_t (
PRIMARY KEY (Gallery_id)
USING INDEX TABLESPACE graphics_index
STORAGE (INITIAL 100k NEXT 100k pctincrease 0))
OBJECT ID PRIMARY KEY
NESTED TABLE contents STORE AS galleries_ntab (
(PRIMARY KEY (NESTED_TABLE_ID, picture#))
ORGANIZATION INDEX COMPRESS)
RETURN AS LOCATOR
TABLESPACE tools
STORAGE (INITIAL 2m NEXT 2m PCTINCREASE 0);
```

Let's look more closely at the CREATE TABLE command as shown above and see what exactly we are telling Oracle to do:

```
CREATE TABLE galleries OF gallery_t (
```

In this statement, we are instructing Oracle to use the defined type gallery_t to create a table using the specified type to define the columns in the table.

```
PRIMARY KEY (Gallery_id)
USING INDEX TABLESPACE graphics_index
STORAGE (INITIAL 100k NEXT 100k pctincrease 0))
OBJECT ID PRIMARY KEY
```

In this next statement, we are telling Oracle to make gallery_id the primary key for galleries, as specified in the gallery_t definition. We are placing the index in the graphics_index tablespace with the specified storage parameters. The OBJECT ID PRIMARY KEY clause tells Oracle that the primary key value is to be used as the row's OID.

```
NESTED TABLE contents STORE AS galleries_ntab (
(PRIMARY KEY (NESTED_TABLE_ID, picture#))
ORGANIZATION INDEX COMPRESS)
RETURN AS LOCATOR
```

This section of the command tells Oracle to store the nested table type values in the nested table named galleries_ntab. This will be a separate table from the galleries table. Note that you cannot specify the location for storing the nested table. If the table is nonpartitioned, it defaults to the same location as the table itself; if the table containing the nested table is partitioned, then the location for the nested table storage defaults to the default tablespace for the schema (user) in which it is created.

The NESTED_TABLE_ID is a special column included in all nested tables; it is used to identify the row in the source table to which the values in the nested table relate. By tying the NESTED_TABLE_ID and the picture# together, we ensure uniqueness in the nested table.

The ORGANIZATION INDEX COMPRESS clause forces the nested table into an IOT configuration, saving space. The COMPRESS keyword suppresses the storage of the NESTED_TABLE_ID in each row, saving more space.

Finally, the RETURN AS LOCATOR clause returns a locator value that can then be decoded with the Oracle Call Interface call, OCICollIsLocator, or a call to the stored package procedure, UTL_COLL.IS_LOCATOR, to return the details of the rows in the nested table. This is important because if you don't specify the RETURN AS LOCATOR, the default is to return VALUE, which returns all values in the nested table that corresponds to your request. If the gallery we were probing was the Metropolitan Museum of Art in New York City, the return values could number in the tens of thousands.

Object Types

If you will be using the type to build an object table that will be REFed by a second table, it must be constructed as an OBJECT type and thus include an object ID (OID). Nested tables and varrays are limited, in that they cannot themselves store a nested table or varray; a second OBJECT table is not limited. In cases where the entity relationship diagram (ERD) shows a series of one-to-many type relationships, OBJECT tables will have to be used to implement this relationship structure under the object-oriented paradigm in Oracle8.

The basic command to create an OBJECT type would be:

```
CREATE OR REPLACE TYPE [schema.]type_name
AUTHID CURRENT_USER|DEFINER
AS OBJECT (element_list)
```

The element_list can consist of:

- Attribute_name Datatype-constraint pairs
- User-defined types
- Method declarations with pragma specification
- MAP or ORDER method specifications

I will refer the reader to the Web documentation in the Oracle technet site for the complete syntax.

NOTE   Object types can be used in partition tables only after release 8*i*.

The possible datatype specifications for a type are:

REF schema.object_type_name

schema.type_name

VARCHAR2(size)

NUMBER (precision, scale)

DATE

RAW(size)

CHAR(size)

CHARACTER(size)

CHAR(size)

CHARACTER VARYING(size)

CHAR VARYING(size)

VARCHAR(size)

The following datatypes are provided for compatibility but internally are treated the same as NUMBER:

NUMERIC(precision, scale)

DECIMAL(precision, scale)

DEC(precision, scale)
INTEGER
INT
SMALLINT
FLOAT(size)
DOUBLE PRECISION
REAL

The following are large object datatypes:

BLOB
CLOB
BFILE

TIP   The NCLOB datatype is also a LOB, but it cannot be used for TYPE definitions.

An object specification can contain only one map method, which must be a function. The resulting type must be a predefined SQL scalar type, and the map function can have no arguments other than the implicit SELF argument.

You can define either the MAP or ORDER method in a type specification, but not both. If a MAP or an ORDER method is not specified, only comparisons for equality or inequality can be performed, thus the object instances cannot be ordered. No comparison method needs to be specified to determine the equality of two object types. If you declare either method, you can compare object instances in SQL. If you do not declare either method, you can compare only object instances for equality or inequality. Note that instances of the same type definition are equal only if each pair of their corresponding attributes is equal. No comparison method needs to be specified to determine the equality of two object types.

5.4 CREATION OF OBJECT TABLES

Object tables differ from relational tables in that an object table has an object identifier that is system-generated and -maintained.

Object Table CREATE Command Definition

Oracle8, Oracle8*i,* and Oracle9*i* allow the creation of OBJECT tables as well as relational tables. An object table is made up of object types or a combination of standard and object types. Prior to Oracle8*i*, an object table could not be partitioned. Object tables have OIDs and can be used for a REF call. To use a standard nonobject relational table in a REF, it must be masked with an object view.

The details of the command to create an object table are contained in the SQL reference in the Web documentation on the Oracle Technet site. Here is a simplified version:

```
CREATE [GLOBAL TEMPORARY] TABLE [schema.]table_name
OF [schema.]object_type [(object_properties)]
[[NOT] SUBSTITUTABLE AT ALL LEVELS]
[ON COMMIT DELETE|PRESERVE ROWS]
[OID_clause][OID_index_clause][physical_properties]
[table_properties];
```

The object_properties clause includes column and attribute information, as well as default value, constraint, and table constraints, along with any REF information. A REF is similar to a foreign key reference in straight relational tables, but instead of holding an actual value used to tie back to the parent table, it holds a pointer (in the form of an OID) to the actual row in the parent table.

The [[NOT] SUBSTITUTABLE AT ALL LEVELS] clause indicates that the object table types are or are not substitutable at all levels. If a column is substitutable, it means that if a TYPE is a subtype or is somewhere in a chain of subtypes, any type or supertype for which this type is a subtype can be inserted to its place in the table simply by calling the supertype or type's constructor rather than the subtype constructor. For example, assume we have the PERSON_T → EMPLOYEE_T → PART TIME_EMP_T type hierarchy, where PERSON_T is the main type, EMPLOYEE_T is a subtype of PERSON_T, and PARTTIME_EMP_T is a subtype of the EMPLOYEE_T type. This would indicate that PARTTIME_PERSON_T has its own attributes, plus all those in EMPLOYEE_T, including any the EMPLOYEE_T inherited from PERSON_T. If a table were defined using the PARTTIME_EMP_T type, you could also use the EMPLOYEE_T or PERSON_T constructor methods to insert a subset of data to the same column location. Using NOT SUBSTITUTABLE turns off this capability.

The ON COMMIT clause is used only if the object table is a GLOBAL TEMPORARY object table.

The OID_clause is used to tell Oracle whether or not the OID is SYSTEM GENERATED (the default) or the PRIMARY KEY. The OID_index_clause specifies how the OID is to be indexed, and specifies the storage parameters for the index.

The physical_properties and table_properties clauses are the same as for a relational table.

5.5 CONVERSION FROM ORACLE7 TO ORACLE9*i*: AN EXAMPLE

You may soon be faced with the prospect of both migrating from Oracle7 to Oracle9*i* as well as converting from the Oracle7 relational table and data structure into the new object-based format for Oracle9*i*.

If you don't intend on taking advantage of the Oracle8, Oracle8*i*, and Oracle9*i* object extensions then this section isn't for you. If you are doing a straight conversion, relational to relational, the conversion from Oracle7 to Oracle9*i* is simply a matter of migration. Even adding partitions to tables or indexes, or converting partition views to partition tables, is pretty straightforward. In fact, if you intend on using partitions, then you cannot use Oracle object types, such as nested tables, varrays, or REFs, as they are not supported for use in partitioned tables in Oracle8. They aren't supported until version 8*i* and 9*i*.

If, on the other hand, you are jumping into the deep end with Oracle8*i* or Oracle9*i*, and will be doing a full conversion into the new object-oriented structure, then by all means read on.

A Concrete Example

I'll use a small sample application fragment to demonstrate how to map it from an Oracle7 relational table format into Oracle9*i* types and objects. The fragment is from a telecommunications application that provides for the tracking of clients, their assigned client numbers, phone numbers, contracts, and related data.

NOTE   For the purpose of this example, I have removed the storage and physical attributes from the application fragment, as they are not germane here.

The Oracle7 structure to be converted consists of 8 tables, 8 primary keys, and 11 foreign keys, with supporting indexes for the primary and foreign keys. The entity relational diagram for this structure is shown in Figure 5.1; the table definitions are given in Source 5.1. This structure shows that the client entity, which maps to the clients table, and the clients_info_number entity, which maps to the clients_info_numbers table, are the two main entities; all of the other entities are dependent upon these two controlling entities. This will evolve under Oracle9*i* into two objects, CLIENTS and CLIENTS_INFO_NUMBERS, which will absorb the other entities into a hierarchical object structure. This is shown in Source 5.2.

As you no doubt noticed, many of the structures in Source 5.1 violate Third Normal Form; unfortunately, certain design restrictions forced this design; specifically, much of this was from a third-party application and therefore verboten to touch. If I could have designed the structure from the ground up, it would have been better normalized.

In order to convert this relational structure into an object-relational structure, we have to know the dependencies. In this case, we are working against the following business rules:

1. Clients and clients_info_numbers can have independent existence; but usually, for every one client, there may be many or no clients_info_number records.

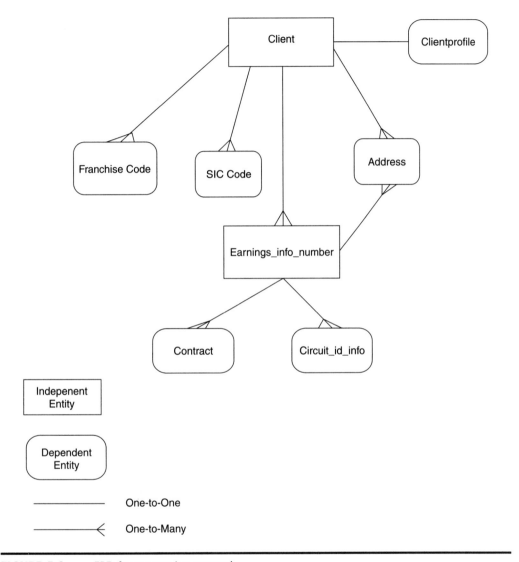

FIGURE 5.1   ERD for conversion example.

2. A clients_info_number can be created without a parent client.
3. The ftx_code and/or sub_code entities are dependent (i.e., they can't exist without the parent) on clients.
4. The contract and/or circuit_id_info are dependent on clients_info_number.
5. In some cases, the records in address are dependent on clients; sometimes they are dependent on clients_info_number.
6. There can be no more than six franchise codes and no more than three ftx_codes per client.

Source 5.1 **Oracle7 creation script for application fragment.**

```
DROP TABLE clients CASCADE CONSTRAINTS;

CREATE TABLE clients (
      clients_id                INTEGER       NOT NULL,
      customer_name             VARCHAR2(35) NOT NULL,
      active_flag               VARCHAR2(1),
      fax                       VARCHAR2(20),
      lookup_no                 VARCHAR2(9) NOT NULL,
      phone                     VARCHAR2(20),
      corporate_name            VARCHAR2(30),
      lookup_parent             VARCHAR2(9),
      lookup_str_adrs           VARCHAR2(25),
      lookup_city               VARCHAR2(20),
      lookup_state              VARCHAR2(2),
      lookup_zip                VARCHAR2(5),
      lookup_zip_ext            VARCHAR2(4),
      lookup_type               CHAR(2),
      lookup_parent_flag        CHAR(1),
      creation_ts               DATE,
      creation_sy_user          INTEGER,
      spp_rating                CHAR(2),
      rating_date               DATE,
      competitor_loss           INTEGER,
      note                      VARCHAR2(250),
      last_contact_ts           DATE,
      delete_status             CHAR(1),
      name_soundex              CHAR(4),
      sales_volume              VARCHAR2(15),
      sales_volume_code         CHAR(1),
      total_employees           VARCHAR2(9),
      line_of_bus               VARCHAR2(19),
      pct_growth_sales          VARCHAR2(4),
      territory_covered         CHAR(1),
      ceo_first_name            VARCHAR2(13),
      ceo_last_name             VARCHAR2(15),
      ceo_middle_initial        VARCHAR2(1),
      ceo_suffix                VARCHAR2(3),
      ceo_prefix                VARCHAR2(10),
      ceo_title                 VARCHAR2(30),
      mrc                       VARCHAR2(4),
      sub_indctr                CHAR(1),
       CONSTRAINT PK_clients
         PRIMARY KEY (clients_id)
             USING INDEX
           TABLESPACE APPL_INDEX
)
TABLESPACE APPL_DATA
;
```

```
DROP TABLE clientprofiles CASCADE CONSTRAINTS;

CREATE TABLE clientprofiles (
    clientprofiles_id       INTEGER NOT NULL,
    clients_id              INTEGER NOT NULL ,
    revnum                  INTEGER,
    created_by              INTEGER,
    creation_ts             DATE,
    delta_sy_user           INTEGER,
    delta_ts                DATE,
    industry                INTEGER,
    business_descrip        VARCHAR2(160),
    primary_contact         INTEGER,
    num_locations           SMALLINT,
    equipment               INTEGER,
    equipment_brand         VARCHAR2(32),
    year_equip_installed    INTEGER,
    voice_network           INTEGER,
    business_strategy       VARCHAR2(160),
    bell_perception         INTEGER,
    lan_info                VARCHAR2(160),
    long_dist_carrier       INTEGER,
    revenue                 NUMBER(9,2),
    internet_flag           CHAR(1),
    isp                     VARCHAR2(32),
    home_page               VARCHAR2(50),
    cust_market_info        VARCHAR2(160),
    co_type                 INTEGER,
    msa_flag                CHAR(1),
    msa_term                SMALLINT,
    csa_flag                CHAR(1),
    maint_provider          VARCHAR2(32),
    telecom_budget          NUMBER(9,2),
    fiscal_end              DATE,
    equip_vendor            VARCHAR2(32),
    long_dist_bill          NUMBER(10,2),
    contact_frequency       INTEGER,
    video_flag              CHAR(1),
 CONSTRAINT PK_clientprofiles
  PRIMARY KEY (clientprofiles_id)
     USING INDEX
     TABLESPACE APPL_INDEX,
  CONSTRAINT fk_clientprofiles_1
  FOREIGN KEY (clients_id)
     REFERENCES clients
)
TABLESPACE APPL_DATA
;

CREATE INDEX Fk_clientprofiles_1 ON clientprofiles
```

continues

Source 5.1 Continued.

```
(
     clients_id
)
TABLESPACE APPL_INDEX
;

DROP TABLE clients_info_nmbrs CASCADE CONSTRAINTS;

CREATE TABLE clients_info_numbers (
     clients_info_nmbrs_id    INTEGER NOT NULL ,
     userid                   INTEGER,
     clients_id               INTEGER,
     listing_name             VARCHAR2(100),
     clients_number           CHAR(13),
     service_class            VARCHAR2(5),
     installed_lines          NUMBER(4),
     restrict_code_1          VARCHAR2(14),
     restrict_code_2          VARCHAR2(14),
     restrict_code_3          VARCHAR2(14),
     restrict_code_4          VARCHAR2(14),
     restrict_code_5          VARCHAR2(14),
     billing_name             VARCHAR2(40),
     phone                    VARCHAR2(10),
     disconnect_reason        CHAR(2),
     disconnect_date          DATE,
     btn                      CHAR(13),
     old_clients_number       CHAR(13),
     service_address          VARCHAR2(100),
     con_ctrl_number          CHAR(15),
     term_agreement           CHAR(13),
     shared_tenant_svcs       VARCHAR2(10),
     installation_date        DATE,
 CONSTRAINT pk_clients_info_nmbrs
  PRIMARY KEY (clients_info_nmbrs_id)
     USING INDEX
     TABLESPACE APPL_INDEX,
     CONSTRAINT fk_clients_info_nmbrs_1
  FOREIGN KEY (userid)
     REFERENCES users,
 CONSTRAINT fk_clients_info_nmbrs_2
  FOREIGN KEY (clients_id)
     REFERENCES clients
)
TABLESPACE APPL_DATA
;

CREATE INDEX Fk_clients_info_nmbrs_2 ON clients_info_nmbrs
(
     clients_id
```

```
)
 TABLESPACE APPL_INDEX
;

CREATE INDEX FK_clients_info_nmbrs_1 ON clients_info_nmbrs
(
     userid
)
TABLESPACE APPL_INDEX
;

DROP TABLE addresses CASCADE CONSTRAINTS;

CREATE TABLE addresses (
     addresses_id            INTEGER NOT NULL ,
     addrtype                INTEGER NOT NULL ,
     clients_info_nmbrs_id   INTEGER,
     clients_id              INTEGER,
     address1                VARCHAR2(80),
     address2                VARCHAR2(80),
     address3                VARCHAR2(80),
     address4                VARCHAR2(80),
     address5                VARCHAR2(80),
     address6                VARCHAR2(80),
     address7                VARCHAR2(80),
     address8                VARCHAR2(80),
     address9                VARCHAR2(80),
     address10               VARCHAR2(80),
     address11               VARCHAR2(80),
     address12               VARCHAR2(80),
     address13               VARCHAR2(80),
     address14               VARCHAR2(80),
     address15               VARCHAR2(80),
 CONSTRAINT pk_addresses
  PRIMARY KEY (addresses_id)
     USING INDEX
     TABLESPACE APPL_INDEX
 CONSTRAINT fk_addresses_1
  FOREIGN KEY (userid)
     REFERENCES users,
 CONSTRAINT fk_addresses_2
  FOREIGN KEY (clients_id)
     REFERENCES clients(clients_id),
 CONSTRAINT fk_addresses_3
  FOREIGN KEY (clients_info_nmbrs_id)
     REFERENCES clients_info_nmbrs
)
TABLESPACE APPL_DATA
;
```

continues

Source 5.1   Continued.

```
CREATE INDEX FK_addresses_3 ON addresses
(
     clients_info_nmbrs_id
)
TABLESPACE APPL_INDEX
;

CREATE INDEX FK_addresses_2 ON addresses
(
     clients_id
)
TABLESPACE APPL_INDEX
;

CREATE INDEX Fk_addresses_1 ON addresses
(
     userid
)
TABLESPACE APPL_INDEX
;

DROP TABLE circuit_id_info CASCADE CONSTRAINTS;

CREATE TABLE circuit_id_info (
     circuit_id_info_id          INTEGER NOT NULL,
     clients_info_nmbrs_id       INTEGER,
     connect_type                CHAR(1),
     connected_number            VARCHAR2(36) NOT NULL,
 CONSTRAINT PK_circuit_id_info
  PRIMARY KEY (circuit_id_info_id)
     USING INDEX
     TABLESPACE APPL_INDEX,
 CONSTRAINT fk_circuit_id_info_1
  FOREIGN KEY (clients_info_nmbrs_id)
   REFERENCES clients_info_nmbrs
)
TABLESPACE APPL_DATA
;

DROP TABLE sub_codes CASCADE CONSTRAINTS;

CREATE TABLE sub_codes (
     sub_codes_id               INTEGER NOT NULL,
     sub_code                   VARCHAR2(8) NOT NULL,
     clients_id                 INTEGER NOT NULL,
 CONSTRAINT PK_sub_codes
  PRIMARY KEY (clients_id,sub_codes_id)
     USING INDEX
     TABLESPACE APPL_INDEX,
```

```
  CONSTRAINT fk_sub_codes
   FOREIGN KEY (clients_id)
     REFERENCES clients
)
TABLESPACE APPL_DATA
;

CREATE INDEX FK_sub_codes_1 ON sub_codes
(
     clients_id
)
TABLESPACE APPL_INDEX
;

DROP TABLE ftx_codes CASCADE CONSTRAINTS;

CREATE TABLE ftx_codes (
     ftx_codes_id          INTEGER NOT NULL,
     ftx_code              CHAR(8) NOT NULL,
     clients_id            INTEGER,
     ftx_code_desc         VARCHAR2(32),
     primary_ftx_code_ind  CHAR(1),
 CONSTRAINT PK_ftx_codes
  PRIMARY KEY (clients_id,ftx_codes_id)
     USING INDEX
     TABLESPACE APPL_INDEX,
 CONSTRAINT fk_ftx_codes
  FOREIGN KEY (clients_id)
     REFERENCES clients
)
TABLESPACE APPL_DATA
;

CREATE INDEX FK_ftx_codes_1 ON ftx_codes
(
 clients_id
)
TABLESPACE APPL_INDEX
;

DROP TABLE contracts CASCADE CONSTRAINTS;

CREATE TABLE contracts (
     contacts_id            INTEGER NOT NULL,
     clients_info_nmbrs_id  INTEGER,
     contract_no            CHAR(15),
 CONSTRAINT PK_contracts
  PRIMARY KEY (clients_info_nmbrs_id,contacts_id)
     USING INDEX
     TABLESPACE APPL_INDEX,
```

continues

Source 5.1   Continued.

```
CONSTRAINT fk_contracts_1
  FOREIGN KEY (clients_info_nmbrs_id)
     REFERENCES clients_info_nmbrs
)
TABLESPACE APPL_DATA
;

CREATE INDEX Fk_contracts_1 ON contracts
(
 clients_info_nmbrs_id
)
TABLESPACE APPL_INDEX
;
```

7. Up to three addresses can tie to a clients_info_number, but only one can tie to the client.
8. A single clients_info_number can be tied to multiple contracts.
9. A single clients_info_number can be tied to multiple circuit/phone numbers.
10. A restrict_code indicator (up to 5) is used on a per-clients_info_number basis to restrict access to that number's information (this promulgates back up to any client information as well).
11. A client may have one client profile.

Under Oracle's implementation of object-oriented design in versions 8, 8*i,* and 9*i* object relationships are shown by use of REF statements. REF relationships are one-to-one. Since we can't make clients_info_number dependent on the client (see rule 1 in the previous list), we need the two main object structures, CLIENTS and CLIENTS_ INFO_NUMBERS. CLIENTS and CLIENTS_INFO_NUMBERS will relate by a REF from CLIENTS_INFO_NUMBERS to CLIENTS. All of the other dependent entities will roll up into one of the following: a type, a nested table, or a varray internal object.

For dependent entities whose behavior is limited to a fixed number of occurrences per parent record, Oracle suggests the use of varrays that are stored inline with the parent records in RAW format. However, tests indicates this wastes space, so a nested table may be more efficient. For multiple relations, where the ultimate number is unknown or is extremely high, or the size of the resulting RAW would be too long (i.e., anytime in early releases), I suggest using a nested table. For related one-to-one data, such as the RESTRICT_CODE data and the client profile data, I suggest using a type specification.

These are some rules for using types:

1. A varray or nested table cannot contain a varray or nested table as an attribute.
2. When using nested tables, you must specify a store table in which to store their records.
3. Store tables inherit the physical attributes of their parent table.

4. Default values cannot be specified for varrays.
5. Constraints (including NOT NULL) cannot be used in type definitions (they must be specified using an ALTER TABLE command).
6. A table column specified as a varray cannot be indexed.
7. A table using varrays or nested tables cannot be partitioned.
8. Varrays cannot be directly compared in SQL.
9. Incomplete types (forward typing) are allowed, but an incomplete type cannot be used in a CREATE TABLE command until it is complete.
10. The scalar parts of a type can be indexed directly in the parent table object.
11. Varray and nested table subattributes cannot be indexed directly on a parent table object.
12. Nested table store table attributes can be indexed.

Let's take a look at how this maps into the CREATE TYPE, varray, and NESTED TABLEs of Oracle9*i*. Look at Source 5.2, the code to implement the structure as remapped to Oracle8*i*. A simplified UML diagram of the new structure is shown in Figure 5.2; the symbols used are shown in Figure 5.3.

Source 5.2 Oracle9*i* code to implement application fragment.

```
rem
rem First drop then create the types, varrays, and nested table
rem definitions.
rem Order is important; you cannot delete a type with dependent
rem types, varrays, or nested tables.
rem
DROP TABLE clients_info_numbersv9i;
DROP TYPE clients_info_t force;
DROP TABLE clientsv9i;
DROP TYPE client_t force;
DROP TYPE sub_v force;
DROP TYPE ftx_v force;
DROP TYPE ceo_t force;
DROP TYPE restrict_code_t force;
DROP TYPE address_list force;
DROP TYPE address_t force;
DROP TYPE contract_list force;
DROP TYPE contract_t force;
DROP TYPE circuit_list force;
DROP TYPE circuit_t force;
rem
rem There can be multiple contracts so let's
rem make it a nested table
rem
CREATE TYPE circuit_t AUTHID DEFINER AS OBJECT (
     connect_type                    CHAR(1),
     connected_number                VARCHAR2(36)
```

continues

Source 5.2 Continued.

```
);
/

CREATE OR REPLACE TYPE circuit_list AS TABLE OF circuit_t;
/
rem
rem There can be multiple contracts; let's make it a
rem nested table
rem
CREATE OR REPLACE TYPE contract_t AUTHID DEFINER AS OBJECT (
     contract_number         CHAR(15)
);
/
CREATE OR REPLACE TYPE contract_list AS TABLE OF contract_t;
/
rem
rem There was a fixed number of franchise codes allowed and it was small
rem so use a VARRAY
rem
CREATE OR REPLACE TYPE sub_t AUTHID DEFINER AS OBJECT (
     sub_code           VARCHAR2(8)
);
/
rem
rem sub_v is a VARRAY of 10 elements
rem
CREATE OR REPLACE TYPE sub_v AS VARRAY(10) OF sub_t;
/
rem
rem There is a fixed number of SIC codes and it is small
rem so use a VARRAY
rem
CREATE OR REPLACE TYPE ftx_t AUTHID DEFINER AS OBJECT (
     ftx_code                    CHAR(8)  ,
     ftx_code_desc               VARCHAR2(32),
     primary_ftx_code_ind        CHAR(1)
);
/
rem
rem ftx_v is a VARRAY of 6 elements
rem
CREATE OR REPLACE TYPE ftx_v AS VARRAY(6) OF ftx_t;
/
rem
rem The LOOKUP information is a one-to-one type
rem data set so use a type definition directly into the object
rem
CREATE OR REPLACE TYPE lookup_t AUTHID DEFINER AS OBJECT(
```

```
            lookup_no                           VARCHAR2(9) ,
            lookup_parent                       VARCHAR2(9),
            lookup_str_adrs                     VARCHAR2(25),
            lookup_city                         VARCHAR2(20),
            lookup_state                        VARCHAR2(2),
            lookup_zip                          VARCHAR2(5),
            lookup_zip_ext                      VARCHAR2(4),
            lookup_type                         CHAR(2),
            lookup_parent_flag                  CHAR(1)
);
/
rem
rem The address information is fairly long, so even though
rem it is a fixed number of values, let's put it in a nested table.
rem This data is from a legacy system; addresses can have from
rem 5 to 15 lines of data.
rem
CREATE OR REPLACE TYPE address_t AUTHID DEFINER AS OBJECT (
        addrtype              INTEGER ,
        address1              VARCHAR2(80),
        address2              VARCHAR2(80),
        address3              VARCHAR2(80),
        address4              VARCHAR2(80),
        address5              VARCHAR2(80),
        address6              VARCHAR2(80),
        address7              VARCHAR2(80),
        address8              VARCHAR2(80),
        address9              VARCHAR2(80),
        address10             VARCHAR2(80),
        address11             VARCHAR2(80),
        address12             VARCHAR2(80),
        address13             VARCHAR2(80),
        address14             VARCHAR2(80),
        address15             VARCHAR2(80)
);
/
rem
rem address_list is a nested table definition
rem
CREATE OR REPLACE TYPE address_list AS TABLE OF address_t;
/
rem
rem The restrict_code data is a one-to-one type relation
rem so let's use a type definition directly into the object.
rem
CREATE OR REPLACE TYPE restrict_code_t AUTHID DEFINER AS OBJECT(
        restrict_code_1                 VARCHAR2(14),
        restrict_code_2                 VARCHAR2(14),
        restrict_code_3                 VARCHAR2(14),
```

continues

Source 5.2   Continued.

```
        restrict_code_4              VARCHAR2(14),
        restrict_code_5              VARCHAR2(14)
);
/
rem
rem The CEO data is a one-to-one relationship, so just use
rem a type definition directly into the object.
rem
CREATE OR REPLACE TYPE ceo_t AUTHID DEFINER AS OBJECT (
     ceo_first_name              VARCHAR2(13),
     ceo_last_name               VARCHAR2(15),
     ceo_middle_initial          VARCHAR2(1),
     ceo_suffix                  VARCHAR2(3),
     ceo_prefix                  VARCHAR2(10),
     ceo_title                   VARCHAR2(30)
);
/
rem
rem The client table is the master in this set. Now that
rem the dependent types, VARRAYs, nested tables, and
rem REF table have been created, go ahead and create it.
rem
CREATE OR REPLACE TYPE client_t AUTHID DEFINER AS OBJECT (
     clients_id                  INTEGER ,
     addresses                   address_list,
     customer_name               VARCHAR2(35) ,
     active_flag                 VARCHAR2(1),
     fax                         VARCHAR2(20),
     lookups                     lookup_t ,
     phone                       VARCHAR2(20),
     corporate_name              VARCHAR2(30),
     creation_ts                 DATE,
     creation_sy_user            NUMBER(38),
     spp_rating                  CHAR(2),
     rating_date                 DATE,
     competitor_loss             INTEGER,
     last_contact_ts             DATE,
     delete_status               CHAR(1),
     name_soundex                CHAR(4),
     sales_volume                VARCHAR2(15),
     sales_volume_code           CHAR(1),
     total_employees             VARCHAR2(9),
     line_of_bus                 VARCHAR2(19),
     pct_growth_sales            VARCHAR2(4),
     territory_covered           CHAR(1),
     mrc                         VARCHAR2(4),
     ceo                         ceo_t,
     sub_indctr                  CHAR(1),
```

```
    ftx_codes                ftx_v,
    sub_codes                sub_v,
    MEMBER PROCEDURE do_soundex(id IN integer, nor_val IN varchar2)
);
/
rem
rem Now create the object clients, which contain
rem nested tables, types, and normal attributes
rem
CREATE TABLE clientsV9i OF client_t
OIDINDEX oid_clientsV9i (TABLESPACE APPL_INDEX)
NESTED TABLE addresses STORE AS addressesv9i
        PCTFREE 10
        PCTUSED 80
        INITRANS 5
        MAXTRANS 255
        TABLESPACE APPL_DATA
        STORAGE (
                INITIAL 20m
                NEXT 10m
                MINEXTENTS 1
                MAXEXTENTS 10
                PCTINCREASE 0
        )
;
/
ALTER TABLE clientsV9i ADD
        CONSTRAINT PK_clientsv9i
                PRIMARY KEY (clients_id)
        USING INDEX
                PCTFREE 20
                INITRANS 5
                MAXTRANS 255
                TABLESPACE APPL_INDEX
                STORAGE (
                        INITIAL 10m
                        NEXT 10m
                        MINEXTENTS 1
                        MAXEXTENTS 121
                        PCTINCREASE 0
                        FREELISTS 5
                )
;
/
ALTER TABLE clientsV8i MODIFY
     customer_name NOT NULL;/
CREATE OR REPLACE TYPE BODY client_t IS
MEMBER PROCEDURE do_soundex(id IN integer, nor_val IN varchar2) IS
sx_val integer;
```

continues

Source 5.2   Continued.

```
begin
     sx_val:=soundex(nor_val);
     update clientsv9i set name_soundex=sx_val where clients_id=id;
end;
END;
/
rem
rem The clients_info_data is an independent one-to-many
rem from clientsv9i. We will REF client_t and CLIENTSV9i
rem
CREATE OR REPLACE TYPE clients_info_t AUTHID DEFINER AS OBJECT (
     clients_info_nmbrs_id     INTEGER,
     clients_id_r              REF client_t,
     listed_name               VARCHAR2(100),
     earning_number            CHAR(13),
     service_class             VARCHAR2(5),
     restrict_code             restrict_code_t,
     no_of_lines               NUMBER(4),
     disconnect_date           DATE,
     disconnect_reason         CHAR(2),
     billing_name              VARCHAR2(40),
     phone                     VARCHAR2(10),
     btn                       CHAR(13),
     old_clients_number        CHAR(13),
     service_address           VARCHAR2(100),
     con_ctrl_number           CHAR(15),
     term_agreement            CHAR(13),
     shared_tenant_svcs        VARCHAR2(10),
     installation_date         DATE,
     contracts                 contract_list,
     circuits                  circuit_list,
MEMBER PROCEDURE get_client_id_ref
(client_id IN integer, earning_id IN integer)
);
/
rem
rem clients_info_numbers is a table definition
rem
CREATE TABLE  clients_info_numbersV9i OF clients_info_t
     (clients_id_r WITH ROWID
     SCOPE IS tele_dba.clientsv9i)
     OIDINDEX oid_clients_info_nmbrsV9i (TABLESPACE APPL_INDEX)
     NESTED TABLE contracts STORE AS contractsV9i
     NESTED TABLE circuits STORE AS circuitsV9i
     PCTFREE 10
       PCTUSED 80
       INITRANS 5
       MAXTRANS 255
```

```
        TABLESPACE APPL_DATA
        STORAGE (
                INITIAL 20m
                NEXT 10m
                MINEXTENTS 1
                MAXEXTENTS UNLIMITED
                PCTINCREASE 0
        )
;
ALTER TABLE clients_info_numbersV9i ADD
        CONSTRAINT PK_clients_info_numbersV9i
                PRIMARY KEY (clients_info_nmbrs_id)
        USING INDEX
                PCTFREE 20
                INITRANS 5
                MAXTRANS 255
                TABLESPACE APPL_INDEX
                STORAGE (
                        INITIAL 10m
                        NEXT 10m
                        MINEXTENTS 1
                        MAXEXTENTS UNLIMITED
                        PCTINCREASE 0
                        FREELISTS 5
                )
;
CREATE OR REPLACE TYPE BODY clients_info_t AS
MEMBER PROCEDURE get_client_id_ref
(client_id IN integer, earning_id IN integer)
IS
begin
        update CLIENTS_INFO_NUMBERSV9i z
    set z.clients_id_r =
    (SELECT REF(x) FROM clientsv9i x
        WHERE x.clients_id=client_id)
    WHERE z.clients_info_nmbrs_id=earning_id;
end;
END;
/
```

Notice in the code in Source 5.2 the use of the following coding conventions:

- All TYPES end in "_t."
- All varrays end in "_v" (I use "_vw" for views).
- All NESTED TABLES end in "_list."
- When used in a DDL statement, native datatypes are capitalized, while user-defined types are lowercased.

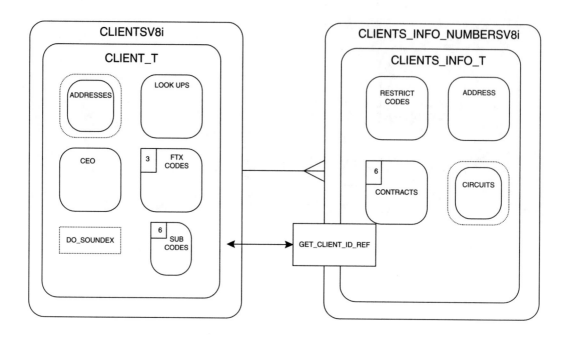

NOTE:

Implicit methods such as the constructor/destructors built by
Oracle internals when the type is created aren't shown.

FIGURE 5.2   Simplified UML diagram of converted Oracle7 application fragment.

- The entities are singular, while the tables or objects that they become are plural or are a plural or neutral form.
- All REF columns end in "_r."
- All primary keys have the prefix "PK_" followed by the table name.
- All foreign keys have the prefix "FK_" followed by the table name and arbitrary integer.
- All lookup keys have the prefix "LU_" followed by the table name and arbitrary integer.
- All unique value keys have the prefix "UK_" followed by the table name and an arbitrary integer.
- All object ID indexes (OID) have the prefix "OID_" followed by the table name.

Also notice that each section is remarked (in the new code) to tell what is going on and why. These are good practices and should be emulated (I don't say this is the best way or the only way; I do recommend that you develop a methodology that makes sense to your environment).

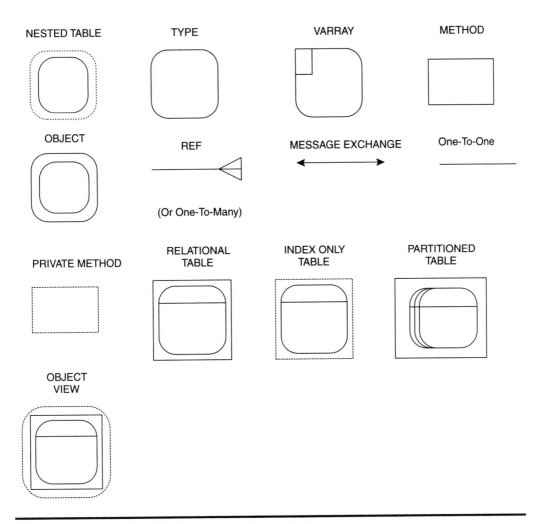

FIGURE 5.3   Symbol definition for simplified UML diagram.

I want to point out here that, in version 8.1.3, the following type creation in the Source 5.2 didn't work, and resulted in an ORA-03113 and forced disconnection. It did, however, work in 8.0.5 and 8.1.5.

```
CREATE OR REPLACE TYPE client_t as object (
        clients_id              INTEGER ,
        addresses               address_list,
        customer_name           VARCHAR2(35) ,
        active_flag             VARCHAR2(1),
        fax                     VARCHAR2(20),
        lookups                 lookup_t ,
        phone                   VARCHAR2(20),
```

```
        corporate_name          VARCHAR2(30),
        creation_ts             DATE,
        creation_sy_user        NUMBER(38),
        spp_rating              CHAR(2),
        rating_date             DATE,
        competitor_loss         INTEGER,
        last_contact_ts         DATE,
        delete_status           CHAR(1),
        name_soundex            CHAR(4),
        sales_volume            VARCHAR2(15),
        sales_volume_code       CHAR(1),
        total_employees         VARCHAR2(9),
        line_of_bus             VARCHAR2(19),
        pct_growth_sales        VARCHAR2(4),
        territory_covered       CHAR(1),
        mrc                     VARCHAR2(4),
        ceo                     ceo_t,
        sub_indctr              CHAR(1),
        ftx_codes               ftx_v,
        sub_codes               sub_v,
        MEMBER PROCEDURE do_soundex(id IN integer, nor_val IN varchar2)
);
```

This next type creation did work. Notice that the record length has been shortened by removing several VARCHAR2 columns. Other than that it is identical, and the changes allowed the rest of the script to complete:

```
CREATE OR REPLACE TYPE client_t as object (
        clients_id              INTEGER ,
        addresses               address_list,
        customer_name           VARCHAR2(35) ,
        active_flag             VARCHAR2(1),
        lookups                 lookup_t ,
        creation_ts             DATE,
        creation_sy_user        NUMBER,
        spp_rating              CHAR(2),
        rating_date             DATE,
        competitor_loss         INTEGER,
        last_contact_ts         DATE,
        delete_status           CHAR(1),
        name_soundex            CHAR(4),
        sales_volume            VARCHAR2(15),
        sales_volume_code       CHAR(1),
        territory_covered       CHAR(1),
        mrc                     VARCHAR2(4),
        ceo                     ceo_t,
        sub_indctr              CHAR(1),
        ftx_codes               ftx_v,
        sub_codes               sub_v,
        MEMBER PROCEDURE do_soundex(id IN integer, nor_val IN varchar2)
);
/
```

This seems to indicate a row length limit when using types in 8*i*, version 8.1.3, which wasn't present in 8.0.5 and isn't present in 8.1.5, so if you use an older release of 8*i*, be careful. It is not present in 9*i*.

If I had included the storage and physical attributes for the standard relational Oracle7 code, this fragment would have been 12 pages long. The object relational Oracle9*i* code (with storage clauses) is only five pages. The Oracle7 DDL must have the primary tables created first, then the related tables (or all tables, then the constraints). The Oracle9*i* code must have all types, varrays, and nested tables, as well as related tables, before the primary tables can be defined. If methods used in the type bodies are dependent on specific existing tables, then those tables must be created before the type bodies. This indicates that the Oracle8, Oracle8*i*, and Oracle9*i* system will require more analysis on the front end to build properly. If this analysis is not done properly, the rebuilding will be more complex than with an Oracle7 database structure, at least in versions prior to Oracle9*i*. In Oracle9*i*, the ability to cascade TYPE changes will make fixing oversights and mistakes easier.

Notice that the number of indexes dropped from 19 to 4. This is because, as tables are made into nested tables, Oracle in its object-oriented paradigm adds another column (SETID$) that is in the structure of their store tables. This SETID$ value is added to the applicable indexes to establish the proper relations. This is done under the covers, and DBAs need not concern themselves with it. The store tables inherit the physical attributes of their master table. The store tables can be modified just as regular tables can; thus, if required, you can add performance-enhancing indexes, as well as alter storage parameters.

Again, the order is critical. Notice that the type bodies come after the table created with the types (for client_t and clients_info_t). This is because the methods included in the bodies are dependent on the clients and clients_info_numbers tables to be valid. Also note that the clients table is created prior to the clients_info_numbers table. This is required because the column clients_id_r references the clients table. (Note that a REF can only refer to one entry in a referenced object; therefore, references always go from the dependent table to the controlling table, from the many side of the relation to the one side.)

In the table definition for the clients_info_numbers table, examine the first couple of lines that follow the CREATE line:

```
clients_id_r WITH ROWID
SCOPE IS tele_dba.clientsv9i
```

These commands "finish" the REF command that was started in the type declaration. Because a type is generic in nature, you cannot limit the scope of a REF value inside a type declaration. Instead, you must restrict the value at point of use, in this case, the table creation. These commands allow the rowid pseudocolumn to be stored with the OID from the REFed object table. This storing of the rowid and OID speeds any UNREF activities. The SCOPE command restricts all REFs from this column to the specified table; this also reduces the space requirements for the REF column value and speeds access.

The OIDINDEX clause in both CREATE TABLE commands creates an index on the object identifier that can then be used to speed REF type queries against the tables. In this situation, the clients_info_numbersV9i object table will be REFing the clientsv9i object table, so placing the clientsv9i OIDs into an index is a performance-enhancing idea. The OIDINDEX on clients_info_numbersV9i is just good form.

Conversion Summary

To summarize the conversion example here are a few guidelines:

1. Attribute sets that are one-to-one with the main object should be placed in a TYPE definition and used directly.
2. Attribute sets that have a low, fixed number of occurrences should be placed into varrays. (But note, this may not be true if constraints or direct comparisons are required.)
3. Attribute sets with many occurrences or that require constraints and value-to-value comparison should be placed in nested tables.
4. If a type is to be used in a REFable object, the object must be created using the AS OBJECT clause.
5. REF clauses in a TYPE declaration must be finished via an ALTER TABLE command on the final object table if scoping or rowid storage is required.
6. Use of WITH ROWID and OIDINDEX clauses should be encouraged to speed access and, in some cases, to reduce storage requirements.
7. Analysis of dependencies is critical to success.
8. In some versions of 8i, be careful of row length; there seems to be an undocumented length limitation.

Oracle8, Oracle8i, and Oracle9i will require a great deal more front-end analysis in order to prevent recoding. To pull together the example in this section, I had to use the DBA, Application Developer, Server Concepts, PL/SQL, and SQL Reference Manuals (Oracle9i beta copies and OracleTechnet, supplied online, 9.0.1 versions; http:// technet. oracle.com/). Even with references, it initially took two days of testing for the Oracle8 rewrite and an additional day with Oracle8i and Oracle9i to get clean builds of the code in Source 5.2 (hence the drop commands at the top of the script). Oracle9i is a new view of the world, and you will have to change your perception of how the database works in order to fully utilize its provided features.

NOTE The DBA should read the SQL reference manual on the Oracle technet Web site concerning constraints, table creation, and use of storage parameters before creating tables.

5.6 INDEX-ONLY TABLE: AN EXAMPLE

In many cases, such as with lookup tables, we end up with a one- or two-column table and an index for that table. This wastes space. Oracle8, Oracle8*i,* and Oracle9*i* allow us to create an index-only table that is stored in B-tree format based on the value of the primary keys. Since the table is stored as an index, there are no rowids, and all access is through the primary key. This reduces space needs and makes access to the table much faster. This should be used for small tables and low update/insert tables. Index-only tables cannot contain LOB or LONG columns, and the following operations are not allowed:

- Creating an index-only table with a subquery clause.
- Indexing an index-only table (other than bitmap indexes on IOTs that have a mapping table specified).
- Imposing UNIQUE constraints on values in an index-only table.
- Composite partitioning of an index-only table.

The following is an example of the creation of an index-only table:

```
CREATE TABLE look_ups (
lookup_code            INTEGER NOT NULL,
lookup_value           VARCHAR2(10),
lookup_descr           VARCHAR2(80),
CONSTRAINT pk_look_ups PRIMARY KEY (lookup_code)
ORGANIZATION INDEX TABLESPACE sales_ts
PCTTHRESHOLD 20 INCLUDING lookup_value
OVERFLOW TABLESPACE sales_ts;
```

You can convert INDEX ONLY tables to regular tables using the Oracle IMPORT/ EXPORT utilities. To convert an INDEX ONLY table to a regular table:

1. Export the INDEX ONLY table data using the conventional path.
2. Create a regular table definition with the same definition.
3. Import the INDEX ONLY table data, making sure IGNORE = y (ensures that "object exists" error is ignored).

After an INDEX ONLY table is converted to a regular table, it can be exported and imported using pre-Oracle8 EXPORT/IMPORT utilities.

5.7 SIZING AN ORACLE9*i* NONCLUSTERED TABLE

The procedures in this section describe how to estimate the total number of data blocks necessary to hold data inserted to a nonclustered table. Typically, the space required to store a set of rows that experience updates, deletes, and inserts will exceed this calculated value. The actual space required for complex workloads is best determined by analyzing an existing table; it is then scaled by the projected number of future rows in the production table. In general, increasing amounts of concurrent activity on the same data block results in additional overhead (for transaction records), so it is important that you take into account such activity when scaling empirical results. (Spreadsheets are available at the Wiley Web site for calculating table and index size.)

NOTE   No allowance is made here for changes to PCTFREE or PCTUSED, due to insert, delete, or update activity. Thus, this reflects a best-case scenario, that is, when users insert rows without performing deletes or updates.

Calculating space required by nonclustered tables is a five-step process:

1. Calculate the total block header size.
2. Calculate the available data space per data block.
3. Calculate the space used per row.
4. Calculate the total number of rows that will fit in a data block.
5. With the rows/block data, calculate the total number of data blocks and convert to kilo- or megabytes.

A Simple Sizing Example

Let's take a more detailed look at the steps using a simple example.

Step 1: Calculate the Total Block Header Size   The space required by the data block header is the result of the following formula:

Space after headers (hsize) =
DB_BLOCK_SIZE – KCBH – UB4 – KTBBH – ((INITRANS – 1) * KTBIT) – KDBH

where:

DB_BLOCK_ SIZE. The database blocksize with which the database was created. It can be viewed in the V$PARAMETER view by selecting:

```
SELECT value FROM v$parameter WHERE name = 'db_block_size';
```

KCBH, UB4, KTBBH, KTBIT, KDBH. Constants whose sizes you can obtain by selecting from entries in the V$TYPE_SIZE view.

- KCBH is the block common header; on NT with a 4-KB blocksize, this is 20.
- UB4 is "either byte 4"; on NT with a 4-KB blocksize, this is 4.
- KTBBH is the transaction fixed-header length; on NT with a 4-KB blocksize, this is 48.

- KTBIT is transaction variable header; on NT with a 4-KB blocksize, this is 24.
- KDBH is the data header; on NT with a 4-KB blocksize, this is 14.

INITRANS. The initial number of transaction entries allocated to the table. For an NT 4.0 platform with a 4-KB blocksize and an INITRANS value of 5, the calculation would be:

DB_BLOCK_SIZE – KCBH – UB4 – KTBBH – ((INITRANS – 1) * KTBIT) – KDBH
hsize = 4192 – 20 – 4 – 48 – ((5–1)*24) – 14 = 4192 – 182 = 4010 bytes

Step 2: Calculate the Available Data Space per Data Block   The space reserved for data in each data block, as specified by PCTFREE, is calculated as follows:

available data space (availspace) =
CEIL(hsize * (1 – PCTFREE/100)) – KDBT

where:

CEIL. A fractional result rounded to the next-highest integer.

PCTFREE. The percentage of space reserved for updates in the table.

KDBT. A constant corresponding to the Table Directory Entry size, which you can obtain by selecting the entry from the V$TYPE_SIZE view. For an NT 4.0 platform with a 4-KB blocksize, this is 4.

TIP   If you are unable to locate the value of KDBT, use the value of UB4 instead.

So, to carry on our example, assuming a PCTFREE of 20 for our table:

CEIL(hsize * (1 – PCTFREE/100)) – KDBT
CEIL(4010*(1 – 20/100)) – 4 = CEIL((4010*.8) – 4) = CEIL(3208 – 4) = 3204

we get an available data size of 3204 bytes per block.

Step 3: Calculate the Space Used per Row   Calculating the amount of space used per row is a multistep task. First, you must calculate the column size, including byte lengths:

Column size including byte length =
column size + (1, if column size < 250, else 3)

I suggest using estimated averages for all variable-length fields, such as numeric, VARCHAR2, and RAW. Remember that number datatypes are stored at a two-to-one ratio in the database (i.e., a NUMBER(30) takes up 15 bytes of storage if each place is filled). The maximum for a NUMBER is 21 bytes. The size for a DATE is 7 bytes. Rowid takes 10 bytes for the extended and 6 bytes for the restricted type of rowid. CHAR always takes its full specified length; VARCHAR2, RAW, and other variable-length fields will use only the space they take up.

TIP   You can also determine column size empirically, by selecting avg(vsize (colname)) for each column in the table.

For example, I have a table TEST with a single VARCHAR2(50) column that has eight rows of various lengths. The return from the select "SELECT AVG(VSIZE (TEST1)) FROM TEST;" is:

```
AVG(VSIZE(TEST1))
-------------------------------
                             29
```

The table also has a number column TEST2:

```
AVG(VSIZE(TEST2))
-------------------------------
                              7
```

Then, calculate the row size:

Rowsize =
row header (3 * UB1) + sum of column sizes including length bytes

UB1 is "UNSIGNED BYTE 1," which is 1 on NT 4.0 with a 4-KB blocksize, so:

Rowsize =
(3*1) + (8 + 30) = 41

Of course, if you have an example table, the quickest way to get average row size is to just analyze it and then select average row size from USER_TABLES:

```
SQL> analyze table test1 compute statistics;
Table analyzed.
SQL> select avg_row_len from user_tables
  2 where table_name='TEST1';

AVG_ROW_LEN
--------------------
                  41
```

Finally, you can calculate the space used per row:

Space used per row (rowspace) =
MIN(UB1 * 3 + UB4 + SB2, rowsize) + SB2

where:

UB1, UB4, SB2. Constants whose size can be obtained by selecting entries from the V$TYPE_SIZE view:

- UB1 is "unsigned byte 1"; it is set to 1 for NT 4.0 with a 4-KB blocksize.
- UB4 is "unsigned byte 4"; it is set to 4 for NT 4.0 with a 4-KB blocksize.
- SB2 is "signed byte 2"; it is set to 2 for NT 4.0 with a 4-KB blocksize.

So this becomes MIN((1*3) + 4 + 2, 41) + 2, or, 41 + 2 = 43.

MIN. Calculated by taking the lesser of either UBI *3 + UB4 + SB2 or the calculated row size value. If the space per row exceeds the available space per data block, but is less than the available space per data block without any space reserved for updates (for example, available space with PCTFREE = 0), each row will be stored in its own block.

When the space per row exceeds the available space per data block, without any space reserved for updates, rows inserted into the table will be chained into two or more pieces; hence, this storage overhead will be higher.

Step 4: Calculate the Total Number of Rows That Will Fit into a Data Block
You can calculate the total number of rows that will fit into a data block using the following equation:

Number of rows in block =
FLOOR(availspace / rowspace)

where:

FLOOR. A fractional result rounded to the next lowest integer.

So for our example this becomes:

```
FLOOR(3204/43) = 74
```

Step 5: Calculate the Total Blocks Required The next step allows calculation of total blocks that then allows us to convert to total size required.

```
total blocks =
(Total Table Rows) / (Rows Per Block)
Total Kilobytes =
```

```
CEIL((total blocks * blocksize) / 1024)
Total Megabytes =
CEIL((total blocks * blocksize) / 1048576)      --(1024^2)
```

For our example, we estimate we will have 42,000 rows in this table over the next year. So, the calculation becomes:

((42000/74)*4192) / 1024 = 2324 KB or 3 MB (rounding up)

This calculation must also be done for each nested table type, and the table storage must be altered accordingly. Remember to add the SETID$ column length of 16 to each row length calculated for a nested table. The size of the RAW required for inline storage of a varray can vary between 2.5 and over 6 times the size of the combined row length times the number of elements. A nested table reference pointer is usually a RAW(36) value. A REF value will vary between 42 and 46 bytes of system storage.

A More Complex Sizing Example

Let's do a complex sizing example before moving on. From our conversion example, we have the following example of an Oracle9*i* complex object:

```
SQL> DESC CLIENTSV9i
 Name                         Null?     Type
 --------------------         -------   ---------------
 CLIENTS_ID                   NOT NULL  NUMBER(38)
 ADDRESSES                              RAW(36)
 CUSTOMER_NAME                          VARCHAR2(35)
 ACTIVE_FLAG                            VARCHAR2(1)
 FAX                                    VARCHAR2(20)
 LOOKUPS                                LOOKUP_T
 PHONE                                  VARCHAR2(20)
 CORPORATE_NAME                         VARCHAR2(30)
 CREATION_TS                            DATE
 CREATION_SY_USER                       NUMBER(38)
 SPP_RATING                             CHAR(2)
 RATING_DATE                            DATE
 COMPETITOR_LOSS                        NUMBER(38)
 LAST_CONTACT_TS                        DATE
 DELETE_STATUS                          CHAR(1)
 NAME_SOUNDEX                           CHAR(4)
 SALES_VOLUME                           VARCHAR2(15)
 SALES_VOLUME_CODE                      CHAR(1)
 TOTAL_EMPLOYEES                        VARCHAR2(9)
 LINE_OF_BUS                            VARCHAR2(19)
 PCT_GROWTH_SALES                       VARCHAR2(4)
 TERRITORY_COVERED                      CHAR(1)
 MRC                                    VARCHAR2(4)
 CEO                                    CEO_T
```

```
SUB_INDCTR                              CHAR(1)
FTX_CODES                               RAW(676)
SUB_CODES                               RAW(560)
```

In this object we have normal attributes, named types, varrays, and a nested table. The named types are LOOK_UPS and CEO. The nested table is addresses, and the varrays are ftx_codes and sub_codes. The first step is to size the nested tables and named types. The nested table is called address_list, and consists of:

```
setid$          RAW(16)
addrtype        INTEGER
address1        VARCHAR2(80)
address2        VARCHAR2(80)
address3        VARCHAR2(80)
address4        VARCHAR2(80)
address5        VARCHAR2(80)
address6        VARCHAR2(80)
address7        VARCHAR2(80)
address8        VARCHAR2(80)
address9        VARCHAR2(80)
address10       VARCHAR2(80)
address11       VARCHAR2(80)
address12       VARCHAR2(80)
address13       VARCHAR2(80)
address14       VARCHAR2(80)
address15       VARCHAR2(80)
```

The address1-15 fields will always be filled with two records, one with 5 fields (average of 10 characters each) plus a single integer value for addrtype and a second with up to 15 fields (average of 7 with 10 characters each) and a single integer value for addrtype. This yields the following row lengths:

$$16 + 1 + (10 * 5) + (1 * 7) = 75$$
$$16 + 1 + (10 * 7) + (1 * 9) = 96$$

We have a 4-KB blocksize, and this is on NT 4.0, so the following calculation from step 1 is still good assuming we use an INITRANS of 5:

DB_BLOCK_SIZE – KCBH – UB4 – KTBBH – ((INITRANS – 1) * KTBIT) – KDBH
hsize = 4192 – 20 – 4 – 48 – ((5–1) * 24) – 14 = 4192 – 182 = 4010 bytes

The calculation from step 2 is valid here, too:

CEIL(hsize * (1 – PCTFREE / 100)) – KDBT
CEIL(4010 * (1 – 20 / 100)) – 4 = CEIL((4010 * .8) – 4) = CEIL(3208 – 4) = 3204

Step 3 becomes:

Rowsize =
row header (3 * UB1) + sum of column sizes including length bytes
3 + 75 = 78
3 + 96 = 99

At this point, let's average these to a single row size and double the expected count (since we will have x occurrences of two rows, if we average the row size, we will have $2x$ of the average size): average = (78 + 99) / 2 = 177/2 = 89 (rounding up).

Step 4 becomes:

Rows per block: =
3204 / 89 = 36

For step 5 we estimate 2.5 million rows, so let's calculate in megabytes only:

((2500000 / 36) * 4196) / 1048576) = 278 meg

This should be the amount of storage required for our nested table store table.

Next, we do the named types. The named types are LOOK_UPS and CEO. Here is CEO:

```
ceo_first_name          VARCHAR2(13),
ceo_last_name           VARCHAR2(15),
ceo_middle_initial      VARCHAR2(1),
ceo_suffix              VARCHAR2(3),
ceo_prefix              VARCHAR2(10),
ceo_title               VARCHAR2(30)
```

with a total length of 72 plus 7 length bytes, for a grand total of 79.

Here is LOOK_UPS:

```
lookup_no               VARCHAR2(9)  ,
lookup_parent           VARCHAR2(9),
lookup_str_adrs         VARCHAR2(25),
lookup_city             VARCHAR2(20),
lookup_state            VARCHAR2(2),
lookup_zip              VARCHAR2(5),
lookup_zip_ext          VARCHAR2(4),
lookup_type             CHAR(2),
lookup_parent_flag      CHAR(1)
```

with a total length of 77 plus 9 length bytes, for a total of 86.

Now we have the data required to finish the calculation:

3 + (35 + 17 + 1 + 20 + 86 + 20 + 10 + 7 + 3 + 2 + 7 + 3 + 7 + 1 + 4 + 7 + 2 + 10 + 3 + 1 + 4 + 79 + 1 + 676 + 560) + (1 * 25) =
1700

> **N**OTE   Some values (most of the VARCHAR2s) were averaged. The number values all correspond to integers that won't exceed six places (6 / 2 = 3), and DATEs are always 7 bytes.

So now we have the 3,204 available-space calculation and the 1,700 row size, which indicates we will have one row per block with a 4-KB blocksize. If we changed the varrays into NESTED TABLE, this requirement would drop by 1,166 and push us down to a row size of 534 and a rows-per-block of 3,204/534, or 6, decreasing the storage requirements by a factor of 6 for the primary object table. Since we are talking about a much smaller row size in the nested table storage tables than would be required with varrays, we would also reduce the overall storage requirements and make better use of available resources.

5.8 TABLE ALTERATION AND TRUNCATION

The ALTER TABLE command was covered in Chapter 4, Section 4.2, on relational tables. The commands for dropping and truncating tables are also covered in Chapter 4.

5.9 SUMMARY

This chapter examined object tables, using examples to show how an application fragment could be converted from Oracle7 relational tables to Oracle9*i* object tables. The chapter also covered the alteration of tables and sizing of both simple and complex object tables.

CHAPTER 6

Administration of Indexes

Indexes can make or break an application. A nonindexed query that takes tens of minutes can be made to return values within seconds if indexes are done properly. A critical subset of the DBA's tasks involves the placement, creation, sizing, and maintenance of the normal, bitmapped, partitioned, function-based, and subpartitioned indexes available in Oracle8, Oracle8*i* and Oracle9*i*.

Oracle8 offered new functionality in the form of partitioned, bitmapped, and reversed key indexes. Oracle8*i* offered all of these plus the capability to do INDEXTYPE, DOMAIN INDEX, and function-based indexes, as well as more advanced partitioning options for indexes. Partitioned indexes allow the spread of index data automatically by data value range across multiple partitions that can be placed on several disk arrays or platters. In Oracle8*i*, these partitions can be further subdivided into subpartitions. Bitmapped indexes allow for indexing of low-cardinality data, a feature that came about in 7.3.2.3 and continued with Oracle8 and its later releases. Bitmapped indexes map data values as binary integers, allowing low-cardinality data to be quickly accessed with sometimes almost quantum decreases in access speed. For some specialized types of query, a reverse key index can improve data access speeds.

In Oracle9*i,* two new types of index are offered: the *bitmap join index* and the *skip scan index*. A bitmap join index acts as an intersection between two tables, in a sense, prejoining them via a bitmap index. A skip scan index is a specially constructed index that allows Oracle to scan independent B-tree levels instead of the normal top-down scan.

Indexes allow queries to rapidly retrieve data, with proper implementation. Single columns, or groups of columns, can be indexed. A DBA can specify whether or not an index is unique. Remember, for proper table design, each table must have a unique identifier. A unique index is automatically created when a unique or primary key constraint clause is used in a CREATE or ALTER TABLE command.

Indexes speed the search for queries when approximately 2 to 7 percent of the table or less is being retrieved. For larger retrievals, inserts, and updates to index columns, and deletes, indexes slow response. An exception to this is if you use a bitmapped index for low-cardinality data.

How columns are indexed affects their efficiency. Order columns should be specified to reflect the way a select will retrieve them. The column accessed most often should be put first. Remember, the leading portion of the index is used to speed queries. A composite index can be created on up to 16 columns. Columns of type LONG and LONG RAW cannot be indexed.

6.1 CREATION OF INDEXES

Oracle8 introduced the concepts of partitioned, bitmapped (available in 7.3.2), and reversed key indexes. These concepts were carried over in Oracle8*i,* which also added functional indexes and descending indexes, as well as index types. In Oracle8*i* and Oracle9*i,* local and global partitioning and subpartitioning are also available for indexes.

NOTE   For this section, refer to the CREATE INDEX command syntax in the SQL reference at http://technet.oracle.com/, or to the Oracle9*i* SQL Reference (Release 9.0.1, Oracle Corporation, June 2002) from the Oracle9*i* documentation CD-ROM.

When an index is created, you should specify the INITRANS and MAXTRANS parameterss, or you will have to drop and re-create the index, or use the index rebuild commands to change them. If you are loading data, create indexes last, as it is more efficient to load data and then create indexes than to update multiple disks concurrently during the load process. If a table is fairly static, then a large number of indexes may be good; however, if you have a table with a large number of inserts and updates, then multiple indexes will cause a performance hit.

The value for PCTFREE should be set according to how much update activity you expect on the table. The space specified as PCTFREE (a percentage of each block) will never be used unless there is update activity against the columns in an index. Therefore, for primary keys whose values you expect never to be updated, set PCTFREE low. For foreign key or lookup indexes, set PCTFREE higher, to allow for expected update activity.

Always specify FREELISTS if the index will be updated by more than one process. The value for FREELISTS will correspond to the number of concurrently updating processes. This is another parameter that requires a rebuild of the index to alter in Oracle versions earlier than 8.1.6.

When creating an index, always specify the tablespace where it is to be placed. If the location is not specified, it goes in your default tablespace, which is probably the location of the table you are indexing as well! Not specifying the tablespace can result in instant contention for disk resources and poor performance. I once saw an application improve query speeds by 300 percent just by placing the indexes in their proper location, as opposed to being in with the tables. The DBA before me had dropped and re-created the primary keys for each of the tables simply by using the DISABLE/ENABLE clause of the ALTER TABLE and without specifying the storage clause.

If you use a parallel server to create your index, remember to set your extent sizes to X/N bytes, where X is the calculated size for the index (maximum expected size) and N is the number of query servers to be used. Each parallel query server takes an extent to do its work above the high-water mark; this is true for table creations and loads in parallel as well.

To further speed index builds, specify the UNRECOVERABLE option so that the index doesn't generate any redo. Remember to immediately do a backup since the creation will not be logged. Use this for large index creations, as it does little good for small indexes.

Composite indexes cannot exceed 32 columns, or half the available data space in a block, whichever comes first.

To create a function-based index in your own schema on your own table, in addition to the prerequisites for creating a conventional index, you must have the QUERY REWRITE system privilege. To create the index in another schema or on another schema's table, you must have the GLOBAL QUERY REWRITE privilege. In both cases, the table owner must also have the EXECUTE object privilege on the function(s) used in the function-based index. The functions used in a function-based index must be DETERMINISTIC (i.e., they always return the same answer for the same input) and be created with the DETERMINISTIC keyword. In addition, in order for Oracle to use function-based indexes in queries, the QUERY_REWRITE_ENABED initialization parameter must be set to TRUE, and the QUERY_REWRITE_INTEGRITY initialization parameter must be set to TRUSTED. Following the function-based indexes creation, both the index and table must be analyzed to enable the CBO to recognize the new index and use it.

B-Tree and Indexes

During any discussion of indexes with Oracle, the subject of B-tree structure is always bandied about as if everyone knew exactly what is being talked about. However, unless you come from a computer science or academic programming background, all you may understand is that a B-tree is a special structure format for an index that allows rapid access of the data in the index. But exactly what is a B-tree? Let's take a quick look at a B-tree structure in Figure 6.1 before we go on. Each upper node is known as a *branch,* while the lowest levels are known as *leaf nodes.* Branches point to other branches or leaf nodes. Leaf nodes store value-rowid pairs.

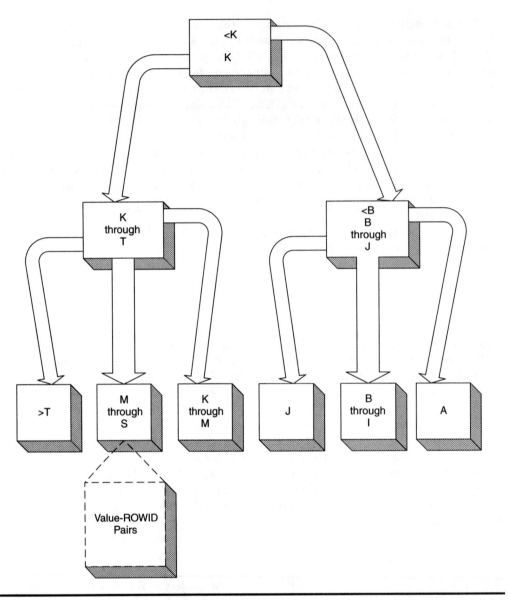

FIGURE 6.1   Example of a B-tree.

The actual distribution will depend on the number of data values in each range of values in a B-tree, with the overall goal to reduce the number of required levels that must be traversed to get to a specific value. The advantages of a B-tree structure are:

- All leaf blocks are of the same depth (number of values).
- In the case of randomly entered data, the B-tree stays balanced automatically.
- All blocks of a B-tree index are three-quarters full (on the average), allowing insertion without rebuild.
- B-trees provide excellent performance for all types of selects.
- Insert, update, and deletes tend to be efficient in a B-tree structure.
- B-tree performance stays optimal even when tables vary from small to large.

Indexes and Their Usage

With concatenated indexes, Oracle8*i* and Oracle9*i* can use *key compression* on the leading index values that show repeating behavior. Key compression reduces the size required for the storage of concatenated indexes. In order to use key compression, the index must be concatenated to show a grouping piece and a unique piece. The grouping piece repeats, while the unique piece will generally vary within a unique group range value. Key compression cannot be used on a primary key or unique index with a single column used as the index value.

Indexes store column values in either B-tree or bitmap format. The B-tree format is used for high-cardinality data (data with many unique values, such as last name, date of birth, part number, etc.). The binary index is used for low-cardinality data (sex, true/false, race, etc.). Indexes improve the performance of queries sometimes one-hundred-fold. Indexes are especially useful for:

- Searching for rows with specified index column values.
- Accessing tables in index column order.

When you initially insert a great number of rows into a new table, such as with import or SQLLOADER, it is generally faster to create the table, insert the rows, and then create the index. If you create the index before inserting the rows, Oracle must update the index for every row inserted. However, if you are inserting using a PL/SQL routine from a flat database table into a more normal structure, indexes can speed the process considerably.

TIP   If you are using a sequence or a call to SYSDATE to populate a column that corresponds to a unique or primary key field, use a reverse key index to prevent "hot spotting" and unbalanced B-trees.

Oracle recommends that you do not explicitly define UNIQUE indexes on tables; uniqueness is strictly a logical concept and should be associated with the definition of a table. Therefore, define UNIQUE integrity constraints on the desired columns. Oracle enforces UNIQUE integrity constraints by automatically defining a unique index on the unique key. Exceptions to this recommendation are usually performance-related. For example, using a CREATE TABLE . . . AS SELECT with a UNIQUE constraint is very much slower than creating the table without the constraint and then manually creating the UNIQUE constraint via an ALTER TABLE command.

If indexes contain NULLs, the NULLs are considered distinct values. There is, however, one exception: If all the non-NULL values in two or more rows of an index are identical, the rows are considered identical; therefore, UNIQUE indexes prevent this from occurring. This does not apply if there are no non-NULL values—in other words, if the rows are entirely NULL.

Use of Normal Unique and Nonunique Indexes

For most situations, a normal index (i.e., not a bitmapped or reverse key) will be used. This type of index can be monolithic (all in one index, albeit with multiple extents) or partitioned and subpartitioned (divided automatically by Oracle into several different identically structured indexes with different data ranges). Another item to note is that, prior to Oracle8*i*, while you could specify the DESC keyword for compatibility reasons, it was ignored in practice. This does not happen in versions of Oracle later than Oracle8*i*, and the index will be built in descending order. The DESC keyword is not applicable to bitmapped indexes. Like function-based indexes, DESC type indexes are not used until they and their base table are analyzed.

A normal index can be unique, which enforces uniqueness on the column it is based on (primary key and unique indexes are of this type), or nonunique. If the primary key constraint, unique constraint, or UNIQUE command option is not specified either during CREATE or ALTER tables or CREATE INDEX, then the index is nonunique.

If an index is being used for high cardinality (few related table rows for a single value) or to enforce uniqueness (primary key or unique index), then for most cases it should be a normal index. However, improvements in performance for high cardinality, low update, or insert indexes have been reported by converting them to bitmapped indexes. Normal indexes should also be used when enforcing a normal relational-type primary-foreign key relationship. One caveat here is that if the column for a unique or primary key index is populated by a call to a sequence or to SYSDATE, then a reverse key index may be advantageous to prevent hot spotting caused by an unbalanced B-tree structure. Bitmapped indexes cannot be UNIQUE indexes.

Normal indexes are subject to *index browning*, a condition where deletes from the underlying tables cause leaf nodes to not be filled, resulting in long search times as Oracle "climbs" the tree to find good values. Generally, this can be determined by analyzing the indexes for a table and examining the DBA_INDEXES or INDEX_ STATS views. The DBA_INDEXES view has one row for each index in the database; the INDEX_STATS view has one row for the most recently analyzed index. I suggest the use of a code fragment like the one shown in Source 6.1 to populate a temporary table so that all of a table's indexes can be examined at one time for problems.

Source 6.1   Code fragment to analyze all the table indexes of an owner.

```
ACCEPT owner PROMPT 'Enter table owner name: '
ACCEPT table PROMPT 'Enter table name: '
SET HEADING OFF FEEDBACK OFF VERIFY OFF ECHO OFF RECSEP OFF PAGES 0
DEFINE cr = 'chr(10)'
SPOOL index_sz.sql
SELECT 'CREATE TABLE stat_temp AS SELECT * FROM index_stats WHERE
orwnum<1;'||&&cr
FROM dual;
SELECT
'ANALYZE INDEX '||owner||'.'||index_name||' VALIDATE STRUCTURE;'||&&cr||
'INSERT INTO stat_temp SELECT * FROM index_stats;'||&&cr||
'COMMIT;'
FROM dba_indexes
WHERE owner=upper('&owner')
AND table_name=upper('&table');
SPOOL OFF
@index_sz.sql
```

Once a table's indexes have been analyzed, you can query the stat_temp table to find the ratio between del_lf_rows_len and the sum of lf_rows_len and del_lf_rows_len. If this ratio exceeds 0.3 (that is, 15 to 30 percent of the leaf rows are probably empty), then more than likely you have a browning problem. The report in Source 6.2 can be run to determine this and other data that will help determine index state.

Source 6.2   Browning report for indexes.

```
rem  ******************************************************************
rem
rem  NAME: brown.sql
rem
rem  HISTORY:
rem  Date              Who             What
rem  --------          ----------      ----------------------------
rem   06/05/97  Mike Ault               Updated for Oracle 7.x
rem   09/27/99  Mike Ault               Verified for 8.x
rem   09/22/99  Mike Ault               Verified for 9.x
rem  FUNCTION:  Will show index browning for all indexes for a
rem                user.
rem  INPUTS:  owner = Table owner name.
rem
rem  ******************************************************************

column value noprint new_value blocksize
define cr=chr(10)
select value from v$parameter where name='db_block_size';
accept tab_owner prompt 'Enter Table Owner for Indexes:'
```

continues

Source 6.2 **Continued.**

```
set heading off verify off termout off pages 0 recsep 0 feedback off
spool index_sz.sql
select
     'create table stat_temp as select * from index_stats;'||&&cr||
     'truncate table stat_temp;'
from dual;
select
     'analyze index '||owner||'.'||index_name||
     ' validate structure;'||&&cr||
     'insert into stat_temp select * from index_stats;'||&&cr||
     'commit;'
from dba_indexes
where
     owner=upper('&&tab_owner');
spool off
set feedback on termout on lines 80
start index_sz.sql
insert into temp_size_table select name,trunc(used_space/&&blocksize)
from stat_temp;
rem drop table stat_temp;
clear columns
column del_lf_rows_len format 999,999,999 heading 'Deleted Bytes'
column lf_rows_len format 999,999,999 heading 'Filled Bytes'
column browning format 999.90 heading 'Percent|Browned'
start ttitle "Index Browning Report"
spool rep_out/browning.lst
select
     name,del_lf_rows_len,lf_rows_len,
     (del_lf_rows_len/decode((lf_rows_len+del_lf_rows_len),0,1,
     lf_rows_len+del_lf_rows_len))*100 browning
from
     stat_temp
where
     del_lf_rows_len>0;
spool off
```

Bitmapped Index Usage

A bitmapped index is used for low-cardinality data such as sex, race, hair color, and so on. If a column to be indexed has a selectivity of greater than 30 to 40 percent of the total data, then it is probably a good candidate for bitmap indexing.

Bitmap indexing is not suggested for high-cardinality, high-update, or high-delete-type data, as bitmap indexes may have to be frequently rebuilt in these type situations.

There are three things to consider when choosing an index method:

- Performance
- Storage
- Maintainability

The major advantages of using bitmapped indexes are performance impact for certain queries and their relatively small storage requirements. Note, however, that bitmapped indexes are not applicable to every query; and bitmapped indexes, like B-tree indexes, can impact the performance of insert, update, and delete statements. Bitmaps store large amounts of data about various rows in each block of the index structure, and because bitmap locking is at the block level, any insert, update, or delete activity may lock an entire range of values.

Bitmapped indexes can provide very impressive performance improvements. Under test conditions, the execution times of certain queries improved by several orders of magnitude. The queries that benefit the most from bitmapped indexes have the following characteristics:

- The WHERE clause contains multiple predicates on low-cardinality columns.
- The individual predicates on these low-cardinality columns select a large number of rows.
- Bitmapped indexes have been created on some or all of these low-cardinality columns.
- The tables being queried contain many rows.

An advantage of bitmapped indexes is that multiple bitmapped indexes can be used to evaluate the conditions on a single table. Thus, bitmapped indexes are very useful for complex ad hoc queries that contain lengthy WHERE clauses involving low-cardinality data.

Bitmapped indexes incur a small storage cost and have a significant storage savings over B-tree indexes. A bitmapped index can require 100 times less space than a B-tree index for a low-cardinality column.

But with all those advantages in mind, you must remember that a strict comparison of the relative sizes of B-tree and bitmapped indexes is not an accurate measure for selecting bitmapped over B-tree indexes. Because of the performance characteristics of bitmapped indexes and B-tree indexes, you should continue to maintain B-tree indexes on your high-cardinality data. Bitmapped indexes should be considered primarily for your low-cardinality data.

The storage savings incurred by bitmapped indexes are so large because they replace multiple-column B-tree indexes. In addition, single-bit values replace possibly long columnar type data. When using only B-tree indexes, you must anticipate the columns that will commonly be accessed together in a single query and then create a multicolumn B-tree index on those columns. Not only does this B-tree index require a large amount of space, but it will also be ordered; that is, a B-tree index on (MARITAL_ STATUS, RACE, SEX) is useless for a query that only accesses RACE and SEX. To completely index the database, you will be forced to create indexes on the other permutations of these columns. In addition to an index on (MARITAL_STATUS, RACE, SEX), there is a need for indexes on (RACE, SEX, MARITAL_STATUS), (SEX, MARITAL_ STATUS, RACE), and so on. For the simple case of three low-cardinality columns, there are six possible concatenated B-tree indexes. This means that you will be forced to decide between disk space and performance when determining which multiple-column B-tree indexes to create.

With bitmapped indexes, the problems associated with multiple-column B-tree indexes are solved because bitmapped indexes can be efficiently combined during query execution. Three small single-column bitmapped indexes are a sufficient functional replacement for six three-column B-tree indexes. Note that while the bitmapped indexes may not be quite as efficient during execution as the appropriate concatenated B-tree indexes, the space savings provided by bitmapped indexes can often more than justify their utilization.

The net storage savings will depend upon a database's current usage of B-tree indexes:

- A database that relies on single-column B-tree indexes on high-cardinality columns will not observe significant space savings (but should see significant performance increases).
- A database containing a significant number of concatenated B-tree indexes could reduce its index storage usage by 50 percent or more, while maintaining similar performance characteristics.
- A database that lacks concatenated B-tree indexes because of storage constraints will be able to use bitmapped indexes and increase performance with minimal storage costs.

Bitmapped indexes are best for read-only or light online transaction-processing (OLTP) environments. Because there is no effective method for locking a single bit, row-level locking is not available for bitmapped indexes. Instead, locking for bitmapped indexes is effectively at the block level, which can impact heavy OLTP environments. Note also that like other types of indexes, updating bitmapped indexes is a costly operation.

Although bitmapped indexes are not appropriate for databases with a heavy load of insert, update, and delete operations, their effectiveness in a data warehousing environment is not diminished. In such environments, data is usually maintained via bulk inserts and updates. For these bulk operations, rebuilding or refreshing the bitmapped indexes is an efficient operation. The storage savings and performance gains provided by bitmapped indexes can provide tremendous benefits to data warehouse users.

In preliminary testing of bitmapped indexes, certain queries ran up to 100 times faster. The bitmapped indexes on low-cardinality columns were also about 10 times smaller than B-tree indexes on the same columns. In these tests, the queries containing multiple predicates on low-cardinality data experienced the most significant speedups. Queries that did not conform to this characteristic were not assisted by bitmapped indexes. Bitmapped composite indexes cannot exceed 30 columns.

Example Index Scenarios

The following sample queries on the CUSTOMERS table demonstrate the variety of query-processing techniques that are necessary for optimal performance.

Example 1: Single Predicate on a Low-Cardinality Attribute

```
select * from customers  where gender = 'male';
```

Best approach: parallel table scan.

This query will return approximately 50 percent of the data. Since we will be accessing such a large number of rows, it is more efficient to scan the entire table rather than use either bitmapped indexes or B-tree indexes. To minimize elapsed time, the server should execute this scan in parallel.

Example 2: Single Predicate on a High-Cardinality Attribute

```
select * from customers where customer# = 101;
```

Best approach: conventional unique index.

This query will retrieve at most one record from the employee table. A B-tree index or hash cluster index is always appropriate for retrieving a small number of records based upon criteria on the indexed columns.

Example 3: Multiple Predicates on Low-Cardinality Attributes

```
select * from customers  where gender = 'male' and region in ('central',
'west') and marital_status in ('married', 'divorced');
```

Best approach: bitmapped index.

Though each individual predicate specifies a large number of rows, the combination of all three predicates will return a relatively small number of rows. In this scenario, bitmapped indexes provide substantial performance benefits.

Example 4: Multiple Predicates on Both High-Cardinality and Low-Cardinality Attributes

```
select * from customers where gender = 'male' and customer# < 100;
```

Best approach: B-tree index on CUSTOMER#.

This query returns a small number of rows because of the highly selective predicate on customer#. It is more efficient to use a B-tree index on customer# than to use a bitmapped index on gender.

In each of the previous examples, the Oracle cost-based optimizer transparently determines the most efficient query-processing technique if the tables and indexes have representative statistics present in the database.

The BITMAP clause (version 7.3.2 and later) causes the index to be stored as a bitmap and should only be used for low-cardinality data such as sex, race, and so on.

The option is available only as beta in pre-7.3.2.2 releases and is bundled with the parallel query option. Several initialization parameters and event settings are required to use the option in earlier versions of 7.3:

Initialization parameters (must be set regardless of version):

```
COMPATIBLE set to 7.3.2 or higher
V733_PLANS_ENABLED set to TRUE
```

Events (must be set prior to 7.3.2.3):

```
event = "10111 trace name context forever"
event = "10112 trace name context forever"
event = "10114 trace name context forever"
```

Creation of a Partitioned Index: An Example

As already noted, Oracle8 introduced the concept of a partitioned index; and Oracle8*i* and Oracle9*i* have continued and expanded upon partitioning concepts related to indexes. A partitioned index goes hand in hand with partitioned tables. In fact, usually a partitioned table will have partitioned indexes by default. A prefixed index is defined as an index whose leftmost columns correspond exactly with those of the partition key. In the arena of partitioned indexes, the concept of prefixed indexes is important because:

- Unique prefixed indexes guarantee that you only need to access one index partition to get the data.
- Nonunique prefixed indexes still guarantee you only need one index partition, if you provide the full partition key as part of the WHERE clause. The caveat to this is that if you provide only part of the partition key, all partitions will be scanned.

Let's look at two quick examples.

```
CREATE TABLE sales
    (acct_no                NUMBER(5) NOT NULL,
    sales_person_id         NUMBER(5) NOT NULL,
    po_number               VARCHAR2(10) NOT NULL,
    po_amount               NUMBER(9,2),
    month_no                NUMBER(2) NOT NULL)
    PARTITION BY RANGE (month_no)
        PARTITION first_qtr    VALUES LESS THAN (4),
        PARTITION sec_qtr      VALUES LESS THAN (7),
        PARTITION thrd_qtr     VALUES LESS THAN(10),
        PARTITION frth_qtr     VALUES LESS THAN(13),
        PARTITION bad_qtr      VALUES LESS THAN (MAXVALUE));
    CREATE INDEX pt_sales
    ON sales (month_no, sales_person_id,acct_no,po_number)
        LOCAL;
```

Notice in this example that we didn't have to specify the index partitions. This is because we used the LOCAL clause that tells Oracle to use the same partition logic as the master table. A suitable prefix is added to differentiate the indexes. One problem is that the indexes, if the location is not specified, will be placed in the same tablespace as the table partitions. A better form to use would be:

```
CREATE INDEX pt_lc_sales
ON sales (month_no, sales_person_id,acct_no,po_number)
      LOCAL(
      PARTITION i_first_qtr      TABLESPACE part_ind_tbsp1,
      PARTITION i_sec_qtr        TABLESPACE part_ind_tbsp2,
      PARTITION i_thrd_qtr       TABLESPACE part_ind_tbsp3,
      PARTITION i_frth_qtr       TABLESPACE part_ind_tbsp4,
      PARTITION i_bad_qtr        TABLESPACE part_ind_tbsp5);
```

The other choice is to use a GLOBAL index; this is a partitioned index that doesn't use the same partitioning as the base table. Let's look at an example:

```
CREATE INDEX pt_gl_sales
ON sales (month_no, sales_person_id,acct_no,po_number)
GLOBAL
      PARTITION BY RANGE (month_no)
(PARTITION i_gl_sales1 VALUES LESS THAN (6)
      TABLESPACE sales_index1,
          PARTITION i_gl_sales2 VALUES LESS THAN (MAXVALUE)
      TABLESPACE sales_index2));
```

Here are some guidelines for the use of partitioned indexes:

- Use local prefixed indexes whenever possible.
- It is more expensive to scan a nonprefixed index, due to more index probes required.
- Unique local nonprefixed indexes are not supported.
- DML operations on global unique indexes are not supported in parallel update.
- Global prefixed indexes can minimize the number of index probes.

Using Function-Based Indexes

Oracle8*i* also introduced the concept of a function-based index. In previous releases of Oracle, if we wanted to have a column that was always searched uppercase (for example, a last name that could have mixed-case, such as McClellum), we had to place the returned value with its mixed-case letters in one column and add a second column that was uppercased to index and use in searches. The double storage of columns required for this type of searching led to the doubling of size requirements for some application fields. The cases where more complex requirements such as the use of SOUNDEX and other functions would also have required the use of a second column. This is not the case with Oracle releases later than and including Oracle8*i*; Oracle-provided functions, user-defined functions, as well as methods, can be used in indexes. Let's look at a simple example using the UPPER function.

```
CREATE INDEX tele_dba.up1_clientsv8i
ON tele_dba.clientsv8i(UPPER(customer_name))
TABLESPACE tele_index
STORAGE (INITIAL 1M NEXT 1M PCTINCREASE 0);
```

In many applications, a column may store a numeric value that translates to a minimal set of text values; for example, a user code that designates functions such as 'Manager', 'Clerk', or 'General User'. In previous versions of Oracle, you had to perform a join between a lookup table and the main table to search for all 'Manager' records. With function indexes, the DECODE function can be used to eliminate this type of join.

```
CREATE INDEX tele_dba.dec_clientsv8i
ON tele_dba.clientsv8i(DECODE(user_code,
1,'MANAGER',2,'CLERK',3,'GENERAL USER'))
TABLESPACE tele_index
STORAGE (INITIAL 1M NEXT 1M PCTINCREASE 0);
```

A query against the clientsv8*i* table that would use the above index would look like:

```
SELECT customer_name FROM tele_dba.clientsv8i
WHERE DECODE(user_code,
1,'MANAGER',2,'CLERK',3,'GENERAL USER')='MANAGER';
```

The execution plan for the above query shows that the index will be used to execute the query:

```
SQL> SET AUTOTRACE ON EXPLAIN
SQL> SELECT customer_name FROM tele_dba.clientsv8i
  2  WHERE DECODE(user_code,
  3* 1,'MANAGER',2,'CLERK',3,'GENERAL USER') = 'MANAGER'

no rows selected


Execution Plan
----------------------------------------------------------------------
   0      SELECT STATEMENT Optimizer=CHOOSE (Cost=1 Card=1 Bytes=526)
   1    0   TABLE ACCESS (BY INDEX ROWID) OF 'CLIENTSV8i' (Cost=1 Card=1
Bytes=526)
   2    1      INDEX (RANGE SCAN) OF 'DEC_CLIENTSV8i' (NON-UNIQUE) (Cost=1
Card=1)
```

The table using function-based indexes must be analyzed, and the optimizer mode must be set to CHOOSE, or the function-based indexes will not be used. The RULE-based optimizer cannot use function-based indexes. Function-based indexes are only available in the Enterprise and Personal Oracle releases, not in Standard Oracle.

If the function-based index is built using a user-defined function, any alteration or invalidation of the user function will invalidate the index. Any user-built functions must not contain aggregate functions and must be deterministic in nature. A deterministic function is one that is built using the DETERMINISTIC keyword in the CREATE FUNCTION, CREATE PACKAGE, or CREATE TYPE commands. As stated earlier, a deterministic function is defined as one that always returns the same set value, given the same input, no matter where the function is executed from within your application. As of 9.0.1, the validity of the DETERMINISTIC keyword usage has not been verified, so it is left up to the programmer to ensure that it is used properly. A function-based index cannot be created on a LOB, REF, or nested table column, or against an object type that contains a LOB, REF, or nested table. A FUNCTION return value may be cached and reused if the call to the FUNCTION looks identical to the optimizer; therefore, if for some reason it will not return the same value (if you use internal package variables for instance), then the changes may not be reliably reported. Let's look at an example of a user-defined type (UDT) method:

```
CREATE TYPE room_t AS OBJECT(
lngth NUMBER,
width NUMBER,
MEMBER FUNCTION SQUARE_FOOT
RETURN NUMBER DETERMINISTIC);
/
CREATE TYPE BODY room_t AS
  MEMBER FUNCTION SQUARE_FOOT
  RETURN NUMBER IS
  area NUMBER;
  BEGIN
   AREA:=lngth*width;
    RETURN area;
  END;
END;
/
CREATE TABLE rooms OF room_t
TABLESPACE test_data
STORAGE (INITIAL 100K NEXT 100K PCTINCREASE 0);

CREATE INDEX area_idx ON rooms r (r.square_foot());
```

NOTE The preceding example is based on those given in the Oracle manuals; when tested on 8.1.3, the DETERMINISTIC keyword caused an error, and dropping the DETERMINISTIC keyword allowed the type to be created. However, the attempted index creation failed on the alias specification. In 8.1.3, the keyword is REPEATABLE, instead of DETERMINISTIC; however, even when specified with the REPEATABLE keyword, the attempt to create the index failed on the alias. On both an 8.1.7 and 9.0.1 instance, all statements in the example work satisfactorily using the DETERMINISTIC keyword (remember that the user that creates the function-based index must have QUERY REWRITE or GLOBAL QUERY REWRITE privilege).

A function-based index either may be a normal B-tree index or be mapped into a bitmapped format.

Using Reverse-Key Indexes

A reverse-key index prevents unbalancing of the B-tree and the resulting hot blocking, which will happen if the B-tree becomes unbalanced. Generally, unbalanced B-trees are caused by high-volume insert activity in a parallel server where the key value is only slowly changing, such as with an integer generated from a sequence or a data value. A reverse key index works by reversing the order of the bytes in the key value; of course, the rowid value is not altered, just the key value. The only way to create a reverse-key index is to use the CREATE INDEX command. An index that is not reverse-key cannot be altered or rebuilt into a reverse-key index; however, a reverse-key index can be rebuilt as a normal index.

One of the major limitations of reverse-key indexes is that they cannot be used in an index range scan, since reversing the index key value randomly distributes the blocks across the index leaf nodes. A reverse-key index can only use the fetch-by-key or full-index(table)scans methods of access. Let's look at an example:

```
CREATE INDEX rpk_po ON tele_dba.po(po_num) REVERSE
TABLESPACE tele_index
STORAGE (INITIAL 1M NEXT 1M PCTINCREASE 0);
```

The above command would reverse the values for the po_num column as it creates the index. This would assure random distribution of the values across the index leaf nodes. But what if we then determine that the benefits of the reverse key do not outweigh the drawbacks? We can use the ALTER command to rebuild the index as a NOREVERSE index:

```
ALTER INDEX rpk_po REBUILD NOREVERSE;
ALTER INDEX rpk_po RENAME TO pk_po;
```

Oracle manuals only discuss the benefits of the reverse-key index in the realm of Oracle Parallel Server, so note that if you experience performance problems after a bulk load of data, it may help to drop and re-create the indexes involved as reverse-key indexes, if the table will continue to be loaded in a bulk fashion.

The major drawback to a reverse-key index is that you are not able to perform range scans against them, so if your table requires the use of index range scans do not use a reverse-key index.

Using DOMAIN Type Indexes

The DOMAIN index is another feature new to Oracle 8*i*. A DOMAIN index is actually an extension to the Oracle index system that allows developers to create their own index type (this is usually done by companies developing commercial applications or cartridges). Index types are created using the CREATE INDEXTYPE command. A DOMAIN index can only be placed on a single column in Oracle8*i*. Multiple DOMAIN indexes can be created on the same column if their index types are different. A DOMAIN index is stored in an index organized table (IOT) or in an external file.

DOMAIN indexes are built against an index type. An index type encapsulates a set of routines that manage access to a domain. This encapsulation allows efficient search and retrieval functions for complex domains such as text, spatial, image, and OLAP data. All of this encapsulation is specified using the Oracle Data Cartridge Interface for indexes (ODCIIndex). These routines can be implemented by type methods. [For a more complete description, refer to the *Oracle9i Data Cartridge Developer's Guide* (Release 1, (9.0.1), PART A88896-01, Oracle Corporation, June 2001) as it is beyond the scope of this book to cover the complete usage of DOMAIN indexes.]

Using Bitmap Join Indexes

In Oracle9*i*, the bitmap join index becomes part of the arsenal of indexes available in Oracle. The bitmap join index allows prejoining of two tables through a bitmap index. The bitmap join index requires a unique constraint be present. For example, notice the boldface code in the execution plan below:

```
SQL> CREATE TABLE EMP1 AS SELECT * FROM SCOTT.EMP;

Table created.

SQL> CREATE TABLE DEPT1 AS SELECT * FROM SCOTT.DEPT;

Table created.

SQL> ALTER TABLE DEPT1 ADD CONSTRAINT DEPT_CONSTR1 UNIQUE (DEPTNO);

Table altered.

SQL> CREATE BITMAP INDEX EMPDEPT_IDX
  1    ON EMP1(DEPT1.DEPTNO)
  2    FROM EMP1, DEPT1
  3*   WHERE EMP1.DEPTNO = DEPT1.DEPTNO;

Index created.

SQL> SELECT /*+ INDEX(EMP1 EMPDEPT_IDX) */ COUNT(*)
  1    FROM EMP1, DEPT1
  2*   WHERE EMP1.DEPTNO = DEPT1.DEPTNO;

COUNT(*)
--------
      14

Elapsed: 00:00:00.67
```

```
Execution Plan
-----------------------------------------------------------
   0        SELECT STATEMENT Optimizer=CHOOSE
   1    0    SORT (AGGREGATE)
   2    1     BITMAP CONVERSION (COUNT)
   3    2      BITMAP INDEX (FULL SCAN) OF 'EMPDEPT_IDX'
```

Now let's play with some real numbers. We'll create emp5/emp6 to have 2 million rows each, with indexes on the empno column:

```
SQL> alter table emp5
  1* add constraint emp5_constr unique (empno);

SQL> create bitmap index emp5_j6
  1  on emp6(emp5.empno)
  2  from emp5,emp6
  3* where emp5.empno=emp6.empno;

Index created.
Elapsed: 00:02:29.91

SQL> select count(*)
  2  from emp5, emp6
  3* where emp5.empno=emp6.empno

  COUNT(*)
----------
   2005007

Elapsed: 00:01:07.18

Execution Plan
-----------------------------------------------------------
   0        SELECT STATEMENT Optimizer=CHOOSE
   1    0    SORT (AGGREGATE)
   2    1     NESTED LOOPS
   3    2      TABLE ACCESS (FULL) OF 'EMP6'
   4    2      INDEX (RANGE SCAN) OF 'EMP5I_EMPNO' (NON-UNIQUE)

Statistics
-----------------------------------------------------------
6026820  consistent gets
7760  physical reads
FORCE THE USE OF THE BITMAP JOIN INDEX:
SQL> select /*+ index(emp6 emp5_j6) */ count(*)
  2  from emp5, emp6
  3* where emp5.empno=emp6.empno

  COUNT(*)
----------
   2005007
```

```
Elapsed: 00:00:00.87! Same as with small tables!

Execution Plan
-----------------------------------------------------------
   0      SELECT STATEMENT Optimizer=CHOOSE
   1   0    SORT (AGGREGATE)
   2   1      BITMAP CONVERSION (COUNT)
   3   2        BITMAP INDEX (FULL SCAN) OF 'EMP5_J6'
Statistics
-----------------------------------------------------------
970  consistent gets
967  physical reads
```

What you should take from the above example is that proper use of this new bitmap join index technology can lead to improvement in query speeds by up to 10,000 times.

Using Skip Scan Indexes

The main strength of the Oracle9*i* skip scan index capability is that you scan the index, not the table, saving a full table scan. Let's take a look at an example:

```
SQL> desc emp5
  Name                                   Null?     Type
  ------------------------------------   ------    ------------
  EMPNO                                            NUMBER(15)
  ENAME                                            VARCHAR2(10)
  JOB                                              VARCHAR2(9)
  MGR                                              NUMBER(4)
  HIREDATE                                         DATE
  SAL                                              NUMBER(7,2)
  COMM                                             NUMBER(7,2)
  DEPTNO                                           NUMBER(2)

SQL> create index skip1 on emp5(job,empno);

Index created.
```

The index skip1 will be a two-level B-tree index. The first level will contain the job value; the second will contain the empno values associated with the jobs. First a select with the normal index:

```
SQL> select count(*)
  1  from emp5
  2* where empno=7900;

Elapsed: 00:00:00.12 (Result is a single row...not displayed)

Execution Plan
   0      SELECT STATEMENT Optimizer=CHOOSE (Cost=2 Card=1 Bytes=5)
   1   0    SORT (AGGREGATE)
   2   1      INDEX (RANGE SCAN) OF 'EMP5I_EMPNO' (NON-UNIQUE)
```

```
Statistics
3   consistent gets
0   physical reads
```

Now, let's see what the execution time is without the index:

```
SQL> select /*+ no_index(emp5 emp5i_empno) */ count(*)
  1  from emp5
  2* where empno=7900;
```

```
Elapsed: 00:00:03.13 (Result is a single row...not displayed)
```

```
Execution Plan
------------------------------------------------------------------
  0        SELECT STATEMENT Optimizer=CHOOSE (Cost=4 Card=1 Bytes=5)
  1    0     SORT (AGGREGATE)
  2    1       INDEX (FAST FULL SCAN) OF 'SKIP1' (NON-UNIQUE)
```

```
Statistics
--------------------
6826  consistent gets
6819  physical reads
```

Now let's force the use of the skip scan index:

```
SQL> select /*+ index(emp5 skip1) */ count(*)
  1  from emp5
  2* where empno=7900;
```

```
Elapsed: 00:00:00.56
```

```
Execution Plan
------------------------------------------------------------------
  0        SELECT STATEMENT Optimizer=CHOOSE (Cost=6 Card=1 Bytes=5)
  1    0     SORT (AGGREGATE)
  2    1       INDEX (SKIP SCAN) OF 'SKIP1' (NON-UNIQUE)
```

```
Statistics
--------------------
21  consistent gets
17  physical reads
```

As you can see a significant performance improvement!

Estimating the Size of an Index

To estimate the size of an index for the storage clause, use the following procedure:

1. Calculate the required database block header size (BHS).

```
BHS = fixed header + variable transaction header
```

where:

fixed header = 113
variable transaction header = 24 * INITRANS

2. Calculate available data space (ADS).

```
ADS = ((Blocksize - BHS)  * (PCTFREE/100))
```

3. Calculate the average data length (ADL) per row.

NOTE   Step 3 is the same as step 3 in the table-sizing section in Chapter 5. However, size only for those columns in the index.

---

4. Calculate the average row length (ARL).

```
bytes/entry = entry header + ROWID length + F + V + D
```

where:

entry header = 2
ROWID = 6
F = Total length of bytes of all columns that store 127 bytes or fewer—one header byte per column.
V = Total length of bytes of all columns that store more than 127 bytes—two header bytes per column.
For UNIQUE indexes, the entry header is 0.

5. Calculate number of blocks for index.

```
# of Blocks = 1.05 * (((# of NOT NULL rows) / (ADS) / ARL))
```

The 1.05 factor allows for branch space and is an empirically (SWAG) derived value.

6. Calculate the number of bytes required.

```
Size in bytes = BLOCKSIZE • number of blocks
```

If the table on which the index is based exists, the script in Source 6.3 in the next section is used to estimate the size of the index that is generated from a given list of columns. The DBA enters the table name, the table owner name, and a list of columns; the procedure does the rest. A spreadsheet to calculate index size based on 8*i* sizing formulas is included in the MISC directory on the Wiley Web site. An example of how this spreadsheet looks is shown in Figure 6.2.

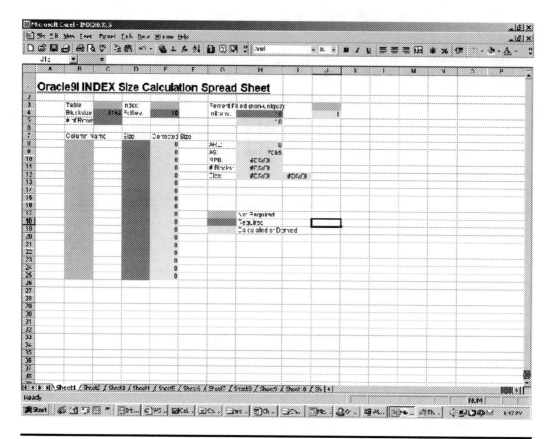

FIGURE 6.2 Example Oracle9*i* index-sizing spreadsheet.

6.2 ANALYZING INDEXES

For Oracle8, Oracle8*i*, and Oracle9*i*, the ANALYZE command can be used to get the average index size from an example index. The format of this command follows. Other statistics are also generated, but these will be covered in Chapter 9.

```
ANALYZE INDEX [schema.]index_name
[PARTITION(partition)]
[SUBPARTITION(subpartition)]
COMPUTE STATISTICS|ESTIMATE STATISTICS [SAMPLE n ROWS|PERCENT]
[VALIDATE STRUCTURE [CASCADE]]
```

where:

   COMPUTE STATISTICS. Calculates statistics based on all rows.

ESTIMATE STATISTICS. Calculates an estimate of the statistics based on n ROWS or PERCENT of rows in table.

VALIDATE STRUCTURE. Validates that the table and its indexes are consistent and not corrupted.

CASCADE. For clusters, validates all tables and indexes in cluster; for tables, validates all indexes.

DELETE STATISTICS. Removes current statistics.

The results appear in the INDEX_STATS view, and some of the statistics also appear in the *_INDEXES series of views (DBA, USER, and ALL). One thing to remember is that, unlike the DBA_TABLES view, only one row at a time is saved in the INDEX_STATS view, the row for the last index analyzed.

The script in Source 6.3 estimates index sizes.

Source 6.3   **Script to calculate index space requirements for a proposed index.**

```
rem *********************************************************
rem NAME:  IN_ES_SZ.sql
rem HISTORY:
rem Date           Who                    What
rem ---------------  ------------------------------------  --------
------------------
rem 01/20/93       Michael Brouillette    Creation
rem 09/22/01       Michael Ault           Upgraded to 9i
rem FUNCTION:  Compute the space used by an entry for an
rem   existing index.
rem NOTES:  Currently requires DBA.
rem INPUTS:
rem        tname  = Name of table.
rem        towner = Name of owner of table.
rem        clist  = List of columns enclosed in quotes.
rem                 i.e., 'ename', 'empno'
rem        cfile  = Name of output SQL Script file
rem *********************************************************
COLUMN name     NEW_VALUE      db NOPRINT
COLUMN dum1     NOPRINT
COLUMN isize    FORMAT 99,999.99
COLUMN rcount   FORMAT 999,999,999 NEWLINE
ACCEPT tname  PROMPT 'Enter table name: '
ACCEPT towner PROMPT 'Enter table owner name: '
ACCEPT clist  PROMPT 'Enter column list: '
ACCEPT cfile  PROMPT 'Enter name for output SQL file: '
SET HEADING OFF VERIFY OFF TERMOUT OFF PAGES 0 EMBEDDED ON
SET FEEDBACK OFF SQLCASE UPPER TRIMSPOOL ON SQLBL OFF
SET NEWPAGE 3
SELECT name FROM v$database;
```

continues

Source 6.3   Continued.

```
SPOOL rep_out/&db/&cfile..sql
SELECT -1 dum1,
       'SELECT ''Proposed Index on table ''||'
FROM dual
UNION
SELECT 0,
       '''&towner..&tname'||' has '',COUNT(*) rcount,
       '' entries of '', ('
FROM dual
UNION
SELECT column_id,
     'SUM(NVL(vsize('||column_name||'),0)) + 1 +'
FROM dba_tab_columns
WHERE table_name = '&tname'
   AND owner = '&towner'
   AND column_name in (upper(&clist))
   AND column_id <> (SELECT MAX(column_id)
                    FROM dba_tab_columns
                     WHERE table_name = UPPER('&tname')
                       AND owner = UPPER('&towner')
                       AND column_name IN (upper(&clist)))
UNION
SELECT column_id,
     'SUM(NVL(VSIZE('||column_name||'),0)) + 1)'
 FROM dba_tab_columns
 WHERE table_name = upper('&tname')
   AND owner = upper('&towner') AND column_name IN (upper(&clist))
   AND column_id = (SELECT MAX(column_id)
                    FROM dba_tab_columns
                     WHERE table_name = upper('&tname')
                       AND owner = upper('&towner')
                       AND column_name IN (upper(&clist)))
UNION
SELECT 997, '/ COUNT(*) + 11 isize, '' bytes each.'''
FROM dual
UNION
SELECT 999,
      'FROM &towner..&tname.;'  FROM dual;
SPOOL OFF
SET TERMOUT ON FEEDBACK 15 PAGESIZE 20 SQLCASE MIXED
SET NEWPAGE 1
START rep_out/&db/&cfile
CLEAR COLUMNS
```

6.3 ALTERATION OF INDEXES

If the DBA suspects that an index's storage clause is improper, he or she can run the script in Source 6.4 to show the space used for the average entry in the index. This data can then be input to the space calculation formula to get a more accurate sizing estimate. The DBA can then use the ALTER INDEX command to alter the index's storage clause for future extents, or drop and re-create the index with better parameters.

Indexes can be altered to change their storage clauses, and in version 7.3.4 and all 8 versions, they can be rebuilt on the fly. Oracle8*i* and Oracle9*i* also allow either online (where table access is permitted) or offline (where table access is restricted). The alteration will affect only the storage allocations of future extents. To alter rows used in the index, unique versus nonunique, or all of the storage extents for an existing index, it must be dropped and re-created. To alter the storage within an existing index, use the ALTER INDEX command.

Source 6.4   **Script to calculate average length of an index entry.**

```
rem   ***********************************************************
rem
rem   NAME:  IN_CM_SZ.sql
rem
rem   HISTORY:
rem   Date            Who            What
rem   --------------- -------------  ----------------
rem   01/20/93  Michael Brouillette  Creation
rem   09/22/01  Mike Ault            Updated to 9i
rem
rem   FUNCTION:  Compute the space used by an entry for an
rem      existing index.
rem
rem   NOTES:  Currently requires DBA.
rem
rem   INPUTS:
rem         tname  = Name of table.
rem         towner = Name of owner of table.
rem         iname  = Name of index.
rem         iowner = Name of owner of index.
rem         cfile  = Name of output file SQL Script.
rem   ***********************************************************
COLUMN dum1       NOPRINT
COLUMN isize        FORMAT 999,999,999.99
COLUMN rcount       FORMAT 999,999,999 NEWLINE
ACCEPT tname  PROMPT 'Enter table name: '
ACCEPT towner PROMPT 'Enter table owner name: '
ACCEPT iname  PROMPT 'Enter index name: '
ACCEPT iowner PROMPT 'Enter index owner name: '
ACCEPT cfile  PROMPT 'Enter name for output SQL file: '
```

continues

Source 6.4 Continued.

```
SET PAGESIZE 0 HEADING OFF VERIFY OFF TERMOUT OFF
SET FEEDBACK OFF TRIMSPOOL ON SQLBL OFF
SET SQLCASE UPPER NEWPAGE 3
SPOOL &cfile..sql
SELECT -1 dum1,
       'SELECT ''Index '||'&iowner..&iname'||' on table '
  FROM dual
UNION
SELECT 0,
       '&towner..&tname'||' has '',
       nvl(COUNT(*),0) rcount,'' entries of '', ('
  FROM dual
UNION
SELECT column_id,
      'SUM(NVL(vsize('||column_name||'),0)) + 1 +'
  FROM dba_tab_columns
 WHERE table_name = '&tname'
   AND owner = upper('&towner') AND column_name IN
                     (SELECT column_name FROM dba_ind_columns
                       WHERE table_name = upper('&tname')
                         AND table_owner = upper('&towner')
                         AND index_name = upper('&iname')
                         AND index_owner = upper('&iowner'))
                       AND column_id <> (select max(column_id)
                                          FROM dba_tab_columns
                                          WHERE table_name = upper('&tname')
                                          AND owner = upper('&towner')
                                          AND column_name IN
                     (SELECT column_name FROM dba_ind_columns
                       WHERE table_name = upper('&tname')
                         AND table_owner = upper('&towner')
                         AND index_name = upper('&iname')
                         AND index_owner = upper('&iowner')))
UNION
SELECT column_id,
      'SUM(NVL(vsize('||column_name||'),0)) + 1)'
  FROM dba_tab_columns
  WHERE table_name = upper('&tname') AND owner = upper('&towner')
   AND column_name IN
                     (SELECT column_name FROM dba_ind_columns
                       WHERE table_name = upper('&tname')
                         AND table_owner = upper('&towner')
                         AND index_name = upper('&iname')
                         AND index_owner = upper('&iowner'))
                       AND column_id = (SELECT MAX(column_id)
                       FROM dba_tab_columns
                       WHERE table_name = upper('&tname')
                         AND owner = upper('&towner')
```

```
                    AND column_name IN
                    (SELECT column_name FROM dba_ind_columns
                      WHERE table_name = upper('&tname')
                        AND table_owner = upper('&towner')
                        AND index_name = upper('&iname')
                        AND index_owner = upper('&iowner')))
UNION
SELECT 997,
       '/ COUNT(*) + 11 isize, '' bytes each.'''  from dual
UNION
SELECT 999,  'FROM &towner..&tname.;'  FROM dual;
SPOOL OFF
SET TERMOUT ON FEEDBACK 15 PAGESIZE 20 SQLCASE MIXED
SET NEWPAGE 1
START &cfile
CLEAR columns
UNDEF tname
UNDEF towner
UNDEF iname
UNDEF iowner
UNDEF cfile
```

The ALTER INDEX command is detailed in the SQL reference manual, in the documentation on http://technet.oracle.com/. Instead of filling pages with syntax and definitions, let's look at some specific ALTER INDEX examples.

The ALTER command can be used to change the storage and physical characteristics of an index, but not the contents of the index. To change the actual columns an index applies to, or to change the order of columns in a concatenated index, the index must be dropped and rebuilt. Changes to storage or physical characteristics apply only to new index extents, not existing extents, unless the index is rebuilt using the REBUILD clause. Let's look at some specific examples using the ALTER INDEX command.

The most simple use of the ALTER INDEX command is to alter an index's storage clause for future extents:

```
ALTER INDEX pk_clientsv8i
STORAGE (NEXT 2m);
```

In some cases, an index may have been misnamed and thus must be renamed to fit into the application's naming guidelines:

```
ALTER INDEX test_new_index RENAME TO lu2_clientsv8i;
```

For a more complex example, assume we want to rebuild an index into a new location. Prior to the addition of the REBUILD clause in late 7.3 versions of Oracle, this would have involved dropping related constraints, dropping the index, and re-creating the index in the new location. Since Oracle8*i*, the index can be rebuilt online with access still available to the underlying tables:

```
ALTER INDEX pk_clientsv8i REBUILD
TABLESPACE tele_index
STORAGE (INITIAL 1M NEXT 1M PCTINCREASE 0)
ONLINE;
```

TIP   To use the ONLINE clause, the COMPATIBLE parameter must be set to 8.1.3.0.0 or later.

Another new clause since Oracle8 is the COALESCE command. In cases where an index has experienced browning, and the percentage of browning exceeds 15 to 30 percent, it is no longer required that the index be dropped and rebuilt; instead, the COALESCE option can be specified with the ALTER INDEX command:

```
ALTER INDEX pk_clientsv9i COALESCE;
```

6.4 REBUILDING INDEXES

Occasionally, the DBA may be required to rebuild indexes. In late Oracle version 7.3 and in Oracle8, Oracle8*i*, and Oracle9*i*, the ALTER INDEX . . . REBUILD command can be used to rebuild indexes on the fly. In releases prior to 8*i*, the rebuild was done offline, restricting access to the table to read-only. The ONLINE clause new in Oracle8*i* allows online rebuild of indexes. In earlier versions (pre-7.3), the indexes have to be rebuilt using drop and re-create scripts. If the scripts used to initially create the system are available, this is a relatively simple matter. If the scripts used to build the indexes are not available, or were never created in the first place, the script IND_RCT9*i*.SQL (available on the Wiley Web site) can be run to create a script that will re-create existing, simple, nonpartitioned indexes when run. For more complex indexes, use the DBMS_METADATA package available in Oracle9*i*. The script will not re-create bitmapped or partition indexes, though it can be modified to create bitmapped indexes by utilizing the INDEX_TYPE column of the USER_INDEXES or DBA_INDEXES views. The re-create script can also flag partition indexes by utilization of the PARTITIONED column of the USER_INDEXES or DBA_INDEXES views. To also rebuild partitioned indexes, the USER_IND_PARTITIONS, USER_PART_KEY_ COLUMNS, or DBA_IND_PARTITIONS and DBA_PART_KEY_ COLUMNS views would have to be queried.

The DBA can use the ANALYZE command to validate an index's structures. The format of this command follows. This data can help the DBA determine if a specific index has become corrupted and must be rebuilt.

```
ANALYZE INDEX [schema.]index
VALIDATE STRUCTURE;
```

The results are supplied to the DBA on-screen and are placed in a view called index_stats, which is dropped upon session exit.

In Oracle9*i,* the new package DBMS_METADATA can be used to get DML to rebuild complex indexes. The DBMS_METADATA function FETCH_DDL returns a CLOB data item that contains the text to rebuild any database object.

6.5 DROPPING INDEXES

Indexes occasionally have to be dropped. Sometimes they are built incorrectly or shouldn't have been built at all. Other times, especially in early Oracle7 releases (prior to 7.3), in order to rebuild an index it had to be dropped first. Finally, dropping an index may be required to speed import or SQLLOADER during large data loads.

The DROP INDEX Command

The DROP INDEX command has the following format:

```
DROP INDEX [schema.]index_name [FORCE];
```

Of course, you must own the index or have the DROP ANY INDEX privilege to drop an index. The FORCE clause only applies to DOMAIN type indexes and forces a drop of the index even if its status is LOADING or its invocation returns an error.

6.6 SUMMARY

This chapter examined the administration of indexes. Traditional B-tree indexes, as well the newer bitmapped, functional, descending, and reverse-key indexes were discussed; examples of their creation and use were shown. The chapter also covered the altering, rebuilding, and dropping of indexes.

CHAPTER 7

Administration of Other Database Objects

Chapters 4, 5, and 6 covered the administration of database tables and indexes. In this chapter, we will discuss the administration of other database objects, which include synonyms, sequences, views, and so on. More specifically, for Oracle8 and Oracle8*i,* we add Java, DIRECTORY, DIMENSION, OUTLINE, CONTEXT, OPERATOR, MATERIALIZED VIEWS, and LIBRARY objects; for Oracle9*i,* we add the ability to create parameter (initialization) and server parameter (dynamically reconfigurable initialization) files.

7.1 ADMINISTRATION OF SYNONYMS

Synonyms are a very powerful feature of Oracle and other SQL-compliant relational database systems. They are used as a database shorthand. They make it possible to shorten the specification of long or complex object names. This is especially useful for shared tables or views. In addition, the use of DATABASE LINKS in synonyms allows transparent access to other databases on other nodes or even other entire systems halfway around the globe.

Creation of Synonyms

Synonyms are created using the CREATE SYNONYM command. Synonyms can be either PRIVATE (the default) or PUBLIC. Private synonyms can only be used by the user creating them. You must have a specific grant or one of the special ROLES assigned to you before you can create synonyms. Only users with appropriate privileges (usually DBAs) can create PUBLIC synonyms. Since only the owner can use them, PRIVATE synonyms are more secure.

The simplified format of the CREATE SYNONYM command follows:

```
CREATE [PUBLIC] SYNONYM [schema.]synonym_name
FOR [schema.]object[@dblink];
```

where:

Synonym. An allowed name. (It cannot be the name of an existing object for this user. For the purposes of uniqueness, the schema name is considered to be a part of the name for an object.)

Schema.object. An existing table, view, package, procedure, function, Java object, materialized view, other synonym, or sequence name. The schema object cannot be contained in a package. A synonym cannot be created for an object type.

Database link. An existing database link (covered in Section 7.3).

Synonyms provide both data independence and location transparency. With proper use and assignment, they allow an application to function regardless of table ownership, location, or even database.

Synonyms can be used in SELECT, INSERT, UPDATE, DELETE, EXPLAIN PLAN, LOCK TABLE, AUDIT, NOAUDIT, GRANT, REVOKE, and COMMENT commands.

Alteration of Synonyms

Synonyms cannot be altered. To change a synonym's definition, it must be dropped and re-created.

Dropping Synonyms

Synonyms are dropped via the DROP command:

```
DROP [PUBLIC] SYNONYM [schema.]synonym_name;
```

Re-creating Synonyms

It is sometimes handy to have a script lying around to rebuild your existing synonyms. The script in Source 7.1 will create a synonym rebuild script for you from your data dictionary.

Source 7.1   Script to generate synonym rebuild script.

```
REM FUNCTION: SCRIPT FOR CREATING SYNONYMS
REM     This script must be run by a user with the DBA role.
REM     This script is intended to run with Oracle7 or Oracle8.
REM     Running this script will in turn create a script to build
```

```
REM     all the synonyms in the database. The created script,
REM     create_synonyms.sql, can be run by any user with the DBA
REM     role or with the 'CREATE ANY SYNONYM' and 'CREATE PUBLIC
REM     SYNONYM' system privileges.
REM NOTE: This script does not capture synonyms for tables owned
REM     by the 'SYS' user.
REM     Only preliminary testing of this script was performed. Be
REM     sure to test it completely before relying on it.
REM
SET VERIFY OFF FEEDBACK OFF TERMOUT OFF ECHO OFF PAGESIZE 0
SET TERMOUT ON
SELECT ''Creating synonym build script...'' FROM dual;
SET TERMOUT OFF
COLUMN dbname NEW_VALUE db NOPRINT
SELECT name dbname FROM v$database;
DEFINE cr=''chr(10)''
SPOOL rep_out\&db\crt_syns.sql

SELECT ''CREATE ''|| DECODE(owner,''PUBLIC'',''PUBLIC '',NULL) ||
'SYNONYM ''|| DECODE(owner,''PUBLIC'',NULL, owner || ''.'') ||
LOWER(synonym_name) || '' FOR '' || LOWER(table_owner) ||
''.'' || LOWER(table_name) ||
DECODE(db_link,NULL,NULL,''@''||db_link) || '';''
FROM sys.dba_synonyms
WHERE table_owner != ''SYS''
ORDER BY owner
/
SPOOL OFF
SET VERIFY ON FEEDBACK ON TERMOUT ON PAGESIZE 22
CLEAR COLUMNS
UNDEF cr
```

7.2 ADMINISTRATION OF SEQUENCES

Sequences are special database objects that provide numbers in sequence for input to a table. They are useful for providing generated primary key values and for input of number type columns such as purchase order, employee number, sample number, and sales order number, where the input must be unique and in some form of numerical sequence.

Creation of Sequences

Sequences are created by use of the CREATE SEQUENCE command. The command's format follows:

```
CREATE SEQUENCE [schema.]sequence_name
[START WITH n]
[INCREMENT BY n]
[MAXVALUE n|NOMAXVALUE]
```

```
[MINVALUE n|NOMINVALUE]
[CYCLE|NOCYCLE]
[CACHE n|NOCACHE]
[ORDER|NOORDER] ;
```

where:

sequence_name. The name you want the sequence to have. This may include the user name if created from an account with DBA privilege.

n. An integer, positive or negative.

INCREMENT BY. Tells the system how to increment the sequence. If it is positive, the values are ascending; if it is negative, the values are descending.

START WITH. Tells the system which integer to start with.

MINVALUE. Tells the system how low the sequence can go. For ascending sequences, it defaults to 1; for descending sequences, the default value is 10e27-1.

MAXVALUE. Tells the system the highest value that will be allowed. For descending sequences, the default is 1; for ascending sequences, the default is 10e27-1.

CYCLE. Causes the sequence to automatically recycle to minvalue when maxvalue is reached for ascending sequences; for descending sequences, it causes a recycle from minvalue back to maxvalue.

CACHE. Caches the specified number of sequence values into the buffers in the SGA. This speeds access, but all cached numbers are lost when the database is shut down. The default value is 20; maximum value is maxvalue-minvalue.

ORDER. Forces sequence numbers to be output in order of request. In cases where they are used for timestamping, this may be required. In most cases, the sequence numbers will be in order anyway, so ORDER will not be required. ORDER is necessary only to guarantee ordered generation if you are using Oracle with the Oracle Real Application Clusters option in parallel mode. If you are using exclusive mode, sequence numbers are always generated in order.

Sequences prevent the performance problems associated with sequencing numbers generated by application triggers of the form:

```
DECLARE
TEMP_NO NUMBER;
BEGIN
LOCK TABLE PO_NUM IN EXCLUSIVE MODE NOWAIT;
SELECT MAX(PO_NUM)+1 INTO TEMP_NO FROM SALES ;
END;
```

If the application requires numbers that are exactly in sequence (for example, 1, 2, 3 . . .) then the trigger shown above may be your only recourse, since if a statement that references a sequence is rolled back (canceled), that sequence number is lost. Likewise, any cached sequence numbers are lost each time a database is shut down. The closest a sequence can get to being fully sequential would be:

```
CREATE SEQUENCE in_order
START WITH 1
INCREMENT BY 1
NOMAXVALUE
ORDER
NOCACHE;
```

If a sequence already exists in a test or development instance, the script SEQ_RCT.SQL, available from the Wiley Web site, can be used to build a script to transfer or document the structure of the sequence.

Alteration of Sequences

There may be times when a sequence must be altered, such as when a maximum or minimum value is reached. The ALTER SEQUENCE command is used to accomplish this. The format of the command follows:

```
ALTER SEQUENCE [schema.]sequence_name
[INCREMENT BY n]
[MAXVALUE n|NOMAXVALUE]
[MINVALUE n|NOMINVALUE]
[CYCLE|NOCYCLE]
[CACHE n|NOCACHE]
[ORDER|NOORDER];
```

Only future sequence numbers are affected by this statement. To alter the START WITH clause, the sequence must be dropped and re-created. For ascending sequences, the MAXVALUE cannot be less than the current sequence value. For descending sequences, the MINVALUE cannot be greater than the current sequence value.

Dropping a Sequence

Sequences are dropped using the DROP SEQUENCE command. The format of this command follows:

```
DROP SEQUENCE [schema.]sequence_name;
```

If triggers and procedures reference the sequence, these triggers and procedures will fail if the sequence is dropped. It may be advisable to add an exception that will perform the trigger creation of sequences in this situation.

Use of Sequences

Sequences are used by selecting, using the sequence name and the parameters CURRVAL AND NEXTVAL. For example:

```
INSERT INTO purchase_orders (po_num, po_date, originator)
VALUES (po_seq.NEXTVAL, SYSDATE, USER) FROM dual;
```

Here, po_seq is the name of a sequence, and INSERT would update the po_num, po_date, and originator fields of the purchase_orders table with the next sequence value from po_seq, the current system date, and the current user name.

CURRVAL will retrieve the same value into multiple fields in the same session. CURRVAL cannot be used unless the NEXTVAL for the sequence has already been referenced in the current session. The following lists itemize the uses and restrictions of NEXTVAL and CURRVAL.

Uses

- Used with the VALUES clause on an INSERT command.
- Used with the SELECT subclause of a SELECT command.
- Used in the SET clause of an UPDATE command.

Restrictions

- Neither can be used in a subquery.
- Neither can be used in a view or snapshot query.
- Neither can be used with a DISTINCT clause.
- Neither can be used with GROUP BY or ORDER BY.
- Neither can be used in a SELECT command in combination with another SELECT using UNION, MINUS, or INTERSECT.
- Neither can be used in the WHERE clause.
- Neither can be used in the DEFAULT column value in a CREATE TABLE or ALTER TABLE command.
- Neither can be used in a CHECK in a constraint.

Sequences and Import, Export, and SQLLOADER

Sequences are ignorant objects, in that they know nothing about the tables or clusters they service; furthermore, they don't care that they don't know. This puts the onus on the DBA to ensure that sequence values and table values are synchronized after the use of imports, manual data insertion, or use of SQLLOADER to load values into tables whose key values depend on sequences.

IMPORT Scenario   For this scenario, assume that a database is being used for testing. The test plan calls for the database to be periodically purged of data by using the combined deletion and truncation of key data tables. After the first test cycle, it is decided that a larger data set is required. A larger, second test database is exported, and its data values are imported with the IGNORE=Y option. What will happen? The following:

- The sequences will be out of sync with the tables.
- The sequences will have a lesser value than the key fields in the database.
- Any attempted insert will most likely result in a duplicate key error being returned.

What can you do to correct it? Actually, the solution is quite simple:

1. Determine the affected tables by doing simple

```
SELECT COUNT(primary key field) FROM table;
```

type selects and comparing them to known data counts before the drop occurred, or by comparing to a

```
SELECT last_number FROM dba_sequences
WHERE
sequence_name = 'affected_sequence'; (Note: name must be uppercase)
```

2. Determine the difference between the affected sequences and the row count of the tables they support.

3. Adjust the sequence parameter INCREMENT_BY to this difference plus one:

```
ALTER SEQUENCE affected_sequence INCREMENT BY difference+1;
```

4. Select the NEXTVAL from the sequence:

```
SELECT affected_sequence.NEXTVAL FROM dual;
```

5. Reset the INCREMENT_BY value to 1 (or whatever it is supposed to be):

```
ALTER SEQUENCE affected_sequence INCREMENT BY 1;
```

For example, let's say that table clients in phase 1 of testing has 1.2 million rows. The table is truncated and reloaded with 2.5 million rows. The clients_seq sequence shows its LAST_VALUE to be 1,200,000, and any attempted inserts generate the duplicate primary key error. To fix this:

```
SQL>ALTER SEQUENCE clients_seq INCREMENT BY 1300001;
SQL>SELECT clients_seq.NEXTVAL FROM dual;
clients_seq.NEXTVAL
25000001
one row returned.
SQL>ALTER SEQUENCE clients_seq INCREMENT BY 1;
```

7.3 ADMINISTRATION OF DATABASE LINKS

Database links allow users to access tables in other databases, even other databases on other computers running different operating systems. To use database links, the systems involved must have the SQL*NET product installed. All systems need to have network links as well.

Creation of Database Links

Database links are created with the CREATE DATABASE LINK command. The format of this command follows:

```
CREATE [SHARED] [PUBLIC] DATABASE LINK dblink
CONNECT TO
```

```
CURRENT_USER|username IDENTIFIED BY password [authenticated_clause]|
Authenticated_clause
USING 'connect string';

Authenticated_clause:
AUTHENTICATED BY username IDENTIFIED BY password
```

where:

> **database link.** Under Oracle7 and Oracle8, the GLOBAL db_name and the DB_DOMAIN.
>
> **DBLINKS.** These are schema-independent.
>
> **SHARED.** Uses a single network connection, which is shared between different users of the link. This clause can only be specified if the server is using the multi-threaded server (MTS) configuration.
>
> **PUBLIC.** Specified for database links that are to be used by all users. The user must have DBA privilege to specify a PUBLIC link.
>
> **CURRENT_USER.** Specifies that the invoking user's user name and password be invoked to connect to the remote instance.
>
> **CONNECT TO.** Used to force connection to a specific database user at the database being connected to. This allows the DBA to restrict access to confidential or sensitive information for one user instead of all users. If this clause isn't specified, the user's user name and password will be used in its place.
>
> **'connect string'.** The protocol-specific connection command. For a version 2 SQL*NET or NET8 connection, the string would be:

```
sid|alias.domain
```

> where:

> > **sid | alias** is either the actual SID for the database or the alias entered in the tnsnames.ora file for the platform or names server.
> >
> > **domain** is the domain to which the instance belongs.

> **Authenticated_clause.** New in Oracle8*i,* allows the specification of a user name and password that must exist on the remote instance. This clause must be used if the database link is created SHARED.

> An example of a database link creation would be:

```
CREATE PUBLIC SHARED DATABASE LINK ortest1.world
CONNECT TO tele_dba IDENTIFIED BY not_the_password
AUTHENTICATED BY security_dba IDENTIFIED BY secure_password
USING 'ortest1';
```

The database link would be used in the following manner:

```
SELECT * FROM emp@ortest1
```

The combination of table name and link can be placed into a single synonym for ease of use:

```
CREATE PUBLIC SYNONYM BOS_EMP FOR EMP@ORPERDB.BOSTON
```

(assuming ORPERDB.BOSTON is a defined alias in the tnsnames.ora file).

To document existing database links, the script DBLINK_RCT.SQL, available from the Wiley Web site can be run to create a database link rebuild script.

Alteration of Database Links

Database links cannot be altered. To modify a database link, it must be dropped and re-created.

Dropping Database Links

Database links are dropped via the DROP DATABASE LINK command. For public database links, the word PUBLIC must be inserted after DROP. Only DBAs can drop public database links. The format of the DROP command follows:

```
DROP [PUBLIC] DATABASE LINK dblink;
```

7.4 ADMINISTRATION OF VIEWS

Views (with the exception of materialized views) offer virtual looks at tables. They don't exist until queried except as a specification statement stored in the database. A single view can be very efficient, but the "stacking" of views—that is, views that reference views that reference views—will cause a performance problem.

Views allow the DBA to restrict access to certain columns within a table or tables. Views can also act as preprocessing for reports, and can be used to perform calculations and display the results alongside of the data as if the results were stored in a table. Views can also be used to "filter" data. A view can be constructed from virtually any SELECT statement. Depending upon how a view is constructed, updates and inserts can be done through them.

Creation of Views

The creation of views is accomplished with the CREATE VIEW command. Let's look at this command:

```
CREATE [OR REPLACE] [[NO] FORCE] VIEW [schema.]viewname
[[(alias list)]|
OF [schema.]type_name
WITH OBJECT IDENTIFIER DEFAULT|(attribute_list)]| UNDER super_view
AS subquery [with clause];
```

```
With clause:
WITH READ ONLY|CHECK OPTION [CONSTRAINT constraint]
```

where:

[NO] FORCE. The force option allows a view to be created even if the creator doesn't have proper access to the tables, types, or views specified. However, before the view can be used, the appropriate grants must be issued.

viewname. The name for the view.

alias list. A valid column name or list of column names; the name isn't required to be the same as the column it is based on. If aliases aren't used, the names of the columns are used. If a column is modified by an expression, it must be aliased. If four columns are in the query, there must be four aliases. Each alias may also include a constraint. In addition, the alias list may also contain table or view constraints.

OF... Used for an object view. The specified type must exist and must contain an attribute for each column in the subquery.

WITH OBJECT IDENTIFIER. Replaces the version 8.0 WITH OBJECT OID clause and specifies that the attribute list specified will be used to generate an object identifier. The specified attribute or attribute list must uniquely identify the row in the view. This clause can be omitted or the DEFAULT clause used if the view is based on an existing object table or another object view.

UNDER super_view. New in Oracle9*i*, allows a view to be created as a subview under a master super_view. To see if a view is a sub- or super_view, use the SUPERVIEW_NAME column in the appropriate VIEW data dictionary view (DBA_VIEWS, USER_VIEWS or ALL_VIEWS).

The restrictions on the UNDER clause are:

- You must create a subview in the same schema as the superview.
- The object type type_name must be the immediate subtype of superview.
- You can create only one subview of a particular type under the same superview.

subquery. Any valid SELECT statement that doesn't include an ORDER BY or FOR UPDATE clause. Other restrictions on a view's query are:

- The view query cannot select the CURRVAL or NEXTVAL pseudocolumns.
- If the view query selects the ROWID, ROWNUM, or LEVEL pseudocolumns, those columns must have aliases in the view query.
- If the view query uses an asterisk (*) to select all columns of a table, and you later add new columns to the table, the view will not contain those columns until you re-create the view by issuing a CREATE OR REPLACE VIEW statement.
- For object views, the number of elements in the view subquery select list must be the same as the number of top-level attributes for the object type.

The datatype of each of the selecting elements must be the same as the corresponding top-level attribute.

- You cannot specify the SAMPLE clause.
- The preceding restrictions apply to materialized views as well.

If you want the view to be inherently updatable, it must not contain any of the following constructs:

- A set operator
- A DISTINCT operator
- An aggregate or analytic function
- An ORDER BY, GROUP BY, CONNECT BY, or START WITH clause
- A collection expression in a SELECT list
- A subquery in a SELECT list
- Joins (with some exceptions)

If an inherently updatable view contains pseudocolumns or expressions, the UPDATE statement must not refer to any of these pseudocolumns or expressions.

- If you want a join view to be updatable, all of the following conditions must be true:
  - The DML statement must affect only one table underlying the join.
  - For an UPDATE statement, all columns updated must be extracted from a key-preserved table. If the view has the CHECK OPTION, join columns and columns taken from tables that are referenced more than once in the view must be shielded from UPDATE.
  - For a DELETE statement, the join can have one and only one key-preserved table. That table can appear more than once in the join, unless the view has the CHECK_OPTION.
  - For an INSERT statement, all columns into which values are inserted must come from a key-preserved table, and the view must not have the CHECK_OPTION.

With clause. Specifies that inserts and updates through the view must be selectable from the view. This can be used in a view based on a view.

READ ONLY. Specifies that the view is READ ONLY and cannot be updated.

CONSTRAINT. Specifies the name associated with the WITH CHECK constraint.

A view can usually be used in the following commands:

COMMENT
DELETE
INSERT
LOCK TABLE

UPDATE

SELECT

A view's SELECT statement in the subquery cannot select a CURRVAL or NEXTVAL from a sequence, or directly access ROWID, ROWNUM, or LEVEL pseudo-columns. To use the pseudocolumns for a table, a view select must alias them.

A normal view is just a window to data; it can't store data itself. Views can be used in an SQL statement, just as a table can, with the following exceptions. You can't update a view if:

- It contains a join.
- It contains a GROUP BY, CONNECT BY, or START WITH clause.
- It contains a DISTINCT clause or expressions like "AMOUNT+10" in the column list.
- It doesn't reference all NOT NULL columns in the table (all NOT NULLs must be in the view and assigned a value by the update).

You can update a view that contains pseudocolumns or columns modified by expressions if the update doesn't affect these columns. A new trigger, called an INSTEAD OF trigger, can be used to update the underlying tables in a view that can't be directly updated. If you base a view on a view with INSTEAD OF triggers, the new view must also contain INSTEAD OF triggers.

You can query the view USER_UPDATABLE_COLUMNS to find out if the columns in a join view are updatable. Generally speaking, as long as all of the NOT NULLs and key columns are included in a join view for a table, then that table may be updated through the view.

A join view can have the commands INSERT, UPDATE, and DELETE used against it under the circumstances described below.

- The DML affects only one of the tables in the join.
- If the command is UPDATE, then all of the columns updated are extracted from a key-preserved table. In addition, if the view has a CHECK OPTION constraint, join columns and columns taken from tables that are referenced more than once in the view are shielded from update.
- If the statement is DELETE, then there is one and only one key-preserved table in the join, and that table can be present more than once if there is no CHECK OPTION constraint on the view.
- If the statement is INSERT, then all of the columns are from a key-preserved table, and the view doesn't have a CHECK OPTION constraint.

Partition Views

Under Oracle7 version 7.3, a new type of view, called the partition view, was allowed. This view joins several tables that have identical structure into a single entity that can be queried as if all of the component parts were actually in one table. The purpose for a partition view is to allow physical partitioning of data into several table partitions (this is pre-Oracle8 and shouldn't be confused with actual partition tables, which aren't available until Oracle8). These table partitions must be hand-built by the DBA to spread data across several disk volumes and to separate data by a preset algorithm that is application-controlled (instead of as in Oracle8, where the partitioning is specified at the table's creation). An example would be an application that breaks down sales data by month and stores it in independent monthly sales tables. A partitioned view could be created to join all of the monthly sales tables in quarterly, yearly, or other views of all sales for that period. All that said, because these views were not widely used, and have been replaced by true partitions, I do not discus them in detail.

Object Views

In order to take advantage of the benefits of the new object paradigm in Oracle8, 8*i*, and 9*i*, a common relational table can be made into a pseudo-object table by creating what is known as an *object view* that is directly based on the relational table. The object ID is not system-generated but is based on columns that you specify.

An example using the emp table would be:

```
CREATE TYPE emp_t AS OBJECT (
empno      NUMBER(5),
ename      VARCHAR2(20),
salary     NUMBER(9,2),
job        VARCHAR2(20));
/
CREATE TABLE emp(
empno      NUMBER(5) CONSTRAINT pk_emp PRIMARY KEY,
ename      VARCHAR2(20),
salary     NUMBER(9,2),
job        VARCHAR2(20));

CREATE VIEW emp_man OF emp_t
WITH OBJECT IDENTIFIER (empno) AS
SELECT empno, ename, salary, job
FROM emp
WHERE job=''MANAGER'';
```

This creates an object view of emp_t (type) objects that correspond to the employees from the emp table who are managers, with empno, the primary key of EMP, as the object identifier.

Example Views

An example view that uses aliases and expressions to modify columns is shown in Source 7.2.

Source 7.2   Example of a view with expressions.

```
CREATE VIEW free_space
(tablespace, file_id, pieces, free_bytes, free_blocks,
largest_bytes,largest_blks) AS
SELECT tablespace_name, file_id, COUNT(*),
SUM(bytes), SUM(blocks),
MAX(bytes), MAX(blocks) FROM sys.dba_free_space
GROUP BY tablespace_name, file_id;
```

In Source 7.2, the SUM, MAX, and COUNT expressions (functions) are used to provide summary data on space usage. This view could not be updated. Further reading will show it is also based upon a view, DBA_FREE_SPACE, that is based on several data dictionary tables owned by the SYS user. An example of a view that performs calculations and filters the data provided is shown in Source 7.3.

Source 7.3   View using expressions and filtering.

```
REM Title    : DD_VIEW.SQL
REM Purpose : View of the Data Dictionary caches
REM     showing only parameters that have usage
REM     and the percent of GETMISSES/GETS
REM USE      : Use as a selectable table only
REM Limitations    : User must have access to V$ views.
REM Revisions:
REM    Date  Modified By Reason For change
REM    4/28/93     Mike Ault   Initial Creation
REM
CREATE VIEW dd_cache
AS SELECT parameter,gets,getmisses,
getmisses/gets*100 percent
,count,usage
FROM v$rowcache
WHERE gets > 100 AND getmisses > 0;
```

To create a script to document and allow rebuild of existing views, the script in Source 7.4 can be used.

Alteration of Views

Under Oracle7, Oracle8, and Oracle8*i*, there is only a single option for the ALTER VIEW command: the COMPILE option. In Oracle9*i*, you can ADD, MODIFY, or DROP view constraints using ALTER VIEW. If a view's underlying views or tables are marked

Source 7.4   Script to rebuild views.

```
REM
REM NAME        :view_rct.sql
REM FUNCTION:re-create database views by owner
REM USE              :Generate a report on database views
REM Limitations :If your view definitions are greater than 5000
REM           characters then increase the set long. This can be
REM           determined by querying the DBA_VIEWS table's
REM           text_length column for the max value: select
REM           max(text_length) from dba_views;
REM
SET PAGES 59 LINES 79 FEEDBACK OFF ECHO OFF VERIFY OFF
DEFINE cr='chr(10)'
COLUMN text        FORMAT a80 word_wrapped
COLUMN view_name       FORMAT a20
COLUMN dbname NEW_VALUE db NOPRINT
UNDEF owner_name
UNDEF view_name
SELECT name dbname from v$database;
SET LONG 5000 HEADING OFF
SPOOL rep_out\&db\cre_view.sql
SELECT
'rem Code for view: '||v.view_name||'instance: '||&&db||&&cr||
'CREATE OR REPLACE VIEW '||v.owner||'.'||v.view_name||' AS '
||&&cr,
v.text
FROM
dba_views v
WHERE
v.owner LIKE UPPER('&&owner_name%')
AND view_name LIKE UPPER('%&&view_name%')
ORDER BY
v.view_name;
SPOOL OFF
SET HEADING ON PAGES 22 LINES 80 FEEDBACK ON
CLEAR COLUMNS
TTITLE OFF
PAUSE Press enter to continue
```

as invalid or changed, the view is marked as invalid and must be recompiled. This can be done automatically when the view is next called, or it can be done explicitly with the ALTER VIEW command. It is best to do this explicitly so that any problems are found before users attempt to use the view. The format for the ALTER VIEW command follows:

```
ALTER VIEW [schema.]view_name COMPILE
[ADD|MODIFY|DROP constraint_clause] (Oracle9i only.)
```

Dropping Views

Views are dropped with the DROP VIEW command. Its format follows:

```
DROP VIEW [schema.]view_name;
```

> **TIP**   Altering or dropping a view will result in invalidation of any dependent packages, functions, or procedures. Be sure to check dependencies before performing these operations.

7.5 ADMINISTRATION OF MATERIALIZED VIEW LOGS IN ORACLE8*i* AND ORACLE9*i*

In order to facilitate fast refreshes of materialized views, you must create a materialized view log. If a materialized view log is not available for a materialized view, a fast refresh cannot be done and a complete refresh is the only refresh mechanism. A complete refresh involves truncating the materialized view table and then repopulating the materialized view by reexecuting its build query. A fast refresh uses the information in the materialized view log to only apply changes to the materialized view.

Creation of a Materialized View Log

The actual syntax of the CREATE MATERIALIZED VIEW LOG command is rather lengthy so though I show an example here of the creation of a materialized view log, I refer you to the SQL manual at the documentation link (technet.oracle.com) for more details.

```
CREATE MATERIALIZED VIEW LOG ON tab_example1
STORAGE (INITIAL 250K NEXT 250K PCTINCREASE 0)
TABLESPACE view_logs
PARALLEL 4
NOLOGGING
NOCACHE
WITH PRIMARY KEY, ROWID (tablespace_name)
INCLUDING NEW VALUES;
```

Don't be confused that it tells you that a snapshot log has been created; remember, snapshots and materialized views are synonymous. This command creates a materialized view log (or snapshot log, if you prefer) on the table tab_example1 using the specified storage parameters and tablespace. The log will use a parallel degree of 4 (normally this is not required since the PARALLEL clause by itself will cause Oracle to calculate the proper degree). The log is not logged; rather, the default is LOGGED (which means it is not recoverable) and will not be cached. The default is CACHED, in the SGA. The log will track both primary key and rowid information, as well as any changes to the filter column TABLESPACE_NAME. Filter columns cannot be part of the primary key and must exist in the master table. If no WITH clause is specified, the primary key values are tracked by default. Materialized view logs can be partitioned just like regular tables.

Altering a Materialized View Log

All aspects of a materialized view log are alterable; these include the adding of filter columns, rowid, or primary key data to that which is already being stored in the log. For this task, too, I refer you to the documentation link at technet.oracle.com for the details.

Dropping a Materialized View Log

The command for dropping a materialized view log is simple:

```
DROP MATERIALIZED VIEW LOG ON [schema.]tablename;
```

7.6 ADMINISTRATION OF MATERIALIZED VIEWS (SNAPSHOTS) IN ORACLE8*i* AND ORACLE9*i*

Another feature of Oracle that needs administration is the *snapshot* (also known as a *materialized view*). Snapshots are copies of an entire single table or set of its rows (simple snapshot), or a collection of tables, views or their rows using joins, grouping, and selection criteria (complex snapshots). Snapshots are very useful in a distributed environment where remote locations need a query-able copy of a table from the master database. Instead of paying the penalty for using the network to send out the query and get back the data, the query is against a local table image and is thus much faster. With later versions of Oracle7 and in Oracle8, Oracle8*i*, and Oracle9*i*, snapshots can be made updatable. As stated in Section 7.5, the new materialized view is actually a special form of "same database" snapshot.

Snapshots and materialized views are asynchronous in nature; that is, they reflect a table's or a collection's state at the time the snapshot was taken. A simple snapshot or materialized view can be periodically refreshed either by use of a snapshot log, containing only the changed rows for the snapshot (fast refresh), or a totally new copy (complete refresh). In most cases, the fast refresh is quicker and just as accurate. A fast refresh, however, can be used only if the snapshot or materialized view has a log, and that log was created prior to the creation or last refresh of the snapshot. For a complex snapshot or materialized view, a complete refresh is required. It is also possible to allow the system to decide which to use, either a fast or complete refresh.

One problem with a snapshot or materialized view log is that it keeps a copy of each and every change to a row. Therefore, if a row undergoes 200 changes between one refresh and the next, there will be 200 entries in the snapshot or materialized view log that will be applied to the snapshot at refresh. This could lead to the refresh of the snapshot or materialized view taking longer than a complete refresh. Every snapshot or materialized view should be examined for the amount of activity it is experiencing, and if this is occurring with any of them, the snapshot or materialized view log should be eliminated or the refresh mode changed to COMPLETE.

 , A materialized view is simply a snapshot that is contained in the current instance instead of a remote instance. Other than the keyword MATERIALIZED VIEW, the CREATE SNAPSHOT and CREATE SNAPSHOT LOG commands are identical to the CREATE MATERIALIZED VIEW and CREATE MATERIALIZED VIEW LOG commands. Since the CREATE MATERIALIZED VIEW command creates a view, table, and an index, to maintain the materialized view, you must have the CREATE VIEW, CREATE TABLE, CREATE INDEX, and CREATE MATERIALIZED VIEW or CREATE SNAPSHOT privileges to create a materialized view. If you wish query rewrite to be available on the materialized views created, the owner of the underlying tables and the materialized view must have the QUERY REWRITE privilege, or the creator of the materialized view must have the GLOBAL QUERY REWRITE privilege.

In a data warehousing situation, a materialized view can be used by Oracle to rewrite queries on the fly that the optimizer determines would profit from using the materialized view rather than the base tables. You should take this into consideration when the concurrency of the data is important, since a materialized view is only as current as its last refresh.

Creating a Materialized View or Snapshot

The format for the CREATE MATERIALIZED VIEW command is complex enough that I refer you once again to the SQL manual for details. However, we will look at a couple of examples. In perusing the manual, at one point it states that the first step in creating a materialized view is to create a DIMENSION. However, in investigating this claim, I found no way to tie a DIMENSION to a MATERIALIZED VIEW; I also learned that DIMENSIONs are really only of use in data warehousing, where rollup and aggregation are of importance. I will touch on DIMENSION creation in a later section of this chapter; for now, note that there are no direct ties between MATERIALIZED VIEWs and DIMENSIONs. Perhaps the Oracle8i or Oracle9i database engine itself ties them together, but one is not required for the other to function, as far as I can determine. Let's get on with some simple examples.

In the first example, let's do some summary work against the DBA_views so we can query about total space, total extents, and so on without having to place the code into our reports. This will actually be a materialized view based on two example tables, TAB_EXAMPLE1 and TAB_EXAMPLE2, that are based on the underlying DBA_views, DBA_TABLES, and DBA_EXTENTS.

```
CREATE MATERIALIZED VIEW table_extents
TABLESPACE tools
```

```
STORAGE (INITIAL 1M NEXT 1M PCTINCREASE 0)
NOLOGGING
BUILD IMMEDIATE
REFRESH COMPLETE START WITH SYSDATE NEXT SYSDATE+1/24
AS
SELECT
  a.owner           owner,
  a.table_name      table_name,
a.tablespace_name tablespace_name,
  count(b.owner)    extents,
  sum(b.bytes)      bytes
FROM
tab_example1 a,
tab_example2 b
WHERE
a.owner <>'SYSTEM'
AND a.owner=b.owner
AND a.table_name=b.segment_name
AND b.segment_type=''TABLE''
GROUP BY
a.owner,a.table_name, a.tablespace_name;
```

What does a materialized view buy us as far as performance? Let's look at the explain plans for a query on a regular view and then one on the materialized view we just created. First we create an identical normal view:

```
CREATE VIEW test_view
AS
SELECT
a.owner owner,
a.table_name table_name,
a.tablespace_name tablespace_name,
count(b.owner) extents,
sum(b.bytes) bytes
FROM
tab_example1 a, tab_example2 b
WHERE
a.owner <>''SYSTEM''
AND a.owner=b.owner
AND a.table_name=b.segment_name
AND b.segment_type=''TABLE''
GROUP BY a.owner,a.table_name, a.tablespace_name;
```

Now let's set autotrace on, with the explain option and see what happens when we select against each of these objects.

```
SQL> set autotrace on explain
SQL> select * from test_view
2*  where extents>1
```

```
OWNER   TABLE_NAME          TABLESPACE_NAME      EXTENTS    BYTES
------- ------------------  ------------------   --------   --------
SYS     ACCESS$             SYSTEM                     8     536576
SYS     ARGUMENT$           SYSTEM                    10    1191936
SYS     COM$                SYSTEM                     7     368640
SYS     CON$                SYSTEM                     3      45056
SYS     DEPENDENCY$         SYSTEM                     7     352256
SYS     ERROR$              SYSTEM                     2      24576
SYS     EXTENT_TO_OBJECT_TAB  SYSTEM                   3      45056
SYS     EXT_TO_OBJ          SYSTEM                     4      86016
SYS     HIST_HEAD$          SYSTEM                     3      45056
SYS     IDL_CHAR$           SYSTEM                     7     368640
SYS     IDL_SB4$            SYSTEM                     9     802816
SYS     IDL_UB1$            SYSTEM                    14    5861376
SYS     IDL_UB2$            SYSTEM                    13    3915776
SYS     OBJ$                SYSTEM                     7     352256
SYS     OBJAUTH$            SYSTEM                     3      45056
SYS     PROCEDURE$          SYSTEM                     2      24576
SYS     SEQ$                SYSTEM                     2      24576
SYS     Source$             SYSTEM                    18   29503488
SYS     SYN$                SYSTEM                     3      45056
SYS     VIEW$               SYSTEM                    10    1191936

20 rows selected.

Execution Plan
    0        SELECT STATEMENT Optimizer=CHOOSE
    1    0    VIEW OF 'TEST_VIEW'
    2    1     FILTER
    3    2      SORT (GROUP BY)
    4    3       MERGE JOIN
    5    4        SORT (JOIN)
    6    5         TABLE ACCESS (FULL) OF 'TAB_EXAMPLE2'
    7    4        SORT (JOIN)
    8    7         TABLE ACCESS (FULL) OF 'TAB_EXAMPLE1'


SQL> select * from table_extents
2* where extents>1
OWNER   TABLE_NAME          TABLESPACE_NAME      EXTENTS    BYTES
------- ------------------  ------------------   --------   --------
SYS     ACCESS$             SYSTEM                     8     536576
SYS     ARGUMENT$           SYSTEM                    10    1191936
SYS     COM$                SYSTEM                     7     368640
SYS     CON$                SYSTEM                     3      45056
SYS     DEPENDENCY$         SYSTEM                     7     352256
SYS     ERROR$              SYSTEM                     2      24576
SYS     EXTENT_TO_OBJECT_TAB  SYSTEM                   3      45056
SYS     EXT_TO_OBJ          SYSTEM                     4      86016
SYS     HIST_HEAD$          SYSTEM                     3      45056
SYS     IDL_CHAR$           SYSTEM                     7     368640
SYS     IDL_SB4$            SYSTEM                     9     802816
```

```
SYS    IDL_UB1$              SYSTEM                    14   5861376
SYS    IDL_UB2$              SYSTEM                    13   3915776
SYS    OBJ$                  SYSTEM                     7    352256
SYS    OBJAUTH$              SYSTEM                     3     45056
SYS    PROCEDURE$            SYSTEM                     2     24576
SYS    SEQ$                  SYSTEM                     2     24576
SYS    Source$              SYSTEM                    18  29503488
SYS    SYN$                  SYSTEM                     3     45056
SYS    VIEW$                 SYSTEM                    10   1191936

20 rows selected.

Execution Plan
   0       SELECT STATEMENT Optimizer=CHOOSE
   1    0    TABLE ACCESS (FULL) OF ''MVIEW_TEST''
```

As you can see, we get identical results; but the second query against the materi-alized view only does a single table scan against the materialized view table, not two table scans against the underlying base tables. The results would be even more advan-tageous for a remote snapshot since no network traffic would be involved. Also notice that in the materialized view we are updating once an hour. While a view will give an instantaneous result (after the view itself is instantiated) the materialized view will only be as current as its last refresh. The materialized view can be created such that any commit against the base table forces a refresh against the materialized view if the materialized view has no aggregations or includes no joins.

Altering a Materialized View or Snapshot

As with snapshots, a materialized view can have its physical attributes altered, its index parameters changed, and its logging and cache parameters changed (look at the syn-tax for the command at the document link for the SQL manual); in addition, a materi-alized view can have the capability to allow query rewrite enabled or disabled.

Dropping a Materialized View

The command to drop a materialized view or snapshot is rather simple:

```
DROP MATERIALIZED VIEW|SNAPSHOT
[schema.]materialized_view_name|snapshot_name;
```

Refreshing Materialized Views

Normally, a materialized view will be refreshed using the DBMS_JOB queues. This means that you must have at least one job queue set up and operating; normally, I suggest at least two queues or more be set up using the JOB_QUEUE_PROCESSES and JOB_QUEUE_INTERVAL initialization parameters. (Note: These parameters are synonymous with the SNAPSHOT_QUEUE_PROCESSES and SNAPSHOT_INTERVAL parameters in prior releases.) A third parameter, JOB_QUEUE_KEEP_CONNECTIONS, forces the database links to be opened for remote snapshots, or for materialized views to be held open between refreshes.

Materialized views can be refreshed using COMPLETE, FAST, FORCE, ON DEMAND, or ON COMMIT, depending on the complexity of the materialized view. A COMPLETE truncates the materialized view table and reloads it from scratch. A FAST uses a materialized view log only to update changed rows. If you intend to use the FAST refresh method, you must create the materialized view log first and then the materialized view. A FORCE will perform a FAST if possible and a COMPLETE if required. ON DEMAND uses the DBMS_MVIEW or DBMS_SNAP packages to complete a refresh, and ON COMMIT refreshes a materialized view or snapshot whenever a commit is executed against the base table (for a simple materialized view with no joins or aggregations).

Oracle8*i* provided the DBMS_MVIEW package, which handles refresh activity on materialized views on demand. This package is covered in the script zip "Oracle9*i* provided PL/SQL Packages and Types Reference Manual" on the Oracle documentation site.

Snapshot Usage

Source 7.5 shows the use of the CREATE SNAPSHOT command for a simple snapshot. It is followed directly by Source 7.6, which shows use of the CREATE SNAPSHOT command with a complex snapshot. The sizing considerations should mirror those for the source table. If the source table is stable, a large initial extent with smaller subsequent extents should be used. Since snapshots will most likely be on slow-growth tables, set pctincrease to 0 in most cases.

In the snapshot in Source 7.5, the entire test_drugs table is used to create a snapshot from its location at a remote database identified in the kcgc connect string into the tablespace clinical_tests in the current database. It will first be refreshed in seven days at 2:00 o'clock in the morning and subsequently at seven-day intervals on every Tuesday thereafter at 2:00 o'clock in the morning. Since no refresh mode is specified, if

Source 7.5   Example of the CREATE SNAPSHOT command for a simple snapshot.

```
CREATE SNAPSHOT new_drugs
PCTFREE 10 PCTUSED 70
TABLESPACE clinical_tests
STORAGE (INITIAL 50K NEXT 50K PCTINCREASE 0)
REFRESH
START WITH ROUND(SYSDATE + 7) + 2/24
NEXT NEXT_DAY(TRUNC(SYSDATE, 'TUESDAY') + 2/24
AS SELECT * FROM appl_dba.test_drugs@kcgc
```

Source 7.6   Script to produce a complex snapshot.

```
CREATE SNAPSHOT trial_summary
PCTFREE 5 PCTUSED 60
TABLESPACE clinical_tests
STORAGE (INITIAL 100K NEXT 50K PCTINCREASE 0)
REFRESH COMPLETE
START WITH ROUND(SYSDATE + 14) + 6/24
NEXT NEXT_DAY(TRUNC(SYSDATE, 'FRIDAY') + 19/24
AS
select td.drug_name, s.trial_number, dr.doctor_id,
s.comment_line,s.comment
from
appl_dba.test_drugs@kcgc   td,
appl_dba.trial_doctors@kcgc dr,
appl_dba.trial_summaries@kcgc s
where
td.drug_id = s.drug_id and
s.trial_id = dr.trial_id and
s.doctor_id = dr.doctor_id;
```

the table has a snapshot log, the fast mode will be used since it is a simple snapshot. If no snapshot log is available, then the complete mode will be used. If you specify the FORCE option, it will always try to do a FAST refresh first.

The script in Source 7.6 produces a complex snapshot called trial_summary with data from the test_drugs, trial_doctors, and trial_summaries tables in the database specified in the connect string kcgc. The snapshot is refreshed using the complete mode since it is a complex query and is created in the clinical_tests tablespace of the local database.

7.7 ADMINISTRATION OF TRIGGERS IN ORACLE9*I*

Database triggers are PL/SQL procedures stored in the database and associated with specific actions on a database level. Beginning with Oracle8, a new type of trigger called an INSTEAD OF trigger could be created exclusively for views. Under Oracle8*i* and Oracle9*i*, the concept of database event triggers has been added. A database event trigger triggers on DDL or database events such as STARTUP, SHUTDOWN, LOGIN, LOGOFF, or server errors.

TIP   Never depend on the order in which triggers fire. This is not guaranteed to always be identical.

Creation of Database Triggers

Database triggers are created using the CREATE TRIGGER command, and are ENABLED upon creation. There were three basic types of triggers in Oracle7: BEFORE, AFTER, and FOR EACH ROW. Under Oracle8, a fourth was added: the INSTEAD OF trigger for views. Since the FOR EACH ROW clause can be combined with the other two non-view triggers, this gives four types of triggers: BEFORE and AFTER statement triggers and BEFORE and AFTER row triggers. In addition, each of the four types can be tied to the three basic actions, DELETE, INSERT, and UPDATE, resulting in 12 possible triggers per table.

A view can only have an INSTEAD OF trigger (under Oracle8 only). The Oracle8*i* DDL and database event triggers are also created using the CREATE TRIGGER command. DDL events that can cause a trigger to fire are CREATE, ALTER, or DROP on clusters, tables, views, procedures, functions, packages, roles, sequences, synonyms, indexes, tablespaces, triggers, types, and users. The database event triggers are LOGON, LOGOFF, SERVERERROR, STARTUP, and SHUTDOWN, with the LOGON, STARTUP, and SERVERERROR coming AFTER event triggers. The LOGOFF and SHUTDOWN are BEFORE event triggers. You can find the exact syntax for the CREATE TRIGGER command in the SQL reference at the techent.oracle.com Web site.

Database triggers are complex, so if you do not save the creation script, it will be very difficult to readily recall the exact command used in many cases. The script in TRIG_RCT.SQL, available from the Wiley Web site, can be used to retrieve trigger definitions for the database.

Prior to the release of Oracle version 7.3, triggers were compiled at runtime. Since 7.3, they are stored in the database as Pcode. This provides significant performance benefits over earlier versions since the overhead of reparsing the trigger for each firing is eliminated. This allows larger and more complex triggers to be created without fear of performance degradation caused by reparsing large sections of code. In versions 8, 8*i*, and 9*i* triggers can be pinned into memory using the DBMS_SHARED_POOL. KEEP('trigger_name', 'T') procedure call.

Conditional Predicates   New to Oracle8 and continued in Oracle8*i* and Oracle9*i* is the concept of a conditional predicate for a trigger that tells the trigger why it is being fired. These conditional predicates are of the form:

INSERTING. Evaluates to TRUE if an insert operation fired the trigger.

DELETING. Evaluates to TRUE if a delete operation fired the trigger.

UPDATING. Evaluates to TRUE if an update operation fired the trigger.

UPDATING(column). Evaluates to TRUE if the operation is an update and the specified column is updated.

LOB Trigger Limitations   You can reference object, varray, nested table, LOB, and REF columns inside triggers, but you cannot modify their values. Triggers based on actions against these types of attributes can be created.

Triggers and Mutating Tables   One recurring problem with triggers is when one tries to reference the table for which it is fired (for example, to check a date range). This self-referencing results in "ORA-04091 table 'table_name' is mutating, trigger/ function may not see it." Usually, this situation can be remedied in one of three ways: by using a temporary PL/SQL table to hold values, by using a temporary table to hold values, or by using a view. The key here is to remove the values to be selected against from the table before you attempt the operation, and then refer to this remote source for any value checking. It might also be possible to create an index that any selects will reference. Any solution that moves the data from the table to a secondary source that can then be used in place of the table itself should correct this problem.

Let's look at an example of a trigger that is set to fire on an insert or update to a purchase_orders table:

```
CREATE OR REPLACE TRIGGER purchase_order_adjust
BEFORE INSERT OR UPDATE ON purchase_orders
FOR EACH ROW
WHEN (new.price>0)
DECLARE
adj_price NUMBER;
RATE number;
BEGIN
SELECT adjust_rate
INTO rate
FROM price_adjust
WHERE state_code = :new.state_code;
adj_price:=:new.price*rate;
:new.adjusted_price:=adj_price;
END;
Here is the result:
SQL>  update purchase_orders set price=2000 where po_num=1
2    and lineno=1;
1 row updated.
SQL> select * from purchase_orders;
LINENO   PRICE    ADJUSTED_PRICE    PO_NUM ST
-------  -------  ----------------  ---------
1        2000            2130          1 GA
```

For both inserts and updates, the adjusted price column is set to the price, times the rate from the price_adjust table, based on the state. See how all of this is hidden from the user? Even at the base SQL level, the user has no indication that any of the trigger activity is occurring. This is a simple form of data hiding. Because the trigger is stored as being associated only with a single table, it is also a simple form of encapsulation (except that they aren't stored together as one entity).

Use of Conditional Predicates   Conditional predicates allow a single trigger to decide which action to take based on the triggering action. For example, different actions could be taken if a table were inserted into, updated, or deleted from. The action could be as simple as inserting a row into an auditing table for each table action or updating multiple tables with the results of a changed calculation.

For our example, we have a purchase_orders table with line number, price, adjusted price, purchase order number, and state code; a price_adjust table with state_code and adjustment rate; and a billings table with a total price, purchase order number, and purchaser name.

The trigger we want to build updates the total price column of the billings table each time a change is made to a purchase order number line item in the purchase_ orders table. I know this wastes resources and calculated values shouldn't be stored in a database, but this is just an example.

Here is the trigger we want to create:

```
CREATE OR REPLACE TRIGGER maintain_total
BEFORE INSERT OR DELETE OR UPDATE
ON purchase_orders FOR EACH ROW
DECLARE
new_total NUMBER;
chg_date DATE;
BEGIN
SELECT SUM(adjusted_price), sysdate
INTO new_total,chg_date
FROM purchase_orders
WHERE po_num=:new.po_num;
IF INSERTING THEN
UPDATE billings
SET po_amount=new_total,
change_date=chg_date,
change_type='INSERT'
WHERE po_num=:new.po_num;
ELSIF DELETING THEN
UPDATE billings
SET po_amount=new_total,
change_date=chg_date,
change_type='DELETE'
WHERE po_num=:new.po_num;
ELSIF UPDATING THEN
UPDATE billings
SET po_amount=new_total,
change_date=chg_date,
change_type='UPDATE'
WHERE po_num=:new.po_num;
END IF;
END;
```

The code compiles fine. Let's run it:

```
SQL> update purchase_orders set price=3000 where po_num=1;
update purchase_orders set price=3000 where po_num=1
        *
```

```
ERROR at line 1:
ORA-04091: table TELE_DBA.PURCHASE_ORDERS is mutating, trigger/function may
not see it
ORA-06512: at "TELE_DBA.MAINTAIN_TOTAL", line 5
ORA-04088: error during execution of trigger 'TELE_DBA.MAINTAIN_TOTAL'
```

What happened? Remember the mutating table errors? This is a classic way of generating them. Essentially, we have a value that we are updating, so it is in a state of flux (our first trigger from the previous guide is firing at the same time this one fires, leaving a value in a transient state; hence, the mutation).

How can we fix this? We must change the trigger to an AFTER type. This means eliminating all OLD and NEW references and using logic closer to that of a stored PROCEDURE using cursors. In pre-7.3 days, we would have done this anyway because PROCEDUREs were compiled and triggers were not. Here is the new trigger code:

```
CREATE OR REPLACE TRIGGER maintain_total
AFTER INSERT OR DELETE OR UPDATE
ON purchase_orders
DECLARE
adj_price NUMBER;
RATE      number;
new_total NUMBER;
chg_date  DATE;
po        NUMBER;
CURSOR get_po IS
SELECT UNIQUE po_num
FROM billings;
CURSOR get_total(po number) IS
SELECT SUM(adjusted_price), sysdate
FROM purchase_orders
WHERE po_num=po;
BEGIN
OPEN get_po;
FETCH get_po into po;
LOOP
EXIT WHEN get_po%NOTFOUND;
OPEN get_total(po);
FETCH get_total INTO new_total,chg_date;
IF INSERTING THEN
UPDATE billings
SET po_amount=new_total,
change_date=chg_date,
change_type='INSERT'
WHERE po_num=po and
po_amount<>new_total;
ELSIF DELETING THEN
UPDATE billings
SET po_amount=new_total,
change_date=chg_date,
change_type='DELETE'
```

```
WHERE po_num=po and
po_amount<>new_total;
ELSIF UPDATING THEN
UPDATE billings
SET po_amount=new_total,
change_date=chg_date,
change_type='UPDATE'
WHERE po_num=po and
po_amount<>new_total;
END IF;
CLOSE get_total;
FETCH get_po INTO po;
END LOOP;
END;
```

So what happens now when we fire off an update into the table?

```
SQL> select * from billings;
PO_NUM PO_AMOUNT         PURCHASER            CHANGE_DA  CHANGE_TYP
------ ---------         -------------        ---------- ----------
1         3195           Georges Shootery     24-JUL-97  Initial
SQL> update purchase_orders set price=2000 where po_num=1;
1 row updated.
SQL> select * from billings;
PO_NUM PO_AMOUNT         PURCHASER            CHANGE_DA  CHANGE_TYP
------ ---------         -------------        ---------- ----------
1         2130           Georges Shootery     24-JUL-97  UPDATE
```

Our trigger works (and, yes, I did check it out on all three actions: insert, update, and delete). What did we change? We made the trigger an AFTER action trigger instead of a BEFORE action. This changed the timing to eliminate the conflict with the other trigger. Because we made the trigger an AFTER action trigger, the capability of using the NEW and OLD qualifiers disappeared, so now we have to use cursor logic instead.

Using cursors, we have to loop through the entire set of purchase orders—not very efficient, but it works. We assumed that a change would affect a total amount. If a change doesn't alter the total, then no processing is done for the purchase order.

Let's look at a simple example of a database trigger. Here we want to capture who has logged in and the date they logged in (yes, I realize the audit trail will allow us to do this, but this is just for demonstration purposes). The trigger would require a table to capture the data:

```
CREATE TABLE GET_LOGINS (login_rec VARCHAR2(60), login_date DATE);
CREATE OR REPLACE TRIGGER capture_logins AFTER LOGON ON DATABASE DECLARE text
VARCHAR2(30);
BEGIN
SELECT user||' logged into '||value
INTO text
FROM v$parameter
WHERE name = 'db_name';
```

```
INSERT INTO get_logins VALUES (text,sysdate);
EXCEPTION
WHEN OTHERS THEN
NULL;
END;
/
```

The above trigger will now fire on each logon to the database and capture all users and their login times. Note the use of the EXCEPTION clause. Especially for LOGON triggers, this is critical since any error in the trigger logic that generates an exception will prevent all users from logging on the system. I had to log in using the SVRMGRL command as INTERNAL and drop the trigger when I misspelled 'db_name' as 'db name', causing a "no rows found" exception.

Let's look at an example of a DDL database-level trigger before we move on:

```
CREATE OR REPLACE TRIGGER test_ddl_trig AFTER DROP ON SCHEMA
DECLARE
text VARCHAR2(255);
BEGIN
SELECT user||' dropped an object'
INTO text FROM dual;
INSERT INTO test_trig VALUES (text,sysdate);
EXCEPTION
WHEN OTHERS THEN
NULL;
END;
```

As a result of this trigger, any drop of any schema object by anyone is monitored.

Alteration of Triggers

As was stated in the "Creation of Database Triggers" section preceding, the CREATE command has the OR REPLACE option to allow a trigger to be re-created without being dropped. Also available is the COMPILE [DEBUG] option that allows recompilation and debug of a trigger that has become invalidated. To alter the contents of a trigger, this create or replace option is used. A trigger has one of two possible states: ENABLED or DISABLED. The ALTER TRIGGER command is limited in functionality:

```
ALTER TRIGGER [schema.]trigger_name ENABLE|DISABLE|COMPILE [DEBUG];
```

One limit on the usefulness of the ALTER TABLE in either disabling or enabling triggers is that it is an all-or-nothing proposition. It is better to use the ALTER TRIGGER command, unless you want all of the triggers on the table enabled or disabled at one time.

The DEBUG option instructs the PL/SQL compiler to generate and store the code for use by the PL/SQL debugger.

Dropping a Trigger

Triggers are dropped using the DROP TRIGGER command:

```
DROP TRIGGER [schema.]trigger_name;
```

TIP   Give careful consideration to all triggers created after Oracle8. Ask whether its function could be better accomplished with a method. If so, use a method. Check for trigger dependencies before dropping a trigger or significantly altering a trigger's actions.

7.8 ADMINISTRATION OF FUNCTIONS AND PROCEDURES

New in Oracle8 was the advance typing that allows a PL/SQL table in functions and procedures to be multidimensional. In contrast, in Oracle7, a PL/SQL table had to be scalar (a single datatype). Oracle8 also offers object support and external procedure and function calls.

Functions and procedures under Oracle7, Oracle8, Oracle8*i*, and Oracle9*i* are virtually identical. The major difference between functions and procedures is that functions always return a single value, whereas procedures may return one, many, or no values. This leads to a second difference: The procedure can use the OUT and IN OUT arguments in the CREATE command, but the function can't. In fact, the function doesn't have to specify the IN argument since input to a function is required. Structurally, procedures and functions didn't change between versions Oracle7 and Oracle8; however, in Oracle8*i*, the AUTHID clause (invoker_rights_clause) and the DETERMINISTIC and PARALLEL_ ENABLE keywords were added, as well as the capability to call C and Java objects. In Oracle9*i*, the capability was added to return PL/SQL tables as either aggregates (must be returned to a PL/SQL table) or PIPELINED (returns individual values).

Why Use Functions and Procedures?

The benefits of functions and procedures are numerous. Functions and procedures provide a consistent means of accessing, altering, and deleting database information. They allow enhanced security by giving the DBA the ability to grant access to the procedures and functions instead of to the actual tables or views. The procedure or functions can have elevated privileges that are in effect while the procedure or function is active but are disabled when it completes.

Functions and procedures enhance productivity by allowing a given process to be coded once and then referenced by all developers. Instead of each form requiring coded triggers for data access, the stored procedures and functions can be referenced instead. This drives consistency down to the database level instead of requiring it from each developer.

Performance is enhanced by allowing multiple users to access the same shared image. Since the procedures and functions are loaded into the cached memory area, only one I/O is required for each procedure or function to be available to all users. In network situations, a function or procedure can be called with a single network call; the function or procedure can then trigger a multitude of database actions and then return, via another single call, the results, thus greatly reducing network traffic.

TIP If a function or procedure affects only one table, then, in Oracle8 and Oracle8*i*, perhaps it should be made into a method. Methods should be used for any internal PL/SQL objects that affect only one table or are used to obtain values from only one table. Using a method instead of a procedure or function will implement the concept of encapsulation in these cases.

Let's look next at the administration of functions and procedures.

Creation of Functions and Procedures

Before a function or procedure can be created, the DBA must run the CATPROC.SQL script. The CATPROC.SQL script is usually run at database creation and, unless you upgrade, you shouldn't have to run it again. The user creating the function or procedure must have the CREATE PROCEDURE privilege to create a procedure or function in his or her own schema, or the CREATE ANY PROCEDURE system privilege.

Any tables, clusters, or views used in the creation of functions and procedures must have direct grants against them issued to the developer who creates the function or procedure. If this is not the case, the errors returned can be as informative as the message that you can't create a stored object with privileges granted through a role, or as frustrating as the message, "ORA-0942—Table or View doesn't exist."

A new entity known as an *external function* is available under Oracle8, 8*i*, and 9*i*. The CREATE FUNCTION command is also used to register this new entity to the database. External functions are 3GL code functions stored in a shared library, which can be called from either SQL or PL/SQL. To call an external function, you must have EXECUTE privileges on the callout library where it resides (this is an external operating system file and OS-level execute permission, not Oracle internal level).

Functions and procedures are created using the CREATE command. The format for each differs slightly, as shown in the two subsequent subsections.

CREATE FUNCTION Command   The CREATE command syntax for functions is:

```
CREATE [OR REPLACE] FUNCTION [schema.]function_name
[(argument [IN|OUT|IN OUT] [NOCOPY] datatype)]
RETURN datatype [invoker_rights_clause]
[DETERMINISTIC] [PARALLEL_ENABLE]
[[AGGREGATE|PIPELINED USING] [schema.]Implementation_type
[PIPELINED IS|AS] pl/sql function_body|external_call
IS|AS
Plsql_body|call_spec;
```

where:

argument. The name given to this argument; this can be any valid variable name.

IN, OUT, or IN OUT. Specifies how the argument is to be treated (strictly input, strictly output, or both). This is optional and will default to IN if not specified.

datatype. The datatype of the argument; this can be any valid scalar datatype.

DETERMINISTIC. Specifies the function will always return the same value(s) from wherever it is called. If a function is to be used in a function-based index, it must be deterministic.

PARALLEL_ENABLE. Allows the function to be processed using multiple parallel query servers.

AGGREGATE I PIPELINE. If the value returned is a PL/SQL table, this tells Oracle to return as one large value (AGGREGATE) or as individual values (PIPELINE); for more details refer to the SQL manual.

The call_spec has the form:

```
LANGUAGE java_declaration|C_declaration
```

The Java_declaration has the form:

```
JAVA NAME 'string'
```

The C_declaration has the form:

```
C [NAME name] LIBRARY lib_name [WITH CONTEXT]
[PARAMETERS (parameters)]
```

The parameters have the form:

```
{{parameter_name [PROPERTY]|RETURN prop } [BY REF] [extern_datatype]|CONTEXT}
```

with the above repeated as many times as is needed.

Finally, prop has the values:

```
INDICATOR, LENGTH, MAXLEN, CHARSETID, or CHARSETFORM
```

CREATE PROCEDURE Command The command for creating a procedure is almost identical to that for a function, except that no RETURN clause is required. The CREATE PROCEDURE command can be used to create either internal standalone procedures or procedures that register calls to external procedures. For procedures, the CREATE command format is:

```
CREATE [OR REPLACE] PROCEDURE [schema.]procedure_name
[(argument [IN|OUT|IN OUT] [NOCOPY] datatype)]
[invoker_rights_clause]
IS|AS
Plsql_body|call_spec;
```

where:

> **argument.** The name given to this argument; this can be any valid variable name.
>
> **IN, OUT, or IN OUT.** Specifies how the argument is to be treated (strictly input, strictly output, or both).
>
> **datatype.** The datatype of the argument; this can be any valid scalar datatype.
>
> The call_spec has the form:

```
LANGUAGE java_declaration|C_declaration
```

> The Java_declaration has the form:

```
JAVA NAME 'string'
```

> The C_declaration has the form:

```
C [NAME name] LIBRARY lib_name [WITH CONTEXT]
[PARAMETERS (parameters)]
```

> The parameters have the form:

```
{{parameter_name [PROPERTY] | RETURN prop } [BY REF] [extern_datatype] |
CONTEXT}
```

with the above repeated as many times as is needed.

> Finally, prop has the values:

```
INDICATOR, LENGTH, MAXLEN, CHARSETID, or CHARSETFORM
```

> For both procedures and functions, the command arguments are listed below:
>
> **OR REPLACE.** (Optional) Specifies that if the procedure or function exists, replace it; if it doesn't exist, create it.
>
> **schema.** The schema to place the procedure or function into. If other than the user's default schema, the user must have the CREATE ANY PROCEDURE system privilege.

Procedure_name or function_name. The name of the procedure or function being created.

argument(s). The argument to the procedure or function; it may be more than one of these.

IN. Specifies that the argument must be identified when calling the procedure or function. For functions, an argument must always be provided.

OUT. Specifies that the procedure passes a value for this argument back to the calling object. Not used with functions.

IN OUT. Specifies that both the IN and OUT features are in effect for the procedure. This is not used with functions.

datatype. The datatype of the argument. Precision, length, and scale cannot be specified; they are derived from the calling object.

PL/SQL body. An embedded SQL and PL/SQL body of statements.

IS or AS. The documentation states that these are interchangeable, but one or the other must be specified. However, Oracle didn't tell this to some of their tools, so if you get an error using one, try the other.

It is suggested that each function and procedure be created under a single owner for a given application. This makes administration easier and allows use of dynamic SQL to create packages. It is also suggested that the procedure or function be created as a text file for documentation and later easy update. The source files for related procedures and functions should be stored under a common directory area.

Alteration of Procedures and Functions

To alter the logic or variables of a procedure or function, use the CREATE OR REPLACE form of the command in the previous subsection. The only option for the ALTER command for functions and procedures is COMPILE. This option recompiles the procedure or function after a modification to their referenced objects has occurred. The format of this command is available in the *SQL Reference Manual*, at the documentation Web site, technet.oracle.com.

If a function or procedure that has been invalidated by a change to a table, view, or other referenced procedure or function is called, it is automatically recompiled. Whenever possible, explicit recompilation via the ALTER command should be used. This will pinpoint any problems before the users find them for you. The script in Source 7.7 will provide a list of invalid database objects upon execution. Use this script to pinpoint which packages, procedures, functions, or views need to be recompiled.

Dropping Procedures or Functions

Periodically, a DBA may be required to remove a function or procedure from the database. This is accomplished with the DROP command. The format of this command follows:

Source 7.7   Example of a script to check on database object status.

```
rem Name: inv_obj.sql
rem Purpose: Show all invalid objects in database
rem Mike Ault 7/2/96 TUSC
rem
COLUMN object_name     FORMAT A30 HEADING 'Object|Name'
COLUMN owner           FORMAT a10 HEADING 'Object|Owner'
COLUMN last_time       FORMAT a20 HEADING 'Last Change|Date'
SET LINES 80 FEEDBACK OFF PAGES 0 VERIFY OFF
START title80 'Invalid Database Objects'
SPOOL rep_out/&db/inv_obj
SELECT
owner,
object_name,
object_type,
TO_CHAR(last_ddl_time,'DD-MON-YY hh:mi:ss') Last_time
FROM
dba_objects
WHERE
status='INVALID'
/
PAUSE Press Enter to continue
SET LINES 80 FEEDBACK ON PAGES 22 VERIFY ON
CLEAR COLUMNS
TTITLE OFF
```

```
DROP PROCEDURE|FUNCTION [schema.]function_name|procedure_name;
```

This will invalidate any related functions or procedures, and they will have to be recompiled before use.

7.9 ADMINISTRATION OF PACKAGES

Under Oracle7, Oracle8, Oracle8*i*, and Oracle9*i,* packages are collections of related functions, variables, procedures, and external calls to functions and procedures. All of the functions and procedures for a specific application can be grouped under one or more packages and handled as units. A package is loaded into shared memory whenever one of its parts is referenced. The package stays in memory until the *least recently used* (LRU) algorithm determines it hasn't been recently used. You, as DBA, can force an object to stay in the SGA by "pinning" it. (Object pinning is covered in Chapter 13.) This use determination applies to all database users, not just the originating user.

Packages allow public and private functions, procedures, and variables. Public functions, procedures, and variables are named in the package definition and are available to all users with the right to access the package. Private procedures, functions, and variables are not referenced in the package definition, but are contained in the package body. Private procedures, functions, and variables are only referenced by the package internal objects. External functions and procedures were new with Oracle8.

As hinted at above, the package consists of two possible parts, a definition and a body, each of which is created separately. The package definition contains the names of all public functions, procedures, and variables; the package body contains the PL/SQL and SQL code for all of the public and private package objects. In the case of a package that has no private functions, procedures, or variables, no package body is required. However, each of the referenced public objects must exist. Not using private objects allows the DBA and developers to maintain the individual objects separately instead of as a single entity. If a package has private objects, it must have a body.

If the DBA has enforced use of script files to create database functions and procedures, creating the package body involves simply concatenating the various scripts together and making minor changes to the syntax of the statements. By the use of the DBA_SOURCE view, the DBA can use dynamic SQL to create script listings. An example of this is shown in Source 7.8.

Source 7.8   Example of a script to rebuild function and procedure or package objects.

```
rem   ******************************************************
rem   NAME:  FPRC_RCT.sql
rem   HISTORY:
rem   Date      Who                What
rem   --------  -----------        --------------------------
rem   05/22/93  Michael Ault       Created
rem   FUNCTION:  Build a script to re-create functions,
rem                  procedures, packages, or package bodies.
rem   ******************************************************
SET VERIFY OFF  FEEDBACK OFF LINES 80 PAGES 0 HEADING OFF
SPOOL cre_fprc.sql
SELECT 'CREATE '||s1.type||' '||s1.owner||'.'||s1.name,
substr(s2.text,1,80)||';'
FROM
dba_source s1,
dba_source s2
WHERE
s1.type = UPPER('&object_type') AND
s1.owner = UPPER('&object_owner') AND
s1.type = s2.type AND
s1.owner = s2.owner AND
s1.name = UPPER('&object_name') AND
s1.name = s2.name
GROUP BY
s1.owner,
s1.name
ORDER BY
s2.line;
rem
SPOOL OFF
```

This will create one large file with all of the types of objects that the DBA specifies for a given owner. This script can also be used to document existing package definitions and package bodies.

Let's now look at the processes and commands used to administer packages.

Creation of Packages

Package creation involves up to two steps. The first step, creation of the package definition (or header), is required for all packages. The second step, creation of the package body, is required only for those packages that have private components. If the use of functions stored in a package is required from outside the package, the functions' purity level must be explicitly stated using the PRAGMA RESTRICT_REFERENCES call, which has the following definition:

```
PRAGMA RESTRICT_REFERENCES( function_or_procedure, rest_code );
```

where:

> **Function_or_procedure.** The name of the function or procedure to which the PRAGMA is to be applied.

> **Rest_code.** One or more of WNDS, RNDS, WNPS, RNPS, which function as follows:

>> **WNDS.** Writes no database state (purity rules 2 and 4).

>> **RNDS.** Reads no database state (purity rules 2, 3, and 4).

>> **WNPS.** Writes no package state (purity rules 1 and 4).

>> **RNPS.** Reads no package state (purity rules 1 and 4).

The purity rules, as enforced through the PRAGMA calls for functions and procedures, are:

1. They cannot insert into, update, or delete from a database table.
2. They cannot be executed remotely or in parallel if they read or write the values of packaged variables.
3. They cannot write the values of packaged variables unless called from a SELECT, VALUES, or SET clause.
4. They cannot call another function, method, or subprogram that breaks one of these rules, nor can they reference views that break any of these rules. (Oracle replaces references to a view with a stored SELECT operation, which can include FUNCTION calls.)

If a stored object (method, procedure, or function) violates its declared PRAGMA level, an error will be returned and the object will be invalid.

The command for creating package definitions follows:

```
CREATE [OR REPLACE] PACKAGE [schema.]package_name
[invoker_rights_clause] IS|AS
PLSQL_package_spec;
```

where:

OR REPLACE. Used when the user wishes to create or replace a package. If the package definition exists, it is replaced; if it doesn't exist, it is created.

schema. The schema in which the package is to be created. If this is not specified, the package is created in the user's default schema.

Package_name. The name of the package to be created.

PLSQL_package_spec. The list of procedures, functions, or variables that make up the package. All components listed are considered to be public in nature.

TIP   You can insert the PRAGMA RESTRICT_REFERENCES call into Oracle-provided package headers for functions that you need to use outside of those packages; however, it may not always work and is not supported by Oracle.

For example:

```
CREATE PACKAGE admin.employee_package
AS
FUNCTION new_emp(ename CHAR, position CHAR, supervisor NUM,
category NUM, hiredate DATE)
RETURN NUMBER;
PRAGMA RESTRICT_REFERENCES( new_emp, WNDS);
FUNCTION fire_them(ename CHAR, reason VARCHAR2, term_date DATE)
RETURN DATE;
PROCEDURE new_dept(ename CHAR, dept CHAR, new_dept CHAR,
date_of_change DATE);
bad_category EXCEPTION;
bad_date EXCEPTION;
END employee_package;
```

This code creates the package employee_package. The package contains the functions new_emp and fire_them, the procedure new_dept, and the exceptions bad_category and bad_date. All of the objects are available to whomever has privileges on employee_package. Notice the PRAGMA call that sets the purity level of new_emp as Writes No Database State (WNDS).

Creation of the Package Body   The package body contains all of the SQL and PL/SQL scripts that make up the procedures, functions, exceptions, and variables used by the package. If the package contains only public items, a package body may not be required. The format for the CREATE PACKAGE BODY command follows:

```
CREATE [OR REPLACE] PACKAGE BODY [schema.]package_name
IS|AS PL/SQL package body;
```

where:

OR REPLACE. When used, if the package body exists, it is replaced; if it doesn't exist, it is created.

schema. Specifies the schema in which to create the package. If this is not specified, the package body is created in the user's default schema.

PL/SQL package body. The collection of all of the SQL and PL/SQL text required to create all of the objects in the package.

Source 7.9 is an example of the use of the CREATE PACKAGE BODY command. The exceptions listed in the package definition are contained within the procedures.

Source 7.9   Example of a format for package body.

```
CREATE OR REPLACE PROCEDURE BODY admin.employee_package AS
FUNCTION new_emp(ename CHAR, position CHAR, supervisor NUM,
category NUM, hiredate DATE)
RETURN NUMBER IS
emp_number number(5);
BEGIN
       .
       .
       .
END;
FUNCTION fire_them(
ename CHAR,reason VARCHAR2,term_date DATE)
RETURN NUMBER AS
years_of_service NUMBER (4,2);
BEGIN
       .
       .
       .
END;
PROCEDURE new_dept(ename CHAR, dept CHAR, new_dept CHAR,
date_of_change DATE)
IS
BEGIN
       .
       .
       .
END;
END  employee_package
```

Alteration of the Package

The DBA will be required to alter a package when there are changes to tables, views, sequences, and so on that the package procedures and functions reference. This is accomplished through the use of the CREATE OR REPLACE PACKAGE [BODY] form of the CREATE PACKAGE command. The format for the command is identical to that of the CREATE PACKAGE [BODY] command. But be aware that all procedures, variables, and functions referenced in the CREATE PACKAGE command must be present in the CREATE OR REPLACE PACKAGE BODY command, for if you just use the command with a single procedure or function you want altered, that will be the only object left in the body when you are finished. Perhaps with a future release we will be able to use the package definition as a link list, and this won't be required. There is also an ALTER PACKAGE BODY command that is used only to recompile the package body. The format of the ALTER command follows.

```
ALTER PACKAGE [schema.]package_name COMPILE
[DEBUG PACKAGE|SPECIFICATION|BODY];
```

The DEBUG clause has been added to compile and store debugging information for the specified area of the package for the PL/SQL debugger.

Dropping a Package

Even such wonderful things as packages have limited lifetimes. Applications are replaced or are no longer needed; entire database practices are rethought and changed. This leads to the requirement to be able to drop packages that are no longer needed. This is accomplished through the DROP PACKAGE command. The format of this command follows:

```
DROP PACKAGE [BODY] [schema.]package_name;
```

Exclusion of the keyword BODY results in the drop of both the definition and the body. Inclusion of BODY drops just the package body, leaving the definition intact.

When a package is dropped, all dependent objects are invalidated. If the package is not re-created before one of the dependent objects is accessed, Oracle tries to recompile the package; this will return an error and cause failure of the command.

7.10 ADMINISTRATION OF SCHEMAS

A feature of Oracle7, Oracle8, Oracle8*i*, and Oracle9*i* that has been mentioned but not explained in the previous sections is the *schema*. Those DBAs familiar with other database systems may recognize this concept as it has been used in systems such as INFORMIX for several years. However, the concept of schemas wasn't introduced to Oracle until Oracle7.

A schema is a logical grouping of related database objects; it roughly compares to the owner of the objects. Objects in a given schema do not have to be in the same tablespace. In fact, each user has a default schema that corresponds to his or her user name in Oracle. A user may only create objects in his or her own schema (that schema named the same as the user he or she is logged in under). Schemas can be populated via the CREATE SCHEMA command or by using individual object CREATE commands.

Creation of Schemas

The CREATE SCHEMA statement can include the creation commands for tables, views, and grants. The user issuing the command must have the appropriate privileges to create each of the objects mentioned in the CREATE SCHEMA command. The format of this command follows:

```
CREATE SCHEMA AUTHORIZATION schema
Create_table_statement|create_view_statement|grant_statement;
```

where:

> **schema.** The user's schema; it must be his or her user name.
>
> ***_statement.** Corresponds to the appropriate CREATE object command.

The individual create commands are not separated with a command terminator; the terminator is placed at the end of the entire create sequence of commands for the schema. Schemas cannot be altered or dropped; only individual schema objects can be altered or dropped. Note that you cannot specify nonstandard SQL in the CREATE SCHEMA command; therefore, clauses such as STORAGE and partitioning logic cannot be used.

7.11 ADMINISTRATION OF LIBRARY OBJECTS

Under Oracle8, a new type of schema object, known as a *library*, was introduced. A library is a schema object that represents an operating system shared library from which calls can be made by SQL and PL/SQL to external functions and procedures. Note that libraries are *not* physical schema objects; they are stored pointers to physical operating system-shared library files.

To create a library, you must have the CREATE ANY LIBRARY internal Oracle system privilege. To use the functions and procedures stored in the library, you must have the execute privilege at the operating system level on the shared library that is referenced. Libraries can only be used on operating systems that allow shared libraries and dynamic linking.

The file specified as the source for the shared library is not verified to exist when the library is initially specified; it is verified at runtime.

The syntax for the CREATE LIBRARY command is:

```
CREATE [OR REPLACE] LIBRARY [schema.]library IS|AS 'filespec';
```

where:

> **schema.** The schema in which the library is to reside. If not specified, it defaults to the user's default schema.
>
> **library.** The name for the schema object; it must comply with object naming standards.
>
> **filespec.** The existing operating system shared library that is to correspond to the internal library name.

Example of the Use of CREATE LIBRARY

The following is an example of the creation of a library:

```
CREATE OR REPLACE LIBRARY dev_c_lib IS
'/users/oracle/c/lib/sharedlibs.so.1.0';
```

Once a library link to an external shared library is created, the functions and procedures inside can be referenced for use from SQL and PL/SQL:

```
CREATE FUNCTION bitand (
left IN BINARY_INTEGER, right IN BINARY_INTEGER)
RETURN BINARY_INTEGER
IS
EXTERNAL
NAME "bitand"
LIBRARY dev_c_lib
PARAMETERS (
left INT,
left INDICATOR long,
right INT,
right INDICATOR short,
RETURN INDICATOR short);
```

An external procedure call is similar:

```
CREATE OR REPLACE PROCEDURE factorial (
input_number IN INTEGER,
number_factorial OUT INTEGER)
IS
EXTERNAL NAME "factorial"
LIBRARY "dev_c_lib"
PARAMETERS (
input_number INDICATOR short,
input_number INT,
```

```
output_factorial INDICATOR long,
output_factorial INT,
RETURN INDICATOR short);
```

Available libraries can be viewed via queries to the DBA_LIBRARIES, ALL_ LIBRARIES, and USER_LIBRARIES views.

Altering Libraries

The CREATE OR REPLACE option of the CREATE command for libraries is used to alter libraries; there is no ALTER LIBRARY command.

Dropping a Library

A library is dropped via the DROP LIBRARY command. The command has the following format:

```
DROP LIBRARY [schema.]library;
```

The drop command removes only the library alias at the database level; it does not affect the status of the operating system shared library.

7.12 ADMINISTRATION OF DIRECTORIES

A directory is an internal Oracle8, 8*i*, and 9*i* database pointer to a physical operating system directory where external files (in Oracle9*i*) and database objects of type BFILE are stored. As noted in Chapter 4, BFILEs are large binary objects such as video segments, which would be impractical to store within the database structure itself. An external file is used to create an external table reference. An internal Oracle directory is an alias that points to the external physical directory.

A directory in Oracle has no size or space requirements other than that for a table entry in the data dictionary. You must have the CREATE ANY DIRECTORY system privilege to create a directory alias in Oracle. The operating system directory must have the proper access permissions (READ) to allow the Oracle process access.

A BFILE column in a database table contains a locator that has the directory alias specified in a CREATE DIRECTORY command and a filename. The locator maintains the directory alias and filename.

A directory is created inside a single namespace; it is not owned by a schema. Therefore, directory names have to be unique across the entire database. You grant access to the BFILEs or external files in a specific directory by granting READ access to the users or roles that require access. When a directory is created by a user, that user automatically receives the READ grant with the admin option so it can be subsequently granted to others.

A directory is created with the CREATE DIRECTORY command; its syntax follows:

```
CREATE [OR REPLACE] DIRECTORY directory_name AS 'path_name';
```

where:

directory_name. Database-unique directory name.

path_name. Operating system directory path (note that if the OS is case-sensitive, the name must be exact).

Use of the CREATE DIRECTORY Command: An Example

The command below associates the directory internal Oracle alias g_vid_lib with the directory '/video/library/g_rated'.

```
CREATE OR REPLACE DIRECTORY g_vid_lib AS '/video/library/g_rated';
```

The path name must be a full path and not use any system logicals or symbols. The directory's existence is not validated until the directory alias is referenced by Oracle.

Altering Directories

There is no ALTER DIRECTORY command. To change a DIRECTORY, you must drop and re-create it.

Dropping Directories

When a directory is no longer needed, it should be dropped with the DROP DIRECTORY command. You must have the DROP ANY DIRECTORY command to drop a directory. The syntax for this command is:

```
DROP DIRECTORY directory_name;
```

Once a directory is dropped, all BFILEs or external tables in that directory location become inaccessible.

7.13 ADMINISTRATION OF JAVA OBJECTS

In Oracle 8*i*, Java must first be loaded to make use of it; Oracle9*i* loads the Java VM automatically through the LoadJava utility, which is described next.

Using LoadJava

Using a built-in PL/SQL package named LoadLobs, the LoadJava utility uploads Java files into a BLOB column in the table create$java$lob$table, which the utility creates in the logon schema. Then it uses the SQL CREATE JAVA statement to load the Java files into the RDBMS.

LoadJava also accepts SQLJ input files (.sqlj files). To process them, it invokes the Server SQLJ Translator, which outputs Java sources and serialized objects for SQLJ profiles (.ser files). Then it invokes the Java compiler, which compiles the Java sources into standard binaries. (For more information, refer to the numerous Java references on the documentation Web site.)

Using a client-side JDBC driver, LoadJava can upload individual Java sources and binaries, SQLJ input files, and entire Java archives (JARs). However, it cannot upload individual resources, so you must put them in a JAR. You can enter .java, .class, .jar, and .sqlj files on the command line in any order. The syntax is:

```
loadjava
[{-h | -help}]
[{-v | -verbose}]
[{-f | -force}]
[{-r | -resolve}]
[{-a | -andresolve}]
[{-S | -schema} schema_name]
[{-d | -definer}]
[{-s | -synonym}]
[{-g | -grant} {username | role_name}[, {username | role_name}]...]
[{-R | -resolver} "resolver_spec"]
[{-e | -encoding} encoding_scheme_name]
[{-t | -thin} | {-o | -oci81}]
[{-u | -user} username/password@host_name:port_number:database_sid]
{filename.java | filename.class | filename.jar | filename.sqlj} ...
```

where:

resolver_spec. Specifies schemas to be searched (in the order listed) for referenced Java fullnames. Its syntax is:

```
((match_string schema_name) (match_string schema_name) ...)
```

where match_string is a Java fullname; the wildcard, an asterisk (*),which matches any name; or a combination, such as home/java/bin/*; and where schema_name is the name of a schema or the wildcard (which indicates that names matching the pattern need not be resolved). The default resolver_spec follows:

```
((* definer's_schema) (* public))
```

The following list presents the LoadJava command-line options:

Option	*Description*
-h	Displays a help screen that lists all the command-line options.
-v	Enables verbose mode, in which progress messages are displayed.

Option	*Description*
-f	Forces the loading of Java classes whether or not they have been loaded before. By default, previously loaded classes are rejected. You cannot force the loading of a binary if you previously loaded the source. You must drop the source first.
-r	Compiles all uploaded sources, then resolves external references in uploaded Java classes. Otherwise, sources are compiled and classes are resolved at runtime or when the Java virtual machine (JVM) needs the definitions to resolve other classes. If errors occur during name resolution, they are displayed.
-a	Works like the -r option except that each uploaded source is compiled and resolved separately. This lets you replace a class that might invalidate other classes.
-S	Assigns newly created Java library units to the specified schema. Otherwise, the logon schema is used.
-d	Specifies that the methods of uploaded classes will execute with the privileges of their definer, not their invoker.
-s	Creates public synonyms for uploaded classes. To specify this option, you must have the CREATE PUBLIC SYNONYM privilege.
-g	Grants the EXECUTE privilege on uploaded classes and resources to the listed users and/or roles. (To call the methods of a class directly, users must have the EXECUTE privilege.)
-R	Specifies a resolver spec, which is bound to newly created Java library units. Because it contains spaces, the resolver spec must be enclosed by double quotation marks.
-e	Sets the encoding option in the database table java$options to the specified value, which must be a standard JDK encoding-scheme name. The encoding of uploaded sources must match the specified encoding.
-t | -o	Selects the client-side JDBC driver used to communicate with Oracle. You can choose the Thin JDBC Driver (the default) or the OCI JDBC Driver. For information about these drivers, see the JDBC reference on the documentation Web site.
-u	Specifies a database connect string without spaces. The string includes a user name, password, host-computer name, port number, and database system identifier. If this option is not specified, the string defaults to internal/oracle@localhost:1521:orcl.

CAUTION   LoadJava uses the hash table java$class$md5$table to track the loading of Java library units into a schema (md5 refers to RSA Data Security's MD5 Message-Digest Algorithm, which does the hashing). If you use LoadJava to load a Java library unit, you must use DropJava to drop the unit. Otherwise, the table will not be updated properly. Also, if you use the SQL DROP JAVA statement to drop a Java class, and then use LoadJava to upload the same class, you must specify the force (-f) command-line option. Otherwise, the upload fails.

LoadJava Examples   In the first example, LoadJava uploads archived Java binaries and resources from an OS file system (> is the prompt). The utility reads the JAR files, stores each binary or resource in a database row keyed by the filename of the class or resource, then uses the SQL CREATE JAVA statement to load the Java files into the RDBMS.

```
> loadjava -u scott/tiger@myComputer:1521:orcl managers.jar
managerText.jar
```

In the next example, operating in verbose mode, LoadJava uploads and resolves a Java source file. The force (-f) option forces the loading of the file. The resolve option (-r) compiles the file and resolves external references; also, by reporting resolution errors, it helps to identify missing classes.

```
> loadjava -v -f -r -u scott/tiger@myComputer:1521:orcl Agent.java
Load Lobs package already installed
loading  : Agent
creating : Agent
resolving: Agent
```

In the following example, a name resolver is specified:

```
> loadjava -R "((/home/java/bin/* scott) (* public))"
-u scott/tiger@myComputer:1521:orcl Swapper.class
```

If the path to a file begins with a slash, LoadJava prefixes the word ROOT to the Java fullname, as the following example shows:

```
> loadjava -v -f -u scott/tiger@myComputer:1521:orcl
/routines/java/src/Alerter.java
Load Lobs package already installed
loading  : ROOT/routines/java/src/Alerter
creating : ROOT/routines/java/src/Alerter
```

Checking Upload Results

To check upload results, you can query the database view user_objects, which contains information about schema objects owned by the user (Scott, in this case). For example, the following SQL*Plus script formats and displays useful information about uploaded Java sources, binaries, and resources:

```
SET SERVEROUTPUT ON
SET VERIFY OFF
PROMPT A)ll or J)ava only?
ACCEPT x CHAR PROMPT 'Choice: '
DECLARE
  choice CHAR(1) := UPPER('&x');
  printable BOOLEAN;
  bad_choice EXCEPTION;
BEGIN
  IF choice NOT IN ('A', 'J') THEN RAISE bad_choice; END IF;
  DBMS_OUTPUT.PUT_LINE(CHR(0));
  DBMS_OUTPUT.PUT_LINE('Object Name                    ' ||
    'Object Type   Status  Timestamp');
  DBMS_OUTPUT.PUT_LINE('----------------------------- ' ||
    '------------- ------- ----------------');
  FOR i IN (SELECT object_name, object_type, status, timestamp
    FROM user_objects ORDER BY object_type, object_name)
  LOOP
    /* Exclude objects generated for LoadJava and DropJava. */
    printable := i.object_name NOT LIKE 'SYS_%'
      AND i.object_name NOT LIKE 'CREATE$%'
      AND i.object_name NOT LIKE 'JAVA$%'
      AND i.object_name NOT LIKE 'LOADLOBS';
    IF choice = 'J' THEN
      printable := i.object_type LIKE 'JAVA %';
    END IF;
    IF printable THEN
      DBMS_OUTPUT.PUT_LINE(RPAD(i.object_name,31) ||
        RPAD(i.object_type,14) ||
        RPAD(i.status,8) || SUBSTR(i.timestamp,1,16));
    END IF;
  END LOOP;
EXCEPTION
  WHEN bad_choice THEN
    DBMS_OUTPUT.PUT_LINE('Bad choice');
END;
/
```

You can choose to display *all* your schema objects or *only* the Java objects:

```
SQL> @usr_obj
A)ll or J)ava only?
Choice: a
```

```
Object Name              Object Type   Status  Timestamp
------------------------------------------------------------
Alerter                  JAVA CLASS    VALID   1998-10-08:13:42
POManager                JAVA CLASS    VALID   1998-10-08:17:14
Alerter                  JAVA Source   VALID   1998-10-08:13:42
POManager                JAVA Source   VALID   1998-10-08:17:11
BONUS                    TABLE         VALID   1998-10-08:14:02
DEPT                     TABLE         VALID   1998-10-08:14:02
EMP                      TABLE         VALID   1998-10-08:14:02
SALGRADE                 TABLE         VALID   1998-10-08:14:02


SQL> @usr_obj
A)ll or J)ava only?
Choice: j


Object Name              Object Type   Status  Timestamp
------------------------------------------------------------
Alerter                  JAVA CLASS    VALID   1998-10-08:13:42
POManager                JAVA CLASS    VALID   1998-10-08:17:14
Alerter                  JAVA Source   VALID   1998-10-08:13:42
POManager                JAVA Source   VALID   1998-10-08:17:11
```

The column object_name stores Java fullnames. However, if a name is longer than 30 characters or contains an untranslatable character, the shortname is stored instead. To convert shortnames to fullnames, you can use the function longname in the utility package DBMS_JAVA, as follows:

```
SQL> SELECT dbms_java.longname(object_name), ... FROM user_objects;
```

Table 7.1 describes all the columns in database view user_objects.

Using DropJava

The DropJava utility drops individual Java sources and binaries and entire JAR files. It also maintains the hash table that LoadJava uses to track the loading of Java library units. You can enter .java, .class, and .jar files on the command line in any order. Here is the syntax:

```
dropjava
[{-v | -verbose}]
[{-t | -thin} | {-o | -oci81}]
[{-u | -user} username/password@host_name:port_number:database_sid]
{filename.java | filename.class | filename.jar} ...
```

TABLE 7.1   USER_OBJECTS View Columns

Column Name	Datatype	Description
OBJECT_NAME	VARCHAR2(128)	Name of the object
SUBOBJECT_NAME	VARCHAR2(30)	Name of any subobject (a partition, for example)
OBJECT_ID	NUMBER	Object number of the object
DATA_OBJECT_ID	NUMBER	Object number of the segment that contains the object
OBJECT_TYPE	VARCHAR2(15)	Type of object (a table or index, for example)
CREATED	DATE	Date on which the object was created
LAST_DDL_TIME	DATE	Date of the last DDL operation on the object
TIMESTAMP	VARCHAR2(19)	Character string containing the date and time the object was created
STATUS	VARCHAR2(7)	Status (valid or invalid) of the object
TEMPORARY	VARCHAR2(1)	Indicator (y/n) of whether or not the current session sees only the data that it stores in the object
GENERATED	VARCHAR2(1)	Indicator of whether or not the name of the object was generated by the system
SECONDARY	VARCHAR2(1)	Indicator of whether or not this is a secondary object created for domain indexes

The following list presents the DropJava command-line options:

Option	Description
-v	Enables verbose mode, in which progress messages are displayed.
-t │ -o	Selects the client-side JDBC driver used to communicate with Oracle. You can choose the Thin JDBC Driver (the default) or the OCI JDBC Driver.
-u	Specifies a database connect string without spaces. The string includes a user name, password, host-computer name, port number, and database system identifier. If this option is not specified, the string defaults to internal/oracle@localhost:1521:orcl.

DropJava Examples   In the first example, DropJava drops various Java binaries and resources. The utility reads the JAR files, then drops each Java class or resource from your schema.

```
> dropjava -u scott/tiger@myComputer:1521:orcl manager.jar
managerText.jar
```

In the next example, operating in verbose mode, DropJava drops a Java class:

```
> dropjava -v -u scott/tiger@myComputer:1521:orcl Calculator.class
...
files:
    Calculator.class
dropping Calculator
```

Using CREATE Java

In Oracle8*i* and Oracle9*i,* Java, an object-oriented development language, was added to the Oracle kernel. In previous versions, Java, JDBC (Java Database Connectivity), and SQLJ, Oracle's PRO*Java product, provided connectivity to the database, but Java was relegated to the outside, along with the other languages, such as C, C++, FORTRAN, and COBOL. Now Java is allowed inside the database. Java can be used for procedures, functions, and methods and will be stored inside the database just like PL/SQL.

However, in order to move Java into the database, a way had to be provided to bridge the gap between the normal database lingua franca, PL/SQL, and the new Java classes. This bridge between Java and PL/SQL is the Java object.

Creation of a Java Object

The Java object is created using the CREATE JAVA command, which is documented in the *SQL Reference Manual* on the documentation Web site. Java is stored in much the same way as PL/SQL in database tables. Once called into memory (by standard function, procedure, and method calls), it is placed in its own area. The area where Java resides is appropriately called the Java Pool and is configured at 20 MB by default but can be increased by use of the JAVA_POOL_SIZE initialization parameter if required. Let's look at an example of the CREATE JAVA command.

NOTE   Java is not available until version 8.1.4.

```
CREATE OR REPLACE JAVA Source NAMED 'Login' AS
PUBLIC CLASS Login (
Public static String Login() (
Return 'You are logged into ORTEST1'; ) );
/
```

Use of the Java Object

A function or procedure call is wrapped around the Java object in order to make it callable:

```
CREATE OR REPLACE FUNCTION login
RETURN VARCHAR2 AS
LANGUAGE JAVA NAME 'Login() return String()';
/
```

Once the Java object is wrapped, it is called just as the function or procedure would be called; in addition, the object can be included in a package specification. The Login Java object would be called like this:

```
SQL> VARIABLE t VARCHAR2;
```

Finally, we are ready to call the function Login. Remember, in a CALL statement, host variables must be prefixed with a colon.

```
SQL> CALL Login() INTO :t;

Call completed.

SQL> PRINT t

t
-------------------------
You are logged into ORTEST1
```

For more complex examples, refer to the *Java Developer's Guide*.

Altering Java Objects

The ALTER JAVA command is used to alter Java objects. The syntax for the ALTER JAVA command is:

```
ALTER JAVA Source|CLASS [schema.]object_name
[RESOLVER ((match_string [,] schema_name|- ))
[COMPILE|RESOLVE] [invoker_rights_clause]
```

The ALTER JAVA command is only used to force resolution of Java objects (compilation). The Java source must be in your own schema, or you must have the ALTER ANY PROCEDURE, or the source must be declared PUBLIC. You must also have EXECUTE privilege on the Java object.

An example use of the ALTER JAVA command is:

```
ALTER JAVA CLASS "Agent"
RESOLVER (("D:\orant81\java\bin\*.*" , tele_dba)(* public))
RESOLVE;
```

Dropping Java Objects

If you don't use the DropJava utility, you may cause inconsistencies in Oracle internal tables; that is, the command for dropping Java objects is:

```
DROP JAVA [schema.]java_name;
```

Memory and Java Objects

Java uses the shared pool and the Java pool. The default in 8.1.3 for the Java pool is almost 10 MB; for the 8.1.4 beta it was upsized to 20 MB, and there it has remained. If you get memory-related errors when dealing with Java objects, increase the size of the Java pool. In Oracle9*i* the Java pool should be near 60 megabytes.

Error reporting in out-of-memory situations is inconsistent and in some cases may result in a core dump. If you suspect that memory usage is the cause of a core dump, adjust the JAVA_POOL_SIZE in the init.ora file. JAVA_POOL_SIZE should be set to 60,000,000 or higher for large applications in Oracle9*i*. The default value of 20,000,000 in 8.1.4 and 8.1.5 should be adequate for typical Java Stored Procedure usage before release 9*i*.

7.14 ADMINISTRATION OF DIMENSION OBJECTS

DIMENSION objects are used in data warehouse, DSS, and datamart-type applications to provide information on how denormalized tables relate to themselves. The CREATE DIMENSION command specifies level and hierarchy information for a table or set of related tables. If you want to use query rewrite with the Oracle optimizer and materialized views, you must specify dimensions that the optimizer then uses to "decrypt" the inter- and intratable levels and hierarchies. As an administrator, you should know how these DIMENSION objects are created, altered, and dropped. To that end, we will discuss these topics and show some simple examples later in this chapter. For information beyond the basics, I suggest reviewing the application development and cartridge developer manuals.

Creation of DIMENSION Objects

The CREATE DIMENSION command is used to create dimensions in Oracle8*i* and Oracle9*i*. The CREATE DIMENSION clause has the following syntax:

```
CREATE [FORCE|NOFORCE] DIMENSION [schema.]dimension_name
Level_clauses
[Hierarchy_clauses]
[attribute_clauuses];
```

For an example of the use of the DIMENSION command, we'll use the PLAN_TABLE implemented by EXPLAIN PLAN, which contains the recursive relationship between ID and PARENT_ID columns.

```
SQL> desc plan_table
 Name                             Null?      Type
 ------------------------------   -------    ------------
  STATEMENT_ID                               VARCHAR2(30)
  TIMESTAMP                                  DATE
  REMARKS                                    VARCHAR2(80)
  OPERATION                                  VARCHAR2(30)
  OPTIONS                                    VARCHAR2(30)
  OBJECT_NODE                                VARCHAR2(128)
  OBJECT_OWNER                               VARCHAR2(30)
  OBJECT_NAME                                VARCHAR2(30)
  OBJECT_INSTANCE                            NUMBER(38)
  OBJECT_TYPE                                VARCHAR2(30)
  OPTIMIZER                                  VARCHAR2(255)
  SEARCH_COLUMNS                             NUMBER
  ID                                         NUMBER(38)
  PARENT_ID                                  NUMBER(38)
  POSITION                                   NUMBER(38)
  COST                                       NUMBER(38)
  CARDINALITY                                NUMBER(38)
  BYTES                                      NUMBER(38)
  OTHER_TAG                                  VARCHAR2(255)
  PARTITION_START                            VARCHAR2(255)
  PARTITION_STOP                             VARCHAR2(255)
  PARTITION_ID                               NUMBER(38)
  OTHER                                      LONG


SQL> create dimension test_dim
  2    level child_id is plan_table.id
  3    level parent_id is plan_table.parent_id
  4    hierarchy plan (child_id child of parent_ID)
  5    attribute parent_id determines plan_table.statement_id
  6    /

Dimension created.

SQL>
```

With the dimension test_dim, if we now created a materialized view on the PLAN_TABLE, any queries attempting to do a ROLLUP or CUBE type operation across the ID-PARENT_ID levels would use the connection information stored in the DIMENSION to rewrite the query. The CREATE DIMENSION command also allows forcing of the creation if the tables don't exist or you don't have permission on them; it also allows join conditions to be specified between child and parent levels.

Oracle does not automatically validate the relationships you declare when creating a dimension. To validate the relationships specified in the hierarchy_clause and the join_clause of CREATE DIMENSION, you must run the DBMS_OLAP.validate_dimension procedure.

Altering DIMENSION Objects

The ALTER DIMENSION command is used to add or drop LEVEL, HIERARCHY, or ATTRIBUTE information for a DIMENSION, as well as to force a compile of the object. An example would be if the PLAN_TABLE in the CREATE example didn't exist and we had used the FORCE keyword in the command. The views DBA_DIMENSIONS, ALL_DIMENSIONS, and USER_DIMENSIONS are used to monitor DIMENSION status; the INVALID (shown as "I" in the example below) tells the state of the DIMENSION, either Y for an INVALID DIMENSION or N for a VALID DIMENSION.

```
SQL> select * from user_dimensions;

OWNER                         DIMENSION_NAME              I   REVISION
----------------------------  --------------------------  -  ----------
SYSTEM                        TEST_DIM                    Y          1

SQL> @d:\orant81\rdbms\admin\utlxplan

Table created.

SQL> alter dimension test_dim compile;

Dimension altered.

SQL> select * from user_dimensions;

OWNER                         DIMENSION_NAME              I   REVISION
----------------------------  --------------------------  -  ----------
SYSTEM                        TEST_DIM                    N          1
```

As noted above, we could also have added or removed levels, hierarchies, or attributes using the ALTER DIMENSION command.

Dropping DIMENSIONS

A DIMENSION object is dropped using the DROP DIMENSION command. The syntax of the DROP command is:

```
DROP DIMENSION [schema.]dimension_name;
```

An example is:

```
SQL> DROP DIMENSION system.test_dim;
Dimension dropped.
```

7.15 ADMINISTRATION OF OUTLINE OBJECTS

An outline is a stored query path or set of attributes that will be used by the optimizer to optimize a specific SQL query. Outlines can be enabled or disabled at both the system and session levels by use of the ALTER SESSION and ALTER SYSTEM commands.

An outline should not be generated until the statement to be outlined has been tuned and you are absolutely sure that it is performing exactly the way you want it to.

In order to create outlines, users must have the CREATE ANY OUTLINE privilege; to create a clone of an existing outline (in Oracle9i) users must have SELECT_CATALOG_ROLE granted.

Storing plan outlines for SQL statements is known as *plan stability*; it ensures that changes in the Oracle environment don't affect the way a SQL statement is optimized by the cost-based optimizer. If you want, Oracle will define plans for all issued SQL statements at the time they are executed, and this stored plan will be reused until altered or dropped. Generally, however, I do not suggest using the automatic outline feature as it can lead to poor plans being reused by the optimizer. It makes more sense to monitor for high-cost statements and tune them as required, storing an outline for them only after they have been properly tuned.

As with the storage of SQL in the shared pool, the storage of outlines depends on the statement being reissued in an identical fashion each time it is used. If even one space is out of place, the stored outline is not reused. Therefore, your queries should be stored as PL/SQL procedures, functions, or packages (or perhaps Java routines), and bind variables should always be used. This allows reuse of the stored image of the SQL as well as reuse of stored outlines.

Remember that to be useful over the life of an application, the outlines will have to be periodically verified by checking SQL statement performance. If performance of SQL statements degrades, the stored outline may have to be dropped and regenerated after the SQL is retuned.

In Oracle9i, the ability to edit a stored outline is provided by means of the DBMS_OTLN_EDIT Oracle-provided package.

You enable or disable the use of stored outlines dynamically for an individual session or for the system:

- Enable the USE_STORED_OUTLINES parameter to use public outlines.
- Enable the USE_PRIVATE_OUTLINES parameter to use private stored outlines.

Creation of an OUTLINE Object

Outlines are created using the CREATE OUTLINE command; the syntax for this command is:

```
CREATE [OR REPLACE] [PUBLIC|PRIVATE] OUTLINE outline_name
[FROM [PUBLIC|PRIVATE] source_outline_name]
[FOR CATEGORY category_name]
ON statement;
```

where:

> **PUBLIC|PRIVATE.** By default all outlines are public. Before first creating a private outline, you must run the DBMS_OUTLN_EDIT.CREATE_EDIT_TABLES procedure to create the required outline tables and indexes in your schema.

Outline_name. A unique name for the outline.

FROM. Use this clause to create a new outline by copying an existing one. By default, Oracle looks for the source category in the public area. If you specify PRIVATE, Oracle will look for the outline in the current schema. If you specify the FROM clause, you cannot specify the ON clause.

[FOR CATEGORY category_name]. (Optional) Allows more than one outline to be associated with a single query by specifying multiple categories, each named uniquely.

ON statement. Specifies the statement for which the outline is prepared.

An example would be:

```
CREATE OR REPLACE PUBLIC OUTLINE get_tables
ON
SELECT
a.owner,
a.table_name,
a.tablespace_name,
SUM(b.bytes),
COUNT(b.table_name) extents
FROM
    dba_tables a,
    dba_extents b
WHERE
    a.owner=b.owner
    AND a.table_name=b.table_name
GROUP BY
    a.owner, a.table_name, a.tablespace_name;
```

Assuming the above select is a part of a stored PL/SQL procedure or perhaps part of a view, the stored outline will now be used each time an exactly-matching SQL statement is issued.

Before a public outline can be created, the user must have access to a PLAN_TABLE.

Altering an OUTLINE Object

Outlines are altered using the ALTER OUTLINE or the CREATE OR REPLACE form of the CREATE command. The format of the command is identical whether it is used for the creation or replacement of an existing outline. For example, assume we want to add SUM(b.blocks) to the previous example.

```
CREATE OR REPLACE PUBLIC OUTLINE get_tables
ON
SELECT
a.owner,
a.table_name,
a.tablespace_name,
```

```
SUM(b.bytes),
COUNT(b.table_name) extents,
SUM(b.blocks)
FROM
     dba_tables a,
     dba_extents b
WHERE
     a.owner=b.owner
     AND a.table_name=b.table_name
GROUP BY
     a.owner, a.table_name, a.tablespace_name;
```

This example has the effect of altering the stored outline get_tables to include any changes brought about by inclusion of the SUM(b.blocks) in the SELECT list. But what if we want to rename the outline or change a category name? The ALTER OUTLINE command has the format:

```
ALTER OUTLINE outline_name
[REBUILD]
[RENAME TO new_outline_name]
[CHANGE CATEGORY TO new_category_name]
```

The ALTER OUTLINE command allows us to rebuild the outline for an existing outline_name as well as rename the outline or change its category. The benefit of using the ALTER OUTLINE command is that we do not have to respecify the complete SQL statement, as we would have to using the CREATE OR REPLACE command.

Dropping an OUTLINE Object

Outlines are dropped using the DROP OUTLINE command; the syntax for this command is:

```
DROP OUTLINE outline_name;
```

7.16 ADMINISTRATION OF CONTEXT OBJECTS

A CONTEXT object associates a package containing variable and constant definitions with a context namespace. The established relationship between a context object and a namespace is then utilized by the SYS_CONTEXT function to validate against the variables or constants defined in the package.

Creating a CONTEXT Object

The first step in creating a CONTEXT object is to decide which context variables your application requires. These CONTEXT variables are then mapped into a set of functions and procedures contained in a stored package that is then associated with a unique context name. CONTEXT objects are owned by the SYS user and reside in the SYS schema. Once a CONTEXT is established, the SYS_CONTEXT function is used to fetch the specified attributes. This serves to encapsulate the attributes used in their own secure database object, which can then be controlled. For a simple example, let's assume your application is restricted to a specific department within your company. By setting up a procedure to get the department number based on the login ID, you can then set a context that can be used for verification inside your application. Let's look at the package, procedure, and context required to do this operation.

```
CREATE OR REPLACE PACKAGE tele_security_context IS
  PROCEDURE set_deptno;
END;
/
CREATE OR REPLACE PACKAGE tele_security_context IS
  PROCEDURE set_deptno
  IS
  Dept_no NUMBER;
  BEGIN
   SELECT dept INTO Dept_no FROM users
   WHERE UPPER(login_name) =
     UPPER(SYS_CONTEXT('USERENV','SESSION_USER'));
   DBMS_SESSION.SET_CONTEXT('tele_security','deptno',Dept_no);
  END;
END;
```

Notice that we used the SYS_CONTEXT system function and the Oracle-provided package/procedure DBMS_ SESSION. SET_CONTEXT. The SYS_CONTEXT function accesses any created CONTEXT; in the above example it accesses the USERENV context to get the value of the SESSION_USER context attribute. The SESSION USER is then used to get the department number from the application's USERS table. Once the department number (DEPT_NO) is fetched into the local variable DEPTNO, DEPTNO is used to set the session context attribute DEPTNO in the context object APP_CONTEXT through the use of the DBMS_SESSION.SET_CONTEXT packaged procedure. The basic syntax for the SYS_CONTEXT call is:

```
SYS_CONTEXT('namespace','attribute')
```

The syntax for the DBMS_SESSION.SET_CONTEXT package call is:

```
DBMS_SESSION.SET_CONTEXT('context_name','atrribute',value)
```

where value is the value to which to set the context attribute.

Once the package has been created, you must associate it with a context name-space. This association is done through the CREATE CONTEXT command:

```
CREATE CONTEXT tele_security USING tele_security_context.set_deptno;
```

The values set with the DBMS_SESSION.SET_CONTEXT package remain set until they are reset or the session ends. The following is an example of the use of our created context:

```
CREATE VIEW show_salary AS
    SELECT a.first_name,a.last_name,b.job_title,a.deptno,c.salary
    FROM users a, assignments b, pay_records c
    WHERE a.emp_no=b.emp_no
    AND a.emp_no=c.emp_no
    AND 99 = SYS_CONTEXT('tele_security','dept_no');
```

In this example, unless the user querying the view had a department number of 99, he or she would receive no rows from his or her query. The full syntax for creating a context is:

```
CREATE OR REPLACE CONTEXT namespace USING [schema.]package;
```

Altering CONTEXT Objects

CONTEXT objects cannot be altered. However, their underlying packages can be rebuilt as required. The CONTEXT object itself is changed by using the OR REPLACE clause of the CREATE OR REPLACE CONTEXT command. An example would be to point the context at a different package:

```
CREATE OR REPLACE CONTEXT tele_security USING temp_security_context;
```

This example would re-create the CONTEXT tele_security to point at the temp_security_context package.

Dropping CONTEXT Objects

A CONTEXT object is dropped using the DROP CONTEXT command:

```
DROP CONTEXT namespace;
```

7.17 ADMINISTRATION OF THE OPERATOR OBJECTS

Oracle8*i* introduced the concept of an OPERATOR object, which is user-defined and can be used as an operator, much the same as +, -, *, and the like. This provides extensibility to the set of standard SQL operators. Operators are used in index types, DML, and SQL statements.

Operators can reference functions, packages, types, and other user-defined objects. To create an operator, you must have the CREATE OPERATOR or CREATE ANY OPERATOR privilege, as well as EXECUTE permission on any underlying objects. New operators are usually defined by data cartridge developers, but may have many uses in database administration and management.

Creation of an OPERATOR Object

OPERATOR objects are created through the CREATE OR REPLACE OPERATOR command. This command is of sufficient complexity that I refer you to the *SQL Reference*

Manual on the documentation Web site for a detailed listing. But here we'll examine an example of the creation of an OPERATOR object.

First, the underlying package and function on which the operator depends must be built. Assuming we're novice DBAs, we don't realize that there is a concatenation operator (| |) already defined for Oracle, so we decide to build one using the nifty new **CREATE OPERATOR** command. First, we must create a package that contains our procedures, which will be used to implement the concatenation operator.

```
CREATE OR REPLACE PACKAGE con AS
FUNCTION concat_string (var1 IN VARCHAR2, var2 IN VARCHAR2)
RETURN VARCHAR2;
END;
/
CREATE OR REPLACE PACKAGE con AS
FUNCTION concat_string (var1 IN VARCHAR2, var2 IN VARCHAR2)
RETURN VARCHAR2 AS
BEGIN
var3:=var1+var2;
RETURN var3;
END concat_string;
END;
/
```

Now that we have our package, we can create an operator that utilizes the package:

```
CREATE OR REPLACE OPERATOR concat
BINDING (VARCHAR2,VARCHAR2) RETURN VARCHAR2
USING con.concat_string;
```

Here is a demonstration of the preceding examples in use:

```
SQL> CREATE OR REPLACE PACKAGE con AS
  2  FUNCTION concat_string (var1 IN VARCHAR2, var2 IN VARCHAR2)
  3  RETURN VARCHAR2;
  4  END;
  5  /

Package created.

SQL> CREATE OR REPLACE PACKAGE BODY con AS
  2  FUNCTION concat_string (var1 IN VARCHAR2, var2 IN VARCHAR2)
  3  RETURN VARCHAR2 AS
  4  var3 VARCHAR2(4000);
  5  BEGIN
  6  select var1||var2 into var3 from dual;
  7  RETURN var3;
  8  END concat_string;
  9  END;
 10  /

Package body created.
```

```
SQL> CREATE OR REPLACE OPERATOR concat
  2   BINDING (VARCHAR2,VARCHAR2) RETURN VARCHAR2
  3   USING con.concat_string;

Operator created.

SQL> select 'test' testit
  2   from dual where concat('test','test')='testtest';

TESTIT
------
test

SQL>
```

What all this does is allow you to use nonpurified functions. Notice what happens if we call the function directly:

```
SQL> select 'Test' testit from dual
  2   where con.concat_string('it ','works')='it works'
where con.concat_string('it ','works')='it works'
        *
ERROR at line 2:
ORA-06571: Function CONCAT_STRING does not guarantee not to update database
```

Even if we add the line PRAGMA RESTRICT_REFERENCES(concat-string, 'WNDS'); to the package specification we, still get:

```
SQL> select 'Test' testit from dual
  2   where con.concat_string('it ','works')='it works';
where con.concat_string('it ','works')='it works'
        *
ERROR at line 2:
ORA-06573: Function CONCAT_STRING modifies package state, cannot be used here
```

One quick note about using the CREATE OR REPLACE OPERATOR command: In version 8.1.3, I was able to use it about three times, then it started returning ORA-06553 errors unless the operator was dropped first.

Altering OPERATOR Objects

Operators can only be dropped and re-created; there is no ALTER OPERATOR command.

Dropping OPERATOR Objects

Operators are dropped using the DROP OPERATOR command; the command syntax is:

```
DROP OPERATOR [schema.]operator_name [FORCE];
```

The FORCE clause forces the drop of the OPERATOR even if it is currently being accessed by one or more schema objects. Any dependent objects are marked as INVALID.

7.18 THE STORAGE CLAUSE

The STORAGE clause is used in table, cluster, index, rollback segment, snapshot, snapshot log, and tablespace creation commands, as well as in their respective ALTER commands. Let's look at the parameters for this clause, as DBAs must become intimately familiar with all aspects of the STORAGE clause.

NOTE   The syntax for the STORAGE clause is shown in detail in the SQL *Reference Manual* on the documentation Web site.

STORAGE Parameters: Definitions

INITIAL. Sets the size in bytes, kilobytes, or megabytes for the initial extent for the object. This should be set to hold the first year's worth of expected data. If you will be loading data using sqlloader parallel inserts, set the initial extent to the size expected for one year, divided by the number of parallel processes, and set NEXT to the same value. This is suggested because all parallel insert processes insert to their own extents. The Oracle process will round up to the next multiple of data blocksize for sizes smaller than five data blocks. The minimum size is two data blocks. The maximum size is operating-system specific.

NEXT. Sets the value for the next extent of the file. It is specified in bytes, kilobytes, or megabytes. The default value is five data blocks. The minimum is one data block. Oracle rounds up to the next whole blocksize for sizes less than five blocks. The maximum size is operating-system specific. For sizes over five blocks, Oracle will resize to minimize fragmentation if possible.

PCTINCREASE. A value is from 0-100; sets the amount that each extension after NEXT will increase in size over the size of NEXT. This factor is applied to the last extent created; it is not calculated based on the size of NEXT after the first extension after NEXT. The default is 50. If you properly size your tables, this should be set to 0. This factor cannot be set for rollback segments. For rollback segments, this factor will be set to 0.

MINEXTENTS. Sets how many initial extents Oracle will create for a specified object. Generally, this is set to the default of 1 (2 for rollback segments). If you use parallel insert processes, you may want to adjust INITIAL, NEXT, PCTINCREASE, and MINEXTENTS to set the size of initial extents to the size corresponding to calculated table size, divided by number of insert processes, and the MINEXTENTS to the number of insert processes. The value for the sizes of the extents is calculated based on INITIAL, NEXT, and PCTINCREASE.

MAXEXTENTS. Determines the maximum number of extents allowed a specific object. The minimum value is 1; the maximum is determined by the size of your data blocksize.

UNLIMITED. Means the object can grow until it runs out of space. This setting is not suggested for use with rollback segments.

FREELIST GROUPS. Used for objects other than tablespaces to set up the number of groups of FREELISTS. The default and minimum for this parameter is 1. Only use this parameter with the parallel server set in parallel mode. This parameter is only used in tables and clusters.

FREELISTS. Used for objects other than tablespaces. The default is 1; the maximum is dependent on your data blocksize. If multiple processes will be updating the same data block, this parameter should be set higher. This parameter is only used in tables, indexes, and clusters.

OPTIMAL. Used with rollback segments and sets the size in bytes, kilobytes, or megabytes for the optimal size of a rollback segment. This is the size that the rollback segment will shrink to when it has expanded because of a large transaction. This cannot be set to less than the amount of space used by the rollback segment via the INITIAL, NEXT, and MINEXTENTS values.

BUFFER_POOL. Has three possible values: KEEP, RECYCLE, and DEFAULT. BUFFER_POOL allows the DBA to specify which buffer pool will hold the data from the object. If KEEP is specified for BUFFER_POOL, then the data is protected from LRU aging. If RECYCLE is specified for the BUFFER_POOL, the data experiences accelerated aging. If no value is set for BUFFER_POOL, or DEFAULT is specified, then behavior is identical to previous releases when multiple buffer pools weren't available.

The High-Water Mark

To view an object's high-water mark, you can use the DBMS_SPACE package, which contains a procedure (UNUSED_SPACE) that returns information about the position of the high-water mark and the amount of unused space in a segment.

Some operations, such as parallel inserts, will only insert into space above the high-water mark. It may be smart to reduce space used to the absolute minimum and then reset NEXT and PCTINCREASE before performing a large parallel insert.

Within a segment, the high-water mark indicates the amount of used space. You cannot release space below the high-water mark (even if there is no data in the space you wish to deallocate). However, if the segment is completely empty, you can release space using the TRUNCATE object DROP STORAGE statement.

The Oracle9*i* PFILE and SPFILE Commands

In Oracle9*i*, the ability to create parameter (initialization) files (called pfiles) and server parameter files (dynamic initialization) called spfiles was added. The commands are:

```
CREATE PFILE [pfile_name] FROM [spfile_name];
CREATE SPFILE [spfile_name] FROM PFILE [pfile_name];
```

If the pfile_name and spfile_names aren't provided, they will be given default names and stored in the default locations for your system.

A PFILE is a standard Oracle initialization file. However, the ability to simply create one from the database was not provided until Oracle9*i*. An SPFILE, on the other hand, is a feature new to Oracle9*i;* it allows the DBA to create a binary file that tracks any ALTER SYSTEM commands that change systemwide initialization parameters (for a complete list, refer back to Chapter 2) and makes it possible to capture and reuse these dynamic changes on the next database startup.

By allowing a PFILE to be created from an SPFILE, Oracle gives a DBA a method for easily dumping the database initialization parameters, editing them, and then reloading them by inverting the command.

7.19 FURTHER DBA READING

The DBA should consult the following references for more detailed information:

- *Oracle9i Database Administrator's Guide*, Release 1 (9.0.1), Part No. A90117-01, Oracle Corporation, June 2001.
- *Oracle9i SQL Reference*, Release 1 (9.0.1), Part No. A90125-01, Oracle Corporation, June 2001.
- *Oracle9i Performance Guide and Reference*, Release 1 (9.0.1), Part no. A87503-01, Oracle Corporation, June 2001.
- *Oracle9i JDBC Developer's Guide and Reference*, Release 1 (9.0.1), Part No. A90211-01, Oracle Corporation, June 2001.
- *Oracle Administrator,* online reference, RevealNet, Inc., version 01-3. www.revealnet.com/.

7.20 SUMMARY

In this chapter we examined the management of many different Oracle objects, including packages, procedures, functions, triggers, and others. The chapter also provided guidelines for using the PRAGMA RESTRICT_REFERENCES call, and introduced additions to various objects and the new objects provided in Oracle9*i*.

CHAPTER 8

Administration of Table Clusters

A cluster can be used when several tables store a row that is of the same datatype and size and is in the same location. This reduces storage requirements and, in some cases, can speed access to data. The major drawback occurs for operations involving updates, inserts, and deletes, in the form of performance degradation. The DBA should evaluate the expected mix of transaction types on the tables to be clustered and only cluster those that are frequently joined and don't have numerous updates, inserts, and deletes.

Clusters store shared data values in the same physical blocks (the cluster key values). For tables that are frequently joined, this can speed access; for tables that are frequently accessed separately, joining is not the answer. An exception is when a single table is clustered. A single table cluster forces the key values for that table into a single set of blocks, thus speeding up accesses of that table. Usually, this single-table clustering also uses a HASH structure to further improve access times.

Under Oracle7, there was an additional cluster feature added, the ability to specify a HASH cluster. A HASH cluster uses a HASH form of storage and no index, rather than the normal B-tree type index. But hash structures should be used only for static tables. Hashing is the process whereby a value, either of a unique or nonunique row, is used to generate a hash value. This hash value is used to place the row into the hashed table. To retrieve the row, the value is simply recalculated. Hashes can only be used for equality operations.

Oracle8 did not add any further functionality to clusters, butOracle8*i* added one feature to clustering: the ability to specify that the cluster is a single-table cluster. If a cluster is specified as a single-table cluster, only one table can be placed in the cluster at any given time; however, the table can be dropped and a different table placed in the cluster as desired. Clusters may not be partitioned.

8.1 CREATION OF CLUSTERS

Cluster creation is a two-step process. The first step is to specify the cluster using the CREATE CLUSTER command. Before any tables in the cluster can be accessed, the cluster index must also be created. Let's look at this process.

1. First create the cluster. The syntax for the CREATE CLUSTER command for Oracle7, Oracle8, Oracle8*i,* and Oracle9*i* is:

```
CREATE CLUSTER [schema.]cluster_name(column_and_datatype_list)
[physical_attributes]
[SIZE n [K|M]]
[TABLESPACE tablespace_name]
[INDEX]|[[SINGLE TABLE] HASHKEYS integer [HASH IS expr]]
[parallel_clause][CACHE|NOCACHE]
```

where:

cluster_name. The name for the cluster; if the user has DBA privilege, a schema or user name may be specified.

column_and_datatype list (column datatype, column datatype . . .). A list of columns and their datatypes, called the *cluster key*. The names for the columns do not have to match the table column names, but the datatypes, lengths, and precisions do have to match.

n. An integer (not all *n*s are of the same value; *n* is used for convenience).

SIZE. The expected size of the average cluster. This is calculated by:

19 + (sum of column lengths) + (1 X num of columns)

SIZE should be rounded up to the nearest equal divisor of your blocksize. For example, if your blocksize is 2,048 and the cluster length is 223, round up to 256.

physical_attributes. Provides physical attributes and the storage clause that will be used as the default for the tables in the cluster.

INDEX. Specifies to create an indexed cluster (default).

SINGLE TABLE. (New to 8*i*) Specifies that the cluster is a SINGLE TABLE cluster; no more than one table can be assigned to the cluster at the same time.

HASH IS. Specifies to create a HASH cluster. The specified column must be a zero-precision number.

HASHKEYS. Creates a HASH cluster and specifies the number (*n*) of keys. The value is rounded up to the nearest prime number.

The other parameters are the same as for the CREATE TABLE command.

2. Create the cluster index:

```
CREATE  INDEX index name ON CLUSTER cluster_name
```

Note that you don't specify the columns; this is taken from the CREATE CLUSTER command that was used to create the named cluster.

3. Create the tables that will be in the cluster:

```
CREATE TABLE cluster_table
    ( column_list)
      CLUSTER cluster_name (cluster_column(s))
```

where:

cluster_table. A name for a table that will be a part of the cluster.

column_list. A list of columns for the table, which is specified identically to the CREATE TABLE command's normal format.

Remember: The cluster columns don't have to have the same name but must be the same data type, size, and precision, and must be specified in the same order as the columns in the CREATE CLUSTER command.

8.2 ESTIMATING SPACE REQUIRED BY CLUSTERS

The procedure given here shows how to estimate the initial amount of space required by a clustered set of tables. This procedure only estimates the initial amount of space required for a cluster. When using these estimates, note that the following factors can affect the accuracy of estimations:

- Trailing nulls are not stored, nor is a length byte. Inserts, updates, and deletes of rows, as well as tables containing rows or columns larger than a single data block, can cause chained row pieces. Therefore, the estimates you derive using the following procedure may tend to be lower than the actual space required if significant row chaining occurs.
- Once you determine an estimate for a table's size using the following procedure, you should add about 10 to 20 percent additional space to calculate the initial extent size for a working table.

To estimate the space required by clusters, perform the following general steps:

1. Calculate total block header size and space available for table data.
2. Calculate the combined average column lengths of the rows per cluster key.
3. Calculate the average row size of all clustered tables.
4. Calculate the average cluster blocksize.
5. Calculate the total number of blocks required for the cluster.

Let's step through a more detailed example.

Step 1: Calculate Total Block Header Size and Space Available for Table Data

The following formula returns the amount of available space in a block:

space left in block after headers (hspace)
hspace = BLOCKSIZE -(KCBH - UB4 - KTBBH - (KTBIT*(INITTRANS - 1)) - KDBH)

The sizes of KCBH, KTBBH, KTBIT, KDBH, and UB4 can be obtained by selecting * from v$type_size table.

Then use the following formula to calculate the space available (s_avail) for table data:

s_avail = (hspace*(1 – PCTFREE/100)) – (4*(NTABLES + 1) * ROWSINBLOCK)

where:

BLOCKSIZE. The size of a data block.

INITTRANS. The initial number of transaction entries for the object.

PCTFREE. The percentage of space to reserve in a block for updates.

NTABLES. The number of tables in the cluster.

ROWS IN BLOCK. The number of rows in a block.

NOTE   Several calculations are required to obtain a final estimate, and several of the constants (indicated by an asterisk [*]) provided are operating system-specific. Your estimates should not significantly differ from actual values. See your operating system–specific Oracle documentation for any substantial deviations from the constants provided in the above procedure.

Step 2: Calculate Space Required by a Row

To calculate this number, use step 3 from the five-step procedure for estimating the space required by nonclustered tables from Chapter 5, Section 5.7, "Sizing an Oracle9*i* Nonclustered Table." Make note of the following caveats:

- Calculate the data space required by an average row for each table in the cluster. For example, in a cluster that contains tables t1 and t2, calculate the average row size for both tables.
- Do not include the space required by the cluster key in any of the above data space calculations. Make note of the space required to store an average cluster key value

for use in step 5. For example, calculate the data space required by an average row in table t1, not including the space required to store the cluster key.

Do not include any space required by the row header (that is, the length bytes for each column); this space is accounted for in the next step. For example, assume two clustered tables are created with the following statements:

```
CREATE TABLE t1 (a CHAR(6), b DATE, c NUMBER(9,2))
              CLUSTER t1_t2 (c);
CREATE TABLE t2 (c NUMBER(9,2), d CHAR(6))
              CLUSTER t1_t2 (c);
```

Notice that the cluster key is column C in each table.

Considering these sample tables, the space required for an average row (D1) of table t1 and the space required for an average row (D2) of table t2 is:

D1 (space/average row) = (a + b) = (9 + 6) bytes = 15 bytes
D2 (space/average row) = (d) = 9 bytes

Step 3: Calculate Total Average Row Size

You can calculate the minimum amount of space required by a row in a clustered table according to the following equation:

$$S_n \text{ bytes/row} = \text{row header} + F_n + V_n + D_n$$

where:

row header. Four bytes per row of a clustered table.

Fn. Total length bytes of all 250 bytes or less. The number of length bytes required by each column of this type is 1 byte.

Vn. Total length bytes of all columns in table n that store more than 250 bytes. The number of length bytes required by each column of this type is 3 bytes.

Dn. Combined data space of all columns in table n (from step 2).

TIP Do not include the column length for the cluster key in variables F or V for any table in the cluster. This space is accounted for in step 5.

For example, the total average row size of the clustered tables t1 and t2 is as follows:

S1 = (4 + (1 * 2) + (3 * 0) + 15) bytes = 21 bytes
S = (4 + (1 * 1) + (3 * 0) + 9) bytes = 14 bytes

TIP   The absolute minimum row size of a clustered row is 10 bytes and is operating system specific. Therefore, if your calculated value for a table's total average row size is less than these absolute minimum row sizes, use the minimum value as the average row size in subsequent calculations.

Step 4: Calculate Average Cluster Blocksize

To calculate the average cluster blocksize, first estimate the average number of rows (for all tables) per cluster key. Once this is known, use the following formula to calculate average cluster block size:

avg. cluster block size (bytes) = ((R1*S1) + (R2*S2) + . . . + (Rn*Sn)) + key header + Ck + Sk + 2Rt

where:

Rn. The average number of rows in table n associated with a cluster key.

Sn. The average row size in table n (see step 3).

key header. This is 19.

Ck. The column length for the cluster key.

Sk. The space required to store average cluster key value.

Rt. The total number of rows associated with an average cluster key (R1 + R2 . . . + Rn). This accounts for the space required in the data block header for each row in the block.

For example, consider the cluster that contains tables t1 and t2. An average cluster key has one row per table t1 and 20 rows per table t2. Also, the cluster key is of datatype NUMBER (column length is 1 byte), and the average number is 4 digits (3 bytes). Considering this information and the previous results, the average cluster key size is:

SIZE = ((1 * 21) + (20 * 14) + 19 + 1 + 3 + (2 * 21)) bytes = 368 bytes

Specify the estimated SIZE in the SIZE option when you create the cluster with the CREATE CLUSTER command. This specifies the space required to hold an average cluster key and its associated rows; Oracle uses the value of SIZE to limit the number of cluster keys that can be assigned to any given data block. After estimating an average cluster key SIZE, choose a SIZE somewhat larger than the average expected size to account for the space required for cluster keys on the high side of the estimate.

To estimate the number of cluster keys that will fit in a database block, use the following formula, which uses the value you calculated in step 2 for available data space, the number of rows associated with an average cluster key (Rt), and SIZE:

cluster keys per block = FLOOR(available data space + 2R / SIZE + 2Rt)

For example, with SIZE previously calculated as 400 bytes (calculated as 368 earlier in this step and rounded up), Rt estimated at 21, and available space per data block (from step 2) calculated as $1,742 - 2R$ bytes, the result is as follows:

cluster keys per block = FLOOR((1936 − 2R + 2R) / (400 + 2 * 21))
= FLOOR(1936 / 442) = FLOOR(4.4) = 4

Note: FLOOR means round down.

Step 5: Calculate Total Number of Blocks

To calculate the total number of blocks for the cluster, you must estimate the number of cluster keys in the cluster. Once this is estimated, use the following formula to calculate the total number of blocks required for the cluster:

blocks = CEIL(# cluster keys / # cluster keys per block)

Note: CEIL means round up.

If you have a test database, you can use statistics generated by the ANALYZE command to determine the number of key values in a cluster key. For example, assume that there are approximately 500 cluster keys in the T1_T2 cluster:

blocks T1_T2 = CEIL(500/3) = CEIL(166.7) = 167

To convert the number of blocks to bytes, multiply the number of blocks by the data block size.

This procedure provides a reasonable estimation of a cluster's size, but not an exact number of blocks or bytes. Once you have estimated the space for a cluster, you can use this information when specifying the INITIAL storage parameter (the size of the cluster's initial extent) in your corresponding CREATE CLUSTER statement.

Space Requirements for Clustered Tables in Use

Once clustered tables have been created and are in use, the space required by the tables is usually higher than the estimate derived by the procedure given in the previous section. More space is required because of the method Oracle uses to manage freespace in the database.

8.3 ESTIMATING SPACE REQUIRED BY HASH CLUSTERS

As with index clusters, it is important to estimate the storage required for the data in a HASH cluster. Use the procedure described in Section 8.2, "Estimating Space Required by Clusters," noting the following additional points:

- A subgoal of the procedure is to determine the SIZE of each cluster key. However, for HASH clusters, the corresponding subgoal is to determine the SIZE of each hash key. Therefore, you must consider not only the number of rows per cluster key value, but also the distribution of cluster keys over the hash keys in the cluster.
- In step 3, make sure to include the space required by the cluster key value. Unlike an index cluster, the cluster key value is stored with each row placed in a hash cluster.
- In step 5, you are calculating the average hash key size, not cluster key size. Therefore, take into account the number of cluster keys that map to each hash value. Also, disregard the addition of the space required by the cluster key value, Ck. This value has already been accounted for in step 3.

8.4 ALTERATION OF CLUSTERS

Only the sizing and storage parameters of clusters may be altered, via the ALTER CLUSTER command. No additional columns may be added to, or removed from, the cluster using the ALTER CLUSTER command. The format of the command follows:

```
ALTER CLUSTER [schema.]cluster_name
[physical_attributes]
[SIZE n [K|M]]
[allocate_extent_clause]
[deallocate_unused_clause]
[parallel_clause]
```

The definitions for the parameters in this code are the same as for the CREATE TABLE, CREATE CLUSTER, and storage clause definitions.

In Oracle, the structure of a cluster and its associated index and tables can be analyzed for consistency and for sizing data using the ANALYZE CLUSTER command. The format of this command follows:

```
ANALYZE CLUSTER [schema.]cluster_name
[COMPUTE STATISTICS]
[ESTIMATE STATISTICS SAMPLE n ROWS|PERCENT]
[VALIDATE STRUCTURE [CASCADE]]
[DELETE STATISTICS]
```

where:

COMPUTE STATISTICS. Calculates statistics based on all rows.

ESTIMATE STATISTICS. Calculates an estimate of the statistics based on n ROWS or PERCENT of rows in table.

VALIDATE STRUCTURE. Validates that the table and its indexes are consistent and not corrupted.

CASCADE. For clusters, validates all tables in cluster.

DELETE STATISTICS. Removes current statistics.

The results appear in the DBA_CLUSTERS view.
To verify a cluster's integrity, use the following version of the ANALYZE command.

```
ANALYZE CLUSTER [schema.]cluster
VALIDATE STRUCTURE   [CASCADE]
```

The CASCADE option forces analysis of all indexes and tables in the cluster.

8.5 DROPPING A CLUSTER

As with the creation of clusters, dropping a cluster is a multistep function. The first step is to drop the tables in the cluster using the DROP TABLE command. Next, the cluster is dropped with the DROP CLUSTER command. An INCLUDING TABLES clause allows the DBA to drop both the cluster and tables at the same time. The format of the command can be found on the documentation Web site at technet.oracle.com.

8.6 DECLUSTERING TABLES

Rather than dropping a cluster's tables completely, it may be desirable to decluster them and then just drop the cluster and cluster index with the DROP CLUSTER command. The procedure to decluster a table follows:

1. Create a new table that is a mirror of the existing clustered table—except, of course, it isn't clustered.

```
CREATE TABLE new table
AS SELECT * FROM cluster table
```

TIP Remember that "new table" is a different name from "cluster table."

2. Drop the clustered table.

```
DROP TABLE cluster table
```

3. Rename the replacement table.

```
RENAME new table TO cluster table
```

4. Reassign all grants; create required indexes and constraints.

TIP   In the sample SQL scripts zip file on the Wiley Web site there is a dynamic SQL script that will create a grant script for a specified database object. The script must, of course, be run before the object is dropped.

---

5. Drop the cluster.

```
DROP CLUSTER [schema.]cluster_name;
```

8.7 SUMMARY

This chapter covered database table clusters, specifically how they are sized, created, altered, and dropped. The chapter also discussed the new ability to specify a single table cluster in Oracle.

CHAPTER 9

User and Security Administration

This chapter first addresses user administration. Database access begins with the creation of users, which are then assigned specific rights to perform actions either directly or through roles. The rights to perform actions are called *system* and *object privileges*. System privileges are rights to perform actions in the database; object privileges are access rights to an object (table, index, synonym, etc.) within the database.

This chapter then covers Oracle8, Oracle8*i,* and Oracle9*i* security-specific topics, such as the use of profiles to control resource usage; password security, contexts, and row-level security; and resource plans and their use in apportioning CPU and parallel server resources.

9.1 ADMINISTRATION OF USERS

In order to access your database, an account must be created in the Oracle database for the user. The exceptions to this are the SYS and SYSTEM users, which are created by Oracle when the database is created. Users can be created, altered, and dropped.

Creating Users

Before you can create a user, you must have the CREATE USER privilege. You can create users with the Oracle Enterprise Manager GUI, at the command line in SQL*Plus, or in Oracle Server Manager versions prior to 9*i*. The command syntax for creating a user is:

```
CREATE USER user IDENTIFIED BY password|EXTERNALLY
[GLOBALLY AS 'external_name']
```

```
[DEFAULT TABLESPACE tablespace]
[TEMPORARY TABLESPACE tablespace]
[QUOTA   n [K|M]|UNLIMITED ON tablespace]
[PROFILE   profile]
[DEFAULT ROLE role_list|ALL [EXCEPT role_list]|NONE]
[PASSWORD EXPIRE]
[ACCOUNT LOCK|UNLOCK]
```

For example:

```
CREATE USER  james  IDENTIFIED BY    abc1
DEFAULT TABLESPACE  users
TEMPORARY TABLESPACE  temp
QUOTA  1M ON  users
QUOTA unlimited ON temp
PROFILE  enduser
DEFAULT ROLE fin_app_user
PASSWORD EXPIRE;
```

You need to assign each new user a password or indicate that operating system authentication will be used. Passwords are stored in the database in encrypted format and cannot be read by any user. The use of operating system authentication means that once your user has logged in at the operating system level, no user name or password will be required when logging in to the Oracle database. Users not assigned an Oracle password are designated as IDENTIFIED EXTERNALLY. Oracle depends upon the operating system for authentication of the user. In order to use external authentication, you must set the OS_AUTHENT_PREFIX in the database parameter file.

Password security features were added to Oracle in versions 8 and 8*i*. In the example, the user's password has been set to expired. This will require the user to reenter a different password on first login. By using a PROFILE with password security features enabled, we can force users to change passwords on a frequent basis and limit password reuse and password complexity.

When you create a user, you can designate a specific tablespace as the DEFAULT tablespace for that user. The designation of a default tablespace means that all the objects created by that user will be placed in that tablespace unless the user specifically indicates that the database object be placed in another tablespace. If no default tablespace is indicated for a user, the SYSTEM tablespace will be the default for that user.

NOTE   I can't caution strongly enough not to allow users to have the SYSTEM tablespace as their temporary or default tablespace assignment. The only users that may have SYSTEM as their default tablespace are SYS and certain special users (such as DBSNMP) created by Oracle install scripts. All other users, including SYSTEM, should have default and temporary tablespaces other than SYSTEM. The SYS user should have a different temporary tablespace from SYSTEM.

When you create a user, you can also designate a specific tablespace to be the TEMPORARY TABLESPACE. This designation specifies the tablespace that will be used for any database actions that require the use of a workspace for the storage of intermediate results for actions such as sorting.

If no temporary tablespace is indicated for a user, the system tablespace will be used. When you designate a default tablespace, temporary tablespace, or quota on a tablespace, this does not implicitly grant any system or object privileges. You can give a user permission to create objects in tablespaces with the QUOTA clause.

To allow a user to create objects in a tablespace, you need to specify a quota for that user on that tablespace. The tablespace quota may be limited to a specific amount of kilobytes or megabytes or may be designated as unlimited. A quota of unlimited indicates that the user can have any portion of a tablespace that is not already in use by another user. If the user is not assigned the UNLIMITED TABLESPACE system privilege, and the assigned limit is reached, the user will no longer be able to create additional objects or insert rows into any objects he or she owns in that tablespace.

NOTE   The role RESOURCE automatically grants UNLIMITED TABLE SPACE, so only use it when absolutely required. A user's temporary tablespace assignment does not require a quota grant for the user to use it.

The DBA_TS_QUOTAS view provides tablespace quota information for all users in the database. The USER_TS_QUOTAS view provides tablespace quota information for the current user. When you query DBA_TS_QUOTAS or USER_TS_QUOTAS, a designation of 1 in the max_bytes and max_blocks columns indicates that the user has an unlimited quota on that tablespace.

Altering Users

To create a user, you must have the ALTER USER privilege. You can alter users with the Oracle Enterprise Manager GUI or at the command line in SQL*Plus or Server Manager (SVRMGRL). The command-line syntax for altering a user is:

```
ALTER user IDENTIFIED  BY password|EXTERNALLY|VALUE
[DEFAULT TABLESPACE tablespace]
[TEMPORARY TABLESAPCE tablespace]
[QUOTA    n [K|M|]|[UNLIMITED] ON tablespace]
[PROFILE  profile]
[DEFAULT ROLE role_list|ALL[EXCEPT rolelist]|NONE]
[PASSWORD EXPIRE]
[ACCOUNT LOCK|UNLOCK]
```

For example:

```
ALTER USER ault IDENTIFIED BY  xyz2
DEFAULT TABLESPACE  users
```

```
TEMPORARY TABLESPACE temp
QUOTA 2M ON user_data
QUOTA UNLIMITED ON temp
PROFILE  appuser
DEFAULT ROLE ALL
ACCOUNT LOCK;
```

Once a user has been created, the only thing that you cannot alter for that user is the user name. The password, default tablespace, temporary tablespace, and the quota on a tablespace, profile, default role, status, and password expiration can all be altered by someone with the ALTER USER system privilege.

Each user can alter the Oracle password you initially assigned to that user upon creation, provided that user is not identified externally (via the operating system). In addition to the end user, users with the ALTER USER system privilege can issue the ALTER USER command to change the user's password. The use of operating system authentication can also be changed by a user with the ALTER USER system privilege. Any changes to the password will take effect the next time that user logs in to Oracle.

When you change the default tablespace for a user, all future objects created by that user will be created in the new default tablespace you designated (unless otherwise specified by the user at the time the object was created). Remember, the user must have a quota in the tablespace to create new objects in that tablespace. If a user reaches the maximum number of bytes assigned (quota), only a user with the ALTER USER system privileges will be able to increase the quota limit for the user.

The undocumented keyword VALUE allows you to specify the encrypted value of a user's password. This can be handy if the DBA needs to temporarily become a user. You simply capture the encrypted value of the user's password from the SYS.USER$ table, alter the user to a password you know, do what you need to do, then reset the password using this command:

```
ALTER USER username IDENTIFIED BY VALUE 'encrypted_password';
```

Dropping Users

In order to drop a user, you must have the DROP USER system privilege. You can drop users with Server Manager or at the command line in SQL*Plus. The command-line syntax for dropping a user is:

```
DROP USER user [CASCADE]
```

For example:

```
DROP USER scott CASCADE;
```

If a user owns any database objects, you can only drop that user by including the CASCADE keyword in the DROP USER command. The DROP USER command with the

CASCADE keyword will drop the user and all objects owned by that user. If you are using Oracle Enterprise Manager (OEM) to drop a user, you need to indicate that the associated schema objects be included in the command to drop the user. If a user owns objects and you fail to include CASCADE, you will receive an error message and the user will not be dropped. If a user is currently connected to the database, you cannot drop that user until he or she exits. Once a user has been dropped, all information on that user and all objects owned by that user are removed from the database.

Once you have issued the command to drop a user, you cannot perform a rollback to re-create the user and his or her objects. DROP USER is a DDL command and DDL commands cannot be rolled back.

If you need the objects created by that user, instead of dropping the user, you can revoke the CREATE SESSION system privilege to prevent the user from logging on. You can also copy the objects to another user by importing the objects from an export made before the user was dropped. In order to avoid the problem of dropping a user without losing your application tables, all application tables should be owned by a separate application schema instead of an actual database user schema.

9.2 ADMINISTRATION OF SECURITY

Security in Oracle has six layers:

- The first layer of security is the raw assignment and management of users, which we have already discussed.
- The second layer is the high-level system grants that give the users already built permission to create, alter, and use database objects such as tables, indexes, and clusters.
- The third layer of security comprises the object-level grants that allow users to interact with database objects.
- The fourth layer is the column grant layer that grants or restricts access to the specific columns inside a database object.
- The fifth layer (new in Oracle8*i*) involves the use of policies and contexts to control row-level access.
- The sixth level of security deals with controlling access to system resources, such as CPUs and parallel query resources, and is accomplished through the use of profiles (Oracle7 and Oracle8) and resource plans and groups (new in Oracle8*i*).

Security in Oracle is becoming a very complex topic, and entire books have been written concerning this one aspect of Oracle.

User Grants and Privileges

As mentioned in the introduction to this chapter, two types of privileges can be granted: system privileges and object privileges.

- System privileges allow a user to perform a particular systemwide action or to perform a particular action on a particular type of object. For example, the privilege to create a table (CREATE TABLE) or insert rows into any table (INSERT ANY TABLE) are system privileges.
- Object privileges allow a user to perform a particular action on a specific object, including tables, views, sequences, procedures, functions, and packages. For example, the privilege to insert rows into a particular table is an object privilege. Object privilege grants always include the name of the object for which the privilege is granted.

System Privileges   All users require the CREATE SESSION privilege to access the database. This privilege is automatically granted to all users when you assign the grants using Oracle Enterprise Manager. But if you create the user in command-line mode, you must remember to explicitly grant each user the CREATE SESSION system privilege, either directly or through a role, as shown here:

```
GRANT system_priv_list|role_list TO user_list|role_list|PUBLIC
[WITH ADMIN OPTION]
```

For example:

```
GRANT create session, create table, dba
TO scott
WITH ADMIN OPTION;
```

System privileges can be granted to other users when the grant made includes the WITH ADMIN OPTION.

There are more than 100 distinct privileges, most of which are self-explanatory. Table 9.1 lists all the system privileges.

TABLE 9.1   System Privileges

Class/Privilege	Description
CLUSTERS	
CREATE CLUSTER	Create clusters in grantee's schema.
CREATE ANY CLUSTER	Create a cluster in any schema except SYS. Behaves similarly to CREATE ANY TABLE.
ALTER ANY CLUSTER	Alter clusters in any schema except SYS.
DROP ANY CLUSTER	Drop clusters in any schema except SYS.
CONTEXTS	
CREATE ANY CONTEXT	Create any context namespace.
DROP ANY CONTEXT	Drop any context namespace.

TABLE 9.1 (*Continued*)

Class/Privilege	Description
DATABASE	
ALTER DATABASE	Alter the database.
ALTER SYSTEM	Issue ALTER SYSTEM statements.
AUDIT SYSTEM	Issue AUDIT sql_statements statements.
DATABASE LINKS	
CREATE DATABASE LINK	Create private database links in grantee's schema.
CREATE PUBLIC DATABASE LINK	Create public database links.
DROP PUBLIC DATABASE LINK	Drop public database links.
DIMENSIONS	
CREATE DIMENSION	Create dimensions in the grantee's schema.
CREATE ANY DIMENSION	Create dimensions in any schema except SYS.
ALTER ANY DIMENSION	Alter dimensions in any schema except SYS.
DROP ANY DIMENSION	Drop dimensions in any schema except SYS.
DIRECTORIES	
CREATE ANY DIRECTORY	Create directory database objects.
DROP ANY DIRECTORY	Drop directory database objects.
INDEXTYPES	
CREATE INDEXTYPE	Create an indextype in the grantee's schema.
CREATE ANY INDEXTYPE	Create an indextype in any schema except SYS.
DROP ANY INDEXTYPE	Drop an indextype in any schema except SYS.
EXECUTE ANY INDEXTYPE	Reference an indextype in any schema except SYS.
INDEXES	
CREATE INDEX	Create in the grantee's schema an index on any table in the grantee's schema or a domain index.
CREATE ANY INDEX	Create in any schema except SYS a domain index or an index on any table in any schema except SYS.
ALTER ANY INDEX	Alter indexes in any schema except SYS.
DROP ANY INDEX	Drop indexes in any schema except SYS.
QUERY REWRITE	Enable rewrite using a materialized view, or create a function-based index, when that materialized view or index references tables and views that are in the grantee's own schema.

continued

TABLE 9.1 (*Continued*)

Class/Privilege	Description
GLOBAL QUERY REWRITE	Enable rewrite using a materialized view, or create a function-based index, when that materialized view or index references tables or views in any schema except SYS.

LIBRARIES

CREATE LIBRARY	Create external procedure/function libraries in grantee's schema.
CREATE ANY LIBRARY	Create external procedure/function libraries in any schema except SYS.
DROP LIBRARY	Drop external procedure/function libraries in the grantee's schema.
DROP ANY LIBRARY	Drop external procedure/function libraries in any schema except SYS.

MATERIALIZED VIEWS (a.k.a. SNAPSHOTS)

CREATE MATERIALIZED VIEW	Create a materialized view in the grantee's schema.
CREATE ANY MATERIALIZED VIEW	Create materialized views in any schema except SYS.
ALTER ANY MATERIALIZED VIEW	Alter materialized views in any schema except SYS.
DROP ANY MATERIALIZED VIEW	Drop materialized views in any schema except SYS.
QUERY REWRITE	Enable rewrite using a materialized view, or create a function-based index, when that materialized view or index references tables and views that are in the grantee's own schema.
GLOBAL QUERY REWRITE	Enable rewrite using a materialized view, or create a function-based index, when that materialized view or index references tables or views in any schema except SYS.

OPERATORS

CREATE OPERATOR	Create an operator and its bindings in the grantee's schema.
CREATE ANY OPERATOR	Create an operator and its bindings in any schema except SYS.
DROP ANY OPERATOR	Drop an operator in any schema except SYS.
EXECUTE ANY OPERATOR	Reference an operator in any schema except SYS.

OUTLINES

CREATE ANY OUTLINE	Create outlines that can be used in any schema that uses outlines.

TABLE 9.1 (*Continued*)

Class/Privilege	Description
ALTER ANY OUTLINE	Modify outlines.
DROP ANY OUTLINE	Drop outlines.
PROCEDURES	
CREATE PROCEDURE	Create stored procedures, functions, and packages in grantee's schema.
CREATE ANY PROCEDURE	Create stored procedures, functions, and packages in any schema except SYS.
ALTER ANY PROCEDURE	Alter stored procedures, functions, or packages in any schema except SYS.
DROP ANY PROCEDURE	Drop stored procedures, functions, or packages in any schema except SYS.
EXECUTE ANY PROCEDURE	Execute procedures or functions (standalone or packaged). Reference public package variables in any schema except SYS.
PROFILES	
CREATE PROFILE	Create profiles.
ALTER PROFILE	Alter profiles.
DROP PROFILE	Drop profiles.
ROLES	
CREATE ROLE	Create roles.
ALTER ANY ROLE	Alter any role in the database.
DROP ANY ROLE	Drop roles.
GRANT ANY ROLE	Grant any role in the database.
ROLLBACK SEGMENTS	
CREATE ROLLBACK SEGMENT	Create rollback segments.
ALTER ROLLBACK SEGMENT	Alter rollback segments.
DROP ROLLBACK SEGMENT	Drop rollback segments.
SEQUENCES	
CREATE SEQUENCE	Create sequences in grantee's schema.
CREATE ANY SEQUENCE	Create sequences in any schema except SYS.
ALTER ANY SEQUENCE	Alter any sequence in the database.
DROP ANY SEQUENCE	Drop sequences in any schema except SYS.
SELECT ANY SEQUENCE	Reference sequences in any schema except SYS.

continued

TABLE 9.1 (*Continued*)

Class/Privilege	Description
SESSIONS	
CREATE SESSION	Connect to the database.
ALTER RESOURCE COST	Set costs for session resources.
ALTER SESSION	Issue ALTER SESSION statements.
RESTRICTED SESSION	Log on after the instance is started using the SQL*Plus STARTUP RESTRICT statement.
SNAPSHOTS (a.k.a. MATERIALIZED VIEWS)	
CREATE SNAPSHOT	Create snapshots in grantee's schema.
CREATE ANY SNAPSHOT	Create snapshots in any schema except SYS.
ALTER ANY SNAPSHOT	Alter any snapshot in the database.
DROP ANY SNAPSHOT	Drop snapshots in any schema except SYS.
GLOBAL QUERY REWRITE	Enable rewrite using a snapshot, or create a function-based index, when that snapshot or index references tables or views in any schema except SYS.
QUERY REWRITE	Enable rewrite using a snapshot, or create a function-based index, when that snapshot or index references tables and views that are in the grantee's own schema.
SYNONYMS	
CREATE SYNONYM	Create synonyms in grantee's schema.
CREATE ANY SYNONYM	Create private synonyms in any schema except SYS.
CREATE PUBLIC SYNONYM	Create public synonyms.
DROP ANY SYNONYM	Drop private synonyms in any schema except SYS.
DROP PUBLIC SYNONYM	Drop public synonyms.
TABLES	
CREATE ANY TABLE	Create tables in any schema except SYS. The owner of the schema containing the table must have space quota on the tablespace to contain the table.
ALTER ANY TABLE	Alter any table or view in the schema.
BACKUP ANY TABLE	Use the Export utility to incrementally export objects from the schema of other users.
DELETE ANY TABLE	Delete rows from tables, table partitions, or views in any schema except SYS.
DROP ANY TABLE	Drop or truncate tables or table partitions in any schema except SYS.

TABLE 9.1 (*Continued*)

Class/Privilege	Description
INSERT ANY TABLE	Insert rows into tables and views in any schema except SYS.
LOCK ANY TABLE	Lock tables and views in any schema except SYS.
UPDATE ANY TABLE	Update rows in tables and views in any schema except SYS.
SELECT ANY TABLE	Query tables, views, or snapshots in any schema except SYS.

TABLESPACES

CREATE TABLESPACE	Create tablespaces.
ALTER TABLESPACE	Alter tablespaces.
DROP TABLESPACE	Drop tablespaces.
MANAGE TABLESPACE	Take tablespaces offline and online and begin and end tablespace backups.
UNLIMITED TABLESPACE	Use an unlimited amount of any tablespace. This privilege overrides any specific quotas assigned. If you revoke this privilege from a user, the user's schema objects remain, but further tablespace allocation is denied unless authorized by specific tablespace quotas. You cannot grant this system privilege to roles.

TRIGGERS

CREATE TRIGGER	Create a database trigger in grantee's schema.
CREATE ANY TRIGGER	Create database triggers in any schema except SYS.
ALTER ANY TRIGGER	Enable, disable, or compile database triggers in any schema except SYS.
DROP ANY TRIGGER	Drop database triggers in any schema except SYS.
ADMINISTER DATABASE TRIGGER	Create a trigger on DATABASE. (You must also have the CREATE TRIGGER or CREATE ANY TRIGGER privilege.)

TYPES

CREATE TYPE	Create object types and object type bodies in grantee's schema.
CREATE ANY TYPE	Create object types and object type bodies in any schema except SYS.
ALTER ANY TYPE	Alter object types in any schema except SYS.

continued

TABLE 9.1   (*Continued*)

Class/Privilege	Description
DROP ANY TYPE	Drop object types and object type bodies in any schema except SYS.
EXECUTE ANY TYPE	Use and reference object types and collection types in any schema except SYS, and invoke methods of an object type in any schema if you make the grant to a specific user. If you grant EXECUTE ANY TYPE to a role, users holding the enabled role will not be able to invoke methods of an object type in any schema.
USERS	
CREATE USER	Create users. This privilege also allows the creator to assign quotas on any tablespace, set default and temporary tablespaces, and assign a profile as part of a CREATE USER statement.
ALTER USER	Alter any user. This privilege authorizes the grantee to change another user's password or authentication method, assign quotas on any tablespace, set default and temporary tablespaces, and assign a profile and default roles.
BECOME USER	Become another user. (Required by any user performing a full database import.)
DROP USER	Drop users.
VIEWS	
CREATE VIEW	Create views in grantee's schema.
CREATE ANY VIEW	Create views in any schema except SYS.
DROP ANY VIEW	Drop views in any schema except SYS.
MISCELLANEOUS	
ANALYZE ANY	Analyze any table, cluster, or index in any schema except SYS.
AUDIT ANY	Audit any object in any schema except SYS using AUDIT schema_objects statements.
COMMENT ANY TABLE	Comment on any table, view, or column in any schema except SYS.
FORCE ANY TRANSACTION	Force the commit or rollback of any in-doubt distributed transaction in the local database. Induce the failure of a distributed transaction.
FORCE TRANSACTION	Force the commit or rollback of grantee's in-doubt distributed transactions in the local database.

TABLE 9.1 (*Continued*)

Class/Privilege	Description
GRANT ANY PRIVILEGE	Grant any system privilege.
SYSDBA	Perform STARTUP and SHUTDOWN operations, ALTER DATABASE; OPEN, MOUNT, BACK UP, or change character set; CREATE DATABASE; ARCHIVELOG and RECOVERY. Includes the RESTRICTED SESSION privilege.
SYSOPER	Perform STARTUP and SHUTDOWN operations; ALTER DATABASE OPEN/MOUNT/BACKUP; ARCHIVELOG and RECOVERY. Includes the RESTRICTED SESSION privilege.

As the DBA, you can access the DBA_SYS_PRIVS view for information on the system privileges granted to users. Users can see information related to them by accessing the corresponding user view: USER_SYS_PRIVS.

Object Privileges   Object privileges define a user's rights on existing database objects. All grants on objects take effect immediately.

To grant an object privilege, you must either be the owner of the object, have been granted WITH GRANT OPTION on that object for that privilege, or have the system privilege GRANT ANY PRIVILEGE. You can also grant access to all users by granting the privilege to PUBLIC, as shown here:

```
GRANT object_priv_list|ALL PRIVILEGES
[(column_list)]
ON [schema.]object|DIRECTORY dir_name|JAVA SOURCE|RESOURCE
    [schema.]object
TO user|role|PUBLIC
[WITH GRANT OPTION]
```

For example:

```
GRANT insert, update, select ON  bob.emp TO  derek;
```

As the DBA, you can access the DBA_TAB_PRIVS view for information on the object privileges granted to users. Note that, although named DBA_TAB_ PRIVS, this view also includes information on views and sequences, as well as tables. By accessing the corresponding user view, USER_TAB_PRIVS, users can see information on objects for which they are the owner, grantor, or grantee. A user can see information for all objects for which that user or PUBLIC is the grantee with the ALL_TAB_ PRIVS view. The ALL_TAB_PRIVS view is slightly different from the USER_TAB_ PRIVS and DBA_TAB_PRIVS.

An object owner can grant the following object privileges to other users:

ALTER

DELETE

INDEX

INSERT

REFERENCES

SELECT

UPDATE

READ

EXECUTE

Grants on objects, and revocation of those grants, are valid immediately, even if a user is currently logged in to the database. The SELECT privilege can be granted only on tables, views, sequences, and snapshots. In fact, the only object-level grants on a sequence are ALTER and SELECT. The EXECUTE privilege is used for libraries, UDTs, operators, indextypes, procedures, and functions (and Java objects). Remember that procedures and functions are always executed with the permissions of the owner of that procedure or function, unless the AUTHID clause specifies AS EXECUTOR. Java objects are treated as a procedure for the purpose of grants.

By granting other users INSERT, UPDATE, DELETE, and SELECT privileges on your table, you allow them to perform the respective action on the table. By granting the ALTER privilege, you can allow another user to modify the structure of your table or sequence or create a trigger on your table. By granting users the INDEX privilege, you can allow them to create indexes on your table. INDEX grants are applicable only to tables.

The REFERENCES privilege differs from the other privileges in that is does not actually grant the right to change the table or data contained in the table; rather, it allows users to create foreign-key constraints that reference your table.

The READ privilege is only applicable to DIRECTORY objects; it cannot be granted on any other object.

Users can access the USER_TAB_PRIVS_RECD view for information on table privileges for which that user is the grantee. The corresponding ALL_TAB_PRIVS_RECD view includes all grants on objects for which that user or PUBLIC is the grantee.

Users can access the USER_TAB_PRIVS_MADE view for information on table privileges that they have granted to others. The corresponding ALL_TAB_PRIVS_MADE view includes information on all the grants that user has made, as well as grants by others on that user's objects.

Column Privileges   Only INSERT, UPDATE, and REFERENCES privileges can be granted at the column level. When granting INSERT at the column level, you must include all the NOT NULL columns in the row.

```
GRANT object_priv|ALL [PRIVILEGES](column_list)
ON [schema.]object TO user_list|role|PUBLIC
[WITH GRANT OPTION]
```

For example:

```
GRANT  update (emp_id,emp_name)
ON  admin.emp
TO scott WITH GRANT OPTION;
```

As the DBA, you can access the DBA_COL_PRIVS view for information on the object privileges granted to users.

Users can access the USER_COL_PRIVS_RECD view for information on column privileges that have been granted to them. The ALL_COL_PRIVS_RECD view includes information on all column privileges that have been granted to them or to PUBLIC.

Users can access the USER_COL_PRIVS_MADE view for information on column privileges that they have granted to others. The corresponding ALL_COL_PRIVS_MADE view includes information on all columns for which the user is the owner or the grantor.

Users can access information on all columns for which they are the grantor, grantee, or owner, or for which access has been granted to PUBLIC with the corresponding ALL_TAB_PRIVS_MADE and ALL_TAB_PRIVS_RECD views.

Revoking Grants   When system privileges are passed to others using the WITH ADMIN OPTION, revoking the system privileges from the original user will not cascade. The system privileges granted to others must be revoked directly. In contrast, when object privileges are passed on to others using the WITH GRANT OPTION, they are revoked when the grantor's privileges are revoked.

NOTE   It is important to remember that only object privileges will cascade when revoked; system privileges will not.

When the WITH ADMIN OPTION or WITH GRANT OPTION has been included in a grant to another user, it cannot be revoked directly. You must revoke the privilege and then issue another grant without the WITH ADMIN OPTION or WITH GRANT OPTION.

The command-line syntax for revoking a system privilege is:

```
REVOKE system_priv_list
FROM user_list|PUBLIC;
```

For example:

```
REVOKE create table
FROM   admin_dba;
```

In order to revoke an object privilege, you must either be the owner of the object, have granted that privilege to that user with the WITH GRANT OPTION, or have the GRANT ANY PRIVILEGE system privilege.

You can revoke object and system privileges with Server Manager or at the command line in SQL*Plus. The command-line syntax for revoking an object privilege is:

```
REVOKE object_priv_list|ALL PRIVILEGES
ON [schema.]object  FROM user_list|role_list|PUBLIC
[CASCADE CONSTRAINTS];
```

For example:

```
REVOKE  select
ON  scott.emp
FROM  admin_user;
```

When the object privilege REFERENCES has been granted, you must specify CASCADE CONSTRAINTS in order to drop the foreign-key constraints that were created.

9.3 USE OF ROLES

Roles are collections of system, object, and row grants. Using roles allows the DBA to collect all related grants for a specific application function (or role, if you wish) under one object that can then be easily granted to your users with a single command. Using roles has several benefits:

- Reduces the number of grants, thereby making it easier to manage security.
- Dynamically changes the privileges for many users with a single grant/revoke.
- Can be selectively enabled/disabled, depending upon the application.
- Roles can be used for most system and object privileges. Privileges granted through a role cannot be used for creating a stored object (views, packages, triggers, Java, procedures, and functions). You need to grant privileges directly to the user for this.

Creating Roles

To implement a role, you first create the role and then grant system and object privileges to that role. When you create the role, there are three password options available:

- No authentication
- Operating system authentication
- Password authentication

You can set operating system authentication when the role is created or by using the database initialization parameters OS_ROLES=TRUE and REMOTE_OS_ROLES=

TRUE. Note, however, if you are using the multithreaded server (MTS) option, you cannot use operating system authentication for roles.

In order to create a role, you must have the CREATE ROLE system privilege. You can create roles with Server Manager or at the command line in SQL*Plus. The command-line syntax for creating a role is:

```
CREATE ROLE role
[NOT IDENTIFIED|IDENTIFIED BY password]
[IDENTIFIED EXTERNALLY|USING schema.package|GLOBALLY]
```

For example:

```
CREATE ROLE appusers
NOT IDENTIFIED;
```

To alter a role, you must have the ALTER ANY ROLE system privilege or have been granted the role with the WITH ADMIN OPTION. The creator of any role automatically has the WITH ADMIN OPTION for that role. Note that this command only creates the role that acts as a tag for later storage of a grants list; it has no implicit grants. The privileges and grants to a role are made identically to the method used to grant to users. Roles may also be granted to other roles in the form of a role hierarchy.

Grants to Roles

To grant a role to a user, you must either be the creator of that role or have the GRANT ANY ROLE privilege. You can grant roles to users with Oracle Enterprise Manager, at the command line in Server Manager (svrmgrl) in versions prior to 9i, or with SQL*Plus. Grants to roles will not take effect for a user if that user is currently logged in to the database with that role. Only when the user exits or sets another role do the changes take effect. Once roles have been granted to a user, they can be enabled and disabled.

The command-line syntax for granting privileges to a role is basically the same as the syntax for granting privileges to a user, as shown here:

```
GRANT role TO user;
```

For example:

```
GRANT appuser TO scott;
```

The following syntax is for granting system privileges to roles:

```
GRANT system_priv_list TO role
```

For example:

```
GRANT create session, create table TO appuser;
```

The following syntax is for granting object privileges to roles:

```
GRANT object_priv_list|ALL PRIVILEGES [(column_list)]
ON [schema.]object TO role
```

For example:

```
GRANT  select, insert, update
ON  scott.emp
TO  appuser;
```

System privileges can be granted to roles, with the exception of the UNLIMITED TABLESPACE system privilege. Grants on objects can be passed to other users or to roles if the grantee has been given the WITH GRANT OPTION. However, you cannot assign a privilege that includes the WITH GRANT OPTION to a role. The INDEX and REFERENCES privileges cannot be granted to a role; they may be granted only to a user. You can grant that role to a user or to another role. However, you cannot grant a role to itself.

Setting Roles

When a user is created, the default for active roles is set to ALL, which means that all the roles granted to a user are active. The DBA can change the default with an ALTER USER command. A user can enable multiple roles at one time and use the SET ROLE command to switch between roles or activate all roles with the command SET ROLE ALL. The SET ROLE ALL command will not work if any of the roles assigned to that user requires either a password or operating system authentication.

The command-line syntax for setting roles is:

```
SET ROLE role_list|ALL|NONE [EXCEPT role_list]
[IDENTIFIED BY password]
```

Users can look at the SESSION_ROLES view to find the roles that are currently enabled for them. Users can look at SESSION_PRIVS view to see the privileges available to their session.

If you determine that all control of roles will be at the operating system level, you can set the database initialization parameter OS_ROLES=TRUE. Again, all roles must still be created first in the database. And though any grants you previously made using the database command line or Server Manager are still listed in the data dictionary, they cannot be used and are not in effect. If the use of roles is determined at the operating system level, the multithreaded server option cannot be used.

You can use the MAX_ENABLED_ROLES parameter in the database initialization file to set the number of roles that you will allow any user to have enabled at one time.

Special Roles   Oracle creates the following two roles when you install the Oracle executables:

- OSOPER
- OSDBA

Oracle may create the following roles when you create the database:

CONNECT
RESOURCE
DBA
DELETE_CATALOG_ROLE (Oracle8 and greater)
EXECUTE_CATALOG_ROLE (Oracle8 and greater)
SELECT_CATALOG_ROLE (Oracle8 and greater)
AQ_USER_ROLE (Oracle8)
AQ_ADMINISTRATION_ROLE (Oracle8 and greater)
SNMPAGENT (Oracle8)
RECOVERY_CATALOG_OWNER (Oracle8 and greater)
HS_ADMIN_ROLE (Oracle8 and greater)

When you execute the catalog.sql script, the following two roles are created:

- EXP_FULL_DATABASE
- IMP_FULL_DATABASE

In the following subsection, I explain these special roles and how they are used for database maintenance.

OSOPER and OSDBA   The OSOPER and OSDBA roles are created at the operating system level when Oracle is installed; they cannot be granted. The OSOPER and OSDBA roles are needed to perform database operations when the database is not mounted and, therefore, the data dictionary is not accessible. It is the OSOPER and OSDBA roles that are used when you CONNECT INTERNAL to the database using Server Manager. The database roles correspond to the operating system level role (or group) assignments of SYSDBA and SYSOPER.

The OSOPER role can perform the following:

STARTUP
SHUTDOWN
ALTER DATABASE OPEN/MOUNT
ALTER DATABASE BACKUP CONTROLFILE
ALTER TABLESPACE BEGIN/END BACKUP
ARCHIVE LOG
RECOVER

The OSDBA role also has the OSOPER role. In addition, the OSDBA role has the WITH ADMIN OPTION to allow it to grant system privileges to other users. This is the role that is used to create the database and to use for time-based recovery processes. Both the OSOPER and OSDBA roles include the RESTRICTED SESSION system privilege.

If you intend to allow remote users to CONNECT INTERNAL, you need to set the REMOTE_LOGIN_PASSWORDFILE option in your database parameter file to either EXCLUSIVE or SHARED. The user will then connect in Server Manager with the AS SYSDBA or AS SYSOPER clause at the end of the CONNECT command (CONNECT SYS AS SYSDBA). The privileges assigned to SYSDBA correspond to those for OSDBA. The privileges assigned to SYSOPER correspond to OSOPER. The operating system verifies the password provided using an external operating system file. This external file is generated using the ORAPWD utility. When the password for the INTERNAL or SYS accounts is changed with the ALTER USER command, the changes are mapped to the operating system password file. The V$PWFILE_USERS view lists users with the SYSDBA and SYSOPER privileges.

*Internal Roles in Oracle8, Oracle8i, and Oracle9*i   Oracle8, Oracle8*i,* and Oracle9*i* have the following internal roles that are created based on the options you select to load during installation:

CONNECT

RESOURCE

DBA

DELETE_CATALOG_ROLE

EXECUTE_CATALOG_ROLE

SELECT_CATALOG_ROLE

AQ_USER_ROLE

AQ_ADMINISTRATION_ROLE

SNMPAGENT

RECOVERY_CATALOG_OWNER

HS_ADMIN_ROLE

The CONNECT, RESOURCE, and DBA roles are predefined roles that are available for backward compatibility. These are generated by Oracle when the database is created. When you create a user with Oracle Enterprise Manager, the CONNECT role is automatically granted to that user. In some releases, the RESOURCE privilege has the hidden grant UNLIMITED TABLESPACE, which allows the user receiving the grant to create objects in any tablespace, including SYSTEM. Table 9.2 lists all the internal roles and the privileges granted to them.

TABLE 9.2 Internal Roles and Their Grants

Role	Grants	Admin Option?
AQ_ADMINISTRATOR_ROLE	DEQUEUE ANY QUEUE	YES
	ENQUEUE ANY QUEUE	YES
	MANAGE ANY QUEUE	YES
CONNECT	ALTER SESSION	NO
	CREATE CLUSTER	NO
	CREATE DATABASE LINK	NO
	CREATE SEQUENCE	NO
	CREATE SESSION	NO
	CREATE SYNONYM	NO
	CREATE TABLE	NO
	CREATE VIEW	NO
DBA	ADMINISTER DATABASE TRIGGER	YES
	ADMINISTER RESOURCE MANAGER	YES
	ALTER ANY CLUSTER	YES
	ALTER ANY DIMENSION	YES
	ALTER ANY INDEX	YES
	ALTER ANY INDEXTYPE	YES
	ALTER ANY LIBRARY	YES
	ALTER ANY OUTLINE	YES
	ALTER ANY PROCEDURE	YES
	ALTER ANY ROLE	YES
	ALTER ANY SEQUENCE	YES
	ALTER ANY SNAPSHOT	YES
	ALTER ANY TABLE	YES
	ALTER ANY TRIGGER	YES
	ALTER ANY TYPE	YES
	ALTER DATABASE	YES
	ALTER PROFILE	YES
	ALTER RESOURCE COST	YES
	ALTER ROLLBACK SEGMENT	YES
	ALTER SESSION	YES
	ALTER SYSTEM	YES

continued

TABLE 9.2 (*Continued*)

Role	Grants	Admin Option?
	ALTER TABLESPACE	YES
	ALTER USER	YES
	ANALYZE ANY	YES
	AUDIT ANY	YES
	AUDIT SYSTEM	YES
	BACKUP ANY TABLE	YES
	BECOME USER	YES
	COMMENT ANY TABLE	YES
	CREATE ANY CLUSTER	YES
	CREATE ANY CONTEXT	YES
	CREATE ANY DIMENSION	YES
	CREATE ANY DIRECTORY	YES
	CREATE ANY INDEX	YES
	CREATE ANY INDEXTYPE	YES
	CREATE ANY LIBRARY	YES
	CREATE ANY OPERATOR	YES
	CREATE ANY OUTLINE	YES
	CREATE ANY PROCEDURE	YES
	CREATE ANY SEQUENCE	YES
	CREATE ANY SNAPSHOT	YES
	CREATE ANY SYNONYM	YES
	CREATE ANY TABLE	YES
	CREATE ANY TRIGGER	YES
	CREATE ANY TYPE	YES
	CREATE ANY VIEW	YES
	CREATE CLUSTER	YES
	CREATE DATABASE LINK	YES
	CREATE DIMENSION	YES
	CREATE INDEXTYPE	YES
	CREATE LIBRARY	YES
	CREATE OPERATOR	YES
	CREATE PROCEDURE	YES
	CREATE PROFILE	YES
	CREATE PUBLIC DATABASE LINK	YES

TABLE 9.2 (*Continued*)

Role	Grants	Admin Option?
	CREATE PUBLIC SYNONYM	YES
	CREATE ROLE	YES
	CREATE ROLLBACK SEGMENT	YES
	CREATE SEQUENCE	YES
	CREATE SESSION	YES
	CREATE SNAPSHOT	YES
	CREATE SYNONYM	YES
	CREATE TABLE	YES
	CREATE TABLESPACE	YES
	CREATE TRIGGER	YES
	CREATE TYPE	YES
	CREATE USER	YES
	CREATE VIEW	YES
	DELETE ANY TABLE	YES
	DEQUEUE ANY QUEUE	YES
	DROP ANY CLUSTER	YES
	DROP ANY CONTEXT	YES
	DROP ANY DIMENSION	YES
	DROP ANY DIRECTORY	YES
	DROP ANY INDEX	YES
	DROP ANY INDEXTYPE	YES
	DROP ANY LIBRARY	YES
	DROP ANY OPERATOR	YES
	DROP ANY OUTLINE	YES
	DROP ANY PROCEDURE	YES
	DROP ANY ROLE	YES
	DROP ANY SEQUENCE	YES
	DROP ANY SNAPSHOT	YES
	DROP ANY SYNONYM	YES
	DROP ANY TABLE	YES
	DROP ANY TRIGGER	YES
	DROP ANY TYPE	YES
	DROP ANY VIEW	YES

continued

TABLE 9.2 (Continued)

Role	Grants	Admin Option?
	DROP PROFILE	YES
	DROP PUBLIC DATABASE LINK	YES
	DROP PUBLIC SYNONYM	YES
	DROP ROLLBACK SEGMENT	YES
	DROP TABLESPACE	YES
	DROP USER	YES
	ENQUEUE ANY QUEUE	YES
	EXECUTE ANY INDEXTYPE	YES
	EXECUTE ANY LIBRARY	YES
	EXECUTE ANY OPERATOR	YES
	EXECUTE ANY PROCEDURE	YES
	EXECUTE ANY TYPE	YES
	FORCE ANY TRANSACTION	YES
	FORCE TRANSACTION	YES
	GLOBAL QUERY REWRITE	YES
	GRANT ANY PRIVILEGE	YES
	GRANT ANY ROLE	YES
	INSERT ANY TABLE	YES
	LOCK ANY TABLE	YES
	MANAGE ANY QUEUE	YES
	MANAGE TABLESPACE	YES
	QUERY REWRITE	YES
	RESTRICTED SESSION	YES
	SELECT ANY SEQUENCE	YES
	SELECT ANY TABLE	YES
	UPDATE ANY TABLE	YES
EXP_FULL_DATABASE	ADMINISTER RESOURCE MANAGER	NO
	BACKUP ANY TABLE	NO
	EXECUTE ANY PROCEDURE	NO
	EXECUTE ANY TYPE	NO
	SELECT ANY TABLE	NO
IMP_FULL_DATABASE	ADMINISTER DATABASE TRIGGER	NO
	ADMINISTER RESOURCE MANAGER	NO
	ALTER ANY PROCEDURE	NO

TABLE 9.2 (*Continued*)

Role	Grants	Admin Option?
	ALTER ANY TABLE	NO
	ALTER ANY TRIGGER	NO
	ALTER ANY TYPE	NO
	AUDIT ANY	NO
	BECOME USER	NO
	COMMENT ANY TABLE	NO
	CREATE ANY CLUSTER	NO
	CREATE ANY CONTEXT	NO
	CREATE ANY DIMENSION	NO
	CREATE ANY DIRECTORY	NO
	CREATE ANY INDEX	NO
	CREATE ANY INDEXTYPE	NO
	CREATE ANY LIBRARY	NO
	CREATE ANY OPERATOR	NO
	CREATE ANY PROCEDURE	NO
	CREATE ANY SEQUENCE	NO
	CREATE ANY SNAPSHOT	NO
	CREATE ANY SYNONYM	NO
	CREATE ANY TABLE	NO
	CREATE ANY TRIGGER	NO
	CREATE ANY TYPE	NO
	CREATE ANY VIEW	NO
	CREATE DATABASE LINK	NO
	CREATE PROFILE	NO
	CREATE PUBLIC DATABASE LINK	NO
	CREATE PUBLIC SYNONYM	NO
	CREATE ROLE	NO
	CREATE ROLLBACK SEGMENT	NO
	CREATE TABLESPACE	NO
	CREATE USER	NO
	DROP ANY CLUSTER	NO
	DROP ANY CONTEXT	NO
	DROP ANY DIMENSION	NO

continued

TABLE 9.2 *(Continued)*

Role	Grants	Admin Option?
	DROP ANY DIRECTORY	NO
	DROP ANY INDEX	NO
	DROP ANY INDEXTYPE	NO
	DROP ANY LIBRARY	NO
	DROP ANY OPERATOR	NO
	DROP ANY OUTLINE	NO
	DROP ANY PROCEDURE	NO
	DROP ANY ROLE	NO
	DROP ANY SEQUENCE	NO
	DROP ANY SNAPSHOT	NO
	DROP ANY SYNONYM	NO
	DROP ANY TABLE	NO
	DROP ANY TRIGGER	NO
	DROP ANY TYPE	NO
	DROP ANY VIEW	NO
	DROP PROFILE	NO
	DROP PUBLIC DATABASE LINK	NO
	DROP PUBLIC SYNONYM	NO
	DROP ROLLBACK SEGMENT	NO
	DROP TABLESPACE	NO
	DROP USER	NO
	EXECUTE ANY PROCEDURE	NO
	EXECUTE ANY TYPE	NO
	GLOBAL QUERY REWRITE	NO
	INSERT ANY TABLE	NO
	MANAGE ANY QUEUE	NO
	SELECT ANY TABLE	NO
OUTLN	EXECUTE ANY PROCEDURE	NO
	UNLIMITED TABLESPACE	NO
RECOVERY_CATALOG_OWNER	ALTER SESSION	NO
	CREATE CLUSTER	NO
	CREATE DATABASE LINK	NO
	CREATE PROCEDURE	NO
	CREATE SEQUENCE	NO

TABLE 9.2 *(Continued)*

Role	Grants	Admin Option?
	CREATE SESSION	NO
	CREATE SYNONYM	NO
	CREATE TABLE	NO
	CREATE TRIGGER	NO
	CREATE VIEW	NO
RESOURCE	CREATE CLUSTER	NO
	CREATE INDEXTYPE	NO
	CREATE OPERATOR	NO
	CREATE PROCEDURE	NO
	CREATE SEQUENCE	NO
	CREATE TABLE	NO
	CREATE TRIGGER	NO
	CREATE TYPE	NO
HS_ADMIN_ROLE	(Only table grants)	N/A
SNMPAGENT	ANALYZE ANY	NO

You can grant additional privileges to, or revoke privileges from, the internal roles, including the CONNECT, RESOURCE, and DBA roles, just as you can any other role that you create.

9.4 AUDITING THE DATABASE

Auditing is a method of recording database activity as part of database security. It allows the DBA to track user activity within the database. The audit records will provide information on who performed what database operation and when it was performed. Records are written to a SYS-owned table named AUD$. The SYS.AUD$ table is commonly referred to as the *audit trail*.

It is advisable to copy the AUD$ table into a separate tablespace from other SYS-owned objects. In some cases, the AUD$ table should be owned by a user other than SYS. There are three reasons for these two statements:

- The AUD$ table, if auditing is used, may grow to a very large size, depending on the audit options selected.
- In some situations, you may want to add a trigger to the AUD$ table to count logins, monitor for specific actions (prior to 8*i*), or perform other security-related functions (such as implement password-checking functionality prior to version 8). Remember, you can't add triggers to catalog objects owned by SYS.

- Since the table will grow and shrink and be high activity, it is advisable to move it from the SYSTEM tablespace to avoid fragmentation.

Auditing information is not collected without some impact on performance and database resources. How much of an impact auditing will have on your system depends largely on the type of auditing you enable. For example, setting high-level auditing such as connection activity will not have as much of a performance impact as tracking all SQL statements issued by all users. It is best to start out with high-level auditing and then refine additional auditing as needed.

You can audit all users with the exception of SYS and CONNECT INTERNAL. Auditing can only be performed for users connected directly to the database, not for actions on a remote database.

On some versions of Oracle7 (7.3.2 to 7.3.3) operating system-level auditing of SYS and INTERNAL logins was initiated automatically on install. Auditing at operating system level (EPC_DISABLE=FALSE) results in a small audit file being generated in an operating system-specific directory location for each use of SYS or INTERNAL. This system-level auditing also may result in longer and longer login times for all users as the files process.dat, regid.dat, and so on, in the $ORACLE_HOME/otrace/admin directory on UNIX, or orant\otrave73\admin on NT, expand in size. This is disabled by dropping the *.dat files in the previously mentioned locations, shutting down the instance, typing otrccref from the command line to reinitiate the files, and then setting the environmental variable EPC_DISABLED to TRUE (EPC_DISABLED=TRUE (Borne shell), setenv EPC_DISABLED TRUE (C shell), and restarting the instance(s).

Auditing should be enabled if the following types of questionable activities are noted:

- Unexplained changes in passwords, tablespace settings, or quotas appear.
- Excessive deadlocks are encountered.
- Records are being read, deleted, or changed without authorization.

There are three types of auditing:

- Statement auditing
- Privilege auditing
- Object auditing

Enabling and Disabling Auditing

The database initialization parameter AUDIT_TRAIL controls the enabling and disabling of auditing. The default setting for this parameter is NONE, which means that no auditing will be performed, regardless of whether or not AUDIT commands are issued. It is important to remember that any auditing statements issued will not be performed if AUDIT_TRAIL=NONE. Unless auditing is enabled in the database parameter initialization file, any auditing options that have been turned on will not create records in the audit trail. Auditing is not completely disabled unless it is set to NONE in the database parameter initialization file.

You must set the database initialization parameter AUDIT_TRAIL to DB or OS in order to enable auditing. The DB setting means the audit trail records are stored in the database in the SYS.AUD$ table. OS will send the audit trail records to an operating system file. The OS setting is operating system-dependent and is not supported on all operating systems.

Auditing can be performed based on whether statements are executed successfully or unsuccessfully. Auditing WHEN SUCCESSFUL inserts records into the audit trail only if the SQL command executes successfully. Auditing WHEN NOT SUCCESSFUL inserts records into the audit trail only when the SQL statement is unsuccessful. If a statement is unsuccessful due to syntax errors, it will not be included in the audit trail. If neither WHEN SUCCESSFUL or WHEN NOT SUCCESSFUL is specified, both successful and unsuccessful actions will be audited.

Auditing can be set BY SESSION or BY ACCESS. When you use the BY SESSION option for statement or privilege auditing, it writes a single record to the audit trail when a connection is made. When the session is disconnected, that record is updated with cumulative information about the session. The information collected includes connection time, disconnection time, and logical and physical I/Os processed. Audit options set BY SESSION for objects insert one record per database object into the audit trail for each session. When you set auditing BY ACCESS, a record is inserted into the audit trail for each statement issued. All auditing of DDL statements will be audited BY ACCESS regardless of whether you have set auditing BY ACCESS or BY SESSION.

The BY USER option allows you to limit auditing to a specific user or list of users. When you do not specify BY USER, all users will be audited.

When you change auditing options, they become active for subsequent sessions, not current sessions. Any existing sessions will continue to use the auditing options in effect when they logged in to the database.

The syntax to enable statement and privilege auditing is:

```
AUDIT system_priv_list|statement_opt_list
[BY user_list|proxy[ ON BEHALF OF user|ANY]]
[BY SESSION|ACCESS] [WHENEVER [NOT]SUCCESSFUL]
```

The following are the options listed in the syntax diagram for statement auditing:

```
statement_opt_list

CREATE|ALTER|DROP|TRUNCATE CLUSTER
CREATE|DROP[PUBLIC}DATABASE LINK
NOT EXISTS
CREATE|ALTER|DROP INDEX
CREATE|DROP PROCEDURE|FUNCTION|LIBRARY|PACKAGE|PACKAGE BODY
CREATE|ALTER|SET|DROP ROLE
CREATE|ALTER|DROP ROLLBACK SEGMENT
CREATE|ALTER|DROP SEQUENCE
```

```
SESSION
CREATE|DROP [PUBLIC]SYNONYM
SYSTEM AUDIT [NO]AUDIT sql_statements
SYSTEM GRANT
     GRANT system_priv_and_roles|REVOKE system_priv_and_roles
CREATE|ALTER|DROP|TRUNCATE|COMMENT ON|DELETE [FROM] TABLE
CREATE|ALTER|DROP TABLESPACE
CREATE|ALTER {ENABLE|DISABLE]|DROP TRIGGER
     (And ALTER TABLE ENABLE|DISABLE ALL TRIGGERS)
CREATE||ALTER|DROP TYPE [BODY] (ALTER TYPE BODY N/A)
CREATE|ALTER|DROP USER
CREATE|DROP VIEW
addl_stmt_opt =
GRANT and REVOKE commands on:
EXECUTE PROCEDURE
INSERT|LOCK|SELECT|DELETE|UPDATE|ALTER TABLE
ALTER|SELECT SEQUENCE
READ DIRECTORY
GRANT TYPE
SELECT SEQUENCE
COMMENT ON TABLE|COMMENT ON COLUMN
```

For example:

```
AUDIT DELETE TABLE, INSERT TABLE,
       EXECUTE ANY PROCEDURE
       BY beth
       BY ACCESS
WHENEVER SUCCESSFUL;
```

The syntax to disable statement and privilege auditing is:

```
NOAUDIT system_priv_list|statement_opt_list
[BY user_list|proxy[ ON BEHALF OF user|ANY]]
[WHENEVER [NOT]SUCCESSFUL]
```

For example:

```
NOAUDIT DELETE TABLE, INSERT TABLE,
       EXECUTE ANY PROCEDURE
BY app_user
WHENEVER SUCCESSFUL;
```

The syntax to enable object auditing is:

```
AUDIT object_opt_list|ALL
ON [schema.]object_name|DIRECTORY dir_name|DEFAULT
[BY SESSION|ACCESS][WHENEVER [NOT]SUCCESSFUL]
```

For example:

```
AUDIT SELECT, INSERT, DELETE
ON scott.dept
WHENEVER NOTSUCCESSFUL;
```

The syntax to disable object auditing is:

```
NOAUDIT object_opt_list|ALL
ON [schema.]object_name|DIRECTORY dir_name|DEFAULT
[BY SESSION|ACCESS][WHENEVER [NOT]SUCCESSFUL]
```

For example:

```
NOAUDIT SELECT, INSERT, DELETE
ON scott.dept
WHENEVER SUCCESSFUL;
```

Using Statement Auditing

Statement auditing involves tracking the SQL statements issued by database users. In order to enable or disable auditing on SQL statements, you must have the AUDIT SYSTEM privilege.

In addition to the statement-auditing options shown previously, there are several options that will create audit records for a combination of statements. These options, sometimes referred to as *audit shortcuts*, are CONNECT, RESOURCE, DBA, and ALL. When these shortcuts are specified, all grants given through the specified role will be audited.

The audit shortcuts are useful for setting up auditing for multiple options with one command. For example:

```
AUDIT RESOURCE
WHENEVER NOT SUCCESSFUL;
```

will audit all the commands listed for ALTER SYSTEM, CLUSTER, DATABASE LINK, PROCEDURE, ROLLBACK SEGMENT, SEQUENCE, SYNONYM, TABLE, TABLE SPACE, TYPE, and VIEW for all users when the command does not successfully complete.

NOTE   Be careful that you do not confuse these shortcuts with the roles named CONNECT, RESOURCE, and DBA. Also note that these shortcuts are provided for compatibility with earlier versions of Oracle and may not be supported in future versions.

Using Privilege Auditing

Privilege auditing involves the tracking of the SQL statements issued by users who have been granted the right to execute that statement through a system privilege. In order to enable or disable auditing on SQL statements, you must have the AUDIT SYSTEM privilege. Privilege audit options match the corresponding system privileges. For example, in order to audit the DELETE ANY TABLE system privilege, you would issue the following command:

```
AUDIT DELETE ANY TABLE
BY ACCESS
WHENEVER SUCCESSFUL;
```

Using Object Auditing

Object auditing involves the tracking of the specific SQL DML statements issued against objects by database users. In order to enable or disable auditing on objects, you must have the AUDIT ANY system privilege or own the object. The following objects can be audited: tables, views, sequences, packages, standalone stored procedures and stand-alone functions, directories, libraries, and types. Since views and procedures may contain statements that reference multiple objects, they may generate multiple records in the audit trail. You cannot limit object auditing with the BY USER clause; all users will be audited for the object.

Managing the Audit Trail

Audit records are written when the statement is executed. Even if a statement or transaction is rolled back, the audit trail record remains. Auditing BY SESSION will write only one record to the audit trail. Auditing BY ACCESS will write multiple records, one for each time the action is executed.

The audit trail grows according to the following factors:

- The number of audit options enabled
- The number of audited actions issued

You need to control the growth of the audit trail with the following methods:

- Enable and disable auditing options.
- Be selective in deciding which auditing to turn on.
- Control who can perform auditing.

In order to control the auditing of objects, Oracle recommends that all objects be owned by a separate schema that does not correspond to an actual user and that is not granted CONNECT SESSION. This will prevent anyone from connecting as the owner of these objects and turning on auditing for the objects. The AUDIT ANY system privilege should not be granted to anyone except the security administrator. An alternate method is to have all the objects owned by the security administrator.

If the audit trail record cannot be written, the audited action will not be executed and errors will be generated. If connections are being audited and the audit trail table (SYS.AUD$) is full, users will not be allowed to log in to the database. The DBA can CONNECT INTERNAL using Server Manager in either GUI or command-line mode and clean out the audit trail.

You should develop an auditing strategy by evaluating the purpose of the auditing and be conservative in the auditing performed. When auditing is being set to investigate possible problems, begin with general auditing and then narrow it down to specific actions. If the purpose of the audit is to provide a record of historical activity, remember to archive (to another table or an export file) and purge data on a regular basis. You can selectively insert records to another table if only a subset needs to be maintained.

Take these recommended steps to truncate the audit trail:

1. Copy any subset of records you may need to keep into a temporary table, or export the entire SYS.AUD$ table.
2. CONNECT INTERNAL.
3. Truncate the SYS.AUD$ table.
4. Insert records from the temporary table back into SYS.AUD$.

To protect the audit trail, AUDIT insert, update, and delete on SYS.AUD$ BY ACCESS (or in whichever user you have created the AUD$ table) so that records cannot be added, changed, or deleted without that action being audited. Even if a user is able to delete records from SYS.AUD$, he or she will not be able to delete the records generated by his or her actions without creating additional audit records. In addition, users should not be granted DELETE ANY TABLE system privilege. Always protect the audit trail (SYS.AUD$).

The maximum size allowed for an audit trail written to the database is determined at the time the database is created. By default, the size reflects the system tablespace default values. The sql.bsq script, which is executed when the database is created, sets the size of the SYS.AUD$ table. It is very important that the audit trail be cleaned up regularly. You should export the data and truncate the SYS.AUD$ table on a regular basis.

If you want to implement processes such as notification when a user logs on, checking of passwords, automated invalidation of passwords, and you don't have Oracle8 or later, you will want to move the AUD$ table out of the SYS user so that triggers can be created against it. By creating an ON INSERT trigger that monitors for specific event codes in the AUD$ table, you can then use that trigger to implement specific database actions.

Follow these steps to create the AUD$ table in a different user:

1. Turn off auditing.
2. Export the current records in the AUD$ table.
3. Drop the SYS.AUD$ table.

4. Create the new AUD$ table either under SYS in a different tablespace or as a different user.

5. If step 4 created an AUD$ table in a different user, grant all on that AUD$ to SYS user.

6. If step 4 created an AUD$ table in a different user, create a private synonym, AUD$, pointing to that user's AUD$ table in the SYS user.

Viewing Audit Trail Information

On most operating systems, special views on SYS.AUD$ are created when the catalog. sql script (which calls several scripts, including cataudit.sql) is executed. For other operating systems, you can create these views by executing the script cataudit.sql. To remove the audit views, you can execute the script catnoaud.sql.

The following notations are used in the audit trail views:

<NULL>. Audit is not set.

S. Audit by SESSION.

A. Audit by ACCESS.

/. Separates the two settings. The first setting is for WHENEVER SUCCESSFUL; the second setting is for WHENEVER NOT SUCCESSFUL.

Examples:

<NULL>/<NULL>. No auditing.

A/<NULL>. Auditing BY ACCESS WHENEVER SUCCESSFUL.

<NULL>/A. Auditing BY ACCESS WHENEVER NOT SUCCESSFUL.

S/<NULL>. Auditing BY SESSION WHENEVER SUCCESSFUL.

<NULL>/S. Auditing BY SESSION WHENEVER NOT SUCCESSFUL.

A/S. Auditing BY ACCESS WHENEVER SUCCESSFUL and BY SESSION WHENEVER NOT SUCCESSFUL.

S/A. Auditing BY SESSION WHENEVER SUCCESSFUL and BY ACCESS WHENEVER NOT SUCCESSFUL.

Several views contain a column called ses_actions. The ses_actions column is a summary for the actions included in that entry. The ses_actions column is an 11-character code, where the letter S means success, F means failure, B means both, and none indicates not audited. The character codes appear in alphabetical order:

Alter, Audit, Comment, Delete, Grant, Index, Insert, Lock, Rename, Select, Update

The audit views fall into several categories: general information on auditing performed, statement audit information, privilege audit information, and object audit information.

There are four general auditing views:

AUDIT_ACTIONS. Maps audit trail action types to codes.

STMT_AUDIT_OPTION_MAP. Maps auditing option types to codes.

DBA_AUDIT_TRAIL. All audit records in the system.

USER_AUDIT_TRAIL. Audit trail entries relevant to the user.

For statement auditing, the following views are useful:

DBA_STMT_AUDIT_OPTS. Information on current system-auditing options across the system and by user.

DBA_AUDIT_STATEMENT. Audit entries for statements with the GRANT, REVOKE, AUDIT, NOAUDIT, and ALTER SYSTEM commands.

USER_AUDIT_STATEMENT. Audit entries for statements issued by the user.

DBA_AUDIT_SESSION. Audit entries for connections and disconnections.

USER_AUDIT_SESSION. Audit entries for connections and disconnections for that user.

DBA_AUDIT_EXISTS. Audit entries created by the AUDIT EXISTS command.

For privilege auditing, the DBA_PRIV_AUDIT_OPTS view shows the privilege option audit entries. There is one entry for each audited privilege. For object auditing, the relevant views are:

DBA_OBJ_AUDIT_OPTS. Auditing options set for all tables and views.

USER_OBJ_AUDIT_OPTS. Auditing options for the owner's tables and views (corresponds to the DBA_OBJ_AUDIT_OPTS view).

ALL_DEF_AUDIT_OPTS. Default audit options for objects being created.

DBA_AUDIT_OBJECT. Audit records for all objects in the system.

USER_AUDIT_OBJECT. Audit trail records for statements concerning objects owned by that user (corresponds to the DBA_AUDIT_OBJECT view).

Auditing by Database Triggers

Enabling auditing options may not always be sufficient to evaluate suspicious activity within your database. When you enable auditing, Oracle places records in the SYS.AUD$ table in accordance with the auditing options that you have specified. One limitation to this type of auditing is that SYS.AUD$ does not provide you with value-based information. You need to write triggers to record the before and after values on a per-row basis.

Auditing with Oracle supports DML and DDL statements on objects and structures. Triggers support DML statements issued against objects, and can be used to record the actual values before and after the statement.

In some facilities, audit commands are considered *security audit utilities*, while triggers are referred to as *financial auditing*. This is because triggers can provide a method to track actual changes to values in a table. Although, similar to the AUDIT command, you can use triggers to record information, you should customize your auditing by using triggers only when you need more detailed audit information.

AFTER triggers are normally used to avoid unnecessary statement generation for actions that fail due to integrity constraints. AFTER triggers are executed only after all integrity constraints have been checked. AFTER ROW triggers provide value-based auditing for each row of the tables and support the use of "reason codes." A reason for the statement or transaction, along with the user, sysdate, and old and new values, can be inserted into another table for auditing purposes.

Oracle auditing can be used for successful and unsuccessful actions, as well as connections, disconnections, and session I/O activities. With auditing, you can decide if the actions should be BY ACCESS or BY SESSION. Triggers can only audit successful actions against the table on which they are created. If auditing is being performed using a trigger, any rollback or unsuccessful action will not be recorded.

Auditing provides an easy, error-free method to tracking, with all the audit records stored in one place. Triggers are more difficult to create and maintain.

9.5 MANAGING RESOURCES WITH PROFILES

You can establish limits on the system resources consumed by setting up profiles with defined limits on resources. Profiles are very useful in large, complex organizations with many users. It allows you, the DBA, to regulate the amount of resources consumed by each database user by creating and assigning profiles to users. Under Oracle8, password attributes were added to the profile capability.

Creation of Profiles

Profiles comprise a named set of resource limits. By default, when you create users, they are given the default profile, which provides unlimited use of all resources.

The syntax to create a profile follows:

```
CREATE PROFILE profile LIMIT resource_parameters|password_parameters;
Resource_parameters:
[SESSIONS_PER_USER n|UNLIMITED|DEFAULT]
[CPU_PER_SESSION n|UNLIMITED|DEFAULT]
[CPU_PER_CALL n|UNLIMITED|DEFAULT]
[CONNECT_TIME              n|UNLIMITED|DEFAULT]
[IDLE_TIME                 n|UNLIMITED|DEFAULT]
[LOGICAL_READS_PER_SESSION n|UNLIMITED|DEFAULT]
[LOGICAL_READS_PER_CALL    n|UNLIMITED|DEFAULT]
[COMPOSITE_LIMIT           n|UNLIMITED|DEFAULT]
[PRIVATE_SGA               n [K|M]|UNLIMITED|DEFAULT]
```

```
Password_parameters (Oracle8 and above):
 [FAILED_LOGIN_ATTEMPTS expr|UNLIMITED|DEFAULT]
 [PASSWORD_LIFE_TIME      expr|UNLIMITED|DEFAULT]
 [PASSWORD_REUSE_TIME     expr|UNLIMITED|DEFAULT]
 [PASSWORD_REUSE_MAX      expr|UNLIMITED|DEFAULT]
 [PASSWORD_LOCK_TIME      expr|UNLIMITED|DEFAULT]
 [PASSWORD_GRACE_TIME     expr|UNLIMITED|DEFAULT]
 [PASSWORD_VERIFY_FUNCTION function_name|NULL|DEFAULT]
```

Restrictions on password parameters are as follows:

- expr must resolve to either an integer value or an integer number of days.
- If PASSWORD_REUSE_TIME is set to an integer value, PASSWORD_REUSE_MAX must be set to UNLIMITED.
- If PASSWORD_REUSE_MAX is set to an integer value, PASSWORD_REUSE_TIME must be set to UNLIMITED.
- If both PASSWORD_REUSE_TIME and PASSWORD_REUSE_MAX are set to UNLIMITED, then Oracle uses neither of these password resources.
- If PASSWORD_REUSE_MAX is set to DEFAULT, and PASSWORD_REUSE_TIME is set to UNLIMITED, then Oracle uses the PASSWORD_REUSE_MAX value defined in the DEFAULT profile.
- If PASSWORD_REUSE_TIME is set to DEFAULT, and PASSWORD_REUSE_MAX is set to UNLIMITED, then Oracle uses the PASSWORD_REUSE_TIME value defined in the DEFAULT profile.
- If both PASSWORD_REUSE_TIME and PASSWORD_REUSE_MAX are set to DEFAULT, then Oracle uses whichever value is defined in the DEFAULT profile.

For example:

```
CREATE PROFILE  enduser  LIMIT
CPU_PER_SESSION  60000
LOGICAL_READS_PER_SESSION   1000
CONNECT_TIME   30
PRIVATE_SGA   102400
CPU_PER_CALL   UNLIMITED
COMPOSITE LIMIT   60000000
FAILED_LOGIN_ATTEMPTS   3
PASSWORD_LIFE_TIME   90
PASSWORD_REUSE_TIME   180
PASSWORD_LOCK_TIME   3
PASSWORD_GRACE_TIME   3
PASSWORD_VERIFY_FUNCTION ;
```

You can assign a profile to a user when you create the user or by altering the user. The syntax to alter the profile for a user is:

```
ALTER USER PROFILE profile;
```

For example:

```
ALTER USER scott
PROFILE appuser;
```

You must have the CREATE PROFILE system privilege to create a profile. To alter a profile you must be the creator of the profile or have the ALTER PROFILE system privilege. To assign a profile to a user, you must have the CREATE USER or ALTER USER system privilege.

Profiles and Resource Limits

The default cost assigned to a resource is unlimited, but you can also assign a composite cost to each profile. By setting resource limits, you can prevent users from performing operations that will tie up the system, and prevent other users from performing operations. You can use resource limits for security, to ensure that users log off the system, so as not to leave the session connected for long periods of time.

The system resource limits can be enforced at the session level, the call level, or both. The session level is calculated from the time the user logs in to the database until the user exits. The call level applies to each SQL command issued. Session-level limits are enforced for each connection. When a session level limit is exceeded, only the last SQL command issued is rolled back; no further work can be performed until a commit, rollback, or exit is performed. Table 9.3 lists the system resources that can be regulated at the session level.

NOTE   If you use parallel query option (PQO), the resources will be applied to each new session, not accumulated over all of the sessions used by a parallel operation.

Call-level limits are enforced during the execution of each SQL statement. When a call-level limit is exceeded, the last SQL command issued is rolled back. All the previous statements issued continue to be valid, and the user can continue to execute other SQL statements. The following system resources can be regulated at the call level:

- CPU_PER_CALL, for the CPU time for the SQL statement
- LOGICAL_READS_PER_CALL, for the number of data blocks read for the SQL statement

The assignment of a cost to a resource can be performed with the ALTER RESOURCE COST command. Resource limits that you set explicitly for a user take precedence over the resource costs in an assigned profile. The command-line syntax for this command is:

TABLE 9.3   Resources Regulated at the Session Level

SYSTEM RESOURCE	*DEFINITION*
CPU_PER_SESSION	Total CPU time in hundreds of seconds
SESSIONS_PER_USER	Number of concurrent sessions for a user
CONNECT_TIME	Allowed connection time in minutes
IDLE_TIME	Inactive time on the server in minutes
LOGICAL_READS_PER_SESSION	Number of data blocks read, including both physical and logical reads from memory and disk
PRIVATE_SGA	Bytes of SGA used in a database with the multithreaded server (in KB or MB)

Note: You can combine the CPU_PER_SESSION, LOGICAL_READS_PER_SESSION, CONNECT_TIME, and PRIVATE_SGA to create a COMPOSITE LIMIT.

```
ALTER RESOURCE COST
[CPU_PER_SESSION n|UNLIMITED|DEFAULT]
[CONNECT_TIME n|UNLIMITED|DEFAULT]
[LOGICAL_READS_PER_SESSION n|UNLIMITED|DEFAULT]
[PRIVATE_SGA  n [K|M]|UNLIMITED|DEFAULT];
```

For example:

```
ALTER RESOURCE COST CONNECT_TIME 100;
```

The use of resource limits is set in the database initialization parameter RESOURCE_LIMIT=TRUE. By default, this parameter is set to FALSE. This parameter can be changed interactively with an ALTER SYSTEM command.

The DBA_PROFILES view provides information on all the profiles and the resource limits for each profile. The RESOURCE_COST view shows the unit cost associated with each resource. Each user can find information on his or her resources and limits in the USER_RESOURCE_LIMITS view.

Altering Profiles

Provided you have the CREATE PROFILE or ALTER PROFILE system privilege, you can alter any profile, including the Oracle-created DEFAULT profile. You can alter a profile to change the cost assigned to each resource. The syntax to alter a profile follows:

```
ALTER PROFILE profile LIMIT resource_parameters|password_parameters;

Resource_parameters:

 [SESSIONS_PER_USER n|UNLIMITED|DEFAULT]
 [CPU_PER_SESSION   n|UNLIMITED|DEFAULT]
```

```
[CPU_PER_CALL          n|UNLIMITED|DEFAULT]
[CONNECT_TIME          n|UNLIMITED|DEFAULT]
[IDLE_TIME             n|UNLIMITED|DEFAULT]
[LOGICAL_READS_PER_SESSION n|UNLIMITED|DEFAULT]
[LOGICAL_READS_PER_CALL    n|UNLIMITED|DEFAULT]
[COMPOSITE_LIMIT           n|UNLIMITED|DEFAULT]
[PRIVATE_SGA               n [K|M|UNLIMITED|DEFAULT]]

Password_parameters (Oracle8 and above):

[FAILED_LOGIN_ATTEMPTS expr|UNLIMITED|DEFAULT]
[PASSWORD_LIFE_TIME     expr|UNLIMITED|DEFAULT]
[PASSWORD_REUSE_TIME    expr|UNLIMITED|DEFAULT]
[PASSWORD_REUSE_MAX     expr|UNLIMITED|DEFAULT]
[PASSWORD_LOCK_TIME     expr|UNLIMITED|DEFAULT]
[PASSWORD_GRACE_TIME    expr|UNLIMITED|DEFAULT]
[PASSWORD_VERIFY_FUNCTION function_name|NULL|DEFAULT]
```

For example:

```
ALTER PROFILE enduser LIMIT
CPU_PER_SESSION 60000
LOGICAL_READS_PER_SESSION 1000
CONNECT_TIME 60
PRIVATE_SGA 102400
CPU_PER_CALL UNLIMITED
COMPOSITE LIMIT 60000000;
```

To disable a profile during a session, you must have the ALTER SYSTEM privilege. A limit that you set for the session overrides the previous limit set by the profile. To reset the profile to the limit originally set by the database, set the limit to DEFAULT.

```
ALTER SYSTEM SET RESOURCE_LIMIT =  TRUE|FALSE;
```

For example:

```
ALTER SYSTEM SET RESOURCE_LIMIT = TRUE ;
```

Profiles and Passwords

The capability to control password expiry and password complexity and validity was added to Oracle8. The capability to control passwords is contained within the purview of the profile. Table 9.4 lists the password control attributes in a profile and their definitions.

Oracle also provides a template PL/SQL procedure for use in creating your own password complexity and verification function. The sample PL/SQL procedure is located in $ORACLE_HOME/rdbms/admin/utlpwdmg.sql on UNIX and in x:\orant\ rdbms\ admin\utlpwdmg.sql on NT. Any script you use must follow the general template shown in Listing 9.1.

TABLE 9.4 Password Control Attributes in a Profile

Attribute	Description
FAILED_LOGIN_ATTEMPTS	Specifies the number of failed attempts to log in to the user account before the account is locked.
PASSWORD_LIFE_TIME	Limits the number of days the same password can be used for authentication. The password expires if it is not changed within this period, and further connections are rejected.
PASSWORD_REUSE_TIME	Specifies the number of days before which a password cannot be reused. If you set PASSWORD_REUSE_TIME to an integer value, then you must set PASSWORD_REUSE_MAX to UNLIMITED.
PASSWORD_REUSE_MAX	Specifies the number of password changes required before the current password can be reused. If you set PASSWORD_REUSE_MAX to an integer value, then you must set PASSWORD_REUSE_TIME to UNLIMITED.
PASSWORD_LOCK_TIME	Specifies the number of days an account will be locked after the specified number of consecutive failed login attempts.
PASSWORD_GRACE_TIME	Specifies the number of days after the grace period begins during which a warning is issued and login is allowed. If the password is not changed during the grace period, the password expires.
PASSWORD_VERIFY_FUNCTION	Allows a PL/SQL password complexity verification script to be passed as an argument to the CREATE PROFILE statement. Oracle provides a default script, but you can create your own routine or use third-party software instead. FUNCTION is the name of the password complexity verification routine. NULL indicates that no password verification is performed.

Listing 9.1   Required function input and return variables.

```
CREATE OR REPLACE FUNCTION <function_name>
(username varchar2,
 password varchar2,
 old_password varchar2)
  RETURN boolean IS
BEGIN
...
RETURN <boolean value>;
END;
```

Other than the required input and return variables, the password verification function can be as simple or as complex as you desire.

9.6 ORACLE RESOURCE GROUPS

Oracle8*i* added the concept of Oracle resource groups. A resource group specification allows you to specify that a given group of database users can use only a certain percentage of the CPU resources on the system. A resource plan must be developed in a waterfall-type structure that defines the various levels within the application and their percentage allotment of CPU resources, where each subsequent level's percentage is based on the previous level.

Creating a Resource Plan

Rather than a simple CREATE RESOURCE PLAN command, Oracle8*i* has a series of packages that must be run in a specific order to create a proper resource plan. All resource plans are created in a pending area before being validated and committed to the database. The requirements for a valid resource plan are outlined later in section titled "DBMS_RESOURCE_MANAGER Package."

Resource plans can have up to 32 levels with 32 groups per level, allowing the most complex resource plan to be easily grouped. Multiple plans, subplans, and groups can all be tied together in an application, spanning CPU resource utilization rule set through the use of directives.

Creating a Resource Plan Manually

By manually creating a resource plan, you can change the resource allocations for the active session pool, which defaults to 1000000; the queuing resources for sessions, which defaults to 1000000; the maximum estimated execution time, which defaults to 1000000; and the undo pool allocation, which, as you have probably guessed, defaults to 1000000. If you use the Oracle Enterprise Manager to create and maintain plans, you are limited to controlling CPU allocation and parallel process allocation only. An example resource plan would be a simple two-tier plan like that shown in Figure 9.1.

An example of how this apportioning of CPU resources works would be to examine what happens in the plan shown in Figure 9.1. There, the top level, called MASTER, will have 100 percent of the CPU. The next level of the plan creates two subplans, USERS and REPORTS, which will get 60 and 20 percent of the CPU, respectively. Under USERS, are two groups, ONLINE_USERS and BATCH_USERS: ONLINE_USERS gets 70 percent of USERS' 60 percent, or an overall percentage of CPU of 42 percent; the other subgroup, BATCH_USERS, gets 30 percent of the 60 percent, for a total overall percentage of 18.

The manual steps for creating a resource plan, its directives, and its groups are shown in Figure 9.2. Notice here that the last step shows several possible packages that can be run to assign or change the assignment of resource groups. The first package

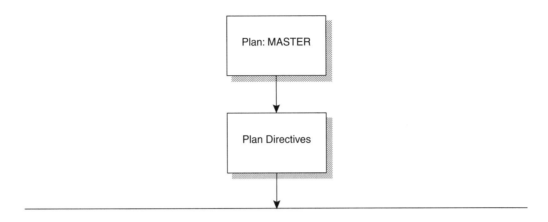

Set level CPU_P1 in directive

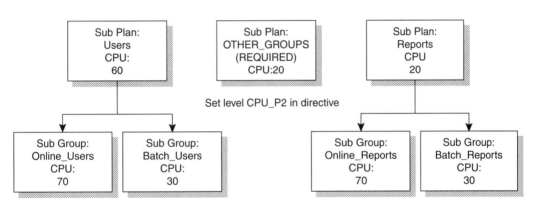

FIGURE 9.1   Example of a resource plan.

listed, DBMS_RESOURCE_MANAGER_PRIVS.GRANT_SWITCH_CONSUMER_GROUP, must be run the first time a user is assigned to a resource group or you won't be able to assign the user to the group. After the user has been given the SWITCH_CON-SUMER_GROUP system privilege, you don't have to rerun the package. Source 9.1 shows the code to manually create the resource plan in Figure 9.2. Listing 9.2 shows the results from running the source in Source 9.1.

Notice that the script in Source 9.1 follows the chart in Figure 9.2. These are the proper steps to create a resource plan.

The other operations allowed against the components of the resource plan are ALTER and DROP. Let's look at a drop example in Source 9.2.

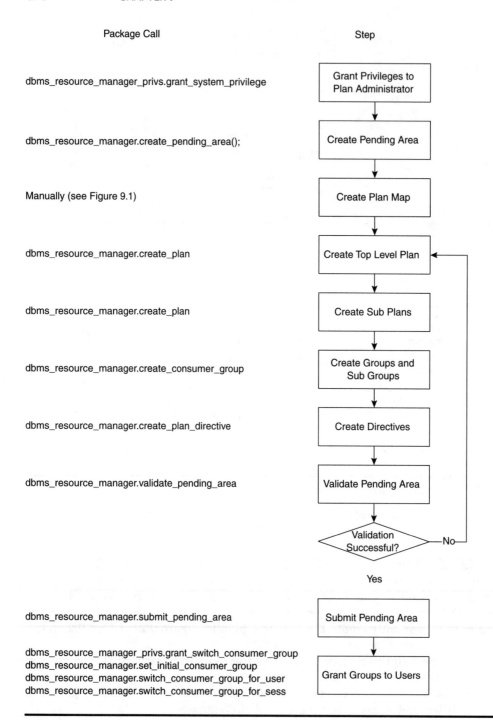

Package Call

Step

dbms_resource_manager_privs.grant_system_privilege → Grant Privileges to Plan Administrator

dbms_resource_manager.create_pending_area(); → Create Pending Area

Manually (see Figure 9.1) → Create Plan Map

dbms_resource_manager.create_plan → Create Top Level Plan

dbms_resource_manager.create_plan → Create Sub Plans

dbms_resource_manager.create_consumer_group → Create Groups and Sub Groups

dbms_resource_manager.create_plan_directive → Create Directives

dbms_resource_manager.validate_pending_area → Validate Pending Area

Validation Successful? —No

Yes

dbms_resource_manager.submit_pending_area → Submit Pending Area

dbms_resource_manager_privs.grant_switch_consumer_group
dbms_resource_manager.set_initial_consumer_group
dbms_resource_manager.switch_consumer_group_for_user
dbms_resource_manager.switch_consumer_group_for_sess → Grant Groups to Users

FIGURE 9.2 Steps to create a resource plan.

Source 9.1   Script to create a sample resource plan.

```
set echo on
spool test_resource_plan.doc
-- Grant system privilege to plan administrator
--
execute
dbms_resource_manager_privs.grant_system_privilege('SYSTEM','ADMINISTER_RESOURCE_
MANAGER',TRUE);
--
--connect to plan administrator
--
CONNECT system/system_test@ortest1.world
--
-- Create Plan Pending Area
--
EXECUTE dbms_resource_manager.create_pending_area();
--
-- Create plan
--
execute dbms_resource_manager.create_plan('MASTER','Example Resource
Plan','EMPHASIS');
execute dbms_resource_manager.create_plan('USERS','Example Resource Sub
Plan','EMPHASIS');
execute dbms_resource_manager.create_plan('REPORTS','Example Resource Sub
Plan','EMPHASIS');
--
--Create tiers of groups in plan
--
EXECUTE dbms_resource_manager.create_consumer_group('ONLINE_USERS','3rd level
group','ROUND-ROBIN');
EXECUTE dbms_resource_manager.create_consumer_group('BATCH_USERS','3rd level
group','ROUND-ROBIN');
EXECUTE dbms_resource_manager.create_consumer_group('ONLINE_REPORTS','2nd
level group','ROUND-ROBIN');
EXECUTE dbms_resource_manager.create_consumer_group('BATCH_REPORTS','2nd
level group','ROUND-ROBIN');
--
-- Create plan directives
--
EXECUTE dbms_resource_manager.create_plan_directive('MASTER', 'USERS',
0,60,0,0,0,0,0,0,NULL);
EXECUTE dbms_resource_manager.create_plan_directive('MASTER', 'REPORTS',
0,20,0,0,0,0,0,0,NULL);
EXECUTE dbms_resource_manager.create_plan_directive('MASTER','OTHER_GROUPS',
0,20,0,0,0,0,0,0,NULL);
EXECUTE dbms_resource_manager.create_plan_directive('USERS',   'ONLINE_USERS',
0,0,70,0,0,0,0,0,NULL);
EXECUTE dbms_resource_manager.create_plan_directive('USERS',   'BATCH_USERS',
0,0,30,0,0,0,0,0,NULL);
```

continues

Source 9.1   Continued.

```
EXECUTE
dbms_resource_manager.create_plan_directive('REPORTS','ONLINE_REPORTS',0,0,70
,0,0,0,0,0,NULL);
EXECUTE
dbms_resource_manager.create_plan_directive('REPORTS','BATCH_REPORTS',
0,0,30,0,0,0,0,0,NULL);
--
-- Verify Plan
--
EXECUTE dbms_resource_manager.validate_pending_area;
--
-- Submit Plan
--
EXECUTE dbms_resource_manager.submit_pending_area;
spool off
set echo off
```

Listing 9.2   Example of a script run to create a sample resource plan.

```
SQL> -- Grant system privilege to plan administrator
SQL> --
SQL> execute
dbms_resource_manager_privs.grant_system_privilege('SYSTEM','ADMINISTER_RESOU
RCE_MANAGER',TRUE);

PL/SQL procedure successfully completed.

SQL> --
SQL> --connect to plan administrator
SQL> --
SQL> CONNECT system/system_test@ortest1.world
Connected.
SQL> --
SQL> -- Create Plan Pending Area
SQL> --
SQL> EXECUTE dbms_resource_manager.create_pending_area();

PL/SQL procedure successfully completed.

SQL> --
SQL> -- Create plan
SQL> --
SQL> execute dbms_resource_manager.create_plan('MASTER','Example Resource
Plan','EMPHASIS');

PL/SQL procedure successfully completed.
```

```
SQL> execute dbms_resource_manager.create_plan('USERS','Example Resource Sub
Plan','EMPHASIS');

PL/SQL procedure successfully completed.

SQL> execute dbms_resource_manager.create_plan('REPORTS','Example Resource
Sub Plan','EMPHASIS');

PL/SQL procedure successfully completed.

SQL> --
SQL> --Create tiers of groups in plan
SQL> --
SQL> EXECUTE dbms_resource_manager.create_consumer_group('ONLINE_USERS','3rd
level group','ROUND-ROBIN');

PL/SQL procedure successfully completed.

SQL> EXECUTE dbms_resource_manager.create_consumer_group('BATCH_USERS','3rd
level group','ROUND-ROBIN');

PL/SQL procedure successfully completed.

SQL> EXECUTE
dbms_resource_manager.create_consumer_group('ONLINE_REPORTS','2nd level
group','ROUND-ROBIN');

PL/SQL procedure successfully completed.

SQL> EXECUTE dbms_resource_manager.create_consumer_group('BATCH_REPORTS','2nd
level group','ROUND-ROBIN');

PL/SQL procedure successfully completed.

SQL> --
SQL> -- Create plan directives
SQL> --
SQL> EXECUTE dbms_resource_manager.create_plan_directive('MASTER', 'USERS',
0,60,0,0,0,0,0,0,NULL);

PL/SQL procedure successfully completed.

SQL> EXECUTE dbms_resource_manager.create_plan_directive('MASTER', 'REPORTS',
0,20,0,0,0,0,0,0,NULL);

PL/SQL procedure successfully completed.

SQL> EXECUTE
dbms_resource_manager.create_plan_directive('MASTER','OTHER_GROUPS',
0,20,0,0,0,0,0,0,NULL);
```

continues

Listing 9.2   Continued.

```
PL/SQL procedure successfully completed.

SQL> EXECUTE dbms_resource_manager.create_plan_directive('USERS',
'ONLINE_USERS',  0,0,70,0,0,0,0,0,NULL);

PL/SQL procedure successfully completed.

SQL> EXECUTE dbms_resource_manager.create_plan_directive('USERS',
'BATCH_USERS',   0,0,30,0,0,0,0,0,NULL);

PL/SQL procedure successfully completed.

SQL> EXECUTE
dbms_resource_manager.create_plan_directive('REPORTS','ONLINE_REPORTS',0,0,70
,0,0,0,0,0,NULL);

PL/SQL procedure successfully completed.

SQL> EXECUTE
dbms_resource_manager.create_plan_directive('REPORTS','BATCH_REPORTS',
0,0,30,0,0,0,0,0,NULL);

PL/SQL procedure successfully completed.

SQL> --
SQL> -- Verify Plan
SQL> --
SQL> EXECUTE dbms_resource_manager.validate_pending_area;

PL/SQL procedure successfully completed.

SQL> --
SQL> -- Submit Plan
SQL> --
SQL> EXECUTE dbms_resource_manager.submit_pending_area;

PL/SQL procedure successfully completed.

SQL> spool off
```

Notice that you must drop *all* parts of the plan. This is because Oracle allows the existence of orphan groups and plans. As you can tell from looking at the scripts, the DBMS_RESOURCE_MANAGER and DBMS_RESOURCE_MANAGER_PRIVS packages are critical to implementing Oracle resource groups. Let's examine these packages.

Source 9.2   Example of a drop procedure.

```
EXECUTE dbms_resource_manager.delete_plan('MASTER');
EXECUTE dbms_resource_manager.delete_plan('USERS');
EXECUTE dbms_resource_manager.delete_plan('REPORTS');
--
--delete tiers of groups in plan
--
EXECUTE dbms_resource_manager.delete_consumer_group('ONLINE_USERS');
EXECUTE dbms_resource_manager.delete_consumer_group('BATCH_USERS');
EXECUTE dbms_resource_manager.delete_consumer_group('ONLINE_REPORTS');
EXECUTE dbms_resource_manager.delete_consumer_group('BATCH_REPORTS');
```

DBMS_RESOURCE_MANAGER Package

The DBMS_RESOURCE_MANAGER package is used to administer the new resource plan and consumer group options since Oracle8*i*. The package contains several procedures that are used to create, modify, drop, and grant access to resource plans, groups, directives, and pending areas. The invoker must have the ADMINISTER_RESOURCE_ MANAGER system privilege to execute these procedures. The procedures to grant and revoke this privilege are in the package DBMS_RESOURCE_MANAGER_PRIVS. The procedures in DBMS_RESOURCE_MANAGER are listed in Table 9.5.

DBMS_RESOURCE_MANAGER Procedure Syntax   The calling syntaxes for all of the DBMS_RESOURCE_MANAGER packages are presented in the following subsections.

CREATE_PLAN Syntax

```
DBMS_RESOURCE_MANAGER.CREATE_PLAN (
    plan                        IN VARCHAR2,
    comment                     IN VARCHAR2,
    cpu_mth                     IN VARCHAR2 DEFAULT 'EMPHASIS',
    max_active_sess_target_mth  IN VARCHAR2 DEFAULT
                                    'MAX_ACTIVE_SESS_ABSOLUTE',
    active_sess_pool_mth        IN VARCHAR2 DEFAULT
                                    'ACTIVE_SESS_POOL_ABSOLUTE',
    parallel_degree_limit_mth   IN VARCHAR2 DEFAULT
                                    'PARALLEL_DEGREE_LIMIT_ABSOLUTE',
    queueing_mth                IN VARCHAR2 DEFAULT 'FIFO_TIMEOUT');
```

where:

> **plan.** The plan name.
>
> **comment.** Any text comment you want associated with the plan name.

TABLE 9.5   DBMS_RESOURCE_MANAGER_PACKAGES

Procedure	Purpose
CREATE_PLAN	Creates entries that define resource plans.
CREATE_SIMPLE_PLAN	Creates a single-level resource plan containing up to eight consumer groups in one step (9*i*).
UPDATE_PLAN	Updates entries that define resource plans.
DELETE_PLAN	Deletes the specified plan as well as all the plan directives to which it refers.
DELETE_PLAN_CASCADE	Deletes the specified plan as well as all its descendants (plan directives, subplans, consumer groups).
CREATE_CONSUMER_GROUP	Creates entries that define resource consumer groups.
UPDATE_CONSUMER_GROUP	Updates entries that define resource consumer groups.
DELETE_CONSUMER_GROUP	Deletes entries that define resource consumer groups.
CREATE_PLAN_DIRECTIVE	Creates resource plan directives.
UPDATE_PLAN_DIRECTIVE	Updates resource plan directives.
DELETE_PLAN_DIRECTIVE	Deletes resource plan directives.
CREATE_PENDING_AREA	Creates a work area for changes to resource manager objects.
VALIDATE_PENDING_AREA	Validates pending changes for the resource manager.
CLEAR_PENDING_AREA	Clears the work area for the resource manager.
SUBMIT_PENDING_AREA	Submits pending changes for the resource manager.
SET_INITIAL_CONSUMER_GROUP	Assigns the initial resource consumer group for a user.
SWITCH_CONSUMER_GROUP_FOR_SESS	Changes the resource consumer group of a specific session.
SWITCH_CONSUMER_GROUP_FOR_USER	Changes the resource consumer group for all sessions with a given user name.

cpu_mth. Either set to EMPHASIS or ROUND-ROBIN.

max_active_sess_target_mth. Allocation method for maximum active sessions.

active_sess_pool_mth. Type of allocation method used for maximum active sessions.

parallel_degree_limit_mth. Allocation method for degree of parallelism.

queueing_mth. Specifies type of queuing policy to use with active session pool feature.

Syntax for the CREATE_SIMPLE_PLAN Procedure   This procedure creates a simplified group in which a top-level group, SYS_GROUP, with 100 percent allocation is created; all named groups are at level 2; and the OTHER_GROUPS is at 100 percent at level 3.

```
DBMS_RESOURCE_MANAGER.CREATE_SIMPLE_PLAN (
    Simple_plan                     IN VARCHAR2,
    Consumer_group1                 IN VARCHAR2,
    group1_cpu                      IN NUMBER,
    Consumer_group2                 IN VARCHAR2,
    group2_cpu                      IN NUMBER,
    Consumer_group3                 IN VARCHAR2,
    group3_cpu                      IN NUMBER,
    Consumer_group4                 IN VARCHAR2,
    group4_cpu                      IN NUMBER,
    Consumer_group5                 IN VARCHAR2,
    group5_cpu                      IN NUMBER,
    Consumer_group6                 IN VARCHAR2,
    group6_cpu                      IN NUMBER,
    Consumer_group7                 IN VARCHAR2,
    group7_cpu                      IN NUMBER,
    Consumer_group8                 IN VARCHAR2,
    group8_cpu                      IN NUMBER);
```

where:

Simple_plan. The plan name.

Consumer_group1-8. The name of the specified consumer group.

Group1-8_cpu. The percentage of CPU to give to the specified group.

UPDATE_PLAN Syntax

```
DBMS_RESOURCE_MANAGER.UPDATE_PLAN (
    plan                            IN VARCHAR2,
    new_comment                     IN VARCHAR2 DEFAULT NULL,
    new_cpu_mth                     IN VARCHAR2 DEFAULT NULL,
    new_max_active_sess_target_mth IN VARCHAR2 DEFAULT
                                    'MAX_ACTIVE_SESS_ABSOLUTE',
    new_active_sess_pool_mth        IN VARCHAR2 DEFAULT
                                    'ACTIVE_SESS_POOL_ABSOLUTE',
    new_parallel_degree_limit_mth  IN VARCHAR2 DEFAULT
                                    'PARALLEL_DEGREE_LIMIT_ABSOLUTE',
    new_queueing_mth                IN VARCHAR2 DEFAULT 'FIFO_TIMEOUT');
```

where:

plan. The plan name.

new_comment. Any new text comment you want associated with the plan name.

new_cpu_mth. Set to either EMPHASIS or ROUND-ROBIN.

new_max_active_sess_target_mth. New allocation method for maximum active sessions.

new_active_sess_pool_mth. New type of allocation method used for maximum active sessions.

new_parallel_degree_limit_mth. New allocation method for degree of parallelism.

new_queueing_mth. Specifies new type of queuing policy to use with active session pool feature.

DELETE_PLAN *Syntax*

```
DBMS_RESOURCE_MANAGER.DELETE_PLAN (
    plan IN VARCHAR2);
```

where:

plan. Name of resource plan to delete.

DELETE_PLAN_CASCADE *Syntax*

```
DBMS_RESOURCE_MANAGER.DELETE_PLAN_CASCADE (
    plan IN VARCHAR2);
```

where:

plan. Name of plan.

CREATE_RESOURCE_GROUP *Syntax*

```
DBMS_RESOURCE_MANAGER.CREATE_CONSUMER_GROUP (
    consumer_group IN VARCHAR2,
    comment        IN VARCHAR2,
    cpu_mth        IN VARCHAR2 DEFAULT 'ROUND-ROBIN');
```

where:

consumer_group. Name of consumer group.

Comment. User's comment.

cpu_mth. Name of CPU resource allocation method.

UPDATE_RESOURCE_GROUP *Syntax*

```
DBMS_RESOURCE_MANAGER.UPDATE_CONSUMER_GROUP (
    consumer_group IN VARCHAR2,
```

```
new_comment      IN VARCHAR2 DEFAULT NULL,
new_cpu_mth      IN VARCHAR2 DEFAULT NULL);
```

where:

plan. Name of resource plan.

new_comment. New user's comment.

new_cpu_mth. Name of new allocation method for CPU resources.

new_max_active_sess_target_mth. Name of new method for maximum active sessions.

new_parallel_degree_limit_mth. Name of new method for degree of parallelism.

DELETE_RESOURCE_GROUP *Syntax*

```
DBMS_RESOURCE_MANAGER.DELETE_CONSUMER_GROUP (
    consumer_group IN VARCHAR2);
```

where:

plan. Name of resource plan.

CREATE_PLAN_DIRECTIVE *Syntax*

```
DBMS_RESOURCE_MANAGER.CREATE_PLAN_DIRECTIVE (
    plan                      IN VARCHAR2,
    group_or_subplan          IN VARCHAR2,
    comment                   IN VARCHAR2,
    cpu_p1                    IN NUMBER    DEFAULT NULL,
    cpu_p2                    IN NUMBER    DEFAULT NULL,
    cpu_p3                    IN NUMBER    DEFAULT NULL,
    cpu_p4                    IN NUMBER    DEFAULT NULL,
    cpu_p5                    IN NUMBER    DEFAULT NULL,
    cpu_p6                    IN NUMBER    DEFAULT NULL,
    cpu_p7                    IN NUMBER    DEFAULT NULL,
    cpu_p8                    IN NUMBER    DEFAULT NULL,
    active_sess_pool_p1       IN NUMBER    DEFAULT 1000000,
    queueing_p1               IN NUMBER    DEFAULT 1000000,
    parallel_degree_limit_p1  IN NUMBER    DEFAULT 1000000,
    switch_group              IN VARCHAR2 DEFAULT NULL,
    switch_time               IN NUMBER    DEFAULT 1000000,
    switch_estimate           IN BOOLEAN   DEFAULT FALSE,
    max_est_exec_time         IN NUMBER    DEFAULT 1000000,
    undo_pool                 IN NUMBER    DEFAULT 1000000);
```

where:

plan. Name of resource plan.

group_or_subplan. Name of consumer group or subplan.

comment. Comment for the plan directive.

cpu_p1. First-level parameter for the CPU resource allocation method.

cpu_p2. Second-level parameter for the CPU resource allocation method.

cpu_p3. Third-level parameter for the CPU resource allocation method.

cpu_p4. Fourth-level parameter for the CPU resource allocation method.

cpu_p5. Fifth-level parameter for the CPU resource allocation method.

cpu_p6. Sixth-level parameter for the CPU resource allocation method.

cpu_p7. Seventh-level parameter for the CPU resource allocation method.

cpu_p8. Eighth-level parameter for the CPU resource allocation method.

active_sess_pool_p1. First parameter for the maximum active sessions allocation method.

queueing_p1. Queue timeout in seconds.

parallel_degree_limit_p1. First parameter for the degree of parallelism allocation method.

switch_group. Group to switch to once switch time is reached.

switch_time. Maximum execution time within a group.

switch_estimate. Execution time estimate to assign a group.

Max_est_exec_time. Maximum estimated execution time in seconds.

Undo_pool. Maximum cumulative undo allocated for consumer groups.

UPDATE_PLAN_DIRECTIVE Syntax

```
DBMS_RESOURCE_MANAGER.UPDATE_PLAN_DIRECTIVE (
    plan                           IN VARCHAR2,
    group_or_subplan               IN VARCHAR2,
    new_comment                    IN VARCHAR2,
    new_cpu_p1                     IN NUMBER    DEFAULT NULL,
    new_cpu_p2                     IN NUMBER    DEFAULT NULL,
    new_cpu_p3                     IN NUMBER    DEFAULT NULL,
    new_cpu_p4                     IN NUMBER    DEFAULT NULL,
    new_cpu_p5                     IN NUMBER    DEFAULT NULL,
    new_cpu_p6                     IN NUMBER    DEFAULT NULL,
    new_cpu_p7                     IN NUMBER    DEFAULT NULL,
    new_cpu_p8                     IN NUMBER    DEFAULT NULL,
    new_active_sess_pool_p1        IN NUMBER    DEFAULT NULL,
    new_queueing_p1                IN NUMBER    DEFAULT NULL,
    new_parallel_degree_limit_p1   IN NUMBER    DEFAULT NULL,
    new_switch_group               IN VARCHAR2 DEFAULT NULL,
    new_switch_time                IN NUMBER    DEFAULT NULL,
    new_switch_estimate            IN BOOLEAN   DEFAULT FALSE,
    new_max_est_exec_time          IN NUMBER    DEFAULT NULL,
    new_undo_pool                  IN NUMBER    DEFAULT NULL);
```

where:

> **plan.** Name of resource plan.
>
> **group_or_subplan.** Name of consumer group or subplan.
>
> **new_comment.** Comment for the plan directive.
>
> **new_cpu_p1.** First-level parameter for the CPU resource allocation method.
>
> **new_cpu_p2.** Second-level parameter for the CPU resource allocation method.
>
> **new_cpu_p3.** Third-level parameter for the CPU resource allocation method.
>
> **new_cpu_p4.** Fourth-level parameter for the CPU resource allocation method.
>
> **new_cpu_p5.** Fifth-level parameter for the CPU resource allocation method.
>
> **new_cpu_p6.** Sixth-level parameter for the CPU resource allocation method.
>
> **new_cpu_p7.** Seventh-level parameter for the CPU resource allocation method.
>
> **new_cpu_p8.** Eighth-level parameter for the CPU resource allocation method.
>
> **new_active_sess_pool_p1.** First parameter for the maximum active sessions allocation method.
>
> **new_queueing_p1.** Queue timeout in seconds.
>
> **new_parallel_degree_limit_p1.** First parameter for the degree of parallelism allocation method.
>
> **new_switch_group.** Group to switch to once switch time is reached.
>
> **new_switch_time.** Maximum execution time within a group.
>
> **new_switch_estimate.** Use execution time estimate to assign a group?
>
> **new_max_est_exec_time.** Maximum estimated execution time in seconds.
>
> **new_undo_pool.** Maximum cumulative undo allocated for consumer groups.

DELETE_PLAN_DIRECTIVE Syntax

```
DBMS_RESOURCE_MANAGER.DELETE_PLAN_DIRECTIVE (
    plan              IN VARCHAR2,
    group_or_subplan IN VARCHAR2);
```

where:

> **plan.** Name of resource plan.
>
> **group_or_subplan.** Name of group or subplan.

CREATE_PENDING_AREA Syntax   This procedure lets you make changes to resource manager objects.

```
DBMS_RESOURCE_MANAGER.CREATE_PENDING_AREA;
```

All changes to the plan schema must be done within a pending area. The pending area can be thought of as a "scratch" area for plan schema changes. The administrator creates this pending area, makes changes as necessary, and possibly validates these changes. Only when the submit is completed do these changes become active.

You may, at any time while the pending area is active, view the current plan schema with your changes by selecting from the appropriate user views.

At any time, you may clear the pending area if you want to stop the current changes. You may also call the VALIDATE procedure to confirm whether the changes you have made are valid. You do not have to do your changes in a given order to maintain a consistent group of entries. These checks are also implicitly done when the pending area is submitted.

TIP Oracle allows "orphan" consumer groups (i.e., consumer groups that have no plan directives that refer to them). This anticipates that an administrator may want to create a consumer group for future use.

VALIDATE_PENDING_AREA Syntax

```
DBMS_RESOURCE_MANAGER.VALIDATE_PENDING_AREA;
```

The following rules must be adhered to validate a pending resource plan area; they are checked whenever the VALIDATE or SUBMIT procedures are executed:

- No plan schema may contain any loops.
- All plans and consumer groups referred to by plan directives must exist.
- All plans must have directives that refer to either plans or consumer groups.
- All the percentages in any given level may not add up to greater than 100 for the emphasis resource allocation method.
- No plan that is currently being used as a top plan by an active instance may be deleted.
- Under Oracle8i, the plan directive parameter, parallel_degree_limit_p1, may appear only in plan directives that refer to consumer groups (i.e., not at subplans).
- There may not be more than 32 plan directives coming from any given plan (i.e., no plan can have more than 32 children).
- There may not be more than 32 consumer groups in any active plan schema.
- Plans and consumer groups use the same namespace; therefore, no plan may have the same name as any consumer group.
- There must be a plan directive for OTHER_GROUPS somewhere in any active plan schema. This ensures that a session not covered by the currently active plan is allocated resources as specified by the OTHER_GROUPS directive.

If any of the above rules are broken when checked by the VALIDATE or SUBMIT procedures, an informative error message is returned. You may then make changes to fix the problem(s) and reissue the VALIDATE or SUBMIT procedures.

CLEAR_PENDING_AREA Syntax This procedure has no arguments it is simply called using:

```
DBMS_RESOURCE_MANAGER.CLEAR_PENDING_AREA;
```

SUBMIT_PENDING_AREA Syntax This procedure has no arguments it is simply called using:

```
DBMS_RESOURCE_MANAGER.SUBMIT_PENDING_AREA;
```

SET_INITIAL_CONSUMER_GROUP Syntax

```
DBMS_RESOURCE_MANAGER.SET_INITIAL_CONSUMER_GROUP (
    user           IN VARCHAR2,
    consumer_group IN VARCHAR2);
```

where:

IOT Overflow. Gives the name of the IOT tables overflow table.

LOG. Does this table use redo logging?

SWITCH_CONSUMER_GROUP_FOR_SESS Syntax

```
DBMS_RESOURCE_MANAGER.SWITCH_CONSUMER_GROUP_FOR_SESS(
    SESSION_ID      IN NUMBER,
    SESSION_SERIAL  IN NUMBER,
    CONSUMER_GROUP  IN VARCHAR2);
```

where:

session_id. SID column from the view V$SESSION.

serial. SERIAL# column from the view V$SESSION.

consumer_group. Name of the consumer group of which to switch.

SWITCH_CONSUMER_GROUP_FOR_USER Syntax

```
DBMS_RESOURCE_MANAGER.SWITCH_CONSUMER_GROUP_FOR_USER (
    user           IN VARCHAR2,
    consumer_group IN VARCHAR2);
```

where:

> **user.** Name of the user.
>
> **consumer_group.** Name of the consumer group to switch to.

DBMS_RESOURCE_MANAGER_PRIVS Package The DBMS_RESOURCE_ MANAGER package has a companion package that grants privileges in the realm of the resource consumer option: DBMS_RESOURCE_MANAGER_ PRIVS. Its procedures are documented in Table 9.6.

DBMS_RESOURCE_MANAGER_PRIVS Procedure Syntax The calling syntaxes for all DBMS_RESOURCE_MANAGER_PRIVS packages are presented in the following subsections.

GRANT_SYSTEM_PRIVILEGE Syntax

```
DBMS_RESOURCE_MANAGER_PRIVS.GRANT_SYSTEM_PRIVILEGE (
   grantee_name   IN VARCHAR2,
   privilege_name IN VARCHAR2 DEFAULT 'ADMINISTER_RESOURCE_MANAGER',
   admin_option   IN BOOLEAN);
```

where:

> **grantee_name.** Name of the user or role to whom privilege is to be granted.
>
> **privilege_name.** Name of the privilege to be granted.
>
> **admin_option.** TRUE if the grant is with admin_option; FALSE otherwise.

REVOKE_SYSTEM_PRIVILEGE Syntax

```
DBMS_RESOURCE_MANAGER_PRIVS.REVOKE_SYSTEM_PRIVILEGE (
   revokee_name   IN VARCHAR2,
   privilege_name IN VARCHAR2 DEFAULT 'ADMINISTER_RESOURCE_MANAGER');
```

TABLE 9.6 DBMS_RESOURCE_MANAGER_PRIVS Procedures

Procedure	Purpose
GRANT_SYSTEM_PRIVILEGE	Performs a grant of a system privilege.
REVOKE_SYSTEM_PRIVILEGE	Performs a revoke of a system privilege.
GRANT_SWITCH_CONSUMER_GROUP	Grants the privilege to switch to resource consumer groups.
REVOKE_SWITCH_CONSUMER_GROUP	Revokes the privilege to switch to resource consumer groups.

where:

> **revokee_name.** Name of the user or role from whom privilege is to be revoked.
>
> **privilege_name.** Name of the privilege to be revoked.

GRANT_SWITCH_CONSUMER_GROUP *Syntax*

```
DBMS_RESOURCE_MANAGER_PRIVS.GRANT_SWITCH_CONSUMER_GROUP (
   grantee_name    IN VARCHAR2,
   consumer_group  IN VARCHAR2,
   grant_option    IN BOOLEAN);
```

where:

> **grantee_name.** Name of the user or role to whom privilege is to be granted.
>
> **consumer_group.** Name of consumer group.
>
> **grant_option.** TRUE if grantee should be allowed to grant access; FALSE otherwise.

When using the GRANT_SWITCH_CONSUMER_GROUP procedure, the following usage notes apply:

- If you grant permission to a user to switch to a particular consumer group, then that user can immediately switch his or her current consumer group to the new consumer group.
- If you grant permission to a role to switch to a particular consumer group, then any users who have been granted that role and have enabled that role can immediately switch their current consumer group to the new consumer group.
- If you grant permission to switch a particular consumer group to PUBLIC, then any user can switch to that consumer group.
- If the grant_option parameter is TRUE, then users granted switch privilege for the consumer group may also grant switch privileges for that consumer group to others.
- In order to set the initial consumer group of a user, you must grant to the user the switch privilege for that group.

REVOKE_SWITCH_CONSUMER_GROUP *Syntax*

```
DBMS_RESOURCE_MANAGER_PRIVS.REVOKE_SWITCH_CONSUMER_GROUP (
   revokee_name    IN VARCHAR2,
   consumer_group  IN VARCHAR2);
```

where:

> **revokee_name.** Name of user/role from which to revoke access.
>
> **consumer_group.** Name of consumer group.

When using the REVOKE_SWITCH_CONSUMER_GROUP procedure, the following usage notes apply.

- If you revoke a user's switch privilege for a particular consumer group, then any subsequent attempts by that user to switch to that consumer group will fail.
- If you revoke the initial consumer group from a user, then that user, upon logging in, will automatically be part of the DEFAULT_CONSUMER_GROUP consumer group.
- If you revoke the switch privilege for a consumer group from a role, then any users who only had switch privilege for the consumer group via that role will be subsequently unable to switch to that consumer group.
- If you revoke the switch privilege for a consumer group from PUBLIC, then any users who could previously only use the consumer group via PUBLIC will not be subsequently able to switch to that consumer group.

Using OEM to Manage Resource Groups and Plans   As an alternative to using manual procedures to create and maintain resource plans and groups, Oracle has created a GUI interface in the OEM that allows the DBA to create and maintain simple resource plans. The OEM Resource Manager interface allows the DBA to create plans and groups, assign CPU and parallel process allocations, and assign users to resource plans. The DBA can also schedule when a resource plan is active via OEM.

TIP   In SuSE 7.2 Linux, I had to edit the oemapp script to remove the "native" setting of the command-line argument since that isn't supported on SuSE. To get OEM working on Linux, search for "native" and comment out the section of the *if* command where it is set to "native."

You can invoke OEM on Linux from a display window using this command:

```
oracle@tuscgalinux> oemapp console
```

The keyword *console* tells OEM that you are not using a service manager. Once OEM starts, you will have to select the Launch Standalone option to show the top-level display that is shown in Figure 9.3.

By clicking on the cross next to the Databases icon, you will see a list of databases. Click on the database icon that corresponds to the database in which you wish to create a resource plan. You will be prompted for the user name and password for the database. Connect as SYS since you will be using DBMS_RESOURCE_MANAGER, and remember to select the "SYSDBA connect as" option. Once all of the icons for the database you chose are displayed, select the Instance icon. From the Instance menu, select the Resource Plans icon; the display for maintaining resource plans will be displayed. The Resource Plans display is shown in Figure 9.4.

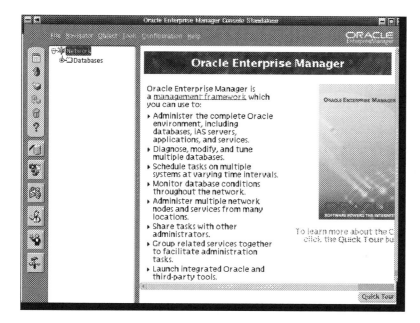

FIGURE 9.3   Example top-level OEM display.

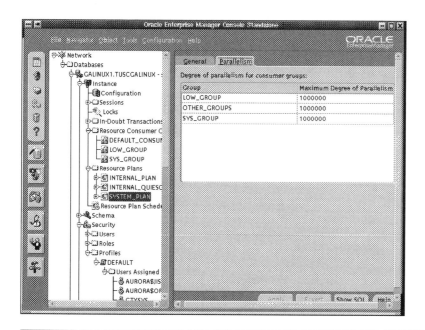

FIGURE 9.4   OEM resource plan display.

By selecting the Object menu item from the top menu bar on the OEM screen, you can choose Create Object, which will allow you to fill in the required dialog boxes to create a resource plan, assign it groups, and assign these groups to users and roles. The top-level display for this resource plan creation wizard is shown in Figure 9.5.

I won't go through an entire resource plan creation using OEM, as the steps are self-explanatory using the wizard, and you shouldn't have any problems with it.

Back in the Instance menu, there is an icon for Resource Consumer Groups. The top-level Resource Consumer Group display is shown in Figure 9.6. Notice that you can choose the group, the users, and roles that belong to it.

If you choose the Object menu item, you can create new resource groups. An example of the Create Resource Consumer Group dialog box is shown in Figure 9.7.

Notice the option at the bottom of the screen in Figure 9.7 that allows the user to see the SQL that will be used to create the resource group. As you can see, I had already selected the user and role from the pick lists under their tabs when the screenshot was taken, as is evident in the resulting SQL commands. These commands should look familiar after stepping through the manual creation method at the start of this section.

When you have completed adding users and roles, you simply click the Create button to generate your new Resource Group. Once you have created a resource group, you will need to assign resources to it; you do this in the Resource Plans area when the group is assigned to a plan.

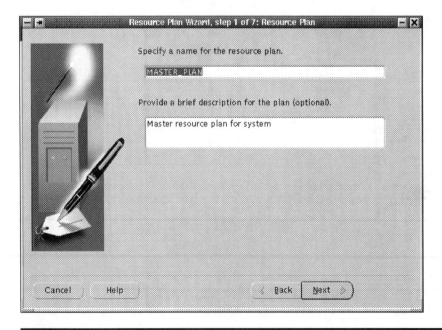

FIGURE 9.5   Example of the Create Resource Plan wizard dialog box.

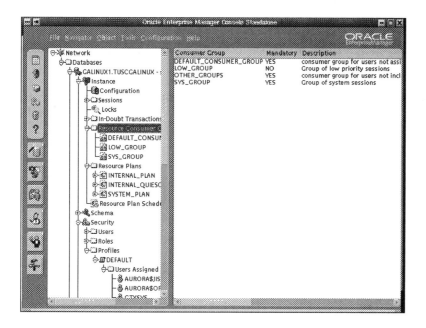

FIGURE 9.6 OEM Resource Manager group display.

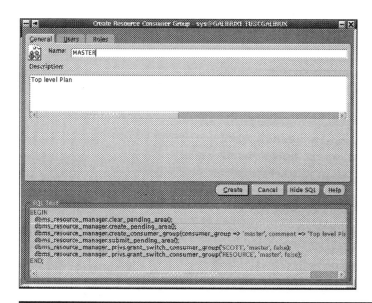

FIGURE 9.7 OEM Create Resource Consumer Group dialog box.

9.7 MANAGING ROW-LEVEL ACCESS

Row-level access, also known as fine-grained security and virtual private databases, is managed using a combination of Oracle8*i* or Oracle9*i* contexts, stored procedures, database-level triggers, and the DBMS_RLS package. Row-level access is used to restrict SELECT, INSERT, UPDATE, and DELETE on table rows based on specific values contained in the rows or specific system-environment-related variables. Generally speaking, a policy will require:

- A context
- A procedure to implement the context
- A database- (Oracle8*i* or Oracle9*i*) level trigger that monitors login activity
- A security procedure to implement the policy
- A policy declaration

A row-level access control depends on certain environment variables known as *contexts* to be set. The DBMS_CONTEXT package is used to set the various context variables used by the RLS policy.

Figure 9.8 shows a flowchart of how to implement a simple security policy. As you can see, the process is not complex. Let's examine each step and see what is really involved.

In the first step, a context package or procedure is developed that will then be used by a login trigger to set each user's context variables. This step is vital in that if the context variables aren't set, it is many times more difficult to implement row-level security using the DBMS_RLS package. The package or procedure used to set the context variables should resemble the one shown in Source 9.3.

Source 9.3   Example of a context-setting procedure.

```
CREATE OR REPLACE PACKAGE graphics_app AUTHID DEFINER AS
PROCEDURE get_graphics_function(usern IN VARCHAR2, graphics_function OUT
VARCHAR2);
PROCEDURE set_graphics_context(usern IN VARCHAR2);
END;
/
SET ARRAYSIZE 1
SHO ERR
CREATE OR REPLACE PACKAGE BODY graphics_app AS
graphics_user VARCHAR2(32);
graphics_function VARCHAR2(32);
PROCEDURE get_graphics_function(usern IN VARCHAR2, graphics_function OUT
VARCHAR2) IS
BEGIN
SELECT user_function INTO graphics_function FROM graphics_dba.graphics_users
WHERE username=usern;
```

```
END get_graphics_function;
PROCEDURE set_graphics_context(usern IN VARCHAR2) IS
BEGIN
graphics_app.get_graphics_function(usern,graphics_function);
DBMS_SESSION.SET_CONTEXT('GRAPHICS_SEC','GRAPHICS_FUNCTION',graphics_function
);
DBMS_SESSION.SET_CONTEXT('GRAPHICS_SEC','GRAPHICS_USER',usern);
END set_graphics_context;
END graphics_app;
/
SHOW ERR
```

In the package in Source 9.3 are two procedures, one that retrieves a user's graphics function from a prebuilt and populated table, and the other that is used to set the user's context variables based on using the DBMS_SESSION.SET_CONTEXT procedure provided by Oracle.

Of course, the procedures in Source 9.3 wouldn't be much use without a trigger that could run it whenever a user logged on to the system. Until Oracle8*i*, this would have involved setting auditing on for login, moving the aud$ table from SYS ownership and setting the ownership to another user, resetting all of the synonyms pointing to aud$, and then building an insert trigger to perform the actual work. Since Oracle8*i*, all we have to do is build a trigger similar to the one shown in Source 9.4.

Once we have an operating context set package and database login trigger, we can proceed to create the required context-checking package and the context it checks. Source 9.5 shows an example context-checking package.

The entire purpose of the package in Source 9.5 is to return a d_predicate value based on a user's graphics_function context value. The d_predicate value is appended to whichever WHERE clause is included with the user's command or is appended as a WHERE clause whenever there is no preexisting clause. It is also possible to use a role

Source 9.4   Example of a database login trigger.

```
CREATE OR REPLACE TRIGGER set_graphics_context AFTER LOGON ON DATABASE
DECLARE
username VARCHAR2(30);
BEGIN
username:=SYS_CONTEXT('USERENV','SESSION_USER');
graphics_app.set_graphics_context(username);
EXCEPTION
WHEN OTHERS THEN
NULL;
END;
/
```

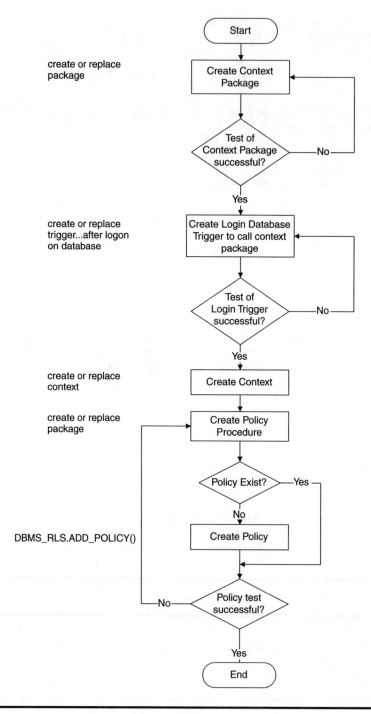

FIGURE 9.8   Steps to implement a security policy.

Source 9.5   Example of a context-checking package.

```
CREATE OR REPLACE PACKAGE graphics_sec AUTHID DEFINER AS
FUNCTION graphics_check(obj_schema VARCHAR2, obj_name VARCHAR2)
 RETURN VARCHAR2;
PRAGMA RESTRICT_REFERENCES(GRAPHICS_CHECK,WNDS);
END;
/
SET ARRAYSIZE 1
SHOW ERR
CREATE OR REPLACE PACKAGE BODY graphics_sec AS
FUNCTION graphics_check(obj_schema VARCHAR2, obj_name VARCHAR2)
 RETURN VARCHAR2 AS
d_predicate VARCHAR2(2000);
user_context VARCHAR2(32);
BEGIN
   user_context:=SYS_CONTEXT('graphics_sec','graphics_function');
   IF user_context = 'ADMIN' THEN
     d_predicate:=' 1=1';
dbms_output.put_line(d_predicate);
   ELSIF user_context = 'GENERAL USER' THEN
     d_predicate:=' graphics_usage='||chr(39)||'UNRESTRICTED'||chr(39);
dbms_output.put_line(d_predicate);
   ELSIF user_context='DEVELOPER' THEN
     d_predicate:=' 1=1';
dbms_output.put_line(d_predicate);
   ELSIF user_context IS NULL THEN
     d_predicate:='1=2';
   END IF;
   RETURN d_predicate;
END graphics_check;
END;
/
SHOW ERR
```

granted to the user to determine row-level access restrictions, but it can result in unpredictable results and should be used with care.

The creation of our graphics security context is rather simple once we have finished the preliminary work. It boils down to one command:

```
CREATE OR REPLACE CONTEXT graphics_sec USING sys.graphics_app;
```

The final step is to set the policy into the database. This is done with the DBMS_RLS package, using the procedure ADD_POLICY:

```
BEGIN
 dbms_rls.add_policy('GRAPHICS_DBA','INTERNAL_GRAPHICS','GRAPHICS_POLICY',
 'GRAPHICS_DBA','GRAPHICS_SEC.GRAPHICS_CHECK','SELECT,INSERT,UPDATE,DELETE',
```

```
TRUE);
END;
```

This policy simply ties the components we previously defined to a coherent entity called GRAPHICS_POLICY and implements this policy against the table INTERNAL_ GRAPHICS, which is in the schema GRAPHICS_DBA. The policy GRAPHICS_POLICY is owned by GRAPHICS_DBA and uses the procedure GRAPHICS_SEC. GRAPHICS_ CHECK to verify that users can perform SELECT, INSERT, UPDATE, and DELETE operations.

Note that the final parameter in the add_policy call is TRUE: It corresponds to the update_check parameter and defaults to FALSE if not set to TRUE. If update_check is set to FALSE, the validity of the INSERT and UPDATE statements will not be verified and no errors or warnings will be generated. The status of the update_check setting for existing policies can be verified by looking in the SYS.EXU81RLS table (named the same in 8*i* and 9*i*) and checking the CHKOPT column: a value of 0 means update_check is set to FALSE; a value of 1 indicates it is set to TRUE. You can also use the DBA_ POLICIES view column CHK_OPTION, which will be either read YES or NO.

The table graphics_users is required in the above example. It contains the user name and the user's graphics function.

NOTE   In version 9.0.1.0, if you create a fine-grained access application and do full restriction, as shown in the preceding example (restrict INSERT, UPDATE, DELETE, and SELECT), any attempt to EXPORT the table(s) involved will fail due to bug 1802004, and you will have to patch the database to use EXPORT.

Policy Usage

Policy usage is controlled internally by the Oracle system and adheres to the following usage guidelines:

- SYS user is not restricted by any security policy.
- The policy functions that generate dynamic predicates are called by the server. The following is the interface for the function:

```
FUNCTION policy_function (object_schema IN VARCHAR2, object_name VARCHAR2)
RETURN VARCHAR2
```

where:

- object_schema is the schema owning the table of view.
- Object_name is the name of table or view that the policy will apply.

- The maximum length of the predicate that the policy function can return is 2,000 bytes.
- The policy functions must have the purity level of WNDS (write no database state).
- Dynamic predicates generated out of different policies for the same object have the combined effect of a conjunction (ANDed) of all the predicates.
- The security check and object lookup are performed against the owner of the policy function for objects in the subqueries of the dynamic predicates.
- If the function returns a zero-length predicate, it is interpreted as no restriction being applied to the current user for the policy.
- When a table alias is required (e.g., parent object is a type table) in the predicate, the name of the table or view itself must be used as the name of the alias. The server constructs the transient view as something like "select c1, c2, . . . from tab where <predicate>."
- The validity check of the function is done at runtime for ease of installation and other dependency issues, such as when the import/export utilities are run.

DBMS_RLS Package　　The entire concept of row-level security is based on the use of policies stored in the database. The only way to store policies in the database is to use the DBMS_RLS package.

The DBMS_RLS procedures cause current DML transactions, if any, to commit before the operation. However, the procedures do not cause a commit first if they are inside a DDL event trigger. With DDL transactions, the DBMS_RLS procedures are part of the transactions.

For example, let's assume you create a trigger for CREATE TABLE and inside the trigger, you add a column through ALTER TABLE; you can also add a policy through DBMS_RLS. All these operations are in the same transaction as CREATE TABLE, even though each one is a DDL statement. Note, however, the CREATE TABLE succeeds only if the trigger is completed successfully.

In Oracle9*i*, three new features have been introduced: the concept of a *static policy*—that is, one that always returns the same predicate; the capability to group related policies for a given table or view; and the ability to add policy contexts via the DBMS_RLS package rather than from a manual command.

All the DBMS_RLS package procedures are shown in Table 9.7, and the syntax for calling these procedures is shown in the subsequent subsections.

ADD_ GROUPED_POLICY Syntax

```
DBMS_RLS.ADD_GROUPED_POLICY (
    object_schema    IN VARCHAR2 := NULL,
    object_name      IN VARCHAR2,
    policy_group     IN VARCHAR2 := 'SYS_DEFAULT',
    policy_name      IN VARCHAR2,
```

TABLE 9.7 DBMS_RLS Package Procedures

Procedure	Purpose
ADD_GROUPED_POLICY	Add a row-level security policy to a policy group for a table or view.
ADD_POLICY	Creates a fine-grained access control policy to a table or view.
ADD_POLICY_CONTEXT	Adds a driving context to a table or view.
CREATE_POLICY_GROUP	Creates a policy group for a table or view.
DELETE_POLICY_GROUP	Deletes a policy group from a table or view.
DISABLE_GROUPED_POLICY	Disables a policy group for a table or view.
DROP_GROUPED_POLICY	Drops a policy group from a table or view.
DROP_POLICY	Drops a fine-grained access control policy from a table or view.
DROP_POLICY_CONTEXT	Drops a driving context from a table or view.
ENABLE_GROUPED_POLICY	Enables a policy group for a table or view.
ENABLE_POLICY	Enables a single policy for a table or view.
REFRESH_GROUPED_POLICY	Recompiles all members of a policy group for a table or view.
REFRESH_POLICY	Causes all the cached statements associated with the policy to be reparsed.

```
function_schema  IN VARCHAR2 := NULL,
policy_function  IN VARCHAR2,
statement_types  IN VARCHAR2 := NULL,
update_check     IN BOOLEAN  := FALSE,
enable           IN BOOLEAN  := TRUE
static_policy    IN BOOLEAN  := FALSE);
```

where:

object_schema. Schema owning the table/view; current user if NULL.

object_name. Name of table or view.

policy_group. Name of the group to which the policy belongs.

policy_name. Name of policy to be added.

function_schema. Schema of the policy function; current user if NULL.

policy_function. Function to generate predicates for this policy.

statement_types. Statement type that the policy applies; default is ANY.

update_check. Policy checked against updated or inserted value? Must be set to TRUE to validate INSERT and UPDATE operations.

enable. Policy is enabled?

static_policy. Is this a static policy?

ADD_POLICY Syntax

```
DBMS_RLS.ADD_POLICY (
    object_schema    IN VARCHAR2 := NULL,
    object_name      IN VARCHAR2,
    policy_name      IN VARCHAR2,
    function_schema  IN VARCHAR2 := NULL,
    policy_function  IN VARCHAR2,
    statement_types  IN VARCHAR2 := NULL,
    update_check     IN BOOLEAN  := FALSE,
    enable           IN BOOLEAN  := TRUE
    static_policy    IN BOOLEAN  := FALSE);
```

where:

object_schema. Schema owning the table/view, current user if NULL.

object_name. Name of table or view.

policy_name. Name of policy to be added.

function_schema. Schema of the policy function, current user if NULL.

policy_function. Function to generate predicates for this policy.

statement_types. Statement type that the policy applies, default is any.

update_check. Policy checked against updated or inserted value? Must be set to TRUE to validate INSERT and UPDATE operations.

enable. Policy is enabled?

static_policy. Is this a static policy? If so, means that the predicate will always be the same.

ADD_POLICY_CONTEXT Syntax

```
DBMS_RLS.ADD_POLICY_CONTEXT (
    object_schema    IN VARCHAR2 := NULL,
    object_name      IN VARCHAR2,
    namespace        IN VARCHAR2,
    attribute        IN VARCHAR2);
```

where:

object_schema. Schema owning the table/view; current user if NULL.

object_name. Name of table or view.

namespace. Namespace of the driving context.

attribute. Attribute of the driving context.

CREATE_POLICY_GROUP Syntax

```
DBMS_RLS.CREATE_POLICY_GROUP (
   Object_schema IN VARCHAR2 := NULL,
   Object_name   IN VARCHAR2,
   policy_group  IN VARCHAR2);
```

where:

>   **object_schema.** Schema owning the table/view; current user if NULL.
>   **object_name.** Name of table or view the group is for.
>   **policy_group.** Name of the policy group to create for the table or view.

DELETE_POLICY_GROUP Syntax

```
DBMS_RLS.DELETE_POLICY_GROUP (
   Object_schema IN VARCHAR2 := NULL,
   Object_name   IN VARCHAR2,
   policy_group  IN VARCHAR2);
```

where:

>   **object_schema.** Schema owning the table/view; current user if NULL.
>   **object_name.** Name of table or view for the group being dropped.
>   **policy_group.** Name of the policy group to drop for the table or view.

DELETE_POLICY_GROUP Syntax

```
DBMS_RLS.DELETE_POLICY_GROUP (
   object_schema IN VARCHAR2 := NULL,
   group_name    IN VARCHAR2,
   policy_name   IN VARCHAR2);
```

where:

>   **object_schema.** Schema owning the table/view; current user if NULL.
>   **group_name.** Name of the group for the policy being disabled.
>   **policy_name.** Name of the policy to disable for the table or view.

DROP_GROUPED_POLICY Syntax

```
DBMS_RLS.DROP_GROUPED_POLICY (
   object_schema IN VARCHAR2 := NULL,
   group_name    IN VARCHAR2,
   policy_name   IN VARCHAR2);
```

where:

> **object_schema.** Schema owning the table/view; current user if NULL.
>
> **group_name.** Name of the group for the policy being dropped.
>
> **policy_name.** Name of the policy to drop for the table or view.

DROP_POLICY Syntax

```
DBMS_RLS.DROP_POLICY (
    object_schema IN VARCHAR2 := NULL,
    object_name   IN VARCHAR2,
    policy_name   IN VARCHAR2);
```

where:

> **object_schema.** Schema containing the table or view; logon user if NULL.
>
> **object_name.** Name of table or view.
>
> **policy_name.** Name of policy to be dropped from the table or view.

DROP_POLICY_CONTEXT Syntax

```
DBMS_RLS.DROP_POLICY_CONTEXT (
    object_schema   IN VARCHAR2 := NULL,
    object_name     IN VARCHAR2,
    namespace       IN VARCHAR2,
    attribute       IN VARCHAR2);
```

where:

> **object_schema.** Schema owning the table/view; current user if NULL.
>
> **object_name.** Name of table or view.
>
> **namespace.** Namespace of the driving context to be dropped.
>
> **attribute.** Attribute of the driving context to be dropped.

ENABLE_ POLICY_GROUP Syntax

```
DBMS_RLS.ENABLE_POLICY_GROUP (
    object_schema IN VARCHAR2 := NULL,
    group_name    IN VARCHAR2,
    policy_name   IN VARCHAR2
    enable        IN BOOLEAN  := TRUE);
```

where:

> **object_schema.** Schema owning the table/view; current user if NULL.
>
> **group_name.** Name of the group for the policy being enabled.

policy_name. Name of the policy to enable for the table or view.

enable. Enable the grouped policy; set to FALSE to disable.

ENABLE_POLICY Syntax

```
DBMS_RLS.ENABLE_POLICY (
    object_schema IN VARCHAR2 := NULL,
    object_name   IN VARCHAR2,
    policy_name   IN VARCHAR2,
    enable        IN BOOLEAN);
```

where:

object_schema. Schema containing the table or view; logon user if NULL.

object_name. Name of table or view with which the policy is associated.

policy_name. Name of policy to be enabled or disabled.

enable. TRUE to enable the policy, FALSE to disable the policy.

REFRESH_GROUPED_POLICY Syntax

```
DBMS_RLS.REFRESH_GROUPED_POLICY (
    object_schema IN VARCHAR2 := NULL,
    object_name   IN VARCHAR2 := NULL,
    group_name    IN VARCHAR2 := NULL,
    policy_name   IN VARCHAR2 := NULL);
```

where:

object_schema. Schema containing the table or view.

object_name. Name of table or view with which the policy is associated.

group_name. Name of group that contains the policy for the table or view.

policy_name. Name of policy to be refreshed.

REFRESH_POLICY Syntax

```
DBMS_RLS.REFRESH_POLICY (
    object_schema IN VARCHAR2 := NULL,
    object_name   IN VARCHAR2 := NULL,
    policy_name   IN VARCHAR2 := NULL);
```

where:

object_schema. Schema containing the table or view.

object_name. Name of table or view with which the policy is associated.

policy_name. Name of policy to be refreshed.

9.8 FURTHER DBA READING

The DBA is encouraged to obtain and review the following resources:

Ault, Michael R. *Exam Cram Oracle8i DBA Test 1: SQL and PL/SQL*, Certification Insider Press, Coriolis Group Books, 2001.

Oracle9i Administrator's Guide, Release 1 (9.0.1), Part No. A90117-01, Oracle Corporation, June 2001.

Oracle9i Concepts, Release 1 (9.0.1), Part No. A88856-01, Oracle Corporation, June 2001.

Oracle Enterprise Manager Administrators Guide, Release 9.0.1, Part No. A88767-02, Oracle Corporation, June 2001.

Oracle9i Reference, Release 1 (9.0.1), Part No. A90190-01, Oracle Corporation, June 2001.

Oracle9i SQL Reference, Release 1 (9.0.1), Part No. A90125-01, Oracle Corporation, June 2001.

Oracle9i Supplied PL/SQL Packages and Types Reference, Release 1 (9.0.1), Part No. A89852-02, Oracle Corporation, June 2001.

9.9 SUMMARY

This chapter delved into issues surrounding the creation and managing of database users, also known as schemas, and how to implement various security and auditing options in Oracle. The chapter also covered changes to the Oracle8i features in Oracle9i, such as the use of row-level security and of resource groups and policies.

CHAPTER 10

Monitoring Database Tables, Indexes, Clusters, Snapshots, and Objects

Since the days of SQLDBA or nothing (for you new folks, that was version 6), Oracle has come a long way with its database monitoring tools. Server Manager, Enterprise Manager, and the numerous other Oracle-provided monitoring tools make the task of monitoring databases easier.

That said, be aware that many of these tools still only monitor the very top level of the data dictionary, to answer questions such as how many users, how many tables, and how many indexes; they do little in the way of in-depth monitoring (to answer questions such as what is user X doing, when will table Y extend next).

NOTE Server Manager (SVRMGR), which was heavily used in Oracle7, 8, and 8*i,* is no longer available in 9*i.*

Several companies offer excellent monitoring tools: Precise, with its Q and Precise* SQL packages; the Quest product suite; Patrol from BMC; ECO Tools; and the many CA offerings spring to mind. All of these tools, however, while freeing some DBAs, end up crippling others because the DBAs never learn the underlying structures of the data dictionary. I am a firm believer in not providing complex, feature-rich tools to inexperienced DBAs, because they need to understand the data dictionary first. The point is, tools only go so far, and a DBA has to be able to dig into the data dictionary to find and correct problems. If you believe great tools make great works, try giving the best materials and the best tools to ineffective or inexperienced workers: the result may be better than with poor materials and tools, but it will probably still be unsatisfactory. As with all things, when using Oracle, knowledge means power: the power to solve problems or, better yet, to prevent them from happening in the first place.

In the past few years, since the publication of my first three books, I have interviewed dozens of candidates for Oracle DBA and developer positions. Some had great resumes, but when I began asking about the data dictionary and V$ tables, really getting under the hood of Oracle, I found many were clueless. To prevent anyone saying that about you, I refer you to the Oracle9i Reference Manual documentation link on the companion Web site; it should become your map, guide, and bible to the Oracle data dictionary and support tables. Also, refer to the documentation (available on the companion Web site) throughout this chapter for definitions of the various views and tables used by the monitoring scripts. I have attempted to provide a "road map" of the views that relate to a specific topic (such as table or indexes). Use this map and the reference manual on the technet.oracle.com Web site to see how the data dictionary views are laid out.

The data dictionary tables (which are usually suffixed with a dollar sign [$], though there are exceptions) are owned by the SYS user and normally shouldn't be accessed except when the supporting views don't have the required data. These are documented in Appendix D. Instead, Oracle has provided DBA_, USER_, and ALL_ views into these tables, which should be used whenever possible; the DBA_ views are documented in Appendix E. In addition, Oracle has provided the dynamic performance tables (DPTs), which provide running statistics and internals information. These DPTs all begin with V$ or, in their pristine form, V_$. The DPTs are also documented in the reference manual.

The data dictionary views are created by the catalog.sql script, located in the $ORACLE_HOME/rdbms/admin directory. The catalog.sql script is a required readme file. The script has numerous remarks and comments that will improve your understanding of the data dictionary views severalfold. I warn you, though, the catalog.sql script is over 200 pages long.

10.1 USING THE ORACLE8, ORACLE8i, AND ORACLE9i DATA DICTIONARY

These tables, views, and DPTs provide detailed information about the system, the data dictionary, and the processes for the Oracle database. Reports can access the data dictionary objects to give the DBA just about any cut on the data he or she desires. Many, if not all, of the reports given in the following sections utilize these objects either directly or indirectly via the $tables, V$ DPTs, or DBA_ views.

The data dictionary objects can also be queried interactively during a DBA user session to find the current status of virtually any system parameter. The use of dynamic SQL against the DBA_ views can shorten a DBA task, such as switching users from one temporary tablespace to another or dropping a set of tables, by a factor of 10 or more.

In the days of SQLDBA, it was often easier to monitor with scripts than with the Oracle-provided monitor screens. The SVRMGR product, with its GUI interface, was an improvement, as was the Enterprise Manager. However, these still don't provide the flexibility available from user-generated scripts. The Performance Pack can be customized to add user-generated monitoring queries. However, the Performance Pack is a cost add-on (and a performance cost) to the system DBA tools.

However, all of the above lack adequate report capabilities. To remedy this shortfall, DBAs must be prepared to create SQL, SQL*Plus, and PL/SQL reports that provide just the cut of information they require. This chapter discusses these reports and shows examples of scripts used to generate them. I suggest that, you, the DBA, review the contents of the V$ and DBA_ views as listed in either the *Oracle, Oracle8i,* or *Oracle9i Administrator's Guide* (Release 1 (9.0.1), June 2001, Part No. A90117-01, Oracle Corporation). Additional information is contained in the *Oracle8, Oracle8i,* or *Oracle9i Reference* (Release 1 (9.0.1), June 2001, Part No. A90190-02, Oracle Corporation).

10.2 USING THE VIEWS AND DYNAMIC PERFORMANCE TABLES TO MONITOR TABLES, CLUSTERS, SNAPSHOTS, TYPES, AND INDEXES

Now that we know all about the views and DPTs, let's look at how they are used to monitor various database table-related constructs.

Monitoring Tables with the V$ and DBA_ Views

Previously, when it came to tables, the DBA had four major concerns: Who owns them? Where were they created? Are they clustered? What is their space utilization? And, since Oracle8, the DBA also has to be concerned with issues such as: Is the table an object or relational table? Does the table contain REFs, VARRAYS, or NESTED TABLES? Is the table (if relational) partitioned? The scripts and techniques in this section will answer these types of questions about tables.

The Oracle Administrator toolbar provides the Schema Manager, which allows GUI-based management of database schema objects. The screen for Oracle version 7.3 of this product is shown in Figure 10.1. The Oracle Administrator product is great for on-screen viewing of database objects, but lacks suitable report capabilities, so the ability to monitor database objects via scripts is still critical. To this end, we will examine a few simple reports; first, though, take a look at Figure 10.2, which shows the cluster of DBA_ views used to monitor tables.

Monitoring Ownership, Placement, and Clustering A single report can determine who owns tables, where they were created, and if they are clustered. This report for tables is shown in Source 10.1. It is important to monitor tables right after they have been created for proper sizing and storage parameters. This can be accomplished through the use of the script in Source 10.1, which documents how a table was created. The Enterprise Manager application provides this data in a very user-friendly format, as demonstrated in Listing 10.1.

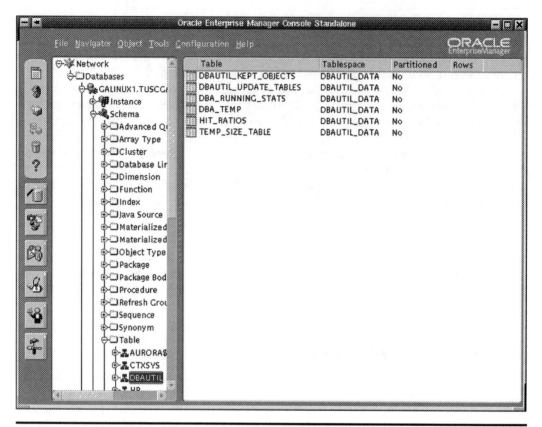

FIGURE 10.1 Oracle Enterprise Manager schema screen.

Notice that the script in Source 10.1 excludes the tables owned by any users other than SYSTEM and SYS. Oracle9*i* has added a plethora of new user names to the list of Oracle-provided users. It seems there must be a new user for each new feature. Since a good DBA never uses these users unless absolutely required, no extraneous tables should be created after product loads; therefore, the data won't change. For the purposes of this report, we are more concerned with new tables. (That said, astute readers will note that I have included the QS user so I can include some other examples in the report.) For Oracle8*i* and earlier, you will need to remove the union clause and the extern column; for Oracle8, you will need to remove the temporary column select; for Oracle7, you will need to remove the temporary, IOT, nested, and partitioned columns. The items the DBA should watch for in the output of the report script shown in Listing 10.1 follow:

- Tables that should belong to a specific application but that belong to a specific user rather than the assigned application owner.

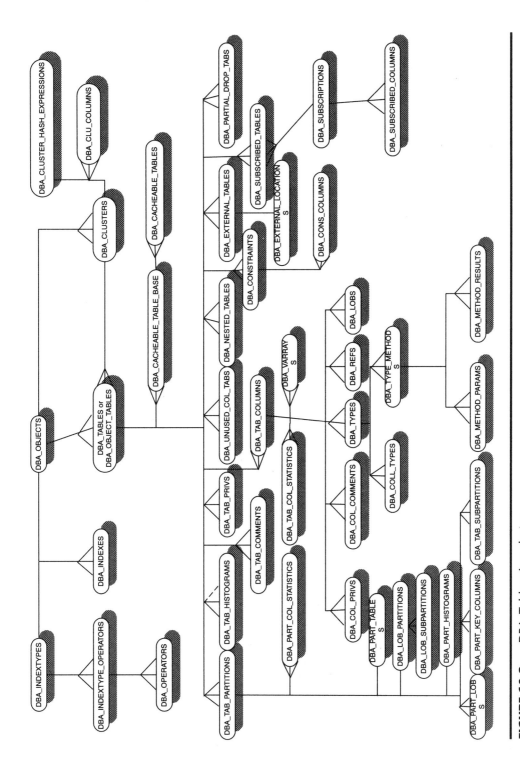

FIGURE 10.2 DBA_Tables view cluster.

511

Source 10.1   Table report script.

```
REM
REM NAME        : TABLE.SQL
REM FUNCTION    : GENERATE TABLE REPORT
REM Limitations : None
clear COLUMNs
COLUMN owner              FORMAT a15      HEADING 'Table | Owner'
COLUMN table_name         FORMAT a18      HEADING Table
COLUMN tablespace_name    FORMAT A13      HEADING Tablespace
COLUMN pct_increase                       HEADING 'Pct|Increase'
COLUMN init                               HEADING 'Initial|Extent'
COLUMN next                               HEADING 'Next|Extent'
COLUMN partitioned        FORMAT a4       HEADING 'Par?'
COLUMN iot_type           FORMAT a4       HEADING 'Iot?'
COLUMN nested             FORMAT a5       HEADING 'Nest?'
COLUMN temporary          FORMAT a5       HEADING 'Temp?'
COLUMN extern             FORMAT a8       Heading 'External?'
BREAK ON owner ON tablespace_name
SET PAGES 48 LINES 132
START TITLE132 "ORACLE TABLE REPORT"
SPOOL rep_out\&db\tab_rep
SELECT
    owner,
    tablespace_name,
    table_name,
    initial_extent Init,
    next_extent Next,
    pct_increase,
    partitioned,
    DECODE(iot_type,NULL,'No','Yes') iot_type,
    nested,
    DECODE(temporary,'N','No','Yes') temporary,
        DECODE(initial_extent, null,
            DECODE(iot_type,null,
            DECODE(temporary,'N','Yes')),'No') extern
FROM
    sys.dba_tables
WHERE
    owner NOT IN  (
'SYSTEM','SYS','DBSNMP','AURORA$JIS$UTILITY$',
'AURORA$ORB$UNAUTHENTICATED','SCOTT','OSE$HTTP$ADMIN',
'OUTLN','LBACSYS','OE','QS','QS_CS','QS_CB','QS_CBADM',
'QS_OS','QS_ES','QS_WS','QS_ADM','SH','HR','WKSYS','ORDSYS',
'ORDPLUGINS','CTXSYS','MDSYS','PM')
ORDER BY
    owner,
    tablespace_name,
    table_name;
SPOOL OFF
```

```
CLEAR COLUMNS
PAUSE Press enter to continue
SET PAGES 22 LINES 80
TTITLE OFF
CLEAR COLUMNS
CLEAR BREAKS
```

Listing 10.1   Example of the table report script output.

```
Date: 10/07/01                                                    Page 1
Time: 09:48 PM                    ORACLE TABLE REPORT              System
                                  galinux1 database


Table
Owner    Tablespace    Table             Initial   Next    Pct
                                         Extent    Extent  Inc Par? Iot? Nest? Temp? External
-------- ------------- ----------------- --------- ------- --- ---- ---- ----- ----- --------
DBAUTIL  DBAUTIL_DATA  DBAUTIL_KEPT_OBJ    16384    204800   0 NO   No   NO    No
                       DBAUTIL_UPD_TABS    57344    204800   0 NO   No   NO    No
                       DBA_RUNNING_STATS 1048576    204800   0 NO   No   NO    No
                       DBA_TEMP            16384    204800   0 NO   No   NO    No
                       HIT_RATIOS          16384    204800   0 NO   No   NO    No
                       TEMP_SIZE_TABLE     16384    204800   0 NO   No   NO    No
         SYSTEM        SQL_SCRIPTS                             NO   No   NO    No    Yes
                       SQL_SCRIPTS2                            NO   No   NO    No    Yes
QS       EXAMPLE       AQ$_AQ$_MEM_MC_S    65536               NO   No   NO    No
                       AQ$_MEM_MC          65536               NO   No   NO    No
                       QS_ORDERS_PR_MQTAB  65536               NO   No   NO    No
                       QS_ORDERS_SQTAB     65536               NO   No   NO    No
                       SYS_IOT_OVER_31044  65536               NO   Yes  NO    No
                       SYS_IOT_OVER_31065  65536               NO   Yes  NO    No
                       AQ$_AQ$_MEM_MC_H                        NO   Yes  NO    No
                       AQ$_AQ$_MEM_MC_I                        NO   Yes  NO    No
                       AQ$_AQ$_MEM_MC_NR                       NO   Yes  NO    No
                       AQ$_AQ$_MEM_MC_T                        NO   Yes  NO    No
```

- Excessive use of clusters.
- Tables that appear in the SYSTEM tablespace or in tablespaces other than where they belong.

You will also note that this report gives no sizing information. This is covered in the next section. Determining whether the sizing of tables is correct is one of the important tasks of the DBA.

Monitoring Size of Tables   One method to determine whether your default storage sizing is correct for a tablespace is to monitor the extents for each of the tables that reside in the tablespace. Another method is to monitor the used space against the available space for each table. Scripts to perform these functions are shown in Sources 10.2 and 10.3; Listing 10.2 shows the output from the report in Source 10.2.

Source 10.2   SQL*Plus report to show extents for each table in each tablespace.

```
REM
REM NAME                : EXTENTS.SQL
REM FUNCTION            : GENERATE EXTENTS REPORT
REM USE                 : FROM SQLPLUS OR OTHER FRONT END
REM LIMITATIONS         : NONE
REM
CLEAR COLUMNS
COLUMN segment_name     HEADING 'Segment'      FORMAT A15
COLUMN tablespace_name  HEADING 'Tablespace'   FORMAT A10
COLUMN owner            HEADING 'Owner'        FORMAT A10
COLUMN segment_type     HEADING 'Type'         FORMAT A10
COLUMN size             HEADING 'Size'          FORMAT 999,999,999
COLUMN extents          HEADING 'Current|Extents'
COLUMN max_extents      HEADING 'Max|Extents'
COLUMN bytes            HEADING 'Size|(Bytes)'
SET PAGESIZE 58 NEWPAGE 0 LINESIZE 130 FEEDBACK OFF
SET ECHO OFF VERIFY OFF
ACCEPT extents PROMPT 'Enter max number of extents: '
BREAK ON tablespace_name SKIP PAGE ON owner
START TITLE132 "Extents Report"
DEFINE output = rep_out\&db\extent
SPOOL &output
SELECT  tablespace_name,
     segment_name,
     extents,
     max_extents,
     bytes,
     owner "owner",
     segment_type
FROM    dba_segments
WHERE extents >= &extents AND owner LIKE UPPER('%&owner%')
ORDER BY tablespace_name,owner,segment_type,segment_name;
SPOOL OFF
CLEAR COLUMNS
CLEAR BREAKS
SET TERMOUT ON FEEDBACK ON VERIFY ON
UNDEF extents
UNDEF owner
TTITLE OFF
UNDEF OUTPUT
PAUSE Press enter to continue
```

Listing 10.2   Example of output from the extents script.

```
Date: 06/12/97                                          Page:   1
Time: 09:55 PM              Extents Report              SYSTEM
                           ORTEST1 database


                           Current   Max   Size
Tablespace Segment         Extents Extents (Bytes) Owner    Type
---------- --------------- ------- ------- ------- --------- -------

SYSTEM     C_OBJ#              10     249 1323008 SYS       CLUSTER
           C_TOID_VERSION#      7     249  352256           CLUSTER
           I_ARGUMENT1          6     249  229376           INDEX
           I_COL1               8     249  565248           INDEX
           I_COL2               6     249  258048           INDEX
           I_COL3               5     249  176128           INDEX
           I_DEPENDENCY1        5     249  147456           INDEX
           I_DEPENDENCY2        5     249  147456           INDEX
           I_OBJ2               5     249  147456           INDEX
           I_Source1           11     249 1765376           INDEX
           SYSTEM              16     249  983040           ROLLBACK
           ACCESS$              6     249  229376           TABLE
           ARGUMENT$            6     249  229376           TABLE
           COM$                 5     249  147456           TABLE
           DEPENDENCY$          5     249  147456           TABLE
           IDL_CHAR$            5     249  147456           TABLE
           IDL_SB4$             6     249  229376           TABLE
           IDL_UB1$             9     249  802816           TABLE
           IDL_UB2$            10     249 1191936           TABLE
           OBJ$                 6     249  229376           TABLE
           Source$             13     249 3915776           TABLE
           VIEW$                9     249  802816           TABLE
```

Source 10.3   Actual size report.

```
rem   *******************************************************
rem
rem   NAME: ACT_SIZE.sql
rem
rem   HISTORY:
rem   Date             Who                 What
rem   --------         -------------------- -----------------------------
rem   09/??/90   Maurice C. Manton     Creation for IOUG
rem   12/23/92   Michael Brouillette   Assume TEMP_SIZE_TABLE exists.Use
rem   DBA info.
rem   Prompt for user name. Spool file = owner.
rem    07/15/96   Mike Ault Updated for Oracle 7.x, added indexes
rem    06/12/97   Mike Ault Updated for Oracle 8.x (use DBMS_ROWID)
```

continues

Source 10.3   Continued.

```
rem  FUNCTION:  Will show actual blocks used vs allocated for all tables rem
for a user
rem  INPUTS:  owner = Table owner name.
rem  ***************************************************************
ACCEPT owner PROMPT 'Enter table owner name: '
SET HEADING OFF FEEDBACK OFF VERIFY OFF ECHO OFF RECSEP OFF PAGES 0
COLUMN db_block_size NEW_VALUE blocksize NOPRINT
TTITLE OFF
DEFINE cr='chr(10)'
DEFINE qt='chr(39)'
TRUNCATE TABLE temp_size_table;
SELECT value db_block_size FROM v$parameter WHERE name='db_block_size';
SPOOL fill_sz.sql
SELECT
 'INSERT INTO temp_size_table'||&&cr||
 'SELECT '||&&qt||segment_name||&&qt||&&cr||
 ',COUNT(DISTINCT(dbms_rowid.rowid_block_number(rowid))) blocks'||&&cr||
 'FROM &&owner..'||segment_name, ';'
FROM
  dba_segments
WHERE
  segment_type ='TABLE'
  AND owner = UPPER('&owner');
SPOOL OFF
SPOOL index_sz.sql
SELECT
    'CREATE TABLE stat_temp AS SELECT * FROM index_stats;'||&&cr||
    'TRUNCATE TABLE stat_temp;'
FROM
    dual;
SELECT
'ANALYZE INDEX '||owner||'.'||index_name||' VALIDATE STRUCTURE;'||&&cr||
'INSERT INTO stat_temp SELECT * FROM index_stats;'||&&cr||
'COMMIT;'
FROM
   dba_indexes
WHERE
   owner=UPPER('&owner');
SPOOL OFF
SET FEEDBACK ON TERMOUT ON LINES 132
START index_sz.sql
INSERT INTO temp_size_table SELECT name,trunc(used_space/&&blocksize)
FROM stat_temp;
DROP TABLE stat_temp;
DEFINE temp_var = &&qt;
START fill_sz
HOST rm fill_size_table.sql
DEFINE bs = '&&blocksize K'
COLUMN t_date       NOPRINT NEW_VALUE t_date
```

```
COLUMN user_id        NOPRINT NEW_VALUE user_id
COLUMN segment_name        FORMAT A25          HEADING "SEGMENT|NAME"
COLUMN segment_type        FORMAT A7           HEADING "SEGMENT|TYPE"
COLUMN extents             FORMAT 999          HEADING "EXTENTS"
COLUMN kbytes              FORMAT 999,999,999 HEADING "KILOBYTES"
COLUMN blocks              FORMAT 9,999,999   HEADING "ALLOC.|&&bs|BLOCKS"
COLUMN act_blocks          FORMAT 9,999,990   HEADING "USED|&&bs|BLOCKS"
COLUMN pct_block           FORMAT 999.99       HEADING "PCT|BLOCKS|USED"
START title132 "Actual Size Report for &owner"
SET PAGES 55
BREAK ON REPORT ON segment_type SKIP 1
COMPUTE SUM OF kbytes ON segment_type REPORT
SPOOL rep_out\&db\&owner
SELECT
    segment_name,
    segment_type,
    SUM(extents) extents,
    SUM(bytes)/1024 kbytes,
    SUM(a.blocks) blocks,
    NVL(MAX(b.blocks),0) act_blocks,
    (MAX(b.blocks)/SUM(a.blocks))*100 pct_block
FROM
    sys.dba_segments a,
    temp_size_table b
WHERE
    segment_name = UPPER( b.table_name )
GROUP BY
    segment_name,
    segment_type
ORDER BY
    segment_type,
    segment_name;
SPOOL OFF
TRUNCATE TABLE temp_size_table;
SET TERMOUT ON FEEDBACK 15 VERIFY ON PAGESIZE 20 LINESIZE 80 SPACE 1
UNDEF qt
UNDEF cr
TTITLE OFF
CLEAR COLUMNS
CLEAR COMPUTES
PAUSE press enter to continue
```

The script to calculate the actual size of a table or index (shown in Source 10.3) uses the TEMP_SIZE_TABLE, which is created with the script shown in Source 10.4. As shown, the act_size script will work only with Oracle8 and Oracle8*i*. To use act_size with Oracle7, replace the call to the dbms_rowid.rowid_block_number procedure with SUBSTR(ROWID,1,8). The act_size.sql report cannot resolve index-only overflow tables or complex objects involving nested tables. Output from the act_size report is shown in Listing 10.3.

Source 10.4   Script to create TEMP_SIZE_TABLE.

```
rem
rem Create temp_size_table for use by actsize.sql
rem
CREATE TABLE temp_size_table (
      table_name VARCHAR2(64),
      blocks NUMBER);
```

Listing 10.3   Example of output of actual size report.

```
Date: 06/12/97                                                      Page:   1
Time: 11:28 PM                    Actual Size Report for tele_dba         SYSTEM
                                    ORTEST1 database
```

SEGMENT NAME	SEGMENT TYPE	EXTENTS	KILOBYTES	ALLOC. 4096 K BLOCKS	USED 4096 K BLOCKS	PCT BLOCKS USED
FK_ACCOUNT_EXECS_1	INDEX	1	12	3	0	.00
FK_ADDRESSES_1		1	10,240	2,560	0	.00
FK_ADDRESSES_2		1	51,200	12,800	2,480	19.38
FK_ADDRESSES_3		1	51,200	12,800	2,967	23.18
FK_FRANCHISE_CODES_1		1	10,240	2,560	461	18.01
FK_SIC_CODES_1		1	51,200	12,800	3,893	30.41
FK_USERS_1		1	102,400	25,600	0	.00
LI_LOAD_TEST		1	40,960	10,240	5,536	54.06
OID_CLIENTSV8		1	20	5	0	.00
OID_EARNINGS_INFO_NMBRS		1	20	5	0	.00
...						
PK_ADDRESSES		1	102,400	25,600	5,203	20.32
PK_CLIENTS		1	102,400	25,600	3,212	12.55
PK_EARNINGS_INFO_NMBRS		1	102,400	25,600	2,780	10.86
PK_FRANCHISE_CODES		1	51,200	12,800	573	4.48
PK_SIC_CODES		1	51,200	12,800	4,863	37.99
UI_EARNINGS_INFO_NMBRS_ID		1	51,200	12,800	4,466	34.89
UK_CLIENTS		1	51,200	12,800	4,292	33.53
UK_LOAD_TEST		1	51,200	12,800	4,650	36.33
	*******		----------			
	sum		1,116,564			
ACCOUNT_EXECS	TABLE	1	12	3	0	.00
ADDRESSES		1	204,800	51,200	32,827	64.12
ADDRESS_TEST		1	20	5	1	20.00
CLIENTS		2	307,200	76,800	61,587	80.19
....						
EARNINGS_INFO_NMBRS		1	204,800	51,200	28,485	55.63
EARNINGS_INFO_NUMBERSV8		1	20,480	5,120	0	.00

EMPLOYEES		1	20	5	0	.00
FRANCHISE_CODES		1	76,800	19,200	803	4.18
INTERACTION_LOG_ACTIVITY		1	12	3	0	.00
LOAD_TEST		3	615,420	153,855	140,441	91.28
LOOKUPS		1	12	3	0	.00
SIC_CODES		1	102,400	25,600	16,765	65.49
USERS		1	204,800	51,200	1	.00
	*******		---------			
	sum		2,036,056			
			---------			
sum			3,152,620			

Each of the above reports gives specific information. In the report from Source 10.2, if a table shows more than 1,000 extents, the DBA should review its size usage via the report in Source 10.3, and rebuild the table with better storage parameters. In the report in Listing 10.3, if a table shows that it is using far less space than it has been allocated, and history has shown it won't grow into the space, it should be re-created accordingly.

Monitoring Table Statistics   Under Oracle7 and Oracle8, the DBA_TABLES view has several additional columns that are populated once a table has been analyzed using the ANALYZE TABLE command. The columns document table-specific data such as number of rows, number of allocated blocks, number of empty blocks, average percentage of free space in a table, number of chained rows, and average row length. In Oracle8*i*, the view gained the avg_space_freelist_blocks and num_freelist_blocks columns. In Oracle9*i*, the dependencies column was added. This provides the DBA with a more detailed view of the tables in the database than ever before. This also shows the need for a new report to document this data in hard-copy format so a DBA can easily track a table's growth, space usage, and chaining. The sample script in Source 10.5 shows such a report. Example output from the report is shown in Listing 10.4.

Source 10.5   Script to report additional table statistics.

```
rem
rem   NAME: tab_stat.sql
rem
rem   FUNCTION:  Show table statistics for user's tables or all tables.
rem   10/08/01 Updated for 9i Mike Ault
rem
 SET PAGES 56 LINES 132 NEWPAGE 0 VERIFY OFF ECHO OFF FEEDBACK OFF
rem
COLUMN owner            FORMAT a12          HEADING "Table Owner"
COLUMN table_name       FORMAT a20          HEADING "Table"
```

continues

Source 10.5   Continued.

```
COLUMN tablespace_name   FORMAT a20              HEADING "Tablespace"
COLUMN num_rows          FORMAT 999,999,999      HEADING "Rows"
COLUMN blocks            FORMAT 999,999          HEADING "Blocks"
COLUMN empty_blocks      FORMAT 999,999          HEADING "Empties"
COLUMN space_full        FORMAT 999.99           HEADING "% Full"
COLUMN chain_cnt         FORMAT 999,999          HEADING "Chains"
COLUMN avg_row_len       FORMAT 99,999,999 HEADING "Avg Length|(Bytes)"
rem
START title132 "Table Statistics Report"
DEFINE OUTPUT = 'rep_out\&db\tab_stat..lis'
SPOOL &output
rem
BREAK ON OWNER SKIP 2 ON TABLESPACE_NAME SKIP 1;
SELECT owner, table_name, tablespace_name, num_rows, blocks,
     empty_blocks,
     100*((num_rows *
     avg_row_len)/((GREATEST(blocks,1)+empty_blocks)*value))
     space_full,
     chain_cnt, avg_row_len
FROM dba_tables, v$parameter
WHERE OWNER NOT IN ('SYS','SYSTEM')
and num_rows>0
and name='db_block_size'
ORDER BY owner, tablespace_name;
SPOOL OFF
PAUSE Press enter to continue
SET PAGES 22 LINES 80 NEWPAGE 1 VERIFY ON FEEDBACK ON
CLEAR COLUMNS
CLEAR BREAKS
TTITLE OFF
```

Listing 10.4   Example of output of report in Source 10.5.

```
Date: 10/07/01
Page:
Time: 11:29 PM                 Table Statistics Report        DBAUTIL
                                  galinux1 database

                                                                 Avg Length
Table Owner  Table           Tablespace     Rows  Blocks Empties % Full Chains  (Bytes)
-----------  --------------- -------------- ------ ------- -------- ------- -------- ----------
DBAUTIL      DBA_TEMP        DBAUTIL_DATA      50      1      23    .74      0       29
HR           REGIONS         EXAMPLE            4      1       6    .12      0       17
             LOCATIONS                         23      1       0  13.76      0       49
             DEPARTMENTS                       27      1       0   6.59      0       20
             EMPLOYEES                        107      2       0  44.41      0       68
             JOB_HISTORY                       10      1       0   3.78      0       31
             JOBS                              19      1       0   7.65      0
```

If indicated by the actual space report, or if the report shown in Source 10.5 shows improper space utilization or excessive chaining, the table(s) involved should be rebuilt. One oddity to notice in the above report is that the Empties columns for many of the HR schema tables show 0 as a value and yet the used space calculations (% Full) show there should be some empty blocks. I analyzed the REGIONS table and, viola! They appeared. Oracle has apparently used the DBMS_STATS package to load statistics in to the data dictionary for their example tables. The selection of the db_block_size will only work in 9*i* if the tablespace in which the table resides is using the default blocksize. If you will be using the new capability of Oracle9*i* to use multiple blocksizes in the same database, change the query to use the block_size column in the DBA_TABLESPACES view instead. Note: I have left this script generic so it can be used with older releases of Oracle.

One method of rebuilding a table is as follows:

1. Using a SQL script, unload the table into a flat file.
2. Drop the table and re-create it with a more representative storage clause.
3. Use SQLLOADER to reload the table data.

A second method is:

1. Using the CREATE TABLE. . .AS SELECT. . .FROM command, build a second table that is a mirror image of the first table (SELECT * FROM first table) with a storage clause that specifies a larger initial extent.
2. Delete the first table.
3. Use the RENAME command to rename the second table with the first table's name.

Of course, the easiest method (since late version 7.3) is to use the Oracle ALTER TABLE...MOVE command without specifying a new tablespace (unless you actually want to move the table to a new tablespace); this will allow the DBA to re-create the table in place, changing the desired storage characteristics.

Monitoring Table Types: Partition, Nested, IOT, External   With Oracle8, the new type of tables caused numerous new columns to be added to the DBA_TABLES view. These rows tell a DBA whether a table is nested or partitioned, whether or not a table is an index-only or overflow table, as well as its logging status. A simple report like that shown in Source 10.6 provides a convenient format for managing this data.

The output from the report on extended table parameters is shown in Listing 10.5. This is about the only place you will find documentation on index-only tables, unless you go back to the XX$ table level. Notice the UNION command: for Oracle8, the first half can be removed and the table name changed to dba_tables. The DBA_OBJECT_TABLES view was added and the type-related columns placed there in Oracle8*i*.

The report output in Listing 10.5 shows the following information for Oracle8, Oracle8*i,* and Oracle9*i* tables. (Note: For Oracle8 and Oracle8*i* tables, you will have to remove sections that don't have counterparts to Oracle9*i*'s new features, such as the UNION to DBA_EXTERNAL_TABLES.)

Source 10.6   Example of script to document extended table parameters.

```
REM
REM      Name:      tab_rep.sql
REM      FUNCTION:  Document table extended parameters
REM      Use:       From SQLPLUS
REM     MRA 6/13/97 Created for ORACLE8
REM    MRA 5/08/99 Updated for ORACLE8i
REM   MRA 10/08/01 Updated for Oracle9i
REM
COLUMN owner            FORMAT a10 HEADING 'Owner'
COLUMN table_name       FORMAT a15 HEADING 'Table'
COLUMN tablespace_name  FORMAT a13 HEADING 'Tablespace'
COLUMN table_type_owner FORMAT a10 HEADING 'Type|Owner'
COLUMN table_type       FORMAT a13 HEADING 'Type'
COLUMN iot_name         FORMAT a10 HEADING 'IOT|Overflow'
COLUMN iot_type         FORMAT a12 HEADING 'IOT or|Overflow'
COLUMN nested           FORMAT a6  HEADING 'Nested'
COLUMN extern           FORMAT a3  HEADING 'Ext'
UNDEF owner
SET LINES 130 VERIFY OFF FEEDBACK OFF PAGES 58
START title132 'Extended Table Report'
SPOOL rep_out\&&db\ext_tab.lis
SELECT
     owner,
     table_name,
     tablespace_name,
     iot_name,
     logging,
     partitioned,
     iot_type,
      'N/A' table_type_owner,
      'N/A' table_type,
     DECODE(temporary,'N','No',temporary),
     nested,
      'N/A' extern
FROM
     dba_tables
WHERE
     owner LIKE UPPER('%&&owner%')
UNION
SELECT
     owner,
     table_name,
     tablespace_name,
     iot_name,
     logging,
     partitioned,
     iot_type,
     table_type_owner,
```

```
        table_type,
        DECODE(temporary,'N','No',temporary),
        nested,
         'N/A' extern
FROM
     dba_object_tables
WHERE
     owner LIKE UPPER('%&&owner%')
UNION
SELECT
     Owner,
     'None' tablespace_name,
      'N/A' Iot_name,
      'N/A' logging,
      'N/A' partitioned,
      'N/A' Iot_type,
      type_owner table_type_owner,
      type_name table_type,
      'N/A' temporary,
      'N/A' nested,
       'Yes' extern
FROM
     Dba_external_tables
WHERE
     Owner LIKE UPPER('%&&owner%');
SPOOL OFF
SET VERIFY ON LINES 80 PAGES 22 FEEDBACK ON
TTITLE OFF
UNDEF OWNER
CLEAR COLUMNS
```

Listing 10.5   Example of output from the extended table parameters report.

```
Date: 10/08/01                                                      Page: 1
Time: 12:06 AM                   Extended Table Report              DBAUTIL
                                  galinux1 database


                                   IOT          IOT or Type
Owner      Table           Tablespace   Ovf  LOG PAR Ovf  Owner   Type          Tmp Nest Ext
---------- --------------- ------------ ---- --- --- ------ ------ ------------- --- ---- ---
DBAUTIL    DBAUTIL_KEPT_OB DBAUTIL_DATA      YES NO          N/A    N/A           No  NO   N/A
DBAUTIL    DBAUTIL_UPD_TAB DBAUTIL_DATA      YES NO          N/A    N/A           No  NO   N/A
DBAUTIL    DBA_RUNNING_STA DBAUTIL_DATA      YES NO          N/A    N/A           No  NO   N/A
DBAUTIL    DBA_TEMP        DBAUTIL_DATA      YES NO          N/A    N/A           No  NO   N/A
DBAUTIL    HIT_RATIOS      DBAUTIL_DATA      YES NO          N/A    N/A           No  NO   N/A
DBAUTIL    SQL_SCRIPTS     None        N/A  N/A N/A N/A     SYS    ORACLE_LOADER N/A N/A  Yes
DBAUTIL    SQL_SCRIPTS     SYSTEM            YES NO          N/A    N/A           No  NO   N/A
```

continues

Listing 10.5 Continued.

DBAUTIL	SQL_SCRIPTS2	None	N/A	N/A N/A N/A		SYS	ORACLE_LOADER	N/A N/A		Yes
DBAUTIL	SQL_SCRIPTS2	SYSTEM		YES NO		N/A	N/A		No NO	N/A
DBAUTIL	STAT_TEMP	DBAUTIL_DATA		YES NO		N/A	N/A		No NO	N/A
DBAUTIL	TEMP_SIZE_TABLE	DBAUTIL_DATA		YES NO		N/A	N/A		No NO	N/A

Owner. The owner of the table.

Table. The table name.

Tablespace. The tablespace name.

IOT Overflow. Gives the name of the IOT tables overflow table.

LOG. Does this table use redo logging?

PAR. Is this table partitioned?

IOT or Overflow. Is this table an IOT or overflow table?

Type Owner. The owner of the type used to build this table.

Type. The main type used to build this table.

Tmp. Is this a temporary table?

Nest. Is this a nested table store table?

Ext. Is this an external table (9*i* only)?

Note that there are entries for the external tables stored in both the DBA_TABLES and DBA_EXTERNAL_TABLES views; in the DBA_TABLES views, the tablespace for all external tables is SYSTEM, and the initial extent, next extent, and pctincrease will be null.

If a table has been analyzed, then its relative statistics will be shown in the DBA_TABLES or DBA_OBJECT_TABLES views. Source 10.7 shows an example of a report for monitoring the statistics of analyzed tables. The DBA should pay attention to the statistics gathered by the analyzer since they are used by the optimizer to tune the queries when Choose mode is set. If rule-based optimization is being used, there should be no statistics present for the tables in the application. The output from the tab_stat. sql report is shown in Listing 10.6.

Source 10.7 Example of script to report table statistics.

```
rem
rem   NAME: tab_stat.sql
rem
rem   FUNCTION:Show table statistics for a user's tables or all tables.
rem
  set pages 56 lines 130 newpage 0 verify off echo off feedback off
```

```
rem
COLUMN owner                FORMAT a12              HEADING "Table Owner"
COLUMN table_name           FORMAT a17              HEADING "Table"
COLUMN tablespace_name      FORMAT a13              HEADING "Tablespace"
COLUMN num_rows             FORMAT 99,999,999       HEADING "Rows"
COLUMN blocks               FORMAT 99,999           HEADING "Blocks"
COLUMN empty_blocks         FORMAT 99,999           HEADING "Empties"
COLUMN space_full           FORMAT 999.99           HEADING "% Full"
COLUMN chain_cnt            FORMAT 99,999           HEADING "Chains"
COLUMN avg_row_len          FORMAT 9,999,999 HEADING "Avg|Length|(Bytes)"
COLUMN num_freelist_blocks FORMAT 99,999 HEADING "Num|Freelist|Blocks"
COLUMN avg_space_freelist_blocks FORMAT 99,999 HEADING "Avg|Space|Freelist
Blocks"
rem
START title132 "Table Statistics Report"
DEFINE OUTPUT = 'rep_out\&db\tab_stat..lis'
SPOOL &output
rem
BREAK ON OWNER SKIP 2 ON TABLESPACE_NAME SKIP 1;
SELECT
   owner, table_name, tablespace_name,
   num_rows, blocks,empty_blocks,
   100*((num_rows * avg_row_len)/((GREATEST(blocks,1) + empty_blocks)
   * 2048)) space_full,
   chain_cnt, avg_row_len,avg_space_freelist_blocks,
   num_freelist_blocks
FROM
   dba_tables
WHERE
  owner NOT IN ('SYS','SYSTEM')
UNION
SELECT
   owner, table_name, tablespace_name,
   num_rows, blocks,empty_blocks,
   100*((num_rows * avg_row_len)/((GREATEST(blocks,1) + empty_blocks)
   * 2048)) space_full,
   chain_cnt, avg_row_len,avg_space_freelist_blocks,
   num_freelist_blocks
FROM
   dba_object_tables
WHERE
  owner NOT IN ('SYS','SYSTEM')
ORDER BY
   owner, tablespace_name;
SPOOL OFF
PAUSE Press enter to continue
SET PAGES 22 LINES 80 NEWPAGE 1 VERIFY ON FEEDBACK ON
CLEAR COLUMNS
CLEAR BREAKS
TTITLE OFF
```

Listing 10.6   Example of table statistics report.

```
Date: 05/09/99                                                          Page:    1
Time: 02:12 PM                  Table Statistics Report                 SYS
                                  ORTEST1 database

                                                           Avg        Avg      Num
                                                           Length     Space    FL
Table Owner   Table           Tablespace    Rows Blocks Empties % Full Chains (Bytes) FL Blocks Blocks
------------  --------------  ------------- ----- ------ ------- ------ ------ ------- --------- ------
GRAPHICS_DBA  BASIC_LOB_TABLE GRAPHICS_DATA     0      0     259    .00      0       0         0      0
              GRAPHICS_TABLE                   32      1     258    .31      0      52     2,276      1
              INTERNAL_GRAPHICS                32      2     257    .93      1     154     2,212      1

MIGRATE       FET$            SYSTEM        5,482     55       0 175.21      0      36     3,768     13
              TS$                              24     55       0   2.22      0     104     3,768     13

OUTLN         OL$             SYSTEM            4      1       1  16.80      0     172     3,308      1
              OL$HINTS                        175      5       0  90.58      0      53     3,168      3

TELE_DBA      ADDRESSESV8i    GRAPHICS_DATA     0      0       4    .00      0       0         0      0
              CIRCUITSV8i                       0      0       4    .00      0       0         0      0
              CLIENTSV8i                        0      0   5,119    .00      0       0         0      0
              CONTRACTSV8i                      0      0       4    .00      0       0         0      0
              DEPT                              1      1       3    .52      0      43     3,959      1
              EMP                               1      1       3    .40      0      33     3,971      1
```

Monitoring Table Columns   To round out the general table reports, we need a report on the columns within a table. The script in Source 10.8 fulfills this need.

Source 10.8   Script to report table columns by owner and table.

```
rem
rem tab_col.sql
rem
rem FUNCTION: Report on Table and View Column Definitions
rem
rem MRA 9/18/96
rem MRA 6/14/97 Added table level selectivity
rem
COLUMN owner              FORMAT a10        HEADING Owner
COLUMN table_name         FORMAT a30        HEADING "Table or View Name"
COLUMN COLUMN_name        FORMAT a32        HEADING "Table or View|Attribute"
COLUMN data_type          FORMAT a15        HEADING "Data|Type"
COLUMN data_type_owner    FORMAT a13        HEADING "Type|Owner"
COLUMN data_length                          HEADING Length
COLUMN nullable           FORMAT a5         HEADING Null
```

```
BREAK ON owner ON table_name SKIP 1
SET LINES 132 PAGES 48 FEEDBACK OFF VERIFY OFF
START title132 "Table Columns Report"
SPOOL rep_out/&db/tab_col
SELECT
        a.owner,
        table_name||' '||object_type table_name,
        column_name,
        data_type,
        data_type_owner,
        data_length,
        DECODE(nullable,'N','NO','YES') nullable
FROM
        dba_tab_columns a, dba_objects b
WHERE
        a.owner=UPPER('&owner') AND
        a.owner=b.owner AND
        a.table_name LIKE UPPER('%&table%') AND
        a.table_name=b.object_name AND
        object_type IN ('TABLE','VIEW','CLUSTER')
ORDER BY
        owner,
        object_type,
        table_name,
        column_id
/
SPOOL OFF
TTITLE OFF
SET LINES 80 PAGES 22 FEEDBACK ON VERIFY ON
```

The script in Source 10.8 allows you to specify for a specific owner the table for which you want to see the columns. If a naming convention that includes prefix or suffix designations is used when naming tables, then the prefix or suffix can be specified to pull the values for a specific type of table. The output from the script is shown in Listing 10.7.

Listing 10.7   Example of the output from the table column report.

```
Enter value for owner: tele_dba
Enter value for table: CLIENTS_INFO_NUMBERSV8i
Date: 05/09/99                                                      Page:   1
Time: 11:43 AM                    Table Columns Report                  SYS
                                   ORTEST1 database
```

continues

Listing 10.7   Continued.

Owner	Table or View Name	Table or View Attribute	Data Type	Type Owner	Length	Null
TELE_DBA	CLIENTS_INFO_NUMBERSV8i TABLE	CLIENTS_INFO_NMBRS_ID	NUMBER		22	NO
		CLIENTS_ID_R	CLIENT_T	TELE_DBA	50	YES
		LISTED_NAME	VARCHAR2		100	YES
		EARNING_NUMBER	CHAR		13	YES
		SERVICE_CLASS	VARCHAR2		5	YES
		NO_OF_LINES	NUMBER		22	YES
		DISCONNECT_DATE	DATE		7	YES
		DISCONNECT_REASON	CHAR		2	YES
		BILLING_NAME	VARCHAR2		40	YES
		PHONE	VARCHAR2		10	YES
		BTN	CHAR		13	YES
		OLD_CLIENTS_NUMBER	CHAR		13	YES
		SERVICE_ADDRESS	VARCHAR2		100	YES
		CON_CTRL_NUMBER	CHAR		15	YES
		TERM_AGREEMENT	CHAR		13	YES
		SHARED_TENANT_SVCS	VARCHAR2		10	YES
		INSTALLATION_DATE	DATE		7	YES
		CONTRACTS	CONTRACT_LIST	TELE_DBA	16	YES
		CIRCUITS	CIRCUIT_LIST	TELE_DBA	16	YES

Monitoring Table Column Statistics   Oracle has provided column-level statistics in the DBA_TAB_COLUMNS view. Several of the statistics, such as average length, number of null values, and so on, are useful to the DBA. These table column statistics aren't populated unless the table is analyzed. Source 10.9 shows a report script for these table column statistics. The output from the script in Source 10.9 is shown in Listing 10.8.

Source 10.9   Example of table column statistics.

```
rem
rem tab_col_stat.sql
rem
rem FUNCTION: Report on Table and View Column Definitions
rem
rem MRA 9/18/96
rem MRA 6/14/97 Added table level selectivity
rem MRA 5/8/99 Converted to do stats
rem
COLUMN owner        FORMAT a12      HEADING Owner
COLUMN table_name   FORMAT a20      HEADING "Table Name"
COLUMN COLUMN_name  FORMAT a13      HEADING "Table|Attribute"
COLUMN data_type    FORMAT a10      HEADING "Data|Type"
COLUMN avg_col_len  FORMAT 99,999   HEADING "Aver|Length"
```

```
COLUMN density              FORMAT 9.9999   HEADING "Density"
COLUMN last_analyzed                        Heading "Analyzed"
COLUMN num_distinct                         HEADING "Distinct|Values"
COLUMN num_nulls                            HEADING "Num.|Nulls"
COLUMN sample_size                          HEADING "Sample|Size"
BREAK ON owner ON table_name SKIP 1
SET LINES 132 PAGES 48 FEEDBACK OFF VERIFY OFF
START title132 "Table Column Stats Report"
SPOOL rep_out/&db/tab_col
SELECT
   owner,table_name,column_name,data_type,
   num_distinct,density,num_nulls,
   TO_CHAR(last_analyzed,'dd-mon-yyyy hh24:mi') last_analyzed,
   sample_size, avg_col_len
FROM
   dba_tab_columns
WHERE
   owner LIKE UPPER('%&owner%')
   and table_name LIKE UPPER('%&tabname%')
/
SPOOL OFF
TTITLE OFF
SET LINES 80 PAGES 22 FEEDBACK ON VERIFY ON
```

Listing 10.8   Example of output from the table column statistics report.

```
Enter value for owner: graphics_dba
Enter value for tabname:
Date: 05/09/99                                                          Page:  1
Time: 01:39 PM               Table Column Stats Report                       SYS
                              ORTEST1 database
```

Owner	Table Name	Table Attribute	Data Type	Distinct Values	Density	Num. Nulls	Analyzed	Sample Size	Aver Length
GRAPHICS_DBA	BASIC_LOB_TABLE	X	VARCHAR2	0	.0000	0	09-may-1999 10:44		0
		B	BLOB						
		C	CLOB						
	GRAPHICS_TABLE	BFILE_ID	NUMBER	32	.0313	0	09-may-1999 10:44	32	2
		BFILE_DESC	VARCHAR2	0	.0313	32	09-may-1999 10:44		0
		BFILE_LOC	BFILE	30	.0333	0	09-may-1999 10:44	32	40
		BFILE_TYPE	VARCHAR2	2	.5000	0	09-may-1999 10:44	32	1
	INTERNAL_GRAPHICS	GRAPHIC_ID	NUMBER	32	.0313	0	09-may-1999 10:45	32	2
		GRAPHIC_DESC	VARCHAR2	31	.0323	0	09-may-1999 10:45	32	18
		GRAPHIC_BLOB	BLOB						
		GRAPHIC_TYPE	VARCHAR2	2	.5000	0	09-may-1999 10:45	32	1

Monitoring Table Keys Per the requirements of Third Normal Form, each table is required to have a unique identifier that consists of one or more of the table's columns. As an alternative, a derived key can be used that consists of a number pulled from an Oracle sequence, but this method should be used only if the key would be excessively long (over three columns). This is called the *primary key* of the table, and it should be identified using a constraint clause when the table is created. A second type of key, called a *foreign key*, is also present in most tables. The foreign key is used to enforce relationships between two or more tables. The foreign key consists of the primary key from the related table. The foreign key, too, should be identified by a constraint clause when the table is created.

If the two types of keys have been identified via the constraint clause during table creation, they can be readily monitored via the PK_FK_RPT.SQL script, which is available on the Wiley Web site. For an example of this script's output, see Listing 10.9.

Monitoring Tables for Chained Rows Row chaining occurs as data is added to an existing record. When there is insufficient room for the addition, the row is chained to another block and added there. Block chaining occurs when a row is too long to fit into a single block (such as with long raw or LOB columns or when a row has more than 255 columns). If chaining is occurring regularly, it can lead to significant performance degradation. This degradation is caused by the requirement to read multiple blocks to retrieve a single record. An example of a script to monitor a single table for chained rows is shown in Source 10.10. Note that this script is limited, in that the table must have a primary or unique key defined in order for it to work. With a companion script, all tables in an application can be checked with this script. As an alternative, you can analyze the tables of concern and use the table statistics report, as described in the following subsection.

Listing 10.9   Example of output of the primary/foreign key report.

```
Date: 05/09/99                                                          Page:    1
Time: 03:13 PM                  Primary Key - Foreign Key Report         SYSTEM
                                     ORTEST1 database


Pri Table   Pri Table          Pri Key             For Table   For Table             For Key
Owner       Name               COLUMNs             Owner       Name                  COLUMNs
----------  ------------------ ------------------  ----------  --------------------  ----------------
TELE_DBA    BBS_DUNS_PROFILE   SITE_ID             TELE_DBA    BBS_FRANCHISE_CODES   SITE_ID
                               SITE_ID                         BBS_SIC_CODES         SITE_ID
            BBS_EARNINGS_INFO  EARNING_NO_DOCID    TELE_DBA    BBS_AUDIT_RECORD      EARNING_NO_DOCID
                               EARNING_NO_DOCID                BBS_CIRCUIT_ID_INFO   EARNING_NO_DOCID
                               EARNING_NO_DOCID                STI_ADDRESS           EARNING_NO_DOCID
            CUSTOMER_SITES     SITE_ID             TELE_DBA    BBS_DUNS_PROFILE      SITE_ID
                               SITE_ID                         BBS_EARNINGS_INFO     SITE_ID
TEMP_USER   DEPT               DEPTNO              TEMP_USER   EMP                   DEPTNO
```

The ANALYZE Command   The ANALYZE command can also be used to generate chained row information into the DBA_TABLES view. Actual chained-row rowids can be listed in a separate table if desired. The general format of this command follows:

```
ANALYZE TABLE_or_CLUSTER [schema.]table_or_cluster
LIST CHAINED ROWS INTO [schema.]table;
```

Under Oracle8, Oracle8*i*, and Oracle9*i*, there is a script called utlchain.sql that will build the chained row table for you. An example of a script to perform a chain analysis of a table for an owner is shown in Source 10.10. Source 10.11 shows a second script, which, with the script in Source 10.10 altered as annotated, will analyze all tables for a specified owner for chains. Listing 10.10 shows the results of this automated chain analysis for an owner's tables.

Source 10.10   Interactive SQL script to determine chained rows in a table.

```
rem  ********************************************************************
rem
rem  NAME:      CHAINING.sql
rem
rem  FUNCTION: Report number of CHAINED rows within a named table
rem
rem  NOTES:  Requires DBA priviledges.
rem         Target table must have column that is the leading portion
rem         of an index and is defined as not null.
rem         Uses the V$SESSTAT table. USERNAME is the current user.
rem         A problem if > 1 session active with that USERID.
rem         V$SESSTAT may change between releases and
rem         platforms.  Make sure that 'table fetch continued row' is
rem         a valid statistic.
rem         This routine can be run by AUTO_CHN.sql by remarking the
rem         two accepts and un-remarking the two defines.
rem
rem  INPUTS: obj_own = the owner of the table.
rem          obj_nam = the name of the table.
rem
rem  ********************************************************************
ACCEPT obj_own PROMPT 'Enter the table owner''s name: '
ACCEPT obj_nam PROMPT 'Enter the name of the table: '

rem DEFINE obj_own = &1    fl Remove comment to use with auto_chain
rem DEFINE obj_nam = &2    fl Remove comment to use with auto_chain

SET TERMOUT OFF FEEDBACK OFF VERIFY OFF ECHO OFF HEADING OFF
SET EMBEDDED ON
COLUMN statistic# NEW_VALUE stat_no NOPRINT
```

continues

Source 10.10   Continued.

```
SELECT
    statistic#
FROM
    v$statname

WHERE
    n.name = 'table fetch continued row'
/
rem  Find out who we are in terms of sid
COLUMN sid NEW_VALUE user_sid
SELECT
    distinct sid
FROM
    v$session
WHERE
    audsid = USERENV('SESSIONID')
/

rem  Find the last col of the table and a not null indexed column
COLUMN column_name      NEW_VALUE last_col
COLUMN name        NEW_VALUE indexed_column
COLUMN value       NEW_VALUE before_count
SELECT
    column_name
  FROM
    dba_tab_columns
 WHERE
    table_name = upper('&&obj_nam')
        and owner = upper('&&obj_own')
 ORDER BY
    column_id
/
SELECT
    c.name
  FROM
    sys.col$ c,
    sys.obj$ idx,
    sys.obj$ base,
    sys.icol$ ic
  WHERE
    base.obj#      = c.obj#
        and ic.bo#     = base.obj#
        and ic.col#    = c.col#
        and base.owner# = (SELECT user# FROM sys.user$
                WHERE name = UPPER('&&obj_own'))
        and ic.obj#    = idx.obj#
        and base.name  = UPPER('&&obj_nam')
        and ic.pos#    = 1
        and c.null$    > 0
```

```
/
SELECT value
  FROM v$sesstat
 WHERE v$sesstat.sid = &user_sid
   AND v$sesstat.statistic# = &stat_no
/
rem  Select every row from the target table
SELECT &last_col xx
  FROM &obj_own..&obj_nam
 WHERE &indexed_column <= (SELECT MAX(&indexed_column)
                  FROM &obj_own..&obj_nam)
/
COLUMN value NEW_VALUE after_count
SELECT value
  FROM v$sesstat
 WHERE v$sesstat.sid = &user_sid
   AND v$sesstat.statistic# = &stat_no
/
SET TERMOUT ON

SELECT
'Table '||UPPER('&obj_own')||'.'||UPPER('&obj_nam')||' contains '||
       (TO_NUMBER(&after_count) - TO_NUMBER(&before_count))||
       ' chained row'||
       DECODE(to_NUMBER(&after_count) - TO_NUMBER(&before_count),1,'.','s.')
  FROM dual
 WHERE RTRIM('&indexed_column') IS NOT NULL
/

rem If we don't have an indexed column this won't work so say so
SELECT 'Table '||
       UPPER('&obj_own')||'.'||UPPER('&obj_nam')||
       ' has no indexed, not null columns.'
  FROM dual
 WHERE RTRIM('&indexed_column') IS NULL
/

SET TERMOUT ON FEEDBACK 15 VERIFY ON PAGESIZE 20 LINESIZE 80 SPACE 1
SET HEADING ON
UNDEF obj_nam
UNDEF obj_own
UNDEF before_count
UNDEF after_count
UNDEF indexed_column
UNDEF last_col
UNDEF stat_no
UNDEF user_sid
CLEAR COLUMNS
CLEAR COMPUTES
```

Source 10.11   The AUTO_CHN.SQL script to automate chaining determination.

```
rem   **************************************************************
rem
rem   NAME: AUTO_CHN.sql
rem
rem   FUNCTION: Run CHAINING.sql for all of a users tables.
rem
rem   NOTES:Requires mod to CHAINING.sql. See CHAINING.sql header
rem
rem   INPUTS:
rem             tabown = Name of owner.
rem
rem   **************************************************************
rem
ACCEPT tabown PROMPT 'Enter table owner: '
rem
SET TERMOUT OFF FEEDBACK OFF VERIFY OFF ECHO OFF HEADING OFF PAGES 999
SET EMBEDDED ON
COLUMN name NEW_VALUE db NOPRINT
SELECT name FROM v$database;
SPOOL rep_out\auto_chn.gql
rem
SELECT 'start chaining &tabown '||table_name
  FROM dba_tables
 WHERE owner = UPPER('&tabown')
/

SPOOL OFF
SPOOL rep_out\&db\chaining
START rep_out\auto_chn.gql
SPOOL OFF
UNDEF tabown
SET TERMOUT ON FEEDBACK 15 VERIFY ON PAGESIZE 20 LINESIZE 80 SPACE 1
SET EMBEDDED OFF
HO del rep_out\auto_chn.gql
PAUSE Press enter to continue
```

Also provided in the DBA_TABLES view is a column showing chained rows for a specific table. If you don't particularly care what rows are chained, just whether you have chaining, a simple query against this view will tell you, if you have analyzed the table.

Monitoring Grants on a Table   The DBA also needs to monitor grants on tables. It is good to know who is granting which privileges to whom. The script to determine this is shown in Source 10.12. Listing 10.11 shows the listing generated from Source 10.12.

Listing 10.10   Example of output when AUTO_CHN.SQL is run against a user's tables.

```
Table SYSTEM.CGS_REFLINE contains 0 chained rows.
Table SYSTEM.CGS_WKSTATION contains 0 chained rows.
Table SYSTEM.CGS_WSATTRIBUTES contains 0 chained rows.
Table SYSTEM.CGS_WSCOLORS contains 0 chained rows.
Table SYSTEM.CGS_WSFONTS contains 0 chained rows.
Table SYSTEM.CGS_WSLNSTYLES contains 0 chained rows.
Table SYSTEM.CGS_WSPATTERNS contains 0 chained rows.
Table SYSTEM.DBA_TEMP has no indexed, not null columns.
Table SYSTEM.DEF$_CALL contains 0 chained rows.
Table SYSTEM.DEF$_CALLDEST contains 0 chained rows.
Table SYSTEM.DEF$_DEFAULTDEST contains 0 chained rows.
```

Source 10.12   SQL script to show object-level grants.

```
rem*********************************************************************
rem   NAME: db_tgnts.sql
rem
rem   FUNCTION: Produce report of table or procedure grants showing
rem   GRANTOR, GRANTEE or ROLE and specific GRANTS.
rem
rem   INPUTS: Owner name
rem *********************************************************************
rem
COLUMN grantee          FORMAT A18      HEADING "Grantee|or Role"
COLUMN owner            FORMAT A18      HEADING "Owner"
COLUMN table_name       FORMAT A30      HEADING "Table|or Proc"
COLUMN grantor          FORMAT A18      HEADING "Grantor"
COLUMN privilege        FORMAT A10      HEADING "Privilege"
COLUMN grantable        FORMAT A19      HEADING "Grant|Option?"
rem
BREAK ON owner SKIP 4 ON table_name SKIP 1 ON grantee ON grantor ON REPORT
rem
SET LINESIZE 130 PAGES 56 VERIFY OFF FEEDBACK OFF
START title132 "TABLE GRANTS BY OWNER AND TABLE"
DEFINE OUTPUT = rep_out/&&db/db_tgnts
SPOOL &output
REM
SELECT
     owner,
     table_name,
     grantee,
     grantor,
     privilege,
     grantable
FROM
     dba_tab_privs
```

continues

Source 10.12   Continued.

```
WHERE
     owner NOT IN ('SYS','SYSTEM')
ORDER BY
     owner,
     table_name,
     grantor,
     grantee;
REM
SPOOL OFF
PAUSE Press enter to continue
```

Listing 10.11   Example of report from grant script.

```
Date: 05/22/96                                              Page:1
Time: 01:49 PM          TABLE GRANTS BY OWNER AND TABLE     SYSTEM
                              ORDSPTD6 database


             Table      Grantee                             Grant
 Owner       or Proc    or Role      Grantor   Privilege    Option?
 --------    --------   -----------  --------- ------------ -------
 DSPTDBA     ACCCAR     DSPT_DEV     DSPTDBA   DELETE       NO
                                               INSERT       NO
                                               SELECT       NO
                                               UPDATE       NO
                                               ALTER        NO
                        DSPT_USER    DSPTDBA   DELETE       NO
                                               UPDATE       NO
                                               SELECT       NO
                                               INSERT       NO
             ACT        DSPT_DEV     DSPTDBA   DELETE       NO
                                               SELECT       NO
                                               UPDATE       NO
                                               ALTER        NO
                                               INSERT       NO
                        DSPT_USER    DSPTDBA   DELETE       NO
                                               UPDATE       NO
                                               SELECT       NO
                                               INSERT       NO
             ADD_REC    DSPT_USER    DSPTDBA   EXECUTE      NO
```

Using the above report makes it is easy to monitor the grants on specific objects. A close look at the generation script shows that this report may be as selective as the individual object level, or as general as the entire database. Using this script, the DBA can find out the level of protection for any and all database objects.

Monitoring Partitioned Tables Partitioned tables and indexes were new in Oracle8. In Oracle8*i*, their functionality has been expanded to include subpartitions and the ability to hash partitions. The DBA will be tasked with monitoring these new types of tables. Essentially, the DBA will want to know which tables are partitioned, the ranges for each partition, and the table fraction locations for each partition. Let's examine a couple of reports that provide this level of information. The first report script provides information on partition names, partitioning value, partition tablespace location, and whether the partition is logging or not. The script is shown in Source 10.13.

Source 10.13   Script to report on partitioned table structure.

```
rem
rem Name: tab_part.sql
rem Function : Report on partitioned table structure
rem History: MRA 6/13/97 Created
rem
COLUMN table_owner      FORMAT a10 HEADING 'Owner'
COLUMN table_name       FORMAT a15 HEADING 'Table'
COLUMN partition_name   FORMAT a15 HEADING 'Partition'
COLUMN tablespace_name FORMAT a15 HEADING 'Tablespace'
COLUMN high_value       FORMAT a10 HEADING 'Partition|Value'
COLUMN subpartition_count FORMAT 9,999 HEADING 'Sub-Partitions'
SET LINES 130
START title132 'Table Partition Files'
BREAK ON table_owner ON table_name
SPOOL rep_out/&&db/tab_part.lis
SELECT
     table_owner,
     table_name,
     partition_name,
     sub_partition_count,
     high_value,
     tablespace_name,
     logging
FROM sys.dba_tab_partitions
ORDER BY table_owner,table_name
/
SPOOL OFF
```

The output from the script in Source 10.13 is shown in Listing 10.12. When looking at the report in this listing, keep in mind that the Partition Value column contains the value that the partition values will be *less than* but won't include.

Listing 10.12   Example of output of the partitioned table structures report.

```
Date: 05/09/99                                                          Page:   1
Time: 03:42 PM                       Table Partition Files              SYSTEM
                                     ORTEST1 database


                                     Partition                              Sub
Owner       Table         Partition  Value      Tablespace   LOGGING Partitions
----------  ------------  ---------- ---------- -----------   ------- ----------
SYSTEM      TEST5         Q1_1997    TO_DATE('  USER_DATA     NONE            5
                                     1997-04-01
                                      00:00:00'
                                     , 'SYYYY-M
                                     M-DD HH24:
                                     MI:SS', 'N
                                     LS_CALENDA
                                     R=GREGORIA

            Q2_1997                  TO_DATE('  USER_DATA     NONE            4
                                     1997-07-01
                                      00:00:00'
                                     , 'SYYYY-M
                                     M-DD HH24:
                                     MI:SS', 'N
                                     LS_CALENDA
                                     R=GREGORIA

            Q3_1997                  TO_DATE('  USER_DATA     NONE            2
                                     1997-10-01
                                      00:00:00'
                                     , 'SYYYY-M
                                     M-DD HH24:
                                     MI:SS', 'N
                                     LS_CALENDA
                                     R=GREGORIA

            Q4_1997                  TO_DATE('  USER_DATA     NONE            8
                                     1998-01-01
                                      00:00:00'
                                     , 'SYYYY-M
                                     M-DD HH24:
                                     MI:SS', 'N
                                     LS_CALENDA
                                     R=GREGORIA

            Q1_1998                  TO_DATE('  USER_DATA     NONE            4
                                     1998-04-01
                                      00:00:00'
                                     , 'SYYYY-M
                                     M-DD HH24:
                                     MI:SS', 'N
                                     LS_CALENDA
                                     R=GREGORIA
```

The second set of data a DBA will want to know about a partition structure is its storage characteristics. The report in Source 10.14 shows an example of a report with this type of information. An example of output from the script in Source 10.14 is shown in Listing 10.13.

Source 10.14   Example of script to report on partition storage characteristics.

```
rem
rem NAME:    Tab_pstor.sql
rem FUNCTION: Provide data on part. table stor. charcacteristics
rem HISTORY: MRA 6/13/97 Created
rem
COLUMN table_owner          FORMAT a6         HEADING 'Owner'
COLUMN table_name           FORMAT a14        HEADING 'Table'
COLUMN partition_name       FORMAT a9         HEADING 'Partition'
COLUMN tablespace_name      FORMAT a11        HEADING 'Tablespace'
COLUMN pct_free             FORMAT 9999       HEADING '%|Free'
COLUMN pct_used             FORMAT 999        HEADING '%|Use'
COLUMN ini_trans            FORMAT 9999      HEADING 'Init|Tran'
COLUMN max_trans            FORMAT 9999      HEADING 'Max|Tran'
COLUMN initial_extent       FORMAT 9999999   HEADING 'Init|Extent'
COLUMN next_extent          FORMAT 9999999   HEADING 'Next|Extent'
COLUMN max_extent                            HEADING 'Max|Extents'
COLUMN pct_increase         FORMAT 999        HEADING '%|Inc'
COLUMN partition_position FORMAT 9999        HEADING 'Part|Nmbr'
SET LINES 130
START title132 'Table Partition File Storage'
BREAK ON table_owner on table_name
SPOOL rep_out/&&db/tab_pstor.lis
SELECT
    table_owner,
    table_name,
    tablespace_name,
    partition_name,
    partition_position,
    pct_free,
    pct_used,
    ini_trans,
    max_trans,
    initial_extent,
    next_extent,
    max_extent,
    pct_increase
FROM sys.dba_tab_partitions
ORDER BY table_owner,table_name
/
SPOOL OFF
```

Listing 10.13   Example of partition storage report output.

```
Date: 06/14/97                                                        Page:   1
Time: 01:16 PM                  Table Partition File Storage          SYSTEM
                                  ORTEST1 database


                                       Part  %    %   Init Max Init   Next     Max    %
Owner  Table        Tablespace Partition Nmbr Free Use Tran Tran Extent Extent  Extents Inc
------ ------------ ---------- --------- ---- ---- --- ---- ---- ------- -------- ------- ---
SYSTEM PART_TEST    RAW_DATA   TEST_P1      1   10  90  1    255  1048576 1048576  249     0
                    RAW_DATA   TEST_P2      2   10  90  1    255  1048576 1048576  249     0
                    RAW_DATA   TEST_P3      3   10  90  1    255  1048576 1048576  249     0
```

Generally speaking, the storage characteristics for your partitions should be similar, if not identical, for a given table. Having said that, let me add that only you know your data, and if, say, you are partitioning a sales table by month, and your particular industry always has a slump in the summer (for example, you sell skis), then your summer months' partitions would be different from those for the peak months.

Monitoring Partition Statistics   Oracle8, Oracle8*i*, and Oracle9*i* partitions store their analysis results in the DBA_TAB_PARTITIONS view. The DBA needs to monitor partitions (and subpartitions) much as he or she would tables for chained rows, extents, and the like. The script in Source 10.15 shows an example of how to retrieve the statistics data in DBA_TAB_PARTITIONS. The report generated by the table partition statistic script is shown in Listing 10.14.

Source 10.15   Example of partitions statistic report.

```
rem
rem Name: tab_part_stat.sql
rem Function : Report on partitioned table statistics
rem History: MRA 6/13/97 Created
rem
COLUMN table_name        FORMAT a15    HEADING 'Table'
COLUMN partition_name    FORMAT a15    HEADING 'Partition'
COLUMN num_rows                        HEADING 'Num|Rows'
COLUMN blocks                          HEADING 'Blocks'
COLUMN avg_space                       HEADING 'Avg|Space'
COLUMN chain_cnt                       HEADING 'Chain|Count'
COLUMN avg_row_len                     HEADING 'Avg|Row|Length'
COLUMN last_analyzed                   HEADING 'Analyzed'
ACCEPT owner1 PROMPT 'Which Owner to report on?:'
SET LINES 130
START title132 'Table Partition Statistics For &owner1'
```

```
BREAK ON table_owner ON table_name ON partition_name
SPOOL rep_out/&&db/tab_part_stat.lis
SELECT
        table_name,
        partition_name,
        num_rows,
        blocks,
        avg_space,
        chain_cnt,
        avg_row_len,
        to_char(last_analyzed,'dd-mon-yyyy hh24:mi') last_analyzed
FROM
        sys.dba_tab_partitions
WHERE
        table_owner LIKE UPPER('%&&owner1%')
ORDER BY
        table_owner,table_name
/
SPOOL OFF
CLEAR BREAKS
CLEAR COLUMNS
TTITLE OFF
UNDEF owner1
```

Listing 10.14   Example of partition statistics report.

```
Date: 05/09/99                                                    Page:   1
Time: 05:27 PM              Table Partition Statistics For system     SYSTEM
                                 ORTEST1 database


                                                   Avg
                     Num              Avg   Chain   Row
Table     Partition  Rows   Blocks   Space Count   Length Analyzed
--------- ---------- ------ -------- ----- ------- ------ --------------------

TEST5     Q1_1997    0      0        0     0       0 09-may-1999 16:40
          Q2_1997    0      0        0     0       0 09-may-1999 16:40
          Q3_1997    0      0        0     0       0 09-may-1999 16:40
          Q4_1997    0      0        0     0       0 09-may-1999 16:40
          Q1_1998    0      0        0     0       0 09-may-1999 16:40
```

The DBA has to pay attention to the chain count. If this column starts showing about a 5 to 10 percent ratio against the Num Rows column, the partition needs to be rebuilt. If any partition shows that it is out of balance (excessive rows when filled in comparison to other partitions), then perhaps that partition needs to be split.

Monitoring Table Subpartitions In Oracle8*i*, the concept of partitions having subpartitions was introduced. Many of the commands, such as ALTER, require the name of the subpartition if you wish to execute commands against a subpartition. Usually, Oracle8*i* will automatically name the partitions created as subpartitions unless you specifically add a subpartition to an existing set of partitions and subpartitions. The report in Source 10.16 demonstrates how to extricate the information about subpartitions from the database data dictionary. An example of a report generated by the script in Source 10.16 is shown in Listing 10.15.

Source 10.16   Example of subpartition report script.

```
rem
rem Name: tab_subpart.sql
rem Function : Report on partitioned table structure
rem History: MRA 6/13/97 Created
rem
COLUMN table_owner NEW_VALUE owner1 NOPRINT
COLUMN table_name        FORMAT a15    HEADING 'Table'
COLUMN partition_name    FORMAT a15    HEADING 'Partition'
COLUMN tablespace_name   FORMAT a15    HEADING 'Tablespace'
COLUMN initial_extent    FORMAT 9,999 HEADING 'Initial|Extent (K)'
COLUMN next_extent       FORMAT 9,999 HEADING 'Next|Extent (K)'
COLUMN pct_increase      FORMAT 999    HEADING 'PCT|Increase'
SET LINES 130
START title132 'Table Sub-Partition Files For &owner1'
BREAK ON table_owner ON table_name ON partition_name
SPOOL rep_out/&&db/tab_subpart.lis
SELECT
    table_owner,
    table_name,
    partition_name,
        subpartition_name,
    tablespace_name,
    logging,
        initial_extent/1024 initial_extent,
        next_extent/1024 next_extent,
        pct_increase
FROM sys.dba_tab_subpartitions
ORDER BY table_owner,table_name,partition_name
/
SPOOL OFF
```

Monitoring Subpartition Statistics Like tables and partitions, statistics are all gathered at the subpartition level. The view DBA_TAB_SUBPARTITIONS contains the statistics for all analyzed subpartitions. Source 10.17 shows a sample report on subpartition statistics in Oracle8*i* and Oracle9*i*.

Listing 10.15   Example of output from subpartition report.

```
Date: 05/09/99                                                        Page:   1
Time: 03:59 PM                Table Sub-Partition Files For SYSTEM           SYSTEM
                                   ORTEST1 database


                                                          Initial     Next      PCT
Table            Partition        SUBPARTITION_NAME Tablespace LOG Extent (K) Extent (K) Increase
---------------- ---------------- ----------------- ----------- --- ------ --- ------ --- --------
TEST5            Q1_1997          SYS_SUBP1         DATA_TBS1   YES       40        40        0
                                  SYS_SUBP2         DATA_TBS2   YES       40        40        0
                                  SYS_SUBP4         DATA_TBS4   YES       40        40        0
                                  SYS_SUBP3         DATA_TBS3   YES       40        40        0
                                  WEEK1             DATA_TBS1   YES       40        40        0
                 Q1_1998          SYS_SUBP17        DATA_TBS1   YES       40        40        0
                                  SYS_SUBP18        DATA_TBS2   YES       40        40        0
                                  SYS_SUBP19        DATA_TBS3   YES       40        40        0
                                  SYS_SUBP20        DATA_TBS4   YES       40        40        0
                 Q2_1997          SYS_SUBP5         DATA_TBS1   YES       40        40        0
                                  SYS_SUBP8         DATA_TBS4   YES       40        40        0
                                  SYS_SUBP7         DATA_TBS3   YES       40        40        0
                                  SYS_SUBP6         DATA_TBS2   YES       40        40        0
                 Q3_1997          Q3_1997_S1        DATA_TBS1   YES       40        40        0
                                  Q3_1997_S2        DATA_TBS2   YES       40        40        0
                 Q4_1997          SYS_SUBP9         Q4_TBS1     YES       40        40        0
                                  SYS_SUBP10        Q4_TBS2     YES       40        40        0
                                  SYS_SUBP11        Q4_TBS3     YES       40        40        0
                                  SYS_SUBP12        Q4_TBS4     YES       40        40        0
                                  SYS_SUBP13        Q4_TBS5     YES       40        40        0
                                  SYS_SUBP14        Q4_TBS6     YES       40        40        0
                                  SYS_SUBP15        Q4_TBS7     YES       40        40        0
                                  SYS_SUBP16        Q4_TBS8     YES       40        40        0
```

Source 10.17   Example of subpartition statistics report.

```
rem
rem Name: tab_subpart_stat.sql
rem Function : Report on partitioned table structure
rem History: MRA 6/13/97 Created
rem
COLUMN table_name          FORMAT a15    HEADING 'Table'
COLUMN partition_name      FORMAT a15    HEADING 'Partition'
COLUMN subpartition_name   FORMAT a15    HEADING 'Sub|Partition'
COLUMN num_rows                          HEADING 'Num|Rows'
COLUMN blocks                            HEADING 'Blocks'
COLUMN avg_space                         HEADING 'Avg|Space'
COLUMN chain_cnt                         HEADING 'Chain|Count'
COLUMN avg_row_len                       HEADING 'Avg|Row|Length'
```

continues

Source 10.17   Continued.

```
COLUMN last_analyzed                        HEADING 'Analyzed'
ACCEPT owner1 PROMPT 'Owner to Report On?: '
SET LINES 130
START title132 'Table Sub-Partition Statistics For &owner1'
BREAK ON table_owner ON table_name ON partition_name
SPOOL rep_out/&&db/tab_subpart_stat.lis
SELECT
    table_owner,
    table_name,
    partition_name,
    subpartition_name,
    num_rows,
    blocks,
    avg_space,
    chain_cnt,
    avg_row_len,
    to_char(last_analyzed,'dd-mon-yyyy hh24:mi') last_analyzed
FROM
    sys.dba_tab_subpartitions
WHERE
    Table_owner LIKE UPPER('%&&owner1%')
ORDER BY
    table_owner,table_name,partition_name
/
SPOOL OFF
CLEAR COLUMNS
TTITLE OFF
UNDEF owner1
```

The output from the report given in Source 10.17 is shown in Listing 10.16. Note that this example isn't highly complex, as I didn't load the subpartitions with data; nevertheless, you should see the value in having a report of this type available.

Listing 10.16   Example of output from subpartition statistics report.

```
Date: 05/09/99                                                          Page:   1
Time: 04:55 PM          Table Sub-Partition Statistics For system          SYSTEM
                            ORTEST1 database


                                                                Avg
                      Sub                     Num    Avg   Chain Row
Table     Partition Partition       Rows    Blocks Space  Count Length Analyzed
--------- --------- --------------- ------- ------ ------ ----- ------ ----------------
TEST5     Q1_1997   SYS_SUBP1          0      0      0       0       0 09-may-1999 16:40
                    SYS_SUBP2          0      0      0       0       0 09-may-1999 16:40
                    SYS_SUBP3          0      0      0       0       0 09-may-1999 16:40
                    SYS_SUBP4          0      0      0       0       0 09-may-1999 16:40
                    WEEK1              0      0      0       0       0 09-may-1999 16:40
```

Q1_1998	SYS_SUBP17	0	0	0	0	0 09-may-1999 16:40
	SYS_SUBP18	0	0	0	0	0 09-may-1999 16:40
	SYS_SUBP20	0	0	0	0	0 09-may-1999 16:40
	SYS_SUBP19	0	0	0	0	0 09-may-1999 16:40
Q2_1997	SYS_SUBP5	0	0	0	0	0 09-may-1999 16:40
	SYS_SUBP6	0	0	0	0	0 09-may-1999 16:40
	SYS_SUBP7	0	0	0	0	0 09-may-1999 16:40
	SYS_SUBP8	0	0	0	0	0 09-may-1999 16:40
Q3_1997	Q3_1997_S1	0	0	0	0	0 09-may-1999 16:40
	Q3_1997_S2	0	0	0	0	0 09-may-1999 16:40
Q4_1997	SYS_SUBP9	0	0	0	0	0 09-may-1999 16:40
	SYS_SUBP10	0	0	0	0	0 09-may-1999 16:40
	SYS_SUBP11	0	0	0	0	0 09-may-1999 16:40
	SYS_SUBP12	0	0	0	0	0 09-may-1999 16:40
	SYS_SUBP13	0	0	0	0	0 09-may-1999 16:40
	SYS_SUBP14	0	0	0	0	0 09-may-1999 16:40
	SYS_SUBP15	0	0	0	0	0 09-may-1999 16:40
	SYS_SUBP16	0	0	0	0	0 09-may-1999 16:40

The DBA must pay attention to the chain count, for if this column starts showing a 5 to 10 percent ratio against the rows column, the subpartition needs to be rebuilt. If any subpartition shows that it is out of balance (excessive rows when filled in comparison to other subpartitions), then perhaps the main partition needs to be resplit using more subpartitions.

Monitoring Nested Tables Another table type new to Oracle8 was the *nested table*, defined as a table called by reference in another table and whose reference value appears as a column. Refer back to the table columns report, shown in Listing 10.7, and note the columns named "xxxx_list"(my self-imposed naming convention): each is an example of a nested table reference column. I suggest that for ease in recognizing a nested table column, you impose a similar convention. Each of these "xxxx_list" columns contains a pointer value that points to a nested table. The DBA_NESTED_ TABLES view provides a convenient place to monitor nested tables. An example of a report run against the DBA_ NESTED_TABLES view is shown in Source 10.18.

Source 10.18   Example of script to monitor nested tables.

```
rem
rem NAME: tab_nest.sql
rem PURPOSE: Report on Nested Tables
rem HISTORY: MRA 6/14/97 Created
rem Updated 5//8/99 to Oracle8i
rem
COLUMN owner                 FORMAT a10 HEADING 'Owner'
COLUMN table_name            FORMAT a15 HEADING 'Store Table'
```

continues

Source 10.18   Continued.

```
COLUMN table_type_owner    FORMAT a10 HEADING 'Type|Owner'
COLUMN table_type_name     FORMAT a15 HEADING 'Type|Name'
COLUMN parent_table_name   FORMAT a25 HEADING 'Parent|Table'
COLUMN parent_table_column FORMAT a12 HEADING 'Parent|Column'
COLUMN storage_spec        FORMAT a15 HEADING 'Storage|Spec'
COLUMN return_type         FORMAT a7  HEADING 'Return|Type'
SET PAGES 58 LINES 132 VERIFY OFF FEEDBACK OFF
START title132 'Nested Tables'
BREAK ON owner
SPOOL rep_out\&db\tab_nest.lis
SELECT
    owner,
    table_name,
    table_type_owner,
    table_type_name,
    parent_table_name,
    parent_table_column,
    LTRIM(storage_spec) storage_spec,
    LTRIM(return_type) return_type
FROM
    sys.dba_nested_tables
ORDER BY
    owner;
SPOOL OFF
```

Notice in this source the use of LTRIM on the storage_spec and return_type fields. For some reason, Oracle8*i*, version 8.1.3, stores these columns left-padded. If you don't institute a proper naming discipline with developers and with yourself under Oracle8, you will quickly become lost when trying to track down various components. The output from the script in Source 10.18 is shown in Listing 10.17.

Listing 10.17   Example of output from nested table script.

```
Date: 05/09/99                                                    Page:   1
Time: 05:47 PM                      Nested Tables                 SYSTEM
                                    ORTEST1 database


                Type     Type      Parent                  Parent   Storage          Return
Owner    Store Table    Owner    Name      Table           Column   Spec             Type
-------- -------------- -------- --------- --------------- -------- --------------- -------
SYSTEM   GALLERIES_NTAB SYSTEM   PICTURE_NT GALLERIES       CONTENTS USER_SPECIFIED LOCATOR
TELE_DBA ADDRESSESV8i   TELE_DBA ADDRESS_LIST CLIENTSV8i    ADDRESSES DEFAULT        VALUE
         CONTRACTSV8i   TELE_DBA CONTRACT_LIST CLIENTS_INFO_NUMBERSV8i CONTRACTS DEFAULT VALUE
         CIRCUITSV8i    TELE_DBA CIRCUIT_LIST CLIENTS_INFO_NUMBERSV8i CIRCUITS DEFAULT VALUE
```

NOTE   I can't stress enough how important a good naming convention is for using the new table types, object types, and various new structures in Oracle8, 8*i*, and 9*i*.

I have included several other table-monitoring scripts in the script zip file on the Wiley Web site, specifically for monitoring bound tables and tables that can't get their next extent.

Monitoring External Tables   In Oracle9*i*, the concept of external tables was introduced. These external tables combine the aspects of an Oracle table, SQLLOADER, and a BFILE, to allow the DBA to access data from a file external to the Oracle9*i* database files as if it were an unindexed normal database table. These new external tables are monitored using the DBA_EXTERNAL_TABLES and DBA_EXTERNAL_LOCATIONS views. Source 10.19 shows an example external tables report script. Sample output from it is shown in Listing 10.18.

Source 10.19   Script to monitor external tables.

```
REM EXT_TAB.SQL
REM MRA 10/08/01 Initial Creation
REM Script to monitor external tables
REM
COLUMN owner FORMAT a8 HEADING 'Owner'
COLUMN table_name FORMAT a15 Heading 'Table'
COLUMN type_owner FORMAT a8 HEADING 'Type|Owner'
COLUMN type_name FORMAT a13 HEADING 'Type|Name'
COLUMN default_directory_owner FORMAT a10 HEADING 'Dir|Owner'
COLUMN default_directory_name FORMAT a10 HEADING 'Dir|Name'
COLUMN reject_limit FORMAT a9 HEADING 'Reject|Limit'
COLUMN access_type FORMAT a6 HEADING 'Access|Type'
COLUMN access_parameters FORMAT a35 WORD_WRAPPED HEADING 'Access Parameters'
SET LINES 132 PAGES 55
START title132 'External Tables'
SPOOL rep_out/&db/ext_tab
SELECT
owner,
table_name,
type_owner,
type_name,
default_directory_owner,
default_directory_name,
reject_limit,
access_type,
```

continues

Source 10.19   Continued.

```
access_parameters
from dba_external_tables
/
SPOOL OFF
SET lines 80 Pages 22
```

Listing 10.18   Example output from external table script.

```
Date: 10/09/01                                                                     Page: 1
Time: 12:16 AM                            External Tables                          SYSTEM
                                          galinux1 database


              Type      Type          Dir       Dir       Reject    Access
Owner  Table  Owner     Name          Owner     Name      Limit     Type   Access Parameters
------ ------ -------   -----------   ------    --------  --------  ------  ---------------------------------
SYSTEM SQL_SCRIPTS  SYS  ORACLE_LOADER SYS      SQL_DIR   0         CLOB   fields terminated by ';' optionally
                                                                           enclosed by "'"
                                                                           (permissions,
                                                                           filetype,owner,group_name,size_in_b
                                                                           ytes, date_edited DATE(19) "Mon dd
                                                                           2001 hh24:mi",
                                                                           script_name)

DBAUTIL SQL_SCRIPTS  SYS  ORACLE_LOADER SYS      SQL_DIR   0         CLOB   fields terminated by ';' optionally
                                                                           enclosed by "'"
                                                                           (permissions,
                                                                           filetype,owner,group_name,size_in_b
                                                                           ytes, date_edited DATE(19) "Mon dd
                                                                           2001 hh24:mi",
                                                                           script_name)

DBAUTIL SQL_SCRIPTS2 SYS  ORACLE_LOADER SYS      SQL_DIR   0         CLOB   fields terminated by ';' optionally
                                                                           enclosed by "'"
                                                                           (permissions,
                                                                           filetype,owner,group_name,size_in_b
                                                                           ytes, date_edited DATE(19) "Mon dd
                                                                           2001 hh24:mi",
                                                                           script_name)

SH      SALES_TRANSACTI SYS  ORACLE_LOADER SYS   DATA_FILE_ UNLIMITED CLOB  RECORDS DELIMITED BY NEWLINE
        ONS_EXT                                   DIR                        CHARACTERSET US7ASCII
                                                                            BADFILE
                                                                            log_file_dir:'sh_sales_ext.bad'
                                                                            LOGFILE
                                                                            log_file_dir:'sh_sales_ext.log'
                                                                            FIELDS TERMINATED BY "|" LDRTRIM
```

Using the V$ and DB_ Views for Monitoring Indexes

In Oracle7 (7.3.2), the bitmapped index was added. Under Oracle8, indexes were expanded to include the concept of partitions, in addition to the old monitoring requirements. In Oracle8*i*, partitioning was expanded to include subpartitions and the additional functionality of function-based indexes, as well as indextypes. Oracle8*i* also added support for descending indexes. To those capabilities, Oracle9*i* added the bitmap join index and the skip scan index.

As for prior versions, in Oracle 9*i*, the DBA will have to monitor table indexes to verify uniqueness, determine if the appropriate columns have been indexed, and determine proper ownership of indexes for a given application. The DBA also needs a convenient reference to show which tables have indexes, as well as what is indexed, in case of the loss of a table or for use during table maintenance. The diagram in Figure 10.3 shows the cluster of DBA_ views that a DBA needs to use for monitoring indexes.

The report in Source 10.20 provides a convenient format for the DBA to use to review indexed tables and columns; it is selective down to the single-table, single-owner level. The report should be run after database maintenance that involves table rebuilds, exports and imports, or database rebuilds. Listing 10.19 is an example of the output from Source 10.20.

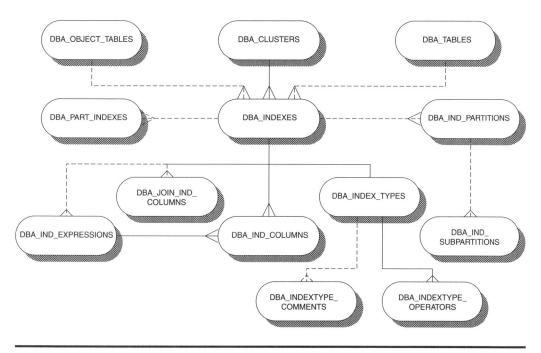

FIGURE 10.3   DBA_View cluster for monitoring indexes.

Source 10.20   SQL script to generate index report.

```
rem
rem NAME: ind_rep.sql
rem FUNCTION: Report on indexes
rem HISTORY: MRA 6/14/97 Creation
rem
COLUMN owner                    FORMAT a8       HEADING 'Index|Owner'
COLUMN index_name               FORMAT a27      HEADING 'Index'
COLUMN index_type               FORMAT a6       HEADING 'Type|Index'
COLUMN table_owner              FORMAT a8       HEADING 'Table|Owner'
COLUMN table_name               FORMAT a24      HEADING 'Table Name'
COLUMN table_type               FORMAT a10      HEADING 'Table|Type'
COLUMN uniqueness               FORMAT a1       HEADING 'U|n|i|q|u|e'
COLUMN tablespace_name          FORMAT a13      HEADING 'Tablespace'
COLUMN column_name              FORMAT a25      HEADING 'Col. Name'
SET PAGES 58 LINES 130 FEEDBACK OFF VERIFY OFF
BREAK ON owner
START title132 'Expandeded Index Report'
SPOOL rep_out\&db\ind_exp.lis
SELECT
    a.owner,
    a.index_name,
    a.index_type,
    a.table_owner,
    a.table_name,
    a.table_type,
    DECODE
    (a.uniqueness, 'UNIQUE', 'U','NONUNIQUE','N') uniqueness,
     a.tablespace_name,
     b.column_name
FROM
    dba_indexes a, dba_ind_columns b
WHERE
    owner LIKE UPPER('%&owner%')
    AND a.owner=b.index_owner(+)
    AND a.index_name=b.index_name(+)
ORDER BY
    owner, index_type;
SPOOL OFF
```

Monitoring Index Statistics   Under Oracle7, the DBA_INDEXES view was extended to include B-tree level, number of leaf blocks, number of distinct keys, average number of leaf blocks per key, average number of data blocks per key, and the index clustering factor. Under Oracle8 and Oracle8*i*, columns covering partitions, domain indexes, and function-based indexes where added. Under Oracle9*i*, columns for index types and join indexes where added, along with a column to show the index status, ei-

Listing 10.19   Example of output from index report.

```
Date: 06/14/97                                                     Page:    1
Time: 04:35 PM                 Expandeded Index Report                SYSTEM
                                  ORTEST1 database


                                                      U
                                                      n
                                                      i
                                                      q
Index                     Type   Table         Table  u
Owner  Index              Index  Owner  Table Name  Type  e Tablespace  Col. Name
------ --------------------- ------ ------ ------------- ------- - ----------- ---------
SYSTEM PK_TEST_IOT         IOT -  SYSTEM TEST_IOT      TABLE   U RAW_DATA    TEST1
                           TOP

       SYS_IL0000001562C00035$ LOB    SYSTEM DEF$_AQCALL    TABLE   U SYSTEM
       SYS_IL0000001571C00035$ LOB    SYSTEM DEF$_AQERROR   TABLE   U SYSTEM
       SYS_IL0000001588C00005$ LOB    SYSTEM DEF$_LOB       TABLE   U SYSTEM
       SYS_IL0000001597C00002$ LOB    SYSTEM DEF$_TEMP$LOB  TABLE   U SYSTEM
       SYS_IL0000001597C00001$ LOB    SYSTEM DEF$_TEMP$LOB  TABLE   U SYSTEM
       SYS_IL0000001588C00006$ LOB    SYSTEM DEF$_LOB       TABLE   U SYSTEM
       SYS_IL0000001588C00004$ LOB    SYSTEM DEF$_LOB       TABLE   U SYSTEM
       SYS_IL0000001597C00003$ LOB    SYSTEM DEF$_TEMP$LOB  TABLE   U SYSTEM
       AQ$_QUEUES_CHECK        NORMAL SYSTEM AQ$_QUEUES     TABLE   U SYSTEM      NAME
       AQ$_QUEUES_PRIMARY      NORMAL SYSTEM AQ$_QUEUES     TABLE   U SYSTEM      OID
       BM_TEST_BITMAP          BITMAP SYSTEM TEST_BITMAP    TABLE   N SYSTEM      TEST_COL1
```

ther DIRECT LOAD or VALID. The TYPE column specifies whether the index is NOR-
MAL, an IOT, an LOB, or a BITMAP index. This is essentially the only indicator for
BITMAP-type indexes.

Index statistics generated from the ANALYZE command are stored in the
INDEX_STATS view. The major limitation of the INDEX_STATS view is that it shows
only the most currently analyzed index. Run the script in Source 10.21 if you want results from all the indexes in a particular schema. An example of a report from the
script in Source 10.21 is shown in Listing 10.20.

**Source 10.21   Script to produce index statistics reports from the ANALYZE INDEX
command.**

```
rem
rem NAME: brown.sql
rem FUNCTION: Analyze indexes and produce stat report
rem FUNCTION: Including browning indicator
rem
```

continues

Source 10.21   Continued.

```
rem HISTORY: MRA 6/15/97 Created
rem
COL del_lf_rows_len FORMAT 999,999,999 HEADING 'Deleted Bytes'
COL lf_rows_len      FORMAT 999,999,999 HEADING 'Filled Bytes'
COL browning         FORMAT 999.90       HEADING 'Percent|Browned'
COL height           FORMAT 999,999      HEADING 'Height'
COL blocks           FORMAT 999,999      HEADING 'Blocks'
COL disti
nct_keys             FORMAT 999,999,999 HEADING '#|Keys'
COL most_repeated_key FORMAT 999999999 HEADING 'Most|Repeated|Key'
COL used_space       FORMAT 999999999   HEADING 'Used|Space'
COL rows_per_key     FORMAT 999999      HEADING 'Rows|Per|Key'
ACCEPT owner PROMPT 'Enter table owner name: '
SET HEADING OFF FEEDBACK OFF VERIFY OFF ECHO OFF RECSEP OFF
SET PAGES 0
TTITLE OFF
DEFINE cr='CHR(10)'
SPOOL index_sz.sql
SELECT
  'CREATE TABLE stat_temp AS SELECT * FROM index_stats;'||&&cr||
  'TRUNCATE TABLE stat_temp;'
FROM dual;
SELECT
'ANALYZE INDEX '||owner||'.'||index_name||
' VALIDATE STRUCTURE;'||&&cr||
    'INSERT INTO stat_temp SELECT * FROM index_stats;'||&&cr||
    'COMMIT;'
FROM
    dba_indexes
WHERE
    owner=UPPER('&owner');
SPOOL OFF
PROMPT 'Analyzing Indexes'
SET FEEDBACK OFF TERMOUT OFF LINES 132 VERIFY OFF
START index_sz.sql
SET TERMOUT ON FEEDBACK ON VERIFY ON LINES 132 PAGES 58
START title132 "Index Statistics Report"
SPOOL rep_out/&db/browning.lst
SELECT
    name,
    del_lf_rows_len,
    lf_rows_len,
(del_lf_rows_len/
DECODE((lf_rows_len+del_lf_rows_len),0,1,lf_rows_len+
del_lf_rows_len))*100 browning,
    height,
    blocks,
    distinct_keys,
    most_repeated_key,
```

```
        used_space,
        rows_per_key
FROM
        stat_temp
WHERE rows_per_key>0;
SPOOL OFF
SET FEEDBACK ON TERMOUT ON LINES 80 VERIFY ON
HOST del stat_temp
```

Listing 10.20   Example of output from index statistics from ANALYZE command report.

```
Date: 06/15/97                                                      Page:   1
Time: 10:31 AM                 Index Statistics Report              SYSTEM
                                  ORTEST1 database


                                                            Most
Rows
                            Percent                 #  Repeat   Used  Per
NAME            Deleted  Filled  Browned Height Blocks  Keys   Key   Space  Key
--------------- -------  ------- ------- ------ ------ ------- ------ ------ ----
FK_ADDRESSES_2      0  10,126,346  .00      3  12800  583996     2 10159315    1
FK_ADDRESSES_3      0  12,115,956  .00      3  12800  758357     1 12153926    1
FK_FRANC_CDS_1      0   1,880,298  .00      3   2560   19619     6  1888613    6
FK_SIC_CODES_1      0  15,896,017  .00      3  12800  875966     3 15948812    1
LI_LOAD_TEST        0  22,568,301  .00      3  10240  875966  8461 22676759    1
PK_ADDRESSES        0  21,249,760  .00      3  25600 1392036     1 21312498    1
PK_CLIENTS          0  13,121,655  .00      3  25600  875966     1 13159342    1
PK_EARNINGS         0  11,357,779  .00      3  25600  758369     1 11390423    1
PK_FRANC_CDS        0   2,340,249  .00      3  12800  117714     1  2349540    1
PK_SIC_CODES        0  19,856,433  .00      3  12800  994826     1 19921338    1
PK_USERS            0          13  .00      1  25600       1     1       13    1
SYS_C00800          0          27  .00      1      5       1     1       27    1
TEST_INDEX          0          17  .00      1      5       1     1       17    1
UI_EARNINGS_1       0  18,200,856  .00      3  12800  758369     1 18295755    1
UK_CLIENTS          0  17,519,320  .00      3  12800  875966     1 17584123    1
16 rows selected
```

If the rows-per-key column in the report in Listing 10.20 exceeds 100, you should consider making the index a bitmap index (post-7.3.2). If the index shows excessive "browning" (30 percent maximum) then a rebuild is in order.

The clustering factor column, in Listing 10.21, shows how well the index is ordered in comparison to the base table. If the value for the clustering factor is near the number of table blocks, it means the index is well ordered; conversely, if the value is near the number of rows in the table, the index is not well ordered (unless the row size is close to blocksize). For indexes with high clustering factors, consider rebuilding, as a high clustering factor indicates that, under index scan conditions, the same blocks will be read numerous times.

A script for reporting some of the statistics stored in the DBA_INDEXES view is shown in Source 10.22. Note that these statistics are not dynamic; they are 100 percent valid only at the time the ANALYZE command is run—which is why I am pleased that Oracle included the last-date-analyzed field in Oracle8. Corresponding sample output is shown in Listing 10.21.

Source 10.22   Example of statistics report for Oracle8, Oracle8i, and Oracle9i indexes.

```
rem   NAME: IN_STAT.sql
rem
rem   FUNCTION: Report on index statistics
rem   INPUTS:    1 = Index owner    2 = Index name
rem
DEF iowner = '&OWNER'
DEF iname  = '&INDEX'
SET PAGES 56 LINES 130 VERIFY OFF FEEDBACK OFF
COLUMN owner                    FORMAT a8           HEADING "Owner"
COLUMN index_name               FORMAT a25          HEADING "Index"
COLUMN status                   FORMAT a7           HEADING "Status"
COLUMN blevel                   FORMAT 9,999        HEADING "Tree|Level"
COLUMN leaf_blocks              FORMAT 999,999,999  HEADING "Leaf Blk"
COLUMN distinct_keys            FORMAT 999,999,999  HEADING "# Keys"
COLUMN avg_leaf_blocks_per_key  FORMAT 9,999        HEADING "Avg.|LB/Key"
COLUMN avg_data_blocks_per_key  FORMAT 9,999        HEADING "Avg.|DB/Key"
COLUMN clustering_factor        FORMAT 999,999      HEADING "Clstr|Factor"
COLUMN num_rows                 FORMAT 999,999,999  HEADING "Number|Rows"
COLUMN sample_size              FORMAT 99,999       HEADING "Sample|Size"
COLUMN last_analyzed                                HEADING 'Analysis|Date'
rem
BREAK ON owner
START title132 "Index Statistics Report"
SPOOL rep_out\&db\ind_stat
rem
SELECT
     owner, index_name, status, blevel, leaf_blocks,
     distinct_keys, avg_leaf_blocks_per_key,
     avg_data_blocks_per_key, clustering_factor,
     num_rows, sample_size, last_analyzed
FROM
     dba_indexes
WHERE
     owner LIKE UPPER('&&iowner')
     AND index_name LIKE UPPER('&&iname')
     AND num_rows>0
```

```
ORDER BY
    1,2;
rem
SPOOL OFF
SET PAGES 22 LINES 80 VERIFY ON FEEDBACK ON
CLEAR COLUMNS
UNDEF iowner
UNDEF iname
UNDEF owner
UNDEF name
TTITLE OFF
```

Listing 10.21   Example of report output from the script in Source 10.22.

```
Date: 06/14/97                                                    Page:   1
Time: 08:22 PM                  Index Statistics Report                SYSTEM
                                  ORTEST1 database


                          Tr. Lf.          Avg.  Avg.  Clstr  Number Sam. Anl.
Owner     Index       Status Lev  Blk   # Keys  LB/Key DB/Key Factor   Rows Size Date
--------  -----------  ------ --- ----  -------  ------ ------ ------   ------ ---- ---------
TELE_DBA FK_ADDRESS_2 VALID   2 2650   583996       1      1  14191   633679    0 14-JUN-97
TELE_DBA FK_ADDRESS_3 VALID   2 3171   758357       1      1  18637   758357    0 14-JUN-97
TELE_DBA FK_FRAN_CD_1 VALID   2  492    19619       1      1    803   117714    0 14-JUN-97
TELE_DBA FK_SIC_CDS_1 VALID   2 4160   875966       1      1  16765   994826    0 14-JUN-97
TELE_DBA LI_LOAD_TEST VALID   2 6474   875966       1      1 140442  1074681    0 14-JUN-97
TELE_DBA PK_ADDRESSES VALID   2 5560  1392036       1      1  32827  1392036    0 14-JUN-97
TELE_DBA PK_CLIENTS   VALID   2 3433   875966       1      1  61587   875966    0 14-JUN-97
TELE_DBA PK_EARNINGS  VALID   2 2972   758369       1      1  28485   758369    0 14-JUN-97
TELE_DBA PK_FRAN_CDS  VALID   2  613   117714       1      1    803   117714    0 14-JUN-97
TELE_DBA PK_SIC_CODES VALID   2 5204   994826       1      1  16765   994826    0 14-JUN-97
TELE_DBA PK_USERS     VALID   0    1        1       1      1      1        1    0 14-JUN-97
TELE_DBA SYS_C00800   VALID   0    1        1       1      1      1        1    0 14-JUN-97
TELE_DBA TEST_INDEX   VALID   0    1        1       1      1      1        1    0 14-JUN-97
TELE_DBA UI_EARNINGs_1 VALID  2 6738   758369       1      1 727251   758369    0 14-JUN-97
TELE_DBA UK_CLIENTS   VALID   2 4493   875966       1      1  61587   875966    0 14-JUN-97
TELE_DBA UK_LOAD_TEST VALID   2 5456   758369       1      1 733393   758369    0 14-JUN-97
```

The various values in the report in Listing 10.21 are interpreted as follows:

Tr. Lev. The depth, or number of levels, from the root block of the index to its leaf blocks. A depth of 1 indicates that they are all on the same level.

LFBLK. The number of leaf blocks in the index.

AVG_LB/KEY. Indicates a nonunique index if its value is greater than 1.

BLOCKS_PER_KEY. If greater than 1, indicates the key has duplicate values.

AVG DB/Key-. Indicates the average number of data blocks in the BLOCKS_PER_KEY indexed table that are pointed to by a distinct value in the index.

CLSTR FACTOR. Indicates the orderliness of the table being indexed. If it is near the number of blocks in table, it indicates a well-ordered table; if it is near the number of rows, it indicates a disorganized table.

SAM. SIZE. Tells the sample size specified if the index was analyzed using the estimate clause.

ANL. DATE. The last date on which the index was analyzed.

Monitoring Partitioned Indexes   Partitioned indexes in Oracle8, Oracle8*i,* and Oracle9*i* also will require monitoring by the DBA. The DBA_IND_PARTITIONS view is almost identical to the DBA_TAB_PARTITIONS view, with the exception of the index/table-specific statistics. The scripts shown here are examples that you can modify for your own needs. The first script, ind_part.sql, is shown in Source 10.23, shows partition file parameters. The output from this script is shown in Listing 10.22.

Source 10.23   Example of script to monitor index partition files.

```
rem
rem Name: ind_part.sql
rem Function : Report on partitioned index structure
rem History: MRA 6/14/97 Created
rem MRA 5/10/99 Updated for Subpartitions
rem
COLUMN index_owner           FORMAT a10 HEADING 'Owner'
COLUMN index_name            FORMAT a15 HEADING 'Index'
COLUMN partition_name        FORMAT a15 HEADING 'Partition'
COLUMN subpartition_name     FORMAT a15 HEADING 'Sub|Partition'
COLUMN tablespace_name       FORMAT a15 HEADING 'Tablespace'
COLUMN high_value            FORMAT a10 HEADING 'Partition|Value'
COLUMN status                FORMAT a10 Heading 'Status'
SET LINES 130
START title132 'Index Partition Files'
BREAK ON index_owner ON index_name
SPOOL rep_out/&&db/ind_part.lis
SELECT
     a.index_owner,
     a.index_name,
     a.partition_name,
     a.high_value,
     b.subpartition_name,
     b.tablespace_name,
     b.logging,
     b.status
```

```
FROM sys.dba_ind_partitions a, sys.dba_ind_subpartitions b
WHERE a.owner=b.owner
    AND a.index_name=b.index_name
    And a.partition_name=b.partition_name
ORDER BY a.index_owner,a.index_name,a.partition_name,
         b.subpartition_position
/
SPOOL OFF
```

Listing 10.22   Example of output from the index partition file script.

```
Date: 06/14/97                                       Page:   1
Time: 08:51 PM            Index Partition Files      SYSTEM
                            ORTEST1 database

                                    Partition
Owner    Index          Partition  Value     Tablespace       LOG Status
-------  -------------- ---------- --------   ---------------  --- ------
SYSTEM   PART_IND_TEST  TEST_P1         10    RAW_DATA         YES VALID
                        TEST_P2         20    RAW_DATA         YES VALID
                        TEST_P3         30    RAW_DATA         YES VALID

3 rows selected
```

The DBA_IND_PARTITIONS view also provides the statistics and storage characteristics for partitioned indexes. Source 10.24 is an example of a script to use for monitoring some of these statistics. The output from this script resembles the report in Listing 10.23.

Source 10.24   Example of script to report on partitioned index storage and statistics.

```
rem
rem NAME:     ind_pstor.sql
rem FUNCTION: Provide data on partitioned index storage charcacteristics
rem HISTORY: MRA 6/13/97 Created
rem
COLUMN owner            FORMAT a6      HEADING 'Owner'
COLUMN index_name       FORMAT a14     HEADING 'Index'
COLUMN partition_name   FORMAT a9      HEADING 'Partition'
COLUMN tablespace_name  FORMAT a11     HEADING 'Tablespace'
COLUMN pct_free         FORMAT 9999    HEADING '%|Free'
```

continues

Source 10.24   Continued.

```
COLUMN ini_trans              FORMAT 9999        HEADING 'Init|Tran'
COLUMN max_trans              FORMAT 9999        HEADING 'Max|Tran'
COLUMN initial_extent         FORMAT 9999999     HEADING 'Init|Extent'
COLUMN next_extent            FORMAT 9999999     HEADING 'Next|Extent'
COLUMN max_extent                                HEADING 'Max|Extents'
COLUMN pct_increase           FORMAT 999         HEADING '%|Inc'
COLUMN distinct_keys          FORMAT 9999999     HEADING '#Keys'
COLUMN clustering_factor      FORMAT 999999      HEADING 'Clus|Fact'
SET LINES 130
START title132 'Index Partition File Storage'
BREAK ON index_owner on index_name
SPOOL rep_out/&&db/ind_pstor.lis
SELECT
     index_owner,
     index_name,
     tablespace_name,
     partition_name,
     pct_free,
     ini_trans,
     max_trans,
     initial_extent,
     next_extent,
     max_extent,
     pct_increase,
     distinct_keys,
     clustering_factor
FROM sys.dba_ind_partitions
ORDER BY index_owner,index_name
/
SPOOL OFF
```

Listing 10.23   Example of output from the partitioned index storage script.

```
Date: 06/14/97                                                         Page:    1
Time: 09:25 PM              Index Partition File Storage               SYSTEM
                                 ORTEST1 database


                                       % Init  Max  Init   Next   Max    %      Clus
Owner   Index      Tablespace Partition Free Tran Tran Extent Extent Extents Inc #Keys Fac
------  ---------- ---------- --------- ---- ---- ---- ------ ------ ------- --- ----- ----
SYSTEM P_IND_TEST  RAW_DATA   TEST_P1    10    2  255  20480  20480     249  50     0    0
                   RAW_DATA   TEST_P2    10    2  255  20480  20480     249  50     0    0
                   RAW_DATA   TEST_P3    10    2  255  20480  20480     249  50     0    0

3 rows selected.
```

The index subpartitions also have statistics collected against them, into the DBA_ IND_SUBPARTITIONS view. The report in Source 10.25 will generate a listing of some of these statistics. Feel free to modify it as needed to monitor the statistics you feel are important. The output from the script in Source 10.25 resembles the report in Listing 10.24.

Source 10.25   Example of script to report on subpartitioned index storage and statistics.

```
rem
rem NAME:      ind_subpstor.sql
rem FUNCTION: Get data on subpartitioned index charcacteristics
rem HISTORY: MRA 5/10/99 Created
rem
COLUMN owner                FORMAT a6         HEADING 'Owner'
COLUMN index_name           FORMAT a14        HEADING 'Index'
COLUMN partition_name       FORMAT a9         HEADING 'Partition'
COLUMN subpartition_name    FORMAT a9         HEADING 'Sub|Partition'
COLUMN tablespace_name      FORMAT a11        HEADING 'Tablespace'
COLUMN pct_free             FORMAT 9999       HEADING '%|Free'
COLUMN ini_trans            FORMAT 9999       HEADING 'Init|Tran'
COLUMN max_trans            FORMAT 9999       HEADING 'Max|Tran'
COLUMN initial_extent       FORMAT 9999999    HEADING 'Init|Extent'
COLUMN next_extent          FORMAT 9999999    HEADING 'Next|Extent'
COLUMN max_extent                             HEADING 'Max|Extents'
COLUMN pct_increase         FORMAT 999        HEADING '%|Inc'
COLUMN distinct_keys        FORMAT 9999999    HEADING '#Keys'
COLUMN clustering_factor    FORMAT 999999     HEADING 'Clus|Fact'
COLUMN num_rows             FORMAT 9999999    HEADING 'Number|Rows'
SET LINES 130
START title132 'Index SubPartition File Storage'
BREAK ON index_owner on index_name
SPOOL rep_out/&&db/ind_pstor.lis
SELECT
    index_owner,
    index_name,
    partition_name,
    sub_partition_name,
    tablespace_name,
    pct_free,
    ini_trans,
    max_trans,
    initial_extent,
    next_extent,
    max_extent,
    pct_increase,
    distinct_keys,
    clustering_factor,
    num_rows
```

continues

Source 10.25   Continued.

```
FROM sys.dba_ind_subpartitions
ORDER BY index_owner,index_name,partition_name,subpartition_position
/
SPOOL OFF
```

Listing 10.24   Example of output from the subpartitioned index storage script.

```
Date: 06/14/97                                                        Page:    1
Time: 09:25 PM                    Index SubPartition File Storage        SYSTEM
                                      ORTEST1 database


                                              % Init  Max   Init   Next   Max   %          Clus
Owner   Index        Tablespace Partition Free Tran  Tran Extent Extent Extents Inc #Keys  Fac
------  ----------   ---------- --------- ---- ---- ---- ------ ------ ------- --- -----  ----
SYSTEM  P_IND_TEST   RAW_DATA   TEST_P1    10    2   255  20480  20480     249  50     0     0
                     RAW_DATA   TEST_P2    10    2   255  20480  20480     249  50     0     0
                     RAW_DATA   TEST_P3    10    2   255  20480  20480     249  50     0     0
```

Monitoring Functional Indexes

The concept of a *functional index* was added to Oracle8*i*. A functional index uses a function or collection of functions to operate on its column, thus allowing the same function or collection of functions to be applied in the WHERE clause of a SELECT that uses the index. A simple example would be a functional index using UPPER on a name field. This would allow selects of the form:

```
SELECT * FROM emp WHERE UPPER(last_name)='AULT';
```

The new functionality will simplify table and application design tremendously in applications that retrieve data based on UPPER, LOWER, SOUNDEX, and other function-based queries.

The DBA will want to know about, and track, the use of function-based indexes in his or her database. The DBA_INDEXES view has a new column that makes this easier, the FUNCIDX_STATUS column. The FUNCIDX_STATUS column contains NULL if the index is not a function-based index, ENABLED if it is a function-based index and is ready for use, and DISABLED if it is a function-based index that is disabled and can't be used. If the value in FUNCIDX_STATUS is not NULL, a join to the DBA_IND_EXPRESSIONS view will provide the information on the expression used to create the function-based column in the index. The script in Source 10.26 demonstrates this type of report; an example of the output from this script is shown in Listing 10.25.

Source 10.26   Example of script to report on functional indexes.

```
rem
rem NAME:      ind_func.sql
rem FUNCTION: Get data on functional index charcacteristics
rem HISTORY: MRA 5/12/99 Created
rem
COLUMN owner              FORMAT a6        HEADING 'Owner'
COLUMN index_name         FORMAT a14       HEADING 'Index'
COLUMN table_name         FORMAT a20       HEADING 'Table'
COLUMN column_expression FORMAT a80 WORD_WRAPPED HEADING 'Expression'
SET LINES 130
START title132 'Functional Index Report'
BREAK ON index_owner on index_name
SPOOL rep_out/&&db/ind_func.lis
SELECT
    Index_owner,
    index_name,
    table_name,
    column_expression
FROM
    Dba_ind_expressions
WHERE
    Index_owner LIKE '%&&owner%'
    And index_name like '%&&index%'
ORDER BY
    Index_owner,index_name,column_position;
SPOOL OFF
TTITLE OFF
```

Listing 10.25   Example of functional index report.

```
Date: 06/14/97                                              Page:  1
Time: 09:45 PM          Functional Index Report            SYSTEM
                           ORTEST1 database


Owner      Index          Table          Expression
_____     _____          _____          _____

TELE_DBA   DEC_CLIENTSV8i  CLIENTSV8i     DECODE ("CREATION_SY_USER",1,'B
                                          OSS',2,'Manager',3,'Clerk','Ev
                                          eryone else')
```

Monitoring Domain Indexes

Also introduced in Oracle8*i* was the concept of *extensible indexing*, also known as *domain indexing*. A domain index is usually used in cartridge development. In fact, a domain index is called so because it is used only within the domain of its parent cartridge. A domain index extends the basic types of hash, bitmapped, and B-tree indexes by allowing the developer to create his or her own index methods and apply them to a specific type of data set.

An example of the use of domain indexing would be the use of R-tree indexes for spatial data. A domain index is based on the concept of an INDEXTYPE, which, like a User Defined Type (UDT), is created and maintained by the user. In order to use a domain index, a data cartridge that implements its structures, methods, and types must be created.

NOTE   The domain indexes in Oracle8*i* are indicated by a non-NULL value in the DOMIDX_STATUS and DOMIDX_OPSTATUS columns in the DBA_INDEXES view. I assume a join can be based on either the INDEX_NAME and INDEXTYPE_NAME in the DBA_INDEXES and DBA_INDEXTYPES table supplemented by the OWNER columns in each or the INDEX_TYPE and INDEXTYPE_NAME columns (even though they don't match in size). I say "assume," because this topic is beyond the scope of this book, so I leave it to the DBA who is involved in a cartridge development effort to actually create the reports required based on the supplied join data.

Monitoring Bitmap Join Indexes

As noted earlier, bitmap join indexes were introduced in Oracle9*i*. If the JOIN_INDEX column in the DBA_INDEXES is set to YES, then the index is a bitmap join index, meaning that a join to the DBA_JOIN_IND_COLUMNS view will produce the data on the tables and columns that are linked through the bitmap join index. You will need to join against the INDEX_OWNER and INDEX_NAME columns.

My testing, however, revealed an apparent flaw in the DBA_JOIN_IND_COLUMNS view—at least based on how I believe it should work. That view seems to have the same number of columns as the DBA_IND_COLUMNS view. In addition, it contains only one row per bitmap join index, when it should show one row for each of the two tables involved in the bitmap join. In tests where I created a bitmap join between two tables with different column names, only one row was displayed. Where the actual information about the second table is stored, if it is, is not clear. Until this is resolved I suggest using naming conventions to clarify the required table-to-table relationship.

Source 10.27 shows an attempt at producing a report against the DBA_INDEXES and DBA_JOIN_IND_COLUMNS views to show the bitmap join indexes in the database. An example output from the script in Source 10.27 is shown in Listing 10.26.

Source 10.27   Example bitmap join table report.

```
REM bmj_Index.sql
REM MRA 10/10/01
COLUMN owner FORMAT a10 HEADING 'Index|Owner'
COLUMN index_name FORMAT a25 HEADING 'Index|Name'
COLUMN table_owner FORMAT a10 HEADING 'Table|Owner'
COLUMN table_name FORMAT a15 HEADING 'Table|Name'
COLUMN column_name FORMAT a15 HEADING 'Column|Name'
SET LINES 132
START title132 'Bitmap Join Indexes'
SPOOL rep_out/&db/bmj_index
select a.owner, a.index_name, b.table_owner, b.table_name, b.column_name
from dba_indexes a, dba_join_ind_columns b
where a.owner = UPPER('&owner')
and a.join_index='YES'
and a.owner=b.index_owner
and a.index_name=b.index_name
/
SPOOL OFF
SET LINES 80
TTITLE OFF
```

Listing 10.26   Example output from bitmap join script.

```
Date: 10/11/01                                                    Page:   1
Time: 00:19 AM                    Bitmap Join Indexes            SYSTEM
                                  ORTEST1 database


Index       Index                 Table      Table            Column
Owner       Name                  Owner      Name             Name
----------  --------------------  ---------- ---------------  ------
DBAUTIL     CONSULTANT_ASSIGMENT_BMJ DBAUTIL   CONSULTANT      CON_ID
```

Monitoring Clusters Using DBA_ and V_$ Views

Clusters can be indexed or hashed in Oracle8, Oracle8*i,* or Oracle9*i,* and using the various views and tables available to the DBA—specifically, DBA_CLUSTERS, DBA_CLU_COLUMNS, DBA_CLUSTER_HASH_FUNCTIONS, and DBA_TABLES—they can be readily monitored

Oracle8*i* added the capability to have a single table cluster, which confers the benefit of storing its key values in physically contiguous blocks, thereby making lookup by cluster key very fast. Clusters haven't changed in Oracle9*i.* Figure 10.4 shows the relationships between the views used to monitor clusters. A script for generating a cluster report is shown in Source 10.28, and the sample report is shown in Listing 10.27.

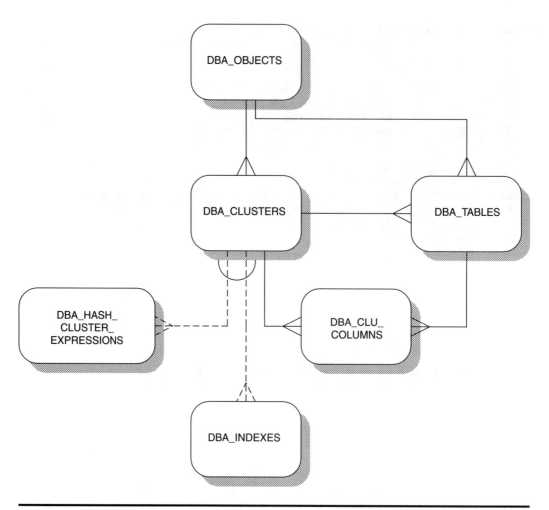

FIGURE 10.4 DBA_CLUSTERS view cluster.

Source 10.28   Example of script to produce a cluster report.

```
rem
rem File:     CLU_REP.SQL
rem Purpose:    Document Cluster Data
rem Use:      From user with access to DBA_ views
rem
rem When       Who        What
rem ----       --------    ------------------------
rem 5/27/93    Mike Ault   Initial Creation
rem 6/15/97    Mike Ault   Verified against Oracle8
```

```
rem 10/11/01    Mike Ault    Verified against oracle9i
rem
COLUMN owner                FORMAT a10
COLUMN cluster_name         FORMAT a15 HEADING "Cluster"
COLUMN tablespace_name      FORMAT a20 HEADING "Tablespace"
COLUMN table_name           FORMAT a20 HEADING "Table"
COLUMN tab_column_name      FORMAT a20 HEADING "Table Column"
COLUMN clu_column_name      FORMAT a20 HEADING "Cluster Column"
SET PAGES 56 LINES 130 FEEDBACK OFF
START title132 "Cluster Report"
BREAK ON owner SKIP 1 ON cluster ON tablespace
SPOOL rep_out\&db\cluster
SELECT
     a.owner,a.cluster_name,tablespace_name,
     table_name,tab_column_name,clu_column_name
FROM
     dba_clusters a,dba_clu_columns b
WHERE
     a.owner = b.owner and
     a.cluster_name=b.cluster_name
ORDER BY 1,2,3,4
/
SPOOL OFF
```

Listing 10.27   Example of output from cluster report.

```
Date: 06/15/97                                               Page:    1
Time: 04:51 PM                   Cluster Report                   SYSTEM
                                 ORTEST1 database


OWNER   Tablespace    Cluster          Table            Table Column     Cluster Column
-------  -------------  ---------------  ---------------  ---------------  --------------

SYS     SYSTEM        C_COBJ#          CCOL$            OBJ#             OBJ#
                                       CDEF$            OBJ#             OBJ#
                      C_FILE#_BLOCK#   SEG$             FILE#            SEGFILE#
                                                        BLOCK#           SEGBLOCK#
                                                        TS#              TS#
                                       UET$             TS#              TS#
                                                        SEGBLOCK#        SEGBLOCK#
                                                        SEGFILE#         SEGFILE#
                      C_MLOG#          MLOG$            MOWNER           MOWNER
                                                        MASTER           MASTER
                                       SLOG$            MASTER           MASTER
                                                        MOWNER           MOWNER
                      C_OBJ#           ATTRCOL$         OBJ#             OBJ#
                                       CLU$             OBJ#             OBJ#
                                       COL$             OBJ#             OBJ#
```

Monitoring Cluster Storage Statistics As a DBA, you may be interested in the storage statistics used to create each cluster. This data is found in the DBA_CLUSTERS view. The script in Source 10.29 is an example of this type of report. An example of the script's output is shown in Listing 10.28.

Source 10.29   Example of script to produce a cluster sizing report.

```
rem Name: clus_siz.sql
rem
rem FUNCTION: Generate a cluster sizing report
rem
COLUMN owner               FORMAT a10
COLUMN cluster_name        FORMAT a15          HEADING "Cluster"
COLUMN tablespace_name     FORMAT a15          HEADING "Tablespace"
COLUMN pct_free            FORMAT 999          HEADING "%|Fre"
COLUMN pct_used            FORMAT 999          HEADING "%|Use"
COLUMN key_size            FORMAT 999999       HEADING "Key Size"
COLUMN ini_trans           FORMAT 999          HEADING "Ini|Trn"
COLUMN max_trans           FORMAT 999          HEADING "Max|Trn"
COLUMN initial_extent      FORMAT 999999999    HEADING "Init Ext"
COLUMN next_extent         FORMAT 999999999    HEADING "Next Ext"
COLUMN min_extents         FORMAT 999          HEADING "Min|Ext"
COLUMN max_extents         FORMAT 999          HEADING "Max|Ext"
COLUMN pct_increase        FORMAT 999          HEADING "%|Inc"
SET PAGES 56 LINES 130 FEEDBACK OFF
START title132 "Cluster Sizing Report"
BREAK ON owner ON tablespace_name
SPOOL rep_out\&db\cls_sze
SELECT
     owner,
     tablespace_name,
     cluster_name,
     pct_free,
     pct_used,
     key_size,
     ini_trans,
     max_trans,
     initial_extent,
     next_extent,
     min_extents,
     max_extents,
     pct_increase
FROM
     dba_clusters
ORDER BY
     1,2,3
/
```

```
SPOOL OFF
CLEAR COLUMNS
CLEAR BREAKS
SET PAGES 22 LINES 80 FEEDBACK ON
PAUSE Press enter to continue
```

Listing 10.28   Example of output of the cluster sizing report.

```
Date: 05/17/96                                                    Page:   1
Time: 04:06 PM                      Cluster Sizing Report                SYS
                                      ORDSPTD6 database


Schema                    %   %         Int Max                 Min Max %
Owner   Tablespace Cluster Fre Use Key Size Trn Trn Init Ext Next Ext  Ext Ext Inc
------  ---------- ------------- --- --- ---- --- --- ---- --- ---- ----- --- --- ---
SYS     SYSTEM     C_COBJ#      10  50  300  2 255   51200    83968  1 121  50
                   C_FILE#_BLOCK# 10  40  225  2 255   20480   190464  1 121  50
                   C_MLOG#      10  40       2 255   10240    10240  1 121  50
                   C_OBJ#        5  40  800  2 255  122880   430080  1 121  50
                   C_RG#        10  40       2 255   10240    10240  1 121  50
                   C_TS#        10  40       2 255   10240    16384  1 121  50
                   C_USER#      10  40  315  2 255   10240    10240  1 121  50
                   HIST$         5  40  200  2 255   10240    10240  1 121  50
```

The reports in Sources 10.28 and 10.29 give the DBA information on cluster keys, cluster columns, cluster tables, and columns and cluster sizing. Combined with the actual size and extent reports previously shown, the DBA can have a complete picture of clusters in his or her database.

Monitoring Cluster Statistics   The DBA_CLUSTERS view in versions after Oracle8 has several additional columns: DBA_CLUSTERS view are AVG_BLOCKS_PER_KEY, CLUSTER_TYPE, FUNCTION, and HASHKEYS. These additional columns provide a more detailed glimpse of cluster status. The report script shown in Source 10.30 can be modified to include these columns (132 is about the widest you can go, and not a good choice) or a new report can be created. An example of the output from Source 10.30 is shown in Listing 10.29.

Source 10.30   Report script for new DBA_CLUSTERS columns.

```
rem Name        : clu_stat.sql
rem Purpose     : Report on new DBA_CLUSTER columns
rem Use         : From an account that accesses DBA_ views
rem
```

continues

Source 10.30 Continued.

```
COLUMN owner                    FORMAT a10      HEADING "Owner"
COLUMN cluster_name             FORMAT a15      HEADING "Cluster"
COLUMN tablespace_name          FORMAT a10      HEADING "Tablespace"
COLUMN avg_blocks_per_key       FORMAT 999999   HEADING "Blocks per Key"
COLUMN cluster_type             FORMAT a8       HEADING "Type"
COLUMN function                 FORMAT 999999   HEADING "Function"
COLUMN hashkeys                 FORMAT 99999    HEADING "# of Keys"
SET PAGES 56 LINES 79 FEEDBACK OFF
START title80 "Cluster Statistics Report"
SPOOL report_output/&db/clu_type
SELECT
     owner,
     cluster_name,
     tablespace_name,
     avg_blocks_per_key,
     cluster_type,
     function,
     hashkeys
FROM
     dba_clusters
ORDER BY 2
GROUP BY  owner, tablespace, type
/
SPOOL OFF
SET PAGES 22 LINES 80 FEEDBACK ON
CLEAR COLUMNS
TTITLE OFF
```

Listing 10.29   Example of output from cluster statistics report script.

```
Date: 05/22/96                                            Page:    1
Time: 12:54 PM                  Cluster Type Report        SYSTEM
                                ORDSPTD6 database


                                Blocks
                                per                        # of
Owner  Cluster          Tablespace Key     Type    Function   Keys
------ ---------------  ---------- ------- -------- ---------------- ----
SYS    C_COBJ#          SYSTEM             INDEX
       C_FILE#_BLOCK#
       C_MLOG#
       C_OBJ#
       C_RG#
       C_TS#
       C_USER#
       HIST$
       C_RG#
```

Monitoring Cluster Hash Expressions As of later versions of Oracle7, including all versions of Oracle8, and Oracle8*i*, and Oracle9*i,* the capability to specify your own hash expressions for a hash cluster has been provided. These hash expressions can be viewed for a specific cluster by querying the DBA_CLUSTER_ HASH_EXPRESSION view. The DBA_CLUSTER_HASH_EXPRESSION view has three columns: OWNER, CLUSTER_NAME, and HASH_EXPRESSION. HASH_EXPRESSION is a LONG, so be sure to allow for extra-length character strings by using the WORD_WRAPPED parameter on a COLUMN command when querying this value.

Monitoring of Materialized Views and Materialized View Logs Using DBA_ and V Type Views

Snapshots and snapshot logs are Oracle7 and Oracle8 features. Under Oracle8*i*, the localized snapshot (materialized views) also became available. Snapshots make it possible to maintain read-only copies of a table or columns from multiple tables in several locations. The refresh rate of the materialized views can be varied and accomplished automatically.

> **NOTE** Remember, as of Oracle8*i*, the term *materialized view* has replaced the term *snapshot*.

The DBA needs tools to monitor materialized views and materialized view logs. The OEM in Oracle8, Oracle8*i*, and Oracle9*i* provide screens that let the DBA see the status of the database's materialized views. The Replication Manager application also provides monitoring and control functionality. At times, however, it is more convenient to have a hard-copy documentation of materialized views and materialized view logs. The script in Source 10.31, the report in Listing 10.30, and Source 10.32 document a database's materialized views and materialized view logs.

Source 10.31   Example of script to document materialized views and materialized view logs.

```
rem
rem Name:     mv_rep.sql
rem Purpose:Report on database Materialized views
rem Use:      From an account that accesses DBA_MVIEWS
rem
rem   When        Who          What
rem   -------     ---------    ----------------
rem   5/27/93     Mike Ault    Initial Creation
rem   10/10/01    Mike Ault    Update to 9i
```

continues

Source 10.31   Continued.

```
rem
SET PAGES 56 LINES 130 FEEDBACK OFF VERIFY OFF
rem
COLUMN mv                  FORMAT a30        HEADING "Materialized|View"
COLUMN source              FORMAT a30        HEADING "Source Table"
COLUMN log                                   HEADING "Use|Log?"
COLUMN type                FORMAT a10        HEADING "Ref|Type"
COLUMN refreshed                             HEADING "Last Refresh"
COLUMN start               FORMAT a13        HEADING "Start Refresh"
COLUMN error                                 HEADING "Error"
COLUMN next                FORMAT a13        HEADING "Next Refresh"
rem
PROMPT Percent signs are wild card
ACCEPT mv_owner PROMPT Enter the materialized view owner
START title132 "Materialized View Report for &mv_owner"
SPOOL rep_out/&db/mv_rep&db
rem
SELECT
    Owner||'.'||mview_name mv, master_view,
    master_link Source,
    substr(query,1,query_len) query,
    updatable,
    update_log Log, last_refresh_date Refreshed,
DECODE(refresh_mode,'FAST','F','COMPLETE','C','FORCE','FR','COMMIT','CM'),
    query,
    master_rollback_segment rbk
FROM dba_mviews
WHERE owner LIKE UPPER('%&mv_owner%')
ORDER BY owner,mview_name;
rem
SPOOL OFF
```

Listing 10.30   Example of output of the script in Source 10.31.

```
Date: 06/10/93                 "Your  Company Name "                  Page:   1
Time: 04:28 PM              Snapshot Report for DEV7_DBA              DEV7_DBA
                              "Your Database"
                           Use          Ref
Snapshot          View   Source   Log Last Ref Typ Next Ref Started  Query
---------------   ------ -------- --- --------- --- -------- -------- ----------------
TEST.SNAP$_TEST MVIEW$_  DEV7_DBA. YES 10-JUN-93 F   SYSDATE+7 10-JUN-93 SELECT CHECK_DATE
      TEST      HIT_RATIO                                FROM  HIT_RATIOS
```

Source 10.32   Example of script to generate materialized view log report.

```
rem
rem Name:      mv_log_rep.sql
rem Purpose:     Report on database materialized view Logs
rem Use:       From an account that accesses DBA_ views
rem
rem   When        Who         What
rem   -------     ---------   -------------------
rem   5/27/93     Mike Ault   Initial Creation
rem   10/10/01    Mike Ault    Updated to oracle9i
rem
SET PAGES 56 LINES 130 FEEDBACK OFF
START title132 "Materialized View Log Report"
SPOOL rep_out/&db/mv_log_rep&db
rem
COLUMN log_owner      FORMAT a10 HEADING "Owner"
COLUMN master         FORMAT a20 HEADING "Master"
COLUMN log_table      FORMAT a20 HEADING "Materialized View"
COLUMN trigger        FORMAT a20 HEADING "Trigger Text"
COLUMN current                   HEADING "Last Refresh"
rem
SELECT
    log_owner, master, log_table table,
    log_trigger trigger, rowids, filter_columns filtered,
    object_id id, sequence seq, Include_new_values new
FROM
    dba_mview_logs
ORDER BY 1;
rem
SPOOL OFF
CLEAR COLUMNS
SET FEEDBACK ON
TTITLE OFF
```

The reports from Sources 10.31 and 10.32 will provide the DBA with hard-copy documentation of all materialized views and materialized view logs in the database. Each can be made more restrictive by using WHERE clauses, by selecting on a specific set of values such as owner or log_owner, type, or date since last refresh (last_refresh > &date or current_snapshots > &date).

Later in this chapter, you will learn how to monitor DIMENSIONS, a new Oracle8*i* feature used with materialized views to provide for query rewrite.

10.3 MONITORING ORACLE8 TYPES, COLLECTIONS, METHODS, AND OPERATORS

Under Oracle8, Oracle added an entirely new set of objects to monitor, which have been called, variously, collections, types, user-defined types, ADTs, and other. I prefer the all-inclusive terms types, collections, and methods. *Types* allow the grouping of related data and, subsequently, the use of these grouped data sets to form more complex objects. For example, a table object might consist of standard columns, a user-defined type, a nested table (built from a type), and a collection (called a VARRAY), which is in itself a type. In order to declare a table to be an object and have its OIDs implicitly defined, it must be created as an object type from a defined type.

As explained in previous sections, there can be types that, while being named, have no other attributes. These are called *incomplete types* and are used where circular references may need to be defined. Of course, these incomplete types must be completed before an object is built from them.

The major view for types is the DBA_TYPES. The cluster of views associated with types is shown in Figure 10.5.

Monitoring Types

A simple report to tell us some basic information about the types stored in our database is shown in Source 10.33. The report uses the DBA_TYPES view. To get detailed information on the attributes for each type, join to the DBA_TYPE_ATTRS view. The script in Source 10.33 produces a report similar to the one shown in Listing 10.31. The only columns not reported are TYPE_OID and TYPEID RAW.

Source 10.33   Example of types report.

```
rem
rem NAME: types.sql
rem FUNCTION: Provide basic report of all database types
rem for a specific owner or all owners
rem HISTORY : MRA 6/15/97 Created
rem
COLUMN owner            FORMAT a10    HEADING 'Type|Owner'
COLUMN type_name        FORMAT a15    HEADING 'Type|Name'
COLUMN typecode         FORMAT a11    HEADING 'Type|Code'
COLUMN predefined       FORMAT a3     HEADING Pre?
COLUMN incomplete       FORMAT a3     HEADING Inc?
COLUMN methods          FORMAT 9999   HEADING '#|Methods'
COLUMN attributes       FORMAT 9999   HEADING '#|Attrib'
COLUMN final            FORMAT A5     HEADING 'Final'
COLUMN instantiable     FORMAT A5     HEADING 'Inst.'
COLUMN supertype_owner  FORMAT a10    HEADING 'SuperType|Owner'
COLUMN supertype_name   FORMAT a15    HEADING 'SuperType|Name'
```

```
COLUMN local_attributes FORMAT 99999  HEADING 'Local|Attri'
COLUMN local_methods FORMAT 99999     HEADING 'Local|Meth'
SET LINES 130 PAGES 58 VERIFY OFF FEEDBACK OFF
BREAK ON owner
START title132 'Database Types Report'
SPOOL rep_out\&db\types.lis
SELECT
    DECODE(owner, null,'SYS-GEN',owner) owner,
    type_name,
    typecode,
    attributes,
    methods,
    predefined,
    incomplete,
    final,
    Instantiable,
    Supertype_owner,
    Supertype_name,
    local_attributes,
    local_methods
FROM dba_types
WHERE owner LIKE '%&owner%'
ORDER BY owner, type_name;
SPOOL OFF
TTITLE OFF
SET VERIFY ON FEEDBACK ON LINES 80 PAGES 22
CLEAR COLUMNS
CLEAR BREAKS
```

Listing 10.31   Example of output from basic types report.

```
Date: 10/10/01                                                      Page: 1
Time: 10:51 PM                    Database Types Report             SYSTEM
                                  galinux1 database


Type   Type          Type          #     #                Super   Super     Local  Local
Owner  Name          Code       Attrib Methods Pre Inc Final Inst. Owner   Name      Attri  Meth
------ ------------- ---------- ------ ------- --- --- ----- ----- ------- --------- ------ ------
SYSTEM ADDRESS_T     OBJECT          9       0 NO  NO  NO    YES
       EMPLOYEE_T    OBJECT          9       0 NO  NO  YES   YES   SYSTEM  PERSON_T       3      0
       GALLERY_T     OBJECT          4       0 NO  NO  YES   YES
       PERSON_T      OBJECT          6       0 NO  NO  NO    YES
       PICTURE_NT    COLLECTION      0       0 NO  NO  YES   YES
       PICTURE_T     OBJECT          6       0 NO  NO  YES   YES
       ROOM_T        OBJECT          2       1 NO  NO  YES   YES
```

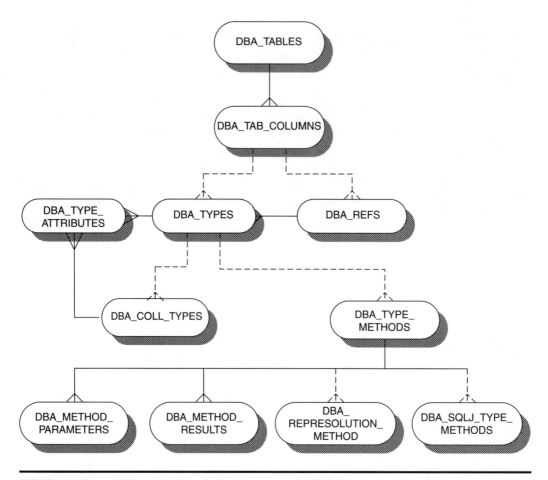

FIGURE 10.5   DBA_TYPES view cluster.

Notice that there are many kinds of types, many of which (those labeled SYSGEN) are system-generated at system build; others, such as OBJECT and COLLECTION, are user-defined. The collection types are further documented in the DBA_COLL_TYPES view.

Monitoring Type Collections   Another kind of type is a collection (such as a VAR-RAY). The script in Source 10.34 generates a simple report that documents the important columns from DBA_COLL_TYPES. If you find you need the other data (for simple scalar collections), then by all means add them to the script. To determine the attributes that map into each collection, join to the DBA_TYPE_ATTRS view.

Source 10.34   This script produces a report similar to that in Listing 10.32.

```
rem
rem NAME: coll_type.sql
rem FUNCTION: Document the collection types in the database
rem for a specified user or all users
rem HISTORY: MRA 6/15/97 Created
rem          MRA 10/10/01 Updated to 9i
rem
COL owner            FORMAT a10 HEADING 'Collec.|Owner'
COL type_name        FORMAT a16 HEADING 'Type|Name'
COL coll_type        FORMAT a15 HEADING 'Collec.|Type'
COL upper_bound                 HEADING 'VARRAY|Limit'
COL elem_type_owner FORMAT a10 HEADING 'Elementary|Type|Owner'
COL elem_type_name  FORMAT a11 HEADING 'Elementary|Type|Name'
SET PAGES 58 LINES 130 VERIFY OFF FEEDBACK OFF
START title132 'Collection Type Report'
SPOOL rep_out\&db\col_type.lis
select
     owner,
     type_name,
     coll_type,
     upper_bound,
     elem_type_mod,
     elem_type_owner,
     elem_type_name,
     length,
     precision,
     scale,
     elem_storage,
     nulls_stored
FROM dba_coll_types
WHERE owner LIKE '%&owner%'
/
SPOOL OFF
CLEAR COLUMNS
CLEAR BREAKS
TTILTE OFF
SET VERIFY ON FEEDBACK ON
```

Monitoring Type Methods   Types can also have methods associated with them. A *type method* is a procedure or function that is intrinsic to (an integral part of) the type and is defined (generally speaking) at the time the type is created. Take a close look at Listing 10.33, it only shows types with defined methods. The methods are documented in the DBA_TYPE_METHODS; additional drill-down information is located in the DBA_METHOD_PARAMS and DBA_METHOD_RESULTS views. A simple report showing the types with methods in the database is given in Source 10.35. The report that results from running this source is shown in Listing 10.33.

Listing 10.32   Example of output from the collection type report.

```
Date: 10/10/01                                              Page:    1
Time: 11:26 PM              Collection Type Report          SYSTEM
                              galinux1 database


                                      Element Element
   Collec.    Type             Collec. VARRAY  Type   Type
   Owner      Name             Type    Limit   Owner  Name      Length  Prec.  Scale  Nulls
   ---------- -------------------- ------- --------- ------- ---------- ------- ------ ------ -----

   SYS        AQ$_SUBSCRIBERS      VARRAY      1024 SYS     AQ$_AGENT                              YES
   SYS        DBMS_DEBUG_VC2COLL   TABLE                    VARCHAR2     1000                      YES
   SYS        ODCIRIDLIST          VARRAY     32767         VARCHAR2     5072                      YES
   SYS        ODCIGRANULELIST      VARRAY     65535         NUMBER                                 YES
   WKSYS      VARCHAR2_TABLE_100   TABLE                    VARCHAR2      100                      YES
   WKSYS      VARCHAR2_TABLE_200   TABLE                    VARCHAR2      200                      YES
   WKSYS      VARCHAR2_TABLE_300   TABLE                    VARCHAR2      300                      YES
   WKSYS      VARCHAR2_TABLE_400   TABLE                    VARCHAR2      400                      YES
   SYSTEM     PICTURE_NT           TABLE            SYSTEM  PICTURE_T                              YES
```

Source 10.35   Example of script to generate type methods report.

```
rem
rem NAME typ_meth.sql
rem FUNCTION : Create a report of type methods for a
rem specific user or all users
rem HISTORY: MRA 6/16/97 Created
rem         MRA 10/10/01 Updated to 9i
rem
COLUMN owner           FORMAT a10        HEADING 'Owner'
COLUMN type_name       FORMAT a25        HEADING 'Type|Name'
COLUMN method_name     FORMAT a25        HEADING 'Method|Name'
COLUMN method_type                       HEADING 'Method|Type'
COLUMN parameters      FORMAT 99999      HEADING '#|Param'
COLUMN results         FORMAT 99999      HEADING '#|Results'
COLUMN method_no       FORMAT 99999      HEADING 'Meth.|Number'
COLUMN final           FORMAT A5         HEADING 'Final'
COLUMN Instantiable    FORMAT A6         HEADING 'Instan'
COLUMN overriding      FORMAT A6         HEADING 'ORide?'
COLUMN Inherited       FORMAT A9         HEADING 'Inherited'
BREAK ON owner ON type_name
SET LINES 132 PAGES 58 VERIFY OFF FEEDBACK OFF
START title132 'Type Methods Report'
SPOOL rep_out\&db\typ_meth.lis
SELECT
     owner,
     type_name,
     method_name,
```

```
        method_no,
        method_type,
        parameters,
        results,
        final,
        Instantiable,
        Overriding,
        Inherited
FROM dba_type_methods
WHERE owner LIKE UPPER('%&owner%')
ORDER BY owner, type_name;
SPOOL OFF
CLEAR COLUMNS
CLEAR BREAKS
SET VERIFY ON FEEDBACK ON LINES 80 pages 22
TTITLE OFF
```

Listing 10.33   Example of output from the type methods report.

```
Date: 10/10/01                                                      Page:  13
Time: 11:44 PM                      Type Methods Report                SYSTEM
                                    galinux1 database


        Type          Method        Meth.  Method    #      #
Owner   Name          Name          Number Type    Param Results Final Instan ORide? Inherited
------- ------------- ------------- ------ ------  ----- ------- ----- ------ ------ ---------
SYS     DBURITYPE     GETCLOB          7 PUBLIC     1      1 NO    YES    YES    NO
                      GETURL           3 PUBLIC     1      1 NO    YES    NO     YES
                      GETEXTERNALURL   2 PUBLIC     1      1 NO    YES    NO     YES
        FTPURITYPE    GETCLOB          1 PUBLIC     1      1 NO    NO     NO     YES
                      CREATEFTPURI     9 PUBLIC     1      1 NO    YES    NO     NO
                      GETBLOB          4 PUBLIC     1      1 NO    NO     NO     YES
                      GETEXTERNALURL   5 PUBLIC     1      1 NO    YES    YES    NO
                      GETURL           6 PUBLIC     1      1 NO    YES    YES    NO
                      GETBLOB          8 PUBLIC     1      1 NO    YES    YES    NO
                      GETCLOB          7 PUBLIC     1      1 NO    YES    YES    NO
                      GETURL           3 PUBLIC     1      1 NO    YES    NO     YES
                      GETEXTERNALURL   2 PUBLIC     1      1 NO    YES    NO     YES
        HTTPURITYPE   GETCLOB          1 PUBLIC     1      1 NO    NO     NO     YES
                      GETBLOB          4 PUBLIC     1      1 NO    NO     NO     YES
                      GETEXTERNALURL   5 PUBLIC     1      1 NO    YES    YES    NO
                      GETCLOB          7 PUBLIC     1      1 NO    YES    YES    NO
                      CREATEURI        9 PUBLIC     1      1 NO    YES    NO     NO
                      GETBLOB          8 PUBLIC     1      1 NO    YES    YES    NO
                      GETURL           6 PUBLIC     1      1 NO    YES    YES    NO
                      GETEXTERNALURL   2 PUBLIC     1      1 NO    YES    NO     YES
                      GETURL           3 PUBLIC     1      1 NO    YES    NO     YES
```

continues

Listing 10.33   Continued.

```
ORACLE_LOADER  ODCIGETINTERFACES      1 PUBLIC   1     1 NO   YES  NO   NO
               ODCIEXTTABLEPOPULATE   4 PUBLIC   3     1 NO   YES  NO   NO
               ODCIEXTTABLECLOSE      5 PUBLIC   3     1 NO   YES  NO   NO
               ODCIEXTTABLEOPEN       2 PUBLIC   7     1 NO   YES  NO   NO
               ODCIEXTTABLEFETCH      3 PUBLIC   5     1 NO   YES  NO   NO
```

Monitoring Type REFs   The only object-oriented method of relating two object tables in Oracle8, Oracle8*i*, and Oracle9*i* is via a REF. A REF internalizes the foreign key relationship between a child and parent table. A REF always goes between child and parent since a REF can only reference one column. The DBA_REFS view documents existing REFs in the database. The script in Source 10.36 shows how a report can be generated to show the REFs in the database. Refer back to Figure 10.2, which shows the relationships between the views used to document REFs in the database, and Listing 10.34 shows an example of a report from the script in Source 10.36.

Source 10.36   Example of REF column report.

```
rem
rem NAME: tab_ref.sql
rem FUNCTION: Generate a lit of all REF columns in the database
rem  for a specific user or all users
rem HISTORY: MRA 6/16/97 Created
rem
COLUMN owner               FORMAT a8   HEADING 'Owner'
COLUMN table_name          FORMAT a23  HEADING 'Table|Name'
COLUMN column_name         FORMAT a15  HEADING 'Column|Name'
COLUMN with_rowid          FORMAT a5   HEADING 'With|Rowid'
COLUMN is_scoped           FORMAT a6   HEADING 'Scoped'
COLUMN scope_table_owner   FORMAT a8   HEADING 'Scope|Table|Owner'
COLUMN scope_table_name    FORMAT a15  HEADING 'Scope|Table|Name'
BREAK ON owner
SET PAGES 58 LINES 130 FEEDBACK OFF VERIFY OFF
START title132 'Database REF Report'
SPOOL rep_out\&db\tab_ref.lis
SELECT
     owner,
     table_name,
     column_name,
     with_rowid,
     is_scoped,
     scope_table_owner,
     scope_table_name
FROM
     dba_refs
```

```
WHERE
      Owner LIKE UPPER('%&owner%')
ORDER BY
      owner;
SPOOL OFF
SET FEEDBACK ON VERIFY ON
CLEAR COLUMNS
CLEAR BREAKS
TTITLE OFF
```

Listing 10.34   Example of output from the database REF report.

```
Date: 06/16/97                                           Page:    1
Time: 01:03 AM               Database REF Report            SYSTEM
                               ORTEST1 database

                                                      Scope    Scope
              Table                   Column    With    Table    Table
Owner         Name                    Name      Rowid Scoped Owner    Name
--------  -------------------------  -----------  -----  ------  --------  --------
TELE_DBA  EARNINGS_INFO_NUMBERSV8    CLIENTS_ID_R YES    YES     TELE_DBA  CLIENTSV8
```

Monitoring Operators

Operators were new to Oracle8*i*. They enable extensibility of Oracle by allowing users to add operators (+, -, AND, OR, BETWEEN) to the database. Operators are also a key component of the Oracle8*i* INDEXTYPE (domain indexes). The views used to monitor operators are DBA_OPERATORS, DBA_OPARGUMENTS, DBA_OPANCILLARY, and DBA_OPBINDINGS. The operators' series of views are diagrammed in Figure 10.6 along with the DIMENSION and OUTLINE views. Source 10.37 shows an example of an operator report. An example of the output from the script in Source 10.37 is shown in Listing 10.35.

Source 10.37   Example of database OPERATOR report.

```
rem
rem NAME: operator.sql
rem FUNCTION: Generate a lit of all OPERATORS in the database
rem for a specific user or all users
rem HISTORY: MRA 5/12/98 Created
rem
COLUMN owner              FORMAT a8    HEADING 'Owner'
COLUMN operator_name      FORMAT a10   HEADING 'Operator|Name'
COLUMN number_of_binds    FORMAT 9999  HEADING 'Binds'
```

continues

Source 10.37 Continued.

```
COLUMN position                          HEADING 'Position'
COLUMN argument_type        FORMAT A20   HEADING 'Argument|Type'
COLUMN function_name        FORMAT A20   HEADING 'Binding|Argument'
COLUMN return_schema        FORMAT A10   HEADING 'Return|Schema'
COLUMN return_type          FORMAT A20   HEADING 'Return|Type'
BREAK ON owner ON operator_name ON number_of_binds
SET PAGES 58 LINES 130 FEEDBACK OFF VERIFY OFF
START title132 'Database OPERATOR Report'
SPOOL rep_out\&db\operator.lis
SELECT
     a.owner,
     a.operator_name,
     a.number_of_bindings,
     b.position,
     b.argument_type,
     c.function_name,
     DECODE(c.return_schema,NULL,'Internal',c.return_schema) return_schema,
     c.return_type
FROM
     Dba_operators a, dba_oparguments b, dba_opbindings c
WHERE
          Owner LIKE '%&owner%'
     AND a.owner=b.owner
     AND a.operator_name=b.operator_name
     AND a.owner=c.owner
     AND a.operator_name=c.operator_name
     AND b.binding#=c.binding#;
SPOOL OFF
CLEAR BREAKS
CLEAR COLUMNS
TTITLE OFF
SET FEEDBACK ON VERIFY ON
```

Listing 10.35 Example of output from database OPERATOR report.

```
Date: 06/17/99                                          Page:   1
Time: 08:45 PM              Database OPERATOR Report          SYSTEM
                              ORTEST1 database


         Operator              Argument Bound            Return  Return
Owner   Name    Binds Position Type     Function         Schema  Type
------  ------  ----- -------- -------- ---------------------- -------- -------
SYSTEM  CONCAT     1         1 VARCHAR2 "CON"."CONCAT_STRING" Internal VARCHAR2
                             2 VARCHAR2 "CON"."CONCAT_STRING" Internal VARCHAR2
```

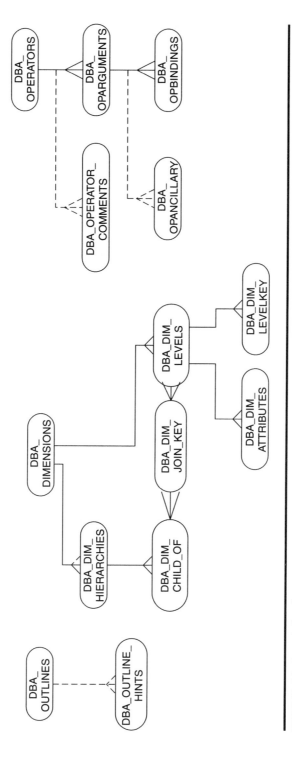

FIGURE 10.6 Miscellaneous DBA_ view clusters.

You should review the operator report to ensure that the operator bindings are properly ascribed and are of the correct type. Also, make sure that the function for the operator is properly assigned and that input and output types are properly defined.

Monitoring Dimensions

Dimensions, new to Oracle8*i*, are usually used in data warehouse applications to allow Oracle to remap queries efficiently against summaries (materialized views). Dimensions describe the relationships in a large denormalized table or a set of quasi-normalized tables such as would be found in a star or snowflake design DSS or data warehouse application. The views used to monitor dimensions are shown in Figure 10.6.

Dimensions contain levels and hierarchies that are linked using join keys. A report showing some of these aspects of dimensions is shown in Source 10.38. An example of the output from Source 10.38 is shown in Listing 10.36. Additional reports showing the relationship of dimension to hierarchy and dimension and attribute are shown in Sources 10.39 and 10.40. Example outputs are shown in Listings 10.36 and 10.37.

Source 10.38   Example of database dimension-level report.

```
rem
rem NAME: dim_level.sql
rem FUNCTION: Generate a lit of all Dimensions and levels in the
rem database for a specific user or all users
rem HISTORY: MRA 5/12/98 Created
rem
COLUMN owner                FORMAT a8   HEADING 'Owner'
COLUMN dimension_name       FORMAT a10  HEADING 'Dimension|Name'
COLUMN level_name           FORMAT a10 HEADING 'Level|Name'
COLUMN column_name          FORMAT a20 HEADING 'Column|Name'
COLUMN key_position         FORMAT 9999 HEADING 'Key|Position'
BREAK ON owner ON operator_name ON number_of_binds
SET PAGES 58 LINES 130 FEEDBACK OFF VERIFY OFF
START title132 'Database Dimension Levels Report'
SPOOL rep_out\&db\dim_level.lis
SELECT
     a.owner,
     a.dimension_name,
     b.level_name,
     c.column_name,
     c.key_position
FROM
     Dba_dimensions a, dba_dim_levels b, dba_dim_level_key c
WHERE
          a.Owner LIKE '%&owner%'
      AND a.owner=b.owner
      AND a.dimension_name=b.dimension_name
```

```
      AND a.owner=c.owner
      AND a.dimension_name=c.dimension_name
      AND b.level_name=c.level_name
ORDER BY
      a.owner,
      a.dimension_name,
      b.level_name;
SPOOL OFF
CLEAR BREAKS
CLEAR COLUMNS
TTITLE OFF
SET FEEDBACK ON VERIFY ON
```

Listing 10.36   Example of output from database dimension-level report.

```
Date: 05/13/99                                               Page:   1
Time: 11:25 PM         Database Dimension Levels Report         SYSTEM
                          ORTEST1 database


          Dimension  Level       Column                   Key
Owner     Name       Name        Name                     Position
--------  ---------  ----------  --------------------     --------
TELE_DBA  TEST_DIM   CHILD_ID    ID                              1
          TEST_DIM   PARENT_ID   PARENT_ID                       1
```

The database dimension-level report should be reviewed to ensure that the levels are assigned to the proper columns.

Source 10.39   Example of database dimension hierarchy report.

```
rem
rem NAME: dim_hierarchies.sql
rem FUNCTION: Generate a lit of all dimensions and hierarchies in the
rem database for a specific user or all users
rem HISTORY: MRA 5/12/98 Created
rem
COLUMN owner             FORMAT a8   HEADING 'Owner'
COLUMN dimension_name    FORMAT a10  HEADING 'Dimension|Name'
COLUMN column_name       FORMAT a10  HEADING 'Column|Name'
COLUMN hierarchy_name    FORMAT a10  HEADING 'Hierarchy|Name'
COLUMN parent_level_name FORMAT a10  HEADING 'Parent|Level'
COLUMN child_level_name  FORMAT a10  HEADING 'Child|Level'
COLUMN join_key_id       FORMAT a20  HEADING 'Join Key|ID'
BREAK ON owner ON dimension_name
```

continues

Source 10.39   Continued.

```
SET PAGES 58 LINES 78 FEEDBACK OFF VERIFY OFF
START title80 'Database Dimension Hierarchy Report'
SPOOL rep_out\&db\dim_hierarchies.lis
SELECT
     a.owner,
     a.dimension_name,
     b.hierarchy_name,
     c.parent_level_name,
     c.child_level_name,
     c.join_key_id
FROM
     Dba_dimensions a, dba_dim_hierarchies b, dba_dim_child_of c
WHERE
          a.Owner LIKE '%&owner%'
     AND a.owner=b.owner
     AND a.dimension_name=b.dimension_name
     AND a.owner=c.owner
     AND a.dimension_name=c.dimension_name
     AND b.hierarchy_name=c.hierarchy_name
ORDER BY
     a.owner,
     a.dimension_name,
     b.hierarchy_name;
SPOOL OFF
CLEAR BREAKS
CLEAR COLUMNS
TTITLE OFF
SET FEEDBACK ON VERIFY ON
```

Listing 10.37   Example of output from database dimension hierarchy report.

```
Date: 05/13/99                                        Page:    1
Time: 11:32 PM      Database Dimension Hierarchy Report     SYSTEM
                          ORTEST1 database


          Dimension  Hierarchy  Parent      Child      Join Key
Owner     Name       Name       Level       Level      ID
--------  ---------- ---------- ----------  ---------- ----------
TELE_DBA  TEST_DIM   PLAN       PARENT_ID   CHILD_ID
```

The database dimension hierarchy report should be reviewed to ensure that the hierarchies are using the proper level assignments and that the parent-child relationships make sense (that is, they aren't inverted).

The database dimension attribute report should be reviewed to be sure that the proper attributes are being ascribed to the proper levels.

Source 10.40   Example of database dimension attribute report.

```
rem
rem NAME: dim_attribute.sql
rem FUNCTION: Generate a lit of all Dimensions and atrributes in the
rem database for a specific user or all users
rem HISTORY: MRA 5/12/98 Created
rem
COLUMN owner            FORMAT a8    HEADING 'Owner'
COLUMN dimension_name   FORMAT a10   HEADING 'Dimension|Name'
COLUMN column_name      FORMAT a20   HEADING 'Column|Name'
COLUMN level_name       FORMAT a20   HEADING 'Level|Name'
COLUMN inferred         FORMAT a10   HEADING 'Inferred'
BREAK ON owner ON level_name
SET PAGES 58 LINES 78 FEEDBACK OFF VERIFY OFF
START title80 'Database OPERATOR Report'
SPOOL rep_out\&db\dim_attribute.lis
SELECT
    a.owner,
    a.dimension_name,
    b.level_name,
    c.column_name,
    c.inferred
FROM
    Dba_dimensions a, dba_dim_levels b, dba_dim_attributes c
WHERE
        a.owner LIKE '%&owner%'
    AND a.owner=b.owner
    AND a.dimension_name=b.dimension_name
    AND a.owner=c.owner
    AND a.dimension_name=c.dimension_name
    AND b.level_name=c.level_name
ORDER BY
    a.owner,
    a.dimension_name,
    b.level_name;
SPOOL OFF
CLEAR BREAKS
CLEAR COLUMNS
TTITLE OFF
SET FEEDBACK ON VERIFY ON
```

Monitoring Outlines

Outlines provide a method for forcing the cost-based optimizer to consistently use the same optimization for a specific SQL statement. The DBA needs to be aware of which outlines are currently stored in the database and if the outline has been used. The views used to monitor the outlines are DBA_OUTLINES and DBA_OUTLINE_HINTS. Note

Listing 10.38   Example of output from database dimension attribute report.

```
Date: 05/13/99                                              Page:    1
Time: 11:34 PM              Database OPERATOR Report         SYSTEM
                               ORTEST1 database


           Dimension  Level                 Column
Owner      Name       Name                  Name            Inferred
--------   ---------  --------------------  --------------  --------

TELE_DBA   TEST_DIM   PARENT_ID             STATEMENT_ID    N
```

that to create an outline (covered in Chapter 7), the PLAN_TABLE must be located in either a publicly available schema or in your own schema. In Oracle9*i*, the OEM tool has been extended to allow for outline editing. There are also new DBMS packages provided for this purpose. The views relationship is shown in Figure 10.6. An example report using the DBA_OUTLINES and DBA_OUTLINE_HINTS views is shown in Source 10.41, with example output from the script following in Listing 10.39.

Source 10.41   Example of database outline report.

```
rem
rem NAME: outline.sql
rem FUNCTION: Generate a lit of all outlines in the
rem database for a specific user or all users
rem HISTORY: MRA 5/13/98 Created
rem
COLUMN owner          FORMAT a8    HEADING 'Owner'
COLUMN name           FORMAT a13   HEADING 'Outline|Name'
COLUMN category       FORMAT a8    HEADING 'Category|Name'
COLUMN used           FORMAT a7    HEADING 'Used?'
COLUMN timestamp      FORMAT a16   HEADING 'Date Last|Used'
COLUMN version        FORMAT a9    HEADING 'Version'
COLUMN sql_text       FORMAT a40   HEADING 'SQL Outlined' WORD_WRAPPED
BREAK ON owner ON category
SET PAGES 58 LINES 130 FEEDBACK OFF VERIFY OFF
START title132 'Database OUTLINE Report'
SPOOL rep_out\&db\outline.lis
SELECT
     owner,
     name,
     category,
     used,
     to_char(timestamp,'dd/mm/yyyy hh24:mi') timestamp ,
     version,
     sql_text
```

```
FROM
     Dba_outlines
WHERE
     Owner LIKE '%&owner%'
ORDER BY
     owner,category;
SPOOL OFF
CLEAR BREAKS
TTITLE OFF
SET FEEDBACK ON VERIFY ON
```

Listing 10.39   Example of output from database outline report.

```
Date: 05/13/99                                                     Page:   1
Time: 11:44 PM                   Database OUTLINE Report                SYSTEM
                                   ORTEST1 database


        Outline        Category        Date Last
Owner   Name           Name     Used?  Used             Version   SQL Outlined
------- -------------- -------- ------ ---------------- --------- ---------------------------
TELE_DBA PROD_OUTLINE1 PROD     UNUSED 13/05/1999 23:39 8.1.5.0.0 select owner,table_name from
                                                                  dba_tables
        PROD_OUTLINE2           UNUSED 13/05/1999 23:39 8.1.5.0.0 select * from dba_data_files
        TEST_OUTLINE1 TEST      UNUSED 13/05/1999 23:39 8.1.5.0.0 select a.table_name,
                                                                  b.tablespace_name,
                                                                  c.file_name from
                                                                  dba_tables a, dba_table
        TEST_OUTLINE2           UNUSED 13/05/1999 23:39 8.1.5.0.0 select * from dba_data_files
```

In the outline report you should monitor for outlines that either haven't been used or haven't been used recently, and review whether they are still pertinent to your database application. The OUTLN_UTL package is used to maintain outlines.

Monitoring Outline Hints   Outlines generate and use outline hints. The outline hints are viewed in the DBA_OUTLINE_HINTS view. The report in Source 10.42 demonstrates the monitoring of the outline hints. Listing 10.40 shows sample output from that report.

Source 10.42   Example of database outline hints report.

```
rem
rem NAME: outline_hint.sql
rem FUNCTION: Generate a lit of all outlines in the
rem database for a specific user and outline or all users
```

continues

Source 10.42   Continued.

```
rem and outlines
rem HISTORY: MRA 5/13/98 Created
rem
COLUMN owner          FORMAT a8    HEADING 'Owner'
COLUMN name           FORMAT a13   HEADING 'Outline|Name'
COLUMN category       FORMAT a10   HEADING 'Category|Name'
COLUMN node           FORMAT 9999  HEADING 'Node'
COLUMN join_pos       FORMAT 9999  HEADING 'Join|Pos'
COLUMN hint           FORMAT A27   HEADING 'Hint Text' WORD_WRAPPED
BREAK ON owner ON category ON name
SET PAGES 58 LINES 78 FEEDBACK OFF VERIFY OFF
START title80 'Database OUTLINE Report'
SPOOL rep_out\&db\outline_hint.lis
SELECT
     a.owner, a.name,
     a.category, b.node,
     b.join_pos, b.hint
FROM
     Dba_outlines a, dba_outline_hints b
WHERE
      a.Owner LIKE UPPER('%&owner%')
      AND a.name LIKE UPPER('%&outline%')
      AND a.owner=b.owner
      AND a.name=b.name
ORDER BY
      owner,category,name,b.node;
SPOOL OFF
CLEAR BREAKS
TTITLE OFF
SET FEEDBACK ON VERIFY ON
```

Listing 10.40   Example of output from database outline hints report.

```
Date: 05/14/99                                               Page:   1
Time: 12:08 AM            Database OUTLINE Report            SYSTEM
                             ORTEST1 databas


          Outline       Category        Join
Owner     Name          Name     Node   Pos Hint Text
--------  ------------- -----------  ------  --- ---- --------------------
TELE_DBA  TEST_OUTLINE2 TEST          1     0 NO_EXPAND
                                      1     0 ORDERED
                                      1     1 NO_ACCESS(DBA_DATA_FILES)
                                      1     0 NOREWRITE
```

```
1    0 NO_FACT(DBA_DATA_FILES)
1    0 NOREWRITE
2    0 NO_EXPAND
2    0 ORDERED
2    0 NOREWRITE
2    0 NOREWRITE
3    0 NO_EXPAND
3    0 PQ_DISTRIBUTE(TS NONE NONE)
3    0 PQ_DISTRIBUTE(HC NONE NONE)
3    0 PQ_DISTRIBUTE(F NONE NONE)
3    0 ORDERED
3    0 NO_FACT(HC)
3    0 NO_FACT(X$KCCFN)
3    3 FULL(HC)
3    1 FULL(X$KCCFN)
3    0 NOREWRITE
3    0 NOREWRITE
3    2 INDEX(F I_FILE1)
3    4 INDEX(TS)
3    0 NO_FACT(F)
3    0 NO_FACT(TS)
3    0 USE_NL(F)
3    0 USE_NL(HC)
3    0 USE_NL(TS)
4    0 NO_EXPAND
4    0 NOREWRITE
4    0 PQ_DISTRIBUTE(TS NONE NONE)
4    0 PQ_DISTRIBUTE(F NONE NONE)
4    0 USE_NL(TS)
4    0 USE_NL(F)
4    0 ORDERED
4    0 NO_FACT(TS)
4    0 NO_FACT(F)
4    0 NO_FACT(X$KCCFN)
4    3 INDEX(TS)
4    2 INDEX(F I_FILE1)
4    1 FULL(X$KCCFN)
4    0 NOREWRITE
5    0 NOREWRITE
6    0 NOREWRITE
7    0 NOREWRITE
8    0 NOREWRITE
```

The output from the database outline hints report should be reviewed to verify that the proper hints are being used for the specific SQL outline.

10.4 FURTHER DBA READING

The DBA may find these references of interest when planning to do monitoring activities:

Oracle9i Database Administrator's Guide, Release 9.0.1, Part No. A90117-01, Oracle Corporation, June 2001.
Oracle9i Database Reference, Release 9.0.1, Part No. A90190-01, Oracle Corporation, June 2001.
Oracle9i PL/SQL User's Guide and Reference, Release 9.0.1, Part No. A89856-01, Oracle Corporation, June 2001.
Oracle9i SQL Reference, Release 9.0.1, Part No. A90125-01, Oracle Corporation, June 2001.
Oracle9i Supplied PL/SQL Packages and Types Reference, Release 9.0.1, Part No. A89852-02, June 2001, Oracle Corporation.

10.5 SUMMARY

This chapter discussed the monitoring of all nontable and nonindex items in an Oracle database. The numerous scripts provided here are designed to make monitoring and documenting these other Oracle structures easier for both the novice and the experienced DBA.

CHAPTER 11

Monitoring Users and Other Database Objects

Chapter 10 covered monitoring of table-related objects in Oracle; this chapter continues to discuss monitoring, but as it applies to virtually all other database objects. And note that because information about users is stored in the database, and because a DBA creates users, I am including users in the "other" database object category. Like tables, clusters, snapshots, types, and indexes, all other database objects are monitored using the data dictionary tables and views.

NOTE Refer to the reference manual on the documentation Web site, technet.oracle.com, as you review the scripts provided here. The data dictionary is a powerful tool in the hands of someone who knows how to use it.

11.1 USING THE V$ AND DBA_ VIEWS FOR MONITORING USERS

What exactly do DBAs need to know about the users of their databases? The DBA needs to keep track of many important facts about each user, including privileges, quotas, tables owned, filespace used, and database default locations, just to name a few. The Oracle Administrator toolbar (part of the Oracle Enterprise Manager toolset) has a nice GUI in its Security Manager section (see Figure 11.1), but it has no report capability.

The DBA_USERS view is the root of a tree of related DBA_ views that give a full picture of the privileges, resources, and roles granted to users. Figure 11.2 diagrams how all these views in the DBA_ user view cluster relate to each other.

How can the DBA keep track of this information for hundreds or possibly thousands of users? Scribble it down as it displays on the SVRMGR or OEM screen? Use some sort

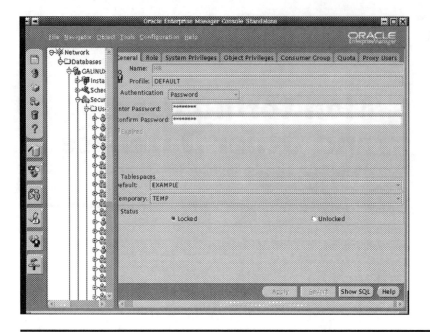

FIGURE 11.1   Oracle Enterprise Manager Security Manager screen.

of screen capture or screen print facility? Hardly. To keep track of this information, the DBA needs reports. Whether a DBA store these reports online or uses a three-ring binder, good reports detail exactly what a DBA needs to know. Let's address the relevant topics.

Monitoring User Setup

The first report we will look at implements the DBA_USERS view to provide information on users, user default and temporary tablespace assignments, and user database-level privileges. The script for this report is shown in Source 11.1.

Several items about this report script bear mentioning. First, notice the header format. Each report should contain a header section similar to this one. It tells what the report script does, who wrote it, and, most important, what changes have been made to it. Next, notice the START command. This command is calling a script that generates a standard 132-column header for use in reports. (Note: This script is located in the zip files on the Wiley Web page.) The report header programs also return the database name so that it may be included in the filename. This report was written for use on the UNIX platform. To use it on other platforms, only the file specification format would have to be modified; no other changes would have to be made. Notice also that LOCK_DATE and EXPIRY_DATE have been moved from this report to the script in Source 11.2. The

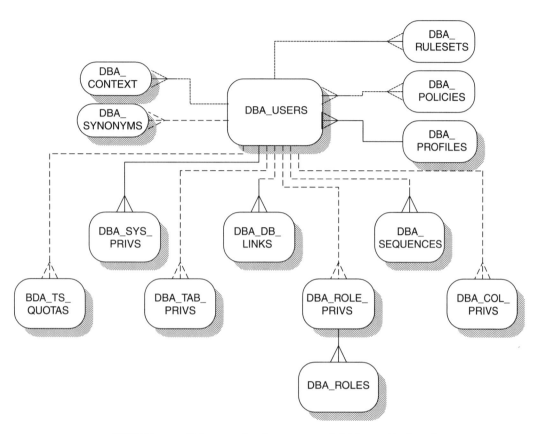

NOTE: Users, which equate to schemas, own all database objects and
thus also have links to all DBA_ views related to objects such as tables,
indexes, clusters, views, etc. However I have chosen for clarity's sake
not to include all of these links on this diagram, please remember them
as implicit.

FIGURE 11.2   DBA_USERS view cluster.

report in Source 11.3 is useful if you invoke the password control options available in
Oracle8, Oracle8*i*, and Oracle9*i*. I have added the resource group to the report in Source
11.1, so if resource groups are implemented, you will have a record of who is assigned
to each resource group. The output from Source 11.2 report is shown in Listing 11.1.

As you can see, this report takes care of several of our requirements: user names,
default tablespace assignments, temporary tablespace assignments, and database roles.
The report is currently sorted, using the ORDER BY command, by user name, tablespace assignments, profile, resource group assignment, and status. If you prefer, it could

Source 11.1   Example of user report listing.

```
REM
REM NAME        : DB_USER.SQL
REM
REM FUNCTION    : GENERATE USER_REPORT
REM Limitations : None
REM
REM Updates     : MRA 6/10/97 added Oracle8 account status
REM               MRA 5/14/99 Added Oracle8i Resource Group
REM               MRA 5/22/99 Removed expiry data to new report
REM
SET PAGESIZE 58  LINESIZE 131 FEEDBACK OFF
rem
COLUMN username                FORMAT a12 HEADING User
COLUMN account_status          FORMAT a6  HEADING Status
COLUMN default_tablespace      FORMAT a14 HEADING Default
COLUMN temporary_tablespace    FORMAT a10 HEADING Temporary
COLUMN granted_role            FORMAT a22 HEADING Roles
COLUMN default_role            FORMAT a8  HEADING Default?
COLUMN admin_option            FORMAT a6  HEADING Admin?
COLUMN profile                 FORMAT a10 HEADING Profile
COLUMN initial_rsrc_consumer_group FORMAT a22 HEADING 'Resource|Group'
rem
START title132 'ORACLE USER REPORT'
DEFINE output = rep_out\&db\db_user
BREAK ON username SKIP 1 ON default_tablespace ON temporary_tablespace ON
profile ON account_status ON initial_rsrc_consumer_group
SPOOL &output
rem
SELECT a.username,
       a.default_tablespace,a.temporary_tablespace,
       a.profile,a.account_status,
       a.initial_rsrc_consumer_group,
       b.granted_role,b.admin_option,
       b.default_role
FROM sys.dba_users a,
     sys.dba_role_privs b
WHERE a.username = b.grantee
ORDER BY username,
         default_tablespace,
         temporary_tablespace,
         profile,
         granted_role;
rem
SPOOL OFF
SET TERMOUT ON FLUSH ON FEEDBACK ON VERIFY ON
CLEAR COLUMNS
CLEAR BREAKS
PAUSE Press Enter to continue
```

Source 11.2   Example user report.

```
REM
REM NAME         : DB_USER.SQL
REM
REM FUNCTION     : GENERATE USER_REPORT
REM Limitations : None
REM
REM Updates      : MRA 6/10/97 added Oracle8 account status
REM                MRA 5/14/99 Added Oracle8i Resource Group
REM
SET PAGESIZE 58  LINESIZE 131 FEEDBACK OFF
rem
COLUMN username                  FORMAT a10 HEADING User
COLUMN account_status            FORMAT a10 HEADING Status
COLUMN default_tablespace        FORMAT a15 HEADING Default
COLUMN temporary_tablespace      FORMAT a15 HEADING Temporary
COLUMN granted_role              FORMAT a21 HEADING Roles
COLUMN default_role              FORMAT a9  HEADING Default?
COLUMN admin_option              FORMAT a7  HEADING Admin?
COLUMN profile                   FORMAT a15 HEADING Profile
COLUMN initial_rsrc_consumer_group FORMAT a10 HEADING 'Resource|Group'
COLUMN lock_date                 HEADING 'Date|Locked'
COLUMN expiry_date               HEADING 'Expiry_date'
rem
START title132 'ORACLE USER REPORT'
DEFINE output = rep_out\&db\db_user
BREAK ON username SKIP 1 ON account_status ON default_tablespace
ON temporary_tablespace ON profile
SPOOL &output
rem
SELECT a.username,
       a.account_status,
       TO_CHAR(a.lock_date,'dd-mon-yyyy hh24:mi') lock_date,
       TO_CHAR(a.expiry_date,'dd-mon-yyyy hh24:mi') expiry_date,
       a.default_tablespace,a.temporary_tablespace,
       a.profile,b.granted_role,
       b.admin_option,b.default_role,
       a.initial_rsrc_consumer_group
FROM sys.dba_users a,
     sys.dba_role_privs b
WHERE a.username = b.grantee
ORDER BY username,
         default_tablespace,temporary_tablespace,
         profile, granted_role;
rem
SPOOL OFF
SET TERMOUT ON FLUSH ON FEEDBACK ON VERIFY ON
CLEAR COLUMNS
CLEAR BREAKS
PAUSE Press Enter to continue
```

Listing 11.1   Example of user report format.

```
Date: 05/22/99                                                    Page:   1
Time: 08:45 AM                    ORACLE USER REPORT                 SYSTEM
                                  ORTEST1 database


                                     Resource
User    Default  Temp   Profile Status Group                  Roles                      Admin? Def?
------- -------- ------ ------- ------ --------------------- --------------------- ------ ----
DBSNMP  SYSTEM   TEMP   DEFAULT OPEN   DEFAULT_CONSUMER_GROUP CONNECT                    NO    YES
                                                              RESOURCE                   NO    YES
                                                              SNMPAGENT                  NO    YES

MIGRATE SYSTEM   TEMP   DEFAULT OPEN   DEFAULT_CONSUMER_GROUP DBA                        NO    YES
                                                              RESOURCE                   NO    YES

ORDSYS  SYSTEM   TEMP   DEFAULT OPEN   DEFAULT_CONSUMER_GROUP CONNECT                    NO    YES
                                                              RESOURCE                   NO    YES

OUTLN   SYSTEM   TEMP   DEFAULT OPEN   DEFAULT_CONSUMER_GROUP CONNECT                    NO    YES
                                                              RESOURCE                   NO    YES

SYS     SYSTEM   TEMP   DEFAULT OPEN   SYS_GROUP              AQ_ADMINISTRATOR_ROLE     YES   YES
                                                              AQ_USER_ROLE              YES   YES
                                                              CONNECT                   YES   YES
                                                              DBA                       YES   YES
                                                              DELETE_CATALOG_ROLE       YES   YES
                                                              EXECUTE_CATALOG_ROLE      YES   YES
                                                              EXP_FULL_DATABASE         YES   YES
                                                              IMP_FULL_DATABASE         YES   YES
                                                              RECOVERY_CATALOG_OWNER    YES   YES
                                                              RESOURCE                  YES   YES
                                                              SELECT_CATALOG_ROLE       YES   YES
                                                              SNMPAGENT                 YES   YES

SYSTEM  TOOLS    TEMP   DEFAULT OPEN   SYS_GROUP              AQ_ADMINISTRATOR_ROLE     YES   YES
                                                              DBA                       YES   YES
                                                              TEST                      YES   YES

TEL_DBA TELE_DATA TEMP  DEFAULT OPEN   DEFAULT_CONSUMER_GROUP CONNECT                    NO    YES
                                                              RESOURCE                   NO    YES
```

be sorted by default or temporary tablespace or by individual role. In this script, there will be one row for each role granted to the user.

In Source 11.3. we examine user expiration information. The report columns will be populated only with date information if you are using the password expiration features in Oracle8 and Oracle8*i* in profiles. The expiry date in a profile will be set based on the last password change. If a user has just been assigned to a profile, I suggest using the ALTER USER command to expire the user's password, forcing him or her to reset it, and set the expiry date. The output from the script in Source 11.3 is shown in Listing 11.2.

Monitoring User Roles

Monitoring user setup is important, but it is only the beginning of user monitoring. A companion script to show roles and administration options is also required. This is

Source 11.3   Example of script to report account expiry status.

```
REM
REM NAME        : USER_EXPIRE.SQL
REM
REM FUNCTION    : GENERATE USER EXPIRY DATA REPORT
REM Limitations : None
REM
REM Updates     : MRA 5/22/99 Created
REM
COLUMN account_status           FORMAT a15 HEADING Status
COLUMN default_tablespace       FORMAT a14 HEADING Default
COLUMN temporary_tablespace     FORMAT a10 HEADING Temporary
COLUMN username                 FORMAT a12 HEADING User
COLUMN lock_date                FORMAT a11 HEADING 'Date|Locked'
COLUMN expiry_date              FORMAT a11 HEADING 'Expiry|Date'
COLUMN profile                  FORMAT a15 HEADING Profile
SET PAGESIZE 58  LINESIZE 131 FEEDBACK OFF
START title132 'ORACLE USER EXPIRATION REPORT'
BREAK ON username SKIP 1 ON default_tablespace ON temporary_tablespace ON
profile ON account_status
SPOOL rep_out\&db\user_expire
rem
SELECT username,
       default_tablespace,temporary_tablespace,
       profile,account_status,
       TO_CHAR(lock_date,'dd-mon-yyyy') lock_date,
       TO_CHAR(expiry_date,'dd-mon-yyyy') expiry_date
FROM sys.dba_users
ORDER BY username,
         default_tablespace,temporary_tablespace,
         profile, account_status;
rem
SPOOL OFF
SET TERMOUT ON FLUSH ON FEEDBACK ON VERIFY ON
CLEAR COLUMNS
CLEAR BREAKS
PAUSE Press Enter to continue
```

Listing 11.2   Example of output from the user expiry report.

```
Date: 05/22/99                                                          Page:   1
Time: 09:47 AM                    ORACLE USER EXPIRATION REPORT               SYS
                                       ORTEST1 database


                                                          Date       Expiry
User           Default          Temporary  Profile        Status    Locked     Date
-----------    --------------   ---------  --------------- ---------- ---------- ----------
DBSNMP         SYSTEM           TEMP       DEFAULT         OPEN

GRAPHICS_DBA   GRAPHICS_DATA    TEMP       DEFAULT         OPEN

MIGRATE        SYSTEM           TEMP       DEFAULT         OPEN

ORDSYS         SYSTEM           TEMP       DEFAULT         OPEN

OUTLN          SYSTEM           TEMP       DEFAULT         OPEN

SYS            SYSTEM           TEMP       DEFAULT         OPEN

SYSTEM         TOOLS            TEMP       DEFAULT         OPEN

TELE_DBA       TELE_DATA        TEMP       TELE_PROFILE    OPEN                  09-aug-1999

TEST1          USER_DATA        TEMP       TELE_PROFILE    OPEN                  20-aug-1999

TEST_IT        USER_DATA        TEMP       TELE_PROFILE    LOCKED(TIMED) 22-may-1999
```

shown in Source 11.4. As you can see, it is very important under Oracle to assign roles to users, due to the large number of required grants for the modern environment.

If you assign each privilege to each user as it is required, you will soon find it impossible to manage your user base. Start by assigning only the default roles, then expand those roles as required. For example, for a user who needs to create tables and indexes, a role called CREATOR could be constructed that has the role CONNECT, plus the CREATE_TABLE and CREATE_INDEX privileges. It should also be obvious that the DBA will need to track the roles and have them available at a moment's notice in hard copy to refer to as users are assigned to the system. See Listing 11.3 for an Oracle roles report.

Monitoring User Profiles

In addition to roles, each user is also assigned profiles. Each user gets the default profile if he or she is not explicitly assigned to a different profile. Profiles control resource usage and, with Oracle8, Oracle8i, and Oracle9i, password security. Source 11.5 is a script that shows the different user profiles. The output of Source 11.5 is shown in Listing 11.4.

Source 11.4   Example of roles report listing for Oracle7, Oracle8, and Oracle8*i*.

```
REM
REM NAME         : sys_role.SQL
REM PURPOSE      : GENERATE SYSTEM GRANTS and ROLES REPORT
REM USE          : CALLED BY SQLPLUS
REM Limitations  : None
REM Revisions    :
REM Date           Modified by  Reason for change
REM 08-Apr-1993    MIKE AULT     INITIAL CREATE
REM 10-Jun-1997    Mike Ault     Update to Oracle8
REM 15-May-1999    Mike Ault     No changes for Oracle8i
REM
SET FLUSH OFF TERM OFF PAGESIZE 58  LINESIZE 78
COLUMN grantee            HEADING 'User or Role'
COLUMN admin_option       HEADING Admin?
START title80 'SYSTEM GRANTS AND ROLES REPORT'
DEFINE output = rep_out\&&db\role_report
SPOOL &output
SELECT
    grantee,
    privilege,
    admin_option
FROM
    sys.dba_sys_privs
GROUP BY
    grantee;
SPOOL OFF
SET FLUSH ON TERM ON
CLEAR COLUMNS
TTITLE OFF
```

Listing 11.3   Example of output from script in Source 11.4.

```
Date: 05/22/99           "Your Company Name"           Page:   1
Time: 03:12 PM            ORACLE ROLES REPORT                SYSTEM
                          "Your Database"


User or Role             PRIVILEGE                      Adm
--------------------     ----------------------------   ---

CONNECT                  ALTER SESSION                  NO
                         CREATE CLUSTER                 NO
                         CREATE DATABASE LINK           NO
                         CREATE SEQUENCE                NO
                         CREATE SESSION                 NO
                         CREATE SYNONYM                 NO
                         CREATE TABLE                   NO
                         CREATE VIEW                    NO
```

continues

Listing 11.3   Continued.

DBA	ALTER ANY CLUSTER	YES
	ALTER ANY INDEX	YES
	ALTER ANY PROCEDURE	YES
	ALTER ANY ROLE	YES
	CREATE SEQUENCE	YES
	CREATE SESSION	YES
	CREATE SNAPSHOT	YES
	.	
	.	
DEV8_DBA	UNLIMITED TABLESPACE	NO

Source 11.5   Script to generate a report on Oracle8, Oracle8_i_, and Oracle9_i_ user resource profiles.

```
REM NAME        : PROFILE_REPORT.SQL
REM PURPOSE     : GENERATE USER PROFILES REPORT
REM Revisions:
REM Date          Modified by       Reason for change
REM 08-Apr-1993   MIKE AULT         INITIAL CREATE
REM 14-May-1999   MIKE AULT         Added resource_type
REM
SET FLUSH OFF TERM OFF PAGESIZE 58 LINESIZE 78 VERIFY OFF FEEDBACK OFF
COLUMN profile          FORMAT a15    HEADING Profile
COLUMN resource_name    FORMAT A25    HEADING 'Resource:'
COLUMN resource_type    FORMAT A9     HEADING 'Resource|Affects'
COLUMN limit            FORMAT a20    HEADING Limit
START title80 'ORACLE PROFILES REPORT'
BREAK ON profile
SPOOL rep_out/&&db/prof_rep
SELECT
    profile,resource_name,
    resource_type,limit
FROM
    sys.dba_profiles
WHERE
    profile LIKE UPPER('%&profile_name%')
ORDER BY
    profile,resource_type,resource_name;
SPOOL OFF
CLEAR COLUMNS
SET FLUSH ON TERM ON VERIFY ON FEEDBACK ON
TTITLE OFF
```

Listing 11.4   Example of output from the report in Source 11.5.

```
Date: 05/22/99                                           Page:   1
Time: 10:13 AM              ORACLE PROFILES REPORT       SYS
                            ORTEST1 database


                                        Resource
Profile          Resource:              Affects    Limit
-------------    -----------------      ---------  ----------------
TELE_PROFILE     COMPOSITE_LIMIT              KERNEL     DEFAULT
                 CONNECT_TIME                 KERNEL     DEFAULT
                 CPU_PER_CALL                 KERNEL     DEFAULT
                 CPU_PER_SESSION              KERNEL     DEFAULT
                 IDLE_TIME                    KERNEL     DEFAULT
                 LOGICAL_READS_PER_CALL       KERNEL     DEFAULT
                 LOGICAL_READS_PER_SESSION    KERNEL     DEFAULT
                 PRIVATE_SGA                  KERNEL     DEFAULT
                 SESSIONS_PER_USER            KERNEL     DEFAULT
                 FAILED_LOGIN_ATTEMPTS        PASSWORD   6
                 PASSWORD_GRACE_TIME          PASSWORD   5
                 PASSWORD_LIFE_TIME           PASSWORD   90
                 PASSWORD_LOCK_TIME           PASSWORD   3
                 PASSWORD_REUSE_MAX           PASSWORD   DEFAULT
                 PASSWORD_REUSE_TIME          PASSWORD   DEFAULT
                 PASSWORD_VERIFY_FUNCTION     PASSWORD   DEFAULT
```

In Listing 11.4, notice that it does not display the values for the DEFAULT profile. You should know that the default profile has unlimited resources. This is fine for DBA type accounts, but for the majority of general users, you will probably want to restrict some of the quotas and define a new profile for them. Remember to set the RESOURCE_ LIMIT parameter in the initialization file to TRUE in order to enable resource quota usage. The RESOURCE_LIMIT parameter does *not* have to be set to use the password features of the profile.

Monitoring User Consumer Groups and Plans

New in Oracle8*i* was the concept of user resource groups. A resource group specifies how much of a particular resource a specific user (or role) is assigned. For example, a CEO group may get a %CPU assignment of 100, while a clerk may get 40. A resource group is set up using resource plans. The DBA_RSRC series of views are used to monitor resource groups, and the DBMS_RESOURCE_MANAGER and DBMS_RESOURCE_ MANAGER_PRIVS packages are used to maintain resource consumer groups and plans.

Monitoring resource plans involves several layers of reports. The top layer will report on the overall structure of the resource plans, directives, subplans, and resource groups. The next level reports on the directive level and the different CPU usage specifications. The final level deals with the group and system-level grants and administration privileges associated with them. Figure 11.3 shows how the PLAN cluster DBA_ views relate to each other. Source 11.6 is an example of a report that shows the structure of a resource plan. The output from the script in Source 11.6 is shown in Listing 11.5.

Once the plans and groups have been documented, it would be nice to know how they relate to each other, wouldn't it? These relationships are called the *plan directives*. The plan directives are documented via a script similar to the one shown in Source 11.7. An example of output from Source 11.7 is shown in Listing 11.6.

Oracle8*i* resource plans are usually maintained by a plan administrator. This administrator is usually a SYSTEM user who has the required privileges through the DBA role. However, you may want to isolate the plan administration functions from the system administration functions by giving other users the required privileges through the use of the DBMS_RESOURCE_MANAGER_PRIVS package procedures. These privilege grants need to be monitored. The script in Source 11.8 is an example of a resource manager system privilege grants monitoring script. Listing 11.7 shows what the output from the script in Source 11.8 looks like.

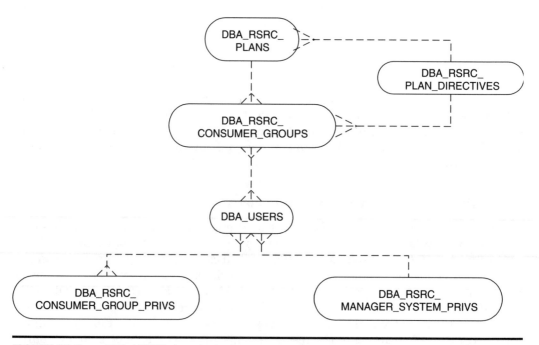

FIGURE 11.3   DBA_USERS view cluster for resource groups.

Source 11.6 **Script to generate a report on Oracle8*i* and Oracle9*i* group resource plans.**

```
REM NAME         : RESOURCE_PLAN.SQL
REM PURPOSE      : GENERATE DATABASE RESOURCE PLAN REPORT
REM Revisions:
REM Date            Modified by      Reason for change
REM 15-May-1999     MIKE AULT        initial creation
REM
COLUMN plan                   FORMAT a16      HEADING 'Plan|Name'
COLUMN cpu_method1            FORMAT a8       HEADING 'CPU|Method'
COLUMN mandatory1            FORMAT a4       HEADING 'Man?'
COLUMN group_or_subplan  FORMAT a12      HEADING 'Group or|Subplan Name'
COLUMN type                   FORMAT a8       HEADING 'Group or|Subplan'
COLUMN cpu_method2            FORMAT a8       HEADING 'CPU|Method2'
COLUMN plan2                  NOPRINT
COLUMN queue_meth1           FORMAT A12
COLUMN queue_meth2           FORMAT A12
COLUMN session_pool1         FORMAT A25 HEADING 'Sessions 1'
COLUMN session_pool2         FORMAT A25 HEADING 'Sessions 2'
REM
SET LINES 228 PAGES 55 VERIFY OFF FEEDBACK OFF
BREAK ON plan ON cpu_method1 ON mandatory1 ON num_plan_directives
START title132 'Resource Plan Report'
SPOOL rep_out\&&db\resource_plan.lis
REM
SELECT DISTINCT
      decode(b.plan,'',a.plan,b.plan) plan,
      a.active_sess_pool_mth session_pool1,
      a.parallel_degree_limit_mth parallel_meth1,
      a.queueing_mth queue_meth1,
      b.plan plan2,
      a.cpu_method cpu_method1,
      a.mandatory mandatory1,
      DECODE(b.group_or_subplan,'',d.consumer_group,
        b.group_or_subplan) group_or_subplan,
      DECODE(b.type,'CONSUMER_GROUP','GROUP',b.type) type,
      c.active_sess_pool_mth session_pool2,
      c.parallel_degree_limit_mth parallel_meth2,
      c.queueing_mth queue_meth2,
      decode(c.cpu_method,'',d.cpu_method,c.cpu_method) cpu_method2
FROM
      dba_rsrc_plans a, dba_rsrc_plan_directives b, dba_rsrc_plans c,
      dba_rsrc_consumer_groups d
WHERE
      a.plan=b.plan
      AND ((b.group_or_subplan = c.plan OR
            b.group_or_subplan = d.consumer_group))
ORDER BY
      2,5;
```

continues

Source 11.6 **Continued.**

```
SPOOL OFF
CLEAR COLUMNS
SET VERIFY ON FEEDBACK ON LINES 80 PAGES 22
TTITLE OFF
```

Listing 11.5 **Output from script to generate a report on Oracle8*i* /Oracle9*i* group resource plans.**

```
Date: 10/13/01
Time: 06:23 PM


Plan                                                                   CPU
Name            Sessions 1              PARALLEL_METH1                 QUEUE_METH1 Method  Man?
--------------- ----------------------- ------------------------------ ----------- -------- ----
INTERNAL_PLAN   ACTIVE_SESS_POOL_ABSOLUTE PARALLEL_DEGREE_LIMIT_ABSOLUTE FIFO_TIMEOUT EMPHASIS YES
INTERNAL_QUIESCE ACTIVE_SESS_POOL_ABSOLUTE PARALLEL_DEGREE_LIMIT_ABSOLUTE FIFO_TIMEOUT EMPHASIS YES
                ACTIVE_SESS_POOL_ABSOLUTE PARALLEL_DEGREE_LIMIT_ABSOLUTE FIFO_TIMEOUT
SYSTEM_PLAN     ACTIVE_SESS_POOL_ABSOLUTE PARALLEL_DEGREE_LIMIT_ABSOLUTE FIFO_TIMEOUT EMPHASIS NO
                ACTIVE_SESS_POOL_ABSOLUTE PARALLEL_DEGREE_LIMIT_ABSOLUTE FIFO_TIMEOUT
                ACTIVE_SESS_POOL_ABSOLUTE PARALLEL_DEGREE_LIMIT_ABSOLUTE FIFO_TIMEOUT
Second Half of report:
                                                                              Page  1
    Resource Plan Report                                                      SYSTEM
    galinux1 database


Group or    Group or                                                       CPU
Subplan Name Subplan Sessions 2            PARALLEL_METH2                 QUEUE_METH2 Method2
------------ ------- ------------------------ ------------------------------ ------------ -------
OTHER_GROUPS GROUP   ACTIVE_SESS_POOL_ABSOLUTE PARALLEL_DEGREE_LIMIT_ABSOLUTE FIFO_TIMEOUT EMPHASIS
OTHER_GROUPS GROUP   ACTIVE_SESS_POOL_ABSOLUTE PARALLEL_DEGREE_LIMIT_ABSOLUTE FIFO_TIMEOUT EMPHASIS
SYS_GROUP    GROUP   ACTIVE_SESS_POOL_ABSOLUTE PARALLEL_DEGREE_LIMIT_ABSOLUTE FIFO_TIMEOUT EMPHASIS
LOW_GROUP    GROUP   ACTIVE_SESS_POOL_ABSOLUTE PARALLEL_DEGREE_LIMIT_ABSOLUTE FIFO_TIMEOUT EMPHASIS
OTHER_GROUPS GROUP   ACTIVE_SESS_POOL_ABSOLUTE PARALLEL_DEGREE_LIMIT_ABSOLUTE FIFO_TIMEOUT EMPHASIS
SYS_GROUP    GROUP   ACTIVE_SESS_POOL_ABSOLUTE PARALLEL_DEGREE_LIMIT_ABSOLUTE FIFO_TIMEOUT EMPHASIS
```

Source 11.7 **Script to generate a report on Oracle8*i* and Oracle9*i* group resource plan directives.**

```
REM NAME        : PLAN_DIRECTIVES.SQL
REM PURPOSE     : GENERATE DATABASE RESOURCE PLAN DIRECTIVES REPORT
REM Revisions:
REM Date            Modified by      Reason for change
REM 15-May-1999     MIKE AULT        initial creation
REM 13-Oct-2001     Mike Ault        Update to 9i
```

```
REM
COLUMN plan                      FORMAT a17       HEADING 'Plan|Name'
COLUMN cpu_method1               FORMAT a8        HEADING 'CPU|Method'
COLUMN mandatory1                FORMAT a3        HEADING 'Man|?'
COLUMN num_plan_directives       FORMAT 999       HEADING 'Num|Dir'
COLUMN group_or_subplan          FORMAT a17       HEADING 'Group or|Subplan
Name'
COLUMN type                      FORMAT a5        HEADING 'Type'
COLUMN cpu_method2               FORMAT a8        HEADING 'CPU|Method'
COLUMN cpu_p1                    FORMAT 999       HEADING 'CPU|1%'
COLUMN cpu_p2                    FORMAT 999       HEADING 'CPU|2%'
COLUMN cpu_p3                    FORMAT 999       HEADING 'CPU|3%'
COLUMN cpu_p4                    FORMAT 999       HEADING 'CPU|4%'
COLUMN cpu_p5                    FORMAT 999       HEADING 'CPU|5%'
COLUMN cpu_p6                    FORMAT 999       HEADING 'CPU|6%'
COLUMN cpu_p7                    FORMAT 999       HEADING 'CPU|7%'
COLUMN cpu_p8                    FORMAT 999       HEADING 'CPU|8%'
COLUMN parallel_degree_limit_p1  FORMAT 9999999   HEADING 'Par|Degree'
COLUMN switch_group              FORMAT a15       HEADING 'Switch|Group'
COLUMN switch_time                                HEADING 'Switch|Time'
COLUMN switch_estimate                            HEADING 'Switch|Estimate'
COLUMN max_est_exec_time                          HEADING 'Max Est|Exec Time'
COLUMN undo_pool                                  HEADING 'Undo|Pool'
COLUMN active_sess_pool_p1                         HEADING 'Active|Session|Pool'
COLUMN queueing_p1                                HEADING 'Queueing'
REM
SET LINES 200 PAGES 55 VERIFY OFF FEEDBACK OFF
BREAK ON plan on cpu_method1 on mandatory1 on num_plan_directives
START title132 'Resource Plan Directives Report'
SPOOL rep_out\&&db\plan_directives.lis
REM
SELECT DISTINCT
     a.plan,
     a.cpu_method cpu_method1,
     a.mandatory mandatory1,
     b.group_or_subplan,
     DECODE(b.type,'CONSUMER_GROUP','GROUP',b.type) type,
     c.cpu_method cpu_method2,
     b.cpu_p1,b.cpu_p2,b.cpu_p3,b.cpu_p4,
     b.cpu_p5,b.cpu_p6,b.cpu_p7,b.cpu_p8,
     b.active_sess_pool_p1,b.queueing_p1,
     b.parallel_degree_limit_p1,
     b.switch_group,b.switch_time,
     b.switch_estimate,b.max_est_exec_time,
     b.undo_pool
FROM
     dba_rsrc_plans a, dba_rsrc_plan_directives b, dba_rsrc_plans c,
     dba_rsrc_consumer_groups d
WHERE
     a.plan=b.plan
```

continues

Source 11.7   Continued.

```
     AND ((b.group_or_subplan = c.plan OR
b.group_or_subplan=d.consumer_group))
AND b.status='ACTIVE'
ORDER BY
     1,4,5;
SPOOL OFF
CLEAR COLUMNS
SET VERIFY ON FEEDBACK ON
TTITLE OFF
```

Listing 11.6   Output from script to generate a report on Oracle8*i* group resource plan directives.

```
First Half of Report:
Date: 10/13/01
Time: 06:50 PM




Plan                CPU      Man Group or                 CPU    CPU CPU CPU CPU
Name                Method   ?   Subplan Name    Type  Method   1%  2%  3%  4%
----------------    -------- --- ---------------- ----- -------- ---- ---- ---- ----
INTERNAL_PLAN       EMPHASIS YES OTHER_GROUPS     GROUP EMPHASIS  0    0   0   0
INTERNAL_QUIESCE    EMPHASIS YES OTHER_GROUPS     GROUP EMPHASIS  0    0   0   0
                                SYS_GROUP         GROUP EMPHASIS  0    0   0   0
SYSTEM_PLAN         EMPHASIS NO  LOW_GROUP        GROUP EMPHASIS  0    0  100  0
                                OTHER_GROUPS      GROUP EMPHASIS  0   100  0   0
                                SYS_GROUP         GROUP EMPHASIS 100   0   0   0
Second Half of Report:
                                                                              Page:   1
 Resource Plan Directives Report                                              SYSTEM
     galinux1 database


                        Active
CPU CPU CPU CPU Session                Par Switch          Switch   Switch   Max Est     Undo
5%  6%  7%  8%  Pool    Queueing Degree Group              Time     Estimate Exec Time   Pool
---- ---- ---- ---- --------- --------- -------- ---------------- ------- --------- --------- ---------
  0    0    0    0  1000000  1000000  1000000                    1000000        0  1000000  1000000
  0    0    0    0        0  1000000  1000000                    1000000        0  1000000  1000000
  0    0    0    0  1000000  1000000  1000000                    1000000        0  1000000  1000000
  0    0    0    0  1000000  1000000  1000000                    1000000        0  1000000  1000000
  0    0    0    0  1000000  1000000  1000000                    1000000        0  1000000  1000000
  0    0    0    0  1000000  1000000  1000000                    1000000        0  1000000  1000000
```

Source 11.8   Script to generate a report on Oracle8*i* and Oracle9*i* group resource plan system-level grants.

```
REM NAME          : PLAN_SYS_GRANTS.SQL
REM PURPOSE       : GENERATE DATABASE RESOURCE PLAN SYSTEM GRANTS REPORT
REM Revisions:
REM Date          Modified by      Reason for change
REM 15-May-1999    MIKE AULT       initial creation
REM
COLUMN privilege      FORMAT a30    HEADING 'Plan System Privilege'
COLUMN grantee        FORMAT a30    HEADING 'User or Role'
COLUMN admin_option   FORMAT a7     HEADING 'Admin?'
BREAK ON privilege
SET LINES 78 VERIFY OFF FEEDBACK OFF
START title80 'Resource Plan System Grants'
SPOOL rep_out\&&db\plan_sys_grants.lis
REM
SELECT
    privilege, grantee, admin_option
FROM
    Dba_rsrc_manager_system_privs
ORDER BY
    Privilege;
SPOOL OFF
SET VERIFY ON FEEDBACK ON
TTITLE OFF
```

Listing 11.7   Output from script to generate a report on Oracle8*i* and Oracle9*i* user resource plan system-level grants.

```
Date: 05/22/99                                          Page:   1
Time: 02:34 PM        Resource Plan System Grants       SYSTEM
                          ORTEST1 database


Plan System Privilege         User or Role              Admin?
---------------------------   -----------------------   ------
ADMINISTER RESOURCE MANAGER   DBA                       YES
                              EXP_FULL_DATABASE         NO
                              IMP_FULL_DATABASE         NO
                              SYSTEM                    YES
```

Each user can also be granted some privileges via the DBMS_RESOURCE_
MANAGER_PRIVS package, such as the right to switch resource plans. These user-level
plan grants also need to be monitored. The script in Source 11.9 should be used to monitor the user-level privileges granted in your database. An example of output from the
script in Source 11.9 is shown in Listing 11.8.

Source 11.9 **Script to generate a report on Oracle8*i* and Oracle9*i* group resource plan user grants.**

```
REM NAME          : PLAN_GROUP_GRANTS.SQL
REM PURPOSE       : GENERATE DATABASE RESOURCE PLAN GROUP GRANTS REPORT
REM Revisions:
REM Date            Modified by       Reason for change
REM 15-May-1999     MIKE AULT         initial creation
REM
COLUMN granted_group    FORMAT a30    HEADING 'Granted Group'
COLUMN grantee          FORMAT a30    HEADING 'User or Role'
COLUMN grant_option     FORMAT a7     HEADING 'Admin?'
COLUMN initial_group    FORMAT a8     HEADING 'Initial?'
BREAK ON granted_group
SET LINES 78 VERIFY OFF FEEDBACK OFF
START title80 'Resource Plan Group Grants'
SPOOL rep_out\&&db\plan_group_grants.lis
REM
SELECT
    Granted_group, grantee, grant_option, initial_group
FROM
    Dba_rsrc_consumer_group_privs
ORDER BY
    Granted_group;
SPOOL OFF
SET VERIFY ON FEEDBACK ON
TTITLE OFF
```

Listing 11.8 **Output from script to generate a report on Oracle8*i* and Oracle9*i* group resource plan user grants.**

```
Date: 05/22/99                                            Page:   1
Time: 02:49 PM           Resource Plan Group Grants       SYSTEM
                             ORTEST1 database

Granted Group           User or Role                  Admin?  Initial?
--------------------    ----------------------------  ------- --------
DEFAULT_CONSUMER_GROUP  PUBLIC                         YES     YES
LOW_GROUP               PUBLIC                         NO      NO
ONLINE_USERS            TELE_DBA                       NO      YES
SYS_GROUP               SYSTEM                         NO      YES
```

Monitoring User Table and Column Grants

Keeping track of which users and roles have access to which objects in the database is a vital part of the process of monitoring users. Two reports, one on table-level grants and one on column-level grants, are required to monitor the users' permissions and grants profile. Source 11.10 shows a script to generate information on a user's table-level grants. For the output, see Listing 11.9.

Source 11.10   Example of script to generate a table grants report for Oracle9*i*.

```
rem   PURPOSE: Produce report of table grants showing
rem            GRANTOR, GRANTEE and specific GRANTS.
rem   LIMITATIONS: User must have access to DBA_TAB_PRIVS
rem   INPUTS: Owner name
rem   OUTPUTS: Report of table grants
rem
rem   HISTORY:
rem Who:            What:                Date:
rem Mike Ault       Initial creation     3/2/95
rem Mike Ault       Oracle8 verified     6/10/97
rem Mike Ault       Oracle8i verified    5/15/99
rem Mike Ault       Oracle9i Updated     13/10/01
rem
rem
COLUMN GRANTEE          FORMAT A19   HEADING "Grantee"
COLUMN OWNER            FORMAT A10   HEADING "Owner"
COLUMN TABLE_NAME       FORMAT A26   HEADING "Table"
COLUMN GRANTOR          FORMAT A10   HEADING "Grantor"
COLUMN PRIVILEGE        FORMAT A10   HEADING "Privilege"
COLUMN GRANTABLE        FORMAT A6    HEADING "With|Grant|Option?"
COLUMN HIERARCHY        FORMAT A3    HEADING 'HRY'
REM
BREAK ON owner SKIP 2 ON table_name ON grantee ON grantor ON REPORT
REM
SET LINESIZE 100 PAGES 56 VERIFY OFF FEEDBACK OFF
START title132 "TABLE GRANTS BY OWNER AND TABLE"
SPOOL rep_out\&db\tab_grants
REM
SELECT
    owner,table_name,grantee,grantor,
    privilege,grantable,hierarchy
  FROM
    dba_tab_privs
  WHERE
    owner LIKE UPPER('%&owner&')
    AND privilege !='EXECUTE'
  ORDER BY
    owner,table_name,grantor,grantee;
REM
```

continues

Source 11.10   Continued.

```
SPOOL OFF
PAUSE Press Enter to continue
SET LINESIZE 80 PAGES 22 VERIFY ON FEEDBACK ON
CLEAR BREAKS
CLEAR COLUMNS
TTITLE OFF
```

Notice that the report in Source 11.10 excludes grants of EXECUTE. The EXECUTE grant is given only on stored objects such as packages, functions, and procedures (also Java stored objects); because this is a table grant report, I excluded them. Also, you will have to remove the call for the hierarchy column if you want to run this report on earlier versions of Oracle. Listing 11.9 shows example output from the script in Source 11.10.

Listing 11.9   Example of output from table grant script.

```
Date: 10/13/01                                                         Page 1
Time: 07:17 PM              TABLE GRANTS BY OWNER AND TABLE            SYSTEM
                                 galinux1 database


                                                              With
                                                              Grant
Owner       Table               Grantee            Grantor    Privilege  Option HRY
----------  ------------------  -----------------  ---------  ---------- ------ ---
OE          CUSTOMERS           PM                 OE         SELECT     NO     NO
                                QS_ADM             OE         SELECT     NO     NO
                                                              REFERENCES NO     NO
            INVENTORIES         PM                 OE         SELECT     NO     NO
            ORDERS              PM                 OE         SELECT     NO     NO
            ORDER_ITEMS         PM                 OE         SELECT     NO     NO
            PRODUCT_DESCRIPTIONS PM                OE         SELECT     NO     NO
            PRODUCT_INFORMATION PM                 OE         SELECT     NO     NO
                                                              REFERENCES NO     NO
                                QS_ADM             OE         SELECT     NO     NO
                                                              REFERENCES NO     NO
            WAREHOUSES          PM                 OE         SELECT     NO     NO


ORDSYS      DBA_CARTRIDGES      SELECT_CATALOG_ROLE ORDSYS    SELECT     NO     NO
            DBA_CARTRIDGE_COMPONENTS SELECT_CATALOG_ROLE ORDSYS SELECT   NO     NO


OUTLN       OL$                 SELECT_CATALOG_ROLE OUTLN     SELECT     NO     NO
            OL$HINTS            SELECT_CATALOG_ROLE OUTLN     SELECT     NO     NO
            OL$NODES            SELECT_CATALOG_ROLE OUTLN     SELECT     NO     NO
```

Another bit of data to be gathered on user (or role) table grants is whether they have column-level grants. Column-level grants don't seem to be used much in Oracle. Perhaps this is because SELECT and DELETE privileges cannot be granted in this manner (they are considered table-level grants). A script to re-create table column-level grants is shown in Source 11.11. Of course, since Oracle8*i*, there are row-level grants and security options. These row-level security options are known as *policies* and are maintained through the use of the DBMS_CONTEXT and DBMS_RLS package procedures.

The output from the table column grant-capture script is shown in Listing 11.10.

Source 11.11   Example of script to capture table column grants.

```
REM FUNCTION:    SCRIPT FOR CAPTURING TABLE COLUMN GRANTS
REM
REM
REM This script is intended to run with Oracle7,Oracle8 or Oracle9.
REM
REM Running this script will create a script of all the grants
REM on columns
REM
REM Grants must be made by the original grantor so the script
REM connects as that user using the username as the password
REM edit the proper password in at time of running
REM
REM NOTE:  Grants made to 'SYS','CONNECT','RESOURCE','DBA',
REM     'EXP_FULL_DATABASE','IMP_FULL_DATABASE' are not captured.
REM
REM      Only preliminary testing of this script was performed.
REM      Be sure to test it completely before relying on it.
REM
SET VERIFY OFF FEEDBACK OFF TERMOUT OFF ECHO OFF PAGESIZE 0
SET EMBEDDED ON HEADING OFF
SET TERMOUT ON
PROMPT Creating table grant script...
SET TERMOUT OFF
DEFINE cr=CHR(10);
BREAK ON line1
COLUMN dbname NEW_VALUE db NOPRINT
SELECT name dbname FROM v$database;
SPOOL rep_out\&db\grt_cols.sql
rem
SELECT
  'CONNECT '||grantor||'/'||grantor line1,
  'GRANT '||&&cr||lower(privilege)||'('||column_name||
  ') ON  '||owner||'.'||table_name||&&cr||
  ' TO '|| lower(grantee) ||&&cr||
  decode(grantable,'YES',' WITH ADMIN OPTION;',';')
FROM
  sys.dba_col_privs
```

continues

Source 11.11 Continued.

```
WHERE
  grantee NOT IN ('SYS','CONNECT','RESOURCE','DBA',
'EXP_FULL_DATABASE','IMP_FULL_DATABASE')
ORDER BY grantor, grantee
/
SPOOL OFF
SET VERIFY ON FEEDBACK ON TERMOUT ON PAGESIZE 22 EMBEDDED OFF
CLEAR COLUMNS
CLEAR COMPUTES
CLEAR BREAKS
```

Listing 11.10 Example of output from table column grant capture script.

```
CONNECT TELE_DBA/TELE_DBA
GRANT
insert(DELETE_STATUS) ON TELE_DBA.CLIENTS
 TO system
;

GRANT
update(DELETE_STATUS) ON TELE_DBA.CLIENTS
 TO system
;
```

In most environments, weekly monitoring of users is sufficient. In some high-use, rapidly changing environments, where several DBAs or other types of administrative personnel are adding users, the reports may have to be run more frequently. Source 11.12 shows an example of a script to monitor row-level security policies. Output from Source 11.12 is shown in Listing 11.11.

Source 11.12 Example of row-level security-monitoring policy report script.

```
rem   PURPOSE: Produce report of db policies
rem            used to implement row level grants
rem
rem   LIMITATIONS: User must have access to DBA_POLICIES
rem
rem   HISTORY:
rem Who:           What:            Date:
rem Mike Ault      Initial creation     5/23/99
rem Mike Ault      Updated to Oracle9i  10/13/01
rem
COLUMN object_owner    FORMAT A10    HEADING 'Object|Owner'
COLUMN object_name     FORMAT A19    HEADING 'Object|Name'
COLUMN policy_group    FORMAT A12    HEADING 'Policy|Group'
COLUMN policy_name     FORMAT A16    HEADING 'Policy|Name'
```

```
COLUMN pf_owner       FORMAT A10    HEADING 'Policy|Function|Owner'
COLUMN function       FORMAT A15    HEADING 'Function|Name'
COLUMN sel            FORMAT A3    HEADING 'Sel|?'
COLUMN ins            FORMAT A3    HEADING 'Ins|?'
COLUMN upd            FORMAT A3    HEADING 'Upd|?'
COLUMN del            FORMAT A3    HEADING 'Del|?'
COLUMN chk_option     FORMAT A3    HEADING 'Check|Option'
COLUMN enable         FORMAT A3    HEADING 'Enabled?'
COLUMN static_policy  FORMAT A7    HEADING 'Static?'
SET LINES 132 VERIFY OFF FEEDBACK OFF PAGES 47
START title132 'DB Policies Report'
BREAK ON object_owner
SPOOL rep_out\&db\db_policies
SELECT
  object_owner, object_name,policy_group,
  policy_name,pf_owner,function,
  sel,ins,upd,del,chk_option,
  enable,static_policy
FROM
  dba_policies
ORDER BY
  1,2,3;
SPOOL OFF
SET LINES 80 VERIFY ON FEEDBACK ON PAGES 22
CLEAR BREAKS
CLEAR COLUMNS
TTITLE OFF
```

**Listing 11.11   Example of output of row-level security-monitoring policy report
script.**

```
Date: 10/13/01                                                          Page: 1
Time: 07:35 PM                        DB Policies Report                 SYSTEM
                                      galinux1 database


                                      Policy
Object    Object           Policy     Policy    Function  Function      Sel Ins Upd Del Che
Owner     Name             Group      Name      Owner     Name          ?   ?   ?   ?   Opt Ena Static?
--------- ---------------- ---------- --------------- --------- --------------- --- --- --- --- --- --- -------
WKSYS     WK$ATTRIBUTE     SYS_DEFAULT WK$INSTADMIN_POL WKSYS     WK$INSTADMIN_PF YES YES YES YES YES YES NO
          WK$ATTR_MAPPING  SYS_DEFAULT WK$INSTADMIN_POL WKSYS     WK$INSTADMIN_PF YES YES YES YES YES YES NO
          WK$CRAWLER_CONFIG SYS_DEFAULT WK$INSTADMIN_POL WKSYS     WK$INSTADMIN_PF YES YES YES YES YES YES NO
          WK$CRAWLER_SCHED SYS_DEFAULT WK$INSTADMIN_POL WKSYS     WK$INSTADMIN_PF YES YES YES YES YES YES NO
          WK$CRAWLER_STAT  SYS_DEFAULT WK$INSTADMIN_POL WKSYS     WK$INSTADMIN_PF YES YES YES YES YES YES NO
          WK$DATA_SOURCE   SYS_DEFAULT WK$INSTADMIN_POL WKSYS     WK$INSTADMIN_PF YES YES YES YES YES YES NO
          WK$GROUP_DS_MAPPING SYS_DEFAULT WK$INSTADMIN_POL WKSYS  WK$INSTADMIN_PF YES YES YES YES YES YES NO
          WK$JOB_INFO      SYS_DEFAULT WK$INSTADMIN_POL WKSYS     WK$INSTADMIN_PF YES YES YES YES YES YES NO
          WK$MAILLIST      SYS_DEFAULT WK$INSTADMIN_POL WKSYS     WK$INSTADMIN_PF YES YES YES YES YES YES NO
          WK$SCHED_MAPPING SYS_DEFAULT WK$INSTADMIN_POL WKSYS     WK$INSTADMIN_PF YES YES YES YES YES YES NO
          WK$SOURCE_GROUP  SYS_DEFAULT WK$INSTADMIN_POL WKSYS     WK$INSTADMIN_PF YES YES YES YES YES YES NO
          WK$SYSINFO       SYS_DEFAULT WK$SYSINFO_POL   WKSYS     WK$SYSINFO_PF   YES YES YES YES YES YES NO
          WK$SYS_ADMIN     SYS_DEFAULT WK$INSTADMIN_POL WKSYS     WK$INSTADMIN_PF YES YES YES YES YES YES NO
          WK$TDS_LOG       SYS_DEFAULT WK$INSTADMIN_POL WKSYS     WK$INSTADMIN_PF YES YES YES YES YES YES NO
          WK$TRACE         SYS_DEFAULT WK$INSTADMIN_POL WKSYS     WK$INSTADMIN_PF YES YES YES YES YES YES NO
```

Monitoring Currently Logged-in User Processes

A final report in this section that I have found useful lists currently logged-in processes, their user IDs, and operating system IDs, as well as any programs they are currently running. Of course, the Q product on the Precise Web site does a better job, but I don't always have time to start it up just to check on users. The script, called pid.sql, is shown in Source 11.13, and an example of its output is shown in Listing 11.12.

Source 11.13   Example of script to show active users.

```
REM
REM   Name:      pid.sql
REM
REM   FUNCTION: Generate a list of current oracle sids/pids
REM
COLUMN terminal FORMAT a10    HEADING 'Terminal'
COLUMN program FORMAT  a30    HEADING 'Program'
COLUMN pid      FORMAT  9999  HEADING 'Process|ID'
COLUMN sid      FORMAT  9999  HEADING 'Session|ID'
COLUMN osuser   FORMAT  A15   HEADING 'Operating|System|User'
COLUMN spid     FORMAT  A7    HEADING 'OS|Process|ID'
COLUMN serial# FORMAT  99999 HEADING 'Serial|Number'
SET LINES 132 PAGES 58
BREAK ON username
COMPUTE COUNT OF pid ON username
START title132 "Oracle Processes"
SPOOL rep_out\&db\cur_proc
SELECT
     NVL(a.username,'Null') username,
     b.pid,a.sid,
     DECODE(a.terminal,'?','Detached',a.terminal) terminal,
     b.program,b.spid,a.osuser,a.serial#
 FROM
     v$session a,
     v$process b
WHERE
     a.PADDR = b.ADDR
ORDER by
     a.username,
     b.pid
/
SPOOL OFF
CLEAR BREAKS
CLEAR COLUMNS
SET PAGES 22
TTITLE OFF
PAUSE Press Enter to continue
```

Listing 11.12   Example of output of the current users report (pid.sql).

```
Date: 10/13/01                                                            Page:   1
Time: 07:45 PM                          Oracle Processes                  SYSTEM
                                        galinux1 database

                                                        OS      Operating
                       Process Session                  Process System     Serial
USERNAME                    ID      ID Terminal  Program          ID User  Number
--------------------   ------- ------- --------  -------   ------- -------  ------
DBAUTIL                     12       7 pts/1     oracle@tuscgalinux (TNS V1-V3) 1182 oracle  46
******************************* -------
count                        1
SYSTEM                      13       8 pts/3     oracle@tuscgalinux (TNS V1-V3) 15885 oracle 3146
                            14      10 MRAMOBILE oracle@tuscgalinux (TNS V1-V3) 19156 Administrator 191
******************************* -------
count                        2
Null                         2       1 UNKNOWN   oracle@tuscgalinux (PMON)  147 oracle     1
                             3       2 UNKNOWN   oracle@tuscgalinux (DBW0)  149 oracle     1
                             4       3 UNKNOWN   oracle@tuscgalinux (LGWR)  151 oracle     1
                             5       4 UNKNOWN   oracle@tuscgalinux (CKPT)  153 oracle     1
                             6       5 UNKNOWN   oracle@tuscgalinux (SMON)  155 oracle     1
                             7       6 UNKNOWN   oracle@tuscgalinux (RECO)  157 oracle     1
******************************* -------
count                        6
```

11.2 USING THE V$ AND DB_ VIEWS TO MONITOR TABLESPACES

The DBA needs to monitor more than just users. Tablespaces also require watching, because they are not unchanging objects. They are subject to becoming filled and/or fragmented. The Oracle Administrator toolbar provides for a GUI-based monitoring of tablespaces via the Storage Manager (see Figure 11.4). Unfortunately, it provides no report output. Luckily, it is a fairly easy thing to monitor tablespaces using the V$ and DB_ views. Look at Figure 11.5, which shows the DBA_ views that relate to tablespaces, as we examine a script or two that provide us with information we can put our hands on.

Monitoring Tablespace Freespace and Fragmentation

Let's begin by examining a report that covers two critical parameters, available space and fragmentation. The OEM GUI includes a tablespace map feature that gives this information graphically and can be printed in a report format; this is shown in Figure 11.6. An example of the OEM tablespace analysis report is shown in Figure 11.7. For a manual report, see Source 11.14.

The report in Source 11.14 uses the view FREE_SPACE, which is based on the DBA_ view DBA_FREE_SPACE. This view is shown in Source 11.15. The freespace report is shown in Listing 11.13.

In an ideal situation, the tablespace data file(s) will show one extent (there will be one line in the report for each tablespace data file), and the biggest area will match

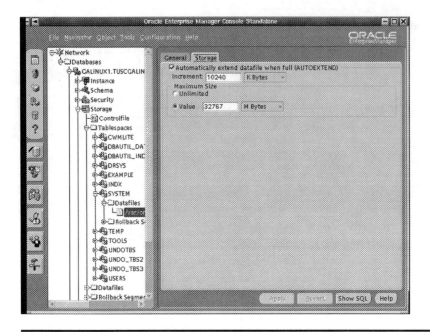

FIGURE 11.4   Oracle Enterprise Manager Storage Manager screen.

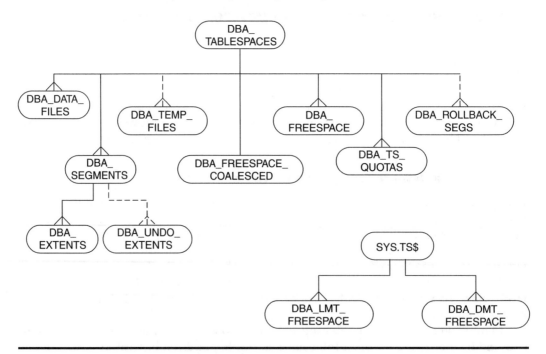

FIGURE 11.5   DBA_TABLESPACES view cluster.

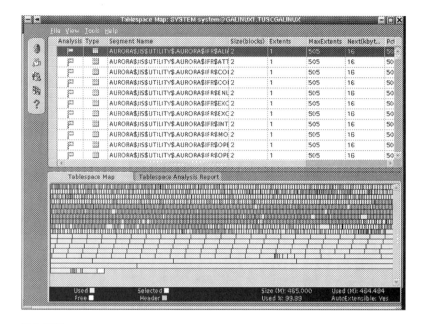

FIGURE 11.6   OEM tablespace map.

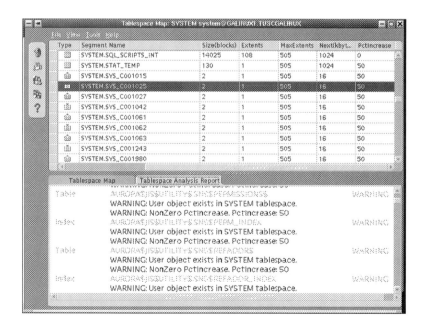

FIGURE 11.7   OEM tablespace analysis report.

Source 11.14   A report on tablespace space usage and fragmentation.

```
rem
rem Name:        free_space.sql
rem
rem FUNCTION: Provide data on tablespace extent status
rem FUNCTION: this report uses the free_space2 view
rem FUNCTION: includes fsfi from DBA Handbook
rem
SET FEED OFF
SET FLUSH OFF
SET VERIFY OFF
set pages 58 LINES 132
COLUMN tablespace        HEADING Name              FORMAT a30
COLUMN files             HEADING '#Files'          FORMAT 9,999
COLUMN pieces            HEADING 'Frag'            FORMAT 9,999
COLUMN free_bytes        HEADING 'Free|Byte'       FORMAT 9,999,999,999
COLUMN free_blocks       HEADING 'Free|Blk'        FORMAT 999,999
COLUMN largest_bytes     HEADING 'Biggest|Bytes'   FORMAT 9,999,999,999
COLUMN largest_blks      HEADING 'Biggest|Blks'    FORMAT 999,999
COLUMN ratio             HEADING 'Percent'         FORMAT 999.999
COLUMN average_fsfi      HEADING 'Average|FSFI'    FORMAT 999.999
START title132 "FREE SPACE REPORT"
DEFINE 1 = report_output/&&db/free_spc
SPOOL &1
SELECT
        tablespace,
        COUNT(*) files,
        SUM(pieces) pieces,
        SUM(free_bytes) free_bytes,
        SUM(free_blocks) free_blocks,
        SUM(largest_bytes) largest_bytes,
        SUM(largest_blks) largest_blks,
        SUM(largest_bytes)/sum(free_bytes)*100 ratio,
        SUM(fsfi)/COUNT(*) average_fsfi
FROM
        free_space
GROUP BY
        tablespace;
SPOOL OFF
CLEAR COLUMNS
TTITLE OFF
SET FEED ON
SET FLUSH ON
SET VERIFY ON
SET PAGES 22 LINES 80
PAUSE Press Enter to continue
```

Source 11.15   Freespace view listing.

```
rem
rem Name:      free_space_view.sql
rem
rem FUNCTION: Create free_space view for use by freespc reports
rem
CREATE VIEW free_space
    (tablespace, file_id, pieces, free_bytes, free_blocks,
     largest_bytes,largest_blks, fsfi) AS
SELECT tablespace_name, file_id, COUNT(*),
    SUM(bytes), SUM(blocks),
    MAX(bytes), MAX(blocks),
    SQRT(MAX(blocks)/SUM(blocks))*(100/SQRT(SQRT(COUNT(blocks))))
FROM sys.dba_free_space
GROUP BY tablespace_name, file_id, relative_fno;
```

Listing 11.13   Example of report from freespace report script.

```
Date: 10/14/01                                                    Page:   1
Time: 12:41 PM                    FREE SPACE REPORT               DBAUTIL
                                 galinux1 database

                            Free      Free    Biggest  Biggest              Average
Name         #Files  Frag   Byte      Blk      Bytes     Blks  Percent        FSFI
------------ ------  ----  ----------- -------  ----------- ------- --------  --------
CWMLITE          1     1   20,905,984   2,552   20,905,984   2,552  100.000   100.000
DBAUTIL_DATA     1     1    5,939,200     725    5,939,200     725  100.000   100.000
DBAUTIL_INDEX    1     1    9,625,600   1,175    9,625,600   1,175  100.000   100.000
DRSYS            1     1   12,845,056   1,568   12,845,056   1,568  100.000   100.000
EXAMPLE          1     1      262,144      32      262,144      32  100.000   100.000
INDX             1     1   26,148,864   3,192   26,148,864   3,192  100.000   100.000
SYSTEM           1     1      540,672      66      540,672      66  100.000   100.000
TOOLS            1     3    8,192,000   1,000    7,274,496     888   88.800    71.602
UNDOTBS          1     4  208,338,944  25,432  114,098,176  13,928   54.766    52.329
UNDO_TBS2        1     1   19,595,264   2,392   19,595,264   2,392  100.000   100.000
UNDO_TBS3        1     1   19,595,264   2,392   19,595,264   2,392  100.000   100.000
USERS            1     1   25,952,256   3,168   25,952,256   3,168  100.000   100.000
```

the free area. In most cases, if the tablespace has been used for any length of time, there will be several extents, and the free area (which corresponds to total freespace in the tablespace) and the biggest area (which corresponds to the biggest area of contiguous free space) will not be equal. If, after a coalesce, the number of extents isn't large, say, fewer than 20, and the mismatch between the two sizes is small, say, less than 10 percent difference between biggest and free, then there is probably nothing to worry about.

If, on the other hand, either of these values is exceeded, the DBA should consider using the defragmentation methods described earlier. This report will not cover temporary tablespaces that are created as CREATE TEMPORARY TABLESPACE using tempfiles.

Under Oracle8, Oracle8*i*, and Oracle9*i*, the tablespaces will be automatically defragmented by the SMON process if the value for the default storage parameter PCT INCREASE is set to greater than 0. The Free Space Fragmentation Index (FSFI) tells how much the freespace in a tablespace is fragmented—and comes to us by way of the *Oracle DBA Handbook,* by Kevin Loney (Oracle Press, 1994). A high value is good (with 100 the best); a low value is bad.

If you find yourself adding several data files to a single tablespace in a relatively short period of time, it may be wise to extrapolate the growth and then export, drop, and re-create the tablespace to the size required to prevent excessive addition of data files. Though Oracle suggests using autoextend data files for tablespaces with expected growth, I still prefer manual control of tablespace growth so I am not surprised due to a runaway insert or other database mishap that causes the tablespace to grow unpredictably. However, turning on autoextend for a stable production environment may be the way to go if you understand the way the tablespaces are likely to grow.

Spreading data files for large databases across several drives may be desirable for equalizing disk I/O. This is, however, a database-specific question, which has to be answered on a case-by-case basis. If you have several large tables that would benefit from being spread across several disks, you might consider placing them in their own tablespaces, then sizing the data files for the tablespaces such that the data contained in the tables is spread. For instance, if you have a single table that contains a gigabyte of data, it may be advisable to spread this file across several platters. To do this in Oracle7, create a table-specific tablespace on each of the platters that will hold the file, with each tablespace a fraction of the total size of the table; that is, if you want to spread the file across four drives, each data file would be 250 megabytes in size. Then, when you import the table, it will be spread across the four drives. The database will treat the table as one contiguous entity, but you will gain I/O speed by having spread the table across the available drives. Under Oracle8, Oracle8*i*, and Oracle9*i*, this can be accomplished with table partitioning, which allows a single table to be spread, by value range, across several files. Of course with RAID 1, RAID01/10, or RAID5, the spreading is done quasi-automatically so you would partition only for use of partition elimination or the benefits of parallel query and independent partition maintenance.

You should create each tablespace with a default storage parameter that takes into account the performance-critical tables in the application that resides in it. You should also do the best job you can estimating the size requirements for the tables as they are created and only default to the default storage for minor tables. Ideally, this size estimation should be pushed down to the developers of the applications.

To avoid fragmentation issues altogether, you can use the fixed-size extent model for your tablespaces. The fixed-size extent model states that, for any tablespace, all objects in that tablespace will have initial extent sizes that are multiples of a fixed default value, and next extent sizes that are equal to the default extent value for the tablespace. In the fixed-extent-size model, you have several tablespaces—usually a small extent, medium extent, and large extent—each sized according to the needs of your application. By using the fixed-size-extent model, any extents that are released due to table or index maintenance will be reusable by any other object in the table. By allowing freed-extent reuse, fragmentation is no longer a concern in fixed-extent-size model tablespaces.

Monitoring Tablespace Autoextend Settings

In addition to space usage and fragmentation monitoring, if you use the autoextend feature, you need to monitor database autoextend status and data file locations. Source 11.16 shows the SQL to create a view that monitors autoextend data for pre-Oracle8. In pre-Oracle8 versions, the only way to get this information was to query the SYS table FILEXT$, which, unfortunately, looks like this:

```
Name                                   Null?           Type
------------------------------------   --------------  ------
FILE#                                  NOT NULL        NUMBER
MAXEXTEND                              NOT NULL        NUMBER
INC                                    NOT NULL        NUMBER
```

This structure means that, in order to get back to the actual filename and tablespace, you need to join to several other tables, namely, FILE$, TS$, and V$DBFILE. A script to create a data file view is shown in Source 11.16.

Source 11.16   Script to create a data file view.

```
CREATE VIEW dba_file_data AS
SELECT
  a.name tablespace,a.dflminext min_extents,
  a.dflmaxext max_extents,
  a.dflinit init,a.dflincr next,
  a.dflextpct pct_increase, d.name datafile,
  b.blocks datafile_size, c.maxextend max_extend,
  c.inc ext_incr
FROM ts$ a, file$ b, filext$ c, v$dbfile d
WHERE
  a.ts#=b.ts# and b.file#=c.file# and b.file#=d.file#
/
```

This script creates the view DBA_FILE_DATA, which will look like this when queried:

```
Name                                Null?          Type
-------------------------------     ---------      ------------
TABLESPACE                          NOT NULL       VARCHAR2(30)
MIN_EXTENTS                         NOT NULL       NUMBER
MAX_EXTENTS                         NOT NULL       NUMBER
INIT                                NOT NULL       NUMBER
NEXT                                NOT NULL       NUMBER
PCT_INCREASE                        NOT NULL       NUMBER
DATAFILE                                           VARCHAR2(257)
DATAFILE_SIZE                       NOT NULL       NUMBER
MAX_EXTEND                          NOT NULL       NUMBER
EXT_INCR                            NOT NULL       NUMBER
```

Using this view, it is then easy to create a simple SELECT that gets autoextend and data file location information from a single view, along with all of the pertinent sizing information. The Oracle Administrator Storage Manager does show this information under the data files section. In Oracle8i, the view DBA_DATA_FILES contains the columns AUTOEXTENSIBLE (YES or NO), MAXBYTES, MAXBLOCKS, and INCREMENT_BY, which allow for ease of report generation and monitoring of the autoextension capabilities of all data files.

Monitoring Tablespace Data Files

As the DBA, you should also monitor the size and location of the data files associated with the tablespaces under your control. If for no other reason than to prevent yourself from placing index tablespace data files alongside those that deal with table data, you need to have an accurate map of data files. A script to document tablespace data files is shown in Source 11.17; it produces the report in Listing 11.14 that provides this data file map.

Source 11.17   Script to document tablespace data files.

```
REM
REM      Name:      dbfiles.sql
REM      FUNCTION:  Document  file sizes and locations
REM      Use:       From SQLPLUS
REM  MRA 05/16/99 Added autoextend monitoring
REM  MRA 10/14/99 Added temp file monitoring 9i
REM
CLEAR COMPUTES
COLUMN file_name            FORMAT A51          HEADING 'File Name'
COLUMN tablespace_name      FORMAT A15          HEADING 'Tablespace'
```

```
COLUMN meg               FORMAT 99,999.90  HEADING 'Megabytes'
COLUMN status            FORMAT A10        HEADING 'Status'
COLUMN autoextensible    FORMAT A3         HEADING 'AE?'
COLUMN maxmeg            FORMAT 99,999      HEADING 'Max|Megabytes'
COLUMN Increment_by      FORMAT 9,999        HEADING 'Inc|By'
SET LINES 130 PAGES 47 VERIFY OFF FEEDBACK OFF
START title132 'DATABASE DATA FILES'
SPOOL rep_out\&db\datafile
BREAK ON tablespace_name SKIP 1 ON REPORT
COMPUTE SUM OF meg ON tablespace_name
COMPUTE SUM OF meg ON REPORT
SELECT
     tablespace_name,file_name,
     bytes/1048576 meg,
     status,autoextensible,
     maxbytes/1048576 maxmeg,
     increment_by
FROM
     dba_data_files
UNION
SELECT
     tablespace_name,file_name,
     bytes/1048576 meg,
     status,autoextensible,
     maxbytes/1048576 maxmeg,
     increment_by
FROM
     dba_temp_files
ORDER BY
     tablespace_name
/
SPOOL OFF
SET VERIFY ON FEEDBACK ON
TTITLE OFF
CLEAR COLUMNS
CLEAR COMPUTES
PAUSE Press Enter to continue
```

Monitoring Tablespace Extent Mapping

A final set of freespace information that is handy to have around (OEM and many third-party tools will provide a GUI-based map) is the location of the freespace in a tablespace and the size of the fragments themselves. The script in Source 11.18 provides this data. The output from the script in Source 11.18 is shown in Listing 11.15.

Listing 11.14   Example of output from data file report.

```
Date: 10/14/01                                                           Page:   1
Time: 12:59 PM                        DATABASE DATA FILES                 DBAUTIL
                                       galinux1 database


                                                                  Max      Inc
Tablespace     File Name                    Megabytes Status   AE? Megabytes  By
-------------- ------------------------------------- --------- ---------- --- --------- -------
CWMLITE        /var/oracle/oradata/galinux1/cwmlite01.dbf   20.00 AVAILABLE YES   32,768    80
**************                                            ----------
sum                                                          20.00


DBAUTIL_DATA   /opt/oracle/oradata/galinux1/dbt1_dat1.dbf   10.00 AVAILABLE NO        0     0
**************                                            ----------
sum                                                          10.00


DBAUTIL_INDEX  /opt/oracle/oradata/galinux1/dbt1_idx1.dbf   10.00 AVAILABLE NO        0     0
**************                                            ----------
sum                                                          10.00


DRSYS          /var/oracle/oradata/galinux1/drsys01.dbf     20.00 AVAILABLE YES   32,768    80
**************                                            ----------
sum                                                          20.00


EXAMPLE        /var/oracle/oradata/galinux1/example01.dbf   36.25 AVAILABLE YES   32,768    80
**************                                            ----------
sum                                                          36.25


INDX           /var/oracle/oradata/galinux1/indx01.dbf      25.00 AVAILABLE YES   32,768   160
**************                                            ----------
sum                                                          25.00


SYSTEM         /var/oracle/oradata/galinux1/system01.dbf   465.00 AVAILABLE YES   32,768 1,280
**************                                            ----------
sum                                                         465.00


TEMP           /var/oracle/oradata/galinux1/temp01.dbf      40.00 AVAILABLE NO        0     0
               /var/oracle/oradata/galinux1/temp02.dbf      50.00 AVAILABLE NO        0     0
**************                                            ----------
sum                                                          90.00


TOOLS          /var/oracle/oradata/galinux1/tools01.dbf     10.00 AVAILABLE YES   32,768    40
**************                                            ----------
sum                                                          10.00


UNDOTBS        /var/oracle/oradata/galinux1/undotbs01.dbf  200.00 AVAILABLE YES   32,768   640
**************                                            ----------
sum                                                         200.00
```

```
UNDO_TBS2      /opt/oracle/oradata/galinux1/undo_tbs2.dbf      20.00 AVAILABLE  YES     32,768        1
*************                                             ----------
sum                                                           20.00


UNDO_TBS3      /opt/oracle/oradata/galinux1/undo_tbs3.dbf      20.00 AVAILABLE  YES         30        1
*************                                             ----------
sum                                                           20.00


USERS         /var/oracle/oradata/galinux1/users01.dbf        25.00 AVAILABLE  YES     32,768      160
*************                                             ----------
sum                                                           25.00


                                                         ----------
sum                                                          951.25
```

Source 11.18   Script to document freespace extents inside a tablespace.

```
rem
rem Name: mapper.sql
rem Function: create an extent map for a specific tablespace
rem  Based on a technique from DBA Handbook
rem Mike Ault 7/19/96 TUSC
rem
SET PAGES 47 LINES 132 VERIFY OFF FEEDBACK OFF
COLUMN file_id        HEADING 'File|id'
COLUMN value          NEW_VALUE dbblksiz NOPRINT
COLUMN meg            FORMAT 9,999.99 HEADING 'Meg'
COLUMN partition_name FORMAT a30      HEADING 'Partition|Name'
SELECT value FROM v$parameter WHERE name='db_block_size';
START title132 '&&ts Mapping Report'
SPOOL rep_out/&db/ts_map
SELECT
    'free space' owner, '      ' object,'Not Part.' partition
    file_id, block_id, blocks,
    (blocks*&dbblksiz)/(1024*1024) meg
FROM
    dba_free_space
WHERE
    tablespace_name=UPPER('&&ts')
UNION
SELECT
    SUBSTR(owner,1,20), SUBSTR(segment_name, 1,32),partition_name
    file_id, block_id, blocks,
    (blocks*&dbblksiz)/(1024*1024) meg
FROM
    dba_extents
WHERE
    tablespace_name = UPPER('&&ts')
```

continues

Source 11.18   Continued.

```
ORDER BY 3,4;
SPOOL OFF
UNDEF ts
SET PAGES 22 LINES 80 VERIFY ON FEEDBACK ON
CLEAR COLUMNS
TTITLE OFF
```

Listing 11.15   Example of output of the mapper script.

```
Date: 06/13/97                                          Page:   1
Time: 07:29 PM          raw_data Mapping Report          SYSTEM
                        ORTEST1 database

                                 File
OWNER       OBJECT             id  BLOCK_ID    BLOCKS      MEG
----------  ---------------   ----  --------   ------    ------
TELE_DBA    LOAD_TEST          11         2    102655    401.00
TELE_DBA    LOAD_TEST          11    102657     25600    100.00
TELE_DBA    LOAD_TEST          11    128257     25600    100.00
SYSTEM      PARTITION_TEST     11    153857       260      1.02
SYSTEM      PARTITION_TEST     11    154117       260      1.02
SYSTEM      PARTITION_TEST     11    154377       260      1.02
free space                     11    154637     24564     95.95
```

11.3 USING THE V$ AND DB_ VIEWS FOR MONITORING SEQUENCES

Sequences are used to generate integer numbers for use in keys or in any other column that requires either repeating or nonrepeating numbers. No changes were made to sequences under Oracle8, Oracle8*i*, and Oracle9*i*. Essentially, therefore, the only monitoring that the DBA can do is to identify the sequences, their owners, and so on. The DBA can query the sequence's values, but then those values are lost. The view used in the SQL script in Source 11.19 holds the last value written to disk; this is all the data on the actual sequence value that the DBA can get nondestructively (use of the NEXTVAL function destroys the value selected).

> **TIP**   One technique I have found useful is to use a SELECT against the DBA_SEQUENCES table LAST_NUMBER column when I use a sequence for the primary key of a table I am loading, instead of using a COUNT(*) to determine the progress of the load. This technique provides a virtually instantaneous return of the value and doesn't contend with the load process. Of course, this only applies if the sequence is used as a part of a SQLLOADER load or an SQL load, and is reset to start at 1 at the beginning of the load.

The DBA should monitor the last value written against the maximum value for ascending sequences and the minimum value for descending. If the sequence is near its limit, and is not a cycled sequence, the DBA will have to alter the minimum or maximum values using the ALTER SEQUENCE command if the sequence value is approaching the minimum or maximum value. If this isn't done, the tables depending on the sequence will fail any selects to retrieve sequence values.

Source 11.19   SQL script to generate a sequence report.

```
rem  NAME: Seq_rep.sql
rem
rem  HISTORY:
rem  Date            Who                         What
rem  --------        ----------------------      --------------
rem  5/10/93         Mike Ault                   Creation
rem  5/16/99         Mike Ault                   Verified for Oracle8i
rem  FUNCTION: Generate report on Sequences
rem  INPUTS:
rem
rem     1 - Sequence Owner or Wild Card
rem     2 - Sequence Name or Wild Card
rem
rem  ****************************************************************
SET HEADING OFF VERIFY OFF PAUSE OFF
PROMPT ** Sequence Report **
PROMPT
PROMPT Percent signs are wild
ACCEPT sequence_owner char  PROMPT 'Enter account to report on (or pct
sign):';
ACCEPT sequence_name char  PROMPT 'Enter sequence to report on (or pct
sign):';
PROMPT
PROMPT Report file name is SEQUENCE.LIS
SET HEADING ON
SET LINESIZE 80 PAGESIZE 56 NEWPAGE 0 TAB OFF SPACE 1
SET TERMOUT OFF VERIFY OFF FEEDBACK OFF
BREAK ON sequence_owner SKIP 2
COLUMN sequence_owner      FORMAT A10      HEADING 'Sequence|Owner'
COLUMN sequence_name       FORMAT A16      HEADING 'Sequence|Name'
COLUMN min_value                           HEADING 'Minimum'
COLUMN max_value                           HEADING 'Maximum'
COLUMN increment_by        FORMAT 999      HEADING 'Inc'
COLUMN cycle_flag                          HEADING 'Cycle'
COLUMN order_flag                          HEADING 'Order'
COLUMN cache_size          FORMAT 99999    HEADING 'Cache'
COLUMN last_number         FORMAT 99999    HEADING 'Last|Value'
START title80 "SEQUENCE REPORT"
SPOOL rep_out/&&db/seq_rep
```

continues

Source 11.19   Continued.

```
SELECT
    sequence_owner,sequence_name,
    min_value,max_value,
    increment_by,
    DECODE(cycle_flag,'Y','YES','N','NO') cycle_flag,
    DECODE(order_flag,'Y','YES','N','NO') order_flag,
    cache_size,last_number
FROM
    dba_sequences
WHERE
    sequence_owner LIKE UPPER('&sequence_owner') AND
    sequence_name LIKE UPPER('&sequence_name')
ORDER BY
    1,2;
SPOOL OFF
SET LINESIZE 80 PAGESIZE 22 NEWPAGE 0 TAB ON SPACE 1
SET TERMOUT ON VERIFY ON FEEDBACK ON
CLEAR BREAKS
CLEAR COLUMNS
TTITLE OFF
```

Listing 11.16   Example of report format from sequence script.

```
Date: 10/14/01                                          Page:    1
Time: 01:45 PM              SEQUENCE REPORT            DBAUTIL
                           galinux1 databa

Sequence   Sequence                                          Last
Owner      Name            Minimum   Maximum   Inc Cyc Ord Cache Value
---------- --------------- --------- --------- --- --- --- ------ ------

WKSYS      WK$ATTR_SEQ           1 1.000E+27    1 NO  NO     20      1
           WK$CHARSET_SEQ       1 1.000E+27    1 NO  NO     20     58
           WK$CRAWLERID_SEQ     1 1.000E+27    1 NO  NO     20   1000
           WK$DS_ID_SEQ         1 1.000E+27    1 NO  NO     20      1
           WK$INST_SEQ          1 1.000E+27    1 NO  NO     20      1
           WK$JOB_ID_SEQ        1 1.000E+27    1 NO  NO     20      1
           WK$MAILLIST$SEQ      1 1.000E+27    1 NO  NO     20      1
           WK$MIMETYPES_SEQ     1 1.000E+27    1 NO  NO     20     36
           WK$SCHED_ID_SEQ      1 1.000E+27    1 NO  NO     20      1
           WK$SG_ID_SEQ         1 1.000E+27    1 NO  NO     20      1
           WK$TRACE_SEQ         1 1.000E+27    1 NO  NO     20     11
```

As with other objects, if sequences are used in applications, they should be owned by a central DBA account for the application. This report, if used with the wild card (%) option, will report on all sequences, thus showing privately owned sequences. To alter the ownership of a sequence, it must either be dropped and re-created, with possible loss of continuity in sequence numbers, or exported and then imported into the new owner with no loss of values.

In addition, the DBA should monitor the number of values being cached. If this value is excessive, large numbers of cached sequence values are lost during shutdown. If the value is too small, and the sequence is accessed frequently, performance can suffer. The default value for cache is 20.

A heads-up is also required for the following scenario: If someone adds a value or values to the DUAL table (this is a SYS-owned table with a single column, DUMMY, and a single value, X), then any selects in PL/SQL against DUAL to fetch a NEXTVAL or CURRVAL will error out with "ORA-01422: exact fetch returns more than the requested number of rows." In addition, several of the DBMS_ packages depend on this table, so if they start returning ORA-01422 errors, check this table immediately. Source 11.19 shows a report format from a sequence report. Listing 11.16 shows the output from the script in Source 11.19.

11.4 MONITORING SYNONYMS USING THE V$ AND DBA_ VIEWS

Synonyms remain the same in Oracle8, Oracle8*i*, and Oracle9*i*. The major changes that have affected synonyms are those to the structure of the connection strings from SQL*NET V1 to V2 to NET8. Despite the fact that synonyms are the key to providing cross-database access for queries, and a means of implementing distributed data across nodes, systems, and databases, in all the reports reviewed for this book, not one seemed to cover synonyms. Recall that a synonym allows a shorthand version of an object name to be specified. The parts of a synonym are the object name (which usually includes an owner) and, possibly, a database link that will also provide an Oracle user name and password to a remote system. A complete report will show all of these items.

Why is it important to monitor synonyms? Synonyms can be used to access data, sometimes data that shouldn't be accessed if object grants have been too widely granted. In addition, they are the means for reaching other nodes and databases. If a connect string becomes invalid, a user name is disconnected or its password changes or node name changes, it is good to be able to see which object synonyms will be affected. Source 11.20 shows a script for a synonym report, and Listing 11.17 shows an example of output from a synonym script.

Source 11.20   Script for synonym report.

```
REM
REM NAME        : SYNONYM.SQL
REM PURPOSE     : GENERATE REPORT OF A USERS SYNONYMS
REM USE         : FROM SQLPLUS
REM Limitations : None
REM Revisions:
REM Date                    Modified by Reason for change
```

continues

Source 11.20   Continued.

```
REM 12/MAY/93      Mike Ault      Initial Creation
REM 15/Jun/97      Mike Ault      Verified for Oracle8
REM 16/May/99      Mike Ault      Verified for Oracle8i
REM
PROMPT Percent signs are Wild Cards
PROMPT
ACCEPT own PROMPT 'Enter the user who owns synonym: '
SET PAGES 56 LINES 130 VERIFY OFF FEEDBACK OFF TERM OFF
START title132 "Synonym Report"
SPOOL rep_out/&&db/synonym
COLUMN host             FORMAT a24 HEADING "Connect String"
COLUMN owner            FORMAT a15
COLUMN table            FORMAT a35
COLUMN db_link          FORMAT a6  HEADING Link
COLUMN username         FORMAT a15
SELECT
     a.owner, synonym_name ,
     table_owner ||'.'|| table_name "Table" ,
     b.db_link,username,host
FROM
     dba_synonyms a,
     dba_db_links b
WHERE
     a.db_link = b.db_link(+) AND
     a.owner LIKE UPPER('&own');
SPOOL OFF
SET PAGES 22 LINES 80 VERIFY ON FEEDBACK ON TERM ON
CLEAR COLUMNS
CLEAR BREAKS
TTITLE OFF
```

Listing 11.17   Example of output from synonym script.

```
Date: 10/14/01                                                    Page:   1
Time: 01:57 PM                      Synonym Report                DBAUTIL
                                    galinux1 database


                             Table or
Owner      Synonym           Object Name                Link   Username  Host
---------  ----------------  -------------------------- ------ --------- --------
SYSTEM     CATALOG           SYS.CATALOG
SYSTEM     COL               SYS.COL
SYSTEM     PRODUCT_USER_PROFILE  SYSTEM.SQLPLUS_PRODUCT_PROFILE
SYSTEM     PUBLICSYN         SYS.PUBLICSYN
SYSTEM     SYSCATALOG        SYS.SYSCATALOG
SYSTEM     SYSFILES          SYS.SYSFILES
SYSTEM     TAB               SYS.TAB
SYSTEM     TABQUOTAS         SYS.TABQUOTAS
```

11.5 MONITORING DATABASE LINKS USING V$ AND DBA_ VIEWS

Database links provide connection paths to external databases. They specify user name, password, and connection string data. In earlier versions, a protocol had to be specified; now, protocol-specific data is placed in the TNSNAMES.ORA file and is hidden from the user. Database links can be either private, used by a single user, or public, and accessible by all users. Database links can be used on the fly in queries or can be made invisible to the common user by using synonyms. The DBA_DB_LINKS view is used to monitor them. Source 11.21 shows an example of a database link report, and Listing 11.18 shows an example of a listing from a DB link report script.

Source 11.21   Example of database links report.

```
REM
REM NAME          : DBLINK_REP.SQL
REM FUNCTION      : GENERATE REPORT OF DATABASE LINKS
REM USE           : FROM SQLPLUS
REM Limitations   : None
REM   MRA 10/14/01 Verified for Oracle9i
REM
SET PAGES 58 LINES 80 VERIFY OFF TERM OFF
START title80 "Db Links Report"
SPOOL rep_out/&db/dblink_rep
COLUMN host              FORMAT a18      HEADING "Connect|String"
COLUMN owner             FORMAT a8       HEADING "Creator"
COLUMN db_link           FORMAT a19      HEADING "DB Link|Name"
COLUMN username          FORMAT a8       HEADING "Connect|User"
COLUMN created           FORMAT a15      HEADING "Date|Created"
SELECT
      host,owner,db_link,username,
      to_char(created,'dd-mon-yy hh24:mi') created
FROM
      dba_db_links
ORDER BY
      owner,
      host;
SPOOL OFF
SET PAGES 22 LINES 80 VERIFY ON FEEDBACK ON TERM ON
CLEAR COLUMNS
TTITLE OFF
PAUSE Press Enter to continue
```

Listing 11.18   Example of listing from DB links report script.

```
Date: 10/14/01                                    Page:    1
Time: 02:21 PM              Db Links Report       DBAUTIL
                           galinux1 databa


Connect                    DB Link        Connect Date
String          Creator    Name           User    Created
--------------- --------   -------------------- ------- ---------------
aultdb1.mramobile  DBAUTIL  AULTDB1.TUSCGALINUX DBAUTIL  14-oct-01 14:01
```

11.6 MONITORING DATABASE ROLLBACK SEGMENTS USING V$ AND DBA_ VIEWS

Rollback segments and the new Oracle9*i* UNDO segments must be monitored. Though their tablespace area is monitored through the freespace and extents reports shown in previous sections, it would be helpful to have a report just for rollback segments to present rollback-related data in one convenient location. Even in Oracle9*i*, information on UNDO usage is helpful to the DBA in tuning the Oracle UNDO tablespace. The same views as with Oracle7, Oracle8, and Oracle8*i* are used to monitor UNDO segments in Oracle9*i*.

Monitoring Rollback Usage and Statistics

Unfortunately, the DBA_ROLLBACK_SEGS view is just too large to allow a single report to cover all of the parameters it shows. Therefore, two views and two reports are required to adequately cover the DBA_ROLLBACK_SEGS view and the monitoring of rollback segments. The scripts in Source 11.22 create two views, ROLLBACK1 and ROLLBACK2, both based on the V$ROLLSTAT and V$ROLLNAME views, which are very important for monitoring rollback activity. The DBA_ view, DBA_ROLLBACK_SEGS, is based on these two tables. In Oracle9*i*, a new V$ view was added to allow monitoring of the UNDO segment usage statistics; this new view is called V$UNDOSTAT.

Source 11.22   SQL scripts to generate ROLLBACK1 and ROLLBACK2 views.

```
REM
REM FUNCTION: create views required for rbk1 and rbk2 reports.
REM
REM
CREATE OR REPLACE VIEW rollback1 AS
SELECT
      d.segment_name, extents, optsize, shrinks,
      aveshrink, aveactive, d.status
```

```
FROM
     v$rollname n,
     v$rollstat s,
     dba_rollback_segs d
WHERE
     d.segment_id=n.usn(+)
     AND d.segment_id=s.usn(+)
;

CREATE OR REPLACE VIEW rollback2 AS
SELECT
     d.segment_name,extents,xacts,hwmsize,
     rssize,waits,wraps,extends,d.status
FROM
     v$rollname n,
     v$rollstat s,
     dba_rollback_segs d
WHERE
     d.segment_id=n.usn(+)
     AND d.segment_id=s.usn(+);
```

Once the ROLLBACK1 and ROLLBACK2 views have been created, two simple SQL scripts are used to monitor rollback segments. These scripts are shown in Source 11.23; their output is shown in Listing 11.19.

Source 11.23   Example of rollback report scripts.

```
REM NAME              : RBK1.SQL
REM FUNCTION          : REPORT ON ROLLBACK SEGMENT STORAGE
REM FUNCTION          : USES THE ROLLBACK1 VIEW
REM USE               : FROM SQLPLUS
REM Limitations       : None
REM
COLUMN hwmsize            FORMAT 9999999999      HEADING 'LARGEST TRANS'
COLUMN tablespace_name    FORMAT a10             HEADING 'TABLESPACE'
COLUMN segment_name       FORMAT A10             HEADING 'ROLLBACK'
COLUMN optsize            FORMAT 9999999999      HEADING 'OPTL|SIZE'
COLUMN shrinks            FORMAT 9999            HEADING 'SHRINKS'
COLUMN aveshrink          FORMAT 9999999999      HEADING 'AVE|SHRINK'
COLUMN aveactive          FORMAT 9999999999      HEADING 'AVE|TRANS'
COLUMN waits              FORMAT 99999           HEADING 'WAITS'
COLUMN wraps              FORMAT 99999           HEADING 'WRAPS'
COLUMN extends            FORMAT 9999            HEADING 'EXTENDS'
rem
BREAK ON REPORT
COMPUTE AVG OF AVESHRINK ON REPORT
```

continues

Source 11.23 Continued.

```
COMPUTE AVG OF AVEACTIVE ON REPORT
COMPUTE AVG OF SHRINKS ON REPORT
COMPUTE AVG OF WAITS ON REPORT
COMPUTE AVG OF WRAPS ON REPORT
COMPUTE AVG OF EXTENDS ON REPORT
COMPUTE AVG OF HWMSIZE ON REPORT
SET FEEDBACK OFF VERIFY OFF LINES 132 PAGES 58
@title132 "ROLLBACK SEGMENT STORAGE"
SPOOL rep_out\&db\rbk1
rem
SELECT
  a.SEGMENT_NAME,a.OPTSIZE,a.SHRINKS,
  a.AVESHRINK,a.AVEACTIVE,b.HWMSIZE,
  b.WAITS,b.WRAPS,b.EXTENDS,A.STATUS
FROM rollback1 a, rollback2 b
WHERE A.SEGMENT_NAME=B.SEGMENT_NAME
ORDER BY segment_name;
SPOOL OFF
CLEAR COLUMNS
TTITLE OFF
SET FEEDBACK ON VERIFY ON LINES 80 PAGES 22
PAUSE Press enter to continue

REM
REM NAME        : RBK2.SQL
REM FUNCTION    : REPORT ON ROLLBACK SEGMENT STATISTICS
REM FUNCTION    : USES THE ROLLBACK2 VIEW
REM USE         : FROM SQLPLUS
REM Limitations : None
REM
COLUMN segment_name     FORMAT A8              HEADING 'ROLLBACK'
COLUMN extents          FORMAT 99999           HEADING 'EXTENTS'
COLUMN xacts            FORMAT 9999            HEADING 'TRANS'
COLUMN hwmsize          FORMAT 9999999999      HEADING 'LARGEST TRANS'
COLUMN rssize           FORMAT 9999999999      HEADING 'CUR SIZE'
COLUMN waits            FORMAT 99999           HEADING 'WAITS'
COLUMN wraps            FORMAT 99999           HEADING 'WRAPS'
COLUMN extends          FORMAT 9999            HEADING 'EXTENDS'
rem
SET FEEDBACK OFF VERIFY OFF lines 132 pages 58
BREAK ON REPORT
COMPUTE AVG OF WAITS ON REPORT
COMPUTE AVG OF WRAPS ON REPORT
COMPUTE AVG OF EXTENDS ON REPORT
COMPUTE AVG OF HWMSIZE ON REPORT
rem
@title132 "ROLLBACK SEGMENT STATISTICS"
SPOOL rep_out\&db\rbk2
```

```
rem
SELECT * FROM rollback2 ORDER BY segment_name;
SPOOL OFF
SET LINES 80 PAGES 20 FEEDBACK ON VERIFY ON
TTITLE OFF
CLEAR COLUMNS
PAUSE Press enter to continue
REM
REM NAME                  : RBK3.SQL
REM FUNCTION              : REPORT ON ROLLBACK SEGMENT HEALTH
REM FUNCTION              : USES THE ROLLBACK1 and ROLLBACK2 VIEWs
REM USE                   : FROM SQLPLUS
REM Limitations           : None
REM
COLUMN hwmsize           FORMAT 9999999999         HEADING 'LARGEST TRANS'
COLUMN tablespace_name   FORMAT a10                HEADING 'TABLESPACE'
COLUMN segment_name      FORMAT A10                HEADING 'ROLLBACK'
COLUMN optsize           FORMAT 9999999999         HEADING 'OPTL|SIZE'
COLUMN shrinks           FORMAT 9999               HEADING 'SHRINKS'
COLUMN aveshrink         FORMAT 9999999999         HEADING 'AVE|SHRINK'
COLUMN aveactive         FORMAT 9999999999         HEADING 'AVE|TRANS'
COLUMN waits             FORMAT 99999              HEADING 'WAITS'
COLUMN wraps             FORMAT 99999              HEADING 'WRAPS'
COLUMN extends           FORMAT 9999               HEADING 'EXTENDS'
rem
BREAK ON REPORT
COMPUTE AVG OF AVESHRINK ON REPORT
COMPUTE AVG OF AVEACTIVE ON REPORT
COMPUTE AVG OF SHRINKS ON REPORT
COMPUTE AVG OF WAITS ON REPORT
COMPUTE AVG OF WRAPS ON REPORT
COMPUTE AVG OF EXTENDS ON REPORT
COMPUTE AVG OF HWMSIZE ON REPORT
SET FEEDBACK OFF VERIFY OFF LINES 132 PAGES 47
@title132 "ROLLBACK SEGMENT HEALTH"
SPOOL rep_out\&db\rbk3
rem
SELECT c.tablespace_name, a.segment_name, a.optsize, a.shrinks, a.aveshrink,
a.aveactive,
        b.hwmsize, b.waits, b.wraps, b.extends
FROM rollback1 a, rollback2 b, dba_rollback_segs c
where a.segment_name=b.segment_name
and c.segment_name=a.segment_name
ORDER BY tablespace_name, segment_name;
SPOOL OFF
CLEAR COLUMNS
TTITLE OFF
SET FEEDBACK ON VERIFY ON LINES 80 PAGES 22
PAUSE Press enter to continue
```

The report in listing 11.19 is from an Oracle9*i* database: notice that all of the segments have those wonderful system-generated names and that all are in the UNDOTBS tablespace. In the reports shown in this listing, the parameters of concern to the DBA are location, status, and sizing data. The DBA needs to verify that no rollback segments

Listing 11.19   Example of rollback segment reports output.

```
Date: 10/14/01                                                        Page:   1
Time: 03:21 PM                  ROLLBACK SEGMENT STORAGE              DBAUTIL
                                   galinux1 database


                OPTL              AVE       AVE
ROLLBACK        SIZE SHRINKS      SHRINK    TRANS LARGEST TRANS  WAITS  WRAPS EXTENDS STATUS
-----------     ---- -------      ------    ----- -------------  -----  ----- ------- ------

SYSTEM             0      0            0        0        401408      0      0       0 ONLINE
_SYSSMU1$          0      0            0     6553        122880      0      1       0 ONLINE
_SYSSMU10$         0      0            0        0        122880      0      0       0 ONLINE
_SYSSMU2$          0      0            0        0        122880      0      0       0 ONLINE
_SYSSMU3$          0      0            0        0        122880      0      0       0 ONLINE
_SYSSMU4$          0      0            0        0        122880      0      0       0 ONLINE
_SYSSMU5$          0      0            0     6553        122880      0      1       0 ONLINE
_SYSSMU6$          0      0            0     6553        122880      0      1       0 ONLINE
_SYSSMU7$          0      0            0     6553        122880      0      1       0 ONLINE
_SYSSMU8$          0      0            0        0        122880      0      0       0 ONLINE
_SYSSMU9$          0      0            0     5734        122880      0      1       0 ONLINE
                 ---- -------      ------    ----- -------------  -----  ----- ------- ------
avg                0      0            0     2904        148201      0      0       0
Press enter to continue


Date: 10/14/01                                                        Page:   1
Time: 03:24 PM                  ROLLBACK SEGMENT STATISTICS           DBAUTIL
                                   galinux1 database


ROLLBACK     EXTENTS TRANS LARGEST TRANS   CUR SIZE  WAITS  WRAPS EXTENDS
-----------  ------- ----- -------------   --------  -----  ----- -------

SYSTEM             5     0        401408     401408      0      0       0
_SYSSMU1$          2     0        122880     122880      0      1       0
_SYSSMU10$         2     0        122880     122880      0      0       0
_SYSSMU2$          2     0        122880     122880      0      0       0
_SYSSMU3$          2     0        122880     122880      0      0       0
_SYSSMU4$          2     0        122880     122880      0      0       0
_SYSSMU5$          2     0        122880     122880      0      1       0
_SYSSMU6$          2     0        122880     122880      0      1       0
_SYSSMU7$          2     0        122880     122880      0      1       0
_SYSSMU8$          2     0        122880     122880      0      0       0
_SYSSMU9$          2     0        122880     122880      0      1       0
                               -------------   --------  -----  ----- -------
avg                            148201                    0      0       0
Press enter to continue
```

```
Date: 10/14/01                                                      Page:   1
Time: 03:25 PM                    ROLLBACK SEGMENT HEALTH           DBAUTIL
                                    galinux1 database


                        OPTL            AVE       AVE
TABLESPACE ROLLBACK     SIZE SHRINKS   SHRINK    TRANS LARGEST TRANS WAITS WRAPS EXTENDS
---------- ----------   ---- -------  ------- -------- ------------- ----- ----- -------
SYSTEM     SYSTEM          0       0        0        0        401408     0     0       0
UNDOTBS    _SYSSMU1$       0       0        0     6553        122880     0     1       0
UNDOTBS    _SYSSMU10$      0       0        0        0        122880     0     0       0
UNDOTBS    _SYSSMU2$       0       0        0        0        122880     0     0       0
UNDOTBS    _SYSSMU3$       0       0        0        0        122880     0     0       0
UNDOTBS    _SYSSMU4$       0       0        0        0        122880     0     0       0
UNDOTBS    _SYSSMU5$       0       0        0     6553        122880     0     1       0
UNDOTBS    _SYSSMU6$       0       0        0     6553        122880     0     1       0
UNDOTBS    _SYSSMU7$       0       0        0     6553        122880     0     1       0
UNDOTBS    _SYSSMU8$       0       0        0        0        122880     0     0       0
UNDOTBS    _SYSSMU9$       0       0        0     5734        122880     0     1       0
                        ---- -------  ------- -------- ------------- ----- ----- -------
avg                        0       0        0     2904        148201     0     0       0
Press enter to continue
```

have been created outside of the prescribed tablespaces. In addition, the DBA should verify that all rollback segments that are supposed to be online are in fact online, and that those that are supposed to be offline are offline. Excessive waits indicate the need for more rollback segments. Excessive extends indicate you may need larger extent sizes. If optimal is set, and you get excessive shrinks, this indicates that you need larger rollback segment extents. Usually, wraps aren't of concern, although excessive wraps may be indicative of a too-small rollback segment extent size. If you are using Oracle-managed UNDO, then the reports in Listing 11.19 are informational only.

A report similar to Source 11.24 should be used to monitor undo usage. The UNDO_RETENTION parameter should be based on desired undo retention time, in minutes multiplied by the undo usage showed in this report. The output from the report in Source 11.24 is shown in Listing 11.20.

Source 11.24   Example UNDO usage report.

```
REM undo_usage.sql
REM Function: reports undo usage for Oracle9i
REM
REM MRA 10/14/01 Initial Creation
REM
COLUMN undo_usage FORMAT 99,999,999.999 HEADING 'Undo Usage|Blocks/Min'
COLUMN oer_old_errors FORMAT 99,999,999 HEADING 'Undo|Old Errors'
COLUMN oer_space_errors FORMAT 9,999,999,999 HEADING 'Undo|Space Errors'
```

continues

Source 11.24   Continued.

```
SET FEEDBACK OFF
@title80 'Undo Usage'
spool rep_out/&db/undo_usage
select
  sum(undoblks)/sum((end_time-begin_time)*24*60) undo_usage,
  sum(ssolderrcnt) OER_old_errors,
  sum(nospaceerrcnt) OER_space_errors
from
  v$undostat
where
  undoblks>0
/
spool off
SET FEEDBACK ON
TTITLE OFF
```

Listing 11.20   Example UNDO usage report.

```
Date: 10/14/01                                       Page:   1
Time: 03:43 PM              Undo Usage               DBAUTIL
                        galinux1 database


    Undo Usage        Undo            Undo
    Blocks/Min    Old Errors    Space Errors
    -------------  ------------  --------------
          .123            0               0
```

Monitoring Rollback Current Usage

To identify which users are using which rollback segments, run the script in Source 11.25. The report generated shows the Oracle Process ID, the System Process ID, and the rollback segment in use. Listing 11.21 shows an example of output from an active rollback report.

Source 11.25   Example of SQL script to generate active rollback report.

```
rem    Name    : TX_RBS.SQL
rem    Purpose: Generate a report of active rollbacks
rem    Use     : From SQL*Plus
rem    History:
rem    Date        Who              What
rem    Sept 91     Lan Nguyen       Presented in paper at IOUG
rem                Walter Lindsey
rem    5/15/93     Mike Ault        Added Title80, sets and output
rem    1/04/97     Mike Ault        Verified against 7.3
rem    5/16/99     Mike Ault        Verified against Oracle8i
```

```
rem    10/14/01    Mike Ault       Verified against Oracle9i
rem                                reformated added curext, curblk
rem*********************************************************
COLUMN  name FORMAT a10         HEADING "Rollback|Segment"
COLUMN  pid  FORMAT 99999       HEADING "Oracle|PID"
COLUMN  spid FORMAT 99999       HEADING "Sys|PID"
COLUMN  curext FORMAT 999999    HEADING "Current|Extent"
COLUMN  curblk FORMAT 999999    HEADING "Current|Block"
COLUMN transaction FORMAT A15   Heading 'Transaction'
COLUMN program FORMAT a10 HEADING 'Program'
SET PAGES 56  LINES 80 VERIFY OFF FEEDBACK OFF
START title80 "Rollback Segments in Use"
SPOOL rep_out\&db\tx_rbs
SELECT
    r.name, l.Sid, p.spid,
    NVL(p.username, 'no transaction') "Transaction",
    p.program "Program",
    s.curext,s.curblk
FROM
    v$lock l,
    v$process p,
    v$rollname r,
    v$rollstat s
WHERE
        l.Sid = p.pid (+)
    AND TRUNC(l.id1(+) / 65536) = r.usn
    AND l.type(+) = 'TX'
    AND l.lmode(+) = 6
    AND r.usn=s.usn
    AND p.username is not null
ORDER BY r.name;
SPOOL OFF
SET PAGES 22  LINES 80 VERIFY ON FEEDBACK ON
CLEAR COLUMNS
TTITLE OFF
```

Listing 11.21   Example of output from active rollback report.

```
Date: 10/14/01                                       Page:   1
Time: 03:56 PM           Rollback Segments in Use      DBAUTIL
                            galinux1 databa

Rollback            Sys                            Current Current
Segment         SID PID     Transaction    Program  Extent   Block
---------- --------- --------- ------------- ---------- ------- -------
_SYSSMU6$         7 157     oracle          oracle@tus      0       2
                                            cgalinux (
                                            RECO)
```

Monitoring Rollback Transaction Size

To determine if your rollback segments are properly sized, you can run some sample transactions through the script in Source 11.26. To do so, simply place the SQL from the transaction or the call to the transaction into the script where indicated and execute the script. Note: Make sure that your transaction is the only one running when you do the test, or the results will be invalid.

Source 11.26   Script to generate total rollback bytes used in a transaction.

```
rem*****************************************************************
rem  Name       : UNDO.SQL
rem  Purpose: Document rollback usage for a single
rem     transaction
rem  Use  : Note: You must alter the UNDO script and add a
rem     call to the transaction at the indicated line
rem  Restrictions:     : The database should be placed in DBA mode and
rem     this transaction should be the only one running.
rem  History:
rem   Date                 Who          What
rem   Sept 91         Lan Nguyen         Presented in paper at IOUG
rem                   Walter Lindsey
rem   5/15/93         Mike Ault Changed to use one table
rem
SET FEEDBACK OFF  TERMOUT OFF
COLUMN name FORMAT a40
DEFINE undo_overhead=54
DROP TABLE undo_data;
CREATE TABLE undo_data
     (
     tran_no number, start_writes number, end_writes number
     );
INSERT INTO undo_data
SELECT 1, SUM(writes),0 from v$rollstat;
SET FEEDBACK ON  TERMOUT ON
rem
rem    INSERT TRANSACTION HERE
rem
SET FEEDBACK OFF  TERMOUT OFF
UPDATE undo_data SET end_writes = SUM(writes) FROM v$rollstat;
  WHERE tran_no=1;
SET FEEDBACK ON  TERMOUT ON
SELECT  ((end-writes - start_writes) - &undo_overhead)
"Number of Rollback Bytes Generated"
FROM undo_data;
SET TERMOUT OFF FEEDBACK OFF
DROP TABLE undo_data;
```

If the DBA has one transaction whose rollback usage he or she is concerned about, the script in Source 11.25 can be run with the transaction in question executed in the indicated spot in the script. The data generated will tell the DBA the exact amount of rollback usage for the transaction. This data can then be used to create a custom rollback segment that can be brought online and used during that transaction. Again, the script and test run of the transaction must be the only active transactions in the database when the test is run.

Monitoring Deferred Rollback Segments

If a rollback segment is taken offline, its transactions may be placed in a temporary segment in the rollback segment's tablespace. These temporary segments are referred to as *deferred rollback segments*. The following SQL code will list any deferred rollbacks in your 7.x , 8.x, or 9.x database:

```
SELECT segment_name, segment_type, tablespace_name
FROM sys.dba_segments
WHERE segment_type = 'DEFERRED ROLLBACK';
```

Example output from the preceding select statement:

```
SEGMENT_NAME    SEGMENT_TYPE       TABLESPACE_NAME
------------    -----------------  ---------------
RBK1            DEFERRED ROLLBACK  USERS
```

Under Oracle7, if a rollback segment is taken offline, its status will be changed to PENDING OFFLINE, and it will be taken offline as soon as its pending transactions are complete. The preceding SELECT statement could be used to determine if any of these active transactions are in a deferred state. To determine if a rollback segment under Oracle7 has outstanding transactions, the following SELECT statement is used.

```
SELECT name, xacts 'ACTIVE TRANSACTIONS'
FROM     v$rollname, v$rollstat
WHERE status = 'PENDING OFFLINE'
AND         v$rollname.usn = v$rollstat.usn;
```

TIP Be sure your database has a sufficient number of online rollback segments. If the ratio TRANSACTIONS/TRANSACTIONS_PER_ROLLBACK is exceeded, the system automatically brings online any available public rollback segments. If the only available public rollback happens to be the maintenance segment in the system space, it will be brought online and could cause havoc in the system tablespace as it extends to accommodate transactions.

Monitoring Redo Activity with V$ and DBA_ Views

The redo logs provide the information required to redo transactions performed on the database. For an Oracle8, Oracle8*i,* or Oracle9*i* database, redo logs are placed in log groups whose members consist of individual log files. For Oracle8, Oracle8*i,* or Oracle9*i*, there should be at least two mirrored groups of log files on separate drives to start up; three are highly recommended. In high-activity environments, the use of five mirrored groups of 5 megabytes each will ensure that there is no log contention. Sizing redo logs and number required is not an exact science; it must be done by trial and error. Monitor the alert log for waits on log switches or checkpoints to see if your logs are large enough or if you have enough of them.

Monitoring Redo Log Status

DBAs should monitor redo log status to determine which logs are in use and if there are any odd status codes such as stale log indications or indications of corrupt redo logs. The log files can have the following status values:

USED. Indicates status of a log that has just been added (never used) or that a RESETLOGS command has been issued.

CURRENT. Indicates a valid log that is in use.

ACTIVE. Indicates a valid log file that is not currently in use.

CLEARING. Indicates log is being re-created as an empty log due to DBA action.

CLEARING CURRENT. Means that current log is being cleared of a closed thread. If a log stays in this status, it could indicate there is some failure in the log switch.

INACTIVE. Means that log is no longer needed for instance recovery but may be needed for media recovery.

The v$logfile table has a status indicator that gives these additional codes:

INVALID. File is inaccessible.

STALE. File contents are incomplete (such as when an instance is shut down with SHUTDOWN ABORT or due to a system crash).

DELETED. File is no longer used.

The script in Source 11.27 provides some basic information on log status. Listing 11.22 shows an example of output from LOG_STAT.SQL script.

Source 11.27   Example LOG_STAT.SQL script.

```
rem
rem Name:     log_stat.sql
rem
rem FUNCTION: Provide a current status for redo logs
rem
rem
COLUMN first_change#  FORMAT 99999999   HEADING Change#
COLUMN group#         FORMAT 9,999      HEADING Grp#
COLUMN thread#        FORMAT 999        HEADING Th#
COLUMN sequence#      FORMAT 999,999    HEADING Seq#
COLUMN members        FORMAT 999        HEADING Mem
COLUMN archived       FORMAT a4         HEADING Arc?
COLUMN first_time     FORMAT a21        HEADING 'Switch|Time'
BREAK ON thread#
SET PAGES 60 LINES 131 FEEDBACK OFF
START title132 'Current Redo Log Status'
SPOOL rep_out\&db\log_stat
SELECT thread#,group#,sequence#,bytes,
       members,archived,
       status,first_change#,
       TO_CHAR(first_time, 'DD-MM-YYYY HH24:MI:SS') first_time
  FROM
       sys.v_$log
  ORDER BY
       thread#,
       group#;
SPOOL OFF
PAUSE Press Enter to continue
SET PAGES 22 LINES 80 FEEDBACK ON
CLEAR BREAKS
CLEAR COLUMNS
TTILE OFF
```

Listing 11.22   Example output of script to monitor redo log status.

```
Date: 06/15/97                                          Page:   1
Time: 01:39 PM           Current Redo Log Status           SYSTEM
                           ORTEST1 database


                                        Switch
Th# Grp#  Seq#      BYTES Mem Arc? STATUS   Change# Time
--- ----  -----    ------- -------- -------- ------- -----------------
  1    1 4,489    1048576    2 NO    INACTIVE  719114 15-JUN-97 16:54:23
       2 4,490    1048576    2 NO    INACTIVE  719117 15-JUN-97 16:56:10
       3 4,491    1048576    2 NO    CURRENT   719120 15-JUN-97 17:02:22
```

Monitoring Redo Log Switches

In addition to the alert logs, the frequency of log switches can also be monitored via the v$log_history and v$archived_log DPTs. A script that uses these DPTs for this purpose is shown in Source 11.28. Listing 11.23 shows an example of output from an archive log switch script.

Source 11.28   Script to monitor archive log switches.

```
REM
REM NAME          :log_hist.sql
REM PURPOSE       :Provide info on logs for last 24 hours since last
REM PURPOSE       :log switch
REM USE           : From SQLPLUS
REM Limitations   : None
REM MRA 10/14/01 Updated for Oracle9i
REM
COLUMN thread#               FORMAT 999      HEADING 'Thrd#'
COLUMN sequence#             FORMAT 99999    HEADING 'Seq#'
COLUMN first_change#                         HEADING 'SCN Low#'
COLUMN next_change#                          HEADING 'SCN High#'
COLUMN archive_name          FORMAT a50      HEADING 'Log File'
COLUMN first_time            FORMAT a20      HEADING 'Switch Time'
COLUMN name                  FORMAT a30      HEADING 'Archive Log'
SET LINES 132 FEEDBACK OFF VERIFY OFF
START title132 "Log History Report"
SPOOL rep_out\&db\log_hist
REM
SELECT
     X.recid,a.thread#,
     a.sequence#,a.first_change#,
     a.switch_change#,
     TO_CHAR(a.first_time,'DD-MON-YYYY HH24:MI:SS') first_time,
     x.name
FROM
 v$loghist a, v$archived_log x
WHERE
  a.first_time>
   (SELECT b.first_time-1
   FROM v$loghist b WHERE b.switch_change# =
    (SELECT MAX(c.switch_change#) FROM v$loghist c)) AND
    x.recid(+)=a.sequence#;
SPOOL OFF
SET LINES 80 VERIFY ON FEEDBACK ON
CLEAR COLUMNS
TTITLE OFF
PAUSE Press Enter to continue
```

Listing 11.23   Example of output from archive log switch script.

```
Date: 10/14/01                                                    Page:   1
Time: 04:10 PM                     Log History Report             DBAUTIL
                                   galinux1 database


   RECID Thrd#   Seq#   SCN Low# SWITCH_CHANGE# Switch Time        Archive Log
--------- ----- ------ --------- -------------- ------------------ ----------------------------
          1      8     375520          409741 05-SEP-2001 08:18:06
Press Enter to continue
```

Monitoring Redo Statistics

There are no views in Oracle that allow the user to look directly at a log file's statistical data. Instead, we must look at statistics based on redo log and log writer process statistics. These statistics are in the views V$STATNAME, V$SESSION, V$PROCESS, V$SESSTAT, V$LATCH, and V$LATCHNAME. An example of a report that uses these views is shown in Source 11.29; an example of the script's output is shown in Listing 11.24.

Source 11.29   Script to generate reports on redo statistics.

```
REM
REM NAME         : rdo_stat.sql
REM PURPOSE      : Show REDO latch statistics
REM USE          : from SQLPlus
REM Limitations  : Must have access to v$_ views
REM
SET PAGES 56 LINES 78 VERIFY OFF FEEDBACK OFF
START title80 "Redo Latch Statistics"
SPOOL rep_out/&&db/rdo_stat
rem
COLUMN name     FORMAT a30          HEADING Name
COLUMN percent  FORMAT 999.999      HEADING Percent
COLUMN total                        HEADING Total
rem
SELECT
    l2.name,
    immediate_gets+gets Total,
    immediate_gets "Immediates",
    misses+immediate_misses "Total Misses",
    DECODE (100.*(GREATEST(misses+immediate_misses,1)/
    GREATEST(immediate_gets+gets,1)),100,0) Percent
FROM
    v$latch l1,
    v$latchname l2
```

continues

Source 11.29 Continued.

```
WHERE
    l2.name like '%redo%'
    and l1.latch#=l2.latch# ;
rem
PAUSE Press Enter to continue
rem
rem Name: Redo_stat.sql
rem
rem Function: Select redo statistics from v$sysstat
rem History:
rem Who             What              Date
rem ---------       ----------------  -------
rem Mike Ault       Revised from V6   1/04/97
rem Mike Ault       Verified Oracle8  6/15/97
rem
COLUMN name     FORMAT a30          HEADING 'Redo|Statistic|Name'
COLUMN value    FORMAT 999,999,999 HEADING 'Redo|Statistic|Value'
SET PAGES 80 LINES 60 FEEDBACK OFF VERIFY OFF
START title80 'Redo Log Statistics'
SPOOL rep_out/&&db/redo_stat
SELECT
    name,
    value
FROM
    v$sysstat
WHERE
    name LIKE '%redo%'
ORDER BY statistic#;
SPOOL OFF
SET LINES 24 FEEDBACK ON VERIFY ON
TTITLE OFF
CLEAR COLUMNS
CLEAR BREAKS
```

Listing 11.24 Example of output from redo report scripts.

```
Date: 10/14/01                                      Page:   1
Time: 04:14 PM       Redo Latch Statistics        DBAUTIL
                      galinux1 databa

Name                      Total Immediates Total Misses  Percent
------------------------- --------- ---------- ------------ --------
redo allocation           172438             0            0
redo copy                   6259          6231            0
redo writing              672470             0            0
Press Enter to continue
```

```
Date: 10/14/01                                          Page:   1
Time: 04:14 PM            Redo Log Statistics           DBAUTIL
                            galinux1 databa

Redo                               Redo
Statistic                          Statistic
Name                               Value
------------------------------  ------------
redo synch writes                      250
redo synch time                         72
redo entries                         6,231
redo size                        1,569,816
redo buffer allocation retries           0
redo wastage                     1,200,696
redo writer latching time                0
redo writes                          3,635
redo blocks written                  5,586
redo write time                        151
redo log space requests                  0
redo log space wait time                 0
redo log switch interrupts               0
redo ordering marks                      0
```

Of course, right about now you are probably asking, what good all these numbers will do you. Let's look at what they mean and how you can use them. The first section of the report in Source 11.29 should be self-explanatory. The redo logs use two latches: REDO ALLOCATION and REDO COPY.

In general, if the PERCENT statistic (actually, the ratio of total misses to total gets) is greater than 10 percent, contention is occurring, and the DBA needs to examine the way he or she is doing redo logs (more about this in a second). The initial latch granted for redo is the REDO_ALLOCATION latch. The REDO_COPY latch is granted to a user when the size of his or her entry is greater than the _LOG_SMALL_ENTRY_MAX_SIZE parameter in the initialization file. If you see REDO_ALLOCATION latch contention, decrease the value of _LOG_SMALL_ENTRY_MAX_SIZE. If there is more than one user that requires the REDO_COPY latch, you get contention on single-CPU systems. The number of REDO_COPY latches is limited to twice the number of CPUs on the system. If you have a single CPU, only one is allowed. It is normal to see high contention for this latch on single-CPU systems, and there is nothing the DBA can do to increase the number of REDO_COPY latches. However, even on single-CPU systems, you can force Oracle to prebuild redo entries, thereby reducing the number of latches required. This is accomplished by setting the _LOG_ENTRY_ PREBUILD_THRESHOLD entry in the initialization file higher. On multiple-CPU systems, increase the number of REDO_COPY latches to twice the number of CPUs.

In the second half of the report, statistics from the caches that affect redo operations are shown. Let's look at what these numbers tell us. The most important of the listed statistics are *redo blocks written*, *redo entries linearized*, *redo small copies*, and *redo writes*.

- *redo blocks written* is useful when two entries are compared for a specified time period. This will indicate how much redo is generated for the period between the two checks.
- *redo small copies* tells how many times the entry was effectively written on a redo allocation latch. This indicates that a redo copy latch was not required for this entry. This statistic should be compared with the redo entries parameter. If there is close to a one-to-one relationship, then your system is making effective use of the redo allocation latch. If there is a large difference, then the LOG_SMALL_ENTRY_MAX_SIZE INIT.ORA parameter should be increased. If the LOG_SIMULTANEOUS_COPIES parameter is 0, this value is ignored.
- *redo writes* is the total number of redo writes to the redo buffer. If this value is too large compared to the redo entries parameter value, then the DBA should tune the INIT.ORA parameters mentioned in the previous sections to force prebuilding of the entries. If the entries are not prebuilt, the entry may require several writes to the buffer before it is fully entered; if it is prebuilt, it requires only one.
- *redo log space wait* is the statistic that tells you if users are having to wait for space in the redo buffer. If this value is nonzero, increase the size of the LOG_BUFFER in the initialization file.
- *redo buffer allocation retries* is the statistic that tells the DBA the number of repeated attempts needed to allocate space in the redo buffer. If this value is high in comparison to redo entries, it indicates that the redo logs may be too small and should be increased in size. Normally, this value should be much less than the redo entries statistic. In the example, it has a value of 5 compared to the entry's value of 1044; this is satisfactory.
- *redo size* tells the total number of redo bytes generated since the database was started. Comparison of two readings will give the amount generated over time. This value can then be used to determine if the log switch interval is proper. Too many log switches over a small amount of time can impair performance.

Use the following formula to look at log switches over time:

$$(X / (dN / dt)) / \text{interval of concern}$$

where:

X is the value of LOG_CHECKPOINT_INTERVAL or size of the redo log in system blocks.

dN is the change in the redo size over the time interval.

dt is the time differential for the period (usually minutes).

Once the number of log switches is known, the DBA can use this value to determine the size of redo logs based on system I/O requirements. If you need to reduce the number of log switches, increase the redo log size; of course, this may impact system availability since it takes longer to write out a large redo log buffer than a small one to disk. A balance must be struck between undersizing the redo logs and taking a database performance hit and making the logs too large and taking an I/O hit.

Monitoring Directories and Libraries

Directories and libraries were internal database structures new to Oracle8. Libraries are pointers to external sharable libraries of 3GL routines that can be called via the external procedures call option, also new to Oracle8. Directories, as their name implies, are pointers to external directories, where BFILE and other LOB data objects can be stored outside the database.

Monitoring Directories

Directory information is available from the DBA_DIRECTORIES view. This view has three columns. A simple report to show everything the database knows about directories is shown in Source 11.30.

Source 11.30   Example of script to report on database directories.

```
rem NAME: dir_rep.sql
rem FUNCTION: Report on directories known by the database
rem HISTORY: MRA 6/16/97 Created for Oracle8
rem          MRA 5/16/99 Verified for Oracle8i
rem          MRA 10/14/01 Verified for Oracle9i
rem
COLUMN owner              FORMAT a10 HEADING 'Owner'
COLUMN directory_name     FORMAT a15 HEADING 'Directory'
COLUMN directory_path     FORMAT a45 HEADING 'Full Path'
SET VERIFY OFF PAGES 58 LINES 78 FEEDBACK OFF
START title80 'Database Directories Report'
SPOOL rep_out\&db\dir_rep.lis
SELECT
     owner,directory_name,directory_path
FROM
     dba_directories
ORDER BY
     owner;
SPOOL OFF
SET VERIFY ON FEEDBACK ON
TTITLE OFF
CLEAR COLUMNS
```

Listing 11.25 shows an example of output from the directories report script in Source 11.30. Remember, directories aren't verified for existence until access is attempted.

Listing 11.25   Example of output from the directories report.

```
Date: 10/14/01                                                   Page:    1
Time: 04:18 PM           Database Directories Report       DBAUTIL
                              galinux1 databa

Owner        Directory        Full Path
----------   --------------   -------------------------------------------------
SYS          MEDIA_DIR        /project/linux/install/d2/pse/cus/901/demo/sc
                              hema/product_media/

SYS          LOG_FILE_DIR     /project/linux/install/d2/pse/cus/901/admin/s
                              tp1/create/

SYS          DATA_FILE_DIR    /project/linux/install/d2/pse/cus/901/demo/sc
                              hema/sales_history/

SYS          SQL_DIR          /home/oracle/sql_scripts
```

Monitoring Libraries

Libraries are monitored through the DBA_LIBRARIES view. The DBA_LIBRARIES view contains five fields. An example of a report for monitoring libraries is shown in Source 11.31. The output from the library report script is shown in Listing 11.26.

Source 11.31   Example of script to document external library specifications.

```
rem
rem NAME: lib_rep.sql
rem FUNCTION: Document External Library Entries in Database
rem HISTORY: MRA 6/16/97 Created
rem          MRA 10/14/01 Updated for Oracle9i
rem
COLUMN owner             FORMAT a8     HEADING 'Library|Owner'
COLUMN library_name      FORMAT a15    HEADING 'Library|Name'
COLUMN file_spec         FORMAT a30    HEADING 'File|Specification'
COLUMN dynamic           FORMAT a7     HEADING 'Dynamic'
COLUMN status            FORMAT a10    HEADING 'Status'
BREAK ON owner
SET FEEDBACK OFF VERIFY OFF LINES 78 PAGES 58
START title80 'Database External Libraries Report'
SPOOL rep_out\&db\lib_rep.lis
```

```
SELECT
     owner,library_name,file_spec,dynamic,status
FROM
     dba_libraries
ORDER BY
     owner;
SPOOL OFF
SET VERIFY ON FEEDBACK ON
TTITLE OFF
CLEAR COLUMNS
CLEAR BREAKS
```

Listing 11.26   Example of output from the library report.

```
Date: 10/14/01                                          Page:   1
Time: 04:22 PM        Database External Libraries Report    DBAUTIL
                          galinux1 databa

Library  Library        File
Owner    Name           Specification               Dynamic STATUS
-------- --------       --------------------------- ------- -------
CTXSYS   DR$LIB                                     N       VALID
         DR$LIBX        /var/oracle/OraHome2/ctx/lib/l Y    VALID
                        ibctxx9.so

LBACSYS  LBAC$CACHE_LIBT                            N       VALID
         LBAC$COMPS_LIBT                            N       VALID
         LBAC$EVENT_LIBT                            N       VALID
         LBAC$LABEL_LIBT                            N       VALID
         LBAC$LABLT_LIBT                            N       VALID
         LBAC$PRIVS_LIBT                            N       VALID
         LBAC$RLS_LIBT                              N       VALID
         LBAC$STD_LIBT                              N       VALID
         LBAC$TYPE_LIBT                             N       VALID
         LBAC$USER_LIBT                             N       VALID
```

Remember, as with directories, the existence of the actual libraries isn't tested until they are called by an external procedure.

11.7 MONITORING CONTROL FILES AND INITIALIZATION PARAMETERS

The control files have traditionally been a "don't ask, don't tell" element of Oracle. Everyone knew they were there but weren't sure what they were for or how they could be monitored. Although initialization parameters were easy to monitor, no one did so. Now, in Oracle8, Oracle8*i*, and Oracle9*i*, monitoring both control files and initialization parameters, which are critical to database health and well-being, is much easier.

Monitoring Control Files

Oracle7 (from release 7.3 on) and Oracle8 provide the V$CONTROLFILE view to help keep track of the control files. Oracle8 provides the V$CONTROLFILE_RECORD view that is used with Recovery Manager. In Oracle9i, the V$CONTROLFILE_RECORD view becomes the V$CONTROLFILE_RECORD_SECTION view. The script in Source 11.32 can be used to monitor control file status. Its output is documented in Listing 11.27.

Source 11.32   Script to monitor control file location and status.

```
rem
rem NAME : con_file.sql
rem FUNCTION: Document control file location and status
rem HISTORY: MRA 6/16/97 Creation
rem          MRA 10/14/01 Verified against Oracle9i
rem
COLUMN name    FORMAT a60 HEADING 'Con|File|Location' WORD_WRAPPED
COLUMN status  FORMAT a7  HEADING 'Con|File|Status'
SET LINES 78 FEEDBACK OFF VERIFY OFF
START title80 'Control File Status'
SPOOL rep_out\&db\con_file.lis
SELECT
    name,status
FROM
    v$controlfile;
SPOOL OFF
SET VERIFY ON FEEDBACK ON
TTITLE OFF
CLEAR COLUMNS
```

Listing 11.27   Example of output of control file script.

```
Date: 10/14/01                                          Page:    1
Time: 04:27 PM           Control File Status            DBAUTIL
                          galinux1 databa

Con                                                     Con
File                                                    File
Location                                                Status
------------------------------------------------------- -------
/var/oracle/OraHome2/oradata/galinux1/control01.ctl
/var/oracle/OraHome2/oradata/galinux1/control02.ctl
/var/oracle/OraHome2/oradata/galinux1/control03.ctl
```

Note that the Control File Status should always be blank. If it shows a status, it's an indication that the control file is corrupt. That said, because the database can't start up if the file is corrupt, this is an unlikely occurrence. You should confirm that the files are on separate disks or disk arrays.

TIP   In previous versions of Oracle prior to 8, the control files were usually less than 1 megabyte in size. From Oracle8 on, they can be tens of megabytes in size due to the extra backup material monitored. Be careful to allow for this in your file systems.

The v$controlfile_record_section gives statistics on each type of record contained in the control file. Recall that, in Chapter 2, we used this view to generate the MAX set of parameters for the CREATE DATABASE command. A script to monitor this table is shown in Source 11.33. The output from this script is shown in Listing 11.28.

Source 11.33   Script to monitor the control file record sections.

```
rem
rem NAME: con_rec.sql
rem FUNCTION: Provide documentation of control file record stats
rem HISTORY: MRA 6/16/97 Creation
rem          MRA 10/14/01 Verified for Oracle9i
rem
COLUMN type          FORMAT a18        HEADING 'Record Type'
COLUMN record_size   FORMAT 999999     HEADING 'Record|Size'
COLUMN records_used  FORMAT 999999     HEADING 'Records|Used'
COLUMN first_index   FORMAT 9999999    HEADING 'First|Index'
COLUMN last_index    FORMAT 9999999    HEADING 'Last|Index'
COLUMN last_recid    FORMAT 999999     HEADING 'Last|Record|ID'
SET LINES 80 PAGES 58 FEEDBACK OFF VERIFY OFF
START title80 'Control File Records'
SPOOL rep_out\&db\con_rec.lis
SELECT
     type,record_size,records_total,records_used,first_index,
     last_index,last_recid
FROM
     v$controlfile_record_section;
SPOOL OFF
CLEAR COLUMNS
SET FEEDBACK ON VERIFY ON
TTITLE OFF
```

Listing 11.28   Results from the control file records report.

```
Date: 10/14/01                                              Page:   1
Time: 04:31 PM              Control File Records        DBAUTIL
                              galinux1 databa


                                                              Last
                    Record              Records    First    Last  Record
Record Type          Size RECORDS_TOTAL   Used     Index   Index     ID
-----------------  ------ ------------- -------  -------- -------- -------
DATABASE              192             1       1         0        0       0
CKPT PROGRESS        4084             4       0         0        0       0
REDO THREAD           104             1       1         0        0       0
REDO LOG               72            50       3         0        0       3
DATAFILE              180           100      12         0        0      19
FILENAME              524           351      17         0        0       0
TABLESPACE             68           100      13         0        0       7
TEMPORARY FILENAME     56           100       2         0        0       2
RMAN CONFIGURATION   1108            50       0         0        0       0
LOG HISTORY            36           226       8         1        8       8
OFFLINE RANGE          56           145       0         0        0       0
ARCHIVED LOG          584            13       0         0        0       0
BACKUP SET             40           204       0         0        0       0
BACKUP PIECE          736           210       0         0        0       0
BACKUP DATAFILE       116           211       0         0        0       0
BACKUP REDOLOG         76           107       0         0        0       0
DATAFILE COPY         660           210       0         0        0       0
BACKUP CORRUPTION      44           185       0         0        0       0
COPY CORRUPTION        40           204       0         0        0       0
DELETED OBJECT         20           408       0         0        0       0
PROXY COPY            852           306       0         0        0       0
RESERVED4               1          8168       0         0        0       0
```

The control file records report can tell you the number of data files, redo logs, archived logs, and a plethora of other information about your database. The Records Used column indicates how many of a particular type has been assigned for your database.

Monitoring Database Initialization Parameters

The database initialization parameters are critical parts of the database. I have seen many installations where administrators were very diligent about database back-ups but neglected to document the settings of their initialization parameters. At some installations DBAs—or should I say DBBSs (database babysitters)—didn't even know the location of the init<SID>.ora file.

The documentation of the parameters has been covered in earlier sections; with the advent of Oracle9*i*, the v$parameter file provides the source for discovering the value and status of any documented initialization file parameter in effect for the current session (previously it was for the instance). Oracle9*i* also added the V$PARAMETER2, V$SYSTEM_PARAMETER, and V$SYSTEM_PARAMETER2 views. The V$SYSTEM_PARAMETERS view shows the instancewide parameter values. The V$PARAMETER2 and V$SYSTEM_PARAMETER2 views show the same parameters as their nonnumbered counterparts, except that any multivalues string (such as CONTROL_FILE or ROLLBACK_SEGMENT) will have an individual listing for each value of the string, differentiated by an ORDINAL column to tell you the order that the substring occurred within the master string. A simple script to generate a nearly ready-for-prime-time init <SID>.ora file is listed in Source 11.34. Of course, with Oracle9*i*, you can use the CREATE PFILE command if you have a current SPFILE to generate a parameter file listing. An example of output from this script is shown in Listing 11.29.

Source 11.34   Script to re-create the init<SID>.ora file.

```
REM
REM NAME        : init_ora_rct.sql
REM FUNCTION    : Re-create the instance init.ora file
REM USE         : GENERAL
REM Limitations : None
REM History: MRA 11/7/95  Initial creation
REM          MRA 10/14/01  Updated for Oracle9i
REM
SET NEWPAGE 0 VERIFY OFF
SET ECHO OFF FEEDBACK OFF TERMOUT OFF PAGES 300 LINES 80 HEADING OFF
COLUMN name  FORMAT a80 WORD_WRAPPED
COLUMN dbname NEW_VALUE db NOPRINT
SELECT name dbname FROM v$database;
DEFINE OUTPUT = 'rep_out\&db\init.ora'
SPOOL &OUTPUT
SELECT '# Init.ora file FROM v$system_parameter' name FROM dual
UNION
SELECT '# generated on:'||sysdate name FROM dual
UNION
SELECT '# script by MRA 10/14/01 TUSC' name FROM dual
UNION
SELECT '#' name FROM dual
UNION
SELECT name||' = '||value name  FROM v$system_parameter
WHERE value IS NOT NULL and Isdefault='FALSE';
SPOOL OFF
CLEAR COLUMNS
SET NEWPAGE 0 VERIFY OFF
SET TERMOUT ON PAGES 22 LINES 80 HEADING ON
SET TERMOUT ON
UNDEF OUTPUT
PAUSE Press Enter to continue
```

Listing 11.29   Example of output from the INIT.ORA re-creation script.

```
#
# Init.ora file FROM v$system_parameter
# generated on:14-OCT-01
# script by MRA 10/14/01 TUSC
background_dump_dest = /var/oracle/OraHome2/admin/galinux1/bdump
compatible = 9.0.0
control_files = /var/oracle/OraHome2/oradata/galinux1/control01.ctl,
/var/oracle/OraHome2/oradata/galinux1/control02.ctl,
/var/oracle/OraHome2/oradata/galinux1/control03.ctl

core_dump_dest = /var/oracle/OraHome2/admin/galinux1/cdump
db_block_size = 8192
db_cache_size = 67108864
db_domain = tuscgalinux
db_name = galinux1
dispatchers = (PROTOCOL=TCP)(SER=MODOSE),
(PROTOCOL=TCP)(PRE=oracle.aurora.server.GiopServer),
(PROTOCOL=TCP)(PRE=oracle.aurora.server.SGiopServer)

fast_start_mttr_target = 300
instance_name = galinux1
java_pool_size = 117440512
large_pool_size = 1048576
open_cursors = 300
processes = 150
remote_login_passwordfile = EXCLUSIVE
resource_manager_plan = SYSTEM_PLAN
shared_pool_size = 117440512
sort_area_size = 524288
timed_statistics = TRUE
undo_management = AUTO
undo_tablespace = UNDOTBS
user_dump_dest = /var/oracle/OraHome2/admin/galinux1/udump
```

Notice that the WHERE clause in the query for the init.ora re-creation script restricts the return values to only those that have been changed from their default settings (isdefault='FALSE'). If you do not restrict the return from the query, you get all hundred-plus parameters.

Monitoring Undocumented Initialization Parameters

There are also undocumented initialization parameters that require monitoring. Undocumented parameters are those that are (a) undergoing testing or (b) were too good to get rid of completely. Unfortunately, the undocumented values are a wee bit more difficult to access. For Oracle7.2 and earlier, the following script would return the values:

```
Rem undoc7.sql
Rem MRA from posting on compuserve orauser forum
COLUMN parameter  FORMAT a40
COLUMN value      FORMAT a30
COLUMN ksppidf                    HEADING 'Is|Default'
SET FEEDBACK OFF VERIFY OFF PAGES 55
START title80 'Undocumented Init.ora Parameters'
SPOOL rep_out/&db/undoc
SELECT
     ksppinm "Parameter",
       ksppivl "Value",
       ksppidf
FROM
     x$ksppi
WHERE
     ksppinm like '/_%' escape '/'
/
SPOOL OFF
TTITLE OFF
```

But because Oracle monkeyed with the structure of the k and x$ tables, frequently you have to use the following script for Oracle7.3 and later:

```
REM undoc.sql
REM Script for getting undocumented init.ora
REM parameters from a 7.3 or greater instance
REM MRA - Revealnet 4/23/97
REM MRA - 10/14/01 verified against Oracle9i
REM
COLUMN parameter          FORMAT a37
COLUMN description        FORMAT a30 WORD_WRAPPED
COLUMN "Session VALUE"    FORMAT a10
COLUMN "Instance VALUE"   FORMAT a10
SET LINES 100 PAGES 0
SPOOL undoc.lis
SELECT
     a.ksppinm  "Parameter",
     a.ksppdesc "Description",
     b.ksppstvl "Session Value",
     c.ksppstvl "Instance Value"
FROM
     x$ksppi a,
     x$ksppcv b,
     x$ksppsv c
WHERE
     a.indx = b.indx
     AND a.indx = c.indx
     AND a.ksppinm LIKE '/_%' escape '/'
/
SPOOL OFF
```

Both these scripts must be run from the SYS user.

NOTE   These parameters are listed in Chapter 2, if you would like to review them. Also, be aware that the preceding scripts have been tested up to Oracle9.0.1, so they aren't guaranteed beyond that.

11.8 MONITORING LOCKS AND LATCHES

Monitoring latches and locks can be a challenge in Oracle. Just for V$LOCK DPT alone, multiple joins are usually required to get to the information you desire. I suggest running the CATBLOCK.SQL script, as it creates several useful views for locks. The CATBLOCK.SQL script is located in the /oracle/rdbms/admin directory on UNIX, and in the c:\orant\rdbmsxx\admin directory on NT. The script creates DBA_KGLLOCK, DBA_LOCK, DBA_LOCK_INTERNAL, DBA_DML_LOCKS, DBA_DDL_LOCKS, DBA_WAITERS, and DBA_BLOCKERS. I suggest executing this script with echo set to ON, since in many releases it contains errors that you must correct before it will run properly. On early Oracle7 releases, there were also problems with permissions on some of the lock views, which required that they be queried from SYS or INTERNAL only. OEM contains a detailed lock screen in the GUI, as well as an HTML-based report for locking. The OEM Lock Manager GUI is shown in Figure 11.8.

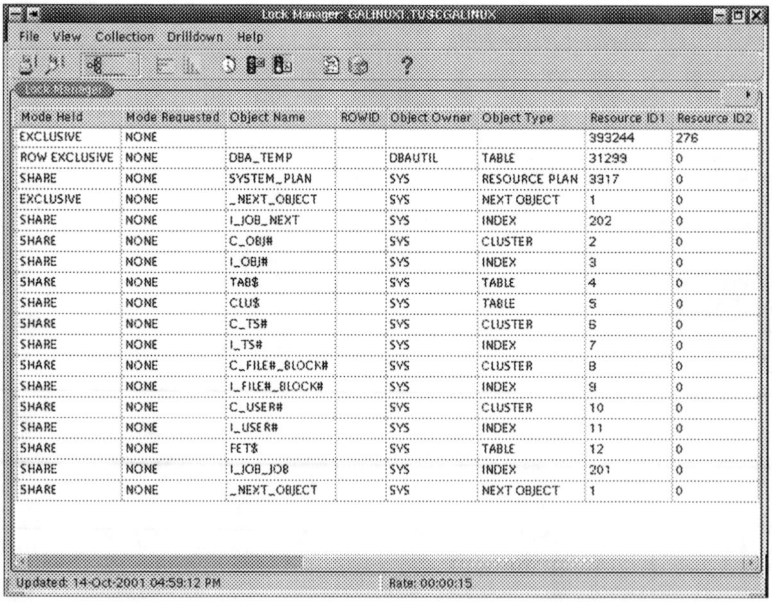

Mode Held	Mode Requested	Object Name	ROWID	Object Owner	Object Type	Resource ID1	Resource ID2
EXCLUSIVE	NONE					393244	276
ROW EXCLUSIVE	NONE	DBA_TEMP		DBAUTIL	TABLE	31299	0
SHARE	NONE	SYSTEM_PLAN		SYS	RESOURCE PLAN	3317	0
EXCLUSIVE	NONE	_NEXT_OBJECT		SYS	NEXT OBJECT	1	0
SHARE	NONE	I_JOB_NEXT		SYS	INDEX	202	0
SHARE	NONE	C_OBJ#		SYS	CLUSTER	2	0
SHARE	NONE	I_OBJ#		SYS	INDEX	3	0
SHARE	NONE	TAB$		SYS	TABLE	4	0
SHARE	NONE	CLU$		SYS	TABLE	5	0
SHARE	NONE	C_TS#		SYS	CLUSTER	6	0
SHARE	NONE	I_TS#		SYS	INDEX	7	0
SHARE	NONE	C_FILE#_BLOCK#		SYS	CLUSTER	8	0
SHARE	NONE	I_FILE#_BLOCK#		SYS	INDEX	9	0
SHARE	NONE	C_USER#		SYS	CLUSTER	10	0
SHARE	NONE	I_USER#		SYS	INDEX	11	0
SHARE	NONE	FET$		SYS	TABLE	12	0
SHARE	NONE	I_JOB_JOB		SYS	INDEX	201	0
SHARE	NONE	_NEXT_OBJECT		SYS	NEXT OBJECT	1	0

Updated: 14-Oct-2001 04:59:12 PM   Rate: 00:00:15

FIGURE 11.8   OEM Lock Manager screen.

Monitoring Sessions Waiting for Locks

If you run the catblock.sql script, which is located in the $ORACLE_HOME/rdbms.
admin directory on UNIX or Linux, you will have access to the dba_waiters view. The
dba_waiters view gives information on sessions waiting for locks held by other sessions.
By joining v$session with dba_waiters, you can obtain detailed information about the
locks and sessions that are waiting. A report on this information is shown in Source
11.35.

Source 11.35   Script to report sessions waiting for locks.

```
rem NAME: waiters.sql
rem FUNCTION: Report on sessions waiting for locks
rem HISTORY: MRA 1/12/96 Creation
rem          MRA 10/14/01 Updated for Oracle9i
rem
COLUMN busername         FORMAT a10      HEADING 'Holding|User'
COLUMN wusername         FORMAT a10      HEADING 'Waiting|User'
COLUMN bsession_id                       HEADING 'Holding|SID'
COLUMN wsession_id                       HEADING 'Waiting|SID'
COLUMN mode_held         FORMAT a10      HEADING 'Mode|Held'
COLUMN mode_requested    FORMAT 999999   HEADING 'Mode|Requested'
COLUMN lock_id1          FORMAT 999999   HEADING 'Lock|ID1'
COLUMN lock_id2          FORMAT a15      HEADING 'Lock|ID2'
COLUMN type                              HEADING 'Lock|Type'
SET LINES 132 PAGES 59 FEEDBACK OFF ECHO OFF
START title132 'Processes Waiting on Locks Report'
SPOOL rep_out/&db/waiters
SELECT
     holding_session bsession_id,
     waiting_session wsession_id,
     b.username busername,
     a.username wusername,
     c.lock_type type,
     mode_held, mode_requested,
     lock_id1, lock_id2
FROM
     sys.v_$session b,
     sys.dba_waiters c,
     sys.v_$session a
WHERE
     c.holding_session=b.sid and
     c.waiting_session=a.sid
/
SPOOL OFF
PAUSE press Enter to continue
CLEAR COLUMNS
SET LINES 80 PAGES 22 FEEDBACK ON
TTITLE OFF
```

In the script in Source 11.35, the lock_id1 and lock_id2 columns map into the object upon which the lock is being held. An example of the report in Source 11.35 output is shown in Listing 11.30.

Listing 11.30   Example waiters report output.

```
Date: 10/14/01                                                          Page:   1
Time: 05:11 PM                  Processes Waiting on Locks Report        SYS
                                      galinux1 database


   Holding    Waiting Holding    Waiting    Lock            Mode       Mode         Lock    Lock
       SID        SID User        User       Type            Held       Requested    ID1     ID2
---------  --------- ----------  ----------  --------------- ----------  ----------  ------- -------
        7         14 DBAUTIL      SYSTEM      Transaction     Exclusive  Exclusive    65580     279
press Enter to continue
```

Monitoring Sessions Causing Blocked Locks

Again, the catblock.sql script must be run in order to create the dba_blockers view. The dba_blockers view indicates all sessions that are currently causing blocks that aren't blocked themselves. Source 11.35 looks at the other side of the coin: it reports on the sessions that are causing blocks by joining against v$session and dba_locks. Example output from Source 11.35 is shown in Listing 11.31.

Source 11.36   Example of script to generate a report of sessions causing blocks.

```
rem NAME: blockers.sql
rem FUNCTION: Show all processes causing a dead lock
rem HISTORY: MRA 1/15/96 Created
rem          MRA 5/21/99 dba_locks becomes dba_lock in 8.1.5
rem          MRA 10/14/01 Verified for oracle9i
rem
COLUMN username          FORMAT a10      HEADING 'Holding|User'
COLUMN session_id                        HEADING 'SID'
COLUMN mode_held         FORMAT a10      HEADING 'Mode|Held'
COLUMN mode_requested    FORMAT a10      HEADING 'Mode|Requested'
COLUMN lock_id1          FORMAT a10      HEADING 'Lock|ID1'
COLUMN lock_id2          FORMAT a10      HEADING 'Lock|ID2'
COLUMN type                              HEADING 'Lock|Type'
SET LINES 132 PAGES 59 FEEDBACK OFF ECHO OFF
START title132 'Sessions Blocking Other Sessions Report'
SPOOL rep_out\&db\blockers
SELECT
     a.session_id, username,type,mode_held,mode_requested,
     lock_id1,lock_id2
```

```
FROM
    sys.v_$session b,
    sys.dba_blockers c,
    sys.dba_lock a
WHERE
    c.holding_session=a.session_id AND
    c.holding_session=b.sid
/
SPOOL OFF
PAUSE press Enter to continue
CLEAR COLUMNS
SET LINES 80 PAGES 22 FEEDBACK ON
```

Listing 11.31   Example blockers report.

```
Date: 10/14/01                                        Page:    1
Time: 05:16 PM     Sessions Blocking Other Sessions Report     SYS
                        galinux1 database

          Holding    Lock       Mode       Mode       Lock     Lock
      SID User       Type       Held       Requested  ID1      ID2
--------- ---------- ---------- ---------- ---------- ---------- -----
        7 DBAUTIL    USER       Row-S (SS) None       31299     0
        7 DBAUTIL    USER       Exclusive  None       65580     279
```

Monitoring DDL and DML Locks

The other aspects of locks are the Data Definition (DDL) and Data Manipulation (DML) locks. The views DBA_DML_LOCKS and DBA_DDL_LOCKS are both created by the catblock.sql script and are used to monitor DML and DDL locks. Let's look at two scripts (Sources 11.37 and 11.38) that report on DDL and DML locks, respectively.

Source 11.37   Example of script to report on Data Definition locks.

```
rem Name: ddl_lock.sql
rem Function: Document DDL Locks currently in use
rem History: MRA 1/15/97 Creation
rem          MRA 5/21/99 Reformat, verify for 8i
rem
COLUMN owner            FORMAT a7    HEADING 'User'
COLUMN session_id       FORMAT 9999  HEADING 'SID'
COLUMN mode_held        FORMAT a7    HEADING 'Lock|Mode|Held'
COLUMN mode_requested   FORMAT a7    HEADING 'Lock|Mode|Request'
COLUMN type             FORMAT a20   HEADING 'Type|Object'
COLUMN name             FORMAT a21   HEADING 'Object|Name'
```

continues

Source 11.37 Continued.

```
SET FEEDBACK OFF ECHO OFF PAGES 48 LINES 79
START title80 'Report on All DDL Locks Held'
SPOOL rep_out\&db\ddl_lock
SELECT
     NVL(owner,'SYS') owner, session_id,name,type,
    mode_held,       mode_requested
FROM
    sys.dba_ddl_locks
ORDER BY 1,2,3
/
SPOOL OFF
PAUSE press Enter/return to continue
CLEAR COLUMNS
SET FEEDBACK ON PAGES 22 LINES 80
TTITLE OFF
```

Listing 11.32 Example of output from the DDL_LOCK report.

```
Date: 10/14/01                                              Page:   1
Time: 05:24 PM            Report on All DDL Locks Held       SYS
                              galinux1 databa


                                                     Lock    Lock
                    Object                           Mode    Mode
User        SID Name                Type             Held    Request
                                    Object
-------     ----- ------------------- -------------------- ------- -------
SYS          11 DBMS_SESSION        Body             Null    None
SYS          11 DBMS_STANDARD       Table/Procedure/Type Null    None
SYS          12 DATABASE            18               Null    None
SYS          12 DBMS_SESSION        Table/Procedure/Type Null    None
SYS          12 DBMS_SESSION        Body             Null    None
SYS          12 DBMS_STANDARD       Table/Procedure/Type Null    None
SYS          13 DATABASE            18               Null    None
SYS          13 DBMS_SESSION        Table/Procedure/Type Null    None
SYS          13 DBMS_SESSION        Body             Null    None
SYS          13 DBMS_STANDARD       Table/Procedure/Type Null    None
SYS          14 DATABASE            18               Null    None
SYS          14 DBMS_APPLICATION_INFO Body           Null    None
SYS          14 DBMS_APPLICATION_INFO Table/Procedure/Type Null    None
SYS          14 DBMS_SESSION        Table/Procedure/Type Null    None
SYS          14 DBMS_SESSION        Body             Null    None
SYS          14 DBMS_STANDARD       Table/Procedure/Type Null    None
SYSTEM        8 SYSTEM              18               Null    None
SYSTEM       11 SYSTEM              18               Null    None
SYSTEM       12 SYSTEM              18               Null    None
SYSTEM       13 SYSTEM              18               Null    None
SYSTEM       14 SYSTEM              18               Null    None
press Enter/return to continue
```

Source 11.38   Script to report DML locks.

```
rem NAME: dml_lock.sql
rem FUNCTION: Document DML locks currently in use
rem HISTORY: MRA 1/15/96 Creation
rem         MRA 5/22/99 Verfied for 8i
rem         MRA 10/14/01 Updated for 9i
rem
COLUMN owner            FORMAT a8       HEADING 'User'
COLUMN session_id                       HEADING 'SID'
COLUMN mode_held        FORMAT a10      HEADING 'Mode|Held'
COLUMN mode_requested   FORMAT a10      HEADING 'Mode|Requested'
SET FEEDBACK OFF ECHO OFF PAGES 59 LINES 80
START title80 'Report on All DML Locks Held'
SPOOL rep_out\&db\dml_lock
SELECT
     NVL(owner,'SYS') owner, session_id, name,
     mode_held, mode_requested
FROM
     sys.dba_dml_locks
ORDER BY 2
/
SPOOL OFF
PAUSE press Enter to continue
CLEAR COLUMNS
SET FEEDBACK ON PAGES 22 LINES 80
TTITLE OFF
```

When contention is suspected, a quick look at these DDL and DML reports can tell the DBA if a session is holding a lock on the table or object involved. A word of caution is in order here, however: Because these reports contain volatile information, they are useful only for pinpoint monitoring (i.e., when there is a problem).

Monitoring Internal Locks

The last type of lock we will look at is the *internal* lock (see Source 11.39). Internal locks are generated by the database's internal processes. The dba_internal_locks view is created by the catblock.sql script.

Source 11.39   Example of script to document internal locks currently held.

```
rem NAME: int_lock.sql
rem FUNCTION: Document current internal locks
rem HISTORY: MRA 1/15/96 Creation
rem
COLUMN username         FORMAT a10      HEADING 'Lock|Holder'
```

continues

Source 11.39   Continued.

```
COLUMN session_id                          HEADING 'User|SID'
COLUMN lock_type          FORMAT a27       HEADING 'Lock Type'
COLUMN mode_held          FORMAT a10       HEADING 'Mode|Held'
COLUMN mode_requested     FORMAT a10       HEADING 'Mode|Requested'
COLUMN lock_id1           FORMAT a30       HEADING 'Lock/Cursor|ID1'
COLUMN lock_id2           FORMAT a10       HEADING 'Lock|ID2'
PROMPT 'ALL is all types or modes'
ACCEPT lock PROMPT 'Enter Desired Lock Type: '
ACCEPT mode PROMPT 'Enter Lock Mode: '
SET LINES 132 PAGES 59 FEEDBACK OFF ECHO OFF VERIFY OFF
BREAK ON username
START title132 'Report on Internal Locks Mode: &mode Type: &lock'
SPOOL rep_out\&db\int_locks
SELECT
     NVL(b.username,'SYS') username,
     session_id,lock_type,mode_held,
     mode_requested,lock_id1,lock_id2
FROM
     sys.dba_lock_internal a, sys.v_$session b
WHERE
     UPPER(mode_held) like UPPER('%&mode%') OR
     UPPER('&mode')='ALL' AND
     UPPER(lock_type) like UPPER('%&lock%') OR
     UPPER(mode_held) like UPPER('%&mode%') OR
     UPPER('&mode')='ALL' AND
     UPPER('&lock')='ALL' AND
     a.session_id=b.sid
ORDER BY 1,2
/
SPOOL OFF
PAUSE press Enter to continue
SET LINES 80 PAGES 22 FEEDBACK ON VERIFY ON
CLEAR COLUMNS
CLEAR BREAKS
UNDEF LOCK
UNDEF MODE
```

A caution is in order here, too: The report in Source 11.39 can run to several pages in an idle instance. An excerpt from the report is shown in Listing 11.33.

Listing 11.33   Example internal lock report output.

```
Date: 10/14/01                                                          Page:   1
Time: 05:30 PM              Report on Internal Locks Mode: ALL Type: ALL      SYS
                                  galinux1 database
```

```
Lock      User                            Mode     Mode       Lock/Cursor                     Lock
Holder    SID Lock Type                   Held     Requested  ID1                             ID2
--------  ----- --------------------      -------- ---------- ------------------------------  ----------
DBAUTIL     7 Cursor Definition Pin       Share    None       table_1_0_139_0_0_              57BFE99C
            7 Cursor Definition Lock      Null     None       table_1_0_139_0_0_              57BFE99C
            7 Cursor Definition Lock      Null     None       SELECT ATTRIBUTE    FROM V$CONT 57B96CF0
                                                              EXT  WHERE NAMESPACE = 'LBAC$L
                                                              ABELS'

            7 Cursor Definition Lock      Null     None       SELECT POL#,PACKAGE   FROM LBA 57B7E728
                                                              C$POL  WHERE BITAND(FLAGS,1) =
                                                              1 ORDER BY PACKAGE

            7 Cursor Definition Lock      Null     None       commit                          57B5ABC0
            7 Cursor Definition Lock      Null     None       SELECT POL#,PACKAGE   FROM LBA 57B96EE4
                                                              C$POL  WHERE BITAND(FLAGS,1) =
                                                              1 ORDER BY PACKAGE

            7 Body Definition Lock        Null     None       SYS.DBMS_SESSION                57B879E8
            7 Body Definition Lock        Null     None       LBACSYS.LBAC_CACHE              57BA1D8C
            7 Cursor Definition Lock      Null     None       SELECT MAX(TAG#)    FROM LBAC$L 57B7C03B
                                                              AB

            7 Cursor Definition Lock      Null     None       select pol#, usr_name, usr_lab 57B91108
                                                              els, package, privs from lbac$
                                                              user_logon where usr_name = :u
                                                              sername
```

11.9 MONITORING EVENTS

As you know, Oracle is an event-driven system. Sessions wait for calls; locks and latches spin; processes wake up and go back to sleep—all based on events. The V$SESSION_ EVENT DPT tracks all current events by session. The report in Source 11.40 will generate a report on current events (Oracle-wise anyway). An example of the event report is shown in Listing 11.34.

Source 11.40   Script to generate an event report.

```
rem
rem FUNCTION: Generate a report on session events by user
rem
rem NAME:events.sql
rem HISTORY: MRA 6/15/97 Created
rem          MRA 5/22/99 Verified on 8i
rem
```

continues

Source 11.40   Continued.

```
COLUMN sid                      HEADING Sid
COLUMN event                    HEADING Event              FORMAT a40
COLUMN total_waits              HEADING Total|Waits
COLUMN total_timeouts           HEADING Total|Timeouts
COLUMN time_waited              HEADING Time|Waited
COLUMN average_wait             HEADING Average|Wait
COLUMN username                 HEADING User
BREAK ON username
START title132 "Session Events By User"
SPOOL rep_out\&db\events
SET LINES 132 PAGES 59 VERIFY OFF FEEDBACK OFF
SELECT
    username, event,total_waits,total_timeouts,
    time_waited,average_wait
FROM
    sys.v_$session_event a,
    sys.v_$session b
WHERE
    a.sid= b.sid
ORDER BY 1;
SPOOL OFF
PAUSE Press Enter to continue
CLEAR COLUMNS
CLEAR BREAKS
SET LINES 80 PAGES 22 VERIFY ON FEEDBACK ON
TTITLE OFF
```

Listing 11.34   Example of output from the session events report.

```
Date: 10/14/01                                               Page:   1
Time: 05:37 PM                Session Events By User          SYS
                                galinux1 database


                                   Total     Total      Time   Average
User        Event                  Waits  Timeouts    Waited      Wait
----------  ----------------------------- --------- --------- ---------
SYSTEM      enqueue                  149       149     44425       298
            control file sequential read    214       0        14         0
            log file sync             61         0        65         1
            SQL*Net message to client        462       0         1         0
            single-task message        2         0         5         2
            SQL*Net break/reset to client    4         0         0         0
            SQL*Net message from client      800       0    735778       920
            SQL*Net message to client         19       0         0         0
            db file sequential read        24987       0     10986         0
            db file sequential read           16       0        10         1
            pmon timer            167133    167130  49031711       293
            rdbms ipc message     163764    163681  49050112       300
```

```
control file sequential read       20        0        2        0
control file parallel write    163663        0    75411        0
direct path read                   14        0        0        0
db file parallel write           3300     3300        8        0
db file scattered read            596        0      750        1
db file sequential read           248        0      232        1
log file parallel write          3760        0     1168        0
log file single write               4        0        0        0
log file sequential read            4        0        2        1
library cache load lock             1        1      299      299
smon timer                       1640     1634 47313312    28850
direct path write                  12        0        0        0
direct path read                   14        0        0        0
control file parallel write         8        0        4        0
control file sequential read    49110        0     1069        0
async disk IO                       1        0        0        0
rdbms ipc message              166085   163858 49051891      295
Press Enter to continue
```

Workspaces in Oracle9*i*

Orcacle9*i* introduced the concept of a database *workspace*. A workspace is an environment for a long-term transaction that allows versioning of objects. A workspace can be shared among multiple users. The concept of workspace management involves a series of short transactions and multiple data versions to implement a complete long-transaction event that maintains atomicity and concurrency.

The Workspace Manager (WKS) is installed by default in all seed and DBCA databases. (If you need it in a manually created database you must install it according with the installation guide in the Oracle9*i Application Developers Guide—Workspace Manager*, Release 1 9.0.1, PART# A88806-01, Oracle Corporation, June 2001.)

Workspaces are monitored using the DBA_ view cluster associated with workspaces shown in Figure 11.9. OEM also provides a Workspace Manager interface accessible from the database listing of the main GUI.

An example report to show workspace status is shown in Source 11.41. An example of the workspace status script output is shown in Listing 11.35.

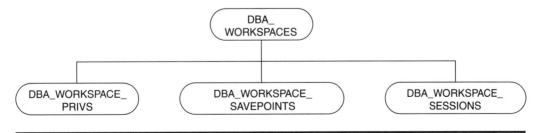

FIGURE 11.9   DBA_ view cluster for workspaces.

Source 11.41   Example workspace status script.

```
rem workspace_status.sql
rem Function: Show status of workspaces in database
rem
rem History: MRA 10/14/2001 Initial Creation
rem
COLUMN WORKSPACE FORMAT a10 HEADING 'Workspace'
COLUMN owner FORMAT a10 HEADING 'Owner'
COLUMN freeze_status FORMAT a8 HEADING 'Freeze|Status'
COLUMN resolve_status FORMAT a8 HEADING 'Resolve|Status'
COLUMN parent_workspace FORMAT a10 HEADING 'Parent|Workspace'
COLUMN freeze_mode FORMAT a8 HEADING 'Freeze|Mode'
start title80 'Workspace Status'
spool rep_out\&db\workspace_status
select
  workspace,
  NVL(parent_workspace,'NONE') parent_workspace,
  owner,
  freeze_status,
  NVL(freeze_mode,'NONE') freeze_mode,
  resolve_status
from
  dba_workspaces
/
spool off
ttitle off
```

Listing 11.35   Example output from workspace status report.

```
Date: 10/14/01                                            Page:    1
Time: 06:25 PM               Workspace Status             SYS
                             galinux1 databa


            Parent               Freeze   Freeze  Resolve
Workspace   Workspace   Owner    Status   Mode    Status
----------  ----------  -------- -------- ------- --------
LIVE        NONE        SYS      UNFROZEN NONE    INACTIVE
```

Other items, such as workspace privileges and savepoints, can also be monitored using the DBA_ series of views.

11.10 MONITORING OTHER DATABASE OBJECTS

Generally speaking, the "other" database objects consist of stored objects such as packages, procedures, and functions. About the only thing for which these stored objects can be monitored (other than tuning stats, which we cover in the next chapter) is status, that is, whether they are either valid or invalid.

Monitoring for Invalid Objects

The script in Source 11.42 generates a listing of invalid database objects. If the object is valid, you don't need to monitor it! Sample output from the object-monitoring script is shown in Listing 11.36.

Source 11.42   Example of script to report object status.

```
rem Name: inv_obj.sql
rem Purpose: Show all invalid objects in database
rem Mike Ault 7/2/96
rem Mike Ault 10/14/01 verified for Oracle9i
rem
COLUMN object_name       FORMAT A20        HEADING 'Object|Name'
COLUMN owner             FORMAT a10        HEADING 'Object|Owner'
COLUMN last_time         FORMAT a18        HEADING 'Last Change|Date'
COLUMN object_type       FORMAT a15        Heading 'Object|Type'
SET LINES 80 FEEDBACK OFF PAGES 0 VERIFY OFF
START title80 'Invalid Database Objects'
SPOOL rep_out/&db/inv_obj
SELECT
    owner,
    object_name,
    object_type,
    TO_CHAR(last_ddl_time,'DD-MON-YY hh:mi:ss') Last_time
FROM
    dba_objects
WHERE
    status='INVALID'
/
PAUSE Press Enter to continue
SET LINES 80 FEEDBACK ON PAGES 22 VERIFY ON
CLEAR COLUMNS
TTITLE OFF
```

Listing 11.36   Example of output from invalid objects script.

```
Date: 10/14/01                                      Page:    1
Time: 06:39 PM           Invalid Database Objects          SYS
                            galinux1 databa


Object      Object               Object          Last Change
Owner       Name                 Type            Date
---------   ------------------   --------------  ------------------
SYS         RECREATE_DB          PROCEDURE       23-AUG-01 01:40:59
WKSYS       WK_CRW               PACKAGE BODY    06-JUN-01 12:54:24
Press Enter to continue
```

If your search reveals that you have invalid objects, then a script similar to that in Source 11.43 can be executed to recompile the objects. The utlrp.sql script, found in the $ORACLE_HOME/rdbms/admin directory, can be used to recompile all invalid PL/SQL objects at any time; there is also the dbms_utility.compile_schema procedure.

Source 11.43   Example of dynamic SQL script to recompile invalid objects.

```
rem Name: com_proc.sql
rem Function: Create a compile list for invalid procedures
rem
rem MRA 5/1/96
rem
DEFINE cr='chr(10)'
SET HEADING OFF PAGES 0 ECHO OFF TERMOUT OFF FEEDBACK OFF VERIFY OFF
SPOOL recompile.sql
SELECT 'ALTER '||object_type||' '||object_name||' COMPILE;'||&&cr||
'SHOW ERROR'
FROM dba_objects WHERE status='INVALID'
/
SPOOL OFF
SET HEADING ON TERMOUT ON FEEDBACK ON VERIFY ON
UNDEF cr
```

11.11 MONITORING MULTIPLE DATABASES

Frequently today, DBAs are called upon to manage multiple instances. In this era of corporate downsizing, what was a manageable job a few years ago has rapidly descended into the chaos of a *Doom* episode gone wrong, as more responsibility is being placed on fewer and fewer people. Thus, it's imperative for DBAs to automate the management of multiple databases, especially if they are physically remote.

To this end, a DBA has several options. If your budget permits (the tools seem to get more expensive as the hardware decreases in cost), purchase a good monitoring tool, such as Patrol by BMC, or Eco-Tools, as well as a "point-and-shoot" monitor, such as Q by Savant Corporation, Platinum Technologies' offerings, or any of the plethora of new tools that seem to spring up each year. If the budget is not there for purchasing tools or, like me, you are a bit of a masochist, you may want to develop your own tools based on the scripts in this book.

To develop your own tools, you must first decide what you want to monitor. Once you have, in a central monitoring database, design and install a small set of database tables to store the data, with an identifier and date stamp for each entry. On each of the remote databases, establish a monitoring user that has select privileges against all required tables. Next, establish a database link from the remote databases to the central monitoring instance. On the central monitoring instance, establish a set of monitoring users with a set of synonyms that point to the remote database tables. Finally, set up a group of monitoring jobs that execute the monitoring scripts via the database links and synonyms against the remote databases, and store the results in the results tables. Once the tables are loaded, you can report against them. Procedurized, the steps are:

1. Establish a user on the remote database that has select privilege on the DBA and V$ views and tables you want to monitor.
2. On the central or monitoring database, establish a corresponding monitoring user that has a database link to the remote database monitoring user.
3. Create synonyms that hide the required database link syntax for a select from the monitoring remote user; for example:

```
CREATE SYNONYM galinux_sessions FOR v$session@galinux;
```

4. Once the synonyms are in place in the monitoring database, create a central repository user that can be used to store statistics (this will depend on what you want to trend; look at the DBA_RUNNING_STATS definition in the DBA_UTILITIES zip file on the Wiley Web site).
5. Use procedures to collect and store information in the central repository for each monitored instance.
6. Generate reports from of the central repository.

The Oracle Enterprise Manager enables remote monitoring for multiple instances.

11.12 SUMMARY

This chapter examined how to monitor users and other objects in the Oracle database. Scripts with example output and monitoring tips were included.

CHAPTER **12**

Oracle Tuning

This chapter and Chapter 13 address Oracle tuning. If you are this far into the book, you are already aware of the structure of Oracle, and you have some idea of the complexities of object creation and monitoring, and probably know what a SQL statement looks like. Now it's time to make Oracle perform.

NOTE   In the previous editions of this book, this chapter was called "Oracle Application Tuning," but now that Oracle Applications have taken on a life of their own, I didn't want to mislead anyone into thinking that this chapter would deal with the Oracle Applications products and how to tune them. While many of the techniques presented in this chapter can be applied to any application, the chapter is not about Oracle Applications tuning.

12.1 ORACLE CORPORATION ON TUNING

To accompany recent releases, Oracle Corporation has completely rewritten its tuning manuals. In fact, Oracle has removed the word "tuning" from its manual titles, which are now called *Oracle9i Performance Guide and Reference* and *Oracle9i Performance Methods*. The Oracle Corporation method has been well thought out and makes sense when you have the time to devote to using it properly. However, often, DBAs don't have the time to utilize a lengthy or vigorous methodology, and instead have to resort to what I refer to as "guerrilla tuning," which hits the high points and moves on to the next engagement. If you have time to use Oracle methodology, do so; as I said, it has been well thought out. In any case, I suggest that all Oracle DBAs read the Oracle performance manuals, as they contain good information for tuning databases. The following is quoted directly from the Oracle performance manuals:

Oracle has come up with an eight-step tuning methodology:

1. **Get candid feedback from users.** Determine the performance project's scope and subsequent performance goals, as well as performance goals for the future. This process is key in future capacity planning.
2. **Get a full set of operating system, database, and application statistics** from the system when the performance is both good and bad. If these are not available, then get whatever is available. Missing statistics are analogous to missing evidence at a crime scene: They make detectives work harder and [the process] is more time-consuming.
3. **Sanity-check the operating systems of all machines** involved with user performance. By sanity-checking the operating system, you look for hardware or operating system resources that are fully utilized. List any overused resources as symptoms for analysis later. In addition, check that all hardware shows no errors or diagnostics.
4. **Check for the top 10 most common mistakes with Oracle** [listed below], and determine if any of these are likely to be the problem. List these as symptoms for analysis later. These are included because they represent the most likely problems.
5. **Build a conceptual model of what is happening on the system** using the symptoms as clues to understand what caused the performance problems.
6. **Propose a series of remedy actions and the anticipated behavior to the system,** and apply them in the order that can benefit the application the most. A golden rule in performance work is that you change only one thing at a time and then measure the differences. Unfortunately, system downtime requirements might prohibit such a rigorous investigation method. If multiple changes are applied at the same time, then try to ensure that they are isolated.
7. **Validate that the changes made have had the desired effect,** and see if the user's perception of performance has improved. Otherwise, look for more bottlenecks, and continue refining the conceptual model until your understanding of the application becomes more accurate.
8. **Repeat the last three steps** until performance goals are met or become impossible due to other constraints.

Additional wisdom from the Oracle manuals comes in the form of a top-10 list of user and designer errors, which are:

1. *Bad connection management.* The application connects and disconnects for each database interaction. This problem is common with stateless middleware in application servers. It has over two orders of magnitude impact on performance, and it is

totally unscalable. This may involve tuning the Apache Web Server. On many platforms, I have seen the keepalive functionality, which is turned on by Apache, choke a system to death with unused processes (usually found in the FIN_WAIT2 state). You may also need to tune the TCP process on the server to reduce its keepalive settings. On many servers, the keepalive is set at two hours; the keepalive settings determine the buildup and die off rates. If your buildup rate for connections exceeds the die-off rate, you will choke the system on processes..

2. *Bad use of cursors and the shared pool.* Not using cursors results in repeated parses. If bind variables are not used, then there is hard parsing of all SQL statements. This has an order of magnitude impact in performance, and it is totally unscalable. Use cursors with bind variables that open the cursor, and reexecute it many times. Be suspicious of applications that generate dynamic SQL. Oracle tests revealed the levels of users that were capable of being supported based on parsing; these results are shown in Table 12.1.

3. *Getting database I/O wrong.* Many sites lay out their databases poorly over the available disks. Other sites specify the number of disks incorrectly, because they configure disks by disk space and not I/O bandwidth. Be wary of SAME configurations (stripe and mirror everything); pieces of every single file can get placed on every single disk. In a situation where a single file is read at one time, a SAME configuration can show significant advantages. However, in Oracle, dozens of files are accessed simultaneously by many processes on behalf of many users, and this leads to instant I/O contention in a SAME configuration.

4. *Redo log setup problems.* Many sites run with too few redo logs that are too small. Small redo logs cause system checkpoints to continuously put a heavy load on the buffer cache and I/O system. If there are too few redo logs, then the archive cannot keep up, and the database will wait for the archive process to catch up. Check the alert log for messages concerning archive waits and log problems.

5. *Serialization of data blocks in the buffer cache due to lack of freelists, freelist groups, transaction slots (INITRANS); or shortage of rollback segments.* This is particularly common on INSERT-heavy applications, in applications that have raised the blocksize to 8K or 16K, or in applications with large numbers of active users and few rollback segments. Set INITRANS to the number of expected simultaneous accesses to

TABLE 12.1   User Load Based on Parsing

Test	Number of Users Supported
No parsing all statements	270
Soft parsing all statements	150
Hard parsing all statements	60
Reconnecting for each transaction	30

a block, and set freelists to the number of expected simultaneous inserts. There should be one rollback extent for each concurrent DML transaction, I don't believe in sharing rollback segments; one segment per each DML transaction can be achieved in most databases. If you must share rollback segments, limit the number of transactions per rollback segment to no more than four.

6. *Long full table scans.* Long full table scans for high-volume or interactive online operations could indicate poor transaction design, missing indexes, or poor SQL optimization. Long table scans, by nature, are I/O-intensive and unscalable. Remember that any form of disk I/O is by nature magnitudes of time slower than memory access.

7. *In-disk sorting.* In-disk sorts for online operations could indicate poor transaction design, missing indexes, or poor SQL optimization. Disk sorts, by nature, are I/O-intensive and unscalable. Consider adding solid-state disks for sorting.

8. *High amounts of recursive (SYS) SQL.* Large amounts of recursive SQL executed by SYS user could indicate space management activities, such as extent allocations, taking place. This is unscalable and impacts user response time. Recursive SQL executed under another user ID is probably SQL and PL/SQL, and this is not a problem. Ensure the use of local extent management whenever possible and that indexes and tables are correctly sized and placed.

9. *Schema errors and optimizer problems.* In many cases, an application uses too many resources because the schema owning the tables has not been successfully migrated from the development environment or from an older implementation. Examples of this are missing indexes or incorrect statistics. These errors can lead to suboptimal execution plans and poor interactive user performance. When migrating applications of known performance, export the schema statistics to maintain plan stability using the DBMS_STATS package.

   Likewise, optimizer parameters set in the initialization parameter file can override proven optimal execution plans. For these reasons, schemas, schema statistics, and optimizer settings should be managed together as a group to ensure consistency of performance.

   An example of a change of execution plans due to change in initialization parameters is in the porting of Oracle8*i* to Oracle9*i*: the _expand_subquery undocumented initialization parameter is changed from a value of FALSE in Oracle8*i* to a value of TRUE in Oracle9*i* by default. This has a negative effect on almost all queries using subqueries and should be set back to TRUE to get proper behavior.

10. *Use of nonstandard initialization parameters.* These might have been implemented based on poor advice or incorrect assumptions. In particular, parameters associated with spin_count on latches and undocumented optimizer features can cause a number of problems that can require considerable investigation. Initialization parameters should be one of your first investigation points; question any that are usually not used. Be aware that the undocumented parameter _unnest_subquery may be set explicitly to FALSE to overcome certain anomalies that occur when it is set to TRUE (as it is by default in Oracle9*i*).

Of these 10 mistakes, the following four are the most likely to occur at many sites:

- Bad use of cursors and the shared pool
- Long full table scans
- In-disk sorting
- Schema errors and optimizer problems

Usually, the shared pool is the most overlooked area of tuning. Many DBAs fall prey to the old-DBA adage that says, to tune the shared pool, just add more to it. But especially in releases prior to Oracle9*i,* adding space to the shared pool beyond 50 to 100 megabytes in excess of pinned objects will result in a net performance decrease. Though Oracle9*i* has improved the performance of the shared pool, oversizing or undersizing the shared pool can still have an impact on performance.

Long full table scans are done from disk; any disk I/O is going to be up to 14,000 times slower than memory access. Proper use of indexes, especially the function-based index and bitmap-join index will greatly reduce the need for full table scans. Where full table scans are a requirement, consider using partitions and parallel query to reduce scan times.

For the same reason that long full table scans cause performance degradation, any form of disk-based sort or hash activity will slow a statement to a crawl. For statements where you know that sorting or hash activity will result in large sort and hash area requirements, consider adding logic to increase the sessions sort area size parameter.

Schema errors and optimizer problems are generally the result of poor design or poor maintenance. Insufficient or bad indexes, or indexes and tables that are the result of insufficient design or maintenance effort, will result in poor performance. Rebuilding indexes that undergo frequent update and delete/insert activity is a must for any database, and should be a regularly scheduled maintenance activity. Fortunately, in Oracle8*i* and Oracle9*i,* rebuilding indexes is not nearly as painful as it was in previous releases, if the activity is scheduled for a nonbusy time; and index rebuilds can be done concurrently with processing. Essentially, any index that shows a deleted leaf node ratio of 10 percent or higher (I coined the term *browning* for this), or any index where the clustering factor exceeds the count of used blocks in the source table by a large ratio (I can't get more specific, as this is very table- and application-specific) should be rebuilt.

I also advise you to implement the Oracle Emergency Performance method. It proceeds as follows:

1. Survey the performance problem and collect the symptoms of the performance problem. This process should include the following:

   - User feedback on how the system is underperforming. Is the problem throughput or response time? To this I add, check the Oracle alert and trace logs, and verify disk space.
   - Ask the question, "What has changed since we last had good performance?" The answer can give clues to the problem; that said, getting unbiased answers

in an escalated situation can be difficult. Obtain any performance data that may be available from before the performance went bad.

- Don't immediately begin chasing symptoms; find the root cause and correct that.

2. Sanity-check the hardware utilization of all components of the application system. Check the point of highest CPU utilization, and check the disk, memory usage, and network performance on all the system components. This quick process identifies which tier is causing the problem. If the problem is in the application, then shift analysis to application debugging. Otherwise, move on to database server analysis. (For example: On one system we were moving from a four-CPU system to an eight-CPU system with disk farms that were essentially identical: performance decreased by 30 percent. Upon investigation, we found I/O waits were the culprit. There was a software resettable option on the disk hardware to enable fast read-ahead buffering, and it had not been switched on for the new system.)

3. Determine if the database server is constrained on CPU or if it is spending time waiting on wait events. If the database server is CPU-constrained, investigate the following:

- Sessions that are consuming large amounts of CPU at the operating system level. In Oracle9*i,* this can be determined by examining the V$SQLAREA view, as it contains both elapsed and CPU time.
- Sessions or statements that perform many buffer gets at the database level (check V$SESSTAT, V$SQL).
- Execution plan changes causing suboptimal SQL execution. These can be difficult to locate. Usually, the statements with the most CPU time or most disk reads will be the ones whose execution plans have changed.
- Incorrect setting of initialization parameters. Look for changes in cache area sizes (for example, a missing or extra zero on a DB_BLOCK_BUFFERS in pre-Oracle9*i,* or bad reset of the DB_CACHE_SIZE in Oracle9*i,* could result in significant reduction, or increase, in memory used by Oracle, one resulting in frequent disk reads, the other in possible swapping).
- Algorithmic issues arising as a result of code changes or upgrades of all components
- If the database sessions are waiting on events, follow the wait events listed in V$SESSION_WAIT to determine what is causing serialization. In cases of massive contention for the library cache, it might not be possible to log on or submit SQL to the database. In this case, use historical data to determine why suddenly there is contention on this latch. If most waits are for I/O, then sample the SQL being run by the sessions that are performing all of the I/Os. I would perform the V$WAITSTAT and V$SESSION_WAIT checks as soon as possible, as they will identify what Oracle is waiting on.

4. Apply emergency action to stabilize the system. This could involve actions that take parts of the application offline or restrict the workload that the system can handle. It could also involve a system restart or the termination of job in process. Of course, these have service-level implications.

5. Validate that the system is stable after making changes and restrictions. Collect a reference set of statistics for the database. Follow the rigorous performance method described earlier in this chapter to bring back all functionality and users to the system. This process may require significant application reengineering before it is complete.

12.2 THE AUTHOR ON ORACLE TUNING

I agree with much of Oracle's approach to tuning. To that approach, however, I add that there are two major items that must be present in a system before tuning can be successful:

- A proper hardware foundation
- Proper design

Any system that is on an improperly sized or configured hardware platform will not perform to its fullest capabilities. Any system that is improperly designed and implemented will not perform adequately. Thus it can be said that the first part of tuning takes place when the database is designed and the hardware against which the database will run is chosen. Therefore, it can also be said that a database administrator should be one of the first brought in on any Oracle project. And this should a *fully qualified Oracle DBA* with several years of experience.

I also suggest that, at least initially, this DBA be an experienced consultant with several successful projects under his or her belt. And I don't say that just because that is how I make my living; I say it because it will prevent lots of headaches down the road. What often happens on large projects is that a relatively inexperienced DBA will be assigned, which means he or she grows with the project, eventually becoming an expert DBA. But after the project is complete and becomes less interesting, the now-expert DBA leaves. A better idea is to bring in an expert DBA from the start; by doing so, the project gets a firm foundation to build upon, and as the project grows, the consultant can be used to transition knowledge to site DBAs. Once the project is in production, the consultant exits and the site DBAs take over. In many cases, the monitoring and maintenance of a production database can even be turned over to a remote database monitoring company, making an expensive on-site DBA unnecessary.

Unfortunately, what usually happens is that a DBA is hired well after the design phase—sometimes not until the system is going live. Thus, the DBA is handed a poorly designed and tuned system and is expected to make it perform. When he or she can't, a high-powered consultant is called in; the design, if possible, is corrected, and after spending much more money than was really required, the system is brought online in production, usually late and still not performing at an optimal level. Then, because of all the manual tweaks needed to keep the system hobbling along, it is nearly impossible to turn over monitoring to a monitoring service. The result? The need for an expensive DBA for the life of the database. This process is analogous to requiring a mechanic to ride with you in your car so he can tune the engine while you are driving down the road. If automobiles were built the same way databases usually are, we would all be walking.

So, to repeat, the first step in tuning any application is to develop a proper logical and physical design. If your design is unsound, tuning will be that much more difficult. Do not simply model an existing system or attempt to duplicate an existing process with a computerized solution. First review existing systems or processes to ascertain what is being done incorrectly and what is being done right. In my first position as an Oracle DBA, I would walk past one set of cubicles whose adjoining hallway was always lined with waist-high stacks of printouts. When I asked about the reports, I was told that people printed entire reports just to get the last page; the rest was waste. When I asked why they didn't print out only the last page, the answer was that this was the way it had always been done. That is the worst reason for doing anything. The point here is, look at the work being accomplished, review the actual needs, then make changes. Find out which reports are actually being used and which are filed circular after a cursory glance. I'm willing to bet you'll discover that half the reports generated by existing systems aren't really needed or wanted.

Always look at disk and file placement to minimize the potential for I/O contention. I already cited the problems with the SAME configuration, so I won't repeat that example here. Just because a new way of doing something is being espoused doesn't mean it is a correct means for laying out an Oracle database. I recommend that you follow Table 1.1 in Chapter 1 that shows the RAID configurations suggested by Oracle for use with various Oracle files. Don't let a system operator force you into a file system arrangement that is suboptimal; he or she won't be the one answering for poor database performance.

Always size tables and indexes, even if you are using the standard extent size model for your tablespaces. Even for locally managed tablespaces, I suggest sizing the tables and indexes so that you can place them into the correct sizing model. I have included spreadsheets on the Wiley Web site to assist you in this effort.

I also recommend that, all developers who will be writing SQL or PL/SQL be required to take an in-house, or third-party-provided, or Oracle training tuning class. The developers also should be equipped with tools that allow explain plans to be run properly; the developers should be familiar with the use of TKPROF, DBMS_PROFILER, and UTL_OUTLN, at a minimum. (Note that OEM allows some of this to be accomplished through use of GUIs.) All SQL should be submitted for review with an explain plan attached, and all PL/SQL should have an output report from DBMS_PROFILER.

Using Good Design Techniques

I've said it a number of times now: Good tuning starts with good design. And good design involves following good relational concepts during the logical design and following good physical layout rules during the physical implementation.

To achieve good logical design:

- Use business rules to establish basic entities and attributes.
- Become familiar with the reports and screens from current applications that really are used.
- Get feedback from users as well as managers. Sometimes managers don't know what their employees use to get them the data they require, although they think they do.
- Use normalization to understand relationships. When using ERDs, try to avoid crossing lines. An entity that has to constantly cross lines to establish relationships is probably not being placed logically where it should in the application.
- Denormalize to enhance performance.
- If tables will always be queried together, combine them. If tables are combined, ensure program logic handles INSERT, UPDATE, and DELETE anomalies that may occur as a result.
- Make sure that each entity has unique primary key.

To achieve good physical design:

- Ensure that all tables have a unique primary key.
- Locate all primary key indexes away from the table they index.
- Index all foreign key relationships.
- Locate all foreign key indexes away from the table they index.
- Size all tables and indexes; apply the sizing information to a standard extent model tablespace layout.
- Use OFA.
- Use locally managed tablespaces whenever possible.

Using My Sizing Spreadsheets

The sizing spreadsheets I include on the Wiley Web site are based on the sizing calculations provided in the Oracle8*i* DBA manual. (Unfortunately, Oracle does not provide sizing calculation examples in Oracle9*i*.) Use the V$TYPE_SIZE table to verify the header values for the various sizing constants before using the sheets. Also, have a good idea of the number of rows and of the values for INITRANS and PCTFREE before attempting to use the sizing estimates. The following subsections detail how to use the spreadsheets.

Using the Table-Sizing Spreadsheet   Here are the steps for using the table-sizing spreadsheet:

1. If your defaults for the basic sizing parameters are different, change the values from their default values as shown in the spreadsheet header; otherwise these are

Oracle9*i* Table Size Calculation Spread sheet										
Table:	SQL_SCRIPTS_INT									
V$TYPE_SIZE Constants:		KDBH:	14	KDBT:		4	UB1:	1	UB4:	4
	SB2:	2	KCBH:	20	UB4:	4	KTBBH:	48	KTBIT:	24
Column		Col Size	Cor Size	Date	Cor Siz	Number	Cor Siz			
		0	0	0	0	0	0			
		0	0	0	0	0	0			
		0	0	0	0	0	0			
		0	0	0	0	0	0			
		0	0	0	0	0	0			
		0	0	0	0	0	0			
		0	0	0	0	0	0			
		0	0	0	0	0	0			
		0	0	0	0	0	0			
		0	0	0	0	0	0			
		0	0	0	0	0	0			
		0	0	0	0	0	0			
		0	0	0	0	0	0			
		0	0	0	0	0	0			
		0	0	0	0	0	0			
		0	0	0	0	0	0			
		0	0	0	0	0	0			
		0	0	0	0	0	0			
	Totals:	0	0	0	0	0	0			
	ARL:	0	ERL:	0						
	DB Bk Sz:	8192		Init Trans:		Pctfree:		Tbl in Cl:		
	TBH(init)	#VALUE!			#VALUE!				1	
	DS in Bk:	#VALUE!		Init RPB:	#VALUE!		Size:	#VALUE!	#VALUE!	
	# of ROW:			Blocks:	#VALUE!					
	FFS:	#VALUE!	#VALUE!							
	V$TYPE_SIZE constant	defaults set to NT values							Not Required	
									Required	
									Calculated or Derived	

FIGURE 12.1   Table-sizing spreadsheet constants.

constants. The constants section in the table v$type_size is highlighted in Figure 12.1 at the top of the spreadsheet. Listing 12.1 is an example SELECT against the v$type_size table.

Listing 12.1   Contents of the V$TYPE_SIZE table.

```
SQL> DESC v$type_size
 Name                                    Null?     Type
 ---------------------------------------- -------- -----------------
 COMPONENT                                         VARCHAR2(8)
 TYPE                                              VARCHAR2(8)
 DESCRIPTION                                       VARCHAR2(32)
 TYPE_SIZE                                         NUMBER
```

```
SQL> SELECT component, type, description, type_size from v$type_size;

COMPONEN TYPE     DESCRIPTION                             TYPE_SIZE
-------- -------  --------------------------------------  ---------
S        EWORD    EITHER WORD                                     4
S        EB1      EITHER BYTE 1                                   1
S        EB2      EITHER BYTE 2                                   2
S        EB4      EITHER BYTE 4                                   4
S        UWORD    UNSIGNED WORD                                   4
S        UB1      UNSIGNED BYTE 1                                 1
S        UB2      UNSIGNED BYTE 2                                 2
S        UB4      UNSIGNED BYTE 4                                 4
S        SWORD    SIGNED WORD                                     4
S        SB1      SIGNED BYTE 1                                   1
S        SB2      SIGNED BYTE 2                                   2
S        SB4      SIGNED BYTE 4                                   4
S        BOOLEAN  BOOLEAN                                         4
S        FLOAT    FLOAT                                           4
S        DOUBLE   DOUBLE                                          8
S        SIZE_T   SIZE_T                                          4
S        PTR_T    PTR_T                                           4
K        KDBA     DATABASE BLOCK ADDRESS                          4
K        KTNO     TABLE NUMBER IN CLUSTER                         1
K        KSCN     SYSTEM COMMIT NUMBER                            8
K        KXID     TRANSACTION ID                                  8
K        KUBA     UNDO ADDRESS                                    8
KCB      KCBH     BLOCK COMMON HEADER                            20
KTB      KTBIT    TRANSACTION VARIABLE HEADER                   24
KTB      KTBBH    TRANSACTION FIXED HEADER                      48
KDB      KDBH     DATA HEADER                                   14
KDB      KDBT     TABLE DIRECTORY ENTRY                          4
KTE      KTECT    EXTENT CONTROL                                44
KTE      KTECH    EXTENT CONTROL                                72
KTE      KTETB    EXTENT TABLE                                   8
KTS      KTSHC    SEGMENT HEADER                                 8
KTS      KTSFS    SEGMENT FREE SPACE LIST                       20
KTU      KTUBH    UNDO HEADER                                   16
KTU      KTUXE    UNDO TRANSACTION ENTRY                        40
KTU      KTUXC    UNDO TRANSACTION CONTROL                     104
KDX      KDXCO    INDEX HEADER                                  16
KDX      KDXLE    INDEX LEAF HEADER                             32
KDX      KDXBR    INDEX BRANCH HEADER                           24

38 rows selected.
```

2. Enter the table constants that affect size, number of rows, PCTFREE, blocksize, INITRANS (if greater than 1). Enter the number of estimated rows, and, if the table is in a cluster, the number of tables in the cluster. Example values have been filled in on Figure 12.2.

Oracle9*i* Table Size Calculation Spread sheet

Table:	SQL_SCRIPTS_INT										
V$TYPE_SIZE Constants:		KDBH:	14	KDBT:	4	UB1:	1	UB4:	4
	SB2:	2	KCBH:	20	UB4:	4	KTBBH:	48	KTBIT:	24
Column		Col Size	Cor Size	Date	Cor Siz	Number	Cor Siz		
		0	0	0	0	0	0		
		0	0	0	0	0	0		
		0	0	0	0	0	0		
		0	0	0	0	0	0		
		0	0	0	0	0	0		
		0	0	0	0	0	0		
		0	0	0	0	0	0		
		0	0	0	0	0	0		
		0	0	0	0	0	0		
		0	0	0	0	0	0		
		0	0	0	0	0	0		
		0	0	0	0	0	0		
		0	0	0	0	0	0		
		0	0	0	0	0	0		
		0	0	0	0	0	0		
		0	0	0	0	0	0		
	Totals:	0	0	0	0	0	0		
	ARL:	0	ERL:	0					
	DB Bk Sz:	8192		Init Trans:	1	Pctfree:	10	Tbl in Cl:	1
	TBH(init)	86			23				1
	DS in Bk:	7298		Init RPB:	#DIV/0!		Size:	#DIV/0!	#DIV/0!
	# of ROW:	1806336		Blocks:	#DIV/0!				
	FFS:	0	K						
	V$TYPE_SIZE constant defaults set to NT values							Not Required	
								Required	
								Calculated or Derived	

FIGURE 12.2 Table constants and number of rows entered.

3. Enter the column names, column sizes (in either the Character type column which is the first column; the Date type column, which is the second column; or in the Number type column, which is the third column. Enter a table name if you are going to use this for documentation; otherwise this isn't required. For the Date column, any entry but Y will result in a 0 entry; enter Y if the column is a date field. Figure 12.3 shows a completed table-sizing spreadsheet.

> **NOTE** For this example, the actual table size was 113 megabytes, arrived at by multiplying BLOCKS from DBA_TABLES, after an ANALYZE COMPUTE, times DB_BLOCK_SIZE; it was 97 megabytes, arrived at by multiplying AVG_ROW_LEN times NUM_ROWS. As you can see, the calculated size is 104 megabytes, which is well within a plus or minus 10-percent margin. Of course, the size estimate will only be as good as your estimates for the variable-size columns (number and varchar2).

Oracle9*i* Table Size Calculation Spread sheet

Table:	SQL_SCRIPTS_INT									
V$TYPE_SIZE Constants:		KDBH:		14	KDBT:		4	UB1:		1	UB4:	4
	SB2:	2	KCBH:		20	UB4:		4	KTBBH:		48	KTBIT:	24
Column		Col Size	Cor Size	Date	Cor Siz	Number	Cor Siz			
PERMISSIONS		12	13	N	0	0	0			
FILETYPE		0	0	N	0	3	3			
OWNER		6	7	N	0	0	0			
GROUP_NAME		3	4	N	0	0	0			
SIZE_IN_BYTES		0	0	N	0	4	3			
DATE_EDITED		0	0	Y	8	0	0			
SCRIPT_NAME		10	11	N	0	0	0			
		0	0		0	0	0			
		0	0		0	0	0			
		0	0		0	0	0			
		0	0		0	0	0			
		0	0		0	0	0			
		0	0		0	0	0			
		0	0		0	0	0			
		0	0		0	0	0			
		0	0		0	0	0			
		0	0		0	0	0			
		0	0		0	0	0			
	Totals:	31	35	0	8	7	8			
	ARL:	54	ERL:	38						
	DB Bk Sz:	8192		Init Trans:	1	Pctfree:	10	Tbl in Cl:	1	
	TBH(init)	86			23				1	
	DS in Bk:	7298		Init RPB:	136		Size:	104	M	
	# of ROW:	1806336		Blocks:	13282					
	FFS:	66	M							
	V$TYPE_SIZE constant defaults set to NT values							Not Required		
								Required		
								Calculated or Derived		

FIGURE 12.3   Filled-out table-sizing spreadsheet.

Using the Index-Sizing Spreadsheet   Here are the steps for using the index-sizing spreadsheet.

1. Fill in the required constants for a given index (these are boldfaced in the example spreadsheet in Figure 12.4).
2. Fill in the table and index names (though not required, doing so is good for documentation).
3. Fill in the column names and sizes. A completed spreadsheet is shown in Figure 12.5.

Using the SGA-Sizing Spreadsheet   Once the physical size of the database is complete, you can size the SGA using the SGA-sizing spreadsheet. Unfortunately, there is no automated way to access such factors as required log buffer size, number and size of redo logs, sort area size, shared pool size, and so on. I suggest starting with a log buffer size of 1 megabyte, a sort area size of 1 megabyte, and a shared pool size of 40 megabytes. Also, there is no good method for determining the number of concurrent users and concurrent sorts until you have an operating system. I suggest using the 10:10:10 ratio; for every 100 users, you will have 10 concurrent users, and for every 10 concurrent users, you will have one sort operation for any given point in time. Adjust upward for all of these, with

Oracle9*i* Index Size Calculation Spread sheet

Table:	SQL_SCRIPTS_INT	Index:	INX_SQL_SCRIPTS_INT		Percent Filled (non-unique) :			1
Blocksize:	8192	Pctfree:	10		Initrans:	2		
# of Rows:	1806336					2		
Column Name		Size	Corrected Size					
SCRIPT_NAMES		10	11		ARL:	19		
		0	0		AS:	7230		
		0	0		RPB:	381		
		0	0		# Blocks:	4742		
		0	0		Size:	38.89921875 M		
		0	0					
		0	0					
		0	0					
		0	0		Not Required			
		0	0		Required			
		0	0		Calculated or Derived			
		0	0					
		0	0					
		0	0					
		0	0					
		0	19					

FIGURE 12.4   Constants for the index-sizing spreadsheet.

the exception of sort area size, which may have to be reduced. Figure 12.6 shows the SGA-sizing spreadsheet; the steps below detail how to use it.

1. Enter the individual index and table names; or just enter the total size value in the Size column.
2. Enter the size of log buffer you want to use (the default is OS-specific; I suggest no more than 1 meg), the number of log buffers (usually 4), the number of redo groups

Oracle9*i* Index Size Calculation Spread sheet

Table:	SQL_SCRIPTS_INT	Index:	INX_SQL_SCRIPTS_INT		Percent Filled (non-unique) :			1
Blocksize:	8192	Pctfree:	10		Initrans:	2		
# of Rows:	0					2		
Column Name		Size	Corrected Size					
		0	0		ARL:	8		
		0	0		AS:	7230		
		0	0		RPB:	904		
		0	0		# Blocks:	0		
		0	0		Size:	0 k		
		0	0					
		0	0					
		0	0					
		0	0		Not Required			
		0	0		Required			
		0	0		Calculated or Derived			
		0	0					
		0	0					
		0	0					
		0	0					
		0	8					

FIGURE 12.5   Completed index spreadsheet.

Oracle9*i* SGA-Sizing Spreadsheet

Table or Index Name	Size (K)
Total:	0
Adjusted Total:	0

Blocksize:	8192	Bytes
DB Block Estimate:	0	Blocks
Log Buffer Size:		Meg
Number of Log Buffers:		
Number of Redo Groups:		
Number of Redo Members:		
Size of Redo Logs:		Meg
Size of Sort Area:		Meg
Size of Shared Pool:		Meg
Number of Users:		
Number of Concurrent Users:		
Number of Concurrent Sorts:		
Size of Java Pool:		Meg
Size of Large Pool:		Meg
Total SGA:	######	Meg
Total Memory:	######	Meg

DB block estimate includes a 25% overage for miscellaneous
  requirements.
Shared Pool is sized for a mixed-usage environment with minimal
  code reusage.
Sort area size is based on average sort sizes from past experience.
Total memory is based only on SGA occupying 60% of total
  physical memory.
Total memory includes 300K per concurrent user, including 12
  Oracle base processes.
DB block estimate is based on 1/20 of physical data size.

  Not Required
  Required
  Calculated or Derived

Adjustment includes 25% for summary tables and 50% for indexes

---

FIGURE 12.6   Example SGA-sizing spreadsheet.

(minimum 2; I suggest 3 to 5), number of log group members (1 is the minimum; I suggest 2), size of logs (start at 1 megabyte), size of sort area desired (defaults to 64K; I suggest 1 meg), size of shared pool (defaults to 7 to 9 meg; I suggest 40), number of users, number of concurrent users and number of concurrent sorts (these are usually in a 10:10:10 ratio; for example, 1,000 total users, 100 concurrent, 10 doing sorts). The Java pool will usually be about 20 megabytes, and the large pool about 600K to start with. A sample completed spreadsheet is shown in Figure 12.7.

NOTE   In Oracle9*i*, any amount of memory specified in MAX_SGA_SIZE that is not explicitly allocated to buffers will be allocated to the shared pool.

Spreadsheet Summary   Once you have designed the database using good techniques, have sized the database properly, and have used good physical implementation

Oracle9*i* SGA-Sizing Spreadsheet

Table or Index Name	Size (K)
All tables	2,000,000
All indexes	1,800,000
Total:	3800000
Adjusted Total:	6650000

Blocksize:	8192	Bytes
DB Block Estimate:	51953	Blocks
Log Buffer Size:	1	Meg
Number of Log Buffers:	4	
Number of Redo Groups:	5	
Number of Redo Members:	2	
Size of Redo Logs:	40	Meg
Size of Sort Area:	1	Meg
Size of Shared Pool:	40	Meg
Number of Users:	1000	
Number of Concurrent Users:	100	
Number of Concurrent Sorts:	10	
Size of Java Pool:	20	Meg
Size of Large Pool:	0.6	Meg
Total SGA:	481	Meg
Total Memory:	995	Meg

DB block estimate includes a 25% overage for miscellaneous requirements.
Shared Pool is sized for a mixed-usage environment with minimal code reusage.
Sort area size is based on average sort sizes from past experience.
Total memory is based only on SGA occupying 60% of total physical memory.
Total memory includes 300K per concurrent user, including 12 Oracle base processes.
DB block estimate is based on 1/20 of physical data size.

Not Required
Required
Calculated or Derived

Adjustment includes 25% for summary tables and 50% for indexes

FIGURE 12.7 Sample completed SGA-sizing spreadsheet.

processes, you will be ready to begin tuning SQL and PL/SQL (assuming your system is properly tuned for Oracle and has adequate resources, topics we will cover in Chapter 13). If you have laid out the disk arrays properly, made sure you have enough memory and CPU resources, and have configured your kernel as per Oracle installation instructions, you should be ready to start the tuning process.

12.3 TUNING SQL AND PL/SQL

In a perfect environment, all developers would fine-tune their code before submitting it to production. Unfortunately, this rarely happens. Usually, the prevailing approach is that the DBA tunes the code only if it has problems. Of course, this ignores the fact that by the time the problem code makes itself known, the system will probably be in production, thereby affecting users and/or clients. Therefore, the DBA must know which views are important for SQL performance monitoring, and understand which values in the views point to potential problems.

Finding Problem Code

The OEM tool provides the Diagnostics packs, which you can use to locate problem code. The Top SQL screen, shown in Figure 12.8, can be used to locate code that has high disk reads and/or high buffer gets. By default, the ordering column supplies disk reads per execution, but a simple mouse click on the Buffer Gets column header will reorder the SQL according to that specification. The data may also be sorted by any of the Returned columns: Execution, Total Disk Reads, or Total Buffer Gets. The Returned columns can be turned off or on by using the options icon at the top of the screen. You may also vary the SQL filtering and the number of values returned. By default, 25 values are returned.

For sites where OEM is not used or is not available, the script in Source 12.1 can be used to return the top SQL statements by number of disk reads.

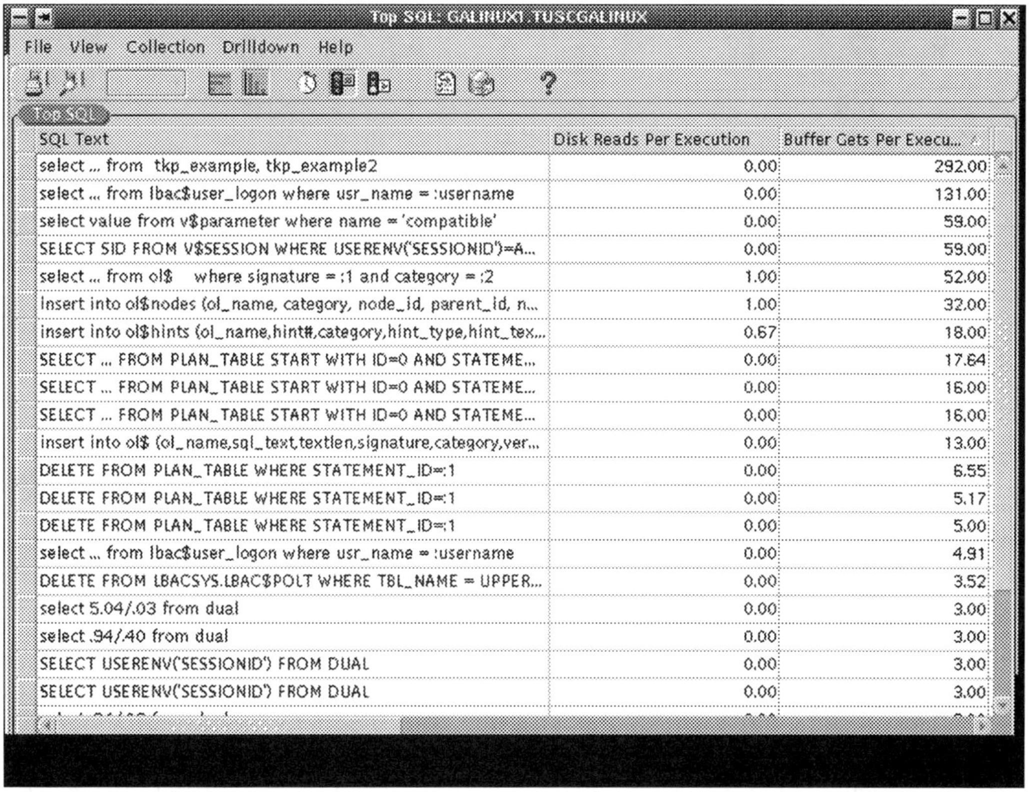
Top SQL: GALINUX1.TUSCGALINUX
File View Collection Drilldown Help
Top SQL
SQL Text
Disk Reads Per Execution
Buffer Gets Per Execu...
select ... from tkp_example, tkp_example2 0.00 292.00
select ... from lbac$user_logon where usr_name = :username 0.00 131.00
select value from v$parameter where name = 'compatible' 0.00 59.00
SELECT SID FROM V$SESSION WHERE USERENV('SESSIONID')=A... 0.00 59.00
select ... from ol$ where signature = :1 and category = :2 1.00 52.00
insert into ol$nodes (ol_name, category, node_id, parent_id, n... 1.00 32.00
insert into ol$hints (ol_name,hint#,category,hint_type,hint_tex... 0.67 18.00
SELECT ... FROM PLAN_TABLE START WITH ID=0 AND STATEME... 0.00 17.64
SELECT ... FROM PLAN_TABLE START WITH ID=0 AND STATEME... 0.00 16.00
SELECT ... FROM PLAN_TABLE START WITH ID=0 AND STATEME... 0.00 16.00
insert into ol$ (ol_name,sql_text,textlen,signature,category,ver... 0.00 13.00
DELETE FROM PLAN_TABLE WHERE STATEMENT_ID=:1 0.00 6.55
DELETE FROM PLAN_TABLE WHERE STATEMENT_ID=:1 0.00 5.17
DELETE FROM PLAN_TABLE WHERE STATEMENT_ID=:1 0.00 5.00
select ... from lbac$user_logon where usr_name = :username 0.00 4.91
DELETE FROM LBACSYS.LBAC$POLT WHERE TBL_NAME = UPPER... 0.00 3.52
select 5.04/.03 from dual 0.00 3.00
select .94/.40 from dual 0.00 3.00
SELECT USERENV('SESSIONID') FROM DUAL 0.00 3.00
SELECT USERENV('SESSIONID') FROM DUAL 0.00 3.00

FIGURE 12.8 OEM Top SQL screen.

Source 12.1   Example SQL to return the top SQL by disk reads.

```
REM Name: sqldrd.sql
REM Function: return the sql statements from the shared area with
REM Function: highest disk reads
REM History: Presented in paper 35 at IOUG-A 1997, converted for
REM use 6/24/97 MRA
REM
DEFINE access_level = 10000 (NUMBER)
COLUMN parsing_user_id FORMAT 9999999 HEADING 'User Id'
COLUMN executions      FORMAT 9999         HEADING 'Exec'
COLUMN sorts           FORMAT 99999        HEADING 'Sorts'
COLUMN command_type    FORMAT 99999        HEADING 'CmdT'
COLUMN disk_reads      FORMAT 999,999,999 HEADING 'Block Reads'
COLUMN sql_text        FORMAT a40          HEADING 'Statement' WORD_WRAPPED
SET LINES 130 VERIFY OFF FEEDBACK OFF
START title132 'SQL Statements With High Reads'
SPOOL rep_out/&db/sqldrd.lis
SELECT * FROM (SELECT
    parsing_user_id, executions,sorts,command_type,
    disk_reads,sql_text
FROM
    v$sqlarea
WHERE
    disk_reads > &&access_level
ORDER BY
    disk_reads) WHERE rownum<26;
SPOOL OFF
SET LINES 80 VERIFY ON FEEDBACK ON
```

Beginning with Oracle9*i*, the code in Source 12.1 can be modified to return results based on CPU time or total elapsed time, because the V$SQLAREA view includes the CPU_TIME and ELAPSED_TIME columns.

Sort Problems

In previous versions of Oracle, locating code with sort problems would involve looking at the V$SQLAREA or V$SYSSTAT table to determine which code was performing sorts. Beginning in later versions of Oracle8*i*, the V$SORT_AREA and V$SORT_USAGE views could capture sorts in progress, to help the DBA determine which code needs attention. Source 12.2 shows an example SQL script for generating information on SQL statements currently using sorts to disk.

Source12.2   Example script to extract sort information.

```
col sql_text format a40 word_wrapped
col username format a15
col sid format 999999
col system_date format a20 heading 'System|Date'
set lines 132 pages 50
@title132 'Sorters Report'
spool rep_out\&db\sorters
select to_char(system_date,'dd-mon-yyyy hh24:mi') system_date,
sid,username,extents,blocks,sql_text from sorters
/
spool off

The view used in the above script looks like:

rem Code for view: SORTERS
CREATE OR REPLACE VIEW sorters as
select
SYSDATE system_date , s.sid, s.username
, b.extents, b.blocks, c.sql_text
from v$session s
, v$sort_usage b, v$sqlarea c
where s.saddr = b.session_addr
and s.sql_address = c.address;
```

Of course, isolating the faulty SQL is only half the battle; winning the war on bad code requires tuning it, so let's get to it.

Tuning Poorly Performing SQL

Essentially, tuning SQL and PL/SQL involves *knowing and understanding access paths*. Access paths determine the speed at which data can be obtained from the Oracle data structures. In the rule-based optimizer (RBO) these paths were mapped into a set of 15 rules that determined, according to their hierarchy, which path a statement would be able to take on execution. If an index was present, it was used with the rule-based optimizer, which always assumed an index was faster than a table scan, even if 100 percent of the table data was returned. Many times in the rule based optimizer, tuning involved *defeating* indexes. The rules went from single-value access via ROWID (the fastest access method) to full table scan (the slowest access method). Table 12.2 ranks the rule-based optimizer path hierarchy.

TABLE 12.2 RBO Path Rankings

Rank	Path
1	Single row by ROWID
2	Single row by cluster join
3	Single row by hash cluster key with unique or primary key
4	Single row by unique or primary key
5	Cluster join
6	Hash cluster key
7	Indexed cluster key
8	Composite index
9	Single-column index
10	Bounded range search on indexed columns
11	Unbounded range search on indexed columns
12	Sort-merge join
13	MAX or MIN on indexed column
14	ORDER BY indexed columns
15	Full table scan

In the cost-based optimizer (CBO), multiple access paths and their computed cost are examined for each statement, and the path with the lowest cost is selected. The cost in Oracle8 and Oracle8*i* is mostly based on I/O. In Oracle9*i*, you can force CPU use to play a more prominent role in cost. As memories and number of CPUs increase, it becomes more likely that after the first read of a table, it will be cached in memory; thus, CPU usage becomes more of a cost factor than disk I/O.

Table Access Methods

Generally, only four types of table access are used by Oracle; these are:

By ROWID. Usually as a result of an index scan. This is the fastest access method for Oracle data contained in a table. A ROWID points directly to a specific row in a table.

Full table scan. Usually due to no indexes, improper indexes, or more than 20 percent of the table's data being accessed (in Oracle9*i;* as little as 5 to 7 percent in Oracle8 and Oracle8*i*). High values for DB_FILE_MULTIBLOCK_READ_COUNT will favor more full table scans, as will large DB block buffer areas.

Cluster scan. Only used with database CLUSTERS. Clusters aren't used very much (except in the data dictionary) so this access method isn't generally used.

Hash scan. Usually due to no indexes, improper indexes, or more than 20 percent of the table's data being accessed (in Oracle9*i;* as little as 5 to 7 percent in Oracle8 and Oracle8*i*). Favored by large SORT_AREA_SIZE values, as the HASH area sizes are derived from SORT_AREA_SIZE.

Index Scan Methods

Indexes are the preferred way to get at data if you are returning less than 20 percent of the table's data, or when histograms indicate that an index would be the best method for data lookup and retrieval. For bitmap indexes, the value for percentage of data returned is much higher. The types of index scans used by Oracle are:

Unique. Used on unique indexes for single-row lookup.

Range. Used when a range of data is requested.

Fast full scan. Can be used in place of a full table scan if the data required is stored in the index.

Full index scan. Can be used when the column used in a comparison is in the index.

Bitmap scan. Used with bitmap indexes.

Skip-scan (9*i* only). Allows a scan of the second tier of a multilevel index.

Bitmap-join (9*i* only). Allows tables to be prejoined via a bitmap index on the join columns.

Table Join Methodology

Numerous table join methods are used by Oracle to satisfy the various join conditions. They are:

Nested loops. One table is chosen as the driving, or outer, table; the other becomes the inner table. The values meeting the join criteria are selected from the outer table; the inner table is then scanned for those values. This is most effective when the driving table is many times smaller than the inner table.

Sort-merge. Both tables are scanned for the rows meeting the join criteria; the results are sorted and then merged.

Cluster joins. Used in Oracle cluster tables

Hash joins. The smaller table is converted into a hash table, with the hash based on the join criteria. The values from the hash table are then used to probe hashed chunks of values from the larger table. The tables are broken up into HASH_AREA_SIZE chunks (HASH_AREA_SIZE is usually twice the size of SORT_AREA_SIZE). This is most effective when the tables are nearly the same size and fairly large.

Cartesian. If insufficient join conditions are specified (there must be n-1 join conditions for n tables in a join), the entire contents of the improperly joined table or tables are joined with the result set.

Index join. New in Oracle8, this allows indexes, rather than tables, to be joined if the data in the query is available in the indexes. Up to 15 indexes may be joined. Indexes participating in the join must be single-column (not concatenated) indexes.

There is another major tuning effort that goes into join order. For example, generally speaking, if the join technique known as a nested loop is used to process a join between tables, you want the smallest table to drive the nested loop; however, under some conditions, such as when the small table can be completely read into memory, it may actually be faster to drive from the larger table.

Oracle Statement Tuning Tools

There are two basic tools every database administrator must know how to use to tune SQL statements: TKPROF and EXPLAIN PLAN. TKPROF is a trace file formatting tool. EXPLAIN PLAN shows you the actual execution plan Oracle will use to execute SQL statements.

In order to use TKPROF, you should have the initialization parameter TIMED_ STATISTICS set to TRUE at either the database or the session level for the session you wish to trace. Likewise, the initialization parameter SQL_TRACE should be set to TRUE, either at the database or session level. Once SQL_TRACE is set to TRUE, trace files showing all actions taken by the traced session are generated into the USER_ DUMP_DEST directory. The trace files created by SQL_TRACE will be named for the session that generated them, based on the session ID of the process. Generally speaking, trace files are not very human-readable, so you must use TKPROF to get a good look at them.

The EXPLAIN PLAN utility can be invoked with TKPROF, as a standalone command from SQL*Plus, or from within the SQL*Plus environment for each and every statement run automatically. In order to run any form of the EXPLAIN PLAN utility, a PLAN_TABLE table must be available for the explaining user to utilize (either shared or owned by the user). The utility script UTLXPLAN.SQL creates the PLAN_TABLE. The UTLXPLAN.SQL script is usually located in the $ORACLE_HOME/rdbms/admin directory or its equivalent on your operating system.

Using TKPROF   First we'll examine TKPROF. Start by looking at the two queries in Listing 12.2.

TKPROF is executed either by moving to the directory where the trace files are located (the value of the initialization parameter user_dump_dest gives this information) or by moving the trace file to a work directory and executing the tkprof command against it:

Listing 12.2   Example queries for TKPROF.

```
Query 1:
SELECT C.OWNER, C.TABLE_NAME, C.CONSTRAINT_NAME,
CC.COLUMN_NAME, R.TABLE_NAME REF_TABLE,
RC.COLUMN_NAME REF_COLUMN
FROM DBA_CONSTRAINTS C, DBA_CONSTRAINTS R, DBA_CONS_COLUMNS CC,
DBA_CONS_COLUMNS RC
WHERE C.R_CONSTRAINT_NAME = R.CONSTRAINT_NAME
AND C.R_OWNER = R.OWNER AND C.CONSTRAINT_NAME = CC.CONSTRAINT_NAME
AND C.OWNER = CC.OWNER AND R.CONSTRAINT_NAME = RC.CONSTRAINT_NAME
AND R.OWNER = RC.OWNER AND CC.POSITION = RC.POSITION
AND C.CONSTRAINT_TYPE = 'R' AND C.OWNER <> 'SYS'
AND C.OWNER <> 'SYSTEM'
ORDER BY C.OWNER, C.TABLE_NAME, C.CONSTRAINT_NAME, CC.POSITION

query 2:
SELECT C.OWNER, C.TABLE_NAME, C.CONSTRAINT_NAME,
CC.COLUMN_NAME, R.TABLE_NAME REF_TABLE,
RC.COLUMN_NAME REF_COLUMN
FROM DBA_CONSTRAINTS C, DBA_CONSTRAINTS R, DBA_CONS_COLUMNS CC,
DBA_CONS_COLUMNS RC
WHERE C.CONSTRAINT_TYPE = 'R'
AND C.OWNER NOT IN ('SYS','SYSTEM')
AND C.R_OWNER = R.OWNER
and C.R_CONSTRAINT_NAME = R.CONSTRAINT_NAME
AND C.CONSTRAINT_NAME = CC.CONSTRAINT_NAME
AND C.OWNER = CC.OWNER
AND R.CONSTRAINT_NAME = RC.CONSTRAINT_NAME
AND R.OWNER = RC.OWNER
AND CC.POSITION = RC.POSITION
ORDER BY C.OWNER, C.TABLE_NAME, C.CONSTRAINT_NAME, CC.POSITION
```

```
tkprof input output explain=user/password sort=(sort options)
```

Both of these examples are complex queries against views, and both retrieve the same information from the database. Close examination reveals that the only difference between them is the order of the WHERE clause columns. Listing 12.3 shows the results of analyzing these queries with the TKPROF tool. As you can see, the second query performs better. This is due to the placement of the most restrictive columns first, thus reducing the volume of subsequent merges and sorts. The explain plan generated is huge, because this is a multitable and multiview join. Unfortunately, a query against views that are not owned by the user running TKPROF cannot be run through the EXPLAIN PLAN option, so if the queries you analyze involve views from multiple owners, an explain plan output will not be available.

Listing 12.3   Example output of TKPROF.

```
*******************************************************

select c.owner,c.table_name,c.constraint_name,
cc.column_name,r.table_name ref_table,
rc.column_name ref_column
from dba_constraints c, dba_constraints r, dba_cons_columns cc,
dba_cons_columns rc
where c.r_constraint_name=r.constraint_name
and c.r_owner=r.owner and c.constraint_name=cc.constraint_name
and c.owner=cc.owner and r.constraint_name=rc.constraint_name
and r.owner=rc.owner and cc.position=rc.position
and c.constraint_type='R' and c.owner<>'SYS'
and c.owner<>'SYSTEM'
order by c.owner, c.table_name, c.constraint_name,cc.position


call     count    cpu   elapsed   disk      query    current      rows
-------  -----   -----  --------  ------  ---------- ----------  ----------
Parse        1    2.84     5.58       0           0          1           0
Execute      1    0.00     0.00       0           0          0           0
Fetch        8    8.22    16.88      63      112469          5          92
-------  -----   -----  --------  ------  ---------- ----------  ----------
total       10   11.06    22.47      63      112469          6          92

Misses in library cache during parse: 1
Optimizer goal: CHOOSE
Parsing user id: 5  (SYSTEM)

Rows     Row Source Operation
-------  --------------------------------------------------------------
     92  SORT ORDER BY
     92   NESTED LOOPS OUTER
     92    NESTED LOOPS
     92     NESTED LOOPS
     92      NESTED LOOPS
     92       NESTED LOOPS OUTER
     92        NESTED LOOPS OUTER
     92         NESTED LOOPS OUTER
     92          NESTED LOOPS OUTER
     92           NESTED LOOPS
     92            NESTED LOOPS OUTER
     92             NESTED LOOPS
     92              NESTED LOOPS
     92               NESTED LOOPS
     92                NESTED LOOPS
     92                 NESTED LOOPS
     92                  NESTED LOOPS
     92                   NESTED LOOPS OUTER
     92                    NESTED LOOPS OUTER
```

```
    92                    NESTED LOOPS OUTER
    92                    NESTED LOOPS OUTER
    92                     NESTED LOOPS
    92                      NESTED LOOPS OUTER
    92                       NESTED LOOPS
   840                       NESTED LOOPS
   840                       NESTED LOOPS
  2384                        NESTED LOOPS
  2384                         NESTED LOOPS
  2384                          NESTED LOOPS OUTER
  2384                           NESTED LOOPS
  2384                            NESTED LOOPS
  2384                             NESTED LOOPS
 31183                             TABLE ACCESS FULL OBJ$
  2384                              TABLE ACCESS CLUSTER CCOL$
   591                             INDEX UNIQUE SCAN (object id 30)
  2384                           TABLE ACCESS BY INDEX ROWID CDEF$
  2384                            INDEX UNIQUE SCAN (object id 50)
  2384                          TABLE ACCESS BY INDEX ROWID COL$
  2384                           INDEX UNIQUE SCAN (object id 47)
     0                           TABLE ACCESS CLUSTER ATTRCOL$
  2384                          TABLE ACCESS BY INDEX ROWID CON$
  2384                           INDEX UNIQUE SCAN (object id 49)
  2384                         TABLE ACCESS CLUSTER USER$
  2384                          INDEX UNIQUE SCAN (object id 11)
   840                        TABLE ACCESS BY INDEX ROWID USER$
   840                         INDEX UNIQUE SCAN (object id 44)
   840                       TABLE ACCESS BY INDEX ROWID CON$
   840                        INDEX UNIQUE SCAN (object id 48)
    92                       TABLE ACCESS BY INDEX ROWID CDEF$
   840                        INDEX UNIQUE SCAN (object id 50)
    91                      TABLE ACCESS BY INDEX ROWID OBJ$
    91                       INDEX UNIQUE SCAN (object id 36)
    92                     TABLE ACCESS BY INDEX ROWID OBJ$
    92                      INDEX UNIQUE SCAN (object id 36)
    92                    INDEX UNIQUE SCAN (object id 36)
    92                    TABLE ACCESS BY INDEX ROWID CON$
    92                     INDEX UNIQUE SCAN (object id 49)
    91                   TABLE ACCESS CLUSTER USER$
    91                    INDEX UNIQUE SCAN (object id 11)
    92                   TABLE ACCESS CLUSTER USER$
    92                    INDEX UNIQUE SCAN (object id 11)
    92                  TABLE ACCESS BY INDEX ROWID USER$
    92                   INDEX UNIQUE SCAN (object id 44)
    92                 TABLE ACCESS BY INDEX ROWID USER$
    92                  INDEX UNIQUE SCAN (object id 44)
    92                 TABLE ACCESS BY INDEX ROWID CON$
    92                  INDEX UNIQUE SCAN (object id 48)
    92                TABLE ACCESS BY INDEX ROWID CON$
    92                 INDEX UNIQUE SCAN (object id 48)
```

continues

Listing 12.3   Continued.

```
    92                      TABLE ACCESS BY INDEX ROWID CDEF$
    92                        INDEX UNIQUE SCAN (object id 50)
    92                      TABLE ACCESS BY INDEX ROWID CDEF$
    92                        INDEX UNIQUE SCAN (object id 50)
    92                    TABLE ACCESS BY INDEX ROWID OBJ$
    92                      INDEX UNIQUE SCAN (object id 36)
    92                    TABLE ACCESS BY INDEX ROWID OBJ$
    92                      INDEX UNIQUE SCAN (object id 36)
     0                    INDEX UNIQUE SCAN (object id 36)
     0                  TABLE ACCESS BY INDEX ROWID CON$
     0                    INDEX UNIQUE SCAN (object id 49)
    92                  TABLE ACCESS CLUSTER USER$
    92                    INDEX UNIQUE SCAN (object id 11)
     0                  TABLE ACCESS CLUSTER USER$
     0                    INDEX UNIQUE SCAN (object id 11)
    92                 TABLE ACCESS BY INDEX ROWID CCOL$
   124                   INDEX RANGE SCAN (object id 55)
    92               INDEX UNIQUE SCAN (object id 36)
    92             TABLE ACCESS BY INDEX ROWID COL$
    92               INDEX UNIQUE SCAN (object id 47)
     0         TABLE ACCESS CLUSTER ATTRCOL$


****************************************************************************

select c.owner,c.table_name,c.constraint_name,
cc.column_name,r.table_name ref_table,
rc.column_name ref_column
from dba_constraints c, dba_constraints r, dba_cons_columns cc,
dba_cons_columns rc
where c.constraint_type='R'
and c.owner <> 'SYS'
and c.owner <> 'SYSTEM'
and c.r_owner=r.owner
and c.r_constraint_name=r.constraint_name
and c.constraint_name = cc.constraint_name
and c.owner=cc.owner
and r.constraint_name=rc.constraint_name
and r.owner=rc.owner
and cc.position=rc.position
order by c.owner, c.table_name, c.constraint_name,cc.position
```

call	count	cpu	elapsed	disk	query	current	rows
Parse	1	1.96	3.88	0	0	0	0
Execute	1	0.00	0.00	0	0	0	0
Fetch	8	7.93	15.92	0	112467	5	92
total	10	9.89	19.80	0	112467	5	92

```
Misses in library cache during parse: 1
Optimizer goal: CHOOSE
Parsing user id: 5  (SYSTEM)


Rows      Row Source Operation
-------   -------------------------------------------------------
     92   SORT ORDER BY
     92    NESTED LOOPS OUTER
     92     NESTED LOOPS
     92      NESTED LOOPS
     92       NESTED LOOPS
     92        NESTED LOOPS OUTER
     92         NESTED LOOPS OUTER
     92          NESTED LOOPS OUTER
     92           NESTED LOOPS OUTER
     92            NESTED LOOPS
     92             NESTED LOOPS OUTER
     92              NESTED LOOPS
     92               NESTED LOOPS
     92                NESTED LOOPS
     92                 NESTED LOOPS
     92                  NESTED LOOPS
     92                   NESTED LOOPS
     92                    NESTED LOOPS OUTER
     92                     NESTED LOOPS OUTER
     92                      NESTED LOOPS OUTER
     92                       NESTED LOOPS OUTER
     92                        NESTED LOOPS
     92                         NESTED LOOPS OUTER
     92                          NESTED LOOPS
    840                         NESTED LOOPS
    840                        NESTED LOOPS
   2384                       NESTED LOOPS
   2384                      NESTED LOOPS
   2384                     NESTED LOOPS OUTER
   2384                    NESTED LOOPS
   2384                   NESTED LOOPS
   2384                  NESTED LOOPS
  31183                   TABLE ACCESS FULL OBJ$
   2384                   TABLE ACCESS CLUSTER CCOL$
    591                 INDEX UNIQUE SCAN (object id 30)
   2384              TABLE ACCESS BY INDEX ROWID CDEF$
   2384               INDEX UNIQUE SCAN (object id 50)
   2384             TABLE ACCESS BY INDEX ROWID COL$
   2384              INDEX UNIQUE SCAN (object id 47)
      0             TABLE ACCESS CLUSTER ATTRCOL$
   2384             TABLE ACCESS BY INDEX ROWID CON$
   2384              INDEX UNIQUE SCAN (object id 49)
   2384            TABLE ACCESS CLUSTER USER$
```

continues

Listing 12.3   Continued.

```
2384                         INDEX UNIQUE SCAN (object id 11)
 840                TABLE ACCESS BY INDEX ROWID USER$
 840                    INDEX UNIQUE SCAN (object id 44)
 840                TABLE ACCESS BY INDEX ROWID CON$
 840                    INDEX UNIQUE SCAN (object id 48)
  92                TABLE ACCESS BY INDEX ROWID CDEF$
 840                    INDEX UNIQUE SCAN (object id 50)
  91                TABLE ACCESS BY INDEX ROWID OBJ$
  91                    INDEX UNIQUE SCAN (object id 36)
  92                TABLE ACCESS BY INDEX ROWID OBJ$
  92                    INDEX UNIQUE SCAN (object id 36)
  92                INDEX UNIQUE SCAN (object id 36)
  92              TABLE ACCESS BY INDEX ROWID CON$
  92                  INDEX UNIQUE SCAN (object id 49)
  91              TABLE ACCESS CLUSTER USER$
  91                INDEX UNIQUE SCAN (object id 11)
  92            TABLE ACCESS CLUSTER USER$
  92              INDEX UNIQUE SCAN (object id 11)
  92            TABLE ACCESS BY INDEX ROWID USER$
  92              INDEX UNIQUE SCAN (object id 44)
  92            TABLE ACCESS BY INDEX ROWID USER$
  92              INDEX UNIQUE SCAN (object id 44)
  92            TABLE ACCESS BY INDEX ROWID CON$
  92              INDEX UNIQUE SCAN (object id 48)
  92            TABLE ACCESS BY INDEX ROWID CON$
  92              INDEX UNIQUE SCAN (object id 48)
  92            TABLE ACCESS BY INDEX ROWID CDEF$
  92              INDEX UNIQUE SCAN (object id 50)
  92            TABLE ACCESS BY INDEX ROWID CDEF$
  92              INDEX UNIQUE SCAN (object id 50)
  92            TABLE ACCESS BY INDEX ROWID OBJ$
  92              INDEX UNIQUE SCAN (object id 36)
  92            TABLE ACCESS BY INDEX ROWID OBJ$
  92              INDEX UNIQUE SCAN (object id 36)
   0          INDEX UNIQUE SCAN (object id 36)
   0        TABLE ACCESS BY INDEX ROWID CON$
   0          INDEX UNIQUE SCAN (object id 49)
  92        TABLE ACCESS CLUSTER USER$
  92          INDEX UNIQUE SCAN (object id 11)
   0        TABLE ACCESS CLUSTER USER$
   0          INDEX UNIQUE SCAN (object id 11)
  92      TABLE ACCESS BY INDEX ROWID CCOL$
 124        INDEX RANGE SCAN (object id 55)
  92    INDEX UNIQUE SCAN (object id 36)
  92  TABLE ACCESS BY INDEX ROWID COL$
  92    INDEX UNIQUE SCAN (object id 47)
   0  TABLE ACCESS CLUSTER ATTRCOL$
****************************************************************************
```

As you can see, the rearrangement of the WHERE clause has reduced the CPU and elapsed statistics for both the parse and execute phases of the query processing. You may find it difficult to get valid results unless your datasets are large or your processor is slow.

To use the TKPROF tool, and get timing results, you must set the TIMED_STATISTICS parameter in the INIT.ORA file to TRUE. To limit the size of the generated trace file, set the INIT.ORA parameter MAX_DUMP_FILE_SIZE to the desired file size limit. If you want the files to be created in other than the ORA_INSTANCE, ORA_TRACE or the $ORACLE_HOME directory, set the USER_DUMP_DEST to the desired file location. For these parameters to take effect, the instance has to be shut down and restarted. Since the performance penalty is slight, and the benefits derived potentially great, leave the TIMED_STATISTIC parameter set to TRUE.

NOTE   On some Oracle8*i* versions, the TIMED_STATISTICS parameter can cause performance problems. This is a known bug. For those versions, set this parameter to FALSE.

Setting TIMED_STATISTICS to TRUE will allow individual users to set the SQL_TRACE value for their process to TRUE, which will then generate a trace file in the ORA_TRACE or selected directory. The users should then execute the statements from within SQLPLUS. To use the trace facility in SQL*Plus, use the ALTER SESSION command; for example:

```
ALTER SESSION SET SQL_TRACE TRUE;
```

Once the SQL statements or applications have been run, exit SQLPLUS or the forms-based application and look for the proper trace file that corresponds to the PID of the process that generated it. For example, if the database is testb, the PID in Oracle is 5, and the program being run is SQLPLUS, the trace file will be SQLPLUS_F30_TESTB_005.TRC. On your system, the file naming may be different, but usually the name will contain the PID. If you try to look at this file without processing through TKPROF, you will receive little benefit. TKPROF formats the trace files into a user-readable form. I suggest turning off the multithreaded server (MTS) while tuning with TKPROF since you cannot control which sessions will be threaded into a single process stream.

Invoke TKPROF using this syntax:

```
>--tkprof -- trace_file - output_file ----------------------------->>
                                       |---SORT =-----------------|
                                       |      v----,-----|    |
                                       |--(-- option -----)-|
```

```
>--------------------------------------------------->>
  |- PRINT = integer --|          |-INSERT = filename --|       |- SYS = YES|NO ---|
>--------------------------------------------------->>
        |----------------------------EXPLAIN = user/password---|
           |-- TABLE = schema.table ---|
>--------------------------------------------------->< 
      |-- RECORD = filename--|
```

NOTE   If you invoke TKPROF with no arguments, online help is displayed.

Use the following arguments with TKPROF:

trace file. Specifies the input file, a trace file containing statistics produced by the SQL trace facility. This file can be either a trace file produced for a single session or a file produced by concatenating individual trace files from multiple sessions.

output file. Specifies the file to which TKPROF writes its formatted output.

AGGREGATE. If you specify AGGREGATE = NO, TKPROF does not aggregate multiple users of the same SQL text.

EXPLAIN. Determines the execution plan for each SQL statement in the trace file and writes these execution plans to the output file. TKPROF determines execution plans by issuing the EXPLAIN PLAN command after connecting to Oracle with the user and password specified in this parameter. The specified user must have CREATE SESSION system privileges. TKPROF will take longer to process a large trace file if the EXPLAIN option is used.

TABLE. Specifies the schema and name of the table into which TKPROF temporarily places execution plans before writing them to the output file. If the specified table already exists, TKPROF deletes all rows in the table, uses it for the EXPLAIN PLAN command (which writes more rows into the table), and then deletes those rows. If this table does not exist, TKPROF creates it, uses it, and then drops it.

The specified user must be able to issue INSERT, SELECT, and DELETE statements against the table. If the table does not already exist, the user must also be able to issue CREATE TABLE and DROP TABLE statements. (For the privileges to issue these statements, refer to the ORACLE9*i* SQL Reference.)

This option allows multiple individuals to run TKPROF concurrently using the same user in the EXPLAIN value. These individuals can specify different TABLE values and avoid interfering with each other's processing on the temporary plan table.

If you use the EXPLAIN parameter without the TABLE parameter, TKPROF uses the table PROF$PLAN_TABLE in the schema of the user specified by the

EXPLAIN parameter. If you use the TABLE parameter without the EXPLAIN parameter, TKPROF ignores the TABLE parameter.

INSERT. Creates an SQL script that stores the trace file statistics in the database. TKPROF creates this script with the name filename3. This script creates a table and inserts a row of statistics for each traced SQL statement in the table.

SYS. Enables and disables the listing of SQL statements issued by the user SYS, or recursive SQL statements in the output file. The default value of YES causes TKPROF to list these statements. The value of NO causes TKPROF to omit them. Note that this parameter does not affect the optional SQL script. The SQL script always inserts statistics for all traced SQL statements, including recursive SQL statements.

SORT. Sorts the traced SQL statements in descending order of the specified sort option before listing them in the output file. If more than one option is specified, the output is sorted in descending order by the sum of the values specified in the sort options. If you omit this parameter, TKPROF lists statements in the output file in order of first use. The sort options are as follows:

EXECNT: Number of executes

EXECPU: CPU time spent executing

EXECU: Number of current mode block reads during execute

EXEDSK: Number of physical reads from disk during execute

EXEELA: Elapsed time spent executing

EXEMIS: Number of library cache misses during execute

EXEQRY: Number of consistent mode block reads during execute

EXEROW: Number of rows processed during execute

FCHCNT: Number of fetches

FCHCPU: CPU time spent fetching

FCHCU: Number of current mode block reads during fetch

FCHDSK: Number of physical reads from disk during fetch

FCHELA: Elapsed time spent fetching

FCHQRY: Number of consistent mode block reads during fetch

FCHROW: Number of rows fetched

PRSCNT: Number of times parsed

PRSCPU: CPU time spent parsing

PRSCU: Number of current mode block reads during parse

PRSDSK: Number of physical reads from disk during parse

PRSELA: Elapsed time spent parsing

PRSMIS: Number of consistent mode block reads during parse

PRSMIS: Number of library cache misses during parse

USERID: User ID of the user that parsed the row

PRINT. Lists only the first integer-sorted SQL statements in the output file. If you omit this parameter, TKPROF lists all traced SQL statements. Note that this parameter does not affect the optional SQL script. The SQL script always inserts statistics for all traced SQL statements.

RECORD. Creates an SQL script with the specified filename with all of the non-recursive SQL in the trace file. This can be used to replay the user events from the trace file.

The TKPROF EXPLAIN Option   To use the EXPLAIN option, a user must have quota on a tablespace to create the needed tables. The command is issued at the operating system level. To split the command on multiple lines, in VMS, place a dash at the end of each line. For UNIX, simply place a backslash (/) character at the end of the line to be continued.

This command will generate a file named whatever you specified the output file to be. If you include the SORT qualifier, the output will be sorted accordingly. If you include the EXPLAIN qualifier, a temporary table will be created in the user's default tablespace and the various SQL statements will be "explained" in accordance with the formats of the explain plan command.

TKPROF Statistics   Each line of TKPROF statistics will correspond to the parse, execute, or fetch part of the query operation. These parts of a query occur as follows:

1. *Parse.* The query is translated into an execution plan. If the user doesn't have the proper security or table authorization, or the objects in the query don't exist, this step will catch it as well.
2. *Execute.* The execution plan is executed against the ORDBMS.
3. *Fetch.* In this final step, all rows that satisfy the query are retrieved from the database.

For each step, the following parameters are traced:

Count. The number of times this step was repeated.

cpu. The total CPU time for the step in hundredths of a second.

Elapsed. The total elapsed time for the step in hundredths of a second.

Disk. The total number of database blocks read from disk for the step.

Query. The number of buffers retrieved in a consistent read mode.

Current. The number of buffers retrieved in current mode.

Rows. The number of rows processed during the SQL statement execution step.

TKPROF Example Tuning Session　　Let's look at some example outputs from TKPROF using EXPLAIN. We will run through some tuning scenarios on an example query. The descriptions for tables being used for these examples are shown in Listing 12.4.

Listing 12.4　　Tables used in TKPROF example.

```
SQL> desc tkp_example
 Name                                    Null?    Type
 --------------------------------------- -------- ------------------
 USERNAME                                NOT NULL VARCHAR2(30)
 USER_ID                                 NOT NULL NUMBER
 PASSWORD                                         VARCHAR2(30)
 ACCOUNT_STATUS                          NOT NULL VARCHAR2(32)
 LOCK_DATE                                        DATE
 EXPIRY_DATE                                      DATE
 DEFAULT_TABLESPACE                      NOT NULL VARCHAR2(30)
 TEMPORARY_TABLESPACE                    NOT NULL VARCHAR2(30)
 CREATED                                 NOT NULL DATE
 PROFILE                                 NOT NULL VARCHAR2(30)
 INITIAL_RSRC_CONSUMER_GROUP                      VARCHAR2(30)
 EXTERNAL_NAME                                    VARCHAR2(4000)

Number of records in tkp_example: 26

SQL> desc tkp_example2
 Name                                    Null?    Type
 --------------------------------------- -------- ------------------
 OWNER                                            VARCHAR2(30)
 OBJECT_NAME                                      VARCHAR2(128)
 OBJECT_TYPE                                      VARCHAR2(18)
 TABLESPACE_NAME                                  VARCHAR2(30)

Number of records in tkp_example2: 31034
```

In the first example, let's look at the TKPROF output from some queries using these tables without having indexes. Of course, we expect that the ORDBMS will do full table scans no matter how complex the query. (Keep in mind that it isn't always bad to a full table scan; the decision depends entirely upon the selectivity of your query. If you are returning only a few rows, index use is advised. The old rule of thumb for pre-Oracle9*i* is that, if your query returns less than 7 to 10 percent of rows in the table, use an index; in Oracle9*i*, this leaps to 15 to 20 percent. However, with the new parallel capabilities in Oracle8*i* and Oracle9*i*, full table scans may actually be the fastest method to return data for a broader range of queries.) The SELECT statement in Listing 12.5 is a two-table join of the two tables in Listing 12.4, stripping out system tables. Experienced system managers will recognize these tables as a copy of portions of the DBA_USERS, DBA_OBJECTS, DBA_INDEXES, and the DBA_ALL_TABLES views. They were created using the CREATE TABLE command with the AS clause (CTAS) and several UPDATE/INSERT commands, as shown in Listing 12.5.

Listing 12.5   Creation of the test tables.

```
SQL> create table tkp_example as select * from dba_users;

Table created.

SQL> select count(*) from tkp_example;

  COUNT(*)
----------
        26
SQL> create table tkp_example2 (owner varchar2(64),object_name
  2  varchar2(64), object_type varchar2
  3  storage (initial 1m next 1m pctincrease 0)
  4* /
Table created.

SQL> insert into tkp_example2 SELECT a."OWNER", a.object_name,
  2  a.object_type, b.tablespace_name
  3  FROM dba_objects a, dba_all_tables b
  4  WHERE a."OWNER" = b."OWNER"
  5    AND a.object_type = 'TABLE'
  6    AND a.object_name = b.table_name
  7  UNION
  8  SELECT a."OWNER", a.object_name, a.object_type,
  9  b.tablespace_name
 10  FROM dba_objects a, dba_indexes b
 11  WHERE a."OWNER" = b."OWNER"
 12    AND a.object_type = 'INDEX'
 13    AND a.object_name = b.index_name
 14  UNION
 15 SELECT "OWNER", object_name, object_type, 'None'
 16  FROM dba_objects
 17  WHERE NOT object_type IN ('TABLE', 'INDEX')
 18* /

31019 rows created.
```

Using Listing 12.6, let's look at an example query against these tables and attempt some tuning.

Listing 12.6   Example query to be tuned.

```
select
     username,
     default_tablespace,
     tablespace_name,
     object_name
from
     tkp_example, tkp_example2
where
     username != 'SYS' and
     username != 'SYSTEM' and
     default_tablespace=tablespace_name and
     owner=username


call     count     cpu elapsed   disk      query      current       rows
-------  -----   ----- -------  ------  ---------  ----------  ----------
Parse        1    0.01    0.00       0          0           0           0
Execute      1    0.00    0.00       0          0           0           0
Fetch       20    0.81    0.93       0        214          10         280
-------  -----   ----- -------  ------  ---------  ----------  ----------
total       22    0.82    0.94       0        214          10         280

Misses in library cache during parse: 1
Optimizer goal: CHOOSE
Parsing user id: 5  (SYSTEM)


Rows      Row Source Operation
-------   -------------------------------------------------------
   280    MERGE JOIN
 31019      SORT JOIN
 31019        TABLE ACCESS FULL TKP_EXAMPLE2
   280      SORT JOIN
    24        TABLE ACCESS FULL TKP_EXAMPLE
```

As you can see, the performance isn't as bad as we thought it might be. Even with stripping out the system tables and other objects, there were still 280 rows returned. As we expected, the query performed two full table scans. But what is the significance of MERGE JOIN, SORT(JOIN), and so on? These are part of the execution plan generated by the parse step. In addition to the information presented in Listing 12.6, ORACLE9*i*'s TKPROF also provides the number of misses in the library cache during the parse step and adds a ROWS column to the query plan. When you look at a full plan report, you will get two plans for each SQL, one based on what the system knew the conditions were when the query was executed and one based on current conditions. This is a very powerful feature; in previous TKPROF versions, you had to be very careful not to change anything that would affect the query between the time the trace file was created and TKPROF was executed.

Notice that even though the optimizer goal is CHOOSE, no cost information is displayed; this indicates that the tables have not been analyzed, so RULE mode was actually used to optimize the queries. Let's look at the possible outputs from the EXPLAIN (Row Source Operation) portion of the TKPROF output, shown in Table 12.3.

TABLE 12.3 Contents of the EXPLAIN Portion of TKPROF

Action	Explanation
AND-EQUAL	If the WHERE clause contains references only to unique indexed columns, the system will choose to use the ROWIDs from the indexes to perform the table intersections. This is faster than a full table scan type of intersection.
CONNECT-BY	This shows up only in queries that use a CONNECT clause. When a CONNECT-BY is executed, it forces a tree-walk of the table structure to perform the operation.
CONCATENATION	This is a full union of two or more tables. For small tables, it won't hurt; for large tables, it can kill you.
COUNT	This action happens if the query uses the COUNT aggregate to return the number of rows. The STOPKEY value, if returned, shows that a ROWNUM was used to limit the number of returns.
FILTER	This is a process by which rows not meeting the selection criteria are removed from the returned set of values.
FIRST ROW	This shows that only the first row of a query was returned, along with activity with a cursor.
FOR UPDATE	This shows that the query operation involved a possible update situation (such as in a form or SELECT...FOR UPDATE). This indicates that the rows involved were write-locked during the operation.
INDEX (UNIQUE or RANGE SCAN)	This action shows that a query used and index to resolve the needed values. The UNIQUE qualifier shows that the index was scanned for specific unique values. The RANGE qualifier shows that a specific range of values was searched such as that specified in a BETWEEN or less-than-greater-than construct. The RANGE SCAN may also have the DESCENDING qualifier.
INTERSECTION	This shows that the query retrieved the rows from the tables in the query that were common to each of the tables based on the conditions in the WHERE clause. The rows are sorted.
MERGE JOIN (OUTER)	This shows that two sorted sets of operations were joined to resolve the query. The OUTER qualifier shows that an outer join was performed.

TABLE 12.3 (*Continued*)

Action	Explanation
CONNECT BY	Shows a retrieval of rows in hierarchical order for a query containing a CONNECT BY clause.
MINUS	This shows that an INTERSECTION type operation was performed, but instead of similar rows being returned, only rows that didn't match the specified criteria were returned.
NESTED LOOPS (OUTER)	This shows that for each of the first child operations, one or more of the other child operations, which follow it, were performed. If the OUTER qualifier is present, it signifies that an outer join was performed between the results.
PROJECTION	This shows that a subset of a table's columns was returned.
REMOTE	This shows that a retrieval from other than the current database was performed to resolve the query.
SEQUENCE	This shows that a sequence was accessed during a query.
SORT (UNIQUE GROUP BY JOIN ORDER BY AGGREGATE)	This shows a query used one of the ordering clauses; the type of clause will be listed as a qualifier.
TABLE ACCESS (BY ROWID FULL CLUSTER HASH)	This shows that a table access was performed. Some queries can be resolved by an INDEX scan only. The type of access performed is showed by the included qualifier. ROWID is generally the fastest form of table access and shows an index scan was also used.
UNION	This shows that a retrieval of unique rows from each table was performed with the duplicates removed from the output.
VIEW	This shows the query accessed a view to resolve the query.

Let's look at this first query's EXPLAIN output in light of the above.

Execution Plan

MERGE JOIN. Shows that the results from the following operations were merged.

SORT (JOIN). Shows that the results were sorted before being passed to the MERGE.

TABLE ACCESS (FULL) OF 'TKP_EXAMPLE2'. Indicates the full table was scanned.

SORT (JOIN). Shows that the results were sorted before being passed to the MERGE.

TABLE ACCESS (FULL) OF 'TKP_EXAMPLE'. Indicates the full table was scanned.

So what does this tell us? First, that both tables were fully scanned to retrieve the rows that met the WHERE clause's criteria. Next, the results from each were sorted. Finally, the results were merged based on the selection criteria. Can these results be improved upon for this type of query? Let's add some indexes (shown in Listing 12.7) and find out. Note: An attempt has been made to ensure the indexes have high selectivity and that columns most accessed in the tables are the leading portion of one or more indexes. Let's reissue the SELECT in Listing 12.6 and see what happens.

Listing 12.7   Indexes for the example tables.

```
CREATE  UNIQUE INDEX TKP_EXP_INDEX ON
TKP_EXAMPLE (
USERNAME,
DEFAULT_TABLESPACE,
TEMPORARY_TABLESPACE) ;

CREATE  UNIQUE INDEX TKP_EXP_INDEX2 ON
TKP_EXAMPLE (
TEMPORARY_TABLESPACE,
USERNAME,
DEFAULT_TABLESPACE) ;

CREATE  UNIQUE INDEX TKP_EXP_INDEX3 ON
TKP_EXAMPLE (
DEFAULT_TABLESPACE,
TEMPORARY_TABLESPACE,
USERNAME) ;

CREATE UNIQUE INDEX TKP_EXP2_INDEX ON
TKP_EXAMPLE2 (
OWNER,
OBJECT_NAME
OBJECT_TYPE) ;

CREATE UNIQUE INDEX TKP_EXP2_INDEX2 ON
TKP_EXAMPLE2 (
OWNER,
TABLESPACE_NAME,
OBJECT_NAME,
OBJECT_TYPE) ;

CREATE UNIQUE INDEX TKP_EXP2_INDEX3 ON
TKP_EXAMPLE2 (
TABLESPACE_NAME,
OWNER,
OBJECT_NAME,
OBJECT_TYPE) ;
```

Listing 12.8   Initial TKPROF results after adding indexes.

```
call      count    cpu   elapsed   disk      query     current      rows
-------   -----   -----  --------  ------  ----------  ----------  ----------
Parse        1    0.01    0.00        0          0          0           0
Execute      1    0.00    0.00        0          0          0           0
Fetch       20    5.17    5.23        0      31266          4         280
-------   -----   -----  --------  ------  ----------  ----------  ----------
total       22    5.18    5.24        0      31266          4         280

Misses in library cache during parse: 1
Optimizer goal: CHOOSE
Parsing user id: 5  (SYSTEM)


Rows       Row Source Operation
-------    ------------------------------------------------------------
   280     NESTED LOOPS
 31019       TABLE ACCESS FULL TKP_EXAMPLE2
   280       INDEX RANGE SCAN TKP_EXP_INDEX (UNIQUE)
```

As you can see, the indexes didn't improve performance; in fact, they made performance worse by over 559 percent! A key indicator that something is wrong is that the
query parameter jumped by several orders of magnitude. This is an example of a query
that returns more than 15 percent of a table. In the RULE-based optimizer, if an index
can be used, it will be used regardless of the number of rows returned from a table. How
can we restore performance? If we use the NOT or LIKE clause instead of the comparison operators (!=, =) are indexes used? Let's look at the same query with the NOT clause
replacing the != in the SELECT statement. Listing 12.9 shows the TKPROF results from
this query.

Listing 12.9   TKPROF using NOT in SELECT statement.

```
select
        username,
        default_tablespace,
        tablespace_name,
        object_name
from
        tkp_example, tkp_example2
where
        username not in ('SYS','SYSTEM') and
        default_tablespace=tablespace_name and
        owner=username
```

continues

Listing 12.9   Continued.

```
call     count     cpu  elapsed   disk        query    current       rows
-------  ------  ------  -------  ------   ----------  ---------  ----------
Parse        1    0.01     0.00       0            0          0           0
Execute      1    0.00     0.00       0            0          0           0
Fetch       20    5.30     5.39       0        31266          4         280
-------  ------  ------  -------  ------   ----------  ---------  ----------
total       22    5.31     5.40       0        31266          4         280

Misses in library cache during parse: 1
Optimizer goal: CHOOSE
Parsing user id: 5  (SYSTEM)

Rows     Execution Plan
-------  -----------------------------------------------------------
      0  SELECT STATEMENT    GOAL: CHOOSE
    280   NESTED LOOPS
  31019    TABLE ACCESS (FULL) OF 'TKP_EXAMPLE2'
    280    INDEX (RANGE SCAN) OF 'TKP_EXP_INDEX' (UNIQUE)
```

Did performance improve? No, in fact, the results are almost identical, down to the execution plan. NOT and != are treated identically. Why are the results the same for the queries in Listing 12.8 and 12.9? In the query in Listing 12.9, the controlling table will be TKP_EXAMPLE2 OT doesn't affect the TKP_EXAMPLE2 table, which was already using a full table scan.

Let's replace the = operator with a LIKE statement and see what happens; look at Listing 12.10.

Listing 12.10   Effect of using LIKE.

```
select
        username,
        default_tablespace,
        tablespace_name,
        object_name
from
        tkp_example, tkp_example2
where
        username not in ('SYS','SYSTEM') and
        default_tablespace like tablespace_name and
        owner like username
```

```
call      count    cpu  elapsed  disk      query     current      rows
-------   -----   ----  -------  ------  ---------  ----------  ----------
Parse         1   0.00     0.00       0          0           0           0
Execute       1   0.00     0.00       0          0           0           0
Fetch        20   5.64     5.70       0      31268           4         280
-------   -----   ----  -------  ------  ---------  ----------  ----------
total        22   5.64     5.71       0      31268           4         280

Misses in library cache during parse: 1
Optimizer goal: CHOOSE
Parsing user id: 5  (SYSTEM)


Rows      Execution Plan
-------   -------------------------------------------------------------
      0   SELECT STATEMENT     GOAL: CHOOSE
    280    NESTED LOOPS
  31019     TABLE ACCESS (FULL) OF 'TKP_EXAMPLE2'
    280     INDEX (RANGE SCAN) OF 'TKP_EXP_INDEX3' (UNIQUE)
```

Even by replacing the = operator with LIKE, we have not forced full table scans, and performance still isn't as good as with the original nonindexed tables. The index scanned was changed from TKP_EXP_INDEX to TKP_EXP_INDEX3. The performance is still poor because for each row of the TKP_EXAMPLE2 table, there is a scan of the TKP_EXP_INDEX3 index, with the scans rejecting tables owned by SYS and SYSTEM. Notice that CPU and elapsed increased. This was due to the increased number of index scans.

To achieve the results from the first query, supposedly we can defeat the use of indexes by adding a zero to a number column or by concatenating a null to a character column. Let's do this and see if we can achieve the performance we want. Look at Listing 12.11.

Listing 12.11   Results of using null concatenation.

```
select
        username,
        default_tablespace,
        tablespace_name,
        object_name
from
        tkp_example, tkp_example2
```

continues

Listing 12.11   Continued.

```
where
        username not in ('SYS','SYSTEM') and
        default_tablespace||''=tablespace_name and
        owner||''=username

call     count    cpu   elapsed    disk       query     current        rows
-------  -----  -----  --------  ------  ----------  ----------  ----------
Parse        1   0.01      0.00       0           0           0           0
Execute      1   0.00      0.00       0           0           0           0
Fetch       20   5.86      5.95       0       31266           4         280
-------  -----  -----  --------  ------  ----------  ----------  ----------
total       22   5.87      5.96       0       31266           4         280

Misses in library cache during parse: 1
Optimizer goal: CHOOSE
Parsing user id: 5  (SYSTEM)

Rows     Execution Plan
-------  -------------------------------------------------------
      0  SELECT STATEMENT    GOAL: CHOOSE
    280   NESTED LOOPS
  31019    TABLE ACCESS (FULL) OF 'TKP_EXAMPLE2'
    280    INDEX (RANGE SCAN) OF 'TKP_EXP_INDEX' (UNIQUE)
```

As you can see, the index was still used and performance worsened. Look at the last section of the WHERE clause. The order compares OWNER to USERNAME, which causes the TKP_EXAMPLE2 table to drive the query. If we switch the order of this comparison, we can use the shorter table TKP_EXAMPLE instead of TKP_EXAMPLE2. The index is still used, but the shorter table significantly reduces the query execution time. Look at Listing 12.12.

Listing 12.12   Results of rearranging WHERE clause columns.

```
select
        username,
        default_tablespace,
        tablespace_name,
        object_name
from
        tkp_example, tkp_example2
where
        username not in ('SYS','SYSTEM') and
        default_tablespace||''=tablespace_name and
        username||''=owner
```

```
call       count     cpu  elapsed   disk      query     current      rows
-------   ------   -----  -------  ------  ---------  ---------  ---------
Parse         1    0.01     0.00       0          0          0          0
Execute       1    0.00     0.00       0          0          0          0
Fetch        20    5.51     5.59       0      31268          4        280
-------   ------   -----  -------  ------  ---------  ---------  ---------
total        22    5.52     5.60       0      31268          4        280

Misses in library cache during parse: 1
Optimizer goal: CHOOSE
Parsing user id: 5  (SYSTEM)


Rows      Execution Plan
-------   ---------------------------------------------------------
      0   SELECT STATEMENT   GOAL: CHOOSE
    280   NESTED LOOPS
  31019    TABLE ACCESS (FULL) OF 'TKP_EXAMPLE2'
    280    INDEX (RANGE SCAN) OF 'TKP_EXP_INDEX3' (UNIQUE)
```

As you can see, performance is still not back to the level we had before we created the indexes. Did the use of null concatenation really affect performance for this query? Leaving the WHERE clause the same, let's go back to the standard comparison and see if the results change. Look at Listing 12.13.

Listing 12.13   Removing null concatenation.

```
select
        username,
        default_tablespace,
        tablespace_name,
        object_name
from
        tkp_example, tkp_example2
where
        username not in ('SYS','SYSTEM') and
        default_tablespace=tablespace_name and
        username=owner

call       count     cpu  elapsed   disk      query     current      rows
-------   ------   -----  -------  ------  ---------  ---------  ---------
Parse         1    0.01     0.00       0          0          0          0
Execute       1    0.00     0.00       0          0          0          0
Fetch        20    4.98     5.04       0      31266          4        280
-------   ------   -----  -------  ------  ---------  ---------  ---------
total        22    4.99     5.04       0      31266          4        280
```

continues

Listing 12.13 Continued.

```
Misses in library cache during parse: 1
Optimizer goal: CHOOSE
Parsing user id: 5  (SYSTEM)

Rows      Execution Plan
-------   --------------------------------------------------------
      0   SELECT STATEMENT   GOAL: CHOOSE
    280    NESTED LOOPS
  31019     TABLE ACCESS (FULL) OF 'TKP_EXAMPLE2'
    280     INDEX (RANGE SCAN) OF 'TKP_EXP_INDEX' (UNIQUE)
```

The results look virtually identical to those we had before we switched the WHERE clause. So for this type of statement, it would be best to defeat as many indexes as possible and force execution driven by the shortest table. When I say "force execution to be driven by the smallest table," I am talking about within any loop. In the above examples, we used predominantly the nested-loop access method; but notice that, in each case, we used the TKP_EXAMPLE2 as the driving table. Now let's switch the order of the tables in the FROM clause and see what type of results we get. Look at Listing 12.14.

Listing 12.14 Changing the driving table.

```
select
  username,
  default_tablespace,
  tablespace_name,
  object_name
from
  tkp_example2, tkp_example
where
  username not in ( 'SYS', 'SYSTEM') and
  tablespace_name=default_tablespace and
  username=owner

call     count   cpu  elapsed   disk      query   current      rows
-------  -----  -----  --------  ------  ----------  ----------  ----------
Parse        1   0.00    0.00       0          0          0           0
Execute      1   0.00    0.00       0          0          0           0
Fetch       20   0.04    0.02       3         83          6         280
-------  -----  -----  --------  ------  ----------  ----------  ----------
total       22   0.04    0.03       3         83          6         280

Misses in library cache during parse: 1
Optimizer goal: CHOOSE
Parsing user id: 5  (SYSTEM)
```

```
Rows       Execution Plan
-------    -----------------------------------------------------
      0    SELECT STATEMENT    GOAL: CHOOSE
    280     NESTED LOOPS
     24      TABLE ACCESS (FULL) OF 'TKP_EXAMPLE'
    280      INDEX (RANGE SCAN) OF 'TKP_EXP2_INDEX3' (UNIQUE)
```

As you can see, by switching the order of the tables in the FROM clause, we have substantially improved performance of the example query by changing the driving table to the TKP_EXAMPLE table, which has only 26 rows, versus using the TKP_EXAMPLE2 table, which has over 30,000 rows. In fact, the performance is over 3,133 percent improved (.03 seconds) over our initial query (.94 seconds), where we didn't use indexes at all and performed a sort merge-join operation.

The final example shows that even when the operation is a sort merge-join, placing the TKP_EXAMPLE table in the driving position performs 235 percent better than with TKP_EXAMPLE2 in the driving position. Look at Listing 12.15.

Listing 12.15   Original query with new driving table.

```
select
  username,
  default_tablespace,
  tablespace_name,
  object_name
from
  tkp_example2, tkp_example
where
  username != 'SYS' and
  username != 'SYSTEM' and
  default_tablespace=tablespace_name and
  owner=username

call     count     cpu   elapsed    disk       query     current      rows
-------  -----   -----  --------   ------  ----------  ----------  ----------
Parse        1    0.11      0.01        0          64           4           0
Execute      1    0.00      0.00        0           0           0           0
Fetch       20    0.37      0.38        0         214          10         280
-------  -----   -----  --------   ------  ----------  ----------  ----------
total       22    0.48      0.40        0         278          14         280

Misses in library cache during parse: 1
Optimizer goal: CHOOSE
Parsing user id: 5 (SYSTEM)
```

continues

Listing 12.15   Continued.

```
Rows      Row Source Operation
-------   ------------------------------------------------------
    280   MERGE JOIN
     24    SORT JOIN
     24     TABLE ACCESS FULL TKP_EXAMPLE
    280    SORT JOIN
  31019     TABLE ACCESS FULL TKP_EXAMPLE2
```

Beginning with late Oracle7, and in every release since Oracle8, the cost-based optimizer (CBO) is also available. To use the cost-based optimizer, all tables in the application that contain data should be analyzed. If even a single table in a query is analyzed when using the CHOOSE, FIRST_ROWS, or ALL_ROWS optimizer modes, then the CBO will be used to resolve the query using default statistics for any nonanalyzed table, cluster, or index in the query. The default table and index statistics are shown in Tables 12.3 and 12.4, respectively.

For larger tables, consider sampling only about 30 percent of the rows. In my experience, using a sample level of less than 20 to 30 percent results in errors in the row count. For small tables, analyze the entire table. For our example, we will analyze the

TABLE 12.4   Default Table Statistics

Statistic	Value
Cardinality	100 rows
Average row length	20 bytes
Number of blocks	100
Remote cardinality	2000 rows
Remote average row length	100 bytes

TABLE 12.5   Default Index Statistics

Statistic	Value
Levels	1
Leaf blocks	25
Leaf blocks/keys	1
Data blocks/keys	1
Distinct keys	100
Clustering factor	800 (8 × number of blocks)

entire tables. In Listing 12.16, we will use our worst-performing query, from Listing 12.10 and see what results we get with the optimizer using cost instead of rule-based optimization.

Listing 12.16   Rerunning worst query using CBO.

```
select
  username,
  default_tablespace,
  tablespace_name,
  object_name
from
  tkp_example, tkp_example2
where
  username not in ( 'SYS', 'SYSTEM') and
  tablespace_name like default_tablespace and
  username like owner

call     count    cpu  elapsed   disk      query       current      rows
-------  -----  -----  --------  ------  ----------  ----------  ----------
Parse        1   0.01     0.01       0           0           0           0
Execute      1   0.00     0.00       0           0           0           0
Fetch       20   1.87     2.24       0        5098         102         280
-------  -----  -----  --------  ------  ----------  ----------  ----------
total       22   1.88     2.26       0        5098         102         280

Misses in library cache during parse: 1
Optimizer goal: CHOOSE
Parsing user id: 5  (SYSTEM)


Rows      Execution Plan
-------   -------------------------------------------------------------
      0   SELECT STATEMENT   GOAL: CHOOSE
    280    NESTED LOOPS
     24      TABLE ACCESS   GOAL: ANALYZED (FULL) OF 'TKP_EXAMPLE'
    280      TABLE ACCESS   GOAL: ANALYZED (FULL) OF 'TKP_EXAMPLE2'
```

As you can see, the CBO does a good job of performing optimization if its statistics are good. The performance here is better than our midrange, but worse than our best performance.

These results underscore the need to understand the application, the size and use of its tables, and how its indexes are constructed. If the DBA doesn't understand the application, the tuning of the application should be the developer's job with the DBA assisting.

When do indexes do us any good? If the query returns a small percent of the table values, an index will improve performance. Compare an example of a restricted query with no index, shown in Listing 12.17, with a restricted query with an index, shown in Listing 12.18.

Listing 12.17   Restricted query with no index.

```
select
  username,
  default_tablespace,
  tablespace_name,
  object_name
from
  tkp_example, tkp_example2
where
  username = 'SYSTEM' and
  default_tablespace = tablespace_name and
  owner = username

call     count    cpu   elapsed   disk      query    current      rows
-------  -----  -----  --------  ------  ----------  ----------  ----------
Parse        1   0.07      0.08       0           1           4           0
Execute      1   0.00      0.00       0           0           0           0
Fetch       11   0.77      0.79       0         214          10         147
-------  -----  -----  --------  ------  ----------  ----------  ----------
total       13   0.84      0.87       0         215          14         147

Misses in library cache during parse: 1
Optimizer goal: CHOOSE
Parsing user id: 5   (SYSTEM)

Rows      Execution Plan
-------   -------------------------------------------------------------
      0   SELECT STATEMENT    GOAL: CHOOSE
    147   MERGE JOIN
  31019    SORT (JOIN)
  31019     TABLE ACCESS (FULL) OF 'TKP_EXAMPLE2'
    147    SORT (JOIN)
      1     TABLE ACCESS (FULL) OF 'TKP_EXAMPLE'
```

Listing 12.18   Restricted query with indexes.

```
select
  username,
  default_tablespace,
  tablespace_name,
  object_name
from
  tkp_example, tkp_example2
```

```
where
  username = 'SYSTEM' and
  owner = username

call     count    cpu  elapsed  disk      query    current        rows
-------  -----  -----  -------  ------  ---------  ---------  ----------
Parse        1   0.00     0.00       0          0          0           0
Execute      1   0.00     0.00       0          0          0           0
Fetch       23   0.03     0.01       0         28          0         321
-------  -----  -----  -------  ------  ---------  ---------  ----------
total       25   0.03     0.02       0         28          0         321

Misses in library cache during parse: 1
Optimizer goal: CHOOSE
Parsing user id: 5  (SYSTEM)

Rows       Execution Plan
-------    ------------------------------------------------------------
      0    SELECT STATEMENT   GOAL: CHOOSE
    321    NESTED LOOPS
      1      INDEX (RANGE SCAN) OF 'TKP_EXP_INDEX' (UNIQUE)
    321      INDEX (RANGE SCAN) OF 'TKP_EXP2_INDEX2' (UNIQUE)
```

As you can see, the performance gains (in this case over 300 percent), even for these small tables, is rather large, especially in regard to the number of rows processed per step.

An additional indicator of problems with a query is a high current-to-rows ratio. If this value exceeds 15, the query needs tuning.

So, what have we learned? First, that statement tuning is complex. The optimizer built into the SQL processor makes choices based on built-in optimization rules, which in turn are based on statement rank in the rule-based optimizer, or on cost under the cost-based optimizer. At times, this optimizer doesn't always use the right index, or truly optimize the statement. If statistics are stale or available only on a few tables, the optimizer will not be able to cost-optimize a query properly.

For unrestricted queries that return most, if not all, of the values in a table or group of tables, use methods to restrict the use of indexes as much as possible. With unrestricted queries, start the WHERE clause by restricting as much as possible and as rapidly as possible the values to be retrieved. Try to get full table scans on small tables first, and use their results to search other tables.

There is some debate as to whether placing the small table as the controlling table really does improve performance. If the small table can be completely cached in memory, it may make more sense to drive from the larger table, since multiblock reads can then be used rather than random reads, which may reread the same block several times. This would have the effect of reducing time-consuming physical block reads for the query. In our example, both tables were cached; and having the driving table as the smaller table improved performance by a large percentage. Since this will be application- and index-controlled, in situations where this happens, use TKPROF to find out the facts before following a possibly outmoded rule.

Using the Standalone EXPLAIN PLAN   The EXPLAIN PLAN program can be used in standalone fashion without the TKPROF application. In order to use EXPLAIN PLAN in this way, the user must create a PLAN table in his or her tablespace or have been granted access to a central plan table. This can either be done with the supplied SQL script UTLXPLAN.SQL, which is located in the $ORACLE_HOME/rdbms/admin directory on most UNIX systems. In all 8 versions and in Oracle9*i*, the user can also use the SET AUTOTRACE ON EXPLAIN command in SQL*Plus to generate explain plans as the user enters and executes SQL statements; in addition, SET, SET TIMING ON will generate elapsed time counts between the start and end of a transaction.

The UTLXPLAN.SQL procedure creates the PLAN_TABLE. As an alternative, users can create a table with any name they choose, but the table must have the columns and data types shown in Listing 12.19.

Listing 12.19   Characteristics of file to hold EXPLAIN PLAN output.

```
CREATE TABLE plan_table
    (statement_id    VARCHAR2(30),
    timestamp        DATE,
    remarks          VARCHAR2(80),
    operation        VARCHAR2(30),
    options          VARCHAR2(30),
    object_node      VARCHAR2(128),
    object_owner     VARCHAR2(30),
    object_name      VARCHAR2(30),
    object_instance  NUMERIC,
    object_type      VARCHAR2(30),
    optimizer        VARCHAR2(255),
    search_columns   NUMERIC,
    id               NUMERIC,
    parent_id        NUMERIC,
    position         NUMERIC,
    cost             NUMERIC,
    cardinality      NUMERIC,
    bytes            NUMERIC,
    other_tag        VARCHAR2(255)
    other            LONG);
```

The PLAN_TABLE used by the EXPLAIN PLAN command contains the following columns:

STATEMENT_ID. The value of the option STATEMENT_ID parameter specified in the EXPLAIN PLAN statement.

TIMESTAMP. The date and time when the EXPLAIN PLAN statement was issued.

REMARKS. Any comment (up to 80 bytes) you wish to associate with each step of the explain plan. If you need to add or change a remark on any row of the PLAN_TABLE, use the UPDATE statement to modify the rows of the PLAN_TABLE.

OPERATION. The name of the internal operation performed in this step. In the first row generated for a statement, the column contains one of the following values:

DELETE STATEMENT

INSERT STATEMENT

SELECT STATEMENT

UPDATE STATEMENT

OPTIONS. A variation on the operation described in the OPERATION column.

OBJECT_NODE. The name of the database link used to reference the object (a table name or view name). For local queries using the parallel query option, this column describes the order in which output from operations is consumed.

OBJECT_OWNER. The name of the user that owns the schema containing the table or index.

OBJECT_NAME. The name of the table or index.

OBJECT_INSTANCE. A number corresponding to the ordinal position of the object as it appears in the original statement. The numbering proceeds from left to right, outer to inner, with respect to the original statement text. Note that view expansion will result in unpredictable numbers.

OBJECT_TYPE. A modifier that provides descriptive information about the object; for example, NON-UNIQUE for indexes.

OPTIMIZER. The current mode of the optimizer.

SEARCH_COLUMNS. Not currently used.

ID. A number assigned to each step in the execution plan.

PARENT_ID. The ID of the next execution step that operates on the output of the ID step.

POSITION. The order of processing for steps that all have the PARENT_ID.

OTHER. Other information specific to the execution step that a user may find useful.

OTHER_TAG. Describes the contents of the OTHER column. See below for more information on the possible values for this column.

PARTITION_START. The start partition of a range of accessed partitions.

PARTITION_STOP. The stop partition of a range of accessed partitions.

PARTITION_ID. The step that has computed the pair of values of the PARTITION_START and PARTITION_STOP columns.

DISTRIBUTION. Shows the distribution method.

IO_COST. The cost of the operation as estimated by the optimizer's cost-based approach. For statements that use the rule-based approach, this column is null. Cost is not determined for table access operations. The value of this column does not have any particular unit of measurement; it is merely a weighted value used to compare costs of execution plans.

CPU_COST. The cost of the operation in CPU time.

CARDINALITY. The estimate by the cost-based approach of the number of rows accessed by the operation.

BYTES. The estimate by the cost-based approach of the number of bytes accessed by the operation.

TEMP_SPACE. The amount of temporary space required for the operation.

Table 12.6 describes the values that may appear in the OTHER_TAG column.

The TKPROF section lists each combination of OPERATION and OPTION values produced by the EXPLAIN PLAN command and its meaning within an execution plan.

When TKPROF is run using the EXPLAIN option, the table is created and dropped automatically; when it is created for use in EXPLAIN PLAN, it is permanent. Issue the DELETE command against the table between runs of EXPLAIN PLAN or duplicate rows will be inserted to the table and to any output generated based on the table.

TABLE 12.6 Contents of the OTHER_TAG Column

OTHER_TAG Text	Interpretation
(blank)	Serial execution.
serial_from_remote	Serial execution at a remote site.
serial_to_parallel	Serial execution. Output of step is partitioned or broadcast to parallel query servers.
Parallel_to_parallel	Parallel execution. Output of step is repartitioned to second set of parallel query servers.
Parallel_to_serial	Parallel execution. Output of step is returned to serial "query coordinator" process.
Parallel_combined_with_parent	Parallel execution. Output of step goes to next step in same parallel process. No interprocess communication to parent.
Parallel_combined_with_child	Parallel execution. Input of step comes from prior step in same parallel process. No interprocess communication from child.

Once this table is generated, the user issues the EXPLAIN PLAN command from within SQLPLUS to generate output to the table. The EXPLAIN PLAN command format follows.

```
EXPLAIN PLAN [SET STATEMENT_ID = 'descriptor']
        [INTO table]

FOR SQL statement;
```

where:

descriptor. A short name by which to identify the SQL statement. If not specified, the entire statement will be used as the identifier.

Table. If other than the PLAN_TABLE is used, this is where it is named.

SQL statement. The SQL statement to analyze.

An example of the use of the EXPLAIN PLAN command is shown in Listing 12.20.

Listing 12.20   Example EXPLAIN PLAN command.

```
SQL> explain plan
  2  set statement_id='EXP PLAN EXAMPLE'
  3  for
  4  select t.owner,t.table_name,t.tablespace_name,
  5  i.index_name,i.tablespace_name
  6  from tkp_example t, tkp_example2 i
  7  where
  8  t.table_name=i.table_name and
  9  t.owner not in ('SYS','SYSTEM')
 10*

Explained.
```

To get the results of the EXPLAIN PLAN command, the table PLAN_TABLE, or whichever table was specified in the EXPLAIN PLAN command, must be queried. Let's look at a simple query of this table for the above SQL statement. The query and output from the query are shown in Listing 12.21. While this type of query will provide useful information, it leaves the logical arrangement of that information to the user. With use of the padding options and connect features available in SQL, the user can generated a pseudo-execution plan comparable to the one generated in the TKPROF command. The query used for this, and the output generated in place of the tabular information in Listing 12.21, is shown in Listing 12.22.

The new format shown in Listing 12.22 is easier to understand. Remember to review the TKPROF output for each statement, as shown in the first part of this chapter. Just because an index, rather than a table scan, is used doesn't mean the query will execute faster. If the index is not bitmapped and is not selective, it can actually slow a query.

Keep in mind that these plans have to be read from the inside out, from the bottom up; for example, in the plan in Listing 12.22, the TKP_EXAMPLE table is accessed and

Listing 12.21   Tabular EXPLAIN PLAN output.

```
SQL> column position format 99999999
SQL> column object_name format a12
SQL> column options format a7
SQL> column operation format a15
SQL> select operation, options, object_name, id,  parent_id,
  2  position
  3  from plan_table
  4  where statement_id='EXP PLAN EXAMPLE'
  5* order by id

OPERATION          OPTIONS  OBJECT_NAME    ID  PARENT_ID POSITION
---------------    -------  -----------    ---- --------- ---------
SELECT STATEMENT                           0
MERGE JOIN                                 1       0        1
SORT               JOIN                    2       1        1
TABLE ACCESS       FULL     TKP_EXAMPLE2   3       2        1
SORT               JOIN                    4       1        2
TABLE ACCESS       FULL     TKP_EXAMPLE    5       4        1

6 rows selected
```

Listing 12.22   Formatted EXPLAIN PLAN output.

```
SQL> column query_plan format a60
SQL> select lpad(' ',2*level)||operation||' '||object_name query_plan
  2  from plan_table where statement_id is not null
  3  connect by prior id=parent_id
  4  start with id=0;

QUERY_PLAN
----------------------------------
  SELECT STATEMENT
    MERGE JOIN
      SORT
        TABLE ACCESS TKP_EXAMPLE2
      SORT
        TABLE ACCESS TKP_EXAMPLE

6 rows selected.
```

all rows that don't have the OWNER SYS or SYSTEM are retrieved. Then the TKP_
EXAMPLE2 table is accessed for each row in the TKP_EXAMPLE table and all rows
that have matches in the TABLE_NAME column are selected. The results for both accesses are then sorted and merged to form the final output.

The ORACLE8 table also has columns to document whether partitions are being
used, and this data can be added to the select if desired, as well as a number of other
columns that you may find useful. For the I/O and CPU cost, distribution and temporary space were added in Oracle9*i* columns.

Example Use of Command-Line Explain Plan   As mentioned earlier, the SQL*Plus
program allows use of the explain plan facility. To implement the automatic explain
plan, either users must have a plan_table in their schema or a public plan_table must
be made available to all users. The SET AUTOTRACE ON command turns on tracing
for a session. With just the ON option, the results, explain plan, and related statistics
are generated for each statement executed, as shown in Listing 12.23.

Listing 12.23   Example use of AUTOTRACE ON EXPLAIN.

```
SQL> set autotrace on explain
SQL> set timing on
SQL> select a.tablespace_name, b.file_name, a.initial_extent
  2  from test2 a,
  3  test1 b
  4  where a.tablespace_name=b.tablespace_name
  5* order by a.tablespace_name
... Statement executes
12 rows selected.

 real: 160

Execution Plan
----------------------------------------------------------
   0       SELECT STATEMENT Optimizer=CHOOSE
   1    0  MERGE JOIN
   2    1   SORT (JOIN)
   3    2    TABLE ACCESS (FULL) OF 'TEST1'
   4    1   SORT (JOIN)
   5    4    TABLE ACCESS (FULL) OF 'TEST2'
```

The SET AUTOTRACE command has several additional arguments:

ON EXPLAIN. Generates only the results and explain plan output.

TRACEONLY. Generates only the trace output, no results.

ON STATISTICS. Generates only the results and statistics output.

Another SET command, SET TIMING ON, allows collection of query and statement timing information to the user's screen. By using both AUTOTRACE and TIMING, the user can get many of the benefits of TKPROF, without using it.

OEM also provides an explain plan function. By double-clicking on the SQL statements listed in the TOP SQL display (accessed by selecting an instance, then the Diagnostic Pack icon, and finally the Top SQL display icon), you invoke the Oracle Performance Manager (OPM) for the SQL that was chosen. In OPM, select the Drilldown menu and select Explain Plan to see the explain plan for the chosen SQL statement. An example is shown in Figure 12.9.

Using Hints in Oracle8, Oracle8*i*, and Oracle9*i* to Force Behavior

One important feature of Oracle is the ability to issue *hints* to the optimizer. In Oracle8, Oracle8*i*, and Oracle9*i*, you can direct the optimizer to use a specific type of action for

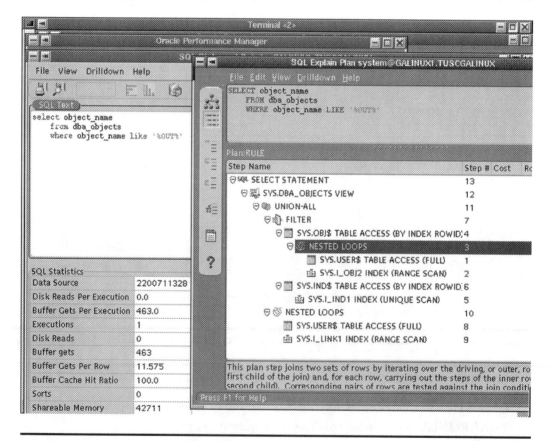

FIGURE 12.9   Example OEM Explain Plan screen.

your queries. This gives the DBA or application developer more control than was possible in earlier versions. Let's look at how to use this feature.

Hints are enclosed within comments to the SQL commands DELETE, SELECT, or UPDATE, or are designated by two dashes (--) and a plus sign (+). (Note: For demonstration purposes here, only the SELECT statement format will be shown, as the format is identical for all three commands.)

```
SELECT          /*+ hint --or-- text */
statement body
    - or -
SELECT          --+ hint --or-- text
statement body
```

where:

/*, */ — are the comment delimiters for multiline comments.

— — is the comment delimiter for a single-line comment (not usually used for hints).

+ — tells Oracle a hint follows (it must come immediately after the /*).

hint is one of the allowed hints.

text is the comment text

Table 12.7 lists the Oracle9*i* hints and their meanings.

TABLE 12.7   Hints and Their Meanings

Hint	Meaning
+	Must appear immediately after comment indicator. Tells Oracle this is a list of hints.
ALL_ROWS	Use the cost-based approach for best throughput.
CHOOSE	Default; if statistics are available, it will use cost, if not, rule.
FIRST_ROWS	Use the cost-based approach for best response time.
RULE	Use rules-based approach. This cancels any other hints specified for this statement.
Access Method Hints	
CLUSTER(table)	Tells Oracle to do a cluster scan to access the table.
FULL(table)	Tells the optimizer to do a full scan of the specified table.
HASH(table)	Tells Oracle to explicitly choose the hash access method for the table.

continued

TABLE 12.7   (Continued)

Access Method Hints

HASH_AJ(table)	Transforms a NOT IN subquery to a hash antijoin.
ROWID(table)	Forces a rowid scan of the specified table.
INDEX(table [index])	Forces an index scan of the specified table using the specified index(s). If a list of indexes is specified, the optimizer chooses the one with the lowest cost. If no index is specified, the optimizer chooses the available index for the table with the lowest cost.
INDEX_ASC (table [index])	Same as INDEX, but performs an ascending search of the index chosen. Functionally identical to the INDEX statement.
INDEX_DESC(table [index])	Same as INDEX, but performs a descending search. If more than one table is accessed, this is ignored.
INDEX_COMBINE(table index)	Combines the bitmapped indexes on the table if the cost shows that to do so would give better performance.
INDEX_FFS(table index)	Performs a fast full index scan rather than a table scan.
MERGE_AJ (table)	Transforms a NOT IN subquery into a merge antijoin.
AND_EQUAL(table index index [index index index])	Causes a merge on several single-column indexes. Two must be specified, five can be.
NL_AJ	Transforms a NOT IN subquery into an NL antijoin (nested loop).
HASH_SJ(t1, t2)	Inserted to the EXISTS subquery, converts the subquery into a special type of hash join between t1 and t2, which preserves the semantics of the subquery. That is, even if there is more than one matching row in t2 for a row in t1, the row in t1 will be returned only once.
MERGE_SJ (t1, t2)	Inserted to the EXISTS subquery, converts the subquery into a special type of merge join between t1 and t2, which preserves the semantics of the subquery. That is, even if there is more than one matching row in t2 for a row in t1, the row in t1 will be returned only once.
NL_SJ	Inserted to the EXISTS subquery, converts the subquery into a special type of nested loop join between t1 and t2, which preserves the semantics of the subquery. That is, even if there is more than one matching row in t2 for a row in t1, the row in t1 will be returned only once.

Hints for Join Orders and Transformations

ORDERED	Forces tables to be joined in the order specified. If you know that table X has fewer rows, ordering it first may speed execution in a join.

TABLE 12.7   *(Continued)*

Hints for Join Orders and Transformations

STAR	Forces the largest table to be joined last, using a nested_loops join on the index.
STAR_TRANSFORMATION	Makes the optimizer use the best plan in which a start transformation is used.
FACT(table)	Says that when performing a star transformation, use the specified table as a fact table.
NO_FACT(table)	Says that when performing a star transformation, do not use the specified table as a fact table.
PUSH_SUBQ	Causes nonmerged subqueries to be evaluated at the earliest possible point in the execution plan.
REWRITE(mview)	If possible, forces the query to use the specified materialized view; if no materialized view is specified, the system chooses what it calculates to be the appropriate view.
NOREWRITE	Turns off query rewrite for the statement. Use this hint when the data returned must be concurrent and can't come from a materialized view.
USE_CONCAT	Forces combined OR conditions and IN processing in the WHERE clause to be transformed into a compound query using the UNION ALL set operator.
NO_MERGE (table)	Causes Oracle to join each specified table with another row source without a sort-merge join.
NO_EXPAND	Prevents OR and IN processing expansion.

Hints for Join Operations

USE_HASH (table)	Causes Oracle to join each specified table with another row source with a hash join.
USE_NL(table)	Forces a nested loop using the specified table as the controlling table.
USE_MERGE(table,[table,...])	Forces a sort-merge-join operation of the specified tables.
DRIVING_SITE	Forces query execution to be done at a different site than that selected by Oracle. This hint can be used with either rule-based or cost-based optimization.
LEADING(table)	Causes Oracle to use the specified table as the first table in the join order.

continued

TABLE 12.7   (*Continued*)

Hints for Parallel Operations	
[NO]APPEND	Specifies that data is to be or not to be appended to the end of a file, rather than into existing freespace. Use this hint only with INSERT commands.
NOPARALLEL (table)	Specifies the operation is not to be done in parallel.
PARALLEL(table, instances)	Specifies the operation is to be done in parallel.
PARALLEL_INDEX	Allows parallelization of a fast full index scan on any index.

Other Hints	
CACHE	Specifies that the blocks retrieved for the table in the hint will be placed at the most recently used end of the LRU list when the table is full table scanned.
NOCACHE	Specifies that the blocks retrieved for the table in the hint will be placed at the least recently used end of the LRU list when the table is full table scanned.
[NO]APPEND	For insert operations, appends data at the HWM of table.
UNNEST	Turns on the UNNEST_SUBQUERY option for statement if UNNEST_SUBQUERY parameter is set to FALSE.
NO_UNNEST	Turns off the UNNEST_SUBQUERY option for statement if UNNEST_SUBQUERY parameter is set to TRUE.
PUSH_PRED	Pushes the join predicate into the view.
NO_PUSH_PRED	Prevents the predicate from being pushed into the view.
ORDERED_PREDICATES	Forces the optimizer to preserve the order of predicate evaluation, except for predicates used as index keys. Use this hint in the WHERE clause of SELECT statements.
CURSOR_SHARING_EXACT	If the CURSOR_SHARING initialization parameter is set to FORCE or SIMILAR, resets it to EXACT for this query (no bind variable substitution).

As you can see, the dilemma with the stubborn index usage demonstrated in the first part of this chapter could have been easily solved using FULL or NO_INDEX hints. Again I say: You must know the application to be tuned. Though the DBA can provide guidance to developers, in all but the smallest development projects, it will be nearly impossible for a DBA to know everything about each application. It is clear that responsibility for application tuning rests solely on the developer's shoulders, with help and guidance from the DBA.

Using Global Hints   Hints normally refer to table in the query, but it is also possible to specify a hint for a table within a view through the use of what are known as *global* *hints.* Any table hint can be transformed into a global hint. Doing so requires using the global hint syntax, shown here:

```
/*+ hint(view_name.table_in_view) */
```

For example:

```
/*+ full(sales_totals_vw.s_customer) */
```

If the view is an inline view, place an alias on it, then use the alias to reference the inline view in the global hint.

Using Stealth Hints (OUTLINES)   In versions of Oracle prior to Oracle8*i,* the only ways to stabilize an execution plan was to ensure that tables were analyzed frequently and that the relative ratios of rows in the tables involved stayed relatively stable. Moreover, neither of these options in pre-Oracle8*i* for stabilizing execution plans worked 100 percent of the time. In Oracle8*i,* a new feature, the OUTLINE capability, has been added. And in Oracle9*i,* the capability to edit the actual outlines produced was provided.

The outline feature allows the DBA to tune a SQL statement and then store the optimizer plan for the statement in what is known as an OUTLINE. From that point forward, whenever an identical SQL statement to the one in the OUTLINE is used, it will use the optimizer instructions contained in the OUTLINE. I refer to this process as using *stealth hints,* because what actually happens beneath the covers is that Oracle stores a series of hints tied to the hash value of the SQL statement; and whenever Oracle sees the hash value, it automatically applies the hints it has stored.

Storage of plan outlines for SQL statements is known as *plan stability;* it ensures that changes in the Oracle environment don't affect the way an SQL statement is optimized by the cost-based optimizer. If you want, Oracle will define plans for all issued SQL statements at the time they are executed; these stored plans will be reused until altered or dropped. That said, generally I do not suggest using the automatic outline feature, as it can lead to poor plans being reused by the optimizer. It makes more sense to monitor for high cost statements and tune them as required, storing an outline for them only once they have been properly tuned.

As with the storage of SQL in the shared pool, outline storage depends on the statement being reissued in an identical fashion each time it is used. If even one space is out of place, the stored outline will not be reused. Therefore, your queries should be stored as PL/SQL procedures, functions, or packages (or perhaps Java routines), and bind variables should always be used. This allows reuse of the stored image of the SQL, as well as reuse of stored outlines.

NOTE   To be useful over the life of an application, outlines have to be periodically verified by checking SQL statement performance. If performance of SQL statements degrades, the stored outline may have to be dropped and regenerated after the SQL is retuned.

Creating an OUTLINE Object   Outlines are created using the CREATE OUTLINE command, or via the OUTLINE editor in OEM. The syntax for the CREATE OUTLINE command is:

```
CREATE [OR REPLACE] OUTLINE outline_name
[FOR CATEGORY category_name]
ON statement;
```

where:

> **Outline_name.** A unique name for the outline.
>
> **[FOR CATEGORY category_name].** (Optional) Allows more than one outline to be associated with a single query by specifying multiple categories, each of which is named uniquely.
>
> **ON statement.** Specifies the statement for which the outline is prepared.

An example is shown in Listing 12.24.

Listing 12.24   Example outline creation.

```
CREATE OR REPLACE OUTLINE get_tables
ON
SELECT
a.owner,
a.table_name,
a.tablespace_name,
SUM(b.bytes),
COUNT(b.table_name) extents
FROM
     dba_tables a,
     dba_extents b
WHERE
     a.owner=b.owner
     AND a.table_name=b.table_name
GROUP BY
     a.owner, a.table_name, a.tablespace_name;
```

Assuming the above select is a part of a stored PL/SQL procedure, or perhaps part of a view, the stored outline will now be used each time an exactly matching SQL statement is issued.

Altering an Outline   Outlines are altered using the ALTER OUTLINE or CREATE OR REPLACE form of the CREATE command, or via the OEM GUI interface. The format of the command is identical whether it is used for initial creation or replacement of an existing outline. For example, to add SUM(b.blocks) to the previous example, we would use the format shown in Listing 12.25.

Listing 12.25   Example replacement of an outline.

```
CREATE OR REPLACE OUTLINE get_tables
ON
SELECT
a.owner,
a.table_name,
a.tablespace_name,
SUM(b.bytes),
COUNT(b.table_name) extents,
SUM(b.blocks)
FROM
     dba_tables a,
     dba_extents b
WHERE
     a.owner=b.owner
     AND a.table_name=b.table_name
GROUP BY
     a.owner, a.table_name, a.tablespace_name;
```

The above example has the effect of altering the stored outline get_tables to include any changes brought about by inclusion of the SUM(b.blocks) in the SELECT list.

If we want to rename the outline or change a category name, we use the ALTER OUTLINE command in this format:

```
ALTER OUTLINE outline_name
[REBUILD]
[RENAME TO new_outline_name]
[CHANGE CATEGORY TO new_category_name]
```

The ALTER OUTLINE command allows us to rebuild the outline for an existing outline_name, as well as rename the outline or change its category. The benefit of using the ALTER OUTLINE command is that we do not have to respecify the complete SQL statement as we would have to do using the CREATE OR REPLACE command.

Dropping an OUTLINE   Outlines are dropped using the DROP OUTLINE command or through OEM. The syntax for the DROP OUTLINE command is:

```
DROP OUTLINE outline_name;
```

Using the OUTLN_PKG to Manage SQL Stored Outlines   The OUTLN_PKG package (now synonymous with DBMS_OUTLINE) enables the management of *stored* *outlines.* A stored outline is an execution plan for a specific SQL statement, which permits the optimizer to stabilize an SQL statement's execution plan by giving repeatable execution plans even when data and statistics change. In Oracle9*i,* the OEM Outline Management wizard can be used to manage outlines. Figure 12.10 shows the Outline Management screens in OEM.

NOTE   The DBA should take care when granting the EXECUTE privilege on the OUTLN_PKG. By default, it is not granted to the public user group, nor is a public synonym created.

The following subsections describe the components of OUTLN_PKG.

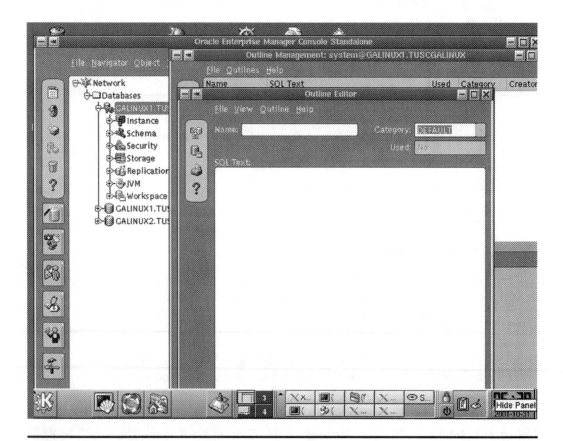

FIGURE 12.10   OEM Outline Management screens.

DROP_EXTRAS   The DROP_EXTRAS procedure drops any extra hints that are a result of an import from another database schema. The hints are dropped because they aren't accounted for by the hintcount. The procedure, shown here, has no arguments and returns no variables.

```
SQL> EXECUTE DBMS_OUTLINE.DROP_EXTRAS;

PL/SQL procedure successfully executed.
```

DROP_UNREFD_HINTS   The DROP_UNREFD_HINTS procedure drops any hints that aren't referred to in any outlines in the OUTLN.OL$ table (note that the tables used to produce outlines are owned by the OUTLN user, not SYS). The procedure, shown below, has no arguments and returns no variables.

```
SQL> EXECUTE DBMS_OUTLINE.DROP_UNREFD_HINTS;

PL/SQL procedure successfully executed.
```

DROP_COLLISION   The DBMS_OUTLINE.DROP_COLLISION precedure drops an outline with an ol$.hintcount value that does not match the number of hints for that outline in ol$.hintcount. This rare condition can occur if the outline is being modified at the same time it is being imported. The procedure DROP_COLLISION has no arguments and returns no variables, as shown here.

```
SQL> EXECUTE DBMS_OUTLINE.DROP_COLLISION;

PL/SQL procedure successfully executed.
```

DROP_UNUSED   The DROP_UNUSED procedure is used to drop outlines that have not been used in the compilation of SQL statements. The DROP_UNUSED procedure has no arguments and returns no variables.

```
SQL> EXECUTE DBMS_OUTLINE.DROP_UNUSED;

PL/SQL procedure successfully executed.
```

To determine whether an SQL statement OUTLINE is unused, perform a SELECT against the DBA_OUTLINES view, as shown in Listing 12.26.

Listing 12.26   Example SELECT against DBA_OUTLINES.

```
SQL> desc dba_outlines;
 Name                                    Null?    Type
 --------------------------------------- -------- ------------
 NAME                                             VARCHAR2(30)
 OWNER                                            VARCHAR2(30)
 CATEGORY                                         VARCHAR2(30)
```

```
    USED                              VARCHAR2(9)
    TIMESTAMP                         DATE
    VERSION                           VARCHAR2(64)
    SQL_TEXT                          LONG
    SIGNATURE                         RAW(16)

SQL> set long 1000
SQL> select name, owner, category, used, timestamp, version, sql_text
  2  from dba_outlines where used='UNUSED';

NAME            OWNER CATEGORY  USED   TIMESTAMP   VERSION            SQL_TEXT
------------    ------ -------- ------ --------- ----------   --------------------
TEST_OUTLINE SYSTEM TEST       UNUSED 04-NOV-01 9.0.1.0.0   select a.table_name,
                                                            b.tablespace_name,
                                                            c.file_name from
                                                            dba_tables a,
                                                            dba_tablespaces b,
                                                            dba_data_files c
                                                            where
                                                            a.tablespace_name =
                                                            b.tablespace_name
                                                            and b.tablespace_name
                                                            = c.tablespace_name
                                                            and c.file_id =
                                                            (select
                                                            min(d.file_id) from
                                                            dba_data_files d
                                                            where
                                                            c.tablespace_name =
                                                            d.tablespace_name)

1 row selected.

SQL> execute sys.outln_pkg.drop_unused;

PL/SQL procedure successfully completed.

SQL> select * from dba_outlines where used='UNUSED';

no rows selected
```

NOTE   Remember, the DROP_UNUSED procedure drops all unused outlines, so use it carefully.

DROP_BY_CAT   The DROP_BY_CAT procedure drops all outlines that belong to a specific category. The procedure has one input variable, cat, a VARCHAR 2 that corresponds to the name of the category you want to drop. See Listing 12.27 for an example.

Listing 12.27   Example use of DROP_BY_CAT.

```
SQL> create outline test_outline for category test on
  2  select a.table_name, b.tablespace_name, c.file_name from
  3  dba_tables a, dba_tablespaces b, dba_data_files c
  4  where
  5  a.tablespace_name=b.tablespace_name
  6  and b.tablespace_name=c.tablespace_name
  7  and c.file_id = (select min(d.file_id) from dba_data_files d
  8  where c.tablespace_name=d.tablespace_name)
  9  ;
Outline created.

SQL> select name, owner, category, used, timestamp, version, sql_text
  2  from dba_outlines where category='TEST';

NAME          OWNER CATEGORY USED  TIMESTAMP  VERSION            SQL_TEXT
------------  ----- -------- ----- ---------  ----------  ----------------------
TEST_OUTLINE SYSTEM TEST     UNUSED 04-NOV-01 9.0.1.0.0   select a.table_name, b.ta
                                                          blespace_name, c.file_nam
                                                          e from
                                                          dba_tables a, dba_tablesp
                                                          aces b, dba_data_files c
                                                          where
                                                          a.tablespace_name=b.table
                                                          space_name
                                                          and b.tablespace_name=c.t
                                                          ablespace_name
                                                          and c.file_id = (select m
                                                          in(d.file_id) from dba_da
                                                          ta_files d
                                                          where c.tablespace_name=d
                                                          .tablespace_name)




1 row selected.

SQL> execute sys.outln_pkg.drop_by_cat('TEST');

PL/SQL procedure successfully completed.

SQL> select * from dba_outlines where category='TEST';

no rows selected
```

UPDATE_BY_CAT   The UPDATE_BY_CAT procedure changes all of the outlines in one category to a new category. If the SQL text in an outline already has an outline in the target category, then it is not merged into the new category. The procedure has two input variables, oldcat VARCHAR2 and newcat VARCHAR2, where oldcat corresponds to the category to be merged, and newcat is the new category with which oldcat is to be merged. Listing 12.28 shows an example using UPDATE_BY_CAT.

Listing 12.28   Example use of UPDATE_BY_CAT.

```
SQL> create outline test_outline for category test on
  2  select a.table_name, b.tablespace_name, c.file_name from
  3  dba_tables a, dba_tablespaces b, dba_data_files c
  4  where
  5  a.tablespace_name=b.tablespace_name
  6  and b.tablespace_name=c.tablespace_name
  7  and c.file_id = (select min(d.file_id) from dba_data_files d
  8  where c.tablespace_name=d.tablespace_name)
  9  ;

Outline created.

SQL> create outline test_outline2 for category test on
  2  select * from dba_data_files;

Outline created.

SQL> create outline prod_outline1 for category prod on
  2  select owner,table_name from dba_tables;

Outline created.

SQL> create outline prod_outline2 for category prod on
  2  select * from dba_data_files;

Outline created.

SQL>  select name,category from dba_outlines order by category
NAME             CATEGORY
---------------- --------
PROD_OUTLINE1    PROD
PROD_OUTLINE2    PROD
TEST_OUTLINE2    TEST
TEST_OUTLINE     TEST

4 rows selected.

SQL> execute sys.outln_pkg.update_by_cat('TEST','PROD');
```

```
PL/SQL procedure successfully completed.

SQL> select name,category from dba_outlines order by category;
NAME               CATEGORY
---------------    --------
TEST_OUTLINE       PROD
PROD_OUTLINE1      PROD
PROD_OUTLINE2      PROD
TEST_OUTLINE2      TEST

4 rows selected.
```

As a result of the UPDATE_BY_CAT procedure call, the TEST_OUTLINE outline was moved into the PROD category, but TEST_OUTLINE2, because it is a duplicate of PROD_OUTLINE2, was not merged.

GENERATE_SIGNATURE   The GENERATE_SIGNATURE package accepts an input variable of an SQL statement and returns a RAW signature value. The signature value can then be used to locate the SQL's outline, if it exists in the DBA_OUTLINES table. (Note: Testing on Oracle9i version 9.0.1.0 revealed this procedure was not present. The SQL_TEXT is a VARCHAR2; the SIGNATURE is a RAW. This procedure is, however, present in the next package described, DBMS_OUTLN_EDIT.)

```
DBMS_OUTLINE.GENERATE_SIGNATURE(sql_text, signature);
```

Using the DBMS_OUTLN_EDIT Package to Change Stored OUTLINES   Though it was possible in Oracle8i to alter stored outlines, by manually manipulating the base tables owned by the OUTLN user, this process was not supported and was fraught with complexity and pitfalls. To remedy those problems, in Oracle9i Oracle Corporation has provided the DBMS_OUTLN_EDIT package, which allows for the manual manipulation of outlines, and the Outline Editor in the OEM (shown in Figure 12.11), which is a GUI interface for editing outlines. The subsections to follow cover the use of the DBMS_OUTLN_EDIT package.

NOTE   The OEM interface is essentially self-explanatory, so I will not detail its use here. I will, however, point out that, to use the OEM outline editor, you must have EXECUTE privileges on OUTLN_PKG and on DBMS_OUTLN_EDIT, as well as the CREATE ANY OUTLINE and ALTER ANY OUTLINE system privileges.

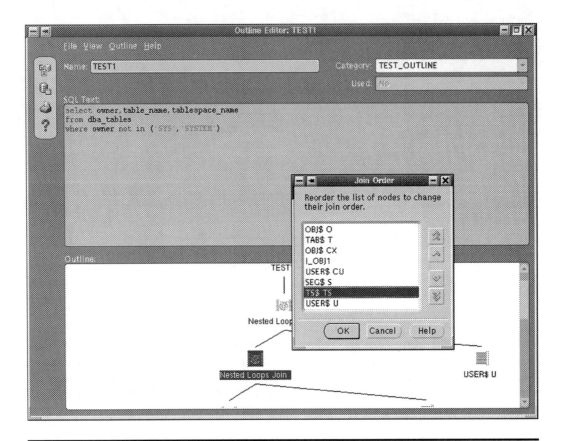

FIGURE 12.11 OEM Outline Editor.

The DBMS_OUTLN_EDIT package consists of several procedures that allow for the following: the creation and drop of the required support tables for the edit operation, the ability to change the position of a particular join, and the ability to generate signatures and refresh private outlines. These procedures are described in the following subsections.

NOTE The DBMS_OUTLN_EDIT package can only be used on private outlines. To edit join methods or the table order of anything more complex than join position, you must use the OEM Outline Editor.

Using DBMS_OUTLN_EDIT.CREATE_EDIT_TABLES If you are starting an edit session in a user that has not created outlines, you will need to create the edit tables.

The DBMS_OUTLN_EDIT.CREATE_EDIT_TABLES procedure is used to create the required outline edit support tables. The CREATE_EDIT_TABLES procedure performs the same actions as the UTLEDITOL.SQL script located in the $ORACLE_HOME/rdbms/admin directory or its equivalent on your system. (Note: The UTLEDITOL.SQL script may not be present on 9.0.1.0 version systems.)

There are no arguments or return variables for CREATE_EDIT_TABLES, whose syntax is shown here:

```
SQL> DBMS_OUTLN_EDIT.CREATE_EDIT_TABLES;

Procedure successfully executed.
```

Once the tables have been created, you need to create the base outlines you will be editing.

Creating Outlines   As shown earlier, Oracle outlines are created with the CREATE OUTLINE command. For example:

```
SQL> CREATE OUTLINE TEST1 FOR CATEGORY TEST_OUTLINE ON
  2  select owner, table_name, tablespace_name
  3  from dba_tables
  4  where
  5  owner not in ('SYS','SYSTEM');

Outline created.
```

Once the outlines have been created, you can select their signature based on what you know the outlines' names to be; or, if you don't know the outline names, use the GENERATE_SIGNATURE package to generate a signature for a statement to be used to retrieve its information from the DBA_OUTLINES view.

Using DBMS_OUTLN_EDIT.GENERATE_SIGNATURE   When using GENERATE_SIGNATURE, it is probably easiest to create an anonymous PL/SQL script to return the signature or the SQL and OUTLINE name to you. The signature is a RAW, so in the example, shown in Listing 12.29, we return the outline name.

Listing 12.29   Example use of the GENERATE_SIGNATURE procedure.

```
SQL> set serveroutput on

SQL> declare
2   sql_text varchar2(200);
3   ret_sql_text varchar2(200);
4   ret_outline_name varchar2(32);
5   gen_sig raw(16);
```

continues

Listing 12.29   Continued.

```
6  begin
7    sql_text := 'select owner, table_name, tablespace_name
8       from
9         dba_tables
10      where owner not in '
11    ('||chr(39)||'SYS'||chr(39)||','||chr(39)||'SYSTEM'||chr(39)||')';
12    dbms_outln_edit.generate_signature(sql_text,gen_sig);
13    select a.sql_text, a.name into ret_sql_text, ret_outline_name
14    from dba_outlines a where signature=gen_sig;
15    dbms_output.put_line('Sql text for '||name||': '||ret_sql_text);
16  end;
17* /

Sql text for TEST1: select owner,table_name,tablespace_name
from dba_tables
where
owner not in ('SYS','SYSTEM')

PL/SQL procedure successfully completed.
```

Once you have identified the SQL statement for which you want to edit the hint structure, you use the DBMS_OUTLN_EDIT procedure.

Using the DBMS_PROFILER Package

The DBMS_PROFILER package is similar to a UTLESTAT/UTLBSTAT for PL/SQL. Just as UTLESTAT and UTLEBSTAT collect database-level statistics for later analysis, the DBMS_PROFILER package does the same for PL/SQL. The package allows you to start, stop, and flush statistics to persistent storage. It is created using the PROFLOAD. SQL script, located in the $ORACLE_HOME/rdbms/admin directory on UNIX, and the ORACLE_HOME\rdbms\admin directory on NT. The required storage tables for persistent data retention are created using the PROFTAB.SQL script, which is collocated with the PROFLOAD.SQL script. If the data collected by DBMS_PROFILER packages is not flushed to the persistent tables created with PROFTAB.SQL, the data will be erased at the end of the monitoring session.

NOTE   DBMS_PROFILER must be installed as the SYS user.

Data is flushed only when the explicit call to the flush_data procedure is made or when the stop_profiler function is executed. To ensure collection of proper statistics, put the application though a complete cycle before invoking the start_profiler function, otherwise startup noise of the PL/SQL portions of the application may mask, or indicate nonexistent, problems.

The Profiler gathers the following information about each line of PL/SQL code:

- Total elapsed time in execution
- Number of times line has been executed
- Minimum and maximum times spent executing line

Based on this information, the DBA and developers can concentrate their efforts on the PL/SQL statements that are the most costly.

The functions in the DBMS_PROFILER package have the following return codes:

ERROR_PARAM. Indicates that an incorrect parameter was sent to the function; it corresponds to a one (1).

ERROR_IO. Shows that a data flush operation failed, usually due to permission or tables not being present; it corresponds to a two (2).

ERROR_VERSION. Indicates there is a mismatch between the version of Profiler and the database; it corresponds to a negative one (-1).

START_PROFILER The START_PROFILER function has a single input variable: run_comment VARCHAR2, which defaults to the value of SYSDATE. The function starts a collection of PL/SQL statistics (it should not be invoked until the application has been run through once to avoid startup noise). The function returns a BINARY_INTEGER, which will be 0 if the call was successful; otherwise, it will relate to one of the standard DBMS_PROFILER error codes.

```
DBMS_PROFILE.START_PROFILER(run_comment IN VARCHAR2:=SYSDATE)
RETURN BINARY_INTEGER;
```

STOP_PROFILER The STOP_PROFILER function has no input variables and returns a BINARY_INTEGER, which will be 0 if the call was successful; otherwise, it will relate to one of the standard DBMS_PROFILER error codes. STOP_PROFILER flushes statistics to the predefined flush tables and stops PL/SQL statistics from gathering.

```
DBMS_PROFILER.STOP_PROFILER RETURN BINARY_INTEGER;
```

PAUSE_PROFILER The PAUSE_PROFILER function call temporarily halts Profiler data collection. Use it in lengthy procedures or functions, to pause data collection for long sections of code that can't be tuned.

```
DBMS_PROFILER.PAUSE_PROFILER RETURN BINARY_INTEGER;
```

RESUME_PROFILER The RESUME_PROFILER function call restarts data collection.

```
DBMS_PROFILER.RESUME_PROFILER RETURN BINARY_INTEGER;
```

FLUSH_DATA The FLUSH_DATA function has no input variables and returns a BINARY_INTEGER, which will be 0 if the call was successful; otherwise, it will relate to one of the standard DBMS_PROFILER error codes. The FLUSH_DATA function flushes statistics to the predefined flush tables, and can be used at anytime during statistics gathering to provide intermediate looks at PL/SQL statistics. To use FLUSH_DATA, the PROFTAB.SQL script must have been run and the tables must be available to the executing user.

```
DBMS_PROFILE.FLUSH_DATA RETURN BINARY_INTEGER;
```

GET_VERSION   The GET_VERSION procedure gets the version of the DBMS_PROFILER API to ensure that there isn't a version mismatch. The procedure GET_VERSION has the following output variables:

- major BINARY_INTEGER
- minor BINARY_INTEGER

```
DBMS_PROFILER.GET_VERSION(major VARCHAR2, minor VARCHAR2);
```

INTERNAL_VERSION_CHECK   The INTERNAL_VERSION_CHECK function verifies that this version of DBMS_PROFILER will work with the version of the database. The function has no input variables and returns a BINARY_INTEGER, which will be 0 if the call was successful; otherwise, it will relate to one of the standard DBMS_PROFILER error codes.

```
DBMS_PROFILER.INTERNAL_VERSION_CHECK RETURNS BINARY_INTEGER;
```

Implementing DBMS_PROFILER   In order to use DBMS_PROFILER, you must insert calls to the various functions inside DBMS_PROFILER into your package. Look at Listing 12.30, which shows a simple PL/SQL anonymous block.

Listing 12.30   Example anonymous PL/SQL block.

```
declare
x integer;
begin
x:=dbms_profiler.start_profiler('Test Profiler');
DBA_UTILITIES.just_statistics;
x:=dbms_profiler.flush_data;
x:=dbms_profiler.stop_profiler;
end;
/
```

In this listing, we start the Profiler with the call to DBMS_PROFILER.START_PROFILER, execute the script we want monitored, then issue an implicit data flush (DBMS_PROFILER.FLUSH_DATA), and, finally, issue the call to DBMS_PROFILER.STOP_PROFILER to stop the Profiler from collecting data. However, this use is incorrect; to find out why, read on.

The procedure we want to evaluate is contained in the DBA_UTILITIES package and is called JUST_STATISTICS. It gathers various statistics about the Oracle database and writes them into a temporary file for review. The results of the operation, as gleaned from the PL/SQL_PROFILER tables, is shown in Listing 12. 31.

Listing 12.31   Output from DBMS_PROFILER tables.

```
SQL> col run_comment format a20
SQL> select runid, run_date, run_total_time, run_comment from plsql_profiler_runs;

     RUNID RUN_DATE RUN_TOTAL_TIME   RUN_COMMENT
---------- --------- -------------- -------------
         1 05-SEP-99      6.802E+11 Test Profiler
         2 05-SEP-99         533133

SQL> col unit_name format a15
SQL> col unit_type format a15
SQL> column unit_owner format a11
SQL> select runid,unit_number,unit_type,unit_owner, unit_name, unit_timestamp,
  2  total_time from plsql_profiler_units where runid=2;

     RUNID UNIT_NUMBER UNIT_TYPE       UNIT_OWNER      UNIT_NAME UNIT_TIME TOTAL_TIME
---------- ----------- --------------- ----------- --------------- --------- ----------
         2           1 ANONYMOUS BLOCK <anonymous> <anonymous>     00-DECEMB          0
         2           2 PACKAGE BODY    SYS             DBMS_PROFILER 05-SEP-99        0

2 rows selected.


SQL> select runid,unit_number, line#,total_occur, total_time, min_time, max_time
  2  from plsql_profiler_data where runid=2

     RUNID UNIT_NUMBER     LINE# TOTAL_OCCUR TOTAL_TIME  MIN_TIME  MAX_TIME
---------- ----------- --------- ----------- ---------- --------- ---------
         2           1         4           0          0         0         0
         2           1         5           0          0         0         0
         2           1         6           1      20117     20117     20117
         2           1         7           1      37566     37566     37566
         2           2         8           2     125887      4158    121728
         2           2        51           2       7301      2917      4383
         2           2        57           0          0         0         0
         2           2        58           0          0         0         0
         2           2        60           1      19431     19431     19431
         2           2        65           2      15498      6135      9362
         2           2        66           0          0         0         0
         2           2        68           1       2001      2001      2001
         2           2        73           0          0         0         0
         2           2        74           0          0         0         0
         2           2        76           0          0         0         0
         2           2        82           0          0         0         0
         2           2        83           0          0         0         0

17 rows selected.
```

Not a lot of information about DBA_UTILITIES is shown, is there? Why not? Remember, the calls to DBMS_PROFILER have to be inside the object being profiled. In this case, we placed the calls inside the PL/SQL anonymous block, but not inside DBA_UTILITIES, so all we profiled was the execution of the PL/SQL block.

Now look at Listing 12.32: it shows the (partial) results for the same run with the calls to DBMS_PROFILER placed in both the anonymous PL/SQL block and DBA_UTILITIES.JUST_STATISTICS.

Listing 12.32   Results with properly placed calls.

```
SQL> @test_profiler
SQL> declare
2   x integer;
3   begin
4   x:=dbms_profiler.start_profiler('Test Profiler2');
5   DBA_UTILITIES.just_statistics;
6   x:=dbms_profiler.flush_data;
7   x:=dbms_profiler.stop_profiler;
8   end;
9   /

PL/SQL procedure successfully completed.

SQL> col run_comment format a20
SQL> select runid, run_date, run_total_time, run_comment from plsql_profiler_runs;

     RUNID RUN_DATE  RUN_TOTAL_TIME    RUN_COMMENT
---------- --------- ---------------- ----------------
         1 05-SEP-99      6.802E+11 Test Profiler
         2 05-SEP-99         533133
         3 05-SEP-99      1.393E+09 Test Profiler2
         4 05-SEP-99         522158

SQL> select runid,unit_number,unit_type,unit_owner, unit_name, unit_timestamp,
  2  total_time from plsql_profiler_units where runid>2;

RUNID UNIT_NUMBER UNIT_TYPE        UNIT_OWNER      UNIT_NAME UNIT_TIME TOTAL_TIME
----- ----------- --------------- ----------- ---------------- --------- ----------
    3           1 PACKAGE BODY    SYS             DBMS_PROFILER 05-SEP-99          0
    3           2 ANONYMOUS BLOCK <anonymous> <anonymous>       00-DECEMB          0
    3           3 PACKAGE BODY    SYSTEM          DBA_UTILITIES 05-SEP-99          0
    4           1 ANONYMOUS BLOCK <anonymous> <anonymous>       00-DECEMB          0
    4           2 PACKAGE BODY    SYS             DBMS_PROFILER 05-SEP-99          0

21 rows selected.

SQL> select runid,unit_number, line#,total_occur, total_time, min_time, max_time
  2  from plsql_profiler_data where runid>2;
```

```
RUNID UNIT_NUMBER  LINE#  TOTAL_OCCUR  TOTAL_TIME   MIN_TIME   MAX_TIME
----- -----------  -----  -----------  ----------   --------   --------
    1           1      9            2       74000      19000      55000
    1           1     16            3    13308000      72000   12600000
    1           1     24            2        9000       4000       5000
    1           1     25            2     2467000    1086000    1381000
    1           1     26            2       94000      30000      64000
    1           1     27            4      132000       3000      62000
    1           1     42            2       12000       5000       7000
    1           1     43            1       15000      15000      15000
    1           1     84            1        4000       4000       4000
    1           1     88            1    19449000   19449000   19449000
    1           1     89            1       52000      52000      52000
...
    1           1    656            1       33000      33000      33000
    1           1    657            2       39000      13000      26000


816 rows selected.
```

As you can see, we now have full details about DBA_UTILITIES. To make this work, you place the first call (DBMS_PROFILER.START_PROFILER) just inside the first BEGIN block of the section of code you want to trace, and the second call (DBMS_PROFILER.END_PROFILER) just before the END. For an example see Listing 12.33.

Listing 12.33   Placement of DBMS_PROFILER calls.

```
...
PROCEDURE just_statistics AS
     Start_date    DATE;
     Dd_ratio      NUMBER :=0;
     ...
BEGIN
  DBMS_PROFILER.START_PROFILER;
...
  DBMS_PROFILER.FLUSH_DATA;
  DMBS_PROFILER.STOP_PROFILER;
END just_statistics;
```

Note that I removed all of the rows that corresponded to unused sections of code (zero times and executions). Using the Oracle9i version, I could go back and reinstrument, using the PAUSE_PROFILER and RESUME_PROFILER function calls. I suggest doing a preliminary run to determine the sections of code that don't require monitoring and use the new pause and resume functionality to remove their data collection. The lines with executions map back into the definitions and code for the JUST_STATISTICS procedure. Now, using the SYS.SOURCE$ table and the above data, we should be able to pull the lines that have the most numbers of executions, enabling us to determine if we can reduce the executions or time required by reworking the specific lines where performance is being taxed. For example, in Listing 12.32 the lines shown in Listing 12.34 should be looked at first.

Listing 12.34   Important lines from Listing 12.32.

RUNID	UNIT_NUMBER	LINE#	TOTAL_OCCUR	TOTAL_TIME	MIN_TIME	MAX_TIME
1	1	16	3	13308000	72000	12600000
1	1	241	55	245540000	17000	244362000
1	1	606	1	5078898000	5078898000	5078898000
1	1	618	9	232648000	669000	223666000
1	1	648	21	2494449000	472000	2484483000

Since the major problem seems to be with DBA_UTILITIES.JUST_STATISTICS (runid 1, unit_number 1) in line 606, let's pull that line from the SOURCE$ table and take a quick look at it. Look at Listing 12.35 to see the results from selecting line 606.

Listing 12.35   Line showing performance problem.

```
SQL> desc source$
 Name                            Null?    Type
 ------------------------------- -------- -------------------------------
 OBJ#                            NOT NULL NUMBER
 LINE                            NOT NULL NUMBER
 SOURCE                                   VARCHAR2(4000)

SQL> desc obj$
 Name                            Null?    Type
 ------------------------------- -------- -------------------------------
 OBJ#                            NOT NULL NUMBER
 DATAOBJ#                                 NUMBER
 OWNER#                          NOT NULL NUMBER
 NAME                            NOT NULL VARCHAR2(30)
 NAMESPACE                       NOT NULL NUMBER
 SUBNAME                                  VARCHAR2(30)
 TYPE#                           NOT NULL NUMBER
 CTIME                           NOT NULL DATE
 MTIME                           NOT NULL DATE
 STIME                           NOT NULL DATE
 STATUS                          NOT NULL NUMBER
 REMOTEOWNER                              VARCHAR2(30)
 LINKNAME                                 VARCHAR2(128)
 FLAGS                                    NUMBER
 OID$                                     RAW(16)
 SPARE1                                   NUMBER
```

```
    SPARE2                              NUMBER
    SPARE3                              NUMBER
    SPARE4                              VARCHAR2(1000)
    SPARE5                              VARCHAR2(1000)
    SPARE6                              DATE

SQL> select obj#, name, namespace from obj$
  2  where name ='DBA_UTILITIES';
    OBJ# NAME                            NAMESPACE
--------- ------------------------------ ---------
    31417 DBA_UTILITIES                          1
    31418 DBA_UTILITIES                          2 (Package Body)

SQL> col source format a60
SQL>select source from source$ where obj#=31418 and line=606 /

SOURCE
------------------------------------------------------------
     FETCH get_good INTO stat_val;

SQL> select line, source from source$ where obj#=3315
  2  and line between 915 and 925;

     LINE SOURCE
---------- ------------------------------------
      600      write_one(stat_name,0,37);
      601    COMMIT;
      602  END;
      603 BEGIN
      604   stat_name:='Shared SQL%';
      605   OPEN get_good;
      606   FETCH get_good INTO stat_val;
      607   write_one(stat_name, stat_val,37);
      608   CLOSE get_good;
      609   COMMIT;
      610   EXCEPTION
      611     WHEN NO_DATA_FOUND THEN
      612       write_one(stat_name,0,37);
      613       COMMIT;
      614   END;
      615 BEGIN
      616 OPEN get_latch;

17 rows selected.
```

Notice in Listing 12.35 that the first select, which just pulled back the single line, doesn't tell us much. Once we broaden the scope of the net a bit, we can see why that statement is using up the most time: it is calling a cursor. Further investigation shows that the cursor calls a view that adds up all of the reused SQL in the shared pool! To see this for yourself, look at the listing for DBA_UTILITIES9.SQL on the Wiley Web site. Though this is just a simple example, I hope you can see how this type of data could be useful in your PL/SQL tuning work.

12.4 OTHER SQL STATEMENT TUNING OPTIONS

So far in this chapter, I have explained how to add indexes; change statement structures; force the use of different indexes, join orders, and join methods by use of hints; and lock down performance plans using outlines. That's a lot to learn about tuning. But there still more tuning options to consider. You should also learn to use many of the new features of Oracle9*i*, as well as some of the existing Oracle8*i* features, to improve Oracle statement performance, because at some point, depending on the complexity of the SQL or PL/SQL you are trying to tune, you will find that nothing you do to the statement itself will improve performance; or you will discover that the returns are so minimal as to make your efforts useless. What do you do then? You look at other database options that will reduce the required disk I/O, reduce CPU usage, or make for a more efficient join methodology.

The features that that I suggest you consider (ideally before statement tuning is attempted, but even for that last bit of performance boost) are:

External tables. Useful for tuning Oracle data loads by reducing the number of steps required to complete tasks.

Multitable INSERT. Useful for complex uploads that formerly required multiple statements. By combining multiple INSERT statements into a single transaction, you can reduce overall overhead and improve performance.

MERGE command. Useful for complex loads where records may or may not exist. Allows UPDATE to existing records and INSERT for records that don't yet exist. By reducing the number of statements and achieving improved optimization from the cost-based optimizer, overhead is reduced and performance increased.

Index-only table (IOT). Useful for tables that are searched on the primary key and whose data rows can fit into a single Oracle database block.

Single-table cluster. Useful for tables that are primarily searched by primary key (cluster key), as it allows storage of key values in the same physical blocks for the entire table.

Bitmap-join index. Used to prejoin two tables that are frequently joined via a bitmap index. Can speed table joins by thousands of percentage points.

Skip-scan index. Used to avoid a full table scan by implementing a specially designed two-level index; the index's second level is scanned, thereby avoiding the full table scan.

SORT area. Dynamically alters SORT_AREA_SIZE. By increasing SORT_AREA_SIZE using ALTER SESSION or PL/SQL package calls, the sort area used by a sort-intensive SQL or PL/SQL routine can be dramatically increased for a single session, allowing a process that might take hours to be completed in minutes.

Materialized views. Useful for preprocessing queries. For reports required by many users, and where data doesn't have to be concurrent, materialized views can provide preprocessed reports and queries. By enabling QUERY_REWRITE capabilities, hours of processing time can be saved.

To get expanded benefits, the diligent DBA will also perform the following maintenance operations:

Tune internals. As explained in Chapter 13 on Oracle internals tuning, if the SQL or PL/SQL routines don't have enough resources, no amount of tuning will enable them to run faster. Oracle internals tuning ensures that Oracle processes have enough resources to run efficiently.

Perform frequent index maintenance. An index that has too many levels or too many leaf nodes can kill database performance. Look at percent browning and clustering factors, and rebuild if an index exceeds 15 to 30 percent browning or whose clustering factor is several times the number of used blocks in the base table.

Set table parameters. Make sure there are enough transaction slots and freelists. For tables (and indexes) that undergo inserts or updates from multiple processes to the same blocks, increase the INITRANS and FREELISTS values to be equal to the number of expected simultaneous processes. Improper transaction slots and freelists can cause serialization of operations and bad performance.

Use partitioning. Use range and list partitions to enable partition elimination, hash, and composite partitioning to spread disk I/O. By allowing only subsets of data to be scanned (via partition pruning), and allowing parallel query processing by use of range partitions, you improve the efficiency and speed of processing. By spreading IO across multiple disk assets (single disks or sets of arrays), you improve parallel operations and speed data access.

Use APPEND. If you are not space-constrained as far as disk assets, use the APPEND hint to ignore freelists, and simply add data above the high-water mark.

Waste space. If you are in an insert-intensive environment, waste space in blocks to make sure that partial, nonreusable blocks don't end up on the freelist. Set PCTUSED and PCTFREE such that a block can only be placed on the freelist if there is room for an entire row left in it.

Use proper caching. Use the multiple buffer pool options, place frequently accessed data and indexes in the KEEP pool and infrequently used, scanned objects in the RECYCLE POOL. This works for individual partitions as well, place older, less frequently used partitions in the RECYCLE pool and current more frequently used partitions in the KEEP pool. Also consider changing the tablespace that contains non-updated partitions to READ-ONLY.

12.5 FURTHER DBA READING

The DBA may find these references of interest when planning SQL and PL/SQL tuning activities:

Feuerstein, Steven, Charles Dye, and John Beresniewicz. *Oracle Built-in Packages.* (Sebastopol, California: O'Reilly and Associates, Inc.), April 1998.

Oracle9i Administrator's Guide, Release 1 9.0.1, Part No. A90117-01, Oracle Corporation, June 2001.

Oracle9i Concepts, Release 1 9.0.1, Part No. A88856-02, Oracle Corporation, June 2001.

Oracle9i Database Performance Guide and Reference, Release 1 9.0.1, Part No. A87503-02, Oracle Corporation, June 2001.

Oracle9i Database Performance Methods, Release 1 9.0.1, Part No. A87504-01, Oracle Corporation, June 2001.

Oracle9i Reference, Release 1, 9.0.1, Part No. A90190-01, Oracle Corporation, June 2001.

Oracle9i SQL Reference, Release 8.1.5, Part No. A90125-01, Oracle Corporation, June 2001.

Oracle9i Supplied PL / SQL Packages and Types Reference, Release 1, (9.0.1), Part No. A89852-02, Oracle Corporation, June 2001.

PL / SQL User's Guide and Reference, Release 1 9.0.1, Part No. A89856-01, Oracle Corporation, June 2001.

12.6 SUMMARY

This chapter explained the importance of tuning SQL and PL/SQL; it also detailed how to do this tuning. With this chapter as a guide, the DBA should be able to use the methods and references provided to tune virtually any SQL or PL/SQL code that is causing performance problems. The next chapter covers tuning the internals of Oracle9*i*.

CHAPTER 13

Database Internals Tuning

This chapter deals with the tuning of Oracle internal structures. Oracle uses memory to speed processing by use of the System Global Area, or Shared Global Area (depending on who you ask), or, the SGA. The SGA consists of several cache areas and pool areas, and each needs to be tuned to obtain optimal performance. An additional complexity, the capability to have SGA areas with different-sized db_block_buffers, makes SGA tuning even more fun.

13.1 MEMORY TUNING

Database internals tuning is a complex topic. Just when you think you have Oracle internals figured out, Oracle slips in some new features, takes old ones away, or, just for some perverse form of fun, changes the structures of tried-and-true tables and views. Actually it is all a secret plot between senior Oracle DBAs and Oracle to maintain job security.

This section will cover one of the more challenging and critical aspects of the DBA job: analyzing, diagnosing, and fixing database internals performance problems. The last chapter discussed application tuning. You will get a majority of the performance gains in an application from proper database configuration and application tuning. However, where you will be most exposed will be in the area of internals tuning. Squeezing that last bit of performance from the database seems to be the one area managers like to focus on (they forgot the bit about application tuning and now expect you to work miracles) when there are problems.

Steps to Internals Tuning

As was said at the end of the last chapter, once the application has been tuned, the DBA's job really begins. Now you can begin tuning the Oracle system itself to take advantage of the tuned application. This step of the tuning process is typically a five-part process:

1. Review and set all initialization parameters for your application and operating system.
2. Tune memory allocation.
3. Eliminate I/O bottlenecks.
4. Tune resource contention.
5. Tune sorts, freelists, and checkpoints.

The first step involves reading the operating system-specific release manual and database readme files for any new, changed, or improved initialization parameters. Using your knowledge of the number of users, size of the system memory, number and configuration of disks, sizing of tables, and other system and application parameters, you must do your best to set all of the initialization parameters that will help your system perform better. Parameters can be reviewed by looking at initialization file or by querying V$PARAMETER file. (Note: The Wiley Web site includes a script to report on changed initialization parameters (param9.sql).) You should also perform a control file dump using the command:

```
ALTER DATABASE BACKUP CONTROLFILE TO TRACE;
```

The second step requires an up-and-operating database against which you run various performance-monitoring scripts and tools; then you readjust the initialization parameters. You should also examine database and session level waits using queries against V$WAITSTAT and V$SESSION_WAIT dynamic performance views.

The third step requires monitoring your disk assets and their performance. Your system administrator will be critical to assuring the success of this step. Hopefully, if you were able to have a hand in designing the system layout, you won't have much I/O-related tuning. An inherited database (especially those from aftermarket products) usually requires extensive file movements and optimizations, so this step could actually give the most performance gains.

In one system I inherited, a well-meaning DBA had rebuilt the application indexes, by disabling and then reenabling the primary keys, without specifying the location for the indexes. Of course, you will remember what this causes: all of the indexes were in the same tablespace as the data tables. Simply moving the indexes to their (empty) tablespace resulted in an over 300 percent performance gain (one 30-minute query dropped to less than a minute). I was an instant hero. What this anecdote should tell you is to carefully examine any inherited database for badly placed indexes, tablespaces, rollback segments, and redo logs. Just putting everything where it should be can provide dramatic improvements in performance for badly laid-out systems.

Step 4 involves more monitoring with tools or scripts. Contention for system resources (latches, rollbacks, logs, memory, etc.) can be a real performance drain. Always review the alert log for all databases you inherit, as they will tell you if there are some forms of contention such as for redo logs. The scripts that follow will help determine if there are other types of contention.

Step 5 will involve monitoring system statistics on a running application. There are numerous tools, as well as the scripts included in this section, that will tell you if you have problems with sorts, freelists, and checkpoints. Tuning sorts is especially important in DSS and reporting databases. In one case, a 10-minute sort dropped to less than a minute by bumping up the SORT_AREA_SIZE parameter 2 to 3 megabytes, thus preventing disk sorts.

Each of the following sections addresses a specific area, and includes reports and scripts to help you monitor your database.

13.2 USING STATSPACK FOR INTERNALS TUNING

The STATSPACK utility was introduced in Oracle8*i* 8.1.6, but with various kludges, it can be made to work with releases as far back as 8.0.6. (If you have a release older than 8.1.6 and want to install STATSPACK, I suggest going to ww.oracle.com/oracle/00-Mar/statspack-other.html and downloading the various scripts as required to load into your version.) You install STATSPACK into a PERFSTAT user, which is created for you during the install. The PERFSTAT user should have his or her own tablespace; I suggest using at least a 500-megabyte locally managed tablespace with uniform extent allocations of 500K to start.

Installation and Use of STATSPACK   This procedure is for a Windows 2000 install; however, installations on UNIX or other platforms should be nearly identical.

1. Create the STATSPACK tablespace (note, you cannot use the SYSTEM tablespace for STATSPACK results).

```
: sqlplus /nolog

SQL*Plus: Release 9.0.1.0.1 - Production on Wed Nov 7 11:11:21 2001

(c) Copyright 2001 Oracle Corporation.  All rights reserved.

SQL> connect sys as sysdba
Password:
Connected.
SQL> CREATE TABLESPACE perfstat
DATAFILE 'c:\oracle\ora9i\oradata\perfstat01.dbf' SIZE 500m
EXTENT MANAGEMENT LOCAL UNIFORM SIZE 500k;

Tablespace created.
```

2. Run the spcreate.sql script for Oracle9*i;* it is located in the $ORACLE_HOME/ rdbms/admin directory. (Note: This was called statscre.sql in previous releases.) In

Oracle9*i*, it also automatically runs dbmspool.sql and dbmsjob.sql as a part of the spcusr.sql script. If you have already installed dbmspool.sql (dbms_shared_pool) and dbmsjob.sql (dbms_job), then you may wish to comment-out the calls to these packages in the spcusr.sql script. All STATSPACK scripts are located in the same directory as the spcreate.sql script, so you may wish to move them to a STATSPACK or reporting-specific directory. I have removed all of the creating-this and creating-that messages for the sake of brevity; however, you should know this script creates numerous views, tables, and packages.

```
SQL> @spcreate

... Installing Required Packages
... Creating PERFSTAT user

Below are the list of online tablespaces in this database.
Decide which tablespace you wish to create the STATSPACK tables
and indexes.  This will also be the PERFSTAT user's default tablespace.

Specifying the SYSTEM tablespace will result in the installation
FAILING, as using SYSTEM for performance data is not supported.


TABLESPACE_NAME                        CONTENTS
------------------------------   ---------
DRSYS                                  PERMANENT
INDX                                   PERMANENT
PERFSTAT                               PERMANENT
RBS                                    PERMANENT
TEMP                                   TEMPORARY
TOOLS                                  PERMANENT
USERS                                  PERMANENT

7 rows selected.

Specify PERFSTAT user's default   tablespace
Enter value for default_tablespace: perfstat
Using perfstat for the default tablespace

Choose the PERFSTAT user's temporary tablespace.

Specifying the SYSTEM tablespace will result in the installation
FAILING, as using SYSTEM for the temporary tablespace is not recommended.

Specify PERFSTAT user's temporary tablespace.
Enter value for temporary_tablespace: temp
Using temp for the temporary tablespace

NOTE:
SPCUSR complete. Please check spcusr.lis for any errors.

If this script is automatically called from spcreate (which is
the supported method), all STATSPACK segments will be created in
the PERFSTAT user's default tablespace.

Using perfstat tablespace to store Statspack objects
```

```
NOTE:
SPCTAB complete. Please check spctab.lis for any errors.

Creating Package STATSPACK...

Package created.

No errors.
Creating Package Body STATSPACK...

Package body created.

No errors.

NOTE:
SPCPKG complete. Please check spcpkg.lis for any errors.
```

3. Test the installation by running a couple of statistics snapshots and generating a report. The report will depend on two or more "snapshots" having been taken of your instance. Snapshots are taken using the statspack.snap procedure, which is built automatically during the install process:

```
SQL> connect perfstat/perfstat
Connected.

SQL> execute statspack.snap;

PL/SQL procedure successfully completed.

Note: You may want to wait a couple of minutes and maybe run a few scripts or
some of the application for the instance.

SQL> execute statspack.snap;

PL/SQL procedure successfully completed.
```

4. Next, you run the report using the spreport.sql script. It will generate its output to the directory where it is run, so it would be a good idea to move at least spreport.sql into its own reporting directory. Also, all of the output for the spreport.sql script comes to the screen.

```
SQL> @spreport

Current Instance

   DB Id     DB Name      Inst Num Instance
----------- ------------ -------- -----------
  980691836 AULTDB1             1 aultdb1

Instances in this Statspack schema
~~~~~~~~~~~~~~~~~~~~~~~~~~~~~~~~~~~

   DB Id     Inst Num DB Name      Instance     Host
----------- -------- ------------ ------------ ----------
  980691836        1 AULTDB1      aultdb1      TUSCGA-PC2

Using  980691836 for database Id
```

```
Using           1 for instance number
Completed Snapshots

                             Snap                      Snap
Instance      DB Name        Id    Snap Started        Level Comment
------------  -----------    ------ -----------------  ----- --------------------
aultdb1       AULTDB1          1 07 Nov 2001 09:55      5
                              2 07 Nov 2001 09:59      5

Specify the Begin and End Snapshot Ids
~~~~~~~~~~~~~~~~~~~~~~~~~~~~~~~~~~~~~~~~
Enter value for begin_snap: 1
Begin Snapshot Id specified: 1

Enter value for end_snap: 2
End   Snapshot Id specified: 2


Specify the Report Name
~~~~~~~~~~~~~~~~~~~~~~~~~
The default report file name is sp_1_2.  To use this name,
press <return> to continue, otherwise enter an alternative.
Enter value for report_name:

Using the report name sp_1_2

STATSPACK report for

DB Name         DB Id    Instance        Inst Num Release       Cluster Host
---------------  --------  -------------  -------- -----------  ------- ----------
AULTDB1         980691836 aultdb1              1 9.0.1.1.1     NO      TUSCGA-PC2

               Snap Id     Snap Time        Sessions Curs/Sess Comment
               -------  -----------------   -------- --------- --------------------
Begin Snap:       1 07-Nov-01 09:55:29         9       5.2
  End Snap:       2 07-Nov-01 09:59:06         9       5.6
   Elapsed:              3.62 (mins)

Cache Sizes (end)
~~~~~~~~~~~~~~~~~
               Buffer Cache:        47M    Std Block Size:         8K
          Shared Pool Size:        72M        Log Buffer:        32K

Load Profile
~~~~~~~~~~~~                        Per Second        Per Transaction
                                   ---------------    ---------------
                  Redo size:         1,321.68           286,804.00
              Logical reads:            11.72             2,544.00
              Block changes:             2.40               520.00
             Physical reads:             0.73               159.00
            Physical writes:             0.83               180.00
                 User calls:             0.04                 9.00
                    Parses:             0.41                90.00
               Hard parses:             0.06                14.00
                     Sorts:             0.57               123.00
```

```
          Logons:              0.00            0.00
        Executes:              1.16          251.00
    Transactions:              0.00
```

```
% Blocks changed per Read:   20.44    Recursive Call %:   99.39
Rollback per transaction %:   0.00       Rows per Sort:   86.98
```

Instance Efficiency Percentages (Target 100%)
~~~~~~

```
        Buffer Nowait %:  100.00      Redo NoWait %:   99.66
        Buffer  Hit  %:  100.00    In-memory Sort %:   95.93
        Library Hit  %:   87.74       Soft Parse %:   84.44
      Execute to Parse %:   64.14       Latch Hit %:  100.00
Parse CPU to Parse Elapsd %:           % Non-Parse CPU:
```

```
Shared Pool Statistics       Begin   End
                             ------  -----
          Memory Usage %:    38.60   39.46
   % SQL with executions>1:  43.16   47.60
   % Memory for SQL w/exec>1: 46.36   59.20
```

Top 5 Wait Events
~~~~~~~~~~~~~~~~~

| | | Wait | % Total |
Event	Waits	Time (s)	Wt Time
control file sequential read	58	0	36.03
control file parallel write	79	0	19.44
log file switch completion	1	0	12.60
async disk IO	152	0	10.86
db file parallel write	8	0	8.13

Wait Events for DB: AULTDB1 Instance: aultdb1 Snaps: 1 -2
-> s - second
-> cs - centisecond -   100th of a second
-> ms - millisecond -   1000th of a second
-> us - microsecond - 1000000th of a second
-> ordered by wait time desc, waits desc (idle events last)

| | | | Avg | |
| | | Total Wait | wait | Waits |
Event	Waits	Timeouts	Time (s)	(ms)	/txn
control file sequential read	58	0	0	7	58.0
control file parallel write	79	0	0	3	79.0
log file switch completion	1	0	0	147	1.0
async disk IO	152	0	0	1	152.0
db file parallel write	8	8	0	12	8.0
direct path read	72	0	0	1	72.0
log file parallel write	18	14	0	3	18.0
direct path write	18	0	0	2	18.0
log file sequential read	1	0	0	8	1.0
log file single write	2	0	0	0	2.0
log file sync	1	0	0	1	1.0

```
LGWR wait for redo copy              1           0         0        0     1.0
SQL*Net message from client          5           0       381    76296     5.0
virtual circuit status               8           8       240    30001     8.0
SQL*Net message to client            5           0         0        0     5.0
                        --------------------------------------------------------
```

Background Wait Events for DB: AULTDB1 Instance: aultdb1 Snaps: 1 -2
-> ordered by wait time desc, waits desc (idle events last)

```
                                                                 Avg
                                                  Total Wait   wait   Waits
Event                        Waits   Timeouts   Time (s)   (ms)   /txn
---------------------------- ------------ ----------  ----------  ------ ------
control file sequential read     39          0         0        8    39.0
control file parallel write      79          0         0        3    79.0
db file parallel write            8          8         0       12     8.0
log file parallel write          19         15         0        4    19.0
async disk IO                     3          0         0       11     3.0
direct path write                 8          0         0        4     8.0
log file sequential read          1          0         0        8     1.0
log file single write             2          0         0        0     2.0
direct path read                  8          0         0        0     8.0
LGWR wait for redo copy           1          0         0        0     1.0
rdbms ipc message               245        231       646     2637   245.0
smon timer                        1          1       307   ######     1.0
pmon timer                       72         72       216     3001    72.0
                        --------------------------------------------------------
```

SQL ordered by Gets for DB: AULTDB1 Instance: aultdb1 Snaps: 1 -2
-> End Buffer Gets Threshold: 10000
-> Note that resources reported for PL/SQL includes the resources used by
   all SQL statements called within the PL/SQL code. As individual SQL
   statements are also reported, it is possible and valid for the summed
   total % to exceed 100

```
                                               CPU     Elapsd
  Buffer Gets  Executions Gets per Exec  %Total Time (s)  Time (s) Hash Value
-------------- ---------- -------------- ------ -------- --------- ----------
          84          42           2.0    3.3     0.00      0.00 2963598673
```
select job, nvl2(last_date, 1, 0) from sys.job$ where (((:1 <= n
ext_date) and (next_date < :2))   or ((last_date is null) and
(next_date < :3))) and (field1 = :4 or (field1 = 0 and 'Y' = :5)
) and (this_date is null) order by next_date, job

```
          42          42           1.0    1.7     0.00      0.00 2964743345
```
select count(*) from sys.job$ where (next_date > sysdate) and (n
ext_date < (sysdate+5/86400))

```
          20           4           5.0    0.8     0.00      0.00 2085632044
```
select intcol#,nvl(pos#,0),col# from ccol$ where con#=:1

```
          15           5           3.0    0.6     0.00      0.00 1705880752
```
select file# from file$ where ts#=:1

```
           9           2           4.5    0.4     0.00      0.00 1536916657
```

```
select con#,type#,condlength,intcols,robj#,rcon#,match#,refact,n
vl(enabled,0),rowid,cols,nvl(defer,0),mtime,nvl(spare1,0) from c
def$ where obj#=:1
```

```
             3           1          3.0    0.1    0.00      0.00  931956286
select grantee#,privilege#,nvl(col#,0),max(mod(nvl(option$,0),2)
)from objauth$ where obj#=:1 group by grantee#,privilege#,nvl(co
l#,0) order by grantee#
```

```
             2           2          1.0    0.1    0.00      0.00  114078687
select con#,obj#,rcon#,enabled,nvl(defer,0) from cdef$ where rob
j#=:1
```

```
             2           1          2.0    0.1    0.00      0.00 1453445442
select col#, grantee#, privilege#,max(mod(nvl(option$,0),2)) fro
m objauth$ where obj#=:1 and col# is not null group by privilege
#, col#, grantee# order by col#, grantee#
```

```
             ------------------------------------------------------------
SQL ordered by Reads for DB: AULTDB1  Instance: aultdb1  Snaps: 1 -2
-> End Disk Reads Threshold:     1000
```

				CPU	Elapsd	
Physical Reads	Executions	Reads per Exec	%Total	Time (s)	Time (s)	Hash Value
---------------	-----------	---------------	------	---------	--------	----------

```
             0           2          0.0    0.0    0.00      0.00  114078687
select con#,obj#,rcon#,enabled,nvl(defer,0) from cdef$ where rob
j#=:1
```

```
             0           1          0.0    0.0    0.00      0.00  931956286
select grantee#,privilege#,nvl(col#,0),max(mod(nvl(option$,0),2)
)from objauth$ where obj#=:1 group by grantee#,privilege#,nvl(co
l#,0) order by grantee#
```

```
             0           1          0.0    0.0    0.00      0.00 1453445442
select col#, grantee#, privilege#,max(mod(nvl(option$,0),2)) fro
m objauth$ where obj#=:1 and col# is not null group by privilege
#, col#, grantee# order by col#, grantee#
```

```
             0           2          0.0    0.0    0.00      0.00 1536916657
select con#,type#,condlength,intcols,robj#,rcon#,match#,refact,n
vl(enabled,0),rowid,cols,nvl(defer,0),mtime,nvl(spare1,0) from c
def$ where obj#=:1
```

```
             0           5          0.0    0.0    0.00      0.00 1705880752
select file# from file$ where ts#=:1
```

```
             0           4          0.0    0.0    0.00      0.00 2085632044
select intcol#,nvl(pos#,0),col# from ccol$ where con#=:1
```

```
             0          42          0.0    0.0    0.00      0.00 2963598673
select job, nvl2(last_date, 1, 0) from sys.job$ where (((:1 <= n
ext_date) and (next_date < :2))    or  ((last_date is null) and
(next_date < :3))) and (field1 = :4 or (field1 = 0 and 'Y' = :5)
) and (this_date is null) order by next_date, job
```

```
        0          42              0.0     0.0     0.00      0.00 2964743345
select count(*) from sys.job$ where (next_date > sysdate) and (n
ext_date < (sysdate+5/86400))
```

SQL ordered by Executions for DB: AULTDB1 Instance: aultdb1 Snaps: 1 -2
-> End Executions Threshold: 100

| | | | CPU per | Elap per | |
Executions	Rows Processed	Rows per Exec	Exec (s)	Exec (s)	Hash Value

```
       42           0              0.0     0.00       0.00 2963598673
select job, nvl2(last_date, 1, 0) from sys.job$ where (((:1 <= n
ext_date) and (next_date < :2))    or ((last_date is null) and
(next_date < :3))) and (field1 = :4 or (field1 = 0 and 'Y' = :5)
) and (this_date is null) order by next_date, job

       42          42              1.0     0.00       0.00 2964743345
select count(*) from sys.job$ where (next_date > sysdate) and (n
ext_date < (sysdate+5/86400))

        5           5              1.0     0.00       0.00 1705880752
select file# from file$ where ts#=:1

        4           6              1.5     0.00       0.00 2085632044
select intcol#,nvl(pos#,0),col# from ccol$ where con#=:1

        2           0              0.0     0.00       0.00  114078687
select con#,obj#,rcon#,enabled,nvl(defer,0) from cdef$ where rob
j#=:1

        2           4              2.0     0.00       0.00 1536916657
select con#,type#,condlength,intcols,robj#,rcon#,match#,refact,n
vl(enabled,0),rowid,cols,nvl(defer,0),mtime,nvl(spare1,0) from c
def$ where obj#=:1

        1           1              1.0     0.00       0.00  931956286
select grantee#,privilege#,nvl(col#,0),max(mod(nvl(option$,0),2)
)from objauth$ where obj#=:1 group by grantee#,privilege#,nvl(co
l#,0) order by grantee#

        1           0              0.0     0.00       0.00 1453445442
select col#, grantee#, privilege#,max(mod(nvl(option$,0),2)) fro
m objauth$ where obj#=:1 and col# is not null group by privilege
#, col#, grantee# order by col#, grantee#
```

SQL ordered by Parse Calls for DB: AULTDB1 Instance: aultdb1 Snaps: 1 -2
-> End Parse Calls Threshold: 1000

| | | % Total | |
Parse Calls	Executions	Parses	Hash Value

```
        5           5         0.06 1705880752
select file# from file$ where ts#=:1
```

```
        0           0     0.00    29771263
insert into argument$( obj#,procedure$,procedure#,overload#,posi
tion#,sequence#,level#,argument,type#,default#,in_out,length,pre
cision#,scale,radix,charsetid,charsetform,properties,type_owner,
type_name,type_subname,type_linkname,pls_type) values (:1,:2,:3,
:4,:5,:6,:7,:8,:9,:10,:11,:12,:13,:14,:15,:16,:17,:18,:19,:20,:2

        0           0     0.00    58950663
select con# from con$ where owner#=:1 and name=:2

        0           0     0.00    79934617
select ts#,file#,block#,nvl(bobj#,0),nvl(tab#,0),intcols,nvl(clu
cols,0),audit$,flags,pctfree$,pctused$,initrans,maxtrans,rowcnt,
blkcnt,empcnt,avgspc,chncnt,avgrln,analyzetime, samplesize,cols,
property,nvl(degree,1),nvl(instances,1),avgspc_flb,flbcnt,kernel
cols,nvl(trigflag, 0),nvl(spare1,0),nvl(spare2,0),spare4 from ta

        0           2     0.00    114078687
select con#,obj#,rcon#,enabled,nvl(defer,0) from cdef$ where rob
j#=:1

        0           0     0.00    181436173
select /*+ index(idl_sb4$ i_idl_sb41) +*/ max(version)   from id
l_sb4$ where obj#=:1 and version<=:2 and   (part=0 or part=2) an
d piece#=0

        0           0     0.00    189272129
select o.owner#,o.name,o.namespace,o.remoteowner,o.linkname,o.su
bname,o.dataobj#,o.flags from obj$ o where o.obj#=:1

        0           0     0.00    199702406
select i.obj#,i.ts#,i.file#,i.block#,i.intcols,i.type#,i.flags,
i.property,i.pctfree$,i.initrans,i.maxtrans,i.blevel,i.leafcnt,i
.distkey, i.lblkkey,i.dblkkey,i.clufac,i.cols,i.analyzetime,i.sa
mplesize,i.dataobj#, nvl(i.degree,1),nvl(i.instances,1),i.rowcnt
,mod(i.pctthres$,256),i.indmethod#,i.trunccnt,nvl(c.unicols,0),n

        0           0     0.00    315090940
update con$ set con#=:3 where owner#=:1 and name=:2

        0           0     0.00    411033441
insert into dependency$(d_obj#,d_timestamp,order#,p_obj#,p_times
tamp,d_owner#, property)values (:1,:2,:3,:4,:5,:6, :7)

        0           0     0.00    528349613
delete from uet$ where ts#=:1 and segfile#=:2 and segblock#=:3 a
nd ext#=:4

        0           0     0.00    636388251
insert into ccol$(con#,obj#,intcol#,pos#,col#) values(:1,:2,:3,d
ecode(:4,0,null,:4),:5)
SQL ordered by Parse Calls for DB: AULTDB1  Instance: aultdb1  Snaps: 1 -2
-> End Parse Calls Threshold:      1000
```

```
                              % Total
   Parse Calls  Executions   Parses  Hash Value
   ------------ ------------ -------- ----------

            0            0     0.00  641766606
insert into col$(obj#,name,intcol#,segcol#,type#,length,precisio
n#,scale,null$,offset,fixedstorage,segcollength,deflength,defaul
t$,col#,property,charsetid,charsetform,spare1,spare2,spare3)valu
es(:1,:2,:3,:4,:5,:6,decode(:7,0,null,:7),decode(:5,2,decode(:8,
-127/*MAXSB1MINAL*/,null,:8),178,:8,179,:8,180,:8,181,:8,182,:8,

            0            0     0.00  858169104
BEGIN  dbms_java.server_startup; END;

            0            1     0.00  931956286
select grantee#,privilege#,nvl(col#,0),max(mod(nvl(option$,0),2)
)from objauth$ where obj#=:1 group by grantee#,privilege#,nvl(co
l#,0) order by grantee#

            0            0     0.00  957616262
select /*+ index(idl_char$ i_idl_char1) +*/ piece#,length,piece
from idl_char$ where obj#=:1 and part=:2 and version=:3 order by
 piece#

            0            0     0.00 1142460911
insert into idl_ub2$(obj#,part,version,piece#,length,piece) valu
es(:1,:2,:3,:4,:5,:6)

            0            0     0.00 1428100621
select /*+ index(idl_ub2$ i_idl_ub21) +*/ piece#,length,piece fr
om idl_ub2$ where obj#=:1 and part=:2 and version=:3 order by pi
ece#

            0            1     0.00 1453445442
select col#, grantee#, privilege#,max(mod(nvl(option$,0),2)) fro
m objauth$ where obj#=:1 and col# is not null group by privilege
#, col#, grantee# order by col#, grantee#

            0            0     0.00 1468559776
insert into con$(owner#,name,con#)values(:1,:2,:3)

            0            0     0.00 1499458452
insert into obj$(owner#,name,namespace,obj#,type#,ctime,mtime,st
ime,status,remoteowner,linkname,subname,dataobj#,flags,oid$,spar
e1,spare2)values(:1,:2,:3,:4,:5,:6,:7,:8,:9,:10,:11,:12,:13,:14,
:15,:16, :17)

            0            2     0.00 1536916657
select con#,type#,condlength,intcols,robj#,rcon#,match#,refact,n
vl(enabled,0),rowid,cols,nvl(defer,0),mtime,nvl(spare1,0) from c
def$ where obj#=:1

            0            0     0.00 1819073277
select owner#,name,namespace,remoteowner,linkname,p_timestamp,p_
obj#, d_owner#, nvl(property,0),subname from dependency$,obj$ wh
ere d_obj#=:1 and p_obj#=obj#(+) order by order#
```

SQL ordered by Parse Calls for DB: AULTDB1 Instance: aultdb1 Snaps: 1 -2
-> End Parse Calls Threshold: 1000

```
                          % Total
 Parse Calls  Executions  Parses  Hash Value
------------ ------------ -------- ----------
          0            0    0.00 1839874543
select file#,block#,length from uet$ where ts#=:1 and segfile#=:
2 and segblock#=:3 and ext#=:4
```

Instance Activity Stats for DB: AULTDB1 Instance: aultdb1 Snaps: 1 -2

Statistic	Total	per Second	per Trans
CR blocks created	15	0.1	15.0
DBWR checkpoint buffers written	21	0.1	21.0
DBWR checkpoints	1	0.0	1.0
DBWR transaction table writes	1	0.0	1.0
DBWR undo block writes	11	0.1	11.0
...			
messages received	26	0.1	26.0
messages sent	26	0.1	26.0
no buffer to keep pinned count	1,340	6.2	1,340.0
no work - consistent read gets	250	1.2	250.0
opened cursors cumulative	90	0.4	90.0
parse count (failures)	0	0.0	0.0
parse count (hard)	14	0.1	14.0
parse count (total)	90	0.4	90.0
physical reads	159	0.7	159.0
physical reads direct	159	0.7	159.0
physical writes	180	0.8	180.0
physical writes direct	159	0.7	159.0

Instance Activity Stats for DB: AULTDB1 Instance: aultdb1 Snaps: 1 -2

Statistic	Total	per Second	per Trans
physical writes non checkpoint	177	0.8	177.0
prefetched blocks	0	0.0	0.0
recovery blocks read	0	0.0	0.0
recursive calls	1,459	6.7	1,459.0
redo blocks written	605	2.8	605.0
redo buffer allocation retries	2	0.0	2.0
redo entries	291	1.3	291.0
...			
table scans (long tables)	0	0.0	0.0
table scans (short tables)	3	0.0	3.0
user calls	9	0.0	9.0
user commits	1	0.0	1.0
write clones created in backgroun	0	0.0	0.0
write clones created in foregroun	0	0.0	0.0

```
Tablespace IO Stats for DB: AULTDB1  Instance: aultdb1 Snaps: 1 -2
->ordered by IOs (Reads + Writes) desc

Tablespace
----------------------------
```

	Reads	Av Reads/s	Av Rd(ms)	Av Blks/Rd	Writes	Av Writes/s	Buffer Waits	Av Buf Wt(ms)
TEMP								
	112	1	0.0	1.3	151	1	0	0.0
RBS								
	1	0	0.0	1.0	13	0	0	0.0
SYSTEM								
	1	0	0.0	1.0	10	0	0	0.0
DRSYS								
	1	0	0.0	1.0	1	0	0	0.0
INDX								
	1	0	0.0	1.0	1	0	0	0.0
PERFSTAT								
	1	0	0.0	1.0	1	0	0	0.0
TOOLS								
	1	0	0.0	1.0	1	0	0	0.0
USERS								
	1	0	0.0	1.0	1	0	0	0.0

```
          -------------------------------------------------------------
File IO Stats for DB: AULTDB1  Instance: aultdb1  Snaps: 1 -2
->ordered by Tablespace, File

Tablespace              Filename
----------------------  ------------------------------------------------
```

	Reads	Av Reads/s	Av Rd(ms)	Av Blks/Rd	Writes	Av Writes/s	Buffer Waits	Av Buf Wt(ms)
DRSYS			C:\ORACLE\ORADATA\AULTDB1\DR01.DBF					
	1	0	0.0	1.0	1	0	0	
INDX			C:\ORACLE\ORADATA\AULTDB1\INDX01.DBF					
	1	0	0.0	1.0	1	0	0	
PERFSTAT			C:\ORACLE\ORADATA\AULTDB1\PERFSTAT.DBF					
	1	0	0.0	1.0	1	0	0	
RBS			C:\ORACLE\ORADATA\AULTDB1\RBS01.DBF					
	1	0	0.0	1.0	13	0	0	
SYSTEM			C:\ORACLE\ORADATA\AULTDB1\SYSTEM01.DBF					
	1	0	0.0	1.0	10	0	0	
TEMP			C:\ORACLE\ORADATA\AULTDB1\TEMP01.DBF					
	112	1	0.0	1.3	151	1	0	
TOOLS			C:\ORACLE\ORADATA\AULTDB1\TOOLS01.DBF					
	1	0	0.0	1.0	1	0	0	

```
USERS                      C:\ORACLE\ORADATA\AULTDB1\USERS01.DBF
                  1       0    0.0    1.0          1          0          0
```

```
                  ------------------------------
```

Buffer Pool Statistics for DB: AULTDB1 Instance: aultdb1 Snaps: 1 -2
-> Standard block size Pools D: default, K: keep, R: recycle
-> Default Pools for other block sizes: 2k, 4k, 8k, 16k, 32k

						Free	Write	Buffer
	Number of	Cache	Buffer	Physical	Physical	Buffer	Complete	Busy
P	Buffers	Hit %	Gets	Reads	Writes	Waits	Waits	Waits
--	----------	-----	-------	--------	--------	---------	--------	------
D	6,018	100.0	2,494	0	21	0	0	0

```
                  ------------------------------
```

Instance Recovery Stats for DB: AULTDB1 Instance: aultdb1 Snaps: 1 -2
-> B: Begin snapshot, E: End snapshot

	Targt MTTR (s)	Estd MTTR (s)	Recovery Estd IOs	Actual Redo Blks	Target Redo Blks	Log File Size Redo Blks	Log Ckpt Timeout Redo Blks	Log Ckpt Interval Redo Blks
B	0	101	0	2434	1836	1836	4095	10000
E	0	104	0	2313	1836	1836	4257	10000

```
            ------------------------------------------------------------
```

PGA Memory Stats for DB: AULTDB1 Instance: aultdb1 Snaps: 1 -2
-> WorkArea (W/A) memory is used for: sort, bitmap merge, and hash join ops

Statistic	Begin (M)	End (M)	% Diff
maximum PGA allocated	14.967	14.967	.00
total PGA allocated	14.967	14.967	.00

```
            ------------------------------------------------------------
```

Rollback Segment Stats for DB: AULTDB1 Instance: aultdb1 Snaps: 1 -2
->A high value for "Pct Waits" suggests more rollback segments may be required
->RBS stats may not be accurate between begin and end snaps when using Auto Undo
  managment, as RBS may be dynamically created and dropped as needed

RBS No	Trans Table Gets	Pct Waits	Undo Bytes Written	Wraps	Shrinks	Extends
0	2.0	0.00	0	0	0	0
1	8.0	0.00	0	0	0	0
2	10.0	0.00	138	0	0	0
3	7.0	0.00	1,496	0	0	0
4	8.0	0.00	0	0	0	0
5	13.0	0.00	0	0	0	0
6	6.0	0.00	0	0	0	0
7	42.0	0.00	81,700	0	0	0

```
            ------------------------------------------------------------
```

Rollback Segment Storage for DB: AULTDB1 Instance: aultdb1 Snaps: 1 -2
->Optimal Size should be larger than Avg Active

```
RBS No   Segment Size    Avg Active    Optimal Size    Maximum Size
------   -------------   ------------   -------------   -------------
    0        401,408           0                            401,408
    1      4,186,112        52,428        4,194,304       4,186,112
    2      4,186,112        52,428        4,194,304       4,186,112
    3      4,186,112        52,428        4,194,304       4,186,112
    4      4,186,112           0          4,194,304       4,186,112
    5      4,186,112        52,428        4,194,304       4,186,112
    6      4,186,112        52,428        4,194,304       4,186,112
    7      4,186,112        52,428        4,194,304       4,186,112
         -------------------------------------------------------------
```

Undo Segment Summary for DB: AULTDB1 Instance: aultdb1 Snaps: 1 -2
-> Undo segment block stats:
-> uS - unexpired Stolen,   uR - unexpired Released,   uU - unexpired reUsed
-> eS - expired   Stolen,   eR - expired   Released,   eU - expired   reUsed

```
Undo        Undo     Num Max Qry    Max Tx Snapshot Out of uS/uR/uU/
TS#         Blocks   Trans Len (s)  Concurcy Too Old Space eS/eR/eU
----    --------------- ---------- -------- ---------- -------- ----- -----------
  0           0          0         0          0         0       0 0/0/0/0/0/0
         -------------------------------------------------------------
```

Undo Segment Stats for DB: AULTDB1 Instance: aultdb1 Snaps: 1 -2
-> ordered by Time desc

```
                 Undo    Num Max Qry   Max Tx  Snap   Out of uS/uR/uU/
End Time         Blocks  Trans Len (s)  Concy Too Old Space eS/eR/eU
-----------  ----------- ----- ------- -------- ------- ------ -----------
07-Nov 09:55     0        0      0        0        0       0 0/0/0/0/0/0
         -------------------------------------------------------------
```

Latch Activity for DB: AULTDB1 Instance: aultdb1 Snaps: 1 -2
->"Get Requests", "Pct Get Miss" and "Avg Slps/Miss" are statistics for
  willing-to-wait latch get requests
->"NoWait Requests", "Pct NoWait Miss" are for no-wait latch get requests
->"Pct Misses" for both should be very close to 0.0
-> ordered by Wait Time desc, Avg Slps/Miss, Pct NoWait Miss desc

Latch	Get Requests	Pct Get Miss	Avg Slps /Miss	Wait Time (s)	NoWait Requests	Pct NoWait Miss
cache buffers chains	6,141	0.0		0	48	0.0
redo copy	0			0	298	0.0
FIB s.o chain latch	4	0.0		0	0	
FOB s.o list latch	5	0.0		0	0	
cache buffers lru chain	124	0.0		0	0	
...						
session allocation	11	0.0		0	0	
sequence cache	3	0.0		0	0	
ktm global data	1	0.0		0	0	
file number translation	11	0.0		0	0	
enqueue hash chains	532	0.0		0	0	
child cursor hash table	163	0.0		0	0	

```
channel operations paren        70    0.0           0           0
SQL memory manager worka        67    0.0           0           0
active checkpoint queue         78    0.0           0           0
         ------------------------------------------------------------
```

Dictionary Cache Stats for DB: AULTDB1 Instance: aultdb1 Snaps: 1 -2
->"Pct Misses" should be very low (< 2% in most cases)
->"Cache Usage" is the number of cache entries being used
->"Pct SGA"   is the ratio of usage to allocated size for that cache

Cache	Get Requests	Pct Miss	Scan Reqs	Pct Miss	Mod Reqs	Final Usage	Pct SGA
dc_free_extents	27	0.0	7	0.0	7	345	96
dc_object_ids	39	0.0	0		0	387	99
dc_objects	77	0.0	0		0	1,211	100
dc_rollback_segments	24	0.0	0		0	13	72
dc_segments	70	0.0	0		7	151	99
dc_tablespaces	29	0.0	0		0	10	50
dc_used_extents	7	100.0	0		7	15	75
dc_usernames	19	0.0	0		0	14	64
dc_users	22	0.0	0		0	25	83

Library Cache Activity for DB: AULTDB1 Instance: aultdb1 Snaps: 1 -2
->"Pct Misses" should be very low

Namespace	Get Requests	Pct Miss	Pin Requests	Pct Miss	Reloads	Invali-dations
SQL AREA	96	1.0	583	7.9	0	0
TABLE/PROCEDURE	215	1.4	347	19.6	0	0

SGA Memory Summary for DB: AULTDB1 Instance: aultdb1 Snaps: 1 -2

SGA regions	Size in Bytes
Database Buffers	50,331,648
Fixed Size	282,476
Redo Buffers	77,824
Variable Size	142,606,336
sum	193,298,284

SGA breakdown difference for DB: AULTDB1 Instance: aultdb1 Snaps: 1 -2

Pool	Name	Begin value	End value	% Diff
java	free memory	53,600,256	53,600,256	0.00
java	memory in use	5,120,000	5,120,000	0.00
shared	1M buffer	1,049,088	1,049,088	0.00
shared	Checkpoint queue	721,248	721,248	0.00
...				
shared	miscellaneous	2,641,428	2,641,428	0.00
shared	parameters	8,352	8,352	0.00
shared	sessions	395,760	395,760	0.00

```
shared sql area                          3,119,712      3,671,572    17.69
shared table definiti                          840          1,680   100.00
shared transaction                         182,376        182,376     0.00
shared transaction_branches                368,000        368,000     0.00
shared trigger defini                        1,720          1,720     0.00
shared trigger inform                          508            508     0.00
shared trigger source                          512            512     0.00
    db_block_buffers                    50,331,648     50,331,648     0.00
    fixed_sga                              282,476        282,476     0.00
    log_buffer                              66,560         66,560     0.00
          ------------------------------------------------------------------

init.ora Parameters for DB: AULTDB1   Instance: aultdb1 Snaps: 1 -2

                                                            End value
Parameter Name                Begin value                   (if different)
-------------------------     -------------------------     --------------
background_dump_dest          C:\oracle\admin\aultdb1\bdump
compatible                    9.0.1
control_files                 C:\oracle\oradata\aultdb1\control
db_block_buffers              6018
...
os_authent_prefix
parallel_max_servers          5
processes                     150
remote_login_passwordfile     EXCLUSIVE
service_names                 aultdb1.tusc.ga
sga_max_size                  193298284
shared_pool_size              75497472
sort_area_retained_size       65536
sort_area_size                65536
user_dump_dest                C:\oracle\admin\aultdb1\udump
utl_file_dir                  *
          --------------------------------

End of Report
```

The report is called whatever you told the procedure, but will default to sp_x_y.lst where *x* is the minimum snapshot ID specified and *y* is the maximum snapshot ID specified.

As you can see, the report generated contains much richer information than was contained in the utlbstat/utlestat reports. You can also query the statspack tables independently, since they are permanent and will hold all snapshot runs until manually cleaned out. The sppurge.sql script is provided to facilitate manual cleanout of the statspack tables. An example run of the spurge.sql script is shown in Listing 13.1.

Unfortunately, it is beyond the scope of this book to cover the reports in detail; I will point out, however, that the major difference between the utlestat report and the spreport report is that spreport is more detailed and contains information not only on the statistics but also on problem SQL statements, SGA memory structure use, PGA structure usage, and buffer pool usage. In addition, the ratios that you have to calculate by hand from the utlestat report are calculated for you, such as hit ratio, latch ratios, and other vital performance-calculated statistics.

Listing 13.1   Example run of the SPPURGE.SQL script.

```
SQL> connect perfstat/perfstat
Connected.
SQL> @sppurge


Database Instance currently connected to
=========================================

                                Instance
   DB Id    DB Name    Inst Num Name
----------- ---------- -------- --------------------
  980691836 AULTDB1           1 aultdb1


Snapshots for this database instance
=====================================

          Snap
 Snap Id Level Snapshot Started      Host             Comment
-------- ----- -------------------- ---------------- -----------
       1     5 07 Nov 2001 09:55:29 TUSCGA-PC2
       2     5 07 Nov 2001 09:59:06 TUSCGA-PC2
       3     5 07 Nov 2001 10:00:05 TUSCGA-PC2
       4     5 07 Nov 2001 11:00:02 TUSCGA-PC2


Warning
~~~~~~~
sppurge.sql deletes all snapshots ranging between the lower and
upper bound Snapshot Id's specified, for the database instance
you are connected to.

You may wish to export this data before continuing.


Specify the Lo Snap Id and Hi Snap Id range to purge
~~~~~~~~~~~~~~~~~~~~~~~~~~~~~~~~~~~~~~~~~~~~~~~~~~~~~~~
Enter value for losnapid: 1
Using 1 for lower bound.

Enter value for hisnapid: 2
Using 2 for upper bound.

Deleting snapshots 1 - 2.


Purge of specified Snapshot range complete.  If you wish to ROLLBACK the
purge, it is still possible to do so.  Exiting from SQL*Plus will
automatically commit the purge.
```

13.3 OEM AND ORACLE INTERNALS TUNING

In early versions of OEM, I would not have suggested using its tuning tools because many times they ended up causing more problems than they helped to cure. The SQL generated by OEM was inefficient and often popped to the top as problem SQL. Not so in OEM on Oracle9*i* and later versions of Oracle8*i*; the code and processing have been made more efficient, so I have no problem recommending that you use the tools for your tuning. OEM still suffers (as do many third-party tools as well) from sampling via live database connections and using Oracle tables and views to generate reports. In contrast, tools such as those provided by Quest and Precise use an advanced memory sampling, which requires no database connection to gather database statistics.

Tools that use advanced memory-sampling techniques can sample many times per second (for example, Precise allows sampling at 99 times per second if desired) with little (maybe up to 5 percent) hit on database performance. Try sampling 99 times per second with tools that must make a database connection (I think the best I have seen was in the Q product from Savant, which now belongs to Precise, at once per minute); I can assure you, they can't do it.

Anyway, OEM can now be used for spot monitoring, although I would not use it for continuous monitoring due to the overhead it places on the system. OEM monitoring is done using the performance pack (not STATSPACK). The OEM base installation for Oracle Enterprise includes:

From the Diagnostics Packs Icon

Lock Monitor

Performance Manager

Performance Overview

Top Sessions

Top SQL

Trace Data Viewer

From the Tuning Pack Icon

Oracle Expert

Outline Manager

SQL Analyzer

Tablespace Map

Many of the OEM tools will require a full repository to be operational, including Oracle Expert; others, such as the Tablespace Mapper, Top Sessions, Top SQL, and Lock Monitor don't. For the ones that require a repository, you can use a local repository.

When attempting to test the tools, I found it nearly impossible to use SYS as the explain plan user; and deciphering the requirements for other users to get at all of the underlying tables proved formidable. I granted the RESOURCE privilege, as well as a direct grant of SELECT ANY TABLE, to my repository user, in addition to the required direct grants CREATE TRIGGER, CREATE TYPE, and EXECUTE ANY TYPE. This was to no avail; unless, for example, I was doing a simple explain of a table owned by the repository owner from the SQL Analyzer tool, it would give me insufficient privileges errors. Even when I could generate an explain plan, attempting to use the Index wizard failed with selects against SYS-owned tables. To correct this, I ended up granting select on all SYS owned table via:

```
: sqlpus /nolog
SQL> connect sys as sysdba
password:
Connected.
SQL> set heading off termout off feedback off pages 0
SQL> spool grant_sys.sql
SQL> select 'grant select on '||table_name||' to &rep_owner;'
  2  from user_tables;
SQL> @grant_sys
```

Once the repository user had select on all SYS-owned objects, I could explain away, and run the wizards. I do not, however, recommend this solution for all users!

13.4 OTHER TOOLS FOR INTERNALS TUNING

The UTLBSTAT/UTLESTAT and STATSPACK series of reports are a great source of information for tuning your database. However, using them on a day-to-day basis would be a bit much for most DBAs to handle. Therefore, in this section I describe several additional tuning and reporting tools that DBAs can add to their tuning toolbox.

The tuning guides for Oracle list several areas where tuning is required, including:

Tuning Memory Allocation

SQL and PL/SQL areas

Shared pool

Database buffer cache

Tuning Input and Output

Disk I/O

Space allocation

Dynamic extension

Tuning Contention

Rollback segments

Redo logs

Multithread server

Other Tuning Areas

Sorts

Freelists

Checkpoints

Tools for Tuning Memory Contention

Memory contention will cause the best-tuned application to perform poorly. If the application constantly has to go to disk to get data dictionary and actual data, then performance will suffer. Remember, the SGA is divided into three major areas: the shared pool, the redo log buffer, and the database buffers. Under ORACLE8, Oracle8*i*, and Oracle9*i*, there are these additional areas in the SGA: the large pool (Oracle8), for databases using the multithreaded server, parallel query and rman, and the Java Pool (Oracle8*i* and Oracle9*i*) for all databases.

Tuning the Shared Pool
Missing a get on the data dictionary or shared pool area of the SGA is more costly than missing a get on a data buffer or waiting for a redo buffer. Therefore, here we will look at an SQL script that allows the DBA to examine the current status of the data dictionary or shared pool area. This SQL script is shown in Source 13.1.

Notice the following in Source 13.1: First, the script only selects statistics that have been used more than 100 times and where getmisses occurred. Obviously, if the parameter has had no getmisses, it should be satisfactory. (The factor of 100 gets was selected to ensure that the parameter has had enough activity to generate valid statistics.) Also notice that the percentage of misses is automatically calculated and reported for each parameter. If the DBA desires, the percent value could be used to generate a decoded value of RAISE if the percent is greater than 10, or LOWER if the value is less than a predetermined value. An example of this script's output is shown in Listing 13.2.

Source 13.1   Data dictionary cache report.

```
REM
REM NAME          : DD_CACHE.SQL
REM FUNCTION      : GENERATE REPORT ON DATA DICTIONARY CACHE
REM                 CONDITION
REM USE           : FROM SQLPLUS
REM Limitations   : None
REM Revisions:
REM Date          Modified By      Reason For change
REM 21-AUG-1991   MIKE AULT        INITIAL CREATE
REM 27-NOV-1991   MIKE AULT        ADD % CALCULATION TO REPORT
REM 28-OCT-1992   MIKE AULT        ADD CALL TO TITLE PROCEDURE
REM 21-Jun-1997   MIKE AULT        Updated to ORACLE8
```

```
REM 07-nov-2001      MIKE AULT      Tested on 9i, reformatted
REM SET FLUSH OFF
REM SET TERM OFF
SET HEAD ON
SET PAGESIZE 59
SET LINESIZE 79
COLUMN parameter FORMAT A20
COLUMN type FORMAT a11
COLUMN percent FORMAT 999.99 HEADING "%";
COLUMN gets FORMAT 999,999 HEADING 'Gets'
COLUMN getmisses FORMAT 999,999 heading 'Get|Misses'
COLUMN count FORMAT 999,999 heading 'Count'
COLUMN usage FORMAT 999,999 HEADING 'Usage'
ttitle "DATA DICTIONARY CACHE STATISTICS"
SPOOL rep_out/ddcache.lis
SELECT
    parameter,
    type,
    gets,
    getmisses,
    ( getmisses / gets * 100) percent,
    count,
    usage
FROM
    v$rowcache
WHERE
    gets > 100 AND
    getmisses > 0
ORDER BY parameter;
SPOOL OFF
```

Listing 13.2   Example output from DD_CACHE script.

```
Wed Nov 07                                              page     1
                   DATA DICTIONARY CACHE STATISTICS


                                       Get
PARAMETER             TYPE       Gets Misses     % Count    Usage
-------------------- ----------- ------ ------ ----- ----- --------
dc_constraints        PARENT      1,004    503 50.10   509      503
dc_files              PARENT        178      2  1.12    11        2
dc_free_extents       PARENT      2,413    825 34.19    30       23
dc_global_oids        PARENT        114     30 26.32    35       30
dc_histogram_defs     PARENT      1,124    165 14.68   166      165
dc_object_ids         PARENT     11,498  1,516 13.18 1,397    1,391
dc_objects            PARENT     12,232  2,696 22.04 2,749    2,746
dc_rollback_segments PARENT        738     12  1.63    18       13
```

continues

Listing 13.2 Continued.

```
dc_segments          PARENT        7,915  1,070 13.52 1,076    1,068
dc_sequences         PARENT          277     53 19.13    58       53
dc_tablespace_quotas PARENT        3,013      2   .07    24        2
dc_tablespaces       PARENT       10,281      5   .05     6        5
dc_used_extents      PARENT          805    804 99.88   811      801
dc_user_grants       SUBORDINATE 13,576     16   .12    16       14
dc_usernames         PARENT        4,993     14   .28    21       14
dc_users             PARENT       20,200     26   .13    29       26

16 rows selected.
```

In reviewing this report, check the following:

- Review Count and Usage columns: If Usage is equal to Count, the cache area is being fully utilized.
- If Usage is consistently low compared to Count, consider reducing the INIT.ORA parameter that controls the caches (SHARED_POOL).
- If Count and Usage are nearly equal and the percents are greater than 10, consider increasing the INIT.ORA parameter that controls the caches (SHARED_POOL_SIZE).

Since we are actually concerned only with an aggregate look at the cache area performance, the following query can be substituted into the report to give you an overall health indicator:

```
SELECT (SUM(getmisses) / SUM(gets)) 'DD CACHE MISS RATIO'
FROM V$ROWCACHE;
```

This substitution simplifies the report into:

```
Wed Nov 07                                           page    1
                    DATA DICTIONARY CACHE STATISTICS

DD CACHE MISS RATIO:
--------------------
          .085476693
```

The usual guidelines state that, if this ratio gets above 10 percent, take action by increasing the shared pool size parameter; that said, I have not seen this ratio greater than 1 percent on a properly tuned instance, so I would recommend earlier action. In our example instance, therefore, we may need to increase the shared pool size; however, we first need to look at other factors such as frequency of shared pool flushes (if any) and how the pool is actually being used before we just start adding to it.

Advanced Tuning of the Shared Pool

Perhaps one of the least-understood aspects of Oracle Shared Global Area tuning is tuning the shared pool. The generally accepted tuning methodology involves throwing memory into the pool until either the problem goes under or the problem is masked. Here we will examine the shared pool and define a method for tuning it that uses measurement, not guesswork, to drive the tuning methodologies. Numerous scripts for examining the shared pool are provided.

What Is the Shared Pool?   Many people know that the shared pool is a part of the Oracle SGA but little else, so to begin this discussion it's necessary to answer exactly, What is the shared pool? The shared pool contains several key Oracle performance-related memory areas. If the shared pool is improperly sized, then overall database performance will suffer, sometimes dramatically. Figure 13.1 diagrams the shared pool structure located inside Oracle 8*i* and 9*i* SGAs.

As you can see from the structures pictured in Figure 13.1, the shared pool is separated into many substructures. The substructures of the shared pool fall into two broad areas: the fixed-size areas, which, for a given database at a given point in time stay relatively constant in size, and the variable-size areas, which grow and shrink according to user and program requirements.

In Figure 13.1, the areas inside the library caches' substructure are variable in size, while those outside the library caches (with the exception of the request and response queues used with MTS) stay relatively fixed in size. The sizes are determined based on an Oracle internal algorithm that ratios out the fixed areas based on overall shared pool size, a few of the initialization parameters, and empirical determinations from previous versions. In early versions of Oracle (notably 6.2 and earlier), the dictionary caches could be sized individually allowing a finer control of this aspect of the shared pool. With Oracle 7, the internal algorithm for sizing the data dictionary caches took control from the DBA.

The major difference between the shared pools in Oracle8*i* and Oracle9*i* is that any excess memory specified by the SGA_MAX_CACHE parameter and not used in the actual cache and buffer definitions will be placed in the miscellaneous area of the shared pool.

The shared pool is used for objects that can be shared among all users, such as table definitions, reusable SQL (although nonreusable SQL is also stored there), PL/SQL packages, procedures, and functions. Cursor information is also stored in the shared pool. At a minimum, the shared pool must be sized to accommodate the needs of the fixed areas, plus a small amount of memory reserved for use in parsing SQL and PL/SQL statements. If this is not done, ORA-04031 and ORA-07445 errors will result.

Monitoring and Tuning the Shared Pool   Let me begin this subsection by stating that the default values for the shared pool size initialization parameters are almost always too small by at least a factor of 4. Unless your database is limited to the basic

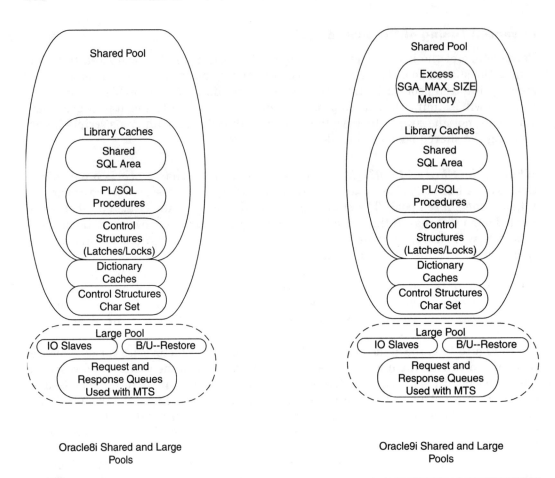

FIGURE 13.1 Shared pools in Oracle8*i* and Oracle9*i*.

scott/tiger type schema, and your overall physical data size is less than a couple of hundred megabytes, even the "large" parameters are far too small. Which parameters control the size of the shared pool? Essentially, only one: SHARED_POOL_SIZE. The other shared-pool parameters control how the variable-space areas in the shared pool are parsed out, but not overall shared pool size. In Oracle8, a new area, the large pool, controlled by the LARGE_POOL_SIZE parameter, is also present. The large pool shares latch structures with the shared pool, so proper sizing of the large pool is critical to help maintain shared pool health.

Generally speaking, I suggest you start at a shared-pool size of 40 megabytes and move up from there. The large pool size will depend on the number of concurrent users, number of multithreaded server servers and dispatchers and the sort requirements for the application.

What should you monitor to determine if the shared pool is too small? For this, you need to wade into the data dictionary tables, specifically the V$SGASTAT and V$SQLAREA views. Source 13.2 is a report that shows how much of the shared pool is in use at any given time the script is run.

Source 13.2   Script to report on shared pool usage.

```
REM Script to report on shared pool usage
REM
column shared_pool_used  format 9,999.99
column shared_pool_size  format 9,999.99
column shared_pool_avail format 9,999.99
column shared_pool_pct   format 999.99
@title80 'Shared Pool Summary'
spool rep_out\&db\shared_pool
select  sum(a.bytes)/(1024*1024) shared_pool_used,
        max(b.value)/(1024*1024) shared_pool_size,
        (max(b.value)/(1024*1024))-(sum(a.bytes)/(1024*1024))
shared_pool_avail,
        (sum(a.bytes)/max(b.value))*100 shared_pool_pct
    from v$sgastat a, v$parameter b
where a.pool = 'shared pool' and a.name != 'free memory'
and b.name = 'shared_pool_size'
spool off
ttitle off
```

Run the script in Source 13.2 periodically during times of normal and high usage of your database. The results will be similar to those in Listing 13.3. If your shared_pool_pct figures stay in the high nineties, then you may need to increase the size of your shared pool; however, this isn't always the case.

Listing 13.3   Example shared-pool summary.

```
Date: 11/08/01                                        Page:   1
Time: 03:50 PM              Shared Pool Summary         SYSTEM
                              aultdb1 databas


SHARED_POOL_USED SHARED_POOL_SIZE SHARED_POOL_AVAIL FULL_POOL_PCT
---------------- ---------------- ----------------- -------------
          22.46            48.00             25.54    46.8008439
```

Too often, all that is monitored is how much of the shared pool is filled; few check *how* is it filled: with good, reusable SQL or bad throwaway SQL. You must examine how the space is being used before you can decide whether the shared pool should be increased or decreased in size or a periodic flush schedule should be set up with the size remaining the same. So how can we determine what is in the shared pool and whether it is being properly reused or not? Let's look at a few more reports.

The first report we will examine shows how individual users are utilizing the shared pool. Before we can run the report, though, we must create a summary view of the V$SQLAREA view. I unimaginatively call this the SQL_SUMMARY view. The code for it is shown in Source 13.3.

Source 13.3   Script to create SQL summary view.

```
rem FUNCTION: Creates summary of v_$sqlarea and dba_users for use
rem           in sqlmem.sql and sqlsummary.sql reports
rem
rem
create or replace view sql_summary as
select username, sharable_mem, persistent_mem, runtime_mem
from   sys.v_$sqlarea a, dba_users b
where  a.parsing_user_id = b.user_id;
```

Once the SQL_SUMMARY view has been created, the report in Source 13.4 is run to generate a summary report of SQL areas used by user. This shows the distribution of SQL areas and may show you that some users are hogging a disproportionate amount of the shared-pool area. Usually, a user that is hogging a large volume of the shared pool is not using good SQL coding techniques and so is generating a large number of nonreusable SQL areas.

Source 13.4   Script to generate SQL summary report.

```
rem FUNCTION: Generate a summary of SQL Area Memory Usage
rem FUNCTION: uses the sqlsummary view.
rem            showing user SQL memory usage
rem sqlsum.sql
rem
column areas                                 heading Used|Areas
column sharable    format 999,999,999        heading Shared|Bytes
column persistent  format 999,999,999        heading Persistent|Bytes
column runtime     format 999,999,999        heading Runtime|Bytes
column username    format a15                heading "User"
column mem_sum     format 999,999,999         heading Mem|Sum
start title80 "Users SQL Area Memory Use"
spool rep_out\&db\sqlsum
set pages 59 lines 80
break on report
compute sum of sharable on report
```

```
compute sum of persistent on report
compute sum of runtime on report
compute sum of mem_sum on report
select username,
 sum(sharable_mem) Sharable,
 sum( persistent_mem) Persistent,
 sum( runtime_mem) Runtime ,
 count(*) Areas,
 sum(sharable_mem+persistent_mem+runtime_mem) Mem_sum
from  sql_summary
group by username
order by 2;
spool off
pause Press enter to continue
clear columns
clear breaks
set pages 22 lines 80
ttitle off
```

Example output from the report in Source 13.4 is shown in Listing 13.4. In the example report, no one user is really hogging the SQL area. If there were, you could use the script in Source 13.5 to show you which SQL areas the user has and what is in them. This report on the actual SQL area contents can then be used to help teach the user how to better construct reusable SQL statements.

Listing 13.4   Example SQL summary report.

```
Date: 01/28/00                                            Page:   1
Time: 10:06 AM            Users SQL Area Memory Use       MAULT
                              dw database

                Shared   Persistent    Runtime    Used        Mem
User             Bytes        Bytes      Bytes   Areas        Sum
---------- ----------- ------------ ----------- ------- -----------
JSMITH     408,211,332   12,876,752  58,737,832   13814 479,825,916
SYS          7,458,619       86,912     350,088    2791   7,895,619
PRECISE     45,392,274    1,155,440  12,562,016     322  59,109,730
DWPROC       6,710,324      239,128   1,194,792     205   8,144,244
DSSUSER      4,985,220      174,304     742,136      97   5,901,660
NETSPO       5,907,293       86,032     657,384      51   6,650,709
...
DEMERY          59,205        1,752       6,760       1      67,717
BSNMP           14,416          816       5,840       1      21,072
           ----------- ------------ ----------- ------- -----------
sum        489,039,559   14,826,608  75,968,544   17427 579,834,711
```

In the example output, we see that the user JSMITH holds the most SQL areas and the application DBA user, DWPROC, holds a great deal less. In a well-designed system, usually, the application owner will hold the largest section of memory, followed by ad hoc users who are using properly designed SQL. Where users aren't using properly designed SQL statements, the ad hoc users will usually have the largest number of SQL areas and show the most memory usage, as is the case in the example report.

I have found that if a shared pool contains greater than 5,000 to 10,000 SQL areas, which maps to well over 100,000 areas in the x$ksmsp structure, then performance will suffer; for example, at one client installation, I recorded that 170 meg = 5038 SQL Areas = 131319 x$ksmsp records. If there are too many x$ksmsp records, the pool latches have difficulty in keeping up, so performance suffers. The report in Source 13.5 shows the actual in memory SQL areas for a specific user. Listing 13.5 shows the example output from a report run against a user on my test system, GRAPHICS_DBA, using the report in Source 13.5.

Source 13.5   Example SQL area report.

```
rem FUNCTION: Generate a report of SQL Area Memory Usage
rem            showing SQL Text and memory catagories
rem sqlmem.sql
rem
column sql_text        format a60    heading Text word_wrapped
column sharable_mem                  heading Shared|Bytes
column persistent_mem                heading Persistent|Bytes
column loads                         heading Loads
column users           format a15    heading "User"
column executions                    heading "Executions"
column users_executing               heading "Used By"
start title132 "Users SQL Area Memory Use"
spool rep_out\&db\sqlmem
set long 2000 pages 59 lines 132
break on users
compute sum of sharable_mem on users
compute sum of persistent_mem on users
compute sum of runtime_mem on users
select username users, sql_text, Executions, loads, users_executing,
  sharable_mem, persistent_mem
from   sys.v_$sqlarea a, dba_users b
where  a.parsing_user_id = b.user_id
  and b.username like upper('%&user_name%')
order by 3 desc,1;
spool off
pause Press enter to continue
clear columns
clear computes
clear breaks
set pages 22 lines 80
```

Listing 13.5   Example SQL area report for a single user.

```
Date: 11/18/98                                                              Page:    1
Time: 04:19 PM                      Users SQL Area Memory Use                 SYSTEM
                                       ORTEST1 database


                                                                    Shared  Per.
User        Text                          Executions Loads Used By  Bytes  Bytes
----------- ------------------------------------------ ----------- ----- ------- ------ -----

GRAPHICS_DBA  BEGIN dbms_lob.read (:1, :2, :3, :4); END;      2121     1      0   10251   488
              alter session set nls_language= 'AMERICAN' nls_territory=      7     1      0    3975   408
              'AMERICA' nls_currency= '$' nls_iso_currency= 'AMERICA'
              nls_numeric_characters= '.,' nls_calENDar= 'GREGORIAN'
              nls_date_format= 'DD-MON-YY' nls_date_language= 'AMERICAN'
              nls_sort= 'BINARY'
              BEGIN :1 := dbms_lob.getLength (:2); END;         6     1      0    9290   448
              SELECT TO_CHAR(image_seq.nextval) FROM dual      6     1      0    6532   484
              SELECT graphic_blob FROM internal_graphics WHERE   2     1      0    5863   468
              graphic_id=10
              SELECT RPAD(TO_CHAR(graphic_id),5)||':           1     1      0    7101   472
              '||RPAD(graphic_desc,30)||' : '||RPAD(graphic_type,10) FROM
              internal_graphics ORDER BY graphic_id
              SELECT graphic_blob FROM internal_graphics WHERE   1     1      0    6099   468
              graphic_id=12
              SELECT graphic_blob FROM internal_graphics WHERE   1     1      0    6079   468
              graphic_id=32
              SELECT graphic_blob FROM internal_graphics WHERE   1     1      0    6074   468
              graphic_id=4
              SELECT graphic_blob FROM internal_graphics WHERE   1     1      0    5962   468
              graphic_id=8
***************                                                          ------ -----
sum                                                                      67226  4640
```

One warning about the report generated by Source 13.5: it can run to several hundred pages for a user with a large number of SQL areas (for example, the JSMITH user in the previous report). What should you watch for in a user's SQL areas? First, watch for the nonuse of bind variables; bind variable usage is shown by the inclusion of variables such as ":1" or ":B" in the SQL text. Notice in the example report in Figure 13.5 that the first four statements use bind variables, and, consequently are reusable. Nonbind usage means hard-coded values such as "Missing" or "10" are used. For most of the rest of the statements, in the report no bind variables are used even though many of the SQL statements are nearly identical. This is one of the leading causes of shared-pool misuse, resulting in useful SQL being drowned in tons of nonreusable garbage SQL.

The problem with nonreusable SQL is that it must still be looked at by any new SQL inserted into the pool (actually, its hash value is scanned). While a hash value scan may seem a small cost item, if your shared pool contains tens of thousands of SQL areas, it can add up to a performance bottleneck. In Oracle9*i*, all SQL is uppercased and then squeezed for whitespace (all excessive spaces, tab characters, carriage returns, and linefeeds are removed); then the hash is calculated, which leads to better comparisons and fewer code redundancies. How can we determine, without running the report in Source 13.5 for each of possibly hundreds of users, if we have garbage SQL in the shared pool?

The report in Source 13.6 shows a view that provides details on individual user's SQL area reuse. The view can be tailored to your environment if the limit on reuse (currently set at 1—see the boldface portions of the code) is too restrictive. For example, in a recent tuning assignment, resetting the value to 12 resulted in nearly 70 percent of the SQL being rejected as garbage SQL. In DSS or data warehouse systems, where rollups are performed by the month, bimonthly, or weekly, values of 12, 24, or 52 might be advisable. Source 13.7 shows a report script that uses the view created in Source 13.6.

Source 13.6   SQL garbage view.

```
REM View to sort SQL into GOOD and GARBAGE
REM
CREATE OR REPLACE VIEW sql_garbage AS
SELECT  b.username users,
        SUM(a.sharable_mem+a.persistent_mem) Garbage,
        TO_NUMBER(null) good
FROM    sys.v_$sqlarea a, dba_users b
WHERE   (a.parsing_user_id = b.user_id and a.executions<=1)
GROUP BY b.username
  UNION
SELECT DISTINCT b.username users,
        TO_NUMBER(null) garbage,
        SUM(c.sharable_mem+c.persistent_mem) Good
FROM    dba_users b, sys.v_$sqlarea c
WHERE   (b.user_id = c.parsing_user_id and c.executions>1)
GROUP BY b.username;
```

Source 13.7   Example SQL garbage report script.

```
column garbage format a14 heading 'Non-Shared SQL'
column good format a14 heading 'Shared SQL'
column good_percent format a14 heading 'Percent Shared'
column users format a14 heading users
column nopr noprint
set feedback off
@title80 'Shared Pool Utilization'
spool rep_out\&db\sql_garbage
select 1 nopr, a.users users,
      to_char(a.garbage,'9,999,999,999') garbage,
      to_char(b.good,'9,999,999,999') good,
```

```
        to_char((b.good/(b.good+a.garbage))*100,'9,999,999.999')
         good_percent
from   sql_garbage a, sql_garbage b
where  a.users=b.users
        and a.garbage is not null and b.good is not null
union
select 2 nopr, '-------------' users,
        '--------------' garbage,
        '--------------' good,
        '--------------' good_percent
from   dual
union
select 3 nopr, to_char(count(a.users)) users,
        to_char(sum(a.garbage),'9,999,999,999') garbage,
        to_char(sum(b.good),'9,999,999,999') good,
        to_char(((sum(b.good)/(sum(b.good)+sum(a.garbage)))*100),
         '9,999,999.999') good_percent
from   sql_garbage a, sql_garbage b
where  a.users=b.users
and     a.garbage is not null and b.good is not null
order by 1,3 desc
/
spool off
```

The report in Source 13.7 shows at a glance (well, maybe a long glance for a system with hundreds of users) which users aren't making good use of reusable SQL. An example report output is shown in Listing 13.6.

Listing 13.6   Example SQL garbage report output.

```
Date: 01/28/00                                          Page:   1
Time: 10:45 AM             Shared Pool Utilization       MAULT
                              dw database

users            Non-Shared SQL Shared SQL   Percent Shared
-------------    -------------- --------------  --------------
JSMITH            371,387,006     1,007,366          .271
NETSPO             10,603,456       659,999         5.860
DCHUN               6,363,158       151,141         2.320
DSSUSER             5,363,057       824,865        13.330
MRCHDXD             4,305,330       600,824        12.246
DWPROC              2,690,086     4,901,400        64.564
CWOOD                 946,199       239,604        20.206
TMANCEOR              877,644        93,323         9.611
GCMATCH               604,369     1,637,788        73.045
MAULT                 445,566     3,737,984        89.350
PRECISE               205,564    46,342,150        99.558
```

continues

Listing 13.6   Continued.

BKUEHNE	154,754	35,858	18.812
SYS	146,811	9,420,434	98.465
SMANN	102,460	8,523,746	98.812
MRCHPHP	56,954	59,069	50.911
MRCHAEM	42,465	65,017	60.491
----------	----------	----------	----------
16	404,553,888	78,358,468	16.226

Notice in Listing 13.6 that the JSMITH user shows only 0.271 percent shared SQL use based on memory footprints. From the report in Source 13.5, we would expect a low reuse value for JSMITH.

A final report in Source 13.8 shows what SQL is being generated over and over again based on the first x characters where x is input at runtime as the chars variable. Of course, you can make it look at longer or shorter pieces of code simply by changing the call to the substr( ) function. A sample report generated by Source 13.8 is shown in Listing 13.7.

Source 13.8   The similar SQL report.

```
set lines 140 pages 55
col num_of_times heading 'Number|Of|Repeats'
col text heading 'SubString - &&chars Characters'
col username format a10 heading 'User'
@title132 'Similar SQL'
spool rep_out\&db\similar_sql
select b.username,substr(a.sql_text,1,&&chars) text, count(a.sql_text) num_of_times from v$sqlarea
a, dba_users b
where a.parsing_user_id=b.user_id
group by b.username,substr(a.sql_text,1,&&chars) having count(a.sql_text)>1
order by 3 desc
/
spool off
```

Listing 13.7   Example of the similar SQL report.

```
Date: 01/18/00                                              Page:   1
Time: 09:10 AM                    Similar SQL               MAULT
                                  dw database


                                                           Number
                                                             Of
User        SubString - 60 Characters                      Repeats
--------    ----------------------------------------------- -------
SMITHJ      select a.TitleStatus,b.ProductLine,a.Category from UserArea.    4960
SMITHJ      select sum(a.OHQty + a.OOQty) from UserArea.InventoryPP a,us     4885
```

```
BKUEHNE   select b.OrderNum, b.OrderLineNum, b.VendorID, c.ProductShor      676
DWPROC    declare  1ERROR_ROW DATAWHSE.ERROR_LOG%ROWTYPE;  1DBCallOK n       660
DWPROC    declare  1LLogSeqNum number;  1ERROR_ROW DATAWHSE.ERROR_LOG%       660
DWPROC    declare    LPLogSeqNum number;      1ERROR_ROW DATAWHSE.ERRO       630
DWPROC    declare  1DBCallOK number := 0;  1FatalError number := 16;         615
DSSUSER   SELECT COUNT(*)   FROM DATAWHSE.LOADER_LOG  WHERE DATACOLLEC        571
DSSUSER   Select  Sum(TotalSales + Estimate),sum(TAStoreSales.FieldPla       199
DSSUSER   select logging from sys.dba_tablespaces where tablespace_nam       194
PRECISE   SELECT COMMENTS FROM ALL_COL_COMMENTS WHERE TABLE_NAME = 'PO        82
DWPROC      Select  TAStore.DistrictNo,Sum(TotalSales + Estimate),sum(TA      82
PRECISE   SELECT COMMENTS FROM ALL_COL_COMMENTS WHERE TABLE_NAME = 'CO        65
DWPROC      declare  1DBCallOK number := 0;  begin    :1ParmResult := 1DB     64
CWOOD     Select  TAStore.RegionNo,Sum(TotalSales + Estimate),sum(TASt        56
CWOOD     Select (LastName || ' ' || FirstName) From UserArea.WaldensB        51
CWOOD     Select Subject From UserArea.FFCTitleCTCurrent where SKU = '        51
MRCHPHP   Select ProductLongName From UserArea.FFCTitleCTCurrent where        51
MRCHPHP   Select AuthorName From UserArea.FFCTitleCTCurrent where SKU         51
MRCHPHP   Select BuyerName From UserArea.TitleCurrent Where Bkey in (S        51
MRCHPHP   Select FFCBuyerCode From   UserArea.FFCTitleInvMgmt where SK        51
MRCHPHP   Select  TAStore.StoreNo,Sum(TotalSales + Estimate),sum(TASto        46
```

When we tracked the first two lines of the report in Listing 13.7 back to the user, guess who we found? Yep, JSMITH. (Names changed to protect the not so innocent.)

Shared Pool Summary Let's review what we have seen so far. We have examined reports that show both gross and detailed shared-pool usage and whether or not shared areas are being reused. What can we do with this data? Ideally, we will use the results to size our shared pool properly. I'll set seven general guidelines for shared-pool sizing:

- *Guideline 1:* If gross usage of the shared pool *not* in an ad hoc environment exceeds 95 percent (rises to 95 percent or greater and stays there), establish a shared-pool size large enough to hold the fixed-size portions, pin reusable packages and procedures, and then increase shared pool by 20 percent increments until usage drops below 90 percent on the average.
- *Guideline 2:* If the shared pool shows a mixed ad hoc and reuse environment, establish a shared-pool size large enough to hold the fixed-size portions, pin reusable packages, and establish a comfort level above this required level of pool fill, then establish a routine flush cycle to filter nonreusable code from the pool.
- *Guideline 3:* If the shared pool shows that no reusable SQL is being used, establish a shared pool large enough to hold the fixed-size portions, plus a few megabytes (usually not more than 40), and allow the shared-pool-modified least recently used (LRU) algorithm to manage the pool.

In guidelines 1, 2, and 3, start at around 40 megabytes for a standard-size system. Notice that guideline 2 states that a routine flush cycle should be instituted. This flies in the face of what Oracle Support used to push in their shared-pool white papers; however, they were working from the assumption that proper SQL is being generated, whereas you want to reuse the SQL present in the shared pool. Oracle's latest paper acknowledges that there are times when a shared-pool flush is beneficial. In a mixed environment, where there is a mixture of reusable and nonreusable SQL, the nonreusable SQL will act as a drag against the other SQL (I call this *shared-pool thrashing*) unless it is periodically removed by flushing. The DBA_UTILITIES package contains a PL/SQL package called FLUSH_IT, which can be used by the DBMS_JOB job queues to periodically flush the shared pool, but only when it exceeds a specified percent.

Because there is always a debate as to whether this really does help performance, I set up a test on a production instance: on day 1, I did no automated flushing; on day 2, I instituted the automated flushing. Figure 13.2 shows the graphs of performance indicators, flush cycles, and users.

In the graphs in Figure 13.2, pay particular attention to the overall trend of the performance indicator between day 1 and day 2. On day 1 (the day with an initial flush, as indicated by the steep plunge on the pool utilization graph, followed by the buildup to maximum and the flattening of the graph), the performance indicator shows an upward trend. The performance indicator is a measure of how long the database takes to do a specific set of tasks (from the Q Diagnostic tool from Savant Corporation). Therefore, an increase in the performance indicator shows a net decrease in performance. On day 2, the overall trend is downward, with the average value less than the average value from day 1. Overall, the flushing improved the performance, as shown by the performance indicator, by 10 to 20 percent. Depending on the environment, I have seen improvements of up to 40 to 50 percent.

One thing that made the analysis difficult was that, on day 2, several large batch jobs were run, which weren't run on day 1. The results still show that flushing has a positive effect on performance when the database is a mixed-SQL environment with a large percentage of nonreusable SQL areas.

Guideline 3 also brings up an interesting point: you may have already overallocated the shared pool. In this case, guideline 3 may result in your decreasing the size of the shared pool. In this situation, the shared pool becomes a cesspool filled with nothing but garbage SQL. After allocating enough memory for dictionary objects and other fixed areas, and ensuring that the standard packages and such are pinned, you should maintain only a few megabytes above and beyond this level of memory for SQL statements. Since none of the code is being reused, you want to reduce the hash search overhead as much as possible. You do this by reducing the size of the available SQL area memory so as few a number of statements as possible are kept.

What to Pin   In all of the rules stated so far, I mention that the memory is usually allocated above and beyond that needed for fixed-size areas and pinned objects. How do you determine what to pin? Generally speaking, any package, procedure, function, or cursor that is frequently used by your application should be pinned into the shared pool when the database is started.

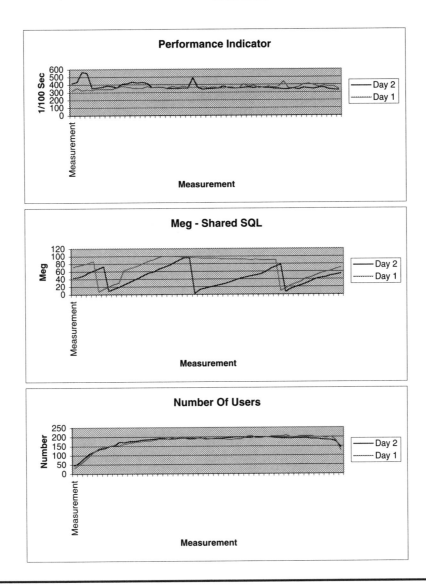

FIGURE 13.2   Graphs showing the effects of flushing.

Packages, cursors, sequences, triggers, procedures, and functions may be pinned in Oracle databases using the DBMS_SHARED_POOL package. The DBMS_SHARED_POOL package may have to be built in earlier releases of Oracle. This is done using the DBMSPOOL.SQL and PRVTPOOL.PLB scripts, located in (UNIX) $ORACLE_HOME/ rdbms/admin or (NT) x:\ora9*i*\rdbms\admin, where x: is the home drive for your install.

How do you determine which packages, procedures, or functions to pin? Actually, Oracle has made this easy by providing the V$DB_OBJECT_CACHE view that shows all objects in the pool, and, more importantly, how they are being utilized. The report in Source 13.9 provides a list of objects that have been loaded more than once and have executions greater than 1. Some example output from this script is shown in Listing 13.8. A rule of thumb is that if an object is being frequently executed and frequently reloaded, it should be pinned into the shared pool.

Source 13.9   **Stored object statistics report.**

```
rem FUNCTION: Report Stored Object Statistics
rem
column owner            format a11            heading Schema
column name             format a30            heading Object|Name
column namespace                              heading Name|Space
column type                                   heading Object|Type
column kept             format a4             heading Kept
column sharable_mem     format 999,999        heading Shared|Memory
column executions       format 999,999        heading Executes
set lines 132 pages 47 feedback off
@title132 'Oracle Objects Report'
break on owner on namespace on type
spool rep_out/&db/o_stat
select OWNER, NAMESPACE, TYPE, NAME, SHARABLE_MEM, LOADS,
       EXECUTIONS, LOCKS, KEPT
from   v$db_object_cache
where type not in (
'NOT LOADED','NON-EXISTENT','VIEW','TABLE','SEQUENCE','PACKAGE BODY')
     and executions>0 and loads>1 and kept='NO'
order by owner,namespace,type,executions desc;
spool off
set lines 80 pages 22 feedback on
clear columns
clear breaks
ttitle off
```

Listing 13.8   **Object statistics report.**

```
Date: 12/16/99                                                           Page:   1
Time: 12:54 PM                      Oracle Should Keep Report             SYSTEM
                                     SBSFAPRD database


          Name       Object      Should Keep        Shared
Schema    Space      Type        Object Name        Memory    LOADS Executes  LOCKS Kept
........  .........  ..........  ................  .......  ..... ........  ..... ....

SIEBEL    TABLE/PROCEDURE PROCEDURE  NGS_EXPORT_PROC    63,310      51    5,471     72 NO
          TRIGGER    TRIGGER     S_OPTY_ESCL_T1      6,733     130 ########     92 NO
```

		S_OPTY_POSTN_ESCL_T2	7,035	635	94,678	41	NO
		S_OPTY_PROD_ESCL_T1	6,466	110	78,297	151	NO
		S_ACCNT_POSTN_ESCL_T1	6,308	674	40,756	10	NO
		S_OPTY_POSTN_ESCL_T3	2,971	60	38,236	1	NO
		S_ACCNT_POSTN_ESCL_T2	6,308	674	36,428	12	NO
		S_OPTY_CON_ESCL_T3	6,481	792	3,669	5	NO
		S_SRV_REQ_ESCL_T1	6,984	678	3,429	6	NO
		S_OPTY_PROD_ESCL_T3	6,602	420	2,393	2	NO
		S_ADDR_ORG_ESCL_T2	7,473	203	1,987	9	NO
		NGS_U_TR	5,743	39	1,515	28	NO
		S_ORG_EXT_ESCL_T3	6,016	140	443	2	NO
		S_ORG_EXT_T_ESCL_T3	6,162	81	194	2	NO
		S_ADDR_ORG_ESCL_T3	6,409	38	114	3	NO
		S_ORG_INDUST_ESCL_T3	6,331	33	102	2	NO
SYS	TABLE/PROCEDURE PACKAGE	STANDARD	120,844	107	397,486	170	NO
		DBMS_APPLICATION_INFO	12,161	278	173,486	2	NO
		DBMS_STANDARD	15,097	109	161,973	234	NO
		DBMS_OUTPUT	14,615	148	100,434	1	NO
		UTL_FILE	3,596	82	7,210	73	NO

To really show the concept, the example report in Listing 13.8 was taken from one of the more active instances I have monitored. What's interesting to note about this report is that the majority of objects are triggers: you can pin triggers, cursors, packages, procedures, or functions. Also note that you have to pin only the package, not the package and package body.

Another criterion for determining if an object should be pinned into the shared pool is its size. The DBMS_SHARED_POOL.SIZES procedure searches the shared pool for any objects larger than the size in kilobytes of the argument it is passed. Generally, the larger the size, the more likely that the object is a package, meaning you will want to keep it in the pool; smaller objects tend to be individual queries and can be aged out of the pool. Remember that, generally, the DBMS_SHARED_POOL procedure is not automatically loaded when an instance is built; the DBMSPOOL.SQL and PRVTPOOL.PLB scripts must be run from INTERNAL or SYS users for it to be created. The use of DBMS_SHARED_POOL.SIZES is shown in Listing 13.9.

Listing 13.9   Use of DBMS_SHARED_POOL.SIZES.

```
SQL> set serveroutput on size 4000;
SQL> execute sys.dbms_shared_pool.sizes(10);
SIZE(K) KEPT   NAME
------- ------ ------------------------------------------------------------
139            SYS.STANDARD                    (PACKAGE)
56             SYS.DBMS_SHARED_POOL            (PACKAGE BODY)
31             SELECT TO_CHAR(SHARABLE_MEM / 1000 ,'999999')
```

continues

Listing 13.9   Continued.

```
                   SZ,DECODE(KEPT_VERSIONS,0,'
                   ',RPAD('YES(' || TO_CHAR(KEPT_VERSIONS) |
                   | ')',6)) KEEPED,RAWTOHEX(ADDRESS) || ',' || TO_CHAR(HASH
                   _VALUE)  NAME,SUBSTR(SQL_TEXT,1,354) EXTRA   FROM V$SQLAREA
                   WHERE SHARABLE_MEM > :b1 * 1000   UNION SELECT TO_CHAR(SH
                   ARABLE_MEM / 1000 ,'999999') SZ,DECODE(KEPT,'YES','YES
                   (004D7F84,2008220828)         (CURSOR)
30                 SYS.STANDARD                  (PACKAGE BODY)
27                 SYS.DBMS_SHARED_POOL              (PACKAGE)
17                 SYS.V$SQLAREA                 (VIEW)
16                 SYS.V$DB_OBJECT_CACHE         (VIEW)
15                 insert into idl_ub2$(obj#,part,version,piece#,length,piece)
val
                   ues(:1,:2,:3,:4,:5,:6)
                   (0027BA44,-512326869)         (CURSOR)
PL/SQL procedure successfully completed.
```

The "set serveroutput on size 4000" command in Listing 13.9 limits the size of the output buffer to 4,000 bytes. The "set serveroutput" command is required. Perhaps in the future, if we all bug Oracle for an enhancement, they will incorporate the use of UTIL_FILE and generate us a report listing we can review as we desire. As you can see from this listing, there is one large package in shared memory. Let's issue a keep against this package to retain it. Listing 13.10 shows the results from this action.

Listing 13.10   Example DBMS_SHARED_POOL.KEEP.

```
SQL> execute dbms_shared_pool.keep('sys.standard');
PL/SQL procedure successfully completed.
SQL> execute dbms_shared_pool.sizes(130);
SIZE(K) KEPT    NAME

------- ------  ------------------------------------------------------------
139     YES     SYS.STANDARD                  (PACKAGE)
PL/SQL procedure successfully completed.
```

By issuing keeps against large packages to hold them in memory, you can mitigate shared-pool fragmentation that results in the ORA-04031 error. Pinning the packages so they don't age out prevents smaller queries, cursors, and procedures from taking their areas; then, when the packages are reloaded, viola! An ORA-04031 as the package seeks a large enough group of areas in which to install itself. Under ORACLE8, this was supposed to be eliminated due to the way the shared-memory area is now used; however, I have had some reports on as late a version as 8.1.7.2. Oracle9*i* has promised better memory management of the shared pool, but the jury is still out, as there aren't many large-scale production databases running Oracle9*i* as of this writing.

- *Guideline 4:* Always determine usage patterns of packages, procedures, functions, triggers, and cursors, and pin those that are frequently used.

The Shared Pool and MTS   The use of the multithreaded server option (MTS) in Oracle requires a sometimes dramatic increase in the size of the shared pool. This increase in the size of the shared pool caused by MTS is due to the addition of the user global areas (UGAs) required for sorting and message queues. If you are using MTS, you should monitor the V$SGASTAT values for MTS-related memory areas, and adjust the shared-pool memory allocations accordingly.

Note that in Oracle 8 and greater, if MTS is being used, you should make use of the large pool feature to pull the user global areas and MTS queues out of the shared-pool area. This prevents the fragmentation problems that have been reported in shared pools when MTS is used without allocating the large pool.

Large Pool Sizing   Sizing the large pool can be complex. The large pool, if configured, must be at least 600 kilobytes in size. Usually, for most MTS applications, 600 is enough. However, if PQO (parallel query option) is also used in your Oracle8, Oracle8*i*, or Oracle9*i* environment, then the size of the large pool will increase dramatically. The V$SGASTAT dynamic performance view has a new column in Oracle8 called POOL. It is used to contain the pool area where that particular type of object is being stored. By issuing a summation select against the V$SGASTAT view, a DBA can quickly determine the size of the large pool area currently being used.

```
SELECT name, SUM(bytes) FROM V$SGASTAT WHERE pool='LARGE POOL' GROUP BY
ROLLUP(name);
```

The above select should be used when an "ORA-04031:Unable to allocate 16084 bytes of shared memory ('large pool', 'unknown object', 'large pool hea', 'PX large pool')" error is received during operation with a large pool configured (the number of bytes specified may differ). When the above select is run, the resulting summary number of bytes will indicate the current size of the pool and show how close you are to your maximum, as specified in the initialization parameter LARGE_POOL_SIZE. Generally, increasing the large_pool by up to 100 percent will eliminate the ORA-04031 errors.

In an undocumented (as of this writing) bug in 8.1.7.1 if you have large complex SQL statements, such as a 15 table join, and nothing to force large pool usage you can get excessive CPU times, ORA-04031 and ORA_01037 errors. If you get ORA-04031, or ORA-01037 errors and aren't using the large pool try turning on parallel query by setting the parallel query processes to minimum values to force use of the large pool.

Oracle8*i* provides for automated sizing of the large pool. If PARALLEL_AUTOMATIC_TUNING is set to TRUE, or if PARALLEL_MAX_SERVERS is set to a nonzero value, then the LARGE_POOL_SIZE will be calculated; however, it can be overridden with a manually specified entry in the initialization file. Indeed, if an "ORA-27102: Out of Memory" error is received when you set either of these parameters (or both), you must either manually set LARGE_POOL_SIZE or reduce the value for

PARALLEL_MAX_SERVERS. The following formula determines the set point for the LARGE_POOL_SIZE if it is not manually set:

```
(DOP^2*(4I-1)+2*DOP*3+4*DOP(I-1))*PEMS*USERS
```

where

> **DOP.** Degree of parallel calculated from #CPU/NODE * #NODES.
>
> **I.** Number of threads/CPU.
>
> **PEMS.** Parallel execution message size, set with the PARALLEL_EXECUTION_MESSAGE_SIZE initialization parameter; this usually defaults to 2K or 4K but can be larger.
>
> **USERS.** Number of concurrent users using parallel query.

For a 2D PEMS with four concurrent users, for a steadily increasing value for DOP, the memory size is a quadratic function ranging from around 4 meg with 10 CPUs to 120 meg with 70 CPUs. This memory requirement is demonstrated in Figure 13.3.

On my NT4.0 Oracle8*i*, 8.1.3 test system, I have two CPUs, set at two threads per CPU (DOP of 4) and four threads per CPU (DOP of 8), message buffer of 4K, and I performed multiple tests increasing the PARALLEL_MAX_SERVERS initialization parameter to see what the resulting increase in LARGE_POOL_SIZE would be. Those results are shown in Table 13.1

Notice that for a small number of CPUs, the large pool size increase from an increase in parallel max servers isn't affected by changes in the number of parallel threads until the value of threads is large in respect to the number of CPUs.

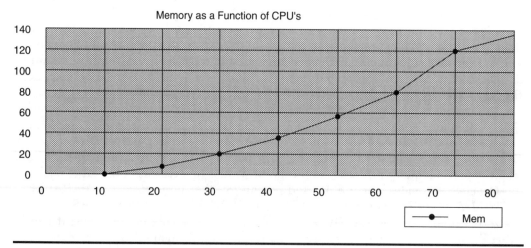

FIGURE 13.3   Charting 2K PEMS and four concurrent users, showing memory requirements as number of CPUs increases.

TABLE 13.1 Parallel Max Servers versus Large Pool Size

PARALLEL_MAX_SERVERS	DOP 4 LARGE_POOL_SIZE	DOP 8 LARGE_POOL_SIZE
4	685,024 bytes	685,024 bytes
8	857,056 bytes	857,056 bytes
16	1,151,968 bytes	1,545,184 bytes

For non-PQO systems, a general rule of thumb is 5K of memory for each MTS user for the large pool area.

■ *Guideline 5*: In Oracle7, when using MTS, increase the shared pool size to accommodate MTS messaging and queuing, as well as UGA requirements. In Oracle8, use the large pool to prevent MTS from affecting the shared-pool areas. If using PQO, the large pool is required in Oracle8.

Disk I/O and the Shared Pool   The shared SQL area contains the Pcode versions of all of the current SQL commands that haven't been aged out of the shared pool. Numerous statistics are available via the v$sqlarea DPT. The text of SQL statements in the shared pool can be retrieved (at least the first tens of bytes) from the v$sqltext and v$sqlarea DPTs. Let's look at a report that displays the SQL statements in the SQL area with the greatest number of disk reads (these will probably be the ones you will want to review and tune). Look at the report in Source 13.10. Output from this report is shown in Listing 13.11.

Source 13.10   SQL versus disk reads report.

```
REM Name: sqldrd.sql
REM Function: return the sql statements from the shared area with
REM Function: highest disk reads
REM History: Presented in paper 35 at IOUG-A 1997, converted for
REM use 6/24/97 MRA
REM
DEFINE access_level = 1000 (NUMBER)
COLUMN parsing_user_id FORMAT 9999999 HEADING 'User Id'
COLUMN executions      FORMAT 9999        HEADING 'Exec'
COLUMN sorts           FORMAT 99999       HEADING 'Sorts'
COLUMN command_type    FORMAT 99999       HEADING 'CmdT'
COLUMN disk_reads      FORMAT 999,999,999 HEADING 'Block Reads'
COLUMN sql_text        FORMAT a40         HEADING 'Statement' WORD_WRAPPED
SET LINES 130 VERIFY OFF FEEDBACK OFF
START title132 'SQL Statements With High Reads'
SPOOL rep_out/&db/sqldrd.lis
```

continues

Source 13.10 Continued.

```
SELECT
    parsing_user_id, executions,
    sorts,command_type,
    disk_reads,sql_text
FROM
    v$sqlarea
WHERE
    disk_reads > &&access_level
ORDER BY
    disk_reads;
SPOOL OFF
SET LINES 80 VERIFY ON FEEDBACK ON
```

Listing 13.11   Example SQLDRD.SQL output.

```
Date: 06/24/97                                              Page:   1
Time: 11:35 PM            SQL Statements With High Reads       SYSTEM
                                 ORTEST1 database
User
Id   Exec Sorts CmdT Block Reads Statement
---- ---- ----- ---- ----------- ------------------------------------
   0  403     0    3        1111 select f.file#, f.block#, f.ts#,
                                 f.length from fet$ f, ts$ t where
                                 t.ts#=f.ts# and t.dflextpct!=0

   0   11     0    3        1104 select order#,columns,types from
                                 access$ where d_obj#=:1

   0   12     0    3         912 select /*+ index(idl_ub1$ i_idl_ub11)
                                 +*/ piece#,length,piece from idl_ub1$
                                 where obj#=:1 and part=:2 and
                                 version=:3 order by piece#

   5   34     0    3          13 SELECT NAME,VALUE   FROM V$SYSSTAT
                                 WHERE NAME = 'db block gets'

   0   12     0    3          14 select /*+ index(idl_ub2$ i_idl_ub21)
                                 +*/ piece#,length,piece from idl_ub2$
                                 where obj#=:1 and part=:2 and
                                 version=:3 order by piece#

   0   17     0    3          27 select file#, block#, ts# from seg$
                                 where type# = 3

   0    1     1    3          79 select distinct d.p_obj#,d.p_timestamp
                                 from sys.dependency$ d, obj$ o where
                                 d.p_obj#>=:1 and d.d_obj#=o.obj# and
                                 o.status!=5
```

```
   5   34    0   47           90 DECLARE job BINARY_INTEGER := :job;
                                 next_date DATE := :mydate;   broken
                                 BOOLEAN := FALSE; BEGIN hitratio;
                                 :mydate := next_date; IF broken THEN
                                 :b:= 1; ELSE :b := 0; END IF; END;
```

By tuning those statements that show large numbers of disk reads, the overall performance of the application is increased.

Monitoring Library and Data Dictionary Caches   I've spent most of this section discussing the shared SQL area of the shared pool. Let's wrap up with a high-level look at the library and data dictionary caches. The library cache area is monitored via the V$LIBRARYCACHE view, which contains the SQL area, PL/SQL area, table, index, and cluster cache areas. The data dictionary caches contain cache area for all data dictionary-related definitions.

Source 13.11 creates a report on the library caches. The items of particular interest in the report generated by Source 13.11 (shown in Listing 13.12) are the various ratios.

Source 13.11   Library caches report.

```
rem Title: libcache.sql
rem FUNCTION: Generate a library cache report
column namespace                      heading "Library Object"
column gets             format 9,999,999 heading "Gets"
column gethitratio      format 999.99   heading "Get Hit%"
column pins             format 9,999,999 heading "Pins"
column pinhitratio      format 999.99   heading "Pin Hit%"
column reloads          format 99,999   heading "Reloads"
column invalidations    format 99,999   heading  "Invalid"
column db format a10
set pages 58 lines 80
start title80 "Library Caches Report"
define output = rep_out\&db\lib_cache
spool &output
select  namespace, gets, gethitratio*100 gethitratio,
        pins, pinhitratio*100 pinhitratio, RELOADS,
        INVALIDATIONS
from v$librarycache;
spool off
pause Press enter to continue
set pages 22 lines 80
ttitle off
undef output
```

In Listing 13.12 we see that all Get Hit% (gethitratio in the view), except for indexes, are greater than 80 to 90 percent. This is the desired state; the value for indexes is low because of the few accesses of that type of object. Notice that the Pin Hit% is also greater than 90 percent (except for indexes) this is also desirable. The other goals of tuning this area are to reduce reloads to as small a value as possible (this is done by proper sizing and pinning) and to reduce invalidations. Invalidations happen when, for one reason or another, an object becomes unusable. However, if you must use flushing of the shared pool, reloads and invalidations may occur as objects are swapped in and out of the shared pool. Proper pinning can reduce the number of objects reloaded and invalidated.

- *Guideline 6*: In a system where there is no flushing, increase the shared-pool size to reduce reloads and invalidations and to increase hit ratios.

Listing 13.12   Example library caches report.

```
Date: 11/08/01                                              Page:    1
Time: 04:57 PM              Library Caches Report           DBAUTIL
                              aultdb1 database


Library Object     Gets Get Hit%       Pins Pin Hit% Reloads Invalid
---------------    ---- --------   --------- -------- ------- -------
SQL AREA          4,523    94.10      19,395    97.91      13       0
TABLE/PROCEDURE   5,835    80.19       3,423    50.16       0       0
BODY                 22    63.64          21    57.14       0       0
TRIGGER               1      .00           1      .00       0       0
INDEX                29      .00          29      .00       0       0
CLUSTER             174    96.55         234    97.01       0       0
OBJECT                0   100.00           0   100.00       0       0
PIPE                  0   100.00           0   100.00       0       0
JAVA SOURCE           0   100.00           0   100.00       0       0
JAVA RESOURCE         2    50.00           2    50.00       0       0
JAVA DATA             1      .00           6    66.67       0       0
```

Formerly, the data dictionary caches were individually tunable through several initialization parameters; now they are internally controlled. The report in Source 13.12 can be used to monitor the overall hit ratio for the data dictionary caches. The output from Source 13.12 is shown in Listing 13.13.

SOURCE 13.12 Monitoring Data Dictionary hit ratio.

```
rem
rem title:    ddcache.sql
rem FUNCTION: report on the v$rowcache table
```

```
rem HISTORY:  created sept 1995 MRA
rem
start title80 "DD Cache Hit Ratio"
spool rep_out\&db\ddcache
SELECT (SUM(getmisses)/SUM(gets))*100 RATIO
FROM   v$rowcache;
spool off
pause Press enter to continue
ttitle off
```

Listing 13.13   Sample Data Dictionary hit ratio report.

```
Date: 11/21/98                                    Page:   1
Time: 02:59 PM              DD Cache Hit Ratio       SYSTEM
                             ORTEST1 database


    RATIO
   --------
   1.273172
```

The ratio reported from the script in Source 13.12 should always be less than 1. The ratio corresponds to the number of times out of 100 that the database engine sought something from the cache and missed. A dictionary cache miss is more expensive than a data block buffer miss, so if your ratio gets near 1, increase the size of the shared pool, since the internal algorithm isn't allocating enough memory to the data dictionary caches.

- *Guideline 7*: In any shared pool in the data dictionary cache ratio is greater than 1.0, increase the size of the shared pool.

Using these guidelines and the scripts and techniques covered in this section, you should be well on the way toward achieving a well-tuned and well-performing shared pool.

Tuning the Buffer Cache

The buffer cache is the area in memory where data is stored from data tables, indexes, rollback segments, clusters, and sequences. By ensuring that enough buffers are available for storage of these data items, you can speed execution by reducing required disk reads. In Oracle7 and early Oracle8 releases, you only had the "normal" buffer area to worry about. To Oracle8*i* was added the capability to subdivide this buffer area into KEEP and RECYCLE buffer areas. Later in this section, we will examine how these areas interact and how they should be tuned and sized. To add to the complexity you can, in Oracle9*i*, also have multiple areas inside the buffers that do not have the same blocksize as the rest of the database. We will cover that in the Oracle9*i* tuning section.

If DB_BLOCK_BUFFERS is set too high, you may exceed shared memory size on UNIX or NT for your instance. Another possible result is that the entire Oracle process could be swapped out due to memory contention with other processes. In either case, it is not a desirable condition. To avoid exceeding shared memory area size, be sure you set these operating system values (on UNIX) high when the instance is created. To avoid swapping, know how much memory you are able to access; talk with your system administrator to find this out.

Tuning the Multipart Oracle8, Oracle8i, and Oracle9i Buffer Cache   In Oracle8 and Oracle8*i*, the database block buffer has been split into three possible areas: the default, keep, and recycle buffer pool areas. It is not required that these three pools be used, only one: the default pool, which must be configured with the DB_BLOCK_ BUFFERS or DB_CACHE_SIZE (in Oracle9*i*, this should be used instead of DB_ BLOCK_BUFFERS) initialization parameters; the others are "sub" pool to this main pool.

How the various pools are used is covered in the following subsections.

Use of the Default Pool   If a table, index, or cluster is created specifying that the KEEP or RECYCLE pool be used for its data, then it is placed in the default pool when it is accessed. This is standard Oracle7 behavior; and if no special action is taken to use the other pools, then this is also standard Oracle8, Oracle8*i,* and Oracle9*i* behavior. The initialization parameters DB_BLOCK_BUFFERS and DB_BLOCK_LRU_LATCHES must be set if multiple pools are to be used:

```
DB_BLOCK_BUFFERS = 2000
DB_BLOCK_LRU_LATCHES = 9

NOTE: In Oracle9i DB_BLOCK_BUFFERS should not be used, Instead set
DB_CACHE_SIZE. Also, DB_BLOCK_LRU_LATCHES will be determined Internally.
```

Use of the KEEP Pool   The KEEP database buffer pool is configured using the BUFFER_POOL_KEEP initialization parameter, which looks like this:

```
BUFFER_POOL_KEEP = '100,2'
```

In Oracle9*i,* this becomes DB_KEEP_CACHE_SIZE and is specified in megabytes.

The two specified parameters are, respectively, the number of buffers from the default pool to assign to the KEEP pool and the number of LRU (least recently used) latches to assign to the KEEP pool. The minimum number of buffers assigned to the pool is 50 times the number of assigned latches. The KEEP pool, as its name implies, is used to store object data that shouldn't be aged out of the buffer pool, such as lookup information and specific performance-enhancing indexes. The objects are assigned to the KEEP pool either through their creation statement or by specifically assigning them to the pool using the ALTER command. Blocks already in the default pool are not affected by the ALTER command, only subsequently accessed blocks are.

The KEEP pool should be sized such that it can hold all the blocks from all of the tables created with the buffer pool set to KEEP.

Use of the RECYCLE Pool   The RECYCLE database buffer pool is configured using the BUFFER_POOL_RECYCLE initialization parameter, which looks like this:

```
BUFFER_POOL_RECYCLE = '1000,5'
```

In Oracle9*i,* this becomes DB_RECYCLE_CACHE_SIZE and is specified in megabytes.

The two specified parameters are, respectively, the number of buffers from the default pool to assign to the RECYCLE pool and the number of LRU (least recently used) latches to assign to the KEEP pool. The minimum number of buffers assigned to the pool is 50 times the number of assigned latches. The RECYCLE pool, as its name implies, is used to store object data that should be aged out of the buffer pool rapidly, such as searchable LOB information. The objects are assigned to the RECYCLE pool either through their creation statement or by specifically assigning them to the pool using the ALTER command. Blocks already in the default pool are not affected by the ALTER command, only subsequently accessed blocks are.

As long as the RECYCLE pool shows low block contention, it is sized correctly. With the above setpoints for the default, KEEP and RECYCLE pools, the default pool would end up with 900 buffers and 3 LRU latches.

Tuning the Three Pools   In Oracle8*i,* the classic method of tuning the shared pool is not available, so we must examine alternative methods to achieve the same ends. This involves looking at what Oracle has provided for tuning the pools. A script, catperf.sql, offers several views for tuning the Oracle buffer pools. These views are:

V$BUFFER_POOL. Provides static information on pool configuration.

V$BUFFER_POOL_STATISTICS. Provides pool-related statistics.

V$DBWR_WRITE_HISTOGRAM. Provides summary information on DBWR write activities.

V$DBWR_WRITE_LOG. Provides write information for each buffer area.

Of these four views, V$BUFFER_POOL_STATISTICS seems the most useful for tuning the buffer pool. It contains statistics such as buffer_busy_waits, free_buffer_inspected, dirty_buffers_inspected, and physical write-related data.

If a buffer pool shows excessive numbers of dirty_buffers_inspected, and high amounts of buffer_busy_waits, then it probably needs to be increased in size.

In Oracle9*i,* the V$DB_CACHE_ADVISE view is available for tuning the buffer areas, which is described in the next subsection.

When configuring LRU latches and DBWR processes, remember that the latches are assigned to the pools sequentially and to the DBRW processes in round-robin fashion.

The number of LRU processes should be equal to or a multiple of the value of DBWR processes to ensure that the DBRW load is balanced across the processes.

Using the V$DB_CACHE_ADVICE View to Tune the Caches   The V$DB_CACHE_ ADVICE view is populated when the DB_CACHE_ADVICE initialization parameter is set to ON. The view shows the estimated miss rates for 20 potential buffer cache sizes, ranging from 10 percent to 200 percent of the current size. Each of the 20 projected cache sizes has its own row in this view, with the predicted physical I/O activity that would take place for that cache size. The DB_CACHE_ADVICE parameter is dynamic, so the advisory can be enabled and disabled dynamically to allow you to collect advisory data for a specific workload. (If this sounds familiar to the old hands out there, it's probably because you remember the X$KCBRBH and X$KCBCBH tables in days of yore.)

There are two minor overheads associated with this advisory process:

- *CPU load.* When the advisory is on, there is a small increase in CPU usage, because additional bookkeeping is required.
- *Memory.* The advisory requires memory to be allocated from the shared pool (on the order of 100 bytes per projected buffer). This memory is preallocated on instance startup if DB_CACHE_ADVICE is set to READY in anticipation of collecting advisory statistics, or if the parameter is set to ON. If the parameter is set to OFF (the default setting), on instance startup, then the memory is dynamically allocated from the shared pool at the time the parameter value is modified to a value other than OFF.

The parameter DB_CACHE_ADVICE should be set to ON, and a representative workload should then be run on the instance. Allow the workload to stabilize before querying the V$DB_CACHE_ADVICE view.

The SQL report in Source 13.13 returns the predicted I/O requirement for the default buffer pool for various cache sizes (based on a script taken from the *Oracle9i Performance Guide and Reference*, Release 1 (9.0.1), Part # 87503-02, Oracle Corporation, June 2001).

Source 13.13   DB cache advice report.

```
Rem db_cache_ad.sql
Rem from Oracle9i tuning
Rem Mike Ault Initial creation
Rem
col size_est    format 999,999,999,999 heading 'Cache Size (m)'
col buf_est     format 999,999,999       heading 'Buffers'
col estd_rf format 999.90        heading 'Estd Phys|Read Factor'
column estd_pr format 999,999,999       heading 'Estd Phys| Reads'
SET LINES 80 PAGES 55
@title80 'DB Cache Advisor Report'
```

```
SPOOL rep_out/&db/db_cache_ad
SELECT
    size_for_estimate size_est,
    buffers_for_estimate buf_est,
    estd_physical_read_factor est_rf,
    estd_physical_reads est_pr
 FROM V$DB_CACHE_ADVICE
 WHERE name = 'DEFAULT'
    AND block_size = (SELECT value FROM V$PARAMETER
                       WHERE name = 'db_block_size')
    AND advice_status = 'ON';
SPOOL OFF
SET PAGES 22
TTITLE OFF
```

In an effort to generate some sort of meaningful report, I attempted to load my server enough, but was only able to get results up to the second level. Listing 13.14 shows sample output from the DB cache advisor report.

Listing 13.14   Example DB cache advice output.

```
Date: 11/08/01                                        Page:   1
Time: 06:09 PM        DB Cache Advisor Report         SYS
                         aultdb1 database

                                 Estd Phys    Estd Phys
     Cache Size (m)     Buffers Read Factor       Reads
    --------------- ------------ ----------- ------------
                  6          802        2.42          996
                 13        1,604        1.03          423
                 19        2,406        1.00          411
                 25        3,208        1.00          411
                 31        4,010        1.00          411
                 38        4,812        1.00          411
                 44        5,614        1.00          411
                 50        6,416        1.00          411
                 56        7,218        1.00          411
                 63        8,020        1.00          411
                 69        8,822        1.00          411
                 75        9,624        1.00          411
                 81       10,426        1.00          411
                 88       11,228        1.00          411
                 94       12,030        1.00          411
                100       12,832        1.00          411
                107       13,634        1.00          411
                113       14,436        1.00          411
                119       15,238        1.00          411
                125       16,040        1.00          411
```

To interpret the results in Listing 13.14, look at the Est Phys Read Factor column:, if this value is greater then 1, then the buffer at that size will perform worse than the current buffer size; if the number is less than 1, then the buffer at that size will perform better than the current buffer size; and if the value is 1, then the performance will not change if you set the buffer size to that size.

Using V$BH and X$BH to Monitor Buffer Use   In versions prior to Oracle9*i*, you may have to run the catparr.sql script, located in ORACLE_HOME/rdbms/admin, to create the v$bh view. The v$bh view, and its parent x$bh, are very important for monitoring buffer usage. Rather then depending on hit ratio, which is prone to miscalculation, problems with nonselective indexes, and other woes, the v$bh and x$bh tables can be used to tell you exactly what is happening with your buffer areas. Look at the report in Source 13.14.

Source 13.14   Block usage script.

```
rem block_usage.sql
rem
rem Mike AUlt - TUSC
rem
@title80 'Block Usage Inside SGA Block Buffers'
spool rep_out\&db\block_usage
SELECT decode(c.name,null,'UNUSED',c.name) ts_name,
       a.file# file_number,
       COUNT(a.block#) Blocks,
       COUNT (DISTINCT a.file# || a.block#) Distinct_blocks
   FROM V$BH a, file$ b, ts$ c
   WHERE a.file#=b.file#(+)
         AND b.ts#=c.ts#(+)
   GROUP BY a.file#,decode(c.name,null,'UNUSED',c.name)
/
spool off
```

The script in Source 13.14 used the v$bh SYS view to show which tablespaces have blocks inside the SGA and how many blocks are free. An example block usage report is shown in Listing 13.15.

Listing 13.15   Example block usage report.

```
Date: 11/09/01                                      Page:    1
Time: 06:05 PM        Block Usage Inside SGA Block Buffers    SYS
                              aultdb1 databas
```

TS_NAME	FILE_NUMBER	BLOCKS	DISTINCT_BLOCKS
UNUSED	0	7177	3791
SYSTEM	1	3149	3138
RBS	2	707	707
TOOLS	5	441	225
PERFSTAT	8	333	333
TEST_2K	9	2	2

As you can see in my SGA, I have nearly 50 percent of my blocks free. If I am running under a normal load, in Oracle9*i*, this would indicate I may have overallocated my DB_CACHE_SIZE or, in earlier versions, that I have allocated too many DB_BLOCK_BUFFERS. This type of information is not available from a mere hit ratio. Another quick look at the v$bh view is obtained by the report in Source 13.15. The output from the report in this source is shown in Listing 13.16 for the same SGA as in Listing 13.15.

Source 13.15   V$BH status script.

```
rem vbh_status.sql
rem
rem Mike Ault -- Tusc
rem
@title80 'Status of DB Block Buffers'
spool rep_out\&db\vbh_status
select status,count(*) number_buffers from v$bh group by status;
spool off
ttitle off
```

Listing 13.16   V$BH status listing.

```
Date: 11/09/01                                        Page:   1
Time: 06:10 PM        Status of DB Block Buffers        SYS
                          aultdb1 databas


STATU NUMBER_BUFFERS
----- --------------
cr              227
free           7177
xcur           4405
```

If we add the cr and xcur values to obtain the dirty blocks, and compare this to the free value listing, we can see that this SGA has well over 50 percent of its blocks free. Generally speaking, if, at two hours, after a normal load is placed on a database, more than 20 percent of its database base buffer blocks are free, you probably have overallocated the number of DB_BLOCK_BUFFERS in pre-Oracle9*i* instances or overstated the DB_CACHE_SIZE in Oracle9*i*.

Tools for Tuning I/O Contention

Once the shared SQL areas and buffer caches have been tuned, the DBA must turn his or her eyes to the I/O performance of the disks and files associated with the Oracle system to realize further performance gains.

Tuning I/O to Avoid Bottlenecks   Once the application and memory areas have been tuned, the next potential performance bottleneck may be the disk subsystem. This system is addressed by tuning the input and output processes that Oracle uses, reducing contention for disk resources, and reducing or eliminating dynamic space allocation within database data files.

Tuning the DBWR Process   The DBWR process manages the buffer cache. In this capacity, it writes filled buffers from the buffer cache in the SGA to the disks. Obviously, a properly tuned DBWR process will be the first step in tuning I/O for the Oracle system. The DBWR process, as described in the section on UTLBSTAT and UTLESTAT, uses the hidden INIT.ORA parameters _DB_BLOCK_WRITE_BATCH and _DB_BLOCK_MAX_SCAN_CNT in Oracle8 to determine when it should write used, or dirty, buffers to the disk, thus freeing them for further use. DBWR triggers on the following conditions:

1. A user process writes a used buffer to the dirty buffer list and finds it is _DB_BLOCK_WRITE_BATCH / 2 long.
2. A user process searches _DB_BLOCK_MAX_SCAN_CNT buffers without finding a clean one.
3. The DBWR has been inactive for three seconds.
4. When a checkpoint occurs, LGWR signals DBWR to trigger it to write.

The DBWR writes out _DB_BLOCK_WRITE_BATCH buffers each time it is triggered. If there aren't that many buffers in the dirty buffer list, the buffers on the LRU list are written until _DB_BLOCK_WRITE_BATCH buffers are written.

NOTE   In Oracle8*i* and Oracle9*i*, you can no longer tune the parameters mentioned above because they have been deprecated. In Oracle8*i* and Oracle9*i*, the parameter _DB_WRITER_MAX_WRITES controls the maximum number of outstanding I/Os that a database writer can issue, but you should not touch this parameter unless instructed to by Oracle Support.

An example report that pulls the DBWR related statistics from the V$SYSSTAT, V$WAITSTAT, and V$BUFFER_POOL_STATISTICS tables is shown in Source 13.16. The report generated from Source 13.16 is shown in Listing 13.17.

Source 13.16   Report to pull DBWR statistics.

```
rem dbwr_stat.sql
rem Mike Ault - TUSC 11/09/01 Created
rem
col name format a46 heading 'DBWR Statistic'
col value format 9,999,999,999 heading 'Statistic Value'
set pages 40
@title80 'DBWR Statistic Report'
spool rep_out\&db\dbwr_stat
select a.name,a.value
from  (select name, value from v$sysstat
       where name not like '%redo%' and name not like '%remote%') a
where (a.name like 'DBWR%' or a.name like '%buffer%'
       or a.name like '%write%' or a.name like '%summed%')
union
select class name, count value from v$waitstat
where class='data block''
union
select name||' '||to_char(block_size/1024)||'K hit ratio',
   round(((1 - (physical_reads / (db_block_gets + consistent_gets))) *
100),3) value
from V$buffer_pool_statistics
union
select name||' '||to_char(block_size/1024)||'K free buffer
wait',free_buffer_wait value
from V$buffer_pool_statistics
union
select name||' '||to_char(block_size/1024)||'K buffer busy
wait',buffer_busy_wait value
from V$buffer_pool_statistics
union
select name||' '||to_char(block_size/1024)||'K write complete
wait',write_complete_wait value
from V$buffer_pool_statistics
/
spool off
set pages 22
ttitle off
```

Pay attention to the following in the report in Listing 13.17:

DBWR checkpoints. Number of checkpoint requests sent to DBWR since startup.
DBWR buffers scanned. Number of DB buffers scanned since startup.

Listing 13.17   Example DBWR statistics report.

```
Date: 11/09/01                                           Page:    1
Time: 04:44 PM              DBWR Statistic Report        DBAUTIL
                              aultdb1 database


DBWR Statistic                                  Statistic Value
-------------------------------------------     ---------------
DBWR buffers scanned                                          0
DBWR checkpoint buffers written                          2,601
DBWR checkpoints                                            18
DBWR cross instance writes                                   0
DBWR free buffers found                                     0
DBWR fusion writes                                          0
DBWR lru scans                                              0
DBWR make free requests                                     0
DBWR revisited being-written buffer                         0
DBWR summed scan depth                                      0
DBWR transaction table writes                              95
DBWR undo block writes                                  1,156
DEFAULT 2K buffer busy wait                                 0
DEFAULT 2K free buffer wait                                 0
DEFAULT 2K hit ratio                                       98
DEFAULT 2K write complete wait                             0
DEFAULT 8K buffer busy wait                                 3
DEFAULT 8K free buffer wait                                0
DEFAULT 8K hit ratio                                      99
DEFAULT 8K write complete wait                            0
buffer is not pinned count                           570,196
buffer is pinned count                               392,710
change write time                                        340
commit cleanout failures: buffer being written           0
commit cleanout failures: write disabled                  0
data block                                                3
dirty buffers inspected                                   0
free buffer inspected                                     0
free buffer requested                                 5,054
hot buffers moved to head of LRU                          0
no buffer to keep pinned count                      208,657
physical writes                                       4,792
physical writes direct                                2,056
physical writes direct (lob)                              0
physical writes non checkpoint                        3,476
pinned buffers inspected                                  0
summed dirty queue length                               122
switch current to new buffer                            219
write clones created in background                        4
write clones created in foreground                        7
```

Summed dirty queue length. Length of the dirty buffer queue. If this gets over 50, Oracle says to add DB_WRITER_PROCESSES..

Physical writes. Number of physical writes performed by the DBWR. If this is high, then there may be insufficient buffers allocated. In Oracle9*i,* increase DB_CACHE_SIZE; in pre-Oracle9*i,* increase DB_BLOCK_BUFFERS.

Data block. A statistic harvested from the V$WAITSTAT table; shows if there are any data block waits occurring. Excessive data block waits when the hit ratio is high can indicate need for more DBWR processes.

Hit ratios. A hit ratio will be calculated for each buffer pool and each separate block size in the default pool. Generally speaking, high hit ratios are desirable, low are not; but hit ratio is not the end-all/be-all statistics for buffer health.

Waits. Various waits will be reported for all pools and all areas of the default buffer with different block sizes. Pay attention to waits that deal with writes; if write-type waits are excessive, then more DBWR processes are in order. Buffer busy waits may indicate a need for more buffers.

There is no need to modify the DBWR internal batch size in Oracle9*i.* The write sizes performed by DBWR are automatically calculated by DBWR in Oracle9*i.* The write size depends on the number of dirty blocks to be written, and is tempered with the maximum number of writes (which is operating system-specific). The values chosen by DBWR are not configurable in Oracle9*i.*

DBWR is monitored using the statistic-free buffer waits. The free buffer waits statistic (available from the V$SYSSTAT table) should be as low as possible and should remain at a slowly increasing value. This means that, for your system, you have to decide: If you see spikes when database activity is high, consider using either more DB writers by setting the initialization parameter DB_WRITERS (Oracle7), DB_WRITER_IO_SLAVES (Oracle8) DB_WRITER_PROCESSES and DBWR_IO_SLAVES (Oracle8*i,* Oracle9*i*) equal to the number of disks used by Oracle, if your system doesn't support asynchronous I/O; or setting the ASYNC_IO initialization parameter to TRUE, if your system supports asynchronous I/O. If setting either the parameter that controls DBWR processes or ASYNC_IO doesn't help reduce the spikes on free buffer waits, verify that _DB_BLOCK_MAX_SCAN_CNT (pre-Oracle8*i* and Oracle9*i*) is set at 30 or greater. Normally, the default value of 30 is fine for this parameter. If you are dissatisfied with the performance of DBWR, first try increasing the INIT.ORA parameter _DB_BLOCK_WRITE_BATCH (on non-Oracle8*i,* or non-Oracle9*i* databases). Increasing this parameter improves DBWR's ability to use operating system facilities to write to multiple disks and write adjacent blocks in a single I/O operation. Increasing the number of DB block buffers may also be in order if DBWR performance is poor.

On many platforms, Oracle can use the built-in asynchronous ability of the operating system to multithread the DBWR process. On platforms where asynchronous I/O is not possible, multiple DBWR processes should be started using the DB_WRITERS initialization parameter. On some systems, such as HP, it has been shown that multiple

DBWR processes may have a positive effect, even with asynchronous I/O set. Note that in Oracle8*i,* the parameter changed: it is DB_WRITER_PROCESSES; an additional parameter, DBWR_IO_SLAVES, also is used. The difference between processes and I/O slaves is that if an I/O slave terminates, the instance continues to run. You cannot run multiple DBWR processes and DBWR I/O slaves on the same instance. You may need to increase the number of DB_BLOCK_LRU_LATCHES to increase the number of DB_WRITER_PROCESSES. (Note that in Oracle9*i,* DB_BLOCK_LRU_LATCHES has changed to _DB_BLOCK_LRU_LATCHES, and becomes undocumented.)

Two additional undocumented parameters that may assist in DBWR tuning are _DB_BLOCK_HASH_BUCKETS and _DB_BLOCK_HASH_LATCHES. The _DB_BLCOK_HASH_BUCKETS parameter should be set to the nearest prime number greater than twice the number of DB_BLOCK_BUFFERS on pre-Oracle9*i* systems. In Oracle9*i,* this parameter is correctly set, but on older systems, it may be set to twice the value of DB_BLOCK_BUFFERS and will have to be adjusted. The other parameter, _DB_BLOCK_HASH_LATCHES, is set to 1,024, but you may see better performance on some releases of Oracle8*i* if this is increased to 32,768. The other undocumented parameters dealing with the DBWR and DB blocks should not be touched.

Another way to improve the performance of DBWR on older systems is to enable the checkpoint process by using the CHECKPOINT_PROCESS initialization parameter. This frees DBWR from checkpoint duties, allowing it to concentrate on buffers only. In Oracle8 and later releases, the checkpoint process is automatically started.

Disk Contention   Once DBWR has been tuned, the DBA needs to look at disk contention. Disk contention happens when one or more users attempt to read the same disk at the same time, or in some cases, access a different disk through the same controller path at the same time. Spreading Oracle-related files across several platters or sets of platters—the more the better—prevents this. The new RAID options don't relieve the DBA of file placement concerns. You should be sure that the RAID volumes are properly set. I had one system where a system administrator set up multiple RAID5 volumes using two disks for each volume (a hint: the 5 is a meaningful number for RAID5).

The report in Source 13.17 can be used to monitor relative-fill I/O efficiency—essentially, how many reads are being performed per request as a percent. The more times the process has to access the same datafile to get the same information, the less efficient the datafile is. This could be caused by collocation of indexes and tables, a poorly ordered table that is scanned frequently, or having temporary or undo segments in with data or index segments.

Source 13.17   File efficiency report.

```
REM
REM NAME      :FILE_EFF.SQL
REM PURPOSE     :GENERATE FILE IO EFFICIENCIES REPORT
REM USE         :FROM STATUS_REPORTS.COM
```

```
REM Limitations :MUST BE RUN FROM ORACLE DBA ACCOUNT
REM Revisions:
REM Date            Modified By        Reason For change
REM 10-JUL-1992     M. AULT            INITIAL CREATE
REM 07-JUN-1993     M.AULT             Added reads to writes, reformatted
REM 23-Jun-1997     M.Ault             kcffio went away, rewrote to use
REM                 existing views/tables
SET PAGES 58 NEWPAGE 0
SET LINES 131
COLUMN eff      FORMAT A6             HEADING '% Eff'
COLUMN rw       FORMAT 9,999,999      HEADING 'Phys Block|read/writes'
COLUMN ts       FORMAT A22            HEADING 'Tablespace Name'
COLUMN name     FORMAT A40            HEADING 'File Name'
START title132 "FILE IO EFFICIENCY"
BREAK ON ts
DEFINE OUTPUT = 'rep_out/&db/file_io.lis'
SPOOL &OUTPUT
SELECT
    f.tablespace_name ts,
    f.file_name name,
    v.phyreads+v.phywrts rw,
    TO_CHAR(DECODE(v.phyblkrd,0,null,
    ROUND(100*(v.phyrds+v.phywrts)/(v.phyblkrd+v.phyblkwrt),2))) eff
FROM dba_data_files f, v$filestat v
WHERE f.file_id=v.file#
ORDER BY 1,file#;
SPOOL OFF
PAUSE Press return to continue
```

This is a cumulative report that gives information based on I/O since the Oracle instance was started. The report generated will list physical block reads and efficiency level (the efficiency number measures the percent of time Oracle asked for and got the right block the first time, which is a function of type of table scan and indexing). An example report is shown in Listing 13.18.

Listing 13.18   File I/O efficiency report.

```
Date: 11/09/01                                                  Page: 1
Time: 06:25 PM              FILE IO EFFICIENCY                   SYS
                              aultdb1 database


     Tablespace                                     Phys Block
Disk name        File Name                          read/writes % Eff
----- ---------- ---------------------------------- ----------- -----
C:\0  SYSTEM     C:\ORACLE\ORADATA\AULTDB1\SYSTEM01.DBF   3,260 63.74
      RBS        C:\ORACLE\ORADATA\AULTDB1\RBS01.DBF      1,351 100
      USERS      C:\ORACLE\ORADATA\AULTDB1\USERS01.DBF       40 100
```

continues

Listing 13.18   Continued.

```
        TEMP         C:\ORACLE\ORADATA\AULTDB1\TEMP01.DBF          4,252 85.25
        TOOLS        C:\ORACLE\ORADATA\AULTDB1\TOOLS01.DBF           891 78.9
        INDX         C:\ORACLE\ORADATA\AULTDB1\INDX01.DBF             40 100
        DRSYS        C:\ORACLE\ORADATA\AULTDB1\DR01.DBF               40 100
        PERFSTAT     C:\ORACLE\ORADATA\AULTDB1\PERFSTAT.DBF        1,206 100
        TEST_2K      C:\ORACLE\ORADATA\AULTDB1\TEST_2K.DBF            42 100
     *****                                                        -------------
     sum                                                           11,122
     9 rows selected.
```

Points of interest in Listing 13.34 are:

- In general, the relatively low efficiency of the SYSTEM and TOOLS areas. This is due to indexes and tables being mixed together in the SYSTEM and TOOLS tablespaces. A classic example, on Oracle's part, of "Do what we say, not what we do."
- Rollback efficiency should always be 100 percent; if not, someone is using the rollback area for tables.
- Index tablespace should always show high efficiencies; if they don't, then either the indexes are bad or someone is using the index areas for normal tables.
- An attempt should be made to even-out I/O. In the above example, too much I/O is being done on C:\; some of these data files should be spread to other disks.
- This report shows total I/O for the time frame beginning with the Oracle system startup. The results could be stored for two or more dates and times and then subtracted to show the disk I/O for a selected period of time. STATSPACK should be used for this type of measurement.

Running this report before and after doing an application test run will give you an idea of the disk I/O profile for the application. This profile, combined with information concerning the maximum I/O supported by each disk or each controller, can help the DBA determine how best to split out the application's files between disks.

In a RAID situation, where tracking disk I/O can be problematic, I suggest using one of the tools from Quest or Precise that allow you to track I/O down to the spindle, even in RAID configurations.

Tuning to Prevent Contention   Contention occurs when a number of users attempt to access the same resource at the same time. This can occur for any database object but is most noticeable when the contention is for rollback segments, redo logs, latches, or locks. You may also experience contention during the processes involved with the multithreaded server.

To correct contention, you must first realize that it is occurring. The procedure called in the script shown in Source 13.18 can be used to monitor for contention. The procedure called is a part of the DBA_UTILITIES package, described later in this chapter, in Section 13.8, "Using the DBA_UTILITIES Package." (Note, this package is over 1,200 lines long; if you want to look at it, download it from the Wiley Web site.) The report generated by this script is shown in Listing 13.19.

Source 13.18   The RUNNING_STATS calling script.

```
REM
REM NAME      : DO_CALSTAT.SQL
REM FUNCTION :Generate calculated statisitics report using
REM FUNCTION :just_statistics procedure
REM USE       :FROM STATUS.SQL or SQLPLUS
REM Limitations       :
REM Revisions:
REM Date            Modified By       Reason For change
REM 05-MAY-1992       Mike Ault       Initial Creation
REM 23-JUN-1997       Mike Ault       Updated to V8
REM
SET PAGES 58  NEWPAGE 0
EXECUTE dba_utilities.running_stats(TRUE);
START title80 "CALCULATED STATISTICS REPORT"
DEFINE output = rep_out\&db\cal_stat.lis
SPOOL &output
SELECT * FROM dba_temp;
SPOOL OFF
```

The DBA_UTILITIES package called in Source 13.18 retrieves contention and database health-related statistics, then calculates other statistics based upon those it retrieves.

Listing 13.19   Sample output from running stats listing.

```
Date: 11/07/01                                        Page:   1
Time: 03:35 PM        CALCULATED STATISTICS REPORT      DBAUTIL
                         aultdb1 database


NAME                                VALUE
-------------------------------- -----
Startup Date: 07-nov-01 15:22:57        0
CUMMULATIVE HIT RATIO           .982755488
sorts (memory)                       4891
sorts (disk)                            6
redo log space requests                 1
redo log space wait time               25
Rollback Wait %                         0
Shared Pool Available           56.4824371
Shared SQL%                     44.0445754
```

continues

Listing 13.19   Continued.

```
Shared Pool Used                 31.4790573
Data Dictionary Miss Percent      9.64587019
Library Reload %                  .039244203
table fetch by rowid                   14930
table scans (long tables)                 85
table scans (short tables)               694
table fetch continued row                383
Non-Index Lookups Ratio          .109677419
RECURSIVE CALLS PER USER          35.1794083
SYS UNDO HDR WAIT CONTENTION               0
SYS UNDO BLK WAIT CONTENTION               0
UNDO BLK WAIT CONTENTION                   0
UNDO HDR WAIT CONTENTION                   0
Free List Contention Ratio                 0
library cache                    .000266132
cache buffers chains             .001655418
cache buffers lru chain          .009571759
redo writing                     .038273117
redo allocation                  .012726424
FUNCTION                                   6
LIBRARY                                   16
TRIGGER                                   22
TABLE                                    426
SYNONYM                                13226
SEQUENCE                                  59
PROCEDURE                                  3
PACKAGE BODY                             125
PACKAGE                                  140
OPERATOR                                  21
LOB                                        9
VIEW                                     165
TYPE BODY                                 23
TYPE                                      75
JAVA RESOURCE                             16
INDEX                                    478
JAVA CLASS                               847
INDEXTYPE                                  7
TOTAL ALLOCATED MEG                   1106.5
TOTAL USED MEG                    520.320313
TOTAL SGA SIZE                     260407308
Press enter to continue
```

Let's examine the various statistics gathered by the do_calst2.sql report and see what each means in respect to the database.

The first value reported is just the startup time for the instance. Since many of the following statistics are cumulative from the time the instance was started, it was deemed necessary to have a timestamp showing the startup date.

```
Startup Date: 07-nov-01 15:22:57        0
```

The next value, the cumulative hit ratio, is used to get a feel for performance over time. The cumulative hit ratio is the "average" hit ratio since the database was started, thus it may be low if taken too soon after startup. Usually, you should look for the cumulative hit ratio to be in the range of 0.85 to 1.0 for an OLTP system and 0.6 to 1.0 for a batch system. Generally speaking, if this value is below the applicable range, an increase in the number of db_block_buffers is indicated.

```
CUMMULATIVE HIT RATIO           .982755488
```

The next two statistics deal with how the database is performing sorts. Essentially, you want to minimize disk sorts. Disk sorts are reduced by increasing the size of the sort_area_size initialization parameter. If disk sorts exceed 1 to 2percent of total sorts, tune your sort areas. If disk sorts are required, look into using direct writes to speed sort processing to disks.

```
sorts (memory)                  4891
sorts (disk)                       6
```

The next two statistics deal directly with redo log contention. If redo log space waits become excessive (into the hundreds), and wait time is excessive, consider tuning log_buffers and possibly resizing or increasing the number of redo logs. Actually, you would increase the number of redo log groups or the size of individual redo log members. All redo logs should be of equal size. It is suggested that the redo logs be sized such that loss of the online redo log will lose only X amount of data, where X is the critical amount of data for your application (say, an hour's worth, day's worth, ten minutes' worth, etc.).

```
redo log space requests         25
redo log space wait time         0
```

The next statistic, "Rollback Wait %," tells how often a process had to wait for a rollback segment. If this value gets near 1.0, consider rollback segment tuning.

```
Rollback Wait %                  0
```

The next set of statistics deal with shared-pool health. The "Shared SQL %" statistic shows the ratio of total SQL areas in the library cache that can't be reused against the total number of SQL areas (by memory). If more than 40 to 50 percent of your SQL is not reusable, and your used area is greater than 40 to 60 meg, you may suffer performance problems due to shared-pool thrashing. Shared-pool thrashing can be reduced by automated flushing or by reducing the shared-pool size, depending on the amount of nonreusable SQL.

```
Shared Pool Available           56.4824371
Shared SQL%                     44.0445754
Shared Pool Used                31.4790573
```

The next statistic, "Data Dictionary Miss Percent," shows the miss percents for attempts to read values from the dictionary caches and fails. Dictionary cache misses can be quite expensive, so if this value exceeds 10 percent, you probably need to increase the size of your shared pool, because the individual dictionary caches haven't been tunable since Oracle 6 (unless you count undocumented parameters).

```
Data Dictionary Miss Percent     9.64587019
```

The next value, "Library Reload %," shows how often your library cache has to reload objects that have been aged (or flushed) out of the shared pool. If this value nears 1 percent, look at resizing the shared pool in most systems. In systems where the percentage of reusable SQL is low, this value may be high due to shared pool thrashing.

```
Library Reload %                 .039244203
```

The next values deal with table fetch efficiencies: "table fetch by rowid" shows how many rows were fetched due to direct statement of rowid in the select or via index lookups resulting in rowid fetches. This value should be used in concert with the "table fetch continued rows" statistic, to determine if your system is experiencing a high level of row/block chaining. If the ratio between the two values (table fetch continued rows/table fetch by rowid) times 100 reaches whole percentage points, examine frequently searched tables containing VARCHAR2 or numeric values that are frequently updated. Columns with LOB, LONG, or LONG RAW values can also result in chaining if their length exceeds the db_block_size. The table scans (long tables) tell how many long full table scans were performed. Ideally, table scans (long tables) should be as small as possible; I try to keep it in a 10:1 ratio with table scans (short tables). The table scans (short_tables) are scans of tables that are less than 2 percent of the value DB_CACHE_SIZE; or, for pre-Oracle9i databases, the product of DB_BLOCK_SIZE and DB_BLOCK_BUFFERS.

```
table fetch by rowid          14930
table scans (long tables)        85
table scans (short tables)      694
table fetch continued row       383
```

The next statistic, "Non-Index Lookups Ratio," is a ratio between long table scans and short table scans, and is based on the assumption that a short table scan will most likely be an index scan. The short table versus long table scan is based on a short table being less than 10 percent of the total of db_block_buffers times db_block_size on most systems. The undocumented initialization parameter, "_small_table_threshold" will override this 10 percent rule if it is set for your system. Generally speaking, this value should always be much less than 1.0. If this value even approaches 0.1, look at the number of full table scans being performed on your system. It is suggested that this number be trended so that you know what is normal for your system and can take action if it changes. For a well-tuned system, this value should remain relatively stable.

```
Non-Index Lookups Ratio          .109677419
```

The next statistic, "RECURSIVE CALLS PER USER," shows how many times, on average, a user process had to repeat a request for information. These repeat calls can be due to dynamic object extension, reparse of SQL statements, or several other recursive database actions. Generally speaking, you want this number as small as possible. On well-tuned systems, I have seen this as low as 7 to 10 per user or lower.

```
RECURSIVE CALLS PER USER         35.1794083
```

The next four statistics deal with UNDO (rollback) segment contention. Usually these numbers will be at or near 0 for a well-tuned database. Generally, any value approaching 1 indicates the need for rollback segment resizing/tuning.

```
SYS UNDO HDR WAIT CONTENTION            0
SYS UNDO BLK WAIT CONTENTION            0
UNDO BLK WAIT CONTENTION                0
UNDO HDR WAIT CONTENTION                0
```

The next statistic, "Free List Contention Ratio," is applicable to Oracle Parallel Server only. If the ratio reaches whole percentages, then look at major tables and rebuild them with better freelist and freelist group structure. This is applicable only if you have freelist groups defined in OPS or RAC, or in Oracle8*i* or Oracle9*i* with freelist groups configured in a normal database.

```
Free List Contention Ratio              0
```

The next set of statistics varies in number from 0 (none shown) to as many as there are latch types in the database. If there is any latch contention for a specific latch, it will be shown in this listing. Generally, these will be in the .001 or less range; if they get into the 0.1 to .01 range, consider tuning the latch that is showing the large contention value, if possible. It is normal for redo copy or redo allocation latches to show contention on RS6000 or single CPU machines. The parallel query latches may also show contention (even Oracle Support can't tell why; surprise, surprise).

```
library cache              .000266132
cache buffers chains       .001655418
cache buffers lru chain    .009571759
redo writing               .038273117
redo allocation            .012726424
```

The next set of statistics give general database object counts. You should be cognizant of the usual values and be aware if any get out of normal bounds.

```
FUNCTION                    6
LIBRARY                    16
TRIGGER                    22
```

```
TABLE                           426
SYNONYM                       13226
SEQUENCE                         59
PROCEDURE                         3
PACKAGE BODY                    125
PACKAGE                         140
OPERATOR                         21
LOB                               9
VIEW                            165
TYPE BODY                        23
TYPE                             75
JAVA RESOURCE                    16
INDEX                           478
JAVA CLASS                      847
INDEXTYPE                         7
```

The next two statistics deal with how allocated filespace is being utilized by the database; they measure the total sum of datafile sizes against the total size of all allocated extents in the database. If you see that your used space is exceeding 90 percent of the total space allocated, then look at a more detailed report of space usage (which follows later in the report list) to see which tablespaces may need additional files allocated.

```
TOTAL ALLOCATED MEG            1106.5
TOTAL USED MEG               520.320313
```

The final statistic, "TOTAL SGA SIZE," calculates a total size of the SGA based on the V$SGA view. This is strictly an informational statistic.

```
TOTAL SGA SIZE               260407308
```

There may be an additional set of statistics that deal with database block contention. The "waits" statistics tell how many waits occurred for a given block type, and the "time" statistics tell how long the waits took for each type of block. The data statistics deal with database blocks; the undo statistics deal with rollback segment blocks; and if you get system statistics, they deal with the system rollback segment. If data block waits or data block header waits exceed 100, then look at increasing the number of database block buffers (note that hit ratio can be satisfactory even with significant contention, so both statistics should be used to determine database block buffer health). If undo block waits are indicated, increase the size of the rollback segment extents; if undo header waits are indicated, increase the number of rollback segment extents. If system block or system header waits are indicated, there may be users other than SYS or SYSTEM assigned to the SYSTEM tablespace.

```
data block waits               396
undo header time                 0
data block time                324
undo header waits                8
```

Tools for Additional Tuning Concerns

Once the DBA has tuned memory, tuned I/O, and tuned contention, there are still a couple of minor items that he or she needs to consider. Though these items will improve performance, if the other tuning areas are not taken care of first, any improvement to these areas would be masked—which is why they are addressed last. The final tuning areas concern sorts, freelists, checkpoints, and processes.

Sorts, Freelists, Checkpoints, and Processes Improvement of sort speed provides obvious benefits. Freelists provide information on the free blocks inside database tables. If there aren't enough freelists, this can have an impact on performance. Checkpoints are writes from buffers to disk. Checkpoints, if excessive, can adversely effect performance as well; if there aren't enough checkpoints, recovery from disasters can be impeded.

The DBA needs to monitor these items on a regular basis and tune them as needed to get peak performance from the database.

Tuning Oracle Sorts Sorts are done when Oracle performs operations that retrieve information and requires the information retrieved to be an ordered set—in other words, sorted. Sorts are done when the following operations are performed:

Index creation

Group by or Order by statements

Use of the distinct operator

Join operations

Union, Intersect and Minus set operators

Each of these operations requires a sort. Primarily, there is one indicator that your sorts are going to disk and therefore your sort area in memory is too small. This area is defined by the initialization parameters SORT_AREA_SIZE and SORT_AREA_RETAINED_SIZE in Oracle8, Oracle8*i*, and Oracle9*i*.

The primary indicator is the sorts (disk) statistic shown in Figure 13.19. If this parameter exceeds 10 percent of the sum of sorts(memory) and sorts(disk), increase the SORT_AREA_SIZE parameter. Large values for this parameter can induce paging and swapping, so be careful not to overallocate. In Oracle8*i* and Oracle9*i*, you can increase the SORT_AREA_SIZE for a specific session by using the ALTER SESSION SET SORT_AREA_SIZE = x, where x is the size in bytes for the new sort area allocation. This dynamic sort area allocation allows the developer or DBA to tune the sort needs on a per-session or per-transaction basis.

For standard sorts, you should set the SORT_AREA_SIZE to the average sort size for your database. The temporary tablespaces initial and next default storage parameters should be set to the value of SORT_AREA_SIZE. For use with parallel query sorts, a temporary tablespace should be spread (striped) across as many disks as the degree of parallelism.

The initialization parameter SORT_MULTIBLOCK_READ_COUNT does for sorts what DB_MULTIBLOCK_READ_COUNT does for full table scans: it forces Oracle to read at least that amount of data specified per merge read pass.

The views that are used to help in the sort tuning process are V$SORT_SEGMENT and V$SORT_USAGE. These views are not populated unless disk sorts occur. The V$SORT_SEGMENT view contains a single line for each sort operation that gives detailed information about segment size in blocks. If you are getting excessive disk sorts, you should query this view to calculate the best possible sort area size. An example query to give average sort area size is shown in Source 13.19.

Source 13.19   Example sorts report.

```
REM
REM FUNCTION: Generate a summary of Disk Sort Area Usage
REM
REM disksort.sql
REM
COLUMN value NEW_VALUE bs NOPRINT
SELECT value FROM v$parameter WHERE name='db block size';
START title80 "Instance Disk Area Average Sizes"
SPOOL rep_out\&&db\disk_sort
SELECT
     Tablespace_name,
     COUNT(*) areas,
     (SUM(total_blocks)/COUNT(*))*&&bs avg_sort_bytes
FROM v$sort_segment
GROUP BY tablespace_name;
SPOOL OFF
```

Reducing Freelist Contention   As stated above, a freelist is a list of data blocks that contain freelists. Every table has one or more freelists. This is determined by the storage clause parameter FREE_LISTS and FREE_LIST_GROUPS; FREE_LISTS has its default value set to 1. The maximum value of FREE_LISTS is blocksize-dependent and should be set to the number of simultaneous update processes that will be inserting to or updating the table. The setting of this parameter at the time the table is created determines the number of freelists for the table. The FREE_LIST_GROUPS parameter is used in only parallel server (not parallel query!) installations and should be set equal to the number of instances accessing the table. Both parameters apply to tables, only FREE_LISTS applies to indexes.

Under ORACLE7, each table specifies its own number of freelists by use of the FREELISTS parameter of the CREATE TABLE command; this parameter will default to 1 if not specified explicitly.

Freelist contention is shown by contention for data blocks in the buffer cache and/or the existence of freelist waits.

Tuning Checkpoints Checkpoints provide for rolling forward after a system crash. Data is applied from the time of the last checkpoint forward from the redo entries. Checkpoints also provide for reuse of redo logs. When a redo log is filled, the LGWR process automatically switches to the next available log. All data in the now-inactive log is written to disk by an automatic checkpoint. This frees the log for reuse or for archiving.

Checkpoints occur when a redo log is filled, when the INIT.ORA parameter LOG_CHECKPOINT_INTERVAL ORACLE7 is reached (total bytes written to a redo log), or the elapsed time has reached the INIT.ORA parameter LOG_CHECKPOINT_TIMEOUT, expressed in seconds, or every three seconds, or when an ALTER SYSTEM command is issued with the CHECKPOINT option specified.

While frequent checkpoints will reduce recovery time, they will also degrade performance. Infrequent checkpoints will increase performance but also increase required recovery times. To reduce checkpoints to occur only on log switches, set LOG_CHECKPOINT_INTERVAL to larger than your redo log size, and set LOG_CHECKPOINT_TIMEOUT to 0.

If checkpoints still cause performance problems, set the INIT.ORA parameter CHECKPOINT_PROCESS to TRUE to start the CKPT process running. This will free the DBWR from checkpoint duty and improve performance. The INIT.ORA parameter PROCESSES may also have to be increased. Note that on Oracle8 and later, the checkpoint process is not optional and is started along with the other Oracle instance processes.

Another option new with Oracle8*i* was the concept of fast-start checkpointing. In order to configure fast-start checkpointing, you set the initialization parameter FAST_START_IO_TARGET. The FAST_START_IO_TARGET parameter sets the number of I/O operations that Oracle will attempt to limit itself to before writing a checkpoint. This feature is available only with Oracle Enterprise Edition.

Tuning LGWR The LGWR process is tuned by sizing the LOG_BUFFER parameter and by starting the checkpoint process on non-Oracle8 versions of Oracle. An additional option on Oracle8 is the LGWR_IO_SLAVES parameter, which is are manually configured under Oracle8.0 and automatically configured under Oracle8.1 if DBWR_IO_SLAVES is set to greater than 1 or Oracle parallel query is enabled. The default value for this parameter is 4.

Under Oracle8.1, a feature called *incremental checkpointing* was provided. By setting the DB_BLOCK_MAX_DIRTY_TARGET initialization parameter, you limit the number of blocks the recovery process must read from disk during a recovery process. DB_BLOCK_MAX_DIRTY setpoints affect the speed of recovery and may have a detrimental affect on normal runtime performance.

13.5 ORACLE8 AND ORACLE8*i* TUNING OPTIONS

With later versions of ORACLE8 and ORACLE8*i* came numerous new tuning areas and capabilities: use of histograms, anti-joins, hash-joins, all of which can be used to improve the performance of Oracle—not to mention using bitmapped indexes and partitioned tables and indexes.

Using Histograms

Histograms help optimize queries and other actions against data that is nonuniformly distributed about a mean. The common term for poorly distributed data is *skewed data*. In particular, in earlier versions of ORACLE7, the cost-based optimizer would go out to lunch if you handed it skewed data. There is a cost associated with histograms, so they should be used only for badly skewed data. Histograms are static and must be periodically renewed just like table statistics.

Histograms should not be used when:

- All predicates on the column use bind variables.
- The column data is uniformly distributed.
- The column is not used in WHERE clauses of queries.
- The column is unique and is used only in equality predicates.

Histograms are created in "bands" of value ranges. For example, if the data in your test_result tables measurement column is skewed into six general ranges, then you would want to create six bands of history:

```
ANALYZE TABLE test_result
COMPUTE STATISTICS FOR COLUMNS measurement SIZE 6;
```

If you know the exact number of keys, and the value is less than 255, set the size to that value; otherwise, set it to 255. Histogram statistics are stored in the DBA_, USER_, and ALL_ HISTOGRAMS views. Additional row statistics appear in the USER_TAB_COLUMNS, ALL_TAB_COLUMNS, and DBA_TAB_COLUMNS views.

New Types of Joins

Two new types of joins became available in late ORACLE7 and ORACLE8: ANTI-JOIN and HASH-JOIN.

Hash-Joins The hash-join has nothing to do with hash clusters or TABLE ACCESS HASH method. A hash-join compares two tables in memory. The first table is full table scanned, and a hashing function is applied to the data in memory. Then the second table is full table scanned and the hashing function is used to compare the values. Matching values are returned to the user. The user usually has nothing to do with this process; it is completely optimizer-controlled. However, it can be used only by the cost-based optimizer. Generally, hash-joins will gain something for you only if you are using parallel query. Typically, the optimizer will use hash-joins for small tables that can be scanned quickly. To use hash-joins, the HASH_JOIN_ENABLED initialization parameter must be set to TRUE.

Several HASH parameters affect how hash-joins are used. These are:

HASH_JOIN_ENABLED. Set to TRUE to use hash-joins

HASH_AREA_SIZE. Large value reduces cost of hash-joins, so they are used more frequently (set to half the square root of the size of the smaller of the two objects, but not less than 1 megabyte). Suggested range is between 8 and 32 megabytes. Defaults to twice SORT_AREA_SIZE.

HASH_MULTIBLOCK_IO_COUNT. Large value reduces cost of hash-joins, so they are used more frequently. Suggested size is 4.

Anti-Joins To use anti-joins, you must set the initialization parameter ALWAYS_ANTI_JOIN to HASH or MERGE. This causes the NOT IN clause in queries to always be resolved using a parallel-hash or parallel-merge anti-join. If the ALWAYS_ANTI_JOIN parameter is set to anything other than HASH or MERGE, the NOT IN clause will be evaluated as a correlated subquery. You can force Oracle to perform a specific query as an ANTI-JOIN by using the MERGE_AJ or HASH_AJ hints.

Multitier Statement Tuning

More and more, Oracle is being used in multitier client/server applications. If you don't take care when designing the queries used in these client/server applications, your performance will be terrible. You still want the server to do the processing of the result set and just pass the result set back to the client. An improperly designed query can return the entire contents of the source tables to your PC and expect the PC to process the data, something you don't want in most situations. The bane of many networks is excessive packet traffic soaking up bandwidth. To prevent bandwidth absorption, you want to encapsulate SQL statements as much as possible. There are some general rules to follow when designing applications for client/server applications:

1. Push processing to the server, pull results back.
2. Use views to prebuild queries.
3. Use MTS only when your number of connections exceeds 50 to 100 users.
4. Use PL/SQL blocks, stored procedures, and functions on both client and server.

How we accomplish these steps is generally easy, although for specific applications it can be complex and in an ad hoc environment impossible. Let's examine some general techniques.

Push Processing to the Server, Pull Results Back   The first rule—push processing to the server, pull results back—is accomplished using of views and PL/SQL encapsulation.

When using views, if you issue:

```
SELECT * FROM EMP WHERE DEPTNO=10;
```

in an ad hoc query, chances are the contents of EMP may get passed back to you to be processed. However, if a server view is created:

```
CREATE VIEW EMP10 AS SELECT * FROM EMP WHERE DPTNO=10;
```

and then you issue:

```
SELECT * FROM EMP10;
```

you get the same result set, but it is processed on the server and passed back to you.

When using PL/SQL encapsulation, if you have several related commands, it will be best to encapsulate them in a PL/SQL block rather than issue each individual command. A PL/SQL block is treated as a single statement by NET8, so a single packet set is used to transfer it to the server, greatly reducing network travel. Lets look at a status report that selects several statistics into a temporary table and then generates a report. The script to run this report looks like this:

```
INSERT INTO dba_temp
   SELECT name, value, 1
   FROM v$sysstat
   WHERE name='consistent gets';
INSERT INTO dba_temp
   SELECT name, value, 2
   FROM v$sysstat
   WHERE name='physical reads';
INSERT INTO dba_temp
   SELECT name, value, 3
   FROM v$sysstat
   WHERE name='db block gets';
INSERT INTO dba_temp
   SELECT 'Hit Ratio',(a.value+b.value)-c.value/(a.value+b.value)
   FROM v$sysstat a, v$sysstat b, v$sysstat c
   WHERE a.name='consistent gets' and
   b.name='db block gets' and
   c.name='physical reads';
SELECT * FROM DBA_TEMP;
```

In it we have five calls to the database, five parses, and five statements stored in the shared pool. Not very efficient; and the network round trips can get significant. Let's see if a PL/SQL routine to perform this (at least the initial processing) can be written:

```
CREATE OR REPLACE PROCEDURE hitratio
p_reads number;
db_gets number;
con_gets number;
h_ratio number;
param varchar2(32);
CURSOR get_param (stat_name varchar2) IS
SELECT value FROM v$sysstat WHERE name=stat_name;
PROCEDURE write_it (stat_name VARCHAR2,p_value NUMBER,
  reporder INTEGER) IS
    BEGIN
    INSERT INTO dba_temp
    VALUES (stat_name, p_value, reporder);
    END;
BEGIN
  param:='consistent gets';
  OPEN get_param(param);
  FETCH get_param INTO con_gets;
  CLOSE get_param;
  write_it(param, con_gets, 1);
  param:='db block gets';
  OPEN get_param(param);
  FETCH get_param INTO db_gets;
  write_it(param, db_gets, 2);
  param:='physical reads';
  OPEN get_param(param);
  FETCH get_param INTO p_reads;
  write_it(param, p_reads, 3);
  h_ratio:=((con_gets+db_gets)-
      p_reads)/(con_gets+db_reads);
  param:='Hit Ratio';
  write_it(param, h_ratio, 4);
  COMMIT:
END;
```

Once the above procedure is compiled on the server, the previous SQL script becomes:

```
EXECUTE hitratio;
SELECT * FROM dba_temp;
```

Now we have reduced the round trips to two; and since the stored procedure is on the server, we may not even have to parse the statement. All of the actions between the BEGIN and END are treated as a single transaction. If we make the call to dba_temp a call to a view, we can be sure that any processing is done for that table on the server. There is also a method that uses the UTLFILE package to output directly to a file on a client, but it would result in more net round trips in this situation.

More complex processing using variables could be done using the DBMS_SQL package and dynamic SQL.

Use Views to Prebuild Queries   I have already discussed this trick. Essentially, if you have a standard data set that is repeatedly selected against, create a view to preprocess this dataset and select against the view. This ensures that processing is pushed to the server, not to the client.

Use MTS When Connections Exceed 50 to 100   The multithreaded server (MTS) allows for large numbers of users to connect through a limited number of database connections. This is great for large environments where it would be impossible for everyone to connect if they had to use individual connect processes. However, unless you normally run with at least 50 to 100 concurrent processes accessing Oracle at the same time, MTS can hurt your performance. Using parallel query just about guarantees that you should use MTS.

In a test using a multigig database and 10 users, a standard set of queries generated over 200 separate processes using dedicated connections. Some queries required over 30 minutes to complete. After switching on MTS and running the same queries, none took over five minutes; the SGA utilization (it had been running 100 percent for DB block buffers) dropped to 75 percent (as shown by the Q monitor system from Savant); and login times dropped to zero (using dedicated server resulted in up to five-minute delays logging in to the machine). The machine was an E6000 from Sun with 9 CPUs, 3 gigabytes of memory, and a 600-gig disk farm using RAID0-1 and RAW disks. Access was over a normal Ethernet type network from PC clients using TCPIP protocols.

MTS is a queuing system for database connections; it allows multiple users to share the same single connection to the database by a time-sharing mechanism. If only 5 to 10 users are connecting, they may actually see delays in statement execution and processing due to this queuing mechanism.

Use PL/SQL Blocks, Procedures and Functions on Both Server and Client   Always look at multistep SQL scripts, whether they are standalone or embedded in an application, and ask yourself if they could be changed into a stored procedure, function, or anonymous PL/SQL block. Even with 3GL programs running from a client to a database server, if you encapsulate the SQL with BEGIN-END block construction (assuming this can be done; some statements can't be done this way), then they will be passed as a single network transaction to the server.

As demonstrated above, a complex set of SQL statements can be converted into a PL/SQL procedure or function, and the procedure or function stored on the server, allowing a simple EXECUTE or direct function call. For example, about the only way for SQL to get the bytes of a table's records is to issue a SUM(bytes) type statement against the tables entry in DBA_EXTENTS. If you want to include a count of the rows in a report, you either have to ANALYZE the table and pull the count from out of DBA_TABLES as a join or use a local variable and do the SELECT COUNT into the local variable. This results in more network round trips and server work. However, if you create a function that does this type of operation for you, then you can issue the call to the function directly from a BEGIN-END block or even from the SELECT itself. For example:

```
CREATE OR REPLACE FUNCTION get_sum(table_name VARCHAR2)
RETURN NUMBER AS
sum_bytes NUMBER;
BEGIN
   SELECT SUM(bytes) INTO sum_bytes FROM dba_extents
   WHERE segment_name=UPPER(table_name) AND
      segment_type='TABLE';
   RETURN sum_bytes;
END;
```

Using the above function (compiled and stored on the server), we can now select the sum of bytes used by any table, just like a regular column (purity restrictions were relaxed in Oracle8*i*):

```
SELECT table_name, get_sum(table_name) tab_size FROM dba_tables;
```

Techniques like this can reduce network traffic substantially. Use of functions and procedures force processing to the server and return only results to the client. Your goal as a DBA tuning in a multitier environment is to pack as much content into each piece of network traffic as possible. To do this, you have to move more into the object paradigm by passing messages (such as just a procedure or function call), rather than an entire procedural structure such as an SQL routine. This also ensures proper use of the shared pool and SGA resources, since multiple "almost virtually" identical statements won't end up being stuffed into your SGA.

Other Oracle8*i* Tuning Features

I have already discussed the use of function-based indexes and reverse-key indexes in Chapter 6; refer to the index if you haven't read those sections yet.

13.6 ORACLE9*i* TUNING FEATURES

Oracle9i offers many new tuning features, which I touch on here. For the details of their usage, refer to the *Oracle9i Database Performance Guide and Reference*.

Using Multiple-Sized DB Block Buffer

Oracle9i allows the use of multiple database block sizes. Set the old DB_BLOCK_BUFFERS parameter should to 0 and instead set the DB_CACHE_SIZE to the desired buffer size. The _DB_BLOCK_BUFFERS parameter is then calculated by dividing the DB_CACHE_SIZE by the DB_BLOCK_SIZE parameter. The SGA_MAX_SIZE parameter controls the maximum size the SGA may reach; any unallocated space goes into the shared pool as unused.

To prepare for using multiple blocksizes, you set one or more of the following parameters:

DB_2K_CACHE_SIZE

DB_4K_CACHE_SIZE

DB_8K_CACHE_SIZE

DB_16K_CACHE_SIZE

DB_32K_CACHE_SIZE

You can set any of them except the one that corresponds to the default blocksize for your database; for example, if you have 8K- (8192) size blocks as set in DB_BLOCK_SIZE, you are not allowed to set the DB_8K_CACHE_SIZE parameter.

First, verify that DB_CACHE_SIZE+SHARED_POOL_SIZE+LARGE_POOL_SIZE+ JAVA_ POOL_SIZE+LOG_BUFFER is less than SGA_MAX_SIZE; if it is not, either increase SGA_MAX_SIZE or deallocate memory from the other structures until the sum of the parameters plus the size set for the new cache is less than SGA_MAX_SIZE. Remember that if SGA_MAX_SIZE is less than 128 megabytes, then the sizes specified must be in 4-megabyte multiples; otherwise they must be in 16-megabyte multiples or Oracle will round up to the next appropriate size.

Next, set DB_xK_CACHE_SIZE to the size you desire. Note: You may have to set it at a multiple of the increment size minus 1 byte, as it seems to round up to the next value at the current value. For example, I tried setting it exactly at 4194304 bytes (4 megabytes) and it rounded it to 8 megabytes.

If you have upgraded the database you are using from a previous versions, make sure and track through all the ifiles in the initialization file(s); for example, in Windows 2000, there were three different ifiles, and in the middle one (created by ODMA) was a DB_BLOCK_BUFFER setting. You cannot have DB_BLOCK_BUFFERS set to anything but 0, or not set at all, or you will get a conflict between the new settings and the old—you can't have both. Make sure and check all of the files. I suggest merging them into one central file.

Once the initialization file settings are correct, then you can shut down and restart the database to have them take effect. I didn't have much luck setting them dynamically due to the aforementioned problems with the initialization files.

Once the database has been restarted with the proper buffer settings, then you simply create a tablespace, adding the BLOCKSIZE parameter and setting it to the desired size. In OEM, this process would be:

1. Log in to OEM console as SYS AS SYSDBA to your database.
2. Select the Instance icon.
3. Select the Configuration icon

4. Select the All Initialization parameters button.

5. Set:

- DB_BLOCK_BUFFERS 0
- SGA_MAX_SIZE to whatever you want max size
- DB_CACHE_SIZE to SGA_MAX_SIZE - SHARED_POOL_SIZE - LARGE_POOL_SIZE - LOG_BUFFERS - DB_xK_CACHE_SIZE-JAVA_POOL_SIZE (x is 2, 4, 8, 16, 32)
- DB_xK_CACHE_SIZE to 1 less than a multiple of 4m or 16m (if SGA_MAX_SIZE > 128m 16 m)

6. Shut down and restart. Note that for a migrated instance, there may be up to three ini files that need to be looked at to eliminate all settings for DB_BLOCK_BUFFERS; again, you cannot have DB_BLOCK_BUFFERS set to anything but null or 0.

7. Restart OEM, if needed, and log in as SYSTEM to your database.

8. Select Object → Create → Tablespace → Create from the top menu bar.

9. Fill in general tablespace parameters.

10. Select the Storage tab and select DB blocksize (if the parameters took, you should see a down arrow to the right of the DB blocksize button; if not, return to step 6. You can use see SQL text button to see actual SQL text used.

11. Select the Create button.

12. Voila! A xK tablespace in a yK database.

Why Have Multiple Blocksizes? In the pre-Oracle9*i* environment, it was necessary to choose a single blocksize for the entire database. The choice usually was based on index retrieval efficiency, to get the best performance (which also helped optimize full table scans); and in most cases, this meant choosing the largest blocksize available. However, in many OLTP or mixed-mode databases, it might be more efficient to use smaller blocksizes for when we want to return only a small amount of information from the database.

Now, in Oracle9*i,* we can place OLTP data in 2K blocks, the indexes for that data in 8K or 16K blocks, and the full table scan tables in 32K blocks if we wish. This allows us to custom-tailor the blocksize based on how the data it contains will be used the majority of the time. Another example is for bitmapped indexes: we would want the blocksize in a bitmapped index to be as small as possible, especially if the index undergoes INSERT, UPDATE, and DELETE operations on a frequent basis. This allows you to tune data accessibility.

Other New Tuning Features

I covered the use of external tables, the MERGE command, the multitable INSERT command, bitmap-join indexes and skip-scan indexes in Chapter 6. Refer to the index to locate their sections if you have not read about them already.

13.8 USING THE DBA_UTILITIES PACKAGE

The Wiley Web site includes a number of SQL, PL/SQL, and UNIX shell scripts. Chief among the SQL and PL/SQL scripts is the core package, DBA_UTILITIES. The DBA_UTILITIES package has evolved over the last few years from a loosely connected group of functions and procedures to an integrated package of functions and procedures that can greatly assist the DBA in the day-to-day database operations.

Installing DBA_UTILITIES Package

The DBA_UTILITIES package is dependent upon a set of grants and a set of tables and views. I suggest that you create a separate monitoring user with its own tablespace (about 10 megabytes in size) and its own index area of about 5 meg in size (not critical, but nice) to hold the DBA_UTILITIES package definition and support tables. This set of tablespaces will be created if the cre_dbautil_tbsp.sql script is executed from the SYS user. (Note: It is assumed monitoring will be done using my scripts through a Windows-compliant workstation running SQLPLUS. See Section 13.9, "Evaluating the Results of the Ault Status.sql Reports" later in this chapter.) The grants required by the DBA_UTILITIES (and other scripts) are contained in the DBAUTIL_GRANTS.SQL script. The tables and views are created via the CREA_DBAUTIL_TAB.SQL script. The general procedure for installing the package is:

1. Install the files from the DBAUTIL.ZIP file into an SQL_SCRIPTS directory.
2. Verify or install SQLPLUS and NET8 on the workstation where the scripts reside.
3. Create the DBAUTIL_DATA and DBAUTIL_INDEX tablespaces (10 and 5 meg, respectively) using the cre_dbautil_tbsp.sql procedure.
4. From the SYS user on the HOST machine, verify that the DBMS_SHARED_POOL package (dbmspool.sql and prvtpool.plb in ORACLE_HOME/rdbms/admin), the DBMS_REPAIR (dbmsrpr.sql and prvtrpr.plb in ORACLE)HOME/rdbms/admin), and the CATBLOCK.SQL script are installed on your database. Create a public synonym on the DBMS_SHARED_POOL and DBMS_REPAIR packages.
5. From the SYS or INTERNAL Oracle user, create the monitoring user (usually called DBAUTIL), give it the CONNECT role, with the DBAUTIL_DATA tablespace as a default tablespace, and unlimited quota on DBAUTIL_DATA and DBAUTIL_INDEX tablespaces. Ensure that a suitable temporary tablespace is also assigned. This is done using the cre_dbautil_user.sql.
6. From the SYS or INTERNAL user, run the dbautil_grants.sql script. (Note: If you're using versions prior to 8*i*, email me at mikerault@earthlink.net for the proper scripts; I may still have them.)

NOTE: I suggest making a copy of the SQLPLUS icon and changing its "start in" directory, via the PROPERTIES-SHORTCUT menus, to the location of the SQL scripts.

---

7. Once the dbautil_grants.sql script has been run against the user created in step 4, log in to the instance as that user and run the crea_dbautil_tab.sql script to create the required support tables.

8. Run the dba_utilities9.sql script to create the DBA_UTILITIES package. (This should work for all versions from 7.3.4 on up.)

NOTE As supplied, the version of DBA_UTILITIES may differ and may not run on the latest version of Oracle; if this is the case, contact me at mikerault@earthlink.net and a proper version will be emailed to you. Once a successful compilation of the DBA_UTILITIES script is completed, you are ready to begin using the package and related scripts to perform monitoring and tuning.

The directories used by the DBA_UTILITIES scripts require that the following structure be in place for your system:

```
Upper level SQL directory\rep_out\instance1_name
                                 \instance2_name
                  ...
                                 \instancex_name
```

The upper-level SQL directory is the same as the directory used in step 6.

Functions and Procedures in the DBA_UTILITIES Package

The best place to start when looking at any package is the package header. A properly written package header will provide documentation on each object contained in the package. The header for the DBA_UTILITIES package contains most of the information given in this section should you lose this book. Let's look at each function and procedure in the package and see what it does for a DBA (or developer):

Function start_it. I suggest that every package have a function similar to start_it. The function does nothing, it consists of a begin, NULL, return, and end sequence. The return variable just shows successful calling of the package. So what the heck does this do for us? By calling any part of a package, the entire package is loaded into the shared library. This allows us to pin it into the shared pool. By having a null function in the package, you can construct a simple script to load and pin all of your in-house-designed packages into memory. In versions after Oracle8*i*, the act of pinning automatically calls an object into the pool, but what the heck, I'll leave this in here and have those folks who don't read documentation scratching their heads over it.

Function return_version. The return_version function looks at the v$version internal view and returns a string that contains the Oracle database version. This string can then be used by the calling procedure to decide which features to use or monitor, since some of the internal tables change from one version to another.

Procedure startup_date. The startup_date procedure returns the date the instance was started. This startup date is then added to all statistics reports where startup date makes a difference. This procedure changes from Oracle 7.2 to 7.3 so this requires two versions of the DBA_UTILITIES package (the actual structure of the v$instance table changes, so a single version is not possible).

Procedure change_role. The change_role procedure allows a role to by dynamically assigned during operation. It uses the DBMS_SQL package, which expects a role and role password and then uses the DBMS_SQL and DBMS_SESSION packages to reset the user's role to the requested role. Designed to be used from within an application.

Procedure change_pwd. The change_pwd procedure allows a user to change his or her password with a procedure call. The procedure uses the DBMS_SQL package to execute a dynamic ALTER USER command. The change_pwd procedure is designed to be used by an application.

Procedure kill_session. The procedure kill_session is passed the session ID and serial number and then uses DBMS_SQL to issue an ALTER SYSTEM KILL SESSION command. The kill_session procedure is designed for use from an application or script to do bulk killing of user sessions prior to maintenance operations. Take care when automating session killing using kill_session to avoid killing sessions owned by SYS or NULL. The ORA_KILL.SQL script shows an example use of this procedure.

Procedure just_statistics. The just_statistics procedure calculates a set of database health statistics. Various ratios, percentages, counts are performed to pull vital database statistics into the dba_temp table; from there a report can be created. The do_cals2.sql script executes this procedure and generates a report. The just_ statistics procedure uses a less complex algorithm that utilizes cursors to simplify the statistics-gathering process and make better use of reusable SQL areas in the shared pool. The status.sql script calls the do_cals2.sql script to run this procedure and generate a report. The procedure uses the dba_temp table.

Function get_avble_bytes. The function get_avble_bytes accepts a tablespace name as an input and returns the free bytes available for the specified tablespace in all of its datafiles. The function uses the dba_free_space view.

Functions get_start and get_end. The functions get_start and get_end generate the starting and ending byte positions at which a specified columns column ID would either start or end in a specified table. The functions are designed to be used in generating control files for a table for use in SQLLOADER.

Function get_bytes. The function get_bytes is used to return the number of bytes allocated to a tablespace over all of its available datafiles. The function uses the dba_free_space view to generate these values.

Procedure get_count. The procedure get_count is used to get the row count for a specified table. It is used in various table-checking routines to perform automated analysis of the table.

Procedures update_column and update_tables. The procedures update_ column and update_tables are designed to be used with a trigger to perform cascade updates to a set of tables. The trigger must be of the form:

```
create or replace trigger cascade_update_<tabname>
  after update of <column> on <table>
  referencing new as upd old as prev
    for each row
      begin
dba_utilities.update_tables('<table>',:prev.<column>,:upd.<column>);
      end;
```

The table name is passed to the update_tables procedure, as is the previous and updated values of the column the trigger is for. The update_tables procedure then looks at the dbautil_update_tables table to get the name of all tables and columns that need to be updated. The tables are called and the update_column procedure is executed to cascade the update to the dependent tables.

Procedure check_tables. The check_tables procedure uses the statistics in the DBA_TABLES view and a row count generated by DBA_UTILITIES.GET_COUNT to determine if a table's contents have changed by greater than plus or minus the percent change entered; if so, the table is analyzed. If the table has less than lim_ rows rows, a complete analysis is done of all rows; if more than lim_rows rows are present, a 30 percent sample is performed. This procedure is designed for use in the DBMS_JOB package to be run automatically on a periodic basis. Any table that is analyzed and any errors encountered are logged in the DBA_RUNNING_ STATS table.

Procedures redo_pin and chk_pin. The procedures redo_pin and chk_pin are used with the dbautil_kept_objects table to verify that kept objects (using the DBMS_SHARED_POOL package) are still valid; if not, the objects are unkept and the pool is flushed, then the objects are repinned. Designed for use in a development environment where objects may be made invalid on a periodic basis.

Procedure running_stats. The running_stats procedure is a modified version of the just_statistics package that is designed to be run on a periodic, automated basis using the DBMS_JOB package. The running_stats procedure inserts records into the DBA_RUNNING_STATS table to allow trending of results. Delta values are also calculated and stored. The procedure can be run in interactive mode if a Boolean TRUE is passed as its sole argument or as a background procedure, if the default value of FALSE is passed. If TRUE is passed, DBA_TEMP is deleted and then re-loaded. If the procedure is run with FALSE as its Boolean argument, the DBA_ RUNNING_STATS table is updated.

Procedure flush_it. The flush_it procedure is designed to be run on an automated, periodic basis using the DBMS_JOB package. The flush_it procedure is provided a percent full value that it uses to check the shared pool. If the shared pool exceeds the specified percent full, the ALTER SYSTEM FLUSH SHARED_POOL command is issued to flush nonpinned SQL areas from the pool. The flush_it procedure is designed for use in systems where ad hoc SQL or poorly designed applications result in high percentages of nonreusable code; it should not be used on systems where a majority of code is reused. The SQL_GARBAGE.SQL report, which uses the sql_garbage view (created by CREA_TAB.SQL), should be used to determine your system's reusable code ratios before considering using the flush_it procedure. If a system is virtually 100 percent ad hoc with no reusable code, consider a reduced shared-pool size rather than automated flushing. The flush_it procedure has been updated to include pinning of cursors (based on a minimum number of reuses), packages, and procedures, as well as sequences.

Procedure hitratio. The hitratio procedure calculates cumulative hit ratio, period hitratio, number of concurrent users, and usage (total I/Os) and sorts these values in the HIT_RATIO table. The procedure is designed to be run hourly, and must be modified if a greater or lesser periodicity is desired. The procedure is designed to be run from the DBMS_JOB package.

Function gen_pword. The gen_pword function returns a randomized six-character password. The gen_pword function is designed for use in bulk loading of users or application-driven user creation. There is some chance that the function will not return a fully unique password for each execution, but the chance is small enough to be ignored. The function uses a 14-place pi value, the v$timer view and the POWER function to derive a password.

Procedure auto_defrag. The auto_defrag procedure is used to defragment honeycomb fragmentation in tablespaces. If the value of PCTINCREASE is set to 0 for the default storage in a tablespace, that tablespace is not automatically coalesced by SMON. The auto_defrag procedure allows a DBA to keep the default value of PCTINCREASE set to 0 and still get automated coalescence of adjacent areas of freespace. The auto_defrag procedure uses the FREE_SPACE view. If used, I suggest that the auto_defrag procedure be called from the DBA_JOB package on an automated periodic basis during off-hours.

Function hextointeger. The function hextointeger takes in a hexadecimal value and converts it to an integer. This function is useful when Oracle internally stores a value as hex and you need it as a decimal (such as with thread numbers in NT).

Function integertohex. The function integertohex converts an integer value to a hexadecimal equivalent.

Procedure check_corrupt. The check_corrupt procedure uses the DBMS_REPAIR package (new in Oracle8*i*) to check a schema for data corruption.

13.9 EVALUATING THE RESULTS OF THE AULT STATUS.SQL REPORTS

The Wiley Web site includes a bundled set of reports known collectively as the Status collection. Run on a daily basis, the Status series of scripts give a view into the health of the Oracle database. This section describes the major reports available in the Status series and how to interpret them.

Evaluating Tuning Scripts Run from status.sql

Many times a novice or even an intermediate-level DBA won't know what to monitor on an ongoing basis. In an attempt to make this monitoring of databases more routine and standard, I have provided a set of scripts that can be used as-is or be modified to suit an individual DBA's needs. One of these scripts, status.sql, groups some of the monitoring scripts into a set of daily reports.

Reports in Status.SQL

The reports in STATUS.SQL fall into three general categories: Internals Monitoring, Space Utilization Monitoring, and Object Status Monitoring. In the subsections that follow, the output from each of the included scripts is covered in detail, to identify what to look for in each report.

Status.sql This report explains the different scripts contained in the status.sql grouping and how to interpret their results.

The status.sql script calls the scripts listed in Table 13.2. The purpose of these scripts is also listed in the table.

I have grouped these scripts in a single wrapper because they give a good representation of what your database status is for a given point in time. If you find other scripts, either from TUSC or other sources, that you wish to add to this list, please feel free to do so; however, if you do, I suggest that the script be renamed to prevent it from being overwritten during upgrades.

The reports run by the CHECK_POOL.SQL script have the functions shown in Table 13.3.

The following subsections examine the various output reports from these scripts and explain what the various statistics indicate.

Do_cals2.sql The first script called by status.sql, do_calst2.sql, runs the DBA_UTILITIES.running_stats procedure, which calculates numerous useful database-level statistics and places them in a temporary file called DBA_TEMP. The do_calst2.sql script next generates a report based on the contents of the DBA_TEMP table. The results of a do_cals2.sql report are shown in Listing 13.9 (I already covered its meanings in the tuning contention section).

TABLE 13.2   Scripts in Status.sql

Script	Purpose
do_cals2.sql	Calls the DBA_UTILITIES.just_statistics procedure to calculate several database statistics.
libcache.sql	Reports library cache statistics relating to pins, hits, reloads.
Free2_spc.sql	Reports on freespace and fragmentation status for all tablespaces.
extents.sql	User provides number of extents and script shows objects with >= that number of extents.
Rbk1.sql	Shows first set of redo log storage and usage statistics.
Rbk2.sql	Shows second set of redo log storage and usage statistics.
Rbk3.sql	Summarizes rollback segment health.
Log_stat.sql	Shows redo log statistics.
Inv_obj.sql	Shows stored objects that have been marked invalid.
Systabs.sql	Shows tables stored in the SYSTEM tablespace that do not belong to SYS schema.
Check_pool.sql	Runs several shared-pool health reports.
Cpu.sql	Reports on SQL usage sorted by CPU usage.

TABLE 13.3   Scripts Called from CHECK_POOL.SQL

Script	Purpose
Test_pool.sql	Gives current used size, max size, and percent used for shared pool.
Sql_garbage.sql	Shows for each user the total amount of reusable and nonreusable code.
Reuse_sql2.sql	Gives the amount of reusable code by user.

Libcache.sql   The next report is generated by the libcache.sql script. An example of the output from the libcache.sql script is shown in Listing 13.20. As its name implies, the libcache.sql report generates statistics on the library cache contents. Other scripts I provide to look at the library area are o_cache.sql, o_cache2.sql, o_kept.sql, and obj_stat.sql. The output from the libcache.sql script is shown in Listing 13.20.

The report is based on the v$library view. Essentially, you want the GET HIT% and PIN HIT% values to be as high as possible, preferably greater than 95 percent. The RELOADS value should be as low as possible, as should the invalidations indicated by the INVALID column. Note that if automated flushing is used, or if the size of the

Listing 13.20   Output from libcache.sql script.

```
Date: 11/07/01                                          Page:   1
Time: 03:37 PM          Library Caches Report           DBAUTIL
                          aultdb1 database
Library Object      Gets Get Hit%   Pins Pin Hit%  Reloads Invalid
----------------   ------ -------- ------ -------- -------- -------
SQL AREA           22,585   95.29 76,547   97.79       22     365
TABLE/PROCEDURE    13,423   88.24 10,756   74.09       12       0
BODY                   30   40.00     42   23.81        0       0
TRIGGER                26   15.38     45    8.89        0       0
INDEX                 355    1.13    355    1.13        0       0
CLUSTER               429   98.14    431   97.45        0       0
OBJECT                  0  100.00      0  100.00        0       0
PIPE                    0  100.00      0  100.00        0       0
JAVA SOURCE             0  100.00      0  100.00        0       0
JAVA RESOURCE           2   50.00      2   50.00        0       0
JAVA DATA               1     .00      4   50.00        0       0
```

shared pool is reduced to counter thrashing, the RELOADS value for the SQL AREA may increase, but this is normal under these conditions. To decrease RELOADS in systems where reusable SQL forms a major portion of SQL areas, use the DBMS_ SHARED_POOL package to pin packages (and cursors and triggers in later than version 7.3) and increase the shared-pool size. Pinning objects prevents their being aged. Also consider using the SHARED_POOL_RESERVED_SIZE and SHARED_POOL_ RESERVED_SIZE_MIN_ALLOC parameters to reserve space for large packages.

Free2_spc.sql   The next report shows database tablespace size, freespace, and fragmentation status. The report name is free2_spc.sql, and it uses the FREE_SPACE view that is a summary of the DBA_FREE_SPACE master view; an example output is shown in Listing 13.21. The Free Space report shows: number of files, number of fragments, maximum free megabytes, biggest contiguous chunk of freespace in megabytes, the percentage of available freespace the largest chunk occupies, the total megabytes in the tablespace, the total amount of used megabytes in the tablespace, and the percentage of the total megabytes that is free.

If the number of fragments exceeds the number of files (an example is the TEMP tablespace shown in the Listing 13.21), then you should consider an export/import from the users in that tablespace to consolidate the freespace into a contiguous chunk. Consolidation should definitely be considered when the biggest contiguous chunk is not a major percentage of the total freespace; an example would be the TEMP tablespace in Listing 13.21. You should be able to glance at the freespace report and tell if there are problems. The total used meg should be trended for your major tablespaces so growth rate can be predicted and allowed for. I provide several freespace reports showing various cuts on the freespace data. Additional information on datafiles can be generated using datafile.sql; tablespace-specific information can be obtained by using tbsp_rct.sql or tablesp.sql scripts.

Listing 13.21   Example freespace report.

```
Date: 11/07/01                                                Page:    1
Time: 06:15 PM                 FREE SPACE REPORT              DBAUTIL
                                aultdbl database

                            Biggest Percent of   Total    Total Percent Free
Name      FILES  Frag Free Meg Free Meg  Free Meg     Meg Used Meg   Total Meg
--------  -----  ---- -------- -------- ---------- ------- -------- ------------
DRSYS       1      1    15.43    15.43   100.000   20.000     4.57       77.15
INDX        1      1    19.99    19.99   100.000               .01       99.96
PERFSTAT    1      1   389.81   389.81   100.000  500.000   110.19       77.96
RBS         1     13    41.99    15.50    36.912   70.000    28.01       59.99
SYSTEM      1      6    12.33     7.42    60.203  344.000   331.67        3.58
TEMP        1   1465    91.80      .30      .332   93.750     1.95       97.93
TOOLS       1      1      .22      .22   100.000   45.625    45.41        .48
USERS       1      1    13.12    13.12   100.000   20.000     6.88       65.59
```

Extents_chk.sql   The next report is generated by the extents_chk.sql report and shows, for a specified number of extents, the database tables and indexes that exceed this number of extents. The user against which the extent report is run can also be specified. In a single-owner environment, running the report against only that user can save time. In this report, you are concerned with the total number of extents. If they get to be more than 1,000 or so, or more than you have used to partition the table or index, I suggest you consolidate the objects involved (Oracle suggests 4,000 but that seems a bit heavy to me). I provide several scripts to monitor tables, indexes, and clusters: tab_col. sql, tab_grnt.sql, tab_rct.sql, table.sql, tab_stat.sql, in_rep.sql, in_rct.sql, in_size.sql, in_stat.sql, brown.sql, clu_typ.sql, clus_rep.sql, and act_size.sql. An example extents report is shown in Listing 13.22.

Listing 13.22   Example extents report.

```
Date: 11/07/01                                          Page: 1
Time: 06:25 PM               EXTENTS REPORT             DBAUTIL
                              aultdbl database

Tablespace Segment     Extents Max Extents        Size Owner  Type
---------- ----------  ------- -----------  ----------- ------ -----
SYSTEM     I_SOURCE1      108  2147483645    28,065,792 SYS    INDEX
           IDL_UB1$       903  2147483645   118,243,328        TABLE
           IDL_UB2$        79  2147483645    10,240,000        TABLE
           SOURCE$        282  2147483645    73,678,848        TABLE
```

Rollback Segment Report rbk3_sql   The rollback segment report breaks out important information from the DBA_ROLLBACK_SEGS view. The vital stats on the report are the optimal size (OPTL SIZE), shrinks, average shrinks, and average transaction size. You are looking to see that shrinks are minimized and that the optimal size is greater than the average transaction size. Usually, it is suggested that the initial and next extents be sized for the average of the average transaction sizes, and that optimal is set to the max transaction size (also shown on the report). If you are getting shrinks, it indicates that the transaction sizes are exceeding the extent sizes, meaning, perhaps, that the initial and next sizes need to be better thought out. Additional reports include: rbk1.sql, rbk2.sql, rbk_rct.sql, rbk_wait.sql, tx_rbs.sql, and rollback.sql.

The rollback segment report shows transactional statistics for all online rollback segments as well. The statistics reported show if there are any current transactions, the largest transaction size, the current rollback segment size, and the number of waits, wraps, and extents.

If the number of waits is excessive, increase the number of extents available by increasing optimal size or by adding rollback segments. If the number of wraps is excessive, increase the size of the initial and next extents; and, finally, if the number of extends is excessive, either increase the size of initial and next extents or increase the value for optimal size. The optimal size should be at or a multiple of the max transaction size.

An example of the report is shown in Listing 13.23.

Listing 13.23   Rollback health report.

```
Date: 11/07/01                                              Page: 1
Time: 06:35 PM              ROLLBACK SEGMENT HEALTH          DBAUTIL
                             aultdbl database


                       OPTL            AVE    AVE  LARGEST
TABLESPACE ROLLBACK     SIZE SHRINKS  SHRINK  TRANS   TRANS  WAITS WRAPS EXTENDS
---------- --------  ------- -------  ------- ------- ------- ----- ----- -------
RBS        RBS0      4194304       0        0  142081 4186112     0     3       0
RBS        RBS1      4194304       0        0  141262 4186112     0     3       0
RBS        RBS2      4194304       0        0  142081 4186112     0     3       0
RBS        RBS3      4194304       0        0  179637 4186112     0     4       0
RBS        RBS4      4194304       0        0  141417 4186112     0     3       0
RBS        RBS5      4194304       0        0  179704 4186112     0     4       0
RBS        RBS6      4194304       0        0  180301 4186112     0     4       0
SYSTEM     SYSTEM                  0        0       0  401408     0     0       0
---------- --------  ------- -------  ------- ------- ------- ----- ----- -------
avg                                  0        0  138310 3713024     0     3       0
```

Log_stat.sql   The next report is generated by the log_stat.sql script, and it shows current redo log status. An example of the output from the log_status.sql script is shown in Listing 13.24. The report shows one line per redo log group and a status line for each. The status should be one of inactive, current, or stale; any other status needs to be investigated. This report should be monitored to ensure the logs are all a standard size. This report also shows if the redo logs have been archived and gives the system change number (SCN) and date when the log was switched. Check that redo log switches aren't happening too frequently or too slowly. Additional reports include: log_hist.sql, log_file.sql, and redo.sql.

Listing 13.24   Redo log status report.

```
Date: 11/07/01                                              Page: 1
Time: 06:40 PM              Current Redo Log Status          DBAUTIL
                              aultdb1 database


                                                     First
Th# Grp#  Seq#    BYTES Mem Arc? STATUS      Change# Time
--- ----  -----  ------- --- ---- -------- ---------- ----------------
  1    1  1,426 1048576   1 NO   CURRENT   2,441,716 07-nov-2001 16:47
       2  1,424 1048576   1 NO   INACTIVE  2,441,492 07-nov-2001 16:31
       3  1,425 1048576   1 NO   INACTIVE  2,441,618 07-nov-2001 16:44
```

Inv_obj.sql   The next report is generated by the inv_obj.sql script. Sample output from it is shown in Listing 13.25. The invalid objects report shows invalid database objects. Ideally, all objects in a production database should be valid and this report shouldn't appear. However, sometimes packages, procedures, functions, or views can become invalid and may need to be recompiled. The com_proc.sql procedure can facilitate the recompilation effort; or you can use the Oracle-provided dbms_utility.compile_schema() procedure. There is also the utlrp.sql script, which will recompile all invalid PL/SQL objects in the database.

Listing 13.25   Invalid objects report.

```
Date: 11/07/01                                       Page:    1
Time: 06:46 PM      Invalid Database Objects          DBAUTIL
                      aultdb1 database

Object  Object           Object        Last Change
Owner   Name             Type          Date
------- ---------------- ------------- ------------------
SYS     DBMS_AQADM_SYS   PACKAGE BODY  15-OCT-01 10:41:12
SYS     DBMS_IREFRESH    PACKAGE BODY  15-OCT-01 10:43:15
SYS     DBMS_JOB         PACKAGE BODY  15-OCT-01 10:37:48
```

```
SYS        DBMS_PCLXUTIL      PACKAGE BODY  15-OCT-01 10:37:22
SYS        DBMS_PRVTAQIP      PACKAGE BODY  15-OCT-01 10:39:58
SYS        DBMS_SNAPSHOT      PACKAGE BODY  15-OCT-01 10:57:17
SYS        DBMS_STATS         PACKAGE BODY  15-OCT-01 10:38:36
ORDSYS     ORDTEXP            PACKAGE BODY  15-OCT-01 12:04:21
ORDSYS     ORDTGET            PACKAGE BODY  15-OCT-01 12:04:45
ORDSYS     TIMESCALE          PACKAGE BODY  15-OCT-01 12:04:48
MDSYS      MDGEN              PACKAGE BODY  15-OCT-01 12:03:29
MDSYS      MDLEXR             PACKAGE BODY  15-OCT-01 12:04:09
MDSYS      RTREE_IDX          PACKAGE BODY  15-OCT-01 12:04:04
MDSYS      SDO_3GL            PACKAGE BODY  15-OCT-01 12:03:51
MDSYS      SDO_CATALOG        PACKAGE BODY  15-OCT-01 12:03:59
MDSYS      SDO_GEOM           PACKAGE BODY  15-OCT-01 12:03:56
CTXSYS     DRIDDL             PACKAGE BODY  15-OCT-01 12:04:06
CTXSYS     DRIDDLR            PACKAGE BODY  15-OCT-01 12:05:04
DBAUTIL    SMP_VDG            PACKAGE       07-NOV-01 03:30:38
DBAUTIL    SMP_VDG            PACKAGE BODY  07-NOV-01 03:30:38
DBAUTIL    SMP_VDI            PACKAGE BODY  07-NOV-01 03:30:50
DBAUTIL    SMP_VDJ            PACKAGE BODY  07-NOV-01 03:31:19
```

Systabs.sql   The next report is generated by the systabs.sql script; it shows non-SYSTEM-owned tables that reside in the SYSTEM tablespace. Listing 13.26 shows an example of the output from systabs.sql. SYS should own all objects in SYSTEM; all other objects should be located in other tablespaces. Sometimes, SYSTEM-owned objects are allowed in SYSTEM tablespace; however, it is best to add a TOOLS tablespace and create all of SYSTEM-owned objects there. There can be problems exporting items in the SYSTEM tablespace. In addition, all objects in the SYSTEM tablespace use the SYSTEM rollback segment, which can result in fragmentation of the SYSTEM tablespace. Never allow users to have SYSTEM as either a default or temporary tablespace, and never create users without specifying their default and temporary tablespace assignments.

Listing 13.26   Example SYSTEM tables report.

```
Date: 11/07/01                            Page:   1
Time: 06:43 PM Non-SYS Owned Tables in SYSTEM DBAUTIL
                 aultdb1 database


OWNER              TABLE_NAME                    TABLESPACE
-------------      ----------------------------  ----------
OUTLN              OL$                           SYSTEM
OUTLN              OL$HINTS                      SYSTEM
SYSTEM             AQ$_QUEUE_TABLES              SYSTEM
SYSTEM             AQ$_QUEUES                    SYSTEM
```

continues

Listing 13.26   Continued.

```
SYSTEM              AQ$_SCHEDULES              SYSTEM
SYSTEM              DEF$_AQCALL                SYSTEM
SYSTEM              DEF$_AQERROR               SYSTEM
SYSTEM              DEF$_ERROR                 SYSTEM
SYSTEM              DEF$_DESTINATION           SYSTEM
SYSTEM              DEF$_CALLDEST              SYSTEM
SYSTEM              DEF$_DEFAULTDEST           SYSTEM
SYSTEM              DEF$_LOB                   SYSTEM
SYSTEM              DEF$_TEMP$LOB              SYSTEM
SYSTEM              DEF$_PROPAGATOR            SYSTEM
SYSTEM              DEF$_ORIGIN                SYSTEM
SYSTEM              DEF$_PUSHED_TRANSACTIONS   SYSTEM
SYSTEM              SQLPLUS_PRODUCT_PROFILE    SYSTEM
SYSTEM              REPCAT$_REPCAT             SYSTEM
SYSTEM              REPCAT$_FLAVORS            SYSTEM
```

Test_pool.sql   The Test_pool.sql report is the first from the CHECK_POOL.SQL calling script. It gives a summary of shared-pool usage. I discussed all of the reports run by the CHECK_POOL.SQL script in the section on shared-pool tuning.

CPU.SQL   The CPU.SQL script generates a report of the top CPU-using SQL statements. This report should be used to find and correct problem SQL. Listing 13.27 shows an example CPU report. (Note: This can only be used on Oracle9*i* or later database versions.)

Listing 13.27   Example SQL by CPU report.

```
Date: 11/07/01                                              Page: 1
Time: 06:59 PM              SQL By CPU Usage                 DBAUTIL
                           aultdb1 database

SQL                                 CPU Elapsed  Disk  Buffer     Rows
Text                                Time    Time Reads    Gets Processed
-----------------------------    ------- ------- ------ ------ ---------
select 1 nopr, a.users users,    2483571 4396000   2080 309258        10
to_char(a.garbage,'9,999,999,999')
garbage, to_char(b.good,'9,999,999,999')
good,
to_char((b.good/(b.good+a.garbage))*100,
'9,999,999.999') good_percent from
sql_garbage a, sql_garbage b where
a.users=b.users and a.garbage is not
null and b.good is not null union select
2 nopr, '-------------'
users,'-------------'
```

```
garbage,'--------------' good,
'--------------' good_percent from dual
union select 3 nopr,
to_char(count(a.users)) users,
to_char(sum(a.garbage),'9,999,999,999')
garbage,
to_char(sum(b.good),'9,999,999,999')
good,
to_char(((sum(b.good)/(sum(b.good)+sum(a
.garbage)))*100),'9,999,999.999')
good_percent from sql_garbage a,
sql_garbage b where a.users=b.users and
a.garbage is not null and b.good is not
null order by 1,3 desc

SELECT                          1191714 1583000  5106  792136       11
(sum(b.good)/(sum(b.good)+sum(a.garbage)
))*100 from sql_garbage a, sql_garbage b
where a.users=b.users and a.garbage is
not null and b.good is not null
```

13.10 FURTHER DBA READING

The DBA may find these references of interest when planning to do Oracle internals tuning activities:

Adams, Steve. *Oracle8i Internal Services for Waits, Latches, Locks, and Memory.* Sebastopol, CA: O'Reilly and Associates Inc., 1999.

Alomari, Ahmed. *Oracle8i & UNIX Performance Tuning.* Upper Saddle River, NJ: Prentice-Hall, 2001.

Burleson, Donald K. *Oracle High-Performance Tuning with STATSPACK.* Berkeley, CA: Osborne/McGraw-Hill, 2001.

Feuerstein, Steven, Charles Dye, and John Beresniewicz. *Oracle Built-in Packages.* Sebastopol, CA: O'Reilly and Associates, Inc., 1998.

Oracle9i Administrator's Guide, Release 1 9.0.1, Part No. A90117-01, Oracle Corporation, June 2001.

Oracle9i Concepts, Release 1 9.0.1, Part No. A88856-02, Oracle Corporation, June 2001.

Oracle9i Database Performance Guide and Reference, Release 1 9.0.1, Part No. A87503-02, June 2001, Oracle Corporation, June 2001.

Oracle9i Database Performance Methods, Release 1 9.0.1, Part No. A87504-01, Oracle Corporation, June 2001.

Oracle9i Reference, Release 1, 9.0.1, Part No. A90190-01, , Oracle Corporation, June 2001.

Oracle9i SQL Reference, Release 8.1.5, Part No. A90125-01, Oracle Corporation, June 2001.

Oracle9i Supplied PL / SQL Packages and Types Reference, Release 1, (9.0.1), Part No. A89852-02, Oracle Corporation, June 2001.

PL / SQL User's Guide and Reference, Release 1 9.0.1, Part No. A89856-01, Oracle Corporation, June 2001.

13.11 SUMMARY

Using the reports and techniques shown in this chapter, the DBA can quickly determine the status of his or her database. The script outputs help the DBA to pinpoint areas where additional investigation is required. The DBA should run the STATUS.SQL script periodically during the day to check on the status of his or her database and to catch problems before they become significant.

I strongly suggest getting Don Burleson's book on STATSPACK and using STATSPACK to help monitor and maintain your database.

CHAPTER 14

Distributed Database Management

This chapter covers the Oracle distributed database setup, including myriad topics such as Oracle Net, multithreaded server, and real application clusters (RAC), as well as distributed databases. In it, I do not attempt to cover every possible Oracle Net, NET8, or SQLNET option; that is what the Oracle manuals are for. Rather, I provide a basic setup for a standard server and discuss the tuning of what will be a new environment to most DBAs: the Apache Web Server environment.

When I say "distributed database," I mean either a set of databases that are connected via a standard interface protocol, such as TCP/IP, or a set of instances that may connect to a single set of database files that communicates through a high-speed interconnect.

A distributed database allows users who are physically remote from one another to share the same data. A distributed database makes it possible to have a central set of data that all the company uses, or a disbursed set of databases that share information.

14.1 SETUP OF A DISTRIBUTED DATABASE

The usual interpretation of a distributed database is as a nonshared database. In a typical distributed database, there are two or more remote (i.e., on separate servers) databases that are connected via a LAN a WAN or the Internet. The distributed databases, if they are Oracle databases, communicate via Oracle Net through database links. If non-Oracle-based databases are included in the distributed database, then these databases are connected via the Oracle heterogeneous database services. Figure 14.1 shows a typical "pure" Oracle distributed database.

In the setup shown in Figure 14.1 the manuf, sales, and price databases each reside on an independent node of a distributed database. By defining database links between

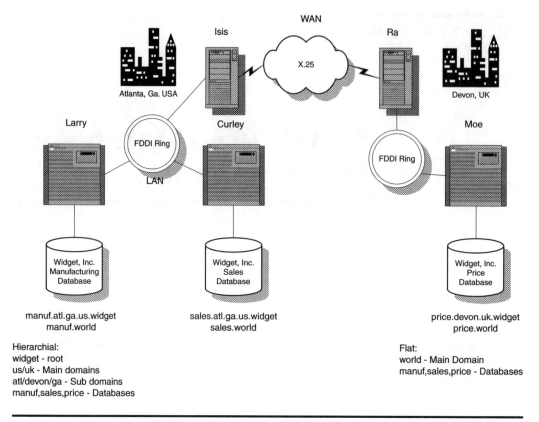

FIGURE 14.1 An Oracle distributed database.

the databases in a distributed database tables and other objects in the remote databases become visible to users in the local databases.

If we assume that the listener.ora and tnsnames.ora files (covered in a latter section of this chapter) have been set up so that the aliases for the databases are MANUF, SALES, and PRICE, then it is a simple matter to set up database links between the separate databases. For example, to set up a link from the MANUF database to the PRICE database:

```
sqlplus john/hungry
connected.
SQL> CREATE DATABASE LINK price
  2   CONNECT TO devon_user IDENTIFIED BY low_privs
  3   USING 'price';

Database Link Created.
```

Now we have a path directly into the tables and objects that the devon_user has access to. For example, say we wanted to check on the price of fish and chips and we know that devon_user for some arcane reason tracks his lunches in a table called LUNCH, we also know he always has fish and chips. We can either use the SELECT ... FROM table@db_link; format for our SELECT or we can hide the link via a synonym. If the selection is one we will do frequently, I suggest creating a SYNONYN:

```
CREATE SYNONYM lunch FOR lunch@price;
```

Once we have a synonym pointing at the remote database we can issue SELECT statements just like the table was a local table:

```
SQL> SELECT cost, food_type
  2  FROM lunch@price
  3  WHERE food_type='FISH AND CHIPS'
  4  AND date_of_price=TRUNC(sysdate);

      COST FOOD_TYPE
---------- -----------------------------------
       1.5 FISH AND CHIPS
```

If you need to access several remote databases at one time, then you may need to bump up the initialization parameter OPEN_LINKS from its default value of 4.

If you will be doing complex INSERT, UPDATE, and DELETE operations across the distributed database, then you will need to set several initialization parameters that help control distributed transactions. These parameters are:

COMMIT_POINT_STRENGTH. This determines the commit point site for a distributed transaction. In a two-phase commit, the commit point site must be able to commit or the entire distributed transaction will rollback. The highest value becomes the commit point site and the transaction coordinator.

DB_DOMAIN. This sets the location of the database within the processing network. For example, our database name (DB_NAME) may be SALES while our database domain name (DB_DOMAIN) is ATL.GA.US.WIDGET. If a database will ever become part of a distributed structure, set this accordingly.

DB_NAME. Sets up the database name. Usually this is the same as the instance name.

DISTRIBUTED_TRANSACTIONS. Determines the maximum number of distributed transactions, should not be set to more than 75 percent of the TRANSACTIONS parameter. If set to zero prohibits distributed transactions in the specific database. If set to zero the RECO process is not started.

GLOBAL_NAMES. Set to either TRUE or FALSE. If set to TRUE, the database link must use the same name as the database it is connecting to; if set to FALSE then any name can be used for the database link. If multiple links will be made to the same database, then I suggest setting it to FALSE (for example, a PRICE link to the PRICES schema, a GRAPHICS link to the GRAPHICS schema); if only one link will be made to a database then I suggest setting it to TRUE.

OPEN_LINKS. Specifies the maximum number of concurrent open connections to remote databases in one session. These connections include database links, as well as external procedures and cartridges, each of which uses a separate process.

REMOTE_DEPENDENCIES_MODE. Specifies how Oracle should handle dependencies upon remote PL/SQL stored procedures.

Values

TIMESTAMP (default). The client running the procedure compares the timestamp recorded on the server-side procedure with the current timestamp of the local procedure and executes the procedure only if the timestamps match.

SIGNATURE. Oracle allows the procedure to execute as long as the signatures are considered safe. This setting allows client PL/SQL applications to be run without recompilation.

Once the parameters are correctly set, Oracle will use the two-phase commit mechanism to control transaction commit and rollback across the distributed database system.

Classical Client Server with Oracle

In a classical client-server setup, multiple clients talk to a single server via a network protocol such as TCP/IP. In Oracle, the client would contact the port configured as the listener port for the NET8 or Oracle Net listener process (usually port 1521). The listener process picks up the connection request and passes it either to a dedicated connection or to a dispatcher process that then passes it along to a shared server (if multi-threaded server option is enabled). The dedicated or shared server process then connects to the database.

Inter- and Intranet Connections

In recent years the Internet and company intranets have virtually taken over the domain of the Oracle NET8 and Oracle Net processes. Actually, I should say they have added to the process stack. Let me explain. In an Inter- or intranet connection, an Application Server (usually Apache, since that is what is shipped with Oracle) is configured to listen for HTTP protocol connection requests (usually on port 8088). When one is received, it is passed on as a connection to the database server (identified in a DAD configuration file). Once the database server receives it, the connection request is processed in the same way as a client server connection request.

The addition of the Application server adds another layer of complexity to the management of the Oracle connection process. If not properly set up and tuned, the Apache server can be a performance nightmare for the Oracle DBA. Usually the Oracle DBA will be saddled with the care and feeding of the Apache server, as it is supplied with the Oracle software.

In dealing with several Apache server installations I have come across a couple of tips that I want to share in regard to Apache service performance. The techniques appear valid on both HP and Sun installs, but I have not seen the problems discussed on Windows or Linux based platforms. In general the problems deal with the usage of the KeepAlive variables and how the clients, servers, and application servers signal that a process is finished.

Essentially, when the server closes a TCP connection, it sends a packet with the FIN bit set to the client, which then responds with a packet with the ACK bit set. The client then sends a packet with the FIN bit set to the server, which responds with an ACK, and the connection is closed. The state that the connection is in during the period between when the server gets the ACK from the client and the server gets the FIN from the client is known as FIN_WAIT_2. At least on HP and Solaris this final FIN from the client doesn't seem to be being sent when the Apache server is used. I discovered this first on an HP client running Oracle Financials.

The server was a HP9000 L2000 with 4 gig of memory and 4 processors. It was running 8.1.6.1 and 11.5.2 of Apps on B11.0.0 U HPUX. When I got here they could run 10 processes against the Oracle DB and would peak out memory and then CPU at 4-hour intervals when they would have to bounce the webserver/forms server and do some zombie slaying to get back memory.

After a couple of false starts, I did some Web research and found out that Apache clients may have memory leaks (of course they blame it on the OS libraries) and JDBC may as well. The lack of the FIN_WAIT_2 processes from closing and the multiple connection attempts to the clients filled process slots and ate memory until reboot was required.

I edited the httpd.conf file and adjusted MaxRequestsPerChild (which is actually MaxConnectionsPerChild) from its default of 0, which means UNLIMITED, to 2500 (some people have adjusted this down as far as 300). Each time a process connected, the memory leak caused the child process to grow until finally all memory disappears (gee sounds like real kids . . .). This solved the memory leak problem, but what about the FIN_WAIT_2 processes?

The killing of FIN_WAIT_2 depends on either the KeepAlive option in httpd.conf (which defaults to ON) or the TCP server value for tcp_keepalive_interval (which defaults usually to 7200000 milliseconds, or 2 hours). I set KeepAlive to OFF and the TCP setting to 45000 milliseconds. The problem was that the quasi-zombies where hanging around for two hours holding resources, but the rate at which they where being killed was slower than the buildup rate. By adjusting the timing of the kill process, we balanced the create/destroy so that they didn't build up past a certain point.

On HP you can reset the kernel parameters to help control the FIN_WAIT_2 processes by running the following commands:

```
ndd -set /dev/tcp tcp_fin_wait_2_timeout 60000
ndd -set /dev/tcp tcp_ip_abort_interval 2000
```

Then place these entries in your /etc/rc.config/nddconf so they are reset with each reboot.

For Solaris, as root run the following commands to determine and set the interval:

```
ndd /dev/tcp tcp_keepalive_interval
```

should tell you what it is, and

```
ndd -set /dev/tcp tcp_keepalive_interval NNN
```

will set it.

Times are in milliseconds, and the default is 2 hours (7200000ms). You'll probably also want to add the reset command to an rc init script.

Listing 14.1 is a little script for HP UNIX you may find useful. It tracks down and kills excessive FIN_WAIT_2 processes. You can probably modify it for other UNIX flavors as needed.

Listing 14.1   Script to detect hung TCP and kill them.

```ksh
#!/bin/ksh
# Hewlett-Packard Corporation
# This script is UNSUPPORTED. Use at own risk.
# @(#)$Revision: 1.3 $ $Author: scotty $ $Date: 98/08/25 17:55:01 $
#
# This script will query the system for any TCP connections that
# are in the FIN_WAIT_2 state and forcibly disconnect them. It
# uses netstat(1) to find the FIN_WAIT_2 connections and calls
# ndd with the correct hexidecimal representation of the connection
# to close the connection.
#


#
# Temporary files used to compare netstat output
#
MYSCRIPTNAME=${0##*/}
TMPFILE1=/var/tmp/$MYSCRIPTNAME.1
TMPFILE2=/var/tmp/$MYSCRIPTNAME.2


#
# Create a log file to keep track of connection that were removed
```

```
#
LOGFILE=/var/adm/$MYSCRIPTNAME.log


function getFinWait2 {

/usr/bin/printf "%.2x%.2x%.2x%.2x%.4x%.2x%.2x%.2x%.2x%.4x\n"
${/usr/bin/netstat -an -f inet | /usr/bin/grep FIN_WAIT_2 | /usr/bin/awk
'{print $4,$5}' | /usr/bin/sed 's/\./ /g') > $TMPFILE1
}

function compareFinWait2 {

FIRST_TIME=1

cp $TMPFILE1 $TMPFILE2
getFinWait2

comm -12 $TMPFILE1 $TMPFILE2 | while read CONN
do
if [[ $CONN != "00000000000000000000000000" ]]
then

if [ $FIRST_TIME -eq 1 ]
then
print >> $LOGFILE
date >> $LOGFILE
FIRST_TIME=0
fi

print "/usr/bin/ndd -set /dev/tcp tcp_discon_by_addr
\"$CONN\""
>> $LOGFILE
/usr/bin/ndd -set /dev/tcp tcp_discon_by_addr $CONN
fi
done

getFinWait2
}

#
# Main
#

touch $TMPFILE1
touch $TMPFILE2

compareFinWait2
```

14.2 OVERVIEW OF ORACLE NET SETUP

There are several files that must either be set up manually or can be set up via the Oracle Net Configuration Assistant. These are divided between the server and the client.

Server Oracle Net Files

On the server, the listener.ora, sqlnet.ora, and maybe the onames.ora files need to be configured depending on whether Oracle Names is being used or not. If other options such as LDAP are configured, other files may also be required.

The Listener.ora File

The Listener.ora file tells the listener what instances are available for connection on the server. Beginning in Oracle8*i* the instances will auto-register when they start if the listener is started. This auto registration of database instances means you no longer have to populate the listener.ora file with entries when new instances are added to a server. However, this is only for Oracle8*i* and greater versions of Oracle, all other versions of Oracle must be manually entered into the file either via an editor or through the GUI interface provided.

Before you can configure the listener.ora file, you must decide whether you want to use a flat model for your Oracle instance structure or the structured model. If you use the flat model (suggested for small Oracle installations where there aren't multiple databases, divisions, or offices) then your instance tree begins at WORLD as the root and ends with WORLD, essentially more of an instance lawn than an instance tree.

On the other hand, if you have multiple databases spread across multiple divisions and offices, then a more structured instance tree is required. For a more structured instance tree, begin with the name of the company or organization as the root of the tree, then each office becomes a branch, as does each division inside each office. finally, the leaves of the tree are the database instances. The structured instance network is similar to the structure of the Internet, except that whereas the address in the Internet would be www.tusc.com, an example instance address in Oracle would be consult.chicago.tusc, where consult is the instance name, Chicago is the office, and tusc is the company. Before beginning to set up the listener.ora file for each office or division, you would need to know where on the instance hierarchy it falls.

For example for my test environment I have chosen a root of TUSC, main branches will be the server or computer names and the end leaves will of course be the database name. I have a LINUX server called TUSCGALINUX and a laptop called MRAMOBILE. On TUSCGALINUX I have a database GALINUX1 and on MRAMOBILE I have a database called AULTDB1. Figure 14.2 shows what this configuration looks like graphically.

The listener.ora file for the TUSCGALINUX Oracle9*i* host is shown in Listing 14.2.

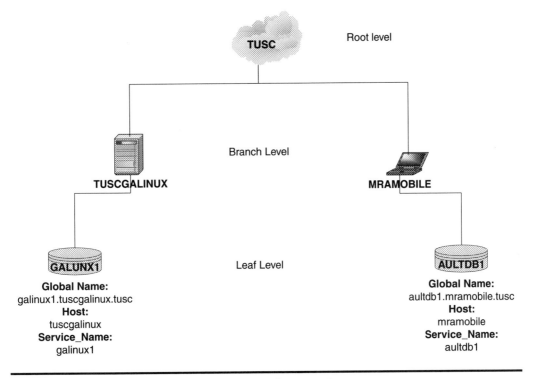

FIGURE 14.2   Graphic Representation of Example Network.

Listing 14.2   Example listener.ora file.

```
# LISTENER.ORA Network Configuration File:
/var/oracle/OraHome2/network/admin/listener.ora
# Generated by Oracle configuration tools.

LISTENER =
  (DESCRIPTION_LIST =
    (DESCRIPTION =
      (ADDRESS_LIST =
        (ADDRESS = (PROTOCOL = TCP)(HOST = tuscgalinux)(PORT = 1521))
      )
    )
  )

SID_LIST_LISTENER =
  (SID_LIST =
    (SID_DESC =
```

continues

Listing 14.2   Continued.

```
      (SID_NAME = PLSExtProc)
      (ORACLE_HOME = /var/oracle/OraHome2)
      (PROGRAM = extproc)
   )
   (SID_DESC =
      (GLOBAL_DBNAME = galinux1.tuscgalinux.tusc)
      (ORACLE_HOME = /var/oracle/OraHome2)
      (SID_NAME = galinux1)
   )
)
```

After configuring the listener.ora file, the listener process needs to be started. On Linux and UNIX, the lsnrctl program is used to start, stop, and reload the listener. On Windows-based platforms, the command line version of this program can be used or the service can be stopped and restarted from the control panel services icon. If the listener process is already running (use: lsnrctl status listener_name to find out, default listener name is *listener*) then you can issue a reload command to reread the listner.ora for all changes except a change in the listing port. To start a listener process the command

```
oracle@tuscgalinux: lsnrctl start
```

is issued, where the appropriate listener name is appended to the command if other than *listener* is used. To stop a listener process the command

```
oracle@tucgalinux: lsnrctl stop
```

is issued, where the appropriate listener name is appended to the command if other than *listener* is used.

Once the listener file is established and the listener process is running, the tnsnames.ora file needs to be populated with the connection information for all databases that you wish to connect with from the server or client. An example tnsnames.ora file for the example network is shown in Listing 14.3.

Listing 14.3   Example tnsnames.ora file.

```
# TNSNAMES.ORA Network Configuration File:
/var/oracle/OraHome2/network/admin/tnsnames.ora
# Generated by Oracle configuration tools.

EXTPROC_CONNECTION_DATA.LOCAL =
  (DESCRIPTION =
    (ADDRESS_LIST =
```

```
      (ADDRESS = (PROTOCOL = IPC)(KEY = EXTPROC))
    )
    (CONNECT_DATA =
      (SID = PLSExtProc)
      (PRESENTATION = RO)
    )
  )

AULTDB1.MRAMOBILE =
  (DESCRIPTION =
    (ADDRESS_LIST =
      (ADDRESS = (PROTOCOL = TCP)(HOST = mramobile)(PORT = 1521))
    )
    (CONNECT_DATA =
      (SERVICE_NAME = aultdb1.mramobile.tusc)
    )
  )

AULTDB1.LOCAL =
  (DESCRIPTION =
    (ADDRESS_LIST =
      (ADDRESS = (PROTOCOL = TCP)(HOST = mramobile)(PORT = 1521))
    )
    (CONNECT_DATA =
      (SERVICE_NAME = aultdb1.mramobile.tusc)
    )
  )

GALINUX1.LOCAL =
  (DESCRIPTION =
    (ADDRESS_LIST =
      (ADDRESS = (PROTOCOL = TCP)(HOST = tuscgalinux)(PORT = 1521))
    )
    (CONNECT_DATA =
      (SERVICE_NAME = galinux1.tuscgalinux.tusc)
    )
  )

INST1_HTTP.TUSCGALINUX =
  (DESCRIPTION =
    (ADDRESS_LIST =
      (ADDRESS = (PROTOCOL = TCP)(HOST = tuscgalinux)(PORT = 1521))
    )
    (CONNECT_DATA =
      (SERVER = SHARED)
      (SERVICE_NAME = MODOSE)
      (PRESENTATION = http://HRService)
    )
  )
```

Notice in Listing 14.2 that there is a listing qualified with either local or the host value for each database. The listener will attach the value specified in the sqlnet.ora parameter NAMES.DEFAULT_DOMAIN to any unqualified name. So GALINUX1 becomes GALINUX1.LOCAL if it cannot locate an unqualified name or one that matches the sid.default_domain, then it will try to resolve the name based on the order of naming method values in the sqlnet.ora parameter NAMES.DIRECTORY_PATH, which defaults to TNSNAMES, ONAMES, or HOSTNAME. An example sqlnet.ora file is shown in Listing 14.4.

Listing 14.4   Example SQLNET.ORA file.

```
# SQLNET.ORA Network Configuration File:
/var/oracle/OraHome2/network/admin/sqlnet.ora
# Generated by Oracle configuration tools.
NAMES.DEFAULT_DOMAIN = local
NAMES.DIRECTORY_PATH= (TNSNAMES, ONAMES, HOSTNAME)
```

As you can see from examining Listing 14.4, there isn't much to a SQLNET.ORA default file; however, this file can be used to add auditing and tracing options.

Connectivity to a remote or local database can be tested using the tnsping program. To use the tnsping program, you simply issue the tnsping command followed by the sid of the database for which you wish to test connectivity.

Oracle Net Configuration Assistant

I have mentioned the Oracle Net Configuration assistant (NETCA) several times in the last few sections. The NETCA is a Java-based GUI that makes configuring and testing Oracle Net connections very easy. Figure 14.3 shows the top-level screen of the NETCA GUI. If you are only configuring a simple Oracle Net setup, there are only two options on this NETCA GUI you will need to bother with. For the server setup, you will use the Listener Configuration and Local Net Service Name Configuration options; for the client, you need only use the Local Net Service Name Configuration option.

The NETCA GUI can be invoked from the command line using netca as the command, from the OEM Service Manager—Oracle Net manager selection, or in Windows from the *Start–Programs–Oracle–Network Administration* menu. The OEM Oracle Net Manager is shown in Figure 14.4. In the OEM Oracle Net manager, for a simple topology you should just use the *Profile, Service Naming,* and *Listeners* configuration options under the *Local Configuration* icon. The top-level screen for the Oracle Net Configuration Assistant is shown in Figure 14.3. The top-level screen of the OEM Oracle net manager is shown in Figure 14.4.

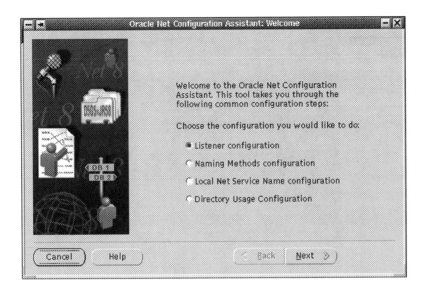

FIGURE 14.3   Top-level NETCA GUI screen.

The interfaces are really rather intuitive once you get into them and understand exactly what you want to do. I suggest overlooking the Oracle Net manuals before attempting to configure your system if it is more complex than a couple of databases, a server, and a flat network topology.

Client Configuration An Oracle client can be one of two basic types, either they are connecting directly to the database through an Oracle Net connection or they are connecting through some server, whether it be an application, forms or reports server through a Net Browser such as Navigator or Internet Explorer for example.

Use of Oracle Applications may also require the downloading and installation of the Jinitiator, a JAVA runtime environment; however, the Jinitiator requires little if any configuration. If the client will attach strictly through the Internet or a company intranet, then all that is needed is the capability to execute JAVA and the Web interface; no further client configuration is required.

A normal Oracle Net connection will require the installation of the appropriate protocol, usually TCP/IP, and installation and configuration of the Oracle Net client software formally called SQLNET or NET8. The configuration of the Oracle Net client usually will consist of setting up the proper database addresses in the tnsnames.ora file. If you will be installing on several clients, either carry a copy of the proper tnsnames.ora file with you on a floppy, or have it readily available on the network someplace. Some shops use a centrally defined tnsnames.ora file for ease of administration.

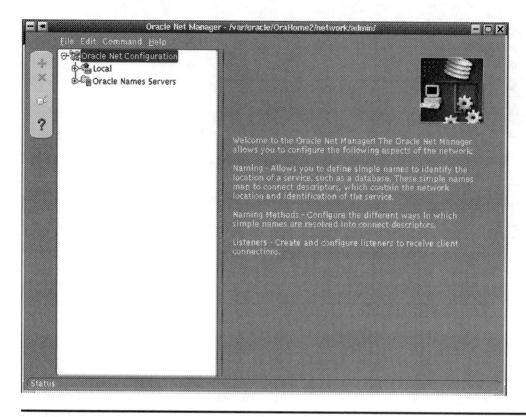

FIGURE 14.4   Top-level OEM Net Manager GUI screen.

Net-Based Connection   As was stated above, the easiest of the client installations involves the net-based connection. Essentially once the net browser (usually Internet Explorer is suggested) is installed, the Jinitiator installed, and the address for the Oracle applications server loaded into the address listing for the browser, the configuration is complete.

Dedicated Connection   In a dedicated connection the client must have an application that can use Oracle Net, Oracle Net and a network transport protocol such as TCP/IP. Once the required software is installed the DBA edits or installs a proper tnsname.ora file in the ORACLE_HOME\network\admin directory and the user should be able to connect. You can test connectivity on a TCP/IP network using the ping system utility and the network address or name of the server to see if the server can be reached from the current client. Once the Oracle Net application is installed and configured you can test connectivity using the tnsping utility and the database connection alias (service name).

In a dedicated connection, the client requests a connection at the specified port (usually 1521), the listener process accepts the request, checks to see if it has the database in its list of instances, and then passes the connection directly to the database. There are no special initialization parameters required for a dedicated connection.

Shared Server Connection   In a shared server or multithreaded server connection, the listener passes the connection request to a dispatcher process that then passes it to one of several shared services in a round-robin least-busy methodology. Multiple users share the same server process that connects to the database. For a shared server connection, the configuration of the client is identical to the configuration of a dedicated client. The real changes are in the database initialization file.

Under a multithreaded server there are several server database initialization parameters that must be set properly for MTS to work. These parameters are:

MTS_CIRCUITS. This is a derived value from the value of SESSIONS. It defaults to 0 if MTS is not configured. The Oracle9*i* parameter is CIRCUITS and should be used as this form is deprecated. The CIRCUITS parameter controls the total number of virtual circuits allowed in the database.

MTS_DISPATCHERS. This parameter tells Oracle the type and number of dispatchers to create for each network protocol. This parameter becomes DISPATCHERS in Oracle9*i* and this new form of the parameter should be used beginning with Oracle9*i* release 9.0.1.

MTS_MAX_DISPATCHERS. Sets the maximum number of dispatcher processes to be allowed to run concurrently. In Oracle9*i* this becomes MAX_DISPATCHERS. This defaults to 5, but there should be at least one dispatcher for each protocol defined in the MTS_DISPATCHERS parameter. The default value applies only if dispatchers have been configured for the system. The value of MAX_DISPATCHERS should at least equal the maximum number of concurrent sessions divided by the number of connections for each dispatcher. For most systems, a value of 250 connections for each dispatcher provides good performance.

MTS_MAX_SERVERS. Sets the maximum number of shared server processes. In Oracle9*i* this becomes MAX_SHARED_SERVERS and defaults to either 20 or to twice the value of SHARED_SERVERS (MTS_SERVERS). If artificial deadlocks occur too frequently on your system, you should increase the value of MAX_SHARED_SERVERS.

MTS_SERVERS. Sets the number of shared connection servers to start when the database is started. Defaults to 1 on a MTS configured system, 0 on a normal system. In Oracle9*i* this becomes SHARED_SERVERS. Oracle will automatically increase this value up to MAX_SHARED_SERVERS, so unless you know you will need more than the default, leave it set at the default.

MTS_SESSIONS. Defines the soft limit on MTS sessions, defaults to 5 less than the greater of CIRCUITS or SESSIONS. In Oracle9*i* you should use SHARED_ SERVER_SESSIONS. This allows some dedicated connections to be reserved.

Monitoring Multithreaded Server   The DBA will be tasked with monitoring the multithreaded server dispatchers and servers and ensuring that there are adequate numbers of each to serve the database and its users. To this end, the V$DISPATCHER, V$QUEUE, VMTS, VSHARED_SERVER, V$SHARED_SERVER_MONITOR, V$CIRCUIT, and V$DISPATCHER_RATE views have been provided by Oracle. For their complete descriptions, I will refer you to the Oracle Reference Manual. Let's look at a couple of reports that will give you a look into the MTS performance.

Monitoring Percent Busy   The DBA needs to monitor the percent busy of the dispatcher processes. If they exceed 50 percent busy then more dispatchers should be started using the

```
ALTER SYSTEM SET MTS_DISPATCHERS
```

command. You monitor percent busy using the V$DISPATCHER view. Source 14.1 shows an example report against the V$DISPATCHER view.

An example report from Source 14.1 is shown in Listing 14.5.

Source 14.1   Example dispatcher percent busy report.

```
rem
rem Name: mts_disp.sql
rem Function: generate percent busy report for dispatchers
rem History: MRA 10/11/96 Created
rem          MRA 11/24/01 Verified and formatted for Oracle9i
rem
COL protocol FORMAT a60 HEADING 'Dispatcher|Protocol'
COL busy     FORMAT 999.99 HEADING 'Percent|Busy'
rem
SET FEEDBACK OFF VERIFY OFF LINES 78 PAGES 58
START title80 'Dispatcher Status'
SPOOL rep_out\&db\mts_disp
rem
SELECT network protocol,
      ((SUM(busy)/(SUM(busy)+SUM(idle)))*100) busy
FROM v$dispatcher
GROUP BY network;
rem
SPOOL OFF
SET FEEDBACK ON VERIFY ON LINES 22
TTITLE OFF
```

Listing 14.5   Example percent busy report.

```
Date: 11/25/01                                              Page:    1
Time: 12:07 PM                   Dispatcher Status         SYSTEM
                                 galinux1 databa


Dispatcher                                                Percent
Protocol                                                  Busy
------------------------------------------------------------- --------
(ADDRESS=(PROTOCOL=tcp)(HOST=tuscgalinux.local)(PORT=32780))    .00
(DESCRIPTION=(ADDRESS=(PROTOCOL=tcp)(HOST=tuscgalinux.local)    .00
(PORT=32782))(PRESENTATION=oracle.aurora.server.GiopServer)(
SESSION=

(DESCRIPTION=(ADDRESS=(PROTOCOL=tcp)(HOST=tuscgalinux.local)    .00
(PORT=32783))(PRESENTATION=oracle.aurora.server.SGiopServer)
(SESSION
```

Monitoring Average Wait Time   The DBA also needs to monitor the average wait time in relation to the dispatchers. If the wait time gets excessive (for example the users complain about long connect times to the database) the DBA should use the V$DISPATCHER and V$QUEUE views to monitor the dispatcher wait times. An example wait time monitoring script is shown in Source 14.2.

Source 14.2   Average wait time report.

```
rem
rem Name: mts_wait.sql
rem Function: Generate Wait time report for the dispatchers
rem History: MRA 10/11/96 Created
rem          MRA 11/25/01 Verified against Oracle9i
rem
COLUMN network FORMAT a40 HEADING 'Dispatcher|Protocol'
COLUMN aw      FORMAT a32 HEADING 'Average Wait|Time %'
SET FEEDBACK OFF VERIFY OFF LINES 78 PAGES 55
START title80 'Dispatcher Wait Times'
SPOOL rep_out\&db\mts_wait
SELECT
   NETWORK,
   DECODE (SUM(totalq),0,'no responses',
           SUM(wait)/SUM(totalq)*100||' sec wait/response') aw
FROM v$queue q, v$dispatcher d
WHERE q.type='DISPATCHER' AND
      q.paddr = d.paddr
GROUP BY network;
SPOOL OFF
SET FEEDBACK ON VERIFY ON PAGES 80 LINES 22
TTITLE OFF
```

An example output from the report in Source 14.2 is shown in Listing 14.6.

Listing 14.6   Example MTS wait report.

```
Date: 11/25/01                                      Page:   1
Time: 11:44 AM          Dispatcher Wait Times       SYSTEM
                         galinux1 database


Dispacther                              Average Wait
Protocol                                Time %
------------------------------------    ----------------------
(ADDRESS=(PROTOCOL=tcp)(HOST=tuscgalinux no responses
.local)(PORT=32780))

(DESCRIPTION=(ADDRESS=(PROTOCOL=tcp)(HOS no responses
T=tuscgalinux.local)(PORT=32782))(PRESEN
TATION=oracle.aurora.server.GiopServer)(
SESSION=

(DESCRIPTION=(ADDRESS=(PROTOCOL=tcp)(HOS no responses
T=tuscgalinux.local)(PORT=32783))(PRESEN
TATION=oracle.aurora.server.SGiopServer)
(SESSION
```

Monitoring for Server Process Contention   We have discussed monitoring the dispatchers, now let's turn our attention to the shared servers. An example report using the V$SHARED_SERVER view is shown in Source 14.3. If the percent busy for all servers is greater than 50 percent and the number of server processes is equal to the initialization parameter MAX_SHARED_SERVERS, then the MAX_SHARED_SERVERS parameter needs to be increased. If the value is less than MAX_SHARED_SERVERS, then the Oracle kernel should automatically start more server processes up to the value of MAX_SHARED_SERVERS. If you feel the need to manually start more server processes, you can use the command

```
ALTER SYSTEM SET SHARED_SERVERS=n
```

where *n* is the current number of processes plus the number you wish to add.

Source 14.3   Script to monitor shared server processes.

```
rem
rem Name: mts_serv.sql
rem Function: generate percent busy report for shared servers
rem History: MRA 11/24/01 Verified and formatted for Oracle9i
rem
COL name     FORMAT a4      HEADING 'Name'
```

```
COL busy    FORMAT 999.99 HEADING 'Percent|Busy'
COL status FORMAT a13    HEADING 'Server Status'
COL messages            HEADING 'Meassages'
COL bytes               HEADING 'Bytes'
COL requests            HEADING 'Requests'
rem
SET FEEDBACK OFF VERIFY OFF LINES 78 PAGES 58
START title80 'Server Status'
SPOOL rep_out\&db\mts_disp
rem
SELECT name,
     ((SUM(busy)/(SUM(busy)+SUM(idle)))*100) busy,
     MAX(status) status, MAX(messages) messages,
     MAX(bytes) bytes, MAX(requests) requests
FROM v$shared_server
GROUP BY name;
rem
SPOOL OFF
SET FEEDBACK ON VERIFY ON LINES 22
TTITLE OFF
```

An example output from Source 14.3 is shown in Listing 14.7.

Listing 14.7   Example shared server report.

```
Date: 11/25/01                                  Page:   1
Time: 12:01 PM          Server Status           SYSTEM
                        galinux1 database


       Percent
Name    Busy Server Status Meassages      Bytes  Requests
----  ------- ------------- --------- --------- ---------
S000    .00 WAIT(COMMON)           0         0         0
```

Monitoring and Configuring MTS Other than the scripts shown, above I haven't found a tool that allows you to monitor the MTS system from Oracle. Several third-party tools such as Precise*Q Monitor provide this functionality. The Database Configuration Assistant (DBCA) allows configuration of the Shared Server Mode if you select the Configure database options in a database option from the top-level screen. Once you have selected an instance from the pick list, you get a set of available options. All will be gray. Choose the next button, select the Shared Server Mode option, and then click on the Edit Shared Connections Parameters button.

Once the Shared Server Mode edit box is displayed you can choose from TCP, IPC, or TCPS protocols and then select the initial number of dispatchers, connections per dispatcher, max number of dispatchers, initial number of servers, and max number of servers from the Basic edit tab. From the advanced edit tab you can configure multiplexing, connection pooling, and maximum number of network sessions. Figure 14.5 shows the basic edit screen for the MTS (now to be called shared server) option.

Before you attempt a manual configuration of Oracle Shared Server (the option formerly known as MTS), I suggest you consult the Oracle Database Administrators Guide for detailed instructions.

14.3 OVERVIEW OF PARALLEL SERVER

Oracle parallel server (OPS) has undergone extreme changes in Oracle9*i*. Other than bug fixes, not much happened with OPS from version 7 (where it was introduced) up to Oracle8*i*. In Oracle8*i* the first foundations of the Real Applications Clusters was laid, and finally with Oracle9*i* they were realized.

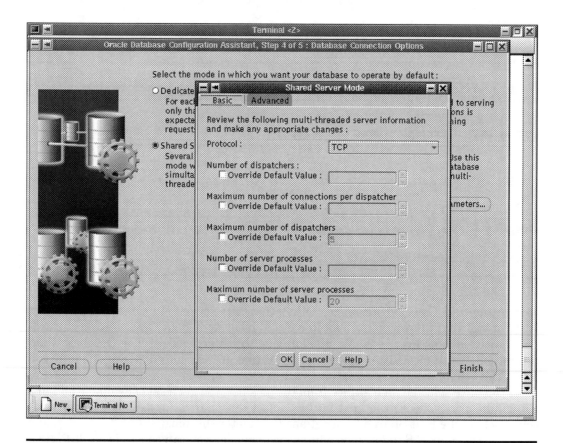

FIGURE 14.5   MTS configuration screen From DBCA.

Real Application Clusters (RAC) Overview

Oracle has had the ability to run in parallel server mode since versions 7. In Oracle, *parallel server mode* means that two or more Oracle instances share a single set of database files. An instance of Oracle is the executable image, background processes, instance-specific initialization file, control files, redo log thread, and a set of either shared or private rollback segments. A shared database consists of the datafiles that make up all tablespaces in the database. Until later versions of Oracle8*i*, a shared Oracle database system had to use a laborious process of copying blocks into and out of memory and to and from disk in order to share information in a single block between the multiple instances. This complex sharing mechanism resulted in performance issues if the database itself didn't practice data partitioning. Oracle9*i* relieves DBAs and designers from these limitations and problems.

Benefits of RAC   In the beginning was OPS. Now we have Real Application Clusters (RAC). It is more than just a name change. RAC provides a process known as cache-fusion, which allows direct sharing of Oracle database blocks between cache areas of Oracle instances participating in RAC via a high-speed interconnect. This direct sharing eliminates the biggest performance robbers in the OPS architecture, the DB block PING.

A DB block PING would occur when an instance participating in an OPS database would have a block in its cache that another participating instance required. In OPS, if another instance required the block in the cache of a second instance, the block would have to be written out to disk, the locks transferred, and then the block reread into the requesting instance. As you can imagine, all of this IO was expensive in terms of time and performance.

The new RAC with cache fusion exploits the new high-speed buses and architectures available in the new servers. By eliminating the blockage caused by pinging, RAC enables better, more efficient scaling. In order to add more processing or user capacity, you simply add a server to the LAN, load the appropriate software, and Oracle9*i* and you are up and operating.

What Is a DB Cluster?   A DB cluster consists of a group of independent servers, connected via a LAN that shares a set of disk assets via the LAN and has a high-speed cluster interconnect that allows connection of its processors to the other processors in the cluster. The clusters do not share memory and act as independent servers. The servers can either be single processor or Symmetric Multi-Processor (SMP) nodes. A DB cluster provides fault-tolerance and allows for modular growth. By having the built-in redundancies of multiple servers, the chance that a single point of failure will prevent database access is unlikely.

DB Cluster Architectures   Essentially there are only two basic architectures used in DB clusters: the shared-nothing and shared-disk. The shared-nothing cluster uses dedicated disk assets for each server in the cluster. The shared-disk cluster uses a SAN-type storage array to serve the cluster.

Examples of systems that use the shared-nothing architecture are the IBM RS/6000 SP and the federated database approach used by SQL Server. This architecture is rapidly losing ground to the shared-disk architecture.

The shared-disk architecture is being adopted almost 100 percent by IBM, SUN, HP, and other vendors. It offers better redundancy and better connectivity through technologies such as fiber-channel, hub, and shared SCSI.

What Is a Cluster Interconnect?   The cluster interconnect is a high-speed (usually optical fiber) connection directly between the servers involved in a DB cluster. The bandwidth is usually large in a cluster interconnect (unlike the previous Ethernet or other connections used in early architectures), thus allowing transfers of blocks instead of just latch and lock information. This high-speed connection allows direct transfer of blocks, eliminating the PING method of block transfer to and from disk.

Oracle's cache fusion process utilizes the high-speed cluster interconnect to form a virtual DB block cache that is the combination of the entire DB block caches of all of the participating Oracle9*i* instances in the RAC.

Problems with Other Architectures   Other architectures for database clusters use either the shared-nothing disk setup, or use a database setup that restricts the database in the areas of referential integrity and ease of use. Let's examine the major vendor implementations.

IBM Shared-Nothing Configuration   IBM has traditionally used the shared-nothing disk architecture for all versions of its DB2 shared database except OS/390 (see Figure 14.6).

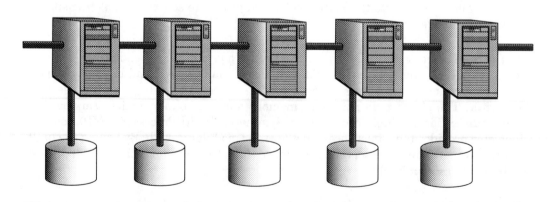

FIGURE 14.6   IBM's shared-nothing configuration.

The shared-nothing configuration utilizes isolated disk assets for each server, and the database in the IBM implementation is hashed across all of the servers. The database image is perceived by the users to be a single database, and each machine has access to its own data. However, this implementation of the parallel database server falls prey to what is known as the "convoy effect." In a convoy of trucks or ships, the speed of the convoy is limited by the speed of the convoy's slowest member. It is the same with a database that is spread across isolated disk assets by hashing—the speed of database processing is limited by the speed of the slowest member of the cluster.

Another problem with the hashed spread of a database across multiple isolated disk assets is that the loss of one of the servers means loss of the entire database until the server or its disk assets are rebuilt and/or reassigned.

In addition, due to the way the data is hashed across the servers and disks, standard methods for maintaining data integrity won't work. This indicates that for a hashed-storage database cluster, much if not all of the data integrity constraints must be programmed into the applications using complex two-phase commit algorithms instead of relying on built-in constraint mechanisms.

The final problem with the shared-nothing approach used by IBM is that to add a new cluster member, the data must be re-hashed across all members requiring database down time.

Microsoft Federated Servers Databases   Microsoft actually has two architectures that they support. The first is limited to a two-node structure if you use WIN2000 Advanced Server, and a four node structure if you use a WIN2000 Datacenter implementation. This initial configuration allows for automatic failover of one server to another and is shown in Figure 14.7.

While this architecture allows for failover, it doesn't improve scalability because each cluster member acts independently until the need for failover, then the server that receives the failover activity essentially has to double its processing load. Each server in this configuration maintains an independent copy of the database that must be maintained in sync with the other copies and has the same restrictions to referential integrity as the DB2 database architecture. Another constraint of this architecture is that to add a server, the databases have to be properly resynced and balanced.

The second architecture used by Microsoft is the SQL Server 2000 federated databases architecture (shown in Figure 14.8).

In this architecture, the data from a single database is spread across multiple separate databases. Again, if you want to guarantee data integrity you will have to implement it by:

- Replication of all data used for integrity such as lookup tables across all databases in the cluster
- Ensure all changes to lookup tables are replicated across the cluster
- Create triggers in each database that ensure integrity is maintained across all databases in the cluster

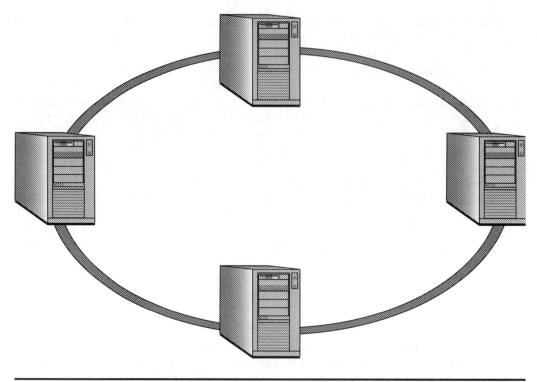

FIGURE 14.7   Example of Microsoft's failover cluster.

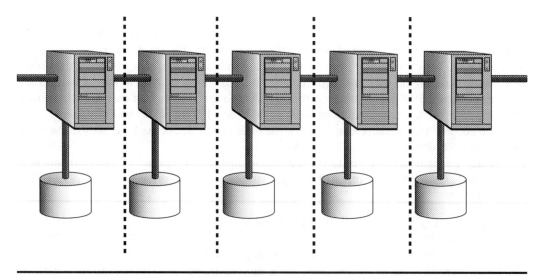

FIGURE 14.8   Microsoft federated databases.

- Create application triggers that check the federated database for integrity violations—but be aware that this may fail in certain multiuser situations

However, even the most complex schemes of referential triggers and replication have been known to fail in federated systems.

Seeing the High Availability Spectrum All database systems fall somewhere on the high availability spectrum (see Figure 14.9). From low-criticality and low-availability systems to systems that absolutely, positively cannot fail. You must be aware of where your system falls, whether it is at the low end of the spectrum, or at the mythical 5–9's end, or beyond.

Many systems that claim to be high-availability, mission-critical systems really aren't. If a system by its nature cannot be high on the high-availability spectrum, you cannot force it to be. If you try, you are opening yourself up for many frustrations and

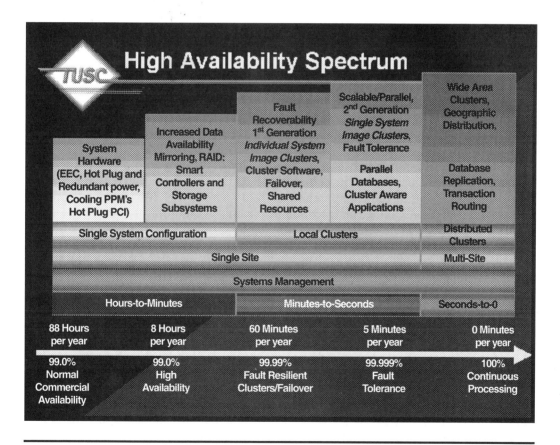

FIGURE 14.9 The high availability spectrum.

failures. In order to meet the requirements of a high-availability system, a database must have the architectural components shown under each area of the high-availability spectrum shown in Figure 14.9. In other words without using distributed DB RAC clusters in a multisite configuration, you would be hard-pressed to be able to guarantee zero minutes per year downtime. If you can handle 60 minutes per year downtime, then local DB clusters on a single site, barring site disasters, would be adequate. And if you can stomach greater than 60 minutes of downtime per year then various implementations of a single server database will meet your requirements.

Real Application Clusters   Let's take a more detailed look at Oracle9*i* RAC. The RAC architecture provides:

- Cache fusion
- True scalability
- Enhanced reliability

RAC allows the DBA true transparent scalability. In order to increase the number of servers in almost all other architectures, including Oracle's previous OPS, data and application changes were required or else performance would actually get worse in many cases. With RAC:

- All applications scale—no tuning required
- No physical data partitioning required
- ISV applications scale out of the box

This automatic, transparent scaling is due almost entirely to the RAC's cache fusion and the unique parallel architecture of the RAC implementation on Oracle9*i*. Because the processing of requests is spread evenly across the RAC instances and all access a single database image instead of multiple images, addition of a server or servers requires no architecture changes, no remapping of data, and no recoding. In addition, failure of a single node results in only loss of its addition to scalability, not in loss of its data, as a single database image is utilized. This is demonstrated in Figure 14.10.

The cache fusion is implemented through the high-speed cluster interconnect that runs between the servers. This is demonstrated in Figure 4.11. Without the high-speed interconnect, cache fusion would not be possible. Each instance in Oracle RAC is independent in that it uses its own shared memory area (which can be structured differently for each instance), its own processes, redo logs, control files, and so forth. However, the cache fusion unites these shared memory structures so that block images are rapidly transferred from one shared memory area to another through the high-speed interconnect, providing a virtual shared area that is the sum of the individual areas.

Each query is divided amongst the parallel instances, and processing is done in parallel. Loss of a single server spreads the processing across all nodes, not just a single designated failure target node. Addition of a processor is quick and easy.

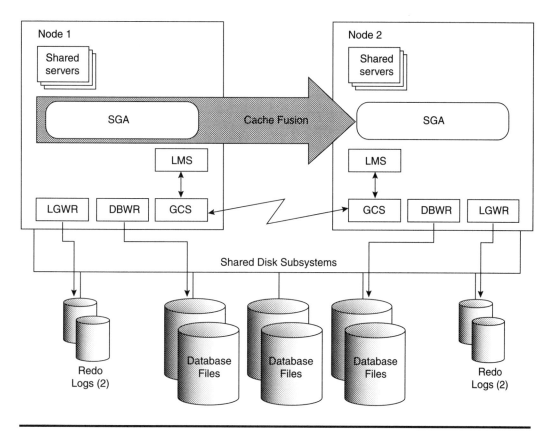

FIGURE 14.10   RAC architecture.

Processing Prior to Cache Fusion   Prior to the introduction of cache fusion, disks had to be ping-ponged between instances as they were needed. For example, if a block would be read by Instance A and then if Instance B required the same block then:

- Instance A would get the request from Instance B
- Instance A would write the block to disk and notify Instance B
- Instance B would then read the block from disk into its cache

This was called a block PING, and as you can imagine was horrible for performance. Data had to be partitioned to the Instance where it was used most.

Processing with to Cache Fusion   Cache fusion replaces older methods of concurrency that required disk writes and reads between instances. Each time a block had to be written to disk so it could be re-read, it was considered a ping and a performance hit.

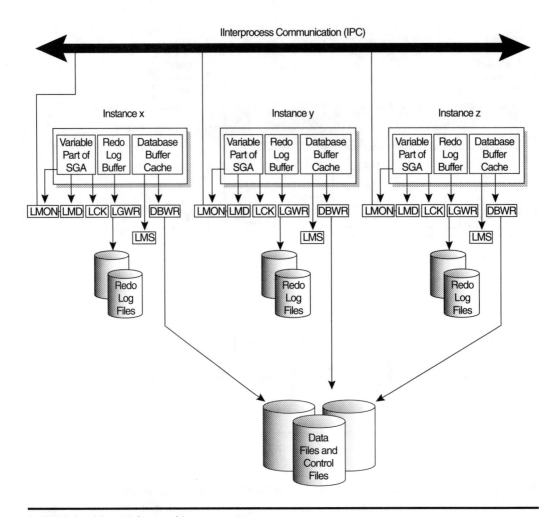

FIGURE 14.11 High-speed interconnect.

By sharing blocks between caches of multiple instances in a RAC environment through the high-speed interconnect and controlling access to the block through cache latches, enqueues, and locks, performance is similar to a single instance.

Be careful if you are upgrading from OPS to RAC. Cache fusion only works with the default resource control scheme. If GC_FILES_TO_LOCKS is set, the old pre-cache fusion behavior is utilized. In other words, forced disk-writes will be used resulting in pings.

Cache fusion all but eliminates the need for data partitioning that was required in OPS early releases. You see data was partitioned by use, so all of account receivable data was isolated to a set of tablespaces, as was general ledger and other application subsets. Then the node that processed that data could be relatively assured that pinging would not occur.

Oracle9i Real Application Clusters   Previous versions of Oracle OPS were not really good for OLTP systems due to pinging and performance issues. Not only performance is improved with RAC, reliability is as well. In order to lose the DB with an Oracle9*i* RAC you would have to either lose the entire LAN, lose the SAN drives, or lose all servers that are running RAC. With modern built-in redundancies for network, SAN drives, and servers, loss of everything is unlikely.

Attributes of an Oracle RAC Cluster   The Oracle9*i* RAC allows for a single or multisystem image. This means the root and other system files can either be localized to internal or non-shared disks for each server in the RAC, or else each can load the operating system from a central set of disks.

If the RAC cluster uses a SAN or other network storage device, this is known as a shared system disk (root) system.

A RAC system must use a cluster file system, in which any server can read or write to any disk in the shared disk subsystem. This allows access to all datafiles, control files, and redo and rollback areas by any instance. This ability to access all disks allows for instance recovery after an instance failure has occurred. The work of the failed instance is automatically absorbed by all surviving nodes until the failed instance is brought back online, at which time it is fully synchronized and restored to service automatically.

A RAC cluster provides for automatic shared execution of Oracle applications. This means that for any Oracle instance application, all queries and other processing is automatically shared among all of the servers in the RAC cluster.

The sharing of application processing to all servers in the RAC cluster leads to automatic load balancing across all cluster members.

The ability of a RAC cluster to provide shared application execution and automatic load balancing leads to the true scalability of applications without code or data changes.

One limit on shared-none or federated databases was the amount of time required for failover. Due to the requirements for rebuild or rehash of data, failover time in a non-shared disk environment can be prohibitive. In a RAC cluster failover time is virtually null because Oracle handles the redistribution of work automatically. No rehash of data is required because the same data files are shared by all participating nodes in the RAC cluster.

The number of nodes in a RAC cluster is only limited by the number of servers that your LAN architecture allows to connect into the disk farm. In the SQL Server 2000, in the cluster database you have a hard limit of two or four servers, depending on what level of server license for Windows 2000 you have loaded on your server. The convoy effect limits the number of servers that an IBM-type structure allows. Due to the cache fusion and the high-speed cluster interconnect, the Oracle9*i* RAC allows for a virtually unlimited number of nodes in a RAC cluster.

Oracle9*i* RAC allows for TCP/IP/ UDP/ VIA for the protocol used by the cluster interconnect. The speed of the interconnect should be at a minimum of 100 mbit/sec. The maximum number of instances that can be interconnected is OS platform dependent. The distance allowed between nodes on a cluster interconnect is system and LAN specific.

Oracle RAC displays great disaster tolerance. If a single or multiple nodes fail, the load is redistributed between all of the remaining nodes. If the database is globally distributed then a disaster to a single site will not affect other sites.

Building an Oracle RAC Cluster   The first step in building a RAC cluster is to establish the LAN with the connection to a SAN or other network storage device via a HUB, Fiber channel switch, or shared SCSI. Once the LAN and SAN is configured, a server can be attached and configured. If the root, user, and other systems are moved into the shared storage and shared among all cluster members, it greatly reduces the amount of system management overhead and database overhead.

Once the first server is installed and then the Oracle RAC software, cluster interconnect, and control software and applications are installed, it is a simple matter to initially configure the first host with the clu_create package. You then add additional nodes to the cluster by using the clu_add_member procedure. You can continue to add members up to the limits of your SAN hardware.

Addition of new nodes is simple and automatic. Memory and CPU capacity are automatically registered with the Oracle RAC software. As soon as their instance is created, they can begin participating in cluster applications load balancing.

RAC Performance and Scalability   In benchmarks performed by Compaq, Oracle RAC clusters were shown to provide a 1.81 scalability index. This means that 2 nodes performed the operation at 1.81 times the speed of a single node. In multi-node performance tests, up to a 278 times performance improvement was demonstrated for operations such as a 5-way table join. Of course the amount of performance improvement seen is directly dependent on how well an operation will parallelize.

RAC Installation   The Oracle9*i* RAC is easily installed using the Oracle Universal Installer. The install is almost identical to a normal installation, with the exception that you install the clusterware for your system first. If the appropriate clusterware is not installed, the Oracle Database Configuration Assistant will not show the nodes available for database installation. You must also configure the appropriate number and size of raw devices before attempting a RAC database install.

The basic steps for installing RAC are:

1. Install OSD clusterware
2. Configure shared disks (must be raw)
3. Use OUI to install Oracle9*i* Enterprise Version and Oracle9*i* RAC
4. Create and configure databases using DBCA (or manual scripts)

Once the RAC database system is installed, the OEM management tools provide expanded coverage with a series of new screens and numerous RAC specific reports.

RAC Backup The rman tool provides automatic coverage of the Rac system through its normal scripting language and interface. The major difference with rman for clusters is that you must make allowances for all redo and archive log locations as well as control file locations. For example for a three-node cluster, the one-time initialization step required at the rman prompt would be:

```
CONFIGURE DEVICE TYPE sbt PARALLELISM 3;
CONFIGURE DEFAULT DEVICE TYPE TO sbt;
CONFIGURE CHANNEL 1 DEVICE TYPE sbt CONNECT 'user1/password1@node1';
CONFIGURE CHANNEL 2 DEVICE TYPE sbt CONNECT 'user2/password2@node2';
CONFIGURE CHANNEL 3 DEVICE TYPE sbt CONNECT 'user3/password3@node3';
```

This would allow for proper backup of the three nodes using a command script similar to:

```
RUN
  {
  ALLOCATE CHANNEL db1tape1 DEVICE TYPE sbt;
  BACKUP DATABASE;
  BACKUP ARCHIVELOG ALL:
  }
```

If the initial configuration is not performed, the above script would result in an error since the archive logs on nodes 2 and 3 would not be accessible.

14.4 FURTHER DBA READING

Niemiec, Rich, *Oracle9i New Features*, TUSC Presentation, September 2001.

Oracle. *Managing Oracle9i Real Application Clusters*, A White Paper, March 2001.

Oracle. *Oracle9i Real Application Clusters—Cache Fusion Delivers Scalability*, A White Paper, May 2001.

Oracle. *Building Highly Available Database Servers Using Oracle Real Application Clusters*, A White Paper, May 2001.

Oracle9i Database Real Application Clusters—Architecture of IBM Clustered Databases, www.oracle.com/ip/deploy/database/oracle9i/rc_arch_ibm.html

Oracle9i Database Real Application Clusters—Architecture of Microsoft Clustered Databases, www.oracle.com/ip/deploy/database/oracle9i/rc_arch_ms.html

Oracle9i Net Services Reference Guide, Release 1 (9.0.1), Part Number A90155-01, , Oracle Corporation, June 2001

Oracle9i Net Services Administrator's Guide, Release 1 (9.0.1), Part Number A90154-01, Oracle Corporation, June 2001.

Oracle9i Real Application Cluster Documentation Set, Oracle Corporation, June 2001.

Sybase. *Setting Keepalive to Detect Client Disconnects,* White paper, http://my.sybase.com/detail?id=611

14.5 SUMMARY

In order to have a distributed database, whether it be a simple set of instances sharing information via database links or a global network of interconnected systems using real application clusters and database link interconnects, the DBA must be aware of the limits and challenges involved in operating a distributed database and the network issues involved.

Backup and Recovery Procedures for Oracle

By now you should be aware that Oracle is a complex, interrelated set of files and executables. With the release of Oracle8*i* and Oracle9*i*, it hasn't gotten any simpler. The database files include data segments, redo logs, rollback segments, control files, bfiles, libraries, LOBs, and system areas. None of these files is a separate entity, but is tightly linked to the others. For instance, the datafiles are repositories for all table data; the datafile structure is controlled by the control file, implemented by the system areas, and maintained by a combination of the executables, redo, and rollback segments. Datafiles reference bfiles that are tied to external procedures stored in libraries, which are referenced in procedures stored in datafiles.

This complexity leads to the requirement of a threefold backup recovery methodology to ensure that data recovery can be made. The threefold recovery methodology consists of:

1. Normal backups using system backups, Oracle Backup Manager, Recovery Manager, or a third-party tool that has been tested against Oracle.
2. Exports and imports.
3. Archive logging of redo logs.

Let's look at each of these procedures and how they are used. Figure 15.1 shows a basic flowchart for determining your backup strategy.

15.1 BACKUPS

Normal system backups, referred to as either *hot* or *cold backups*, are used to protect the system from media failure. Each can and should be used when required.

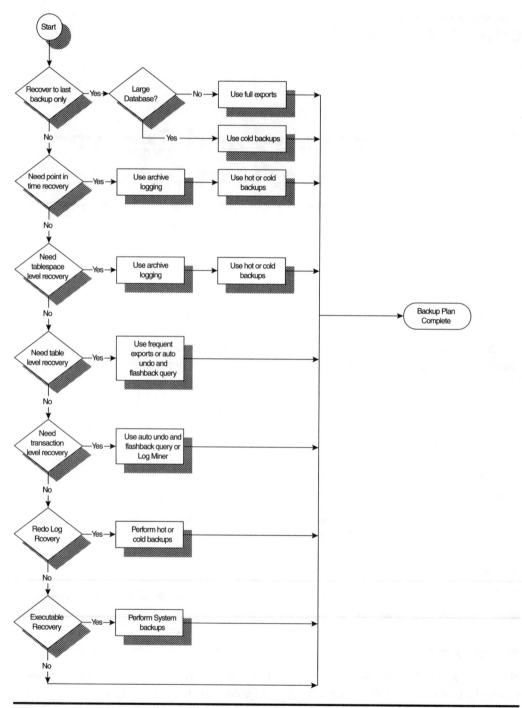

FIGURE 15.1 Backup recovery strategy flowchart.

Cold Backups

A cold backup, that is, one done with the database in a shutdown state, provides a complete copy of the database that can be restored exactly. The procedure for using a cold backup is as follows:

1. Using the shutdown script(s) provided, shut down the Oracle instance(s) to be backed up.
2. Ensure that there is enough backup media to back up the entire database.
3. Mount the first volume of the backup media (9-track, WORM, 4mm, 8mm, etc.) using the proper operating system mount command. For example, On UNIX:

   ```
   $ umount  /dev/rmt0 /tape1
   ```

4. Issue the proper operating system backup command to initiate the backup. On UNIX, the backup command to initiate the backup is as follows:

   ```
   $ tar -cvf /tape1 /ud*/oracle*/ortest1/*
   ```

   for all Oracle data, log, and trace files, assuming an OFA installation, where:

   > **tar.** Short for tape archiver. This is the default backup command on UNIX. RAW volumes may require "dd."
   >
   > **-cvf.** These arguments tell tar to: c: create a new archive, v: tell us what it is doing, and f: use the device specification that follows (we could have *not* specified a device, and it would default to the default tape drive).

5. Once the backup is complete, be sure all backup volumes are properly labeled and stored, away from the computer. The final volume is dismounted from the tape drive using the appropriate operating system DISMOUNT command. For example, on UNIX:

   ```
   $ umount /tape1
   ```

6. Restart the Oracle instances using the appropriate startup script(s).

Hot Backups

A hot backup, or one taken while the database is active, can only give a read-consistent copy; it doesn't handle active transactions. You must ensure that all redo logs archived during the backup process are also backed up. The hot backup differs from the cold backup in that only sections of the database are backed up at one time. This is accomplished by using the ALTER command to modify a tablespace's status to backup. Be sure that you restore the status to normal once the database is backed up or else redo log mismatch and improper archiving/rollbacks can occur.

While it is quite simple (generally speaking) to do a cold backup by hand, a hot backup can be quite complex, hence should be automated. The automated procedure should then be thoroughly tested on a dummy database for both proper operation and the ability to restore prior to its use on the production database(s).

The following are limitations on hot, or online, backups:

- The database must be operating in ARCHIVELOG mode for hot backups to work.
- Hot backups should only be done during off-hours or low-use periods.
- During the hot backups, the entire block containing a changed record, not just the changed record, is written to the archive log, requiring more archive space for this period.

The hot backup consists of three processes:

1. The tablespace datafiles are backed up.
2. The archived redo logs are backed up.
3. The control file is backed up.

The first two parts have to be repeated for each tablespace in the database. For small databases, this is relatively easy. For large, complex databases with files spread across several drives, this can become a nightmare if not properly automated in operating system-specific command scripts. An example of this type of a backup shell script is shown in Source 15.1.

As you can see, this is a bit more complex than a full cold backup and requires more monitoring than a cold backup. Recovery from this type of backup consists of restoring all tablespaces and logs and then recovering. You only use the backup of the control file if the current control file was also lost in the disaster; otherwise, be sure to use the most current copy of the control file for recovery operations.

TIP   In a number of computer facilities, backups are kept close at hand, sometimes in the same room as the computer. What would happen if a site disaster destroyed the computer room? Not only the hardware, but all of the system backups and your data, could be lost. The point is: Store backups in another building or even totally off-site. This assures that come fire, flood, or typhoon, you should be able to get backup one way or another.

Source 15.1   Example of hot backup script for UNIX KORNE shell.

```
#**********************************************************************
# Name       : hot_backup
# Purpose    : Perform a hot backup of an Oracle Database
# Use        : sh hot_backup
# Limitations : Creates a read-consistent image, but doesn't back
#               up in-process transactions
#
#
```

```
# Revision History:
# Date          Who             What
# ---------     ----------      --------------------------------
# June 1993     K. Loney        Featured in Oracle Mag. Article
# 29-Jun-93     M. Ault         Modified, commented
# 02-Aug-93     M. Ault         Converted to UNIX script
# 03-Aug-93     M. Phillips     Added error detection
#****************************************************************
#
ERROR="FALSE"
LOGFILE="$ORACLE_HOME/adhoc/scripts/hot_back_log"
while [ "$error"=FALSE ]
do
svrmgrl << ending1
    connect internal
    alter tablespace system begin backup;
    exit
ending1
    if ( tar cfv /oracle/backup /data/ORA_SYSTEM_1.DBF )
    then
        :
    else
        ERROR="TRUE";
            echo "Tar backup failed for ora_system1.dbf" >$LOGFILE
    fi
svrmgrl << ending2
connect internal
    alter tablespace system end backup;
    exit
ending2

dup_it="tar rv /oracle/backup"
svrmgrl << ending3
    connect internal
    alter tablespace user_tables begin backup;
    exit
ending3
if ( $dup_it /data/ora_user_tables_1.dbf )
then
    :
else
    ERROR="TRUE";echo "Tar backup failed for ora_user_tables_1.dbf">>$LOGFILE
fi #we must still end backup for tablespaces
svrmgrl << ending4
    connect internal
    alter tablespace user_tables end backup;
    exit
ending4
# force write of all archive logs
svrmgrl << ending5
```

continues

Source 15.1   Continued.

```
        connect internal
        alter system switch logfile;
        archive log all;
        exit
ending5
if ( cp /usr/oracle/oracle7/db_example.archives/*.arc *.oldarc )
then
        :
else
    ERROR="TRUE";echo "Copy of archive logs failed">>$LOGFILE
fi
# Now backup a control file
svrmgrl << ending6
        connect internal
        alter database example
        backup controlfile to
        '/usr/oracle/oracle7/db_example/ora_control.bac
        reuse;
        exit
ending6
if ( $dup_it /usr/oracle/oracle7/db_example/ora_control.bac )
then
        :
else
    ERROR="TRUE";echo "Tar backup failed for control file">>$LOGFILE
fi
# now backup all archive logs
if ( $dup_it /usr/oracle/oracle7/db_example.archives/*.oldarc )
then
        :
else
    ERROR="TRUE";echo "Tar backup failed for archive files">>$LOGFILE
fi
# Now delete logs
if ( rm /usr/m_oracle/oracle7/db_examples.archives/*.oldarc;* )
then
    ERROR="TRUE"
else
    ERROR="TRUE";echo "Delete of archive files failed">>$LOGFILE
fi
done
exit
done
```

One problem with a canned script of the type shown for UNIX hot backup is that it doesn't automatically reconfigure itself to include new tablespaces—or redo logs. The script in Source 15.2 is an example of how to let Oracle build its own hot backup script using dynamic SQL and the data dictionary. The output from the script for my test database is shown in Source 15.3.

Source 15.2   Example of script to generate a hot backup script on UNIX.

```
REM Script to create a hot backup script on UNIX
REM Created 6/23/98 MRA
REM
create table bu_temp (line_no number,line_txt varchar2(2000))
storage (initial 1m next 1m pctincrease 0);
truncate table bu_temp;
set verify off embedded off lines 1000 termout off long 1000
define dest_dir=&1;
declare
--
-- Declare cursors
--
-- Cursor to get all tablespace names
--
cursor get_tbsp is
select tablespace_name from dba_tablespaces;
--
-- cursor to create BEGIN BACKUP command
--
cursor bbu_com (tbsp varchar2) is
select
'alter tablespace '||tablespace_name||' begin backup;'
from dba_tablespaces where tablespace_name=tbsp;
--
-- Cursor to create HOST backup commands
--
cursor tar1_com (tbsp varchar2) is
select '! /bin/tar cvf - '||file_name
from dba_data_files where tablespace_name=tbsp
and file_id=(select min(file_id)from dba_data_files
where tablespace_name=tbsp);
--
cursor tar2_com (tbsp varchar2) is
select
file_name
from dba_data_files where tablespace_name=tbsp
and file_id>(select min(file_id) from dba_data_files
where tablespace_name=tbsp);
--
cursor tar3_com (tbsp varchar2) is
select '! /bin/tar cvf - '||file_name
from dba_data_files where tablespace_name=tbsp
and file_id=(select min(file_id)from dba_data_files
where tablespace_name=tbsp);
--
cursor comp_com (tbsp varchar2) is
select
'|compress -c
```

continues

Source 15.2   Continued.

```
>&&dest_dir/'||tablespace_name||'_'||to_char(sysdate,'dd_mon_yy')||'.Z'||chr(
10)
from dba_tablespaces where tablespace_name=tbsp;

--
-- Cursor to create END BACKUP command
--
cursor ebu_com (tbsp varchar2) is
select
'alter tablespace '||tablespace_name||' end backup;' from
dba_tablespaces
where tablespace_name=tbsp;
--
-- Cursor to create redo log HOST backup commands
--
cursor tar1_rdo is
select '! /bin/tar cvf - '
from dual;
--
cursor tar2_rdo is
select
member||' '
from v$logfile;
--
cursor comp_rdo is
select
'|compress -c
>&&dest_dir/redo_logs_'||to_char(sysdate,'dd_mon_yy')||'.Z'||chr(10)
from dual;
--
-- Temporary variable declarations
--
tbsp_name varchar2(64);
line_num number:=0;
line_text varchar2(2000);
fetch_text varchar2(2000);
min_value number;
first_tbsp boolean;
temp_var varchar2(128);
--
-- Begin build of commands into temporary table
--
begin
--
-- first, create script header
--
line_num := line_num+1;
select 'REM Online Backup Script for '||name||' instance'
into line_text from v$database;
insert into bu_temp values (line_num,line_text);
```

```
line_num := line_num+1;
select 'REM Script uses UNIX tar format backup commands'
into line_text from dual;
insert into bu_temp values (line_num,line_text);
line_num := line_num+1;
select 'REM created on '||to_char(sysdate, 'dd-mon-yyyy hh24:mi')||' by user
'||user
into line_text from dual;
insert into bu_temp values (line_num,line_text);
line_num := line_num+1;
select 'REM developed by Mike Ault - TUSC 2-May-2001'
into line_text from dual;
insert into bu_temp values (line_num,line_text);
line_num := line_num+1;
select 'REM Script expects to be fed backup directory location on execution.'
into line_text from dual;
insert into bu_temp values (line_num,line_text);
line_num := line_num+1;
select 'REM Script should be re-run anytime physical structure of database
altered.'
into line_text from dual;
insert into bu_temp values (line_num,line_text);
line_num := line_num+1;
select 'REM '
into line_text from dual;
insert into bu_temp values (line_num,line_text);
line_num := line_num+1;
select 'spool &&dest_dir/log/hot_bu'||to_char(sysdate,'dd_mon_yy')||'.log'
into line_text from dual;
insert into bu_temp values (line_num,line_text);
line_num := line_num+1;
--
-- Now get tablespace names and loop through until all are handled
--
commit;
open get_tbsp;
first_tbsp:=TRUE;
loop
--
-- Get name
--
    fetch get_tbsp into tbsp_name;
    exit when get_tbsp%NOTFOUND;
--
-- Add comments to script showing which tablespace
--
    select 'REM' into line_text from dual;
    insert into bu_temp values (line_num,line_text);
    line_num:=line_num+1;
    select 'REM Backup for tablespace '||tbsp_name into line_text from dual;
```

continues

Source 15.2   Continued.

```
      insert into bu_temp values (line_num,line_text);
      line_num:=line_num+1;
      select 'REM' into line_text from dual;
      insert into bu_temp values (line_num,line_text);
      line_num:=line_num+1;
--
-- Get begin backup command built for this tablespace
--
      open bbu_com (tbsp_name);
      fetch bbu_com into line_text;
      insert into bu_temp values (line_num,line_text);
      line_num:=line_num+1;
      close bbu_com;
--
-- The actual backup commands are per datafile, open cursor and loop
--
      open tar1_com (tbsp_name);
      open tar2_com (tbsp_name);
      open tar3_com (tbsp_name);
      open comp_com (tbsp_name);
      min_value:=1;
         line_text:=NULL;
      loop
         if min_value=1
         then
         if first_tbsp THEN
                 fetch tar1_com into fetch_text;
                 select trim(fetch_text) into line_text from dual;
                 else
                 fetch tar3_com into fetch_text;
                 select trim(fetch_text) into line_text from dual;
         end if;
         else
         fetch tar2_com into fetch_text;
                 exit when tar2_com%NOTFOUND;
                 select trim(line_text)||' '||trim(fetch_text) into line_text
from dual;
         end if;
           first_tbsp:=FALSE;
        min_value:=min_value+1;
      end loop;
      fetch comp_com into fetch_text;
      select trim(line_text)||' '||trim(fetch_text) into line_text from dual;
        insert into bu_temp values (line_num,line_text);
        line_num:=line_num+1;
    close tar1_com;
    close tar2_com;
    close tar3_com;
    close comp_com;
```

```
--
-- Build end backup command for this tablespace
--
  open ebu_com(tbsp_name);
  fetch ebu_com into line_text;
  insert into bu_temp values (line_num,line_text);
  line_num:=line_num+1;
  close ebu_com;
end loop;
  close get_tbsp;
--
-- Backup redo logs, normally you won't recover redo logs you
-- will use your current redo logs so current SCN information not lost
-- commands just here for completeness
--
  select 'REM' into line_text from dual;
  insert into bu_temp values (line_num,line_text);
  line_num:=line_num+1;
  select 'REM Backup for redo logs' into line_text from dual;
  insert into bu_temp values (line_num,line_text);
  line_num:=line_num+1;
  select 'REM Normally you will not recover redo logs' into line_text from
dual;
  insert into bu_temp values (line_num,line_text);
  line_num:=line_num+1;
  select 'REM' into line_text from dual;
  insert into bu_temp values (line_num,line_text);
  line_num:=line_num+1;
--
-- Create host backup commands for all redo logs
--
  open tar1_rdo;
  open tar2_rdo;
  open comp_rdo;
  min_value:=1;
  loop
     if min_value=1
     then
      fetch tar1_rdo into fetch_text;
         select trim(fetch_text) into line_text from dual;
         else
        fetch tar2_rdo into fetch_text;
         select trim(line_text)||' '||trim(fetch_text) into line_text from
dual;
       exit when tar2_rdo%NOTFOUND;
     end if;
         min_value:=min_value+1;
  end loop;
  fetch comp_rdo into fetch_text;
  select trim(line_text)||' '||trim(fetch_text) into line_text from dual;
```

continues

Source 15.2   Continued.

```
    insert into bu_temp values (line_num,line_text);
    line_num:=line_num+1;
    close tar1_rdo;
    close tar2_rdo;
    close comp_rdo;
--
-- Now get all archive logs, performing a switch to be sure all
-- required archives are written out
--
    select 'REM' into line_text from dual;
    insert into bu_temp values (line_num,line_text);
    line_num:=line_num+1;
    select 'REM Backup for archive logs' into line_text from dual;
    insert into bu_temp values (line_num,line_text);
    line_num:=line_num+1;
    select 'REM' into line_text from dual;
    insert into bu_temp values (line_num,line_text);
    line_num:=line_num+1;
    select 'alter system switch logfile;' into line_text from dual;
    insert into bu_temp values (line_num,line_text);
    line_num:=line_num+1;
    select 'alter system archive log all;' into line_text from dual;
    insert into bu_temp values (line_num,line_text);
    line_num:=line_num+1;
--
-- The next command builds the actual backup command based on the
-- value of the log_archive_dest initialization parameter, it looks for the
-- last right square bracket in the name and just uses that section with
-- a wildcard
--
    temp_var:=null;
    select substr (value,1,instr(value,'/',-1,1)) into temp_var
     from v$parameter where name='log_archive_dest';
    if temp_var is not null
    then
    select '! compress '||substr (value,1,instr(value,'/',-1,1))||'/*'
    into line_text from v$parameter where name='log_archive_dest';
    insert into bu_temp values (line_num,line_text);
    line_num:=line_num+1;
    select '! tar cvf - '||substr (value,1,instr(value,'/',-1,1))||'/*.Z'||
    '|compress -c >&&dest_dir/'||
    substr (value,instr(value,'/',-
1,1)+1,length(value))||'_'||to_char(sysdate,'dd_mon_yy')||'.Z'
    into line_text from v$parameter where name='log_archive_dest';
    insert into bu_temp values (line_num,line_text);
    line_num:=line_num+1;
    else
      select 'REM no log_archive_dest specified' into line_text from dual;
```

```
  insert into bu_temp values (line_num,line_text);
  line_num:=line_num+1;
 end if;
 temp_var:=null;
 select substr (value,10,instr(value,'/',-1,1)) into temp_var
  from v$parameter where name='log_archive_dest_1';
 if temp_var is not null
 then
 select '! compress '||substr (value,10,instr(value,'/',-1,1))||'/*'
 into line_text from v$parameter where name='log_archive_dest_1';
 insert into bu_temp values (line_num,line_text);
 line_num:=line_num+1;
 select '! tar cvf - '||substr (value,10,instr(value,'/',-1,1))||'/*.Z'||
 '|compress -c >&&dest_dir/'||
 substr (value,instr(value,'/',-
1,1)+1,length(value))||'_'||to_char(sysdate,'dd_mon_yy')||'.Z'
 into line_text from v$parameter where name='log_archive_dest_1';
 insert into bu_temp values (line_num,line_text);
 line_num:=line_num+1;
  else
  select 'REM no log_archive_dest_1 specified' into line_text from dual;
  insert into bu_temp values (line_num,line_text);
  line_num:=line_num+1;
 end if;
--
-- Next, backup a control file just to be sure
-- we have a good one available that is current with this backup
--
  select 'alter database backup controlfile to
'||chr(39)||'&&dest_dir'||'/ora_cnbkp_'||to_char(sysdate,'dd_mon_yy')||'.bac'
||chr(39)||';'
  into line_text from dual;
  insert into bu_temp values (line_num,line_text);
  line_num:=line_num+1;
  select 'spool off'||chr(10) into line_text from dual;
  insert into bu_temp values (line_num,line_text);
  line_num:=line_num+1;
  commit;
end;
/
rem
rem Now generate output based on bu_temp table contents
rem
set verify off feedback off heading off termout off pages 0
set embedded on lines 1000
column line_no noprint
column dbname new_value db noprint
select value dbname from v$parameter where name='db_name';
spool rep_out/&db/thot_bu.sql
```

continues

Source 15.2 **Continued.**

```
select * from bu_temp order by line_no;
spool off
rem directory syntax for UNIX
rem
! sed '1,$ s/ *$//g' rep_out/&db/thot_bu.sql>rep_out/&db/hot_bu.sql
rem
drop table bu_temp;
set verify on feedback on heading on termout on pages 22
set embedded off lines 80
clear columns
undef dest_dir
```

Source 15.3 **Example output from the hot backup script generator.**

```
REM Online Backup Script for AULTDB1 instance
REM Script uses UNIX tar format backup commands
REM created on 27-nov-2001 11:21 by user SYSTEM
REM developed by Mike Ault - TUSC 2-May-2001
REM Script expects to be fed backup directory location on execution.
REM Script should be re-run anytime physical structure of database altered.
REM
spool /opt/backup/aultdb1/log/hot_bu27_nov_01.log
REM
REM Backup for tablespace SYSTEM
REM
alter tablespace SYSTEM begin backup;
! /bin/tar cvf - /ora1/ORACLE/ORADATA/AULTDB1/SYSTEM01.DBF |compress -c
>/opt/backup/aultdb1/SYSTEM_27_nov_01.Z
alter tablespace SYSTEM end backup;
REM
REM Backup for tablespace RBS
REM
alter tablespace RBS begin backup;
! /bin/tar cvf - /ora2/ORACLE/ORADATA/AULTDB1/RBS01.DBF |compress -c
>/opt/backup/aultdb1/RBS_27_nov_01.Z
alter tablespace RBS end backup;
REM
REM Backup for tablespace USERS
REM
alter tablespace USERS begin backup;
! /bin/tar cvf - /ora3/ORACLE/ORADATA/AULTDB1/USERS01.DBF |compress -c
>/opt/backup/aultdb1/USERS_27_nov_01.Z
alter tablespace USERS end backup;
REM
REM Backup for tablespace TEMP
REM
alter tablespace TEMP begin backup;
```

```
! /bin/tar cvf - /ora4/ORACLE/ORADATA/AULTDB1/TEMP01.DBF |compress -c
>/opt/backup/aultdb1/TEMP_27_nov_01.Z
alter tablespace TEMP end backup;
REM
REM Backup for tablespace TOOLS
REM
alter tablespace TOOLS begin backup;
! /bin/tar cvf - /ora5/ORACLE/ORADATA/AULTDB1/TOOLS01.DBF |compress -c
>/opt/backup/aultdb1/TOOLS_27_nov_01.Z
alter tablespace TOOLS end backup;
REM
REM Backup for tablespace INDX
REM
alter tablespace INDX begin backup;
! /bin/tar cvf - /ora5/ORACLE/ORADATA/AULTDB1/INDX01.DBF |compress -c
>/opt/backup/aultdb1/INDX_27_nov_01.Z
alter tablespace INDX end backup;
REM
REM Backup for tablespace DRSYS
REM
alter tablespace DRSYS begin backup;
! /bin/tar cvf - /ora1/ORACLE/ORADATA/AULTDB1/DR01.DBF |compress -c
>/opt/backup/aultdb1/DRSYS_27_nov_01.Z
alter tablespace DRSYS end backup;
REM
REM Backup for tablespace PERFSTAT
REM
alter tablespace PERFSTAT begin backup;
! /bin/tar cvf - /ora1/ORACLE/ORADATA/AULTDB1/PERFSTAT.DBF |compress -c
>/opt/backup/aultdb1/PERFSTAT_27_nov_01.Z
alter tablespace PERFSTAT end backup;
REM
REM Backup for tablespace TEST_2K
REM
alter tablespace TEST_2K begin backup;
! /bin/tar cvf - /ora2/ORACLE/ORADATA/AULTDB1/TEST_2K.DBF |compress -c
>/opt/backup/aultdb1/TEST_2K_27_nov_01.Z
alter tablespace TEST_2K end backup;
REM
REM Backup for redo logs
REM Normally you will not recover redo logs
REM
! /bin/tar cvf - /ora6/ORACLE/ORADATA/AULTDB1/REDO011.LOG
/ora6/ORACLE/ORADATA/AULTDB1/REDO032.LOG
/ora7/ORACLE/ORADATA/AULTDB1/REDO021.LOG
/ora7/ORACLE/ORADATA/AULTDB1/REDO012.LOG
/ora8/ORACLE/ORADATA/AULTDB1/REDO031.LOG
/ora8/ORACLE/ORADATA/AULTDB1/REDO022.LOG |compress -c
>/opt/backup/aultdb1/redo_logs_27_nov_01.Z
```

continues

Source 15.3   Continued.

```
REM
REM Backup for archive logs
REM
alter system switch logfile;
alter system archive log all;
host compress /ora9/ORACLE/ORADATA/AULTDB1/ARCHIVE/*
host tar cvrf - *.Z|compress>/tape1/_25_may_99.Z
alter database backup controlfile to
'/opt/backup/aultdb1/ora_cnbkp_27_nov_01.bac';
spool off
```

Similar scripts are provided on the Wiley Web site for both OpenVMS and NT. You will need to verify that the target directories exist, or you will have to modify the scripts before running them. The NT script assumes a backup staging area is being used, which is then backed up to tape.

I suggest generating the backup script at the same time as the recovery script. Source 15.4 shows an example of a recovery script generator for NT.

Source 15.4   Example of recovery script generator for NT.

```
REM Script to create a hot backup recovery script on NT using ocopy
REM Created 6/23/98 MRA
REM
create table bu_temp (line_no number,line_txt varchar2(2000));
truncate table bu_temp;
set verify off embedded off esc ^
REM &&ora_home &&dest_dir
column dup new_value dup_it noprint
select ''||chr(39)||'&&ora_home'||'\ocopy '||chr(39)||'' dup
from dual;

declare
--
-- Declare cursors
--
-- Cursor to get all tablespace names
--
cursor get_tbsp is
select tablespace_name from dba_tablespaces;
--
-- Cursor to create recovery commands
--
cursor rec_com (tbsp varchar2) is
select
&&dup_it||' '||'&&dest_dir'||'\datafiles\'||tbsp||file_id||'.bck '||file_name
from dba_data_files where tablespace_name=tbsp;
```

```
--
-- Cursor to create redo log recovery commands
--
cursor rec_rdo (num number) is
select
&&dup_it||
'
'||'&&dest_dir'||'\logs'||substr(member,instr(member,'\LOG',2,1),instr(member
,'.',1,1))||' '||
member
from v$logfile order by group#;
--
-- Temporary variable declarations
--
tbsp_name varchar2(64);
line_num number:=0;
line_text varchar2(2000);
num number:=0;
--
-- Begin build of commands into temporary table
--
begin
--
-- first, create script header
--
line_num := line_num+1;
select 'REM Recovery Script for '||name||' instance'
into line_text from v$database;
insert into bu_temp values (line_num,line_text);
line_num := line_num+1;
select 'REM Script uses ocopy - NT format backup commands'
into line_text from dual;
insert into bu_temp values (line_num,line_text);
line_num := line_num+1;
select 'REM created on '||to_char(sysdate, 'dd-mon-yyyy hh24:mi')||' by user
'||user
into line_text from dual;
insert into bu_temp values (line_num,line_text);
line_num := line_num+1;
select 'REM developed for RevealNet by Mike Ault - DMR Consulting 15-Dec-
1998'
into line_text from dual;
insert into bu_temp values (line_num,line_text);
line_num := line_num+1;
select 'REM '
into line_text from dual;
insert into bu_temp values (line_num,line_text);
line_num := line_num+1;
select 'REM Script should be re-run anytime physical structure of database
altered.'
```

continues

Source 15.4   Continued.

```
into line_text from dual;
insert into bu_temp values (line_num,line_text);
line_num := line_num+1;
select 'REM '
into line_text from dual;
insert into bu_temp values (line_num,line_text);
line_num := line_num+1;
--
-- Now get tablespace names and loop through until all are handled
--
open get_tbsp;
loop
--
-- Get name
--
    fetch get_tbsp into tbsp_name;
    exit when get_tbsp%NOTFOUND;
--
-- Add comments to script showing which tablespace
--
    select 'REM' into line_text from dual;
      insert into bu_temp values (line_num,line_text);
    line_num:=line_num+1;
    select 'REM Recovery for tablespace '||tbsp_name into line_text from
dual;
      insert into bu_temp values (line_num,line_text);
    line_num:=line_num+1;
    select 'REM' into line_text from dual;
      insert into bu_temp values (line_num,line_text);
    line_num:=line_num+1;
--
-- The actual recovery commands are per datafile, open cursor and loop
--
        open rec_com (tbsp_name);
        loop
                fetch rec_com into line_text;
              exit when rec_com%NOTFOUND;
          line_num:=line_num+1;
          insert into bu_temp values (line_num,line_text);
        end loop;
      close rec_com;
end loop;
  close get_tbsp;
--
-- Recover redo logs, normally you won't recover redo logs you
-- will use your current redo logs so current SCN information not lost
-- commands just here for completeness uncomment commands below to
-- enable redo log recovery (not advised)
--
```

```
  select 'REM' into line_text from dual;
  insert into bu_temp values (line_num,line_text);
  line_num:=line_num+1;
  select 'REM Recovery for redo logs' into line_text from dual;
  insert into bu_temp values (line_num,line_text);
  line_num:=line_num+1;
  select 'REM Normally you will not recover redo logs' into line_text from
dual;
  insert into bu_temp values (line_num,line_text);
  line_num:=line_num+1;
  select 'REM' into line_text from dual;
  insert into bu_temp values (line_num,line_text);
  line_num:=line_num+1;
--
-- Create host backup commands for all redo logs
--
  /*open rec_rdo(num);
  loop
     fetch rec_rdo into line_text;
     exit when rec_rdo%NOTFOUND;
     num:=num+1;
     line_num:=line_num+1;
     insert into bu_temp values (line_num,line_text);
  end loop;
  close rec_rdo;*/
--
-- Now recover all archive logs
--
  line_num:=line_num+1;
  select 'REM' into line_text from dual;
  insert into bu_temp values (line_num,line_text);
  line_num:=line_num+1;
  select 'REM Recovery for archive logs' into line_text from dual;
  insert into bu_temp values (line_num,line_text);
  line_num:=line_num+1;
  select 'REM' into line_text from dual;
  insert into bu_temp values (line_num,line_text);
  line_num:=line_num+1;
--
-- The next command builds the actual recovery command based on the
-- value of the log_archive_dest initialization parameter, it looks for the
-- last right square bracket in the name and just uses that section with
-- a wildcard
--
  select &&dup_it||' '||'&&dest_dir'||'\archives\*.* '||value||'\*.*'
  into line_text from v$parameter where name='log_archive_dest';
  line_num:=line_num+1;
  insert into bu_temp values (line_num,line_text);
end;
/
```

continues

Source 15.4   Continued.

```
rem
rem Now generate output based on bu_temp table contents
rem
set verify off feedback off heading off termout off pages 0
set embedded on lines 132
column db_name new_value db noprint
column line_no noprint
select name db_name from v$database;
spool rep_out\&&db\rec_db.bat
select * from bu_temp order by line_no;
spool off
rem
rem get rid of bu_temp table
rem
drop table bu_temp;
set verify on feedback on heading on termout on pages 22
set embedded off lines 80 esc \
clear columns
undef ora_home
undef dest_dir
exit
```

A script for UNIX is also provided on the Wiley Web site. Once you have generated the scripts to generate the online backup and recovery files, document them. The next section presents an example of the documentation procedure for the NT online backup and recovery scripts.

Example of Documentation Procedure for NT Online Backup and Recovery Scripts

This section shows a sample set of procedures for using the NT Oracle hot backup and recovery scripts.

Backup   In order to use the supplied backup scripts for NT, the following procedure must be followed.

1. Run nt_oline_bu.sql from SQL*Plus DBA account.
2. Run nt_rec_db.sql script from SQL*Plus DBA account.
3. Move a copy of the rec_db.bat script generated in step 2 to the backup directory.
4. From an SQ*LPLUS command-line session (using the e:\orant81\bin\sqlplus executable), run the thot_bu.sql script generated in step 1.
5. Once step 4 completes (should take less than two hours), copy the backup directory (i:\backup), using the system backup tool, to tape.
6. Remove the archive logs that were copied from the database archive log destination to tape from the archive log destination.

Recovery In order to perform NT recovery using the provided scripts, the following procedure must be followed:

1. Using the system backup tools, restore the Oracle backup files to the backup location on the database server (for example: i:\backup).
2. Run the recovered copy of the rec_db.bat script to restore the backup files to their proper locations.
3. Manually start the Oracle services and the tns listener process using the Control Panel Services icon.
4. From the command line, use the svrmgrl executable to start up and mount (but not open) the database:

```
>svrmgrl
svrmgrl>connect internal@fsys.world
password: xxxxxxxxx
connected to an idle instance
svrmgrl>startup mount pfile=e:\orant\database\init<SID>.ora  (Be sure to use
the location of your initialization file)
<will see normal startup messages>
svrmgrl> recover
<server will prompt for needed files; they should be already copied to
machine, so just press Return at each prompting>
        media recovery complete
svrmgrl> alter database open
        database altered
```

5. Shut down and perform a cold backup of all database files (essentially, take the ocopy commands from inside the thot_bu.sql script and run them as a .bat file). Do not back up the archive logs; after a cold backup they are not needed anymore.
6. Remove all archive logs from system.
7. Database has been recovered; resume normal operations.

The actual backup process can be automated on NT using the WINAT scheduler, available from the Microsoft Web site or the Microsoft support or toolkit CD-ROM. A script similar to the one shown in Source 15.5 should be used to start the backup.

Source 15.5   Example of NT .bat script to start backup.

```
REM do_hot_bu.bat
REM File to generate and execute hot backup script for Oracle
REM Used for ORTEST1 database only
REM Mike Ault DMR Consulting 1/7/99
REM
REM First, generate the thot_bu.sql script
REM
cd c:\sql_scripts
REM
e:\orant81\bin\sqlplus -s system/manager@ortest1.world
@c:\sql_scripts\nt_oline_bu.sql
```

continues

Source 15.5   Continued.

```
REM
REM Now generate the recovery script so they are in-sync
REM
e:\orant81\bin\sqlplus -s system/manager@ortest1.world
@c:\dmr_temp\nt_rec_db.sql
REM
REM Copy the recovery script to the backup destination
REM
copy c:\sql_scripts\rep_out\ortest1\rec_db.bat i:\backup\rec_db.bat
REM
REM Run the backup script
REM
e:\orant81\bin\sqlplus -s system/manager@ortest1.world
@c:\sql_scripts\rep_out\ortest1\thot_bu.sql
REM
REM End of script
REM
Exit
```

Using NT pass-in variables eliminates the need to store your username and password in the script. For an example of how this is done, look in your database directory for the Oracle shutdown script.

15.2 IMPORTS/EXPORTS

Imports and exports extract or insert an Oracle-readable copy of the actual data and structures in the database. The exports can be used to recover single data structures to the date and time the export was taken. Exports come in three types: full, cumulative, and incremental. Full, as its name implies, provides a full logical copy of the database and its structures. A cumulative provides a complete copy of altered structures since the last full or the last cumulative export. Incremental exports provide a complete copy of altered structures since the last incremental, cumulative, or full export.

Limitations on export/import are as follows:

- A database must be running to perform either an export or import.
- Export files shouldn't be edited and can only be used by import.
- Import only: Imports full tables; it can't be used to do a conditional load.
- Exported data is only a logical copy of the data. An export can only allow recovery to the date and time the export was taken.

Imports and exports are accomplished using the Oracle IMPORT and EXPORT utilities.

EXPORT Utility

For exports, the EXPORT utility is used. The format for using this command follows:

```
Format:  EXP KEYWORD=value -or- KEYWORD=(list of values)
Example: EXP AULT/AUTHOR GRANTS=N TABLES=(CHAPTERS, EDITORS,ADVANCES)
```

Keyword	*Description (Default)*
USERID	User name/password.
BUFFER	Size of data buffer.
FILE	Output file (EXPDAT.DMP).
COMPRESS	Import into one extent (Y).
GRANTS	Export grants (Y).
INDEXES	Export indexes (Y).
ROWS	Export data rows (Y).
CONSTRAINTS	Export table constraints (Y).
CONSISTENT	Cross-table consistency (N).
LOG	Log file of screen output (None).
STATISTICS	Analyze objects (ESTIMATE).
DIRECT	Bypass the SQL command processing layer (N) (new in Oracle8).
FEEDBACK	Show a process meter (a dot) every X rows exported (0 – X value).
HELP	
MLS, MLS_LABEL_FORMAT	Used with secure Oracle; not covered in this text.
FULL	Export entire file (N).
OWNER	List of owner user names.
TABLES	List of table names.
RECORDLENGTH	Length of I/O record.
INCTYPE	Incremental export type.
RECORD	Track incremental export (Y).
PARFILE	Parameter file name.

Exports should be automated and scheduled to run automatically. An export methodology should be worked out such that the DBA is reasonably certain a deleted file can be recovered. The parameters for export can either be placed on the command line or in a parameter file, which can then be accessed using the PARFILE command-line option.

IMPORT

The format of the IMPORT command follows:

```
Format:  IMP KEYWORD=value . . . or . . . KEYWORD=(list of values)
Example: IMP AULT/AUTHOR IGNORE=Y TABLES=(EXPENSES, ADVANCES) FULL=N
```

Keyword	Description (Default)
USERID	User name/password.
BUFFER	Size of data buffer.
FILE	Output file (EXPDAT.DMP).
SHOW	Just list file contents (N).
IGNORE	Ignore create errors (N).
RECORDLENGTH	Length of I/O record.
GRANTS	Import grants (Y).
INDEXES	Import indexes (Y).
ROWS	Import data rows (Y).
LOG	Log file of screen output.
INDEXFILE	Write table/index info to specified file.
FULL	Import entire file (N).
FROMUSER	List of owner user names.
TOUSER	List of user names.
TABLES	List of table names.
FEEDBACK	Provide dot status graph (0).
INCTYPE	Incremental import type.
COMMIT	Commit array insert (N).
PARFILE	Parameter file name.
DESTROY	Overwrite tablespace data (N).
CHARSET	Character set of export file (NLS_LANG).

Under Oracle7, the user must be granted the EXP_FULL_DATABASE role in order to do full exports. In order to perform a full import, the user must have the IMP_FULL_DATABASE role. The users with the DBA role are granted these implicitly.

An example of when the DBA would want to grant these roles to a user would be a user whose password is specified in the command script used for doing the automatic exports. If the only role granted to the user is CREATE_SESSION and EXP_FULL_DATABASE, even if the user's password is compromised, he or she won't be able to do much damage.

15.3 ARCHIVE LOGS

The redo logs store all transactions that alter the database, all committed updates, adds, or deletes of tables, structures, or data. If archiving is disabled, only data in the current offline and online redo logs can be recovered. If the system recycles through all redo logs, the old ones are reused, destroying their contents. If archive logging is enabled, the redo logs are written out to storage before reuse. Archive logging allows recovery to a specific point in time since the last full cold backup or complete offline backup. Under versions after Oracle8*i*, archive logs can be duplexed. The initialization parameters that control archive logging are:

Parameter	*Meaning*
LOG_ARCHIVE_START	If set to TRUE, start archive process.
LOG_ARCHIVE_BUFFERS	Number of log archive buffers.
LOG_ARCHIVE_BUFFER_SIZE	Size of the log archive buffers.
LOG_ARCHIVE_MIN_SUCCEED_DEST	Percentage of archive logs that must reach destinations.
LOG_ARCHIVE_DEST	Primary archive log location.
LOG_ARCHIVE_DUPLEX_DEST	Secondary archive log location.
LOG_ARCHIVE_DEST_1	Archive tertiary location 1.
LOG_ARCHIVE_DEST_2	Archive tertiary location 2.
LOG_ARCHIVE_DEST_3	Archive tertiary location 3.
LOG_ARCHIVE_DEST_4	Archive tertiary location 4.
LOG_ARCHIVE_DEST_5	Archive tertiary location 5.
LOG_ARCHIVE_FORMAT	Specifies the format for archive log names; use the "%s" and "%t" format specifiers to add the sequence and redo thread numbers to the format.

Under Oracle8, Oracle8*i,* and Oracle9*i*, redo logs are specified in groups; each group forms a shadow set and is archived together. Archive logs can also be assigned to threads for use in shared or RAC instances. Individual logs are called members. Threads hold groups that hold members. Each member of a redo log group is the same size and should be on separate physical platters or arrays. Oracle automatically synchronizes members of a group into a shadow set.

Redo logs cannot be used to recover a database brought back from a full export.

To switch a database that is not currently using archive logging to use archive logging, the steps are:

1. Shut down database using immediate or normal options.
2. Edit the initialization parameter file to include appropriate archive log parameters, at a minimum:

```
ARCHIVE_LOG_START = TRUE
ARCHIVE_LOG_DEST1 = destination (operating system specific path to archive
log destination)
ARCHIVE_LOG_FORMAT = arch_%t_%s.arc
```

Usually the defaults for LOG_ARCHIVE_BUFFERS and LOG_ARCHIVE_BUFFER_SIZE are sufficient.

3. Using the appropriate interface (svrmgrl, sqlplus, OEM) start up the database in mounted mode:

```
sqlplus> connect sys/password as sysdba
sqlplus> startup mount (s)pfile=<initialization file location>
```

4. Use the ALTER DATABASE command to reset the ARCHIVELOG mode:

```
sqlplus> ALTER DATABASE ARCHIVELOG;
```

5. Use the ALTER DATABASE command to open the database:

```
sqlplus> ALTER DATABASE OPEN;
```

6. Either shut down and perform a cold backup or perform a hot backup. Since this is the first backup, I would suggest a cold backup be used. This is the baseline backup of your database.
7. Restart the database as you would normally.

Proper use of these backup/recovery tools allows the DBA to recover from any possible failure.

15.4 ORACLE9*i* RECOVERY MANAGER FACILITY

Oracle8 introduced the recovery manager, rman, which can be thought of as the Enterprise Backup Utility on steroids. Oracle8*i* and Oracle9*i* have improved the usability and stability of rman. rman allows the backup of database files at the block level and automatically performs datafile compression by only backing up blocks that have been used or altered. In incremental mode, the rman only backs up blocks that have been altered or added in the database, greatly reducing the size of required backups.

rman also allows the following:

- Scripting with rman script language, backup, and restore operations
- Reports on backup status and backup file status
- Use of a recovery catalog to facilitate backup and restore operations
- Parallelization of backup and restore operations
- Backup based on specified limits (i.e., amount of redo generated against a file)
- Backup of database, tablespace, or individual datafiles
- Batch backup operations

rman uses a recovery catalog. However, you can use rman without a catalog from just the data stored in the control files, but you are restricted to a subset of rman's capabilities in this mode. The catalog contains information on the following:

- Datafile and archive log backup sets and pieces
- Datafile copies
- Archived redo logs and copies of them
- Tablespaces and datafiles at the target database
- Named, user-created sequences of commands called stored scripts

It is a good practice to maintain a small database strictly for the recovery catalog and perhaps the Enterprise Manager catalog files. The catalog should be resynchronized with all remote databases on a periodic basis. If you don't use a catalog, you cannot do the following:

- Point-in-time recovery
- Use stored scripts
- Recovery if a control file is not available

rman creates backup sets that consist of backup pieces. Backup pieces are parts of the backup set at a size that is predetermined and usually based on the backup media capacity of operating system file-size limitations. Backup sets can be written to disk or secondary storage, can include a backup control file, and can span multiple OS files (pieces). Backup devices that are supported on your system are cataloged in the v$backup_device dynamic performance table.

rman backup sets that contain archive logs are called, appropriately enough, archivelog backup sets. With Oracle8, you cannot write archive logs directly to tape, but a job can be scheduled using rman to back archive log backup sets to tape or other storage.

rman produces either full or incremental backups. A full backup is a backup of one or more datafiles that contains all blocks of the datafile(s) that have been modified or changed. Full backups can be created out of:

- Datafiles
- Datafile copies

- Tablespaces (all datafiles for a tablespace)
- Archive logs
- Control files (current or backups)
- Entire databases

An incremental backup is a backup of one or more files and contains only blocks that have been modified. However, only complete control files are backed up in either incremental or full backups. Incremental backups can be made of:

- Datafiles
- Tablespaces
- Databases

The incremental backup allows the leveling of backups. Each level is denoted by an integer value, with the level of backup meaning that any blocks changed since the last incremental backup at this level will be backed up the next time this level is specified. This allows levels to be set based on timeframes; for example, 0 being a monthly full, 1 being a once-a-week incremental, and 2 being a daily incremental. Of course, this also leads to complicated rotation of tapes or backup media, taking us back to the good old towers-of-Hanoi backup scenario nightmares.

rman also allows for image copies of datafiles, archive logs, or control files. Image copies can only be made to disk and cannot contain multiple files.

rman allows report generation. Reports can be generated based on:

- Which files need backup
- Which files haven't been backed up recently
- Which backup files can be deleted

Each backup set can be associated with a tag that can be used to identify it in subsequent operations. The tag doesn't have to be unique. rman selects the most recent backup set in the case of backup sets with duplicate tags.

rman works against running or shutdown databases whether they are in archive log mode or not. However, if the database is not in archive log mode, the entire database can only be backed up if it was shut down cleanly. Tablespaces can only be backed up in NOARCHIVELOG mode if they are offline normal. There are no restrictions of this type on databases in ARCHIVELOG mode.

rman automatically detects corruptions and logs these in v$backup_corruption and v$copy_corruption dynamic performance tables. Corrupt blocks are still backed up.

Installing the rman Catalog

The catalog should be owned by a user with the resource role grant. I suggest a user in a small database dedicated to system administration functions such as the rman catalog and Enterprise Manager catalog. Create a tablespace for use by the rman user and assign that as the user's default tablespace with unlimited quota. For example, if we wanted our user to be named rman_dba, the steps would be as follows:

```
sqlplus system/manager
SQL>CREATE TABLESPACE rman_data DATAFILE 'file_spec' DEFAULT STORAGE
(clause);
SQL>CREATE USER rman_dba IDENTIFIED BY rman_dba
 2: DEFAULT TABLESPACE rman_data
 3: TEMPORARY TABLESPACE  temp
 4: QUOTA UNLIMITED ON rman_data;
SQL>GRANT RESOURCE,CONNECT TO rman_dba;
SQL>CONNECT rman_dba/rman_dba
SQL> CREATE CATALOG
```

Once the catalog has been built, the Recovery Manager can be utilized. The command is rman, rman80, or RMAN80, depending on your Oracle version and operating system (beginning with 8*i*, it will be only rman with no version identifier). There are literally dozens of commands for use with the rman facility. I suggest reviewing the *Oracle9i Backup and Recovery Concepts Release 1 (9.0.1)*, Part Number A90133-02 (or most current release) (Oracle Corporation, June 2001) and *Oracle9i Recovery Manager User's Guide Release 1 (9.0.1)*, Part Number A90135-01 (or most current release) (Oracle Corporation, June 2001) before using RMAN. In the remainder of this section I provide a sample scenario showing how the commands can be made into scripts.

Connection to RMAN in UNIX on early versions can be tricky. On some UNICES, the double quotation (") character has to be escaped, and you need to use the double quotation to log in to rman (at least on early versions). Assuming that the database to be backed up is ORTEST1 with a TNS alias of ORTEST1, the user is as specified earlier, and the catalog database is ORRMAN, the connection to RMAN for the user SYSTEM password MANAGER would look like this:

```
$ rman target ORTEST1 system/manager@ORTEST1  catalog
rman_dbo/rman_dbo@ORRMAN
```

The target database service name in the tnsnames.ora file is ORTEST1. The recovery catalog database service name in the tnsnames.ora file is ORRMAN.

```
% cd $ORACLE_HOME/rdbms/admin
% sqlplus sys/change_on_install@ORRMAN
SQL> grant connect, resource to RMAN_DBA identified by RMAN_DBA;
Grant succeeded.
SQL> connect rman/rman@ORRMAN
Connected.
SQL> CREATE CATALOG
SQL> exit
%
% rman target sys/change_on_install@ORTEST1 catalog rman/rman@ORRMAN
Recovery Manager: Release 8.0.2.0.0 - Beta
RMAN-06005: connected to target database: ORTEST1
```

```
RMAN-06008: connected to recovery catalog database
RMAN> register database;
RMAN-08006: database registered in recovery catalog
RMAN-08002: starting full resync of recovery catalog
RMAN-08004: full resync complete
RMAN> run
2> {
3> allocate channel c1 type disk;

4> backup full format '/oracle16/ORTEST1/amin/backup/backup%s%p' (database);
5> }

RMAN-08030: allocated channel: c1

RMAN-08500: channel c1: sid=12 devtype=DISK

RMAN-08008: channel c1: started datafile backupset
RMAN-08502: set_count=9 set_stamp=280246639

RMAN-08011: channel c1: including current controlfile in backupset
RMAN-08010: channel c1: including datafile number 1 in backupset
RMAN-08010: channel c1: including datafile number 2 in backupset
               .
               .
               .
RMAN-08010: channel c1: including datafile number 11 in backupset
RMAN-08010: channel c1: including datafile number 12 in backupset

RMAN-08013: channel c1: piece 1 created

RMAN-08503: piece handle=/oracle16/ORTEST1/admin/backup/backup91 comment=NONE
RMAN-08003: starting partial resync of recovery catalog
RMAN-08005: partial resync complete
RMAN-10030: RPC call appears to have failed to start on channel default
RMAN-10036: RPC call ok on channel default
RMAN-08031: released channel: c1
RMAN> exit
```

Incomplete Restore Scenario   The following shows the scenario for an incomplete recovery. The following scenario assumes that:

- You wish to do an incomplete recovery due to an application error that was made at a specific time.
- There are three tape drives.
- You are using a recovery catalog.

TIP   It is highly advisable to back up the database immediately after opening the database resetlogs.

The following script restores and recovers the database to the time immediately before the user error occurred. The script does the following:

1. Starts the database mount and restricts connections to DBA-only users.
2. Restores the database files (to the original locations).
3. Recovers the datafiles either by using a combination of incremental backups and redo or just redo. Recovery Manager will complete the recovery when it reaches the transaction from the time specified.
4. Opens the database resetlogs.

Oracle recommends that you back up your database after the resetlogs (this is not shown in the example).

Ensure that you set your NLS_LANG and NLS_DATE_FORMAT environment variables. You can set these to whatever you wish—the date format of the following example is the standard date format used for recovery; for example, for UNIX (csh):

```
> setenv NLS_LANG AMERICAN
> setenv NLS_DATE_FORMAT 'YYYY-MM-DD:hh24:mi:ss'
```

Next, start up SQLPLUS:

```
Sqlplus> connect sys as sysdba
password: xxxxxxx
Connected.
SVRMGR> startup mount restrict
SVRMGR>exit

#  rman target internal/knl@prod1 catalog rman/rman@rcat cmdfile case2.rcv
run {
#  The 'set until time' command is for all commands executed
#  between the { and } braces. Means both restore and recover
#  will both be relative to that point in time.
#  Note that Recovery Manager uses the Recovery Catalog to,
#  determine the structure of the database at that time, and
#  restore it.
#
   set until time '1997-06-23:15:45:00';
#
   allocate channel t1 type 'SBT_TAPE';
   allocate channel t2 type 'SBT_TAPE';
   allocate channel t3 type 'SBT_TAPE';
#
   restore
      (database);
#
#  There is no need to manually catalog logs before recovery,
#  as Recovery Manager does catalog resync from the current
#  control file.
#
```

```
    recover
      database;
 #
    sql 'alter database open resetlogs';
```

The preceding scenario is just an example of how to use the Recovery Manager. Please consult your manual before attempting to use the facility for production work. The RMAN readme file contains valuable insights into RMAN use and has several additional scenarios.

15.5 DB_VERIFY UTILITY

In this section I want to cover the DB_VERIFY utility. The DB_VERIFY utility is an external command line-based utility that is used to perform a physical structure integrity check on an offline (shutdown) database. The utility can be used against backup files and online files or pieces of online files. The utility is used to ensure a backup database or datafile is valid before recovery. The utility can also serve as a diagnostic aid when corruption is suspected.

DB_VERIFY runs against a shutdown database, so it can perform checks significantly faster than export or other utilities. Be aware that the utility is named differently on different platforms; for example, it may be called dbv on Sun, Sequent, Linux, or NT, or something else on your system. Therefore, verify its name with the system-specific documentation you should have received (if you didn't, call your Oracle rep and complain). The utility only verifies cache-managed blocks.

The DB_VERIFY utility has the following general syntax:

```
DBVERIFY: Release 9.0.1.1.1 - Production on Sun Mar 3 16:19:05 2002

(c) Copyright 2001 Oracle Corporation.  All rights reserved.

Keyword      Description                     (Default)
--------------------------------------------------------
FILE         File to Verify                  (NONE)
START        Start Block                     (First Block of File)
END          End Block                       (Last Block of File)
BLOCKSIZE    Logical Block Size              (2048)
LOGFILE      Output Log                      (NONE)
FEEDBACK     Display Progress                (0)
PARFILE      Parameter File                  (NONE)
USERID       Username/Password               (NONE)
SEGMENT_ID   Segment ID (tsn.relfile.block)  (NONE)
```

where:

FILE. The name of the database file to verify.

START. The starting block address to verify. These are Oracle block addresses. If you get an ORA error giving a file number and block that is corrupted, you can use this to check that block.

END. The ending block to verify. This is an Oracle block number.

BLOCKSIZE. The Oracle blocksize if not 2-KB blocks.

LOGFILE. Specifies where logging data should be kept.

FEEDBACK - DB_VERIFY. Shows a dot for each n blocks verified.

HELP. Provides on-screen help.

PARFILE. Specifies the name of the file to read parameters from.

USERID. Specifies the userid and password

SEGMENTID. Specifies the segment to verify in the format tsn.relfile.block (tablespace number, relative file number, and block number).

The following shows an example run of the DB_VERIFY against an Oracle9*i* database file:

```
C:\>dbv file=D:\ORACLE\ORADATA\AULTDB1\MILLMT.ORA blocksize=4096

DBVERIFY: Release 9.0.1.1.1 - Production on Sun Mar 3 16:23:26 2002

(c) Copyright 2001 Oracle Corporation.  All rights reserved.

DBVERIFY - Verification starting : FILE =
D:\ORACLE\ORADATA\AULTDB1\MILLMT.ORA


DBVERIFY - Verification complete

Total Pages Examined        : 51200
Total Pages Processed (Data) : 45989
Total Pages Failing   (Data) : 0
Total Pages Processed (Index): 0
Total Pages Failing   (Index): 0
Total Pages Processed (Other): 20
Total Pages Processed (Seg)  : 0
Total Pages Failing   (Seg)  : 0
Total Pages Empty           : 5191
Total Pages Marked Corrupt  : 0
Total Pages Influx          : 0
```

The following example shows how to get online help:

```
% dbv help=y

DBVERIFY: Release 9.0.1.0.0 - Mon Dec 3 17:09:50 2001

(c) Copyright 2001 Oracle Corporation.  All rights reserved.
```

```
Keyword      Description                      (Default)
------------------------------------------------------------------
FILE         File to Verify                   (NONE)
START        Start Block                      (First Block of File)
END          End Block                        (Last Block of File)
BLOCKSIZE    Logical Block Size               (2048)
LOGFILE      Output Log                       (NONE)
FEEDBACK     Display progress                 (0)
PARFILE      Parameter File                   (NONE)
USERID       Userid/Password                  (NONE)
SEGMENT_ID   Segment ID (tsn.relfile.block)   (NONE)
```

This is sample output of verification for the file, apl_data01.dbf. The feedback parameter has been given the value 100 to display on-screen 1 dot for every 100 blocks processed:

```
% dbv file=apl_data01.dbf feedback=100 blocksize=8192
DBVERIFY: Release Release 9.0.1.0.0 - Mon Dec 3 17:18:32 2001
 (c) Copyright 2001 Oracle Corporation.  All rights reserved.
 DBVERIFY - Verification starting : FILE = tools01.dbf

...............................................................


DBVERIFY - Verification complete

Total Pages Examined       : 1280
Total Pages Processed (Data) : 0
Total Pages Failing   (Data) : 0
Total Pages Processed (Index): 0
Total Pages Failing   (Index): 0
Total Pages Processed (Other): 8
Total Pages Processed (Seg) : 0
Total Pages Failing   (Seg) : 0
Total Pages Empty          : 1272
Total Pages Marked Corrupt : 0
Total Pages Influx         : 0
```

15.6 THE DBMS_REPAIR UTILITY

New in Oracle8*i* was the DBMS_REPAIR utility. The DBMS_REPAIR utility consists of a stored package of procedures and functions that allow the DBA to detect and repair corrupt blocks in tables and indexes. This functionality has been sorely needed in Oracle for a long time. Should a single block become corrupted, now, instead of having to go through a complex recovery procedure, the DBA has the option of attempting to repair it using the DBMS_REPAIR utility.

DBMS_REPAIR Enumeration Types

In Oracle, you can define constants in a package that can then be used throughout the package and database. Oracle has recently taken to calling these constants *enumera-*

tion types. Essentially, an enumeration type is a global variable that defines to a constant numeric value. Enumeration types are used to assign values to specific function and procedure IN-type variables. The DBMS_REPAIR package has the enumeration types shown in Table 15.1.

The default table_name is REPAIR_TABLE when table_type is REPAIR_TABLE; it will be ORPHAN_KEY_TABLE when table_type is ORPHAN.

DBMS_REPAIR Exceptions

The DBMS_REPAIR package can raise several self-declared exceptions. They are all in the 24,000 number range and are shown in Table 15.2.

TABLE 15.1 DBMS_REPAIR Enumeration Types

Variable	Values
Object_type	TABLE_OBJECT, INDEX_OBJECT, CLUSTER_OBJECT
Action	CREATE_ACTION, DROP_ACTION, PURGE_ACTION
Table_type	REPAIR_TABLE, ORPHAN_TABLE
Flags	SKIP_FLAG, NOSKIP_FLAG

TABLE 15.2 DBMS_REPAIR Exceptions

Exception	Purpose
24120	Raised by the package procedures if an invalid parameter is passed.
24122	Raised by the package if an incorrect block range is specified in BLOCK_START or BLOCK_END.
24123	An unimplemented feature was called.
24124	An invalid action was specified.
24125	The target object has been dropped or truncated since DBMS_REPAIR.CHECK_OBJECT was last run.
24127	The TABLESPACE parameter was specified with an action other than CREATE_ACTION.
24128	A partition name was specified for an object that isn't partitioned.
24129	A table name parameter was passed without the appropriate prefix.
24130	The orphan table specified for the repair doesn't exist.
24131	The orphan table specified doesn't have a proper definition.
24132	Table names are limited to 30 characters; the name specified is longer than this.

DBMS_REPAIR Procedures

The BDMS_REPAIR package contains six procedures (as of this writing) that are usable-callable and no-user-callable functions. The procedures are listed in Table 15.3, and the details of their use are delineated in the sections that follow.

ADMIN_TABLES   The ADMIN_TABLES procedure has the following input variables (it has no output variables):

```
Argument Name    Type             In/Out Default Value
---------------  ---------------  ------ --------------------------
TABLE_NAME       VARCHAR2         IN     GENERATE_DEFAULT_TABLE_NAME
TABLE_TYPE       BINARY_INTEGER   IN
ACTION           BINARY_INTEGER   IN
TABLESPACE       VARCHAR2         IN     NULL
```

The procedure is used to create, purge, and drop the REPAIR_TABLE and ORPHAN_KEY_TABLE, which are used during the repair of database tables and indexes. If the TABLE_TYPE is set to REPAIR_TABLE, then the GENERATE_ DEFAULT_ TABLE_NAME setting tells the procedure to set the table name to REPAIR_TABLE. If the TABLE_TYPE is set to ORPHAN_TABLE, then the TABLE_ NAME is set to ORPHAN_KEY_TABLE by the procedure if the GENERATE_ DEFAULT_TABLE_NAME value is entered. This procedure is a good example of why defaulted values should be placed at the end of your argument list. Since the TABLE_ NAME attribute is first, it means that you must specify the positional naming for all other parameters in order to use the default value. To see what I mean, take a look at the DBMS_REPAIR.ADMIN_TABLES that follows.

TABLE 15.3   DBMS_REPAIR Procedures

Procedure Name	Description
ADMIN_TABLES	Enables the administrative functions for the DBMS_REPAIR repair and orphan key tables, such as create, purge, and drop.
CHECK_OBJECT	Used to detect and report corruptions in tables or indexes.
DUMP_ORPHAN_KEYS	Used to report on index entries that point to rows in corrupt table blocks.
FIX_CORRUPT_BLOCKS	Marks blocks as software corrupt that have been flagged as corrupt by CHECK_OBJECT.
REBUILD_FREELISTS	Rebuilds an object's freelists.
SEGMENT_FIX_STATUS	Fixes the corrupted state of a bitmap object.
SKIP_CORRUPT_BLOCKS	For tables and indexes with corrupt blocks, tells Oracle to either ignore the blocks during scans or to raise the ORA-01578 error.

First, let's build a repair table. Note that the name specified for the table is in uppercase. This is required; if you specify the name in lowercase, you will get an error on exception 24129.

```
SQL> execute
dbms_repair.admin_tables('REPAIR_TABLE',dbms_repair.repair_table,dbms_repair.
create_action);

PL/SQL procedure successfully completed.

SQL> desc repair_table
 Name                           Null?    Type
 ---------------------------    -------- ------------
 OBJECT_ID                      NOT NULL NUMBER
 TABLESPACE_ID                  NOT NULL NUMBER
 RELATIVE_FILE_ID               NOT NULL NUMBER
 BLOCK_ID                       NOT NULL NUMBER
 CORRUPT_TYPE                   NOT NULL NUMBER
 SCHEMA_NAME                    NOT NULL VARCHAR2(30)
 OBJECT_NAME                    NOT NULL VARCHAR2(30)
 BASEOBJECT_NAME                         VARCHAR2(30)
 PARTITION_NAME                          VARCHAR2(30)
 CORRUPT_DESCRIPTION                     VARCHAR2(2000)
 REPAIR_DESCRIPTION                      VARCHAR2(200)
 MARKED_CORRUPT                 NOT NULL VARCHAR2(10)
 CHECK_TIMESTAMP                NOT NULL DATE
 FIX_TIMESTAMP                           DATE
 REFORMAT_TIMESTAMP                      DATE
```

Now let's create an orphan key table. The same admonishment about the use of uppercase applies.

```
SQL> execute
dbms_repair.admin_tables('ORPHAN_KEY_TABLE',dbms_repair.orphan_table,dbms_rep
air.create_action);

PL/SQL procedure successfully completed.

SQL> desc orphan_key_table
 Name                           Null?    Type
 ---------------------------    -------- ----------------
 SCHEMA_NAME                    NOT NULL VARCHAR2(30)
 INDEX_NAME                     NOT NULL VARCHAR2(30)
 IPART_NAME                              VARCHAR2(30)
 INDEX_ID                       NOT NULL NUMBER
 TABLE_NAME                     NOT NULL VARCHAR2(30)
 PART_NAME                               VARCHAR2(30)
 TABLE_ID                       NOT NULL NUMBER
 KEYROWID                       NOT NULL ROWID
 KEY                            NOT NULL ROWID
 DUMP_TIMESTAMP                 NOT NULL DATE
```

Here is an example of using the "GENERATE_DEFAULT_TABLE_NAME" default value:

```
SQL> execute
dbms_repair.admin_tables('GENERATE_DEFAULT_TABLE_NAME',dbms_repair.orphan_tab
le, dbms_repair.create_action);

PL/SQL procedure successfully completed.

SQL> desc orphan_key_table;
 Name                           Null?    Type
 ----------------------         -------- -----------------
 SCHEMA_NAME                    NOT NULL VARCHAR2(30)
 INDEX_NAME                     NOT NULL VARCHAR2(30)
 IPART_NAME                              VARCHAR2(30)
 INDEX_ID                       NOT NULL NUMBER
 TABLE_NAME                     NOT NULL VARCHAR2(30)
 PART_NAME                               VARCHAR2(30)
 TABLE_ID                       NOT NULL NUMBER
 KEYROWID                       NOT NULL ROWID
 KEY                            NOT NULL ROWID
 DUMP_TIMESTAMP                 NOT NULL DATE
```

And here is an example using the default value, which requires the positional specification type procedure call. If the defaults had been placed after the required fields, this could have been avoided.

```
SQL> execute
dbms_repair.admin_tables(table_type=>dbms_repair.orphan_table,action=>dbms_re
pair.drop_action);

PL/SQL procedure successfully completed.

SQL> execute
dbms_repair.admin_tables(table_type=>dbms_repair.orphan_table,action=>dbms_re
pair.create_action);

PL/SQL procedure successfully completed.

SQL> desc orphan_key_table
 Name                           Null?    Type
 ----------------------         -------- -----------------
 SCHEMA_NAME                    NOT NULL VARCHAR2(30)
 INDEX_NAME                     NOT NULL VARCHAR2(30)
 IPART_NAME                              VARCHAR2(30)
 INDEX_ID                       NOT NULL NUMBER
 TABLE_NAME                     NOT NULL VARCHAR2(30)
 PART_NAME                               VARCHAR2(30)
 TABLE_ID                       NOT NULL NUMBER
 KEYROWID                       NOT NULL ROWID
 KEY                            NOT NULL ROWID
 DUMP_TIMESTAMP                 NOT NULL DATE
```

The other actions, such as purge, are accessed in the same way as demonstrated in Listing 15.2 for the CREATE_ACTION enumerated type.

CHECK_OBJECT   The CHECK_OBJECT procedure has up to nine possible input values and one output value. Again, due to placement of the arguments, in order to use the default values, you must use positional specifications for any calls to this procedure, unless you specify values for all of the parameters. The following table shows the parameters for the CHECK_OBJECT procedure:

Argument Name	Type	In/Out	Default?
SCHEMA_NAME	VARCHAR2	IN	
OBJECT_NAME	VARCHAR2	IN	
PARTITION_NAME	VARCHAR2	IN	NULL
OBJECT_TYPE	BINARY_INTEGER	IN	TABLE_OBJECT
REPAIR_TABLE_NAME	VARCHAR2	IN	REPAIR_TABLE
FLAGS	BINARY_INTEGER	IN	NULL
RELATIVE_FNO	BINARY_INTEGER	IN	NULL
BLOCK_START	BINARY_INTEGER	IN	NULL
BLOCK_END	BINARY_INTEGER	IN	NULL
CORRUPT_COUNT	BINARY_INTEGER	OUT	

As you can see, the positioning of the CORRUPT_COUNT OUT variable, which appears after all of the values that have default values, will force us to use positional nomenclature or to specify values for all of the required input variables. (Sometimes I wish the guys that write this stuff had to use it on a daily basis.) Another problem is that, if you have more than 32,767 problem entries, this procedure will fail on numeric overflow since the output is specified as a BINARY_INTEGER instead of a plain old NUMBER. A sample run of the procedure CHECK_OBJECT is shown in Listing 15.2.

So, we did all that work just to find out we don't have a problem. Oh well, I guess it is better than finding we did have a problem.

Listing 15.2   Example execution of the CHECK_OBJECT procedure.

```
SQL> execute
dbms_repair.check_object(schema_name=>'GRAPHICS_DBA',object_name=>'INTERNAL_G
RAPHICS', corrupt_count=>:x);

PL/SQL procedure successfully completed.

SQL> print x

        X
---------
        0
```

DUMP_ORPHAN_KEYS If the search with CHECK_TABLE turns up corrupt blocks, the DUMP_ORPHAN_KEYS procedure is used to retrieve key values from the table or index to facilitate the rebuild of the damaged block. Again, notice how the positioning of the KEY_COUNT OUT attribute forces us to use positional nomenclature to use this procedure. The DUMP_ORPHAN_KEYS procedure has seven possible input variables, only the first two of which are required, and one required output variable. Another problem is that if you have more than 32,767 problem entries, this procedure will fail on numeric overflow since the output is specified as a BINARY_INTEGER instead of a plain old NUMBER.

Argument Name	Type	In/Out	Default Value?
SCHEMA_NAME	VARCHAR2	IN	
OBJECT_NAME	VARCHAR2	IN	
PARTITION_NAME	VARCHAR2	IN	NULL
OBJECT_TYPE	BINARY_INTEGER	IN	INDEX_OBJECT
REPAIR_TABLE_NAME	VARCHAR2	IN	REPAIR_TABLE
ORPHAN_TABLE_NAME	VARCHAR2	IN	ORPHAN_KEY_TABLE
FLAGS	BINARY_INTEGER	IN	NULL
KEY_COUNT	BINARY_INTEGER	OUT	

A sample run of this procedure is shown in Listing 15.3.

Listing 15.3   Example run of the DUMP_ORPHAN_KEYS procedure.

```
SQL> execute
dbms_repair.dump_orphan_keys(schema_name=>'GRAPHICS_DBA',object_name=>'PK_INT
ERNAL_GRAPHICS', key_count=>:x);

PL/SQL procedure successfully completed.

SQL> print x

        X
---------
        0
```

Sorry I can't provide more exciting examples, but I don't know of an easy way to generate corrupt blocks to demonstrate actual results.

FIX_CORRUPT_BLOCKS The FIX_CORRUPT_BLOCKS procedure allows you to tell Oracle to mark the blocks as software corrupt and thus skip them, or leave them as-is and generate errors. The procedure has six possible input variables, two of which are required, and one output parameter. Guess what? Yep, the OUT parameter FIX_

COUNT is once again placed so that we have to use positional nomenclature or specify values for all of the input parameters in order to use the procedure. Also, once again, the OUT parameter FIX_COUNT is a BINARY_INTEGER, limiting the number of possible fixes to 32,767. A sample execution of this procedure is shown in Listing 15.4.

```
Argument Name          Type                    In/Out Default Value?
-------------------    ----------------------  ------ ----------------
SCHEMA_NAME            VARCHAR2                IN
OBJECT_NAME            VARCHAR2                IN
PARTITION_NAME        VARCHAR2                IN     NULL
OBJECT_TYPE           BINARY_INTEGER          IN     TABLE_OBJECT
REPAIR_TABLE_NAME     VARCHAR2                IN     'REPAIR_TABLE'
FLAGS                 BINARY_INTEGER          IN     NULL
FIX_COUNT             BINARY_INTEGER          OUT
```

Listing 15.4   Example execution of the FIX_CORRUPT_BLOCKS procedure.

```
SQL> execute
dbms_repair.fix_corrupt_blocks(schema_name=>'GRAPHICS_DBA',object_name=>'INTE
RNAL_GRAPHICS', fix_count=>:x);

PL/SQL procedure successfully completed.

SQL> print x

     X
-----------
     0
```

REBUILD_FREELISTS   The procedure REBUILD_FREELISTS is used to rebuild the freelists of tables that have been repaired to reflect the loss of the corrupt blocks. This procedure has four possible inputs, two of which have default values. Fortunately, for this procedure, Oracle put the defaults at the end of the variable list so positional naming isn't required. However, the developer who created all of these procedures has obviously never heard of the UPPER function, so you must specify your arguments in uppercase or an error will occur. A sample run of this procedure is shown in Listing 15.5.

```
Argument Name          Type                    In/Out Default?
-------------------    ----------------------  ------ -------------
SCHEMA_NAME            VARCHAR2                IN
OBJECT_NAME            VARCHAR2                IN
PARTITION_NAME        VARCHAR2                IN     NULL
OBJECT_TYPE           BINARY_INTEGER          IN     TABLE_OBJECT
```

Listing 15.5   Example run of the REBUILD_FREELISTS procedure.

```
SQL> execute dbms_repair.rebuild_freelists('GRAPHICS_DBA',
'INTERNAL_GRAPHICS');

PL/SQL procedure successfully completed.
```

If there is only one freelist group, the master freelist is updated with all free blocks; the other freelists are zeroed. If the object has multiple freelist groups then the master freelist in each freelist group is updated in a round-robin fashion and the rest of the freelists are zeroed. My question: Since this procedure will be required to be executed after any run of the FIX_CORRUPT_BLOCKS procedure, why wasn't the functionality simply added to that procedure?

SEGMENT_FIX_STATUS   The procedure SEGMENT_FIX_STATUS was added to the DBMS_REPAIR package in version 9*i*. SEGMENT_FIX_STATUS corrects bitmap entry problems caused by corrupt blocks. Oracle took notice of all the complaints generated from its lack of concern for calling values being out of order (nullable intermixed with nonnullable) and have sequenced the nondefault values first. This means you don't have to use the positional calling nomenclature when using SEGMENT_FIX_STATUS. The calling parameters for SEGMENT_FIX_STATUS are:

```
DBMS_REPAIR.SEGMENT_FIX_STATUS (
    segment_owner   IN VARCHAR2,
    segment_name    IN VARCHAR2,
    segment_type    IN BINARY_INTEGER DEFAULT TABLE_OBJECT,
    file_number     IN BINARY_INTEGER DEFAULT NULL,
    block_number    IN BINARY_INTEGER DEFAULT NULL,
    status_value    IN BINARY_INTEGER DEFAULT NULL,
    partition_name  IN VARCHAR2 DEFAULT NULL,);
```

The parameters for the SEGMENT_FIX_STATUS procedure are defined as:

schema_owner. Schema name (owner) of the segment.

segment_name. Segment name.

partition_name. (Optional) Name of an individual partition. NULL for nonpartitioned objects. Default is NULL.

segment_type. (Optional) Type of the segment (for example, TABLE or INDEX). Default is NULL.

file_number. (Optional) The tablespace-relative file number of the data block whose status has to be fixed. If omitted, all the blocks in the segment will be checked for state correctness and fixed.

block_number. (Optional) The file-relative file number of the data block whose status has to be fixed. If omitted, all the blocks in the segment will be checked for state correctness and fixed.

status_value. (Optional) The value to which the block status described by the file_number and block_number will be set. If omitted, the status will be set based on the current state of the block. This is almost always the case, but if there is a bug in the calculation algorithm, the value can be set manually. Status values:

1 = block is full

2 = block is 0-25 percent free

3 = block is 25-50 percent free

4 = block is 50-75 percent free

5 = block is 75-100 percent free

The status for bitmap blocks, segment headers, and extent map blocks cannot be altered. The status for blocks in a fixed hash area cannot be altered. For index blocks, there are only two possible states: 1 = block is full and 3 = block has freespace.

SKIP_CORRUPT_BLOCKS The final procedure in the DBMS_REPAIR package is the SKIP_CORRUPT_BLOCKS procedure. The SKIP_CORRUPT_BLOCKS procedure is used to mark the corrupt blocks software corrupt and tell Oracle to skip those blocks during table and index scans. If the object specified is a cluster, it applies to all of the tables in the cluster and their respective indexes. The SKIP_CORRUPT_BLOCKS procedure has four possible inputs, two of which have default values. Fortunately, Oracle put the defaults at the end of the variable list so positional naming isn't required. However, the developer who created all of these procedures has obviously never heard of the UPPER function, so you must specify your arguments in uppercase or an error will occur. A sample run of the SKIP_CORRUPT_BLOCKS procedure is shown in Listing 15.6.

```
Argument Name        Type                       In/Out  DefaultValue?
----------------     -----------------------    ------  -------------
SCHEMA_NAME          VARCHAR2                    IN
OBJECT_NAME          VARCHAR2                    IN
OBJECT_TYPE          BINARY_INTEGER             IN       TABLE_OBJECT
FLAGS                BINARY_INTEGER             IN       SKIP_FLAG
```

Listing 15.6   Example run of the SKIP_CORRUPT_BLOCKS procedure.

```
SQL> execute dbms_repair.skip_corupt_blocks('GRAPHICS_DBA',
'INTERNAL_GRAPHICS');

PL/SQL procedure successfully completed.
```

Using Flashback Query

In the chart in Figure 15.1, several types of recovery, such as table-level recovery, can be dependent upon using *flashback query*. In essence, flashback query allows a DBA to recover data that has been deleted, revert data that has been updated to its former state, and undo inserts, as long as the data involved is still available in the undo structures in the undo tablespace. This retention of values in the undo tablespace is based on the amount of available space in the undo tablespace and the UNDO_RETENTION initialization parameter. If there is enough space in the undo tablespace, then the data contained in the undo segments will not be overwritten until at least UNDO_RETENTION (which defaults to 900 in seconds) amount of time has passed.

This new capability, to go back in time via the undo retention feature, allows DBAs to be able to fix those oops-type errors, such as deleting all the rows in a table, updating all the rows in a table, dropping a table, and other such things that we DBAs "never" do.

In order to use the flashback query option the following initialization parameters must be set:

UNDO_MANAGEMENT. Set to AUTO.

UNDO_RETENTION. Leave at default (900) or set to a precalculated value.

UNDO_SUPPRESS_ERRORS. Set to FALSE.

UNDO_TABLESPACE. Set to the name of the undo tablespace (default is UNDOTBS).

In addition to setting the initialization parameters, any user who wants to use the DBMS_FLASHBACK package must have the EXECUTE privilege on the DBMS_FLASHBACK package. The DBMS_FLASHBACK package is useful only if a snapshot of the proper data has been maintained before it is needed. Therefore, I suggest that any major transaction should include a call to the DBMS_FLASHBACK.GET_SYSTEM_CHANGE _NUMBER (RETURN NUMBER); function and that the SCN returned be stored in a temporary table until the transaction has been verified. This will allow the DBA to use the DBMS_FLASHBACK.ENABLE_AT_SYSTEM_CHANGE (query_scn IN NUMBER); procedure to reset the database to the values held at the SCN before any changes occurred. Once the database session has been reset to the SCN just prior to the transaction, the DBA can open a cursor to retrieve the required data to rebuild a table or repair damaged entries and then issue a call to DBMS_FLASHBACK.DISABLE; to return the database session to normal mode. Once in normal mode, any data placed into a cursor prior to the return to normal mode will stay at the pre-SCN values and allow the DBA to recover the information. In procedural form this would be:

1. In the transaction that will be causing changes to data, create a small temporary table, and after a preliminary COMMIT, place the current SCN into the table using a call to the DBMS_ FLASHBACK.GET_SYSTEM_ CHANGE_NUMBER (RETURN NUMBER); function call and INSERT command; commit the entry.

2. Execute the transaction that changes data.

3. Review changes; if improper, then issue a call to DBMS_FLASHBACK. ENABLE_ AT_SYSTEM_CHANGE (query_scn IN NUMBER); to enable flashback processing for the current session at the SCN just prior to the change.

4. Open the required cursors to retrieve the proper versions of the data from the flashback database image.

5. Use a call to DBMS_FLASHBACK.DISABLE to disable the flashback database image and return to normal (current) mode.

6. Use the data in the cursors to restore the proper information into the damaged table or restore the deleted table.

A simple test of the flashback query using time-based flashback processing is shown in Listing 15.7, and the *Oracle9i Supplied PL/SQL Packages and Types Reference*, Release 1 (9.0.1), Part Number A89852-02, manual has other excellent PL/SQL examples of this process.

LISTING 15.7   Use of the flashback query option to restore table data.

```
First, just for this test, let's create a user, normally you could just grant
EXECUTE on the DBMS_FLASHBACK to your transaction user.

SQL> CREATE USER test_flash IDENTIFIED BY flash
  2    DEFAULT TABLESPACE users
  3    TEMPORARY TABLESPACE temp
  4    QUOTA UNLIMITED ON users;

User created.

SQL> GRANT CONNECT, RESOURCE TO test_flash;

Grant succeeded.

SQL> GRANT EXECUTE ON DBMS_FLASHBACK TO test_flash;

Grant succeeded.

Now, we connect to the test user and create and populate a test table.

SQL> CONNECT test_flash/flash
Connected.

SQL> CREATE TABLE test_fb(t number(5), "COMMENT" varchar2(32))
SQL> /

Table created.
```

continues

LISTING 15.7   Continued.

```
SQL> INSERT INTO test_fb values (1, 'inserted at '||to_char(sysdate,'dd-mon-
yyyy hh24:mi:ss'))
SQL> /

1 row created.

SQL> c/1/2
  1* INSERT INTO test_fb values (2, 'inserted at '||to_char(sysdate,'dd-mon-
yyyy hh24:mi:ss'))
SQL> /

1 row created.

SQL> commit;

Commit complete.

SQL> SELECT * FROM test_fb;

        T COMMENT
---------- --------------------------------
        1 inserted at 04-dec-2001 15:04:44
        2 inserted at 04-dec-2001 15:05:20
```

Now let's create a table to track a date where we do our mayhem. The date type flashback will go to the nearest 5 minute interval before the specified date.

```
SQL> CREATE TABLE keep_date (date_scn_tracking date);

Table created.
```

Now we will disable flashback processing. Just to make sure we are in the "current" database environment.

```
SQL> EXECUTE DBMS_FLASHBACK.DISABLE;

PL/SQL procedure successfully completed.
```

We now insert our timestamp (note that the new timestamp datatype is supported as well, but since we are going to the nearest 5 minute interval it seems a bit of overkill).

```
SQL> INSERT INTO keep_date values (sysdate);

1 row created.

SQL> commit;
Commit complete.
```

```
Now let's do something to our test table.

SQL> DELETE FROM test_fb WHERE t=1;

1 row deleted.

SQL> COMMIT;

Commit complete.

Just to show you I didn't stuff the card up my sleeve:

SQL> SELECT * FROM test_fb;

        T COMMENT
---------- --------------------------------
        2 inserted at 04-dec-2001 15:05:20

Now commit to end any transactions and start us fresh:

SQL> COMMIT;

Commit complete.

Create the recovery program. Notice how we get the date value back from the
storage table, use it to set our snapshot into the flashback environment,
then get the row we need and then disable flashback to bring us back into the
current database, we then re-insert the record and everything is back to the
way it was (except row order is changed, but hey, we can't have everything
can we?).

SQL> declare
  2   restore_scn date;
  3   begin
  4   select date_scn_tracking into restore_scn from keep_date;
  5   dbms_flashback.enable_at_time(restore_scn);
  6   end;
  7  /

PL/SQL procedure successfully completed.

Look, nothing up my sleeve and Presto!

SQL> SELECT * FROM test_fb;

        T COMMENT
---------- --------------------------------
        1 inserted at 04-dec-2001 15:04:44
        2 inserted at 04-dec-2001 15:05:20
```

continues

LISTING 15.7   Continued.

```
SQL> declare
  2   cursor c1 is
  3     select * from test_fb where t=1;
  4   c1_rec c1%rowtype;
  5   begin
  6    open c1;
  7    dbms_flashback.disable;
  8    fetch c1 into c1_rec;
  9    insert into test_fb values(c1_rec.t,c1_rec.comment);
 10    commit;
 11*  end;
SQL> /

PL/SQL procedure successfully completed.

Now let's see what the table looks like.

SQL> SELECT * FROM test_fb;

         T COMMENT
---------- --------------------------------
         2 inserted at 04-dec-2001 15:05:20
         1 inserted at 04-dec-2001 15:04:44

Everything is back, except of course the row order is different. Just to be
sure:

SQL> EXECUTE DBMS_FLASHBACK.DISABLE;

PL/SQL procedure successfully completed.

SQL> SELECT * FROM test_fb;

         T COMMENT
---------- --------------------------------
         2 inserted at 04-dec-2001 15:05:20
         1 inserted at 04-dec-2001 15:04:44
```

15.7 FURTHER DBA READING

The DBA is encouraged to obtain and review the following resources:

Oracle9i Backup and Recovery Concepts, Release 1 (9.0.1), Part Number A90133-02, Oracle Corporation, June 2001.

Oracle9i Database Utilities, Release 1 (9.0.1), Part Number A90192-01, Oracle Corporation, June, 2001.

Oracle9i Recovery Manager User's Guide, Release 1 (9.0.1), Part Number A90135-01, Oracle Corporation, June 2001.

Oracle9i Supplied PL/SQL Packages and Types Reference, Release 1 (9.0.1), Part Number A89852-02, Oracle Corporation, June 2001.

PL/SQL User's Guide and Reference, Release 9.0.1, Part Number A89856-01, Oracle Corporation, June 2001.

15.8 SUMMARY

This chapter described various backup and recovery options in Oracle, and showed several scripts to ease the use of hot backups on UNIX and NT. The chapter also covered the use of RMAN from Oracle, along with examples of its use. Finally, the use of the Oracle-provided packages DBMS_REPAIR and DBMS_FLASHBACK was detailed.

INDEX